D0795505

Simply C#

Deitel Books, Cyber Classrooms, Complete Training Courses and Web-Based Training Courses
Published by Prentice Hall

Simply Series

Simply C#®: An Application-Driven Tutorial Approach

Simply Visual Basic® .NET: An Application Driven Tutorial Approach (Visual Studio .NET 2002 Edition)

Simply Java™ Programming: An Application-Driven Tutorial Approach

Simply Visual Basic® .NET: An Application Driven Tutorial Approach (Visual Studio .NET 2003 Edition)

How to Program Series

Advanced Java™ 2 Platform How to Program

C How to Program, 4/E

C++ How to Program, 4/E

C# ® How to Program

e-Business and e-Commerce How to Program

Internet and World Wide Web How to Program, 2/E

Java™ How to Program, 5/E

Perl How to Program

Python How to Program

Visual Basic® 6 How to Program

Visual Basic® .NET How to Program, 2/E

Visual C++® .NET How to Program

Wireless Internet & Mobile Business How to Program

XML How to Program

.NET How to Program Series

C#® How to Program

Visual Basic® .NET How to Program, 2/E

Visual C++® .NET How to Program

Visual Studio Series

C#® How to Program

Getting Started with Microsoft® Visual C++® 6 with an Introduction to MFC

Simply C#®: An Application-Driven Tutorial Approach

Simply Visual Basic® .NET: An Application- Driven Tutorial Approach (Visual Studio .NET 2002 Edition)

Simply Visual Basic® .NET: An Application- Driven Tutorial Approach (Visual Studio .NET 2003 Edition)

Visual Basic® 6 How to Program

Visual Basic® .NET How to Program, 2/E

Visual C++® .NET How to Program

CS1 Programming Series

Java™ Software Design

For Managers Series

e-Business and e-Commerce for Managers

DEITEL® Developer Series

Java™ Web Services for Experienced Programmers

Web Services A Technical Introduction

Multimedia Cyber Classroom Series

C++ Multimedia Cyber Classroom, 4/E

C# Multimedia Cyber Classroom

e-Business and e-Commerce Multimedia Cyber Classroom

Internet and World Wide Web Multimedia Cyber Classroom, 2/E

Java™ 2 Multimedia Cyber Classroom, 5/E

Perl Multimedia Cyber Classroom

Python Multimedia Cyber Classroom

Visual Basic® 6 Multimedia Cyber Classroom

Visual Basic® .NET Multimedia Cyber Classroom, 2/E

Wireless Internet & Mobile Business Programming Multimedia Cyber Classroom

XML Multimedia Cyber Classroom

The Complete Training Course Series

The Complete C++ Training Course, 4/E

The Complete C#® Training Course

The Complete e-Business and e-Commerce Programming Training Course

The Complete Internet and World Wide Web Programming Training Course, 2/E

The Complete Java™ 2 Training Course, 5/E

The Complete Perl Training Course

The Complete Python Training Course

The Complete Visual Basic® 6 Training Course

The Complete Visual Basic® .NET Training Course, 2/E

The Complete Wireless Internet & Mobile Business Programming Training Course

The Complete XML Programming Training Course

Computer Science Series

Operating Systems, 3/E

To communicate with the authors, send e-mail to:

deitel@deitel.com

For information on corporate on-site seminars and public seminars offered by Deitel & Associates, Inc. worldwide, visit:

www.deitel.com

For continuing updates on Prentice Hall and Deitel publications visit:

www.deitel.com,
www.prenhall.com/deitel or
www.InformIT.com/deitel

Simply C#

H. M. Deitel
Deitel & Associates, Inc.

P. J. Deitel
Deitel & Associates, Inc.

T. R. Hoey

C. H. Yaeger
Deitel & Associates, Inc.

PEARSON

Prentice
Hall

Upper Saddle River, NJ 07458

Library of Congress Cataloging-in-Publication Data

On file

Vice President and Editorial Director, ECS: Marcia J. Horton
Senior Acquisitions Editor: Kate Hargett
Assistant Editor: Sarah Parker
Project Manager: Carole Snyder
Vice President and Director of Production and Manufacturing, ESM: David W. Riccardi
Executive Managing Editor: Vince O'Brien
Managing Editor: Tom Manshreck
Production Editor: Chirag Thakkar
Production Editor, Media: Bob Engelhardt
Director of Creative Services: Paul Belfanti
Creative Director: Carole Anson
Chapter Opener and Cover Designer: Dr. Harvey Deitel and David Merrell
Interior Design: Jonathan Boylan, John Root, Dr. Harvey Deitel
Interior Design Assistance: Geoffrey Cassar
Manufacturing Manager: Trudy Pisciotti
Manufacturing Buyer: Lisa McDowell
Marketing Manager: Pamela Shaffer
Marketing Assistant: Barrie Reinhold

© 2004 by Pearson Education, Inc.
Upper Saddle River, New Jersey 07458

Pearson Prentice Hall. All rights reserved. No part of this book may be reproduced, in any form or by any means, without permission in writing from the publisher.

The authors and publisher of this book have used their best efforts in preparing this book. These efforts include the development, research, and testing of the theories and programs to determine their effectiveness. The authors and publisher make no warranty of any kind, expressed or implied, with regard to these programs or to the documentation contained in this book. The authors and publisher shall not be liable in any event for incidental or consequential damages in connection with, or arising out of, the furnishing, performance, or use of these programs.

Many of the designations used by manufacturers and sellers to distinguish their products are claimed as trademarks and registered trademarks. Where those designations appear in this book, and Pearson Education, Inc. and the authors were aware of a trademark claim, the designations have been printed in initial caps or all caps. All product names mentioned remain trademarks or registered trademarks of their respective owners.

Printed in the United States of America

10 9 8 7 6 5 4 3 2 1

ISBN 0-13-142641-9

Pearson Education Ltd., London
Pearson Education Australia Pty. Ltd., Sydney
Pearson Education Singapore, Pte. Ltd.
Pearson Education North Asia Ltd., Hong Kong
Pearson Education Canada, Inc., Toronto
Pearson Educación de Mexico, S.A. de C.V.
Pearson Education–Japan, Tokyo
Pearson Education Malaysia, Pte. Ltd.
Pearson Education, Inc., Upper Saddle River, New Jersey

In loving memory of Morris and Lena Deitel.

Harvey, Barbara, Paul and Abbey

To my grandmother, Helen Kelly:
Your generosity opens doors for so many,
and your warmth touches all who know you.

Tim

In loving memory of David Mosberg.

Cheryl

Trademarks:

DEITEL and the double-thumbs-up bug are registered trademarks of Deitel and Associates, Inc. Dive Into is a trademark of Deitel and Associates, Inc.

Microsoft, Visual Studio .NET and C# are either registered trademarks or trademarks of Microsoft Corporation in the United States and/or other countries.

Brief Table of Contents

xvii

859

860

864

867

868

889

890

890

894

909

ᴅing the type of dia-

⟨m the first
⟨odify-
⟨pro-
⟨l GUI
⟨arn core
⟨ that are
⟨dix C com-
⟨or exams.

⟨ilar to the way
⟨w. This way, stu-
⟨y see on their own
⟨ws:

⟨ppear in black

⟨applications fun to create and
⟨26, we discuss Graphical Device
⟨aphical features used by .NET—to
⟨ck. In Tutorial 27, we use a fun tech-
⟨interactive, animated characters to a
⟨aft Agent, your applications can speak
⟨ase commands!

⟨isual ⟨sinesses today, and we use real-world
(audio⟨ming fundamentals. Tutorials 25 and
Intern⟨resented in the context of two appli-
section⟨kstore.

immed⟨ng is one of the most important top-
⟨d business critical applications. Pro

⟨ply C#   This b⟨ze the exceptions (errors) that could
⟨andle those exceptions effectively,
■ AP⟨   ⟨s and continue executing instead of
rar⟨   ⟨proper use of exception handling,
an⟨   ⟨ption handling, throwing exceptions
wi⟨
an⟨
ri⟨e of four tutorials in which the stu-
w⟨plication. Tutorial 28 familiarizes
ti⟨ation Services (which enables Web
ar⟨simple Web transactions. Tutorials
■ L⟨   ⟨build an application that retrieves
E⟨   ⟨the information in a Web page.
d⟨riented programming is the most
t⟨bust, reusable software, and C#
m⟨mming features. This book intro-
c⟨g objects, laying a solid foundation

■ ⟨
d⟨are programs that help program-
⟨am code. Visual Studio .NET con-
⟨ws programmers to analyze their
⟨aroughout the book, we teach the

Visual Studio .NET Debugger; we explain how to use its key features and offer many debugging exercises.

To the Instructor

Focus of the Book

Our goal was clear: Produce a C# textbook for introductory-level courses in computer programming aimed at students with little or no programming experience. This book teaches computer programming principles and the C# language, including data types, control statements, object-oriented programming, C# classes, GUI concepts, event-driven programming and more. After mastering the material in this book, students will be able to program in C# and to employ many important capabilities of the .NET platform.

We also wanted a textbook that was up-to-date with Microsoft's latest release of Visual Studio—Visual Studio .NET 2003, which includes an updated version of C#. We have built every application in this book using the 2003 software. All applications and solutions have been fully implemented and tested on this new platform.

A Note Regarding Software for the Book

For the educational market only, this textbook is available in a "value pack" with the Microsoft® Visual C# .NET Standard Edition version 2003 integrated development environment as a free supplement. The standard edition is fully functional and is shipped on 5 CDs. There is no time limit for using the software. [*Note:* If you are a professional using this publication, you will have to purchase the necessary software to build and run the applications in this textbook.]

Lab Setup

To install some of the required software for this book, students and instructors will need Administrator-level access to the computer. For university computer labs where students do not have Administrator-level access, instructors and system administrators must ensure that the proper software is installed on the lab computers. In addition, student accounts must have at least the **Debugger Users** access level to build and run applications in a lab environment.

In Tutorial 27, certain Microsoft Agent software components must be installed to execute and develop the **Phone Book** application. If students are not allowed to install software on lab computers, the Microsoft Agent components discussed in Tutorial 27 must be installed in advance. To configure and execute some of the examples and exercises, such as the **Bookstore** case study in Tutorials 28–31, students will need to have Administrator-level access.

Objectives

Each tutorial begins with objectives that inform students of what to expect and give them an opportunity, after reading the tutorial, to determine whether they have met the intended goals.

Outline

The tutorial outline enables students to approach the material in top-down fashion. Along with the tutorial objectives, the outline helps students anticipate future topics and set a comfortable and effective learning pace.

Example Applications (with Outputs)

We present C# features in the context of complete, working C# applications. All examples are available on the CD that accompanies the book or as downloads from our Web site, www.deitel.com/books/csharpSimply1/index.html.

Illustrations/Figures

An abundance of charts, line drawings and program outputs are included. The discussion of control statements, for example, features carefully drawn UML activity diagrams. [*Note:* We do not teach UML diagramming as a program-development tool, but we do use UML diagrams to explain the precise operation of many of C#'s control statements.]

Programming Tips

Hundreds of programming tips help students focus on important aspects of program development. These tips and practices represent the best the authors have gleaned from decades of programming and teaching experience.

 Good Programming Practice

Good Programming Practices highlight techniques that help students write programs that are clear, understandable and maintainable.

 Common Programming Error

Students learning a language—especially in their first programming course—frequently make errors. Pointing out these *Common Programming Errors* in the text reduces the likelihood that students will make the same mistakes.

 Error-Prevention Tip

These tips describe aspects of C# that prevent errors from getting into programs in the first place, which simplifies the testing and debugging process.

 Performance Tip

Teaching students to write clear and understandable programs is the most important goal for a first programming course. But students want to write programs that run the fastest, use the least memory, require the smallest number of keystrokes, etc. *Performance Tips* highlight opportunities for improving program performance.

 Portability Tip

The *Portability Tips* provide insights on how C# achieves its high degree of portability among .NET platforms.

 Software Design Tip

The *Software Design Tips* highlight architectural and design issues that affect the construction of object-oriented software systems.

 GUI Design Tip

The *GUI Design Tips* highlight graphical-user-interface conventions to help students design attractive, user-friendly GUIs and use GUI features.

Skills Summary

Each tutorial includes a bullet-list-style summary of the new programming concepts presented. This reinforces key actions taken to build the application in each tutorial.

Key Terms

Each tutorial includes a list of important terms defined in the tutorial. These terms also appear in the index and in a book-wide glossary, so the student can locate terms and their definitions quickly.

230 Self-Review Questions and Answers

Self-review multiple-choice questions and answers are included after most sections to build students' confidence with the material and prepare them for the regular exercises. Students should be encouraged to attempt all the self-review exercises and check the answers.

604 Exercises (Solutions in Instructor's Manual)

Each tutorial concludes with exercises. Typical exercises include 10 multiple-choice questions, a "What does this code do?" exercise, a "What's wrong with this code?" exercise, three programming exercises and a programming challenge. The questions involve simple recall of important terminology and concepts, writing individual C# statements, writing small portions of C# applications and writing complete C# methods, classes and applications. Every programming exercise uses a step-by-step methodology to suggest how to solve the problems. The solutions for the exercises are *available only to instructors* through their Prentice-Hall representatives. [**NOTE: Please do not write to us requesting the instructor's manual. Distribution of this publication is strictly limited to instructors teaching from the book. Instructors may obtain the solutions manual only from their regular Prentice Hall representatives. We regret that we cannot provide the solutions to professionals.**]

GUI Design Guidelines

Consistent and proper graphical user interface design is crucial to visual programming. In each tutorial, we summarize the GUI design guidelines that were introduced. Appendix C presents a cumulative list of these GUI design guidelines for easy reference.

Controls, Events, Properties & Methods Summaries

Each tutorial includes a summary of the controls, events, properties and methods covered in the tutorial. The summary includes a picture of each control, shows the control "in action" and lists the control's properties, events and methods that were discussed up to and including that tutorial. Appendix E groups the controls by tutorial for easy reference.

Index

The extensive index includes important terms both under main headings and as separate entries so that students can search for any term or concept by keyword. The code examples and the exercises also are included in the index. Every C# source-code program in the book is indexed under the appropriate application and as a subindex item under "Examples." We have also double-indexed features such as controls and properties. This makes it easier to find examples using particular features.

Simply C# Ancillary Package

Simply C# is accompanied by ancillary materials for instructors, including:

- *Instructor's Resource CD (IRCD)* which contains the
  - *Instructor's Manual* with solutions to the end-of-tutorial exercises and
  - *Test-Item File* of multiple-choice questions (approximately two per tutorial section).
- *Customizable PowerPoint® Slides* containing the code and figures in the text, and bulleted items that summarize the key points in the text. The slides are downloadable from www.deitel.com/books/csharpSimply1/index.html and are available at www.prenhall.com/deitel.

Course Management Systems

Selected content from *Simply C#* and other Deitel texts, is available to integrate into various Course Management Systems, including CourseCompass, Blackboard and WebCT. Course Management Systems help faculty create, manage and use sophisticated Web-based educational tools and programs. Blackboard, CourseCompass and WebCT offer:

- Features to create and customize an online course
- Communication tools
- Flexible testing tools
- Support materials

In addition to the tools found in Blackboard and WebCT, CourseCompass from Prentice Hall includes:

- **CourseCompass course home page**, which makes the course as easy to navigate as a book.
- **Hosting on Prentice Hall's centralized servers**, which allows course administrators to avoid separate licensing fees or server-space issues.
- **"How Do I" online-support sections** are available for users who need help personalizing course sites.
- **Instructor Quick Start Guide**

To view free online demonstrations and learn more about Course Management Systems that support Deitel content, visit the following Web sites:

- Blackboard: www.blackboard.com and www.prenhall.com/blackboard.
- WebCT: www.webct.com and www.prenhall.com/webct.
- CourseCompass: www.coursecompass.com and www.prenhall.com/coursecompass.

Acknowledgments

One of the great pleasures of writing a textbook is acknowledging the efforts of many people whose names may not appear on the cover, but whose hard work, cooperation, friendship and understanding were crucial to the production of the book. Many people at Deitel & Associates, Inc., devoted long hours to this project:

- Abbey Deitel, President
- Barbara Deitel, Chief Financial Officer
- Christi Kelsey, Director of Business Development

We also would like to thank Jonathan Henry and Roman Feldman, participants in the Deitel & Associates, Inc., College Internship Program.[1]

We are fortunate to have been able to work on this project with the talented and dedicated team of publishing professionals at Prentice Hall. We especially appreciate the extraordinary efforts of our Computer Science editor, Kate Hargett and her boss—our mentor in publishing—Marcia Horton, Editorial Director of Prentice

---

1. The Deitel & Associates, Inc. College Internship Program offers a limited number of salaried positions to college students majoring in Computer Science, Information Technology, Marketing and English. Students work at our corporate headquarters in Maynard, Massachusetts full-time in the summers and (for those attending college in the Boston area) part-time during the academic year. We also offer full-time internship positions for students interested in taking a semester off from school to gain industry experience. Regular full-time positions are available to college graduates. For more information, please contact Abbey Deitel at deitel@deitel.com, visit our Web site, www.deitel.com, and subscribe to our free e-mail newsletter at www.deitel.com/newsletter/subscribe.html.

Hall's Engineering and Computer Science Team. Tom Manshreck and Vince O'Brien did a marvelous job managing the production of the book. Chirag Thakkar and John Lovell served as production editors and Sarah Parker handled editorial responsibilities on the book's ancillary package. We would like to thank the design team that created a completely new look and feel for the *Simply* series—Carole Anson, Paul Belfanti, Tom Manshreck, Jonathan Boylan, John Root, Gary Gray and Geoffrey Cassar.

We wish to acknowledge the efforts of our reviewers and to thank Carole Snyder and Jennifer Cappello of Prentice Hall, who managed the review process. The reviewers from colleges, industry and Microsoft helped us to "get the book right." Adhering to a tight time schedule, these reviewers scrutinized the text and the applications, providing countless suggestions for improving the accuracy and completeness of the presentation. It is a privilege to have the guidance of such talented and busy professionals.

Simply C# reviewers:
Catherine Wyman (University of DeVry-Phoenix)
Dharmesh Chauhan (Microsoft, Singapore)
Jim Huddleston (Independent Consultant)
Peter van de Goes (Rose State College – Business and IT Division)
Jay Cook (Independent Consultant)

We would sincerely appreciate your comments, criticisms, corrections and suggestions for improving the text. Please address all correspondence to:

deitel@deitel.com

We will respond promptly.

Well, that's it for now. Welcome to the exciting world of C# programming. We hope you enjoy this look at leading-edge computer applications development. Good luck!

Dr. Harvey M. Deitel
Paul J. Deitel
Timothy R. Hoey
Cheryl H. Yaeger

About the Authors

Dr. Harvey M. Deitel, Chairman of Deitel & Associates, Inc., has 42 years experience in the computing field, including extensive industry and academic experience. Dr. Deitel earned B.S. and M.S. degrees from the Massachusetts Institute of Technology and a Ph.D. from Boston University. He worked on the pioneering virtual-memory operating-systems projects at IBM and MIT that developed techniques now widely implemented in systems such as UNIX, Linux and Windows XP. He has 20 years of college teaching experience and served as the Chairman of the Computer Science Department at Boston College before founding Deitel & Associates, Inc., with his son, Paul J. Deitel. He is the author or co-author of several dozen books and multimedia packages. With translations published in numerous foreign languages, Dr. Deitel's texts have earned international recognition. Dr. Deitel has delivered professional seminars to major corporations, government organizations and various branches of the military.

Paul J. Deitel, CEO and Chief Technical Officer of Deitel & Associates, Inc., is a graduate of the Massachusetts Institute of Technology's Sloan School of Management, where he studied information technology. Through Deitel & Associates, Inc., he has delivered professional seminars to numerous industry and government clients and has lectured on C++ and Java for the Boston Chapter of the Association for Computing Machinery. He and his father, Dr. Harvey M. Deitel, are the world's best-selling Computer Science textbook authors.

Timothy R. Hoey is a senior at Harvard College pursuing a degree in Computer Science. His coursework includes graduate-level classes in computer graphics, artificial intelligence and network security. Tim gained previous .NET experience as a member of the Information Technology board at *The Harvard Crimson*.

Cheryl H. Yaeger, Director of Microsoft Software Publications with Deitel & Associates, Inc., is a graduate of Boston University with a degree in Computer Science. Cheryl has co-authored various Deitel & Associates, Inc. publications, including *Simply Visual Basic .NET 2003*, *Visual C++ .NET How to Program*, *C# How to Program*, *C# A Programmer's Introduction*, *C# for Experienced Programmers*, *Visual Basic .NET for Experienced Programmers* and *Simply Java™ Programming* and has contributed to several others.

About Deitel & Associates, Inc.

Deitel & Associates, Inc., is an internationally recognized corporate-training and content-creation organization specializing in computer programming languages education, object technology and Internet/World Wide Web software technology. Through its 28-year publishing partnership with Prentice Hall, Deitel & Associates, Inc. publishes leading-edge programming textbooks, professional books, interactive CD-ROM-based multimedia *Cyber Classrooms*, *Complete Training Courses* and course management systems e-content. To learn more about Deitel & Associates, Inc., its publications and its worldwide corporate on-site curriculum, visit:

```
www.deitel.com
```

Individuals wishing to purchase Deitel books, *Cyber Classrooms* and *Complete Training Courses* can do so through bookstores or online booksellers through:

```
www.deitel.com
www.prenhall.com/deitel
www.InformIT.com/deitel
```

Bulk orders by corporations and academic institutions should be placed directly with Prentice Hall. For ordering information, please visit:

```
www.prenhall.com/deitel
```

The Deitel® Buzz Online Newsletter

Our free e-mail newsletter includes commentary on industry trends and developments, links to articles and resources from our published books and upcoming publications, information on future publications, product-release schedules and more. For opt-in registration, visit www.deitel.com/newsletter/subscribe.html.

P lease follow the instructions in this section to ensure that your computer is set up properly before you begin this book.

Font and Naming Conventions

We use fonts to distinguish between Visual Studio .NET features (such as menu names and menu items) and other elements that appear in Visual Studio .NET. Our convention is to emphasize Visual Studio .NET features in a sans-serif bold **Helvetica** font (for example, **Properties** window) and to emphasize program text in a serif Lucida font (for example, `private bool x = true`).

Software Bundled with *Simply C#*

For the educational market only, this textbook is available in a "value pack" with the Microsoft® Visual C# Standard Edition version 2003 integrated development environment as a free supplement. The standard edition is fully functional and is shipped on 5 CDs. There is no time limit for using the software. [*Note:* If you are a professional using this publication, you will have to purchase the necessary software to build and run the applications in this textbook.]

Hardware and Software Requirements to Run Visual C# .NET 2003

To install and run Visual C# .NET 2003, Microsoft recommends that PCs have these minimum requirements:

- Pentium II 450 MHz processor (Pentium III 600 MHz processor recommended)

- Microsoft Windows® Server 2003, Windows XP Professional, Windows XP Home Edition, Windows 2000 Professional (with Service Pack 3 or later), or Windows 2000 Server (with Service Pack 3 or later) operating system

- 160 megabytes for a Windows Server 2003 or Windows XP Professional computer; 96 MB for a Windows XP Home Edition or Windows 2000 Professional computer; 192 MB for a Windows 2000 Server computer

- 500 megabytes of space on the system drive and 1.5 gigabytes of space on the installation drive (additional 1.9 gigabytes of available space required for optional MSDN Library documentation)

- CD-ROM or DVD-ROM drive

- Super VGA monitor (1024 x 768 or higher-resolution display) with 256 colors

- Mouse or other Microsoft-compatible pointing device

- **You must install Microsoft's Internet Information Services (IIS) before installing Visual Studio .NET.** Otherwise, the Web-based bookstore application in the case study cannot be created or executed. See Appendix G for detailed instructions on installing IIS. [*Note:* The Web-based bookstore application cannot be created or executed on Windows XP Home Edition.]

This book assumes that you are using Windows 2000 or Windows XP, plus Microsoft's Internet Information Services (IIS). Additional setup instructions for Web servers and other software is available on our Web site along with the examples. [*Note:* This is copyrighted material. Feel free to use it as you study, but you may not republish any portion of it in any form without explicit permission from Prentice Hall and the authors.]

Monitor Display Settings

Simply C# includes hundreds of screenshots of applications. Your monitor's display settings may need to be adjusted so that the screenshots in the book will match what you see on your computer screen as you develop each application. [*Note:* We refer to single-clicking with the left mouse button as **selecting**, or **clicking.** We refer to double-clicking with the left mouse button as **double clicking**.] Follow these steps to set your monitor display correctly:

1. Open the **Control Panel** and double click **Display**.
2. Click the **Settings** tab.
3. Click the **Advanced...** button.
4. In the **General** tab, make sure **Small Fonts** is selected; this should indicate that **96 dpi** is now the setting (if you already have this setting, you do not need to do anything else).
5. Click **Apply**.

If you choose to use different settings, the Size and Location values we provide for different GUI elements (such as Buttons and Labels) in each application might not appear correctly on your screen. If so, simply adjust the Size and Location values so that the GUI elements in your application appear similar to those in the screenshots in the book.

Theme Settings for Windows XP Users

If you are using Windows XP, we assume that your theme is set to Windows Classic Style. Follow these steps to set Windows XP to display the Windows Classic theme:

1. Open the **Control Panel**, then double click **Display**.
2. Click the **Themes** tab. Select **Windows Classic** from the **Theme:** dropdown list.
3. Click **OK** to save the settings.

Viewing File Extensions

Several screenshots in *Simply C#* display file names on a user's system, including the file extension of each file. Your settings may need to be adjusted to display file extensions. Follow these steps to set your machine to display file extensions:

1. In the **Start** menu, select **Programs** (**All Programs** in Windows XP), then **Accessories**, then **Windows Explorer**.
2. In the window that appears, select **Folder Options...** from the **Tools** menu.
3. In the dialog that appears, select the **View** tab.
4. In the **Advanced settings:** pane, uncheck the box to the left of the text **Hide file extensions for known file types** (Hide extensions for known

file types in Windows XP). [*Note*: If this item is already unchecked, no action needs to be taken.]

Copying and Organizing Files

All the examples for *Simply C#* are included on the CD-ROM that accompanies this textbook. Follow the steps in the following box to copy the examples directory from the CD-ROM to your hard drive. We suggest that you work from your hard drive rather than your CD drive for two reasons: You cannot save your applications to the book's CD (the CD is read-only), and files can be accessed faster from a hard drive than from a CD. The examples from the book (and our other publications) are also available for download from the following Web sites:

    www.deitel.com
    www.prenhall.com/deitel

Screenshots in the following box might differ slightly from what you see on your computer, depending on whether you are using Windows 2000 or Windows XP. We used Windows 2000 to prepare the screenshots for this book.

Copying the Book Examples from the CD-ROM

1. ***Locating the CD-ROM drive.*** Insert the CD that accompanies *Simply C#* into your computer's CD-ROM drive. The window displayed in Fig. 1 should appear. If the page appears, proceed to *Step 3* of this box. If the page does not appear, proceed to *Step 2*.

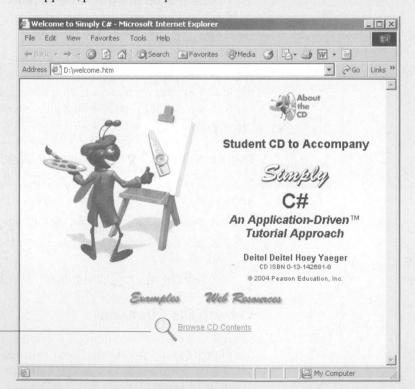

Click the **Browse CD Contents** link to access the CD's contents

Figure 1   Welcome page for *Simply C#* CD.

2. ***Opening the CD-ROM directory using My Computer.*** If the page shown in Fig. 1 does not appear, double click the **My Computer** icon on your desktop. In the **My Computer** window, double click your CD-ROM drive (Fig. 2) to access the CD's contents. Proceed to *Step 4*.

(cont.)

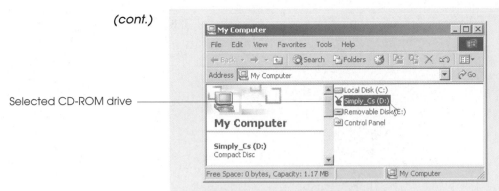

Figure 2   Locating the CD-ROM drive.

Selected CD-ROM drive

3. *Opening the CD-ROM directory.* If the page in Fig. 1 does appear, click the **Browse CD Contents** link to access the CD's contents.

4. *Copying the Examples directory.* Right click the Examples directory (Fig. 3), then select **Copy**. Next, go to **My Computer** and double click the C: drive. Select the **Edit** menu and select **Paste** to copy the directory and its contents from the CD to your C: drive.

    [*Note:* We save the examples to the C: drive and refer to this drive throughout the text. You may choose to save your files to a different drive based on your lab setup or personal preferences. If you are working in a computer lab, please see your instructor to confirm where the examples should be saved.]

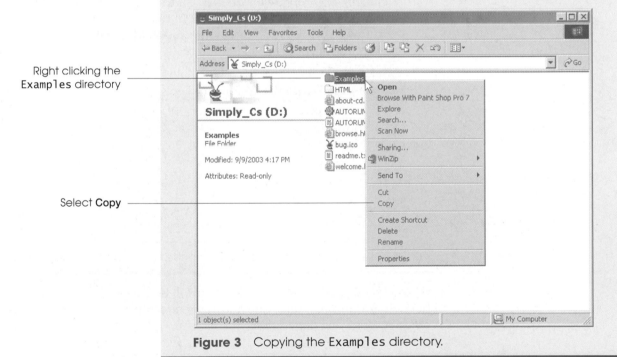

Right clicking the
Examples directory

Select **Copy**

Figure 3   Copying the Examples directory.

The book example files you copied onto your computer from the CD are read-only. To access and modify these files, you must change this property. In the following box, you change the read-only property so that you can run and modify the examples.

Changing the Read-Only Property of Files

1. *Opening the Properties dialog.* Right click the Examples directory and select **Properties** from the menu. The **Examples Properties** dialog appears (Fig. 4).

(cont.)

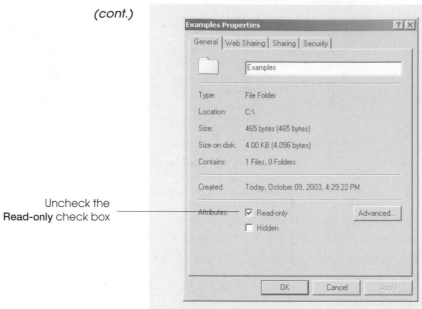

Uncheck the
Read-only check box

Figure 4   Removing the check in the **Read-only** check box.

2. *Changing the read-only property.* In the **Attributes** section of this dialog, click the box next to **Read-only** to remove the check mark. Click **Apply** to apply the changes.

3. *Changing the property for all files.* Clicking **Apply** will display the **Confirm Attribute Changes** window (Fig. 5). In this window, click the radio button next to **Apply changes to this folder, subfolders and files** and click **OK** to remove the read-only property for all the files and folders in the **Examples** directory.

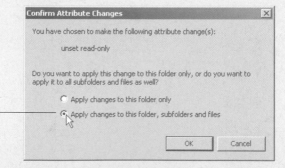

Click this radio button to
remove the read-only
property for all the files

Figure 5   Removing read-only for all the files in the **Examples** directory.

As you work through this book, you will be developing your own applications. In the following box, you create a working directory on your **C:** drive in which you will save all of your applications.

Creating a Working Directory

1. *Selecting the drive.* Double click the **My Computer** icon on your desktop to access a list of your computer drives (Fig. 6). Double click the **C:** drive. The contents of the **C:** drive are displayed.

2. *Creating a new directory.* Select the **File** menu and, under the **New** submenu, select **Folder** (Fig. 7). A new, empty directory appears in your **C:** directory (Fig. 8). [*Note:* From this point onward, we use the **>** character to indicate the selection of a menu command. For example, we use the notation **File > Open** to indicate the selection of the **Open** command from the **File** menu.]

(cont.)

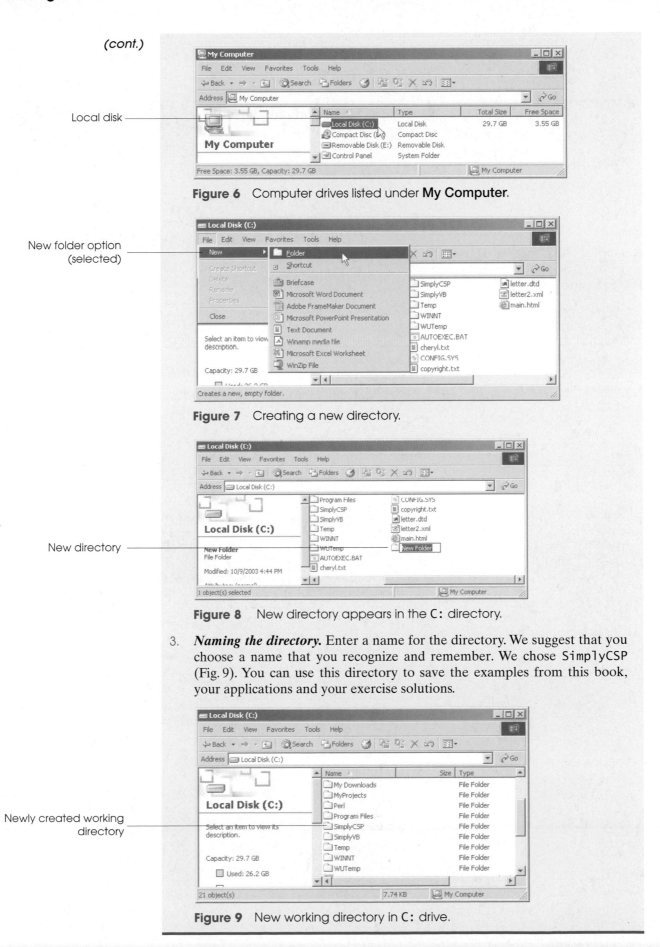

Local disk

Figure 6   Computer drives listed under **My Computer**.

New folder option
(selected)

Figure 7   Creating a new directory.

New directory

Figure 8   New directory appears in the **C:** directory.

3. ***Naming the directory.*** Enter a name for the directory. We suggest that you choose a name that you recognize and remember. We chose `SimplyCSP` (Fig. 9). You can use this directory to save the examples from this book, your applications and your exercise solutions.

Newly created working
directory

Figure 9   New working directory in **C:** drive.

Before you can run the applications in *Simply C#* or build your own applications, you must install Visual C# .NET. The following boxes will guide you through this process.

Installing the
Visual C# .NET
Prerequisites

1. ***Launching the installer.*** Insert the green disc labeled **Visual C# .NET Disc 1** into your CD-ROM drive. The installer should appear after a brief loading period (Fig. 10). If it does not appear, proceed to *Step 2* of this box. Otherwise, proceed to *Step 4*.

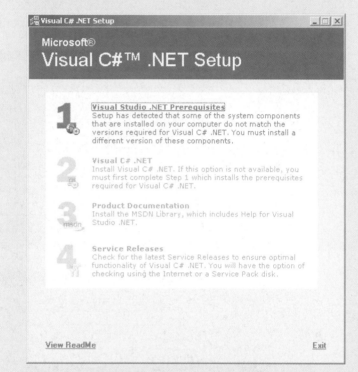

Figure 10   Setup menu for Visual C# .NET.

2. ***Opening the CD-ROM directory using My Computer.*** If the dialog shown in Fig. 10 does not appear, double click the **My Computer** icon on your desktop. In the **My Computer** window, double click your CD-ROM drive (Fig. 11) to access the CD's contents.

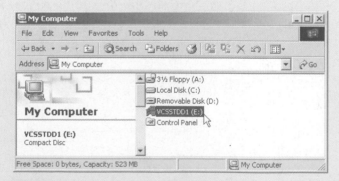

Figure 11   Opening the CD-ROM directory.

3. ***Running the installer.*** Double click the `setup.exe` icon in the **VCSSTDD1** window to launch the installer (Fig. 12). The dialog in Fig. 10 should appear after a brief loading period.

(cont.)

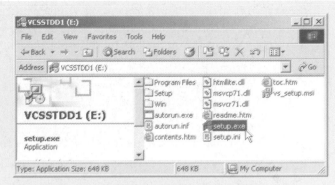

Figure 12 Running the installer.

4. ***Inserting the prerequisites disc.*** Before installing Visual C# .NET, the installer must update certain software components on your system. Click the **Visual Studio .NET Prerequisites** link to begin this process. The installer will prompt you to insert the maroon disc labeled **Visual Studio .NET Prerequisites** (Fig. 13). [*Note:* The CD-ROM drive letter shown might be different on your system.] Insert the disc, then click **OK** to continue.

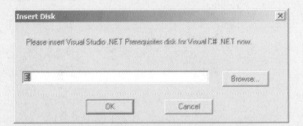

Figure 13 Inserting the prerequisites disc.

5. ***Accepting the license agreement.*** After a brief loading period, the **End User License Agreement** should appear (Fig. 14). Carefully read the license agreement. Click the **I agree** radio button, then click **Continue** to agree to the terms. [*Note:* If you choose not to accept the license agreement, the software will not install, and you will not be able to execute or create C# applications.]

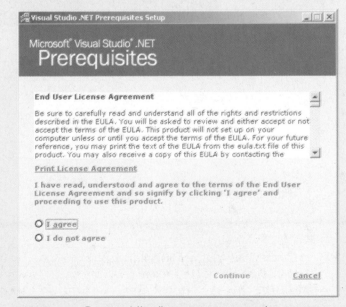

Figure 14 Prerequisites license agreement.

(cont.)   6. ***Installing the prerequisites.*** At this point, the installer will tell you which
           software components need to be updated (Fig. 15). [*Note:* The components
           in the list might be different on your system.] Click **Continue** to proceed
           with the installation.

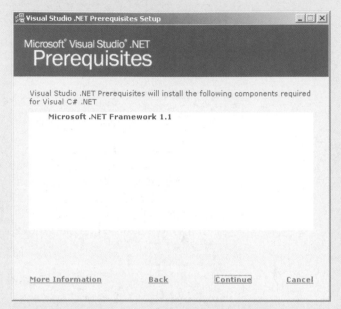

Figure 15   Listing the necessary prerequisites.

7. ***Automatic log on.*** Depending on which components require updates, your
    system might need to restart to complete the process. If you have access to
    your system's password, click the **Automatically log on** check box and enter
    your password twice (to ensure it is entered correctly) (Fig. 16). If you do
    not, you can continue installing Visual Studio .NET, but you might need to
    contact your system administrator if prompted for a password during the
    installation. Click **Install Now!** to continue.

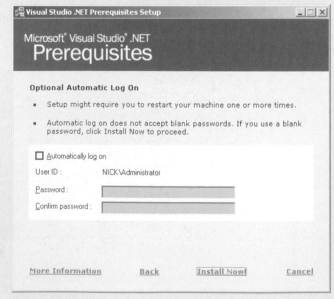

Figure 16   Automatic Log On dialog.

(cont.)   8. ***Finishing the installation.*** The installer will now update your system. When it has finished, click **Done** to return to the main menu (Fig. 17).

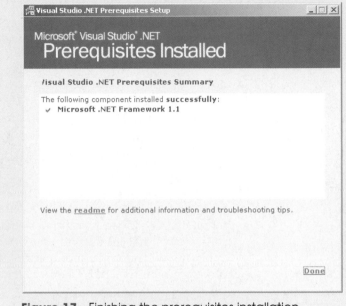

Figure 17   Finishing the prerequisites installation.

You are now ready to begin installing the main portion of the Visual C# .NET software package. The following box will guide you through the necessary steps to complete this part of the installation.

Installing Visual C# .NET   1. ***Beginning the installation.*** Click the **Visual C# .NET** link to begin installing Visual C# .NET (Fig. 18).

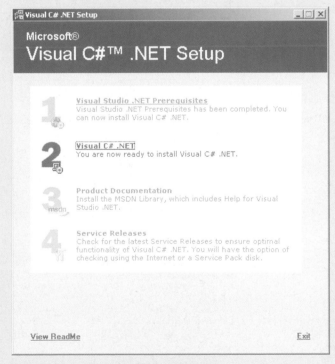

Figure 18   Visual C# .NET installation.

(cont.)   2. ***Inserting the Visual C# .NET disc.*** The installer will prompt you to insert the green disc labeled **Visual C# .NET Disc 1** (Fig. 19). [*Note:* The CD-ROM drive letter shown might be different on your system.] Insert the disc, then click **OK** to continue.

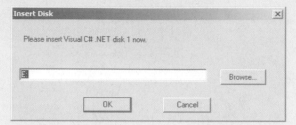

Figure 19   Inserting the Visual C# .NET disc.

3. ***Accepting the license agreement and entering the product key.*** Carefully read the license agreement. Click the **I agree** radio button to agree to the terms (Fig. 20). [*Note:* If you choose not to accept the license agreement, the software will not install, and you will not be able to execute or create C# applications.] Enter your product key (located in a yellow label on the back of your Visual C# .NET CD case) and full name into the boxes provided. Click **Continue** to proceed. [*Note:* If you make a mistake when entering your product key, an error message will be displayed, and you will be asked to correct your information (Fig. 21).]

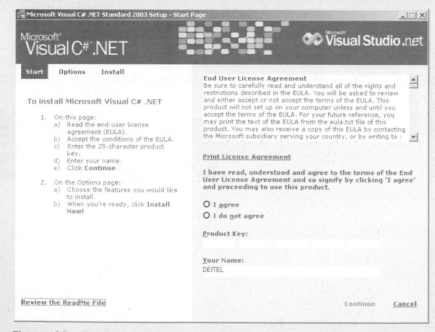

Figure 20   Product key dialog.

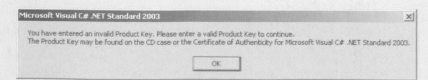

Figure 21   Invalid product key error message.

(cont.)   4. ***Selecting installation options.*** Select all the components of Visual C# .NET Standard Edition (Fig. 22). You can also change the directory where Visual C# .NET will be installed (though we recommend using the default location). After you have selected the desired options, click **Continue** to proceed. [*Note:* Sometimes the checkboxes will be checked, but will have a gray background. This indicates that only a portion of the feature selected will be installed. If this is the case, uncheck and recheck the box. Now, the background of the checkbox should be white, indicating that the entire feature will be installed.]

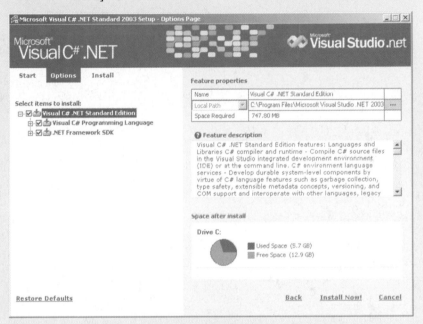

Figure 22   Installation options dialog.

5. ***Finishing the installation.*** The installer will now begin copying the files required by Visual C# .NET. Depending on your system, this process can take up to an hour. When it has finished, click **Done** to return to the main menu (Fig. 23).

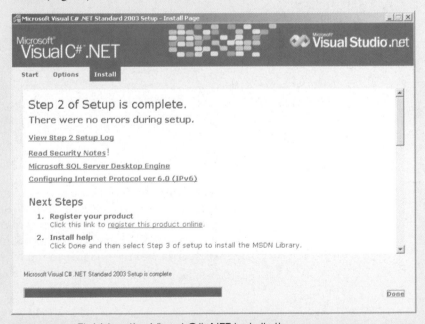

Figure 23   Finishing the Visual C# .NET installation.

Next, you will install the Microsoft Developer Network (MSDN) Library. The MSDN Library contains detailed articles and tutorials on a wide range of topics, including C# reference materials. The following box will guide you through this process.

Installing the MSDN Library

1. ***Beginning the installation.*** Click the **Product Documentation** link to begin installing the MSDN Library (Fig. 24).

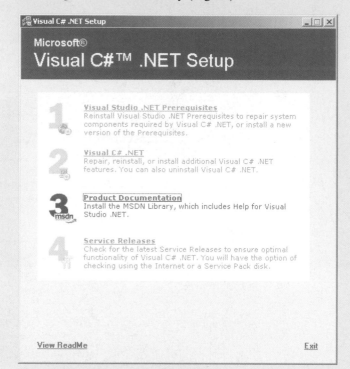

Figure 24   MSDN Library installation.

2. ***Inserting MSDN Library Disc 1.*** The installer will prompt you to insert the dark blue MSDN disc labeled **MSDN Library Disc 1** (Fig. 25). [*Note:* The CD-ROM drive letter shown might be different on your system.] Insert the disc, then click **OK** to continue.

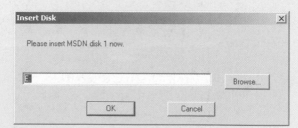

Figure 25   Inserting the first MSDN Library disc.

3. ***Accepting the license agreement.*** After a brief loading period, a dialog welcoming you to the **MSDN Library Setup Wizard** appears. Click **Next >** to proceed to the **License Agreement** dialog. Carefully read the license agreement. Click the **I accept the terms in the license agreement** radio button, then click **Next >** to agree to the terms (Fig. 26). [*Note:* If you choose not to accept the license agreement, the software will not install, and you will not be able to refer to the MSDN documentation for help using C#.]

(cont.)

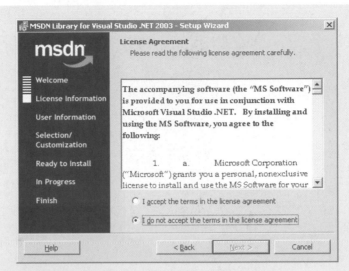

Figure 26   MSDN Library license agreement.

4. ***Entering your information.*** Enter your name and the name of your organization (if any) in the **Customer Information** dialog, then click **Next >** to continue (Fig. 27).

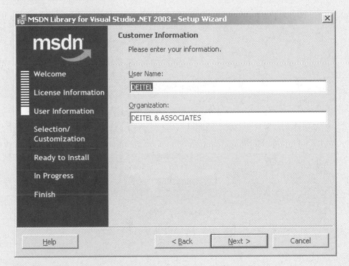

Figure 27   **Customer Information** dialog.

5. ***Selecting an installation type.*** Select an installation type from the list of choices. [*Note:* We recommend a **Full** installation if you have enough disk space, as you will be able to access all the MSDN articles without inserting the CD's in the future.] When you have made a selection, click **Next >** to continue (Fig. 28).

6. ***Selecting a destination directory.*** Select the directory where you would like to install the MSDN Library (we recommend the default location). Click **Next >** to continue (Fig. 29).

7. ***Finishing the installation.*** A dialog informing you that the MSDN Library is ready to install will appear. Click **Install** to begin the installation process. Depending on your system, this could take up to an hour to complete. During the installation, you will be prompted twice to insert the next disc in the series, much like Fig. 25. Insert the requested disc, then click **OK** to continue. When the installation is complete, click **Finish** to return to the main menu (Fig. 30).

(cont.)

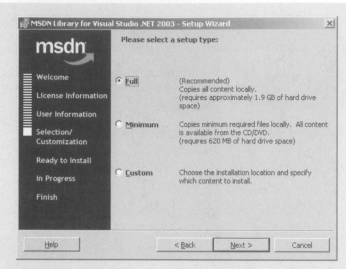

Figure 28 MSDN Library installation type.

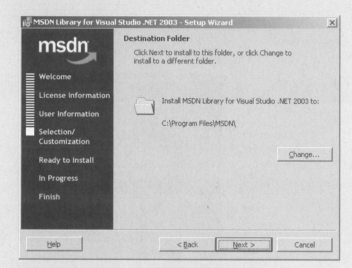

Figure 29 MSDN Library destination directory.

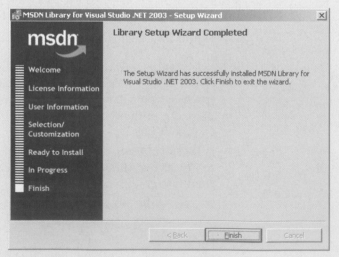

Figure 30 Finishing the MSDN Library installation.

The final step in installing Visual C# .NET is to check for any updates (also called service releases) that Microsoft has released. The following box will guide you through this process.

Checking for Service
Releases

1. **Beginning the update check.** Click the **Service Releases** link to begin the process of checking for updates to Visual C# .NET (Fig. 31).

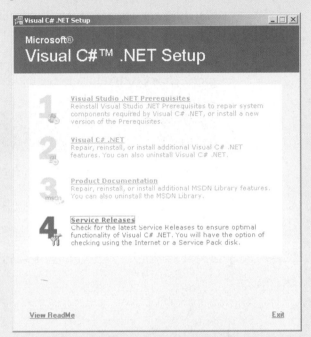

Figure 31   Update check for Visual C# .NET.

2. **Connecting to the Internet.** Make sure your system is connected to the Internet, then click the **Check for Service Releases on the Internet** link (Fig. 32). [*Note:* If you do not have an active Internet connection, you will receive an error repeatedly (Fig. 33), and you cannot complete this step. Click **Cancel** to return to the main menu.]

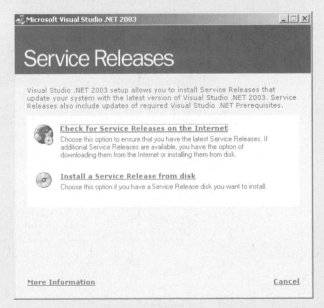

Figure 32   Connecting to the Internet to check for updates.

(cont.)

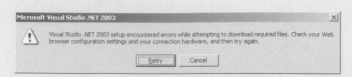

Figure 33   Error connecting to the Internet.

3. ***Finishing the update check.*** The installer will inform you if there are any updates to Visual C# .NET (Fig. 34). If there are, select each item from the list to install it. [*Note:* If you are unsure how to proceed, contact your system administrator.] Once you have applied all the updates (or if there were none), click **OK** to return to the main menu.

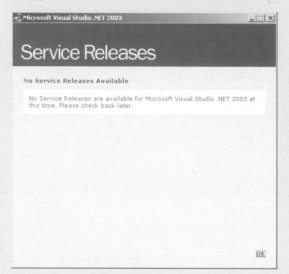

Figure 34   Finishing the update check.

4. ***Finishing the installation.*** The main menu should now indicate that you have completed *Steps 1–4*. Click **Exit** to close the installer (Fig. 35). If prompted to check for Windows security updates, click **No** unless you are already comfortable with this procedure and authorized to do so on your system (Fig. 36).

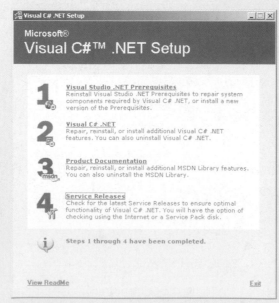

Figure 35   Finishing the installation.

(cont.)

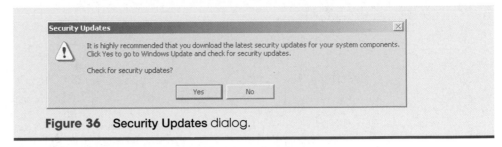

Figure 36 **Security Updates** dialog.

You are now ready to begin your C# studies with *Simply C#*. We hope you enjoy the book! You can reach us easily at deitel@deitel.com.

Objectives

In this tutorial, you will learn to:
- Identify the characteristics of low-level and high-level programming languages.
- Apply the basics of object-oriented programming.
- Run your first C# application.
- Locate additional .NET and C# information.

Outline

Drawing Application

Introducing Computers, the Internet and C#

Welcome to C#! This book uses a straightforward, step-by-step tutorial approach to teach the fundamentals of C# programming. We hope that you will be informed and entertained as you learn the basics of C# programming.

The core of the book teaches C# using our **APPLICATION-DRIVEN approach**, which provides step-by-step instructions for creating and interacting with useful, real-world computer applications. This approach, combined with our signature **LIVE-CODE approach**, which shows dozens of complete, working C# applications and depicts their outputs, will teach you the basic skills that underlie good programming. You will study bonus tutorials on graphics, multimedia and Web programming. All of this book's examples are available on the CD-ROM that accompanies the book and on our Web site, www.deitel.com.

Computer use is increasing in almost every field. In an era of rising costs, computing costs are actually decreasing dramatically because of rapid developments in both hardware and software technology. Silicon chip technology has made computing so economical that hundreds of millions of general-purpose computers are in use worldwide, helping people in business, industry, government and their personal lives.

Reading this text will start you on a challenging and rewarding educational path. If you'd like to communicate with us, send an e-mail to deitel@deitel.com, and we will respond promptly. For more information, visit our Web sites at www.deitel.com, www.prenhall.com/deitel and www.InformIT.com/deitel.

1.1 What Is a Computer?

A **computer** is a device capable of performing computations and making logical decisions at speeds millions and even billions of times faster than humans can. For example, many of today's personal computers can perform billions of additions per second. A person operating a desk calculator might require a lifetime to complete the same number of calculations that a powerful personal computer can perform in one second. Today's fastest supercomputers can perform hundreds of billions of additions per second. Trillion-instructions-per-second computers are already functioning in research laboratories!

Computers process data, or information, using sets of instructions called **computer programs**. These programs guide computers through orderly sets of actions that are specified by people known as **computer programmers**. In this book, we generally use the term "application" instead of the term "program." An application is a program that does something particularly useful. Each tutorial in this book, on average, presents five applications—one in the main example and four in the exercises—for a total of more than 100 applications in the book.

A computer is composed of various devices (such as the keyboard, screen, mouse, hard drive, memory, CD-ROM drive and processing units) known as **hardware**. The programs that run on a computer are referred to as **software**. Object-oriented programming (which models real-world objects with software counterparts), available in C# and other programming languages, is a significant breakthrough that can greatly enhance programmers' productivity.

SELF-REVIEW
1. Computers process data, using sets of instructions called _____.
   a) hardware   b) computer programs
   c) processing units   d) programmers

2. The devices that make up a computer are called _____.
   a) hardware   b) software
   c) programs   d) programmers

Answers: 1) b. 2) a.

1.2 Computer Organization

Computers can be thought of as being divided into six units:

1. **Input unit**. This "receiving" section of the computer obtains information (data and computer programs) from various input devices, such as the keyboard and the mouse. Other input devices include microphones (for recording speech to the computer), scanners (for scanning images) and digital cameras (for taking photographs and making videos).

2. **Output unit.** This "shipping" section of the computer takes information that the computer has processed and places it on various output devices, making the information available for use outside the computer. Output can be displayed on screens, played on audio/video devices and printed on paper, among other things. Output also can be used to control other devices, such as robots used in manufacturing.

3. **Memory unit.** This rapid-access, relatively low-capacity "warehouse" section of the computer stores data temporarily while an application is running. The memory unit retains information that has been entered through input devices, so such information is immediately available for processing. To be executed, computer programs must be in memory. The memory unit also retains processed information until the information can be sent to output devices on which it is made available to users. Often, the memory unit is called either memory or primary memory. Random access memory (RAM) is an example of primary memory. Primary memory is usually **volatile**, which means that it is erased when the machine is powered off.

4. **Arithmetic and logic unit (ALU).** The ALU is the "manufacturing" section of the computer. It performs calculations such as addition, subtraction, multiplication and division. It also makes decisions, allowing the computer to perform tasks such as determining whether two items stored in memory are equal.

5. **Central processing unit (CPU).** The CPU serves as the "administrative" section of the computer, supervising the operation of the other sections. The CPU alerts the input unit when information should be read into the memory unit, instructs the ALU when to use information from the memory unit in calculations and tells the output unit when to send information from the memory unit to certain output devices.

6. **Secondary storage unit.** This unit is the long-term, high-capacity "warehousing" section of the computer. Secondary storage devices, such as hard drives, CD-ROM drives, zip drives and floppy disk drives, normally hold programs or data that other units are not actively using; the computer then can retrieve this information when it is needed—hours, days, months or even years later. Information in secondary storage takes much longer to access than information in primary memory. However, secondary storage is much less expensive than primary memory. Secondary storage is **nonvolatile**, retaining information even when the computer is powered off.

SELF-REVIEW   1. The _____ is responsible for performing calculations and contains decision-making mechanisms.

   a) central processing unit   b) memory unit
   c) arithmetic and logic unit   d) output unit

2. Information stored in _____ is normally erased when the computer is turned off.

   a) primary memory   b) secondary storage
   c) CD-ROM drives   d) hard drives

Answers: 1) c. 2) a.

1.3 Machine Languages, Assembly Languages and High-Level Languages

Programmers write instructions in various programming languages, some of which are directly understandable by computers and others of which require intermediate translation steps. Although hundreds of computer languages are in use today, the diverse offerings can be divided into three general types:

1. Machine languages

2. Assembly languages

3. High-level languages

A computer can directly understand only its own **machine language**. As the "natural language" of a particular computer, machine language is defined by the computer's hardware design. Machine languages generally consist of streams of numbers (ultimately reduced to 1s and 0s) that instruct computers how to perform their most elementary operations. Machine languages are **machine dependent**, which means that a particular machine language can be used on only one type of computer. The following section of a machine-language program, which adds *overtime pay* to *base pay* and stores the result in *gross pay*, demonstrates the incomprehensibility of machine language to humans:

```
+1300042774
+1400593419
+1200274027
```

As the popularity of computers increased, machine-language programming proved to be slow and error prone. Instead of using strings of numbers that computers could directly understand, programmers began using English-like abbreviations to represent the basic operations of the computer. These abbreviations formed the basis of **assembly languages**. Translator programs called **assemblers** convert assembly-language programs to machine language at computer speeds. The following section of an assembly-language program also adds *overtime pay* to *base pay* and stores the result in *gross pay*, but presents the steps somewhat more clearly to human readers than the machine-language example:

```
LOAD    BASEPAY
ADD     OVERPAY
STORE   GROSSPAY
```

This assembly-language code is clearer to humans, but computers cannot understand it until it is translated into machine language by an assembler program.

Although the speed at which programmers could write programs increased rapidly with the creation of assembly languages, these languages still require many instructions to accomplish even the simplest tasks. To speed up the programming process, **high-level languages**, in which single program statements accomplish more substantial tasks, were developed. Translator programs called **compilers** convert high-level-language programs into machine language. High-level languages enable programmers to write instructions that look almost like everyday English and that contain common mathematical notations. For example, a payroll application written in a high-level language might contain a statement such as

```
grossPay = basePay + overTimePay;
```

From these examples, it is clear why programmers prefer high-level languages to either machine languages or assembly languages. In the next section, you will learn about one such high-level language, Microsoft's C#.

SELF-REVIEW

1. The only programming language that a computer can directly understand is its own _____.

   a) high-level language   b) assembly language
   c) machine language   d) English

2. Programs that translate high-level language programs into machine language are called _____.

   a) assemblers   b) compilers
   c) programmers   d) converters

Answers: 1) c. 2) b.

1.4 C, C++, Visual Basic .NET and Java

Although hundreds of high-level languages have been developed, only a few have achieved broad acceptance. IBM Corporation developed Fortran (*fo*rmula *tran*slator) in the mid-1950s to create scientific and engineering applications that require complex mathematical computations. Fortran is still widely used.

COBOL (*Common Business Oriented Language*) was developed in the late 1950s by a group of computer manufacturers in conjunction with government and industrial computer users. COBOL is used primarily for business applications that require the manipulation of large amounts of data. A considerable portion of today's business software is still programmed in COBOL.

The C language, which Dennis Ritchie developed at Bell Laboratories in the early 1970s, gained widespread recognition as the development language of the UNIX operating system. C++, an extension of C, was developed by Bjarne Stroustrup in the early 1980s at Bell Laboratories. Many of today's major operating systems are written in C or C++. C++ provides capabilities for **object-oriented programming (OOP)**. **Objects** are reusable software components that model items in the real world. Object-oriented programs are often easier to understand, correct and modify than programs developed with previous techniques.

Developing Microsoft Windows-based applications in languages such as C and C++, however, proved to be a difficult and cumbersome process. When Bill Gates founded Microsoft Corporation in the 1970s, he implemented BASIC on several early personal computers. BASIC (Beginner's All-Purpose Symbolic Instruction Code) was developed in the mid-1960s by Professors John Kemeny and Thomas Kurtz of Dartmouth College as a language for writing simple programs quickly and easily. BASIC's primary purpose was to teach novices fundamental programming techniques. In the late 1980s and the early 1990s, Microsoft developed the Microsoft Windows **graphical user interface (GUI)**—the visual part of the application with which users interact. With the creation of the Windows GUI, the natural evolution of BASIC was to Visual Basic, introduced by Microsoft in 1991 to make programming Windows applications easier.

Around the same time that Visual Basic was being developed, many organizations, including Sun Microsystems, predicted that intelligent consumer electronic devices would be the next major market in which microprocessors—the chips that make computers work—would have a profound impact. But the marketplace for intelligent consumer electronic devices did not develop as quickly as Sun had anticipated. By sheer good fortune, the World Wide Web exploded in popularity in 1993, and Sun saw an immediate potential for using its new Java programming language to create dynamic content (animated and interactive content) for Web pages. Sun announced Java to the public in 1995, grabbing the immediate attention of the business community because of the widespread interest in the Web. Developers now use Java to create Web pages with dynamic content, to build large-scale enterprise applications, to enhance the functionality of Web servers (the computers that provide the content that is distributed to your Web browser when you browse Web sites), to provide applications for consumer devices (for example, cell phones, pagers and PDAs) and for many other purposes.

The latest version of Visual Basic, called Visual Basic .NET, is designed for Microsoft's new programming platform, **.NET**. Microsoft introduced its .NET (pronounced "dot-net") strategy in 2000. The .NET platform—the set of software components that enables .NET programs to run—allows Web-based applications to be distributed to a variety of devices (such as cell phones) as well as to desktop computers. The .NET platform offers a new programming model that allows programs created in different programming languages to communicate with each other, whether they reside on the same or on different computers connected to a network such as the Internet.

SELF-REVIEW
1. _____ is an extension of C and offers object-oriented capabilities.

    a) Visual Basic   b) C++

    c) assembly language   d) Windows

2. Visual Basic evolved from _____, which was created as a language for writing simple programs quickly and easily.

    a) .NET   b) Windows

    c) Visual Basic .NET   d) BASIC

3. _____, developed in the late 1950s, is still used to produce a considerable portion of today's business software.

    a) COBOL   b) Fortran

    c) Java   d) C

4. _____, developed in the 1950s, is still used to create scientific and engineering applications that require complex mathematical computations.

    a) Visual Basic   b) Fortran

    c) COBOL   d) C#

Answers: 1) b. 2) d. 3) a. 4) b.

1.5 C#

Microsoft announced C# (pronounced "C-Sharp") at the same time the company announced its .NET strategy. The **C# programming language** (sometimes referred to as **Visual C#**) was designed specifically for the .NET platform. C# is object oriented and has access to .NET's powerful library of prebuilt components, enabling programmers to develop applications quickly.

C# is an object-oriented, event-driven (OOED) visual programming language, in which programs are created with the use of a software tool called an **integrated development environment (IDE)**. With Microsoft's **Visual Studio .NET** IDE, a programmer can write, run, test and debug C# programs quickly and conveniently.

C# is fully object oriented—you will encounter a rich treatment of object technology throughout the book. C# is **event-driven**—you will write programs that respond to user-initiated events such as mouse clicks and keystrokes. It is a **visual programming** language—instead of writing detailed program statements to build your applications, you will use Visual Studio .NET's graphical user interface in which you conveniently drag and drop predefined objects into place and label and resize them. Visual Studio .NET will write much of the program for you.

C# has roots in C, C++ and Java, adapting the best features of each. Visual Basic .NET, Java and C# have comparable capabilities, so learning C# may create many opportunities for you.

SELF-REVIEW

1. Microsoft specifically designed _____ in 2000 for its .NET platform.

    a) Windows   b) BASIC

    c) Visual Basic   d) C#

2. Microsoft's _____ allows programmers to write, run, test and debug C# programs quickly and efficiently.

    a) .NET   b) Windows

    c) Visual Studio .NET   d) Visual Basic .NET

Answers: 1) d. 2) c.

1.6 Structured Programming

During the 1960s, software-development efforts often ran behind schedule, costs greatly exceeded budgets and the finished products were unreliable. People began to realize that software development was a far more complex activity than they had imagined. Research activity intended to address these issues resulted in the evolution of **structured programming**—a disciplined approach to the creation of programs that are clear, correct and easy to modify.

One of the results of this research was the development of the Pascal programming language in 1971. Pascal, named after the 17th-century mathematician and philosopher Blaise Pascal, was designed for teaching structured programming and rapidly became the preferred introductory programming language in most colleges. Unfortunately, the language lacked many features needed to make it useful in commercial, industrial and government applications. By contrast, C, which also arose from research on structured programming, did not have the limitations of Pascal, and professional programmers quickly adopted it.

The Ada programming language was developed under the sponsorship of the U.S. Department of Defense (DOD) during the 1970s and early 1980s. The language was named after Lady Ada Lovelace, daughter of the poet Lord Byron. Lady Lovelace is generally credited as being the world's first computer programmer because of an application she wrote in the early 1800s for the Analytical Engine mechanical computing device designed by Charles Babbage.

SELF-REVIEW

1. During the 1960s and 1970s, research to address such software-development problems as running behind schedule, exceeding budgets and creating unreliable products led to the evolution of _____.

    a) multithreading   b) object-oriented programming

    c) Ada   d) structured programming

2. _____ was designed to teach structured programming in academic environments.

    a) C++   b) C

    c) Java   d) Pascal

Answers: 1) d. 2) d.

1.7 Key Software Trend: Object Technology

As the benefits of structured programming were realized in the 1970s, improved software technology began to appear. However, it was not until object-oriented programming became widely used in the 1980s and 1990s that software developers finally felt they had the necessary tools to improve the software development process dramatically.

What are objects, and why are they special? **Object technology** is a packaging scheme for creating meaningful software units. There are date objects, time objects, paycheck objects, invoice objects, automobile objects, people objects, audio objects, video objects, file objects, record objects and so on. In fact, almost any noun can be reasonably represented as a software object. Objects have **properties** (also called **attributes**), such as color, size and weight; and perform actions (also called behaviors or methods), such as moving, sleeping or drawing. Objects can also have events that they can respond to, like a mouse-click. **Classes** represent groups of related objects. For example, all cars belong to the "car" class, even though individual cars vary in make, model, color and options packages. A class specifies the general format of its objects, and the properties and actions available to an object depend on its class. An object is related to its class in much the same way as a building is related to its blueprint.

Before object-oriented languages appeared, **procedural programming languages** (such as Fortran, Pascal, BASIC and C) focused on actions (verbs) rather than things or objects (nouns). This made programming a bit awkward. However, using today's popular object-oriented languages, such as C#, C++, Java and Visual Basic .NET, programmers can program in an object-oriented manner that more naturally reflects the way in which they perceive the world. This has resulted in significant productivity gains.

With object technology, properly designed classes can be reused on future projects. Using libraries of classes can greatly reduce the amount of effort required to implement new systems. Some organizations report that such software reusability is not, in fact, the key benefit that they get from object-oriented programming. Rather, they indicate that object-oriented programming tends to produce software that is more understandable because it is better organized and has fewer maintenance requirements.

Object orientation allows the programmer to focus on the "big picture." Instead of worrying about the minute details of how reusable objects are implemented, the programmer can focus on the behaviors and interactions of objects. A road map that showed every tree, house and driveway would be difficult, if not impossible, to read. When such details are removed and only the essential information (roads) remains, the map becomes easier to understand. In the same way, an application that is divided into objects is easy to understand, modify and update because it hides much of the detail. It is clear that object-oriented programming will be the key programming methodology for at least the next decade.

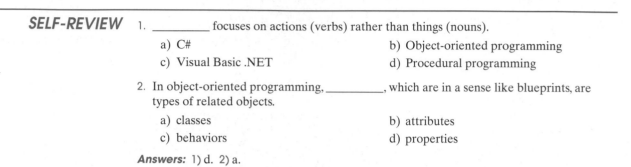

SELF-REVIEW

1. _____ focuses on actions (verbs) rather than things (nouns).

   a) C#
                                    b) Object-oriented programming

   c) Visual Basic .NET
                         d) Procedural programming

2. In object-oriented programming, _____, which are in a sense like blueprints, are types of related objects.

   a) classes
                                   b) attributes

   c) behaviors
                              d) properties

Answers: 1) d. 2) a.

1.8 The Internet and the World Wide Web

In the late 1960s, ARPA—the Advanced Research Projects Agency of the Department of Defense—rolled out the blueprints for networking the main computer systems of approximately a dozen ARPA-funded universities and research institutions. The computers were to be connected with communications lines operating at a then-stunning 56 Kbps (1 Kbps is equal to 1,024 bits per second), at a time when most people (of the few who even had networking access) were connecting over telephone lines to computers at a rate of 110 bits per second. Academic research was about to take a giant leap forward. ARPA proceeded to implement what quickly became called the ARPAnet, the grandparent of today's **Internet**.

Things worked out differently from the original plan. Although the ARPAnet enabled researchers to network their computers, its main benefit proved to be the capability for quick and easy communication via what came to be known as electronic mail (e-mail). This is true even on today's Internet, with e-mail, instant messaging and file transfer allowing hundreds of millions of people worldwide to communicate with each other.

The protocol (in other words, the set of rules) for communicating over the ARPAnet became known as the Transmission Control Protocol (TCP). TCP ensured that messages, consisting of pieces called "packets," were properly routed from sender to receiver and that those messages arrived intact.

In parallel with the early evolution of the Internet, organizations worldwide were implementing their own networks for both intraorganization (that is, within an organization) and interorganization (that is, between organizations) communication. A huge variety of networking hardware and software appeared. One challenge was to enable these different networks to communicate with each other. ARPA accomplished this by developing the Internet Protocol (IP), which created a true "network of networks," the current architecture of the Internet. The combined set of protocols is now commonly called **TCP/IP**.

Businesses rapidly realized that, by using the Internet, they could improve their operations and offer new and better services to their clients. Companies started spending large amounts of money to develop and enhance their Internet presence. This generated fierce competition among communications carriers and hardware and software suppliers to meet the increased infrastructure demand. As a result, **bandwidth**—the information-carrying capacity of communications lines—on the Internet has increased tremendously, while hardware costs have plummeted.

The **World Wide Web (WWW)** is a collection of hardware and software associated with the Internet that allows computer users to locate and view multimedia-based documents (documents with various combinations of text, graphics, animations, audios and videos) on almost any subject. Even though the Internet was developed more than three decades ago, the introduction of the World Wide Web was a relatively recent event. In 1989, Tim Berners-Lee of CERN (the European Organization for Nuclear Research) began to develop a technology for sharing information via "hyperlinked" text documents. Berners-Lee called his invention the **HyperText Markup Language (HTML)**. He also wrote communication protocols to form the backbone of his new hypertext information system, which he referred to as the World Wide Web.

In October 1994, Berners-Lee founded an organization, called the **World Wide Web Consortium** (**W3C**, www.w3.org), devoted to developing technologies for the World Wide Web. One of the W3C's primary goals is to make the Web universally accessible—regardless of a person's disabilities, language or culture.

The Internet and the World Wide Web will surely be listed among the most important creations of humankind. In the past, most computer applications ran on "stand-alone" computers (computers that were not connected to one another). Today's applications can be written with the aim of communicating among the world's hundreds of millions of computers. This is, in fact, as you will see, the focus of Microsoft's .NET strategy. The Internet and World Wide Web make information instantly and conveniently accessible to large numbers of people. They enable even individuals and small businesses to achieve worldwide exposure. They are profoundly changing the way we do business and conduct our personal lives. To highlight the importance of Internet and Web programming, we include four tutorials at the end of the book in which you will actually build and run a Web-based bookstore application.

SELF-REVIEW

1. Today's Internet evolved from the _____, which was a Department of Defense project.

   a) ARPAnet b) HTML
   c) CERN d) WWW

2. The combined set of protocols for communicating over the Internet is now commonly called _____.

   a) HTML b) TCP/IP
   c) ARPA d) TCP

Answers: 1) a. 2) b.

1.9 Introduction to Microsoft .NET

In June 2000, Microsoft announced its .NET initiative, a broad new vision for using the Internet and the Web in the development, engineering, distribution and use of software. Rather than forcing developers to use a single programming language, the .NET initiative permits developers to create .NET applications in any .NET-compatible language (C#, Visual C++ .NET, Visual Basic .NET and others). Part of the initiative includes Microsoft's **Active Server Pages (ASP) .NET** technology, which allows programmers to create applications for the Web. You will be introduced to ASP .NET as you build the Web-based bookstore application later in the book.

The .NET strategy extends the idea of **software reuse** to the Internet, by allowing programmers to concentrate on their specialties without having to implement every component of every application. Instead, companies can buy **Web services**, which are Web-based programs that organizations can incorporate into their systems to speed the Web-application-development process. Visual programming (which you will learn throughout this book) has become popular, because it enables programmers to create applications easily, using such prepackaged graphical components, such as buttons, textboxes and scrollbars, that are popular today in Windows applications.

The Microsoft **.NET Framework** is at the heart of the .NET strategy. This framework executes applications and Web services, contains a class library (called the **Framework Class Library** or **FCL**) and provides many other programming capabilities that you use to build C# applications. In this book, you will learn how to develop .NET software with C#. Steve Ballmer, Microsoft's CEO, stated in May 2001 that Microsoft was "betting the company" on .NET. Such a dramatic commitment surely indicates a bright future for C# programmers.

SELF-REVIEW

1. _____ is a technology specifically designed for the .NET platform and intended for programmers to create Web-based applications.

   a) Visual Basic   b) C++
   c) HTML   d) Active Server Pages .NET

2. _____ are existing Web-based programs that can be incorporated into other applications.

   a) Web services   b) Wire services
   c) Attributes   d) Properties

3. Programmers use the _____, a part of the .NET Framework, to build C# applications.

   a) C# Library (CSL)   b) Framework Class Library (FCL)
   c) Microsoft Class Library (MCL)   d) C# Framework (CSF)

Answers: 1) d. 2) a. 3) b.

1.10 Test-Driving the C# Drawing Application

In this section, you will be introduced to a C# application, using our Application-Driven approach. In each tutorial, you are given a chance to "test-drive" the application. You actually run and interact with the completed application. Then, you will learn the C# features you need to build the application. Finally, you will "put it all together" and actually create your own working version of the application. You begin here in Tutorial 1 simply by running an application that allows the user to draw with "brushes" of four different colors and three different sizes. You will actually build a similar application in Tutorial 21.

The following box, *Test-Driving the **Drawing** Application*, will show you how the application allows the user to draw with different brush styles. The elements and functionality you see in this application are typical of what you will learn to program in this text. [*Note*: We use fonts to distinguish between IDE features (such as menu names and menu items) and other elements that appear in the IDE. Our convention is to emphasize IDE features (such as the **File** menu) in a semibold **sans-serif Helvetica** font and to emphasize other elements, such as file names (for example, Form1.cs), in a sans-serif Lucida font. As you have already noticed, each term that is being defined is set in heavy bold.]

Test-Driving the Drawing Application

1. ***Checking your setup.*** Confirm that you have set up your computer properly by reading the *For Students and Instructors: Important Information before You Begin* section.

2. ***Locating the application directory.*** Open a Windows Explorer window and navigate to the C:\Examples\Tutorial01 directory (Fig. 1.1).

(cont.)

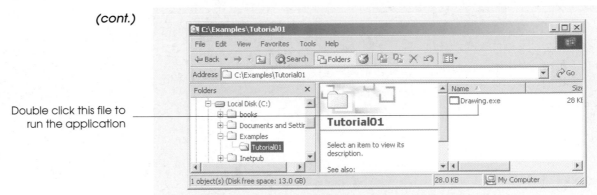

Double click this file to
run the application

Figure 1.1   Contents of `C:\Examples\Tutorial01`.

3. ***Running the Drawing application.*** Now that you are in that directory, double click the file name `Drawing.exe` to run the application (Fig. 1.2).

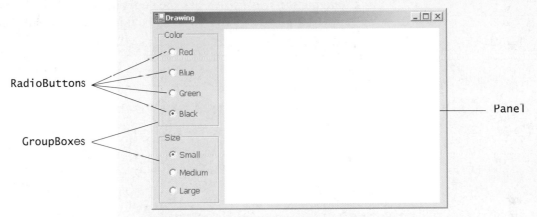

RadioButtons

GroupBoxes

Panel

Figure 1.2   C# **Drawing** application.

In Fig. 1.2, several graphical elements—called **controls**—are labelled. The controls include `GroupBoxes`, `RadioButtons` and a `Panel` (these controls will be discussed in depth later in the text). The application allows you to draw with a black, blue, green or red brush of small, medium or large size. You will explore these options in this test-drive.

Because you can use existing controls—which are objects—you can get powerful applications running in C# much faster than if you had to write all the code yourself. In this text, you will learn how to use many preexisting controls, as well as how to write your own program code to customize your applications.

The brush's properties, selected in the `RadioButtons` labelled **Black** and **Small**, are default settings, which are the initial settings you see when you first run the application. Programmers include default settings to provide visual cues for users to choose their own settings. You will now choose your own settings.

4. ***Changing the brush color.*** Click the `RadioButton` labelled **Red** to change the color of the brush. Click on the `Panel`, and drag the mouse to draw with the brush. Draw flower petals as shown in Fig. 1.3. Then, click the `RadioButton` labelled **Green** to change the color of the brush once again.

(cont.)

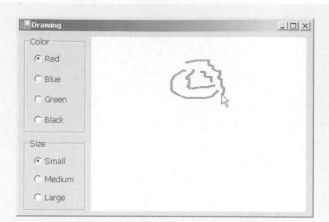

Figure 1.3   Drawing with a new brush color.

5. ***Changing the brush size.*** Click the RadioButton labelled **Large** to change the size of the brush. Draw grass and a flower stem as shown in Fig. 1.4.

Figure 1.4   Drawing with a new brush size.

6. ***Finishing the drawing.*** Click the RadioButton labelled **Blue**. Then, click the RadioButton labelled **Medium**. Draw raindrops as shown in Fig. 1.5 to complete the drawing.

Close box

Figure 1.5   Finishing the drawing.

7. ***Closing the application.*** Close your running application by clicking its **close box**, ⊠ (Fig. 1.5).

1.11 Internet and Web Resources

The Internet and Web are extraordinary resources. This section includes links to interesting and informative Web sites. Hot links to all these sites are included on the CD and at www.deitel.com to save you time. Reference sections like this one are included throughout the book where appropriate.

www.deitel.com
Visit this site for updates, corrections and additional resources for Deitel & Associates publications, including *Simply C#* errata, Frequently Asked Questions (FAQs), hot links, code downloads and PowerPoint® slide downloads.

www.prenhall.com/deitel
The Deitel & Associates page on the Prentice Hall Web site contains information about our publications, code downloads and PowerPoint slides for this book.

www.softlord.com/comp
Visit this site to learn more about the history of computers.

www.elsop.com/wrc/h_comput.htm
This site presents the history of computing. It includes content about famous people in the computer field, the evolution of programming languages and the development of operating systems.

www.w3.org/History.html
Visit this site for the history of the World Wide Web.

www.netvalley.com/intval.html
This site presents the history of the Internet.

msdn.microsoft.com/vcsharp
This is Microsoft's C# Web site.

www.microsoft.com/net
This is Microsoft's .NET Web site.

www.GotDotNet.com
This site has abundant .NET resources.

1.12 Wrap-Up

In this tutorial, you learned about how computers are organized. You studied the levels of programming languages and which kinds of languages, including C#, require translators. You became familiar with some of the most popular programming languages. You learned the importance of structured programming and object-oriented programming. You studied a brief history of the Internet and the World Wide Web, were introduced to Microsoft's .NET initiative and learned some key aspects of .NET.

You took a working C# application out for a "test-drive." In the process of doing this, you learned that .NET provides lots of prebuilt controls that perform useful functions and that, by familiarizing yourself with the capabilities of these controls, you can develop powerful applications much faster than if you tried to build them completely yourself. You were encouraged to explore several Web sites with additional information on this book, computers, the Internet, the Web, .NET and C#.

In the next tutorial, you will learn about the Visual Studio .NET Integrated Development Environment (IDE). This will help you prepare to create your own C# applications. You will continue to learn with our Application-Driven approach, in which you will see all C# features in useful applications and in which you will

1. Study the user requirements for an application.

2. Test-drive a working version of the application.

3. Learn the technologies you'll need to build the application yourself.

4. Build your own version of the application.

As you work through the book, if you have any questions about C#, send an e-mail to `deitel@deitel.com`, and we will respond promptly. We sincerely hope you enjoy learning the latest version of Microsoft's powerful C# language with *Simply C#*. Good luck!

KEY TERMS

Active Server Pages .NET (ASP .NET)—.NET software that helps programmers create applications for the Web.

APPLICATION-DRIVEN approach—Provides step-by-step instructions for creating and interacting with useful, real-world computer applications.

arithmetic and logic unit (ALU)—The "manufacturing" section of the computer that performs calculations such as addition, subtraction, multiplication and division. It also makes decisions, allowing the computer to perform such tasks as determining whether two items stored in memory are equal.

assembler—Translator programs that convert assembly-language programs to machine language at computer speeds.

assembly language—A type of programming language that uses English-like abbreviations to represent the fundamental operations on the computer. Assembly language is easier for a human to understand than machine language, but harder to understand than a high-level language.

attributes—Information about an object, such as its size, color and weight.

bandwidth—The information-carrying capacity of communications lines.

central processing unit (CPU)—The part of the computer's hardware responsible for supervising the operation of the other sections of the computer.

class—Represents a group of related objects. A class specifies the general format of its objects; the properties and actions available to an object depend on its class. An object is to its class much as a house is to its blueprint.

close box—The icon that, when clicked, closes a window.

compiler—A translator program that converts high-level-language programs into machine language.

computer—A device capable of performing computations and making logical decisions at speeds millions and even billions of times faster than the speeds at which human beings carry out those same tasks.

computer program—A set of instructions that guides a computer through an orderly series of actions.

computer programmer—A person who writes computer programs in programming languages.

control—A reusable component, such as a `GroupBox`, `RadioButton` and `Panel`.

C# programming (Visual C#) language—A visual, object-oriented, event-driven programming language designed for Microsoft's .NET platform.

event-driven program—Responds to user-initiated events such as mouse clicks and keystrokes.

Framework Class Library (FCL)—.NET's collection of "prepackaged" classes and methods for performing common mathematical calculations, string manipulations, character manipulations, input/output operations, error checking and many other useful operations.

graphical user interface (GUI)—The visual part of an application with which users interact.

hardware—The various devices that make up a computer, including the keyboard, screen, mouse, hard drive, memory, CD-ROM and processing units.

high-level language—A type of programming language in which a single program statement accomplishes a substantial task. High-level languages use instructions that look almost like everyday English and that contain common mathematical notations.

HyperText Markup Language (HTML)—A language for marking up information to share over the World Wide Web via hyperlinked text documents.

input unit—The "receiving" section of the computer that obtains information (data and computer programs) from various input devices, such as the keyboard and the mouse.

integrated development environment (IDE)—A software tool that enables programmers to write, run, test and debug programs quickly and conveniently.

Internet—A worldwide computer network. Most people today access the Internet through the World Wide Web.

LIVE-CODE approach—Shows dozens of complete, working C# applications and depicts their outputs.

machine dependent—Can be used on only one type of computer.

machine language—A computer's natural language, generally consisting of streams of numbers that instruct the computer how to perform its most elementary operations.

memory unit—The rapid-access, relatively low-capacity "warehouse" section of the computer, which stores data temporarily while an application is running.

Microsoft .NET—Microsoft's vision for using the Internet and the Web in the development, engineering and use of software. .NET includes tools such as Visual Studio .NET and programming languages such as C#.

.NET Framework—Microsoft-provided software that executes applications, provides the Framework Class Library (FCL) and supplies many other programming capabilities.

nonvolatile—Retaining information even when the computer is powered off. Secondary storage is nonvolatile.

object-oriented programming (OOP)—A way of programming that uses objects as reusable components modelling items in the real world. Object-oriented programs are often easier to understand, correct and modify than programs developed with previous techniques.

object technology—A packaging scheme for creating meaningful software units. The units are large and are focused on particular application areas. There are date objects, time objects, paycheck objects and file objects, among others.

objects—Reusable software components that model items in the real world.

output unit—The section of the computer that takes information the computer has processed and places it on various output devices, making the information available for use outside the computer.

procedural programming language—Focuses on actions (verbs) rather than things or objects (nouns). Examples include Fortran, Pascal, BASIC and C.

properties—Object attributes, such as size, color and weight.

secondary storage unit—The long-term, high-capacity "warehousing" section of the computer. Secondary memory takes longer to access information in primary memory but is less expensive and is nonvolatile.

software—The set of applications that run on computers.

software reuse—An approach to software development that enables programmers to avoid "reinventing the wheel" by taking advantage of existing pieces of software, helping them develop new applications faster.

structured programming—A disciplined approach to creating programs that are clear, correct and easy to modify.

TCP/IP—The set of protocols forming the foundation of today's Internet. Transmission Control Protocol (TCP) ensures that messages, consisting of pieces called "packets," are properly routed from sender to receiver and that those messages arrive intact. Internet Protocol (IP) enables many different networks to communicate with each other.

visual programming with C#—Instead of writing detailed program statements, the programmer uses Visual Studio .NET's graphical user interface to conveniently drag and drop predefined objects into place, and to label and resize them. Visual Studio .NET writes much of the C# program, saving the programmer considerable effort.

Visual Studio .NET—An integrated development environment (IDE) for developing C# and other .NET applications.

volatile memory—Memory that is erased when the machine is powered off. Primary memory is volatile.

Web services—Reusable pieces of Web-based software available on the Internet.

World Wide Web Consortium (W3C)—A forum through which qualified individuals and companies cooperate to develop and standardize technologies for the World Wide Web.

World Wide Web (WWW)—A communications system that allows computer users to locate and view multimedia documents (such as documents with text, graphics, animations, audios and videos).

MULTIPLE-CHOICE QUESTIONS

1.1 The HyperText Markup Language was developed _____.
a) by ARPA
b) at CERN by Tim Berners-Lee
c) before the Internet
d) as a replacement for the Internet

1.2 Microsoft's _____ initiative integrates the Internet and the Web into software development.
a) .NET
b) BASIC
c) Windows
d) W3C

1.3 TextBoxes, Buttons and RadioButtons are examples of _____.
a) platforms
b) high-level languages
c) IDEs
d) controls

1.4 _____ is an example of primary memory.
a) TCP
b) RAM
c) ALU
d) CD-ROM

1.5 C# is an example of a(n) _____ language, in which single program statements accomplish more substantial tasks.
a) machine
b) intermediate-level
c) high-level
d) assembly

1.6 Which protocol is primarily intended to create a "network of networks?"
a) TCP
b) IP
c) OOP
d) FCL

1.7 A major benefit of _____ programming is that it produces software that is more understandable and better organized than software produced with previously used techniques.
a) object-oriented
b) centralized
c) procedural
d) HTML

1.8 .NET's collection of prepackaged classes and methods is called the _____.
a) NCL
b) WCL
c) FCL
d) PPCM

1.9 The information-carrying capacity of communications lines is called _____.
a) networking
b) secondary storage
c) traffic
d) bandwidth

1.10 Which of these programming languages was specifically created for .NET?
a) C#
b) C++
c) BASIC
d) Visual Basic

EXERCISES

1.11 Categorize each of the following items as either hardware or software:
a) CPU
b) Compiler
c) Input unit
d) A word-processor program
e) A C# program

1.12 Translator programs, such as assemblers and compilers, convert programs from one language (referred to as the source language) to another language (referred to as the target language). Determine which of the following statements are *true* and which are *false*:

a) A compiler translates high-level-language programs into target-language programs.

b) An assembler translates source-language programs into machine-language programs.

c) A compiler translates source-language programs into target-language programs.

d) Machine languages are generally machine independent.

e) A machine-language program requires translation before it can be run on a computer.

1.13 Computers can be thought of as being divided into six units.

a) Which unit can be thought of as "the boss" of the other units?

b) Which unit is the high-capacity "warehouse" that retains information even when the computer is powered off?

c) Which unit might determine whether two items stored in memory are identical?

d) Which unit obtains information from devices like the keyboard and mouse?

1.14 Expand each of the following acronyms:

a) W3C   b) TCP/IP

c) OOP   d) FCL

e) HTML

1.15 What are the advantages to using object-oriented programming techniques?

T U T O R I A L

Welcome Application

Introducing the Visual Studio .NET IDE

Visual Studio® .NET is Microsoft's integrated development environment (IDE) for creating and running applications written in .NET languages, such as C#. The IDE allows you to create applications by dragging and dropping existing building blocks into place—a technique called visual programming—greatly simplifying application development. In this tutorial, you will learn the Visual Studio .NET IDE features that you will need to create C# applications.

2.1 Test-Driving the Welcome Application

In this section, you continue learning with our Application-Driven approach as you prepare to build an application that displays a welcome message and a picture. This application must meet the following requirements:

> **Application Requirements**
>
> *A software company (Deitel & Associates) has asked you to develop a simple **Welcome** application that includes the greeting "Welcome to C#!" and a picture of the company's bug mascot. To build this application, you must first familiarize yourself with the Visual Studio .NET IDE.*

In this tutorial, you will begin to develop the **Welcome** application. Then, in Tutorial 3, you will "put it all together" and create the **Welcome** application by following our step-by-step boxes. [*Note*: Our convention is to display application names in the **Helvetica** font.] You begin by test-driving the completed application. Then, you will learn the additional C# technologies you will need to create your own version of this application.

Test-Driving the Welcome Application

1. ***Checking your setup.*** Confirm that you have set up your computer properly by reading the *Before You Begin: Important Information for Students and Instructors* section.

2. ***Locating the Welcome application.*** Open Windows Explorer and navigate to the C:\Examples\Tutorial02 directory (Fig. 2.1).

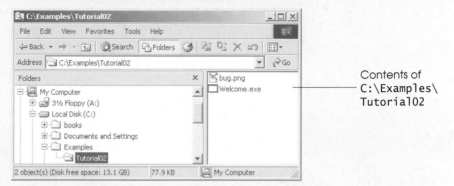

Contents of
C:\Examples\
Tutorial02

Figure 2.1   Contents of C:\Examples\Tutorial02.

3. ***Running the Welcome application.*** Double click Welcome.exe (Fig. 2.1) to run the application (Fig. 2.2).

Close box

Figure 2.2   **Welcome** application running.

4. ***Closing the application.*** Close your running application by clicking its close box, ⊠.

2.2 Overview of the Visual Studio .NET 2003 IDE

This section introduces you to the Visual Studio .NET 2003 IDE. To begin, be certain that you have Visual Studio .NET 2003 installed on your computer. Then, find Visual Studio .NET 2003, and open it; the **Start Page** displays. This page contains three tabs. Select the **Projects** tab (Fig. 2.3).

Depending upon your version of Visual Studio .NET, the **Start Page** might look different from the image in Fig. 2.3. Clicking the **Projects** tab loads a page that contains a table listing the names of recent projects (such as **WageCalculator** and **SecurityPanel** in Fig. 2.4), along with the dates on which these projects were last changed (modified). A **project** is a group of related files and images that make up an application. When you load Visual Studio .NET for the first time, the list of recent projects is empty. There are two Buttons on the page—**New Project** and **Open Project**. They are used to create projects and to open existing projects (such as the ones in the table of recent projects), respectively.

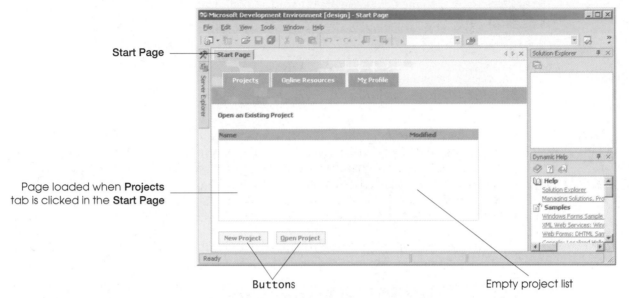

Figure 2.3 **Start Page** in Visual Studio .NET 2003 with an empty project list.

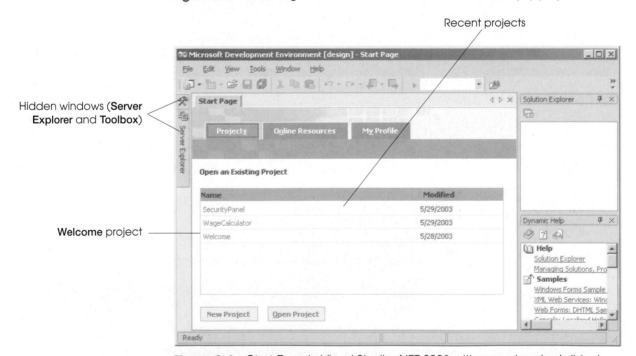

Figure 2.4 **Start Page** in Visual Studio .NET 2003 with recent projects listed.

Click the **Online Resources** tab (Fig. 2.5). The left side of the **Start Page** contains some helpful links, such as **Get Started**, **What's New** and **Online Community**. When you click a link, your computer will display information related to that link. The vast majority of the topics in these links will be more useful to you once you have gained some programming experience. Many of the **Start Page** links require your computer to be connected to the Internet. The following items describe each of the links on the **Start Page**:

Start Page

Start Page links

Page loaded when
Get Started is clicked

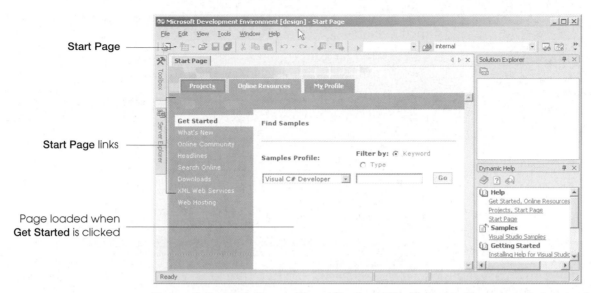

Figure 2.5   **Start Page** in Visual Studio .NET with **Online Resources** tab selected.

■ Clicking the **Get Started** link loads a page that enables the user to search for sample code based on topic. For instance, when you type `Label` into the TextBox provided and click the **Go** Button, links to code samples will be provided for you.

■ Clicking the **What's New** link displays a page that lists new features and updates for Visual Studio .NET, including downloads for C# samples and programming tools. Information is updated frequently on this page.

■ **Online Community** links to online resources for contacting other software developers through newsgroups (organized message boards on the Internet), user groups and Web sites.

■ Clicking **Headlines** displays a page for browsing articles, news and tips for developing applications using Microsoft technologies.

■ To access more extensive information, you can select **Search Online** and begin browsing through the **Microsoft Developer Network (MSDN)** online library, which contains articles and tutorials on technologies of interest to C# programmers.

■ When clicked, **Downloads** displays a page that provides you with access to product updates, code samples and reference materials.

■ The **XML Web Services** page provides you with information about Web services, which are reusable pieces of Web-based software available on the Internet.

■ The **Web Hosting** page allows you to post software (such as Web services) online for public use.

Clicking the final tab, **My Profile**, loads a page where you can adjust and customize various Visual Studio .NET settings, such as the location where various windows should appear in the IDE.

You also can browse the Web from Visual Studio .NET by using Microsoft's Internet Explorer (also called the **internal Web browser** in Visual Studio .NET). Select **View > Web Browser > Show Browser**. Several navigation buttons will be displayed by the top of the IDE (Fig. 2.6). By default, the site `msdn.microsoft.com` will be displayed for you. Enter `www.deitel.com` into the **location bar** (Fig. 2.6), and press the *Enter* key. This causes the DEITEL® home page to be displayed within the Visual Studio .NET IDE. Click the left-arrow Button (in the set of navigation Buttons) to return to `msdn.microsoft.com`. Other windows appear in the IDE in addition to the **Start Page** and the internal Web browser; we discuss several of them later in this tutorial.

Navigation Buttons   Entering in the location bar
                                www.deitel.com

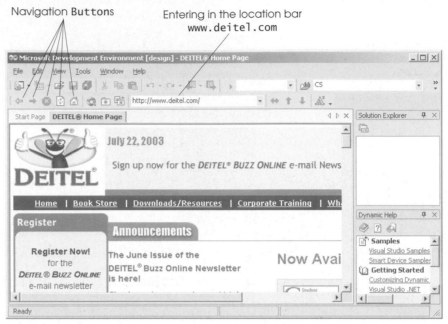

Figure 2.6   DEITEL® home page displayed in the Visual Studio .NET IDE. (Courtesy of Deitel & Associates, Inc.)

SELF-REVIEW   1. When you first open Visual Studio .NET, the _____ displays.

    a) **What's New Page**   b) **Start Page**
    c) **Welcome Page**   d) None of the above.

2. Clicking the _____ tab in the Visual Studio .NET **Start Page** loads a page that contains a table listing the names of recent projects.

    a) **My Profile**   b) **Get Started**
    c) **Projects**   d) **Online Resources**

Answers: 1) b. 2) c.

2.3 Creating a Project for the Welcome Application

In this section, you will create a simple C# Windows application. The Visual Studio .NET IDE organizes applications into projects and **solutions**, which contain one or more projects. Every application always contains exactly one solution. Large-scale applications can contain many projects, in which each project performs a single, well-defined task (Fig. 2.7). Projects in the same solution do not have to be coded in the same language. The .NET platform provides this flexibility so that the programmer can choose the language most appropriate for the task at hand. In this book, each solution you build will contain only one project.

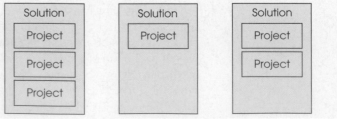

Figure 2.7   Solutions can contain one or more projects.

Creating a Project for the Welcome Application

1. **Creating a new project.** If you have not already done so, start Visual Studio .NET. In the **Projects** tab of the **Start Page**, click the **New Project Button** (Fig. 2.8), causing the **New Project** dialog to display (Fig. 2.9). **Dialogs** (or **message dialogs**) are windows that can display information for, and gather information from the application's user. Like other windows, dialogs are identified by the text in their **title bar**.

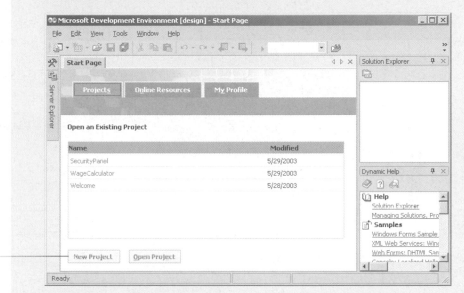

New Project Button

Figure 2.8 New Project Button.

Visual C# Projects directory (selected)

C# Windows Application (selected)

Title bar (displaying **New Project**)

Project Types: pane

Location of the new project

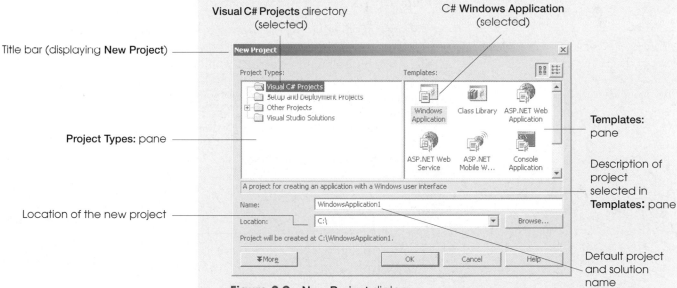

Templates: pane

Description of project selected in **Templates:** pane

Default project and solution name

Figure 2.9 New Project dialog.

2. **Selecting the project type.** The Visual Studio .NET IDE allows you to choose from one of several project types. Click the **Visual C# Projects** directory in the **Project Types:** pane (Fig. 2.9) to display the list of C# project types in the **Templates:** pane. (**Templates** are building blocks for different types of C# applications.) [*Note:* Depending on your version of Visual Studio .NET, the names and number of items shown in the **Project Types:** and **Templates:** panes could differ.]

(cont.)

3. ***Selecting the template.*** Select **Windows Application**, which is a template for an application that displays a GUI. Examples of *Windows applications* include computer games and software products like Microsoft Word, Internet Explorer and Visual Studio .NET. In this book, you concentrate on Windows applications. In the last tutorials, you will also build ASP .NET web applications.

4. ***Changing the name of the project.*** By default, the Visual Studio .NET IDE assigns the name WindowsApplication1 to the project and solution (Fig. 2.9) and places these files in a directory named WindowsApplication1. You can change both the project's name and location. To rename the project, type Welcome in the **Name:** TextBox (Fig. 2.10).

Updated project location

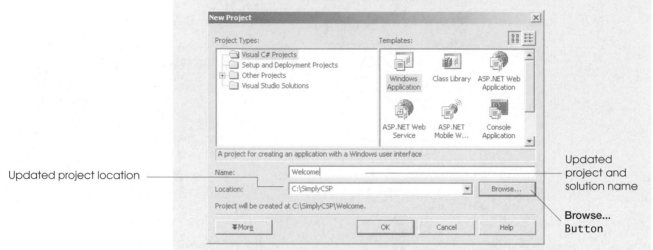

Updated project and solution name

Browse...
Button

Figure 2.10   **New Project** dialog with updated project information.

5. ***Changing the location of the project.*** Save this project in your SimplyCSP directory. To change the project's location, click the **Browse...** Button (Fig. 2.10) to display the **Project Location** dialog (Fig. 2.11). In this dialog, locate your SimplyCSP directory, and click **Open**. After providing the project's name and location in the **New Project** dialog, click **OK**. This displays the IDE in **design view** (or **design mode**) (Fig. 2.12), which contains the features you need to begin creating a Windows application.

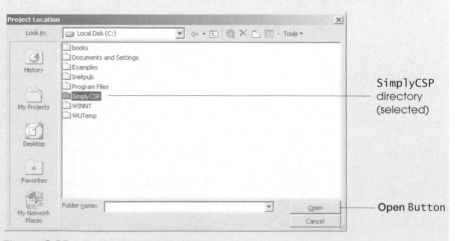

SimplyCSP
directory
(selected)

Open Button

Figure 2.11   **Project Location** dialog.

(cont.)

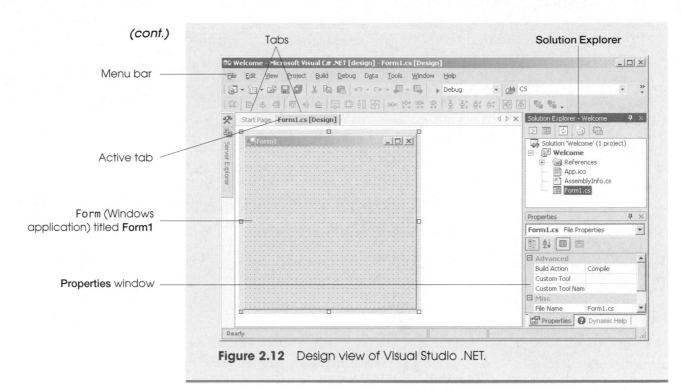

Figure 2.12   Design view of Visual Studio .NET.

The name of each open file is listed on a tab (**Start Page** and **Form1.cs [Design]** in Fig. 2.12). To view a file, click its tab. Tabs provide easy access to multiple files. The **active tab** is displayed in bold text (**Form1.cs [Design]** in Fig. 2.12).

The **Form1.cs [Design]** tab, which includes the gray rectangle (called a **Form**), contains the **Windows Form Designer**. The Form (titled **Form1**) represents the Windows application that you are creating. Forms can be enhanced by adding controls such as Buttons. Together, the Form and controls make up the application's graphical user interface (GUI), which is the visual part of the application. Users enter data (**inputs**) into the application by typing at the keyboard, by clicking the mouse buttons and in a variety of other ways. Applications display instructions and other information (**outputs**) for users to read in the GUI. For example, the **New Project** dialog in Fig. 2.9 is a GUI in which users click with the mouse to select project types and input project names and locations from the keyboard.

GUI controls (such as Buttons) aid both in data entry by users and in formatting and presenting data outputs to users. For example, Internet Explorer (Fig. 2.13) displays Web pages requested by users. Internet Explorer's GUI has a menu bar that contains six menus: **File**, **Edit**, **View**, **Favorites**, **Tools** and **Help**. These menus allow users to print files, save files and more. We discuss menus further in the next section. Below the menu bar is a **toolbar** that contains Buttons. Each Button contains an image (called an **icon**) that identifies the Button. When clicked, toolbar Buttons execute tasks (such as printing and searching). Beneath the toolbar is a ComboBox in which users can type the locations of Web sites to visit. Users also can click the ComboBox's drop-down arrow to select Web sites that they have visited previously. To the left of the ComboBox is a Label (**Address**) that identifies the purpose of the ComboBox. The menus, Buttons and Label are part of Internet Explorer's GUI; they allow users to interact with the Internet Explorer application. Although not part of Internet Explorer's GUI, the Web page's TextBox at the bottom of Fig. 2.13 displays the text **<e-mail>** and allows users to input data. Using C#, you can create your own applications that have all the GUI controls shown in Fig. 2.13 and many more.

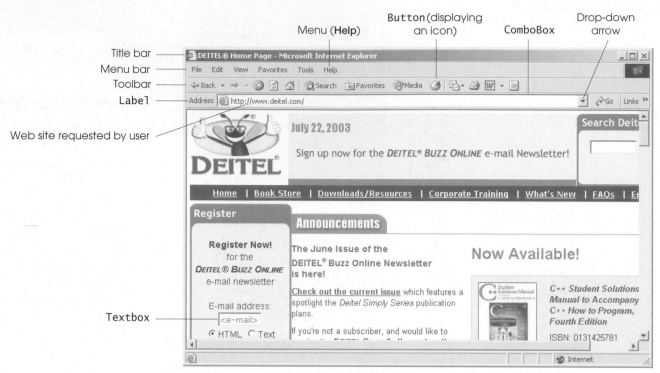

Figure 2.13   Internet Explorer window with GUI controls labelled. (Web site content courtesy of Deitel & Associates, Inc.)

SELF-REVIEW

1. The visual part of the application with which users interact is the application's _____.

   a) graphical user interface
   b) project
   c) solution
   d) title bar

2. A _____ contains one or more projects that collectively form a C# application.

   a) dialog
   b) Form
   c) solution
   d) graphical user interface

Answers: 1) a.   2) c.

2.4 Menu Bar and Toolbar

C# programmers use **menus** (located on the Visual Studio .NET IDE menu bar shown in Fig. 2.14) that contain commands for managing the IDE and for developing and executing applications. Each menu has a group of related commands (also called **menu items**) that, when selected, cause the IDE to perform specific actions, such as opening windows, saving files, printing files and executing applications. For example, to display the **Toolbox** window, select **View > Toolbox**. The menus in Fig. 2.14 are summarized in Fig. 2.15—you will learn to use many of these menus throughout the book. In Tutorial 22, **Typing** Application (Introducing Keyboard Events, Menus and Dialogs), you will learn how to create and add your own menus and menu items to your applications.

Figure 2.14   Visual Studio .NET IDE menu bar.

Menu	Description
File	Contains commands for opening and closing projects, printing project data, etc.
Edit	Contains commands such as **Cut**, **Paste** and **Undo**.
View	Contains commands for displaying IDE windows and toolbars.
Project	Contains commands for managing a solution's projects and their files.
Build	Contains commands for compiling a C# application.
Debug	Contains commands for identifying and correcting problems in applications. Also contains commands for running applications.
Data	Contains commands for interacting with databases, which store the data that an application processes. [*Note*: You will learn database concepts in Tutorial 25, **ATM** Application.]
Format	Contains commands for aligning and spacing a **Form**'s controls.
Tools	Contains commands for accessing additional IDE tools and options that enable customization of the IDE.
Window	Contains commands for hiding, opening, closing and displaying IDE windows.
Help	Contains commands for accessing the IDE's help features.

Figure 2.15 Visual Studio .NET IDE menu summary.

Rather than navigating the menus for certain commonly used commands, you can access those same commands from the IDE toolbar (Fig. 2.16). To execute a command using the IDE toolbar, simply click its **toolbar icon**. Some toolbar icons have associated down arrows that, when clicked, display additional commands.

Toolbar icon indicates a command to open a project or solution

Down arrow indicates additional commands are available

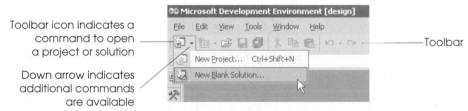

Toolbar

Figure 2.16 IDE toolbar.

Positioning the mouse pointer over an icon highlights the icon and, after a few seconds, displays a description called a **tool tip** (Fig. 2.17). Tool tips help you become familiar with the IDE's features.

Tool tip displays when the mouse pointer has rested on the icon for a few seconds

Figure 2.17 Tool-tip demonstration.

SELF-REVIEW   1. _____ contain groups of related commands.

a) Menu items   b) Menus

c) Tool tips   d) None of the above

2. When the mouse pointer is positioned over an IDE toolbar icon for a few seconds, a
_____ is displayed.

a) toolbox	b) toolbar
c) menu	d) tool tip

Answers: 1) b. 2) d.

2.5 Visual Studio .NET IDE Windows

The IDE provides windows for accessing project files and for customizing Forms
and controls by changing their attributes (names, colors, etc.). These windows provide visual aids for common programming tasks, such as managing files in a project.
In this section, you will become familiar with several windows—**Solution Explorer**,
Properties and **Toolbox**—that are essential for creating C# applications. You can
access these windows by using the IDE toolbar icons (Fig. 2.18) or by selecting the
window name, using the **View** menu. Two of the windows that have icons provided
(the **Object Browser** and **Class View** windows) will not be used in this text. [*Note*:
These icons may not appear if the IDE window has been minimized. If you cannot
view the icons of Fig. 2.18, maximize the IDE window.]

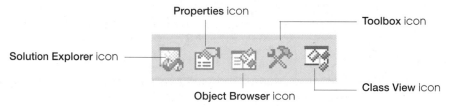

Figure 2.18   Toolbar icons for five Visual Studio .NET IDE windows.

Solution Explorer **Window**

The **Solution Explorer** window (located on the right side of the IDE as shown in
Fig. 2.12) provides access to solution files. This window allows you to manage files
visually. The **Solution Explorer** window displays a list of all the files in a project and
all the projects in a solution. (Remember that a C# solution can contain one or
more projects.) When the Visual Studio .NET IDE is first loaded, the **Solution
Explorer** window is empty; there are no files to display. Once a solution is open, the
Solution Explorer window displays that solution's contents. Figure 2.19 displays the
solution contents for the **Welcome** application.

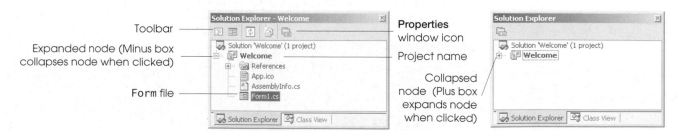

Figure 2.19   **Solution Explorer** with an open solution.

For your single-project solution, **Welcome** is the only project. The file, which
corresponds to the Form shown in Fig. 2.12, is named Form1.cs. (C# Form files use
the .cs file name extension, which is short for "C Sharp.")

The **plus** and **minus** boxes to the left of both the project name and the **References** directory are called **nodes**. The plus and minus boxes expand and collapse
information, respectively.

Navigating a Project with the Solution Explorer

1. **Collapsing a node.** Click the minus box to the left of the project name to collapse the node (Fig. 2.20). The minus box now becomes a plus box (Fig. 2.21).

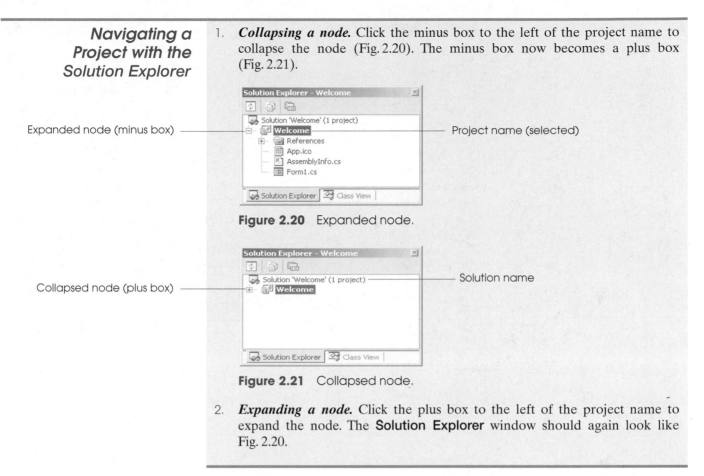

Expanded node (minus box) —— Project name (selected)

Figure 2.20   Expanded node.

Collapsed node (plus box) —— Solution name

Figure 2.21   Collapsed node.

2. **Expanding a node.** Click the plus box to the left of the project name to expand the node. The **Solution Explorer** window should again look like Fig. 2.20.

Toolbox **Window**

Using visual programming, you can "drag and drop" controls onto the Form quickly and easily instead of building them from "scratch," which is a slow and complex process. Just as you do not need to know how to build an engine to drive a car, you do not need to know how to build controls to create effective GUIs. The **Toolbox** (Fig. 2.22) contains a wide variety of controls for building GUIs. You will use the **Toolbox** as you finish creating the **Welcome** application in Tutorial 3. If the **Toolbox** is not visible, select **View > Toolbox**.

The **Toolbox** contains five tabs (three at the top and two at the bottom) that group related controls: **Data**, **Components**, **Windows Forms**, **Clipboard Ring** and **General**. In this book, you will use only the **Windows Forms** tab controls and **Data** tab controls. When you click a tab, the **Toolbox** displays all of the controls in that group. You can scroll through the controls using the black scroll arrows to the right of the **Windows Forms** and **Clipboard Ring** tabs. When there are no more controls to display, the scroll arrow becomes gray, meaning that it is disabled. (It will not perform its normal function if clicked or held down.) The first item in the group is not a control—it is the **mouse pointer**. You will use the mouse pointer to navigate the IDE and to manipulate the Form and its controls. In the remaining tutorials, you will use approximately 20 of the **Toolbox**'s 46 controls.

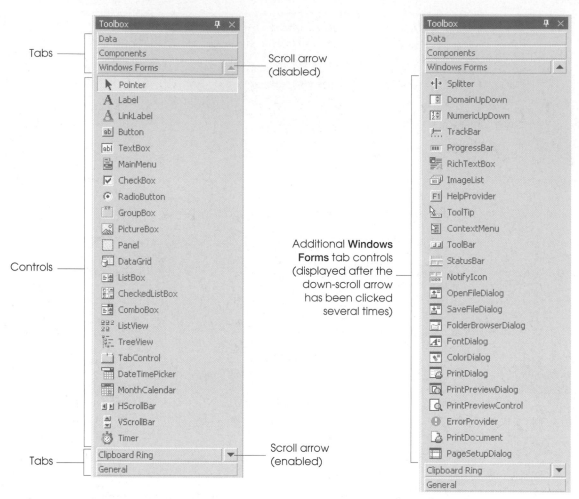

Figure 2.22   **Toolbox** displaying the contents of the **Windows Forms** tab.

Properties **Window**

One of the windows you will use frequently is the **Properties** window, which displays the properties for Form and control objects. Properties specify an object's attributes, such as size, color and position.

The **Properties** window allows you to set object properties visually, without writing code. Setting properties visually provides a number of benefits:

- You can see which properties can be modified and, in many cases, you can learn the acceptable values for a given property.

- You do not have to remember or search the Visual Studio .NET documentation (see Section 2.7) for a property's settings.

- This window displays a brief description of the selected property, so you can understand the property's purpose.

- A property can be set quickly.

All of these features are designed to help you ensure that settings are correct and consistent throughout the project. If the **Properties** window is not visible, select **View > Properties Window** (or right click and select **Properties** from the window that opens). Figure 2.23 shows a Form's **Properties** window:

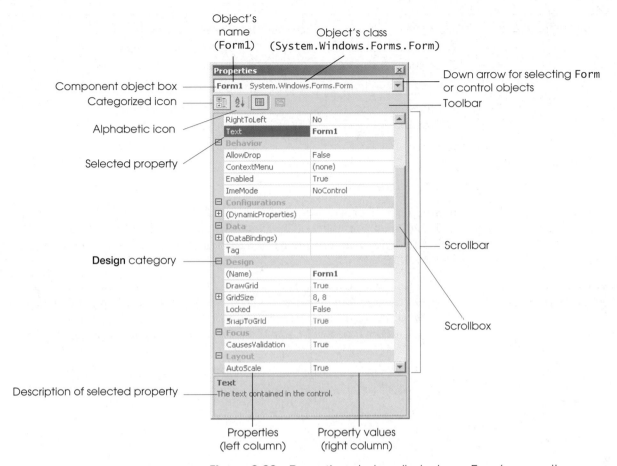

Figure 2.23 **Properties** window displaying a Form's properties.

- Each Form or control object has its own set of properties. At the top of the **Properties** window is the **component object box**, which allows you to select the object whose properties you wish to display in the **Properties** window.

- You can confirm that you are manipulating the correct object's properties because the object's name and class type are displayed in the component object box. Form objects have the System.Windows.Forms.Form class type and are assigned generic names (such as Form1) by Visual Studio .NET. You will learn about the class types for controls in the next tutorial. Icons on the toolbar sort the properties either alphabetically (if you click the **alphabetic icon**) or categorically (if you click the **categorized icon**). Figure 2.23 shows the **Properties** window with its properties sorted categorically. Each gray horizontal bar to the left of the scrollbar is a category that groups related properties. For example, the **Design** category groups five related properties. The categories visible in Fig. 2.23 are **Behavior**, **Configurations**, **Data**, **Design**, **Focus** and **Layout**. Notice that each category is a node, and can thus be collapsed or expanded.

- The left column of the **Properties** window lists the object's property names; the right column displays each property's value. In the next tutorial, you will learn how to set properties for objects.

- You can scroll through the list of properties by dragging the scrollbar's scrollbox up or down.

- Whenever you select a property, a description of the property displays at the bottom of the **Properties** window.

SELF-REVIEW

1. The _____ allows you to add controls to the Form in a visual manner.
   - a) **Solution Explorer**
   - b) **Properties** window
   - c) **Toolbox**
   - d) **Dynamic Help** window

2. The _____ window allows you to view a solution's files.
   - a) **Properties**
   - b) **Solution Explorer**
   - c) **Toolbox**
   - d) None of the above.

Answers: 1) c. 2) b.

2.6 Auto Hide

Visual Studio .NET provides a space-saving feature used for the **Toolbox**, **Properties** and **Dynamic Help** (Section 2.7) windows called **Auto Hide**. When Auto Hide is enabled for one or more of these windows, a toolbar appears along one of the edges of the IDE.

Using Auto Hide

1. ***Displaying a hidden window.*** When Auto Hide is enabled, the toolbar along one of the edges of the IDE contains one or more tabs, each of which identifies a hidden window (Fig. 2.24). Place the mouse pointer over the **Toolbox** tab to display the **Toolbox** (Fig. 2.25).

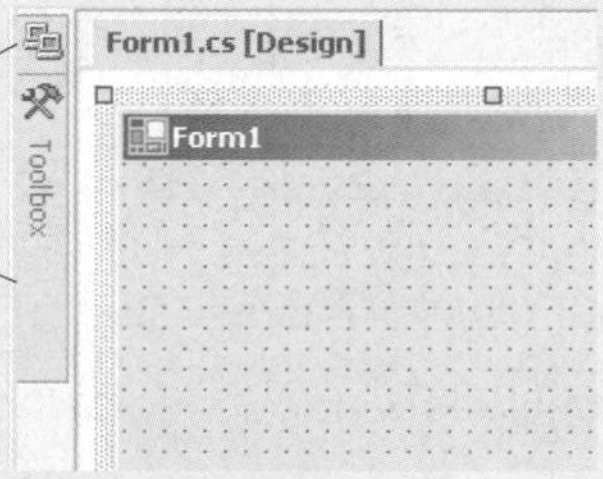

Tabs for hidden windows

Figure 2.24   Hidden-window tabs.

Title bar

Horizontal pin icon (Auto Hide enabled)

Mouse pointer over the tab for the **Toolbox**

Toolbox is displayed when the mouse pointer is placed on the tab for the **Toolbox**

Figure 2.25   Displaying a hidden window with Auto Hide enabled.

2. ***Hiding a window.*** Move the mouse pointer outside the **Toolbox** window's area to hide the **Toolbox** (Fig. 2.26).

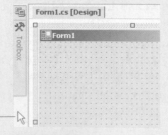

Mouse pointer outside the tab for the **Toolbox** (**Toolbox** window is hidden)

Figure 2.26   Hiding the **Toolbox** by moving the mouse pointer outside the **Toolbox**'s area.

(cont.)

3. ***Disabling Auto Hide.*** To keep the **Toolbox** window open and to disable Auto Hide (called "pinning down" a window), click the **pin icon** (also called the **pushpin icon**) in Fig. 2.25's title bar. Notice that, when a window is "pinned down," the pin icon is vertical (Fig. 2.27), whereas, when Auto Hide is enabled, the pin icon is horizontal.

Vertical pin icon
(Auto Hide is disabled)

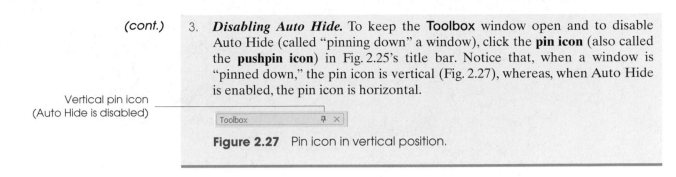

Figure 2.27   Pin icon in vertical position.

SELF-REVIEW

1. Visual Studio .NET provides a space-saving feature used for the _____ window(s).

    a) **Toolbox**   b) **Properties**
    c) **Dynamic Help**   d) All of the above.

2. When Auto Hide is enabled its pin icon is _____.

    a) horizontal   b) vertical
    c) down   d) diagonal

Answers: 1) d 2) a

2.7 Using Help

The Visual Studio .NET IDE provides extensive help features. The **Help** menu commands are summarized in Fig. 2.28. **Dynamic help** (Fig. 2.29) provides links to articles that apply to the current content (that is, the item selected with the mouse pointer). For example, if you have the **Start Page** open, **Dynamic Help** provides links to articles about the **Start Page**, customizing **Dynamic Help** and many other topics. To open the **Dynamic Help** window, select **Help > Dynamic Help**. Then, when you click a word or object (such as a Form or a control), links to relevant help articles appear in the **Dynamic Help** window. The window lists help topics, samples and "Getting Started" information. When you click a link, the help topic appears in a new window. This new window also contains a toolbar that provides access to the **Contents...**, **Index...** and **Search...** help features.

Command	Description
Contents...	Displays a categorized table of contents in which help articles are organized by topic.
Index...	Displays an alphabetized list of topics through which you can browse.
Search...	Allows you to find help articles based on search keywords.

Figure 2.28   **Help** menu commands.

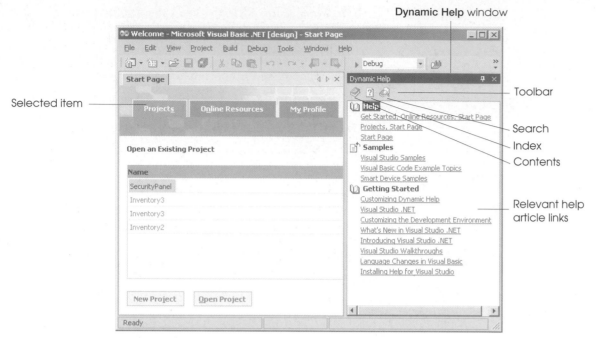

Figure 2.29 **Dynamic Help** window.

SELF-REVIEW 1. _____ displays relevant help articles, based on the selected object.

    a) Internal help   b) Dynamic help

    c) External help   d) Context-driven help

2. **Help** command _____ displays an alphabetized list of topics through which you can browse.

    a) **Search...**   b) **Browse...**

    c) **Contents...**   d) **Index...**

Answers: 1) b. 2) d.

2.8 Saving and Closing Solutions in Visual Studio .NET

Once you are finished with a solution, you will want to save the solution's files and close the solution.

Closing the Solution for the Welcome Application

1. ***Saving the project.*** Before closing the solution for the **Welcome** application, you will want to save the solution's files, ensuring that any changes made to the solution's files are not lost. Although you did not make any changes to the solution's files for this particular tutorial, you will be making such changes in most of the tutorials, so for practice select **File > Save All** to save your changes.

2. ***Closing the solution.*** Select **File > Close Solution**.

3. ***Closing the IDE.*** Close Visual Studio .NET by clicking its close box. [*Note*: You are not required to close the solution before closing the IDE. We include both steps in this instance for demonstration purposes.]

2.9 Internet and Web Resources

Please take a moment to visit each of these sites briefly. To save typing time, use the hot links on the enclosed CD or at `www.deitel.com`.

`www.msdn.microsoft.com/vstudio`
This site is the home page for Microsoft Visual Studio .NET. This site includes news, documentation, downloads and other resources.

`www.worldofdotnet.net`
This site offers a wide variety of information on .NET, including articles, news and links to newsgroups and other resources.

`www.c-sharpcorner.com`
This site has C# articles, reviews of books and software, documentation, downloads, links and more.

`www.msdn.microsoft.com/library/default.asp?url=/library/en-us/`
`vbcon/html/vbconselectingwfcclientcontrol.asp`
This Microsoft site summarizes **Toolbox** controls by function. Each control has a link to a page that contains additional resources for that control.

2.10 Wrap-Up

In this tutorial, you were introduced to the Visual Studio .NET integrated development environment (IDE). You learned key features, including tabs, menus, menu bars, toolbars, icons and Auto Hide.

You created a C# Windows application. The application contained one `Form` object named `Form1`. `Form` objects represent the application's graphical user interface (GUI).

You worked with the **Solution Explorer**, **Toolbox** and **Properties** windows, which are essential to developing C# applications. The **Solution Explorer** window allows you to manage your solution's files visually. The **Toolbox** window contains a rich collection of controls (organized on tabs) that allow you to create GUIs. The **Properties** window allows you to set the attributes of the `Form` and controls.

You explored Visual Studio .NET's help features, including the **Dynamic Help** window and the **Help** menu. The **Dynamic Help** window displays links related to the item you select with the mouse pointer. You learned about Web sites that provide additional C# information.

In the next tutorial, you will begin creating C# applications. You will follow step-by-step instructions for completing the **Welcome** application by using visual programming and the IDE features you learned in this tutorial.

SKILLS SUMMARY

Viewing a Page that Contains a Table Listing Names of Recent Projects
- Click the **Start Page**'s **Projects** tab.

Viewing a Page that Lists New Features and Updates for Visual Studio .NET
- Click the **Start Page**'s **What's New** link.

Viewing a Page that Lists Online Resources for Contacting Other Software Developers
- Click the **Start Page**'s **Online Community** link.

Viewing a Page that Lists News, Articles and Tips for Developing Microsoft Applications
- Click the **Start Page**'s **Headlines** link.

Viewing a Page that Allows Browsing of the Microsoft Developer Network (MSDN) Web Site
- Click the **Start Page**'s **Search Online** link.

Viewing a Page that Lists Product Updates, Code Samples and Reference Materials
- Click the **Start Page**'s **Downloads** link.

Viewing a Page that Allows You to Customize Visual Studio .NET Settings

■ Click the **Start Page**'s **My Profile** link.

Creating a New C# GUI Application

■ Click the **Start Page**'s **New Project** Button to display the New Project dialog.

■ Select **Visual C# Projects** in the **Project Types:** pane.

■ Select **Windows Application** in the **Templates:** pane.

■ Provide the project's name in the **Name:** TextBox.

■ Provide the project's directory information in the **Location:** TextBox.

■ Click the **OK** Button.

Saving a Project

■ Select **File > Save All**.

Viewing a Tool Tip for a Visual Studio .NET Icon

■ Place the mouse pointer on the icon, and keep it there until the tool tip appears.

Collapsing a Node in the Solution Explorer

■ Click the node's minus box.

Expanding a Node in the Solution Explorer

■ Click the node's plus box.

Scrolling Through the List of Windows Forms Controls in the Toolbox

■ Click the scroll arrows.

Viewing the Properties Window

■ Select **View > Properties** Window.

Displaying a Hidden Window

■ Place the mouse pointer over the hidden window's tab.

Disabling Auto Hide and "Pinning Down" a Window

■ Click the window's horizontal pin icon to change it to a vertical pin icon.

Enabling Auto Hide

■ Click the window's vertical pin icon to change it to a horizontal pin icon.

Opening the Dynamic Help Window

■ Select **Help > Dynamic Help**.

KEY TERMS

active tab—The tab of the document currently displayed in the IDE.

alphabetic icon—The icon in the **Properties** window that, when clicked, sorts properties alphabetically.

Auto Hide—A space-saving IDE feature used for windows such as **Toolbox**, **Properties** and **Dynamic Help** that hides a window until the mouse pointer is placed on the hidden window's tab.

categorized icon—The icon in the **Properties** window that, when clicked, sorts properties categorically.

component object box—The ComboBox at the top of the **Properties** window that allows you to select the Form or control object whose properties you want set.

Contents... command—Displays a categorized table of contents in which help articles are organized by topic.

design view (design mode)—IDE view that allows you to create applications using Visual Studio .NET's windows, toolbars and menu bar.

dialog (message dialog)—A window that displays messages to users and gathers input from users.

dynamic help—A help option that provides links to articles that apply to the current content (that is, the item selected with the mouse pointer).

Form—The object that represents the Windows application's graphical user interface (GUI).

icon—The graphical representation of commands in the Visual Studio .NET IDE.

Index... command—Displays an alphabetized list of topics through which you can browse.

input—Data entered by the user into an application by typing at the keyboard, by clicking the mouse buttons and in a variety of other ways.

internal Web browser—The Web browser (Internet Explorer) included in Visual Studio .NET, with which you can browse the Web.

location bar—The ComboBox in Visual Studio .NET where you can enter the name of a Web site to visit.

menu—A group of related commands.

menu item—A command located in a menu that, when selected, causes an application to perform a specific action.

Microsoft Developer Network (MSDN)—An online library that contains articles, downloads and tutorials on technologies of interest to Visual Studio .NET developers.

minus box—The icon that, when clicked, collapses a node.

mouse pointer—Used to navigate the IDE and to manipulate the Form and its controls.

node—An item that can be expanded or collapsed.

output—Instructions and other information displayed by an application for users to read in the application's GUI.

pin (pushpin) icon—An icon that enables or disables the Auto Hide feature.

plus box—An icon that, when clicked, expands a node.

project—A group of related files that make up an application.

Properties window—The window that displays the properties for a Form or control object.

Search... command—Allows you to find help articles based on search keywords.

solution—Contains one or more projects.

Solution Explorer—A window that provides access to all the files in a solution.

Start Page—The initial page displayed when Visual Studio .NET is opened.

template—Building blocks for different types of C# applications.

title bar—Contains text that identifies a window or dialog.

tool tip—The description of an icon that appears when the mouse pointer is held over that icon for a few seconds.

toolbar—A bar that contains Buttons that execute commands.

toolbar icon—A picture on a toolbar Button.

Toolbox—A window that contains controls used to customize Forms.

Tools menu—Contains commands for accessing additional IDE tools and options that enable customization of the IDE.

Visual Studio .NET—Microsoft's integrated development environment (IDE), which allows developers to create applications in a variety of .NET programming languages.

Windows application—A program that displays a GUI.

Windows Form Designer—The Visual Studio .NET interface for designing GUIs.

MULTIPLE-CHOICE QUESTIONS

2.1 The _____ integrated development environment (IDE) is used for creating applications written in .NET programming languages such as C#.

a) **Solution Explorer**   b) Gates

c) Visual Studio .NET   d) Microsoft

2.2 The `.cs` file name extension indicates a _____.

a) C# file   b) dynamic help file

c) help file   d) cool solution file

2.3 The pictures on toolbar Buttons are called _____.

a) prototypes   b) icons

c) tool tips   d) tabs

2.4 The _____ allows programmers to modify controls visually, without writing code.

a) **Properties** window   b) **Solution Explorer**

c) menu bar   d) **Toolbox**

2.5 The _____ hides the **Toolbox** when the mouse pointer is moved outside the **Tool-**
Box's area.

a) component-selection feature   b) Auto Hide feature

c) pinned command   d) minimize command

2.6 A _____ appears when the mouse pointer is positioned over an IDE toolbar icon
for a few seconds.

a) drop-down list   b) menu

c) tool tip   d) down arrow

2.7 The Visual Studio .NET IDE provides _____.

a) help documentation   b) a toolbar

c) windows for accessing project files d) All of the above.

2.8 The _____ contains a list of helpful links, such as **Get Started** and **Online Com-**
munity.

a) **Solution Explorer** window   b) **Properties** window

c) **Start Page**   d) **Toolbox** link

2.9 The **Properties** window contains _____.

a) the component object box   b) a **Solution Explorer**

c) menus   d) a menu bar

2.10 A _____ can be enhanced by adding reusable controls such as Buttons.

a) component   b) Form

c) icon   d) property

2.11 For Web browsing, Visual Studio .NET includes _____.

a) Web View   b) Excel

c) a **Web** tab   d) Internet Explorer

2.12 An application's GUI can include _____.

a) toolbars   b) icons

c) menus   d) All of the above.

2.13 The _____ does not contain a pin icon.

a) **Dynamic Help** window   b) **Solution Explorer** window

c) **Toolbox** window   d) active tab

2.14 When clicked, _____ in the **Solution Explorer** window will expand nodes and
_____ will collapse nodes.

a) minus boxes; plus boxes   b) plus boxes; minus boxes

c) up arrows; down arrows   d) left arrows; right arrows

2.15 Form _____ specify attributes such as size and position.

a) nodes   b) inputs

c) properties   d) title bars

EXERCISES   **2.16** (***Closing and Opening the Start Page***) In this exercise, you will learn how to close and reopen the **Start Page** (Fig. 2.30). To accomplish this task, perform the following steps:

Figure 2.30   Closing the **Start Page**.

a) Close Visual Studio .NET if it is open by clicking its close box.

b) Start Visual Studio .NET.

c) Close the **Start Page** by clicking its close box.

d) Select **Help > Show Start Page** to display the **Start Page**.

2.17 (***Enabling Auto Hide for the Solution Explorer Window***) In this exercise, you will learn how to use the **Solution Explorer** window's Auto Hide feature (Fig. 2.31) by performing the following steps.

Figure 2.31   Enabling Auto Hide.

a) Open the **Start Page**.

b) In the **Projects** tab (displayed by default), click the **Open Project** Button to display the **Open Project** dialog. You can skip to *Step e*) if the **Welcome** application is already open.

c) In the **Open Project** dialog, navigate to C:\SimplyCSP\Welcome, and click **Open**.

d) In the **Open Project** dialog, select Welcome.sln, and click **Open**.

e) Position the mouse pointer on the vertical pin icon in the **Solution Explorer** window's title bar. After a few seconds, a tool tip appears displaying the words **Auto Hide**.

f) Click the vertical pin icon. This action causes a **Solution Explorer** tab to appear on the right side of the IDE. The vertical pin icon changes to a horizontal pin icon (Fig. 2.32). Auto Hide has now been enabled for the **Solution Explorer** window.

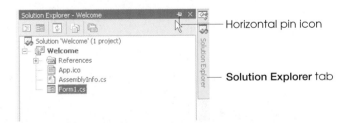

Figure 2.32   **Solution Explorer** window with Auto Hide enabled.

g) Position the mouse pointer outside the **Solution Explorer** window to hide the window.

h) Position the mouse pointer on the **Solution Explorer** tab to view the **Solution Explorer** window.

2.18 (*Sorting Properties Alphabetically in the Properties Window*) In this exercise, you will learn how to sort the **Properties** window's properties alphabetically (Fig. 2.33) by performing the following steps:

Alphabetic icon ———

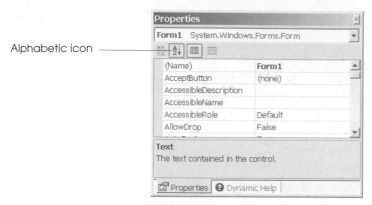

Figure 2.33   Sorting properties alphabetically.

a) Open the **Welcome** application by performing *Steps a–d* of Exercise 2.17. If the **Welcome** application is already open, you can skip this step.

b) Locate the **Properties** window. If it is not visible, select **View > Properties Window** to display the **Properties** window.

c) To sort properties alphabetically, click the **Properties** window's alphabetic icon. The properties will display in alphabetic order.

Objectives

In this tutorial, you will learn to:
- Set the text in the **Form**'s title bar.
- Change the **Form**'s background color.
- Place a **Label** control on the **Form**.
- Display text in a **Label** control.
- Place a **PictureBox** control on the **Form**.
- Display an image in a **PictureBox** control.
- Run an application.

Outline

3.1 Test-Driving the **Welcome** Application
3.2 Constructing the **Welcome** Application
3.3 Objects Used in the **Welcome** Application
3.4 Wrap-Up

Welcome Application

Introduction to Visual Programming

Today, users prefer software with interactive graphical user interfaces (GUIs) that respond to actions such as **Button** clicks and data input. As a result, the vast majority of Windows applications, such as Microsoft Word and Internet Explorer, are GUI based. With C#, you can create Windows applications that input and output information in a variety of ways, which you will learn throughout the book.

In this tutorial, you will use visual programming to complete the **Welcome** application you began creating in Tutorial 2. You will build the application's GUI by placing two controls—a **Label** and a **PictureBox**—on the **Form**. You will use the **Label** control to display text and the **PictureBox** control to display an image. You will customize the appearance of the **Form**, **Label** and **PictureBox** objects by setting their values in the **Properties** window. You will set many property values, including the **Form**'s background color, the **PictureBox**'s image and the **Label**'s text. You also will learn how to run your application from within the Visual Studio .NET IDE.

3.1 Test-Driving the Welcome Application

The last tutorial introduced you to the Visual Studio .NET IDE. In this tutorial, you will use Visual Studio .NET to build the **Welcome** application mentioned in Tutorial 2. This application must meet the following requirements:

Application Requirements

*Recall that a software company (Deitel & Associates) has asked you to develop a simple **Welcome** application that includes the greeting "Welcome to C#!" and a picture of the company's bug mascot. Now that you are familiar with the Visual Studio .NET IDE, your task is to develop this application to satisfy the company's request.*

You begin by test-driving the completed **Welcome** application. Then, you will learn the additional C# technologies you will need to create your own version of this application.

Test-Driving the Welcome Application

1. ***Opening the completed application.*** Start Visual Studio .NET and select **File > Open Solution...** (Fig. 3.1) to display the **Open Solution** dialog (Fig. 3.2). Select the C:\Examples\Tutorial03\CompletedApplication\Welcome directory from the **Look in:** ComboBox. Select Welcome.sln and click the **Open** Button. Double click **Welcome.cs** in the **Solution Explorer** window to open the Form in design view (Fig. 3.3).

Open Solution command (selected) opens an existing solution

Figure 3.1 Opening an existing solution with the **File** menu's **Open Solution...** command.

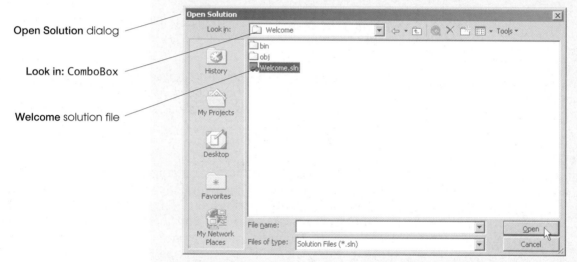

Open Solution dialog

Look in: ComboBox

Welcome solution file

Figure 3.2 **Open Solution** dialog displaying the contents of the **Welcome** solution.

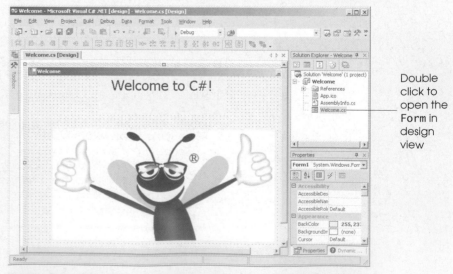

Double click to open the Form in design view

Figure 3.3 **Welcome** application's Form in design view.

(cont.)   2. ***Running the Welcome application.*** Select **Debug > Start** to run the application (Fig. 3.4). The **Start** command runs (executes) the application. The
Welcome Form shown in Fig. 3.5 will appear.

Start command (selected)
runs the application

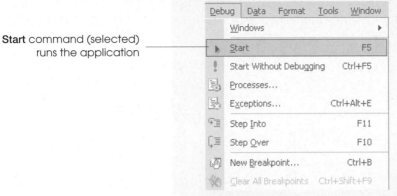

Figure 3.4   Running the **Welcome** application using the **Debug** menu's **Start**
command.

Close
box

Figure 3.5   **Welcome** application running.

3. ***Closing the application.*** Close your running application by clicking its close
box, ☒.

4. ***Closing the IDE.*** Close Visual Studio .NET by clicking its close box.

3.2 Constructing the Welcome Application

In this section, you perform the steps necessary to develop the **Welcome** application. The application consists of a single Form that uses a Label control and a PictureBox control. A **Label** control displays text that the user cannot change. A
PictureBox control displays an image that the user cannot change. You will not
write a single line of code to create this application. Instead, you will use the technique called visual programming, in which Visual Studio .NET processes your programming actions (such as clicking, dragging and dropping controls) and actually
writes the program for you! The box below shows you how to begin constructing
the **Welcome** application, using the solution you created in Tutorial 2 as a starting
point.

Changing the Form's File Name and Title Bar Text

1. *Opening the Welcome application's solution.* Select **File > Open Solution…**. Open the **Welcome** solution file (`Welcome.sln`) in the `C:\SimplyCSP\Welcome` directory to open the application in Visual Studio .NET. If the Windows Form Designer is not open, double click `Form1.cs` in the **Solution Explorer** window to display the blank `Form` in design view (Fig. 3.6).

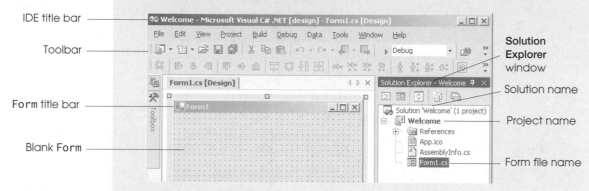

IDE title bar

Toolbar

Form title bar

Blank Form

Solution Explorer window

Solution name

Project name

Form file name

Figure 3.6 Blank `Form`.

2. *Changing the Form's file name.* When a Windows application is created, Visual Studio .NET names the `Form` file `Form1.cs`. Select `Form1.cs` in the **Solution Explorer** window (Fig. 3.6) to display the file's properties in the **Properties** window (the window on the left in Fig. 3.7). If either window is not visible, you can select **View > Properties Window** or **View > Solution Explorer** to display the appropriate window. Double click the field to the right of the `File Name` property's box, and type `Welcome.cs` (Fig. 3.7). Press the *Enter* key to update the `Form`'s file name. Notice that the file name changes in the **Solution Explorer** window (the window on the right in Fig. 3.7).

Good Programming Practice

Change your application's `Form` file name (`Form1.cs`) to a name that describes the application's purpose.

File properties

Selected property

Selected property description

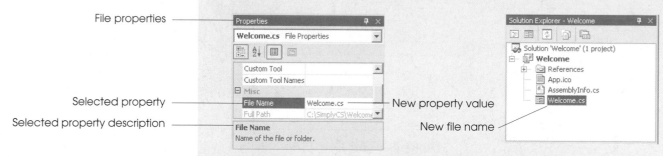

New property value

New file name

Figure 3.7 Changing the `Form`'s file name.

3. *Setting the text in the Form's title bar.* The title bar is the top portion of the window, which contains the window's title. To change the text in the `Form`'s title bar from **Form1** to **Welcome**, use the **Properties** window (Fig. 3.8). Click the `Form`. As in Fig. 3.7, double click the field to the right of the **Text** property in the **Properties** window, then type `Welcome`. Press the *Enter* key to update the `Form`'s title bar (Fig. 3.9).

GUI Design Tip

Choose short and descriptive `Form` titles. Capitalize words that are not articles, prepositions or conjunctions. Do not use punctuation.

(cont.)

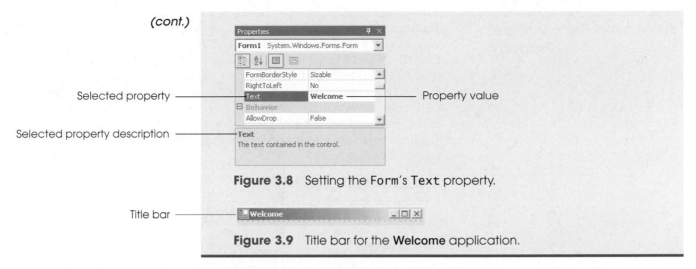

Selected property ——————

Property value

Selected property description ——————

Figure 3.8   Setting the Form's Text property.

Title bar ——————

Figure 3.9   Title bar for the **Welcome** application.

There are several ways to resize the Form. If the resizing does not have to be precise, you can click and drag one of the Form's enabled **sizing handles** (the small white squares that appear along the Form's edges, as shown in Fig. 3.10). The appearance of the mouse pointer changes (that is, it becomes a pointer with one or more arrows) when it is over an enabled sizing handle. The new pointer indicates the direction(s) in which resizing is allowed. Disabled sizing handles appear in gray and cannot be used to resize the Form.

The dots on the background of the Form are called a **grid**. You use the grid to align controls that you place on the Form. The grid is not visible when the application is running (Fig. 3.5).

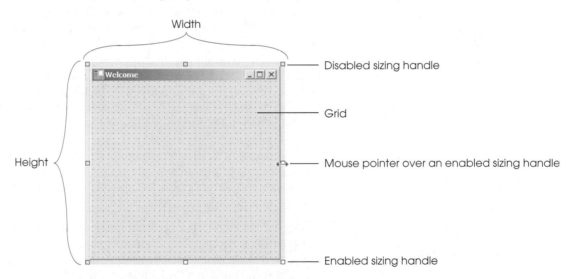

Figure 3.10   Form with sizing handles.

Forms also can be resized by using the **Size** property, which specifies the Form's width and height in units called **pixels** (*pic*ture *el*ements). A pixel is a tiny point on your computer screen that displays a color. The Size property has two members—the **Width** and the **Height** properties. The Width property indicates the width of the Form in pixels, and the Height property specifies the height in pixels. Next, you learn how to set the Form's width and height.

Setting the Form's Size Property

1. *Setting the Form's width and height.* For your **Welcome** application GUI to look exactly like Fig. 3.5, you will need to resize the Form and its controls. Click the Form. Locate the Form's Size property in the **Properties** window (Fig. 3.11). Click the plus box, ⊞, next to this property to expand the node. Type 616 for the Width property value, then press *Enter*. Type 440 for the Height property value, then press *Enter*. Note that the Size property value (616, 440) updated when either the Width or the Height is changed. You also can enter the width and height (separated by a comma) in the Size property's value field.

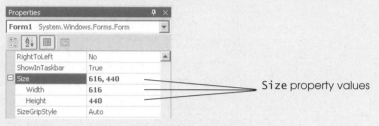

Size property values

Figure 3.11 Size property values for the Form.

Now that you have set the Form's size, you will customize the Form further by changing its background color from gray to yellow.

Setting the Form's Background Color

1. *Exploring the available colors.* Click the Form to ensure that its properties are displayed in the **Properties** window. The **BackColor** property specifies an object's background color. When you click the BackColor property's value in the **Properties** window, a down-arrow (⊻) Button appears (Fig. 3.12). When clicked, the down-arrow Button displays three tabs: **System** (the default), **Web** and **Custom**. Each tab offers a series of colors called a **palette**. The **System** tab displays a palette containing the colors used in the Microsoft Windows GUI. This palette includes the colors for Windows controls and the Windows desktop. The **System** tab's colors are based on the Windows 2000/XP settings in the **Display Properties** dialog. To access this dialog in Windows 2000, right click the desktop and select **Properties**. Click the **Appearance** tab to view the colors used by Windows. The **Web** tab displays a palette of **Web-safe colors**—colors that display the same on different computers. The **Custom** tab palette allows you to choose from a series of predefined colors or to create your own color. Click the **Custom** tab to display its palette as shown in Fig. 3.12.

GUI Design Tip

Use colors in your applications, but not to the point of distracting the user.

2. *Changing the Form's background color.* Right click any one of the 16 white boxes at the bottom of the **Custom** palette to display the **Define Color** dialog (Fig. 3.13). Colors can be created either by entering three values in the **Hue:**, **Sat:** (saturation) and **Lum:** (luminosity) TextBoxes or by providing values for the **Red:**, **Green:** and **Blue:** TextBoxes. The values for the **Red:**, **Green:** and **Blue:** TextBoxes describe the amount of red, green and blue needed to create the custom color and are commonly called **RGB values**. Each red, green and blue value is in the range 0–255, inclusive. We use RGB values in this book. Set the **Red:** value to 255, the **Green:** value to 237 and the **Blue:** value to 169. Click the **Add Color** Button to close the dialog, change the Form's background color and add the color to the **Custom** palette (Fig. 3.14).

(cont.)

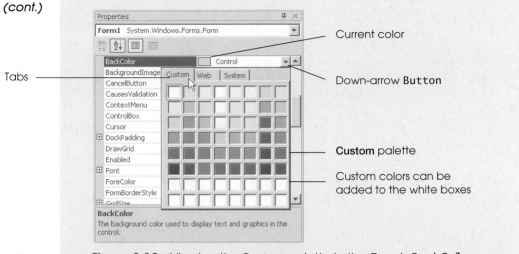

Current color

Tabs

Down-arrow **Button**

Custom palette

Custom colors can be
added to the white boxes

Figure 3.12   Viewing the **Custom** palette in the **Form**'s **BackColor** property value field.

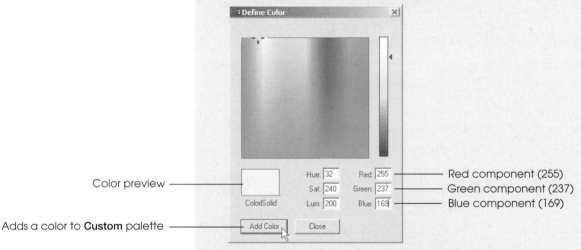

Color preview

Adds a color to **Custom** palette

Red component (255)
Green component (237)
Blue component (169)

Figure 3.13   Adding a color to the **Custom** palette.

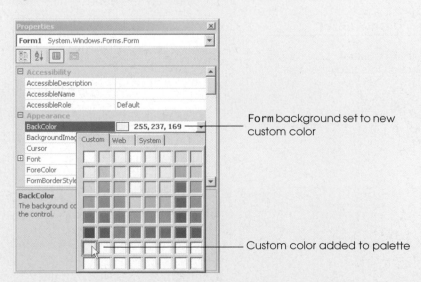

Form background set to new
custom color

Custom color added to palette

Figure 3.14   **Properties** window after the new custom color has been
added.

Now that you have finished customizing the Form, you can add a control to the Form. The box below guides you through adding and customizing a Label that displays a greeting.

Adding a Label to the Form

GUI Design Tip

Use Labels to display text that users cannot change.

1. ***Adding a Label control to the Form.*** Click the **Windows Forms** tab in the **Toolbox** (Fig. 3.15). If the **Toolbox** is not visible, select **View > Toolbox**. Double click the Label control in the **Toolbox**. A Label will appear in the upper-left corner of the Form (Fig. 3.16). You also can "drag" the Label from the **Toolbox** and drop it on the Form. You will use this Label control to display the welcome message. The Label displays the text **label1** by default.

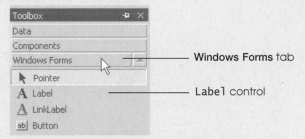

Figure 3.15   Clicking the **Windows Forms** tab in the **Toolbox**.

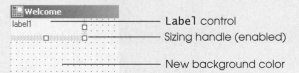

Figure 3.16   Adding a Label to the Form.

Notice that the Label's background color is the same as the Form's background color. When a control is added to the Form, the control's BackColor property value initially is set to the Form's BackColor property value by the Visual Studio .NET IDE.

2. ***Customizing the Label's appearance.*** You will notice that the Label's properties now appear in the **Properties** window. The Label's **Text** property specifies the text (**label1**) that the Label displays. Type Welcome to C#! for the Label's Text property value, then press *Enter*. Notice that if you shrink the Label enough (by using the sizing handles), this text does not fit in the Label (Fig. 3.17). Enlarge the Label until all the text is displayed (Fig. 3.18).

GUI Design Tip

Ensure that all Label controls are large enough to display their text.

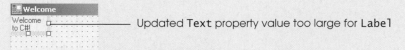

Figure 3.17   Label after updating its **Text** property.

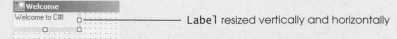

Figure 3.18   Label after it has been resized.

3. ***Aligning the Label.*** Drag the Label to the top center of the Form. You also can center the Label by clicking the Label and selecting **Format > Center In Form > Horizontally**. After centering the Label, the Form should look like Fig. 3.19.

(cont.)

Centered Label

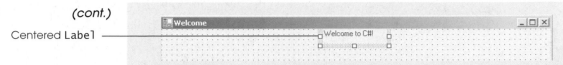

Figure 3.19   Centered Label.

GUI Design Tip

Use **Tahoma** font to improve readability for controls that display text.

4. ***Setting the Label's font.*** Click the value of the **Font** property to cause an ellipsis Button to appear (Fig. 3.20). If you click the ellipsis Button, the **Font** dialog displays (Fig. 3.21). In this dialog, you can select the font name (**Tahoma**, **Times New Roman**, etc.), font style (**Regular**, **Italic**, etc.) and font size (**16**, **18**, etc.) in points (one point equals 1/72 of an inch). The text in the **Sample** Label displays the selected font. Under the **Size:** category, select **24**. Under the **Font** category, select **Tahoma**, then click **OK**. If the Label's text does not fit on a single line, it wraps to the next line. Use the sizing handles to enlarge the Label horizontally so that the text appears on one line. Then, re-center the Label on the Form by clicking the Label and selecting **Format > Center In Form > Horizontally**.

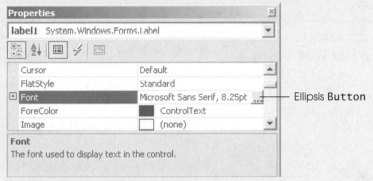

Ellipsis Button

Figure 3.20   **Properties** window displaying the Label's properties.

Font dialog

Current font

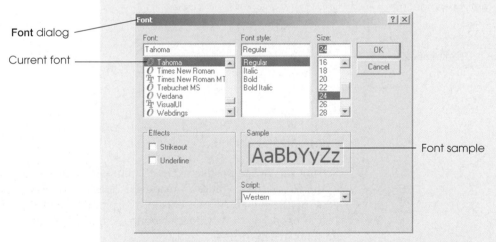

Font sample

Figure 3.21   **Font** dialog for selecting fonts, styles and sizes.

5. ***Aligning the Label's text.*** To align text inside a Label, you will need to use the Label's **TextAlign** property. Clicking the TextAlign property displays a down-arrow Button. Click the down-arrow Button to display a three-by-three grid of Buttons (Fig. 3.22). The position of each Button shows where the text will appear in the Label. Click the top-center Button in the three-by-three grid to align the text at the top-center position in the Label. The value TopCenter is assigned to the TextAlign property.

(cont.)

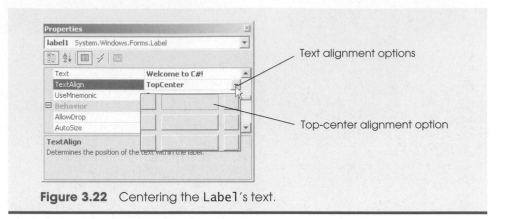

Figure 3.22   Centering the Label's text.

To finish this first C# Windows application, you need to insert an image and run the application. We use a `PictureBox` control to add an image to the Form before running the application. The following box guides you step-by-step through the process of adding an image to your Form.

Inserting an Image and Running the Welcome Application

1. ***Adding a PictureBox control to the Form.*** The `PictureBox` allows you to display an image. To add a `PictureBox` control to the Form, double click the `PictureBox` control icon

in the `Toolbox`. When the `PictureBox` appears, click and drag it to a position centered below the `Label` (Fig. 3.23).

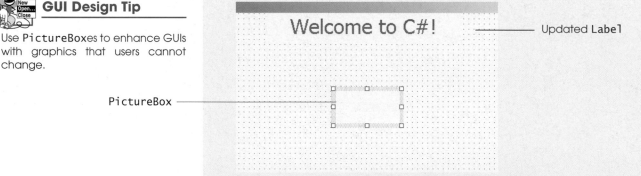

GUI Design Tip

Use `PictureBox`es to enhance GUIs with graphics that users cannot change.

PictureBox —————

Figure 3.23   Inserting and aligning the `PictureBox`.

2. ***Setting the Image property.*** The `PictureBox`'s properties are now displayed in the **Properties** window. Locate the **Image** property, which displays a preview of the image (if one exists). No picture has yet been assigned to the `Image` property, so its value is (none) (Fig. 3.24). You can use any of several popular image formats, including

- *PNG (Portable Network Graphics)*
- *GIF (Graphics Interchange Format)*
- *JPEG (Joint Photographic Experts Group)*
- *BMP (Windows Bitmap)*

(cont.)

For this application, you will use a PNG-format image. Creating new images requires image-editing software, such as Jasc® Paint Shop Pro™ (www.jasc.com), Adobe® Photoshop™ (www.adobe.com), Microsoft Picture It!® (photos.msn.com) or Microsoft Paint (provided with Windows). You will not create images in this book; instead, you will be provided with the images used in the tutorials.

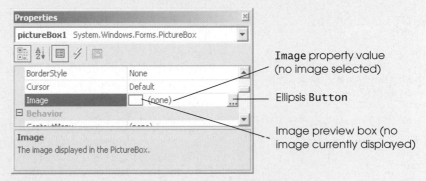

Figure 3.24   Image property of the PictureBox.

3. ***Displaying an image.*** In the **Properties** window, click the value of the Pic-tureBox's Image property to display an ellipsis Button (Fig. 3.24). Click the ellipsis Button to display the **Open** dialog (Fig. 3.25). Navigate to the C:\Examples\Tutorial03\CompletedApplication\Welcome directory. Click bug.png, then click the **Open** Button. Once the image has been selected, the PictureBox displays the image (Fig. 3.26), and the Image property displays a preview of the image (Fig. 3.27). Notice that the PictureBox does not display the entire image (Fig. 3.26). You will solve this problem in the next step.

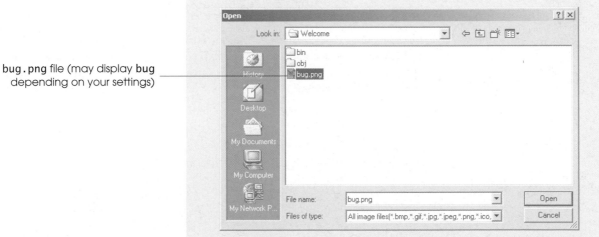

Figure 3.25   **Open** dialog used to browse for a PictureBox image.

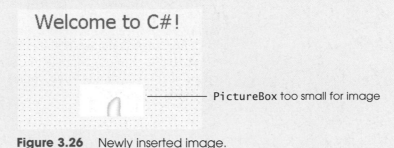

Figure 3.26   Newly inserted image.

(cont.)

Previewed image

Figure 3.27   Image previewed in the **Image** property value field.

4. ***Sizing the image to fit the PictureBox.*** We want the image to fit in the PictureBox. PictureBox property **SizeMode** specifies how an image is displayed in a PictureBox. To size the image to fit in the PictureBox, change the SizeMode property to **StretchImage**, which scales the image (changes its width and height) to the size of the PictureBox. To resize the PictureBox, double click the Size property and enter 500, 250. Center the image horizontally by clicking the PictureBox and selecting **Format > Center in Form > Horizontally**. The Form should now look like Fig. 3.28.

Newly inserted image

Figure 3.28   PictureBox displaying an image.

5. ***Locking the Form controls.*** Often, programmers accidentally alter the size and location of controls on the Form. To ensure that the controls remain in position, use the **Lock Controls** feature. First, select all the controls by using the **Edit > Select All** command. Next, select **Format > Lock Controls** (Fig. 3.29).

Lock Controls option

Figure 3.29   Locking controls by using the **Format** menu.

6. ***Saving the project.*** Select **File > Save All** to save your changes. The solution file (.sln) contains the name(s) and location(s) of its project(s); the project file (.csproj) contains the names and locations of all the files in the project. You should save your solution files to your C:\SimplyCSP directory frequently.

GUI Design Tip

Images should fit inside their PictureBoxes. This can be achieved by setting PictureBox property SizeMode to StretchImage.

(cont.)

7. ***Running the application.*** The text **Microsoft Visual C# .NET [design]** in the IDE's title bar (Fig. 3.6) indicates that we have been working in the IDE design mode. (That is, the application being created is not running.) While in design mode, programmers have access to all the IDE windows (**Toolbox**, **Properties**, etc.), menus and toolbars. In **run mode**, the application is running, and programmers can interact with fewer IDE features. Features that are not available are disabled ("grayed out"). Select **Debug > Start** to run your application. Figure 3.30 shows the IDE in run mode. Note that many toolbar icons and menus are disabled.

IDE title bar displaying **[run]** ⟶

Form (with grid) ⟶

Running application ⟶

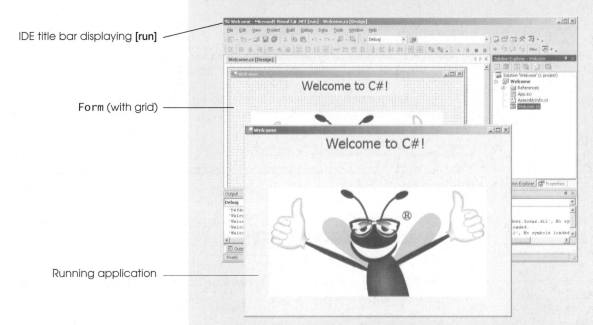

Figure 3.30 IDE in run mode, with the application running in the foreground.

8. ***Closing the application.*** Close your running application by clicking its close box, ⊠. This action returns the IDE to design mode.

9. ***Closing the IDE.*** Close Visual Studio .NET by clicking its close box.

SELF-REVIEW

1. The Form's _____ property specifies the text that is displayed in the Form's title bar.
 a) `Title`   b) `Text`
 c) `(Name)`   d) `Name`

2. The _____ property specifies how text is aligned within a `Label`'s boundaries.
 a) `Alignment`   b) `AlignText`
 c) `Align`   d) `TextAlign`

Answers: 1) b. 2) d.

3.3 Objects Used in the Welcome Application

In Tutorials 1 and 2, you learned that controls are reusable software components called objects. The **Welcome** application used a `Form` object, a `Label` object and a `PictureBox` object to create a GUI that displayed text and an image. Each of these objects is an instance of a class defined in the .NET Framework Class Library (FCL). The `Form` object was created by the Visual Studio .NET IDE. The `Label` and `PictureBox` objects were created when you double clicked their respective icons in the **Toolbox**.

We used the **Properties** window to set the properties (attributes) for each object. Recall that the ComboBox—also called the component object box—at the top of the **Properties** window displays the names and class types of Form and control objects (Fig. 3.31). In Fig. 3.32, the component object box displays the name (Form1) and class type (Form) of the Form object. In the FCL, classes are organized by functionality into directory-like entities called **namespaces**. The namespace of the class types used in this application is System.Windows.Forms. This namespace contains control classes and the Form class. You will learn more about namespaces in later tutorials.

Figure 3.31 Component object box expanded to show the **Welcome** application's objects.

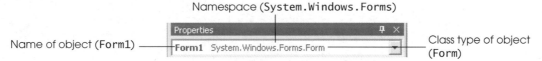

Figure 3.32 The name and class type of an object are displayed in the **Properties** window's component object box.

SELF-REVIEW

1. The ComboBox at the top of the **Properties** window is the _____.
   a) component object box   b) control box
   c) control object box   d) component box

2. The Framework Class Library (FCL) organizes classes into _____.
   a) collections   b) name boxes
   c) namespaces   d) class spaces

Answers: 1) a. 2) c.

3.4 Wrap-Up

This tutorial introduced you to visual programming in C#. You learned that visual programming helps you to design and create the graphical user interface (GUI) portions of applications quickly and easily, by dragging and dropping controls onto Forms.

In creating your **Welcome** application, you used the **Properties** window to set the Form's title-bar text, size (width and height) and background color using the Text, Size (Width and Height) and BackColor properties, respectively. You learned that Labels are controls that display text and that PictureBoxes are controls that display images. You displayed text in a Label by setting its Text and TextAlign properties, and you displayed an image by setting a PictureBox control's Image and SizeMode properties.

You also examined the relationship between controls and classes. You learned that FCL classes are grouped into directory-like entities called namespaces and that controls are instances (objects) of FCL classes. The FCL classes used in this tutorial (Form, Label and PictureBox) belong to the System.Windows.Forms namespace.

You used the **Properties** window's component object box to view an object's name, namespace and class type.

In the next tutorial, you will continue learning visual programming. In particular, you will create an application with controls that are designed to accept user input.

SKILLS SUMMARY

Creating GUIs Quickly and Efficiently
- Use visual programming techniques.

Placing a Control on the Form
- Double click the control in the **Toolbox** to place the control in the upper-left corner of the Form, or drag the control from the **Toolbox** onto the Form.

Aligning Controls
- Use the Form's background grid for alignment. You also can use the **Format** menu's commands.

Resizing the Form or Control with Sizing Handles
- Click and drag one of the object's enabled sizing handles.

Setting the Dimensions of the Form or Control by Using the Size Property
- Enter the height and width of the Form or control in the Size field.

Setting the Width and Height of the Form or Control
- Enter values in the Width and Height property fields (or use the Size property field).

Setting the Form's Background Color
- Set the Form's BackColor property.

Adding a Label Control to the Form
- Double click the Label control in the **Toolbox** to place the control in the upper-left corner of the Form.

Setting the Text Displayed in a Label
- Set the Label's Text property.

Setting a Label's Font Property
- Click the value of the Font property, which causes an ellipsis Button to appear next to the value. When the ellipsis Button is clicked, the **Font** dialog is displayed; it allows programmers to change the font name, style and size of the Label's text.

Aligning Text in a Label
- Use the Label's TextAlign property.

Adding an Image to the Form
- Use a PictureBox control to display the image. Click the ellipsis Button next to the PictureBox Image property's value to browse for an image to insert.
- Scale the image to the size of the PictureBox by setting the SizeMode property to the value StretchImage.

Displaying a Form or Control's Properties in the Properties Window
- Click the Form or a control on the Form.

KEY TERMS

BackColor property of a Form—Specifies the Form's background color.

Font property of a control—Specifies the font name, style and size of any displayed text in the Form or one of its controls.

grid—The dots on the background of a Form that are used to align controls placed on the Form.

Height property—This property, a member of the Size property, indicates the height of the Form or one of its controls in pixels.

Image property of a PictureBox control—Indicates the file name of the image displayed in a

PictureBox.

Label control—Displays text the user cannot modify.

namespace—Classes in the FCL are organized by functionality into these directory-like entities.

palette—A set of colors.

PictureBox control—Displays an image.

pixel—A tiny point on your computer screen that displays a color.

RGB value—The amount of red, green and blue needed to create a color.

run mode—An IDE mode indicating that the application is running (executing).

Size property of a control—Specifies the height and width, in pixels, of the Form or one of its controls.

SizeMode property of a PictureBox control—Specifies how an image is displayed in a PictureBox.

sizing handle—Square that, when enabled, can be used to resize the Form or one of its controls.

StretchImage—The value of PictureBox property SizeMode that scales an image to fill the PictureBox.

Text property of a control—Specifies the text displayed by the Form or a Label.

TextAlign property of a control—Specifies how text is aligned within a Label.

Web-safe colors—Colors that display the same on different computers.

Width property—This property, a member of the Size property, indicates the width of the Form or one of its controls, in pixels.

GUI DESIGN GUIDELINES

Overall Design
- Use colors in your applications, but not to the point of distracting the user.

Forms
- Choose short and descriptive Form titles. Capitalize words that are not articles, prepositions or conjunctions. Do not use punctuation.
- Use **Tahoma** font to improve readability for controls that display text.

Labels
- Use Labels to display text that users cannot change.
- Ensure that all Label controls are large enough to display their text.

PictureBoxes
- Use PictureBoxes to enhance GUIs with graphics that users cannot change.
- Images should fit inside their PictureBoxes. This can be achieved by setting PictureBox property SizeMode to StretchImage.

CONTROLS, EVENTS, PROPERTIES & METHODS

Label   A Label   This control displays on the Form text that the user cannot modify.

- *In action*

- *Properties*
  Text—Specifies the text displayed on the Label.
  Font—Specifies the font name, style and size of the text displayed in the Label.
  TextAlign—Determines how the text is aligned within the Label.

PictureBox PictureBox This control displays an image on the Form.

■ *In action*

■ *Properties*

Image—Specifies the file path of the image.

SizeMode—Specifies how an image is displayed in the PictureBox.

Size—Specifies the height and width (in pixels) of the PictureBox.

MULTIPLE-CHOICE QUESTIONS

3.1 The _____ property determines the Form's background color.

a) BackColor
b) BackgroundColor
c) RGB
d) Color

3.2 To save all the solution's files, select _____.

a) **Save > Solution > Save Files**
b) **File > Save**
c) **File > Save All**
d) **File > Save As...**

3.3 When the ellipsis Button to the right of the **Font** property value is clicked, the _____ is displayed.

a) **Font Property** dialog
b) **New Font** dialog
c) **Font Settings** dialog
d) **Font** dialog

3.4 PictureBox property _____ contains a preview of the image displayed in the PictureBox.

a) Picture
b) ImageName
c) Image
d) PictureName

3.5 The _____ tab allows you to create your own color.

a) **Custom**
b) **Web**
c) **System**
d) **User**

3.6 The PictureBox class belongs to the _____ namespace.

a) System.Windows.Forms
b) System.Form.Form
c) System.Form.Font
d) System.Form.Control

3.7 A Label control displays the text specified by the _____ property.

a) Caption
b) Data
c) Text
d) Name

3.8 In _____ mode, the application is running (executing).

a) start
b) run
c) execute
d) design

3.9 The _____ command prevents programmers from accidentally altering the size and location of the Form's controls.

a) **Lock Controls**
b) **Anchor Controls**
c) **Lock**
d) **Bind Controls**

3.10 Pixels are _____.

a) picture elements
b) controls in the **Toolbox**
c) a set of fonts
d) a set of colors on the **Web** tab

EXERCISES

For Exercises 3.11–3.16, you are asked to create the GUI shown in each exercise. You will use the visual programming techniques presented in this tutorial to create a variety of GUIs. Because you are creating only GUIs, your applications will not be fully operational. For example, the **Calculator** *GUI in Exercise 3.11 will not behave like a calculator when its* Buttons *are clicked. You will learn how to make your applications fully operational in later tutorials. Create each application as a separate project.*

3.11 *(Calculator GUI)* Create the GUI for the calculator shown in Fig. 3.33.

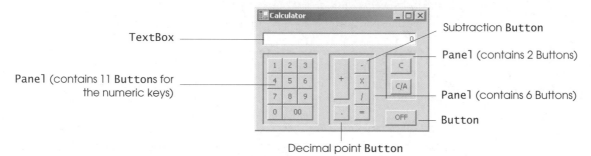

Figure 3.33   **Calculator** GUI.

a) *Creating a new project.* Open Visual Studio .NET. Create a new project in your C:\SimplyCSP directory named Calculator.

b) *Renaming the Form file.* Name the Form file Calculator.cs. Double click the file name to open the Form in design view.

c) *Manipulating the Form's properties.* Change the Size property of the Form to 272, 192. Change the Text property of the Form to Calculator. Change the Font property to **Tahoma**.

d) *Adding a TextBox to the Form.* Add a TextBox control by double clicking it in the **Toolbox**. A TextBox control is used to enter input into applications. Set the TextBox's Text property in the **Properties** window to 0. Change the Size property to 240, 21. Set the TextAlign property to Right; this right aligns text displayed in the TextBox. Finally, set the TextBox's Location property to 8, 16.

e) *Adding the first Panel to the Form.* Panel controls are used to group other controls. Double click the Panel icon (☐ Panel) in the **Toolbox** to add a Panel to the Form. Change the Panel's BorderStyle property to Fixed3D to make the inside of the Panel appear recessed. Change the Size property to 88, 112. Finally, set the Location property to 8, 48. This Panel contains the calculator's numeric keys.

f) *Adding the second Panel to the Form.* Click the Form. Double click the Panel icon in the **Toolbox** to add another Panel to the Form. Change the Panel's BorderStyle property to Fixed3D. Change the Size property to 72, 112. Finally, set the Location property to 112, 48. This Panel contains the calculator's operator keys.

g) *Adding the third (and last) Panel to the Form.* Click the Form. Double click the Panel icon in the **Toolbox** to add another Panel to the Form. Change the Panel's BorderStyle property to Fixed3D. Change the Size property to 48, 72. Finally, set the Location property to 200, 48. This Panel contains the calculator's **C** (clear) and **C/A** (clear all) keys.

h) *Adding Buttons to the Form.* There are 20 Buttons on the calculator. To add a Button to a Panel, double click the Button control (abl Button) in the **Toolbox**. Then add the Button to the Panel by dragging and dropping it on the Panel. Change the Text property of each Button to the calculator key it represents. The value you enter in the Text property will appear on the face of the Button. Finally, resize the Buttons, using their Size properties. Each Button labeled 0–9, x, /, –, = and . should have a size of 24, 24. The **00** and **OFF** Buttons have size 48, 24. The **+** Button is sized 24, 64. The **C** (clear) and **C/A** (clear all) Buttons are sized 32, 24.

i) *Saving the project.* Select **File > Save All** to save your changes.

j) *Closing the IDE.* Close Visual Studio .NET by clicking its close box.

3.12 *(Alarm Clock GUI)* Create the GUI for the alarm clock in Fig. 3.34.

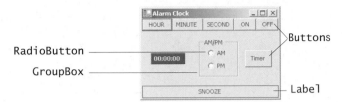

RadioButton

GroupBox

Buttons

Label

Figure 3.34 Alarm Clock GUI.

a) *Creating a new project.* Open Visual Studio .NET. Create a new project in your C:\SimplyCSP directory named AlarmClock.

b) *Renaming the Form file.* Name the Form file AlarmClock.cs. Double click the file name to open the Form in design view.

c) *Manipulating the Form's properties.* Change the Size property of the Form to 256, 176. Change the Text property of the Form to Alarm Clock. Change the Font property to **Tahoma**.

d) *Adding Buttons to the Form.* Add six Buttons to the Form. Change the Text property of each Button to the appropriate text. Change the Size properties of the **Hour**, **Minute** and **Second** Buttons to 56, 23. The **ON** and **OFF** Buttons get size 40, 23. The **Timer** Button gets size 48, 32. Align the Buttons as shown in Fig. 3.34.

e) *Adding a Label to the Form.* Add a Label to the Form. Change the Text property to **Snooze**. Set its Size to 248, 23. Set the Label's TextAlign property to Middle-Center. Finally, to draw a border around the edge of the **Snooze** Label, change the BorderStyle property of the **Snooze** Label to FixedSingle.

f) *Adding a GroupBox to the Form.* **GroupBoxes** are like Panels, except that Group-Boxes can display a title. To add a GroupBox to the Form, double click the GroupBox control (GroupBox) in the **Toolbox**. Change the Text property to **AM/PM**, and set the Size property to 72, 72. To place the GroupBox in the correct location on the Form, set the Location property to 104, 38.

g) *Adding AM/PM RadioButtons to the GroupBox.* Add two RadioButtons to the Form by dragging the RadioButton control (RadioButton) in the **Toolbox** and drop-ping it onto the GroupBox twice. Change the Text property of one RadioButton to AM and the other to PM. Then place the RadioButtons as shown in Fig. 3.34 by setting the Location of the **AM** RadioButton to 16, 16 and that of the **PM** RadioButton to 16, 40. Set their Size properties to 48, 24.

h) *Adding the time Label to the Form.* Add a Label to the Form and change its Text property to 00:00:00. Change the BorderStyle property to Fixed3D and the Back-Color to Black. Set the Size property to 64, 23. Use the Font property to make the time bold. Change the ForeColor to Silver (located in the **Web** tab) to make the time stand out against the black background. Set TextAlign to MiddleCenter to center the text in the Label. Position the Label as shown in Fig. 3.34.

i) *Saving the project.* Select **File > Save All** to save your changes.

j) *Closing the IDE.* Close Visual Studio .NET by clicking its close box.

3.13 *(Microwave Oven GUI)* Create the GUI for the microwave oven shown in Fig. 3.35.

a) *Creating a new project.* Open Visual Studio .NET. Create a new project in your C:\SimplyCSP directory named Microwave.

b) *Renaming the Form file.* Name the Form file Microwave.cs. Double click the file name to open the Form in design view.

c) *Manipulating the Form's properties.* Change the Size property of the Form to 552, 288. Change the Text property of the Form to Microwave Oven. Change the Font property to **Tahoma**.

d) *Adding the microwave oven door.* Add a Panel to the Form by double clicking the Panel (Panel) in the **Toolbox**. Select the Panel and change the BackColor property to Silver (located in the **Web** tab) in the **Properties** window. Then change the Size to 328, 224. Next, change the BorderStyle property to FixedSingle.

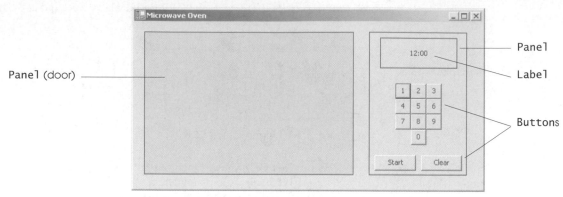

Figure 3.35 Microwave Oven GUI.

e) *Adding another Panel.* Add another Panel and change its Size to 152, 224 and its BorderStyle to FixedSingle. Place the Panel to the right of the door Panel as shown in Fig. 3.35.

f) *Adding the microwave oven clock.* Add a Label to the right Panel by clicking the Label in the **Toolbox** once, then clicking once inside the right Panel. Change the Label's Text to 12:00, BorderStyle to FixedSingle and Size to 120, 48. Change TextAlign to MiddleCenter. Place the clock as shown in Fig. 3.35.

g) *Adding a keypad to the microwave oven.* Place a Button in the right Panel by clicking the Button control in the **Toolbox** once, then clicking inside the Panel. Change the Text to 1 and the Size to 24, 24. Repeat this process for nine more Buttons, changing the Text property in each to the next number in the keypad. Then add the **Start** and **Clear** Buttons, each of Size 64, 24. Do not forget to set the Text properties for each of these Buttons. Finally, arrange the Buttons as shown in Fig. 3.35. The **1** Button is located at 40, 80 and the **Start** Button is located at 8, 192.

h) *Saving the project.* Select **File > Save All** to save your changes.

i) *Closing the IDE.* Close Visual Studio .NET by clicking its close box.

3.14 *(Cell Phone GUI)* Create the GUI for the cell phone shown in Fig. 3.36.

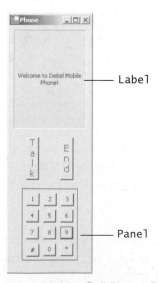

Figure 3.36 Cell Phone GUI.

a) *Creating a new project.* Open Visual Studio .NET. Create a new project in your C:\SimplyCSP directory named Phone.

b) *Renaming the Form file.* Name the Form file Phone.cs. Double click the file name to open the Form in design view.

c) *Manipulating the Form's properties.* Change the Form's Text property to Phone and the Size to 160, 488. Change the Font property to **Tahoma**.

d) *Adding the display Label.* Add a Label to the Form. Change its BackColor to Aqua (in the **Web** tab palette), the Text to Welcome to Deitel Mobile Phone! and the Size to 136, 184. Change the TextAlign property to MiddleCenter. Then place the Label as shown in Fig. 3.36.

e) *Adding the keypad Panel.* Add a Panel to the Form. Change its BorderStyle property to FixedSingle and its Size to 104, 136.

f) *Adding the keypad Buttons.* Add the keypad Buttons to the Form (12 Buttons in all). Each Button on the number pad should be of Size 24, 24 and should be placed in the Panel. Change the Text property of each Button such that numbers 0–9, the pound (#) and the star (*) keys are represented. Then add the final two Buttons such that the Text property for one is Talk and the other is End. Change the Size of each Button to 24, 80, and notice how the small Size causes the Text to align vertically. Change the Font size of these two Buttons to 12.

g) *Placing the controls.* Arrange all the controls so that your GUI looks like Fig. 3.36.

h) *Saving the project.* Select **File > Save All** to save your changes.

i) *Closing the IDE.* Close Visual Studio .NET by clicking its close box.

3.15 *(Vending Machine GUI)* Create the GUI for the vending machine in Fig. 3.37.

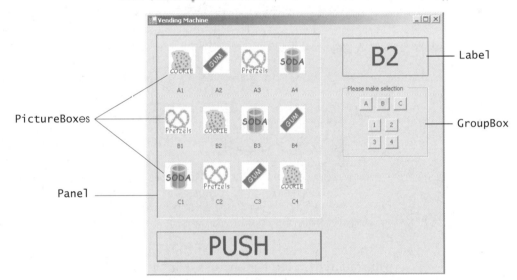

Figure 3.37 Vending Machine GUI.

a) *Creating a new project.* Open Visual Studio .NET. Create a new project in your C:\SimplyCSP directory named VendingMachine.

b) *Renaming the Form file.* Name the Form file VendingMachine.cs. Double click the file name to open the Form in design view.

c) *Manipulating the Form's properties.* Set the Text property of the Form to Vending Machine and the Size to 560, 488. Change the Font property to **Tahoma**.

d) *Adding the food selection Panel.* Add a Panel to the Form, and change its Size to 312, 344 and BorderStyle to Fixed3D. Add a PictureBox to the Panel, and change its Size to 50, 50. Then set the Image property by clicking the ellipsis Button and choosing a file from the C:\Examples\Tutorial03\ExerciseImages\VendingMachine directory. Repeat this process for 11 more PictureBoxes.

e) *Adding Labels for each vending item.* Add a Label under each PictureBox. Change the Text property of the Label to A1, the TextAlign property to TopCenter and the Size to 56, 16. Place the Label so that it is located as in Fig. 3.37. Repeat this process for A2 through C4 (11 Labels).

f) *Creating the vending machine door (as a Button).* Add a Button to the Form by dragging the Button control in the **Toolbox** and dropping it below the Panel. Change the Button's Text property to PUSH, its Font Size to 36 and its Size to 312, 56. Then place the Button on the Form as shown in Fig. 3.37.

g) *Adding the selection display Label.* Add a Label to the Form, and change the Text property to B2, BorderStyle to FixedSingle, Font Size to 36, TextAlign to MiddleCenter and Size to 160, 72.

h) *Grouping the input Buttons.* Add a GroupBox below the Label, and change the Text property to Please make selection and the Size to 160, 136.

i) *Adding the input Buttons.* Finally, add Buttons to the GroupBox. For the seven Buttons, change the Size property to 24, 24. Then change the Text property of the Buttons such that each Button has one of the values A, B, C, 1, 2, 3 or 4, as shown in Fig. 3.37. When you are done, move the controls on the Form so that they are aligned as shown in Fig. 3.37.

j) *Saving the project.* Select **File > Save All** to save your changes.

k) *Closing the IDE.* Close Visual Studio .NET by clicking its close box.

Programming Challenge ▶ **3.16 (Radio GUI)** Create the GUI for the radio in Fig. 3.38. [*Note:* All colors used in this exercises are from the **Web** palette.]

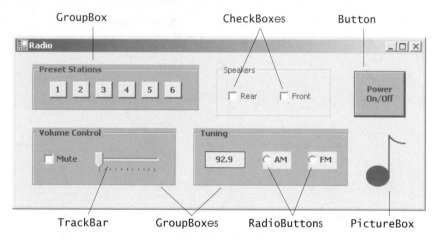

Figure 3.38 Radio GUI.

In this exercise, you will create this GUI on your own. Feel free to experiment with different control properties. For the image in the PictureBox, use the file (MusicNote.gif) found in the C:\Examples\Tutorial03\ExerciseImages\Radio directory.

a) *Creating a new project.* Open Visual Studio .NET. Create a new project in your C:\SimplyCSP directory named Radio.

b) *Renaming the Form file.* Name the Form file Radio.cs. Double click the file name to open the Form in design view.

c) *Manipulating the Form's properties.* Change the Form's Text property to Radio and the Size to 576, 240. Change the Font property to **Tahoma**. Set BackColor to PeachPuff.

d) *Adding the Preset Stations GroupBox and Buttons.* Add a GroupBox to the Form. Set its Size to 232, 64, its Text to Preset Stations, its ForeColor to Black and its BackColor to RosyBrown. Change its Font to bold. Finally, set its Location to 24, 16. Add six Buttons to the GroupBox. Set each BackColor to PeachPuff and each Size to 24, 23. Change the Buttons' Text properties to 1, 2, 3, 4, 5, and 6, respectively.

e) *Adding the Speakers GroupBox and CheckBoxes.* Add a GroupBox to the Form. Set its Size to 160, 72, its Text to Speakers and its ForeColor to Black. Set its Location to 280, 16. Add two CheckBoxes to the Form. Set each CheckBox's Size to 56, 24. Set the Text properties for the CheckBoxes to Rear and Front.

f) *Adding the Power On/Off Button.* Add a Button to the Form. Set its Text to Power On/Off, its BackColor to RosyBrown, its ForeColor to Black and its Size to 72, 64. Change its Font style to Bold.

g) *Adding the Volume Control GroupBox, the Mute CheckBox and the Volume Track-Bar.* Add a GroupBox to the Form. Set its Text to Volume Control, its BackColor to RosyBrown, its ForeColor to Black and its Size to 200, 80. Set its Font style to Bold. Add a CheckBox to the GroupBox. Set its Text to Mute and its Size to 56, 24. Add a TrackBar to the GroupBox.

h) *Adding the Tuning GroupBox, the radio station Label and the AM/FM RadioButtons.* Add a GroupBox to the Form. Set its Text to Tuning, its ForeColor to Black and its BackColor to RosyBrown. Set its Font style to Bold and its Size to 216, 80. Add a Label to the Form. Set its BackColor to PeachPuff, its ForeColor to Black, its BorderStyle to FixedSingle, its Font style to Bold, its TextAlign to Middle-Center and its Size to 56, 23. Set its Text to 92.9. Place the Label as shown in the figure. Add two RadioButtons to the GroupBox. Change the BackColor to Peach-Puff and change the Size to 40, 24. Set one's Text to AM and the other's Text to FM.

i) *Adding the image.* Add a PictureBox to the Form. Set its BackColor to Transparent, its SizeMode to StretchImage and its Size to 56, 72. Set its Image property to C:\Examples\Tutorial03\ExerciseImages\Radio\MusicNote.gif.

j) *Saving the project.* Select **File > Save All** to save your changes.

k) *Closing the IDE.* Close Visual Studio .NET by clicking its close box.

TUTORIAL

4

Objectives

In this tutorial, you will learn to:
- Visually program, using GUI design guidelines.
- Add Labels, TextBoxes and a Button to a Form.
- Use the TextAlign and BorderStyle properties for Labels.

Outline

Designing the Inventory Application

Introducing TextBoxes and Buttons

This tutorial introduces you to the fundamentals of visual programming. You will design the graphical user interface for a simple **Inventory** application. Through each set of steps, you will enhance the application's user interface by adding controls. You will design a Form on which you place Labels, TextBoxes and a Button. You will learn new properties for Labels and TextBoxes, and you will learn how to add a Button to the Form. At the end of the tutorial, you will find a list of new GUI design guidelines to help you create appealing and easy-to-use graphical user interfaces.

4.1 Test-Driving the Inventory Application

In this tutorial, you will create an inventory application that calculates the number of textbooks received by a college bookstore. This application must meet the following requirements:

Application Requirements

A college bookstore receives cartons of textbooks. In a shipment, each carton contains the same number of textbooks. The inventory manager wants to use a computer to calculate the total number of textbooks arriving at the bookstore for each shipment, from the number of cartons and the number of textbooks in each carton. The inventory manager will enter the number of cartons received and the fixed number of textbooks in each carton for each shipment; the application then will calculate the total number of textbooks in a shipment.

This application performs a simple calculation. The user (the inventory manager) inputs into TextBoxes the number of cartons and number of items in each carton. The user then clicks a Button, which causes the application to multiply the two numbers and display the result—the total number of textbooks received. You begin by test-driving the application. Then, you will learn the additional C# technologies you will need to create your own version of this application.

Test-Driving the Inventory Application

1. ***Opening the completed application.*** Open the `C:\Examples\Tutorial04\CompletedApplication\Inventory` directory to locate the **Inventory** application. Double click `Inventory.sln` to open the application in Visual Studio .NET. Depending on your system configuration, you may not see the `.sln` file name extension. In this case, double click the file named `Inventory` that contains a solution file icon, 🖫.

2. ***Running the Inventory application.*** Select **Debug > Start** to run the application. The **Inventory** Form shown in Fig. 4.1 will appear.

TextBoxes

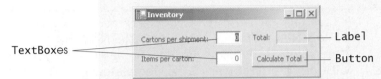

Label

Button

Figure 4.1 **Inventory** application `Form` with the default data displayed by the application.

Notice that there are two controls that you did not use in the **Welcome** application—the `TextBox` and `Button` controls. A **TextBox** is a control that the user can use to enter data from the keyboard and that can display data to the user. A **Button** is a control that allows the application to perform an action when clicked.

3. ***Entering quantities in the application.*** Some controls (such as `TextBoxes`) are not used to display descriptive text for other controls; therefore, we refer to these controls by using the `Labels` that identify them. For example, we will refer to the `TextBox` to the right of the **Cartons per shipment:** `Label` as the **Cartons per shipment:** `TextBox`. Enter 3 in the **Cartons per shipment:** `TextBox`. Enter 15 in the **Items per carton:** `TextBox`. Figure 4.2 shows the `Form` after these values have been entered.

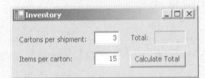

Figure 4.2 **Inventory** application with new quantities entered.

4. ***Calculating the total number of items received.*** Click the **Calculate Total** `Button`. This causes the application to multiply the two numbers you entered and display the result (45) in the `Label` to the right of **Total:** (Fig. 4.3).

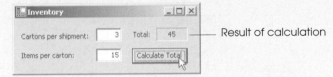

Result of calculation

Figure 4.3 Result of clicking the **Calculate Total** `Button` in the **Inventory** application.

5. ***Closing the application.*** Close your running application by clicking its close box.

6. ***Closing the solution.*** Select **File > Close Solution.**

4.2 Constructing the Inventory Application

Now that you have test-driven the completed application, you will begin creating your own version of the application. In the following box, you will create a new project that contains the Form on which you will place the controls required for the **Inventory** application. Then, you will save the solution containing the Form to your working directory, C:\SimplyCSP (ensuring that you will know which directory contains your solution if you take a break from building the application). Finally, the initial steps conclude with instructions for renaming the C# file.

Creating a New Application

1. ***Creating the new project.*** To create a Windows application, select **File > New > Project…,** to display the **New Project** dialog (Fig. 4.4). Click the **Visual C# Projects** directory in the **Project Types:** pane to retrieve the list of C# project types in the **Templates:** pane. From this list, select **Windows Application**. Type Inventory in the **Name:** Textbox, and leave the dialog open. If your C:\SimplyCSP directory is already displayed in the **Location:** TextBox, you may skip the next step and continue with *Step 3, Viewing the Form.*

Project Types: pane with Visual C# Projects directory selected (your directory list might differ)

Name: TextBox

Location: TextBox

Templates: pane with Windows Application selected

Browse... Button

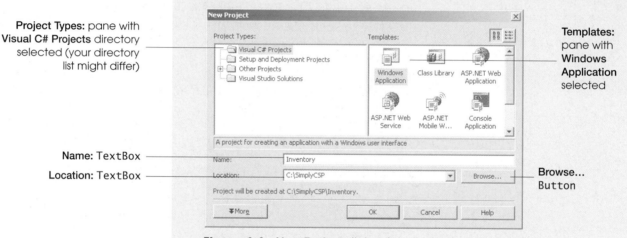

Figure 4.4 New Project dialog for creating new applications.

2. ***Saving the project to your working directory.*** To save the project to your working directory, click the **Browse…** Button (Fig. 4.4). The **Project Location** dialog will appear (Fig. 4.5). Because you already created the SimplyCSP directory, navigate to the C:\SimplyCSP directory. Click **Open** to select the directory and dismiss the dialog. The selected directory will then appear in the **Location:** TextBox.

Working directory

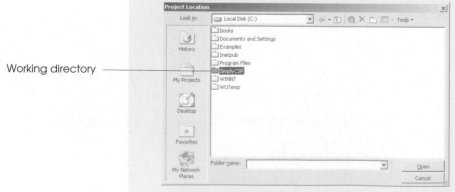

Figure 4.5 Project Location dialog used to specify the directory in which the project files reside.

(cont.)   3. ***Viewing the Form.*** Click the **OK** Button (Fig. 4.4) to close the **New Project** dialog. The IDE will then load the new application, containing a Form named **Form1** (Fig. 4.6). If the Form does not appear as in Fig. 4.6, select **View > Designer**. [*Note:* If the **Solution Explorer** or **Properties** windows do not appear, they can be opened by selecting **View > Solution Explorer** and **View > Properties Window**.]

Form title bar (for **Form1**)

Form file name (**Form1.cs**)

Form

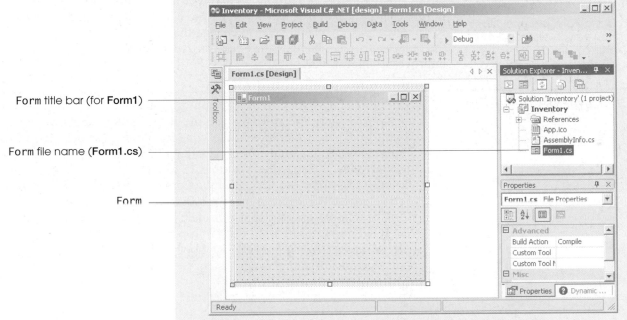

Figure 4.6 New Windows application (**Form1**) in Visual Studio .NET.

4. ***Renaming the Form file.*** It is a good practice to change the Form file name to something more meaningful for your application. To change the Form file name (Fig. 4.7), click its name (**Form1.cs**) in the **Solution Explorer**. Then select **File Name** in the **Properties** window, and type **Inventory.cs** in the field to the right. Press the *Enter* key to update the file name. Unless otherwise noted, you need to press the *Enter* key for changes made in the **Properties** window to take effect.

Form's file name after property change

File **Name** property

Type new **Form** file name here

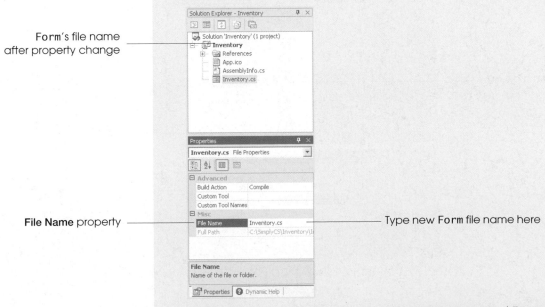

Figure 4.7 Renaming a file in the **Solution Explorer** and **Properties** windows.

(cont.) 5. ***Saving the project.*** Select **File > Save All** to save your changes. Saving your work often will prevent losing changes to the application.

GUI Design Tip

Change the Form's font to **Tahoma** to be consistent with Microsoft's recommended font for Windows.

In the following box, you learn how to modify your Form by setting its font. As in all our examples, you should set the Form's font to **Tahoma**, which is the Microsoft-recommended font for GUIs. Changing the Form's font to **Tahoma** ensures that controls added to the Form use the **Tahoma** font. You will also learn how to change the Form's title and size. Although you already changed the file name to `Inventory.cs`, you still need to change the title bar text to help users identify the Form's purpose. Changing the Form's size to be more appropriate for its content improves its appearance.

Customizing the Form

1. ***Setting the Form's font.*** In the previous tutorial, you used the **Font** dialog to change the font. You will now use the **Properties** window to change the Form's font. Select the Form in the Windows Form Designer. If the **Properties** window is not already open, click the properties icon in the IDE toolbar or select **View > Properties Window**. To change the Form's font to **Tahoma**, click the plus box ⊞ to the left of the **Font** property in the **Properties** window (Fig. 4.8). This causes other properties related to the Form's Font to be displayed. In the list that appears, select the font's **Name** property, and click the down arrow to the right of the property value. In the list that appears, select **Tahoma**. [*Note*: This list may appear slightly different, based on the fonts that are installed on your system.]

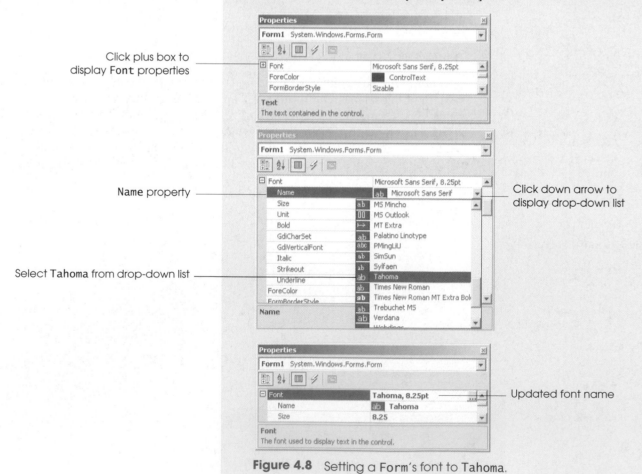

Figure 4.8 Setting a Form's font to Tahoma.

(cont.)

You will notice that several properties, such as Font, have a plus box ⊞ next to the property name to indicate that there are additional properties available for this node. For example, the Name, Size and Bold properties of a Font each have their own listings in the **Properties** window when you click the plus box.

2. ***Setting the text in the Form's title bar.*** The text in the Form's title bar is determined by the Form's Text property. Double click the field to the right of the Text property in the **Properties** window, type Inventory, then press *Enter* (Fig. 4.9). Form titles should use book-title capitalization. **Book-title capitalization** is a style that capitalizes the first letter of each significant word in the text and does not end with any punctuation (for example, *Capitalization in a Book Title*).

GUI Design Tip

Changing the Form's title allows users to identify the application's purpose.

GUI Design Tip

Form titles should use book-title capitalization.

Size property ———

Text property ———

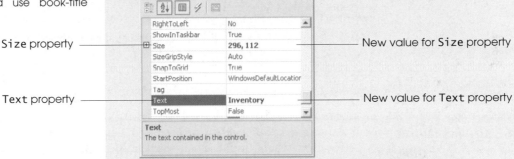

——— New value for Size property

——— New value for Text property

Figure 4.9   Setting the Text property of a Form.

3. ***Resizing the Form.*** Double click the field to the right of the Size property in the **Properties** window, and enter 296, 112 (Fig. 4.9). Notice that the Form is now the same size as in the completed application you test-drove at the beginning of the tutorial (Fig. 4.10). Notice that the title bar is updated based on the changes from *Step 2*.

Title bar renamed to **Inventory** ———

One grid unit ———

Figure 4.10   Resized Form displaying new title bar text.

GUI Design Tip

When sizing a Form, leave approximately two grid units of space between the edges of the Form and the controls that you will later add. This ensures that there is a uniform border around the Form. A grid unit is the distance between two adjacent dots on the Form in design view.

4. ***Saving the project.*** Select **File > Save All** to save your changes.

Now that you have created and modified the Form, you will add controls to the GUI. Labels describe the purpose of controls on the Form and can be used to display results of calculations. In the following box, you learn how to add Label controls and set each Label's name, text and position on the Form.

SELF-REVIEW   1. Change the Form's font to _____ to be consistent with Microsoft's recommended font for Windows.

a) Times New Roman   b) Microsoft Sans Serif

c) Tahoma   d) Courier New

2. The text in the Form's title bar is determined by the Form's _____ property.
    a) Text   b) Title
    c) Name   d) File

Answers: 1) c. 2) a.

4.3 Adding Labels to the Inventory Application

Although you might not have noticed it, there are four Labels in this application. You can easily recognize three of the Labels from the application you designed in Tutorial 3. The fourth Label, however, has a border and contains no text until the user clicks the **Calculate Total** Button (Fig. 4.11). As the control's name indicates, Labels are often used to identify other controls on the Form. **Descriptive Labels** help the user understand each control's purpose, and **output Labels** to display application output.

Figure 4.11   Labels used in the **Inventory** application.

Adding Labels to the Form

1. ***Adding a Label control to the Form.*** Click the **Windows Forms** tab in the **Toolbox**. Then, double click the **Label** control in the **Toolbox** to place a Label on the Form (Fig. 4.12).

Figure 4.12   Adding a Label to the Form.

2. ***Setting the Label's size and location.*** If the **Properties** window is not open, select **View > Properties Window**. In the **Properties** window, set the Label's Size property to 120, 21. Similarly, set the Label's Location property to 8, 18. Using these numbers ensures that the controls will align properly when you have added all of the controls to the Form. As you learned in the previous tutorial, you also can click and drag a control to place it on the Form and use sizing handles to resize it.

The Label's **Location** property specifies the position of the upper-left corner of the control on the Form. Visual Studio .NET assigns the value 0, 0 to the top-left corner of the Form, not including the title bar (Fig. 4.12). A control's Location property is set according to its distance from that point on the Form. As the first number of the Location property increases, the control moves to the right. As the second number of the Location property increases, the control moves toward the bottom of the Form. In this case, the value of 8, 18 indicates that the Label is placed 8 pixels to the right of the top-left corner of the Form and 18 pixels down from the top-left corner of the Form (Fig. 4.14). A Location value of 8, 48 would indicate that the Label is placed 8 pixels to the right of the top-left corner of the Form and 48 pixels down from the top-left corner of the Form.

GUI Design Tip

Use a control's Location property to precisely specify a position on the Form.

GUI Design Tip

A Label used to describe the purpose of a control should use sentence-style capitalization and end with a colon. These types of Labels are called descriptive Labels.

(cont.)

Good Programming Practice

Use standard prefixes for names of objects (controls and `Forms`) so that you can easily tell them apart. Prefix all `Label` control names with `lbl`. Refer to Appendix E for naming conventions used throughout the text.

GUI Design Tip

The `TextAlign` property of a descriptive `Label` should be set to `MiddleLeft` to ensure that text within groups of `Labels` align.

3. ***Setting the Label's Name and Text properties.*** Each control, such as a `Label` object, needs a unique and meaningful name for easy identification. In Visual Studio .NET, you set the `Label`'s name by using the **Name** property, listed as (`Name`). In the **Properties** window, click the field to the right of the `Text` property, and type `Cartons per shipment:`. Set the `Name` property to `lblCartons`.

When entering values for a `Label`'s `Text` property, you should use sentence-style capitalization. **Sentence-style capitalization** means that you capitalize the first letter of the first word in the text. Every other letter in the text is lowercase unless it is the first letter of a proper noun (for example, *Deitel*).

4. ***Modifying the Label's text alignment.*** Select the `TextAlign` property in the **Properties** window. Then, in the field to the right, click the down arrow (Fig. 4.13). The `TextAlign` property sets the alignment of text within a control such as a `Label`. Clicking the down arrow opens a window in which you can select the alignment of the text in the `Label` (Fig. 4.13). In this window, select the middle-left rectangle, which indicates that the `Label`'s text aligns vertically to the middle and horizontally to the left in the control. The value of the property changes to `MiddleLeft`. Figure 4.14 displays the `Label` after you set its properties.

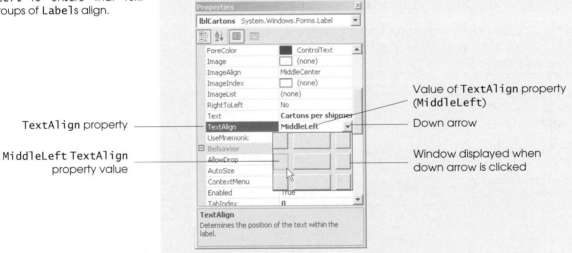

Figure 4.13   Changing the `TextAlign` property of a `Label`.

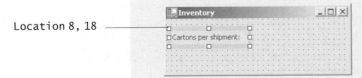

Figure 4.14   GUI after the `Label` has been customized.

5. ***Saving the project.*** Select **File > Save All** to save your changes.

Now you will add the remaining `Labels` to the `Form`. They will help the user understand what inputs to provide and interpret the application's output. These `Labels` will identify the controls that you will add to the `Form` later.

Placing Additional Labels on the Form

GUI Design Tip

Align the left sides of a group of descriptive Labels if the Labels are arranged vertically.

GUI Design Tip

A Label can be used to display output to the user.

GUI Design Tip

Place an application's output below and/or to the right of the Form's input controls.

MiddleCenter TextAlign property value

GUI Design Tip

The TextAlign property of a Label that displays the results of calculations should be set to MiddleCenter to distinguish the value from values in descriptive Labels.

GUI Design Tip

Output Labels should be distinguished from descriptive Labels by setting the BorderStyle property to Fixed3D and the TextAlign property to MiddleCenter.

1. ***Adding a second descriptive Label.*** Double click the Label control on the **Toolbox** to add a second Label. Set the Label's Size property to 104, 21 and the Label's Location property to 8, 48. Set the Label's Text property to Items per carton:, and change the Name property of this Label to lblItems. Then, set the Label's TextAlign property to MiddleLeft.

2. ***Adding a third descriptive Label.*** Double click the Label control on the **Toolbox** to add a third Label. Set the Label's Size property to 40, 21 and the Label's Location property to 184, 16. Set the Label's Text property to Total:, and change the Name property of this Label to lblTotal. Then, set the Label's TextAlign property to MiddleLeft.

3. ***Adding an output Label.*** To add the fourth Label, double click the Label control on the **Toolbox**. Set the Label's Size property to 48, 21 and the Label's Location property to 224, 16. Then, name this Label lblTotal-Result. Set the Label's TextAlign property to MiddleCenter. For the previous Labels, you set this property to MiddleLeft. To select value MiddleCenter, follow the same actions as in *Step 2*, but select the center rectangle shown in Fig. 4.15. You should use MiddleCenter text alignment to display results of calculations because it distinguishes the value in the output Label from the values in the descriptive Labels (whose TextAlign property is set to MiddleLeft).

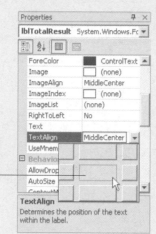

Figure 4.15 Setting the TextAlign property to MiddleCenter.

4. ***Changing a Label's BorderStyle property.*** Label lblTotalResult displays the result of the application's calculation; therefore, you should make this Label appear different from the other Labels. To do this, you will change the appearance of the Label's border by changing the value of the **BorderStyle** property. Assign the value Fixed3D (Fig. 4.16) to lblTotal-Result's BorderStyle property to make the Label seem three-dimensional (Fig. 4.17). [*Note*: If selected, FixedSingle displays a single dark line as a border.]

(cont.)

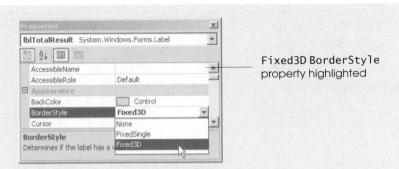

Fixed3D BorderStyle property highlighted

Figure 4.16   Changing a Label's BorderStyle property to Fixed3D.

GUI Design Tip

If several output Labels are arranged vertically to display numbers used in a mathematical calculation (such as in an invoice), set the TextAlign property of these Labels to MiddleRight.

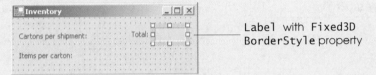

Label with Fixed3D BorderStyle property

Figure 4.17   GUI with all Labels added.

Good Programming Practice

Clear the value of output Labels initially. When the application performs the calculation for that value, the Label's Text property should be updated to the new value. You will learn how to do this in the next tutorial.

5. ***Clearing a Label's Text property.*** When a Label is added to a Form, the Text property is assigned the default name of the Label. In this case, you should clear the text of the Label because you will not be adding meaningful text to the lblTotalResult Label until later. To clear the text of this Label, use the *Delete* or *Backspace* key to delete the text to the right of the Text property in the **Properties** window. Figure 4.17 displays the GUI with all Labels added.

6. ***Saving the project.*** Select **File > Save All** to save your changes.

SELF-REVIEW

1. The value _____ for the Location property indicates the top-left corner (not including the title bar) of the Form.

     a) 1, 1   b) 0, 0
     c) 1, 0   d) 0, 1

2. An output Label should _____.

     a) be distinguishable from other Labels
     b) initially have an empty Text property
     c) use Fixed3D for the BorderStyle property
     d) All of the above.

Answers: 1) b. 2) d.

4.4 Adding TextBoxes and a Button to the Form

The **Inventory** application requires user input to calculate the total number of textbooks that have arrived per shipment. Specifically, the user types in the number of cartons and the fixed number of books per carton. Because this type of data is entered from the keyboard, you use a TextBox control. Next, you will learn how to add TextBoxes to your Form and set their properties. Then, you will add a Button control to complete your GUI.

Adding TextBox es to the Form

Good Programming Practice

Prefix TextBox control names with txt.

GUI Design Tip

Use TextBoxes to input data from the keyboard.

GUI Design Tip

Each TextBox should have a descriptive Label indicating the input expected from the user.

GUI Design Tip

Make TextBoxes wide enough for their expected inputs.

GUI Design Tip

A descriptive Label and the control it identifies should be left aligned if they are arranged vertically.

GUI Design Tip

A descriptive Label should have the same height as the TextBox it describes if the controls are arranged horizontally.

GUI Design Tip

A descriptive Label and the control it identifies should be top aligned if they are arranged horizontally.

1. **Adding a TextBox to the Form.** Double click the TextBox control,

in the **Toolbox** to add a TextBox to the Form. Setting the properties for a TextBox is similar to setting the properties for a Label. To name a TextBox, select the Name property in the **Properties** window, and enter txtCartons in the field to the right of the property (Fig. 4.18). Set the TextBox's Size property to 40, 21 and Location property to 128, 16. These size and location properties will cause the top of the TextBox to align with the top of the Label that describes it. Set the TextBox's Text property to 0 (Fig. 4.19). This will cause the value for your TextBox to be 0 when the application begins running.

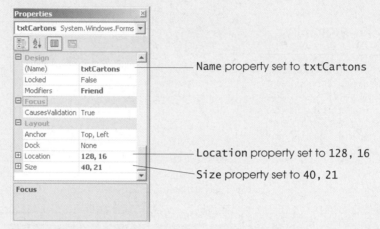

Name property set to txtCartons

Location property set to 128, 16

Size property set to 40, 21

Figure 4.18 Properties window for the txtCartons TextBox.

2. **Changing the TextAlign property of a TextBox.** Change txtCartons's TextAlign property to Right. Notice that, when you click the down arrow to the right of this property, the window in Fig. 4.13 does not appear. This is because TextBoxes have fewer TextAlign options, which are displayed simply as a list. Select Right from this list (Fig. 4.19).

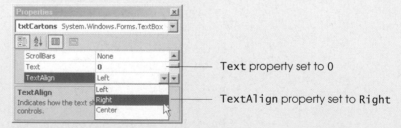

Text property set to 0

TextAlign property set to Right

Figure 4.19 Selecting the value Right of the TextAlign property of a TextBox control.

3. **Adding a second TextBox to the Form.** Double click the TextBox control in the **Toolbox**. Name the TextBox txtItems. Set the Size property to 40, 21 and the Location property to 128, 48. These settings ensure that the left sides of the two TextBoxes align. The settings also align the top of the Text-Box and the top of the Label that describes it. Set the Text property to 0 and the TextAlign property to Right. Figure 4.20 shows the Form after the TextBoxes have been added and their properties have been set.

(cont.)

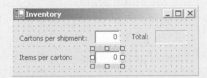

Figure 4.20   GUI after the TextBoxes have been added and modified.

4. ***Saving the project.*** Select **File > Save All** to save your changes.

 GUI Design Tip

Place each descriptive Label either above or to the left of the control (for instance, a TextBox) that it identifies.

 GUI Design Tip

Leave at least two grid units between each group of controls on the Form.

Notice that your controls are aligning horizontally and vertically. In general, you should place each descriptive Label above or to the left of the control it describes (for instance, a TextBox). If you are arranging your controls on the same line, the descriptive Label and the control it describes should be the same height. However, if you arrange your controls vertically, the Label should be placed above the control it describes, and the left sides of the controls should align. Also, leave at least two grid units between each group of controls on your Form. A **grid unit** is the space between two adjacent horizontal (or two adjacent vertical) dots on the Form in design view (Fig. 4.10). Following these simple guidelines will make your applications more appealing visually and easier to use by making the controls on the application less crowded.

Now that the user can enter data using a TextBox, you need a way for the user to command the application to perform the multiplication calculation and display the result. The most common way for a user to do this is by clicking a Button. The box below explains how to add a Button to the **Inventory** application.

Adding a Button to the Form

1. ***Adding a Button to the Form.*** Add a Button to the Form by double clicking the Button control,

in the **Toolbox**. Setting the properties for a Button is similar to setting the properties for a Label or a TextBox. Enter btnCalculate in the Button's Name property. For clarity, you should use btn (short for Button) as the prefix for Buttons.

Set the Button's Size to 88, 24 and Location to 184, 48. Notice that these settings cause the left and right sides of the Button to align with the Labels above it (Fig. 4.21). Enter Calculate Total in the Button's Text property. A Button's Text property displays its value on the face of the Button. You should use book-title capitalization in a Button's Text property. When labelling Buttons, keep the Text as short as possible while still clearly indicating the Button's function.

 GUI Design Tip

Buttons should be stacked downward from the top right of a Form or arranged on the same line starting from the bottom right of a Form.

 Good Programming Practice

Prefix Button control names with btn.

 GUI Design Tip

Buttons are labelled using their Text property. These labels should use book-title capitalization and be as short as possible while still being meaningful to the user.

2. ***Running the application.*** Select **Debug > Start** to run your application (Fig. 4.21). Notice that no action occurs if you click the **Calculate Total** Button. This is because you have not written code to tell the application how to respond to your click. In Tutorial 5, you will write code to display (in lblTotalResult) the total number of books in the shipment when you click the Button.

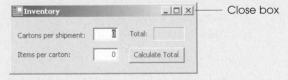

Figure 4.21   Running the application after completing its design.

(cont.)

3. ***Closing the application.*** Close your running application by clicking its close box. You do not need to save your changes, because by running the application, any modified files were saved.

4. ***Closing the IDE.*** Close Visual Studio .NET. by clicking its close box.

SELF-REVIEW

1. A Button's _____ property sets the value on the face of the Button.

   a) Name   b) Text

   c) Title   d) Face

2. Buttons should be _____ of the Form.

   a) on the same line, from the bottom right   b) stacked from the top left

   c) aligned with the title bar text   d) Either a or c.

Answers: 1) b. 2) a.

4.5 Wrap-Up

In this tutorial, you began constructing your **Inventory** application by designing its graphical user interface. You learned how to use Labels to describe controls and how to set a Label's TextAlign and BorderStyle properties. You used these properties to distinguish between descriptive and output Labels.

After labelling your Form, you added TextBoxes to allow users to input data from the keyboard. Finally, you added a Button to the **Inventory** application, allowing a user to signal the application to perform an action (in this case, to multiply two numbers and display the result). While you added controls to the Form, you also learned some GUI design tips to help you create appealing and intuitive graphical user interfaces.

The next tutorial teaches you to program code in C# that will run when the user clicks the **Calculate Total** Button. When the Button is clicked, the application receives a signal called an event. You will learn how to program your application to respond to that event by performing the multiplication calculation and displaying the result.

SKILLS SUMMARY

Creating a New Project

■ Select **File > New > Project...** to create a project.

■ Save a project to your working directory (C:\SimplyCSP) by selecting it from the **Project Location** dialog.

Setting the Application's Font to Tahoma

■ Select Tahoma from the Font's Name property ComboBox in the Form's **Properties** window.

Creating a Descriptive Label

■ Add a Label to your Form, then change the TextAlign property to MiddleLeft.

Creating an Output Label

■ Add a Label to your Form, and change the BorderStyle property to Fixed3D and the TextAlign property to MiddleCenter.

Enabling User Input from the Keyboard

■ Add a TextBox control to your Form.

Signaling that the Application Should Perform an Action

■ Add a Button to the Form, and write application code to perform that action. (You will learn how to add application code in Tutorial 5.)

KEY TERMS	**book-title capitalization**—A style that capitalizes the first letter of each word in the text (for example, **Calculate Total**).

KEY TERMS

book-title capitalization—A style that capitalizes the first letter of each word in the text (for example, **Calculate Total**).

BorderStyle property of the Label control—Specifies the appearance of a Label's border, which allows you to visually distinguish one control from another. The BorderStyle property can be set to None (no border), FixedSingle (a single dark line as a border), or Fixed3D (giving the Label a "sunken" appearance).

Button control—Used to command the application to perform an action.

descriptive Label—Used to describe another control on the Form. This helps users understand a control's purpose.

grid unit—The space between two adjacent horizontal (or vertical) dots on the Form in design view.

Location property of a control—Specifies the location of the upper-left corner of a control. This property is used to place a control on the Form precisely.

Name property of a control—Specifies the name used to access the control programmatically

output Label—Used to display calculation results.

sentence-style capitalization—A style that capitalizes the first letter of the first word in the text. Every other letter in the text is lowercase, unless it is the first letter of a proper noun.

Tahoma font—The Microsoft-recommended font for use in Windows applications.

TextBox control—Used to retrieve user input from the keyboard

GUI DESIGN GUIDELINES

Overall Design

- Leave at least two grid units between each group of controls on the Form.
- Use a control's Location property to precisely specify its position on the Form.
- Place an application's output below and/or to the right of the Form's input controls.

Buttons

- Buttons are labelled using their Text property. These labels should use book-title capitalization and be as short as possible while still being meaningful to the user.
- Buttons should be stacked downward from the top right of a Form or arranged on the same line starting from the bottom right of a Form.

Forms

- Changing the Form's title allows users to identify the application's purpose.
- Form titles should use book-title capitalization.
- When sizing a Form, leave approximately two grid units of space between the edges of the Form and the controls that you will later add. This ensures that there is a uniform border around the Form. A grid unit is the distance between two adjacent dots on the Form in design view.
- Change the Form's font to Tahoma to be consistent with Microsoft's recommended font for Windows.

Labels

- A Label used to describe the purpose of a control should use sentence-style capitalization and end with a colon. These types of Labels are called descriptive Labels.
- A Label can be used to display output to the user.
- Place each descriptive Label either above or to the left of the control (for instance, a TextBox) that it identifies.
- A descriptive Label should have the same height as the TextBox it describes if the controls are arranged horizontally.
- A descriptive Label and the control it identifies should be left aligned if they are arranged vertically.
- Align the left sides of a group of descriptive Labels if the Labels are arranged vertically.
- The TextAlign property of a descriptive Label should be set to MiddleLeft to ensure that text within groups of Labels align.

- The TextAlign property of a Label that displays the results of calculations should be set to MiddleCenter to distinguish the value from values in descriptive Labels.
- Output Labels should be distinguished from descriptive Labels by setting the BorderStyle property to Fixed3D and the TextAlign property to MiddleCenter.
- If several output Labels are arranged vertically to display numbers used in a mathematical calculation (such as in an invoice), set the TextAlign property of these Labels to MiddleRight.
- A descriptive Label and the control it identifies should be top aligned if they are arranged horizontally.

TextBoxes

- Use TextBoxes to input data from the keyboard.
- Each TextBox should have a descriptive Label indicating the input expected from the user.
- Make TextBoxes wide enough for their expected inputs.

CONTROLS, EVENTS, PROPERTIES & METHODS

Button   This control allows the user to raise an action or event.

- *In action*

    Calculate Total

- *Properties*

    Name—Specifies the name used to access the Button programmatically. The name should be prefixed with btn.

    Size—Specifies the height and width (in pixels) of the Button.

    Text—Specifies the text displayed on the Button.

Label A Label This control displays text that the user cannot modify.

- *In action*

    Total:

- *Properties*

    BorderStyle—Specifies the appearance of the Label's border.

    Font—Specifies the font name, style and size of the text displayed in the Label.

    Location—Specifies the location of the Label on the Form relative to the Form's top-left corner.

    Name—Specifies the name used to access the Label programatically (i.e., in a program). The name should be prefixed with lbl.

    Size—Specifies the height and width (in pixels) of the Label.

    Text—Specifies the text displayed in the Label.

    TextAlign—Determines how the text is aligned within the Label.

TextBox   TextBox This control allows the user to input data from the keyboard.

- *In action*

    0

- *Properties*

    Name—Specifies the name used to access the TextBox programmatically. The name should be prefixed with txt.

    Size—Specifies the height and width (in pixels) of the TextBox.

    Text—Specifies the text displayed in the TextBox.

    TextAlign—Specifies how the text is aligned within the TextBox.

MULTIPLE-CHOICE QUESTIONS

4.1 A new Windows application is created by selecting _____ from the **File** menu.

a) **New > Program**
b) **New > File...**
c) **New > Project...**
d) **New > Application**

4.2 A Label's BorderStyle property can be set to _____.

a) Fixed3D
b) Single
c) 3D
d) All of the above.

4.3 When creating a Label, you can specify the _____ of that Label.

a) alignment of the text
b) border style
c) size
d) All of the above.

4.4 Changing the value stored in the _____ property will change the name of the Form file.

a) Name
b) File
c) File Name
d) Full Path

4.5 _____ should be used to prefix all TextBox names.

a) txt
b) tbx
c) frm
d) tbn

4.6 A(n) _____ helps the user understand a control's purpose.

a) Button
b) descriptive Label
c) output Label
d) title bar

4.7 A _____ is a control in which the user can enter data from a keyboard.

a) Button
b) TextBox
c) Label
d) PictureBox

4.8 A descriptive Label uses _____.

a) sentence-style capitalization
b) book-title capitalization
c) a colon at the end of its text
d) Both a and c.

4.9 You should use the _____ font in your Windows applications.

a) Tahoma
b) MS Sans Serif
c) Times
d) Palatino

4.10 _____ should be used to prefix all Button names.

a) but
b) lbl
c) Frm
d) btn

EXERCISES

At the end of each tutorial, you will find a summary of new GUI design tips listed in the GUI Design Guidelines section. A cumulative list of GUI design guidelines, organized by control, appears in Appendix C. In these exercises, you will find C# Forms that do not follow the GUI design guidelines presented in this tutorial. For each exercise, you must modify control properties so that your end result is consistent with the guidelines presented in the tutorial. Note that these applications do not provide any functionality.

4.11 *(Address Book GUI)* In this exercise, you apply the GUI design guidelines you have learned to a graphical user interface for an address book (Fig. 4.22).

a) *Copying the template to your working directory.* Copy the directory C:\Examples\ Tutorial04\Exercises\AddressBook to your C:\SimplyCSP directory.

b) *Opening the application's template file.* Double click AddressBook.sln in the AddressBook directory to open the application. Double click AddressBook.cs in the **Solution Explorer** window to open the Form in design view.

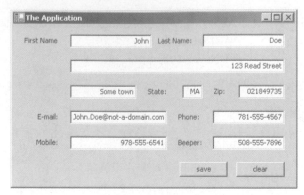

Figure 4.22 **Address Book** application without GUI design guidelines applied.

c) *Applying GUI design guidelines.* Rearrange the controls and modify their properties so that the GUI conforms to the design guidelines you have learned. Add new controls as necessary.

d) *Saving the project.* Select **File > Save All** to save your changes.

e) *Closing the IDE.* Close Visual Studio .NET by clicking its close box.

4.12 *(Mortgage Calculator GUI)* In this exercise, you apply the GUI design guidelines you have learned to a graphical user interface for a mortgage calculator (Fig. 4.23).

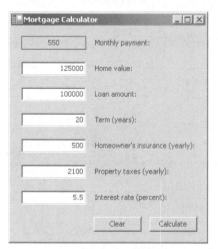

Figure 4.23 **Mortgage Calculator** application without GUI design guidelines applied.

a) *Copying the template to your working directory.* Copy the directory C:\Examples\ Tutorial04\Exercises\MortgageCalculator to your C:\SimplyCSP directory.

b) *Opening the application's template file.* Double click MortgageCalculator.sln in the MortgageCalculator directory to open the application. Double click Mortgage-Calculator.cs in the **Solution Explorer** window to open the Form in design view.

c) *Applying GUI design guidelines.* Rearrange the controls and modify their properties so that the GUI conforms to the design guidelines you have learned.

d) *Saving the project.* Select **File > Save All** to save your changes.

e) *Closing the IDE.* Close Visual Studio .NET by clicking its close box.

4.13 *(Password GUI)* In this exercise, you apply the GUI design guidelines you have learned to a graphical user interface for a password-protected message application (Fig. 4.24).

a) *Copying the template to your working directory.* Copy the directory C:\Examples\ Tutorial04\Exercises\Password to your C:\SimplyCSP directory.

b) *Opening the application's template file.* Double click Password.sln in the Password directory to open the application. Double click Password.cs in the **Solution Explorer** window to open the Form in design view.

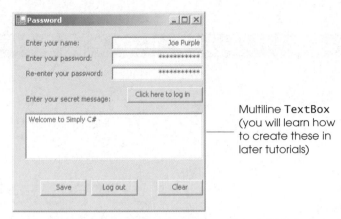

Figure 4.24 **Password** application without GUI design guidelines applied.

c) *Applying GUI design guidelines.* Rearrange the controls and modify their properties so that the GUI conforms to the design guidelines you have learned.

d) *Saving the project.* Select **File > Save All** to save your changes.

e) *Closing the IDE.* Close Visual Studio .NET by clicking its close box.

Programming Challenge ▶ **4.14** *(Monitor Invoice GUI)* In this exercise, you apply the GUI design guidelines you have learned to a graphical user interface for an invoice application (Fig. 4.25).

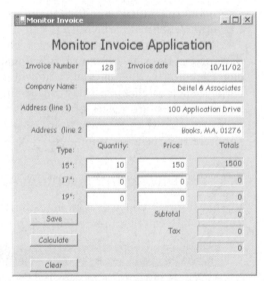

Figure 4.25 **Monitor Invoice** application without GUI design guidelines applied.

a) *Copying the template to your working directory.* Copy the directory `C:\Examples\ Tutorial04\Exercises\MonitorInvoice` to your `C:\SimplyCSP` directory.

b) *Opening the application's template file.* Double click `MonitorInvoice.sln` in the `MonitorInvoice` directory to open the application. Double click `MonitorInvoice.cs` in the **Solution Explorer** window to open the Form in design view.

c) *Applying GUI design guidelines.* Rearrange the controls and modify their properties so that the GUI conforms to the design guidelines you have learned. Add new controls as necessary.

d) *Saving the project.* Select **File > Save All** to save your changes.

e) *Closing the IDE.* Close Visual Studio .NET by clicking its close box.

T U T O R I A L

Objectives

In this tutorial, you will learn to:
- Add an event handler for a **Button** control.
- Insert code into an event handler.
- Access a property's value by using C# code.
- Use the assignment and multiplication operators.

Outline

Completing the Inventory Application

Introducing Programming

This tutorial introduces fundamentals of nonvisual programming to create an application with which users can interact. You will learn these concepts as you add functionality (with C# code) to the **Inventory** application you designed in Tutorial 4. The term **functionality** describes the actions an application can execute. In this tutorial, you will examine **events**, which represent user actions, such as clicking a **Button** or altering a value in a **TextBox**, and **event handlers**, which are pieces of code that are executed (called) when such events occur (that is, when the events are **raised**). You will learn why events and event handlers are crucial to programming Windows applications.

5.1 Test-Driving the Inventory Application

In this tutorial, you will complete the **Inventory** application you designed in Tutorial 4. Recall that this application must meet the following requirements:

Application Requirements

A college bookstore receives cartons of textbooks. In a shipment, each carton contains the same number of textbooks. The inventory manager wants to use a computer to calculate the total number of textbooks arriving at the bookstore for each shipment, from the number of cartons and the number of textbooks in each carton. The inventory manager will enter the number of cartons received and the fixed number of textbooks in each carton for each shipment; the application then will calculate the total number of textbooks in a shipment.

The inventory manager has reviewed and approved your design. Now you must add code that, when the user clicks a **Button**, will make the application multiply the number of cartons by the number of textbooks per carton and display the result—the total number of textbooks received. You begin by test-driving the completed application. Then, you will learn the additional C# technologies you will need to create your own version of this application.

Test-Driving the Completed Inventory Application

1. ***Opening the completed application.*** Open the `C:\Examples\Tutorial05\ CompletedApplication\Inventory2` directory to locate the **Inventory** application. Double click `Inventory.sln` to open the application in Visual Studio .NET.

2. ***Running the Inventory application.*** Select **Debug > Start** to run the application. Enter 3 in the **Cartons per shipment:** TextBox and enter 15 in the **Items per carton:** TextBox (Fig. 5.1).

Figure 5.1   **Inventory** application with quantities entered.

3. ***Calculating the total number of items received.*** Click the **Calculate Total** Button. The application multiplies the two numbers you entered and displays the result (45) in the Label to the right of **Total:** (Fig. 5.2).

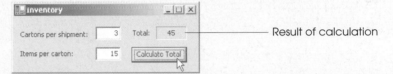
     Result of calculation

Figure 5.2   Result of clicking the **Calculate Total** Button in the **Inventory** application.

4. ***Closing the application.*** Close your running application by clicking its close box.

5. ***Closing the IDE.*** Close Visual Studio .NET by clicking its close box.

5.2 Introduction to C# Code

In Tutorials 3 and 4, you were introduced to a concept called visual programming, which allows you to create GUIs without writing any program code. In this section, you will combine visual programming with conventional programming techniques to enhance the **Inventory** application.

Before you begin to view and edit code, you should customize the way Visual Studio .NET displays and formats your code. In the following box, you open the template application and change display and format settings to make it easier for you to work with code and follow our discussions. Adding line numbers, adjusting tab sizes and setting fonts and colors will help you to navigate your code more easily.

Customizing the IDE

1. ***Copying the template to your working directory.*** Copy the `C:\Examples\ Tutorial05\TemplateApplication\Inventory2` directory to your `C:\SimplyCSP` directory. This directory contains the application created by following the steps in the previous tutorial.

2. ***Opening the Inventory application's template file.*** Double click `Inventory.sln` in the `Inventory2` directory to open the application in Visual Studio .NET.

This is the first tutorial in which you will use our template applications. If an error occurs when you try to copy or modify the template, please consult your system administrator to ensure that you have the proper privileges to edit these applications.

(cont.)   3. ***Displaying line numbers.*** In all of our programming discussions, we refer to specific code elements by line number. To help you locate where you will insert code in the examples, you need to enable Visual Studio .NET's capability to show line numbers in your code.

Select **Tools > Options...**, and in the **Options** dialog that appears (Fig. 5.3), click the **Text Editor** folder icon. Then click the **C#** folder icon (Fig. 5.4) to expand the options for C#. If the arrow is not pointing to the **General** option after you click the **C#** folder, click **General** to display the page in Fig. 5.4. Locate the **Display** header. If the CheckBox next to **Line numbers** is not checked, click inside the box to add a check mark. If the box is already checked, you need not do anything; however, do not close the dialog.

Text Editor folder icon ——————

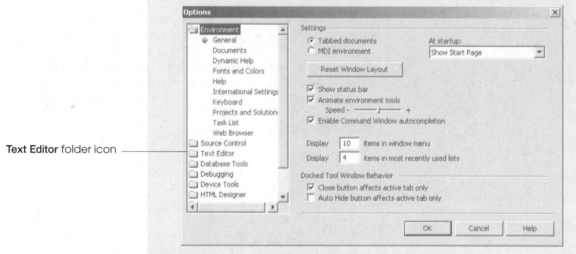

Figure 5.3   **Options** dialog.

C# folder ——————
General item ——————

Line numbers
CheckBox (checked) ——————

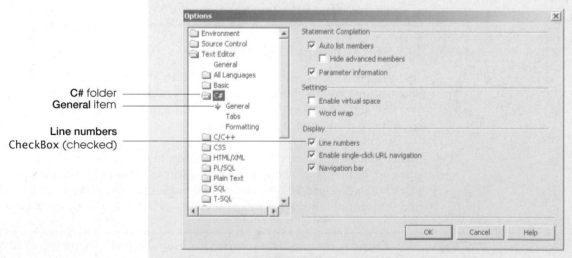

Figure 5.4   **General** settings page for the C# text editor.

(cont.)

4. ***Setting the tab size.*** Just as you indent the first line of each paragraph when writing a letter, it is important to use proper spacing when writing code. Indenting code improves program readability. You can control indents with tabs. Click the **Tabs** item under the **C#** folder (Fig. 5.5). The **Smart** RadioButton, under the **Indenting** header, should be selected by default. If it is not, select the **Smart** RadioButton by clicking inside the white circle. Using this setting, Visual Studio .NET will indent code for you.

Smart indenting (selected) ——————

Tabs item ——————

Insert spaces (selected) ——————

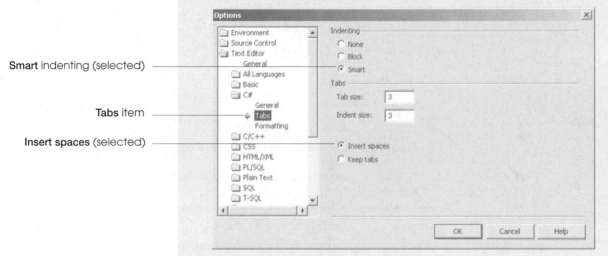

Figure 5.5   Setting the **Tabs** options.

Set **Tab size:** to 3 and **Indent size:** to 3. The **Tab size:** setting indicates the number of spaces each tab character (inserted when you press the *Tab* key) represents. The **Indent size:** setting determines the number of spaces each indent inserted by Visual Studio .NET represents. Visual Studio .NET will now insert three spaces for you if you are using the **Smart** indenting feature; you can insert them yourself with one keystroke by pressing the *Tab* key.

Then, make sure the **Insert spaces** RadioButton is selected (Fig. 5.5), so Visual Studio .NET will insert three one-character spaces (instead of one tab character) to indent lines. If you select the **Keep tabs** RadioButton, each tab or indent will be represented by one tab character. We suggest you select the **Insert spaces** RadioButton.

Good Programming Practice

You can change the font and color settings if you prefer a different appearance for your code. To remain consistent with this book (with the exception of the selected text colors), however, we recommend you do not change the default font and color settings.

5. ***Exploring fonts and colors.*** Click the **Environment** folder icon; then click the **Fonts and Colors** item. The screen that appears allows you to customize fonts and colors used to display code. Visual Studio .NET can apply colors and fonts to make it easier for you to read and edit code. In the book's examples, you will see code with the **Selected Text** background set to yellow for emphasis. The default setting for **Selected Text** is a blue background. You should use the default settings on your machine. If you need to reset your settings to the default for fonts and colors, click the **Use Defaults** Button (Fig. 5.6).

(cont.)

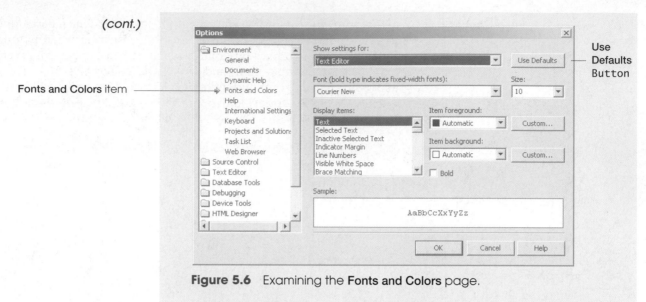

Fonts and Colors item

Use Defaults Button

Figure 5.6 Examining the **Fonts and Colors** page.

6. *Applying your changes.* Click the **OK** Button to apply your changes and dismiss the **Options** dialog.

Visual programming is fun and saves time, but it is insufficient for the vast majority of applications. While you've been programming in a completely visual environment when adding Labels and TextBoxes, Visual Studio .NET has actually been writing code for you in the background. Behind the scenes, everything that your application will do is performed by code written either by you or by the IDE. The key is to develop the right mix of visual programming with code writing ("nonvisual" programming) for each application. In the following box, you will take your first peek at C# code.

Introducing C# Code

Good Programming Practice

Change the Form name to a unique and meaningful name for easy identification.

Good Programming Practice

Prefix Form names with Frm. Capitalize the first letter of the Form name because Form is a class. Objects (such as controls) should be prefixed with lowercase letters.

1. *Renaming the Form object.* If the Windows Form Designer is not open, double click the Inventory.cs file in the **Solution Explorer** window. Before looking at the code, change one final property of the Form. Like each control, each Form object needs a unique and meaningful name for easy identification. By default, the Visual Studio .NET IDE names the Form **Form1**. Click the Form in the Windows Form Designer. In the **Properties** window, double click the field to the right of the Name property, listed as (Name). Type FrmInventory, then press *Enter* to update the name.

2. *Viewing application code.* Switch to **code view** (where the application's code is displayed in an editor window), by selecting **View > Code**. The tabbed window (Inventory.cs) in Fig. 5.7, also called a **code editor**, appears. Note that when select **View > Code**, the Inventory.cs file must be selected in the **Solution Explorer**.

You will notice that the IDE through which we present code to you may appear different than your IDE. To improve readability, we have hidden the **Toolbox** and closed any extra windows, such as the **Solution Explorer**, **Properties** and **Task List** windows.

(cont.)

Inventory.cs tabbed window

Using FCL namespaces

Class is declared in the Inventory namespace

Class declaration

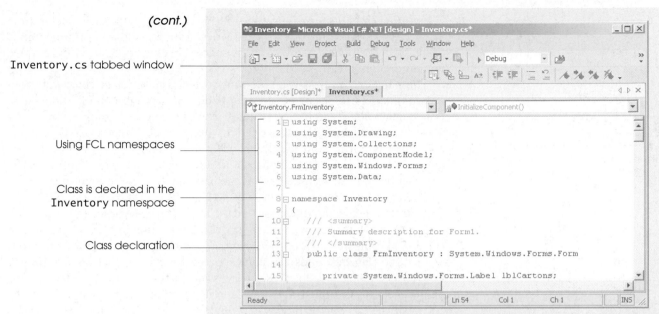

Figure 5.7   IDE showing the uppermost portion of the code for the **Inventory** application.

C# programs consist of pieces called classes, which simplify application organization. Recall from Tutorial 1 that classes contain groups of code statements that perform tasks and return information when the tasks are completed. The code in this application declares your **Inventory** application class. These lines collectively are called a **class declaration** (sometimes called a class definition). Most C# applications consist of a combination of code written by programmers (like you) and preexisting classes written and provided by Microsoft in the Framework Class Library (FCL). Again, the key to successful C# application development is achieving the right mix of the two. You will learn how to use both techniques in your applications.

Recall from Tutorial 3 that classes in the FCL are grouped by functionality in units called namespaces. The System.Drawing namespace, for example, provides classes for using some basic graphics tools. Classes are organized in this way so that programmers like you can locate them easily. The word using, followed by a namespace, indicates that the application uses features of that namespace. The word using appears in blue because it is a keyword, a concept that will be discussed shortly. Visual Studio .NET generates lines 1–6 (Fig. 5.7) for you, because these namespaces are often used in GUI applications. Each of these lines is known as a **using directive**.

You can create your own namespaces as well. By using the **namespace** keyword, line 8 declares the namespace Inventory. By default, Visual Studio .NET uses the project name as the namespace. [*Note:* Although this default namespace is created by the IDE in each Windows application, we will not be making use of these default namespaces in this book.]

(cont.)

Good Programming Practice

Capitalize the first letter of each class identifier, such as the Form name.

Good Programming Practice

Indent the entire body of each class declaration one "level" of indentation between the left brace ({) and the right brace (}) that delimit the class body. This emphasizes the structure of the class declaration and helps make the class declaration easier to read. The same should apply to a namespace. Visual Studio .NET provides indentation in several places as programmers enter code.

Good Programming Practice

Use a name for each identifier that is unique in more than just case. This makes programmers less likely to confuse identifiers with similar names.

3. *Examining class declarations.* Line 13 (Fig. 5.7) begins the class declaration. The **class** keyword introduces a class declaration in C# and is immediately followed by the **class name** (FrmInventory in this application—the value you entered in the Form's Name property).

   The name of the class is an **identifier**, which is a series of characters consisting of letters, digits, underscores (_) and "at" symbols (@). Identifiers cannot begin with a digit and cannot contain spaces. Examples of valid identifiers are intValue1, intLabel_Value and btnExit. The name 7welcome is not a valid identifier, because it begins with a digit, and the name input field is not a valid identifier, because it contains a space. The "at" symbol (@) can be used only as the first character in an identifier.

   The opening **left brace** ({) in line 14 (Fig. 5.7) begins the main part of the class declaration, called the **class body**. The closing **right brace** (}) at line 159 (Fig. 5.8) ends the class declaration. Likewise, the left brace in line 9 (Fig. 5.7) begins the body of the Inventory namespace, while the right brace at line 160 (Fig. 5.8) ends the namespace. Any classes, such as FrmInventory, declared between these braces are assigned to the Inventory namespace. Braces must always occur in matching pairs. Notice how the code between a pair of braces is indented. Indentation improves program readability.

   The class keyword is preceded by the public keyword. The code for every Form you design in Visual Studio .NET begins with the public keyword. You will learn about this keyword in Tutorial 19. **Keywords** (or **reserved words**) are reserved for use by C# (you will learn the various keywords throughout the text). Notice that keywords appear in blue by default in the IDE. A complete list of C# keywords can be found in Appendix F.

   C# keywords and identifiers are **case sensitive**. This means that uppercase and lowercase letters are considered to be different letters; that practice causes FrmInventory and frminventory to be understood by C# as different identifiers. Differentiating identifiers by case only is considered poor programming practice.

4. *Understanding inheriting from the Form class.* Every visual Windows application consists of at least one class that inherits from the Form class (Fig. 5.7, line 13) in the FCL. The colon (:) indicates that the FrmInventory class inherits members from another class. By inheriting from System.Windows.Forms.Form, your application uses the Form class as a "template." A key benefit of inheriting from the Form class is that the FCL previously has declared "what it means to be a Form." The Windows operating system expects every window (for example, a Form) to have certain capabilities. However, because class Form already provides those capabilities, programmers do not need to "reinvent the wheel" by defining all those capabilities themselves. The use of the colon (:) to derive from the Form class enables programmers to create Forms quickly and easily.

5. *Examining the **Main** method.* Lines 155–158 of Fig. 5.8 comprise the **Main** method. Every C# application requires a Main method. The Main method is where the application begins execution. In this book, the Main method simply runs the Form you have created (line 157). The term method will be discussed shortly.

(cont.)

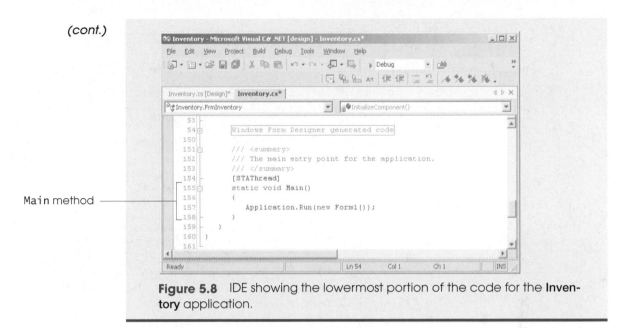

Figure 5.8 IDE showing the lowermost portion of the code for the **Inventory** application.

In the editor window (Fig. 5.8), notice the text Windows Form Designer gener-ated code in line 54, which is surrounded by a gray rectangle and has a plus box, ⊞, next to it. The plus box indicates that this section of code, called a **region**, is **col-lapsed**, as discussed in Tutorial 2. Notice that the line numbers in Fig. 5.8 jump from 54 to 150. The missing line numbers correspond to code hidden from you by Visual Studio .NET. Although collapsed code is not visible, it is still part of the application. Code collapsing allows you to hide code in the editor, so that you can focus on key code segments. Notice that the entire class declaration also can be collapsed by clicking the minus box, ⊟, to the left of public (line 13 of Fig. 5.7). In Fig. 5.8, the description to the right of the plus box indicates that the collapsed code was created by the Windows Form Designer. This region contains the code, inserted by the IDE, that specifies how the GUI will look. In the following box, you explore the code generated by the IDE.

Examining Windows Form Designer Generated Code	1. ***Viewing the generated code.*** In this step, you will view other code that is part of your application. You will not be expected to understand most of the code. Visual programming saves development time by allowing you to build applica-tions without needing to know how every component works "under the hood," just as you don't need to know how an engine works to drive a car.

      You have looked at much of the generated code already (such as the Main method). Click the plus box in line 54 to view the rest of the generated code. The **expanded code** (Fig. 5.9) certainly appears to be complex. The vast majority of the code shown has not been introduced yet. Again, you are not expected to understand how it works.

      This code is created by the IDE and normally is not edited by the pro-grammer. This is Microsoft's intent—you can develop powerful applications without having to worry about the IDE-generated code. This type of code is present in *every* Windows application developed with Visual Studio .NET, saving you a considerable amount of development time. As you read this book, the purpose of much of this code will become clearer.

      Collapse part of the generated code by clicking the node in line 59. Your code should now appear as in Fig. 5.10. A box containing an ellipses appears in place of the code in that region. This area is called **outlined code**. Placing the cursor over the outlined code displays a portion of the collapsed code.

(cont.)

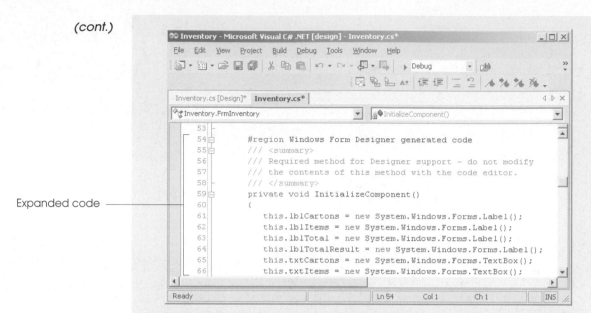

Figure 5.9 Windows **Form** Designer generated code, when expanded.

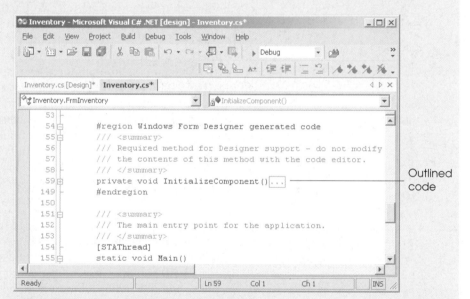

Figure 5.10 Ellipses indicating outlined code.

2. *Viewing the generated code for a specific control.* Expand the code by clicking the node in line 59 once again. Click and drag the scrollbar downward until you reach the code in Fig. 5.11. This region contains code generated by the IDE for setting the lblCarton Label's properties, including the Label's Location, Name, Size, TabIndex (discussed in Tutorial 20), Text and TextAlign properties.

When you designed this application in Tutorial 4, you used the **Properties** window to set properties for the Form, Labels, TextBoxes and Buttons. Once a property was set, the object was updated immediately. Objects (Forms and controls) have **default properties**, which are displayed initially in the **Properties** window when an object is created. These default properties provide the initial characteristics of an object. When a control, such as a Label, is placed on the Form, the IDE adds code to the class (in this case, FrmInventory) that creates the control and sets some of the control's property values, such as the name of the control and its location on the Form.

(cont.)

Property values for `lblCartons`

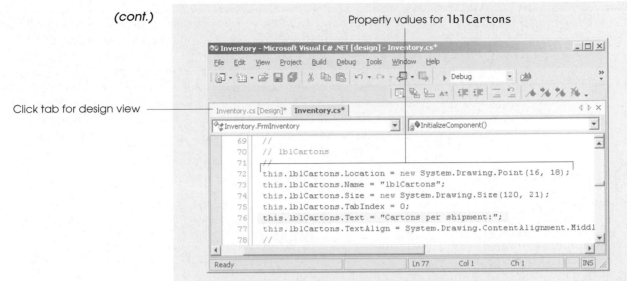

Figure 5.11 Code generated by the IDE for `lblCartons` (with the code setting the `Text` property highlighted).

The values in the code in Fig. 5.11 correspond to what you entered in the **Properties** window in the Windows **Form Designer** in Tutorial 4. Notice that the `Label`'s `Text` property is assigned the text that you entered in the **Properties** window (line 76). When you change a property in design view, the Windows **Form Designer** updates the appropriate line of code in the class to reflect the new value.

3. ***Collapsing code.*** Collapse this application's generated code by clicking the node in line 54.

SELF-REVIEW

1. Identifiers _____.
    a) can begin with any character, but cannot contain spaces
    b) must begin with a digit, but cannot contain spaces
    c) cannot begin with a digit or contain spaces
    d) cannot begin with a digit, but can contain spaces

2. In code view, the plus box shown to the left of a line of code indicates that this region is _____.

    a) positive   b) closed
    c) expanded   d) collapsed

Answers: 1) c. 2) d.

5.3 Inserting an Event Handler

Now that you have finalized the GUI, you are ready to modify your application to respond to user input. You will do this by inserting code manually. Most of the C# applications in this book provide functionality in the form of event handlers. Recall that an event handler is executed when an event occurs, such as the clicking of a `Button`—called a **Click** event. The following box shows you how to add an event handler to your application.

Adding a Button 's Click Event Handler

 Error-Prevention Tip

You should change the name of the Form in the Main method immediately after changing the name of your Form to avoid the "**Form1 not found**" error when the application attempts to run. Also change the name of the Form above the class declaration.

1. **Renaming the Form in code view.** You have already renamed the FrmInventory Form using the Name property. Notice that Visual Studio .NET renames the Form in code view in line 13 of Fig. 5.12, but not in line 11. Change Form1, the default Form name, to FrmInventory, as in Fig. 5.12. Scroll down to the Main method (lines 155–158). Again change Form1 to FrmInventory. These are changes you should make to your code any time you rename a Form. Also, insert a space just inside each of the outer parentheses, (and). This spacing convention will be clarified shortly. Your code should look like line 157 of Fig. 5.13.

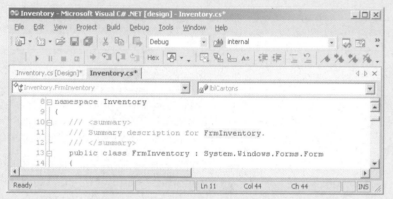

Figure 5.12 Renaming the Form above the class declaration.

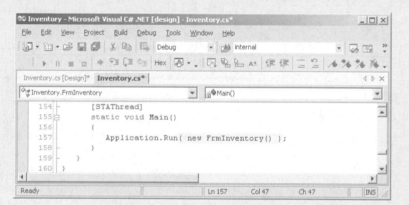

Figure 5.13 Renaming the Form in the Main method and adding spacing.

2. **Adding an event handler for the Button.** In this step, you use the Windows Form Designer to create an event handler and enter code view. Begin by clicking the Inventory.cs [Design] tab to enter the Windows Form Designer. Then, double click the Form's **Calculate Total** Button to enter code view. Notice that the code for the application, which now includes the new event handler on lines 161–164 of Fig. 5.14, is displayed.

Double clicking the **Calculate Total** Button in design view caused Visual Studio .NET to generate the Button's Click event handler—the code that will execute when the user clicks the **Calculate Total** Button. When any control is double clicked in design view, Visual Studio .NET inserts an event handler for that control. The event that the handler is associated with may differ based on the control that is double clicked. For instance, double clicking Button controls causes Click event handlers to be created. Double clicking other types of controls will cause other types of event handlers to be generated. Each control has a default type of event handler that is generated when that control is clicked in design view.

(cont.)

Asterisks indicate unsaved changes to application

Empty event handler

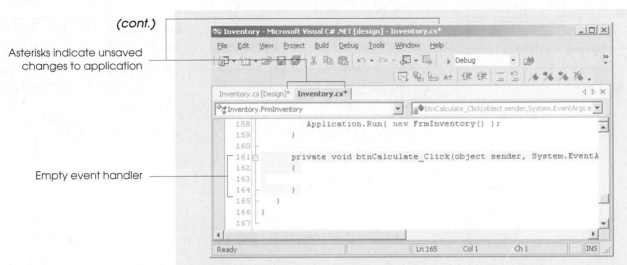

Figure 5.14   Event handler `btnCalculate_Click` before you add your code.

In C#, event handlers by convention follow the naming scheme *controlName_eventName*. The word *controlName* refers to the name of the control provided in its `Name` property (in this case, `btnCalculate`). The name of the event raised by the control (in this case, `Click`) is represented by *eventName*. When event *eventName* occurs, the event handler *controlName_eventName* executes. In this application, the event handler `btnCalculate_Click` handles the **Calculate Total** `Button`'s `Click` event—in other words, the code in `btnCalculate_Click` executes when the user clicks the **Calculate Total** `Button`.

3. **Running the application.** Select **Debug > Start** to run your application (Fig. 5.15). Recall that running your application also saves changes made to your application. Click the **Calculate Total** `Button`. Notice that, although you have added an event handler for the `Button`'s `Click` event, no action occurs when you click the `Button` because you haven't added any code to the event handler yet. In the following box, you add code to the event handler so that, when a user clicks the **Calculate Total** `Button`, text displays in the output `Label` (`lblTotalResult`).

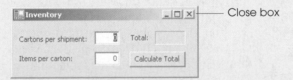

Close box

Figure 5.15   Running the application without functionality.

4. **Closing the application.** Close your running application by clicking its close box.

Now that you have created an event handler for the **Calculate Total** `Button`, you need to insert code to perform an action. Specifically, you need to make the application multiply the number of cartons in a shipment by the fixed number of items per carton when a user clicks the **Calculate Total** `Button`. You write your first C# statement in the following box.

Adding Code to an Empty Event Handler

1. *Changing to code view.* If you are not already in code view, select **View > Code** or click the `Inventory.cs` tab to view the application's code.

2. *Adding code to the event handler.* In the body of the event handler, insert lines 163–164 of Fig. 5.16 by typing the text on the screen.

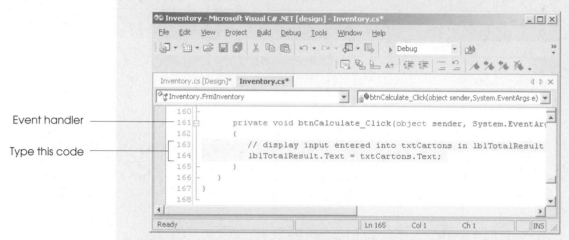

Event handler

Type this code

Figure 5.16 Adding code to the **Calculate Total Button**'s event handler.

Line 163 of Fig. 5.16 begins with a **double slash** (**//**), which indicates that the remainder of the line is a **comment**. Programmers insert comments in programs to improve the readability of their code. These comments explain the code so that other programmers who need to work with the application can understand it more easily. Comments appear in green when displayed in the code editor of Visual Studio .NET. Comments also help you read your own code, especially when you haven't looked at it for a while.

A comment that begins with // is called a single-line comment, because the comment terminates at the end of the line. There is also a way to write a multiple-line comment, or delimited comment, which begins with delimiter /* and ends with delimiter */. All text between these delimiters is treated as a comment and is ignored by the compiler. The C# compiler ignores comments of the form // and /* ... */, which means that comments do not cause the computer to perform any actions when your applications run. Comments can be placed either on their own lines or at the end of a line of C# code. You may have noticed that certain single-line comments follow the opening // with another / (lines 10 and 12 of Fig. 5.12). These are also single-line comments, used by the IDE to create documents providing information about your application. These comments sometimes appear in gray.

The comment in line 163 indicates that the next line displays the value entered into the **Cartons per shipment:** TextBox in the **Total:** Label. Line 164 presents your first executable C# **statement**, which performs an action. Statements end with a **semicolon** (**;**). This statement accesses the `Text` properties of `txtCartons` and `lblTotalResult`. In C#, properties are accessed in code by placing a period between the control name and property name (for example, `lblTotalResult.Text`). This period is called the **member access operator** (**.**), or the **dot operator**. Notice that, when the control name and member access operator are typed, a window appears listing that object's members (Fig. 5.17). This is known as Visual Studio .NET's *IntelliSense* feature, which displays all the members in a class for your convenience. You scroll to the member you are interested in and select it. Click the member name once to display a description of that member; double click it to add the name of the member to your application. *IntelliSense* can be useful in discovering a class's members and their purpose.

Good Programming Practice

Comments written at the end of a line should be preceded by one or more spaces, to enhance program readability.

Good Programming Practice

Precede every full-line comment or group of full-line comments with a blank line. The blank line makes the comments stand out and improves program readability. If the line preceding a comment is a left brace, then no blank line is necessary.

(cont.)

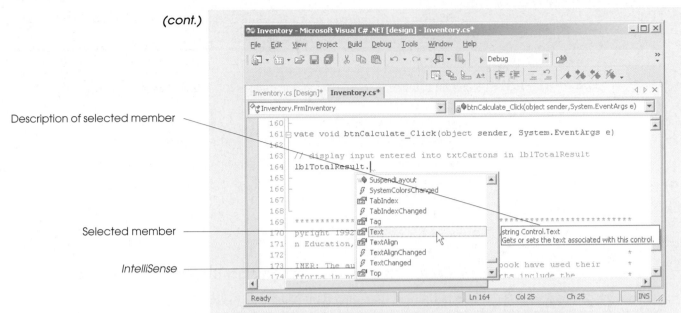

Description of selected member

Selected member

IntelliSense

Figure 5.17   *IntelliSense* activating while entering code.

Let's examine line 164 of Fig. 5.16 more closely. Reading the line from left to right, we see lblTotalResult's Text property, followed by an "equals" sign (=), followed by txtCartons' Text property value. A semicolon ends the statement. The "=" symbol is known as the **assignment operator**. The expressions on either side of the assignment operator are referred to as its **operands**. This assignment operator assigns the value on the right of the operator (the **right operand**) to the variable on the left of the operator (the **left operand**). The assignment operator is known as a **binary operator**, because it has two operands—lblTotalResult.Text and txtCartons.Text. The entire statement is called an **assignment statement**, because it assigns a value to the left operand. In this example, you are assigning the value of txtCartons' Text property to lblTotalResult's Text property. The statement is read as, "The Text property of lblTotal-Result *gets* the value of txtCarton's Text property." Note that the right operand is unchanged by the assignment statement.

When the user clicks the **Calculate Total** Button, the event handler will execute, displaying the value the user entered in the **Cartons per shipment:** TextBox in the output Label lblTotalResult. Clearly, this is not the correct result—the correct result is the number of items per carton times the number of cartons per shipment. In the following box, you correct this error.

3. *Running the application.* Select **Debug > Start** to run your application (Fig. 5.18). Type 5 into the **Cartons per shipment:** TextBox and 10 into the **Items per carton:** TextBox, then click the **Calculate Total** Button. Notice that the text of lblTotalResult now incorrectly displays the data, 5, that was entered into the **Cartons per shipment:** TextBox, rather than displaying the correct result, 50.

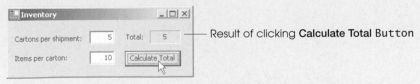

Result of clicking **Calculate Total** Button

Figure 5.18   Running the application with an event handler.

(cont.)   4.   ***Closing the application.*** Close your running application by clicking its close box.

SELF-REVIEW

1. Event handlers generated by Visual Studio .NET follow the naming convention _____.

   a) *controlName_eventName*   b) *eventName_controlName*

   c) *eventNameControlName*   d) *controlNameEventName*

2. The expressions on either side of the assignment operator are referred to as its _____.

   a) operator values   b) results

   c) operands   d) arguments

Answers: 1) a. 2) c.

5.4 Performing a Calculation and Displaying the Result

Now that you are familiar with displaying output in a `Label`, you will complete the **Inventory** application by displaying the product of the number of cartons per shipment and the number of items per carton. In the next box, you will learn how to perform mathematical operations in C#.

Completing the Inventory Application

1. ***Changing the event handler.*** If you are not already in code view, select **View > Code** or click the `Inventory.cs` tab. Add a comment above the event handler (line 161 of Fig. 5.19). Also add a comment indicating the end of the event handler (line 170) and a comment indicating the end of the class (line 172). We often add such comments so that the reader can easily determine which event handler or class is being closed without having to search for the beginning of that event handler or class in the file. Include a blank line before each comment for better readability. Also split the first line of the event handler into two lines for better readability (lines 162–163). Indent line 163, as shown in Fig. 5.19, by placing the cursor at the beginning of the line's text, then pressing *Tab*. Then, replace `btnCalculate_Click`'s body with lines 165–168 of Fig. 5.19. The comment in line 165 indicates that you will be multiplying the two values input by the user and displaying the result in a `Label`.

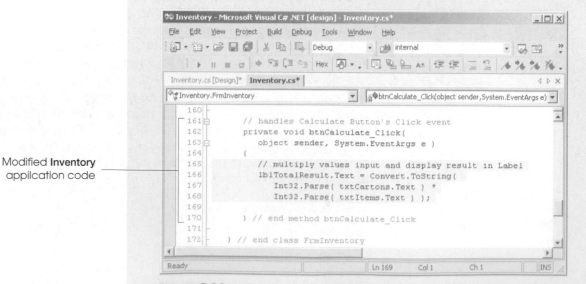

Modified **Inventory** application code

Figure 5.19 Using multiplication in the **Inventory** application.

(cont.)

2. ***Adding multiline code.*** Lines 166–168 perform the multiplication and assignment operations. A single statement can be spread across many lines, because C# ignores the extra spaces, tabs and newline characters in your code. **Newline** characters are inserted when you press *Enter*. Together spaces, tabs and newlines are called **white space**. A programmer typically splits long statements into multiple lines to make the code more readable. You again use the assignment operator to assign a value to lblTotalResult.Text in line 166. The assignment operator in line 166 assigns the result of multiplying the numbers input by the user to lblTotalResult.Text. On lines 167–168, Int32.Parse(txtCartons.Text) is followed by an asterisk (*) and Int32.Parse(txtItems.Text). The asterisk is known as the **multiplication operator**—the operator's left and right operands are multiplied together.

   Lines 167–168 use the Int32.Parse method to turn a string of characters into an integer value. A **method** is a portion of code that performs a task when called (executed) and optionally can send, or return, a value to the location from which it was called. In this case, the values returned by Int32.Parse become the values used to perform multiplication. We call methods (as in line 167–168) by typing their name followed by parentheses. Any values inside the parentheses (for example, txtCartons.Text) are known as method **arguments**. To improve readability, arguments are inputs to the method that provide information that the method needs to perform its task. In this case, the argument specifies which value you want to send to the Int32.Parse method. Arguments should be one space away from their surrounding parentheses. You will learn how to create your own methods in Tutorial 13.

   The **Int32.Parse** method can be used to obtain an integer from a string of characters (keyboard input) that is guaranteed to be digits only. An **integer** is a whole number, such as 919, -11, 0 and 138624. We use Int32.Parse because this application is not intended to perform arithmetic calculations with characters that are not numbers. Your **Inventory** application cannot prevent users from accidentally entering non-numeric input, such as letters and special characters like $ and @. If a user enters a character that is not a digit, the application will not execute correctly. Fortunately, C# provides two ways to handle invalid input. One way is to use C#'s string processing capabilities to examine input. You will learn about such capabilities as you read this book. The other form of handling invalid input is called exception handling, where you write code to handle errors that may be raised as the application executes. You will learn about exception handling in Tutorial 32.

   The Int32.Parse method obtains the integers to be multiplied together from the strings of characters input by the user. After multiplication, the **Convert.ToString** method converts the integer product back into a string of characters, so that the result can be displayed in a Label. This string becomes the value seen in the lblTotalResult TextBox. You will learn more about conversions in Tutorial 6.

3. ***Running the application.*** Select **Debug > Start** to run your application. Now the user can enter data in both TextBoxes. When the **Calculate Total** Button is clicked, the application will multiply the two numbers entered and display the result in lblTotalResult.

4. ***Closing the application.*** Close your running application by clicking its close box.

Figure 5.20 presents the source code for the **Inventory** application. [*Note*: In code listings such as Fig. 5.20, we don't display the Visual Studio .NET generated code. We simply provide a comment (line 50) as a place holder. The line numbers shown in these figures are not intended to match those shown in the IDE. Also, keep in mind that certain generated code that we display may have been broken over multiple lines for formatting purposes, such as lines 34–37.]

```csharp
1   using System;
2   using System.Drawing;
3   using System.Collections;
4   using System.ComponentModel;
5   using System.Windows.Forms;
6   using System.Data;
7
8   namespace Inventory
9   {
10      /// <summary>
11      /// Summary description for FrmInventory.
12      /// </summary>
13      public class FrmInventory : System.Windows.Forms.Form
14      {
15         private System.Windows.Forms.Label lblCartons;
16         private System.Windows.Forms.Label lblItems;
17         private System.Windows.Forms.Label lblTotal;
18         private System.Windows.Forms.Label lblTotalResult;
19         private System.Windows.Forms.TextBox txtCartons;
20         private System.Windows.Forms.TextBox txtItems;
21         private System.Windows.Forms.Button btnCalculate;
22         /// <summary>
23         /// Required designer variable.
24         /// </summary>
25         private System.ComponentModel.Container components = null;
26
27         public FrmInventory()
28         {
29            //
30            // Required for Windows Form Designer support
31            //
32            InitializeComponent();
33
34            //
35            // TODO: Add any constructor code after InitializeComponent
36            // call
37            //
38         }
39
40         /// <summary>
41         /// Clean up any resources being used.
42         /// </summary>
43         protected override void Dispose( bool disposing )
44         {
45            if( disposing )
46            {
47               if (components != null)
48               {
49                  components.Dispose();
50               }
51            }
52            base.Dispose( disposing );
53         }
54
```

Renaming the Form ——— (line 11)

Figure 5.20 **Inventory** application code. (Part 1 of 2.)

```
55          // Windows Form Designer generated code
56
57          /// <summary>
58          /// The main entry point for the application.
59          /// </summary>
60          [STAThread]
61          static void Main()
62          {
63              Application.Run( new FrmInventory() );
64          }
65
66          // handles Calculate Button's Click event
67          private void btnCalculate_Click(
68              object sender, System.EventArgs e )
69          {
70              // multiply values input and display result in Label
71              lblTotalResult.Text = Convert.ToString(
72                  Int32.Parse( txtCartons.Text ) *
73                  Int32.Parse( txtItems.Text ) );
74
75          } // end method btnCalculate_Click
76
77      } // end class FrmInventory
78  }
```

Renaming the Form — 63

Adding an event handler to your code — 70

Adding a comment to your code — 75

Adding a comment to your code — 77

Figure 5.20   **Inventory** application code. (Part 2 of 2.)

SELF-REVIEW   1. _____ provide information that methods need to perform their tasks.

    a) Inputs   b) Arguments

    c) Outputs   d) Both a and b.

2. What method is used to turn a string of characters into an integer?

    a) `Convert.ToString`   b) `Integer.Parse`

    c) `Convert.ToInteger`   d) `Int32.Parse`

Answers: 1) d. 2) d.

5.5 Using the Debugger: Syntax Errors

So far in this book, you have run the applications by selecting **Debug > Start**. This compiles and runs the application. If you do not write your code correctly, errors appear in a window known as the **Task List** when the application is compiled. **Debugging** is the process of fixing errors in an application. There are two types of errors—syntax errors and logic errors.

Syntax errors occur when code statements violate the grammatical rules of the programming language. Examples of syntax errors include omitting a semicolon from the end of a statement. An application cannot be run until all of its syntax errors are corrected. **Compilation errors** are not violations of the language's grammatical rules, but they do prevent the application from compiling successfully. Examples of compilation errors include misspellings of identifiers or method names. Like syntax errors, an application cannot be run until all of its compilation errors are corrected. **Logic errors** do not prevent the application from compiling successfully, but do cause the application to produce erroneous results. Visual Studio .NET contains software called a **debugger**, which allows you to analyze the behavior of your application to determine that it is executing correctly.

You can compile an application without running it by selecting **Build > Build Solution**. Programmers frequently do this when they wish to determine whether there are any syntax errors in their code. Using either **Debug > Start** or **Build > Build Solution** will display any syntax errors in the **Task List** window. The **Output** window will display the result of the compilation. Figure 5.21 displays the output window for an application with no errors.

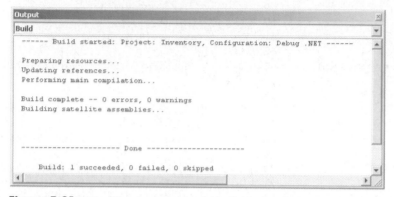

Figure 5.21 Results of a successful build in the **Output** window.

In Visual Studio .NET, syntax errors appear in the **Task List** window along with a description of each error. Figure 5.22 displays the error that appears when a semi-colon is omitted from the end of a statement. For additional information on a syntax error, right click the error statement in the **Task List** window, and select **Show Task Help**. This displays a help page explaining the error message and suggests corrections. In the following box, you will create syntax errors, view the results and fix the errors.

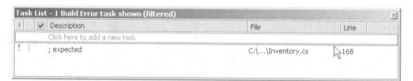

Figure 5.22 **Task List** lists syntax errors.

Using the Debugger: Syntax Errors

1. **Creating your own syntax and compilation errors.** You will now create your own syntax and compilation errors, for demonstration purposes. If you are not in code view, select **View > Code**. Add an additional character (the letter **s**) to `Label lblTotalResult` in line 166 and delete the semicolon at the end of the assignment statement in line 168. Notice the change to the IDE (Fig. 5.23).

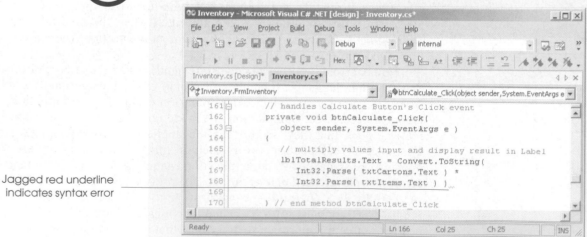

Jagged red underline indicates syntax error

Figure 5.23 IDE with first syntax error.

(cont.)

The Visual Studio .NET IDE can detect syntax errors while you manipulate code in the code editor. After you removed the semicolon on line 168, you might have noticed that this violation of C# syntax was immediately reported in the **Task List**. The precise location of the syntax error in your code is also emphasized by a red jagged line. The missing semicolon is reported in the **Task List** (Fig. 5.24).

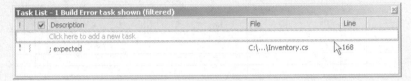

Figure 5.24 **Task List** displaying the syntax error recognized in real time.

These features notify you of possible errors and give you the chance to fix the error before compiling the application. Notice that your changes to lbl-TotalResult, however, have not yet been recognized as an error. An error such as an unrecognized identifier will not appear in real time, because this is a compilation error. Such an error will become apparent only when you attempt to compile your application. The IDE will refuse to run your modified application until *all* syntax and compilation errors have been corrected.

2. ***Locating and fixing the syntax error***. Double clicking an error in the **Task List** window selects the code containing that error. Double click the ';' **expected** error to highlight the error in line 168 (Fig. 5.25). Now type a semicolon to fix the error. Notice how the jagged underline is removed, and the error is removed from the **Task List**.

Highlighted syntax error ——————

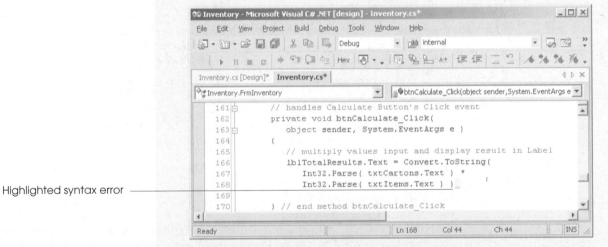

Figure 5.25 Highlighting the portion of code where a syntax error occurs.

3. ***Locating and fixing the compilation error***. Select **Build > Build Solution**. This compiles the code, meaning the high-level C# code is converted to assembly-level code. Now the debugger has found the second error (Fig. 5.26).

The debugger tells you that it cannot find anything with that name. The precise location of the error in your code is now emphasized by a blue jagged line. The blue color indicates a compilation error. This type of error is recognized at compile time. Fix the error by removing the additional character from Label lblTotalResult. Again, notice that the debugger does not acknowledge this change in real time. Select **Build > Build Solution** once again. The task list is now empty, indicating that your application is free of syntax and compilation errors.

(cont.)

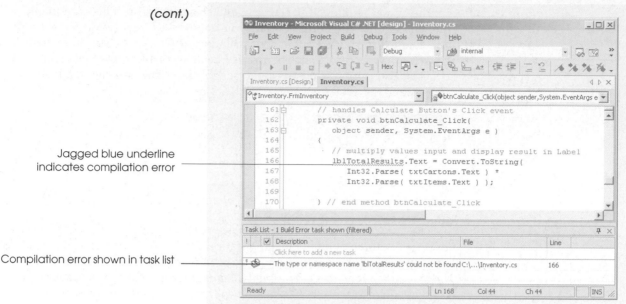

Jagged blue underline indicates compilation error

Compilation error shown in task list

Figure 5.26 IDE with compilation error.

4. **Closing the IDE.** Close Visual Studio .NET by clicking its close box.

In this section, you learned about syntax errors and how to find and correct them. In later tutorials, you will learn to detect and remove logic errors by using the Visual Studio .NET debugger.

SELF-REVIEW

1. If there are syntax or compilation errors in an application, they will appear in a window known as the _____ when the application is compiled.

    a) **Task List**   b) **Output**

    c) **Properties**   d) **Error List**

2. A syntax error occurs when _____.

    a) the application terminates unexpectedly   b) a statement breaks over several lines

    c) a semicolon is omitted   d) All of the above.

Answers: 1) a. 2) c.

5.6 Wrap-Up

In this tutorial, you were introduced to C# programming. You learned how to use a `TextBox` control to allow users to input data and how to use a `Button` control to signal to your running application that it should perform a particular action. You were introduced to the code generated by Visual Studio .NET that creates an application's GUI. Though you are not yet expected to understand the meaning of the Windows `Form` Designer generated code, you learned that the key to good programming is to achieve the right balance between employing visual programming (in which Visual Studio .NET writes code for you) and writing your own code (nonvisual programming).

After learning about operators in C#, you wrote a few lines of code as you added an event handler to your application to perform a simple multiplication calculation and display the result to the user. You also used comments to improve the readability of your code. You learned that placing code in an event handler allows an application to respond to a certain type of event, such as the click of a `Button`.

Finally, you learned about syntax errors and how to use the Visual Studio .NET debugger to reduce the number of errors you see when you try to run an application. In the next tutorial, you will continue developing your **Inventory** application by using identifiers to create variables. You will also enhance your **Inventory** application by using the TextChanged event, which is raised when the user changes the value in a TextBox. After applying your knowledge of variables, you will use the debugger while an application runs to remove a logic error from that application.

SKILLS SUMMARY

Accessing a Property's Value by Using C# Code
- Place the property name after the control name and the member access operator (.). For example, to access the Text property of a TextBox named txtCartons, use txtCartons.Text.

Inserting C# Comments in Code
- Begin a single-line comment with a double slash (//), or use the delimiters /* and */ to enclose a multiple-line comment. A comment can be placed either on its own line or at the end of a line of code.

Inserting an Event Handler for a Button Control's Click Event
- Double click the Button in design view to create an empty event handler; then, insert the code that will execute when the event occurs.

Using an Assignment Statement
- Use the "equals" sign (=) to assign the value of its right operand to its left operand. The entire statement is called an assignment statement, because it assigns a value to the left operand (for example, a property). All statements end with a semicolon.

Using the Multiplication Operator
- Use an asterisk (*) between the two expressions to be multiplied. The multiplication operator multiplies the right and left operands if both operands contain numeric values or variables of numeric types. It is a syntax error to use the multiplication operator on values of nonnumeric types.

Converting an Integer to/from a String of Characters
- Convert a string of characters, such as a TextBox's Text property, to an integer with a call to method Int32.Parse.
- Convert an integer back into a string of characters with a call to method Convert.ToString.

Finding a Syntax or Compilation Error
- Double click the error message in the **Task List** window.
- You may need to build the application for all errors to appear in the **Task List** window.

KEY TERMS

argument—Inputs to the method that provide information that the method needs to perform its task.

assignment operator (=)—Sets its left operand to the value of its right operand.

assignment statement—A unit of code that copies one value to another. An assignment statement contains an "equals"-sign (=) operator that causes the value of its right operand to be copied to its left operand.

binary operator—Requires two operands.

case sensitive—The instance where two words that are spelled identically are treated differently if the capitalization of the two words differs.

class body—The main section of the class declaration, following the class header and enclosed by braces.

class declaration—The code that belongs to a class, beginning with keyword class.

class keyword—Used to begin a class declaration.

class name—The identifier used to identify the name of a class in code.

Click event—Raised when a user clicks a control.

code editor—The window displaying code in the IDE.

code view—Displays the code in an editor window.

collapsed code—Code within a region that has been hidden by clicking on a minus box.

comment—A line of code that follows a double slash (//) or any code that falls between the delimiters /* and */. A comment is inserted to improve an application's readability.

compilation error—Errors that prevent an application from compiling successfully.

Convert.ToString method—Converts its arguments to a string of characters.

debugger—Software that allows you to analyze the behavior of an application to determine that it is executing correctly.

debugging—The process of fixing errors in an application.

default properties—Provide the initial characteristics of an object.

dot operator—*See* member access operator.

double slash (//)—Denotes a single-line comment.

event—A user action that can trigger an event handler.

event handler—A section of code that is executed (called) when a certain event is raised (occurs).

expanded code—Viewed by clicking a plus box.

functionality—The actions an application can execute.

identifier—A series of characters consisting of letters, digits and underscores used to name program units such as classes, controls and variables.

Int32.Parse method—Converts a string of characters to an integer value.

integer—A whole number, such as 919, –11, 0 and 138624.

IntelliSense **feature**—A Visual Studio .NET feature that aids the programmer during development by providing windows listing available class members and pop-up descriptions for those members.

keyword—A word in code reserved for a specific purpose. These words appear in blue in the IDE and cannot be used as identifiers.

left brace ({)—The symbol that denotes the beginning of a block of code.

left operand—Value on the left side of an operand.

logic error—A problem that does not prevent the application from compiling successfully, but does cause the application to produce erroneous results.

Main method—The required starting point in a C# application.

member access operator—Also known as the dot operator (.), allows programmers to access a control's properties using code.

method—A set of instructions for performing a particular task.

multiplication operator—The asterisk (*) used to multiply its two operands, producing their product as a result.

namespace keyword—Used to group classes within the specified namespace.

newline character—Special character that indicates when text should continue on the next line.

operand—An expression subject to an operator.

outlined code—Collapsed code that is represented by ellipses.

raise—Causes to occur (refers to an event).

region—A portion of code that can be collapsed or expanded.

reserved word—*See* keyword.

right brace (})—The symbol that denotes the end of a block of code.

right operand—Value on the right side of an operand.

semicolon (;)—A character used to terminate each statement in an application.

statement—A unit of code that, when compiled and executed, performs an action.

syntax error—An error that occurs when program statements violate the grammatical rules of a programming language.

using directive—Provides access to classes from the specified namespace.

white space—A tab, space or newline.

CONTROLS, EVENTS, PROPERTIES & METHODS

Button `ab] Button` This control allows the user to raise an action or event.

■ *In action*

`Calculate Total`

■ *Event*

Click—Raised when the user clicks the Button.

■ *Properties*

Location—Specifies the location of the Button on the Form relative to the top-left corner.

Name—Specifies the name used to access the Button programmatically. The name should be prefixed with btn.

Size—Specifies the height and width (in pixels) of the Button.

Text—Specifies the text displayed on the Button.

Convert Class containing methods to change between types.

■ *Method*

ToString—Converts its argument into a value of type string.

Int32 This class represents an integer.

■ *Method*

Parse—Converts the given string of characters to a value of type int.

MULTIPLE-CHOICE QUESTIONS

5.1 A(n) _____ represents a user action, such as clicking a Button.

a) statement
b) event
c) application
d) method

5.2 To switch to code view, select _____.

a) **Code > View**
b) **Design > Code**
c) **View > Code**
d) **View > File Code**

5.3 Code that performs the functionality of an application _____.

a) normally is provided by the programmer
b) can never be in the form of an event handler
c) always creates a graphical user interface
d) is always generated by the IDE

5.4 Comments _____.

a) help improve program readability
b) can be placed at the end of a line of code
c) are ignored by the compiler
d) All of the above.

5.5 A _____ typically ends a C# statement.

a) period
b) colon
c) semicolon
d) comma

5.6 A(n) _____ causes an application to produce erroneous results.

a) logic error
b) event
c) assignment statement
d) syntax error

5.7 A portion of code that performs a specific task and returns a value is known as a(n) _____.

    a) variable   b) method

    c) operand   d) identifier

5.8 C# keywords are _____.

    a) identifiers   b) reserved words

    c) case insensitive   d) properties

5.9 Visual Studio .NET allows you to organize code into _____, which you can expand or collapse to facilitate code editing.

    a) statements   b) operators

    c) regions   d) keywords

5.10 An example of a white-space character is a _____ character.

    a) space   b) tab

    c) newline   d) All of the above.

EXERCISES

5.11 *(Inventory Enhancement)* Extend the **Inventory** application to include a TextBox in which the user can enter the number of shipments received in a week (Fig. 5.27). Assume every shipment has the same number of cartons (each of which has the same number of items). Then, modify the code so that the **Inventory** application uses that value in its calculation.

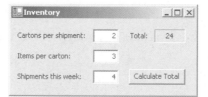

Figure 5.27 Enhanced **Inventory** application GUI.

a) *Copying the template to your working directory.* Copy the directory C:\Examples\ Tutorial05\Exercises\InventoryEnhancement to your C:\SimplyCSP directory.

b) *Opening the application's template file.* Double click Inventory.sln in the InventoryEnhancement directory to open the application.

c) *Resizing the Form.* Resize the Form you used in this tutorial by setting the Size property to 296, 144. Move the Button toward the bottom of the Form, as shown in Fig. 5.27. Its new location should be 184, 78.

d) *Adding a Label.* Add a Label to the Form and change the Text property to Shipments this week:. Set the Location property to 16, 80. Resize the Label so that the entire text displays. Set the Label's Name property to lblShipments.

e) *Adding a TextBox.* Add a TextBox to the right of the Label. Set the Text property to 0 and the Location property to 128, 80. Set the TextAlign and Size properties to the same values as for the other TextBoxes in this tutorial's example. Set the TextBox's Name property to txtShipments.

f) *Modifying the code.* Modify the **Calculate Total** Click event handler so that it multiplies the number of shipments per week with the product of the number of cartons in a shipment and the number of items in a carton.

g) *Running the application.* Select **Debug > Start** to run your application. Enter 2 in the **Cartons per shipment:** TextBox. Enter 3 in the **Items per carton:** TextBox. Enter 4 in the **Shipments this week:** TextBox. Click the **Calculate** Button. The **Inventory** Form in Fig. 5.27 shows the correct result after these values have been entered.

h) *Closing the application.* Close your running application by clicking its close box.

i) *Closing the IDE.* Close Visual Studio .NET by clicking its close box.

5.12 *(Counter Application)* Create a counter application (Fig. 5.28). Your counter application will consist of a Label and Button on the Form. The Label initially displays 0, but, each time a user clicks the Button, the value in the Label is increased by 1. When incrementing the Label, you will need to write a statement such as

```
lblTotal.Text = Convert.ToString( Int32.Parse( lblTotal.Text ) + 1 );
```

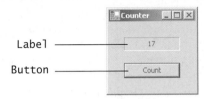

Label
Button

Figure 5.28   Counter GUI.

a) *Creating a new project.* Open Visual Studio .NET. Create a new project in your C:\SimplyCSP directory named Counter.

b) *Modifying a new Form.* Change the Form's Size property to 168, 144. Modify the Form so that the title reads **Counter**. Change the Name property to FrmCounter. Change Form1 to FrmCounter in method Main and in the comments above the class declaration.

c) *Adding a Label.* Add a Label to the Form, and place it as shown in Fig. 5.28. Make sure that the Label's Text property is set to 0 and that TextAlign property is set so that any text will appear in the middle (both horizontally and vertically) of the Label. This can be done by using the MiddleCenter TextAlign property. Also set the BorderStyle property to Fixed3D. Set the Label's Name property to lblCountTotal.

d) *Adding a Button.* Add a Button to the Form. Set the Button's Text property to contain the text **Count**. Set the Button's Name property to btnCount.

e) *Creating an event handler.* Add an event handler to the **Count** Button such that the value in the Label increases by 1 each time the user clicks the **Count** Button.

f) *Running the application.* Select **Debug > Start** to run your application. Click the **Count** Button repeatedly and watch the result.

g) *Closing the application.* Close your running application by clicking its close box.

h) *Closing the IDE.* Close Visual Studio .NET by clicking its close box.

5.13 *(Account Information Application)* Create an application that allows a user to input a name, account number and deposit amount (Fig. 5.29). The user then clicks the **Enter** Button, which causes the name and account number to be copied and displayed in two output Labels. The deposit amount entered will be added to the deposit amount displayed in another output Label. The result is displayed in the same output Label. Every time the **Enter** Button is clicked, the deposit amount entered is added to the deposit amount displayed in the output Label, keeping a cumulative total. When updating the Label, you will need to write a statement such as

```
lblBalance.Text = Convert.ToString(
    Int32.Parse( lblDeposits.Text ) + Int32.Parse( txtDepositAmount ) );
```

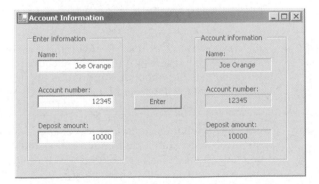

Figure 5.29   Account Information GUI.

a) *Copying the template to your working directory.* Copy the directory C:\Examples\ Tutorial05\Exercises\AccountInformation directory to your C:\SimplyCSP directory.

b) *Opening the application's template file.* Double click AccountInformation.sln in the InventoryEnhancement directory to open the application.

c) *Creating an event handler.* Add an event handler for the **Enter** Button's Click event.

d) *Coding the event handler.* Code the event handler to copy information from the **Name:** and **Account number:** TextBoxes to their corresponding output Labels. Then add the value in the **Deposit amount:** TextBox to the value in **Deposit amount:** output Label, and display the result in the **Deposit amount:** output Label.

e) *Running the application.* Select **Debug > Start** to run your application. Begin with the values in Fig. 5.29 when you test your application.

f) *Closing the application.* Close your running application by clicking its close box.

g) *Closing the IDE.* Close Visual Studio .NET by clicking its close box.

What does this code do? ▶ **5.14** After entering 10 in the txtPrice TextBox and 1.05 in the txtTax TextBox, a user clicks the Button named btnEnter. What is the result of the click, given the following code? Assume that this application has an output Label, lblOutput. [*Note*: The Double.Parse method is similar to the Int32.Parse method, but can convert a string of characters into a number with a decimal point. You will learn more about the Double.Parse method in later tutorials.]

```
1   private void btnEnter_Click( object sender, System.EventArgs e )
2   {
3      lblOutput.Text = Convert.ToString(
4         Double.Parse( txtPrice.Text ) *
5         Double.Parse( txtTax.Text ) );
6
7   } // end method btnEnter_Click
```

What's wrong with this code? ▶ **5.15** The following event handler should multiply two inputs when the user clicks a **Calculate** Button. Identify the error(s) in its code. Assume that this application has a Label, lbl-Result, and two TextBoxes, txtFirst and txtSecond. Also assume that the input entered into txtFirst and txtSecond are integers.

```
1   private void btnCalculate_Click( object sender, System.EventArgs e )
2   {
3      lblResult.Text = txtFirst.Text + txtSecond.Text;
4
5   } // end method btnCalculate_Click
```

Using the Debugger ▶ **5.16** (*Account Information Debugging Exercise*) Copy the directory C:\Examples\ Tutorial05\Exercises\Debugger\AccountInformation to your C:\SimplyCSP directory, and run the **Account Information** application. Remove any syntax and compilation errors so that the application runs correctly.

Programming Challenge ▶ **5.17** (*Account Information Enhancement*) Modify Exercise 5.13 so that it no longer asks for the user's name and account number, but rather asks the user for a withdrawal or deposit amount. The user can enter both a withdrawal and deposit amount at the same time. When the **Enter** Button is clicked, the balance is updated appropriately (Fig. 5.30).

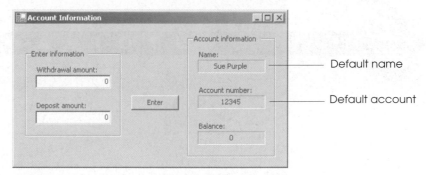

Figure 5.30 Enhanced **Account Information** GUI.

a) ***Copying the template to your working directory.*** If you have not already done so, copy the directory C:\Examples\Tutorial05\Exercises\AccountInformation to your C:\SimplyCSP directory.

b) ***Opening the application's template file.*** Double click AccountInformation.sln in the AccountInformation directory to open the application.

c) ***Modifying the GUI.*** Modify the GUI so that it appears as in Fig. 5.30.

d) ***Setting the default values.*** Set the default name and account number to the values shown in Fig. 5.30 using the **Properties** window.

e) ***Writing code to add functionality.*** Update the account balance for every withdrawal (which decreases the balance) and every deposit (which increases the balance). When the balance is updated, reset the TextBoxes to 0.

f) ***Running the application.*** Select **Debug > Start** to run your application. Begin with the values in Fig. 5.30 when you test your application.

g) ***Closing the application.*** Close your running application by clicking its close box.

h) ***Closing the IDE.*** Close Visual Studio .NET by clicking its close box.

T U T O R I A L

6

Objectives

In this tutorial, you will learn to:
- Create variables.
- Handle the **TextChanged** event.
- Apply basic memory concepts using variables.
- Use the precedence rules of arithmetic operators.
- Set breakpoints to debug applications.

Outline

6.1 Test-Driving the Enhanced **Inventory** Application
6.2 Variables
6.3 Handling the **TextChanged** Event
6.4 Memory Concepts
6.5 Arithmetic
6.6 Using the Debugger: Breakpoints
6.7 Internet and Web Resources
6.8 Wrap-Up

Enhancing the Inventory Application

Introducing Variables, Memory Concepts and Arithmetic

In the previous tutorial, you developed an **Inventory** application that performed a multiplication calculation to determine the number of items received in an inventory. You learned how to create TextBoxes to read user input from the keyboard. You also added a Button to a Form and programmed that Button to respond to a user's click. In this tutorial, you will enhance your **Inventory** application using additional programming concepts, including variables, events and arithmetic.

6.1 Test-Driving the Enhanced Inventory Application

In this tutorial, you will enhance the previous tutorial's **Inventory** application by inserting code rather than dragging and dropping C# controls. You will use variables to perform arithmetic in C#, and study memory concepts to help you understand how applications run on computers. Recall that your **Inventory** application from Tutorial 5 calculated the number of items received, based on information supplied by the user—the number of cartons and the number of textbooks per carton. This application must meet the following requirements:

Application Requirements

*The inventory manager notices a flaw in your **Inventory** application. Although the application calculates the correct result, that result continues to display even after new data is entered. The only time the output changes is when the inventory manager clicks the **Calculate Button** again. You need to alter the **Inventory** application to clear the result as soon as the user enters new information in either of the TextBoxes, to avoid any confusion over the accuracy of your calculated result.*

You begin by test-driving the completed application. Then, you will learn the additional C# technologies you will need to create your own version of this application. At first glance, the application does not seem to operate any differently than the application in the previous tutorial. However, you should notice that the **Total:** Label clears when you enter new data into either of the TextBoxes.

Test-Driving the Enhanced Inventory Application

1. ***Opening the completed application.*** Open the C:\Examples\ Tutorial06\CompletedApplication\Inventory3 directory to locate the **Inventory** application. Double click Inventory.sln to open the application in Visual Studio .NET. If the Form does not appear in design view, double click Inventory.cs in the **Solutions Explorer** window. In general, if Visual Studio .NET does not open the Form in design view, you will need to double click the Form's file name in the **Solution Explorer** window. If the **Solution Explorer** is not open, select **View > Solution Explorer**.

2. ***Running the Inventory application.*** Select **Debug > Start** to run the application (Fig. 6.1).

Figure 6.1   **Inventory** application GUI displayed when the application is running.

3. ***Calculating the number of items in the shipment.*** Enter 5 in the **Cartons per shipment:** TextBox and 6 in the **Items per carton:** TextBox. Click the **Calculate Total** Button. The result will be displayed in the **Total:** output Label (Fig. 6.2).

Figure 6.2   Running the **Inventory** application.

4. ***Entering new quantities.*** After you modify the application, the result displayed in the **Total:** Label will be removed when the user enters a new quantity in either TextBox. Enter 13 as the new number of cartons—the last calculation's result is cleared (Fig. 6.3). This will be explained later in this tutorial.

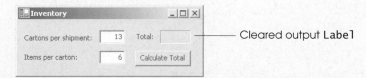
— Cleared output Label

Figure 6.3   Enhanced **Inventory** application clears output Label after new input.

5. ***Closing the application.*** Close your running application by clicking its close box.

6. ***Closing the IDE.*** Close Visual Studio .NET by clicking its close box.

6.2 Variables

Good Programming Practice

By convention, variable-name identifiers begin with a lowercase letter. Every word in the name after the first word should begin with a capital letter—for example, `intFirst-Number`.

Good Programming Practice

Use only letters and digits as characters for your variable names.

A **variable** holds data for your application, much as the Text property of a Label holds the text to be displayed to the user. Unlike the Text property of a Label, however, variable values are not shown to the user by default. Using variables in an application allows you to store and manipulate data without necessarily showing the data to the user and to store data without adding or using controls. Variables store data such as numbers, the date and the time. However, each variable used in C# corresponds to exactly one type of information. For example, a variable that stores a number cannot be used to store text. In C#, all variables must be declared, or reported, to the compiler by using program code. The **declaration** of a variable consists of its type followed by its name.

The following box introduces programming with variables. A variable name can be any valid identifier, which, as you learned in Tutorial 5, is a name that the compiler will recognize (and is not a keyword). As you also learned in the last tutorial, there are many valid characters for identifiers.

Using Variables in the Inventory Application

1. *Copying the template to your working directory.* Copy the `C:\Examples\Tutorial06\TemplateApplication\Inventory3` directory to your `C:\SimplyCSP` directory.

2. *Opening the Inventory application's template file.* Double click `Inventory.sln` in the `Inventory3` directory to open the application in Visual Studio .NET.

3. *Rearranging and commenting the control declarations.* Switch to code view by selecting **View > Code**. Your code, in fact, already contains several variable declarations. Lines 15–21 of Fig. 6.4 are declarations for the controls on the Form. Controls, such as Labels and TextBoxes, are actually variables. Each declaration begins with the `private` keyword, which you will learn more about in Tutorial 19 when you begin to create your own classes. After the `private` keyword is the variable type, followed by the variable name. Both of these terms will be discussed shortly. Rearrange the control declarations and include comments as in Fig. 6.5 (lines 15, 19, 23 and 27). The controls are grouped in the code similarly to how they appear on the Form. The comment above each group of controls explains each one's purpose in the application.

Good Programming Practice

Rearrange control declarations so that they are grouped together in the code as they are on the form. Comment control declarations to clarify the purpose of each one in the application.

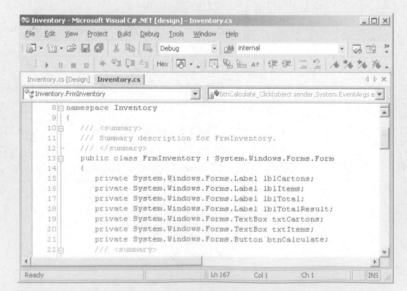

Figure 6.4 The unarranged control declarations.

(cont.)

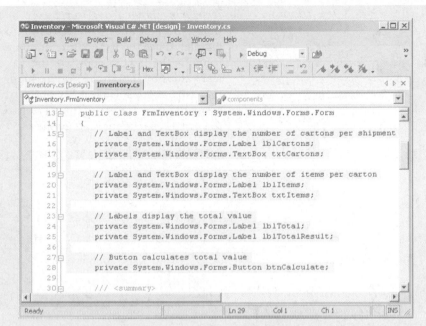

Figure 6.5   Rearranging and commenting the control declarations.

4. **Adding variable declarations to the btnCalculate_Click event handler.**
Add lines 173–176 of Fig. 6.6 to the btnCalculate_Click event handler.
Lines 174–176 are declarations, each of which begin with the variable type.
The variables on these three lines are all of the **int** type. Notice that, when
you type the word int, as with all keywords, Visual Studio .NET colors it
blue by default. Recall that keywords are reserved for use by C#. (A complete list of C# keywords is presented in Appendix F.) The words intCartons, intItems and intResult are the names of the variables. The name
of a variable follows its type. Lines 174–176 declare that the intCartons,
intItems and intResult variables, store data of the int type. Variables of
type int store integer values (whole numbers such as 919, 0 and –11).
Types already defined in C#, such as int, are known as **built-in types**. Built-
in type names are also keywords. The 15 built-in types are listed in Fig. 6.8.
You will use several of these types in the book.

    Built-in types can be called by either their type name (such as int) or
their class name (such as Int32). We use the class name when referring to a
type's methods (such as Int32.Parse).

Good Programming Practice

Prefix all integer variable names with int. Using prefixes that indicate a variable's type makes your code clearer, especially when you
are first learning to program.

Click event handler ————

Variable declarations ————

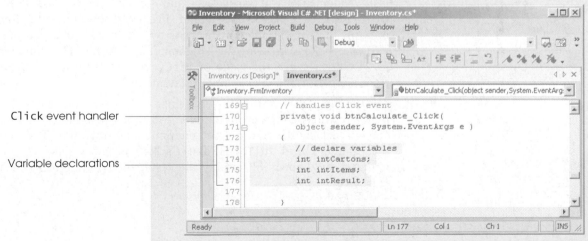

Figure 6.6   Declaring variables in event handler btnCalculate_Click.

(cont.)

5. ***Retrieving input from TextBoxes.*** Skip one line after the variable declarations, and add lines 178–180 of Fig. 6.7 in the `btnCalculate_Click` event handler. Once the user enters numbers and clicks **Calculate Total**, the values found in the `Text` property of the `TextBox` controls are converted to numerical values by the `Int32.Parse` method. Then, the numbers are assigned to the `intCartons` (line 179) and `intItems` (line 180) variables with the assignment operator, `=`. Line 179 is read as "`intCartons` *gets* the result of the `Int32.Parse` method applied to `txtCartons.Text`."

Assigning user input to variables ——

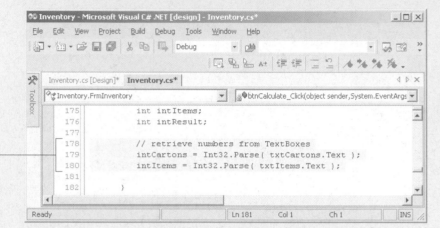

Figure 6.7 Retrieving numerical input from `TextBoxes`.

6. ***Saving the project.*** Select **File > Save All** to save your modified code.

Built-in types

bool	char	float	long	short
byte	decimal	int	ulong	ushort
sbyte	double	uint	object	string

Figure 6.8 C# built-in types.

Now that you have assigned values to your new variables, you use the variables to calculate the number of textbooks received.

Using Variables in a Calculation

1. ***Performing the multiplication operation.*** Skip one line from the end of the last statement you inserted and insert lines 182–183 in the `btnCalculate_Click` event handler (Fig. 6.9). The statement in line 183 will multiply the `int` variable `intCartons` by `intItems` and assign the result to variable `intResult`, using the assignment operator, `=`. The statement is read as, "`intResult` *gets* the value of `intCartons * intItems`." (Most calculations are performed in assignment statements.)

2. ***Displaying the result.*** Add lines 185–186 of Fig. 6.9 to the `btnCalculate_Click` event handler. After the calculation is completed, line 186 will display the result of the multiplication operation. The number sets the value of `Label lblTotalResult`'s `Text` property. Once the property is updated, the `Label` will display the result of the multiplication operation (Fig. 6.10).

(cont.)

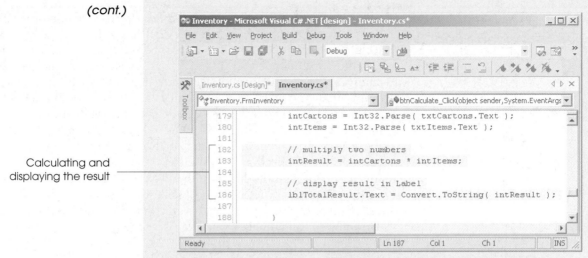

Calculating and displaying the result

Figure 6.9   Multiplication using variables in `btnCalculate_Click`.

Result of calculation

Figure 6.10   Displaying the multiplication result using variables.

3. *Running the application.* Select **Debug > Start** to run your application. Your application should appear as in Fig. 6.1. Enter 5 in the **Cartons per shipment:** TextBox and 6 in the **Items per carton:** TextBox. Then click the **Calculate Total** Button to test your application.

4. *Closing the application.* Close your running application by clicking its close box.

SELF-REVIEW

1. In a declaration, a variable's name follows its _____.

    a) size   b) type

    c) location   d) value

2. Types already defined in C#, such as `int`, are known as _____ types.

    a) provided   b) existing

    c) defined   d) built-in

Answers: 1) b. 2) d.

6.3 Handling the TextChanged Event

You might have noticed that the flaw, or **bug**, mentioned in the application requirements at the beginning of this tutorial remains in your application. Although the `lblTotalResult` Label displays the current result, once you enter a new number into a TextBox, that result is no longer valid. However, the result displayed does not change again until you click the **Calculate Total** Button, potentially confusing anyone using the application. Visual Studio .NET provides a convenient way to deal with this problem, which you will explore in the following box.

Handling the TextChanged Event

1. **Adding an event handler for txtCartons's TextChanged event.** Return to design view by clicking the **Inventory.cs[Design]** tab. Double click the **Cartons per shipment:** TextBox, txtCartons, to generate an event handler for the **TextChanged** event, which is raised when the TextBox's text changes. Visual Studio .NET will then generate an event handler with an empty body (no additional code) and place the cursor in the body. Remember to add a comment (line 191) before the event handler and split the header into two lines (lines 192–193) for better readability. Insert line 195 of Fig. 6.11 in your code. According to the application requirements for this tutorial, the application should clear the value in lblTotalResult every time users change the text in either TextBox. Line 195 clears the value in lblTotalResult. The notation "" (side-by-side double quotes) in line 195 is called an **empty string**, which is a value that does not contain any characters. This empty string replaces whatever is stored in lblTotalResult.Text.

TextChanged event handler

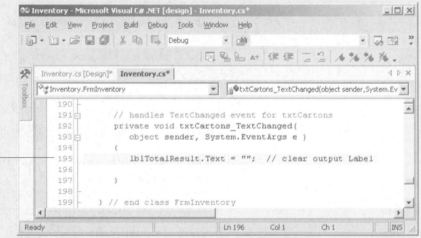

Figure 6.11 TextChanged event handler for **Cartons per shipment:** Text-Box.

Good Programming Practice

If a statement is wider than the code editor window, split the statement into multiple lines

Error-Prevention Tip

Add a comment to the end of each event handler only after all event handlers have been generated. Otherwise, Visual Studio .NET may misinterpret the purpose of such comments and move them to undesired places in your code.

2. **Adding an event handler for txtItems's TextChanged event.** We want the result cleared regardless of which TextBox's value is changed first. Return to design view, then double click the **Items per carton:** TextBox. Format the event handler header and insert line 204 from Fig. 6.12 into the new event handler. Notice that these lines perform the same task as line 195—we want the same action, namely the clearing of a TextBox, to occur. Finally, add comments to the end of each of the three event handlers (lines 93, 101 and 109 of Fig. 6.13). Note that if you had commented the end of one event handler, then generated a second event handler, Visual Studio .NET would have mistakenly moved the comment to the end of the new event handler. For this reason, you should generate all event handlers before commenting the end of each event handler.

3. **Running the application.** Select **Debug > Start** to run your application. To test the application, enter 8 in the **Cartons per shipment:** TextBox and 7 in the **Items per carton:** TextBox. When you click the **Calculate Total** Button, the number 56 should appear in the output Label. Then enter 9 in the **Items per carton:** TextBox. Notice that the TextChanged event handler clears the output Label.

(cont.)

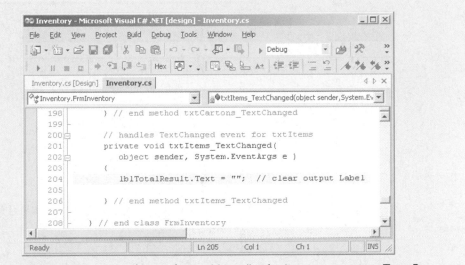

Figure 6.12   TextChanged event handler for **Items per carton:** TextBox.

4. ***Closing the application.*** Close your running application by clicking its close box.

Figure 6.13 presents the source code for the **Inventory** application. The lines of code that contain new programming concepts that you learned in this tutorial are highlighted.

```csharp
1   using System;
2   using System.Drawing;
3   using System.Collections;
4   using System.ComponentModel;
5   using System.Windows.Forms;
6   using System.Data;
7
8   namespace Inventory
9   {
10      /// <summary>
11      /// Summary description for FrmInventory.
12      /// </summary>
13      public class FrmInventory : System.Windows.Forms.Form
14      {
15         // Label and TextBox display the number of cartons per shipment
16         private System.Windows.Forms.Label lblCartons;
17         private System.Windows.Forms.TextBox txtCartons;
18
19         // Label and TextBox display the number of items per carton
20         private System.Windows.Forms.Label lblItems;
21         private System.Windows.Forms.TextBox txtItems;
22
23         // Labels display the total value
24         private System.Windows.Forms.Label lblTotal;
25         private System.Windows.Forms.Label lblTotalResult;
26
27         // Button calculates total value
28         private System.Windows.Forms.Button btnCalculate;
29
```

Rearranging and commenting the control declarations

Figure 6.13   **Inventory** application code. (Part 1 of 3.)

```
30      /// <summary>
31      /// Required designer variable.
32      /// </summary>
33      private System.ComponentModel.Container components = null;
34
35      public FrmInventory()
36      {
37         //
38         // Required for Windows Form Designer support
39         //
40         InitializeComponent();
41
42         //
43         // TODO: Add any constructor code after InitializeComponent
44         // call
45         //
46      }
47
48      /// <summary>
49      /// Clean up any resources being used.
50      /// </summary>
51      protected override void Dispose( bool disposing )
52      {
53         if( disposing )
54         {
55            if (components != null)
56            {
57               components.Dispose();
58            }
59         }
60         base.Dispose( disposing );
61      }
62
63      // Windows Form Designer generated code
64
65      /// <summary>
66      /// The main entry point for the application.
67      /// </summary>
68      [STAThread]
69      static void Main()
70      {
71         Application.Run( new FrmInventory() );
72      }
73
74      // handles Click event
75      private void btnCalculate_Click(
76         object sender, System.EventArgs e )
77      {
78         // declare variables
79         int intCartons;
80         int intItems;
81         int intResult;
82
83         // retrieve numbers from TextBoxes
84         intCartons = Int32.Parse( txtCartons.Text );
85         intItems = Int32.Parse( txtItems.Text );
86
```

Use the **int** keyword to declare variables of type integer

Assigning a property's value to a variable

Figure 6.13 **Inventory** application code. (Part 2 of 3.)

```
87              // multiply two numbers
88              intResult = intCartons * intItems;
89
90              // display result in Label
91              lblTotalResult.Text = Convert.ToString( intResult );
92
93        } // end method btnCalculate_Click
94
95        // handles TextChanged event for txtCartons
96        private void txtCartons_TextChanged(
97           object sender, System.EventArgs e )
98        {
99           lblTotalResult.Text = "";   // clear output Label
100
101       } // end method txtCartons_TextChanged
102
103       // handles TextChanged event for txtItems
104       private void txtItems_TextChanged(
105          object sender, System.EventArgs e )
106       {
107          lblTotalResult.Text = "";   // clear output Label
108
109       } // end method txtItems_TextChanged
110
111    } // end class FrmInventory
112 }
```

Assigning a variable to a property — *(line 90)*

Defining a TextBox's TextChanged event handler — *(lines 96–101)*

Setting a TextBox's Text property to an empty string — *(line 107)*

Figure 6.13 **Inventory** application code. (Part 3 of 3.)

SELF-REVIEW

1. The _____ is represented by "" in C#.

   a) empty character   b) empty string

   c) empty value   d) None of the above.

2. Use the _____ property to remove any text displayed in a TextBox.

   a) `ClearText`   b) `Remove`

   c) `Display`   d) `Text`

Answers: 1) b. 2) d.

6.4 Memory Concepts

Variable names—such as `intCartons`, `intItems` and `intResult`—correspond to actual **locations** in the computer's memory. Every variable has a **name**, **type**, **size** and **value**. In the **Inventory** application code listing in Fig. 6.13, when the assignment statement (line 84)

```
intCartons = Int32.Parse( txtCartons.Text );
```

executes, the user input stored in `txtCartons.Text` is converted to an `int`. This `int` is placed into the memory location to which the name `intCartons` has been assigned by the compiler. Suppose that the user enters the characters 12 in the **Cartons per shipment:** TextBox. This input is stored in `txtCartons.Text`. When the user clicks **Calculate Total**, C# converts the user input to an `int` and places the `int` value 12 into location `intCartons`, as shown in Fig. 6.14.

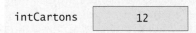

`intCartons`   12

Figure 6.14 Memory location showing the name and value of `intCartons`.

Whenever a value is placed in a memory location, this value replaces the value previously stored in that location. The previous value is overwritten (lost).

Suppose that the user also entered the characters 10 in the **Items per carton:** TextBox. Line 85 of Fig. 6.13

```
intItems = Int32.Parse( txtItems.Text );
```

converts `txtItems.Text` to an `int`, placing the `int` value 10 into location `intItems`, and memory appears as shown in Fig. 6.15.

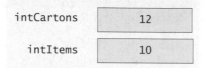

Figure 6.15   Memory locations after values for the `intCartons` and `intItems` variables have been input.

Once the **Calculate Total** Button is clicked, line 88 multiplies these values and places their total into variable `intResult`. The statement

```
intResult = intCartons * intItems;
```

performs the multiplication and replaces (that is, overwrites) `intResult`'s previous value. After `intResult` is calculated, the memory appears as shown in Fig. 6.16. Note that the values of `intCartons` and `intItems` appear exactly as they did before they were used in the calculation of `intResult`. Although these values were used when the computer performed the calculation, they were not destroyed. This illustrates that the process of reading a value from a memory location is **nondestructive** (meaning that the value is not overwritten).

Figure 6.16   Memory locations after a multiplication operation.

SELF-REVIEW

1. When a value is placed into a memory location, the value _____ the previous value in that location.

   a) copies   b) replaces

   c) adds itself to   d) moves

2. When a value is read from memory, that value is _____.

   a) overwritten   b) not overwritten

   c) moved to a new location in memory   d) replaced with a new value

Answers: 1) b. 2) b.

6.5 Arithmetic

Most applications perform arithmetic calculations. In the last tutorial, you performed the arithmetic operation multiplication by using the multiplication operator (*). The **arithmetic operators** are summarized in Fig. 6.17. Note the use of various special symbols not used in algebra. For example, the asterisk (*) indicates multiplication, the percent sign (%) represents the **remainder** (also known as the modulus)

operator and the forward slash (/) represents division. The majority of arithmetic operators in Fig. 6.17 are binary operators, requiring two operands. For example, the expression intSum + intValue contains the binary operator + and the two operands intSum and intValue. C# also provides **unary operators**, which are operators that take only one operand. For example, unary versions of plus (+) and minus (−) are provided so that programmers can write expressions such as +9 (a positive number) and −19 (a negative number).

C# operation	Arithmetic operator	Algebraic expression	C# expression
Addition	+	$f + 7$	f + 7
Subtraction	−	$p - c$	p − c
Multiplication	*	bm	b * m
Division	/	x / y or $\frac{x}{y}$ or $x \div y$	x / y
Remainder	%	r modulo s	r % s
Unary Negative	−	$-e$	−e
Unary Positive	+	$+g$	+g

Figure 6.17 Arithmetic operators.

C# has only one operator, the forward slash (/), for **integer division** and **floating-point division**. Floating-point division divides two numbers (whole or fractional) and returns a floating-point number (a number with a decimal point). The operator for integer division treats its operands as integers and returns an integer result. Integer division takes two int operands and yields an int result. For example, the expression 7 / 4 evaluates to 1, and the expression 17 / 5 evaluates to 3. Note that any fractional part of the integer division result is discarded (this is called truncating)—no rounding occurs. To obtain the exact value of 17 / 5, you must force at least one of the two operands to be a floating-point number. For example, the expression 17.0 / 5 evaluates to 3.4.

The value 17.0 is not an int but a **double**. The double type is used to store both whole and fractional numbers. Normally, doubles store floating-point numbers, which are numbers with decimal points, such as 2.3456 and −845.4680. Variables of the double type can hold values that are much larger than variables of type int. Because doubles and ints are different types of variables, C# performs a conversion from one type to the other before the division can take place. This process is called **implicit conversion** because the conversion takes place without any additional code. Here the value 5 is temporarily converted from the int type to the double type so that floating-point division can be performed.

An int can be implicitly converted to a double, but a double cannot be implicitly converted to an int. C# prevents an implicit conversion from the double type to the int type because information could be lost in such a conversion (here, the fractional part of the floating-point number). To force such a conversion to take place, the **cast operator** is used to perform an **explicit conversion**. The cast operator is a unary operator formed by placing parentheses around a type name. For instance, we can convert the value 17.0 into an int with the expression (int) 17.0. Note that the cast operator, when used on a variable, does not modify the value stored in memory for the variable. Rather it creates a temporary value used only for that particular calculation. Another way to perform explicit conversions is with methods of the Convert class, such as Convert.ToString. You will learn more about conversions in Tutorial 15.

The remainder operator, %, yields the remainder after division. The expression x % y yields the remainder after x is divided by y. Thus, 7 % 4 yields 3, and 17 % 5 yields 2. This operator is used most commonly with int operands, but also can be used with other types. The remainder operator can be applied to several interesting problems, such as discovering whether one number is a multiple of another. If a and b are numbers, a % b yields 0 if a is a multiple of b. 8 % 3 yields 2, so 8 is not a multiple of 3. But 8 % 2 and 8 % 4 each yield 0, because 8 is a multiple both of 2 and of 4.

Neither the division operator nor the remainder operator allows division by zero. If your code divides by zero, a **runtime error** occurs. By default, this error will terminate the application.

Arithmetic expressions in C# must be written in **straight-line form** so that you can type them into a computer. For example, the division of 7.1 by 4.3 cannot be written

$$\frac{7.1}{4.3}$$

but must be written in straight-line form as 7.1 / 4.3.

Parentheses are used in C# expressions in the same manner as in algebraic expressions. For example, to multiply a times the quantity $b + c$, you write

    a * (b + c)

C# applies the operators in arithmetic expressions in a precise sequence, determined by the **rules of operator precedence,** which are generally the same as those followed in algebra. These rules enable C# to apply operators in the correct order.

![Common Programming Error icon] **Common Programming Error**

Attempting to divide by zero is a runtime error (that is, an error that has its effect while the application runs). Dividing by zero terminates an application by default.

Rules of Operator Precedence

1. *Operators in expressions contained within a pair of parentheses are evaluated first*. Thus, parentheses can be used to force the order of evaluation to occur in any sequence desired by the programmer. Parentheses are at the highest level of precedence. With **nested** (or **embedded**) parentheses, the operators contained in the innermost pair of parentheses are applied first. Cast operators are applied after all other parentheses.

2. *Unary positive and negative, + and -, are applied next*. If an expression contains several sign operations, operators are applied from left to right.

3. *Multiplication, division and remainder operations are applied next*. If an expression contains several multiplication, division and remainder operations, operators are applied from left to right.

4. *Addition and subtraction operations are applied last*. If an expression contains several addition and subtraction operations, operators are applied from left to right.

Notice in the previous box that we mention nested parentheses. Not all expressions with several pairs of parentheses contain nested parentheses. For example, although the expression

    a * (b + c) + c * (d + e)

contains multiple pairs of parentheses, none of the parentheses are nested. Rather, these sets are referred to as being "on the same level" and are evaluated from left to right.

Let's consider several expressions in light of the rules of operator precedence. Each example lists an algebraic expression and its C# equivalent.

The following calculates the average of three numbers:

Algebra: $\quad m = \dfrac{(a + b + c)}{3}$

C#: $\quad$ m = (a + b + c) / 3;

The parentheses are required, because division has higher precedence than addition. The entire quantity (a + b + c) is to be divided by 3. If the parentheses are omitted, erroneously, we obtain a + b + c / 3, which evaluates as

$$a + b + \frac{c}{3}$$

The following is the equation of a straight line:

Algebra: $y = mx + b$

C#:   y = m * x + b;

No parentheses are required. The multiplication is applied first, because multiplication has a higher precedence than addition. The assignment occurs last because it has a lower precedence than multiplication and addition.

To develop a better understanding of the rules of operator precedence, consider how the expression $y = ax^2 + bx + c$ is evaluated:

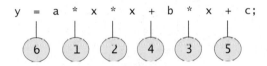

The circled numbers under the statement indicate the order in which C# evaluates the operators. There is no arithmetic operator for exponentiation in C#, so x^2 is represented as x * x. Also, note that the assignment operator is applied last because it has a lower precedence than any of the arithmetic operators.

As in algebra, it is acceptable to place unnecessary parentheses in an expression to make the expression easier to read—these parentheses are called **redundant parentheses**. For example, the preceding assignment statement might use redundant parentheses to emphasize terms:

    y = (a * x * x) + (b * x) + c;

Good Programming Practice

The use of redundant parentheses in complex arithmetic expressions can make the expressions easier to read.

SELF-REVIEW

1. Arithmetic expressions in C# must be written _____ to facilitate entering applications into the computer.

    a) using parentheses   b) on multiple lines
    c) in straight-line form   d) None of the above.

2. The multiplication operator _____.

    a) is applied from left to right
    b) is a unary operator
    c) is applied from right to left
    d) comes before the addition operator in the rules of operator precedence

Answers: 1) c. 2) a.

6.6 Using the Debugger: Breakpoints

The debugger will be one of your most important tools in developing applications, once you become familiar with its features. You were introduced to the debugger in Tutorial 5, where you used it to locate and eliminate syntax and compilation errors. In this tutorial, you continue your study of the debugger, learning about breakpoints, which allow you to examine what your application is doing while it is running. A **breakpoint** is a marker that can be set at any executable line of code. When application execution reaches a breakpoint, execution pauses, allowing you to peek inside your application and ensure that there are no logic errors, such as an incorrect calculation. In the following box, you learn how to use breakpoints in the Visual Studio .NET debugger.

Using the Debugger: Breakpoints

1. **Enabling the debugger.** The debugger is enabled by default. If it is not enabled, you have to change the Solution Configuration ComboBox to **Debug**. To do this, click the ComboBox's down arrow (Fig. 6.18) to access the Solution Configuration ComboBox, and select **Debug**. The IDE toolbar will then display **Debug** in the Solution Configuration ComboBox.

Solution Configuration ComboBox

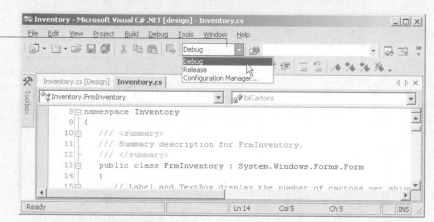

Figure 6.18   Setting the Solution Configuration **ComboBox** to **Debug**.

2. **Inserting breakpoints in Visual Studio .NET.** To insert a breakpoint in Visual Studio .NET, either click inside the **margin indicator bar** (the gray margin indicator at the left of the code window, Fig. 6.19) next to the line of code at which you wish to break or right click that line of code and select **Insert Breakpoint**. You can set as many breakpoints as necessary. Set breakpoints at lines 185 and 188 of your code. A solid maroon circle appears where you clicked, indicating that a breakpoint has been set (Fig. 6.19). When the application runs, it suspends execution at any line that contains a breakpoint. The application is said to be in **break mode** when the debugger pauses the application's execution. Breakpoints can be set in design mode, break mode and run mode.

Margin indicator bar

Breakpoints

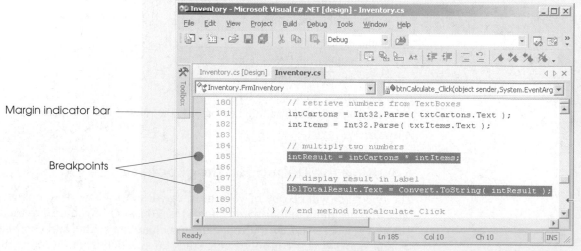

Figure 6.19   Setting two breakpoints.

(cont.)   3. ***Beginning the debugging process.*** After setting breakpoints in the code editor, select **Debug > Start** to begin the debugging process. During debugging of a Windows application, the application window appears (Fig. 6.20), allowing program interaction (input and output). Enter 10 and 7 into the Textboxes and click **Calculate Total** to continue. The title bar of the IDE will now display **[break]** (Fig. 6.21), indicating that the IDE is in break mode.

Figure 6.20   **Inventory** application running.

Title bar displays [break]

Figure 6.21   Title bar of the IDE displaying **[break]**.

4. ***Examining application execution.*** Application execution suspends at the first breakpoint, and the IDE becomes the **active window** (Fig. 6.22). The active window is the window that is currently being used and is sometimes referred to as the window that has the **focus**. The **yellow arrow** to the left of line 185 indicates that this line contains the next statement to execute.

Yellow arrow ———

Breakpoints ———

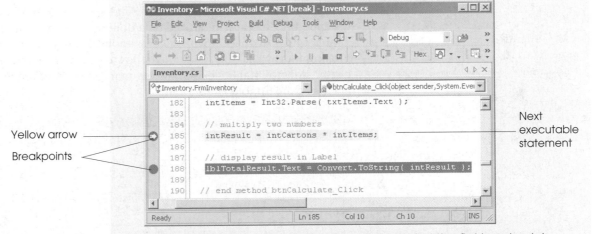

Next executable statement

Figure 6.22   Application execution suspended at the first breakpoint.

5. ***Using the Continue command to resume execution.*** To resume execution, select **Debug > Continue**. The application executes until it stops at the next breakpoint, at line 188. Notice that, when you place your mouse pointer over the variable name intResult, the value that the variable stores is displayed in a *Quick Info* box (Fig. 6.23). In a sense, you are peeking inside the computer at the value of one of your variables. As you'll see, this can help you spot logic errors in your applications.

6. ***Finishing application execution.*** Use the **Debug > Continue** command to complete the application execution. When there are no more breakpoints at which to suspend execution, the application will execute to completion and the output will appear in the **Total:** Label (Fig. 6.24).

(cont.)

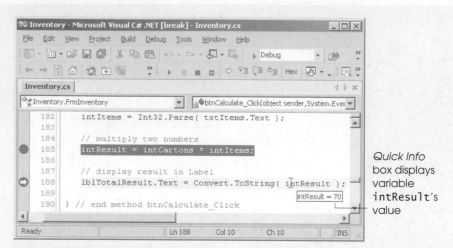

Figure 6.23 Displaying a variable value by placing the mouse pointer over a variable name.

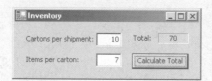

Figure 6.24 Application output.

7. *Disabling a breakpoint.* To disable a breakpoint, right click a line of code on which a breakpoint has been set, and select **Disable Breakpoint**. The disabled breakpoint is indicated by a hollow maroon circle (Fig. 6.25). Disabling rather than removing a breakpoint allows you to re-enable the breakpoint (by clicking inside the hollow circle) in an application. This also can be done by right clicking the line marked by the hollow maroon circle and selecting **Enable Breakpoint**.

Disabled breakpoint

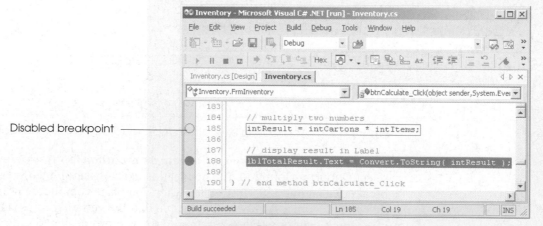

Figure 6.25 Disabled breakpoint.

8. *Removing a breakpoint.* To remove a breakpoint that you no longer need, right click a line of code on which a breakpoint has been set, and select **Remove Breakpoint**. You also can remove a breakpoint by clicking the maroon circle in the margin indicator bar.

9. *Closing the application.* Close your running application by clicking its close box.

10. *Closing the IDE.* Close Visual Studio .NET by clicking its close box.

In this section, you learned how to enable the debugger and set breakpoints so that you can examine the results of code while an application is running. You also learned how to continue execution after an application suspends execution at a breakpoint and how to disable and remove breakpoints.

SELF-REVIEW

1. A breakpoint cannot be set at a(n) _____.

 a) comment   b) executable line of code

 c) assignment statement   d) arithmetic statement

2. When application execution suspends at a breakpoint, the next statement to be executed is the statement _____ the breakpoint.

 a) before   b) after

 c) at   d) None of the above.

Answers: 1) a. 2) c.

6.7 Internet and Web Resources

Please take a moment to visit each of these sites briefly. To save typing time, use the hot links on the enclosed CD or at www.deitel.com.

www.devx.com/dotnet
This Web site contains information about the .NET platform, which includes C#. The site includes links to articles, books and news.

www.c-sharpcorner.com
This site lists numerous links to articles, books and tutorials on C#. The site allows programmers to submit code and have it rated by other developers. This site also contains forums to discuss C# topics.

www.csharphelp.com
This site links to C# tutorials, books, code and more. This site also contains a board for C# questions and answers.

www.codehound.com/csharp
This site offers a search engine designed specifically to discover C# Web sites.

6.8 Wrap-Up

You have now added variables to your **Inventory** application. You began by using variables to produce the same results as your previous **Inventory** application. Then you enhanced the **Inventory** application, using the TextChanged event, which allowed you to execute code that cleared the value in the output Label when the user changed a value in either TextBox.

You learned about memory concepts, including how variables are read and written. You will apply these concepts to the applications that you will build in later tutorials, which rely heavily on the use of variables. You learned how to convert variables from one type to another, both implicitly and explicitly. You learned how to perform arithmetic in C#, and you studied the rules of operator precedence to evaluate mathematical expressions correctly. Finally, you learned how to insert breakpoints in the debugger. Breakpoints allow you to pause program execution and examine variable values. This capability will prove useful to you in finding and fixing logic errors.

In the next tutorial, you will design a graphical user interface and write code to create a wage calculator. You will use pseudocode, an informal language that will help you design the application. You will learn to use to the debugger's **Watch** window, another useful tool that will help you remove logic errors.

SKILLS SUMMARY

Declaring a Variable

- Specify a type, such as `int` or `double`.
- Use a valid identifier as a variable name.

Handling a TextBox's TextChanged Event

- Double click a `TextBox` on a `Form` to generate an empty event handler.
- Insert code into the event handler, which executes when the text in a `TextBox` changes.

Reading a Value from a Memory Location

- Use the variable's name (as it appears in the variable's declaration) on the right side of an assignment statement.

Replacing a Value in a Memory Location

- Use the variable name, followed by the assignment operator (=), followed by an expression giving the new value.

Using the Cast Operator

- Use the cast operator (a type enclosed by parentheses, followed by a variable name) to explicitly convert a variable from one type to another.

Representing Positive and Negative Numbers

- Use the unary versions of plus (+) and minus (-).

Performing Arithmetic Operations

- Write arithmetic expressions in C# in straight-line form.
- Use the rules of operator precedence to determine the order in which operators will be applied.
- Use the + operator to perform addition.
- Use the – operator to perform subtraction.
- Use the * operator to perform multiplication.
- Use the / operator to perform either integer or floating-point division.
- Use the remainder operator, %, to report the remainder after division.

Setting a Breakpoint

- Click the margin indicator bar (the gray margin indicator at the left of the code window) next to the line at which you wish to break or right click a line of code and select **Insert Breakpoint**.

Resuming Application Execution after Entering Break Mode

- Select **Debug > Continue**.

Disabling a Breakpoint

- Right click a line of code containing a breakpoint, and select **Disable Breakpoint**.

Removing a Breakpoint

- Right click a line of code containing a breakpoint, and select **Remove Breakpoint**.
- You also can remove a breakpoint by clicking the maroon circle in the margin indicator bar.

Enabling a Breakpoint

- Enable a disabled breakpoint by clicking inside the hollow circle in the margin indicator bar.
- You also can enable a disabled breakpoint by right clicking the line marked by the hollow maroon circle and selecting **Enable Breakpoint**.

KEY TERMS

active window—The window that is currently being used—sometimes referred to as the window that has the focus.

arithmetic operators—The operators +, -, *, /, and %.

break mode—The IDE mode when application execution is suspended. This mode is entered through the debugger.

breakpoint—A statement where execution is to suspend, indicated by a solid maroon circle.

bug—A flaw that causes an application to run incorrectly.

built-in type—A type (also known as a primitive data type) already defined in C#, such as an `int`.

cast operator—Explicitly converts a variable from one type to another.

declaration—A statement that reports the existence of a variable to the compiler.

double type—Stores floating-point values.

empty string—Does not contain any characters.

explicit conversion—A conversion from one type to another requiring additional code, such as a cast operator.

floating-point division (/)—Incorporates numbers after decimal points (no rounding occurs).

focus—Designates the window currently in use.

implicit conversion—A conversion from one type to another performed by C# without any additional code.

int type—Stores integer values.

integer division (/)—Ignores numbers after decimal points (rounding occurs).

location in computer's memory—Stores a variable.

margin indicator bar—A margin in the IDE where breakpoints are displayed.

name of a variable—The identifier used in an application to access or modify a variable's value.

nested (embedded) parentheses—Located within another set of parentheses.

nondestructive process—Does not overwrite a value.

Quick Info **box**—Displays a variable's name and value when the mouse pointer is placed over the variable name.

redundant parentheses—Unnecessary parentheses that are included to make an expression easier to read.

remainder operator (%)—Yields the remainder after division.

rules of operator precedence—Determine the sequence in which operations in arithmetic expressions are applied.

runtime error—Has its effect at execution time.

size of a variable—The amount of memory required to store the variable.

straight-line form—The way arithmetic expressions must be typed in your code.

TextChanged event—Occurs when the text in a TextBox changes.

type of a variable—Specifies the kind of data that can be stored in a variable and the range of values that can be stored.

unary operator—Requires exactly one operand.

value of a variable—The piece of data that is stored in a variable's location in memory.

variable—A location in the computer's memory where a value can be stored for use by an application.

yellow arrow of debugger—Indicates that the current line contains the next statement to execute.

CONTROLS, EVENTS, PROPERTIES & METHODS

TextBox   [abl TextBox]   This control allows the user to input data from the keyboard.

■ *In action*

[0]

■ *Event*

TextChanged—Raised when the text in the TextBox is changed.

■ *Properties*

Location—Specifies the location of the Label on the Form relative to the top-left corner.

Name—Specifies the name used to access the TextBox programmatically. The name should be prefixed with txt.

Size—Specifies the height and width (in pixels) of the TextBox.

Text—Specifies the text displayed in the TextBox.

TextAlign—Specifies how the text is aligned within the TextBox.

MULTIPLE-CHOICE QUESTIONS

6.1 Parentheses that are added to an expression simply to make it easier to read are known as _____ parentheses.

a) necessary   b) redundant

c) embedded   d) nested

6.2 The _____ operator performs division.

a) /   b) +

c) \   d) ^

6.3 Every variable has a _____.

a) name   b) value

c) type   d) All of the above.

6.4 In C#, arithmetic expressions must be written in _____ form.

a) straight-line   b) top-bottom

c) left-right   d) right-left

6.5 Arithmetic expressions are evaluated _____.

a) from right to left

b) from left to right

c) according to the rules of operator precedence

d) from the lowest level of precedence to the highest level of precedence

6.6 Variable declarations in event handlers begin with their _____.

a) name   b) value

c) type   d) None of the above.

6.7 Entering a character in a TextBox raises the _____ event.

a) TextAltered   b) ValueChanged

c) ValueEntered   d) TextChanged

6.8 The _____ operator makes an explicit conversion from one type to another.

a) cast   b) changetype

c) convert   d) conversion

6.9 Variables used to store integer values should be declared with the _____ keyword.

a) integer   b) int

c) intvariable   d) None of the above.

6.10 The name of a variable in a variable declaration should come directly after its _____.

a) type   b) value

c) size   d) All of the above.

EXERCISES

6.11 *(Simple Encryption Application)* This application uses a simple technique to encrypt a number. Encryption is the process of modifying data so that only those intended to receive it can undo the changes to view the original data. The user enters the data to be encrypted using a `TextBox`. The application then multiplies the number by 7 and adds 5. The application displays the encrypted number in a `Label` as shown in Fig. 6.26.

Figure 6.26   Result of the completed **Simple Encryption** application.

a) ***Copying the template to your working directory.*** Copy the directory `C:\Examples\Tutorial06\Exercises\SimpleEncryption` to your `C:\SimplyCSP` directory.

b) ***Opening the application's template file.*** Double click `SimpleEncryption.sln` in the `SimpleEncryption` directory to open the application.

c) ***Coding the Click event handler.*** Encrypt the number in the `Click` event handler by using the preceding technique. The user input should be stored in an `int` variable (`intNumber`) before it is encrypted. The event handler then should display the encrypted number.

d) ***Clearing the result.*** Add an event handler for the **Enter number to encrypt:** Text-Box's `TextChanged` event. This event handler should clear the **Encrypted number:** `TextBox` whenever the user enters new input.

e) ***Running the application.*** Select **Debug > Start** to run your application. Enter the value 25 into the **Enter number to encrypt:** `TextBox` and click the **Encrypt** `Button`. Verify that the value 180 is displayed in the **Encrypted number:** output `Label`. Enter other values and click the **Encrypt** `Button` after each. Verify that the appropriate encrypted value is displayed each time.

f) ***Closing the application.*** Close your running application by clicking its close box.

g) ***Closing the IDE.*** Close Visual Studio .NET by clicking its close box.

6.12 *(Temperature Converter Application)* Write an application that converts a Celsius temperature, *C*, to its equivalent Fahrenheit temperature, *F*. Figure 6.27 displays the completed application. Use the following formula:

$$F = \frac{9}{5}C + 32$$

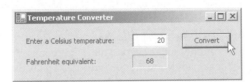

Figure 6.27   Completed **Temperature Converter**.

a) ***Copying the template to your working directory.*** Copy the directory `C:\Examples\Tutorial06\Exercises\TemperatureConversion` to your `C:\SimplyCSP` directory.

b) ***Opening the application's template file.*** Double click `TemperatureConversion.sln` in the `TemperatureConversion` directory to open the application.

c) ***Coding the Click event handler.*** Perform the conversion in the **Convert** `Button`'s `Click` event handler. Define `int` variables to store the user-input Celsius temperature and the result of the conversion. Display the Fahrenheit equivalent of the temperature conversion. Use the cast operator to convert between types. For the most accurate results, make sure you perform floating-point arithmetic and cast to an integer after all calculations have been performed.

d) ***Clearing user input.*** Clear the result in the **Enter a Celsius temperature:** `TextBox`'s `TextChanged` event.

e) ***Running the application.*** Select **Debug > Start** to run your application. Enter the value 20 into the **Enter a Celsius temperature:** `TextBox` and click the **Convert** Button. Verify that the value 68 is displayed in the output Label. Enter other Celsius temperatures, click the **Convert** Button after each. Use the formula provided above to verify that the proper Fahrenheit equivalent is displayed each time.

f) *Closing the application.* Close your running application by clicking its close box.

g) *Closing the IDE.* Close Visual Studio .NET by clicking its close box.

6.13 *(Simple Calculator Application)* In this exercise, you will add functionality to a simple calculator application. The calculator will allow a user to enter two numbers in the Text-Boxes. There will be four Buttons—labelled +, -, / and *. When the user clicks the Button labelled as addition, subtraction, multiplication or division, the application will perform that operation on the numbers in the TextBoxes and display the result. The calculator also should clear the calculation result when the user enters new input. Figure 6.28 displays the completed calculator.

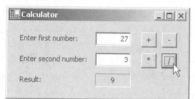

Figure 6.28 Result of the **Simple Calculator** application.

a) *Copying the template to your working directory.* Copy the directory C:\Examples\Tutorial06\Exercises\SimpleCalculator to your C:\SimplyCSP directory.

b) *Opening the application's template file.* Double click SimpleCalculator.sln in the SimpleCalculator directory to open the application.

c) *Coding the addition Click event handler.* This event handler should add the two numbers and display the result.

d) *Coding the subtraction Click event handler.* This event handler should subtract the second number from the first number and display the result.

e) *Coding the multiplication Click event handler.* This event handler should multiply the two numbers and display the result.

f) *Coding the division Click event handler.* This event handler should divide the first number by the second number and display the result.

g) *Clearing the result.* Write event handlers for the TextBoxes' TextChanged events. Write code to clear the result Label (lblResult) after the user enters new input into either TextBox.

h) *Running the application.* Select **Debug > Start** to run your application. Enter a first number and a second number, then verify that each of the Buttons works by clicking each, and viewing the output. Repeat this process with two new values and again verify that the proper output is displayed based on which Button is clicked.

i) *Closing the application.* Close your running application by clicking its close box.

j) *Closing the IDE.* Close Visual Studio .NET by clicking its close box.

What does this code do? ▶ **6.14** This code modifies the values of intNumber1, intNumber2 and intResult. What are the final values of these variables?

```
1  int intNumber1;
2  int intNumber2;
3  int intResult;
4
5  intNumber1 = 5 * ( 4 + 6 );
6  intNumber2 = 2 * 2;
7  intResult = intNumber1 / intNumber2;
```

What's wrong with this code? ▶ **6.15** Find the error(s) in the following code, which uses variables to perform a calculation.

```
1  int intNumber1;
2  int intNumber2;
3  int intResult;
4
5  intNumber1 = 4 * 6 / ( 10 % 4 - 2 );
6  intNumber2 = 16 / 3 * 6 + 1;
7  intResult = intNumber1 - intNumber2;
```

Using the Debugger ▶ **6.16** *(Average Three Numbers Application)* You have just written an application that takes three numbers as input in TextBoxes, stores the three numbers in variables, then finds the average of the numbers. The output is displayed in a Label (Fig. 6.29, which displays the incorrect output). You soon realize, however, that the number displayed in the Label is not the average, but rather a number that does not make sense given the input. Use the debugger to help locate and remove this error.

Figure 6.29   **Average Three Numbers** application running incorrectly.

a) *Copying the template to your working directory.* Copy the directory C:\Examples\ Tutorial06\Exercises\Debugger\AverageDebugging to your C:\SimplyCSP directory.

b) *Opening the application's template file.* Double click AverageDebugging.sln in the AverageDebugging directory to open the application.

c) *Setting breakpoints.* Set a breakpoint in the btnCalculate_Click event handler. Run the application again, and use the debugger to help find the error(s).

d) *Finding and correcting the error(s).* Once you have found the error(s), modify the application so that it correctly calculates the average of three numbers.

e) *Running the application.* Select **Debug > Start** to run your application. Enter the three values from Fig. 6.29 into the input TextBoxes provided and click the **Calculate** Button. Verify that the output now accurately reflects the average of these values, which is 8.

f) *Closing the application.* Close your running application by clicking its close box.

g) *Closing the IDE.* Close Visual Studio .NET by clicking its close box.

Programming Challenge ▶ **6.17** *(Digit Extractor Application)* Write an application that allows the user to enter a five-digit number into a TextBox. The application then separates the number into its individual digits and displays each digit in a Label. The application should look and behave similarly to Fig. 6.30. [*Hint:* You can use the % operator to extract the ones digit from a number. For instance, 12345 % 10 is 5. You can use integer division (/) to "peel off" digits from a number. For instance, 12345 / 100 is 123. This allows you to treat the 3 in 12345 as a ones digit. Now you can isolate the 3 by using the % operator. Apply this technique to the rest of the digits.]

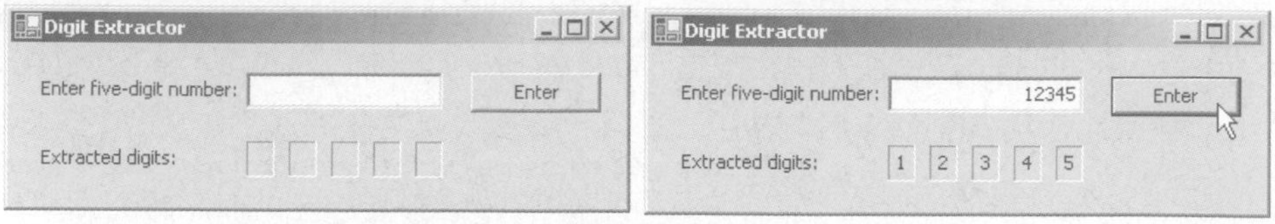

Figure 6.30 **Digit Extractor** application GUI.

a) ***Creating the application.*** Create a new project named DigitExtractor. Rename the Form1.cs file DigitExtractor.cs. Change the name of the Form to FrmDigit-Extractor. Add Labels, a TextBox and a Button to the application's Form. Name the TextBox txtInput and name the Button btnEnter. Name the other controls logically based on the tips provided in earlier tutorials.

b) ***Adding an event handler for btnEnter's Click event.*** In design view, double click btnEnter to create the btnEnter_Click event handler. In this event handler, create five variables of type int. Use the % operator to extract each digit. Store the digits in the five variables created.

c) ***Adding an event handler for txtInput's TextChanged event.*** In design view, double click txtInput to create the txtInput_TextChanged event handler. In this event handler, clear the five Labels used to display each digit. This event handler clears the output whenever new input is entered.

d) ***Running the application.*** Select **Debug > Start** to run your application. Enter a five-digit number and click the **Enter** Button. Enter a new five-digit number and verify that the previous output is cleared.

e) ***Closing the application.*** Close your running application by clicking its close box.

f) ***Closing the IDE.*** Close Visual Studio .NET by clicking its close box.

Wage Calculator Application

Introducing Algorithms, Pseudocode and Program Control

Before writing an application, it is essential to have a thorough understanding of the problem you need to solve. This will allow you to carefully plan an approach to solving the problem. When writing an application, it is equally important to recognize the types of building blocks that are available and to use proven application-construction principles. In this tutorial, you will learn the theory and principles of **structured programming**. Structured programming is a technique for organizing program control to help you develop applications that are easier to debug and modify. The techniques presented are applicable to most high-level languages, including C#.

7.1 Test-Driving the Wage Calculator Application

In this section, we preview this tutorial's **Wage Calculator** application. This application must meet the following requirements:

Application Requirements

A payroll company calculates the gross earnings per week of employees. Employees' weekly salaries are based on the number of hours they work and their hourly wages. Create an application that accepts this information and calculates the employee's total (gross) earnings. The application assumes a standard work week of 40 hours. The wages for 40 or fewer hours are calculated by multiplying the employee's hourly salary by the number of hours worked. Any time worked over 40 hours in a week is considered "overtime" and earns time and a half. Salary for time and a half is calculated by multiplying the employee's hourly wage by 1.5 and multiplying the result of that calculation by the number of overtime hours worked. The total overtime earned is added to the user's gross earnings for the regular 40 hours of work to calculate the total earnings for that week.

This application calculates wages from hourly salary and hours worked per week. If an employee has worked 40 or fewer hours, the employee is paid regular wages. The calculation differs if the employee has worked more than the standard 40-hour work week. In this tutorial, we introduce a programming tool known as a **control statement** that allows us to make this distinction and perform different calculations based on different user inputs. You begin by test-driving the completed application. Then, you will learn the additional C# technologies you will need to create your own version of this application.

Test-Driving the Wage Calculator Application

1. ***Opening the completed application.*** Open the C:\Examples\Tutorial07\ CompletedApplication\WageCalculator directory to locate the **Wage Calculator** application. Double click WageCalculator.sln to open the application in Visual Studio .NET.

2. ***Running the Wage Calculator application.*** Select **Debug > Start** to run the application (Fig. 7.1). Notice that we have placed the TextBoxes vertically, rather than horizontally, in this application. To make our GUI well-organized, we have aligned the right sides of each TextBox and made the TextBoxes the same size. We have also left aligned the TextBoxes' descriptive Labels.

Figure 7.1   **Wage Calculator** application.

3. ***Enter the employee's hourly wage.*** Enter 10 in the **Hourly wage:** TextBox.

4. ***Enter the number of hours the employee worked.*** Enter 45 in the **Weekly hours:** TextBox.

5. ***Calculate the employee's gross earnings.*** Click the **Calculate** Button. The result ($475.00) is displayed in the **Gross earnings:** TextBox (Fig. 7.2). Notice that the employee's salary is the sum of the wages for the standard 40-hour work week (40 * 10) and the overtime pay (5 * 10 * 1.5).

GUI Design Tip

When using multiple TextBoxes vertically, align the TextBoxes on their right sides, and where possible make the TextBoxes the same size. Left-align the descriptive Labels for such TextBoxes

Figure 7.2   Calculating wages by clicking the **Calculate** Button.

6. ***Closing the application.*** Close your running application by clicking its close box.

7. ***Closing the IDE.*** Close Visual Studio .NET by clicking its close box.

7.2 Algorithms

Computing problems can be solved by executing a series of actions in a specific order. A procedure for solving a problem, in terms of:

1. the actions to be executed and
2. the order in which these actions are to be executed

is called an **algorithm**. The following example demonstrates the importance of correctly specifying the order in which the actions are to be executed. Consider the "rise-and-shine algorithm" followed by one junior executive for getting out of bed and going to work: (1) get out of bed, (2) take off pajamas, (3) take a shower, (4) get dressed, (5) eat breakfast and (6) carpool to work. This routine prepares the executive for a productive day at the office.

However, suppose that the same steps are performed in a slightly different order: (1) get out of bed, (2) take off pajamas, (3) get dressed, (4) take a shower, (5) eat breakfast, (6) carpool to work. In this case, our junior executive shows up for work soaking wet.

Indicating the appropriate sequence in which to execute actions is equally crucial in computer programs. **Program control** refers to the task of ordering an application's statements correctly. In this tutorial, you will begin to investigate the program-control capabilities of C#.

SELF-REVIEW

1. _____ refers to the task of ordering an application's statements correctly.

   a) Actions   b) Program control

   c) Control statements   d) Visual programming

2. A(n) _____ is a plan for solving a problem in terms of the actions to be executed and the order in which these actions are to be executed.

   a) chart   b) control statement

   c) algorithm   d) ordered list

Answers: 1) b. 2) c.

7.3 Pseudocode

Pseudocode is an informal language that helps programmers develop algorithms. The pseudocode we present is particularly useful in the development of algorithms that will be converted to structured portions of C# applications. Pseudocode resembles everyday English; it is convenient and user-friendly, but it is not an actual programming language.

Pseudocode statements are not executed on computers. Rather, pseudocode helps you "think out" an application before attempting to write it in a programming language, such as C#. In this tutorial, we provide several examples of pseudocode.

The style of pseudocode that we present consists solely of characters, so you can create and modify pseudocode by using editor programs, such as the Visual Studio .NET code editor or Notepad. A carefully prepared pseudocode program can be converted easily to a corresponding C# application. Much of this conversion is as simple as replacing pseudocode statements with their C# equivalents. Let us look at an example of a pseudocode statement:

    Assign 0 to the counter

This pseudocode statement provides an easy-to-understand task. You can put several such statements together to form an algorithm that can be used to meet application requirements. When the pseudocode algorithm has been completed, the programmer can then convert pseudocode statements to their equivalent C# statements. The pseudocode statement above, for instance, can be converted to the following C# statement:

    intCounter = 0;

Pseudocode normally describes only **executable statements**, which are the actions that are performed when the corresponding C# application is run. One type of programming statement that is not executed is a declaration. The declaration

Software Design Tip

Pseudocode helps the programmer conceptualize an application during the application-design process. The pseudocode statements can be converted to C# at a later point.

```
int intNumber;
```

informs the compiler of `intNumber`'s type and instructs the compiler to reserve space in memory for this variable. The declaration does not cause any action, such as input, output or a calculation, to occur when the application executes, so we would not include this information in the pseudocode.

SELF-REVIEW   1. _____ is an artificial and informal language that helps programmers develop algorithms.

    a) Pseudocode   b) C#-Speak

    c) Notation   d) None of the above.

2. Pseudocode _____.

    a) usually describes only declarations

    b) is executed on computers

    c) usually describes only executable lines of code

    d) usually describes declarations and executable lines of code

Answers: 1) a. 2) c.

7.4 Control Statements

Normally, statements in an application are executed one after another in the order in which they are written. This is called **sequential execution**. However, C# allows you to specify that the next statement to be executed might not be the next one in sequence. A **transfer of control** occurs when an executed statement does not directly follow the previously executed statement in the written application. This is common in computer applications.

All applications can be written in terms of only three forms of control: **sequence**, **selection** and **repetition**. Unless directed to act otherwise, the computer executes C# statements sequentially—that is, one after the other in the order in which they appear in the application. The **activity diagram** in Fig. 7.3 illustrates two statements that execute in sequence. In this case, two calculations are performed in order. The activity diagram presents a graphical representation of the algorithm.

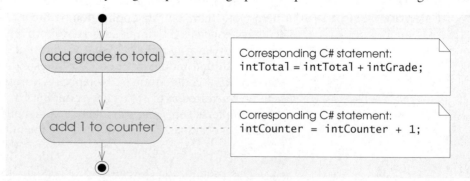

Figure 7.3 Sequence statement activity diagram.

Activity diagrams are part of the **Unified Modeling Language (UML™)**—an industry standard for modeling software systems. An activity diagram models the activity (also called the **workflow**) of a portion of a software system. Such activities may include a portion of an algorithm, such as the sequence of two statements in Fig. 7.3. Activity diagrams are composed of special-purpose symbols, such as **action-state symbols** (a rectangle with its left and right sides replaced with arcs curving outward), diamonds and solid circles. These symbols are connected by **transition arrows**, which represent the flow of the activity. Figure 7.3 does not include any diamond symbols—these will be used in later activity diagrams, beginning with Fig. 7.6.

Like pseudocode, activity diagrams help programmers develop and represent algorithms, although many programmers prefer pseudocode. Activity diagrams clearly show how control statements operate.

Consider the activity diagram for the sequence statement in Fig. 7.3. The activity diagram contains two **action states**, which represent actions to perform. Each action state contains an **action expression**—for example, "add grade to total" or "add 1 to counter"—that specifies a particular action to perform. Other actions might include calculations or input/output operations. The arrows in the activity diagram, called transition arrows, represent **transitions**, which indicate the order in which the actions represented by the action states occur. The application that implements the activities illustrated by the activity diagram in Fig. 7.3 first adds `intGrade` to `intTotal`, then adds `1` to `intCounter`.

The **solid circle** located at the top of the activity diagram represents the activity's **initial state**—the beginning of the workflow before the application performs the modeled activities. The solid circle surrounded by a hollow circle that appears at the bottom of the activity diagram represents the **final state**—the end of the workflow after the program performs its activities.

Notice, in Fig. 7.3, the rectangles with the upper-right corners folded over, looking like sheets of paper. These are called **notes** in the UML. Notes are like comments in C# applications—they are explanatory remarks that describe the purpose of symbols in the diagram. Figure 7.3 uses UML notes to show the C# code that the programmer might associate with each action state in the activity diagram. A **dotted line** connects each note with the element that the note describes. Activity diagrams normally do not show the C# code that implements the activity, but we use notes here to show you how the diagram relates to C# code.

C# provides three types of **selection statements**, which we discuss in this tutorial and in Tutorial 11. The `if` selection statement performs (selects) an action (or sequence of actions) based on a condition. A **condition** is an expression with a true or false value that is used to make a decision. Conditions are evaluated (that is, tested) to determine whether their value is true or false. These values are of the `bool` type and are specified in C# code by using the `true` and `false` keywords. Sometimes we refer to a condition as a boolean expression, or `bool` expression.

If the condition evaluates to true, the actions specified by the `if` statement will execute. If the condition evaluates to false, the actions specified by the `if` statement will be skipped. The `if...else` selection statement performs an action (or sequence of actions) if a condition is true and performs a different action (or sequence of actions) if the condition is false. The `switch` statement, discussed in Tutorial 11, performs one of many actions (or sequences of actions), depending on the value of an expression.

The `if` statement is called a **single-selection statement** because it selects or ignores a single action (or a sequence of actions). The `if...else` statement is called a **double-selection statement** because it selects between two different actions (or sequences of actions). The `switch` statement is called a **multiple-selection statement** because it selects among many different actions or sequences of actions.

C# provides four types of **repetition statements**—`while`, `do...while`, `for` and `foreach`. The `while` repetition statement is covered in Tutorial 9, `do...while` is covered in Tutorial 10, `for` is covered in Tutorial 11, and `foreach` is covered in Tutorial 20. The words `if`, `else`, `switch`, `while`, `do`, `for` and `foreach` are all C# keywords. (Appendix F includes a complete list of C# keywords.)

So, C# has three forms of control—sequence, selection and repetition. Each C# application is formed by combining as many of each type of control statement as is necessary. As with the sequence of statements in Fig. 7.3, each control statement is drawn with two **small circle** symbols—a solid black one to represent the entry point to the control statement and a solid black one surrounded by a hollow circle to represent the exit point.

All C# control statements are **single-entry/single-exit control statement**—each has exactly one entry point and one exit point. Such control statements make it easy to build applications—the control statements are attached to one another by connecting the exit point of one control statements to the entry point of the next. This is similar to stacking building blocks, so we call it **control-statement stacking**. The only other way to connect control statements is through **control-statement nesting**, whereby one control statement can be placed inside another. Thus, algorithms in C# applications are constructed from only eight different types of control statements combined in only two ways. This is a model of simplicity.

SELF-REVIEW

1. All C# applications can be written in terms of _____ forms of control.
    a) one
    b) two
    c) three
    d) four

2. The process of application statements executing one after another in the order in which they are written is called _____.
    a) transfer of control
    b) sequential execution
    c) workflow
    d) None of the above.

Answers: 1) c. 2) b.

7.5 if Selection Statement

A selection statement chooses among alternative courses of action in an application. For example, suppose that the passing grade on a test is 60 (out of 100). The pseudocode statement

> If student's grade is greater than or equal to 60
>   Display "Passed"

determines whether the condition "student's grade is greater than or equal to 60" is true or false. If the condition is true, then "Passed" is displayed, and the next pseudocode statement in order is "performed." (Remember that pseudocode is not a real programming language.) If the condition is false, the display statement is ignored, and the next pseudocode statement in order is performed.

The preceding pseudocode *If* statement may be written in C# as

```
if ( intStudentGrade >= 60 )
    lblGradeDisplay.Text = "Passed";
```

Good Programming Practice

Indent the body of if statements to improve readability.

Notice that the C# code corresponds closely to the pseudocode, demonstrating the usefulness of pseudocode as a program-development tool. The body of the if statement displays the string "Passed" in a Label. The if selection statement normally expects only one statement in its body. To include several statements in the body of an if, enclose these statements in braces ({ and }). A set of statements contained in a pair of braces is called a **block**. For instance, the above statement could be rewritten as

Good Programming Practice

Always include braces around the body of an if statement, even if the body contains only one statement.

```
if ( intStudentGrade >= 60 )
{
    lblGradeDisplay.Text = "Passed";
}
```

Notice the indentation in the if statement. Such indentation enhances application readability. The C# compiler ignores whitespace characters, such as spaces, tabs and newlines, used for indentation and vertical spacing, unless the whitespace characters are contained in strings.

The if keyword must be followed by a set of parentheses that encloses a condition. The condition between the parentheses determines whether the statement(s) within the if statement will execute. If the condition is true, the body of the if

Common Programming Error

It is a syntax error to add spaces between the symbols in the operators !=, >=, <= and == (as in ! =, > =, < =, = =).

Common Programming Error

Reversal of the operators !=, >= and <= (as in =!, =>, =<) is a syntax error.

statement executes. If the condition is false, the body does not execute. Conditions in if statements can be formed by using the **equality operators** and **relational operators** (also called **comparison operators**), which are summarized in Fig. 7.4. The relational and equality operators all have the same level of precedence.

Algebraic equality or relational operators	C# equality or relational operator	Example of C# condition	Meaning of C# condition
Relational operators			
>	>	intX > intY	intX is greater than intY
<	<	intX < intY	intX is less than intY
≥	>=	intX >= intY	intx is greater than or equal to intY
≤	<=	intX <= intY	intX is less than or equal to intY
Equality operators			
=	==	intX == intY	intX is equal to intY
≠	!=	intX !- intY	intX is not equal to intY

Figure 7.4   Equality and relational operators.

Figure 7.5 shows the **syntax** of the if statement. A statement's syntax specifies how the statement must be formed to execute without syntax errors. Let's look closely at the syntax of an if statement. The first line of Fig. 7.5 specifies that the statement must begin with the if kelyword and be followed by a left parenthesis, (, a condition and a right parenthesis,). Notice that we have italicized *condition*. This indicates that, when creating your own if statement, you should replace the text *condition* with the actual condition that you would like to evaluate. The second line indicates that you should replace *statements* with the actual statements that you want to include in the body of the if statement. These statements make up the body of the if statement. Notice that the text *statements* is placed within square brackets. These brackets do not appear in the actual if statement. Instead, the square brackets indicate that certain portions of the statement are optional. In this example, the square brackets indicate that all statements in the if statement's body are optional. Of course, if there are no statements in the body of the if statement, no actions will occur as part of that statement, regardless of the condition's value. The curly braces are required if multiple statements appear in the body of the if statement. For simplicity, we always use braces in our if statements.

Syntax

```
if ( condition )
{
    [ statements ]
}
```

Figure 7.5   if statement syntax.

Figure 7.6 illustrates the single-selection if statement. This activity diagram contains what is perhaps the most important symbol in an activity diagram—the **diamond**, or **decision symbol**, which indicates that a decision is to be made. Note the two sets of square brackets above or next to the arrows leading from the decision symbol—these are called **guard conditions**. A decision symbol indicates that the workflow will continue along a path determined by the symbol's associated guard conditions, which can be true or false. Each transition arrow emerging from a decision symbol has a guard condition (specified in square brackets above or next to the transition arrow). If a given guard condition is true, the workflow enters the action state to which that transition arrow points. For example, in Fig. 7.6, if the grade is greater than or equal to 60, the application displays "Passed", then transitions to the final state of this activity. If the grade is less than 60, the application immediately transitions to the final state without displaying a message. Only one guard condition associated with a particular decision symbol can be true at once.

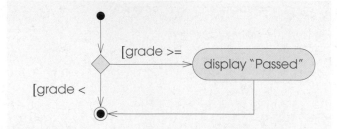

Figure 7.6   if single-selection statement activity diagram.

Note that the if statement (Fig. 7.6), is a single-entry/single-exit statement. The activity diagrams for the remaining control statements also contain (aside from small circle symbols and flowlines called transitions) only action-state symbols, indicating actions to be performed, and diamond symbols, indicating decisions to be made. Representing control statements in this way emphasizes the **action/decision model of programming**. To understand the process of structured programming better, we can envision eight bins, each containing a different type of the eight possible control statements. The control statements in each bin are empty, meaning that nothing is written in the action-state symbols and no guard conditions are written next to the decision symbols. The programmer's task is to assemble an application, using as many control statements as the algorithm demands, combining those control statements in two possible ways (stacking or nesting) and filling in the actions and decisions (with the decisions' guard conditions) in a manner appropriate to the algorithm.

SELF-REVIEW

1. Which of the following if statements correctly displays that a student received an A on an exam if the score was 90 or above?

a) ```
if (intStudentGrade != 90)
{
    lblDisplay.Text = "Student received an A";
}
```

b) ```
if ( intStudentGrade > 90 )
{
    lblDisplay.Text = "Student received an A";
}
```

c) ```
if (intStudentGrade == 90)
{
    lblDisplay.Text = "Student received an A";
}
```

d) ```
if ( intStudentGrade >= 90 )
{
    lblDisplay.Text = "Student received an A";
}
```

2. The _____ symbol is not a C# relational operator.

a) <=   b) >=

c) <>   d) >

Answers: 1) d. 2) c.

7.6 if...else Selection Statement

The if selection statement performs an indicated action (or sequence of actions) only when the condition evaluates to true; otherwise, the action (or sequence of actions) is skipped. The if...else selection statement allows the programmer to specify a different action (or sequence of actions) to be performed when the condition is true than when the condition is false. For example, the pseudocode statement

> If student's grade is greater than or equal to 60
>> Display "Passed"
>
> else
>> Display "Failed"

displays "Passed" if the student's grade is greater than or equal to 60, but displays "Failed" if the student's grade is less than 60. In either case, after output occurs, the next pseudocode statement in sequence is "performed."

The preceding pseudocode *If...Else* statement may be written in C# as

```
if ( intStudentGrade >= 60 )
{
    lblDisplay.Text = "Passed";
}
else
{
    lblDisplay.Text = "Failed";
}
```

Good Programming Practice

Apply a standard indentation convention consistently throughout your applications to enhance readability.

Note that the body of the else block is indented so that it lines up with the indented body of the if block. A standard indentation convention should be applied consistently throughout your applications. It is difficult to read programs that do not use uniform spacing conventions. The if...else selection statement follows the same general syntax as the if statement. The else keyword and any related statements are placed after the if statement as in Fig. 7.7.

Syntax
| ```
if ( condition )
{
    [ statements ]
}
else
{
    [ statements ]
}
``` |

Figure 7.7 if...else statement syntax.

Figure 7.8 illustrates the flow of control in the if...else double-selection statement. Once again, note that (besides the initial state, transition arrows and final state) the only other symbols in the activity diagram represent action states and decisions. In this example, the grade is either less than 60 or greater than or equal to 60. If the grade is less than 60, the application displays "Failed". If the grade is equal to or greater than 60, the application displays "Passed". We continue to emphasize this action/decision model of computing. Imagine again a deep bin containing as many empty double-selection statements as might be needed to build any C# application. Your job as a programmer is to assemble these selection statements (by stacking and nesting) with any other control statements required by the algorithm. You fill in the action states and decision symbols with action expressions and guard conditions appropriate to the algorithm.
```

Good Programming Practice

Indent both body statements of an if...else statement to improve readability.

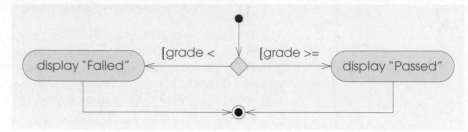

Figure 7.8 if...else double-selection statement activity diagram.

Nested if...else statements test for multiple conditions by placing if...else statements inside other if...else statements. For example, the following pseudocode will display "A" for exam grades greater than or equal to 90, "B" for grades in the range 80–89, "C" for grades in the range 70–79, "D" for grades in the range 60–69 and "F" for all other grades:

```
If student's grade is greater than or equal to 90
    Display "A"

else
        If student's grade is greater than or equal to 80
            Display "B"
        else
            If student's grade is greater than or equal to 70
                Display "C"
            else
                If student's grade is greater than or equal to 60
                    Display "D"
                else
                    Display "F"
```

Good Programming Practice

If there are several levels of indentation, each level should be indented further to the right by the same amount of space.

The preceding pseudocode may be written in C# as follows:

```csharp
if ( intStudentGrade >= 90 )
{
    lblDisplay.Text = "A";
}
else
{
    if ( intStudentGrade >= 80 )
    {
        lblDisplay.Text = "B";
    }
    else
    {
        if ( intStudentGrade >= 70 )
        {
            lblDisplay.Text = "C";
        }
        else
        {
            if ( intStudentGrade >= 60 )
            {
                lblDisplay.Text = "D";
            }
            else
            {
                lblDisplay.Text = "F";
            }
        }
    }
}
```

If `intStudentGrade` is greater than or equal to 90, the first condition evaluates to `true` and the statement `lblDisplay.Text = "A";` is executed. Notice that, with a value for `intStudentGrade` greater than or equal to 90, the remaining three conditions will evaluate to `true`. These conditions, however, are never evaluated, because they are placed within the `else` portion of the outer `if...else` statement. Because the first condition is `true`, all statements within the `else` block are skipped. Let's now assume `intStudentGrade` contains the value 75. The first condition is `false`, so the application will execute the statements within the `else` block of this statement. This `else` block also contains an `if...else` statement, with the condition `intStudentGrade >= 80`. This condition evaluates to `false`, causing the statements in this `if...else` statement's `else` block to execute. This `else` block contains yet another `if...else` statement, with the condition `intStudentGrade >= 70`. This condition is `true`, causing the statement `lblDisplay.Text = "C";` to execute. The `else` block of this `if...else` statement is then skipped.

Most C# programmers prefer to write the preceding `if...else` statement as

```
if ( intStudentGrade >= 90 )
{
    lblDisplay.Text = "A";
}
else if ( intStudentGrade >= 80 )
{
    lblDisplay.Text = "B";
}
else if ( intStudentGrade >= 70 )
{
    lblDisplay.Text = "C";
}
else if ( intStudentGrade >= 60 )
{
    lblDisplay.Text = "D";
}
else
{
    lblDisplay.Text = "F";
}
```

The two statements are equivalent, but the latter statement is popular because it avoids deep indentation of the code. Such deep indentation often leaves little room on a line, forcing lines to be split and decreasing code readability. Notice that the final portion of the `if...else` statement uses the `else` keyword to handle all remaining possibilities. The `else` block must always be last in an `if...else` statement—following an `else` block with another `else` or `else if` is a syntax error.

SELF-REVIEW

1. `if...else` is a _____-selection statement.

   a) single   b) double

   c) triple   d) nested

2. Placing an `if...else` statement inside another `if...else` statement is an example of _____.

   a) nesting `if...else` statements   b) stacking `if...else` statements

   c) creating sequential `if...else` statements   d) None of the above.

Answers: 1) b. 2) a.

7.7 Constructing the Wage Calculator Application

The following section teaches you how to build the **Wage Calculator** by using the `if...else` statement. The `if...else` statement allows you to select between calculating regular wages and including overtime pay based on the number of hours worked. The following pseudocode describes the basic operation of the **Wage Calculator** application, which runs when the user clicks **Calculate**:

When the user clicks the Calculate Button:

    Retrieve the number of hours worked and hourly wage from the TextBoxes
    If the number of hours worked is less than or equal to 40 hours
        Gross earnings equals hours worked times hourly wage
  else
        Gross earnings equals 40 times hourly wage plus hours
            above 40 times wage times 1.5

    Display gross earnings

Before developing each application, you take it for a test drive. Here you interact with the application's GUI and begin to understand the application's purpose. You also learn the GUI components that will be required to obtain user input and display results. Frequently, when determining the requirements of an application, you will design a prototype of the application's GUI. As you develop each application for the remainder of this book, you will use two application development aids—pseudocode and **Action/Control/Event (ACE) tables**. Pseudocode describes the algorithm—that is, the actions to be performed and the order in which those actions should be performed. As you read the pseudocode, you will see that there are specific actions to perform, such as "Calculate gross wages," "Retrieve the number of hours worked" and "Display gross wages." An ACE table helps relate the events that occur on GUI controls with the actions that should be performed in response to those events.

Figure 7.9 presents the Action/Control/Event (ACE) table for the **Wage Calculator** application. Sometimes, when creating an ACE table, actions in the pseudocode can be lifted and inserted directly in the left column of the table—for instance, "Display gross wages." In other cases, one action might be represented with a substantial amount of pseudocode—for instance, calculating an employee's gross wages requires most of the pseudocode that describes the **Wage Calculator** application. It would be tedious to list all this pseudocode in the table. In such cases, you might use a shorthand representation of the action, such as "Calculate gross wages." The left column sometimes includes actions that are not represented in the pseudocode at all. For example, the action "Label the application's controls" is not part of the pseudocode, but is an important part of constructing this application. The middle column specifies the GUI control or class associated with the action. The right column specifies the event that initiates the action.

Action/Control/Event (ACE) Table for the Wage Calculator Application

Action	Control	Event
Label the application's controls	lblWage, lblHours, lblEarnings	Application is run
	btnCalculate	Click
Retrieve the number of hours worked and hourly wage from the TextBoxes	txtWage, txtHours	
If the number of hours worked is less than or equal to 40 hours Gross earnings equals hours worked times hourly wage		
else Gross earnings equals 40 times hourly wage plus hours above 40 times wage times 1.5		
Display gross earnings	lblEarningsResult	

Figure 7.9 Action/Control/Event table for the **Wage Calculator** application.

The Labels in the first row display information about the application to the user. These Labels help guide the user through the application. In the second row, the user clicks btnCalculate to calculate the gross wages for an employee. In the third column of this row, the text Click indicates the event that initializes the calculation. The TextBoxes in the third row will obtain input from the user, accessed through the Text property. The fourth and fifth rows show the if...else statement that determines the gross wages. The final control, lblEarningsResult, is a Label that displays the application's output.

We now apply our pseudocode and the ACE table to complete the **Wage Calculator** application. The following box will guide you through the process of adding a Click event to the **Calculate** Button and declaring the variables you'll need to calculate the employee's wages. If you forget to add code to this Click event, the application will not respond when the user clicks the **Calculate** Button.

Declaring Variables in the Calculate Button's Click Event Handler

1. ***Copying the template application to your working directory.*** Copy the C:\Examples\Tutorial07\TemplateApplication\WageCalculator directory to your C:\SimplyCSP directory.

2. ***Opening the Wage Calculator application's template file.*** Double click WageCalculator.sln in the **WageCalculator** directory to open the application in Visual Studio .NET.

3. ***Adding the Calculate Button's Click event handler.*** In this example, the event handler calculates the gross wages when the **Calculate** Button's Click event occurs. Double click the **Calculate** Button. The default event handler will be generated, and you will be switched to code view. Lines 170–174 of Fig. 7.10 display the generated event handler. Be sure to add the comments and break the header as shown in Fig. 7.10 so that the line numbers in your code match those presented in this tutorial.

Generated event handler ——

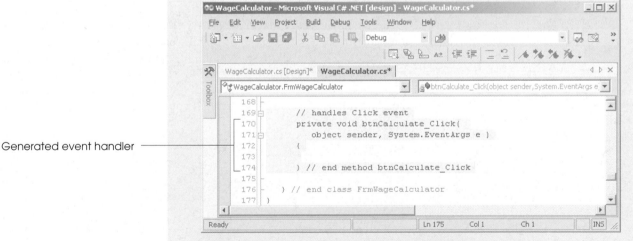

Figure 7.10 Calculate Button event handler.

4. ***Declaring variables.*** As you learned in Tutorial 5, a double holds numbers with decimal points. Because hours and wages are often fractional numbers, ints are not appropriate for this application. Add lines 173–176 of Fig. 7.11 into the body of event handler btnCalculate_Click. Line 174 contains a variable declaration for double dblHours, which holds the number of hours input by the user. Notice that the variable names for doubles are prefixed with dbl.

Good Programming Practice

Prefix double variable names with dbl.

(cont.)

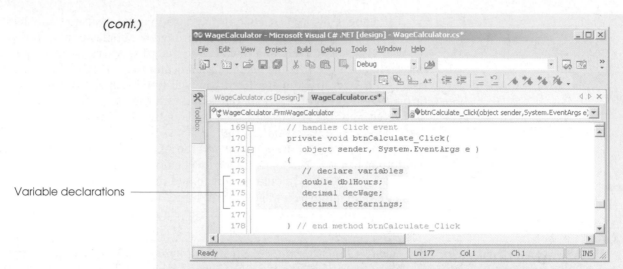

Figure 7.11   Declaring variables of the `double` and `decimal` types.

This application introduces the **decimal** built-in type. The `decimal` type is used to store monetary amounts because it ensures rounding accuracy in arithmetic calculations involving monetary amounts. Lines 175–176 declare `decWage`, which stores the hourly wage input by the user, and `decEarnings`, which stores the total amount of earnings for the week. Notice that `decimal` variable names are prefixed with `dec`.

Good Programming Practice

Prefix `decimal` variable names with `dec`.

5. ***Declaring a constant.*** Add line 178 of Fig. 7.12 to the `btnCalculate_Click` event handler. Line 178 contains a **constant**, a variable whose value cannot be changed after its initial declaration. Constants are declared with the **const** keyword. In this case, we assign to the `intHOUR_LIMIT` constant the maximum number of hours worked before mandatory overtime pay (40). Notice that we prefix this constant with `int` and capitalize the rest of the constant's name to emphasize that it is a constant. Constants are useful because they are more descriptive than explicit values, such as 40. Constants can also reduce your work as a programmer. For example, if you need to change the maximum number of hours worked before mandatory overtime pay from 40 to 35, you would only change 40 to 35 once, in the constant's declaration. If you had not used a constant, you would need to change 40 to 35 every time it appeared in your code.

Good Programming Practice

Capitalize the name of a constant, leaving the prefix indicating the constant's type in lowercase. Separate each word in the name of a constant with an underscore.

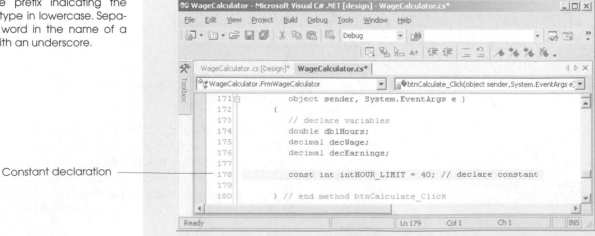

Figure 7.12   Creating a constant.

6. ***Saving the project.*** Select **File > Save All** to save your modified code.

Now that you have declared variables, you can use them to receive input from the user and then use that input to compute and display the user's wages. The following box walks you through using the if...else statement to determine the user's wages.

Determining the User's Wages

1. **Obtaining inputs from the TextBoxes.** Add lines 180–182 of Fig. 7.13 to the end of the btnCalculate_Click event handler. Lines 181–182 assign values to dblHours and decWage from the TextBoxes in which the user enters data. Recall that Int32.Parse converts a string of characters to an int. You can use the **Double.Parse** and **Decimal.Parse** methods to convert a string of characters to a double and to a decimal, respectively (lines 181–182).

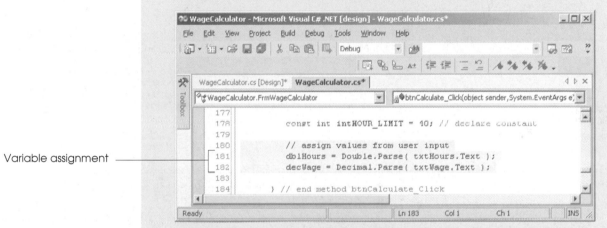

Figure 7.13   Assigning data to variables.

2. **Determining wages based on hours worked.** Begin to add the if...else statement shown in lines 184–199 of Fig. 7.14 to the end of the btnCalculate_Click event handler. You might need to indent as you go. This if...else statement determines whether employees earn overtime in addition to their usual wages. Line 185 determines whether the value stored in dblHours is less than or equal to intHOUR_LIMIT. If it is, then line 188 assigns the value of the product of the hours and the wage to decEarnings. C# does not allow you to multiply a variable of the double type by a variable of the decimal type. The variables must have compatible types. Because the product will be assigned to decEarnings, a variable of type decimal, it makes sense to convert dblHours to a decimal. The cast operator is used to perform the conversion in line 188.

If, on the other hand, dblHours is not less than or equal to intHOUR_LIMIT, then the application proceeds to the else keyword in line 189. Line 193 computes the wage for the hours worked up to the limit set by intHOUR_LIMIT and assigns it to decEarnings. No cast operator is required because an int can be implicitly converted to a decimal. Line 197 determines how many hours over intHOUR_LIMIT there are (by using the expression dblHours - intHOUR_LIMIT) and then converts the result to a decimal. Line 198 calculates the user's time-and-a-half pay for overtime hours, which is 1.5 times the user's hourly wages. The suffix M makes the value 1.5 a decimal. With no such suffix, the value 1.5 is treated as a double. This suffix is another way to convert a value's type. This method can be applied to actual values, such as 1.5, but not to variables. The cast operator can be applied to either values or variables. The decimal result in line 197 is multiplied by the decimal result in line 198. This product is then added to the value of decEarnings, and the result is assigned to decEarnings (line 196).

(cont.)

Added `if...else` statement —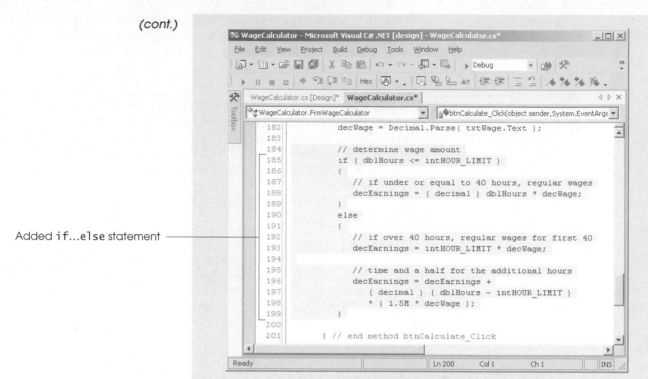

Figure 7.14   `if...else` statement to determine wages.

3. ***Displaying the result.*** Add lines 201–202 of Fig. 7.15 to the end of the `btnCalculate_Click` event handler. Line 202 assigns the value in `decEarnings` to the `Text` property of the `lblEarningsResult` Label, using the `Convert.ToString` method to convert `decEarnings` from a `decimal` to a string.

Displaying output —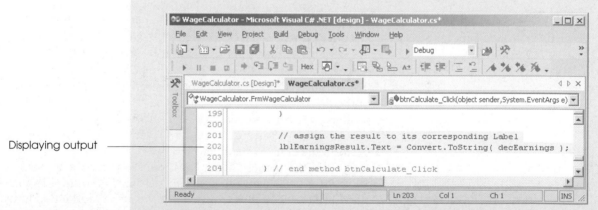

Figure 7.15   Assigning the result to `lblEarningsResult`.

4. ***Running the application.*** Select **Debug > Start** to run your application (Fig. 7.16). Enter 10 in the **Hourly wage:** TextBox, and enter 45 in the **Weekly Hours:** TextBox. Press the **Calculate** Button. Notice that the output is not yet formatted as it should be in the completed application. We will demonstrate how to add this functionality later in this tutorial.

5. ***Closing the application.*** Close your running application by clicking its close box.

(cont.)

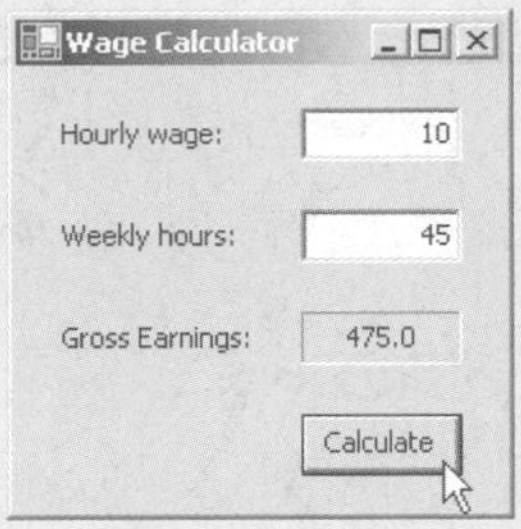

Figure 7.16 Running the application before formatting the output.

SELF-REVIEW 1. The `decimal` type is used to store _____.

   a) letters and digits   b) integers

   c) strings   d) monetary amounts

2. Constants are declared with the _____ keyword.

   a) `fixed`   b) `constant`

   c) `final`   d) `const`

Answers: 1) d. 2) d.

7.8 Assignment Operators

C# provides several **assignment operators** for abbreviating assignment statements. For example, the statement

```
intValue = intValue + 3;
```

which adds 3 to the value in `intValue`, can be abbreviated with the addition assignment operator, `+=`, as

```
intValue += 3;
```

The `+=` operator adds the value of the right operand to the value of the left operand and stores the result in the left operand. C# provides assignment operators for several binary operators, including `+`, `-`, `*` and `/`. When an assignment statement is evaluated, the expression to the right of the operator is always evaluated first, then assigned to the variable on the left. C# also provides special increment (`++`) and decrement (`--`) operators. The `++` operator increases its left operand by one. The `--` operator decreases its left operand by one. Both are unary operators. When the `++` and `--` operators are written immediately to the right of the operand (as in `intC++`), they are called the **postfix increment and decrement operators,** respectively. When these operators are written immediately to the left of the operand (as in `++intC`), they are called the **prefix increment and prefix decrement operators**. If a prefix operator is used, its operand will be incremented or decremented by 1, after which the new value of the operand is used in the expression in which it appears. If a postfix operator is used, its operand will be used in the expression in which it appears, after which the operand's value is incremented or decremented by 1. We predominantly use the postfix operators in this text. Figure 7.17 includes the assignment operators, sample expressions using these operators and explanations.

Assignment operators	Sample expression	Explanation	Assigns
Assume: intC = 4			
+=	intC += 7;	intC = intC + 7;	11 to intC
-=	intC -= 3;	intC = intC - 3;	1 to intC
*=	intC *= 4;	intC = intC * 4;	16 to intC
/=	intC /= 2;	intC = intC / 2;	2 to intC
++	intC++;	intC = intC + 1;	5 to intC
--	intC--;	intC = intC - 1;	3 to intC

Figure 7.17 Assignment operators.

The following box demonstrates abbreviating our time-and-a-half calculation with the += operator. When you run the application again, you will notice that the program runs the same as before—all that has changed is that one of the longer statements was made shorter.

Using the Addition Assignment Operator

1. ***Adding the addition assignment operator.*** Replace lines 196–198 of Fig. 7.14 with lines 196–197 of Fig. 7.18. In this step, we have used the addition assignment operator to make our statement shorter. Notice that the statement still performs the same action—the time-and-a-half pay for the user is calculated and added to the regular wages earned.

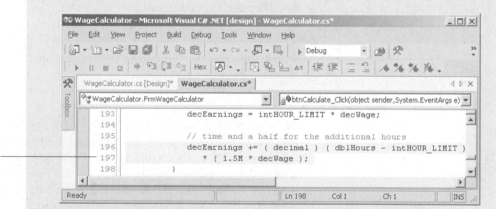

Assignment operator shortens statement

Figure 7.18 Using the addition assignment operator in a calculation.

2. ***Running the application.*** Select **Debug > Start** to run your application. Notice that the application executes as it did in the last box.

3. ***Closing the application.*** Close your running application by clicking its close box.

SELF-REVIEW

1. The *= operator _____.

   a) squares the value of the right operand and stores the result in the left operand

   b) adds the value of the right operand to the value of the left operand and stores the result in the left operand

   c) creates a new variable and assigns the value of the right operand to that variable

   d) multiplies the value of the left operand by the value of the right operand and stores the result in the left operand

2. If `intX` is initialized with the value 5, what value will `intX` contain after the expression `intX -= 3;` is executed?

     a) 3   b) 5

     c) 7   d) 2

Answers: 1) d. 2) d.

7.9 Formatting Text

There are several ways to format output in C#. In this section, we introduce the **String.Format** method to control how text displays. Modifying the appearance of text for display purposes is known as **text formatting**. This method takes as an argument a **format control string**, followed by arguments that indicate the values to be formatted. The format control string argument specifies how the remaining arguments are to be formatted.

Recall that your **Wage Calculator** does not display the result of its calculation with the appropriate decimal and dollar sign that you saw when test-driving the application. In the following box, you learn how to apply currency formatting to the value in the **Gross earnings:** TextBox.

Formatting the Gross Earnings	1. ***Modifying the Calculate Button's Click event.*** Replace line 202 of Fig. 7.15 with lines 201–202 of Fig. 7.19.

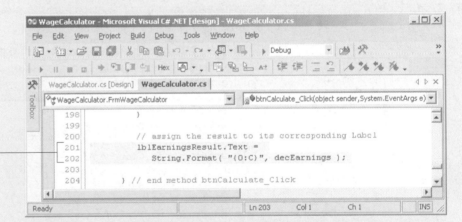

Formatting output as currency

Figure 7.19   Using the `String.Format` method to display the result as currency.

Line 201 sends the format control string, "`{0:C}`", and the value to be formatted, `decEarnings`, to the `String.Format` method. The `0` indicates that argument `zero` (`decEarnings`—the first argument after the format control string) should take the format specified by the letter after the colon; this letter is called the **format specifier**. In this case, we use the format defined by the uppercase letter C, which represents the **currency format**, used to display values as monetary amounts. The effect of the C format specifier varies, depending on the locale setting of your computer. In our case, the result is preceded with a dollar sign ($) and displayed with two decimal places (representing cents), because we are in the United States.

GUI Design Tip

Format all monetary amounts using the C (currency) format specifier.

2. ***Running the application.*** Select **Debug > Start** to run your application. Notice that the output in the **Gross Earnings:** TextBox is properly formatted as in the completed application.

3. ***Closing the application.*** Close your running application by clicking its close box.

Figure 7.20 shows several format specifiers. All format specifiers are case insensitive, so the uppercase letters may be used interchangeably with their lowercase equivalents. Note that format code D may be used only with ints.

Format Specifier	Description
C	Currency. Formats the currency based on the computer's locale setting. For U.S. currency, precedes the number with $, separates every three digits (to the left of the decimal place) with commas and sets the number of decimal places to two.
E	Scientific notation. Displays one digit to the left of the decimal point and six digits to the right of the decimal point, followed by the character E and a three-digit integer representing the exponent of a power of 10. For example, 956.2 is formatted as 9.562000E+002.
F	Fixed point. Sets the number of decimal places to two by default.
G	General. C# chooses either E or F for you, depending on which representation generates a shorter string.
D	Decimal integer. Displays an integer as a whole number in standard base-10 format.
N	Number. Separates every three digits with a comma and sets the number of decimal places to two by default.

Figure 7.20 Format specifiers for strings.

Figure 7.21 presents the source code for the **Wage Calculator** application. The lines of code that contain new programming concepts that you learned in this tutorial are highlighted.

```
1   using System;
2   using System.Drawing;
3   using System.Collections;
4   using System.ComponentModel;
5   using System.Windows.Forms;
6   using System.Data;
7
8   namespace WageCalculator
9   {
10      /// <summary>
11      /// Summary description for FrmWageCalculator.
12      /// </summary>
13      public class FrmWageCalculator : System.Windows.Forms.Form
14      {
15         // Label and TextBox for hourly wage
16         private System.Windows.Forms.Label lblWage;
17         private System.Windows.Forms.TextBox txtWage;
18
19         // Label and Textbox for weekly hours
20         private System.Windows.Forms.Label lbHours;
21         private System.Windows.Forms.TextBox txtHours;
22
23         // Labels to display gross earnings
24         private System.Windows.Forms.Label lblEarnings;
25         private System.Windows.Forms.Label lblEarningsResult;
26
27         // Button to calculate total earnings
28         private System.Windows.Forms.Button btnCalculate;
```

Figure 7.21 **Wage Calculator** application code. (Part 1 of 3.)

```
29
30          /// <summary>
31          /// Required designer variable.
32          /// </summary>
33          private System.ComponentModel.Container components = null;
34
35          public FrmWageCalculator()
36          {
37             //
38             // Required for Windows Form Designer support
39             //
40             InitializeComponent();
41
42             //
43             // TODO: Add any constructor code after InitializeComponent
44             // call
45             //
46          }
47
48          /// <summary>
49          /// Clean up any resources being used.
50          /// </summary>
51          protected override void Dispose( bool disposing )
52          {
53             if( disposing )
54             {
55                if (components != null)
56                {
57                   components.Dispose();
58                }
59             }
60             base.Dispose( disposing );
61          }
62
63          // Windows Form Designer generated code
64
65          /// <summary>
66          /// The main entry point for the application.
67          /// </summary>
68          [STAThread]
69          static void Main()
70          {
71             Application.Run( new FrmWageCalculator() );
72          }
73
74          // handles Click event
75          private void btnCalculate_Click(
76             object sender, System.EventArgs e )
77          {
78             // declare variables
79             double dblHours;
80             decimal decWage;
81             decimal decEarnings;
82
83             const int intHOUR_LIMIT = 40; // declare constant
84
85             // assign values from user input
86             dblHours = Double.Parse( txtHours.Text );
87             decWage = Decimal.Parse( txtWage.Text );
```

The **const** keyword specifies constant

Figure 7.21 **Wage Calculator** application code. (Part 2 of 3.)

```
88
89                  // determine wage amount
90          if ( dblHours <= intHOUR_LIMIT )
91          {
92                  // if under or equal to 40 hours, regular wages
93                  decEarnings = ( decimal ) dblHours * decWage;
94          }
95          else
96          {
97                  // if over 40 hours, regular wages for first 40
98                  decEarnings = intHOUR_LIMIT * decWage;
99
100                 // time and a half for the additional hours
101                 decEarnings += ( decimal ) ( dblHours - intHOUR_LIMIT )
102                     * ( 1.5M * decWage );
103         }
104
105                 // assign the result to its corresponding Label
106         lblEarningsResult.Text =
107                 String.Format( "{0:C}", decEarnings );
108
109         } // end method btnCalculate_Click
110
111     } // end class FrmWageCalculator
112 }
```

Condition after the `if` keyword — 90

`else` body executes when condition evalues to `false` — 95

Assignment operator assigns left operand result of adding left and right operands — 101

Format result as currency — 107

Figure 7.21 Wage Calculator application code. (Part 3 of 3.)

SELF-REVIEW

1. The `String.Format` method is used to _____.

   a) create constant variables   b) control how text is formatted

   c) format C# statements   d) All of the above.

2. The _____ format displays values as monetary amounts.

   a) monetary   b) cash

   c) currency   d) dollar

Answers: 1) b. 2) c.

7.10 Using the Debugger: The Watch Window

Visual Studio .NET includes several debugging windows that are accessible from the **Debug > Windows** submenu. The **Watch** window, which is available only in break mode, allows the programmer to examine the value of a variable or expression. You can use the **Watch** window to view changes in a variable's value as the application executes, or you can change a variable's value yourself by entering the new value directly into the **Watch** window. Each expression or variable that is added to the **Watch** window is called a **watch**. In the following box, we demonstrate how to add, remove and manipulate watches by using the **Watch** window.

Using the Debugger: The Watch Window

1. ***Starting debugging.*** If the IDE is not in code view, switch to code view now. Set breakpoints at lines 182 and 188 (Fig. 7.22). Select **Debug > Start** to run the application. The **Wage Calculator** Form appears. Enter 12 into the **Hourly wage:** TextBox and 40 into the **Weekly hours:** TextBox. Click the **Calculate** Button.

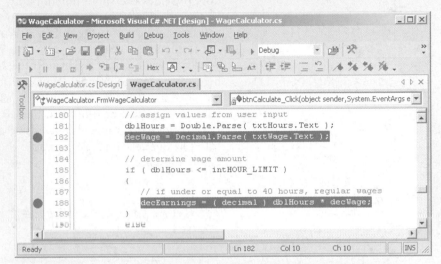

Figure 7.22 Breakpoints added to **Wage Calculator** application.

2. ***Suspending application execution.*** Clicking the **Calculate** Button will cause btnCalculate_Click event handler to run until the breakpoint is reached. When the breakpoint is reached, application execution is paused, and the IDE switches into break mode. Notice that the active window has been changed from the running application to the IDE (Fig. 7.23). The **Wage Calculator** application is still running, but it is hidden behind the IDE.

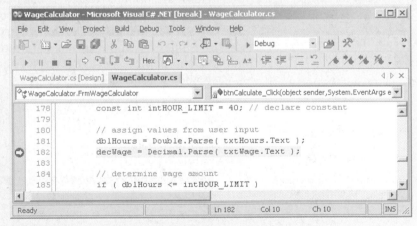

Figure 7.23 Suspending application execution.

(cont.)

3. ***Examining data.*** Once the application has entered break mode, you are free to explore the values of various variables, using the debugger's **Watch** window. To display the **Watch** window, select **Debug > Windows > Watch > Watch 1**. Notice that there are actually four options in the **Debug > Windows > Watch** menu—**Watch 1**, **Watch 2**, **Watch 3** and **Watch 4**. Each window provides the same functionality. The four options simply allow you to have several **Watch** windows open at once. This enables you to display data side-by-side or to set the different **Watch** windows to display data in different formats. The **Watch** window (Fig. 7.24) is initially empty. To add a watch, you can type an expression into the **Name** column. Single click in the first field of the **Name** column. Type dblHours, then press *Enter*. The value and type will be added by the IDE (Fig. 7.24). Notice that this value is 40.0—the value assigned to dblHours in line 182. Type decWage in the next row, then press *Enter*. The value displayed for decWage is 0. The type of decWage is listed as System.Decimal because the decimal type is defined in the System namespace.

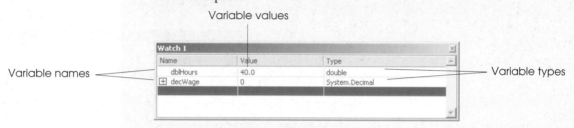

Figure 7.24   **Watch** window.

4. ***Examining different expressions.*** Add the expression (dblHours + 3) * 5 into the **Watch 1** window, then press *Enter*. Notice that the **Watch** window can evaluate arithmetic expressions, returning the value 215.0. Add the expression decWage == 3 into the **Watch 1** window. Expressions containing the == symbol are treated as bool expressions. The value returned is **false**, because decWage does not currently contain the value 3. Add the expression intVariableThatDoesNotExist into the **Watch 1** window. This identifier does not exist in the current application and therefore cannot be evaluated. An appropriate message is displayed in the **Value** field. Your **Watch** window should look similar to Fig. 7.25.

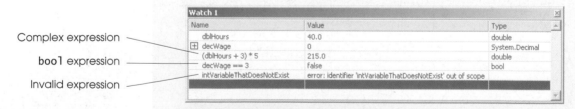

Figure 7.25   Examining expressions.

5. ***Removing an expression from the Watch window.*** At this point, we would like to clear the final expressions from the **Watch** window. To remove an expression, simply right click the expression in the **Watch** window and select **Delete Watch** (Fig. 7.26). Remove the three expressions that you added in *Step 4.*

(cont.)

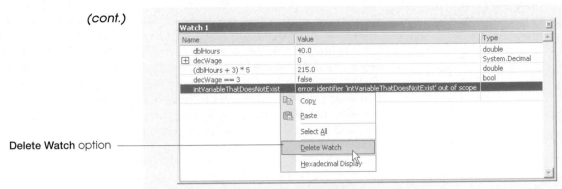

Figure 7.26 Deleting a watch.

6. ***Viewing modified values in a Watch window.*** Continue debugging by
selecting **Debug > Continue.** The application will continue to execute until
the next breakpoint, at line 188. Line 182 executes, assigning the wage
value entered (12) to decWage. The if continuation condition evaluates to
true in line 185, and the application is once again suspended in line 188.
Notice that the value of decWage has changed not only in the application,
but in the **Watch 1** window as well. Because the value has changed since
the last time the application was suspended, the modified value is displayed
in red (Fig. 7.27).

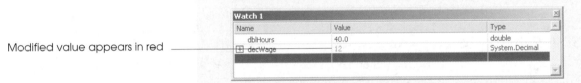

Figure 7.27 Modified values in the **Watch** window.

7. ***Modifying values directly in a Watch window.*** The **Watch** window can be
used to change the value of a variable simply by entering the new value in
the **Value** column. Click in the **Value** field for dblHours, replace 40.0 with
10.0, then press *Enter*. The modified value appears in red (Fig. 7.28). This
option enables you to test various values to confirm the behavior of your
application. If you repeat this exercise multiple times in the same application, a dialog (Fig. 7.29) might appear. Simply disregard this dialog by clicking the **Continue** Button.

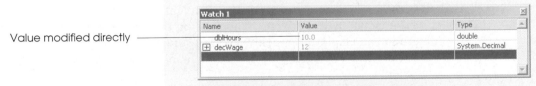

Figure 7.28 Modifying values in a **Watch** window.

Figure 7.29 Dialog to continue running the application after changing
values in the **Watch** window.

(cont.)

8. ***Viewing the application result.*** Select **Debug > Continue** to continue program execution. The `btnCalculate_Click` event handler finishes execution and displays the result in a `Label`. Notice that the result is $120.00, because we changed `dblHours` to 10.0 in the last step. The `TextBox` to the right of **Weekly hours:** still displays the value 40, because we changed the value of `dblHours`, but not the `Text` property of either `TextBox`. Once the application has finished running, the focus is returned to the **Wage Calculator** window, and the final results are displayed (Fig. 7.30).

Figure 7.30 Output displayed after the debugging process.

9. ***Closing the application.*** Close your running application by clicking its close box.

10. ***Closing the IDE.*** Close Visual Studio .NET by clicking its close box.

SELF-REVIEW

1. An application enters break mode when _____.
   a) **Debug > Start** is selected
   b) a breakpoint is reached
   c) the **Watch** window is used
   d) there is a syntax error

2. The **Watch** window allows you to _____.
   a) change variable values
   b) view variable type information
   c) evaluate expressions
   d) All of the above.

Answers: 1) b. 2) d.

7.11 Wrap-Up

In this tutorial, we discussed techniques for solving programming problems. We introduced algorithms, pseudocode, the UML and control statements. We discussed different forms of control and when each might be used.

You began by test-driving an application that used the `if...else` statement to determine an employee's weekly pay. You studied different control statements and used the UML to diagram the decision-making processes of the `if` and `if...else` statements.

You learned how to format text by using the `String.Format` method and how to abbreviate mathematical statements by using the assignment operators.

In the *Using the Debugger* section, you learned how to use the **Watch** window to view an application's data. You learned how to add watches, remove watches and change variable values.

In the next tutorial you will learn how to display message dialogs based on user input. You will study the logical operators, which give you more expressive power for forming the conditions in your control statements. You will use the `CheckBox` control to allow the user to select from various options in a dental payment application.

SKILLS SUMMARY

Choosing Among Alternate Courses of Action

- Use the `if` or `if...else` statements.

Conceptualizing the Application Before Using Visual Studio .NET

- Use pseudocode.
- Create an Action/Control/Event (ACE) table.

Understanding Control Statements

- View the control statement's corresponding UML diagram.

Performing Comparisons

- Use the equality and relational operators.

Creating a Constant

- Use the `const` keyword.
- Assign a value to the constant in the declaration.

Abbreviating Assignment Expressions

- Use the assignment operators.

Formatting a Value as a Monetary Amount

- Use the format code `C` in method `String.Format`.

Examining Data During Application Execution

- Use the debugger to set a breakpoint, and examine the **Watch** window.

KEY TERMS

ACE (Action/Control/Event) table—A program development tool you can use to relate GUI events with the actions that should be performed in response to those events.

action/decision model of programming—A model representing control statements as UML activity diagrams with rounded rectangles, indicating *actions* to be performed, and diamond symbols, indicating *decisions* to be made.

action expression (in the UML)—Used in an action state within a UML activity diagram to specify a particular action to perform.

action state—An action to perform in a UML activity diagram that is represented by an action-state symbol.

action-state symbol—A rectangle with its left and right sides replaced with arcs curving outward that represents an action to perform in a UML activity diagram.

activity diagram—A UML diagram that models the activity (also called the workflow) of a portion of a software system.

algorithm—A procedure for solving a problem, specifying the actions to be executed and the order in which these actions are to be executed.

assignment operators—Operators used for abbreviating assignment statements.

block—A group of code statements.

bool type—Has the value `true` or `false`.

comparison operators—*See* relational operators.

condition—An expression with a true or false value that is used to make a decision.

const keyword—Declares a constant, which is a variable whose value cannot be changed after its initial declaration.

constant—A variable whose value cannot be changed after its initial declaration.

control statement—An application component that specifies the order in which statements execute (also known as the flow of control).

control-statement nesting—Placing one control statement in the body of another control statement.

control-statement stacking—A set of control statements in sequence. The exit point of one control statement is connected to the entry point of the next control statement in sequence.

currency format—Used to display values as monetary amounts.

decimal type—Used to store monetary amounts.

Decimal.Parse method—Converts a given string of characters to a value of type `decimal`.

decision symbol—The diamond-shaped symbol in a UML activity diagram that indicates that a decision is to be made.

diamond—A symbol (also known as the decision symbol) in a UML activity diagram; that indicates that a decision is to be made.

dotted line—A UML activity diagram symbol that connects each UML-style note with the element that the note describes.

double-selection statement—A statement, such as `if...else`, that selects between two different actions or sequences of actions.

Double.Parse method—Converts the given string of characters to a value of type `double`.

equality operator—Operator that compares two values. Returns `true` if the two values are equal; otherwise, returns `false`.

executable statement—Actions that are performed when the corresponding C# application is run.

false keyword—A `bool` value that represents a condition that is false.

format control string—A string that specifies how data should be formatted.

format specifier—Code that specifies the type of format that should be applied to a string for output.

final state—Represented by a solid circle surrounded by a hollow circle in a UML activity diagram—the end of the workflow after a program performs its activities.

guard condition—An expression contained in square brackets above or next to the arrows leading from a decision symbol in a UML activity diagram that determines whether workflow continues along a path.

if selection statement—Performs an action (or sequence of actions) based on a condition. This is also called a single-selection statement.

if...else selection statement—Performs an action (or sequence of actions) if a condition is `true` and performs a different action (or sequence of actions) if the condition is `false`. This is also called a double-selection statement.

initial state—The beginning of the workflow in a UML activity diagram before the program performs the modeled activities.

multiple-selection statement—Selects from among many different actions or sequences of actions.

nested statement—A control statement placed inside another control statement.

note—An explanatory remark (represented by a rectangle with a folded upper-right corner) describing the purpose of a symbol in a UML activity diagram.

postfix increment and decrement operators—The `++` and `--` operators, when they appear to the right of the operand. Causes the operand's value to be used in the expression in which the operand appears, after which the value of the operand is incremented or decremented by 1.

prefix increment and decrement operators—The `++` and `--` operators, when they appear to the left of the operand. Causes the operand's value to be incremented or decremented by 1, after which the operand's value is used in the expression in which the operand appears.

program control—The task of ordering an application's statements in the correct order.

pseudocode—An informal language that helps programmers develop algorithms.

relational operators—Operators < (less than), > (greater than), <= (less than or equal to) and >= (greater than or equal to) that compare two values.

repetition statement—Allows the programmer to specify that an action or sequence of actions should be repeated, depending on the value of a condition.

selection statement—Selects among alternative courses of action.

sequence statement—Built into C#—unless directed to act otherwise, the computer executes C# statements sequentially.

sequential execution—Statements in an application are executed one after another in the order in which they are written.

single-entry/single-exit control statement—A control statement that has one entry point and one exit point. All C# control statements are single-entry/single-exit control statements.

single-selection statement—A control statement that selects or ignores a single action or sequence of actions.

small circles (in the UML)—The solid circle in an activity diagram represents the activity's initial state and the solid circle surrounded by a hollow circle represents the activity's final state.

solid circle (in the UML)—Symbol that represents the activity's initial state.

String.Format method—Formats a string.

structured programming—A technique for organizing program control that helps you develop applications that are easy to understand, debug and modify.

syntax—Specifies how a statement must be formed to execute without syntax errors.

text formatting—Modifying the appearance of text for display purposes.

transfer of control—Occurs when an executed statement does not directly follow the previously executed statement in the written application.

transition—A change from one action state to another, represented by transition arrows in a UML activity diagram.

transition arrow (in the UML)—Symbol that represents a transition.

true keyword—A bool value that represents a condition that is true.

UML (Unified Modeling Language)—An industry standard for modeling software systems graphically.

watch—An expression or variable that is added to the **Watch** window.

Watch window—A Visual Studio .NET window that allows you to view variable values as an application is being debugged.

workflow—The activity of a portion of a software system.

GUI DESIGN GUIDELINES

Overall Design

■ Format all monetary amounts using the C (currency) format specifier.

TextBox

■ When using multiple TextBoxes vertically, align the TextBoxes on their right sides, and where possible make the TextBoxes the same size. Left-align the descriptive Labels for such TextBoxes.

CONTROLS, EVENTS, PROPERTIES & METHODS

Decimal Represents a monetary value.

■ *Method*

   Parse—Converts the given string of characters to a value of type decimal.

Double Represents a floating-point number (one with a decimal point).

■ *Method*

   Parse—Converts the given string of characters to a value of type double.

String Represents a series of characters treated as a single unit.

■ *Method*

   Format—Arranges the string of characters in a specified format.

MULTIPLE-CHOICE QUESTIONS

7.1 The _____ operator returns false if the left operand is larger than the right operand.

a) ==   b) <

c) <=   d) All of the above.

7.2 A _____ occurs when an executed statement does not directly follow the previously executed statement in the written application.

    a) transition   b) flow

    c) logical error   d) transfer of control

7.3 A variable or an expression that is added to the **Watch** window is known as a _____.

    a) watched variable   b) watched expression

    c) watch   d) watched value

7.4 The `if` statement is called a _____ statement because it selects or ignores one action or sequence of actions.

    a) single-selection   b) multiple-selection

    c) double-selection   d) repetition

7.5 The three types of control statements are the sequence statement, the selection statement and the _____ statement.

    a) repeat   b) looping

    c) redo   d) repetition

7.6 In an activity diagram, a rectangle with curved sides represents _____.

    a) a complete algorithm   b) a comment

    c) an action   d) the termination of the application

7.7 The `if…else` selection statement ends with a(n) _____.

    a) right brace (`}`)   b) `endif` statement

    c) `endelse` statement   d) double-selection statement

7.8 A variable of type `bool` can be assigned the _____ keyword or the _____ keyword

    a) `true`, `false`   b) `off`, `on`

    c) `true`, `notTrue`   d) `yes`, `no`

7.9 A variable whose value cannot be changed after its initial declaration is called a _____.

    a) `double`   b) constant

    c) standard   d) `bool`

7.10 The _____ operator assigns the result of adding the left and right operands to the left operand.

    a) `+`   b) `=+`

    c) `+=`   d) `++`

EXERCISES

7.11 *(Currency Converter Application)* Develop an application that functions as a currency converter (Fig. 7.31). Users must provide a number in the **Dollars:** TextBox and a currency name (as text) in the **Convert from Dollars to:** TextBox. Clicking the **Convert** Button will convert the specified amount into the indicated currency and display it in a Label. Limit yourself to the following currencies as user input: Dollars, Euros, Yen and Pesos. Use the following exchange rates: 1 Dollar = 1.02 Euros, 120 Yen and 10 Pesos. Use the M suffix to convert 1.02 to a `decimal`.

Figure 7.31 Currency Converter GUI.

a) *Copying the template to your working directory.* Copy the directory C:\Examples\ Tutorial07\Exercises\CurrencyConverter to your C:\SimplyCSP directory.

b) *Opening the application's template file.* Double click CurrencyConverter.sln in the CurrencyConverter directory to open the application.

c) *Add an event handler for the Convert Button's Click event.* Double click the **Convert** Button to generate an empty event handler for the Button's Click event. The code for *Steps d–f* belongs in this event handler.

d) *Obtaining the user input.* Use the Decimal.Parse method to convert the user input from the **Dollars:** TextBox to a decimal. Assign the decimal to a variable decAmount.

e) *Performing the conversion.* Use an if...else statement to determine which currency the user entered. Assign the result of the conversion to decAmount.

f) *Displaying the result.* Display the result using the String.Format method with the F format specifier F.

g) *Running the application.* Select **Debug > Start** to run your application. Enter a value in dollars to convert and the currency you wish to convert to. Click the **Convert** Button and, using the specified exchange rates, verify that the correct output is displayed.

h) *Closing the application.* Close your running application by clicking its close box.

i) *Closing the IDE.* Close Visual Studio .NET by clicking its close box.

7.12 *(Expanded Wage Calculator that Performs Tax Calculations)* Develop an application that calculates an employee's wages (Fig. 7.32). The user should provide the hourly wage and number of hours worked per week. When the **Calculate** Button is clicked, display the gross earnings in the **Gross earnings:** TextBox. The **Less FWT:** TextBox should display the amount deducted for Federal taxes and the **Net earnings:** TextBox should display the difference between the gross earnings and the Federal tax amount. Assume overtime wages are 1.5 times the hourly wage and Federal taxes are 15% of gross earnings. The **Clear** Button clears all fields.

Figure 7.32 Expanded Wage Calculator GUI.

a) *Copying the template to your working directory.* Copy the directory C:\Examples\ Tutorial07\Exercises\ExpandedWageCalculator to your C:\SimplyCSP directory.

b) *Opening the application's template file.* Double click WageCalculator.sln in the ExpandedWageCalculator directory to open the application.

c) *Modifying the Calculate Button's Click event handler.* Add the code for *Steps d–f* to btnCalculate_Click.

d) *Adding a new variable.* Declare decFederalTaxes to store the amount deducted for Federal taxes.

e) *Calculating and displaying the Federal taxes deducted.* Multiply the total earnings (decEarnings) by 0.15 (that is, 15%) to determine the amount to be removed for taxes. Use the M suffix to convert 0.15 to a decimal. Assign the result to decFederalTaxes. Display this value using the String.Format method with the C format specifier.

f) *Calculating and displaying the employee's net pay.* Subtract decFederalTaxes from decEarnings to calculate the employee's net earnings. Display this value using String.Format method with the C format specifier.

g) *Creating an event handler for the Clear Button.* Double click the **Clear** Button to generate an empty event handler for the Click event. This event handler should clear user input from the two TextBoxes and the results from the three Labels.

h) *Running the application.* Select **Debug > Start** to run your application. Enter an hourly wage and the number of hours worked. Click **Calculate** and verify that the appropriate output is displayed for gross earnings, amount taken out for federal taxes and the net earnings. Click the **Clear** Button and check that all fields are cleared.

i) *Closing the application.* Close your running application by clicking its close box.

j) *Closing the IDE.* Close Visual Studio .NET by clicking its close box.

7.13 *(Credit Checker Application)* Develop an application that determines whether a department-store customer has exceeded the credit limit on a charge account (Fig. 7.33). Each customer enters an account number (an int), a balance at the beginning of the month (a decimal), the total of all items charged for the month (a decimal), the total of all credits applied to the customer's account for the month (a decimal), and the customer's allowed credit limit (a decimal). The application should input each of these facts, calculate the new balance (*beginning balance – credits + charges*), display the new balance and determine whether the new balance exceeds the customer's credit limit. If the customer's credit limit is exceeded, the application should display a message (in a Label at the bottom of the Form) informing the customer of this fact.

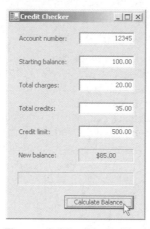

Figure 7.33 Credit Checker GUI.

a) *Copying the template to your working directory.* Copy the directory C:\Examples\ Tutorial07\Exercises\CreditChecker to your C:\SimplyCSP directory.

b) *Opening the application's template file.* Double click CreditChecker.sln in the CreditChecker directory to open the application.

c) *Adding the Calculate Button's Click event handler.* Double click the **Calculate** Button to generate the empty event handler for the Click event. The code for *Steps d–g* is added to this event handler.

d) *Declaring variables.* Declare an int variable to store the account number. Declare four decimal variables to store the starting balance, charges, credits and credit limit. Declare a fifth decimal variable to store the new balance in the account after the credits and charges have been applied.

e) *Obtaining user input.* Obtain the user input from the TextBoxes' Text properties.

f) *Calculating and displaying the new balance.* Calculate the new balance by subtracting the total credits from the starting balance and adding the charges. Assign the result to a variable. Display the result formatted as currency.

g) *Determining if the credit limit has been exceeded.* If the new balance exceeds the specified credit limit, a message should be displayed in lblError.

h) *Handling the Account number: TextBox's TextChanged event.* Double click the **Account number:** TextBox to create its TextChanged event handler. This event handler should clear the other TextBoxes, the error message Label and the result Label.

i) *Running the application.* Select **Debug > Start** to run your application. Enter an account number, your starting balance, the amount charged to your account, the amount credited to your account and your credit limit. Click the **Calculate Balance** Button and verify that the new balance displayed is correct. Enter an amount charged that exceeds your credit limit. Click the **Calculate Balance** Button and ensure that a message is displayed in the lower Label.

   j) *Closing the application.* Close your running application by clicking its close box.

   k) *Closing the IDE.* Close Visual Studio .NET by clicking its close box.

What does this code do? ▶

7.14 Assume that txtAge is a TextBox control and that the user has entered the value 27 into this TextBox. Determine the action performed by the following code:

```
1   int intAge;
2
3   intAge = Int32.Parse( txtAge.Text );
4
5   if ( intAge < 0 )
6   {
7      txtAge.Text = "Enter a value greater than or equal to zero.";
8   }
9   else if ( intAge < 13 )
10  {
11     txtAge.Text = "Child";
12  }
13  else if ( intAge < 20 )
14  {
15     txtAge.Text = "Teenager";
16  }
17  else if ( intAge < 30 )
18  {
19     txtAge.Text = "Young adult";
20  }
21  else if ( intAge < 65 )
22  {
23     txtAge.Text = "Adult";
24  }
25  else
26  {
27     txtAge.Text = "Senior Citizen";
28  }
```

What's wrong with this code? ▶

7.15 Assume that lblAMPM is a Label control. Find the error(s) in the following code.

```
1   int intHour;
2
3   intHour = 14;
4
5   if ( intHour < 0 )
6   {
7      lblAMPM.Text = "Time Error.";
8   }
9   else if ( intHour > 23 )
10  {
11     lblAMPM.Text = "Time Error.";
12  }
13  else
14  {
15     lblAMPM.Text = "PM";
16  }
17  else if ( intHour < 12 )
18  {
19     lblAMPM.Text = "AM";
20  }
```

Using the Debugger ▶

7.16 *(Grade Calculator Application)* Copy the directory C:\Examples\Tutorial07\ Exercises\Debugger\Grades into your C:\SimplyCSP directory. This directory contains the Grades application, which takes a number from the user and displays the corresponding letter grade. For values in the range 90–100 it should display **A**, for 80–89, **B**, for 70–79, **C**, for 60–69, **D** and for anything lower, **F**. Run the application. Enter the value 85 in the TextBox and click **Calculate**. Notice that the application displays **D** when it ought to display **B**. Select **View > Code** to enter the code editor and set as many breakpoints as you feel necessary. Select **Debug > Start** to use the debugger to help you find the error(s). Figure 7.34 shows the incorrect output when the value 85 is input.

Figure 7.34   Incorrect output for **Grade Calculator** application.

Programming Challenge ▶

7.17 *(Encryption Application)* A company transmits data over the telephone, but it is concerned that its phones could be tapped. All its data is transmitted as four-digit ints. The company has asked you to write an application that encrypts its data so that it may be transmitted more securely. Encryption is the process of transforming data for security reasons. Create a Form similar to Fig. 7.35. Your application should read four digits entered by the user and encrypt the information as follows:

a) Replace each digit by *(the sum of that digit plus 7) modulo 10*. We use the term modulo to indicate you are to use the remainder (%) operator.

b) Swap the first digit with the third, and swap the second digit with the fourth.

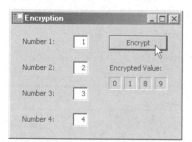

Figure 7.35   **Encryption** application.

Objectives

In this tutorial, you will learn to:
- Use CheckBoxes to allow users to select options.
- Use dialogs to display messages.
- Use logical operators to form more powerful conditions.

Outline

Dental Payment Application

Introducing *CheckBoxes and Message Dialogs*

Many C# applications use **dialogs** (or **message dialogs**), which are windows that display messages to users. You encounter many dialogs while using a computer, from those that instruct you to select files or enter passwords to those that notify you of problems while using an application. In this tutorial, you will learn how to use message dialogs to inform users of input problems.

You may have noticed that TextBoxes allow users to enter nearly any value as input. In some cases, you may want to use to provide users with predefined options. One way to do this is by providing CheckBoxes in your application. You also will learn about logical operators, which you can use in your applications to make more involved decisions based on user input.

8.1 Test-Driving the Dental Payment Application

When you visit the dentist, there are many procedures that the dentist can perform. The office assistant may present you with a bill generated by a computer. In this tutorial, you will program an application that prepares a bill for basic dental procedures. This application must meet the following requirements:

> **Application Requirements**
>
> *A dentist's office administrator wishes to create an application that employees can use to bill patients. The application must allow the user to enter the patient's name and specify which services were performed during the visit. The application will then calculate the total charges. If a user attempts to calculate a bill before any services are specified, or before the patient's name is entered, a message will be displayed.*

In the **Dental Payment** application, you will use CheckBox controls and a message dialog to assist the user in entering data. You begin by test-driving the completed application. Then, you will learn the additional C# technologies you will need to create your own version of this application.

169

Test-Driving the Dental Payment Application

1. **Opening the completed application.** Open the C:\Examples\Tutorial08\ CompletedApplication\DentalPayment directory to locate the **Dental Payment** application. Double click DentalPayment.sln to open the application in Visual Studio .NET.

2. **Running the Dental Payment application.** Select **Debug > Start** to run the application (Fig. 8.1). Notice that there are three square-shaped controls in the left column of the Form. These are known as **CheckBox** controls. A CheckBox is a small white square that either is blank or contains a check mark. When a CheckBox is selected, a black check mark appears in the box (☑). A CheckBox can be selected by clicking within the CheckBox's small white square or by clicking on the text of the CheckBox. A selected Check-Box can be unchecked in the same way. You will learn how to add CheckBox controls to a Form shortly.

CheckBox controls (unchecked)

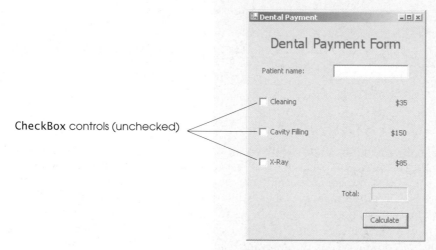

Figure 8.1   **Dental Payment** application without input entered.

3. **Attempting to calculate a total without entering input.** Leave the **Patient name** field blank, and deselect any CheckBoxes that you have selected. Click the **Calculate** Button. Notice that a message dialog appears, indicating that you must enter data (Fig. 8.2). Close this dialog by clicking its **OK** Button.

Figure 8.2   Message dialog appears when no name is entered and/or no CheckBoxes are selected.

4. **Entering quantities in the application.** The **Dental Payment** Form is still displayed. Type Bob Jones in the **Patient name** field. Check all three Check-Boxes by single clicking each one. Notice that a check mark appears in each CheckBox.

5. **Unchecking the Cavity Filling CheckBox.** Click the **Cavity Filling** CheckBox to remove its check mark. Only the **Cleaning** and **X-Ray** CheckBoxes should now be selected (Fig. 8.3).

(cont.)

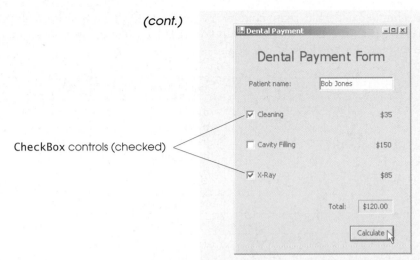

CheckBox controls (checked)

Figure 8.3 **Dental Payment** application with input entered.

6. ***Determining the bill.*** Click the **Calculate** Button. This causes the application to total the price of the services performed during the dentist visit. The result is displayed in the **Total:** field.

7. ***Closing the application.*** Close your running application by clicking its close box.

8. ***Closing the IDE.*** Close Visual Studio .NET by clicking its close box.

8.2 Designing the Dental Payment Application

Now that you have test-driven the **Dental Payment** application, you need to analyze the application components. Recall that pseudocode is an informal language that helps programmers develop algorithms. The following pseudocode describes the basic operation of the **Dental Payment** application:

```
When the user clicks the Calculate Button:
    Clear the previous total

    If the user has not entered a patient name or has not selected any
    CheckBoxes
        Display message in dialog
    else
        Initialize the total to zero

        If the "Cleaning" CheckBox is selected
            Add the cost of a cleaning to the total

        If the "Cavity Filling" CheckBox is selected
            Add the cost of receiving a cavity filling to the total

        If the "X-Ray" CheckBox is selected
            Add the cost of receiving an x-ray to the total

        Format the total to be displayed as currency
        Display the total
```

Now that you have test-driven the **Dental Payment** application and studied its pseudocode representation, you will use an ACE table to help you convert the pseudocode to C#. Figure 8.4 lists the actions, controls and events that will help you complete your own version of this application. Data is input using a TextBox (txt-

Name) and CheckBoxes (chkClean, chkCavity and chkXRay). Output is displayed in the lblTotalResult Label when a Button (btnCalculate) is clicked. Field names are displayed in the Form's other Labels.

Action/Control/Event (ACE) Table for the Dental Payment Application

Action	Control/Class	Event
Label all the application's controls	lblTitle, lblName, lblTotal, lblCleanCost, lblFillingCost, lblXRayCost	Application is run
	btnCalculate	Click
Clear previous total	lblTotalResult	
If the user has not entered a patient name or has not selected any CheckBoxes Display message in dialog	txtName, chkClean, chkCavity, chkXRay, MessageBox	
Else Initialize the a total to zero		
If the "Cleaning" CheckBox is selected Add the cost of a cleaning to the total	chkClean	
If the "Cavity Filling" CheckBox is selected Add the cost of receiving a cavity filling to the total	chkCavity	
If the "X-Ray" CheckBox is selected Add the cost of receiving an x-ray to the total	chkXRay	
Format the total to be displayed as currency	String	
Display the total	lblTotalResult	

Figure 8.4 Action/Control/Event table for the **Dental Payment** application.

8.3 Using CheckBoxes

As mentioned earlier, a CheckBox is a small white square that either is blank or contains a check mark. (A CheckBox is known as a **state button**, because it can be in the on/off [true/false] state.) When a CheckBox is selected, a black check mark appears in the box. Any number of CheckBoxes can be selected at a time, including none at all. The text that appears alongside a CheckBox is called the **CheckBox label**.

 **GUI Design Tip**

A CheckBox's label should be descriptive and as short as possible. When a CheckBox label contains more than one word, use book-title capitalization.

You can determine whether a CheckBox is on (that is, checked) by using the **Checked** property. If the CheckBox is checked, the Checked property returns the bool value true when accessed. If the CheckBox is not checked, the Checked property returns false when accessed.

You will now create the **Dental Payment** application from the template provided. The following box demonstrates how to add the CheckBoxes to your application. The application you will build in the next two boxes will not display a dialog if the TextBox is empty and/or all the CheckBoxes are unchecked when the **Calculate** Button is clicked. You will learn how to display that dialog in Section 8.4.

Adding CheckBoxes to the Form

1. ***Copying the template to your working directory.*** Copy the `C:\Examples\Tutorial08\TemplateApplication\DentalPayment` directory to your `C:\SimplyCSP` directory.

2. ***Opening the Dental Payment application's template file.*** Double click `DentalPayment.sln` in the `DentalPayment` directory to open the application in Visual Studio .NET.

3. ***Adding CheckBox controls to the Form.*** Add a CheckBox to the Form by double clicking the

   icon in the **Toolbox**. Repeat this process until three CheckBoxes have been added to the Form.

4. ***Customizing the CheckBoxes.*** For this application, you will be modifying the `Location`, `Text`, `Size` and `Name` properties of each CheckBox. Change the `Size` property of all three CheckBoxes to `122, 24`. Change the `Name` property of the first CheckBox to `chkClean` and set its `Location` property to `16, 112` and its `Text` property to `Cleaning`. Change the `Name` property of the second CheckBox to `chkCavity`, its `Location` property to `16, 159` and its `Text` property to `Cavity Filling`. Change the `Name` property of the final CheckBox to `chkXRay`, its `Location` property to `16, 206` and its `Text` property to `X-Ray`.

5. ***Rearranging and commenting the control declarations.*** In code view, locate the declarations for the three CheckBoxes you just created (lines 37–39 of your code). Cut these three lines of code and paste them above the declarations of their corresponding Labels as shown in Fig. 8.5. Change the comments in lines 22, 26 and 30 of Fig. 8.5 appropriately.

GUI Design Tip

Align groups of CheckBoxes either horizontally or vertically.

Good Programming Practice

Prefix CheckBox control names with chk.

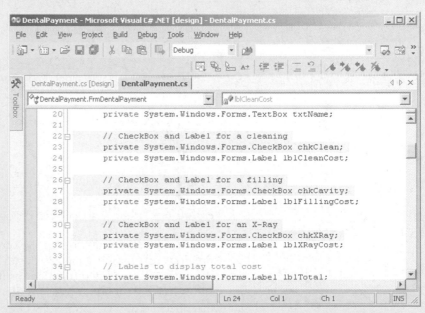

Figure 8.5   Rearranging and commenting the control declarations.

6. ***Saving the project.*** Select **File > Save All** to save your modified code.

After placing the CheckBoxes on the Form and setting their properties, you need to code an event handler to enhance the application's functionality when users select CheckBoxes, then click **Calculate**.

Adding the Calculate Button's Event Handler

1. **Adding an event handler for btnCalculate's Click event.** In design view, double click the **Calculate** Button on the Form to create an event handler for that control's Click event.

2. **Adding if statements to calculate the patient's bill.** Be sure to add the comments and break the header as shown in Fig. 8.6 so that the line numbers in your code match those presented in this tutorial. Then, add lines 235–261 to your application. Be sure to include all blank lines shown in Fig. 8.6 to improve code readability and to ensure that your line numbers correspond to those in the figure.

Calculating and displaying total bill

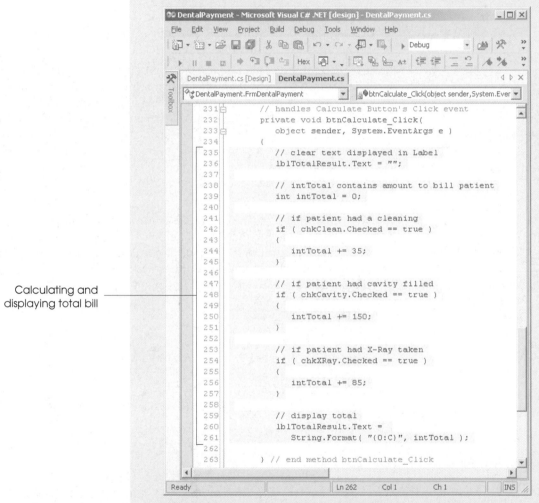

```
231     // handles Calculate Button's Click event
232     private void btnCalculate_Click(
233        object sender, System.EventArgs e )
234     {
235        // clear text displayed in Label
236        lblTotalResult.Text = "";
237
238        // intTotal contains amount to bill patient
239        int intTotal = 0;
240
241        // if patient had a cleaning
242        if ( chkClean.Checked == true )
243        {
244            intTotal += 35;
245        }
246
247        // if patient had cavity filled
248        if ( chkCavity.Checked == true )
249        {
250            intTotal += 150;
251        }
252
253        // if patient had X-Ray taken
254        if ( chkXRay.Checked == true )
255        {
256            intTotal += 85;
257        }
258
259        // display total
260        lblTotalResult.Text =
261            String.Format( "{0:C}", intTotal );
262
263     } // end method btnCalculate_Click
```

Figure 8.6   Using the Checked property.

Line 236 clears any text in the output Label that may be present from a previous calculation. Line 239 declares the intTotal variable, which stores the total charges for the patient as an int. This variable is initialized to 0. Lines 241–257 define three if statements that determine whether the user has checked any of the Form's CheckBoxes. Each if statement's condition compares a CheckBox's Checked property to true. Each if statement adds the dollar value of the service to intTotal if its corresponding CheckBox is checked. The first if statement, for example, adds 35 to intTotal in line 244 if the chkClean CheckBox is selected (line 242). Notice that the numeric values added to intTotal correspond to the monetary values indicated on the GUI to the right of each service. Lines 260–261 display the total (formatted as a currency amount) in lblTotalResult.

(cont.)   3. ***Running the application.*** Select **Debug > Start** to run your application
(Fig. 8.7). Notice that the user is not required to enter a name or select any
CheckBoxes before clicking the **Calculate** Button. If no CheckBoxes are
selected, the bill displays the value $0.00.

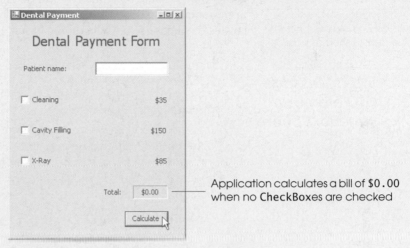

Figure 8.7   Application running without input.

4. ***Selecting a CheckBox.*** Select the **Cleaning** CheckBox, then click the **Calculate** Button. Notice that the **Total:** field now displays $35.00.

5. ***Closing the application.*** Close your running application by clicking its close
box.

1. The _____ property sets a CheckBox's text.

   a) Text   b) Value
   c) Label   d) Checked

2. Which property determines whether a CheckBox is selected?

   a) Selected   b) Checked
   c) Clicked   d) Check

Answers: 1.) a. 2.) b.

8.4 Using a Dialog to Display a Message

In the completed application, a message is displayed in a dialog if the user attempts
to calculate the total charges without specifying which services were performed or
without entering a name. In this section, you will learn how to display a dialog when
a patient name is not input. Later in this tutorial, you will learn how to write code to
determine if at least one CheckBox is checked. When the dialog is closed, control is
returned to the application's Form. The message dialog used in your application is
displayed in Fig. 8.8.

Title bar ———————————— |
Icon indicates the
tone of the message
OK Button allows the user
to close the dialog

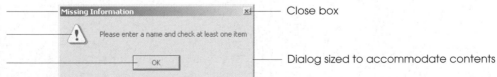

———— Close box
———— Dialog sized to accommodate contents

Figure 8.8   Dialog displayed by the application.

Notice that the message dialog contains a title bar and a close box. This dialog
also contains a message (Please enter a name and check at least one item), an

OK Button that allows the user to **dismiss** (close) the dialog (which the user must do to proceed) and an icon that indicates the tone of the message. (In this case, ⚠ indicates that a problem has occurred.)

Message dialogs are defined by the **MessageBox** class and can be displayed by using the **MessageBox.Show** method. The message dialog is customized by the arguments passed to the **MessageBox.Show** method. The following box demonstrates displaying a message dialog based on a condition.

GUI Design Tip

Text displayed in a dialog should be descriptive and as short as possible.

Displaying a Message Dialog Using MessageBox.Show

1. **Adding an *if* statement to the event handler for *btnCalculate's* Click event.** The message should display only if the user does not enter the patient's name. Add lines 238–240 of Fig. 8.9 to your event handler. Line 239 tests whether data was entered in the **Patient name:** TextBox. If no data has been entered, the expression `txtName.Text == ""` evaluates to `true`. You will add the body of this `if` statement in *Step 2*. Notice that event handler's code following lines 238–240 are not indented. The proper indentation will be applied to the code shortly.

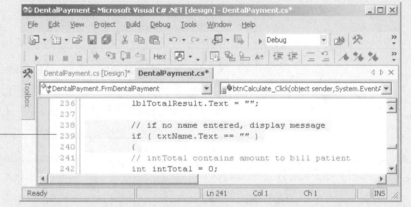

Checking for blank user input

Figure 8.9 Adding an `if` statement to the `btnCalculate` Click event handler to display a message dialog.

2. **Adding code to display a message dialog.** Place the cursor after the { on line 240 and press *Enter*. Add lines 241–246 of Fig. 8.10 to the body of the `if` statement you created in the previous step. Then, add an `else` statement and a left brace ({) as in lines 247–248. Notice that the code you added to the `btnCalculate_Click` event handler earlier (Fig. 8.6) now composes the body of the `else` portion of your `if...else` statement. The `else` statement is now missing a right brace (}). You will add this right brace *Step 3*.

   Lines 242–245 call the `MessageBox.Show` method using four arguments, separated by commas. The first argument specifies the text that displays in the dialog, the second argument specifies the text that appears in its title bar, the third argument indicates which Button(s) to display at the bottom of the dialog and the fourth argument indicates which icon appears at the left of the dialog. We discuss the final two arguments in more detail shortly.

3. **Closing the *if...else* statement.** Scroll to the end of your event handler code. Be sure to close the `if...else` statement by inserting a right brace (}) before the end of the event handler (line 274 of Fig. 8.11). Closing the `if...else` statement will indent lines 249–272 of Fig. 8.6 appropriately. Add a comment and leave a line before and a line after the right brace to maintain clarity in your code (as shown in Fig. 8.11).

(cont.)

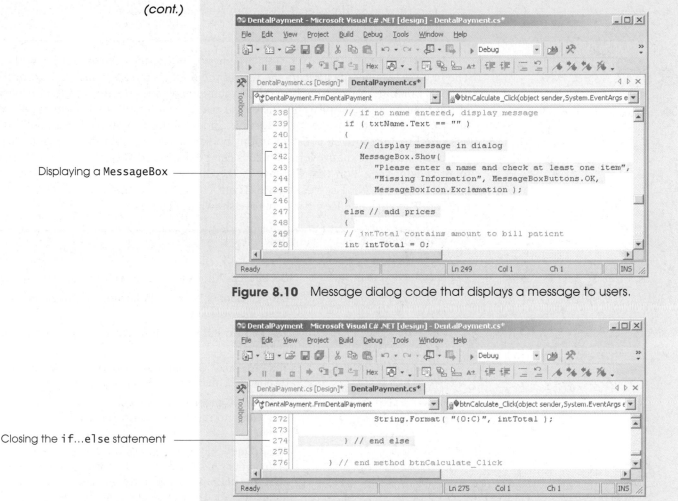

Displaying a MessageBox

Figure 8.10   Message dialog code that displays a message to users.

Closing the if...else statement

Figure 8.11   Ending the if...else statement.

4. ***Running the application.*** Select **Debug > Start** to run your application. Notice that the user does not have to select any CheckBoxes before clicking the **Calculate** Button, but the user must enter a name in the **Patient name:** TextBox. If none of the CheckBoxes is selected, the bill will contain the value $0.00 (Fig. 8.12). In the next section, you will modify the code to test whether the user has selected any CheckBoxes.

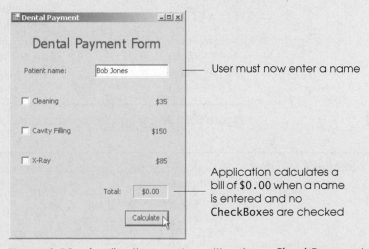

User must now enter a name

Application calculates a bill of $0.00 when a name is entered and no CheckBoxes are checked

Figure 8.12   Application running without any CheckBoxes selected.

(cont.)

5. ***Closing the application.*** Close your running application by clicking its close box.

In this example, you passed four arguments to the `MessageBox.Show` method. The first two arguments indicate the text of the dialog's message and the text of the dialog's title bar, respectively. The third argument specifies the `Button` that displays in the dialog. To accomplish this task, you passed one of the FCL's **MessageBox-Buttons** constants to the `MessageBox.Show` method. You will use only the `MessageBoxButtons.OK` constant in this book. Figure 8.13 lists the available `Button` constants. Note that several `Buttons` can be displayed at once. The fourth argument specifies the icon that displays in the dialog. To set the icon to display, you passed one of .NET's **MessageBoxIcon** constants to the `MessageBox.Show` method. The available icon constants are shown in Fig. 8.14.

MessageBoxButtons Constants	Description
`MessageBoxButtons.OK`	**OK** Button. Allows the user to acknowledge a message.
`MessageBoxButtons. OKCancel`	**OK** and **Cancel** Buttons. Allow the user to either continue or cancel an operation.
`MessageBoxButtons.YesNo`	**Yes** and **No** Buttons. Allow the user to respond to a question.
`MessageBoxButtons. YesNoCancel`	**Yes**, **No** and **Cancel** Buttons. Allow the user to respond to a question or cancel an operation.
`MessageBoxButtons. RetryCancel`	**Retry** and **Cancel** Buttons. Typically used to allow the user either to retry or to cancel an operation that has failed.
`MessageBoxButtons. AbortRetryIgnore`	**Abort**, **Retry** and **Ignore** Buttons. When one of a series of operations has failed, these Buttons allow the user to abort the entire sequence, retry the failed operation or ignore the failed operation and continue.

Figure 8.13 Message dialog **Button** constants.

MessageBoxIcon Constants	Icon	Description
`MessageBox-Icon.Exclamation`	⚠	Icon containing an exclamation point. Typically used to caution the user against potential problems.
`MessageBox-Icon.Information`	ⓘ	Icon containing the letter "i." Typically used to display information about the state of the application.
`MessageBox-Icon.Question`	?	Icon containing a question mark. Typically used to ask the user a question.
`MessageBox-Icon.Error`	⊗	Icon containing an ∞ in a red circle. Typically used to alert the user of errors or critical situations.

Figure 8.14 Message dialog icon constants.

SELF-REVIEW

1. Which constant, when passed to the `MessageBox.Show` method, indicates that a question is being asked?

    a) `MessageBox.Question`   b) `MessageBoxIcon.QuestionMark`

    c) `MessageBox.QuestionMark`   d) `MessageBoxIcon.Question`

2. What is the message dialog icon containing the letter "i" typically used for?

    a) To display information about the state of the application

    b) To caution the user against potential problems

    c) To ask the user a question

    d) To alert the user to critical situations

Answers: 1.) d. 2.) a.

8.5 Logical Operators

So far, you have studied only **simple conditions**, such as `intCount <= 10`, `intTotal > 1000`, and `intNumber != intValue`. Each selection statement that you used evaluated only one condition with one of the operators >, <, >=, <=, == or !=.

To handle multiple conditions more efficiently, C# provides **logical operators**, which can be used to form complex conditions by combining simple ones. The logical operators are **&& (logical AND)**, **|| (logical inclusive OR)**, **∧ (logical exclusive OR)** and **! (logical NOT)**. We will consider examples that use each of these operators. After you learn about logical operators, you will use them to create a complex condition in your **Dental Payment** application to confirm `CheckBox` entries.

Using && (Logical AND)

Error-Prevention Tip

Always write the simplest condition possible by limiting the number of logical operators used. Conditions with many logical operators can be hard to read and can introduce subtle bugs into your applications.

Suppose that you wish to ensure that two conditions are *both* true in an application before choosing a certain path of execution. In that case, you can use the && (logical AND) operator as follows:

```
if ( txtGender.Text == "Female" && intAge >= 65 )
{
    intSeniorFemales += 1;
}
```

This `if` statement contains two simple conditions. The condition `txtGender.Text == "Female"` determines whether a person is female, and the condition `intAge >= 65` determines whether a person is a senior citizen. The == and >= operators are always evaluated before the && operator because the == and >= operators have a higher precedence than the && operator. In this case, the two simple conditions are evaluated first, then the && operator is evaluated using their result. The `if` statement then considers the combined condition

```
txtGender.Text == "Female" && intAge >= 65
```

This condition evaluates to true *if and only if* both of the simple conditions are true, meaning that `txtGender.Text` contains the value `"Female"` and `intAge` contains a value greater than or equal to 65. When this combined condition is true, the count of `intSeniorFemales` is incremented by 1. However, if either or both of the simple conditions are false, the application skips the increment and proceeds to the statement following the `if` statement. The readability of the preceding combined condition can be improved by adding redundant (that is, unnecessary) parentheses:

```
( txtGender.Text == "Female" ) && ( intAge >= 65 )
```

Figure 8.15 illustrates the outcome of using the && operator with two expressions. The table lists all four possible combinations of `true` and `false` values for *expression1* and *expression2*, which represent the left operand and the right operand, respectively. Such tables are called **truth tables**. C# evaluates to `true` or `false` expressions that include relational operators, equality operators and logical operators.

expression1	expression2	expression1 && expression2
false	false	false
false	true	false
true	false	false
true	true	true

Figure 8.15 Truth table for the && operator.

Using || (Logical Inclusive OR)

Now let's consider the || (logical inclusive OR) operator. Suppose that you wish to ensure that either *or* both of two conditions are true before you choose a certain path of execution. You would use the || operator, as in the following application segment:

```
if ( intSemesterAverage >= 90 || intFinalExam >= 90 )
{
   MessageBox.Show( "Student grade is A", "Student Grade",
      MessageBoxButtons.OK, MessageBoxIcon.Information );
}
```

This statement also contains two simple conditions. The condition intSemesterAverage >= 90, is evaluated to determine whether the student deserves an "A" in the course because of an outstanding performance throughout the semester. The condition intFinalExam >= 90 is evaluated to determine whether the student deserves an "A" in the course because of an outstanding performance on the final exam. The if statement then considers the combined condition

```
( intSemesterAverage >= 90 || intFinalExam >= 90 )
```

and awards the student an "A" if either or both of the conditions are true, meaning that the student performed well during the semester, performed well on the final exam or both. Note that the text "Student grade is A" is displayed unless both of the conditions are false. Figure 8.16 provides a truth table for the || operator. Note that the && operator has a higher precedence than the || operator. See Appendix A for a complete listing of operator precedence in C#.

 Error-Prevention Tip

When writing conditions that contain combinations of && and || operators, use parentheses to ensure that the conditions evaluate properly. Otherwise, logic errors could occur because && has a higher precedence than ||.

expression1	expression2	expression1 || expression2
false	false	false
false	true	true
true	false	true
true	true	true

Figure 8.16 Truth table for the || operator.

An expression containing the && operator is evaluated only until truth or falsity is known. For example, evaluation of the expression

```
( txtGender.Text == "Female" && intAge >= 65 )
```

stops immediately if txtGender.Text is not equal to "Female" (which would mean the entire expression is false). In this case, the evaluation of the second expression is irrelevant; once the first expression is known to be false, the whole expression must be false. Evaluation of the second expression occurs if and only if txtGender. Text is equal to "Female" (which would mean that the entire expression could still be true if the condition intAge >= 65 is true).

Similarly, an expression containing || is evaluated only until truth or falsity is known. For example, evaluation of the expression

```
if ( intSemesterAverage >= 90 || intFinalExam >= 90 )
```

stops immediately if intSemesterAverage is greater than or equal to 90 (which would mean the entire expression is true). In this case, the evaluation of the second expression is irrelevant; once the first expression is known to be true, the whole expression must be true.

This way of evaluating logical expressions can require fewer operations, therefore taking less time. This performance feature for the evaluation of && and || expressions is called **short-circuit evaluation**.

Using ∧ (Logical Exclusive OR)

A condition containing the ∧ (logical exclusive OR) operator is true *if and only if one of its operands results in a true value and the other results in a false value.* If both operands are true or both are false, the entire condition is false. Figure 8.17 presents a truth table for the ∧ (logical exclusive OR) operator. This operator always evaluates both of its operands (that is, there is no short-circuit evaluation).

expression1	expression2	expression1 ∧ expression2
false	false	false
false	true	true
true	false	true
true	true	false

Figure 8.17 Truth table for the ∧ (logical exclusive OR) operator.

Using ! (Logical NOT)

C#'s ! (logical NOT, or logical negation) operator enables a programmer to "reverse" the meaning of a condition. Unlike the &&, || and ∧ logical operators, each of which combines two expressions (that is, these are all binary operators), the logical negation operator is a unary operator, requiring only one operand. The logical negation operator is placed before a condition to choose a path of execution if the original condition (without the logical negation operator) is false. The logical negation operator is demonstrated by the following application segment:

```
if ( ! ( intGrade == intValue) )
{
    lblDisplay.Text = "They are not equal!";
}
```

The parentheses around the condition intGrade == intValue are necessary, because the logical negation operator (!) has a higher precedence than the equality operator. Most programmers prefer to write

```
( ! ( intGrade == intValue ) )
```

as

```
( intGrade != intValue )
```

Figure 8.18 provides a truth table for the logical negation operator. The following box provides an example of a complex expression. You will modify your **Dental Payment** application to use a complex expression.

expression	! expression
false	true
true	false

Figure 8.18 Truth table for the ! operator (logical NOT).

Using Logical Operators in Complex Expressions

1. **Inserting a complex expression into the Click event handler.** In design view, double click the **Calculate** Button on the Form. Replace lines 238–239 of Fig. 8.9 with lines 238–243 of Fig. 8.19.

Using logical operators and the Checked property of a CheckBox

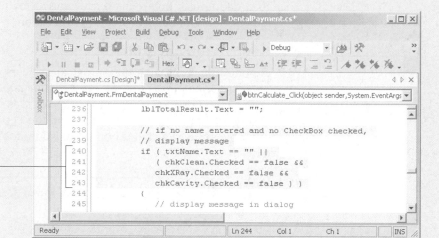

Figure 8.19 Using the && and || logical operators.

Lines 240–243 define a more sophisticated logical expression than others we have used in this book. Notice the use of || and &&. If the name is blank or if no CheckBox is checked, a dialog should appear. After the original expression (txtName.Text == ""), you use || to indicate that either the expression on the left (txtName.Text == "") or the expression on the right (which determines if no CheckBox has been checked) needs to be `true` for the entire expression to evaluate to `true` and execute the body of the `if` statement. The complex expression "on the right" uses && twice to determine if all of the CheckBoxes are unchecked. Note that because && has a higher precedence than ||, the inner set of parentheses in lines 241 and 243 are redundant.

2. **Running the application.** Select **Debug > Start** to run your application. Notice that users must enter a name and select at least one CheckBox before they click the **Calculate** Button. You have finally corrected the weakness from your earlier implementation of the **Dental Payment** application.

3. **Closing the application.** Close your running application by clicking its close box.

4. **Closing the IDE.** Close Visual Studio .NET by clicking its close box.

Figure 8.20 presents the source code for the **Dental Payment** application. The lines of code that contain new programming concepts that you learned in this tutorial are highlighted.

```
 1   using System;
 2   using System.Drawing;
 3   using System.Collections;
 4   using System.ComponentModel;
 5   using System.Windows.Forms;
 6   using System.Data;
 7
 8   namespace DentalPayment
 9   {
10      /// <summary>
11      /// Summary description for FrmDentalPayment.
12      /// </summary>
13      public class FrmDentalPayment : System.Windows.Forms.Form
14      {
15         // Label displaying title
16         private System.Windows.Forms.Label lblTitle;
17
18         // Label and TextBox for patient name
19         private System.Windows.Forms.Label lblName;
20         private System.Windows.Forms.TextBox txtName;
21
22         // CheckBox and Label for a cleaning
23         private System.Windows.Forms.CheckBox chkClean;
24         private System.Windows.Forms.Label lblCleanCost;
25
26         // CheckBox and Label for a filling
27         private System.Windows.Forms.CheckBox chkCavity;
28         private System.Windows.Forms.Label lblFillingCost;
29
30         // CheckBox and Label for an X-Ray
31         private System.Windows.Forms.CheckBox chkXRay;
32         private System.Windows.Forms.Label lblXRayCost;
33
34         // Labels to display total cost
35         private System.Windows.Forms.Label lblTotal;
36         private System.Windows.Forms.Label lblTotalResult;
37
38         // Button to calculate total cost
39         private System.Windows.Forms.Button btnCalculate;
40
41         /// <summary>
42         /// Required designer variable.
43         /// </summary>
44         private System.ComponentModel.Container components = null;
45
46         public FrmDentalPayment()
47         {
48            //
49            // Required for Windows Form Designer support
50            //
51            InitializeComponent();
52
53            //
54            // TODO: Add any constructor code after InitializeComponent
55            // call
56            //
57         }
58
```

Declaration for a **CheckBox** ——— (line 23)

Figure 8.20 Dental Payment application code. (Part 1 of 3.)

```
59      /// <summary>
60      /// Clean up any resources being used.
61      /// </summary>
62      protected override void Dispose( bool disposing )
63      {
64         if( disposing )
65         {
66            if (components != null)
67            {
68               components.Dispose();
69            }
70         }
71         base.Dispose( disposing );
72      }
73
74      // Windows Form Designer generated code
75
76      /// <summary>
77      /// The main entry point for the application.
78      /// </summary>
79      [STAThread]
80      static void Main()
81      {
82         Application.Run( new FrmDentalPayment() );
83      }
84
85      // handles Calculate Button's Click event
86      private void btnCalculate_Click(
87         object sender, System.EventArgs e )
88      {
89         // clear text displayed in Label
90         lblTotalResult.Text = "";
91
92         // if no name entered and no CheckBox checked,
93         // display message
94         if ( txtName.Text == "" ||
95            ( chkClean.Checked == false &&
96            chkXRay.Checked == false &&
97            chkCavity.Checked == false ) )
98         {
99            // display message in dialog
100           MessageBox.Show(
101              "Please enter a name and check at least one item",
102              "Missing Information", MessageBoxButtons.OK,
103              MessageBoxIcon.Exclamation );
104        }
105        else // add prices
106        {
107           // intTotal contains amount to bill patient
108           int intTotal = 0;
109
110           // if patient had a cleaning
111           if ( chkClean.Checked == true )
112           {
113              intTotal += 35;
114           }
115
```

Using logical operators and the Checked property of a CheckBox — (lines 94–97)

Displaying a MessageBox — (lines 100–103)

Using the Checked property of a CheckBox — (line 111)

Figure 8.20 **Dental Payment** application code. (Part 2 of 3.)

```
116              // if patient had cavity filled
117              if ( chkCavity.Checked == true )
118              {
119                  intTotal += 150;
120              }
121
122              // if patient had X-Ray taken
123              if ( chkXRay.Checked == true )
124              {
125                  intTotal += 85;
126              }
127
128              // display total
129              lblTotalResult.Text =
130                  String.Format( "{0:C}", intTotal );
131
132          } // end else
133
134      } // end method btnCalculate_Click
135
136  } // end class FrmDentalPayment
137 }
```

Figure 8.20 Dental Payment application code. (Part 3 of 3.)

SELF-REVIEW

1. A unary operator _____.

    a) requires exactly one operand   b) requires two operands

    c) must use the **&&** operator   d) can have no operands

2. The _____ operator is used to ensure that two conditions are both true.

    a) ∧   b) **&&**

    c) +   d) ||

Answers: 1.) a. 2.) b.

8.6 Wrap-Up

In this tutorial, you used CheckBox controls to provide a series of choices to users in the **Dental Payment** application. CheckBoxes provide options that can be selected by clicking them. When a CheckBox is selected, its white square contains a check mark. You can determine whether a CheckBox is selected in your code by accessing its Checked property.

Your **Dental Payment** application also used message dialogs to display messages to the user when information was not entered properly. To implement dialogs in your application, you used the MessageBox class, which provides methods and constants necessary to display a dialog containing Buttons and an icon. You used an if...else statement to calculate the cost of the dental visit or display a message dialog if the user was missing input. Later in this book you will learn to avoid checking for invalid user input by disabling a control (such as a Button) when its events should not cause any action to occur.

You learned to use the && (logical AND) operator when both conditions must be true for the overall condition to be true—if either condition is false, the overall condition is false. You also learned that the || (logical inclusive OR) operator requires at least one of its conditions to be true for the overall condition to be true—if both conditions are false, the overall condition is false. The ∧ (logical exclusive OR) operator requires that exactly one of its conditions be true for the overall condition to be true—if both conditions are false or if both conditions are true, the overall condition is false. The ! (logical NOT) operator reverses the bool result of a condition—true becomes false, and false becomes true. You then used the && and || operators to form a complex expression.

In the next tutorial, you will learn more about C#'s control statements. Specifically, you will use repetition statements, which allow the programmer to specify that an action or a group of actions should be performed many times.

SKILLS SUMMARY

Adding a CheckBox to a Form
- Double click the CheckBox in the **Toolbox**.

Selecting a CheckBox
- Click the CheckBox, and a check mark will appear in the white box.

Deselecting a CheckBox
- Click a checked CheckBox to remove its check mark.

Determining Whether a CheckBox Is Selected
- Access the CheckBox's Checked property.

Displaying a Dialog
- Use the MessageBox.Show method.

Combining Multiple Conditions
- Use the logical operators to form complex conditions by combining simple ones.

KEY TERMS

&& (logical AND) operator—Used to ensure that two conditions are *both* true before choosing a certain path of execution. Performs short-circuit evaluation.

|| (logical inclusive OR) operator—Used to ensure that either *or* both of two conditions are true in an application before a certain path of execution is chosen.

∧ (logical exclusive OR) operator—Evaluates to true if and only if one of its operands results in true and the other results in false.

! (logical NOT, or logical negation) operator—Enables a programmer to reverse the meaning of a condition: A true condition, when logically negated, becomes false, and a false condition, when logically negated, becomes true.

CheckBox control—A small white square GUI element that either is blank or contains a check mark.

CheckBox label—The text that appears alongside a CheckBox.

Checked property of the CheckBox control—Specifies whether the CheckBox is checked (true) or unchecked (false).

dialog (message dialog)—A window that displays messages to users and gathers input from users.

dismiss—Synonym for close.

logical operators—Operators (for example, &&, ||, ∧ and !) that can be used to form complex conditions by combining simple ones.

MessageBox class—Provides a method for displaying message dialogs.

MessageBoxButtons constants—Identifiers that specify Buttons that can be displayed in a MessageBox dialog.

MessageBoxIcon constants—Identifiers that specify icons that can be displayed in a MessageBox dialog.

MessageBox.Show method—Displays a message dialog.

short-circuit evaluation—The evaluation of the right operand in && and || expressions occurs only if the first condition meets the criteria for the condition.

simple condition—Contains one expression.

state button—Can be in the on/off (true/false) state.

truth table—Displays the boolean result of a logical operator for all possible combinations of true and false values for its operands.

GUI DESIGN GUIDELINES

CheckBoxes

- A CheckBox's label should be descriptive and as short as possible. When a CheckBox label contains more than one word, use book-title capitalization.
- Align groups of CheckBoxes either horizontally or vertically.

Message Dialogs

- Text displayed in a dialog should be descriptive and as short as possible.

CONTROLS, EVENTS, PROPERTIES & METHODS

CheckBox   ☑ CheckBox   This control allows the user to select an option.

- ***In action***

  ☑ Cleaning
  ☐ Cavity Filling

- ***Properties***

  Checked—Specifies whether the CheckBox is checked (true) or unchecked (false).
  Location—Specifies the location of the CheckBox on the Form.
  Name—Specifies the name used to access the CheckBox control programmatically. The name should be prefixed with chk.
  Text—Specifies the text displayed next to the CheckBox.

MULTIPLE-CHOICE QUESTIONS

8.1 How many CheckBoxes in a GUI can be selected at once?

   a) 0   b) 1
   c) 4   d) any number

8.2 The text that appears alongside a CheckBox is referred to as the _____.

   a) CheckBox label   b) CheckBox name
   c) CheckBox value   d) CheckBox data

8.3 The first argument passed to the MessageBox.Show method is _____.

   a) the text displayed in the dialog's title bar
   b) a constant representing the Buttons displayed in the dialog
   c) the text displayed inside the dialog
   d) a constant representing the icon that appears in the dialog

8.4 You can specify the Button(s) and icon to be displayed in a message dialog by using the MessageBoxButtons and _____ constants.

   a) MessageIcon   b) MessageBoxImages
   c) MessageBoxPicture   d) MessageBoxIcon

8.5 _____ are used to create complex conditions.

   a) Assignment operators   b) Activity diagrams
   c) Logical operators   d) Formatting codes

8.6 The && operator _____.

   a) performs short-circuit evaluation
   b) is a keyword
   c) is a comparison operator
   d) evaluates to false if both operands are true

8.7 A CheckBox is selected when its Checked property is set to _____.

   a) on   b) true
   c) selected   d) checked

8.8 The condition *expression1* && *expression2* evaluates to true when _____.

a) *expression1* is true and *expression2* is false

b) *expression1* is false and *expression2* is true

c) both *expression1* and *expression2* are true

d) both *expression1* and *expression2* are false

8.9 The condition *expression1* || *expression2* evaluates to false when _____.

a) *expression1* is true and *expression2* is false

b) *expression1* is false and *expression2* is true

c) both *expression1* and *expression2* are true

d) both *expression1* and *expression2* are false

8.10 The condition *expression1* ^ *expression2* evaluates to true when _____.

a) *expression1* is true and *expression2* is false

b) *expression1* is false and *expression2* is true

c) both *expression1* and *expression2* are true

d) Both a and b.

EXERCISES

8.11 (***Enhanced Dental Payment Application***) Modify the **Dental Payment** application from this tutorial to include additional services, as shown in Fig. 8.21. Add the proper functionality (using if statements) to determine whether any of the new CheckBoxes are selected and, if so, add the price of the service to the total bill.

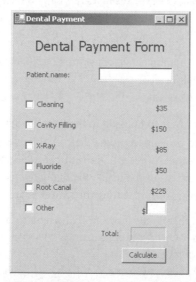

Figure 8.21 Enhanced **Dental Payment** application.

a) ***Copying the template to your working directory.*** Copy the directory C:\Examples\ Tutorial08\Exercises\DentalPaymentEnhanced to your C:\SimplyCSP directory.

b) ***Opening the application's template file.*** Double click DentalPayment.sln in the DentalPaymentEnhanced directory to open the application.

c) ***Adding CheckBoxes and Labels and a TextBox.*** Add two CheckBoxes and two Labels to the Form. The new CheckBoxes should be labelled **Fluoride** and **Root Canal**, respectively. Add these CheckBoxes and Labels beneath the X-Ray CheckBox and its price Label. The price for a Fluoride treatment is $50; the price for a root canal is $225. Add a CheckBox labelled **Other** and a Label containing a dollar sign ($) to the Form, as shown in Fig. 8.21. Then add a TextBox to the right of the $ Label in which the user can enter the cost of the service performed. Rearrange and comment the new control declarations appropriately.

d) *Modifying the Click event handler code.* Add code to the btnCalculate_Click event handler to determine whether the new CheckBoxes have been selected. This can be done using if statements that are similar to the ones already in the event handler. Use the if statements to update the bill amount.

e) *Running the application.* Select **Debug > Start** to run your application. Test your application by checking one or more of the new services. Click the **Calculate** Button and verify that the proper total is displayed. Test the application again by checking some of the services, then checking the **Other** CheckBox and entering a dollar value for this service. Click the **Calculate** Button and verify that the proper total is displayed, and that it includes the price for the "other" service.

f) *Closing the application.* Close your running application by clicking its close box.

g) *Closing the IDE.* Close Visual Studio .NET by clicking its close box.

8.12 (*Fuzzy Dice Order Form Application*) Write an application that allows users to process orders for fuzzy dice, as shown in Fig. 8.22. The application should calculate the total price of the order, including tax and shipping. TextBoxes for inputting the order number, the customer name and the shipping address are provided. Initially, these fields contain text that describes their purpose. Provide CheckBoxes for selecting the fuzzy-dice color and Text-Boxes for inputting the quantities of fuzzy dice to order. The application should also contain a Button that, when clicked, calculates the subtotals for each type of fuzzy dice ordered and the total of the entire order (including tax and shipping). Use 5% for the tax rate. Shipping charges are $1.50 for up to 20 pairs of dice. If more than 20 pairs of dice are ordered, shipping is free. For the total to be calculated, the user must enter an order number, a name and a shipping address. If they have not done so, a message should be displayed in a dialog.

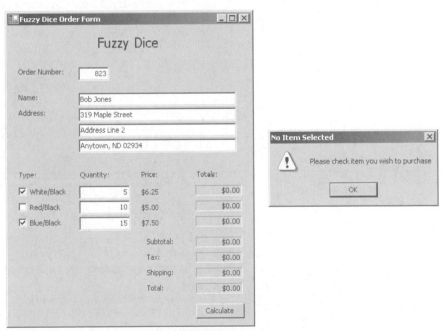

Figure 8.22 **Fuzzy Dice Order Form** application.

a) *Copying the template to your working directory.* Copy the directory C:\Examples\ Tutorial08\Exercises\FuzzyDiceOrderForm to your C:\SimplyCSP directory.

b) *Opening the application's template file.* Double click FuzzyDiceOrderForm.sln in the FuzzyDiceOrderForm directory to open the application.

c) *Adding CheckBoxes to the Form.* Add three CheckBoxes to the Form. Label the first CheckBox **White/Black**, the second one **Red/Black** and the third **Blue/Black**. Rearrange and comment the new control declarations appropriately.

d) *Adding a Click event handler and its code.* Create the Click event handler for the **Calculate** Button. For this application, users should not be allowed to specify an item's quantity unless the item's corresponding CheckBox is checked. For the total to be calculated, the user must enter an order number, a name and a shipping address.

Use logical operators to ensure that these terms are met. If they are not, display a message in a dialog.

e) *Calculating the total cost.* Calculate the subtotal, tax, shipping and total, and display the results in their corresponding Labels.

f) *Running the application.* Select **Debug > Start** to run your application. Test the application by providing quantities for checked items. For instance, ensure that your application is calculating 5% sales tax. If more than 20 pairs of dice are ordered, verify that shipping is free. Also, determine whether your code containing the logical operators works correctly by specifying a quantity for an item that is not checked. For instance, in Fig. 8.22, a quantity is specified for **Red/Black** dice, but the corresponding CheckBox is not selected. This should cause the message dialog in Fig. 8.22 to appear.

g) *Closing the application.* Close your running application by clicking its close box.

h) *Closing the IDE.* Close Visual Studio .NET by clicking its close box.

8.13 (*Modified Fuzzy Dice Order Form Application*) Modify the **Fuzzy Dice Order Form** application from Exercise 8.12 to determine whether customers should receive a 7% discount off their purchase. Customers ordering more than $500 (before tax and shipping) in fuzzy dice are eligible for this discount (Fig. 8.23).

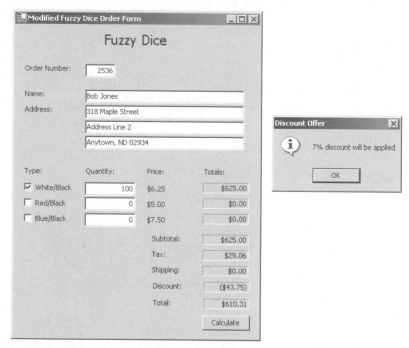

Figure 8.23 Modified **Fuzzy Dice Order Form** application.

a) *Copying the template to your working directory.* Copy the directory C:\Examples\ Tutorial08\Exercises\FuzzyDiceOrderFormModified to your C:\SimplyCSP directory.

b) *Opening the application's template file.* Double click FuzzyDiceOrderForm.sln in the FuzzyDiceOrderFormModified directory to open the application.

c) *Determining whether the total cost is over $500.* Use an if statement to determine if the amount ordered is greater than $500.

d) *Displaying the discount and subtracting the discount from the total.* If a customer orders more than $500, display a message dialog as shown in Fig. 8.23 that informs the user that the customer is entitled to a 7% discount. The message dialog should contain an Information icon and an **OK** Button. Calculate 7% of the total amount, and display the discount amount in the **Discount:** field. Subtract this amount from the total, and update the **Total:** field.

e) *Running the application.* Select **Debug > Start** to run your application. Test your application to ensure that it runs correctly and calculates and displays the discount properly, as shown in Fig. 8.23.

f) *Closing the application.* Close your running application by clicking its close box.

g) *Closing the IDE.* Close Visual Studio .NET by clicking its close box.

What does this code do? ▶   **8.14** Assume that `txtName` is a TextBox and that `chkOther` is a CheckBox next to which is a TextBox, `txtOther`, in which the user should specify a value. What does this code segment do?

```
1  if ( txtName.Text == "" ||
2     ( ( chkOther.Checked == true ) &&
3     ( txtOther.Text == "" ) ) )
4  {
5     MessageBox.Show( "Please enter a name or value",
6        "Input Error", MessageBoxButtons.OK,
7        MessageBoxIcon.Exclamation );
8  }
```

What's wrong with this code? ▶   **8.15** Assume that `txtName` is a TextBox. Find the error(s) in the following code:

```
1  if ( txtName.Text == "John Doe" )
2  {
3     MessageBox.Show( "Welcome, John!",
4        MessageBoxIcon.Exclamation );
5  }
```

Using the Debugger ▶   **8.16** (*Sibling Survey Application*) The **Sibling Survey** application displays the siblings selected by the user in a dialog. If the user checks either the **Brother(s)** or **Sister(s)** Check-Box, and the **No Siblings** CheckBox, the user is asked to verify the selection. Otherwise, the user's selection is displayed in a MessageBox. While testing this application, you noticed that it does not execute properly. Use the debugger to find and correct the logic error(s) in the code. This exercise is located in the `C:\Examples\Tutorial08\Exercises\Debugger\SiblingSurvey` directory. Figure 8.24 shows the correct output for the application.

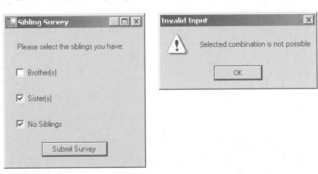

Figure 8.24   Correct output for the **Sibling Survey** application.

Programming Challenge ▶   **8.17** (*Enhanced Fuzzy Dice Order Form Application*) Copy the directory `C:\Examples\Tutorial08\Exercises\FuzzyDiceOrderFormEnhanced` to your `C:\SimplyCSP` directory. Double click `FuzzyDiceOrderForm.sln` in the `FuzzyDiceOrderFormEnhanced` directory to open the application. Enhance the **Fuzzy Dice Order Form** application from Exercise 8.12 by replacing the **Calculate** Button with a **Clear** Button. The application should update the total cost, tax and shipping when the user changes any one of the three **Quantity:** field's values (Fig. 8.25). The **Clear** Button should return all fields to their original values. [*Hint*: You will need to use the CheckBox **CheckedChanged** event for each CheckBox. This event is raised when the state of a CheckBox changes. Double click a CheckBox in design view to create an event handler for that CheckBox's CheckedChanged event. You also will need to assign `bool` values to the CheckBoxes' Checked properties to control their states.]

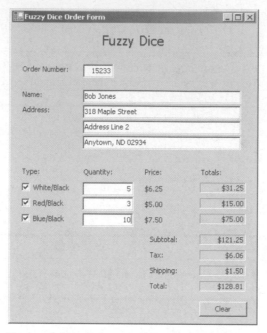

Figure 8.25 Enhanced **Fuzzy Dice Order Form** application.

Objectives

In this tutorial, you will learn to:
- Use the while repetition statement to execute statements in an application repeatedly.
- Use counter-controlled repetition.
- Display information in ListBoxes.

Outline

Car Payment Calculator Application

Introducing the while Repetition Statement

This tutorial continues the discussion of structured programming that we began in Tutorial 7. We introduce repetition statements, which are control statements that can repeat actions on the basis of a condition's value. You perform many repetitive tasks based on conditions. For example, each time you turn a page in this book (while there are more pages to read), you are repeating a simple task—namely turning a page—based on the condition that there are more pages to read.

The ability to perform tasks repeatedly is an important part of structured programming. Repetition statements are used in many types of applications. In this tutorial, you will learn to use the while repetition statement. You will include a repetition statement in the **Car Payment Calculator** application that you build. Later tutorials will introduce additional repetition statements.

9.1 Test-Driving the Car Payment Calculator Application

The following problem statement requires an application that repeats a calculation four times—you will use a repetition statement to solve this problem. This application must meet the following requirements:

Application Requirements

Typically, banks offer car loans for periods ranging from two to five years (24 to 60 months). Borrowers repay the loans in monthly installments. The amount of each monthly payment is based on the length of the loan, the amount borrowed and the interest rate. Create an application to allow the customer to enter the price of a car, the down-payment amount and the annual interest rate of the loan. The application should display the loan's duration in months and the monthly payments for two-, three-, four- and five-year loans. The variety of options allows the user to easily compare their options and choose the payment plan that is most convenient for them.

You begin by test-driving the completed application. Then, you will learn the additional C# technologies you will need to create your own version of this application.

*Test-Driving the Car
Payment Calculator
Application*

1. *Opening the completed application.* Open the C:\Examples\Tutorial09\ CompletedApplication\CarPaymentCalculator directory to locate the **Car Payment Calculator** application. Double click CarPaymentCalculator.sln to open the application in Visual Studio .NET.

2. *Running the Car Payment Calculator application.* Select **Debug > Start** to run the application (Fig. 9.1). Notice a new GUI control—the **ListBox** control, which allows users to view and select from multiple items in a list. Users cannot add items to, or remove items from, a ListBox by interacting directly with the ListBox. The ListBox does not accept keyboard input; users cannot add or delete selected items. You need to add code to your application to add or remove items from a ListBox.

ListBox control —————

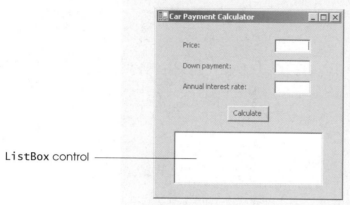

Figure 9.1 **Car Payment Calculator** application before data has been entered.

3. *Entering quantities in the application.* Enter 16900 in the **Price:** TextBox. Enter 6000 in the **Down payment:** TextBox. Enter 7.5 in the **Annual interest rate:** TextBox. The Form appears as in Fig. 9.2.

Figure 9.2 **Car Payment Calculator** application after data has been entered.

4. *Calculating the monthly payment amounts.* Click the **Calculate** Button. The application displays the monthly payment amounts in the ListBox (Fig. 9.3). The information is organized in tabular format.

5. *Closing the application.* Close your running application by clicking its close box.

6. *Closing the IDE.* Close Visual Studio .NET by clicking its close box.

(cont.)

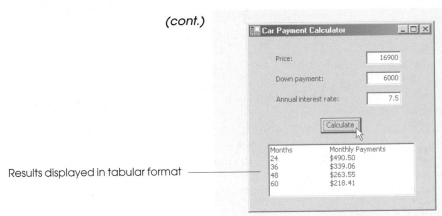

Results displayed in tabular format ——————

Figure 9.3   Car Payment Calculator application displaying calculation results.

9.2 `while` Repetition Statement

A repetition statement can repeat actions, depending on the value of a condition (which can be either true or false). For example, if you go to the grocery store with a list of items to purchase, you go through the list until you have each item. This process is described by the following pseudocode statements:

> While there are still items on my shopping list
>> Add an item to my shopping cart
>> Cross it off my list

These statements describe the repetitive actions that occur during a shopping trip. The condition, "there are still items on my shopping list" can be true or false. If it is true, then the actions, "Add an item to my shopping cart" and "Cross it off my list" are performed in sequence. In an application, these actions execute repeatedly while the condition remains true. The statement(s) indented in this repetition statement constitute its body. When the last item on the shopping list has been placed in the cart and crossed off the list, the condition becomes false. At this point, the repetition terminates, and the first statement after the repetition statement executes. In the shopping example, you would proceed to the checkout station.

As an example of a **while** statement, let's look at an application segment designed to find the first power of 3 greater than 50.

```
int intProduct = 3;

while ( intProduct <= 50 )
{
    intProduct *= 3;
}
```

Common Programming Error

Provide in the body of every `while` statement an action that eventually causes the condition to become false. If you do not, the repetition statement never terminates, causing an error called an infinite loop. When an infinite loop occurs in an application running in Visual Studio .NET, select **Debug > Stop Debugging** to terminate the application.

The application segment initializes the `intProduct` variable to 3, taking advantage of a C# feature that allows variable initialization to be incorporated into a declaration. The condition in the `while` statement, `intProduct <= 50`, is referred to as the **loop-continuation condition**. While the loop-continuation condition remains true, the `while` statement executes its body repeatedly. When the loop-continuation condition becomes false, the `while` statement finishes executing, and `intProduct` contains the first power of 3 larger than 50. If the loop-continuation condition never becomes false, the `while` statement loops forever, creating an error called an **infinite loop**. Let's examine the execution of the preceding code in detail.

When the `while` statement is entered, the value of `intProduct` is 3. Each time the loop executes, the variable `intProduct` is multiplied by 3, successively taking on the values 3, 9, 27 and 81. When `intProduct` becomes 81, the condition in the `while` statement, `intProduct <= 50`, is evaluated to false. When the repetition ends, the final value of `intProduct` is 81, which is, indeed, the first power of 3 greater than 50. Application execution continues with the next statement after the `while` statement. Like the `if` and `if...else` statements, the `while` statement expects only the statement immediately following the condition to be executed each time through the loop. For multiple statements to be executed each time through the loop, enclose the body statements with braces ({ and }). For simplicity, we always use braces in our `while` statements. Note that, if a `while` statement's condition is initially false, the body statement(s) are not performed and your application simply continues executing with the next statement after the right brace (}). The following box describes each step as the above repetition statement executes.

Executing the `while` Repetition Statement	1. The application declares the `intProduct` variable and sets its value to 3.
	2. The application enters the `while` repetition statement.
	3. The loop-continuation condition is checked. The condition evaluates to `true` (`intProduct` is less than or equal to 50), so the application resumes execution at the next statement.
	4. The number (currently 3) stored in `intProduct` is multiplied by 3 and the result is assigned to `intProduct`; `intProduct` now contains the number 9.
	5. The loop-continuation condition is checked. The condition evaluates to `true` (`intProduct` is less than or equal to 50), so the application resumes execution at the next statement.
	6. The number (currently 9) stored in `intProduct` is multiplied by 3 and the result is assigned to `intProduct`; `intProduct` now contains the number 27.
	7. The loop-continuation condition is checked. The condition evaluates to `true` (`intProduct` is less than or equal to 50), so the application resumes execution at the next statement.
	8. The number (currently 27) stored in `intProduct` is multiplied by 3 and the result is assigned to `intProduct`; `intProduct` now contains the number 81.
	9. The loop-continuation condition is checked. The condition evaluates to `false` (`intProduct` is not less than or equal to 50), so the application exits the `while` repetition statement and the application resumes execution at the first statement after the `int *= 3;` statement.

Let's use a UML activity diagram to illustrate the flow of control in the preceding `while` repetition statement. The UML activity diagram in Fig. 9.4 contains an initial state, transition arrows, a merge, a decision, two guard conditions, three notes and a final state. The oval represents the action state in which the value of `intProduct` is multiplied by 3.

The activity diagram clearly shows the repetition. The transition arrow emerging from the action state wraps back to the merge, creating a **loop**. The guard conditions are tested each time the loop iterates until the guard condition `intProduct > 50` eventually becomes true. At this point, the `while` statement is exited, and control passes to the next statement in the application following the loop.

Figure 9.4 introduces the UML's **merge symbol**. The UML represents both the merge symbol and the decision symbol as diamonds. The merge symbol joins two flows of activity into one flow of activity. In this diagram, the merge symbol joins the transitions from the initial state and the action state, so they both flow into the loop-continuation guard decision, which is the decision that determines whether the loop body statement should begin executing (or continue executing). In this case, the UML diagram enters its action state when the loop-continuation guard condition `intProduct <= 50` is true.

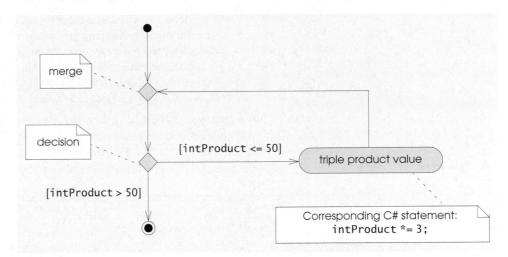

Figure 9.4 while repetition statement UML activity diagram.

Although the UML represents both the decision and the merge symbols with the diamond shape, the symbols can be distinguished by the number of "incoming" and "outgoing" transition arrows. A decision symbol has one transition arrow pointing to the diamond and two (or more) transition arrows pointing out from the diamond to indicate possible transitions from that point. In addition, each transition arrow pointing out of a decision symbol has a guard condition next to it. A merge symbol has two (or more) transition arrows pointing to the diamond and only one transition arrow pointing from the diamond, to indicate multiple activity flows merging to continue the activity.

SELF-REVIEW

1. The body of a while statement executes _____.
   a) at least once
   b) never
   c) if its condition is true
   d) if its condition is false

2. The UML represents both the merge symbol and the decision symbol as _____.
   a) rectangles with rounded sides
   b) diamonds
   c) small black circles
   d) ovals

Answers: 1) c. 2) b.

9.3 Constructing the Car Payment Calculator Application

Now that you have learned the while repetition statement, you are ready to construct the **Car Payment Calculator** application. The following pseudocode describes the basic operation of the **Car Payment Calculator** when the user clicks the **Calculate** Button:

> When the user clicks the Calculate Button:
>   Initialize the loan length to two years
>   Clear the ListBox of any previous calculation results
>   Add a header to the ListBox
>   Get the down payment from a TextBox
>   Get the sticker price from a TextBox
>   Get the interest rate from a TextBox
>   Calculate the loan amount (sticker price – down payment)
>   Calculate the monthly interest rate (interest rate / 12)

> While the loan length is less than or equal to five years
>   Convert the loan length from years to months
>   Calculate the monthly payment based on the loan amount, monthly
>   interest rate and loan length in months
>   Insert the result into the ListBox
>   Increment the loan length in years by one year

Now that you have test-driven the **Car Payment Calculator** application and studied its pseudocode representation, you will use an ACE table to help you convert the pseudocode to C#. Figure 9.5 lists the actions, controls and events that will help you complete your own version of this application.

Action/Control/Event (ACE) Table for the Car Payment Calculator

Action	Control/Class	Event
Label all the application's controls	`lblStickerPrice,` `lblDownPayment,` `lblInterest`	Application is run
	`btnCalculate`	`Click`
Initialize the loan length to two years		
Clear the ListBox of any previous calculation results	`lstPayments`	
Add a header to the ListBox	`lstPayments`	
Get the down payment from a TextBox	`txtDownPayment`	
Get the sticker price from a TextBox	`txtStickerPrice`	
Get the interest rate from a TextBox	`txtInterest`	
Calculate the loan amount		
Calculate the monthly interest rate		
While the loan length is less than or equal to five years		
Convert the loan length from years to months		
Calculate the monthly payment based on the loan amount, monthly interest rate and loan length in months	`Math`	
Insert the result into the ListBox	`lstPayments`	
Increment the loan length in years by one year		

Figure 9.5 ACE table for the **Car Payment Calculator** application.

Notice in the pseudocode that the retrieval of the user input and the calculations of the loan amount and the monthly interest rate occur before the repetition statement because they need to be performed only once. The statements that have different results in each iteration are included in the repetition statement. The repetition statement's body includes: converting the loan length from years to months, calculating the monthly payment amount, displaying the calculation's result and incrementing the loan length in years.

The application displays the calculation results in a `ListBox`. Next, you will add and customize the `ListBox` that displays the results.

*Adding a **ListBox** to the **Car Payment Calculator** Application*

1. ***Copying the template to your working directory.*** Copy the `C:\Examples\ Tutorial09\TemplateApplication\CarPaymentCalculator` directory to your `C:\SimplyCSP` directory.

(cont.)

2. ***Opening the Car Payment Calculator application's template file.*** Double click CarPaymentCalculator.sln in the CarPaymentCalculator directory to open the application in Visual Studio .NET. Open the Form in design view (Fig. 9.6). Notice that the TextBoxes for user input and the **Calculate** Button are provided to you.

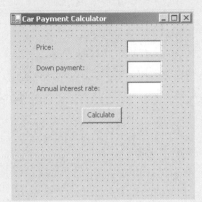

Figure 9.6   **Car Payment Calculator** application in design view.

3. ***Adding a ListBox control to the Form.*** Double click the ListBox control,

in the **Toolbox**. Change the Name property of the ListBox to lstPayments. Set the Location property to 28, 168 and the Size property to 232, 82. Figure 9.7 shows the Form with the ListBox control. In design view, the ListBox control displays the value of its Name property. This text will not appear when the application runs.

ListBox's control name
displayed in design view ————

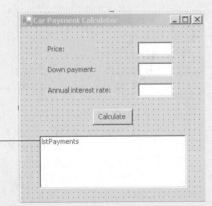

Figure 9.7   ListBox added to the **Car Payment Calculator** application's Form.

4. ***Saving the project.*** Select **File > Save All** to save your modified code.

After adding the ListBox, you must add an event handler to the application so that the application can respond to the user's clicking the **Calculate** Button. The btnCalculate_Click event handler updates the ListBox's contents. The following box describes how to add items to a ListBox and how to clear a ListBox.

Good Programming Practice

Prefix ListBox control names with lst.

GUI Design Tip

A ListBox should be large enough to display all of its contents or large enough that scrollbars can be used easily.

**Using Code to Change a
ListBox's Contents**

1. ***Rearranging and commenting the control declarations.*** In code view, locate the declaration for the `ListBox` you just created (line 29 of your code). Add a comment to describe the role of the `ListBox` in your application, as in line 30 of Fig. 9.8. Be sure to add spaces before and after each group of control declarations.

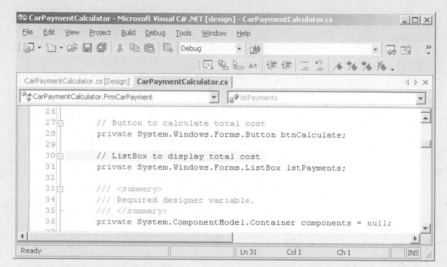

Figure 9.8 Rearranging and commenting the `ListBox` control declaration.

2. ***Adding the Calculate Button's event handler.*** In design view, double click the **Calculate** Button to generate the empty event handler `btnCalculate_Click`.

3. ***Clearing the ListBox control.*** Be sure to add the comments (lines 181 and 190) and break the header as shown in Fig. 9.9 so that the line numbers in your code match those presented in this tutorial. Then, add lines 185–186 of Fig. 9.9 to `btnCalculate_Click`. Each time users click the **Calculate** Button, any content previously displayed in the `ListBox` is removed. To remove all content from the `ListBox`, call the **Clear** method of the **Items** property (line 186). Content can be added and deleted from the `ListBox` by using its `Items` property. The `Items` property returns an object that contains a list of items displayed in the `ListBox`.

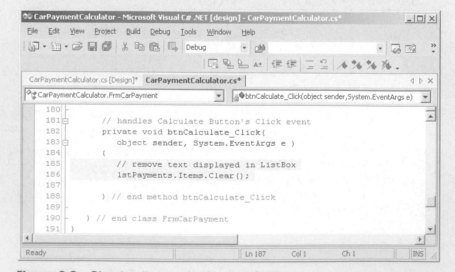

Figure 9.9 Clearing the contents of a `ListBox`.

(cont.)

4. ***Adding content to the ListBox control.*** Add lines 188–189 of Fig. 9.10 to `btnCalculate_Click`. The `ListBox` displays the number of monthly payments and the amount per payment. To clarify what information is being displayed, a line of text—called a **header**—needs to be added to the `ListBox`. The **Add** method (line 189 of Fig. 9.10) adds the header—consisting of the column headings `"Months"` and `"Monthly Payment"`—to the `ListBox`'s `Items` property.

GUI Design Tip

Use headers in a `ListBox` when you are displaying tabular data. Adding headers improves readability by indicating the information that will be displayed in the `ListBox`.

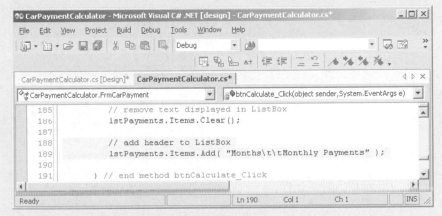

Figure 9.10 Adding a header to a `ListBox`.

In line 189, the header is created by joining the values `"Months"` and `"Monthly Payments"` with the characters `\t`. The backslash (`\`) in line 189 is called an **escape character**, and is used to display special characters. When a backslash is encountered in a string of characters, the next character is combined with the backslash to form an **escape sequence**. The escape sequence `\t` represents the tab character. It inserts a whitespace tab into the string. The application uses two tab characters of separation. Some common escape sequences are listed in Fig. 9.11.

5. ***Saving the project.*** Select **File > Save All** to save your modified code.

Escape sequence	Description
`\t`	Horizontal tab. Move the screen cursor to the next tab stop.
`\n`	Newline. Position the screen cursor at the beginning of the next line.
`\r`	Carriage return. Position the screen cursor at the beginning of the current line; do not advance to the next line.
`\\`	Backslash. Used to print a backslash character.
`\"`	Double quote. Used to print a double quote (") character.

Figure 9.11 Some common escape sequences.

Now that you have learned how to change a `ListBox`'s contents, you need to declare variables and obtain user input for the calculation. The following box shows you how to initialize the **Car Payment Calculator** application's variables. The box also guides you through converting the annual interest rate to the monthly interest rate and shows you how to calculate the amount of the loan.

Declaring Variables and Receiving User Input

1. ***Declaring variables.*** Add lines 185–192 of Fig. 9.12 to the application above the code you added in the previous box. The `intYears` and `intMonths` variables store the length of the loan in years and months. The calculation requires the length in months, but the loop-continuation condition will use the number of years. Variables `intPrice`, `intDownPayment` and `dblInterest` store the user input from the TextBoxes. Normally `intPrice` and `intDownPayment` would be represented as type `decimal`, because they represent monetary values. For simplicity in this application, we have used `int`s. Variables `decMonthlyPayment`, `intLoanAmount` and `dblMonthlyInterest` store calculation results.

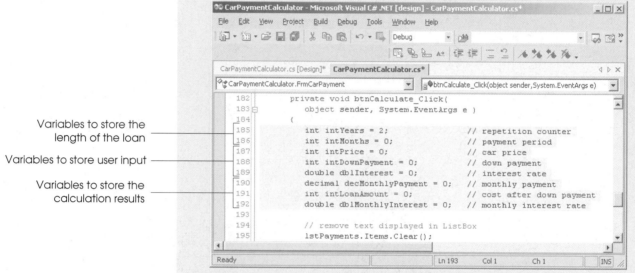

Variables to store the length of the loan

Variables to store user input

Variables to store the calculation results

Figure 9.12 Variables for the **Car Payment Calculator** application.

2. ***Retrieving user input needed for the calculation.*** Add lines 200–204 of Fig. 9.13 below the code you added in the previous box. Lines 202–204 receive the down payment (`intDownPayment`), the price (`intPrice`) and the annual interest rate (`dblInterest`) provided by the user. Notice that line 204 divides the interest rate by 100 to obtain the decimal equivalent (for example, 5% becomes `.05`)

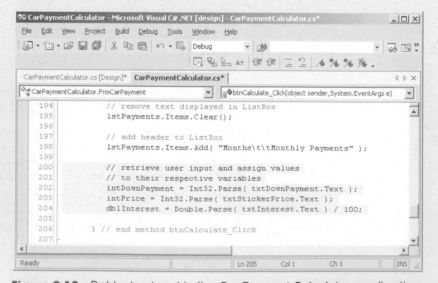

Figure 9.13 Retrieving input in the **Car Payment Calculator** application.

(cont.)

3. ***Calculating values used in the calculation.*** The application computes the amount of the loan by subtracting the down payment from the price. Add lines 206–208 of Fig. 9.14 to calculate the amount borrowed (line 207) and the monthly interest rate (line 208). Because these calculations need to occur only once, they are placed before the `while` statement. The `intLoan-Amount` and `dblMonthlyInterest` variables will be used in the calculation of monthly payments, which will be added to your application shortly.

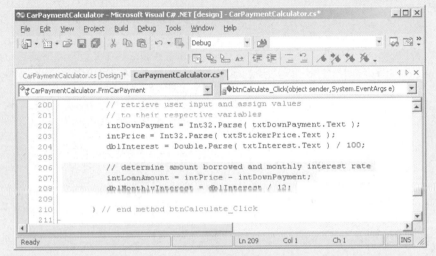

Figure 9.14   Determining the amount borrowed and monthly interest rate.

4. ***Saving the project.*** Select **File > Save All** to save your modified code.

The following box adds a repetition statement to the application to calculate the monthly payment for four loans. The repetition statement performs this calculation for loans that last two, three, four and five years.

Calculating the Monthly Payment Amounts with a `while` Repetition Statement

1. ***Setting the loop-continuation condition.*** Add lines 210–214 of Fig. 9.15 to the application below the lines that calculate the amount of the loan (`intLoanAmount`) and the monthly interest rate (`dblMonthlyInterest`).

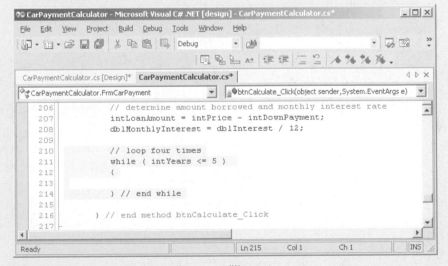

Figure 9.15   Loop-continuation condition.

(cont.)

Recall that the shortest loan in this application lasts two years, so you initialized `intYears` to 2 (line 185 of Fig. 9.12). The loop-continuation condition (`intYears <= 5`) in Fig. 9.15 specifies that the `while` statement executes while `intYears` remains less than or equal to 5. This loop is an example of **counter-controlled repetition**. This technique uses a variable called a **counter** (`intYears`) to control the number of times that a set of statements will execute. Counter-controlled repetition also is called **definite repetition**, because the number of repetitions is known before the loop begins executing. In this example, repetition terminates when the counter (`intYears`) exceeds 5.

2. *Calculating the payment period.* Add lines 213–214 of Fig. 9.16 to the `while` repetition statement to calculate the number of payments (that is, the length of the loan in months). The number of months changes with each iteration of the loop, and the calculation result changes as the length of the payment period changes. The `intMonths` variable will have the values 24, 36, 48 and 60 on successive iterations of the loop.

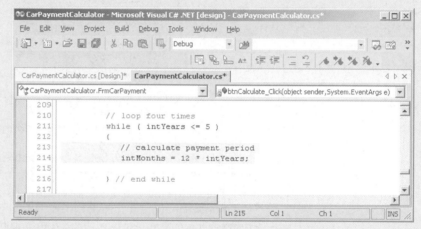

Figure 9.16 Converting the loan duration from years to months.

3. *Computing the monthly payment.* Add lines 216–222 of Fig. 9.17 to the `while` repetition statement. Lines 218–222 use a complex mathematical formula to calculate the user's monthly payment, given a loan amount (`intLoanAmount`), a constant interest rate (`dblMonthlyInterest`) and a given time period (`intMonths`).

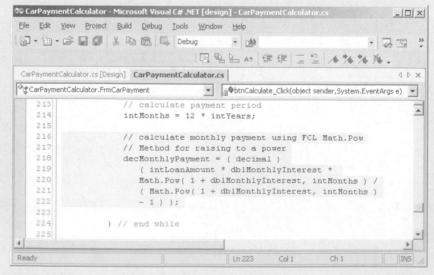

Figure 9.17 Calculating the monthly payment.

(cont.)

The **Math.Pow** method raises a number to a power. Line 220 and line 221 each pass to Math.Pow the value 1 + dblMonthlyInterest as the base and the value intMonths as the power, or exponent. The return value of Math.Pow is a double. Because monetary amounts are stored in decimal variables, a cast operator converts the result of the formula from the double type to the decimal type and assigns this value to decMonthlyPayment.

4. *Displaying the monthly payment amount.* Add lines 224–226 of Fig. 9.18 to the application. The number of monthly payments and the monthly payment amounts are displayed beneath the header. To add this content to the List-Box, call the Add method (lines 225–226). Line 226 uses the String.Format method to display decMonthlyPayment in currency format. The plus sign (+) in line 225 is called the **string-concatenation operator**. This operator combines (or concatenates) its two operands into one value. Lines 225–226 concatenate the value of intMonths with two tab characters and with the formatted value of decMonthlyPayment. Notice that the two tab characters ensure that the monthly payment amount is placed in the second column. The space provided by the extra tab characters makes the application output more readable.

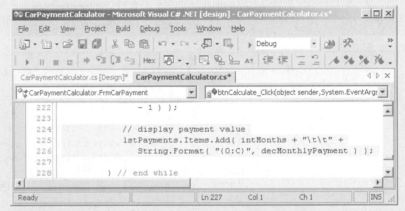

Figure 9.18   Displaying the number of months and the amount of each monthly payment.

5. *Incrementing the counter variable.* Add line 228 of Fig. 9.19 before the closing right brace of the repetition statement. Line 228 increments the counter variable (intYears) by 1 using the ++ operator. The intYears variable will be incremented until it equals 6. Then, the loop-continuation condition (intYears <= 5) will evaluate to false and the repetition will end.

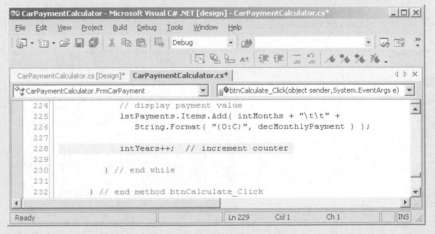

Figure 9.19   Incrementing the counter.

(cont.)

6. ***Running the application.*** Select **Debug > Start** to run your application. The application should calculate and display monthly payments. Enter values for a car's price, down payment and annual interest rate and click the **Calculate** **Button** to verify that the application is working correctly.

7. ***Closing the application.*** Close your running application by clicking its close box.

8. ***Closing the IDE.*** Close Visual Studio .NET by clicking its close box.

Figure 9.20 presents the source code for the **Car Payment Calculator** application. The lines of code that contain new programming concepts that you learned in this tutorial are highlighted.

```
1   using System;
2   using System.Drawing;
3   using System.Collections;
4   using System.ComponentModel;
5   using System.Windows.Forms;
6   using System.Data;
7
8   namespace CarPaymentCalculator
9   {
10     /// <summary>
11     /// Summary description for FrmCarPayment.
12     /// </summary>
13     public class FrmCarPayment : System.Windows.Forms.Form
14     {
15        // Label and TextBox for sticker price
16        private System.Windows.Forms.Label lblStickerPrice;
17        private System.Windows.Forms.TextBox txtStickerPrice;
18
19        // Label and TextBox for down payment
20        private System.Windows.Forms.Label lblDownPayment;
21        private System.Windows.Forms.TextBox txtDownPayment;
22
23        // Label and textbox for interest rate
24        private System.Windows.Forms.TextBox txtInterest;
25        private System.Windows.Forms.Label lblInterest;
26
27        // Button to calculate total cost
28        private System.Windows.Forms.Button btnCalculate;
29
30        // ListBox to display total cost
31        private System.Windows.Forms.ListBox lstPayments;
32
33        /// <summary>
34        /// Required designer variable.
35        /// </summary>
36        private System.ComponentModel.Container components = null;
37
38        public FrmCarPayment()
39        {
40           //
41           // Required for Windows Form Designer support
42           //
43           InitializeComponent();
44           //
```

Declaration for a ListBox control → *(line 31)*

Figure 9.20 **Car Payment Calculator** application code. (Part 1 of 3.)

```
45              // TODO: Add any constructor code after InitializeComponent
46              // call
47              //
48          }
49
50          /// <summary>
51          /// Clean up any resources being used.
52          /// </summary>
53          protected override void Dispose( bool disposing )
54          {
55              if( disposing )
56              {
57                  if (components != null)
58                  {
59                      components.Dispose();
60                  }
61              }
62              base.Dispose( disposing );
63          }
64
65          // Windows Form Designer generated code
66
67          /// <summary>
68          /// The main entry point for the application.
69          /// </summary>
70          [STAThread]
71          static void Main()
72          {
73              Application.Run( new FrmCarPayment() );
74          }
75
76          // handles Calculate Button's Click event
77          private void btnCalculate_Click(
78              object sender, System.EventArgs e )
79          {
80              int intYears = 2;                  // repetition counter
81              int intMonths = 0;                 // payment period
82              int intPrice = 0;                  // car price
83              int intDownPayment = 0;            // down payment
84              double dblInterest = 0;            // interest rate
85              decimal decMonthlyPayment = 0;     // monthly payment
86              int intLoanAmount = 0;             // cost after down payment
87              double dblMonthlyInterest = 0;     // monthly interest rate
88
89              // remove text displayed in ListBox
90              lstPayments.Items.Clear();
91
92              // add header to ListBox
93              lstPayments.Items.Add( "Months\t\tMonthly Payments" );
94
95              // retrieve user input and assign values
96              // to their respective variables
97              intDownPayment = Int32.Parse( txtDownPayment.Text );
98              intPrice = Int32.Parse( txtStickerPrice.Text );
99              dblInterest = Double.Parse( txtInterest.Text ) / 100;
100
101             // determine amount borrowed and monthly interest rate
102             intLoanAmount = intPrice - intDownPayment;
```

Using the **Clear** method of property **Items** of a **ListBox** *(points to line 90)*

Using the **Add** method of property **Items** of a **ListBox** *(points to line 93)*

Figure 9.20 Car Payment Calculator application code. (Part 2 of 3.)

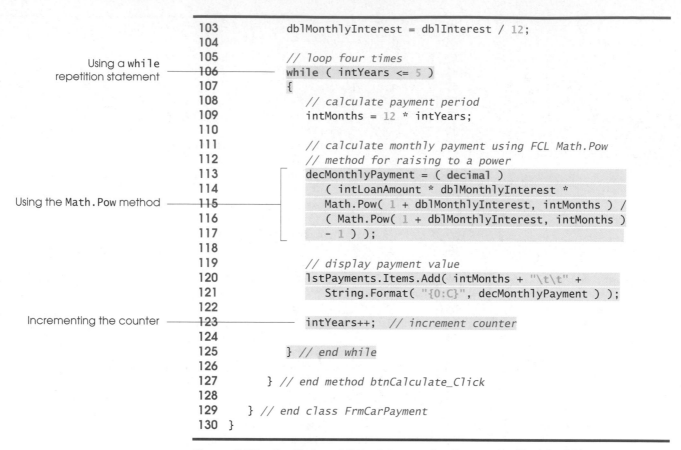

```
103         dblMonthlyInterest = dblInterest / 12;
104
105         // loop four times
106         while ( intYears <= 5 )
107         {
108             // calculate payment period
109             intMonths = 12 * intYears;
110
111             // calculate monthly payment using FCL Math.Pow
112             // method for raising to a power
113             decMonthlyPayment = ( decimal )
114                 ( intLoanAmount * dblMonthlyInterest *
115                 Math.Pow( 1 + dblMonthlyInterest, intMonths ) /
116                 ( Math.Pow( 1 + dblMonthlyInterest, intMonths )
117                 - 1 ) );
118
119             // display payment value
120             lstPayments.Items.Add( intMonths + "\t\t" +
121                 String.Format( "{0:C}", decMonthlyPayment ) );
122
123             intYears++;   // increment counter
124
125         } // end while
126
127     } // end method btnCalculate_Click
128
129     } // end class FrmCarPayment
130 }
```

Using a `while` repetition statement — line 106

Using the `Math.Pow` method — line 115

Incrementing the counter — line 123

Figure 9.20   Car Payment Calculator application code. (Part 3 of 3.)

SELF-REVIEW   1. Counter-controlled repetition is also called _____ because the number of repetitions
is known before the loop begins executing.

    a) definite repetition   b) known repetition

    c) sequential repetition   d) counter repetition

2. The line of text that is added to a `ListBox` to clarify the information that will be displayed
is called a _____.

    a) title   b) starter

    c) header   d) clarifier

Answers: 1) a. 2) c.

9.4 Wrap-Up

In this tutorial, you began using repetition statements. You used the `while` statement to repeat actions in an application, depending on a loop-continuation condition. The `while` repetition statement executes as long as its loop-continuation condition is `true`. When the loop-continuation condition becomes `false`, the repetition terminates. An infinite loop occurs if this condition never becomes `false`.

You learned about counter-controlled repetition, in which a repetition statement "knows" the number of times it will iterate because a variable known as a counter precisely counts the number of iterations. You used a repetition statement to develop a **Car Payment Calculator** application in which you calculated the monthly payments for a given loan amount and a given interest rate for loan durations of two, three, four and five years.

In the **Car Payment Calculator** application, you used the `ListBox` control to display several payment options on a car loan. You learned about the `ListBox` control, which is used to maintain a list of items. Items can be added and removed from the `ListBox` programmatically. Values are added to a `ListBox` control by invoking the `Add` method of the `ListBox` control's `Items` property. The `Items` property returns an object that contains all the values displayed in the `ListBox`.

In the next tutorial, you will learn another repetition statement and you will continue exploring counter-controlled repetition. The **Car Payment Calculator** application demonstrated one common use of repetition statements—performing a calculation for several different values. The next application introduces another common application of repetition statements—summing a series of numbers.

SKILLS SUMMARY

Displaying Values in a `ListBox`

- Use `Items` property of the `ListBox` control to return an object that contains the values to be displayed in a `ListBox`.
- Invoke the `Add` method to add values to the `Items` property.

Clearing a `ListBox`'s Contents

- Use the `Clear` method of the `Items`'s property to delete (clear) all the values in the `ListBox`.

Repeating Actions in an Application

- Use a repetition statement that depends on the true or false value of a loop-continuation condition.

Executing a Repetition Statement for a Known Number of Repetitions

- Use counter-controlled repetition with a counter variable to determine the number of times that a set of statements will execute.

Using the `while` Repetition Statement

- This repetition statement executes while the loop-continuation condition is `true`.
- An infinite loop occurs if the condition never becomes `false`.

KEY TERMS

Add method of the `Items` control property—Adds an item to a `ListBox` control.

Clear method of the `Items` control property—Deletes all the values in a `ListBox`'s control.

counter—A variable often used to determine the number of times a block of statements in a loop will execute.

counter-controlled repetition—A technique (also called definite repetition) that uses a counter variable to determine the number of times that a block of statements will execute.

definite repetition—*See* counter-controlled repetition.

escape character—The backslash (\) character that is used to form escape sequences.

escape sequence—The backslash (\) and the character next to it, when used within a `string`, represent a special character, such as a newline (\n) or a tab (\t).

header—A line of text in that clarifies what information is being displayed.

infinite loop—An error in which a repetition statement never terminates.

`Items` property of the `ListBox` control—Returns an object containing all the values in the `ListBox`.

`ListBox` control—Allows the user to view items in a list. Items can be added to or removed from the list programmatically.

loop—Another name for a repetition statement.

loop-continuation condition—In a repetition statement (such as a `while` statement), enables repetition to continue while the condition is `true` and that causes repetition to terminate when the condition becomes `false`.

merge symbol—In the UML, this symbol joins two flows of activity into one flow of activity.

`Math.Pow` method—Raises a given base to a given exponent and returns the result as a `double` value.

string-concatenation operator (+)—Combines (or concatenates) its two operands into one string of characters.

`while` repetition statement—A control statement that executes a set of body statements while its loop-continuation condition is `true`.

GUI DESIGN GUIDELINES	**ListBox**

- A `ListBox` should be large enough to display all of its contents or large enough that scrollbars may be used easily.
- Use headers in a `ListBox` when you are displaying tabular data. Adding headers improves readability by indicating the information that will be displayed in the `ListBox`.

CONTROLS, EVENTS, PROPERTIES & METHODS	**Math** The `Math` class performs mathematical operations.

- *Method*

  Pow—Raises a given base (first argument) to a given exponent (second argument) and returns the result as a `double`.

ListBox `ListBox` This control allows the user to view and select from items in a list.

- *In action*

Months	Monthly Payments
24	$490.50
36	$339.06
48	$263.55
60	$218.41

- *Properties*

  `Items`—Returns an object that contains the items displayed in the `ListBox`.

  `Location`—Specifies the location of the `ListBox` on the `Form`.

  `Name`—Specifies the name used to access the properties of the `ListBox` programatically. The name should be prefixed with `lst`.

  `Size`—Specifies the height and width (in pixels) of the `ListBox`.

- *Methods*

  `Items.Add`—Adds an item to the `Items` property.

  `Items.Clear`—Deletes all the values in the `ListBox`'s `Items` property.

MULTIPLE-CHOICE QUESTIONS	**9.1** If a `while` statement's loop-continuation condition is initially false, how many times will the body execute?

    a) 0   b) 1

    c) infinite   d) There is no way to know in advance.

9.2 The _____ statement executes until its loop-continuation condition becomes `false`.

    a) `while`   b) `until`

    c) `loop`   d) `whileTrue`

9.3 A(n) _____ loop occurs when a condition in a `while` loop never becomes `false`.

    a) infinite   b) undefined

    c) nested   d) indefinite

9.4 A _____ is a variable that helps control the number of times that a set of statements will execute.

    a) repeater   b) counter

    c) loop   d) repetition control statement

9.5 The _____ control allows users to add and view items in a list.

   a) `ListItems`
               b) `SelectBox`

   c) `ListBox`
               d) `ViewBox`

9.6 In a UML activity diagram, a(n) _____ symbol joins two flows of activity into one flow of activity.

   a) merge
               b) combine

   c) action state
               d) decision

9.7 The _____ property returns an object containing all the values in a `ListBox`.

   a) `All`
               b) `List`

   c) `ListItemValues`
               d) `Items`

9.8 The _____ method deletes all the values in a `ListBox`.

   a) `Remove`
               b) `Delete`

   c) `Clear`
               d) `Del`

9.9 The _____ method of property `Items` adds an item to a `ListBox`.

   a) `Include`
               b) `Append`

   c) `Add`
               d) `Insert`

9.10 The _____ method raises a number to an exponent.

   a) `Math.Exp`
               b) `Math.Exponent`

   c) `Math.Power`
               d) `Math.Pow`

EXERCISES

9.11 *(Table of Powers Application)* Write an application that displays a table of numbers from 1 to an upper limit, along with each number's squared value (for example, the number n to the power 2, or $n \wedge 2$) and cubed value (the number n to the power 3, or $n \wedge 3$). The users should specify the upper limit, and the results should be displayed in a `ListBox`, as in Fig. 9.21.

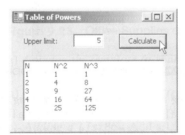

Figure 9.21   **Table of Powers** application.

a) *Copying the template to your working directory.* Copy the directory `C:\Examples\Tutorial09\Exercises\TableOfPowers` to your `C:\SimplyCSP` directory.

b) *Opening the application's template file.* Double click `TableOfPowers.sln` in the `TableOfPowers` directory to open the application.

c) *Adding a ListBox.* Add a `ListBox` to the application, as shown in Fig. 9.21. Name the `ListBox` `lstResults`. Rearrange and comment the new control declaration appropriately.

d) *Adding the Upper limit: TextBox event handler.* Double click the **Upper limit:** Text-Box to generate an event handler for this TextBox's TextChanged event. In this event handler, clear the `ListBox`.

e) *Adding the Calculate Button event handler.* Double click the **Calculate** Button to generate the empty event handler `btnCalculate_Click`. Add the code specified by the remaining steps to this event handler.

f) *Clearing the ListBox.* Use the `Clear` method on the `Items` property to clear the `ListBox` from any previous data.

What does this code do? ▶   **9.14** What value does `intMysteryValue` contain when the following code is completed?

```
1   int intX = 1;
2   int intMysteryValue = 1;
3
4   while ( intX < 6 )
5   {
6       intMysteryValue *= intX;
7       intX++;
8   }
```

What's wrong with this code? ▶   **9.15** Find the error(s) in the following code:

a) Assume that the `intX` variable is declared and initialized to 1. The loop should total the numbers from 1 to 10.

```
1   while ( !( intX <= 10 ) )
2   {
3       intTotal += intX;
4       intX++;
5   }
```

b) Assume that the `intCounter` variable is declared and initialized to 1. The loop should sum the numbers from 1 to 100.

```
1   int intCounter = 1;
2
3   while ( intCounter <= 100 )
4   {
5       intTotal += intCounter;
6   }
7
8   intCounter++;
```

c) Assume that the `intCounter` variable is declared and initialized to 1000. The loop should iterate from 1000 to 1.

```
1   intCounter = 1000;
2
3   while ( intCounter > 0 )
4   {
5       lblDisplay.Text = Convert.ToString( intCounter );
6       intCounter++;
7   }
```

d) Assume that the `intCounter` variable is declared and initialized to 1. The loop should execute five times, adding the numbers 1–5 to a `ListBox`.

```
1   intCounter = 1;
2
3   while ( intCounter < 5 )
4   {
5       lstNumbers.Items.Add( intCounter );
6       intCounter++;
7   }
```

Using the Debugger ▶ **9.16** (*Odd Numbers Application*) The **Odd Numbers** application should display all of the odd integers between one and the number input by the user. Copy the directory `C:\Examples\Tutorial09\Exercises\Debugger\OddNumbers` to your `C:\SimplyCSP` directory. Run the application. Notice that, after you enter a value into the **Upper limit:** TextBox and click the **View** Button, an infinite loop occurs (your application will not respond). Use the debugger to find and fix the error(s) in the application. Figure 9.24 displays the correct output for the application.

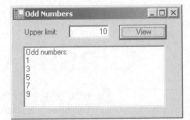

Figure 9.24   Correct output for the **Odd Numbers** application.

Programming Challenge ▶ **9.17** (*To Do List Application*) Use a ListBox as a to do list. Enter each item in a TextBox, and add it to the ListBox by clicking a Button. The item should be displayed in a numbered list as in Fig. 9.25. To do this, we introduce the Count method, which returns the number of items in a ListBox's Items property. The following is a sample call to assign the number of items displayed in the lstSample ListBox to an int variable:

```
intCount = lstSample.Items.Count();
```

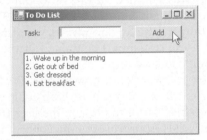

Figure 9.25   **To Do List** application.

10

TUTORIAL

Class Average Application

Introducing the do...while Repetition Statement

Objectives

In this tutorial, you will learn to:
- Use the **do...while** statement.
- Understand counter-controlled repetition.
- Transfer the focus to a control.
- Enable and disable **Buttons**.

Outline

10.1 Test-Driving the **Class Average** Application

10.2 **do...while** Repetition Statement

10.3 Creating the **Class Average** Application

10.4 Wrap-Up

T his tutorial continues our discussion of repetition statements that we began in Tutorial 9, focusing on a **Class Average** application. In the previous tutorial, we examined the while repetition statement, which tests its loop-continuation condition before each iteration. This tutorial introduces an additional repetition statement, do...while, which performs its test after each iteration. As a result, the statements contained in the body of this repetition statement are performed at least once.

You will also learn how to disable and enable controls on a Form. When a control, such as a Button, is disabled, it will no longer respond to the user. You will use this feature to prevent the user from causing errors in your applications. This tutorial also introduces the concept of transferring the focus of the application to a control. Proper use of focus makes an application easier to use.

10.1 Test-Driving the Class Average Application

This application must meet the following requirements:

Application Requirements

A teacher regularly issues quizzes to a class of ten students. The grades on these quizzes are integers in the range 0 to 100 (0 and 100 are each valid grades). The teacher would like you to develop an application that computes the class average for a quiz.

The class average is equal to the sum of the grades divided by the number of students who took the quiz. The algorithm for solving this problem on a computer must input each of the grades, total the grades, perform the averaging calculation and display the result. You begin by test-driving the completed application. Then, you will learn the additional C# technologies you will need to create your own version of this application.

Test-Driving the Class Average Application

1. *Opening the completed application.* Open the `C:\Examples\ Tutorial10\CompletedApplication\ClassAverage` directory to locate the **Class Average** application. Double click `ClassAverage.sln` to open the application in Visual Studio .NET.

2. *Running the Class Average application.* Select **Debug > Start** to run the application (Fig. 10.1).

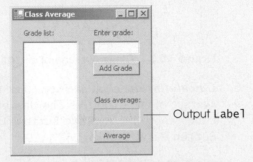

Figure 10.1   **Class Average** application's **Form** in run mode.

3. *Entering quiz grades.* Enter 85 as the first quiz grade in the **Enter grade:** TextBox, then click the **Add Grade** Button. The grade entered will display in the ListBox as in Fig. 10.2. Notice that, after you click the **Add Grade** Button, the cursor appears in the **Enter grade:** TextBox. When a control is selected (for example, the **Enter grade:** TextBox), it is said to have the **focus** of the application. You will learn to set the focus as you build this tutorial's application. As a result of the application's focus being transferred to the **Enter grade:** TextBox, you can type another grade without navigating to the TextBox with the mouse or the *Tab* key. Transferring the focus to a particular control tells the user what information the application expects next. [*Note*: If you click the **Average** Button before 10 grades have been input, an error occurs. In the dialog that displays, click **Continue** to return to design view. Repeat *Step 2* and *Step 3*. You will fix this problem in the exercises at the end of this tutorial.]

Figure 10.2   Entering quiz grades in the **Class Average** application.

4. *Repeat* **Step 3** *nine more times.* Enter nine other grades between 0 and 100, and click the **Add Grade** Button after each entry. After 10 grades are displayed in the **Grade list:** ListBox, the **Add Grade** Button is disabled (Fig. 10.3). That is, its color is gray (including the Button's text), and clicking the Button does not invoke its event handler.

(cont.)

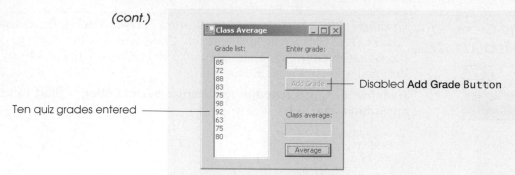

Figure 10.3   **Class Average** application after 10 grades have been input.

5. ***Calculating the class average.*** Click the **Average** Button to calculate the average of the 10 quizzes. The class average will be displayed in an output Label above the **Average** Button (Fig. 10.4). Notice that the **Add Grade** Button is now enabled.

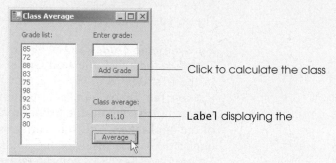

Figure 10.4   Displaying the class average.

6. ***Entering another set of grades.*** You can calculate the class average for another set of 10 grades without restarting the application. Enter a grade in the TextBox, then click the **Add Grade** Button. Notice that the **Grade list:** ListBox and the **Class average:** field are cleared when you start entering another set of grades (Fig. 10.5).

Figure 10.5   Entering a new set of grades.

7. ***Closing the application.*** Close your running application by clicking its close box.

8. ***Closing the IDE.*** Close Visual Studio .NET by clicking its close box.

10.2 do...while Repetition Statement

The **do...while** repetition statement is similar to the while statement; both statements iterate while their loop-continuation conditions are true. In the while statement, the loop-continuation condition is tested at the beginning of the loop, before

**Common
Programming Error**

An infinite loop occurs when the loop-continuation condition in a do...while statement never becomes false.

the body of the loop is performed. The do...while statement performs the loop-continuation condition *after* the loop body is performed. Therefore, in a do...while statement, the loop body always executes at least once. Recall that a while executes only if its loop-continuation condition evaluates to true. When a do...while statement terminates, execution continues with the statement after the while clause.

To illustrate the do...while repetition style, consider the example of packing a suitcase: Before you begin packing, the suitcase is empty. You place an item in the suitcase, then determine whether the suitcase is full. As long as the suitcase is not full, you continue to put items in the suitcase. As an example of a do...while statement, let's look at the following application segment designed to display the numbers 1 through 3 in a ListBox:

```
int intCounter = 1;

do
{
    lstDisplay.Items.Add( intCounter )
    intCounter++;
} while ( intCounter <= 3 );
```

The application segment initializes the counter intCounter to 1. The loop-continuation condition in the do...while statement is intCounter <= 3. While the loop-continuation condition is true, the do...while statement executes. When the loop-continuation condition becomes false (that is, when intCounter is greater than 3), the do...while statement finishes executing and lstDisplay contains the numbers 1 through 3. Braces are used to execute multiple statements each time through the loop. For simplicity, we always use braces in our do...while statements. Note the semicolon (;) following the loop-continuation condition. The semicolon is used to end the do...while statement. No such semicolon is necessary in a while statement. The following box describes each step as the above repetition statement executes.

***Executing the
do...while Repetition
Statement***

1. The application declares the intCounter variable and sets its value to 1.

2. The application enters the do...while repetition statement.

3. The number (currently 1) stored in intCounter is Added to the lstDisplay ListBox's Items property.

4. The value of intCounter is increased by 1; intCounter now contains the number 2.

5. The loop-continuation condition is checked. The condition evaluates to true (intCounter is less than or equal to 3), so the application resumes execution at the first statement after the do statement.

6. The number (currently 2) stored in intCounter is Added to the lstDisplay ListBox's Items property.

7. The value of intCounter is increased by 1; intCounter now contains the number 3.

8. The loop-continuation condition is checked. The condition evaluates to true (intCounter is less than or equal to 3), so the application resumes execution at the first statement after the do statement.

9. The number (currently 3) stored in intCounter is Added to the lstDisplay ListBox's Items property.

10. The value of intCounter is increased by 1; intCounter now contains the number 4.

11. The loop-continuation condition is checked. The condition evaluates to false (intCounter is not less than or equal to 3), so the application exits the do...while repetition statement.

Notice that, if you mistyped the loop-continuation condition as intCounter < 3 or intCounter <= 2, the ListBox would display only 1 and 2. Including an incorrect relational operator (such as the less than sign in intCounter < 3) or an incorrect final value for a loop counter (such as the 2 in intCounter <= 2) in the condition of any repetition statement can cause **off-by-one errors**, which occur when a loop executes for one more or one fewer iterations than is necessary.

Figure 10.6 illustrates the UML activity diagram for the preceding do...while statement. This diagram makes it clear that the loop-continuation guard condition ([intCounter <= 3]) does not evaluate until after the loop performs the action state at least once. Recall that action states can include one or more C# statements executed sequentially, as in the preceding example. When you use a do...while repetition statement in building an application, provide the appropriate action state and the guard conditions for your application.

Error-Prevention Tip

Including a final value in the condition of a repetition statement (and choosing the appropriate relational operator) can reduce the occurrence of off-by-one errors. For example, in a while statement used to print the values 1–10, the loop-continuation condition should be intCounter <= 10, rather than intCounter < 10 (which is an off-by-one error) or intCounter < 11 (which is correct, but less clear).

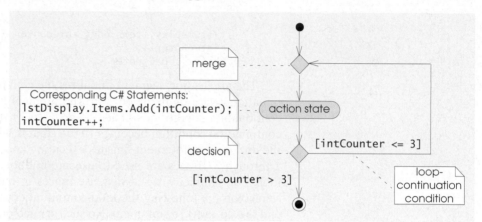

Figure 10.6 do...while repetition statement UML activity diagram.

SELF-REVIEW

1. A _____ must immediately follow the loop-continuation condition in a do...while statement.

    a) colon

    b) left brace

    c) semicolon

    d) right brace

2. An infinite loop occurs when the loop-continuation condition in a while or do...while statement _____.

    a) never becomes true

    b) never becomes false

    c) is false

    d) is tested repeatedly

Answers: 1) c. 2) b.

10.3 Creating the Class Average Application

Now that you have learned the do...while repetition statement, you can begin to develop the **Class Average** application. First, you will use pseudocode to list the actions to be executed and to specify the order of execution. You will use counter-controlled repetition to input the grades one at a time. Recall that this technique uses a variable called a counter to determine the number of times a set of statements executes. In this example, repetition terminates when the counter exceeds 10 because we are assuming, for simplicity, that the user will only enter 10 grades. The following pseudocode describes the basic operation of the **Class Average** application:

When the user clicks the Add Grade Button:

> If an average has already been calculated for a set of grades
> > Clear the output Label and the ListBox
>
> Retrieve the grade entered by the user in the Enter grade: TextBox
> Display the grade in the ListBox
> Clear the Enter grade: TextBox
> Transfer the focus to the Enter grade: TextBox
>
> If the user has entered 10 grades
> > Disable the Add Grade Button
> > Transfer the focus to the Average Button

When the user clicks the Average Button:
> Set the total to zero
> Set the grade counter to zero
>
> Do
> > Read the next grade in the ListBox
> > Add the grade to the total
> > Add one to the grade counter
> While the grade counter is less than 10
>
> Calculate the class average by dividing the total by 10
> Display the class average
> Enable the Add Grade Button
> Transfer the focus to the Enter grade: TextBox

Now that you have test-driven the **Class Average** application and studied its pseudocode representation, you will use an ACE table to help you convert the pseudocode to C#. Figure 10.7 lists the actions, controls and events that will help you complete your own version of this application.

Action/Control/Event
Table for the Class
Average Application

Event	Control	Event
Label all the application's controls	lblPrompt, lblGradeList, lblDescribeOutput	Application is run
	btnAdd	Click
If an average has already been calculated for a set of grades Clear the output Label and the ListBox	lblOutput, lstGrades	
Retrieve the grade entered by the user in the Enter grade: TextBox	txtInput	
Display the grade in the ListBox	lstGrades	
Clear the Enter grade: TextBox	txtInput	
Transfer the focus to the Enter grade: TextBox	txtInput	
If the user has entered 10 grades Disable the Add Grade Button	lstGrades, btnAdd	
Transfer the focus to the Average Button	btnAverage	

Figure 10.7   ACE table for the **Class Average** application. (Part 1 of 2.)

Event	Control	Event
	`btnAverage`	`Click`
Set the total to zero		
Set the grade counter to zero		
Do		
Read the next grade in the ListBox	`lstGrades`	
Add the grade to the total		
Add one to the grade counter		
While the grade counter is less than 10		
Calculate the class average by dividing the total by 10		
Display the class average	`lblOutput`	
Enable the Add Grade Button	`btnzAdd`	
Transfer the focus to the Enter grade: TextBox	`txtInput`	

Figure 10.7   ACE table for the **Class Average** application. (Part 2 of 2.)

We label the application's GUI, using the `lblPrompt`, `lblDescribeOutput` and `lblGradeList` Labels. The user enters grades in the `txtInput` TextBox and clicks the `btnAdd` Button. The `Click` event then Adds the value that the user entered in the `txtInput` TextBox to the ListBox, using the `lstGrades.Items.Add` method. When the user has entered 10 grades and clicked the `btnAverage` Button, the application will retrieve each value from the ListBox, add it to the total and compute the class average by dividing by 10. The class average then will be displayed in the `lblOutput` Label.

Now that we have formulated an algorithm for solving the **Class Average** problem, we can begin adding functionality to the template application. To display in the **Grade list:** ListBox a grade entered in the **Enter grade:** TextBox, the user clicks the **Add Grade** Button. If the application is already displaying grades in the **Grade list:** ListBox and the class average in the **Class average:** Label, the values are first cleared. The following box guides you through adding this functionality to the **Add Grade** Button's event handler.

Entering Grades in the Class Average Application	1. ***Copying the template to your working directory***. Copy the `C:\Examples\Tutorial10\TemplateApplication\ClassAverage` directory to your `C:\SimplyCSP` directory. 2. ***Opening the Class Average template application***. Double click `ClassAverage.sln` in the `ClassAverage` directory to open the application in Visual Studio .NET. Double click `ClassAverage.cs` in the **Solution Explorer** to display the Form (Fig. 10.8).

Figure 10.8   **Class Average** application's Form in design view.

(cont.)

3. **Adding an event handler for the Add Grade Button.** Each time users enter grades in the **Class Average** application, they must click the **Add Grade** Button. Double click the **Add Grade** Button to create the btnAdd_Click event handler.

4. **Clearing the ListBox and the Class average: Label of any output from a previous calculation.** Add lines 182–187 of Fig. 10.9 to the btnAdd_Click event handler. Be sure to add the comments and break the header as shown in Fig. 10.9 so that the line numbers in your code match those presented in this tutorial. To determine whether there was a previous calculation, test whether lblOutput displays any text by comparing the Text property's value to the empty string (line 183). If the lblOutput Label displays the result of a previous calculation, set its Text property to the empty string (line 185). Line 186 clears the grades from the ListBox.

Clearing the grade list and class average

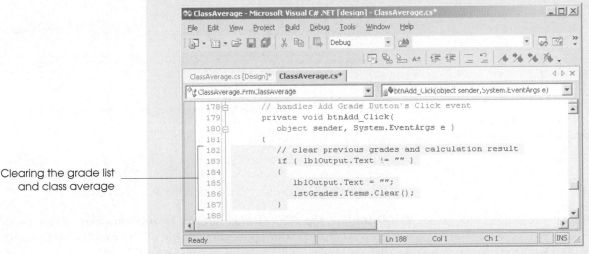

Figure 10.9 Clearing the ListBox and output Label after a calculation.

5. **Displaying each grade in the ListBox control.** Add lines 189–191 of Fig. 10.10 to the btnAdd_Click event handler below the if statement. Line 190 Adds the grade entered in txtInput to ListBox lstGrades's Items property. The grade is displayed in the ListBox.

Adding a numeric grade to the ListBox and clearing the user input from the TextBox

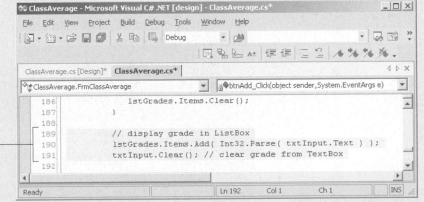

Figure 10.10 Adding the grade input to the ListBox and clearing the **Enter grade:** TextBox.

6. **Preparing for the next grade to be entered.** The **Clear** method (line 191 of Fig. 10.10) deletes the grade from the TextBox to prepare the application for the next grade to be entered.

7. **Saving the project.** Select **File > Save All** to save your modified code.

You have added the code to display the grade entered in the **Enter grade:** TextBox in the ListBox when the user clicks the **Add Grade** Button. The following box shows you how to transfer the focus to the TextBox for the next grade entry after the user clicks the **Add Grade** Button. The box also shows you how to disable the **Add Grade** Button after 10 grades have been entered, because its functionality is no longer needed.

Transferring the Focus to a Control and Disabling a Button

1. ***Transferring the focus to a control.*** Add line 192 (Fig. 10.11) to event handler btnAdd_Click. Line 192 calls txtInput's **Focus** method to place the cursor in the TextBox for the next grade input. This process is called **transferring the focus**. Here the focus is transferred from the Button to the TextBox.

Transferring the focus of the application to the TextBox

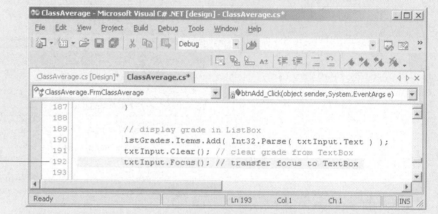

Figure 10.11 Transferring the focus to the **TextBox** control.

2. ***Disabling the Add Grade Button to prohibit users from entering more than 10 grades.*** Your application should accept exactly 10 grades. If the number of grades already entered by the user is equal to 10, the application should prevent the user from entering more grades. Add lines 194–199 of Fig. 10.12 to the btnAdd_Click event handler. Line 195 determines whether 10 grades have been entered, using the == comparison operator. The **Count** property of Items returns the number of items displayed in the **Grade list:** ListBox. If 10 grades have been entered, line 197 disables the btnAdd Button by setting its **Enabled** property to false. Clicking the disabled **Add Grade** Button will not cause the btnAdd_Click event handler to execute. Add the comment on line 201 after you have completed the next box (as we will be adding another event handler shortly).

GUI Design Tip

Disable **Buttons** when their function should not be available to the user.

Disabling the **Add grade** Button and transferring the focus to the **Average** Button

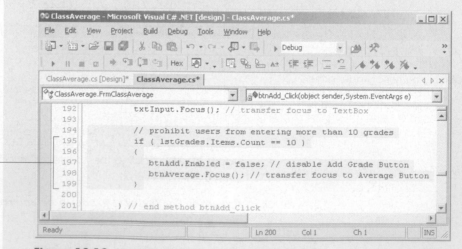

Figure 10.12 Application accepts only 10 grades.

(cont.)

3. ***Transferring the focus to the Average Button after 10 grades have been entered.*** After 10 grades have been entered, it does not make sense for the application to transfer the focus to the TextBox. Instead, line 198 invokes the Focus method to transfer the focus to the **Average** Button. This way, you can press *Enter* to invoke the **Average** Button's event handler, without navigating to the Button or using the mouse pointer.

4. ***Saving the project.*** Select **File > Save All** to save your modified code.

After 10 grades have been entered and displayed in the ListBox, the **Add Grade** Button's event handler transfers the focus to the **Average** Button. When the user clicks the **Average** Button, the application calculates and displays the average of the 10 grades. The following box shows you how to sum the grades with a do…while repetition statement before the calculating of the average. The box also covers displaying the result in the **Class average:** Label.

Calculating the Class Average

1. ***Adding an event handler for the Average Button.*** Switch to design view, then double click the **Average** Button to generate event handler btnAverage_Click.

2. ***Initializing variables used in the class-average calculation.*** Add lines 208–212 of Fig. 10.13 to the btnAverage_Click event handler. Be sure to add the comments and break the header as shown in Fig. 10.13 so that the line numbers in your code match those presented in this tutorial. Line 209 declares int variable intTotal. You will use intTotal to calculate the sum of 10 grades (you will need this sum later when you calculate the average grade). Line 210 declares the counter (intGradeCounter) and initializes it to 0. It is important for variables used as totals and counters to have appropriate initial values before they are used. The intGrade variable (line 211) temporarily stores each grade read from the ListBox. Although the grades entered are ints, the result of calculating the average can be a floating-point value (such as the 81.1 result in Fig. 10.4); therefore, you declare double variable dblAverage (line 212) to store the class average.

Initializing variables ————

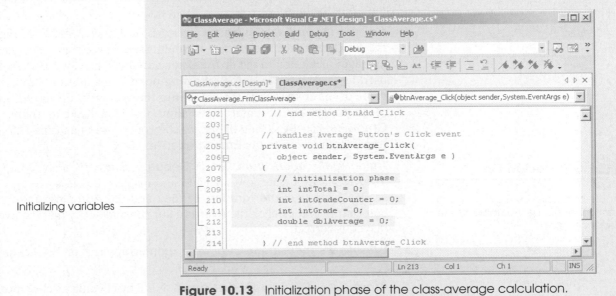

Figure 10.13 Initialization phase of the class-average calculation.

(cont.)

3. ***Summing the grades displayed in the ListBox.*** Add lines 214–222 of Fig. 10.14 to the btnAverage_Click event handler. The do...while statement (lines 215–222) sums the grades that it reads from the ListBox. Line 222 indicates that the statement should iterate while the value of intGradeCounter is less than 10.

Using the do...while repetition statement to sum grades in the ListBox

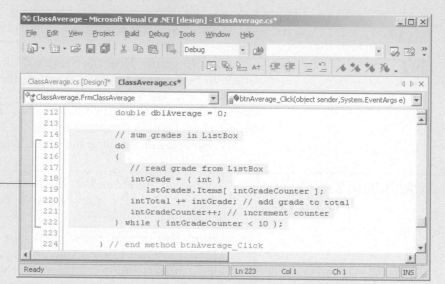

```
212             double dblAverage = 0;
213
214             // sum grades in ListBox
215             do
216             {
217                 // read grade from ListBox
218                 intGrade = ( int )
219                     lstGrades.Items[ intGradeCounter ];
220                 intTotal += intGrade; // add grade to total
221                 intGradeCounter++; // increment counter
222             } while ( intGradeCounter < 10 );
223
224         } // end method btnAverage_Click
```

Figure 10.14 do...while summing grades.

Lines 218–219 read the current value from the ListBox using the Items and property square brackets ([]), converts that value to an int using the cast operator and stores that value in intGrade. This notation will be explored in Tutorial 17 and Tutorial 20. Line 220 adds intGrade to the previous value of intTotal and assigns the result to intTotal, using the += assignment operator. The intGradeCounter variable is incremented (line 221) to indicate that another grade has been processed. (Incrementing the counter ensures that the condition in line 222 eventually becomes true, terminating the loop.)

4. ***Calculating and displaying the average.*** Add lines 224–227 of Fig. 10.15 to the btnAverage_Click event handler. Line 224 assigns the result of the average calculation to the dblAverage variable. The value 10.0, a double, is used as the divisor to enforce floating-point division. Line 225 displays the value of the dblAverage variable. After the average is displayed, another set of 10 grades can be entered. To allow this, you need to enable the **Add Grade** Button, by setting the Enabled property to true (line 226). Line 227 transfers the focus to the **Enter grade:** TextBox.

GUI Design Tip

Enable a disabled Button when its function should be available to the user once again.

5. ***Running the application.*** Select **Debug > Start** to run your application. Your application can now calculate and display the class average. Enter 10 grades using the **Enter grade:** TextBox and the **Add Grade** Button. After entering 10 grades, click the **Average** Button and verify that the average displayed is correct.

6. ***Closing the application.*** Close your running application by clicking its close box.

7. ***Closing the IDE.*** Close Visual Studio .NET by clicking its close box.

(cont.)

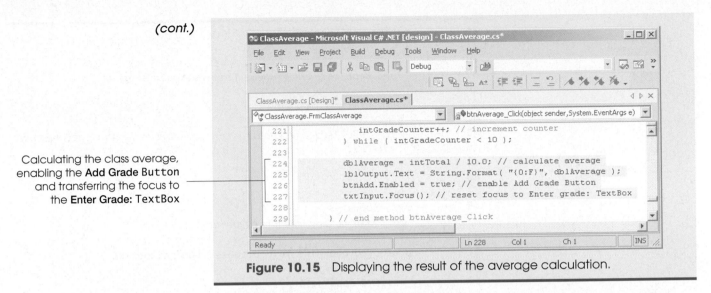

Calculating the class average, enabling the **Add Grade** Button and transferring the focus to the **Enter Grade:** TextBox

Figure 10.15   Displaying the result of the average calculation.

Figure 10.16 presents the source code for the **Class Average** application. The lines of code that use new programming concepts that you learned in this tutorial are highlighted.

```
1   using System;
2   using System.Drawing;
3   using System.Collections;
4   using System.ComponentModel;
5   using System.Windows.Forms;
6   using System.Data;
7
8   namespace ClassAverage
9   {
10      /// <summary>
11      /// Summary description for FrmClassAverage.
12      /// </summary>
13      public class FrmClassAverage : System.Windows.Forms.Form
14      {
15         // Label and ListBox to display grades
16         private System.Windows.Forms.Label lblGradeList;
17         private System.Windows.Forms.ListBox lstGrades;
18
19         // Label, TextBox and Button to add a grade
20         private System.Windows.Forms.Label lblPrompt;
21         private System.Windows.Forms.TextBox txtInput;
22         private System.Windows.Forms.Button btnAdd;
23
24         // Labels to display the average grade
25         private System.Windows.Forms.Label lblDescribeOutput;
26         private System.Windows.Forms.Label lblOutput;
27
28         // Button to compute the average grade
29         private System.Windows.Forms.Button btnAverage;
30
31         /// <summary>
32         /// Required designer variable.
33         /// </summary>
34         private System.ComponentModel.Container components = null;
35
```

Figure 10.16   **Class Average** application code. (Part 1 of 3.)

```
36        public FrmClassAverage()
37        {
38           //
39           // Required for Windows Form Designer support
40           //
41           InitializeComponent();
42           //
43           // TODO: Add any constructor code after InitializeComponent
44           // call
45           //
46        }
47
48        /// <summary>
49        /// Clean up any resources being used.
50        /// </summary>
51        protected override void Dispose( bool disposing )
52        {
53           if( disposing )
54           {
55              if (components != null)
56              {
57                 components.Dispose();
58              }
59           }
60           base.Dispose( disposing );
61        }
62
63        // Windows Form Designer generated code
64
65        /// <summary>
66        /// The main entry point for the application.
67        /// </summary>
68        [STAThread]
69        static void Main()
70        {
71           Application.Run( new FrmClassAverage() );
72        }
73
74        // handles Add Grade Button's Click event
75        private void btnAdd_Click(
76           object sender, System.EventArgs e )
77        {
78           // clear previous grades and calculation result
79           if ( lblOutput.Text != "" )
80           {
81              lblOutput.Text = "";
82              lstGrades.Items.Clear();
83           }
84
85           // display grade in ListBox
86           lstGrades.Items.Add( Int32.Parse( txtInput.Text ) );
87           txtInput.Clear(); // clear grade from TextBox
88           txtInput.Focus(); // transfer focus to TextBox
89
90           // prohibit users from entering more than 10 grades
91           if ( lstGrades.Items.Count == 10 )
92           {
```

Using the **Focus** method ——— 88

Figure 10.16 Class Average application code. (Part 2 of 3.)

Disabling the **Add Grade**
Button and transferring the
focus to the **Average** Button

```
93        btnAdd.Enabled = false; // disable Add Grade Button
94        btnAverage.Focus(); // transfer focus to Average Button
95     }
96
97  } // end method btnAdd_Click
98
99  // handles Average Button's Click event
100 private void btnAverage_Click(
101    object sender, System.EventArgs e )
102 {
103    // initialization phase
104    int intTotal = 0;
105    int intGradeCounter = 0;
106    int intGrade = 0;
107    double dblAverage = 0;
108
109    // sum grades in ListBox
110    do
111    {
112       // read grade from ListBox
113       intGrade = ( int )
114          lstGrades.Items[ intGradeCounter ];
115       intTotal += intGrade; // add grade to total
116       intGradeCounter++; // increment counter
117    } while ( intGradeCounter < 10 );
118
119    dblAverage = intTotal / 10.0; // calculate average
120    lblOutput.Text = String.Format( "{0:F}", dblAverage );
121    btnAdd.Enabled = true; // enable Add Grade Button
122    txtInput.Focus(); // reset focus to Enter grade: TextBox
123
124 } // end method btnAverage_Click
125
126 } // end class FrmClassAverage
127 }
```

Using a do...while statement to
calculate the class average

Enabling the **Add Grade** Button
and transferring the focus to the
Enter grade: TextBox

Figure 10.16   **Class Average** application code. (Part 3 of 3.)

SELF-REVIEW   1. If you do not want a Button to call its event handler when the Button is clicked, set the
_____ property to _____.

a) Enabled, false   b) Enabled, true

c) Disabled, true   d) Disabled, false

2. _____ a TextBox selects that TextBox to receive user input.

a) Enabling   b) Clearing

c) Transferring the focus to   d) Disabling

Answers: 1) a. 2) c.

10.4 Wrap-Up

In this tutorial, you learned how to use the do...while repetition statement. We provided the syntax and included UML activity diagrams to explain how the statement executes. You used the do...while statement in the **Class Average** application that you developed.

The do...while repetition statement executes as long as its loop-continuation condition is true. This repetition statement always executes at least once. When the loop-continuation condition becomes false, the repetition terminates. This repetition statement enters an infinite loop if the loop-continuation condition never becomes `false`.

You also learned more sophisticated techniques for creating more polished graphical user interfaces for your applications. You now know how to invoke the `Focus` method to transfer the focus in an application, indicating that the next action the user takes should involve a given control. You also learned how to disable `Buttons` that should not be available to a user at certain times during an application's execution and you learned how to enable those `Buttons` again.

In the next tutorial, you will continue studying repetition statements. You will learn how to use the `for` repetition statement, which is particularly useful for counter-controlled repetition.

SKILLS SUMMARY

do...while Repetition Statement

- Iterates while its loop-continuation condition is `true`.
- Tests the loop-continuation condition after the loop body is performed.
- Always executes the loop at least once.
- Becomes an infinite loop if the loop-continuation condition can never become `false`.

Disabling a Button

- Set Button property `Enabled` to `false`.

Enabling a Button

- Set Button property `Enabled` to `true`.

Transferring the Focus to a Control

- Call the Focus method.

KEY TERMS

Clear method of class TextBox—Removes the text in the TextBox.

Count property of Items—Returns the number of ListBox items.

do...while repetition statement—A control statement that executes a set of statements while the loop-continuation condition is `true`; the condition is tested after the loop executes.

Enabled property—Specifies whether a control, such as a `Button`, appears enabled (`true`) or disabled (`false`).

focus—When a control is selected, it is said to have the focus of the application.

Focus method—Transfers the focus of the application to the control, on which the method is called.

off-by-one error—Occurs when a loop executes for one more or one fewer iterations than is necessary.

transferring the focus—Selecting a control in an application.

GUI DESIGN GUIDELINES

Button

- Disable `Buttons` when function should not be available to the user.
- Enable a disabled `Button` when its function should be available to the user once again.

CONTROLS, EVENTS, PROPERTIES & METHODS

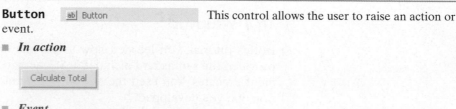

Button   This control allows the user to raise an action or event.

- *In action*

- *Event*

  `Click`—Raised when the user clicks the `Button`.

■ *Properties*

Enabled—Determines whether the Button's event handler executes when the Button is clicked.

Location—Specifies the location of the Button on the Form relative to the top-left corner.

Name—Specifies the name used to access the Button programmatically. The name should be prefixed with btn.

Size—Specifies the height and width (in pixels) of the Button.

Text—Specifies the text displayed on the Button.

■ *Method*

Focus—Transfers the focus of the application to the Button that calls it.

ListBox   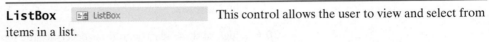   This control allows the user to view and select from items in a list.

■ *In action*

Months	Monthly Payments
24	$490.50
36	$339.06
48	$263.55
60	$218.41

■ *Properties*

Items—Returns an object that contains the items displayed in the ListBox.

Items.Count—Returns the number of items in the ListBox.

Location—Specifies the location of the ListBox on the Form relative to the top-left corner.

Name—Specifies the name used to access the ListBox programmatically. The name should be prefixed with lst.

Size—Specifies the height and width (in pixels) of the ListBox.

■ *Methods*

Items.Add—Adds an item to the Items property.

Items.Clear—Deletes all the values in the ListBox's Items property.

TextBox   abl TextBox   This control allows the user to input data from the keyboard.

■ *In action*

■ *Event*

TextChanged—Raised when the text in the TextBox is changed.

■ *Properties*

Location—Specifies the location of the TextBox on the Form relative to the top-left corner.

Name—Specifies the name used to access the TextBox programmatically. The name should be prefixed with txt.

Size—Specifies the height and width (in pixels) of the TextBox.

Text—Specifies the text displayed in the TextBox.

TextAlign—Specifies how the text is aligned within the TextBox.

■ *Methods*

Clear—Removes the text in the TextBox.

Focus—Transfers the focus of the application to the TextBox that calls it.

MULTIPLE-CHOICE QUESTIONS

10.1 A(n) _____ occurs when a loop-continuation condition in a while loop never becomes false.

a) infinite loop

b) counter-controlled loop

c) control statement

d) nested control statement

10.2 Set the _____ property to true to enable a Button.

a) Disabled

b) Focus

c) Enabled

d) ButtonEnabled

10.3 The _____ statement executes at least once and continues executing until its loop-continuation condition becomes false.

a) do...loop

b) while

c) do...while

d) loop...while

10.4 Which of these loop conditions describes the loop "repeat until i is greater than five"?

a) **do...until (i > 5)**

b) **while (i <= 5)**

c) **while (i < 5)**

d) **do...while (i == 5)**

10.5 The _____ method transfers the focus to a control.

a) GetFocus

b) Focus

c) Transfer

d) Activate

10.6 A _____ contains the sum of a series of values.

a) total

b) counter

c) condition

d) loop

10.7 The _____ property of _____ property contains the number of items in a ListBox.

a) Count, ListBox

b) ListCount, Items

c) ListCount, ListBox

d) Count, Items

10.8 A(n) _____ occurs when a loop executes for one more or one less iteration than is necessary.

a) infinite loop

b) counter-controlled loop

c) off-by-one error

d) nested control statement

10.9 When a GUI element (such as a Button) should no longer be accessible by the user, it should be _____.

a) deleted

b) hidden

c) disabled

d) All of the above.

10.10 If its loop-continuation condition is initially false, a do...while repetition statement _____.

a) never executes

b) executes while the condition is false

c) executes until the condition becomes true

d) executes only once

EXERCISES

10.11 *(Modified Class Average Application)* Modify the **Class Average** application, as in Fig. 10.17, so that **Average** Button is disabled until 10 grades have been entered.

a) *Copying the template to your working directory.* Copy the directory C:\Examples\ Tutorial10\Exercises\ModifiedClassAverage to your C:\SimplyCSP directory.

b) *Opening the application's template file.* Double click ClassAverage.sln in the ModifiedClassAverage directory to open the application.

c) *Initially disabling the Average Button.* Use the **Properties** window to modify the **Average** Button in the Form so that it is disabled when the application first runs by setting its Enabled property to false.

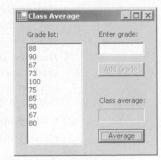

Figure 10.17   Modified **Class Average** application.

d) *Enabling the Average Button after 10 grades have been entered.* Add code to the btnAdd_Click event handler so that the **Average** Button becomes enabled when 10 grades have been entered.

e) *Disabling the Average Button after the calculation has been performed.* Add code to the btnAverage_Click event handler so that the **Average** Button is disabled once the calculation result has been displayed.

f) *Running the application.* Select **Debug > Start** to run your application. Enter 10 grades and ensure that the **Average** Button is disabled until all 10 grades are entered. Verify that the **Add Grade** Button is disabled after 10 grades are entered. Once the **Average** Button is enabled, click it and verify that the average displayed is correct. The **Average** Button should then become disabled again, and the **Add Grade** Button should be enabled.

g) *Closing the application.* Close your running application by clicking its close box.

h) *Closing the IDE.* Close Visual Studio .NET by clicking its close box.

10.12 *(Undetermined Class Average Application That Handles Any Number of Grades)* Rewrite the **Class Average** application to handle any number of grades, as in Fig. 10.18. Note that, because the application does not know how many grades the user will enter, the Buttons must be enabled at all times.

Figure 10.18   Undetermined **Class Average** application handling an unspecified number of grades.

a) *Copying the template to your working directory.* Copy the directory C:\Examples\ Tutorial10\Exercises\UndeterminedClassAverage to your C:\SimplyCSP directory.

b) *Opening the application's template file.* Double click ClassAverage.sln in the UndeterminedClassAverage directory to open the application.

c) *Never disabling the Add Grade Button.* Remove code from the btnAdd_Click event handler so that the **Add Grade** Button is not disabled after entering 10 grades.

d) *Summing the grades in the ListBox.* Modify code in the btnAverage_Click event handler so that intGradeCounter is incremented until it is equal to the number of grades entered. Use lstGrades.Items.Count to determine the number of items in the ListBox. The number returned by the Count property will be zero if there are no grades entered. Use an if selection statement to avoid division by zero and display a message dialog to the user if there are no grades entered when the user clicks the **Average** Button.

e) *Calculating the class average.* Modify the code in the btnAverage_Click event handler so that dblAverage is computed by using intGradeCounter rather than the value 10.

f) *Running the application.* Select **Debug > Start** to run your application. Enter 10 grades and click the Average Button. Verify that the average displayed is correct. Follow the same actions but this time for 15 grades, then for 5 grades. Each time, verify that the appropriate average is displayed.

g) *Closing the application.* Close your running application by clicking its close box.

h) *Closing the IDE.* Close Visual Studio .NET by clicking its close box.

10.13 *(Arithmetic Calculator Application)* Write an application that allows users to enter a series of numbers and manipulate them. The application should provide users with the option of adding or multiplying the numbers. Users should enter each number in a TextBox. After entering each number, users should click a Button, then the number should be inserted in a ListBox. The GUI should appear as shown in Fig. 10.19.

Figure 10.19 **Arithmetic Calculator** application.

a) *Copying the template to your working directory.* Copy the directory C:\Examples\Tutorial10\Exercises\ArithmeticCalculator to your C:\SimplyCSP directory.

b) *Opening the application's template file.* Double click ArithmeticCalculator.sln in the ArithmeticCalculator directory to open the application.

c) *Add a ListBox to display the entered numbers.* Add a ListBox. Place and size it as in Fig. 10.19. Rearrange and comment the control declarations appropriately.

d) *Creating an event handler for the Enter Button.* Create the Click event handler for the **Enter** Button. If the result of a previous calculation is displayed, this event handler should clear the result and disable the addition and multiplication Buttons. It should then insert the current number in the **Operands list:** ListBox. When the ListBox contains at least two numbers, the event handler should then enable the addition and multiplication Buttons.

e) *Summing the grades in the ListBox.* Define the Click event handler for the **Add** Button. This event handler should compute the sum of all of the values in the **Operands list:** ListBox and display the result in a Label, lblResult. Use the square bracket notation to access each item in the ListBox. Use the cast operator to convert the ListBox items into doubles.

f) *Define the Click event handler for the Multiply Button.* This event handler should compute the product of all of the values in the **Operands list:** ListBox and display the result in the lblResult Label. Use the square bracket notation to access each item in the ListBox. Use the cast operator to convert the ListBox items into doubles.

g) *Running the application.* Select **Debug > Start** to run your application. Enter two values, then click the **Add** and **Multiply** Buttons. Verify that the results displayed are correct. Also, make sure that the **Add** and **Multiply** Buttons are not enabled until two values have been entered.

h) *Closing the application.* Close your running application by clicking its close box.

i) *Closing the IDE.* Close Visual Studio .NET by clicking its close box.

What does this code do? ▶ **10.14** What is the result of the following code?

```
1   int intY;
2   int intX;
3   int intMysteryValue;
4
5   intX = 1;
6   intMysteryValue = 0;
7
8   do
9   {
10      intY = ( int ) Math.Pow( intX, 2 );
11      lstDisplay.Items.Add( intY );
12      intMysteryValue++;
13      intX++;
14
15  } while ( intX <= 10 );
16
17  lblResult.Text = Convert.ToString( intMysteryValue );
```

What's wrong with this code? ▶ **10.15** Find the error(s) in the following code. This code should add 10 to the value in intY and store it in intZ. It then should reduce the value of intY by one and repeat until intY is less than 10. The output Label lblResult should display the final value of intZ.

```
1   int intY = 10;
2   int intZ = 2;
3
4   do
5   {
6       intZ = intY + 10;
7
8   } while ( !( intY < 10 ) );
9
10  intY--;
11
12  lblResult.Text = Convert.ToString( intZ );
```

Using the Debugger ▶ **10.16** (*Factorial Application*) The **Factorial** application calculates the factorial of an integer input by the user. The factorial of an integer is the product of the integers from one to that number. For example, the factorial of 3 is 6 ($1 \times 2 \times 3$). Copy the directory C:\Examples\ Tutorial10\Debugger\Factorial to your C:\SimplyCSP directory. Run the application. While testing the application you noticed that it does not execute correctly. Use the debugger to find and correct the logic error(s) in the application. Figure 10.20 displays the correct output for the **Factorial** application.

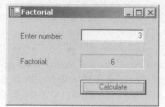

Figure 10.20 Correct output for the **Factorial** application.

Programming Challenge ▶ **10.17** (*Restaurant Bill Application*) Develop an application that calculates a restaurant bill. The user should be able to enter the item ordered, the quantity of the item ordered and the price per item. When the user clicks the **Add Item** Button, your application should display the number ordered, the item ordered and the price per unit in three ListBoxes as shown in Fig. 10.21. When the user clicks the **Total Bill** Button, the application should calculate the total cost. For each entry in the ListBox, multiply the cost of each item by the number of items ordered. Use the square bracket notation to access each item in a ListBox.

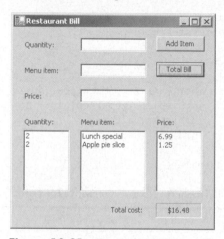

Figure 10.21 **Restaurant Bill** application.

Objectives

In this tutorial, you will learn to:
- Execute statements repeatedly with the **for** repetition statement.
- Obtain user input with the **NumericUpDown** control.
- Display information using a multiline **TextBox**.

Outline

11.1 Test-Driving the **Interest Calculator** Application

11.2 Essentials of Counter-Controlled Repetition

11.3 Introducing the **for** Repetition Statement

11.4 Examples Using the **for** Statement

11.5 Constructing the **Interest Calculator** Application

11.6 Wrap-Up

Interest Calculator Application

Introducing the for *Repetition Statement*

As you learned in Tutorial 9 and Tutorial 10, applications are often required to repeat actions. Using a `while` or `do...while` repetition statement allowed you to specify a condition and test that condition either before entering the loop or after execution of the body of the loop. In the **Car Payment Calculator** application and the **Class Average** application, a counter was used to determine the number of times the loop should iterate. In fact, the use of counters in repetition statements is so common in applications that C# provides an additional control statement specially designed for such cases—the `for` repetition statement. In this tutorial, you will use the `for` repetition statement to create an **Interest Calculator** application.

11.1 Test-Driving the Interest Calculator Application

The **Interest Calculator** application calculates the amount of money in your savings account after you begin with a certain amount of money and are paid a certain interest rate for a certain amount of time. Users specify the principal amount (the initial amount of money in the account), the interest rate and the number of years for which interest will be calculated. The application then displays the results. This application must meet the following requirements:

> **Application Requirements**
>
> *You are considering investing $1000.00 in a savings account that yields 5% interest, and you want to forecast how your investment will grow. Assuming that you will leave all interest on deposit, calculate and print the amount of money in the account at the end of each year over a period of n years. To compute these amounts, use the following formula:*
>
> $$a = p \, (1 + r)^n$$
>
> *where*
>
> *p is the original amount of money invested (the principal)*
> *r is the annual interest rate (for example, .05 is equivalent to 5%)*
> *n is the number of years*
> *a is the amount on deposit at the end of the nth year.*

You begin by test-driving the completed application. Then, you will learn the additional C# technologies you will need to create your own version of this application.

Test-Driving the *Interest* **Calculator** *Application*

1. ***Opening the completed application.*** Open the `C:\Examples\Tutorial11\` `CompletedApplication\InterestCalculator` directory to locate the **Interest Calculator** application. Double click `InterestCalculator.sln` to open the application in Visual Studio .NET.

2. ***Running the Interest Calculator application.*** Select **Debug > Start** to run the application (Fig. 11.1).

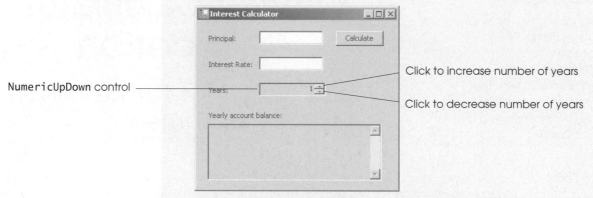

NumericUpDown control ⸺

Click to increase number of years

Click to decrease number of years

Figure 11.1   Completed **Interest Calculator** application.

3. ***Providing a principal value.*** Once the application is running, provide a value in the **Principal:** TextBox. Input 1000, as specified in the problem statement.

4. ***Providing an interest-rate value.*** We specified the interest rate 5% in the problem statement, so enter 5 in the **Interest Rate:** TextBox.

5. ***Providing the duration of the investment.*** Now you should choose the number of years for which you want to calculate the amount in the savings account. In this case, select 10 by clicking the up arrow in the **Years:** NumericUpDown control repeatedly until the value reads 10. We will discuss this type of control in more detail shortly.

6. ***Calculating the amount.*** Click the **Calculate** Button. The amount of money in your account at the end of each year during a period of 10 years displays in the multiline TextBox. The application should look similar to Fig. 11.2.

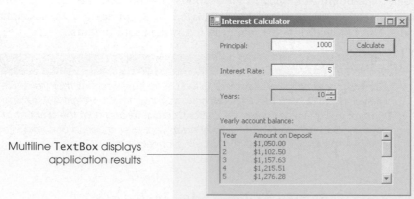

Multiline **TextBox** displays application results ⸺

Figure 11.2   Output of completed **Interest Calculator** application.

(cont.)   7. ***Closing the application.*** Close your running application by clicking its close
box.

8. ***Closing the IDE.*** Close Visual Studio .NET by clicking its close box.

11.2 Essentials of Counter-Controlled Repetition

In Tutorial 10, you were introduced to counter-controlled repetition. The four essential elements of counter-controlled repetition are

1. the **name** of a **control variable** (or loop counter) that is used to determine whether the loop continues to iterate;

2. the **initial value** of the control variable;

3. the **increment** (or **decrement**) by which the control variable is modified during each iteration of the loop (that is, each time the loop is performed); and

4. the condition that tests for the **final value** of the control variable (to determine whether looping should continue).

The example of Fig. 11.3 uses the four elements of counter-controlled repetition. This `while` statement is similar to the **Car Payment Calculator** application's loop in Tutorial 9.

```
1   int intCounter = 2; // repetition counter
2
3   while ( intCounter <= 5 )
4   {
5      intMonths = 12 * ( intCounter + 1 ); // calculate payment period
6
7      // calculate payment value
8      decValue = ( decimal )
9         ( intLoanAmount * dblMonthlyInterest *
10        Math.Pow( 1 + dblMonthlyInterest, intMonths ) /
11        ( Math.Pow( 1 + dblMonthlyInterest, intMonths )
12           1 ) );
13
14     // display payment value
15     lstPayments.Items.Add( intMonths + "\t\t" +
16        String.Format( "{0:C}", decValue ) );
17
18     intCounter++; // increment counter
19  }
```

Figure 11.3 Counter-controlled repetition example.

Recall that the **Car Payment Calculator** application calculates and displays monthly car payments over periods of two to five years. The declaration in line 1 *names* the control variable (`intCounter`), indicating that it is of the `int` type. This declaration includes an initialization, which sets the variable to an *initial value* of 2.

Consider the `while` statement (lines 3–19). Line 5 uses the `intCounter` variable to calculate the number of months over which car payments are to be made. Lines 8–12 use a mathematical formula to determine the monthly payment for the car. This value depends on the car's price, the interest rate, the duration of the loan in months and the down-payment amount. Lines 15–16 display the amount in a `ListBox`. Line 18 increments the `intCounter` control variable by 1 for each iteration of the loop. The condition in the `while` statement (line 3) tests for whether the value of the control variable is less than or equal to 5, meaning that 5 is the *final value* for which the condition is true. The body of this `while` is performed even when the control variable is 5. The loop terminates when the control variable exceeds 5 (that is, when `intCounter` has a value of 6).

SELF-REVIEW

1. The control variable's _____ is not one of the four essential elements of counter-controlled repetition.

    a) name   b) initial value

    c) type   d) final value

2. What aspect of the control variable determines whether looping should continue?

    a) name   b) final value

    c) type   d) None of the above.

Answers: 1) c. 2) b.

11.3 Introducing the for Repetition Statement

The **for** repetition statement makes it easier for you to write code to perform counter-controlled repetition. This statement specifies all four elements essential to counter-controlled repetition. The `for` statement takes less time to code and is easier to read than an equivalent `while` or `do...while` repetition statement.

Let's examine the first line of the `for` repetition statement (Fig. 11.4), which we call the `for` header. The **for header** specifies all four essential elements for counter-controlled repetition. The line should be read "*for each value of `intCounter` starting at 2 and ending at 10, do the following statements, then add two to `intCounter`.*"

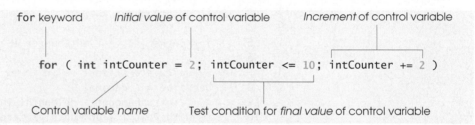

Figure 11.4 `for` header components.

Each `for` statement begins with the **for** keyword. Then, the statement declares and initializes a control variable (in this case, `intCounter` is set to 2). You may declare the counter variable before the `for` statement if desired. In that case, the name of the variable would still be required, but the type would not. When it is declared inside the `for` header, the control variable can be used only in the header or the body of the `for` statement. When the body of the `for` statement ends, the variable will no longer be recognized by the C# compiler.

Following the initial value of the control variable is a semicolon (;), followed by the condition that tests for the final value of the control variable to be used in the loop and a second semicolon. Finally, you can specify the amount by which to increase (or decrease) the control variable each time the loop body completes execution.

The `for` header is followed by statements to be executed each time through the loop. As with other repetition statements, braces ({ and }) are required to define the loop's body if there is more than one statement to be executed. For simplicity, we always use braces in our `for` statements. The following box describes each step as the above repetition statement executes, ignoring any body statements.

Executing the for Repetition Statement

1. The application declares the `intCounter` variable and sets its value to 2.

2. The loop-continuation condition is checked. The condition evaluates to true (`intCounter` is 2, which is less than or equal to 10), so the application executes the body of the `for` statement.

3. The value of `intCounter` is increased by 2; `intCounter` now contains the number 4.

4. The loop-continuation condition is checked. The condition evaluates to `true` (`intCounter` is less than 10), so the application executes the body of the `for` statement.

5. The value of `intCounter` is increased by 2; `intCounter` now contains the number 6.

6. The loop-continuation condition is checked. The condition evaluates to `true` (`intCounter` is less than 10), so the application executes the body of the `for` statement.

7. The value of `intCounter` is increased by 2; `intCounter` now contains the number 8.

8. The loop-continuation condition is checked. The condition evaluates to `true` (`intCounter` is less than 10), so the application executes the body of the `for` statement.

9. The value of `intCounter` is increased by 2; `intCounter` now contains the number 10.

10. The loop-continuation condition is checked. The condition evaluates to `true` (`intCounter` is equal to 10), so the application executes the body of the `for` statement.

11. The value of `intCounter` is increased by 2; `intCounter` now contains the number 12.

12. The loop-continuation condition is checked. The condition evaluates to `false` (`intCounter` is not less than or equal to 10), so the application exits the `for` repetition statement.

Good Programming Practice

Place a blank line before and after each control statement to make it stand out in your code.

In many cases, the `for` statement can be represented by another repetition statement. For example, an equivalent `while` statement for Fig. 11.4 would be of the form

```
int intCounter = 2;

while ( intCounter <= 10 )
{
    body statement(s)
    intCounter += 2;
}
```

Notice that the second part of the `for` statement's header (Fig. 11.4) contains the same loop-continuation condition (`intCounter <= 10`) found in the preceding `while` statement. The starting value, ending value and increment portions of a `for` statement can contain arithmetic expressions. The expressions are evaluated anew on each iteration. For example, the following header is valid:

```
for ( int intI = intA; intI <= 4 * intA * intB; intI += intB / intA )
```

If the implied loop-continuation condition is initially `false` (for example, if the starting value is greater than the ending value and the increment value is positive), the `for` statement's body is not performed. Instead, execution proceeds with the statement after the `for` statement.

The control variable frequently is displayed or used in calculations in the `for` body, but it does not have to be. It is common to use the control variable only to control repetition and not in the `for` body.

The three parts of the `for` header are actually optional. A programmer might omit the initialization of the control variable if the application initializes the control variable before the `for` statement. Omitting the loop-continuation condition is generally less useful. If the condition is omitted, C# assumes that the condition is always true, thus creating an infinite loop. The increment (or decrement) expression might be omitted if statements in the body of the `for` calculate the increment or decrement, or if no increment or decrement is necessary. The two semicolons in the `for` header, however, are required. Thus, the following header is syntactically correct (it will not cause a syntax error), although it will result in an infinite loop:

```
for ( ; ; )
```

Error-Prevention Tip

Although the value of the control variable can be changed in the body of a `for` loop, avoid doing so, because this practice can lead to subtle errors.

The UML activity diagram for the `for` statement is similar to that of the `while` statement. For example, the UML activity diagram of the `for` statement

```
for ( int intCounter = 1; intCounter <= 10; intCounter++ )
{
    lstDisplay.Items.Add( intCounter * 10 );
}
```

is shown in Fig. 11.5. This activity diagram shows that the initialization occurs only once and that incrementing occurs *after* each execution of the body statement. Note that, besides small circles and flowlines, the activity diagram contains only rounded rectangle symbols and small diamond symbols. The rounded rectangle symbols are filled with the actions, and the flowlines coming out of the small diamond symbols are labelled with the appropriate guard conditions for this algorithm.

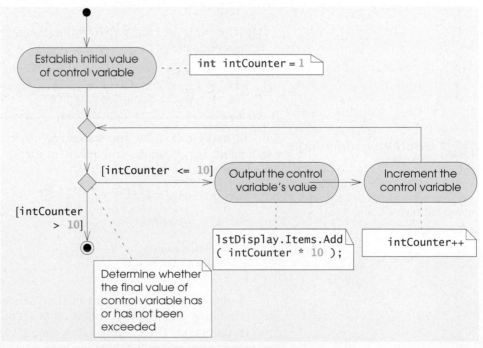

Figure 11.5 `for` repetition statement UML activity diagram.

Good Programming Practice

Vertical spacing above and below control statements, as well as indentation of the bodies of control statements, enhances readability.

Notice that the `for` header indicates each item needed to conduct counter-controlled repetition with a control variable. To help solidify your understanding of this new repetition statement, you will now learn how the `while` statement of Fig. 11.3 can be replaced by a `for` statement.

The converted code is shown in Fig. 11.6. When the `for` statement begins execution, line 3 of Fig. 11.6 initializes control variable `intCounter` to 2. Note the two semicolons separating the header into three sections.

The loop-continuation condition `intCounter <= 5` is tested in line 3. The initial value of `intCounter` is 2, so the loop-continuation condition is satisfied and the payment calculations within the `for` body are executed.

The right brace (}) in line 17 marks the end of the `for` repetition statement. When the end of the `for` body is reached, `intCounter` is incremented by 1, and the loop begins again with the loop-continuation condition test.

The preceding two steps repeat until the implied loop-continuation condition becomes `false` as `intCounter` becomes greater than 5. Repetition then terminates.

Error-Prevention Tip

If you use a `for` loop for counter-controlled repetition, off-by-one errors are normally avoided, because the terminating value is clear.

Common Programming Error

Counter-controlled loops should not be controlled with floating-point variables. These are represented only approximately in the computer's memory, possibly resulting in imprecise counter values and inaccurate tests for termination that could lead to logic errors.

```
1   int intCounter;
2
3   for ( intCounter - 2; intCounter <= 5; intCounter++ )
4   {
5       intMonths = 12 * ( intCounter + 1 ); // calculate payment period
6
7       // calculate payment value
8       decValue = ( decimal )
9           ( intLoanAmount * dblMonthlyInterest *
10          Math.Pow( 1 + dblMonthlyInterest, intMonths ) /
11          ( Math.Pow( 1 + dblMonthlyInterest, intMonths )
12          - 1 ) );
13
14      // display payment value
15      lstPayments.Items.Add( intMonths + "\t\t" +
16          String.Format( "{0:C}", decValue ) )
17  }
```

Figure 11.6   Code segment for the **Car Payment Calculator** application that demonstrates the **for** statement.

SELF-REVIEW

1. The _____ portion of a `for` statement determines the amount of each increment (or decrement).

   a) first   b) second

   c) third   d) the increment amount is always one.

2. The first portion of a `for` statement indicates the _____.

   a) initial value of the counter variable   b) loop-continuation condition

   c) increment size   d) number of times the statement iterates

Answers: 1) c. 2) a.

11.4 Examples Using the for Statement

The following examples demonstrate different ways of varying the control variable in a `for` statement. In each case, we write the appropriate `for` header:

a) Vary the control variable from 1 to 100 (inclusive) in increments of 1.

   ```
   for ( intI = 1; intI <= 100; intI++ )
   ```

b) Vary the control variable from 100 to 1(inclusive) in increments of –1 (decrements of 1).

   ```
   for ( intI = 100; intI >= 1; intI-- )
   ```

c) Vary the control variable from 7 to 77(inclusive) in increments of 7.

   ```
   for ( intI = 7; intI <= 77; intI += 7 )
   ```

d) Vary the control variable from 20 to 2 (inclusive) in increments of -2 (decrements of 2).

```
for ( intI = 20; intI >= 2; intI -= 2 )
```

e) Vary the control variable over the sequence of the following values: 2, 5, 8, 11, 14, 17, 20.

```
for ( intI = 2; intI <= 20; intI += 3 )
```

f) Vary the control variable over the sequence of the following values: 99, 88, 77, 66, 55, 44, 33, 22, 11, 0.

```
for ( intI = 99; intI >= 0; intI -= 11 )
```

SELF-REVIEW

1. Which of the following is the appropriate **for** header for varying the control variable over the following sequence of values: 25, 20, 15, 10, 5?

   a) **for** (i = 5; i < 25; i += 5)   b) **for** (i = 25; i >= 5; i -= 5)
   c) **for** (i = 5; i < 25; i -= 5)   d) **for** (i = 25; i > 5; i += 5)

2. Which of the following statements describes the **for** header

   ```
   for ( i = 81; i < 103; i++ )?
   ```

   a) Vary the control variable from 81 to 102 in increments of 1.
   b) Vary the control variable from 81 to 102 in increments of 2.
   c) Vary the control variable from 102 to 81 in increments of -1.
   d) Vary the control variable from 81 to 102 in increments of 2.

Answers: 1) b. 2) a.

11.5 Constructing the Interest Calculator Application

Our solution to this tutorial's problem statement computes interest over a given number of years by using the **for** statement. This repetition statement will perform the calculation for every year that the money remains on deposit.

The following pseudocode describes the basic operation of the **Interest Calculator** application when the **Calculate** Button is clicked:

> When the user clicks the Calculate Button:
>   Get the values for the principal, interest rate and years entered by the user
>   Store a header to be added to the output TextBox
>
>   For each year (starting at 1 and ending with the number of years entered)
>   Calculate the current value of the investment
>   Display the year and the current value of the investment

The template application we provide for this tutorial contains the **Calculate** Button, plus two Labels and their corresponding TextBoxes—**Principal:** and for **Interest Rate:**. The Form has a **Years:** Label, but you will insert the NumericUp-Down control for this input. The **NumericUpDown** control limits a user's choices for the number of years to a specific range. You will then create a **multiline TextBox** with a scrollbar and add it to the application's GUI. Finally, you will add functionality with a **for** statement. Now that you have test-driven the **Interest Calculator** application and studied its pseudocode representation, you will use an ACE table to help you convert the pseudocode to C#. Figure 11.7 lists the actions, controls and events that will help you complete your own version of this application.

<table>
<tr><td colspan="2">*Action/Control/Event
(ACE) Table for the
Interest Calculator
Application*
</td><td>

Action	Control	Event

Label the application's fields	`lblPrincipal,`
	`lblRate,`
	`lblYears,`
	`lblYearlyAccount`
		Application is run

	`btnCalculate`	`Click`

Get the values for the principal, interest rate and years entered by the user	`txtPrincipal,`
	`txtRate,`
	`updYear`	

Store a header to be added to the output TextBox		
For each year (starting at 1 and ending with the number of years entered)		
Calculate current value of the investment		
Display the year and the current value of the investment	`txtResult`	

</td></tr>
</table>

Figure 11.7   ACE table for **Interest Calculator** application.

To begin building the **Interest Calculator** application, follow the steps in the next box. First, you will add a `NumericUpDown` control to allow the user to specify the number of years. This control provides up and down arrows to allow the user to scroll through the control's range of values. The following box shows you how to set the limits of the range (maximum and minimum values). We will use 10 as the maximum value and 1 as the minimum value for this control. The **Increment** property specifies by how much the current number in the `NumericUpDown` control changes when the user clicks the control's up (for incrementing) or down (for decrementing) arrow. This application uses the `Increment` property's default value, 1.

---

*Adding and Customizing
a NumericUpDown
Control*

1. ***Copying the template to your working directory.*** Copy the `C:\Examples\Tutorial11\TemplateApplication\InterestCalculator` directory to your `C:\SimplyCSP` directory.

2. ***Opening the Interest Calculator application's template file.*** Double click `InterestCalculator.sln` in the `InterestCalculator` directory to open the application in Visual Studio .NET (Fig. 11.8).

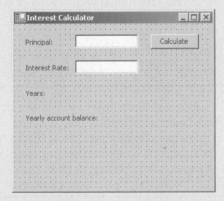

Figure 11.8   **Interest Calculator** application **Form** in design view.

(cont.)

3. ***Adding a NumericUpDown control.*** Double click the NumericUpDown control,

in the **Toolbox** to add it to your Form (Fig. 11.9). Change the control's Name property to updYear. To improve code readability, you should prefix NumericUpDown control names with upd, which is short for up-down.

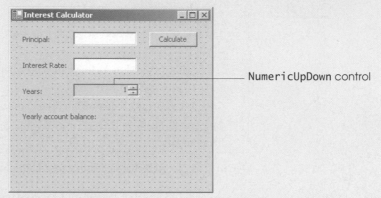

Figure 11.9 NumericUpDown control added to **Interest Calculator** application.

GUI Design Tip

A NumericUpDown control should follow the same GUI Design Guidelines as a single-line TextBox. (See Appendix C.)

Good Programming Practice

Prefix NumericUpDown control names with upd.

GUI Design Tip

Use a NumericUpDown control to limit the range of user input.

4. ***Setting the NumericUpDown control's location and size.*** Set updYear's Location property to 96, 96 and its Size property to 104, 21 so that it aligns horizontally and vertically with the TextBoxes above it.

5. ***Setting the TextAlign property.*** Set the TextAlign property to Right. The number now appears right-aligned in the control.

6. ***Setting property ReadOnly.*** To ensure that the user cannot enter invalid values in the **Years:** NumericUpDown control, set the ReadOnly property to true. The **ReadOnly** property changes the background color of the control to gray, indicating that the user can change its value only by using the up and down arrows.

7. ***Setting range limits for the NumericUpDown control.*** By default, this control sets 0 as the minimum and 100 as the maximum. You will change these values. Set updYear's **Maximum** property to 10. Then, set its **Minimum** property to 1. This (combined with setting its ReadOnly property to true) limits users to selecting values between 1 and 10 for the number of years. Notice that the NumericUpDown control displays 1, the value of its Minimum property. Your Form should now look like Fig. 11.9.

8. ***Saving the project.*** Select **File > Save All** to save your modified code.

The **Interest Calculator** application displays the results of its calculations in a multiline TextBox, which is simply a TextBox that can display more than one line of text. You can configure the TextBox to have a scrollbar, so if the TextBox is too small to display its contents, the user can scroll up and down to view the entire contents of the box. You will create this TextBox in the following box.

Adding and Customizing a Multiline TextBox with a Scrollbar

1. ***Adding a TextBox to the Form.*** Double click the TextBox control in the **Toolbox** to add a TextBox to the Form. Name the TextBox txtResult.

2. ***Creating a multiline TextBox.*** Change the TextBox's **Multiline** property to true. Doing so allows the TextBox to contain multiple lines.

GUI Design Tip

If a TextBox will display multiple lines of output, set the Multiline property to true and left align the output by setting the TextAlign property to Left.

GUI Design Tip

If a multiline TextBox will display many lines of output, limit the Text-Box height and use a vertical scroll bar to allow users to view additional lines of output.

(cont.)

3. ***Setting the location and size of the TextBox.*** Set the TextBox's Location property to 16, 160 and the Size property to 272, 88 so that it aligns horizontally with the controls above it.

4. ***Setting the text appearance in the TextBox.*** Initially, txtResult should not display any text. Clear the Text property. Set the TextAlign property to Left if it is not already set to Left. This left aligns text in the TextBox.

5. ***Setting property ReadOnly.*** To ensure that the user cannot change the output in the **Yearly account balance:** TextBox, set the ReadOnly property of txtResult to true.

6. ***Inserting a vertical scrollbar.*** Using scrollbars allows you to keep the size of a TextBox small while still allowing the user to view all the information in that TextBox. Because the length of the text could exceed the height of the TextBox, enable the vertical scrollbar by setting txtResult's **ScrollBars** property to **Vertical**. A vertical scrollbar appears on the right side of the TextBox. By default, the ScrollBars property is set to None. Note that the scrollbar is disabled on your Form. A scrollbar is enabled only when it is needed (that is, when there is enough text in the TextBox). Your Form should look like Fig. 11.10.

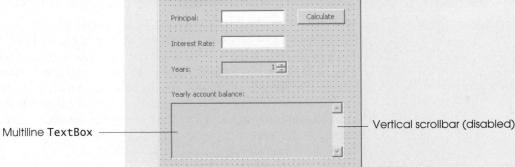

Multiline TextBox ——————

——— Vertical scrollbar (disabled)

Figure 11.10   Multiline TextBox with a vertical scrollbar added to the Form.

7. ***Saving the project.*** Select **File > Save All** to save your modified code.

Now that you have finished designing the GUI, you will add functionality to your application. When the user clicks the **Calculate** Button, you want the application to retrieve the input, then output a table containing the amount on deposit at the end of each year. You will do this by adding code to the **Calculate** Button's Click event handler.

Adding a Click Event Handler

1. ***Rearranging and commenting the controls.*** In code view, move the declaration for the updYear NumericUpDown control from line 31 of your code to line 25 of Fig. 11.11. Update the comment in line 23. The declaration for the txtResult multiline TextBox should now be at line 32. Update the comment in line 30.

2. ***Creating the event handler.*** In design view, double click the **Calculate** Button to generate the **Calculate** Button's Click event handler.

(cont.)

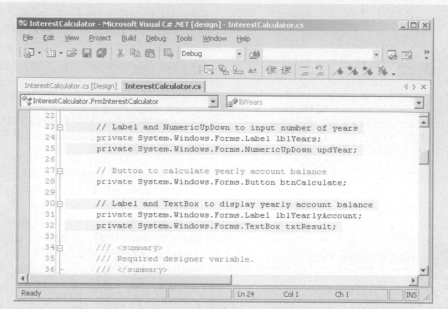

Figure 11.11 Rearranging and commenting the new control declarations.

3. **Adding code to the btnCalculate_Click event handler.** Be sure to add the comments and break the header as shown in Fig. 11.12 so that the line numbers in your code match those presented in this tutorial. Add lines 215–226 to the event handler. Lines 216–221 declare the variables needed to store user inputs, calculation results and the output. The decPrincipal variable stores the amount of the principal as entered by the user, dblRate stores the interest rate and intYear stores the number of years the user selected in the NumericUpDown control. The decAmount variable stores the result of the interest calculation.

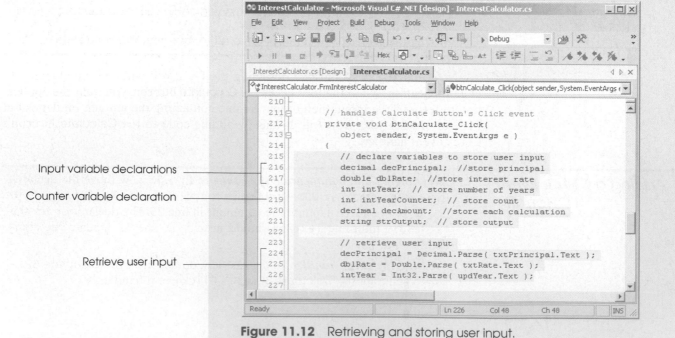

Figure 11.12 Retrieving and storing user input.

(cont.)

Good Programming Practice

Prefix `string` variable names with `str`.

Line 221 declares a `string` variable `strOutput`. A **string** variable stores a series of characters. The most commonly used characters are letters and numbers, though `strings` also include many special characters such as $, *, ^, tabs and newlines. A list of characters you are likely to use is found in Appendix B. You actually have been using `strings` all along—`Labels` and `TextBoxes` both store values in the `Text` property as values of the **string** data type. When you have assigned a numeric type, such as an `int`, to the `Text` property of a `Label`, you have used the `Convert.ToString` method to convert the numerical value to a `string`.

Lines 224–225 retrieve the principal and the interest rate from `TextBoxes`. Line 226 uses the `NumericUpDown` control's `Text` property to obtain the user's selection.

4. ***Displaying a header in a multiline TextBox.*** The multiline `TextBox` should display the results in two columns. A header is used to label the two columns `Year` and `Amount on Deposit`, respectively. Add lines 228–229 of Fig. 11.13 to assign the header to `strOutput`. In the next box, you will display `strOut-put` in the multiline `TextBox`. Add the comment on line 231 to your code.

Assigning header text to the output `string`

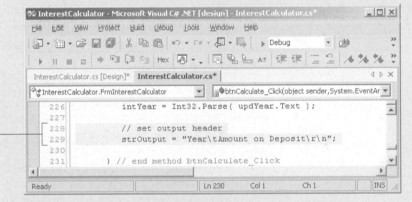

Figure 11.13 Displaying a header in a multiline `TextBox`.

Recall from Tutorial 6 that you cleared values in a `Label` by setting the `Text` property to the empty string (`""`), which represents a `string` value with no characters. When assigning new text to a `string` variable, you must begin and end the text with a double quotation mark (`"`). For example, the following statement stores the word `Year` in the `string` variable `strYear`:

```
strYear = "Year";
```

In line 229 of Fig. 11.13, we use the `\t` escape sequence to insert a tab character between the word `Year` and the text `Amount on Deposit`. We then insert a carriage return (escape sequence `\r`) and a newline character (escape sequence `\n`), so the next series of text will appear on the next line of output.

5. ***Saving the project.*** Select **File > Save All** to save your modified code.

Now that you have retrieved user input and created the output header, you will use a `for` statement to perform the interest calculations for the specified number of years.

Calculating Cumulative Interest with a for Statement

1. ***Creating the for header.*** Add lines 231–234 of Fig. 11.14 to the btnCalculate_Click event handler. Lines 232–233 constitute the for header, which initializes the control variable intYearCounter to 1. The header also contains the loop-continuation condition (intYearCounter <= intYear). This loop continues until the control variable is less than or equal to the number of years specified by the user. The control variable will increment by 1 each time through the loop.

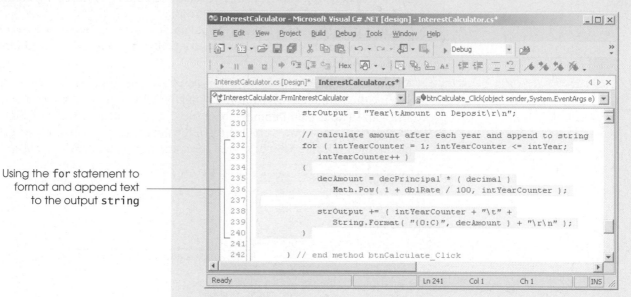

Using the for statement to format and append text to the output string

Figure 11.14 Coding a for statement.

2. ***Performing the interest calculation.*** The for statement executes its body once for each year up to the value of intYear, varying the control variable intYearCounter from 1 to intYear in increments of 1. Add lines 235–236 of Fig. 11.14 to perform the calculation from the formula

$$a = p \ (1 + r)^{\,n}$$

where a is decAmount, p is decPrincipal, r is dblRate and n is intYearCounter.

Notice that the calculation in line 236 also divides the rate, dblRate, by 100. This implies that the user must enter an interest rate value in percentage format (for example, the user should enter the number 5.5 to represent 5.5%).

3. ***Appending the calculation to the output string.*** Add lines 238–240 of Fig. 11.14. These lines append additional text to the end of strOutput, using the + (concatenation) and += (concatenation and assignment) string operators. The += string operator (which behaves much like the += operator for adding numerical values) appends the right operand to the text in the left operand. That new value is then assigned to the variable in the left operand. The text includes the current intYearCounter value, a tab character (\t) to position to the second column, the result of the call String.Format("{0:C}", decAmount) and, finally, a carriage return (\r) and a newline character (\n) to start the next output on the next line. Recall that the C (for "currency") formatting code indicates that its corresponding argument (decAmount) should be displayed in monetary format.

(cont.)

After the body of the loop is performed, application execution reaches the right brace (}) on line 240. The counter (intYearCounter) is incremented by 1, and the loop begins again with the loop-continuation test. The for statement executes until the control variable exceeds the number of years specified by the user.

4. ***Displaying the result of the calculations.*** After exiting the for statement, strOutput is ready to be displayed to the user in the txtResult TextBox. Add line 242 of Fig. 11.15 to display the header and the results in the multi-line TextBox.

Displaying in the multiline TextBox the result of the calculations performed in the for statement

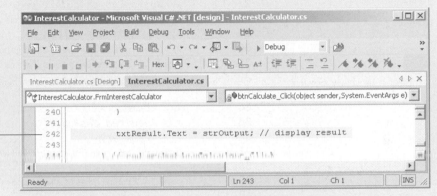

Figure 11.15   Displaying calculation results.

5. ***Running the application.*** Select **Debug > Start** to run your application. Your application can now calculate and display the amount on deposit for each year. Enter 1000 in the **Principal:** TextBox, 5 in the **Interest Rate:** TextBox and 10 in the **Years:** NumericUpDown control. Click the **Calculate** Button and verify that the results are the same as those displayed in Fig. 11.2.

6. ***Closing the application.*** Close your running application by clicking its close box.

7. ***Closing the IDE.*** Close Visual Studio .NET by clicking its close box.

Figure 11.16 presents the source code for the **Interest Calculator** application. The lines of code that contain new programming concepts that you learned in this tutorial are highlighted.

```
1   using System;
2   using System.Drawing;
3   using System.Collections;
4   using System.ComponentModel;
5   using System.Windows.Forms;
6   using System.Data;
7
8   namespace InterestCalculator
9   {
10      /// <summary>
11      /// Summary description for FrmInterestCalculator.
12      /// </summary>
13      public class FrmInterestCalculator : System.Windows.Forms.Form
14      {
15          // Label and TextBox to input principal
16          private System.Windows.Forms.Label lblPrincipal;
```

Figure 11.16   Interest Calculator application code. (Part 1 of 3.)

```
17        private System.Windows.Forms.TextBox txtPrincipal;
18
19        // Label and TextBox to input interest rate
20        private System.Windows.Forms.Label lblRate;
21        private System.Windows.Forms.TextBox txtRate;
22
23        // Label and NumericUpDown to input number of years
24        private System.Windows.Forms.Label lblYears;
25        private System.Windows.Forms.NumericUpDown updYear;
26
27        // Button to calculate yearly account balance
28        private System.Windows.Forms.Button btnCalculate;
29
30        // Label and TextBox to display yearly account balance
31        private System.Windows.Forms.Label lblYearlyAccount;
32        private System.Windows.Forms.TextBox txtResult;
33
34        /// <summary>
35        /// Required designer variable.
36        /// </summary>
37        private System.ComponentModel.Container components = null;
38
39        public FrmInterestCalculator()
40        {
41           //
42           // Required for Windows Form Designer support
43           //
44           InitializeComponent();
45           //
46           // TODO: Add any constructor code after InitializeComponent
47           // call
48           //
49        }
50
51        /// <summary>
52        /// Clean up any resources being used.
53        /// </summary>
54        protected override void Dispose( bool disposing )
55        {
56           if( disposing )
57           {
58              if (components != null)
59              {
60                 components.Dispose();
61              }
62           }
63           base.Dispose( disposing );
64        }
65
66        // Windows Form Designer generated code
67
68        /// <summary>
69        /// The main entry point for the application.
70        /// </summary>
71        [STAThread]
72        static void Main()
73        {
74           Application.Run( new FrmInterestCalculator() );
75        }
```

Declaration for a
NumericUpDown control → (line 25)

Declaration for a
multiline TextBox control → (line 32)

Figure 11.16   **Interest Calculator** application code. (Part 2 of 3.)

```
76
77          // handles Calculate Button's Click event
78          private void btnCalculate_Click(
79             object sender, System.EventArgs e )
80          {
81             // declare variables to store user input
82             decimal decPrincipal;  //store principal
83             double dblRate;  //store interest rate
84             int intYear;  // store number of years
85             int intYearCounter;  // store count
86             decimal decAmount;  //store each calculation
87             string strOutput;  // store output
88
89             // retrieve user input
90             decPrincipal = Decimal.Parse( txtPrincipal.Text );
91             dblRate = Double.Parse( txtRate.Text );
92             intYear = Int32.Parse( updYear.Text );
93
94             // set output header
95             strOutput = "Year\tAmount on Deposit\r\n";
96
97             // calculate amount after each year and append to string
98             for ( intYearCounter = 1; intYearCounter <= intYear;
99                intYearCounter++ )
100            {
101               decAmount = decPrincipal * ( decimal )
102                  Math.Pow( 1 + dblRate / 100, intYearCounter );
103
104               strOutput += ( intYearCounter + "\t" +
105                  String.Format( "{0:C}", decAmount ) + "\r\n" );
106            }
107
108            txtResult.Text = strOutput; // display result
109
110         } // end method btnCalculate_Click
111
112      } // end class FrmInterestCalculator
113 }
```

Declaration for a **string** variable — 87

Assigning a value to a **string** — 95

Using a **for** statement to
calculate amount on deposit — 102

Displaying a **string** in
a multiline TextBox — 108

Figure 11.16   Interest Calculator application code. (Part 3 of 3.)

SELF-REVIEW   1. The _____ property determines by how much the current number in a NumericUp-
Down control changes when the user clicks the up arrow or the down arrow.

    a) Amount   b) Step

    c) Increment   d) Next

2. Which for header alters the control variable from 1 to 50 in increments of 5?

    a) for (i = 1; i <= 50; i += 50)   b) for (5; i < 50; i += 5)

    c) for (i = 1; i < 50; i + 5)   d) for (i = 1; i <= 50; i += 5)

Answers: 1) c. 2) d.

11.6 Wrap-Up

In this tutorial, you learned that the essential elements of counter-controlled repetition are the name of a control variable, the initial value of the control variable, the
increment (or decrement) by which the control variable is modified each time
through the loop and the condition that tests the final value of the control variable.

You then explored the for repetition statement, which combines these essentials of counter-controlled repetition in its header.

After becoming familiar with the for repetition statement, you changed the **Car Payment Calculator** application's while statement into a for statement. You then built an **Interest Calculator**, after analyzing the pseudocode and ACE table for this application. In the **Interest Calculator**'s GUI, you added new design elements, including a NumericUpDown control and a multiline TextBox that contained a vertical scrollbar.

In the next tutorial, you will learn to use the switch multiple-selection statement. You have learned that the if selection statement can be used in code to select between multiple courses of action on the value of a condition. You will see that a switch multiple selection statement can save development time and improve code readability if the number of conditions is large. You will then use a switch multiple selection statement to build a **Security Panel** application.

SKILLS SUMMARY

Using the for Repetition Statement

- First, specify the initial value of the control variable, followed by a semicolon.
- Second, specify the loop-continuation condition, followed by a semicolon.
- Third, specify the increment (or decrement).
- Use braces to enclose multiple statements in the body of the for statement.
- Using the for statement helps eliminate off-by-one errors.

Creating a Multiline TextBox with a Vertical Scrollbar

- Insert a TextBox onto the Form.
- Set TextBox property Multiline to true.
- Set TextBox property ScrollBars to Vertical.

Specifying a NumericUpDown Control's Maximum Value

- Use NumericUpDown property Maximum.

Specifying a NumericUpDown Control's Minimum Value

- Use NumericUpDown property Minimum.

Changing the Current Number in a NumericUpDown Control

- Click the NumericUpDown control's up or down arrow.

Specifying by How Much the Current Number in a NumericUpDown Control Changes When the User Clicks an Arrow

- Use NumericUpDown property Increment.

KEY TERMS

control variable—A variable used to control the number of iterations of a counter-controlled loop.

final value of a control variable—The last value a control variable will hold before a counter-controlled loop terminates.

for header—The first line of a for repetition statement. The for header specifies all four essential elements for the counter-controlled repetition of a for repetition statement.

for keyword—Begins the for statement.

for repetition statement—Handles the details of counter-controlled repetition. The for statement uses all four elements essential to counter-controlled repetition in one line of code (the name of a control variable, the initial value, the increment or decrement value and the condition to test for the final value) in one line of code.

increment (or decrement) of a control variable—The amount by which the control variable's value changes during each iteration of the loop.

Increment property of NumericUpDown control—Specifies by how much the current number in the NumericUpDown control changes when the user clicks the control's up (for incrementing) or down (for decrementing) arrow.

initial value of a control variable—The value of a control variable will hold when counter-controlled repetition begins.

Maximum property of NumericUpDown control—Determines the maximum input value in a particular NumericUpDown control.

Minimum property of NumericUpDown control—Determines the minimum input value in a particular NumericUpDown control.

Multiline TextBox control—Provides the ability to enter or display multiple lines of text. If the text exceeds the size of the TextBox, the control can be set to display a scrollbar.

Multiline property of TextBox control—Specifies whether the TextBox is capable of displaying multiple lines of text. If the value of the property is true, the TextBox may contain multiple lines of text; if the value of the property is false, the TextBox can contain only one line of text.

name of a control variable—Identifier used to reference the control variable of a loop.

NumericUpDown control—Allows you to specify maximum and minimum numeric input values. Also allows you to specify an increment (or decrement) when the user clicks the up (or down) arrow.

ReadOnly property of a NumericUpDown control—Determines whether the input value can be typed by the user.

ScrollBars property of TextBox control—Specifies whether a TextBox has a scrollbar and, if so, of what type. By default, the ScrollBars property set to None. Setting the value to Vertical places a scrollbar along the right side of the TextBox.

string type—Contains a series of characters (letters, numbers, etc.).

Vertical value of ScrollBars property—Places a scrollbar along the right side of a TextBox when assigned to property ScrollBars.

GUI DESIGN GUIDELINES

TextBox

- If a TextBox will display multiple lines of output, set the Multiline property to true and left align the output by setting the TextAlign property to Left.
- If a multiline TextBox will display many lines of output, limit the TextBox height and use a vertical scrollbar to allow users to view additional lines of output.

NumericUpDown

- A NumericUpDown control should follow the same GUI Design Guidelines as a TextBox.
- Use a NumericUpDown control to limit the range of user input.

CONTROLS, EVENTS, PROPERTIES & METHODS

NumericUpDown      This control allows you to specify maximum and minimum numeric input values.

- *In action*

- *Properties*

   Increment—Specifies by how much the current number in the NumericUpDown control changes when the user clicks the control's up (for incrementing) or down (for decrementing) arrow.

   Location—Specifies the location of the NumericUpDown control on the Form relative to the top-left corner.

   Maximum—Determines the maximum input value in a particular NumericUpDown control.

   Minimum—Determines the minimum input value in a particular NumericUpDown control.

   Name—Specifies the name used to access the NumericUpDown control programmatically. The name should be prefixed with upd.

   ReadOnly—Determines whether the input value can be typed by the user.

   Size—Specifies the height and width (in pixels) of the NumericUpDown control.

   TextAlign—Specifies how the text is aligned within the NumericUpDown control.

TextBox   abl TextBox   This control allows the user to input data from the keyboard.

■ *In action*

```
     0
```

■ *Event*

TextChanged—Raised when the text in the TextBox is changed.

■ *Properties*

Location—Specifies the location of the TextBox on the Form relative to the top-left corner.

Multiline—Specifies whether the TextBox is capable of displaying multiple lines of text.

Name—Specifies the name used to access the TextBox programmatically. The name should be prefixed with txt.

ReadOnly—Determines whether the value of a TextBox can be changed.

ScrollBars—Specifies whether a TextBox has a scrollbar and, if so, of what type. By default, the ScrollBars property set to None. Setting the value to Vertical places a scrollbar along the right side of the TextBox.

Size—Specifies the height and width (in pixels) of the TextBox.

Text—Specifies the text displayed in the TextBox.

TextAlign—Specifies how the text is aligned within the TextBox.

■ *Method*

Focus—Transfers the focus of the application to the TextBox that calls it.

MULTIPLE-CHOICE QUESTIONS

11.1 "Hello" has a _____ type.

   a) string   b) stringliteral

   c) char   d) stringtext

11.2 A _____ provides the ability to enter or display multiple lines of text in the same control.

   a) TextBox   b) NumericUpDown

   c) multiline TextBox   d) multiline NumericUpDown

11.3 The NumericUpDown control allows you to specify _____.

   a) a maximum value the user can select   b) a minimum value the user can select

   c) an increment for the values presented to the user   d) All of the above.

11.4 The _____ is often omitted from a for header when the control variable has already been assigned a value.

   a) semicolon   b) initial value of the control variable

   c) for keyword   d) final value of the control variable

11.5 Setting TextBox property ScrollBars to _____ creates a vertical scrollbar.

   a) true   b) Vertical

   c) Up   d) Down

11.6 _____ is used to determine whether a for loop continues to iterate.

   a) The initial value of the control variable   b) The for keyword

   c) The increment value   d) The loop-continuation condition

11.7 In a for loop, the control variable is incremented (or decremented) _____.

   a) after the body of the loop executes

   b) the first time through only

   c) while the loop-continuation condition is false

   d) while the body of the loop executes

11.8 Setting a NumericUpDown control's _____ property to true ensures that the user cannot enter invalid values in the control.

a) Increment

b) ScrollBars

c) ReadOnly

d) Invalid

11.9 The _____ and _____ properties limit the values users can select in the NumericUpDown control.

a) Maximum, Minimum

b) Top, Bottom

c) High, Low

d) Max, Min

11.10 The for header _____ can be used to vary the control variable over the odd numbers between 1 and 10.

a) for (i = 1 ; i <= 10; i++)

b) for (i = 1 ; i <= 10; i += 2)

c) for (i = 1 ; i <= 10; i--)

d) for (i = 1 ; i <= 10; i -= 2)

EXERCISES

11.11 *(Present Value Calculator Application)* A bank wants to show its customers how much they would need to invest to achieve a specified financial goal (future value) in 5, 10, 15, 20, 25 or 30 years. Users must provide their financial goal (the amount of money desired after the specified number of years has elapsed), an interest rate and the length of the investment in years. Create an application that calculates and displays the principal (initial amount to invest) needed to achieve the user's financial goal. Your application should allow the user to invest money for 5, 10, 15, 20, 25 or 30 years. For example, if a customer wants to reach the financial goal of $15,000 over a period of five years when the interest rate is 6.6%, the customer would need to invest $10,896.96 as shown in Fig. 11.17.

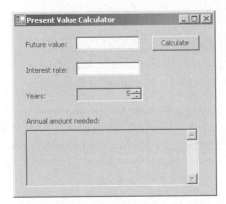 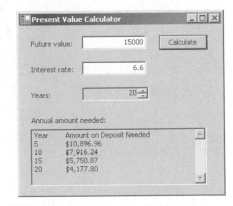

Figure 11.17   Present Value Calculator GUI.

a) *Copying the template to your working directory.* Copy the directory C:\Examples\ Tutorial11\Exercises\PresentValue to your C:\SimplyCSP directory.

b) *Opening the application's template file.* Double click PresentValue.sln in the PresentValue directory to open the application.

c) *Adding the NumericUpDown control.* Place and size the NumericUpDown so that it follows the GUI Design Guidelines. Set the NumericUpDown control's Name property to updYear. Set the NumericUpDown control to allow only multiples of five for the number of years. Also, allow the user to select only a duration that is in the specified range of values.

d) *Adding a multiline TextBox.* Add a TextBox to the Form below the NumericUpDown control. Change the size to 272, 88 and position the TextBox on the Form so that it follows the GUI Design Guidelines. Then, set that TextBox to display multiple lines and a scrollbar. Also ensure that the user cannot modify the text in the TextBox. Rearrange and comment the new control declarations appropriately.

e) *Creating a Click event handler and adding code.* Add a Click event handler for the **Calculate** Button. Once in code view, add code to the application such that, when the **Calculate** Button is clicked, the multiline TextBox displays the necessary principal for each five-year interval. Use the following version of the present-value calculation formula:

$$p = a / (1 + r)^n$$

where

p is the amount needed to achieve the future value
r is the annual interest rate (for example, .05 is equivalent to 5%)
n is the number of years
a is the future-value amount.

f) *Running the application.* Select **Debug > Start** to run your application. Enter amounts for the future value, interest rate and number of years. Click the **Calculate** Button and verify that the year intervals and the amount on deposit needed for each is correct. Test the application again, this time entering 30 for the number of years. Verify that the vertical scrollbar appears to display all of the output.

g) *Closing the application.* Close your running application by clicking its close box.

h) *Closing the IDE.* Close Visual Studio .NET by clicking its close box.

11.12 (Comparing Rates Application) Write an application that calculates the amount of money in an account after 10 years for interest rate amounts of 5%–10% (Fig. 11.18). For this application, users must provide the initial principal.

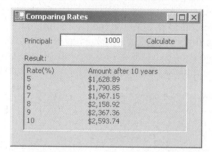

Figure 11.18 Comparing Rates GUI.

a) *Copying the template to your working directory.* Copy the directory `C:\Examples\Tutorial11\Exercises\ComparingRates` to your `C:\SimplyCSP` directory.

b) *Opening the application's template file.* Double click `ComparingRates.sln` in the `ComparingRates` directory to open the application.

c) *Adding a multiline TextBox.* Add a TextBox to the Form below the **Result:** Label control. Change the size to `256, 104`, and position the TextBox on the Form so that it follows the GUI Design Guidelines (Fig. 11.18). Then, set that TextBox to display multiple lines. Also ensure that the user cannot modify the text in the TextBox. Rearrange and comment the new control declaration appropriately.

d) *Creating a Click event handler and adding code.* Add a Click event handler for the **Calculate** Button. Once in code view, add code to the application such that, when the **Calculate** Button is clicked, the multiline TextBox displays the amount in the account after 10 years for interest rates of 5, 6, 7, 8, 9 and 10 percent. Use the following version of the interest-calculation formula:

$$a = p (1 + r)^n$$

where

p is the original amount invested (the principal)
r is the annual interest rate (for example, .05 is equivalent to 5%)
n is the number of years
a is the investment's value at the end of the nth year.

e) *Running the application.* Select **Debug > Start** to run your application. Enter the principal amount for an account and click the **Calculate** Button. Verify that the correct amounts after 10 years are then displayed, based on interest rate amounts of 5–10%.

f) *Closing the application.* Close your running application by clicking its close box.

g) *Closing the IDE.* Close Visual Studio .NET by clicking its close box.

11.13 *(Enhanced Interest Calculator Application to Validate Input)* Enhance the **Interest Calculator** application with error checking. Test for whether the user has entered valid values for the principal and interest rate. If the user enters an invalid value, display a message in the multiline TextBox. Figure 11.19 demonstrates the application handling an invalid input.

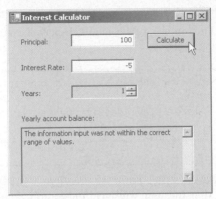

Figure 11.19 Enhanced **Interest Calculator** application with error checking.

a) *Copying the template to your working directory.* Copy the directory C:\Examples\ Tutorial11\Exercises\InterestCalculatorEnhancement to your C:\SimplyCSP directory.

b) *Opening the application's template file.* Double click InterestCalculator.sln in the InterestCalculatorEnhancement directory to open the application.

c) *Adding code to the Click event handler.* Modify the Click event handler for the **Calculate** Button so that it validates the input. The principal should be a positive amount greater than 0. Also, the interest rate should be greater than 0, but less than 100.

d) *Displaying the error message.* Display the text "The information was not within the correct range of values." in txtResult if the values are not valid.

e) *Running the application.* Select **Debug > Start** to run your application. Enter invalid data for the principal and interest rate. The invalid data can include negative numbers and letters. Verify that entering invalid data and clicking the **Calculate** Button results in the error message displayed in Fig. 11.19.

f) *Closing the application.* Close your running application by clicking its close box.

g) *Closing the IDE.* Close Visual Studio .NET by clicking its close box.

What does this code do? ▶ **11.14** What is the value of intResult after the following code executes? Assume that intPower, intI, intResult and intNumber are all declared as ints.

```
1   intPower = 5;
2   intNumber = 10;
3   intResult = intNumber;
4
5   for ( intI = 1; intI <= ( intPower - 1 ); intI++ )
6   {
7       intResult *= intNumber;
8   }
```

What's wrong with this code? ▶ **11.15** Assume that the intCounter variable is declared as an int for both a and b. Identify and correct the error(s) in each of the following:

a) This statement should display in a ListBox all numbers from 100 to 1 in decreasing order.

```
1   for ( intCounter = 100; intCounter >= 1 )
2   {
3       lstDisplay.Items.Add( intCounter );
4   }
```

b) The following code should display in a ListBox the odd ints from 19 to 1 in decreasing order.

```
1   for ( intCounter = 19; intCounter >= 1; intCounter-- )
2   {
3       lstDisplay.Add( intCounter );
4   }
```

Using the Debugger ▶ **11.16** (*Savings Calculator Application*) The **Savings Calculator** application calculates the amount that the user will have on deposit after one year. The application gets the initial amount on deposit from the user, and assumes that the user will add $100 to the account every month for the entire year. No interest is added to the account. Copy the directory C:\Examples\Tutorial11\Debugger\SavingsCalculator to your C:\SimplyCSP directory. Run the application. While testing the application, you noticed that the amount calculated by the application was incorrect. Use the debugger to locate and correct any logic error(s). Figure 11.20 displays the correct output for this application.

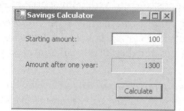

Figure 11.20 Correct output for the **Savings Calculator** application.

Programming Challenge ▶ **11.17** (*Pay Raise Calculator Application*) Develop an application that computes the amount of money an employee makes each year over a user-specified number of years (Fig. 11.21). The employee receives an hourly wage and a pay raise once every year. The user specifies the hourly wage and the amount of the raise (in percentages per year) in the application.

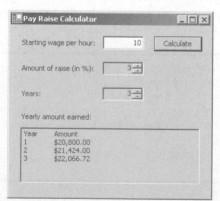

Figure 11.21 **Pay Raise** application's GUI.

a) *Copying the template to your working directory.* Copy the directory C:\Examples\ Tutorial11\Exercises\PayRaise to your C:\SimplyCSP directory.

b) *Opening the application's template file.* Double click PayRaise.sln in the PayRaise directory to open the application.

c) *Adding controls to the Form.* Add two NumericUpDown controls to the Form. The first NumericUpDown control should be provided to allow the user to specify the pay raise percentage. The user should only be able to specify percentages in the range 3–8 percent. Create the second NumericUpDown control for users to select the number of years in the range 1–50. Then add a multiline TextBox control to the application. Ensure that the user cannot modify the text in the NumericUpDown and TextBox controls. Resize and move the controls you created so that they follow the GUI Design Guidelines as in Fig. 11.21. Rearrange and comment the new control declarations appropriately.

d) *Creating a Click event handler and adding code.* Add a Click event handler for the **Calculate** Button. Once in code view, add code to use the for statement to compute the yearly salary amounts, based on the yearly pay raise.

e) *Running the application.* Select **Debug > Start** to run your application. Enter a starting wage per hour, the size of the yearly raise and the number of years worked. Click the **Calculate** Button and verify that the correct amount after each year is displayed in the **Yearly amount earned:** TextBox.

f) *Closing the application.* Close your running application by clicking its close box.

g) *Closing the IDE.* Close Visual Studio .NET by clicking its close box.

TUTORIAL 12

Objectives

In this tutorial, you will learn to:
- Use the `switch` multiple-selection statement.
- Use `case`s.
- Use the `default` keyword.
- Display a date and time.
- Use TextBox property `PasswordChar`.

Outline

Security Panel Application

Introducing the *switch* Multiple-Selection Statement

In the last tutorial, you learned how to use the `for` statement, which is the most concise statement for performing counter-controlled repetition. In this tutorial, you will learn about the `switch` multiple-selection statement. The `switch` statement is used to simplify code that uses several `else if` statements sequentially when an application must choose among many possible actions to perform.

12.1 Test-Driving the Security Panel Application

In this tutorial, you will use the `switch` multiple-selection statement to construct a **Security Panel** application. This application must meet the following requirements:

Application Requirements

A lab wants to install a security panel outside a laboratory room. Only authorized personnel may enter the lab, using their security codes. The following are valid security codes (also called access codes) and the groups of employees they represent:

Values	Groups
1645 or 1689	Technicians
8345	Custodians
9998, 1006–1008	Scientists

Once a security code is entered, access is either granted or denied. All access attempts are written to a window below the keypad. If access is granted, the date, time and group (scientists, custodians, etc.) are written to the window. If access is denied, the date, the time and a message, "Access Denied," are written to the window. Furthermore, the user can enter any one-digit access code to summon a security guard for assistance. The date, the time and a message, "Restricted Access," then are written to the window to indicate that the request has been received.

You begin by test-driving the completed application. Then, you will learn the additional C# technologies you need to create your own version of this application.

Test-Driving the Security Panel Application

1. *Opening the completed application.* Open the C:\Examples\Tutorial12\ CompletedApplication\SecurityPanel directory to locate the **Security Panel** application. Double click SecurityPanel.sln to open the application in Visual Studio .NET.

2. *Running the Security Panel application.* Select **Debug > Start** to run the application (Fig. 12.1). At the top of the Form, you are provided with a Text-Box that displays an asterisk for each digit in the security code entered using the GUI keypad. Notice that the GUI keypad looks much like a real-world keypad. (We will mimic real-world conditions when possible.) The **C** Button clears your current input, and the **#** Button causes the application to process the security code entered. Results are displayed in the ListBox at the bottom of the Form.

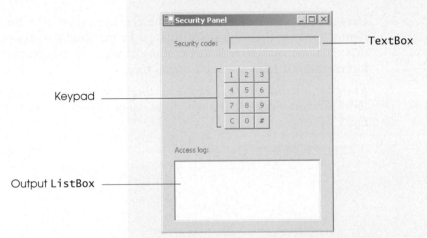

Keypad

Output ListBox

Figure 12.1   **Security Panel** application running.

 **GUI Design Tip**

If your GUI is modeling a real-world object, its design should mimic the physical appearance of the object.

3. *Entering an invalid security code.* Use the keypad to enter the invalid security code 1212. Notice that an asterisk (*) is displayed in the TextBox (Fig. 12.2) for each numeric key pressed (by clicking its Button on the Form). These characters do not allow other people to see the code entered. When finished, click the **#** Button. A message indicating that access is denied will appear in the ListBox, as in Fig. 12.3. Notice that the TextBox is cleared when the **#** Button is pressed.

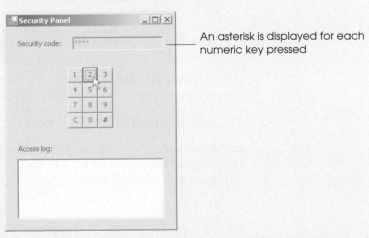

An asterisk is displayed for each numeric key pressed

Figure 12.2   Asterisks displayed in the **Security code:** field.

(cont.)

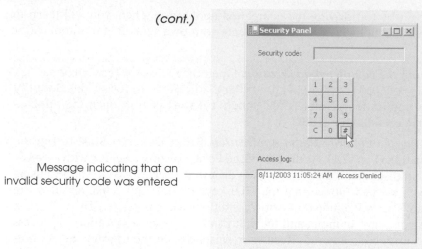

Figure 12.3 **Security Panel** displaying the **Access Denied** message.

Message indicating that an invalid security code was entered

4. ***Using the C Button***. Press a few numeric keys, then click the **C** Button. Notice that all the asterisks displayed in the TextBox disappear. Users often make mistakes when keystroking or when clicking Buttons, so the **C** Button allows users to make a "fresh start."

5. ***Entering a valid security code***. Use the keypad to enter 1006, then click the **#** Button. Notice that a second message appears in the ListBox, as in Fig. 12.4.

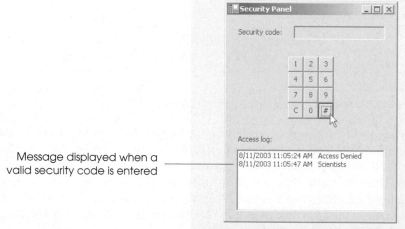

Message displayed when a valid security code is entered

Figure 12.4 **Security Panel** application confirming a valid security-code entry.

6. ***Closing the application***. Close your running application by clicking its close box.

7. ***Closing the IDE***. Close Visual Studio .NET by clicking its close box.

12.2 Introducing the `switch` Multiple-Selection Statement

In this section, you will learn how to use the **switch** multiple-selection statement. For comparison purposes, we will first provide a nested `if...else` statement that displays a text message based on a student's grade:

```
if ( strGrade == 'A' )
{
    lblDisplay.Text = "Excellent!";
}
```

```
        else if ( strGrade == 'B' )
        {
            lblDisplay.Text = "Very good!";
        }
        else if ( strGrade == 'C' )
        {
            lblDisplay.Text = "Good.";
        }
        else if ( strGrade == 'D' )
        {
            lblDisplay.Text = "Poor.";
        }
        else if ( strGrade == 'F' )
        {
            lblDisplay.Text = "Failure.";
        }
        else
        {
            lblDisplay.Text = "Invalid grade.";
        }
```

This statement can be used to produce the correct output when selecting among multiple values of strGrade. However, by using the switch statement, you can simplify every instance like

```
        if ( strGrade == 'A' )
```

to one like

```
        case 'A':
```

and eliminate the if and else keywords.

In this example, grade is of type **char**, which is one of C#'s built-in types. The value of a variable of the char type is a **character constant** (or **character literal**) which is a single character or escape sequence within single quotes. Character constants include letters (such as 'A'), digits (such as '5'), special characters (such as ','—the comma), whitespace (such as ' '—a space) and escape sequences (such as '\n'—the newline character).

The following switch multiple-selection statement performs the same functionality as the preceding if...else statement:

```
        switch ( strGrade )
        {
            case 'A':
                lblDisplay.Text = "Excellent!";
                break;

            case 'B':
                lblDisplay.Text = "Very good!";
                break;

            case 'C':
                lblDisplay.Text = "Good.";
                break;

            case 'D':
                lblDisplay.Text = "Poor.";
                break;

            case 'F':
                lblDisplay.Text = "Failure.";
                break;

            default:
                lblDisplay.Text = "Invalid grade.";
                break;
        }
```

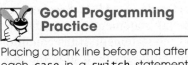

Good Programming Practice

Placing a blank line before and after each case in a switch statement improves readability.

Good Programming Practice

Indenting the statements in the body of a case improves readability.

Good Programming Practice

Although the cases in a switch statement can occur in any order, it is considered a good programming practice to place the default case last.

Good Programming Practice

Placing a blank line before and after each `case` in a `switch` statement improves readability.

Good Programming Practice

Indenting the statements in the body of a `case` improves readability.

Common Programming Error

Specifying two or more `cases` with the same constant expression is a syntax error.

Common Programming Error

Not including a `break` statement at the end of each `case` in a `switch` is a syntax error. The exception to this rule is the empty `case`.

The `switch` statement begins with the keyword `switch`, followed by a **controlling expression** inside parentheses and a left brace, then terminates with a right brace. The preceding `switch` contains five **case labels** and the optional **default case**, which will execute if the controlling expression's value does not match any of the other `cases`. Each `case` label contains the `case` keyword, followed by a **constant expression** and a colon. The constant expression can be a character literal, such as `'A'` (which is a `char` type), a string literal, such as `"Hello"`, or an integer literal, such as `707`, but cannot be a floating-point literal such as `9.9`. The constant expression also can be a variable that contains a character or integer constant (that is, a `const` variable). Only values of types `char`, `string`, `byte`, `sbyte`, `short`, `ushort`, `int`, `uint`, `long` and `ulong` can be tested in a `switch` statement. Although a `switch` statement can have any number of `case` labels, it can have at most one `default` case, and no two `cases` can specify the same constant expression.

Following the colon (`:`) for a `case` is a series of statements to be executed if the value of the controlling expression matches the `case` label. It is important to notice that the `switch` statement is different from other selection or repetition statements in that braces are not required around multiple actions in a `case` of a `switch`. Instead, the body of a `case` begins after the colon and ends with a **break** statement. The `break` statement causes program control to proceed with the first statement after the `switch` statement.

The `break` statement is required for each `case` (including the `default case`) that contains statements. A `case` with no statements is considered an **empty case**, and can omit the `break` statement. The last `case` in a `switch` statement must not be an empty `case`. If the `case` label for an empty case matches the controlling expression, **fall through** occurs. This means that the `switch` statement executes the statements in the next `case`. If that `case` is also empty, this process will continue until a non-empty `case` is found, then that `case`'s statements will execute. This provides the programmer with a way to specify statements to be executed for several different labels.

If no match occurs between the controlling expression's value and a `case` label, the `default case` executes. Note that the `default case` is optional in the `switch` statement. If the controlling expression does not match a `case` and there is no `default case`, program control proceeds with the first statement after the `switch` statement. It is also important to understand that in C# the statements for only one `case` can be executed in one `switch` statement.

Figure 12.5 shows the UML activity diagram for this `switch` multiple-selection statement. The first condition to be evaluated is `strGrade == 'A'`. If this condition is `true`, the text `"Excellent!"` is displayed, the `break` statement is executed and control proceeds to the first statement after the `switch` statement. If the condition is `false` (that is, `strGrade != 'A'`), the statement continues by testing the next condition, `strGrade = 'B'`. If this condition is `true`, the text `"Very good!"` is displayed, the `break` statement is executed and control proceeds to the first statement after the `switch` statement. If the condition is `false` (that is, `strGrade != 'B'`), the statement continues to test the next condition. This process continues until a matching `case` is found or until the final condition evaluates to `false` (`strGrade != 'F'`). If the latter occurs, the `default case`'s body is executed, and the text `"Invalid grade."` is displayed. The `break` statement is then executed, and the application continues with the first statement after the `switch` statement.

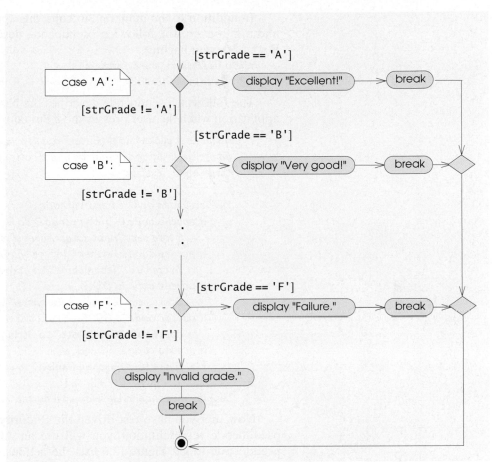

Figure 12.5   UML activity diagram for the **switch** multiple-selection statement.

---

1. A switch statement is a _____-selection statement.

   a) multiple   b) double
   c) single   d) None of the above.

2. When does the default body execute?

   a) Every time a switch statement executes
   b) When more than one case is matched
   c) When all cases are matching cases in a switch statement
   d) None of the above.

Answers: 1) a. 2) d.

12.3 Constructing the Security Panel Application

The **Security Panel** application contains 10 Buttons that display digits. (We call these numeric Buttons.) You will create an event handler for each Button's Click event. These Buttons make up the GUI keypad. The following pseudocode describes the basic operation of the Click event handler for each of these numeric Buttons:

> *When the user clicks a numeric Button:*
>> *Concatenate the Button's digit to the TextBox's Text property value*

Later in this tutorial, you will convert this pseudocode into C# code and create the Click event handlers for each numeric Button. The user then will be able to use the numeric Buttons to enter digits and have those digits concatenated to the text in a TextBox.

In addition to the numeric Buttons, this application also contains a **C** Button and a **#** Button. The following pseudocode describes the basic operation of the **C** Button's event handler:

> When user clicks the C Button:
>> Clear Input TextBox

The following pseudocode describes the basic operation of the **Security Panel** application when the user presses the **#** Button:

> When the user clicks the # (Enter) Button:
>> Store security code input by user (currently in the TextBox) to a variable
>> Clear input TextBox
>>
>> Switch based on the security code
>>> If access code is in the range 0 to 9
>>>> Store text "Restricted Access" to string variable
>>> If access code is either 1645 or 1689
>>>> Store text "Technicians" to string variable
>>> If access code is 8345
>>>> Store text "Custodial Services" to string variable
>>> If access code is 9998 or is in the range 1006 to 1008
>>>> Store text "Scientists" to string variable
>>> If access code is invalid
>>>> Store text "Access Denied" to string variable
>>
>> Display message in ListBox with current time and string variable's contents

Now that you have test-driven the **Security Panel** application and studied its pseudocode representation, you will use an ACE table to help you convert the pseudocode to C#. Figure 12.6 lists the actions, controls and events that will help you complete your own version of this application.

	Action	Control/Class/Object	Event
Action/Control/Event (ACE) Table for the Security Panel Application	Label all the application's controls	lblSecurityCode, lblAccessCode	Application is run
		btnZero, btnOne, btnTwo, btnThree, btnFour, btnFive, btnSix, btnSeven, btnEight, btnNine	Click
	Concatenate Button's digit to the TextBox's Text property value	txtSecurityCode	
		btnEnter	Click
	Store security code input by user to a variable	txtSecurityCode	
	Clear TextBox	txtSecurityCode	
	Switch based on the security code		
	If access code is in the range 0 to 9 Store text "Restricted Access" to string variable	strMessage (string)	
	If access code is either 1645 or 1689 Store text "Technicians" to string variable	strMessage (string)	

Figure 12.6 ACE table for **Security Panel** application. (Part 1 of 2.)

Action	Control/Class/Object	Event

If access code is 8345
    Store text "Custodial
       Services" to string variable
	strMessage (string)	

If access code is 9998 or is in
the range 1006 to 1008
    Store text "Scientists" to
       string variable
	strMessage (string)	

If access code is invalid
    Store text "Access Denied" to
       string variable
	strMessage (string)	

Display message in ListBox with current time and string variable's contents	lstLogEntry, strMessage (string)	
	btnClear	Click
Clear Input TextBox	txtSecurityCode	

Figure 12.6 ACE table for **Security Panel** application. (Part 2 of 2.)

Now that you are familiar with the switch multiple-selection statement, you will use it to build the **Security Panel** application.

Using the PasswordChar Property

GUI Design Tip

Mask passwords and other sensitive pieces of information in TextBoxes.

1. **Copying the template to your working directory.** Copy the C:\Examples\ Tutorial12\TemplateApplication\SecurityPanel directory to your C:\SimplyCSP directory.

2. **Opening the Security Panel application's template file.** Double click SecurityPanel.sln in the SecurityPanel directory to open the application in Visual Studio .NET.

3. **Displaying the * character in the TextBox.** In design view, select the **Security code:** TextBox at the top of the Form, then set its TextBox's Password-Char property to * in the **Properties** window. Text displayed in a TextBox can be hidden or **masked** with the character specified in the **PasswordChar** property. Rather than displaying the actual TextBox text that the user types, **masking characters** are displayed. However, the TextBox's Text property does contain the text the user typed. For example, if a user enters 5469, the TextBox displays ****, yet stores "5469" in its Text property. Now any character displayed in your interface's TextBox displays as the * character.

4. **Disabling the TextBox.** The primary reason for using a TextBox instead of a Label to display the access code is to use the PasswordChar property. To prevent users from modifying the text in the TextBox, set its **Enabled** property to false.

5. **Create the btnEnter_Click event handler.** Double click the # Button to create the btnEnter_Click event handler.

6. **Declaring and initializing variables.** Be sure to add the comments and break the header as shown in Fig. 12.7 so that the line numbers in your code match those presented in this tutorial. Add lines 267–271 to the event handler. Lines 267–268 declare the intAccessCode and strMessage variables. The intAccessCode variable will be used to store the user's security code (access code), and the strMessage variable will store the message that will be displayed to the user, based on the access code entered. Line 270 sets the intAccessCode variable to the security code input by the user. Line 271 clears the **Security code:** TextBox.

(cont.)

Declaring an event handler's variables

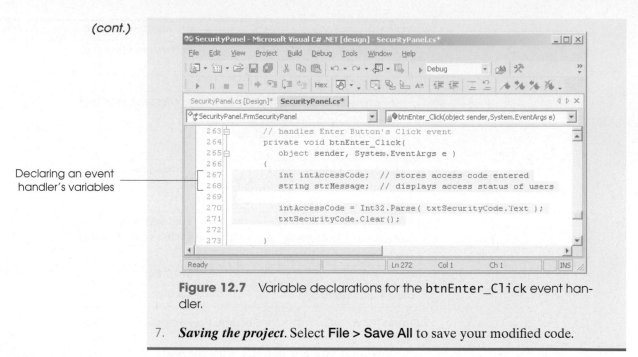

Figure 12.7 Variable declarations for the btnEnter_Click event handler.

7. **Saving the project.** Select **File > Save All** to save your modified code.

Now that you have designed the GUI for your application and initialized the variables for your event handler, let's continue by creating your switch statement, as shown in the following box. This statement will determine the user's access level based on the code input.

Adding a switch Statement to the Application

1. **Adding a switch statement to btnEnter_Click.** Add lines 273–276 from Fig. 12.8 to the btnEnter_Click event handler. Line 273 begins the switch statement, which contains the controlling expression intAccessCode—the access code entered by the user. Remember that this expression (the value intAccessCode) is compared sequentially with each case until either a match occurs or the end of the switch statement is reached. If a matching case is found, the body of that case executes and program control proceeds to the first statement after the right brace (}) that ends the switch statement. Ignore the syntax error that appears, as you will now fill the body of the switch statement. [*Note*: If you add the closing right brace after adding the cases, Visual Studio .NET may indent your comments incorrectly. Readjust them according to the code presented in Fig. 12.9, Fig. 12.10 and Fig. 12.11.]

Creating a switch statement

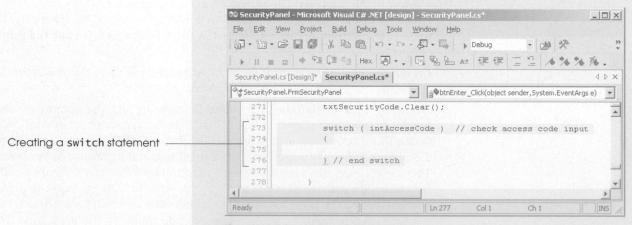

Figure 12.8 switch statement.

(cont.)   2. ***Adding first cases to the switch statement***. Add lines 275–287 from
Fig. 12.9 to the switch statement.

Empty cases fall through ——————

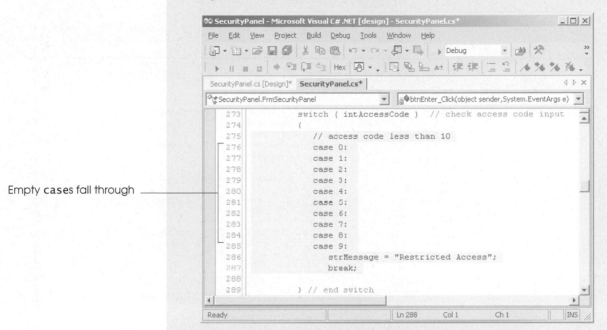

Figure 12.9   First cases added to the switch statement.

The first group of cases test whether intAccessCode is less than 10.
Note that cases 0 through 8 are empty cases. If the value of the controlling
expression matches any of these cases, program control falls through to the
statements under case 9. Thus, if the value in intAccessCode is between 0
and 9 inclusive, the code in the body of that group of cases will execute and
strMessage will be assigned the string "Restricted Access", which will be
displayed after the body of the switch statement completes. The break
statement will transfer program control out of the switch statement.

3. ***Specifying cases for the remaining access codes***. Add lines 289–307 from
Fig. 12.10 to the switch statement. Indent your code as shown in Fig. 12.10.

The cases in lines 290–293 determine whether the value of intAccess-
Code is either 1645 or 1689. The empty case 1645 falls through to the body
of case 1689. If the user enters either of these access codes in this range, the
body of case 1689 sets strMessage to "Technicians".

The next case (lines 296–298) checks for a specific number. If intAccessCode matches the value 8345, then the statement in that case executes.

The next group of cases (lines 302–307) determine whether intAccess-
Code is 9998 or a number in the range 1006 to 1008, inclusive. It is set up
like the first group of cases.

4. ***Adding a default case to the switch statement***. Add lines 309–312 from
Fig. 12.11 to the switch statement. These lines contain the optional default
case, which is executed when the controlling expression does not match any
of the previous cases. It is good programming practice to place the default
case, if used, after all other cases. This increases the readability of your
code. In your application, the body of the default statement sets the
strMessage variable to "Access Denied". The default case, like all other
cases, requires a break statement to end the case body.

The required right brace (}) (line 314 of Fig. 12.11) terminates the switch
statement. Note the indentation of the switch statement to improve the
readability of your code.

(cont.)

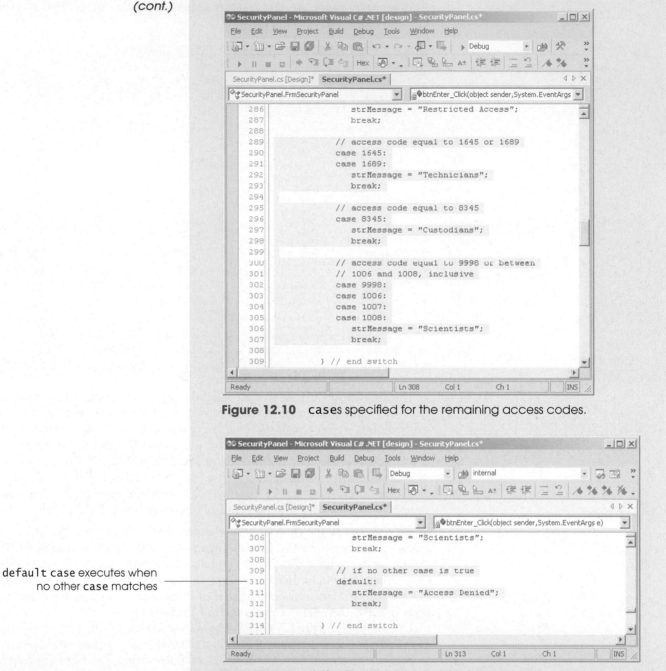

Figure 12.10 cases specified for the remaining access codes.

default case executes when
no other case matches

Figure 12.11 default case of the switch statement.

5. ***Displaying results in the ListBox.*** Insert lines 316–318 of Fig. 12.12 after the switch statement. The statement in lines 317–318 displays a string in lstLogEntry consisting of the current system date and time, followed by three spaces and the value assigned to strMessage.

(cont.)

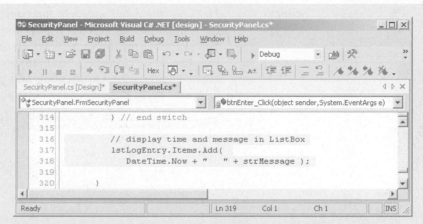

Figure 12.12 Updating the **Security Panel** application's **ListBox**.

The first part of the Add method's argument contains the **DateTime.Now** expression. The Framework Class Library (FCL) provides a **DateTime** structure that can be used to store and display date and time information. A structure is similar to a class. Like objects that you have used in this book, structure members, such as properties, are accessed by using the dot operator (**.**). The **DateTime** property Now returns the system time and date. Passing this value as a **string** in the argument to the Add method (line 317) causes this value to be converted and displayed as a **string**. You will learn about how a date is stored using the **DateTime** structure in Tutorial 14.

6. ***Saving the project***. Select **File > Save All** to save your modified code.

Now that you have defined the btnEnter_Click event handler, you will focus on the numeric Buttons. You will create event handlers for each numbered Button and for the **C** Button in the following box.

Programming the Remaining Event Handlers

1. ***Creating the btnZero_Click event handler***. In design view, double click the **0** Button (btnZero) to create the btnZero_Click event handler.

2. ***Coding the btnZero_Click event handler***. Be sure to add the comments and break the header as shown in Fig. 12.13 so that the line numbers in your code match those presented in this tutorial. Then, add line 327 to the event handler. Line 327 appends the **string** "0" to the end of txtSecurityCode's Text property value. You do this to append the numeric Button's value to the access code in the TextBox.

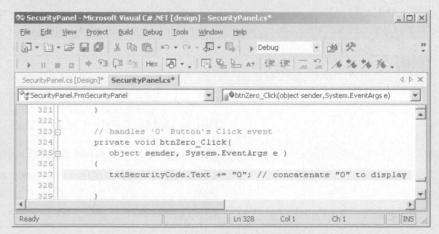

Figure 12.13 The btnZero_Click event handler.

(cont.)

3. ***Defining the other numeric Buttons' event handlers.*** Repeat *Steps 1–2* for the remaining numeric Buttons (**1** through **9**). Be sure to substitute the Button's number for the value between the quotes (for example, `btnOne_Click` sets `txtSecurityCode`'s `Text` property value as 1). Figure 12.15 shows the event handlers for the `btnOne` and `btnTwo` Buttons after all the numeric Buttons' event handlers have been defined.

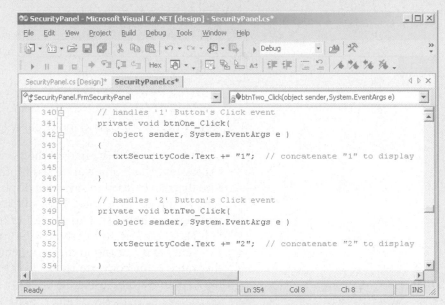

Figure 12.14 The `btnOne_Click` and `btnTwo_Click` event handlers.

4. ***Defining the `btnClear_Click` event handler.*** Double click the **C** Button, and add line 417 as shown in Fig. 12.15. Line 417 clears the **Security code:** TextBox. Add a comment to the end of each event handler you have generated (for example, lines 411 and 419 of Fig. 12.15).

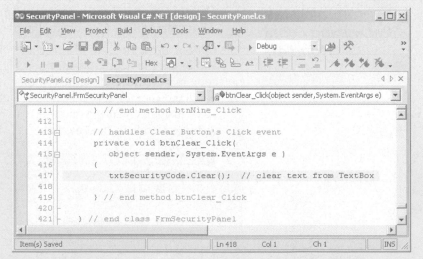

Figure 12.15 The `btnClear_Click` defined Event handler.

5. ***Running the application.*** Select **Debug > Start** to run your application.

6. ***Closing the application.*** Close your running application by clicking its close box.

7. ***Closing the IDE.*** Close Visual Studio .NET by clicking its close box.

Figure 12.16 presents the source code for the **Security Panel** application. The lines of code that contain new programming concepts that you learned in this tutorial are highlighted. Look over the code carefully to make sure that you have added all of the event handlers correctly.

```
1   using System;
2   using System.Drawing;
3   using System.Collections;
4   using System.ComponentModel;
5   using System.Windows.Forms;
6   using System.Data;
7
8   namespace SecurityPanel
9   {
10     /// <summary>
11     /// Summary description for FrmSecurityPanel.
12     /// </summary>
13     public class FrmSecurityPanel : System.Windows.Forms.Form
14     {
15        // Label and TextBox to display security code
16        private System.Windows.Forms.Label lblSecurityCode;
17        private System.Windows.Forms.TextBox txtSecurityCode;
18
19        // Buttons to input security code
20        private System.Windows.Forms.Button btnOne;
21        private System.Windows.Forms.Button btnTwo;
22        private System.Windows.Forms.Button btnThree;
23        private System.Windows.Forms.Button btnFour;
24        private System.Windows.Forms.Button btnFive;
25        private System.Windows.Forms.Button btnSix;
26        private System.Windows.Forms.Button btnSeven;
27        private System.Windows.Forms.Button btnEight;
28        private System.Windows.Forms.Button btnNine;
29        private System.Windows.Forms.Button btnZero;
30        private System.Windows.Forms.Button btnClear;
31        private System.Windows.Forms.Button btnEnter;
32
33        // Label and ListBox to display access log
34        private System.Windows.Forms.Label lblAccessLog;
35        private System.Windows.Forms.ListBox lstLogEntry;
36
37        /// <summary>
38        /// Required designer variable.
39        /// </summary>
40        private System.ComponentModel.Container components = null;
41
42        public FrmSecurityPanel()
43        {
44           //
45           // Required for Windows Form Designer support
46           //
47           InitializeComponent();
48           //
49           // TODO: Add any constructor code after InitializeComponent
50           // call
51           //
52        }
53
```

Figure 12.16 Security Panel application code. (Part 1 of 4.)

```
54          /// <summary>
55          /// Clean up any resources being used.
56          /// </summary>
57          protected override void Dispose( bool disposing )
58          {
59             if( disposing )
60             {
61                if (components != null)
62                {
63                   components.Dispose();
64                }
65             }
66             base.Dispose( disposing );
67          }
68
69          // Windows Form Designer generated code
70
71          /// <summary>
72          /// The main entry point for the application.
73          /// </summary>
74          [STAThread]
75          static void Main()
76          {
77             Application.Run( new FrmSecurityPanel() );
78          }
79
80          // handles Enter Button's Click event
81          private void btnEnter_Click(
82             object sender, System.EventArgs e )
83          {
84             int intAccessCode;  // stores access code entered
85             string strMessage;  // displays access status of users
86
87             intAccessCode = Int32.Parse( txtSecurityCode.Text );
88             txtSecurityCode.Clear();
89
90             switch ( intAccessCode )  // check access code input
91             {
92                // access code less than 10
93                case 0:
94                case 1:
95                case 2:
96                case 3:
97                case 4:
98                case 5:
99                case 6:
100               case 7:
101               case 8:
102               case 9:
103                  strMessage = "Restricted Access";
104                  break;
105
106               // access code equal to 1645 or 1689
107               case 1645:
108               case 1689:
109                  strMessage = "Technicians";
110                  break;
111
```

Declaring variables — (lines 84–85)

Retrieving the access code and clearing the `TextBox` — (lines 87–88)

Using a `switch` statement to determine user access level — (line 90)

Empty `cases` fall through — (line 97)

Figure 12.16   Security Panel application code. (Part 2 of 4.)

```
112              // access code equal to 8345
113              case 8345:
114                 strMessage = "Custodians";
115                 break;
116
117              // access code equal to 9998 or between
118              // 1006 and 1008, inclusive
119              case 9998:
120              case 1006:
121              case 1007:
122              case 1008:
123                 strMessage = "Scientists";
124                 break;
125
126              // if no other case is true
127              default:
128                 strMessage = "Access Denied";
129                 break;
130
131           } // end switch
132
133           // display time and message in ListBox
134           lstLogEntry.Items.Add(
135              DateTime.Now + "    " + strMessage );
136
137        } // end method btnEnter_Click
138
139        // handles '0' Button's Click event
140        private void btnZero_Click(
141           object sender, System.EventArgs e )
142        {
143           txtSecurityCode.Text += "0"; // concatenate "0" to display
144
145        } // end method btnZero_Click
146
147        // handles '1' Button's Click event
148        private void btnOne_Click(
149           object sender, System.EventArgs e )
150        {
151           txtSecurityCode.Text += "1";  // concatenate "1" to display
152
153        } // end method btnOne_Click
154
155        // handles '2' Button's Click event
156        private void btnTwo_Click(
157           object sender, System.EventArgs e )
158        {
159           txtSecurityCode.Text += "2";  // concatenate "2" to display
160
161        } // end method btnTwo_Click
162
163        // handles '3' Button's Click event
164        private void btnThree_Click(
165           object sender, System.EventArgs e )
166        {
167           txtSecurityCode.Text += "3";  // concatenate "3" to display
168
169        } // end method btnThree_Click
```

default case executes when no other **case** matches — (annotation pointing to line 127)

Appending the numeric **Button** value to the text stored in the TextBox — (annotation pointing to lines 139–145)

Figure 12.16   **Security Panel** application code. (Part 3 of 4.)

```
170
171         // handles '4' Button's Click event
172         private void btnFour_Click(
173            object sender, System.EventArgs e )
174         {
175            txtSecurityCode.Text += "4";   // concatenate "4" to display
176
177         } // end method btnFour_Click
178
179         // handles '5' Button's Click event
180         private void btnFive_Click(
181            object sender, System.EventArgs e )
182         {
183            txtSecurityCode.Text += "5";   // concatenate "5" to display
184
185         } // end method btnFive_Click
186
187         // handles '6' Button's Click event
188         private void btnSix_Click(
189            object sender, System.EventArgs e )
190         {
191            txtSecurityCode.Text += "6";   // concatenate "6" to display
192
193         } // end method btnSix_Click
194
195         // handles '7' Button's Click event
196         private void btnSeven_Click(
197            object sender, System.EventArgs e )
198         {
199            txtSecurityCode.Text += "7";   // concatenate "7" to display
200
201         } // end method btnSeven_Click
202
203         // handles '8' Button's Click event
204         private void btnEight_Click(
205            object sender, System.EventArgs e )
206         {
207            txtSecurityCode.Text += "8";   // concatenate "8" to display
208
209         } // end method btnEight_Click
210
211         // handles '9' Button's Click event
212         private void btnNine_Click(
213            object sender, System.EventArgs e )
214         {
215            txtSecurityCode.Text += "9";   // concatenate "9" to display
216
217         } // end method btnNine_Click
218
219         // handles Clear Button's Click event
220         private void btnClear_Click(
221            object sender, System.EventArgs e )
222         {
223            txtSecurityCode.Clear();   // clear text from TextBox
224
225         } // end method btnClear_Click
226
227      } // end class FrmSecurityPanel
228 }
```

Clearing the TextBox ——— 223

Figure 12.16   Security Panel application code. (Part 4 of 4.)

1. To handle multiple `cases` with one block of code, it is possible to _____.

    a) list each `case`, separated by a comma   b) use fall through from empty `cases`

    c) use the `case x to y` structure   d) None of the above.

2. Which one of the following `cases` is valid?

    a) `case intI < 3:`   b) `case 15 to 48:`

    c) `case 1:`   d) `case default:`

Answers: 1) b. 2) c.

12.4 Wrap-Up

In this tutorial, you learned how to use the `switch` multiple-selection statement and discovered its similarities to the `if...else` statement. You studied a UML activity diagram that illustrates the flow of control in `switch` statements.

You then applied what you learned to create your **Security Panel** application. You used a `switch` statement to determine whether the user input a correct security code. You also defined several `cases` and included a `default case`, which executes if a valid security code is not provided.

In the next tutorial, you will learn how to construct applications from small, manageable pieces of reusable code called methods, which you have already been using extensively throughout the book. You will use this capability to enhance an example you created earlier in the book.

SKILLS SUMMARY

Creating a `switch` Statement

- Use the `switch` keyword, followed by a controlling expression.
- Use the `case` keyword, followed by an expression to compare with the controlling expression. Place a colon (`:`) after the expression.
- Define the statements that execute if the `case`'s expression matches the controlling expression.
- Use the `default` label followed by statements to execute if the controlling expression does not match any of the provided `cases`.
- Use the `break` statement to end the body of each `case`, including the `default` case.
- Use the fall-through technique on empty cases to group multiple `cases` together.

Masking User Input in a TextBox

- Set the `TextBox`'s `PasswordChar` property to the desired character, typically the asterisk (`*`), to mask the user input.
- Retrieve the value typed by the user in the `Text` property.

Retrieving the Current Date and Time

- Use the `Now` property of the `DateTime` structure, which, when converted to a `string`, displays the current date in the format `12/31/2003 11:59:59 P.M.`

KEY TERMS

break statement—Required at the end of each `case`. This statement immediately terminates the `switch`, and program control continues with the next statement after the `switch`.

case label—Precedes the statements that will execute if the `switch`'s controlling expression matches the expression for a specific `case`.

char type—Used to store character values.

character constant—Another name for a character literal.

character literal—The value of a variable of type `char`, it is represented by a character within single quotes, such as `'A'`, `'d'`, `'*'`, `'.'` and the like.

constant expression—A value that cannot be changed. A `case` label consists of the keyword `case` followed by a constant expression. This constant expression must be a character literal or an integer literal.

controlling expression—The expression in a `switch` statement whose value is compared sequentially with each `case` until either a match occurs, the `default` case is executed or the right brace is reached.

`DateTime` structure—A structure whose properties can be used to store and display date and time information.

`default` case—The optional `case` whose statements execute if the `switch`'s controlling expression does not match any of the `cases`' values.

empty case—A case with no statements.

`Enabled` property of a `TextBox`—Determines whether the `TextBox` will respond to user input.

fall through—Occurs when program control follows an empty case in a `switch` statement by continuing with another `case` rather than exiting the `switch` statement.

masking—Hiding text such as passwords or other sensitive pieces of information that should not be observed by other people as they are typed. Masking is achieved by using the `PasswordChar` property of the `TextBox` for which you would like to hide data. The actual data entered is retained in the `TextBox`'s `Text` property.

masking character—Used to replace each character displayed in a `TextBox` when the `TextBox`'s data is masked for privacy.

`Now` property of `DateTime` statement—The current system time and date.

`PasswordChar` property of a `TextBox`—A property that specifies the masking character for a `TextBox`.

`switch` statement—Multiple-selection statement used to make a decision by comparing an expression to a series of values.

GUI DESIGN GUIDELINES

Overall Design

■ If your GUI is modeling a real-world object, its design should mimic the physical appearance of the object.

TextBox

■ Mask passwords and other sensitive pieces of information in `TextBox`es.

CONTROLS, EVENTS, PROPERTIES & METHODS

TextBox   `abl TextBox`   This control allows the user to input data from the keyboard.

■ *In action*

```
0
```

■ *Event*

`TextChanged`—Raised when the text in the `TextBox` is changed.

■ *Properties*

`Enabled`—Determines whether the user can enter data (`true`) in the `TextBox` or not (`false`).

`Location`—Specifies the location of the `TextBox` on the `Form` relative to the top-left corner.

`Multiline`—Specifies whether the `TextBox` is capable of displaying multiple lines of text.

`Name`—Specifies the name used to access the `TextBox` programmatically. The name should be prefixed with `txt`.

`PasswordChar`—Specifies the masking character to be used when displaying data in the `TextBox`.

`ReadOnly`—Determines whether the value of a `TextBox` can be changed.

`ScrollBars`—Specifies whether the `TextBox` contains a scrollbar.

`Size`—Specifies the height and width (in pixels) of the `TextBox`.

`Text`—Specifies the text displayed in the `TextBox`.

`TextAlign`—Specifies how the text is aligned within the `TextBox`.

■ *Method*

`Focus`—Transfers the focus of the application to the `TextBox` that calls it.

MULTIPLE-CHOICE QUESTIONS

12.1 The _____ symbol signifies the end of a `switch` statement.

a) right brace (})
b) right square bracket (])
c) newline (\n)
d) backslash (\)

12.2 The _____ expression returns the current system time and date.

a) `DateTime.DateTime`
b) `DateTime.SystemDateTime`
c) `DateTime.Now`
d) `DateTime.SystemTimeDate`

12.3 You can hide information entered into a `TextBox` by setting that `TextBox`'s _____ property to a character—that character will be displayed for every character entered by the user.

a) `PrivateChar`
b) `Mask`
c) `MaskingChar`
d) `PasswordChar`

12.4 Which of the following is a syntax error?

a) Having duplicate `cases` in the same `switch` statement.
b) Using an `int` variable in the test expression of a `switch` statement.
c) Having a `default` case in a `switch` statement.
d) Using a `string` variable in the test expression of a `switch` statement.

12.5 The _____ technique is used to specify multiple values for a `case`.

a) multiple selection
b) nested `switch`
c) fall-through
d) `default`

12.6 The _____ keyword is required at the end of each non-empty `case`.

a) `endcase`
b) `default`
c) `switch`
d) `break`

12.7 An empty `case` of a `switch` statement _____.

a) contains only the `break` statement
b) does not contain any statements
c) never matches the controlling expression
d) None of the above.

12.8 Forgetting the `break` keyword in a non-empty `case` of a `switch` statement results in _____.

a) a logic error
b) a syntax error
c) an infinite loop
d) the next `case` executing

12.9 The expression following the `switch` keyword is called a _____.

a) guard condition
b) controlling expression
c) selection expression
d) `case` expression

12.10 To prevent a user from modifying text in a `TextBox`, set its _____ property to `false`.

a) `Enabled`
b) `Text`
c) `TextChange`
d) `Editable`

EXERCISES

12.11 *(Sales Commission Calculator Application)* Develop an application that calculates a salesperson's commission from the number of items sold (Fig. 12.17). Assume that all items have a fixed price of 100 dollars per unit. Use a `switch` statement to implement the following sales commission schedule:

Fewer than 10 items sold = 1% commission
Between 10 and 39 items sold = 2% commission
Between 40 and 99 items sold = 3% commission
More than 99 items sold = 4% commission

Figure 12.17   Sales Commission Calculator application.

a) **Copying the template to your working directory.** Copy the directory `C:\Examples\Tutorial12\Exercises\SalesCommissionCalculator` to your `C:\SimplyCSP` directory.

b) **Opening the application's template file.** Double click `SalesCommissionCalculator.sln` in the `SalesCommissionCalculator` directory to open the application.

c) **Defining an event handler for the Button's Click event.** Create an event handler for the **Calculate** Button's `Click` event.

d) **Calculate the gross sales.** In your new event handler, convert the user's input to an `int` value and assign the value to the `intItems` local variable. Then insert a statement that multiplies the number of items that the salesperson has sold by the cost per item and assigns the result to `double` variable `dblSales`.

e) **Determine the salesperson's commission percentage.** Declare `int` local variable `intCommission` to store the commission percentage. Next, insert a `switch` statement to determine the salesperson's commission percentage from the number of items sold. In this `switch` statement, assign the commission percentage as a whole number to the `intCommission` variable. For example, if the commission percentage is 2%, assign 2 to `intCommission`. The controlling expression should be `intItems / 10`. Because this is integer arithmetic, any number of items in the range 0–9 will result in 0, any number of items in the range 10–19 will result in 1, etc. Inside the `switch` statement, provide `cases` that enable the `switch` to test for values in the ranges specified by the problem statement.

f) **Calculate the salesperson's earnings.** Insert a statement that multiplies `intSales` by `intCommission` (divided by `100.0`) and assigns the result to `double` local variable `dblEarnings`.

g) **Display the gross sales, the commission percentage and the salesperson's earnings.** Display the values of the `dblSales`, `intCommission` and `dblEarnings` variables in their corresponding TextBoxes. For the sales and earnings values, format the values as dollar amounts.

h) **Running the application.** Select **Debug > Start** to run your application. Enter a value for the number of items sold and click the **Calculate** Button. Verify that the gross sales displayed is correct, that the percentage of commission is correct and that the earnings displayed is correct based on the commission assigned.

i) **Closing the application.** Close your running application by clicking its close box.

j) **Closing the IDE.** Close Visual Studio .NET by clicking its close box.

12.12 **(Cash Register Application)** Use the numeric keypad from the **Security Panel** application to build a **Cash Register** application (Fig. 12.18). In addition to numbers, the cash register should include a decimal point Button. Apart from this numeric operation, there should be **Enter, Delete, Clear** and **Total** Buttons. Sales tax should be calculated on the amount purchased. Use a `switch` statement to compute sales tax. Add the tax amount to the subtotal to calculate the total. Display the tax and total for the user. Use the following sales-tax percentages, which are based on the amount of money spent:

Amounts under $100 = 5% (.05) sales tax
Amounts between $100 and $499 = 7.5% (.075) sales tax
Amounts above $499 = 10% (.10) sales tax

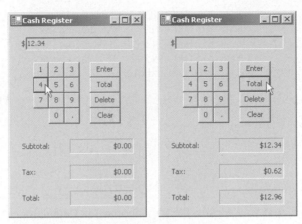

Figure 12.18 Cash Register application.

a) *Copying the template to your working directory.* Copy the directory `C:\Examples\Tutorial12\Exercises\CashRegister` to your `C:\SimplyCSP` directory.

b) *Opening the application's template file.* Double click `CashRegister.sln` in the `CashRegister` directory to open the application.

c) *Define event handlers for the numeric Buttons and decimal point in the keypad.* Create event handlers for the `Click` events each of these `Button`'s. Have each event handler concatenate the proper value to the `TextBox` at the top of the `Form`.

d) *Define an event handler for the Enter Button's Click event.* Create an event handler for this `Button`'s `Click` event. Have this event handler add the current amount to the subtotal and display the new subtotal. Use the expression `Decimal.Parse( lblSubTotalValue.Text.Substring( 1 ) )` to skip over the dollar sign and extract the subtotal from its `Label`. [*Note:* You will learn more about `String` method `Substring` in later tutorials.]

e) *Define an event handler for the Total Button's Click event.* Create an event handler for this `Button`'s `Click` event. Have this event handler use the value in the **Subtotal** `Label` to compute the tax amount. Extract the subtotal value as you did in *Step d*, and assign it to `decimal` variable `decSubTotal`. Insert a `switch` statement that uses the controlling expression `( int ) decSubTotal / 100`, which converts the subtotal to an `int`, then divides the subtotal by 100. The value of this expression will be 0 for subtotals less than $100 and 1–4 for subtotals in the range $100–499. All other values should be handled by the `default case` in this exercise. Calculate the tax amount and total amount based on the subtotal and tax rate. Display these values in their corresponding `Label`s.

f) *Define an event handler for the Clear Button's Click event.* Create an event handler for this `Button`'s `Click` event. Have this event handler clear the user input and display the value `$0.00` for the subtotal, sales tax and total.

g) *Define an event handler for the Delete Button's Click event.* Create an event handler for this `Button`'s `Click` event. Have this event handler clear only the data in the `TextBox`.

h) *Running the application.* Select **Debug > Start** to run your application. Use the keypad to enter various dollar amounts, clicking the **Enter** `Button` after each. After several amounts have been entered, click the **Total** `Button` and verify that the appropriate sales tax and total are displayed. Enter several values again and click the **Delete** `Button` to clear the current input. Click the **Clear** `Button` to clear all the output values.

i) *Closing the application.* Close your running application by clicking its close box.

j) *Closing the IDE.* Close Visual Studio .NET by clicking its close box.

12.13 (Income Tax Calculator Application) Create an application that computes the amount of income tax that a person must pay, depending upon that person's salary. Your application should perform as shown in Fig. 12.19. Use the following income ranges and corresponding tax rates:

Under $25,000 = 2% income tax
$25,000 – 49,999 = 5% income tax
$50,000 – 74,999 = 10% income tax
$75,000 – 99,999 = 15% income tax
$100,000 and over = 20% income tax

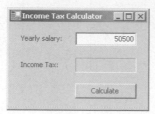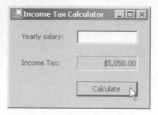

Figure 12.19 Income Tax Calculator application.

a) *Copying the template to your working directory.* Copy the directory `C:\Examples\Tutorial12\Exercises\IncomeTaxCalculator` to your `C:\SimplyCSP` directory.

b) *Opening the application's template file.* Double click `IncomeTaxCalculator.sln` in the `IncomeTaxCalculator` directory to open the application.

c) *Define an event handler for the Calculate Button's Click event.* Use the designer to create an event handler for this `Button`'s `Click` event. Have this event handler convert the user's input to an `int` value and assign the value to the local variable `intSalary`. Then use a `switch` statement to determine the user's income-tax percentage. Use the controlling expression `intSalary / 25000` to determine the tax rate. If the salary is less than $25,000, the controlling expression's value will be 0. For salaries in the range $25,000–49,999, the controlling expression's value will be 1. For salaries in the range $50,000–74,999, the controlling expression's value will be 2. For salaries in the range $75,000–99,999, the controlling expression's value will be 3. For all other salaries, use the `default case`. The tax rate should then be multiplied by the user's salary and displayed in the output `Label`. Clear the input `TextBox` when the output is displayed.

d) *Running the application.* Select **Debug > Start** to run your application. Enter a yearly salary and click the **Calculate** `Button`. Verify that the appropriate income tax is displayed, based on the ranges listed in the exercise description.

e) *Closing the application.* Close your running application by clicking its close box.

f) *Closing the IDE.* Close Visual Studio .NET by clicking its close box.

What does this code do? ▶

12.14 What is output by the following code? Assume that `btnDonation` is a `Button`, `txtDonation` is a `TextBox` and `lblMessage` is an output `Label`.

```
1   private void btnDonation_Click(
2      object sender, System.EventArgs e )
3   {
4      if ( Int32.Parse( txtDonationAmount.Text ) <= 0 )
5      {
6         lblMessage.Text = "Please enter a donation.";
7      }
8      else
9      {
10        switch ( Int32.Parse( txtDonationAmount.Text ) / 100 )
11        {
12           case 0:
13              lblMessage.Text = "Thank you for your donation.";
14              break;
15
```

(Part 1 of 2.)

```
16                  case 1:
17                      lblMessage.Text =
18                          "Thank you very much for your donation!";
19                      break;
20
21                  default:
22                      lblMessage.Text =
23                          "Wow! Thank you for your generosity!";
24                      break;
25              }
26          }
27
28      } // end method btnDonation_Click
```

(Part 2 of 2.)

What's wrong with this code? ▶ **12.15** This `switch` statement should determine whether the `int` variable `intValue` is even or odd. Assume that `txtInput` is a `TextBox` and `lblOutput` is an output `Label`. Find the error(s) in the following code:

```
1   intValue = Int32.Parse( txtInput.Text );
2
3   switch ( intValue % 2 )
4   {
5     case 0 :
6        lblOutput.Text = "Odd Integer";
7        break;
8
9     case 1 :
10       lblOutput.Text = "Even Integer";
11       break;
12  }
```

Using the Debugger ▶ **12.16** (*Discount Calculator Application*) The **Discount Calculator** application determines the discount the user will receive, based on how much money the user spends. A 15% discount is received for purchases of $150 or more, a 10% discount is received for purchases from $100 to $149 and a 5% discount is received for purchases from $50–$99. Purchases less than $50 do not receive a discount. While testing your application, you notice that the application is not calculating the discount properly for some values. Use the debugger to find and fix the logic error(s) in the application. Figure 12.20 displays the correct output for the application.

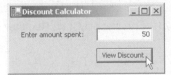

Figure 12.20 Correct output for the **Discount Calculator** application.

a) *Copying the template to your working directory.* Copy the directory `C:\Examples\Tutorial12\Exercises\Debugger\DiscountCalculator` to your `C:\SimplyCSP` directory.

b) *Opening the application's template file.* Double click `DiscountCalculator.sln` in the `DiscountCalculator` directory to open the application.

c) *Finding and correcting the error(s).* Use the debugging skills learned in previous tutorials to determine where the application's logic errors exist.

d) *Running the application.* Select **Debug > Start** to run your application. Test your application with at least one value in each range.

e) *Closing the application.* Close your running application by clicking its close box.

f) *Closing the IDE.* Close Visual Studio .NET by clicking its close box.

Programming Challenge ▶

12.17 (Enhanced Cash Register Application) Modify the **Cash Register** application (Exercise 12.12) to include the addition, subtraction and multiplication operations. Remove the **Enter** Button, and replace it with the addition (**+**), subtraction (**–**) and multiplication (*****) Buttons. These Buttons should take the value displayed in the **Subtotal:** field and the value displayed in the upper `Label` and perform the operation of the clicked Button. The result should be displayed in the **Subtotal:** field. Figure 12.21 displays the enhanced **Cash Register** application. [*Note*: You need only deal with positive values. To prevent negative subtotals, set the subtotal to zero if a subtraction would otherwise result in a negative value.]

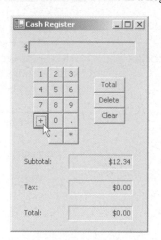

Figure 12.21 Enhanced **Cash Register** application.

Objectives

In this tutorial, you will learn to:
- Construct applications modularly from pieces called methods.
- Work with "built-in" methods.
- Determine when methods should be used.
- Create your own methods.

Outline

Enhancing the Wage Calculator Application

Introducing Methods

Most software applications that solve real-world problems are much larger than the applications presented in the first few tutorials of this text. Experience has shown that the best way to develop and maintain a large application is to construct it from smaller, more manageable pieces. This technique is known as **divide and conquer**. These manageable pieces include application components, known as methods, that simplify the design, implementation and maintenance of large applications. In this tutorial, you will learn how to create methods.

13.1 Test-Driving the Enhanced Wage Calculator Application

Next, you will use methods to enhance the **Wage Calculator** application that you created in Tutorial 7. This application must meet the following requirements:

Application Requirements

Recall the problem statement from Tutorial 7: A payroll company calculates the gross earnings per week of employees from the number of hours they worked and their hourly wages. Create an application that takes this information and calculates the gross earnings by multiplying the employee's hourly wages by the number of hours worked. The application assumes a standard work week of 40 hours. Any hours worked over 40 hours in a week are considered overtime and earn time and a half (that is, one and one-half times the hourly wage). Use a method to determine whether the employee has earned overtime pay. Salary for time and a half is calculated by multiplying the employee's hourly wage by 1.5 and multiplying the result of that calculation by the number of overtime hours worked. This value is then added to the user's earnings for the regular 40 hours of work to calculate the total earnings for that week. Use another method to display the user's pay.

The completed application has the same functionality as that of the application in Tutorial 7, but uses methods to better organize the code. This application calculates wages that are based on an employee's hourly salary and the number of hours worked per week. Normally, an employee who works 40 or fewer hours earns the hourly wage multiplied by the number of hours worked. The calculation differs if the employee has worked more than the standard 40-hour work week. In this tutorial, you learn about methods that perform calculations based on input values that may differ each time the application is run. You begin by test-driving the completed application. Then, you will learn the additional C# technologies you will need to create your own version of this application.

<table>
<tr>
<td>

Test-Driving the Wage Calculator Application

</td>
<td>

1. ***Opening the completed application.*** Open the C:\Examples\Tutorial13\ CompletedApplication\WageCalculator2 directory to locate the **Wage Calculator** application. Double click WageCalculator2.sln to open the application in Visual Studio .NET.

2. ***Running the Wage Calculator application.*** Select **Debug > Start** to run the application.

3. ***Entering the employee's hourly wage and hours worked.*** Enter 10 in the **Hourly wage:** TextBox, then enter 45 in the **Weekly hours:** TextBox (Fig. 13.1).

Figure 13.1 **Wage Calculator** running.

4. ***Calculating wages earned.*** Click the **Calculate** Button. The result ($475.00) is displayed in the **Gross earnings:** Label.

5. ***Closing the application.*** Close your running application by clicking its close box.

6. ***Closing the IDE.*** Close Visual Studio .NET by clicking its close box.

</td>
</tr>
</table>

13.2 Classes and Methods

The key to creating large applications is to break the applications into smaller pieces. In object-oriented programming, these pieces consist primarily of classes, which consist of members (data) and methods (behavior).

Programmers typically combine **programmer-defined** classes and methods with preexisting (also predefined) code available in the FCL. Using preexisting code saves time, effort and money. This concept of reusing code increases efficiency for application developers. Figure 13.2 explains and demonstrates several preexisting C# methods.

You have already used several preexisting classes and methods in the FCL. For example, all the GUI controls you have used in your applications are defined in the FCL as classes. You have also used FCL class methods, such as method Format of class String, to display output properly in your applications. Without method String.Format, you would have needed to code this functionality yourself—a task that would have included many lines of code and programming techniques that have not been introduced yet. You will learn many more FCL classes and methods in this book.

Method	Description	Example
`Int32.Parse( x )`	Returns the given string as an `int`	`Int32.Parse( "5" )` is `5` `Int32.Parse( "58" )` is `58`
`Math.Max( x, y )`	Returns the larger value of x and y	`Math.Max( 2.3, 9.7 )` is `9.7` `Math.Max( -2.3, -9.7 )` is `-2.3`
`Math.Min( x, y )`	Returns the smaller value of x and y	`Math.Min( 2.3, 9.7 )` is `2.3` `Math.Min( -2.3, -9.7 )` is `-9.7`
`Math.Sqrt( x )`	Returns the square root of x	`Math.Sqrt( 9 )` is `3.0` `Math.Sqrt( 2 )` is `1.4142135623731`
`String.Format( x, y )`	Returns string values where x is a format string, and y is a value to be formatted as a `string`	`String.Format( "{0:C}", 1.23 )` is `"$1.23"`

Figure 13.2 Some predefined C# methods.

However, the FCL cannot provide every conceivable feature that you might want, so C# allows you to create your own programmer-defined methods to meet the unique requirements of your particular applications. In the next section, you will learn about writing your own methods.

SELF-REVIEW

1. The _____ provides the programmer with preexisting classes that perform common tasks.

    a) Framework Class Library   b) `PreExisting` keyword

    c) Framework Code Library   d) `Library` keyword

2. Programmers normally use _____.

    a) programmer-defined methods

    b) preexisting methods

    c) both programmer-defined and preexisting methods

    d) neither programmer-defined nor preexisting methods

Answers: 1) a. 2) c.

13.3 Methods

The applications presented earlier in this book have called FCL methods (such as `String.Format`) to help accomplish the applications' tasks. You will now learn how to write your own programmer-defined methods. You will first learn how to create methods in the context of two small applications, before you create the enhanced **Wage Calculator** application. The first application uses the Pythagorean Theorem to calculate the length of the hypotenuse of a right triangle, and the second application determines the maximum of three numbers. Let's begin by reviewing the Pythagorean Theorem. A right triangle (which is a triangle with a 90-degree angle) always satisfies the following relationship—the sum of the squares of the two smaller sides of the triangle equal the square of the largest side of the triangle, which is known as the hypotenuse. In this application, the two smaller sides are called sides A and B, and their lengths are used to calculate the length of the hypotenuse. The steps in the following box will begin to create the application.

Creating the Hypotenuse
Calculator Application

1. ***Copying the template to your working directory.*** Copy the C:\Examples\ Tutorial13\TemplateApplication\HypotenuseCalculator directory to your C:\SimplyCSP directory.

2. ***Opening the Hypotenuse Calculator application's template file.*** Double click HypotenuseCalculator.sln in the HypotenuseCalculator directory to open the application in Visual Studio .NET (Fig. 13.3). When this application is running, the user enters the lengths of a triangle's two shorter sides into the **Length of side A:** and **Length of side B:** TextBoxes, then clicks the **Calculate Hypotenuse** Button. The completed application will calculate the length of the hypotenuse at this time and display the result in the **Length of hypotenuse:** output Label.

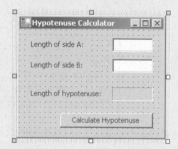

Figure 13.3   **Hypotenuse Calculator** GUI.

Software Design Tip

Use methods to increase the clarity and organization of your applications. This not only helps others understand your applications, but it also helps you develop, test and debug your applications.

3. ***Viewing the template application code.*** Switch to code view, and examine the code provided in the template, shown in Fig. 13.4. We have provided an incomplete event handler for the **Calculate Hypotenuse** Button.

Lengths for sides A, B and hypotenuse

Square of lengths for sides A, B and hypotenuse

Message dialog displays if negative values (or zero) are entered

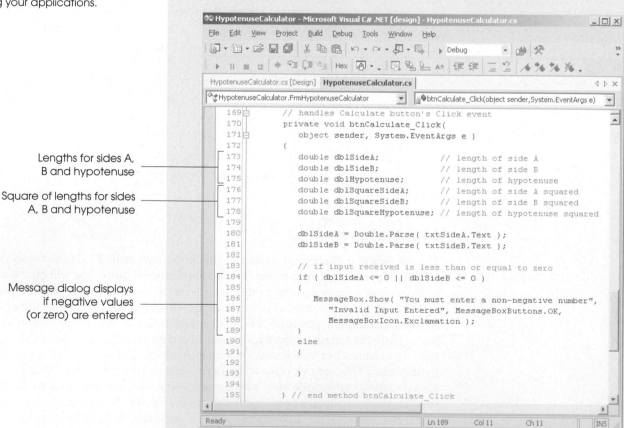

Figure 13.4   **Hypotenuse Calculator** template code.

(cont.)

This event handler contains six declarations (lines 173–178). Variables `dblSideA` and `dblSideB` will contain the lengths of sides A and B, entered by the user. Variable `dblHypotenuse` will contain the length of the hypotenuse, which will be calculated shortly. Variable `dblSquareSideA` will be used to store the length of side A, squared. Similarly, variables `dblSquareSideB` and `dblSquareHypotenuse` will be used to store the squares of the lengths of side B and the hypotenuse, respectively. Lines 180–181 store the user input for the lengths of sides A and B. Lines 184–193 contain an `if...else` statement. The `if` statement's body displays a message dialog if a negative value (or zero) is input as the length of side A or side B, or both. The `else`'s body, which will execute if values greater than zero are entered, will be used to calculate the length of the hypotenuse.

4. ***Creating an empty method.*** Add lines 197–202 of Fig. 13.5 after event handler `btnCalculate_Click`. Notice that we have added a comment (line 202) to identify the method being terminated.

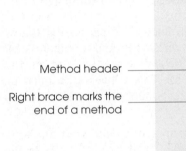

Good Programming Practice

Add comments at the end of your methods, indicating which method is being terminated. Such comments remind the reader of the method that is being terminated.

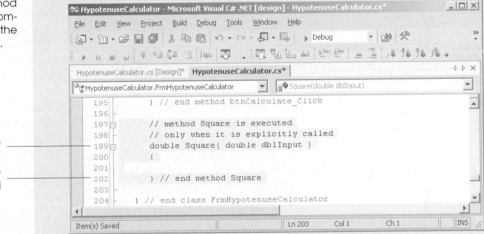

Method header ⎯⎯⎯

Right brace marks the end of a method ⎯⎯⎯

Figure 13.5 Method `Square`.

5. ***Understanding the method.*** The method begins on line 199 (Fig. 13.5) with the type `double`. The type that begins a method is known as the **return type**, which indicates the type of the result returned from the `method` (in this case, `double`).

The return type is followed by a **method name** (in this case, `Square`). The method name can be any valid identifier. The method name is followed by a set of parentheses containing a variable declaration.

Good Programming Practice

Choosing meaningful method names and parameter names makes applications more readable and reduces the need for excessive comments.

The declaration within the parentheses is known as the **parameter list**, where variables (called **parameters**) are declared. Although this parameter list contains only one declaration, the parameter list can contain multiple declarations separated by commas. The parameter list declares each parameter's name and type. Parameter variables are used in the method body.

The first line of a method (including the return type, the method name, the parameter list and the return type) is often called the **method header**. The method header for `Square` declares one parameter variable, `dblInput`, to be of type `double` and sets the return type of `Square` to be `double`.

Software Design Tip

To promote reusability, each method should perform a single, well-defined task, and the method name should express that task effectively.

A left brace (`{`) follows the method header. The method ends with a corresponding right brace (`}`) The declarations and statements that appear between the braces form the **method body**. The method body contains C# code that performs actions, generally by manipulating or interacting with the parameters from the parameter list. In the next step, you will add statements to the body of method `Square`. The method header, the body and the braces collectively make up the **method declaration**.

(cont.)

6. ***Adding code to the body of a method.*** You want your method to perform the squaring functionality needed in this application. Add lines 201–202 of Fig. 13.6 to Square's body.

Good Programming Practice

Method names should be verbs and should begin with an uppercase first letter. Each subsequent word in the name should begin with an uppercase first letter.

Calculating squares by using multiplication

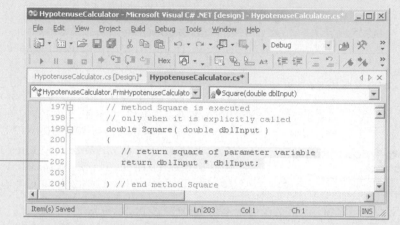

Figure 13.6 Square method declaration.

Good Programming Practice

Placing a blank line between method declarations enhances application readability.

Line 202 uses multiplication to calculate the square of dblInput—the parameter of this method. Line 202 uses a **return statement** to return this value. This statement begins with the keyword return, followed by an expression. The return statement evaluates the expression following keyword return, in this case dblInput * dblInput, and terminates execution of the method. The value of this expression is then sent back, or returned, to the point at which the method was called. This value's type must match the return type found in the method header (double). You will write the code to call the method in the next step.

7. ***Calling method Square.*** Now that you have created your method, you will need to call it from your event handler. Add lines 192–194 of Fig. 13.7 to your application, in the else block of the if...else statement. These lines call Square by using the method name followed by a set of parentheses that contain the method's argument. In this case, the arguments are the result of Double.Parse(txtSideA.Text) and Double.Parse(txtSideB.Text) (lines 180–181 of Fig. 13.4).

Calling method Square

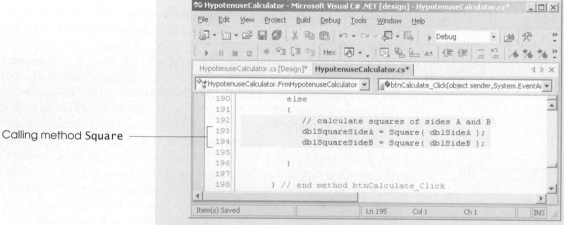

Figure 13.7 Invoking method Square.

(cont.)

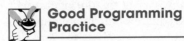

Good Programming Practice

Selecting descriptive parameter names makes the information provided by the *Parameter Info* feature more meaningful.

Notice that typing the opening parenthesis after a method name causes Visual Studio .NET to display a window containing the method's argument names and types (Fig. 13.8). This is the ***Parameter Info*** feature of the IDE, which provides you with information about methods and their arguments. The *Parameter Info* feature displays information for programmer-defined methods as well as for FCL methods. If the *Parameter Info* window does not appear, it may have been disabled. You can enable *Parameter Info* by selecting **Tools > Options**. In the dialog that appears, select the **Text Editor** folder in the left pane, then select the **C#** folder. Select the **General** option found below the C# folder. In the right portion of the dialog, check the **Parameter information** CheckBox.

Parameter Info window

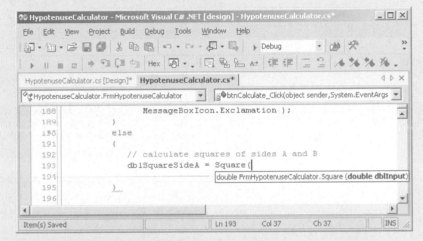

Figure 13.8   *Parameter Info* window.

A method is **invoked** (that is, made to perform its designated task) by a **method call**. The method call specifies the method name and provides information (arguments) that the **callee** (the method being called) requires to do its job. When the called method completes its task, it returns control to the **caller** (the calling method). For example, we have typically called method `Int32.Parse` as follows:

```
intResult = Int32.Parse( txtInput.Text );
```

where `Int32.Parse` is the name of the method, and `txtInput.Text`'s value is the argument passed to this method. The method uses this value to perform its defined task (returning the value of `txtInput.Text` as a number).

When program control reaches line 193 of Fig. 13.7, the application calls method `Square`. At this point, the application makes a copy of the value entered into the **Length of side A:** TextBox (after this value has been converted to a `double`), and program control transfers to the first line of `Square`.

`Square` receives the copy of the value input by the user and stores it in the parameter `dblInput`. When the `return` statement in `Square` is reached, the value to the right of keyword `return` is returned to the point in line 191 where `Square` was called, and the method's execution completes (any remaining statements of the method's body will not be executed). Program control will also be transferred to this point, and the application will continue by assigning the return value of `Square` to variable `dblSquareSideA`. These same actions will occur again when program control reaches the second call to `Square` in line 194. With this call, the value passed to `Square` is the value entered into the **Length of side B:** TextBox (after this value has been converted to a `double`), and the value returned is assigned to variable `dblSquareSideB`.

(cont.)

8. ***Calling a preexisting method of the FCL.*** Add lines 196–204 of Fig. 13.9 to the `else`'s body of the `if...else` statement in your application. Line 198 adds the square of side A and the square of side B, resulting in the square of the hypotenuse, which is assigned to variable `dblSquareHypotenuse`. Line 202 then calls FCL method **Sqrt** of class `Math` (by using the dot operator). This method will calculate the square root of the square of the hypotenuse to find the length of the hypotenuse.

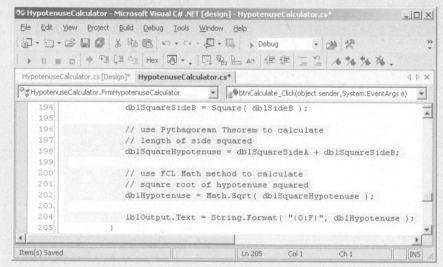

Figure 13.9 Completing the `btnCalculate_Click` event handler.

9. ***Running the application.*** Select **Debug > Start** to run your application. Enter 3 into the **Length of side A:** TextBox and 4 into the **Length of side B:** TextBox. Click the **Calculate Hypotenuse** Button. The output is shown in Fig. 13.10.

Error-Prevention Tip

Small methods are easier to test, debug and understand than are large ones.

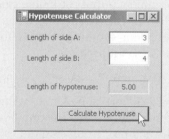

Figure 13.10 Hypotenuse Calculator application running.

10. ***Closing the application.*** Close your running application by clicking its close box.

11. ***Closing the IDE.*** Close Visual Studio .NET by clicking its close box.

You have now successfully created a method. You have also tested this method (by running the application) to confirm that it works correctly. This method can now be used in any C# application where you wish to calculate the square of a `double`. All you need to do is include the method declaration in your application. This is an example of code reuse, which helps programmers create application's faster.

As demonstrated in the **Hypotenuse Calculator** application, a method call follows the format

name(argument list)

There must be one argument in the argument list of the method call for each parameter in the parameter list of the method header. The arguments also must be compatible with the parameters' types (that is, C# must be able to assign the value of the argument to its corresponding parameter variable). For example, a parameter of type `double` could receive the value of 53547.350009, 22 or -.03546, but not "hello", because a `double` variable cannot contain a `string`. If a method does not receive any values, the parameter list is empty (that is, the method name is followed by an empty set of parentheses). You will study method parameters in detail in Tutorial 15.

As you saw in the previous example, the statement

```
return expression;
```

can occur anywhere in a method body and returns the value of *expression* to the caller. If necessary, C# attempts to convert the value of *expression* to the method's return type. Methods `return` at most one value. When a `return` statement is executed, control returns immediately to the point at which that method was called.

A method need not return a result. In such a case, the `return` statement is not required. Control returns to the caller when the application reaches the method-ending right brace or when the statement

```
return;
```

executes. This statement returns control to the caller without returning any value. The **void** keyword is used in place of the return type when the method does not return a result.

You will now create another method. This method, which is part of the **Maximum** application, returns the largest of three numbers input by the user. In the following box, you will create the **Maximum** application.

Creating a Method That Returns the Largest of Three Numbers

1. ***Copying the template to your working directory.*** Copy the C:\Examples\ Tutorial13\TemplateApplication\Maximum directory to your C:\SimplyCSP directory.

2. ***Opening the Maximum application's template file.*** Double click Maximum.sln in the Maximum directory to open the application in Visual Studio .NET (Fig. 13.11)

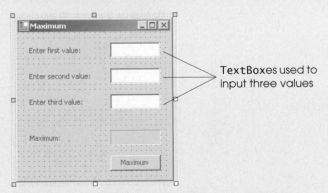

TextBoxes used to input three values

Figure 13.11   **Maximum** application in design view.

3. ***Creating an event handler for the Maximum Button.*** Double click the **Maximum** Button to create an event handler for this Button's Click event. Be sure to add the comments and break the header as shown in Fig. 13.12 so that the line numbers in your code match those presented in this tutorial. Then, add lines 197–200 to the event handler. These lines call method Maximum and pass it the three values the user has input into the application's TextBoxes.

(cont.)

Calling a method that has not yet been defined is an error

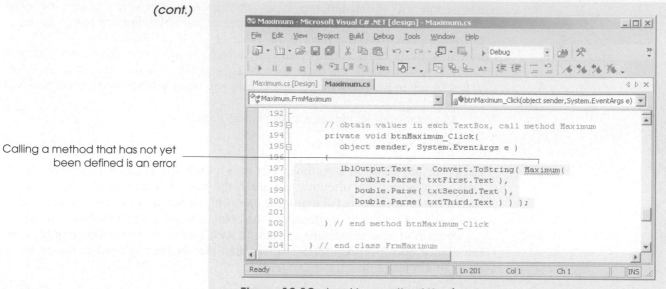

Figure 13.12 Invoking method `Maximum`.

Common Programming Error

Calling a method that does not yet exist, or misspelling the method name in a method call results in a syntax error.

Select **Build > Build Solution** to compile your application. Notice that `Maximum` is underlined in blue, indicating a syntax error. This occurs because method `Maximum` has not yet been defined. You will define `Maximum` in the next step. This syntax error will occur whenever you call a method that is not recognized by Visual Studio .NET. Misspelling the name of a method in a method call will likewise cause a syntax error.

4. *Creating method `Maximum`.* Add lines 204–209 of Fig. 13.13 after event handler `btnMaximum_Click`. The return type `double` begins the method header. The parameter list specifies that the values of the three arguments passed to `Maximum` will be stored in parameters `dblOne`, `dblTwo` and `dblThree`.

Empty method `Maximum`

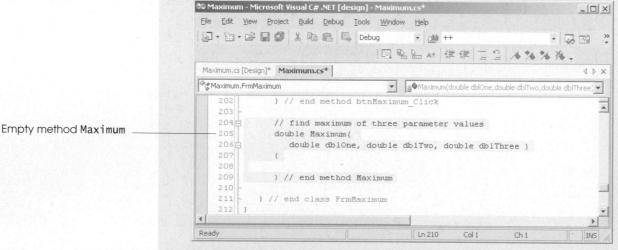

Figure 13.13 `Maximum` method.

(cont.)

5. **Adding functionality to method Maximum.** Add lines 208–214 of Fig. 13.14 to the body of Maximum. Line 208 declares a variable that will contain the maximum of the first two numbers passed to this method. This maximum is determined in line 211 by using the Max method of FCL class Math. This method takes two doubles and returns the maximum of those two values. The value returned is assigned to variable dblTemporaryMaximum in line 211. You then compare that value to method Maximum's third parameter, dblThree, in line 212. The maximum determined on this line, dblFinalMaximum, is the maximum of the three values. Line 214 uses a return statement to return this value. The return statement terminates execution of the method and returns the result of dblFinalMaximum to the calling method. The result is returned to the point (line 197 of Fig. 13.12) where Maximum was called. This result is converted to a string using FCL method Convert.ToString and is assigned to lblOutput's Text property.

Calling Math.Max to determine the maximum of two values

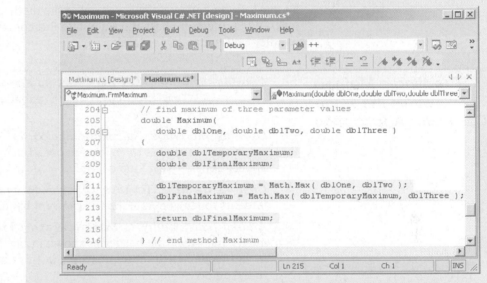

Figure 13.14   Math.Max returns the larger of its two arguments.

6. **Running the application.** Select **Debug > Start** to run your application (Fig. 13.15). Enter a numeric value into each TextBox, then click the **Maximum** Button. Notice that the largest of the three values is displayed in the output Label.

Figure 13.15   **Maximum** application running.

7. **Closing the application.** Close your running application by clicking its close box.

8. **Closing the IDE.** Close Visual Studio .NET by clicking its close box.

SELF-REVIEW

1. A method is invoked by a(n) _____.

    a) callee   b) caller

    c) argument   d) parameter

2. The _____ statement in a method sends a value back to the calling method.

    a) `return`   b) `back`

    c) `end`   d) None of the above.

Answers: 1) b. 2) a.

13.4 Using Methods in the Wage Calculator Application

The **Calculate** `Button`'s `Click` event handler in the original version of the **Wage Calculator** application (Tutorial 7) calculated the wages and displayed the result in a `Label`. In the following box, you will write method `DisplayPay` to perform these tasks. When the user clicks the **Calculate** `Button`, the `btnCalculate_Click` event handler calls method `DisplayPay`.

Creating a Method within the Wage Calculator Application

1. ***Copying the template to your working directory.*** Copy the `C:\Examples\Tutorial13\TemplateApplication\WageCalculator2` directory to your `C:\SimplyCSP` directory.

2. ***Opening the Wage Calculator application's template file.*** Double click `WageCalculator2.sln` in the `WageCalculator2` directory to open the application in Visual Studio .NET.

3. ***Creating the btnCalculate_Click event handler.*** Double click the **Calculate** `Button` to generate the `Click` event handler.

4. ***Adding functionality to btnCalculate_Click.*** Be sure to add the comments and break the header as shown in Fig. 13.16 so that the line numbers in your code match those presented in this tutorial. Then, add lines 173–182 to the empty event handler.

Call to `DisplayPay`

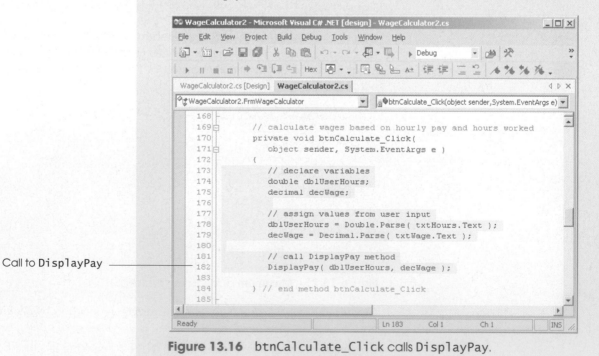

Figure 13.16 `btnCalculate_Click` calls `DisplayPay`.

(cont.)

This code calls method `DisplayPay` to calculate and display the wages. Lines 178–179 retrieve the user input from the `TextBoxes` and assign the values to variables declared in lines 174–175. Line 182 calls method `Display-Pay`, which you will define shortly. This method call takes two arguments: the hours worked (`dblUserHours`) and the hourly wage (`decWage`). Notice that the method's arguments in this example are variables. Arguments also can be constants or expressions.

5. ***Creating a method.*** After event handler `btnCalculate_Click`, add method `DisplayPay` to your application (lines 186–213 of Fig. 13.17).

Method `DisplayPay` →

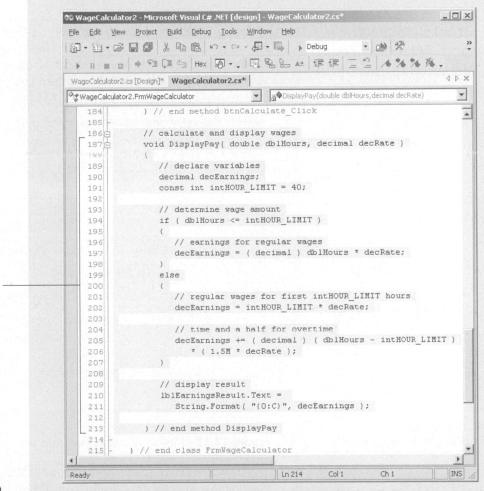

Figure 13.17 Method `DisplayPay` declaration.

Method `DisplayPay` receives the argument values and stores them in the parameters `dblHours` and `decRate`. The `void` keyword in line 187 indicates that this method does not return a value.

Note that the variable `decEarnings` and the constant `intHOUR_LIMIT` have been moved to the `DisplayPay` method. (In Figs. 7.14 and 7.15 of Tutorial 7, they were located within the `btnCalculate_Click` event handler.) They are no longer needed in `btnCalculate_Click`, so they should be removed from that event handler.

Lines 194–207 define the `if...else` statement that determines whether overtime must be calculated. The condition for this statement determines whether `dblHours` is less than or equal to constant `intHOUR_LIMIT`. If it is, then the employee's earnings without overtime are calculated. Otherwise, the employee's earnings including overtime are calculated. Lines 210–211 display the result (formatted as currency) in a `Label`.

Software Design Tip

The method header and method calls all must agree with regard to the number, types and order of parameters.

Common Programming Error

Declaring a variable in the method's body with the same name as a parameter variable in the method header is a syntax error.

(cont.)

> When the right brace in line 213 is encountered, control is returned to the calling method, btnCalculate_Click (line 182 in Fig. 13.16). Notice that no return statement is required because the void keyword was used in place of the return type.
>
> 6. **Saving the project.** Select **File > Save All** to save your modified code.

The following box shows you how to add method CheckOvertime to the **Wage Calculator** application. CheckOvertime will be used to determine whether an employee has worked overtime.

Creating a Second Method within the Wage Calculator Application

1. **Creating a second method.** Add method CheckOvertime (lincs 215–227 of Fig. 13.18) to your application, after the DisplayPay method declaration. Notice that the return type of the method is bool. This indicates that the value returned by the method must be a bool (that is, a constant, variable or expression that evaluates to true or false).

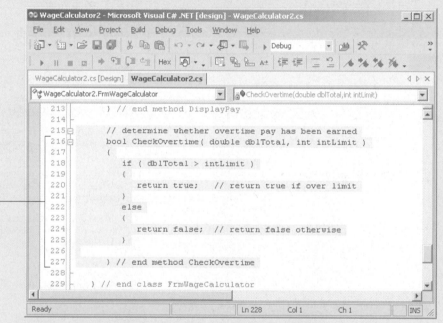

Method CheckOvertime

Figure 13.18   Method CheckOvertime declaration.

When CheckOvertime is called, program control is transferred to the beginning of this method in line 216. The arguments passed to this method (passed in the method call, which you will write in the next step) are stored in the parameter variables dblTotal and intLimit. Line 220 returns the bool value true, to indicate that the employee has worked overtime; line 224 returns the bool value false, to indicate that the employee has not worked any overtime. Program control and the value (either true or false) are returned to the line where CheckOvertime was initially called.

2. **Modifying method DisplayPay.** In method DisplayPay, replace the statement (line 194 of Fig. 13.17)

```
if ( dblHours <= intHOUR_LIMIT )
```

with line 194 from Fig. 13.19. We modify DisplayPay so that it now calls method CheckOvertime to determine whether the employee qualifies for overtime pay.

Common Programming Error

Failure to return a value from a method that is supposed to return a value is a syntax error. If a return type other than void is specified, the method must contain a return statement that returns a value.

(cont.)

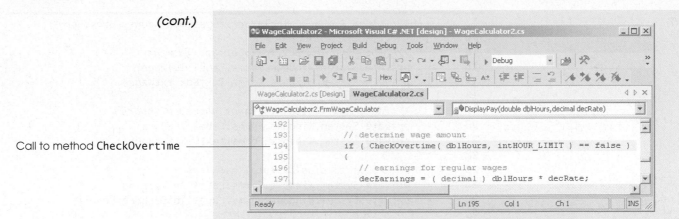

Call to method CheckOvertime

Figure 13.19 DisplayPay calls method CheckOvertime.

Method CheckOvertime is called (line 194) with the method call Check-Overtime(dblHours, intHOUR_LIMIT). When program control reaches this expression, the application calls method CheckOvertime. At this point, the application makes a copy of the value of dblHours and intHOUR_LIMIT (the arguments in the method call), and control transfers to the header of method CheckOvertime.

The parameter variables in CheckOvertime's header are initialized to copies of dblHours's value and intHOUR_LIMIT's value. The value returned from CheckOvertime is compared to the value false in line 194.

Now when the **Calculate Hypotenuse** Button is clicked, DisplayPay is called and executed. Recall that method CheckOvertime is called by the DisplayPay method. This sequence of calls is repeated every time the user clicks the **Calculate** Button.

3. *Running the application.* Select **Debug > Start** to run your application. Enter an hourly wage and number of hours worked (under 40), then click the **Calculate** Button. Verify that the appropriate earnings are displayed. Change the number of hours worked to a value over 40 and click the **Calculate** Button again. Verify that the appropriate output is displayed.

4. *Closing the application.* Close your running application by clicking its close box.

5. *Closing the solution.* Select **File > Close Solution**.

Figure 13.20 presents the source code for the **Wage Calculator** application. The lines of code that contain new programming concepts that you learned in this tutorial are highlighted.

```
1   using System;
2   using System.Drawing;
3   using System.Collections;
4   using System.ComponentModel;
5   using System.Windows.Forms;
6   using System.Data;
7
8   namespace WageCalculator2
9   {
10      /// <summary>
11      /// Summary description for FrmWageCalculator.
12      /// </summary>
```

Figure 13.20 **Wage Calculator** application code. (Part 1 of 4.)

```
13      public class FrmWageCalculator : System.Windows.Forms.Form
14      {
15          // Label and TextBox to input hourly wage
16          private System.Windows.Forms.Label lblWage;
17          private System.Windows.Forms.TextBox txtWage;
18
19          // Label and TextBox to input number of hours
20          private System.Windows.Forms.Label lbHours;
21          private System.Windows.Forms.TextBox txtHours;
22
23          // Labels to display total earnings
24          private System.Windows.Forms.Label lblEarnings;
25          private System.Windows.Forms.Label lblEarningsResult;
26
27          // Button to calculate total earnings
28          private System.Windows.Forms.Button btnCalculate;
29
30          /// <summary>
31          /// Required designer variable.
32          /// </summary>
33          private System.ComponentModel.Container components = null;
34
35          public FrmWageCalculator()
36          {
37              //
38              // Required for Windows Form Designer support
39              //
40              InitializeComponent();
41              //
42              // TODO: Add any constructor code after InitializeComponent
43              // call
44              //
45          }
46
47          /// <summary>
48          /// Clean up any resources being used.
49          /// </summary>
50          protected override void Dispose( bool disposing )
51          {
52              if( disposing )
53              {
54                  if (components != null)
55                  {
56                      components.Dispose();
57                  }
58              }
59              base.Dispose( disposing );
60          }
61
62          // Windows Form Designer generated code
63
64          /// <summary>
65          /// The main entry point for the application.
66          /// </summary>
67          [STAThread]
68          static void Main()
69          {
70              Application.Run( new FrmWageCalculator() );
71          }
```

Figure 13.20 Wage Calculator application code. (Part 2 of 4.)

```
72
73            // calculate wages based on hourly pay and hours worked
74            private void btnCalculate_Click(
75               object sender, System.EventArgs e )
76            {
77               // declare variables
78               double dblUserHours;
79               decimal decWage;
80
81               // assign values from user input
82               dblUserHours = Double.Parse( txtHours.Text );
83               decWage = Decimal.Parse( txtWage.Text );
84
85               // call DisplayPay method
86               DisplayPay( dblUserHours, decWage );
87
88            } // end method btnCalculate_Click
89
90            // calculate and display wages
91            void DisplayPay( double dblHours, decimal decRate )
92            {
93               // declare variables
94               decimal decEarnings;
95               const int intHOUR_LIMIT = 40;
96
97               // determine wage amount
98               if ( CheckOvertime( dblHours, intHOUR_LIMIT ) == false )
99               {
100                  // earnings for regular wages
101                  decEarnings = ( decimal ) dblHours * decRate;
102               }
103               else
104               {
105                  // regular wages for first intHOUR_LIMIT hours
106                  decEarnings = intHOUR_LIMIT * decRate;
107
108                  // time and a half for overtime
109                  decEarnings += ( decimal ) ( dblHours - intHOUR_LIMIT )
110                     * ( 1.5M * decRate );
111               }
112
113               // display result
114               lblEarningsResult.Text =
115                  String.Format( "{0:C}", decEarnings );
116
117            } // end method DisplayPay
118
119            // determine whether overtime pay has been earned
120            bool CheckOvertime( double dblTotal, int intLimit )
121            {
122               if ( dblTotal > intLimit )
123               {
124                  return true;   // return true if over limit
125               }
126               else
127               {
128                  return false;  // return false otherwise
129               }
```

Labels (left margin):
- Call to method `DisplayPay` → line 86
- `DisplayPay` method header → line 91
- Call to method `CheckOvertime` → line 98
- `CheckOvertime` method header → line 120
- Returning a value → line 124

Figure 13.20   Wage Calculator application code. (Part 3 of 4.)

```
130
131         } // end method CheckOvertime
132
133     } // end class FrmWageCalculator
134 }
```

Figure 13.20 **Wage Calculator** application code. (Part 4 of 4.)

SELF-REVIEW

1. Arguments to a method can be _____.

   a) constants   b) expressions

   c) variables   d) All of the above.

2. The _____ is a comma-separated list of declarations in a method header.

   a) argument list   b) parameter list

   c) value list   d) variable list

Answers: 1) d. 2) b.

13.5 Using the Debugger: Debug Toolbar

Now, you continue your study of the debugger by learning about the debug toolbar, which contains Buttons for controlling the debugging process. These Buttons provide convenient access to actions in the **Debug** menu. In this section, you will learn how to use the debug toolbar's Buttons to verify that a method's code is running correctly. In the following box, we use the debug toolbar Buttons to examine the WageCalculator2 application.

Using the Debugger: Debug Toolbar

1. ***Opening the debug toolbar.*** The debug toolbar contains Buttons for controlling the debugging process. These Buttons provide easy access to the **Debug** menu commands. To display the debug toolbar (Fig. 13.21), select **View > Toolbars > Debug**. The debug toolbar appears below the IDE menu bar (Fig. 13.21).

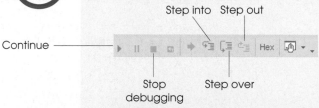

Figure 13.21 Debug toolbar.

2. ***Setting a breakpoint.*** Set a breakpoint in line 182 by clicking in the margin indicator bar (Fig. 13.22).

3. ***Starting the debugger.*** To start the debugger, select **Debug > Start**. The WageCalculator2 application executes. Enter the value 7.50 in the **Hourly wage:** TextBox, and enter 35 in the **Weekly hours:** TextBox. Click the **Calculate** Button.

4. ***Using the Step Into Button.*** The **Step Into Button** (Fig. 13.21) executes the next statement (the yellow highlighted line) in the application. If the next statement to execute is a method call (Fig. 13.23) and the Step Into Button is clicked, control is transferred to the called method. The Step Into Button allows you to enter a method and confirm the method's execution. Click the Step Into Button to enter method DisplayPay (Fig. 13.24). Notice that control is transferred to line 194, which is the first executable statement within the method (declarations are not considered executable statements).

(cont.)

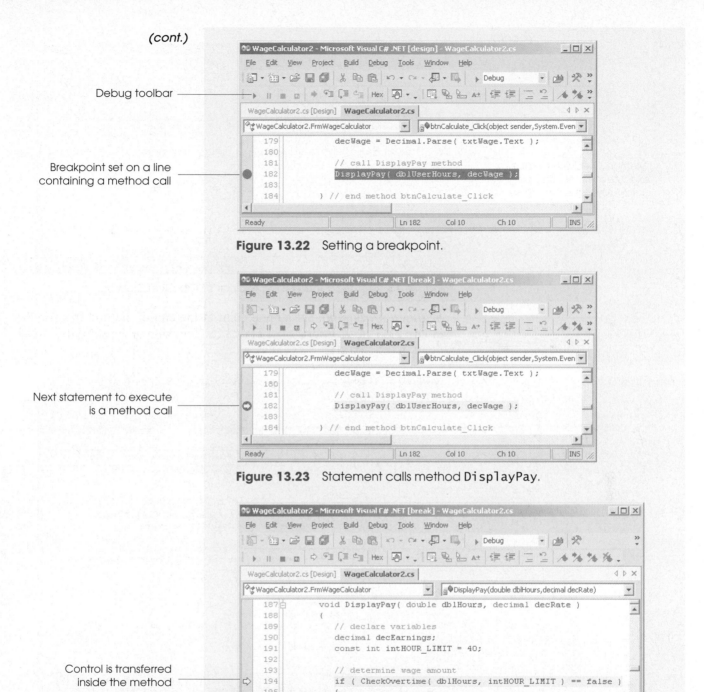

Debug toolbar

Breakpoint set on a line
containing a method call

Figure 13.22 Setting a breakpoint.

Next statement to execute
is a method call

Figure 13.23 Statement calls method `DisplayPay`.

Control is transferred
inside the method

Figure 13.24 Using the debug toolbar's Step Into `Button`.

5. ***Clicking the Step Over Button***. Click the **Step Over Button**. This `Button` behaves like the Step Into `Button` when the next statement to execute does not contain a method call. If the next statement to execute contains a method call, the called method executes in its entirety (without transferring control and entering the method), and the yellow arrow advances to the next executable line in the current method (Fig. 13.25).

(cont.)

Method `CheckOverTime` is executed without stepping into it when the Step Over **Button** is clicked

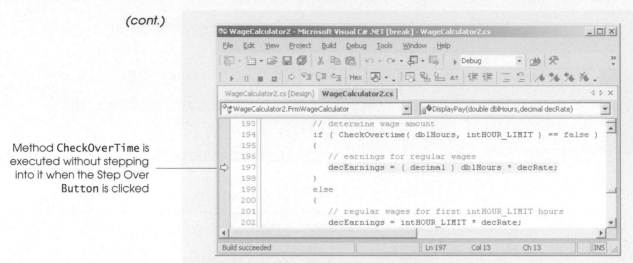

Figure 13.25 Using the debug toolbar's Step Over **Button**.

6. **Setting a breakpoint**. Set a breakpoint at the end of method `DisplayPay` in line 213 (the right brace) of Fig. 13.26. You will make use of this breakpoint in the next step.

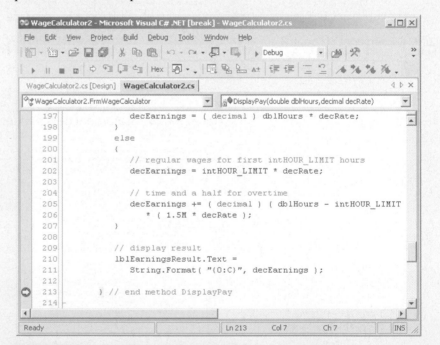

Figure 13.26 Using the debug toolbar's Continue **Button**.

7. **Using the Continue Button.** Clicking the **Continue Button** will execute any statements between the next executable statement and the next breakpoint or the end of the current event handler, whichever comes first. Notice that there is one executable statement (lines 210–211) before the breakpoint that was set in *Step 7*. Click the Continue **Button**. The next executable statement is now line 213 (Fig. 13.26). This feature is particularly useful when you have many lines of code before the next breakpoint that you do not want to step through line by line.

(cont.)

8. ***Using the Stop Debugging Button***. The **Stop Debugging Button** ends the debugging session and returns the IDE to design mode. Click the Stop Debugging `Button`.

9. ***Starting the debugger***. We have one last feature we wish to present that will require you to start the debugger again. Start the debugger, as you did in *Step 4*, entering the same values as input.

10. ***Using the Step Into Button***. Keep the breakpoint in line 182 (Fig. 13.22) and remove the breakpoint from line 213. Repeat *Step 4*.

11. ***Clicking the Step Out Button***. After you have stepped into the `DisplayPay` method, click the Step Out `Button` to execute the statements in the method and return control to line 182, which contains the method call. Often, in lengthy methods, you will want to look at a few key lines of code, then continue debugging the caller's code. This feature is useful for such situations, where you do not want to continue stepping through the entire method line by line.

12. ***Clicking the Stop Debugging Button***. Click the Stop Debugging `Button` to end the debugging session.

13. ***Closing the IDE***. Close Visual Studio .NET by clicking its close box.

SELF-REVIEW

1. During debugging, the _____ `Button` executes the remaining statements in the current method call and returns program control to the place where the method was called.

   a) Step Into   b) Step Out

   c) Step Over   d) Steps

2. The _____ `Button` behaves like the Step Into `Button` when the next statement to execute does not contain a method call.

   a) Step Into   b) Step Out

   c) Step Over   d) Steps

Answers: 1) b. 2) c.

13.6 Wrap-Up

In this tutorial, you learned how methods can be used to better organize an application. This tutorial introduced you to the concept called code reuse, showing how time and effort can be saved by using preexisting code. You used preexisting code provided by the FCL and learned to create your own code that can be used in other applications.

You were introduced to the syntax for creating and invoking methods. You learned the components of a method, including the method header, parameter list and the (sometimes optional) `return` statement. After learning how to develop and write methods, you learned about the order of execution that occurs from the line where a method is called (invoked) to the method declaration, and returning control back to the point of invocation. In this tutorial's applications, you created four methods—`Square`, `Maximum`, `CheckOvertime` and `DisplayPay`.

After creating the methods in this tutorial, you learned how to debug the methods in the application by using the `Buttons` in debug toolbar. These `Buttons` (including the Step Into, Step Out and Step Over `Buttons`) can be used to determine whether a method is executing correctly.

In the next tutorial, you learn about such controls as `GroupBoxes` and `DateTimePickers` and use them to build a **Shipping Time** application. This application controls information about a package being shipped from one location to another.

SKILLS SUMMARY

Invoking a Method

- Specify the method name and any arguments in parentheses.
- Ensure that the arguments passed match the method declaration's parameters in number, type and order.

Defining a Method

- Use the return type (or keyword `void`) to begin the method header, followed by the method name.
- Specify a parameter list declaring each parameter's name and type.
- Use braces to define the method body.
- Add code to the method's body to perform a specific task.
- Return a value with the `return` statement if the return type is not `void`.

Returning a Value From a Method

- Use the `return` keyword followed by the value to be returned.

KEY TERMS

callee—The method being called.

caller—The method that calls another method.

Continue Button—Executes any statements between the next executable statement and the next breakpoint or the end of the current event handler, whichever comes first.

divide-and-conquer technique—Constructing large applications from small, manageable pieces to make development and maintenance of large applications easier.

invoke—Cause a method to perform its designated task.

Math.Sqrt method—Returns the square root of a numeric value.

method body—The declarations and statements that appear between the set of braces that follow the method header. The method body contains C# code that performs actions, generally by manipulating or interacting with the parameters from the parameter list.

method call—Invokes a method, specifying the method name and providing information (arguments) that the callee (the method being called) requires to perform its task.

method declaration—The method header, body and braces surrounding the body.

method header—The first line of a method (including the return type, the method name and the parameter list).

method name—Follows the return type in a method header and distinguishes one method from another. A method name can be any valid identifier.

Parameter Info **feature of Visual Studio .NET**—Provides the programmer with information about methods and their arguments.

parameter list—A comma-separated list in which the method declares each parameter variable's name and type.

parameter variable—Declared in a method's parameter list that can be used in the body of the method.

programmer-defined method—Created by a programmer to meet the unique needs of a particular application.

return statement—Sends a value back to the method's caller.

return type—Type of the result returned from method.

Step Into Button—Executes the next statement in the application. If the next statement to execute is a method call, control is transferred to the called method.

Step Over Button—Executes the next statement in the application. If the next statement to execute is a method call, the called method executes in its entirety.

Stop Debugging Button—Ends the debugging session and returns the IDE to design mode.

void keyword—Used in place of the return type to indicate that a method will return no value.

CONTROLS, EVENTS, PROPERTIES & METHODS

Math This class provides methods used to perform common arithmetic calculations.

■ *Methods*

Min—Returns the smaller of two numeric values.

Max—Returns the larger of two numeric values.

Pow—Raises a given base (first argument) to a given exponent (second argument) and returns the result as a double.

Sqrt—Returns the square root of a numeric value.

MULTIPLE-CHOICE QUESTIONS

13.1 A method defined with keyword void _____.

    a) must specify a return type   b) does not accept arguments

    c) returns a value   d) does not return a value

13.2 The technique of developing large applications from small, manageable pieces is known as _____.

    a) divide and conquer   b) returning a value

    c) click and mortar   d) a building-block algorithm

13.3 What is the difference between void and non-void methods?

    a) void methods return values, non-void methods do not.

    b) non-void methods return values, void methods do not.

    c) void methods accept parameters, non-void methods do not.

    d) non-void methods accept parameters, void methods do not.

13.4 What occurs after a method call is made?

    a) Control is given to the called method. After the method is run, the application continues execution at the point where the method call was made.

    b) Control is given to the called method. After the method is run, the application continues execution with the statement after the called method's declaration.

    c) The statement before the method call is executed.

    d) The application terminates.

13.5 Methods can return _____ value(s).

    a) zero or one   b) exactly one

    c) one or more   d) any number of

13.6 Which of the following must be true when making a method call?

    a) The number of arguments in the method call must match the number of parameters in the method header.

    b) The argument types must be compatible with their corresponding parameter types.

    c) Both a and b.   d) None of the above.

13.7 Which of the following statements correctly returns the variable intValue from a method?

    a) `return int intValue;`   b) `return void intValue;`

    c) `intValue return;`   d) `return intValue;`

13.8 The Step Into and _____ Buttons execute the next statement in the application.

    a) Step Onto   b) Step Out

    c) Step Over   d) Steps

13.9 The first line of a method (including the return type, the method name and the parameter list) is known as the method _____.

    a) body   b) title

    c) caller   d) header

13.10 Math method _____ calculates the square root of the value passed as an argument.

a) SquareRoot

b) Root

c) Sqrt

d) Square

EXERCISES

13.11 (*Temperature Conversion Application*) Write an application that performs temperature conversions (Fig. 13.27). The application should be capable of onverting from degrees Fahrenheit to degrees Celsius and from degrees Celsius to degrees Fahrenheit.

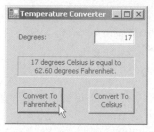 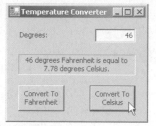

Figure 13.27 Temperature Conversion GUI.

a) *Copying the template to your working directory.* Copy the directory C:\Examples\ Tutorial13\Exercises\TemperatureConversion to your C:\SimplyCSP directory.

b) *Opening the application's template file.* Double click TemperatureConversion.sln in the TemperatureConversion directory to open the application.

c) *Convert Fahrenheit to Celsius.* To convert degrees Fahrenheit to degrees Celsius, use this formula:

```
dblCelsius = ( 5.0 / 9 ) * ( dblFahrenheit - 32 );
```

d) *Convert Celsius to Fahrenheit.* To convert degrees Celsius to degrees Fahrenheit, use this formula:

```
dblFahrenheit = ( 9.0 / 5 ) * dblCelsius + 32;
```

e) *Adding event handlers to your application.* Double click each Button to add the proper event handlers to your application. These event handlers will call methods (that you will define in the next step) to convert the degrees entered to either Fahrenheit or Celsius. Each event handler will display the result in the application's output Label.

f) *Adding methods to your application.* Create methods to perform each conversion, using the formulas above. The user should provide the temperature to convert.

g) *Formatting the temperature output.* To format the temperature information, use the String.Format method. Use F as the formatting code to limit the temperature to two decimal places.

h) *Running the application.* Select **Debug > Start** to run your application. Enter a temperature value. Click the **Convert to Fahrenheit** Button and verify that correct output is displayed based on the formula given. Click the **Convert to Celsius** Button and again verify that the output is correct.

i) *Closing the application.* Close your running application by clicking its close box.

j) *Closing the IDE.* Close Visual Studio .NET by clicking its close box.

13.12 (*Display Square Application*) Write an application that displays a solid square composed of a character input by the user (Fig. 13.28). The user also should input the size.

a) *Copying the template to your working directory.* Copy the directory C:\Examples\ Tutorial13\Exercises\DisplaySquare to your C:\SimplyCSP directory.

b) *Opening the application's template file.* Double click DisplaySquare.sln in the DisplaySquare directory to open the application.

c) *Adding a method.* Write a method DisplaySquare of void return type to display the solid square. The size should be specified by the int parameter intSize. The character that fills the square should be specified by the string parameter strFillCharacter. You should use a for statement nested within another for statement to create the square. The outer for specifies what row is currently being displayed. The inner for appends all the characters that form the row to a display string.

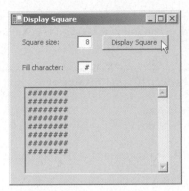

Figure 13.28 **Display Square** application.

d) *Adding an event handler for your Button's Click event.* Double click the **Display Square** Button to create the event handler. Program the event handler to call method `DisplaySquare`.

e) *Displaying the output.* Use the multiline `TextBox` provided to display the square. For example, if `intSize` is 8 and `strFillCharacter` is #, the application should look similar to Fig. 13.28.

f) *Running the application.* Select **Debug > Start** to run your application. Enter a size for the square (the length of each side) and a fill character. Click the **Display Square** Button. A square should be displayed of the size you specified, using the character you specified.

g) *Closing the application.* Close your running application by clicking its close box.

h) *Closing the IDE.* Close Visual Studio .NET by clicking its close box.

13.13 (*Miles Per Gallon Application*) Drivers often want to know the miles per gallon their cars get so they can estimate gasoline costs. Develop an application that allows the user to input the numbers of miles driven and the number of gallons used for a tank of gas (Fig. 13.29).

Figure 13.29 **Miles Per Gallon** application.

a) *Copying the template to your working directory.* Copy the directory `C:\Examples\Tutorial13\Exercises\MilesPerGallon` to your `C:\SimplyCSP` directory.

b) *Opening the application's template file.* Double click `MilesPerGallon.sln` in the `MilesPerGallon` directory to open the application.

c) *Calculating the miles per gallon.* Write a method `MilesPerGallon` that takes the number of miles driven and gallons used (entered by the user), calculates the amount of miles per gallon and returns the miles per gallon for a tankful of gas.

d) *Displaying the result.* Create a `Click` event handler for the **Calculate MPG** Button that invokes the method `MilesPerGallon` and displays the result returned from the method.

e) *Running the application.* Select **Debug > Start** to run your application. Enter a value for the number of miles driven and the amount of gallons used. Click the **Calculate MPG** Button and verify that the correct output is displayed.

f) *Closing the application.* Close your running application by clicking its close box.

g) *Closing the IDE.* Close Visual Studio .NET by clicking its close box.

What does this code do? ▶ **13.14** What does the following code do? Assume this method is invoked by using `Mystery ( 70, 80 )`.

```
1   void Mystery( int intNumber1, int intNumber2 )
2   {
3      int intX;
4      double dblY;
5
6      intX = intNumber1 + intNumber2;
7      dblY = intX / 2;
8
9      if ( dblY <= 60 )
10     {
11        lblResult.Text = "<= 60 ";
12     }
13     else
14     {
15        lblResult.Text = " Result is " + dblY;
16     }
17
18  } // end method Mystery
```

What's wrong with this code? ▶ **13.15** Find the error(s) in the following code, which should take an `int` value as an argument and `return` the value of that argument multiplied by two.

```
1   int TimesTwo( int intNumber )
2   {
3      int intResult;
4
5      intResult = intNumber * 2;
6
7   } // end method TimesTwo
```

Using the Debugger ▶ **13.16** (*Gas Pump Application*) The **Gas Pump** application calculates the cost of gas at a local gas station (Fig. 13.30). This gas station charges $1.41 per gallon for **Regular** grade gas, $1.47 per gallon for **Special** grade gas and $1.57 per gallon for **Super+** grade gas. The user enters the number of gallons to purchase and clicks the desired grade. The application calls a method to compute the total cost from the number of gallons entered and the selected grade. While testing your application, you noticed that one of your totals was incorrect, given the input.

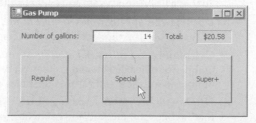

Figure 13.30 **Gas Pump** application running correctly.

a) *Copying the template to your working directory.* Copy the directory C:\Examples\ Tutorial13\Exercises\Debugger\GasPump to your C:\SimplyCSP directory.

b) *Opening the incorrect application.* Double click GasPump.sln in the GasPump directory to open the application.

c) *Running the application.* Run the application and determine which total is incorrect.

d) ***Setting a breakpoint.*** Set a breakpoint at the beginning of the event handler that is providing incorrect output. For instance, if the **Regular** Button is providing incorrect output when clicked, add a breakpoint at the beginning of that Button's Click event handler. Use the debugger to help find any logic error(s) in the application.

e) ***Modifying the application.*** Once you have located the error(s), modify the application so that it behaves correctly.

f) ***Running the corrected application.*** Select **Debug > Start** to run your application. Enter a number of gallons and click the **Regular, Special** and **Super+** Buttons. After each Button is clicked, verify that the total displayed is correct based on the prices given in this exercise's description.

g) ***Closing the application.*** Close your running application by clicking its close box.

h) ***Closing the IDE.*** Close Visual Studio .NET by clicking its close box.

Programming Challenge ▶

13.17 *(Prime Numbers Application)* An int greater than 1 is said to be prime if it is divisible by only 1 and itself. For example, 2, 3, 5 and 7 are prime numbers, but 4, 6, 8 and 9 are not. Write an application that takes two numbers (representing a lower bound and an upper bound) and determines all the prime numbers within the specified bounds, inclusive (Fig. 13.31).

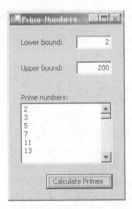 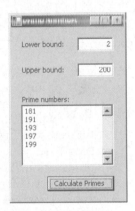

Figure 13.31   **Prime Numbers** application.

a) ***Creating the application.*** Create an application named PrimeNumbers in your C:\SimplyCSP directory and have its GUI appear as shown in Fig. 13.31. Rearrange and comment the control declarations appropriately. Add an event handler for the **Calculate Primes** Button's Click event.

b) ***Checking for prime numbers.*** Write a method Prime that returns true if a number is prime, false otherwise.

c) ***Limiting user input.*** Allow users to enter a lower bound (intLower) and an upper bound (intUpper). Prevent the user from entering bounds less than 2 (the smallest prime), or an upper bound that is smaller than the lower bound.

d) ***Displaying the prime numbers.*** Call method Prime from your event handler to determine which numbers between the lower and upper bounds are prime. Then have the event handler display the prime numbers in a multiline, scrollable TextBox, as in Fig. 13.31.

e) ***Running the application.*** Select **Debug > Start** to run your application. Enter a lower bound and an upper bound that is smaller than the lower bound. Click the **Calculate Primes** Button. You should receive an error message. Enter negative bounds and click the **Calculate Primes** Button. Again, you should receive an error message. Enter valid bounds and click the **Calculate Primes** Button. This time, the primes within that range should be displayed.

f) ***Closing the application.*** Close your running application by clicking its close box.

g) ***Closing the IDE.*** Close Visual Studio .NET by clicking its close box.

Objectives

In this tutorial, you will learn to:
- Create and manipulate `DateTime` variables.
- Execute code at regular intervals using a `Timer` control.
- Retrieve `DateTime` input with a `DateTimePicker` control.
- Group controls using a `GroupBox` control.

Outline

Shipping Time Application

Using DateTimes and Timers

Many companies, from airlines to shipping companies, rely on date and time information in daily operations. These companies often require applications that reliably perform date and time calculations. In this tutorial, you will create an application that performs calculations using the `DateTime` structure, which allows you to store and manipulate date and time information. You will also learn how to use a `DateTimePicker` control to retrieve date and time information from the user. Finally, you will learn how to use a `Timer`—a C# control that allows you to execute code at specified time intervals.

14.1 Test-Driving the Shipping Time Application

In this tutorial, you will build the **Shipping Time** application. This application must meet the following requirements:

Application Requirements

A seafood distributor has asked you to create an application that will calculate the delivery time for fresh seafood shipped from Portland, Maine to its distribution center in Las Vegas, Nevada, where only the freshest seafood is accepted. The distributor has arrangements with local airlines to guarantee that seafood will ship on either flights that leave at noon or ones that leave at midnight. However, for security reasons, the airport requires the distributor to drop off the seafood at the airport at least one hour before each flight. When the distributor specifies the drop-off time, the application should display the delivery time in Las Vegas. This application should take into account the 3-hour time difference (it's 3 hours earlier in Las Vegas) and the 6-hour flight time between the two cities. The application should allow the user to select drop-off times within the current day (seafood must be shipped within a day to guarantee freshness). The application should also include a running clock that displays the current time.

This application calculates the shipment's delivery time from the user's drop-off time, taking into account factors such as transit time and time zones. You will use the DateTimePicker control to enable the user to enter the drop-off time. You will use the DateTime structure properties and methods to calculate the delivery time. You begin by test-driving the completed application. Then, you will learn the additional C# technologies you will need to create your own version of this application.

Test-Driving the Shipping Time Application

1. ***Opening the completed application.*** Open the C:\Examples\Tutorial14\ CompletedApplication\ShippingTime directory to locate the **Shipping Time** application. Double click ShippingTime.sln to open the application in Visual Studio .NET.

2. ***Running the Shipping Time application.*** Select **Debug > Start** to run the application (Fig. 14.1).

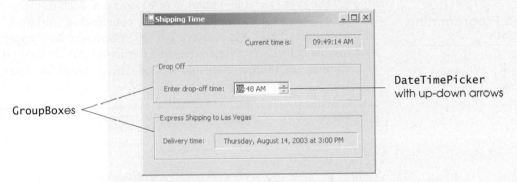

GroupBoxes

DateTimePicker with up-down arrows

Figure 14.1 Shipping Time application.

3. ***Entering a drop-off time.*** Notice that the default drop-off time is set to your computer's current time when the application is loaded (opened). When you change the drop-off time, the Label displaying the delivery time will display the delivery time based on the new time. Notice that if you select a time before 11:00 A.M., the shipment will arrive in Las Vegas at 3:00 P.M. If you specify a time between 11:00 A.M. and 11:00 P.M., the shipment will arrive in Las Vegas at 3:00 A.M. the following day. Finally, if you specify a time after 11:00 P.M., the shipment will not arrive until 3:00 P.M. the following day.

   The time displayed in the **Current time is:** Label will update to the current time once each second. However, the drop-off time displayed in the DateTimePicker will change only if you select different values by using the up and down arrows or by typing in a new value.

4. ***Closing the application.*** Close your running application by clicking its close box.

5. ***Closing the IDE.*** Close Visual Studio .NET by clicking its close box.

14.2 DateTime Variables

Choosing the correct type in which to store information can decrease development time by simplifying code. For example, if you are counting whole numbers, variables of type int are your best choice; if you need to store monetary values, you should use variables of type decimal. However, if you want to store date information (such as the day, month, year and time), there is no obvious built-in type. For example, if you used an int to count days, you would also need separate variables to keep track of the month, day of the week, year and other date-related information. Keeping track of all of these variables would be a complicated task and could slow the development of applications that require date and time information.

Declaring a DateTime Variable

The DateTime structure in C# simplifies manipulation, storage and display of date (and time) information. A DateTime variable, which is created from the DateTime structure, stores information about a point in time (for example, 12:00:00 A.M. on January 1, 2003). Using code, you can access a DateTime's properties, including the day, the hour and the minute. Your **Shipping Time** application requires calculations involving time, so you will use DateTime variables to store and manipulate this information.

The DateTime type is not a built-in type, so you must use the new operator when creating a DateTime value. In the code,

DateTime constructor ———

DateTime variable ———

```
DateTime dtmDelivery = new DateTime( 2003, 1, 1, 0, 0, 0 );
```

a new DateTime variable named dtmDelivery is declared. The **new** operator calls the DateTime structure's constructor. A **constructor** initializes a class object or structure value when it is created. You will also learn how to write your own constructors in Tutorial 19. Notice that this particular constructor takes six arguments: year, month, day, hour, minute and second. These values are described in Fig. 14.2.

Good Programming Practice

Prefix DateTime variable names with dtm (short for date/time).

Argument	Range	Description
Initializing a DateTime variable using new DateTime(year, month, day, hour, minute, second)		
year	int values 1–9999	Specifies the year.
month	int values 1–12	Specifies the month of the year.
day	int values 1–*number of days in month*	Specifies the day of the month. Each month has 28 to 31 days depending on the month and year.
hour	int values 0–23	Specifies the hour of the day. The value 0 represents 12:00 A.M.
minute	int values 0–59	Specifies the minute of the hour.
second	int values 0–59	Specifies the number of elapsed seconds in the current minute.

Figure 14.2 DateTime constructor arguments.

Using DateTime Members

After assigning a value to a DateTime variable, you can access that variable's properties using the member-access (dot) operator, as follows:

```
intYear = dtmDelivery.Year;      // retrieves dtmDelivery's year
intMonth = dtmDelivery.Month;    // retrieves dtmDelivery's month
intDay = dtmDelivery.Day;        // retrieves dtmDelivery's day
intHour = dtmDelivery.Hour;      // retrieves dtmDelivery's hour
intMinute = dtmDelivery.Minute;  // retrieves dtmDelivery's minute
intSecond = dtmDelivery.Second;  // retrieves dtmDelivery's second
```

In this tutorial, you will use several DateTime properties and methods that can be accessed through the member-access operator.

Values in DateTime variables cannot be added like numeric built-in types such as ints and decimals. Instead of using arithmetic operators to add or subtract values in DateTime variables, you must call the correct method, using the member-access operator. Figure 14.3 demonstrates how to perform various calculations with DateTime variables.

C# statement	Result
Assume dtmDelivery has been initialized with a DateTime value.	
dtmDelivery = dtmDelivery.AddYears(2);	Add 2 years.
dtmDelivery = dtmDelivery.AddMonths(-5);	Subtract 5 months.
dtmDelivery = dtmDelivery.AddDays(1);	Add 1 day.
dtmDelivery = dtmDelivery.AddHours(3);	Add 3 hours.
dtmDelivery = dtmDelivery.AddMinutes(30);	Add 30 minutes.
dtmDelivery = dtmDelivery.AddSeconds(-12);	Subtract 12 seconds.

Figure 14.3 DateTime methods that perform various calculations.

Note that each "add" method does not actually change the value of the DateTime variable on which that method is called. Instead, each "add" method returns a DateTime value containing the result of the calculation. To change the value of DateTime variable dtmDelivery, you must assign to dtmDelivery the value returned by the "add" method, as in Fig. 14.3.

C# provides a simple way to assign the current date and time to a DateTime variable. You can use the Now property to assign your computer's current date and time to a DateTime variable:

```
DateTime dtmCurrentTime = DateTime.Now;
```

Much like methods MessageBox.Show and String.Format, you can access the Now property of the DateTime structure by following the name of the structure with the member-access operator and the name of the property. Notice that this assignment does not require the new operator. This is because the DateTime.Now property returns a DateTime value.

Now that you are familiar with DateTime variables, you will design the **Shipping Time** application by using two new controls—the GroupBox control and the DateTimePicker control. A **GroupBox** control groups related controls visually by drawing a labelled box around them. The **DateTimePicker** control allows users to enter date and time information.

SELF-REVIEW

1. The _____ property of the DateTime structure retrieves your computer's current date and time.

   a) Time
   b) Now
   c) CurrentTime
   d) DateTime

2. The fourth argument to the DateTime constructor specifies the variable's _____.

   a) day
   b) year
   c) hour
   d) minute

Answers: 1) b. 2) c.

14.3 Building the Shipping Time Application: Design Elements

You are now ready to begin analyzing the problem statement and developing pseudocode. The following pseudocode describes the basic operation of the **Shipping Time** application:

When the Form loads:
    Set range of possible drop off times to any time in the current day
    Determine the shipment's delivery time

Display the shipment's delivery time
When the user changes the drop-off time:
    Determine the shipment's delivery time
    Display the shipment's delivery time

After one second has elapsed:
    Update the current time displayed

When the DisplayDeliveryTime method gets called:
    Determine the time the shipment's flight will depart
    Add three hours to determine the delivery time (takes into account 6 hours
        for time of flight minus 3 hours for the time difference)
    Display the delivery time

When the DepartureTime method gets called:

    Switch based on the hour the shipment was dropped off

        If the drop off hour is between the values 0 and 10
            Delivery set to depart on noon flight of current day

        If the drop off hour is 23
            Delivery set to depart on noon flight of next day

        If none of the preceding Cases match
            Delivery set to depart on midnight flight of current day

Now that you have test-driven the **Shipping Time** application and studied its pseudocode representation, you will use an ACE table to help you convert the pseudocode to C#. Figure 14.4 lists the actions, controls and events that will help you complete your own version of this application.

Action	Control	Event/Method
Label the application's controls	lblCurrentTime, lblDropOff, lblDeliveryTime	Application is run
	FrmShippingTime	Load
Set range of possible drop off times to any time in the current day	dtpDropOff	
Determine the shipment's delivery time	dtpDropOff	
Display the shipment's delivery time	lblLasVegasTime	
	dtpDropOff	ValueChanged
Determine the shipment's delivery time	dtpDropOff	
Display the shipment's delivery time	lblLasVegasTime	
	tmrClock	Tick
Update and display the current time	lblCurrentTime	
		Display-DeliveryTime
Determine the time the shipment's flight will depart	dtpDropOff	
Add three hours to determine the delivery time		
Display the delivery time	lblLasVegasTime	

Action/Control/Event (ACE) Table for the Shipping Time Application

Figure 14.4 ACE table for the **Shipping Time** application. (Part 1 of 2.)

Action	Control	Event/Method
		Departure-Time
Switch based on the hour the shipment was dropped off	dtpDropOff	
If drop off hour is 0–10 Delivery set to depart on noon flight	dtmDepartureTime	

If drop off hour is 23
    Delivery set to depart on noon flight
    of next day
	dtmDepartureTime	

If none of the preceding Cases match Delivery set to depart on midnight flight	dtmDepartureTime	

Figure 14.4   ACE table for the **Shipping Time** application. (Part 2 of 2.)

Now, you will begin building the **Shipping Time** application from the template provided. The following box demonstrates how to insert a GroupBox control into your application.

Placing Controls in a GroupBox

1. **Copying the template to your working directory.** Copy the `C:\Examples\Tutorial14\TemplateApplication\ShippingTime` directory to your `C:\SimplyCSP` directory.

2. **Opening the Shipping Time application's template file.** Double click Ship-pingTime.sln in the ShippingTime directory to open the application in Visual Studio .NET.

3. **Inserting a GroupBox control in the Form.** The template Form includes a GroupBox that displays the seafood shipment delivery time. Add a second GroupBox for the drop-off time by double clicking the **GroupBox** control

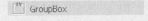

in the **Toolbox**. Change the Text property to Drop Off and the Name property to fraDropOff. Change the Location property to 16, 56 and the Size property to 328, 64. After these modifications, your Form should look like Fig. 14.5.

Good Programming Practice

Prefix GroupBox control names with fra (short for frame, the name of GroupBoxes in earlier languages).

Newly created GroupBox displaying the text **Drop Off**

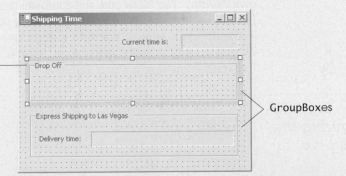

Figure 14.5   GroupBox controls on the **Shipping Time** Form.

GUI Design Tip

GroupBox titles should be concise and should use book-title capitalization.

4. **Creating Labels inside the GroupBox.** To place a Label inside the Group-Box, click the **Label** tab in the **Toolbox**, then click inside the GroupBox to place the Label inside the GroupBox (Fig. 14.6).

(cont.)

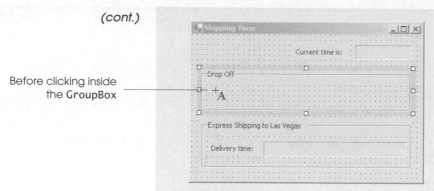

Before clicking inside
the GroupBox

Figure 14.6 Adding a Label to a GroupBox.

Change the Text property of the Label to Enter drop-off time: and the Name property to lblDropOff. Change the Label's Location property to 40, 32 and its Size property to 104, 21. Finally, change the Label's TextAlign property to MiddleLeft.

Notice that the Location values you entered are measured from the top-left corner of the GroupBox and not from the top-left corner of the Form. Objects, such as Forms, GroupBoxes and Panels (which you'll use in Tutorial 19), that contain controls are called **containers**. Location values for controls in an application are measured from the top-left corner of the object that contains them.

If a GroupBox is placed over a control that is already on the Form, the control will be behind the GroupBox (that is, the GroupBox hides the control by covering it). To avoid this problem, remove all controls from the area in which you wish to place the GroupBox control before inserting it. You can then either drag and drop existing controls into the GroupBox or add new controls as needed by using the method described earlier.

GUI Design Tip

Use GroupBoxes to group related controls on the Form visually.

5. **Saving the project.** Select **File > Save All** to save your modified code.

You have now added a GroupBox and a Label to the **Shipping Time** application to display the drop-off time. In the following box, you will add a DateTimePicker control to retrieve the drop-off time from the user.

Recall that the DateTimePicker retrieves date and time information from the user. The DateTimePicker allows you to select from a variety of predefined date and time formats to present to the user (for example, date formats like 12/31/03 and December 31, 2003; and time formats like 2:00 PM and 14:00) or you can create your own format. The date and time information is then stored in a variable of type DateTime, which you can manipulate using DateTime methods. Note that the format limits the date and/or time information the user can specify. However, the format used to present the date and/or time does not alter the value stored in the DateTime-Picker.

Creating and Customizing the DateTimePicker

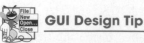

GUI Design Tip

Use a DateTimePicker to retrieve date and time information from a user.

1. **Adding the DateTimePicker.** To add a DateTimePicker to your application, click the **DateTimePicker** control,

DateTimePicker

in the **Toolbox**, then click to the right of lblDropOff to place the DateTimePicker. Your Form should look similar to Fig. 14.7. (Your control will contain your computer's current date.)

2. **Modifying the DateTimePicker.** With the DateTimePicker selected, change the Name property of the DateTimePicker to dtpDropOff.

(cont.)

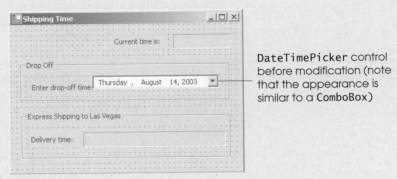

Figure 14.7 DateTimePicker control on the Form.

GUI Design Tip

Each DateTimePicker should have a corresponding descriptive Label.

Good Programming Practice

Prefix DateTimePicker control names with dtp.

Align the DateTimePicker with its Label by setting its Size property to 88, 21 and its Location property to 144, 32. Next, change its **Format** property to Custom. This indicates that you will specify how the date will appear in the DateTimePicker.

3. *Specifying a custom display format.* When the DateTimePicker's Format property is set to Custom, it uses the custom format that you specify in the **CustomFormat** property. Notice that the DateTimePicker now displays the date in the format 1/1/2003, the default format when the CustomFormat property has not been set.

Set the value of the CustomFormat property to hh:mm tt. The "hh" displays the hour as a number from 01 to 12, the ":" inserts a colon and the "mm" indicates that the number of minutes from 00 to 59 should follow the colon. The "tt" indicates that AM or PM should appear, depending on the time of day. Note that this property eliminates the problem of a user entering a letter or symbol when the application expects a number—the DateTimePicker will not allow values in any format other than what you specify in the CustomFormat property.

GUI Design Tip

If the user should specify a time of day or a date and time, set the DateTimePicker's ShowUpDown property to true. If the user should specify only a date, set the DateTimePicker's ShowUpDown property to false to allow the user to select a day from the month calendar.

4. *Using up-down arrows in the DateTimePicker.* Set the DateTimePicker's **ShowUpDown** property to true. This setting allows the user to select the date or time by clicking the up or down arrows that appear on the right side of the control, much like a NumericUpDown control. When the property is set to false (which is the default), a down arrow will appear on the right side of the control (Fig. 14.7), much like a ComboBox. Clicking the down arrow will cause a month calendar to appear, allowing the user to select a date (but not a time). A demonstration of the month calendar is shown in the Controls, Events, Properties & Methods section at the end of this tutorial and in Appendix E. The user needs to enter only the time of day, so you will use up-down arrows to display the time.

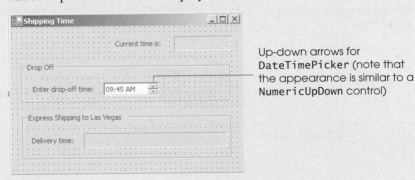

Figure 14.8 Customized DateTimePicker control on the Form.

Error-Prevention Tip

If the user should specify a date and/or time, use a DateTimePicker control to prevent the user from entering invalid date and/or time values.

5. *Saving the project.* Select **File > Save All** to save your modified code.

The final control you will add to the Form is a Timer. In the following box, you will use the Timer to place a clock on the Form so that users can see the current time of day while using the application.

Creating a Timer Control

1. **Adding a Timer control.** A **Timer** control is an object that can "wake up" at specified time intervals by generating a **Tick** event. By default, the Timer "wakes up" every 100 milliseconds (1/10 of a second). Each time the Tick event is generated, its event handler is executed. You can customize the "wake period" (the amount of time between each instance of the Timer's Tick event) and the code that it executes (the event handler for the Tick event) so that a certain task is performed once every "wake up" period.

   Add a Timer to the Form by clicking the **Timer** control,

   in the **Toolbox** and dragging and dropping it anywhere on the Form. Notice that the Timer does not actually appear on the Form; it appears below the Windows Form Designer in an area called the **component tray** (Fig. 14.9). The Timer control is placed in the component tray because it is not part of the graphical user interface—users never see the Timer control.

   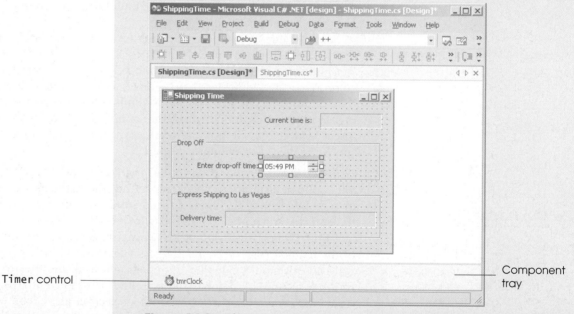

   Timer control

   Component tray

   Figure 14.9 Timer control is displayed in the component tray.

Good Programming Practice

Prefix Timer control names with tmr.

2. **Customizing the Timer control.** Rename the Timer by setting its Name property to tmrClock. To allow the Timer's Tick event to be raised, set the Timer's Enabled property to true. Then, set the Timer's **Interval** property to 1000, which specifies the number of milliseconds between Tick events (1,000 milliseconds = 1 second).

3. **Saving the project.** Select **File > Save All** to save your modified code.

SELF-REVIEW

1. If a GroupBox is placed over a control that is already on the Form, the control will be _____ the GroupBox.

   a) replaced by   b) inside
   c) behind   d) in front of

2. Setting the Format property of the DateTimePicker control to _____ indicates that you will specify how the date will appear in the DateTimePicker.

    a) Custom   b) Unique

    c) User   d) Other

Answers: 1) c. 2) a.

14.4 Creating the Shipping Time Application: Inserting Code

Now that you have completed the visual design of the **Shipping Time** application, you will complete the application by inserting code. You will begin coding the application's functionality by inserting code to create a clock on the application that updates the current time every second. You will then write code that displays the delivery time from Portland to Las Vegas. You will implement this feature by inserting code that is executed when the Form loads or whenever the user specifies a new drop-off time. In the following box, you will write the code to create the clock.

Coding the Shipping Time Application's Clock

1. ***Rearranging and commenting the control declarations.*** In code view, rearrange and comment the control declarations so that they appear as in lines 15–32 of Fig. 14.10. Be sure to add spaces before and after each group of control declarations to increase the clarity of your code.

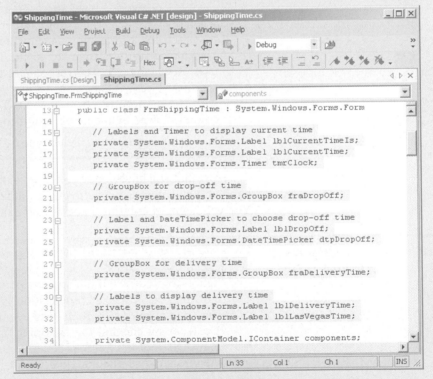

Figure 14.10 Rearranging and commenting the control declarations.

2. ***Inserting code to handle the Timer's Tick event.*** In design view, double click the Timer control in the component tray to generate the empty event handler for the Tick event. (A Tick event is raised once per Interval, as set in the Timer's Interval property.) Be sure to add the comment and break the header as shown in Fig. 14.11 so that the line numbers in your code match those presented in this tutorial. Add lines 197–199 of Fig. 14.11 to the body of the event handler.

(cont.)

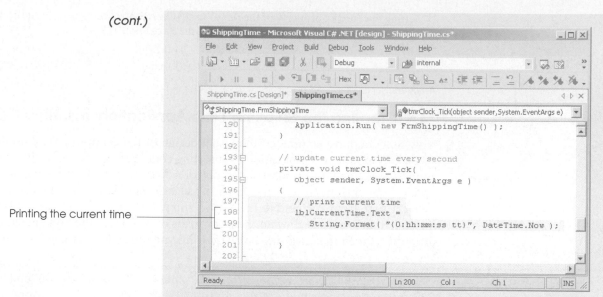

Printing the current time

Figure 14.11 Inserting code for a Tick event.

Lines 194–199 display the event handler for the Tick event, which executes every second. DateTime property Now retrieves your computer's time when it is accessed. The event handler takes this information and formats it to match the format you specify, "hh:mm:ss tt". The Text property of lblCurrentTime is then set to the formatted string for display to the user. Recall that the 0 corresponds to DateTime.Now and the text following the first colon contains your format information. You are already familiar with the purpose of hh:mm and tt. The :ss following mm indicates that a colon followed by the number of seconds (00–59) should be displayed.

3. **Saving the application.** Select **File > Save All** to save your modified code.

Now that you have coded your application's clock using the Timer's Tick event handler, you will insert code to display a delivery time when the application opens. You will begin by creating a Load event handler for your application.

Using Code to Display a Delivery Time

1. **Adding the FrmShippingTime_Load event handler.** When an application executes, the Form is displayed. However, sometimes you also want a specific action to occur when the application opens but before the Form displays. To execute code when the application first opens, create an event handler for the **Load** event. To create a Load event handler, return to the Windows Form Designer by clicking the **ShippingTime.cs [Design]** tab. Double click an empty area of the Form to generate the Load event handler and enter code view. Make sure that you do not click inside a GroupBox or other control.

2. **Storing the current date.** Add lines 208–209 of Fig. 14.12 to the Load event handler. Line 209 stores the current date in variable dtmCurrentTime. (You will store the date as a variable so that you can preserve information about the current date for use later in the event handler.) Be sure to add the comment (line 204) and break the header as shown in Fig. 14.12 so that the line numbers in your code match those presented in this tutorial. Also add the comment shown in line 202 to the end of the tmrClock_Tick event handler.

(cont.)

Storing the current time in
`dtmCurrentTime`

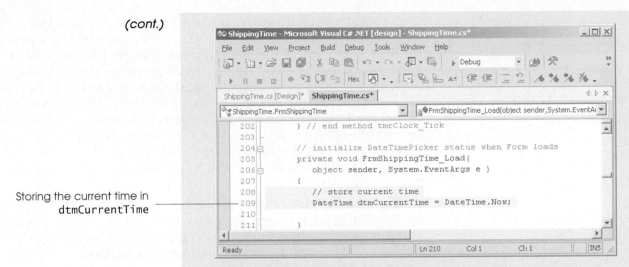

Figure 14.12 Storing the current time.

3. ***Setting the drop-off hours.*** Add lines 211–215 of Fig. 14.13 to the
    FrmShippingTime_Load event handler. These lines set the MinDate and
    MaxDate properties for dtpDropOff. The **MinDate** property specifies the
    earliest value that the DateTimePicker will allow the user to enter. The
    MaxDate property specifies the latest value that the DateTimePicker will
    allow the user to enter. Together, these two properties set the range of
    drop-off times from which the user can select.

    To guarantee freshness, the seafood shipment should be dropped off at
    the airline within the current day; therefore, the earliest drop-off time
    (MinDate) is set to 12:00 A.M. of the current day (lines 212–213), and the
    latest drop-off time (MaxDate) is set to 12:00 A.M. the following day (line
    215). Notice that the MaxDate value is calculated by adding one day to the
    MinDate value using the AddDays method. Recall that the AddDays
    method does not change the DateTime value on which it operates—it
    returns a new DateTime value. This value is assigned to the MaxDate prop-
    erty on line 215.

Setting the range of drop-off times

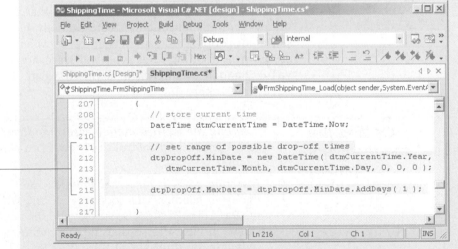

Figure 14.13 Setting the MinDate and MaxDate properties.

(cont.)

The DateTime constructor (called in line 212) creates a value that stores a time. Recall that the first parameter is the year, the second is the month and the third is the day. The last three parameters specify the hour, minute and number of seconds. A DateTime variable's Year property returns the value of its year as an int (for example, 2003). Its Month property returns the value of the DateTime variable's month as an int (for example, 6 for June). Finally, the DateTime variable's Day property returns the day of the month (an int between 1 and 31, depending on the month and year). You assigned to the dtmCurrentTime variable the value of the current time (using DateTime.Now); therefore, the first three arguments combine to specify the current date.

4. **Calling the DisplayDeliveryTime method.** Add lines 217–218 of Fig. 14.14 to call the DisplayDeliveryTime method. You will write this method later in this tutorial. The DisplayDeliveryTime calculates the delivery time in Las Vegas and displays the result in the **Delivery time:** Label.

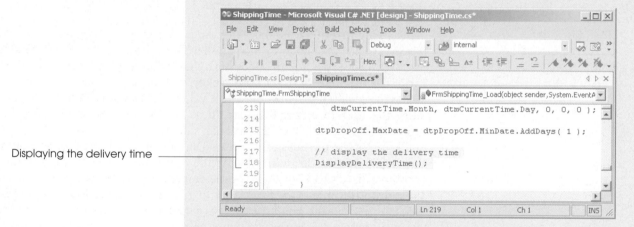

Displaying the delivery time

Figure 14.14 Calling the DisplayDeliveryTime method.

5. **Saving the application.** Select **File > Save All** to save your modified code.

So far, you have added functionality that calculates and displays the delivery time when the application executes initially. However, you should allow a user to select any drop-off time and instantly see when the seafood shipment will be delivered. In the following box, you will learn how to handle the DateTimePicker's **ValueChanged** event, which is raised when the user changes the time in the DateTimePicker.

Coding the ValueChanged Event Handler

1. **Creating the ValueChanged event handler.** In design view, double click the DateTimePicker control dtpDropOff to generate the ValueChanged event handler.

2. **Inserting code in the event handler.** Insert lines 227–228 of Fig. 14.15 into the event handler. This code will execute when the user changes the time in the DateTimePicker. Be sure to add the comments and break the header as shown in Fig. 14.15 so that the line numbers in your code match those presented in this tutorial.

The ValueChanged event handler also uses the DisplayDeliveryTime method to calculate and display the delivery time in Las Vegas. In the next box, you will write the DisplayDeliveryTime method.

3. **Saving the project.** Select **File > Save All** to save your modified code.

(cont.)

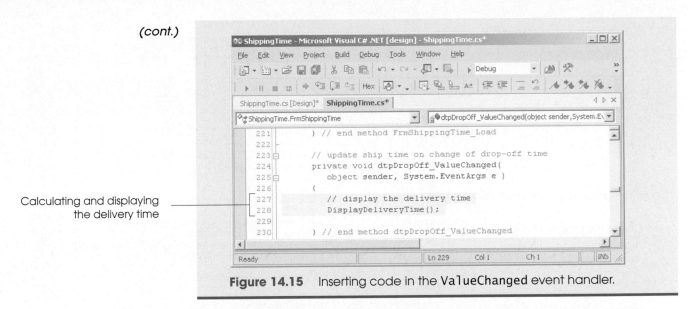

Calculating and displaying
the delivery time

Figure 14.15   Inserting code in the `ValueChanged` event handler.

Though you have called the `DisplayDeliveryTime` method in two event handlers, you still need to write the method. Next, you will use `DateTime` methods to display the delivery time in an output `Label`.

Coding the `DisplayDeliveryTime` *Method*	1. ***Creating the*** `DisplayDeliveryTime` ***method.*** Add lines 232–243 of Fig. 14.16 below the `ValueChanged` event handler. Line 236 calls the `DepartureTime` method. You will write this method in the next box. The `DepartureTime` method determines which flight (midnight or noon) the seafood shipment will use. It returns a `DateTime` value representing the flight's departure time. Line 236 stores this value in the `DateTime` variable `dtmDelivery`.

2. ***Calculating and displaying the delivery time.*** Line 239 calculates the delivery time by adding 3 hours to the departure time (see the discussion following this box). Lines 240–241 display the Las Vegas delivery time by calling the `DateTime` structure's `ToLongDateString` and `ToShortTimeString` methods. A `DateTime` variable's **`ToLongDateString`** method returns the date as a `string` in the format `"Thursday, August 14, 2003"`. A `DateTime` variable's **`ToShortTimeString`** method returns the time as a `string` in the format `"10:00 AM"`. |

(cont.)

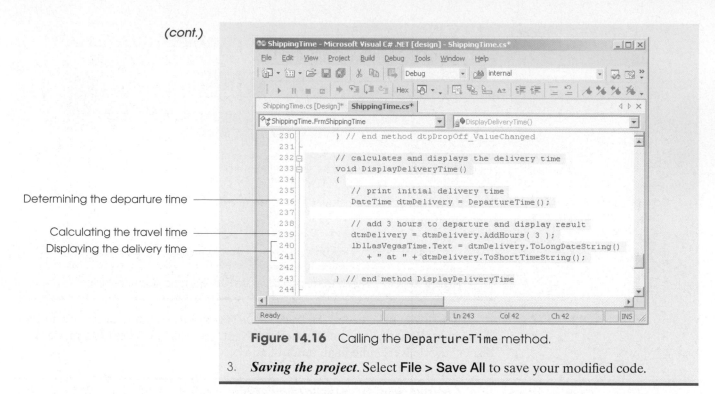

Determining the departure time ⎯⎯⎯⎯⎯⎯⎯⎯⎯⎯⎯⎯

Calculating the travel time ⎯⎯⎯⎯⎯⎯⎯⎯⎯⎯⎯⎯⎯
Displaying the delivery time ⎯⎯⎯⎯⎯⎯⎯⎯⎯⎯⎯

Figure 14.16   Calling the `DepartureTime` method.

3. ***Saving the project.*** Select **File > Save All** to save your modified code.

When calculating the shipment's delivery time, you must account for the time-zone difference and the flight time. For instance, if you send a shipment from Portland, Maine to Las Vegas, Nevada, it will travel west three time zones (the time in Las Vegas is 3 hours earlier) and spend 6 hours in transit. If you drop off the shipment at 5:00 P.M. in Portland, the shipment will leave on the midnight flight and arrive in Las Vegas at

12:00 A.M. + *(time zone change + flight time)* = 12:00 A.M. + (-3 + 6) *hours,*

which is 3:00 A.M. Las Vegas time. Similarly, if the shipment takes the noon flight to Las Vegas, it will arrive at 3 P.M. in Las Vegas.

To complete the application, you need to code the `DepartureTime` method. You will use a `switch` statement and `DateTime` methods to return a `DateTime` containing the departure time (noon or midnight) for the seafood shipment's flight.

Coding the DepartureTime Method

1. ***Writing the DepartureTime method and declaring variables.*** Add lines 245–252 of Fig. 14.17 to your code below the `ValueChanged` event handler. Line 249 stores the current date in the `DateTime` variable `dtmCurrentDate`. Line 250 declares the `DateTime` variable `dtmDepartureTime`, the variable you will use to store the `DepartureTime` method's return value.

2. ***Determining which flight the shipment uses.*** Add lines 252–279 of Fig. 14.18 after the variable declarations and before the right brace that ends the method body. The `switch` statement that begins on line 253 uses the hour specified by the user in the `DateTimePicker` as the controlling expression. The value selected by the user in the `DateTimePicker` is located in its **Value** property. The `DateTime` structure's `Hour` property returns the hour of the `DateTime` stored in the `DateTimePicker`'s `Value` property.

(cont.)

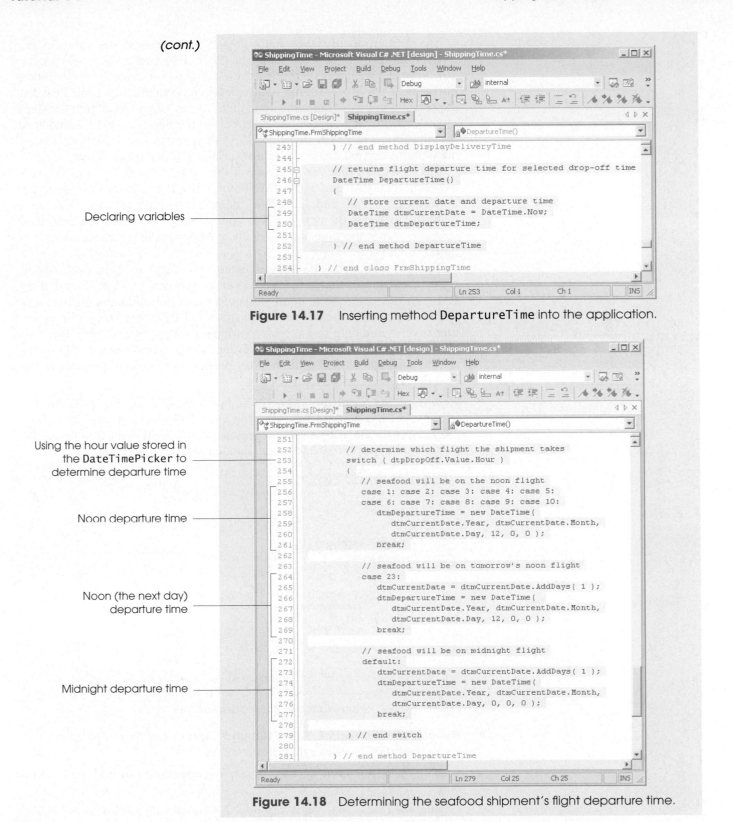

Figure 14.17   Inserting method `DepartureTime` into the application.

Figure 14.18   Determining the seafood shipment's flight departure time.

(cont.)

The first group of cases (lines 256–257) executes if the value in the DateTimePicker is between midnight (Hour = 0) and 10:59 A.M. (Hour = 10). Note that we have compressed these cases to two lines for presentation purposes. If the drop-off time occurs between midnight and 10:59:59 A.M., the seafood shipment takes the noon flight to Las Vegas (recall that the shipment leaves for the airport one hour before the flight leaves). The body of the first group of cases (lines 258–261) then stores the departure time of noon on the current day in the return variable dtmDepartureTime.

The next case (line 264) executes if the value in the DateTimePicker is between 11:00 P.M. and 11:59 P.M. (Hour = 23). If the drop-off time occurs between 11:00 P.M. and 11:59 P.M, the seafood shipment takes the noon flight to Las Vegas the next day. The body of this case (lines 265–269) then stores the departure time of noon on the next day in the return variable dtmDepartureTime.

The default case (line 272) executes if no previous case evaluates to true (the value in the DateTimePicker is between 11:00 A.M. and 10:59 P.M.). In this case, the seafood shipment takes the midnight flight to Las Vegas. The body of the default case (lines 273–277) then stores the departure time of midnight in the return variable dtmDepartureTime. Note that because midnight occurs on the following day, the DateTime variable representing midnight should contain a Day property value corresponding to the next day. Line 273 ensures this occurs.

3. ***Returning the departure time.*** Add lines 281–282 of Fig. 14.19 to the DepartureTime method following the end of the switch statement. Line 282 returns the DateTime value representing the flight departure time. Add a comment to the end of each event handler you have generated.

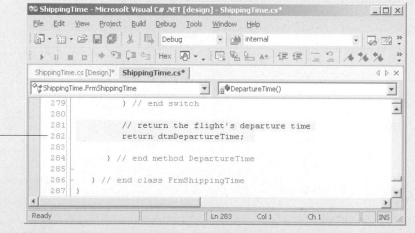

Returning the departure time

Figure 14.19   Returning the flight departure time.

4. ***Running the application.*** Select **Debug > Start** to run your application. Test your application to ensure that it runs correctly.

5. ***Closing the application.*** Close your running application by clicking its close box.

6. ***Closing the IDE.*** Close Visual Studio .NET by clicking its close box.

Figure 14.20 presents the source code for the **Shipping Time** application. The lines of code that contain new programming concepts that you learned in this tutorial are highlighted.

```
1   using System;
2   using System.Drawing;
3   using System.Collections;
4   using System.ComponentModel;
5   using System.Windows.Forms;
6   using System.Data;
7
8   namespace ShippingTime
9   {
10     /// <summary>
11     /// Summary description for FrmShippingTime.
12     /// </summary>
13     public class FrmShippingTime : System.Windows.Forms.Form
14     {
15        // Labels and Timer to display current time
16        private System.Windows.Forms.Label lblCurrentTimeIs;
17        private System.Windows.Forms.Label lblCurrentTime;
18        private System.Windows.Forms.Timer tmrClock;
19
20        // GroupBox for drop-off time
21        private System.Windows.Forms.GroupBox fraDropOff;
22
23        // Label and DateTimePicker to choose drop-off time
24        private System.Windows.Forms.Label lblDropOff;
25        private System.Windows.Forms.DateTimePicker dtpDropOff;
26
27        // GroupBox for delivery time
28        private System.Windows.Forms.GroupBox fraDeliveryTime;
29
30        // Labels to display delivery time
31        private System.Windows.Forms.Label lblDeliveryTime;
32        private System.Windows.Forms.Label lblLasVegasTime;
33
34        private System.ComponentModel.IContainer components;
35
36        public FrmShippingTime()
37        {
38           //
39           // Required for Windows Form Designer support
40           //
41           InitializeComponent();
42
43           //
44           // TODO: Add any constructor code after InitializeComponent
45           // call
46           //
47        }
48
49        /// <summary>
50        /// Clean up any resources being used.
51        /// </summary>
52        protected override void Dispose( bool disposing )
53        {
54           if( disposing )
55           {
56              if (components != null)
57              {
```

Figure 14.20 **Shipping Time** application code. (Part 1 of 3.)

```
58                    components.Dispose();
59                 }
60              }
61              base.Dispose( disposing );
62           }
63
64           // Windows Form Designer generated code
65
66           /// <summary>
67           /// The main entry point for the application.
68           /// </summary>
69           [STAThread]
70           static void Main()
71           {
72              Application.Run( new FrmShippingTime() );
73           }
74
75           // update current time every second
76           private void tmrClock_Tick(
77              object sender, System.EventArgs e )
78           {
79              // print current time
80              lblCurrentTime.Text =
81                 String.Format( "{0:hh:mm:ss tt}", DateTime.Now );
82
83           } // end method tmrClock_Tick
84
85           // initialize DateTimePicker status when Form loads
86           private void FrmShippingTime_Load(
87              object sender, System.EventArgs e )
88           {
89              // store current time
90              DateTime dtmCurrentTime = DateTime.Now;
91
92              // set range of possible drop-off times
93              dtpDropOff.MinDate = new DateTime( dtmCurrentTime.Year,
94                 dtmCurrentTime.Month, dtmCurrentTime.Day, 0, 0, 0 );
95
96              dtpDropOff.MaxDate = dtpDropOff.MinDate.AddDays( 1 );
97
98              // display the delivery time
99              DisplayDeliveryTime();
100
101           } // end method FrmShippingTime_Load
102
103           // update ship time on change of drop-off time
104           private void dtpDropOff_ValueChanged(
105              object sender, System.EventArgs e )
106           {
107              // display the delivery time
108              DisplayDeliveryTime();
109
110           } // end method dtpDropOff_ValueChanged
111
112           // calculates and displays the delivery time
113           void DisplayDeliveryTime()
114           {
```

Displaying current time — (lines 80–81)

Setting the DateTimePicker's minimum and maximum values — (lines 93–96)

Figure 14.20   Shipping Time application code. (Part 2 of 3.)

<table>
<tr><td></td><td>115</td><td>// print initial delivery time</td></tr>
<tr><td></td><td>116</td><td>DateTime dtmDelivery = DepartureTime();</td></tr>
</table>

```
115                // print initial delivery time
116                DateTime dtmDelivery = DepartureTime();
117
118                // add 3 hours to departure and display result
119                dtmDelivery = dtmDelivery.AddHours( 3 );
120                lblLasVegasTime.Text = dtmDelivery.ToLongDateString()
121                   + " at " + dtmDelivery.ToShortTimeString();
122
123          } // end method DisplayDeliveryTime
124
125          // returns flight departure time for selected drop-off time
126          DateTime DepartureTime()
127          {
128                // store current date and departure time
129                DateTime dtmCurrentDate = DateTime.Now;
130                DateTime dtmDepartureTime;
131
132                // determine which flight the shipment takes
133                switch ( dtpDropOff.Value.Hour )
134                {
135                   // seafood will be on the noon flight
136                   case 1: case 2: case 3: case 4: case 5:
137                   case 6: case 7: case 8: case 9: case 10:
138                      dtmDepartureTime = new DateTime(
139                         dtmCurrentDate.Year, dtmCurrentDate.Month,
140                         dtmCurrentDate.Day, 12, 0, 0 );
141                      break;
142
143                   // seafood will be on tomorrow's noon flight
144                   case 23:
145                      dtmCurrentDate = dtmCurrentDate.AddDays( 1 );
146                      dtmDepartureTime = new DateTime(
147                         dtmCurrentDate.Year, dtmCurrentDate.Month,
148                         dtmCurrentDate.Day, 12, 0, 0 );
149                      break;
150
151                   // seafood will be on midnight flight
152                   default:
153                      dtmCurrentDate = dtmCurrentDate.AddDays( 1 );
154                      dtmDepartureTime = new DateTime(
155                         dtmCurrentDate.Year, dtmCurrentDate.Month,
156                         dtmCurrentDate.Day, 0, 0, 0 );
157                      break;
158
159                } // end switch
160
161                // return the flight's departure time
162                return dtmDepartureTime;
163
164          } // end method DepartureTime
165
166    } // end class FrmShippingTime
167 }
```

Calculating and displaying the delivery time in Las Vegas — *(lines 119–121)*

Using a **switch** statement to determine departure time — *(line 133)*

Figure 14.20 **Shipping Time** application code. (Part 3 of 3.)

SELF-REVIEW

SELF-REVIEW
1. The `ToShortTimeString` method is called on a `DateTime` variable to return its value in the format _____.

a) `11 o'clock`   b) `23:00`

c) `11:00`   d) `11:00 PM`

2. `DateTimePicker` properties _____ and _____ specify the earliest and latest dates that can be selected, respectively.

a) `MinDate, MaxDate`   b) `Now, Later`

c) `Minimum, Maximum`   d) `Early, Late`

Answers: 1) d. 2) a.

14.5 Wrap-Up

In this tutorial, you learned how to use the `DateTime` type, a structure for manipulating time and date information. You used variables of this type to calculate and display delivery times in your **Shipping Time** application. To help users enter date and time information, you used a `DateTimePicker` control. You observed how a `DateTimePicker` control can display custom date and time formats and limit user input. To help you group controls on the `Form` visually, you used the `GroupBox` control. You also learned how to use the `Timer` control on the `Form`, which allowed your application to execute code once every second.

You then learned how to use three new event handlers to help you complete the **Shipping Time** application. You learned that the `Form`'s `Load` event handler allows your application to execute code when the application is opened initially. You used this event to set initial values in your application. You then learned how to use the `DateTimePicker` control's `ValueChanged` event handler, which allows you to execute code when the control's value changes. You used this event handler to update the delivery time each time the user entered a new time. Finally, you learned about the `Timer`'s `Tick` event handler, which you used to update and display the current time in a `Label` that serves as a clock.

In the next tutorial, you will use the **Fund Raiser** application to introduce two programming concepts: arguments and scope rules. Learning these concepts will help you build more powerful and dependable applications because you will understand how C# keeps track of variables throughout your application.

SKILLS SUMMARY

Storing and Manipulating Date and Time Information

▪ Use a `DateTime` variable to store and manipulate date and time information. A `DateTime` variable stores information about a point in time (for example, 12:00:00 A.M. on January 1, 2003). This information can be formatted for display in predefined long or short formats or in custom (programmer-defined) formats.

Using DateTime Variables

▪ Use the `new` operator to declare a new `DateTime` value.

▪ Use property `DateTime.Now` to obtain your computer's current date and time.

▪ Use the member-access operator to access properties of a `DateTime` variable.

▪ Use `DateTime` methods, such as `AddHours` and `AddDays`, to add or subtract time from values in `DateTime` variables. Then assign the value returned by the method to a `DateTime` variable.

Using a GroupBox Control

▪ Use a `GroupBox` control to group related controls visually. To add a `GroupBox` to the `Form`, double click the **GroupBox** control in the **Toolbox**.

Placing Controls Inside a GroupBox

▪ Place a control inside the `GroupBox` by clicking the control's name in the **Toolbox** and clicking inside the `GroupBox`.

Using the DateTimePicker Control

■ Use a DateTimePicker control to get date and time information from the user.

■ Set property Format to Custom to indicate that you will specify how the date will appear in the DateTimePicker. The format is specified in property CustomFormat.

■ Set property ShowUpDown to true to allow the user to select the date or time by clicking an up or down arrow. If this property's value is false, a monthly calendar will drop down, allowing the user to pick a date.

Using the Timer Control

■ Use a Timer control to execute code (the Tick event handler) at specified intervals. To add a Timer control to the Form, click **Timer** in the **Windows Forms** tab of the **Toolbox**, and click anywhere on the Form. The Timer control will appear in the component tray.

■ Customize the time between Tick events by using the Interval property, which specifies the number of milliseconds between each Tick event.

■ Set the Enabled property to true so that the Tick event is raised once per Interval.

KEY TERMS

component tray—The area below the Windows Form Designer that contains controls, such as Timers, that are not part of the graphical user interface.

constructor—Initializes a class object or structure value when it is created.

container—An object that contains controls.

CustomFormat property of a DateTimePicker control—Contains the format string used to display the date and/or time when the Format property is set to Custom.

DateTimePicker control—Retrieves date and time information from the user.

Format property of a DateTimePicker control—Allows the programmer to specify a predefined or custom format with which to display the date and/or time.

GroupBox control—Groups related controls visually.

Interval property of a Timer control—Specifies the number of milliseconds between each Tick event.

Load event—Raised when an application initially executes.

MaxDate property of a DateTimePicker control—DateTimePicker maximum allowed date.

MinDate property of a DateTimePicker control—DateTimePicker minimum allowed date.

new operator—Returns a reference to a newly created object.

ShowUpDown property of a DateTimePicker control—When true, allows the user to specify the time using up and down arrows.

Tick event of a Timer controlt—Raised after the number of milliseconds specified in the Interval property has elapsed.

Timer control—Wakes up at specified intervals to execute code in its Tick event handler.

ToLongDateString method of type DateTime—Returns a string containing the date in the format "Thursday, August 14, 2003".

ToShortTimeString method of type DateTime—Returns a string containing the time in the format "10:00 AM".

Value property of a DateTimePicker control—Stores the date and time in a DateTime-Picker control.

ValueChanged event of a DateTimePicker control—Raised when a user selects a new day or time.

GUI DESIGN GUIDELINES

DateTimePicker

■ Use a DateTimePicker to retrieve date and time information from the user.

■ Each DateTimePicker should have a corresponding descriptive Label.

■ If the user should specify a time of day or a date and time, set the DateTimePicker's ShowUpDown property to true. If the user should specify a date, set the DateTimePicker's ShowUpDown property to false to allow the user to select a day from the month calendar.

GroupBox

- GroupBox titles should be concise and should use book-title capitalization.
- Use GroupBoxes to group related controls on the Form visually.

CONTROLS, EVENTS, PROPERTIES & METHODS

DateTime This structure provides properties and methods to store and manipulate date and time information.

- *Properties*

  Day—Returns the day stored in a DateTime variable.

  Hour—Returns the hour stored in a DateTime variable.

  Month—Returns the month stored in a DateTime variable.

  Now—Returns the system's current date and time.

  Year—Returns the year stored in a DateTime variable.

- *Methods*

  AddDays—Creates a new DateTime value that is the specified number of days later (or earlier) in time.

  AddHours—Creates a new DateTime value that is the specified number of hours later (or earlier) in time.

  AddMinutes—Creates a new DateTime value that is the specified number of minutes later (or earlier) in time.

  ToLongDateString—Returns a string containing the date in the format "Wednesday, October 30, 2002."

  ToShortTimeString—Returns a string containing the time in the format "4:00 PM."

DateTimePicker  This control is used to retrieve date and time information from the user.

- *In action*

  DateTimePicker using default format

- *Event*

  ValueChanged—Raised when the Value property is changed.

- *Properties*

  CustomFormat—Sets which format string to use when displaying the date and/or time.

  Format—Specifies the format in which the date and time are displayed on the control.

  Long—Specifies that the date should be displayed in the format "Monday, December 09, 2002."

  Short—Specifies that the date should be displayed in the format "12/ 9/2002."

  Time—Specifies that the time should be displayed in the format "8:39:53 PM."

  Custom—Allows the programmer to specify a custom format in which to display the date and/or time.

  Hour—Stores the hour in the DateTimePicker control.

  Location—Specifies the location of the DateTimePicker control on its container relative to the container's top-left corner.

  MinDate—Specifies the minimum date and/or time that can be selected when using this control.

MaxDate—Specifies the maximum date and/or time that can be selected when using this control.

Name—Specifies the name used to access the DateTimePicker control programmatically. The name should be prefixed with dtp.

ShowUpDown—Specifies whether the up-down arrows are displayed on the control for time values (true). If false, a down arrow is displayed for accessing a drop-down calendar.

Value—Stores the date and/or time in the DateTimePicker control.

GroupBox   GroupBox   This control groups related controls visually.

■ *In action*

■ *Properties*

Name—Specifies the name used to access the GroupBox control programmatically. The name should be prefixed with fra.

Location—Specifies the location of the GroupBox control on the Form.

Size—Specifies the height and width (in pixels) of the GroupBox control.

Text—Specifies the text displayed on the GroupBox.

Timer   Timer   This control wakes up at specified intervals of time to execute code in its Tick event handler.

■ *Event*

Tick—Raised after the number of milliseconds specified in the Interval property has elapsed.

■ *Properties*

Enabled—Determines whether the Timer is running (true). The default is false.

Interval—Determines the time interval between Tick events.

Name—Specifies the name used to access the Timer control programmatically. The name should be prefixed with tmr.

MULTIPLE-CHOICE QUESTIONS

14.1 The _____ allows you to store and manipulate date information easily.

     a) DateTime structure   b) DatePicker control

     c) GroupBox control   d) Now property

14.2 You can _____ to a DateTime variable.

     a) add hours   b) add days

     c) subtract hours   d) All of the above.

14.3 To subtract one day from DateTime variable dtmDay's value, assign the value returned by _____ to dtmDay.

     a) dtmDay.AddHours(-24);   b) dtmDay.SubtractDays(1);

     c) dtmDay.AddDays(-1);   d) Both a and c.

14.4 The time 3:45 and 35 seconds in the afternoon would be formatted as 03:45:35 PM according to the format string _____.

     a) "hh:mm:ss"   b) "hh:mm:ss tt"

     c) "hh:mm:ss am:pm"   d) "h:m:s tt"

14.5 A(n) _____ event occurs before the Form is displayed.

     a) LoadForm   b) InitializeForm

     c) Load   d) FormLoad

14.6 Timer property Interval sets the rate at which Tick events occur in _____.

a) nanoseconds
b) microseconds
c) milliseconds
d) seconds

14.7 To set DateTime dtmNow's time five hours earlier, use _____.

a) `dtmNow = dtmNow.SubHours( 5 );`
b) `dtmNow = dtmNow.AddHours( -5 );`
c) `dtmNow = dtmNow.AddHours( 5 );`
d) `dtmNow.AddHours( -5 );`

14.8 A _____ is a container.

a) GroupBox
b) Form
c) Timer
d) Both a and b.

14.9 A DateTime variable stores hour values in the range _____.

a) 1 to 12
b) 0 to 12
c) 0 to 24
d) 0 to 23

14.10 A DateTimePicker's _____ property specifies the format string with which to display the date.

a) CustomFormat
b) FormatString
c) Format
d) Text

EXERCISES

14.11 (*World Clock Application*) Create an application that displays the current time in Los Angeles, Atlanta, London and Tokyo. Use a Timer to update the clock every second. Assume that your local time is the time in Atlanta. Atlanta is three hours later than Los Angeles. London is five hours later than Atlanta. Tokyo is eight hours later than London. The application should look similar to Fig. 14.21.

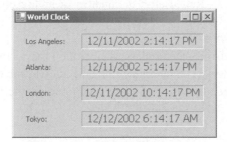

Figure 14.21 World Clock GUI.

a) *Copying the template to your working directory.* Copy the directory C:\Examples\ Tutorial14\Exercises\WorldClock to your C:\SimplyCSP directory.

b) *Opening the application's template file.* Double click WorldClock.sln in the WorldClock directory to open the application.

c) *Adding a Timer to the Form.* Add a Timer control to the **World Clock** application. Set the Timer control's name property to tmrClock. Rearrange and comment the new control declaration appropriately.

d) *Adding a Tick event handler for tmrClock.* Add a Tick event handler for Timer tmrClock. The event handler should calculate and display the current times for Los Angeles, Atlanta, London and Tokyo. Use the DateTime variable's ToShortDate-String and ToLongTimeString methods to create the display text.

e) *Running the application.* Select **Debug > Start** to run your application. Look at the clock on your machine to verify that the time for Los Angeles is three hours earlier, the time in Atlanta is the same as what your clock says, the time in London is five hours later, and the time in Tokyo is 13 hours later (eight hours later than London).

f) *Closing the application.* Close your running application by clicking its close box.

g) *Closing the IDE.* Close Visual Studio .NET by clicking its close box.

14.12 (*Shipping Time Application Enhancement*) During the winter, a distribution center in Denver, Colorado needs to receive seafood shipments to supply the local ski resorts.

Enhance the **Shipping Time** application by adding Denver, Colorado as another shipping destination (Fig. 14.22). Denver is two time zones west of Portland, meaning time is two hours earlier than Portland, Maine. There are no direct flights to Denver, so shipments from Portland will take 8 hours.

Figure 14.22   Enhanced **Shipping Time** GUI.

a) *Copying the template to your working directory.* Copy the directory C:\Examples\ Tutorial14\Exercises\ShippingTimeEnhanced to your C:\SimplyCSP directory.

b) *Opening the application's template file.* Double click ShippingTime.sln in the ShippingTimeEnhanced directory to open the application.

c) *Inserting a GroupBox.* Resize the Form to fit the **Express Shipping to Denver** GroupBox as shown in Fig. 14.22. Add a GroupBox to the Form. Change the Text property of the GroupBox to indicate that it will contain the delivery time in Denver. Resize and move the GroupBox so that it resembles the GUI shown in Fig. 14.22.

d) *Inserting Labels.* In the GroupBox you just created, add an output Label to display the delivery time for a seafood shipment to Denver and a corresponding descriptive Label. Rearrange and comment the new control declarations appropriately.

e) *Inserting code to the DisplayDeliveryTime method.* Add code to Display-DeliveryTime method to compute and display the delivery time in Denver.

f) *Running the application.* Select **Debug > Start** to run your application. Select various drop-off times and ensure the delivery times are correct for Las Vegas and Denver.

g) *Closing the application.* Close your running application by clicking its close box.

h) *Closing the IDE.* Close Visual Studio .NET by clicking its close box.

14.13 (*Pop-Up Reminder Application*) Create an application that allows the user to set an pop-up reminder (Fig. 14.23). The application should allow the user to set the exact time of that a pop-up message should appear by using a DateTimePicker. While the time for the reminder is set, the user should not be able to modify the DateTimePicker. If the time for the reminder is set and the current time matches the time in the DateTimePicker, display a MessageBox as a reminder for the user. The user should be able to cancel a reminder by using a **Reset** Button. This Button is disabled when the application starts.

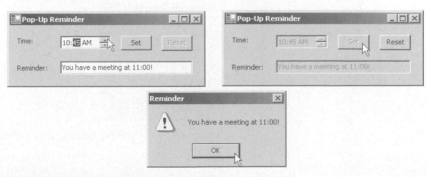

Figure 14.23   Pop-Up Reminder GUI.

a) *Copying the template to your working directory.* Copy the directory C:\Examples\ Tutorial14\Exercises\Reminder to your C:\SimplyCSP directory.

b) *Opening the application's template file.* Double click Reminder.sln in the Reminder directory to open the application.

c) *Inserting a DateTimePicker.* Add a DateTimePicker control to the Form. Set the DateTimePicker to display only the time, as is shown in Fig. 14.23. Set the DateTimePicker control's Size property to 80, 20, and move the control so that it appears as it does in Fig. 14.23. Rearrange and comment the new control declaration appropriately.

d) *Coding the Set Button's Click event handler.* Add a Click event handler for the **Set** Button. This event handler should disable the **Set** Button, the **Reminder:** TextBox and the DateTimePicker and enable the **Reset** Button.

e) *Coding the Timer's Tick event handler.* Define the Tick event handler for the Timer. A Tick event should occur every 1000 milliseconds (one second). If the reminder time is set and the current time matches the time in the DateTimePicker (with a seconds value of 0), display the text from the **Reminder:** TextBox in a MessageBox.

f) *Coding the Reset Button's Click event handler.* Define the Click event handler for the **Reset** Button. When the **Reset** Button is clicked, the GUI should be set back to its original state.

g) *Running the application.* Select **Debug > Start** to run your application. Use the DateTimePicker and the **Set** Button to set a time for the reminder to display. Wait for that time to verify that the MessageBox appears. Click the **Reset** Button to set a new time for the reminder to display.

h) *Closing the application.* Close your running application by clicking its close box.

i) *Closing the IDE.* Close Visual Studio .NET by clicking its close box.

What does this code do? ▶ **14.14** This code creates a DateTime variable. What date does this variable contain?

```
DateTime dtmTime = new DateTime( 2003, 1, 2, 3, 4, 5 );
```

What's wrong with this code? ▶ **14.15** The following lines of code are supposed to create a DateTime variable and increment its hour value by two. Find the error(s) in the code.

```
DateTime dtmNow = DateTime.Now;
dtmNow.AddHours( 2 );
```

Programming Challenge ▶ **14.16** (*Parking Garage Fee Calculator Application*) Create an application that computes the fee for parking a car in a parking garage (Fig. 14.24). The user should provide the **Time In:** and **Time Out:** values by using DateTimePickers. The application should calculate the cost of parking in the garage for the specified amount of time. Assume that parking costs three dollars an hour. When calculating the total time spent in the garage, you can ignore the seconds value, but treat the minutes value as a fraction of an hour (1 minute is 1/60 of an hour). For simplicity, assume that no overnight parking is allowed, so each car leaves the garage on the same day in which it arrives.

Figure 14.24 Parking Garage Fee Calculator GUI.

a) *Copying the template to your working directory.* Copy the directory C:\Examples\ Tutorial14\Exercises\ParkingGarageFeeCalculator to your C:\SimplyCSP directory.

b) *Opening the application's template file.* Double click ParkingGarageFeeCalculator.sln in the ParkingGarageFeeCalculator directory to open the application.

c) *Inserting the DateTimePicker controls.* Add two DateTimePicker controls to the Form. Set the DateTimePickers so that they show the time only. Set the Size property of each DateTimePicker control to 80, 20, and move the DateTimePickers so that they are positioned as in Fig. 14.24. Rearrange and comment the new control declarations appropriately.

d) *Writing the method Fee.* Define a method Fee that accepts four ints as parameters—the hour value of the **Time In:**, the hour value of the **Time Out:**, the minute value of the **Time In:** and the minute value of the **Time Out:**. Using this information, method Fee should calculate the fee for parking in the garage. The method should then return this value as a decimal.

e) *Coding the Calculate Button's Click event handler.* Add the Click event handler for the **Calculate** Button. If the time out is earlier than the time in, disallow the input and display a MessageBox to the user. Otherwise, this event handler should call Fee to obtain the amount due. It should then display the amount (formatted as currency) in a Label.

f) *Running the application.* Select **Debug > Start** to run your application. Use the DateTimePickers' up and down arrows to select a time the car was placed in the garage and the time the car was taken out of the garage. Click the **Calculate** Button and verify that the correct fee is displayed.

g) *Closing the application.* Close your running application by clicking its close box.

h) *Closing the IDE.* Close Visual Studio .NET by clicking its close box.

Objectives

In this tutorial, you will learn to:
- Change a value from one type to another, using conversions.
- Create variables that can be used in all the Form's methods.
- Pass arguments by reference, using keywords ref and out, so that the called method can modify the caller's variables.

Outline

15.1 Test-Driving the Fund Raiser Application

15.2 Conversions

15.3 Constructing the Fund Raiser Application

15.4 Passing Arguments: Pass-by-Value vs. Pass-by-Reference

15.5 Wrap-Up

Fund Raiser Application

Introducing Scope and Pass-by-Reference

In this tutorial, you will learn several important C# concepts. First, you will learn how the C# compiler handles conversions between different types. Next, you will learn how to declare variables that can be referenced from any method within your Form's code. In addition, you will learn another technique for passing arguments to methods. In the methods you have created so far, the application has made a copy of the argument's value, and any changes the called method made to the copy did not affect the original variable's value. You will learn how to pass an argument to a method—using a technique called pass-by-reference—so that changes made to the parameter's value in the method are also made to the original variable in the caller.

15.1 Test-Driving the Fund Raiser Application

In this tutorial, you will create a **Fund Raiser** application that determines how much donated money is available after operating costs. This application must meet the following requirements:

Application Requirements

An organization is hosting a fund raiser to collect donations. A portion of each donation is used to cover the operating expenses of the organization; the rest of the donation goes to the charity. Create an application that allows the organization to keep track of the total amount of money raised. The application should deduct 17% of each donation for operating costs; the remaining 83% is given to the charity. The application should display the amount of each donation after the 17% operating expenses are deducted; it also should display the total amount raised for the charity (that is, the total amount donated less all operating costs) for all donations up to that point.

The user inputs the amount of a donation into a TextBox and clicks a Button to calculate the net amount of that donation the charity receives after operating expenses have been deducted. In addition, the total amount of money raised for charity is updated and displayed. You begin by test-driving the completed application. Then, you will learn the additional C# technologies you will need to create your own version of this application.

Test-Driving the Fund Raiser Application

1. ***Opening the completed application.*** Open the `C:\Examples\Tutorial15\CompletedApplication\FundRaiser` directory to locate the **Fund Raiser** application. Double click `FundRaiser.sln` to open the application in Visual Studio .NET.

2. ***Running the Fund Raiser application.*** Select **Debug > Start** to run the application (Fig. 15.1).

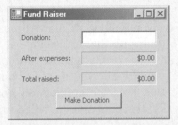

Figure 15.1   **Fund Raiser** application's **Form**.

3. ***Entering a donation in the application.*** Enter 1500 in the **Donation:** Text-Box. Click the **Make Donation** Button. The application calculates the amount of the donation after the operating expenses have been deducted and displays the result ($1245.00) in the **After expenses:** field. Because this is the first donation entered, this amount is repeated in the **Total raised:** field (Fig. 15.2).

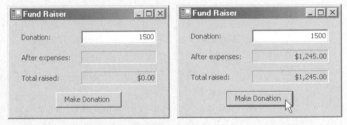

Figure 15.2   **Fund Raiser** application's **Form** with first donation entered.

4. ***Entering additional donations.*** Enter more donations, then click the **Make Donation** Button. Notice that the total raised increases with each additional donation (Fig. 15.3).

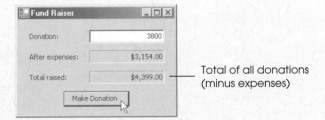

Total of all donations (minus expenses)

Figure 15.3   Making further donations.

5. ***Closing the application.*** Close your running application by clicking its close box.

6. ***Closing the IDE.*** Close Visual Studio .NET by clicking its close box.

15.2 Conversions

When the computer accesses data, it needs to know what type that data is for the data to make sense. Imagine you are purchasing a book from an online store that ships internationally. You notice that the price for the book is 20, but no currency is associated with the price; it could be dollars, euros, pesos, yen or some other currency. Therefore, it is important to know what type of currency is being used. If the currency is different from the one that you normally use, you will need to perform a conversion to get the price.

Similar conversions occur many times in an application. The computer determines a type, and, with that knowledge, it adds two `int`s or combines two `strings` of text. C# can convert one type to another, as long as the conversion makes sense. For example, you are allowed to assign an `int` value to a `double` variable without writing code that tells the application how to do the conversion. These types of assignments perform conversions called implicit conversions. You have already performed implicit conversions in this text. When an attempted conversion doesn't make sense, such as assigning `"hello"` to an `int` variable, an error occurs. Figure 15.4 lists C#'s built-in types and their allowed implicit conversions. [*Note:* We do not discuss every built-in type in detail in this book. Consult the C# documentation to learn more about C#'s built-in types.]

Type	Can be implicitly converted to these (larger) types
`bool`	`object`
`byte`	`short`, `ushort`, `int`, `uint`, `long`, `ulong`, `decimal`, `float`, `double` or `object`
`sbyte`	`short`, `int`, `long`, `decimal`, `float`, `double` or `object`
`char`	`ushort`, `int`, `uint`, `long`, `ulong`, `decimal`, `float`, `double` or `object`
`decimal`	`object`
`double`	`object`
`float`	`double` or `object`
`int`	`long`, `decimal`, `float`, `double` or `object`
`uint`	`long`, `ulong`, `decimal`, `float`, `double` or `object`
`long`	`decimal`, `float`, `double` or `object`
`ulong`	`decimal`, `float`, `double` or `object`
`object`	none
`short`	`int`, `long`, `decimal`, `float`, `double` or `object`
`ushort`	`int`, `uint`, `long`, `ulong`, `decimal`, `float`, `double` or `object`
`string`	`object`

Figure 15.4 Types and their allowed conversions.

The types listed in the right column are "larger" types, in that they can store more data than the types in the left column. For example, `int` types (left column) can be converted to `long` types (right column, which includes four other types). An `int` variable can store values in the approximate range ±2.1 billion; a `long` variable can store numbers in the approximate range $\pm 9 \times 10^{18}$ (9 followed by 18 zeros). This means that any `int` value can be assigned to a `long` variable without losing any data. These kinds of conversions are called **widening conversions**, because the value of a "smaller" type (`int`) is being assigned to a variable of a "larger" type (`long`).

When a "larger" type, such as `double`, is assigned to a "smaller" type, such as `int`, either a run-time error will occur because the value being assigned is too large to be stored in the "smaller" type or the assignment will be permitted. Consider the following code:

```
double dblValue = 4.6;
int intValue = dblValue;
```

Common Programming Error

Narrowing conversions can result in loss of data, which can cause subtle logic errors.

If the code above were allowed, intValue would be assigned 4—the result of implicitly converting the double value 4.6 to an int. These types of conversions are called implicit **narrowing conversions**. These types of conversions can introduce subtle errors in applications, because the actual value being assigned could have been altered without you being aware of it—a dangerous practice. For example, if the programmer was expecting variable intValue to be assigned a value other than 5 (such as 4.6 or 4), a logic error would occur.

Implicit narrowing conversions are not allowed in C#. Instead, narrowing conversions in C# require you to explicitly specify the conversion. That is why these conversions are called explicit conversions (or casting). Explicit conversions require a cast operator (or cast) which is a type name contained in parentheses. According to Fig. 15.4, C# does not allow the implicit conversion of double values to int values (because information could be lost). You can force this conversion to take place using a cast. For example, if intValue is of type int and dblValue is of type double, you can write

```
intValue = ( int ) dblValue;
```

without causing a compilation error. Note that the value stored in dblValue may lose some precision when it is cast to an int. If there is a fractional part of dblValue, it will be truncated (that is, discarded).

Certain explicit conversions, such as converting a string to an int, cannot be performed with the cast operator. C# provides methods in class Convert (Fig. 15.5) for performing additional explicit conversions.

Convert To	Use Convert Method	Sample Statement
int	ToInt32	intValue = Convert.ToInt32(txtInput.Text);
decimal	ToDecimal	decValue = Convert.ToDecimal(50.2);
double	ToDouble	dblRate = Convert.ToDouble(txtRate.Text) / 100;
string	ToString	strResult = Convert.ToString(intTotal);

Figure 15.5 Four of class Convert's methods.

The name of each conversion method is the word To, followed by the name of the type to which the method converts its argument. For example, to convert a string input by the user in TextBox txtInput to an int (represented in C# as type Int32) use the statement

```
intNumber = Convert.ToInt32( txtInput.Text );
```

SELF-REVIEW

1. C# always requires the programmer to explicitly perform _____.
   a) narrowing conversions
   b) widening conversions
   c) all type conversions
   d) no conversions

2. The methods in _____ are used to change types explicitly.
   a) class Strict
   b) class Change
   c) class Convert
   d) class Conversion

Answers: 1) a. 2) c.

15.3 Constructing the Fund Raiser Application

Now that you have test-driven the application, you're ready to begin developing the **Fund Raiser** application. The following pseudocode describes the basic operation of the **Fund Raiser** application:

> *When the user changes the current donation amount in the TextBox:*
> > *Clear Label that displays amount of current donation that goes to charity*
>
> *When the user clicks the Make Donation Button:*
> > *Obtain amount of current donation from TextBox*
> > *Calculate amount of current donation that goes to charity (amount after operating costs)*
> > *Display amount of current donation that goes to charity*
> > *Update total amount raised for charity (from all donations received)*
> > *Display total amount raised for charity*
>
> *When the CalculateDonation method gets called:*
> > *Calculate operating costs (multiply the donated amount by the operating cost percentage)*
> > *Calculate amount of donation that goes to charity (Subtract operating costs from donated amount)*

Now that you have test-driven the **Fund Raiser** application and studied its pseudocode representation, you will use an ACE table to help you convert the pseudocode to C#. Figure 15.6 lists the actions, controls and events that will help you complete your own version of this application.

Action/Control/Event Table for the Fund Raiser *Application*

Action	Control	Event/Method
Label all the application's controls	lblDonations, lblDonated, lblTotal	Application is run
	txtDonation	TextChanged
Clear Label that displays amount of current donation that goes toward charity	lblDonatedValue	
	btnDonate	Click
Obtain user donation from TextBox	txtDonation	
Calculate amount of current donation that goes toward charity		
Display amount of current donation that goes toward charity	lblDonatedValue	
Update total amount raised for charity		
Display total amount raised for charity	lblTotalValue	
		Calculate-Donation
Calculate operating costs		
Calculate amount of donation that goes to charity		

Figure 15.6 **Fund Raiser** application's ACE table.

You're now ready to begin programming the **Fund Raiser** application. First, you will declare the variables needed in the application. In this discussion, you will learn a new concept—scope. The **scope** of an identifier is the portion of an application in which the identifier can be referenced. Some identifiers can be referenced throughout an application; others can be referenced only from limited portions of an application (such as within a single method). You will now add code to your application to illustrate these various scopes.

Examining Scope with the *Fund Raiser* Application

1. ***Copying the template to your working directory.*** Copy the `C:\Examples\Tutorial15\TemplateApplication\FundRaiser` directory to your `C:\SimplyCSP` directory.

2. ***Opening the Fund Raiser application's template file.*** Double click `Fund-Raiser.sln` in the `FundRaiser` directory to open the application in Visual Studio .NET (Fig. 15.7).

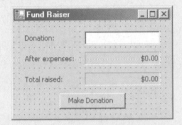

Figure 15.7 Fund Raiser template application's Form.

3. ***Placing declarations in the code file.*** Select **View > Code**, then add lines 35–36 of Fig. 15.8 to `FundRaiser.cs`. Variable `m_decTotalRaised` stores the total amount of money raised for charity.

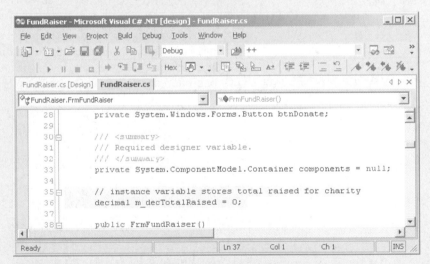

Figure 15.8 Declaring an instance variable in the application.

This variable is initialized when the application first executes and must retain its value while the application executes (that is, it cannot be created each time a method is invoked). Variable `m_decTotalRaised` is an **instance variable**—a variable declared inside a class, but outside any method declarations of that class. All methods in class `FrmFundRaiser` will have access to this variable and will be able to modify its value. The controls, whose declarations you are already familiar with (for example, line 28 of Fig. 15.8), are also instance variables.

Instance variables have **class scope**. Class scope begins at the opening left brace of the class declaration and terminates at the closing right brace. This scope enables any method in the same class to access all instance variables declared in that class. Form instance variables with class scope are created when the application begins running.

Good Programming Practice

Prefix instance variables with `m_` (for class member) to distinguish them from other variables.

(cont.)

4. ***Creating the Click event handler for the Make Donation Button.*** Return to design view and double click the **Make Donation** Button to generate its Click event handler btnDonate_Click. Be sure to add the comments and break the header as shown in Fig. 15.9 so that the line numbers in your code match those presented in this tutorial.

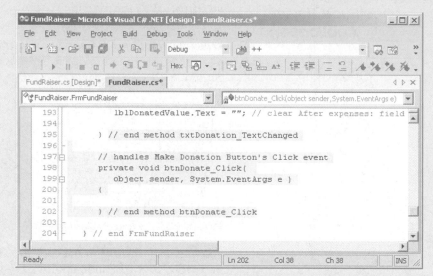

Figure 15.9 Adding a Click event handler to the application.

5. ***Declaring local variables in event handler btnDonate_Click.*** Add lines 201–202 of Fig. 15.10 to event handler btnDonate_Click. Variable decDonation (line 201) stores the donation amount. Variable decAfterCosts (line 202) stores the donation amount after the operating expenses have been deducted. Line 202 initializes decAfterCosts to 0.

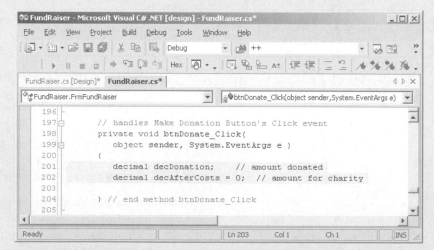

Figure 15.10 Declaring local variables in the **Fund Raiser** application.

In C#, identifiers, such as decDonation and decAfterCosts, that are declared inside a method are known as **local variables**, and have **block scope**. Local variables cannot be referenced outside of the method in which they are declared. Parameters to methods are also considered to have block scope.

Identifiers declared inside control statements, such as inside a for statement, also have block scope. The scope of such variables begins at the identifier's declaration and ends at the block's terminating right brace.

(cont.)

If a local variable has the same name as an instance variable (that is, a variable with class scope), the instance variable is hidden in that method or block. Any expression containing the variable name will use the local variable's value and not the instance variable's value. The instance variable's value is not destroyed, though—it is still available for access outside that method or block.

6. ***Examining the CalculateDonation method.*** The template application provides the CalculateDonation method (lines 175–187 of Fig. 15.11). Line 178 declares constant dblCOSTS, which stores the operating-cost percentage. This constant also is "local" to the method and cannot be used elsewhere. The method accepts one parameter value—the total donation amount (dec-DonatedAmount). The amount of the donation that goes toward operating costs is 17% of the initial donation. The net donation (the amount that goes toward charity) is calculated by multiplying local constant dblCOSTS, whose value is 0.17, by the initial donation amount. A cast operator is required to convert dblCOSTS to a decimal before multiplication.

Method CalculateDonation subtracts the operating cost from the initial donation amount (decDonatedAmount) and assigns the result to decNetDonation (lines 182–183). The method then returns the decimal result (line 185).

Error-Prevention Tip

Hidden variable names can sometimes lead to subtle logic errors. Use unique names for all variables, regardless of scope, to prevent an instance variable from becoming hidden.

Parameter **decDonatedAmount** has block scope because it is declared in the method header

Local variable **decNetDonation** has block scope because it is declared in the method body

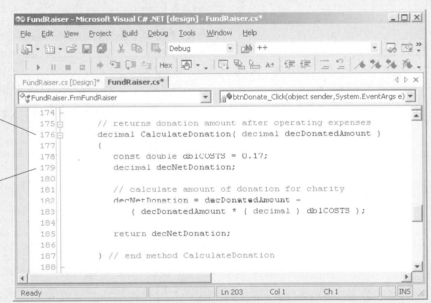

Figure 15.11   Method CalculateDonation provided by the template application.

7. ***Demonstrating the difference between class scope and block scope.*** Now you are going to demonstrate the limits of block scope. Temporarily replace constant dblCOSTS with decDonation, btnDonate_Click's local variable (line 183 in Fig. 15.12). Select **Build > Build Solution** to compile the solution.

Notice the jagged line that appears under decDonation to indicate an error. Variables with block scope can be accessed and modified only in the block in which they are declared. The error message displayed when the mouse pointer rests on decDonation indicates that variable decDonation does not exist. Because this variable is "local" to btnDonate_Click, method CalculateDonation cannot "see" the declaration of decDonation. Replace decDonation with dblCOSTS.

(cont.)

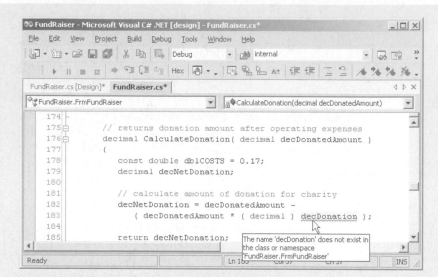

Figure 15.12 Demonstrating block scope.

8. ***Obtaining the donation amount.*** Add lines 204–205 of Fig. 15.13 to event handler btnDonate_Click. You obtain the total donation amount from TextBox txtDonation (line 205).

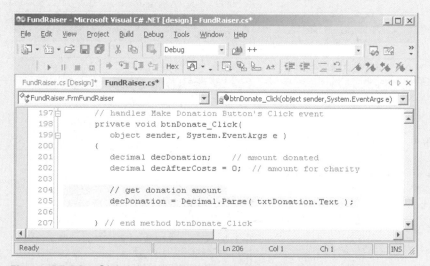

Figure 15.13 Obtaining the donation amount.

9. ***Calculating and displaying the donation amount after the operating expenses.*** Add lines 207–212 of Fig. 15.14 to the event handler. Line 208 invokes method CalculateDonation with the amount of the donation (decDonation). The result of this method—the net amount that goes to charity after the deduction for operating costs—is assigned to variable decAfterCosts. The donation amount after expenses is formatted as a currency string and displayed in the **After expenses:** field (lines 211–212).

10. ***Updating and displaying the fund raiser total.*** Add lines 214–219 of Fig. 15.15 to the event handler. Line 215 updates instance variable m_decTotalRaised, which stores the total amount given to the charity after the operating costs have been deducted. Lines 218–219 display the total amount raised for charity.

(cont.)

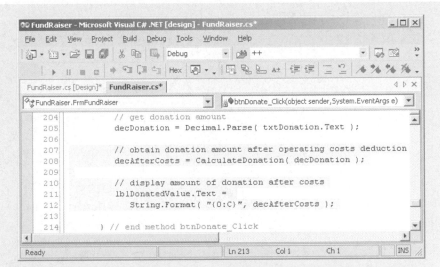

Figure 15.14 Calculating and displaying the donation amount after operating expenses.

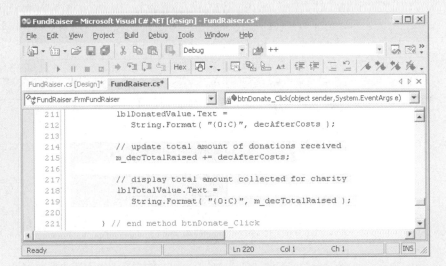

Figure 15.15 Updating and displaying the total amount raised for charity.

Notice that m_decTotalRaised is not declared as a local variable in this event handler. Recall that m_decTotalRaised is an instance variable, declared on line 36 of Fig. 15.8. Instance variables may be used in any of the class's methods. [*Note:* There is an exception to this rule—classes may contain what is known as static methods. Methods that are declared static do not have access to a class's instance variables.]

Because m_decTotalRaised has class scope, it maintains its value between method calls. Local variables do not retain their values between method calls, and therefore must be re-initialized each time their method is invoked.

11. ***Clearing the After expenses: field to display the next result.*** The template application includes event handler txtDonation_TextChanged (lines 189–195 of Fig. 15.16) for the **Donation:** TextBox's TextChanged event. When the user enters data into the TextBox, the TextChanged event occurs and line 193 clears the donation for charity from the **After expenses:** field.

(cont.)

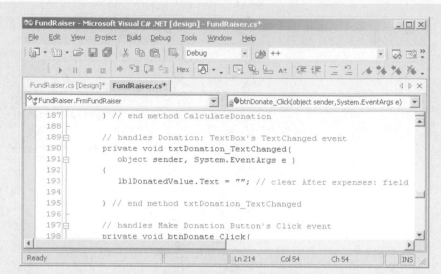

Figure 15.16 Clearing the **Donation:** TextBox.

12. *Running the application.* Select **Debug > Start** to run your application. Test your application to ensure that it runs correctly.

13. *Closing the application.* Close your running application by clicking its close box.

SELF-REVIEW

1. Instance variables have _____ scope.

    a) block

    c) class

    b) method

    d) None of the above.

2. Variables declared in a method are called _____.

    a) instance variables

    c) class variables

    b) local variables

    d) hidden variables

Answers: 1) c. 2) b.

15.4 Passing Arguments: Pass-by-Value vs. Pass-by-Reference

Arguments are passed to methods in one of two ways: **pass-by-value** and **pass-by-reference** (also called **call-by-value** and **call-by-reference**). By default, a variable is passed by value. We have passed by value in all our methods until now. When an argument is passed by value, the application makes a copy of the argument's value and passes that copy to the called method. Changes made to the copy in the called method do not affect the original variable's value in the calling method.

In contrast, when an argument is passed by reference, the original data can be accessed and modified directly by the called method. This is useful in some situations, such as when a method needs to produce more than one result. However, it can cause subtle errors and is used largely only by experienced programmers. To pass by reference, C# provides the **ref** and **out** keywords. There is only a minor difference between these two methods of pass-by-reference. The ref keyword is used for a variable that already has been initialized before the method call. The out keyword is used for a variable that might not have been initialized before the method call; the variable will be initialized within the called method. Normally, when a method receives an uninitialized value, the compiler generates an error. The out keyword is used to prevent this error from occurring. In the following box, you will learn to use keywords ref and out to pass an argument by reference to the method that calculates the donation amount after operating costs. Note that the changes made in the next box should not alter the functionality of your application.

<table>
<tr><td>

*Passing Arguments by
Reference in the Fund
Raiser Application*

</td><td>

1. ***Passing variable decAfterCosts by reference with keyword ref.*** Replace line 208 in event handler btnDonate_Click with line 208 of Fig. 15.17. The method call in line 208 of Fig. 15.17 passes two variables to method CalculateDonation. In the following steps, you will rewrite method CalculateDonation so that it accepts two arguments. The first argument (in this case, decDonation) will be passed by value; the second argument (in this case, decAfterCosts) will be passed by reference, using keyword ref. We use ref here rather than out because decAfterCosts has been initialized (line 202) prior to the call to method CalculateDonation. When the CalculateDonation method returns, variable decAfterCosts will contain the portion of the donation that the charity receives.

</td></tr>
</table>

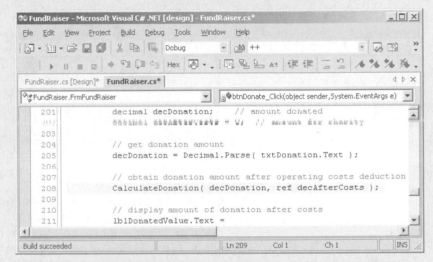

Figure 15.17   Passing variable decAfterCosts with keyword ref.

2. ***Removing the old CalculateDonation method.*** Delete the CalculateDonation method (lines 176–187 of Fig. 15.18) from FundRaiser.cs.

Delete these lines of code —

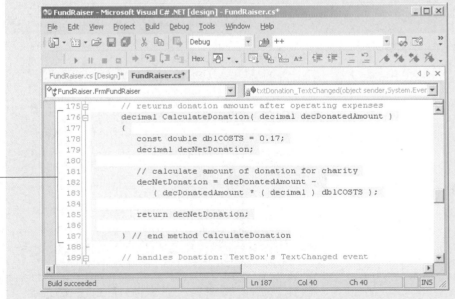

Figure 15.18   Method CalculateDonation to be removed.

(cont.)

3. ***Coding the new CalculateDonation method.*** Add lines 176–180 of Fig. 15.19 to your code. Line 176 specifies method CalculateDonation's header. Keyword ref (line 177) indicates that variable decNetDonation is passed by reference. This means that any changes made to variable decNet-Donation in CalculateDonation affect btnDonate_Click's local variable decAfterCosts. Because it is no longer necessary for CalculateDonation to return a value, CalculateDonation now has void return type, rather than decimal.

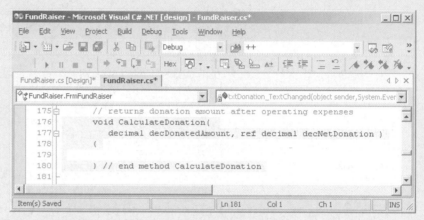

Figure 15.19 CalculateDonation method.

4. ***Calculating the donation amount for charity after operating costs.*** Add lines 179–183 of Fig. 15.20 to method CalculateDonation. Lines 182–183 calculate the amount of the donation that goes toward charity after operating costs have been deducted. Notice that this is the same calculation that was performed in lines 182–183 of the method CalculateDonation in Fig. 15.18. The only difference is that assigning the calculation result to variable decNetDonation actually assigns the value to btnDonate_Click's local variable decAfterCosts. You do not need to return the calculation result.

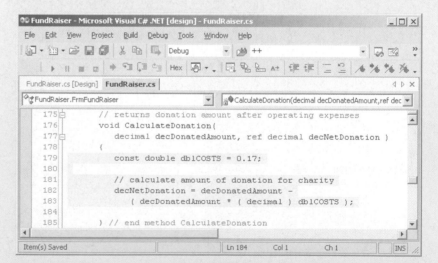

Figure 15.20 Calculating the donation that goes toward charity after operating costs have been deducted.

5. ***Running the application.*** Select **Debug > Start** to run your application. Your application should behave exactly as it did in the previous box. You have changed the application's code but not its functionality.

(cont.)

6. ***Closing the application.*** Close your running application by clicking its close box.

7. ***Passing variable decAfterCosts by reference with keyword out.*** We now demonstrate the difference between keyword ref and keyword out. Notice that method CalculateDonation assigns a value to decNetDonation (line 182 of Fig. 15.20). For this reason, it is not necessary to initialize decNetDonation before the call to method CalculateDonation. Modify the declaration in line 200 of Fig. 15.21 so that decNetDonation is uninitialized. To eliminate the syntax error that would result from passing an uninitialized variable to a method, modify the method call in line 206 by replacing keyword ref with keyword out.

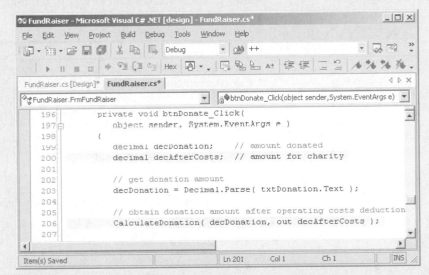

Figure 15.21   Passing variable decAfterCosts with keyword out.

8. ***Modifying the CalculateDonation method header.*** Parameter decNetDonation is passed uninitialized to method CalculateDonation. Modify line 177 of Fig. 15.22 by replacing keyword ref with keyword out. Method CalculateDonation assigns a value to the uninitialized decNetDonation in line 182.

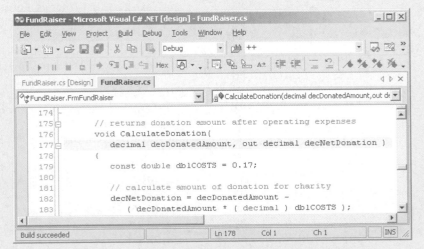

Figure 15.22   Replacing keyword ref with keyword out.

(cont.)

9. ***Running the application.*** Select **Debug > Start** to run your application. Enter a donation amount and click the **Make Donation** Button. Verify that the total raised and the amount after expenses is correct. Enter more donations, each time verifying the output. Note that the total amount raised should also reflect previous donation amounts.

10. ***Closing the application.*** Close your running application by clicking its close box.

11. ***Closing the IDE.*** Close Visual Studio .NET by clicking its close box.

Figure 15.23 presents the source code for the **Fund Raiser** application. The lines of code that contain new programming concepts that you learned in this tutorial are highlighted.

```
1   using System;
2   using System.Drawing;
3   using System.Collections;
4   using System.ComponentModel;
5   using System.Windows.Forms;
6   using System.Data;
7
8   namespace FundRaiser
9   {
10      /// <summary>
11      /// Summary description for FrmFundRaiser.
12      /// </summary>
13      public class FrmFundRaiser : System.Windows.Forms.Form
14      {
15         // Label and TextBox to input donation
16         private System.Windows.Forms.Label lblDonation;
17         private System.Windows.Forms.TextBox txtDonation;
18
19         // Labels to display value of donation after expenses
20         private System.Windows.Forms.Label lblDonated;
21         private System.Windows.Forms.Label lblDonatedValue;
22
23         // Labels to display total raised so far minus expenses
24         private System.Windows.Forms.Label lblTotal;
25         private System.Windows.Forms.Label lblTotalValue;
26
27         // Button to make a donation
28         private System.Windows.Forms.Button btnDonate;
29
30         /// <summary>
31         /// Required designer variable.
32         /// </summary>
33         private System.ComponentModel.Container components = null;
34
35         // instance variable stores total raised for charity
36         decimal m_decTotalRaised = 0;
37
38         public FrmFundRaiser()
39         {
40            //
41            // Required for Windows Form Designer support
42            //
43            InitializeComponent();
```

Declaring an instance variable — (lines 35–36)

Figure 15.23 Fund Raiser application code. (Part 1 of 3.)

```
44
45            //
46            // TODO: Add any constructor code after InitializeComponent
47            // call
48            //
49         }
50
51      /// <summary>
52      /// Clean up any resources being used.
53      /// </summary>
54      protected override void Dispose( bool disposing )
55      {
56         if( disposing )
57         {
58            if (components != null)
59            {
60               components.Dispose();
61            }
62         }
63         base.Dispose( disposing );
64      }
65
66      // Windows Form Designer generated code
67
68      /// <summary>
69      /// The main entry point for the application.
70      /// </summary>
71      [STAThread]
72      static void Main()
73      {
74         Application.Run( new FrmFundRaiser() );
75      }
76
77      // returns donation amount after operating expenses
78      void CalculateDonation(
79         decimal decDonatedAmount, out decimal decNetDonation )
80      {
81         const double dblCOSTS = 0.17;
82
83         // calculate amount of donation for charity
84         decNetDonation = decDonatedAmount -
85            ( decDonatedAmount * ( decimal ) dblCOSTS );
86
87      } // end method CalculateDonation
88
89      // handles Donation: TextBox's TextChanged event
90      private void txtDonation_TextChanged(
91         object sender, System.EventArgs e )
92      {
93         lblDonatedValue.Text = ""; // clear After expenses: field
94
95      } // end method txtDonation_TextChanged
96
97      // handles Make Donation Button's Click event
98      private void btnDonate_Click(
99         object sender, System.EventArgs e )
100     {
101        decimal decDonation;     // amount donated
```

Keyword **out** indicates argument passed by reference — (pointing to lines 78–79)

Figure 15.23   **Fund Raiser** application code. (Part 2 of 3.)

Passing an argument by reference

```
102        decimal decAfterCosts;   // amount for charity
103
104        // get donation amount
105        decDonation = Decimal.Parse( txtDonation.Text );
106
107        // obtain donation amount after operating costs deduction
108        CalculateDonation( decDonation, out decAfterCosts );
109
110        // display amount of donation after costs
111        lblDonatedValue.Text =
112           String.Format( "{0:C}", decAfterCosts );
113
114        // update total amount of donations received
115        m_decTotalRaised += decAfterCosts;
116
117        // display total amount collected for charity
118        lblTotalValue.Text =
119           String.Format( "{0:C}", m_decTotalRaised );
120
121     } // end method btnDonate_Click
122
123  } // end class FrmFundRaiser
124 }
```

Figure 15.23 **Fund Raiser** application code. (Part 3 of 3.)

SELF-REVIEW

1. Keywords _____ indicate pass-by-reference.

   a) `ref` and `val`   b) `ref` and `out`

   c) `val` and `out`   d) `byref` and `byout`

2. When an argument is passed by reference, the called method can access and modify

_____.

   a) the caller's original data directly   b) a copy of the caller's data

   c) other methods' local variables   d) None of the above.

Answers: 1) b. 2) a.

15.5 Wrap-Up

In this tutorial, you learned concepts about types and variables, and you built the **Fund Raiser** application to demonstrate these concepts.

    You learned about data-type conversions. You learned that narrowing conversions (such as converting a `double` to an `int`) can result in data loss and that widening conversions (such as a conversion from `int` to `double`) don't have this problem. You learned that narrowing conversions must be performed explicitly, by using the cast operator or methods from class `Convert`.

    You learned how to create instance variables, which are declared inside a class, but outside any method declarations. Instance variables have class scope, which means that they are accessible to all methods in the class in which they are declared. In this tutorial, you declared your instance variable in the `FrmFundRaiser` class. In Tutorial 19, you will learn how to create your own classes and how to declare instance variables in them. Until now, all the variables you have declared have been local variables—that is, variables with block scope. Variables with block scope are modifiable only within the block in which they are declared.

    You also learned the difference between passing arguments by reference and passing arguments by value. When using pass-by-value, the calling method makes a copy of the argument's value and passes the copy to the called method. Changes to the called method's copy do not affect the original variable value in the calling method. When using pass-by-reference, the original data can be accessed and modified directly by the called method. You now know to use keywords `ref` and `out` to pass arguments by reference. Keyword `ref` is used when the parameter has been initialized before the method call. Keyword `out` is used when the parameter may not have been initialized before the method call, but will be initialized inside the called method.

In the next tutorial, you will learn about random-number generation, and you will create an application that simulates the dice game called Craps.

SKILLS SUMMARY

Understanding Scope

- You have learned the differences between class scope and block scope.
- Instance variables have class scope and can be accessed by all methods in the same class.
- Local variables have block scope.
- Local variables cannot be referenced outside the block in which they are declared.
- Block scope begins at the identifier's declaration and ends at the block's closing right brace.

Passing Arguments

- Arguments can be passed in two ways: pass-by-value (default) and pass-by-reference (using keyword `ref` or `out`).

Passing Arguments by Value

- By default, C# passes arguments by value. No additional code is necessary.
- The application makes a copy of the argument's value and passes the copy to the called method.
- Changes to the called method's copy do not affect the original argument value.

Passing Arguments by Reference

- In the method call, place keyword `ref` or keyword `out` before the name of each argument that should be passed by reference.
- In the method header, place keyword `ref` or keyword `out` before the name of each argument that should be passed by reference.
- Keyword `ref` should be used before parameters that are initialized before the method call.
- Keyword `out` should be used before parameters that are not initialized before the method call, but will be initialized inside the called method.
- Called methods can access and modify original arguments directly.

KEY TERMS

block scope—Variables declared inside control statements, such as a `for` statement, or methods have block scope. Block scope begins at the identifier's declaration and ends at the block's closing right brace.

call-by-reference—*See* pass-by-reference.

call-by-value—*See* pass-by-value.

class scope—Enables all methods in the same class to access all instance variables declared in that class. Begins at the opening left brace of the class declaration and terminates at closing right brace.

instance variable—Declared inside a class but outside any method of that class. Instance variables have class scope.

local variable—Declared inside a block, such as a method or a `for` statement. Local variables have block scope.

narrowing conversion—Changes a value's type to a smaller type. Loss of data can occur. C# requires narrowing conversions to be performed explicitly.

out keyword—Passes an uninitialized parameter by reference.

pass-by-reference—When an argument is passed by reference, the called method can access and modify the caller's original data directly. Keywords `ref` and `out` indicate pass-by-reference (also called call-by-reference).

pass-by-value—When an argument is passed by value, the application makes a copy of the argument's value and passes that copy to the called method. With pass-by-value, changes to the called method's copy do not affect the original variable's value. By default, C# uses pass-by-value (also called call-by-value).

ref keyword—Passes an initialized parameter by reference.

scope—The portion of an application in which an identifier (such as a variable name) can be referenced. Some identifiers can be referenced throughout an application; others can be referenced only from limited portions of an application (such as within a single method or block).

widening conversion—Changes a value's type to a larger type. C# allows widening conversions to be performed implicitly.

MULTIPLE-CHOICE QUESTIONS

15.1 Trying to convert from a `double` to an `int` without any special code causes _____.

  a) a syntax error   b) nothing unusual
  c) a logic error   d) data loss

15.2 To carry out some conversions, C# requires that variables _____.

  a) are passed by value   b) are passed by reference
  c) be explicitly converted to a different type to avoid unintended data loss
  d) are used only within the block in which the variables are declared

15.3 A variable declared inside a class, but outside a method, is called a(n) _____.

  a) local variable   b) hidden variable
  c) instance variable   d) constant variable

15.4 C# provides methods in class _____ to convert from one type to another.

  a) `ChangeTo`   b) `Convert`
  c) `ConvertTo`   d) `ChangeType`

15.5 Referencing a variable with block scope outside the block in which the programmer declared it is _____.

  a) a logic error   b) allowed, but not recommended
  c) a syntax error   d) None of the above.

15.6 When using pass-by-reference, keyword _____ should be used before parameters that are initialized before the method call.

  a) `out`   b) `ref`
  c) `val`   d) `byref`

15.7 With _____, changes made to parameter variables' values do not affect the value of the variables in the calling method.

  a) explicit conversions   b) pass-by-value
  c) pass-by-reference   d) None of the above.

15.8 Instance variables _____.

  a) are members of a class   b) should be prefixed by `m_`
  c) can be accessed by a method in the same class
  d) All of the above.

15.9 Assigning a "smaller" type to a "larger" type is a _____ conversion.

  a) narrowing   b) shortening
  c) widening   d) lengthening

15.10 A value of type `bool` can be implicitly converted to _____.

  a) `int`   b) `string`
  c) `object`   d) None of the above.

EXERCISES   **15.11** (*Task List Application*) Create an application that allows users to add items to a daily task list (Fig. 15.24). The application should also display the number of tasks to be performed. Use method `Convert.ToString` to display the number of tasks in a `Label`.

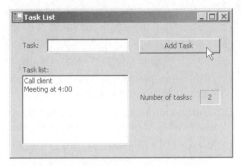

Figure 15.24   Task List application.

a) *Copying the template to your working directory.* Copy the directory `C:\Examples\Tutorial15\Exercises\TaskList` to your `C:\SimplyCSP` directory.

b) *Opening the application's template file.* Double click `TaskList.sln` in the `TaskList` directory to open the application.

c) *Declaring an instance variable.* Declare instance variable `intCounter` of type `int` and initialize its value to 0.

d) *Adding the Add Task Button's `Click` event handler.* Double click the **Add Task** `Button` to generate the empty event handler `btnAdd_Click`. This event handler should display the user input in the `ListBox` and clear the user input from the `TextBox`. The event handler should Increment the instance variable you created in the previous step and update the `Label` that displays the number of tasks. Use method `Convert.ToString` to display the number of tasks in the `Label`. Finally, the event handler should transfer the focus to the `TextBox`.

e) *Running the application.* Select **Debug > Start** to run your application. Enter several tasks, click the **Add Task** `Button` after each. Verify that each task is added to the **Task list:** `ListBox`, and that the number of tasks is incremented with each new task.

f) *Closing the application.* Close your running application by clicking its close box.

g) *Closing the IDE.* Close Visual Studio .NET by clicking its close box.

15.12 (*Quiz Average Application*) Develop an application that computes a student's average quiz score for all of the quiz scores entered. The application should look like the GUI in Fig. 15.25. Use method `Convert.ToInt32` to convert the user input to an `int`. Use instance variables with class scope to keep track of the sum of all the quiz scores entered and the number of quiz scores entered.

Figure 15.25   Quiz Average application.

a) *Copying the template to your working directory.* Copy the directory `C:\Examples\Tutorial15\Exercises\QuizAverage` to your `C:\SimplyCSP` directory.

b) *Opening the application's template file.* Double click `QuizAverage.sln` in the `QuizAverage` directory to open the application.

c) *Adding instance variables.* Add two instance variables—`m_intTotalScore`, which keeps track of the sum of all the quiz scores entered, and `m_intTaken`, which keeps track of the number of quiz scores entered.

d) *Adding the Grade Quiz Button's event handler.* Double click the **Submit Score** `Button` to generate the empty event handler `btnCalculate_Click`. The code required in *Steps e–j* should be placed in this event handler.

e) *Obtaining user input.* Use method `Convert.ToInt32` to convert the user input from the `TextBox` to an `int`.

f) *Updating the number of quiz scores entered.* Increment the number of quiz scores entered.

g) *Updating the sum of all the quiz scores entered.* Add the current quiz score to the current total to update the sum of all the quiz scores entered.

h) *Calculating the average score.* Divide the sum of all the quiz scores entered by the number of quiz scores entered to calculate the average score.

i) *Displaying the average score.* Use method `Convert.ToString` to display the average quiz grade in the **Average:** field.

j) *Displaying the number of quizzes taken.* Use method `Convert.ToString` to display the number of quiz scores entered in the **Number taken:** field.

k) *Running the application.* Select **Debug > Start** to run your application. Enter several quiz scores, clicking the **Submit Score** Button after each. With each new score, verify that the **Number taken:** field is incremented and that the average is updated correctly.

l) *Closing the application.* Close your running application by clicking its close box.

m) *Closing the IDE.* Close Visual Studio .NET by clicking its close box.

15.13 (*Maximum Application*) Modify the **Maximum** application from Tutorial 13 (Fig. 15.26) to use keyword `out` to pass a fourth argument to method `Maximum` by reference. Also, use methods from class `Convert` to perform any necessary type conversions.

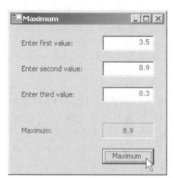

Figure 15.26 **Maximum** application.

a) *Copying the template to your working directory.* Copy the directory `C:\Examples\Tutorial15\Exercises\Maximum` to your `C:\SimplyCSP` directory.

b) *Opening the application's template file.* Double click `Maximum.sln` in the `Maximum` directory to open the application.

c) *Adding a local variable.* Add local variable `dblMaximum` of type `double` to event handler `btnMaximum_Click`. The code required in *Steps d–e* should be placed in this event handler.

d) *Passing four arguments to method `Maximum`.* Use method `Double.Parse` to convert the user input from the `TextBox`es to `double`s. Pass these three values as the first three arguments to method `Maximum`. Pass local variable `dblMaximum` as the fourth argument to method `Maximum`.

e) *Displaying the maximum value.* Use method `Convert.ToString` to display local variable `dblMaximum` in the **Maximum:** field.

f) *Changing the return type of `Maximum`.* Change the return type of `Maximum` to `void`. Make sure that method `Maximum` no longer returns a value and does not specify a return type.

g) *Adding a fourth parameter to method `Maximum`.* Add a fourth parameter `dblFinalMaximum` of type `double` to `Maximum`'s method header. Use keyword `out` to specify that this argument will be passed by reference uninitialized. Remove the declaration of variable `dblFinalMaximum` from the body of method `Maximum`.

h) *Running the application.* Select **Debug > Start** to run your application. Enter three different values into the input fields and click the **Maximum** Button. Verify that the largest value is displayed in the **Maximum:** field.

i) *Closing the application.* Close your running application by clicking its close box.

j) *Closing the IDE.* Close Visual Studio .NET by clicking its close box.

What does this code do? ▶ **15.14** What is displayed in Label lblDisplay when the following code is executed? Assume these variables and methods are declared inside the class FrmScopeTest.

```
1   int intValue2 = 5;
2
3   private void btnEnter_Click( object sender, System.EventArgs e )
4   {
5      int intValue1 = 10;
6      int intValue2 = 3;
7
8      Test( ref intValue1 );
9
10     lblDisplay.Text = Convert.ToString( intValue1 );
11
12  } // end method btnEnter_Click
13
14  void Test( ref int intValue1 )
15  {
16     intValue1 *= intValue2;
17
18  } // end method Test
```

What's wrong with this code? ▶ **15.15** Find the error(s) in the following code (the method should assign the value 14 to variable intResult).

```
1   int Sum()
2   {
3      string strNumber = "4";
4      int intNumber = 10;
5      int intResult;
6
7      intResult = strNumber + intNumber;
8
9      return intResult;
10
11  } // end method Sum
```

Programming Challenge ▶ **15.16** (*Schedule Book Application*) Develop an application that allows a user to enter a schedule of appointments and their respective times. Create the Form in Fig. 15.27 and name the application **Schedule Book**. Add a method called TimeTaken that returns a bool value. Each time a user enters a new appointment, method TimeTaken determines if the user has scheduled more than one appointment at the same time. If TimeTaken returns true, the user will be notified via a message dialog. Otherwise, the appointment should be added to the ListBoxes. Use methods from class Convert as necessary. Use the Items property of the ListBoxes along with the square bracket ([]) notation from Tutorial 10 to access the members of the ListBoxes.

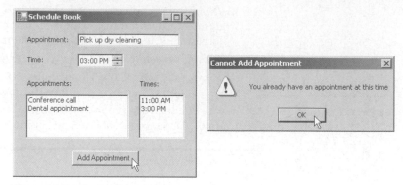

Figure 15.27 Schedule Book application.

Objectives

In this tutorial, you will learn to:
- Code simulation techniques that employ random-number generation.
- Use class **Random** methods.
- Generate random numbers.
- Use enumerations to enhance code readability.

Outline

Craps Game Application

Introducing Random-Number Generation

You will now be introduced to a popular type of application—simulation and game playing. In this tutorial, you will develop a **Craps Game** application. There is something in the air of a gambling casino that invigorates each person—from the high rollers at the plush mahogany-and-felt Craps tables to the quarter-poppers at the one-armed bandits. Many of these individuals are drawn by the element of chance—the possibility that luck will convert a pocketful of money into a mountain of wealth.

The element of chance can be introduced into computer applications using random numbers. This tutorial's **Craps Game** application introduces several new concepts, including random-number generation and enumerations. It also uses important concepts that you learned earlier in this book, including instance variables, methods and the switch multiple-selection control statement.

16.1 Test-Driving the Craps Game Application

One of the most popular games of chance is a dice game known as Craps, played in casinos throughout the world. This application must meet the following requirements:

Application Requirements

Create an application that simulates playing the game of "Craps." In this game, a player rolls two dice. Each die has six faces. Each face contains 1, 2, 3, 4, 5 or 6 spots. After the dice have come to rest, the sum of the spots on the two top faces is calculated. If the sum is 7 or 11 on the first throw, the player wins. If the sum is 2, 3 or 12 on the first throw (called "craps"), the player loses (the "house" wins). If the sum is 4, 5, 6, 8, 9 or 10 on the first throw, that sum becomes the player's "point." To win, a player must continue rolling the dice until the player rolls the point value. The player loses by rolling a 7 before rolling the point.

Creating this application will teach you two important concepts; random-number generation and enumerations. You begin by test-driving the completed application. Then, you will learn the additional C# technologies you will need to create your own version of this application.

Test-Driving the Craps Game Application

1. ***Opening the completed application.*** Open the C:\Examples\Tutorial16\ CompletedApplication\CrapsGame directory to locate the **Craps Game** application. Double click CrapsGame.sln to open the application in Visual Studio .NET.

2. ***Running the Craps Game application.*** Select **Debug > Start** to run the application (Fig. 16.1).

Figure 16.1   **Craps Game** application initial appearance.

3. ***Starting the game.*** Click the **Play** Button. There are three possible outcomes at this point: The player wins by rolling a 7 or an 11 (Fig. 16.2). The player loses by rolling 2, 3 or 12 (Fig. 16.3). Otherwise, the roll becomes the player's point (4, 5, 6, 8, 9 or 10), which is then displayed for the remainder of the game (Fig. 16.4). Note that unlike the real game of Craps, the value of the roll is computed using the forward-facing die faces instead of the top faces in this application.

Figure 16.2   Player wins on first roll by rolling 7 or 11.

Figure 16.3   Player loses on first roll by rolling 2, 3 or 12.

(cont.)

Figure 16.4   First roll sets the point that the player must match to win.

4. ***Continuing the game.*** If the application displays **Roll again!**, as in Fig. 16.4, click the **Roll** Button repeatedly until either you win—by matching your point value (Fig. 16.5)—or you lose—by rolling a 7 (Fig. 16.6). When the game ends, you can click **Play** to start over.

Figure 16.5   Winning the game by matching your point before rolling a 7.

Figure 16.6   Losing by rolling a 7 before matching your point.

5. ***Closing the application.*** Close your running application by clicking its close box.

6. ***Closing the IDE.*** Close Visual Studio .NET by clicking its close box.

16.2 Random-Number Generation

Now you will learn how to use an object of class **Random** to introduce the element of chance into your computer applications. You will learn more about working with objects of existing classes over the next few tutorials, then you will learn to create your own classes and create objects of those classes in Tutorial 19. Consider the following statements:

```
Random objRandom = new Random();
int intRandomNumber = objRandom.Next();
```

Good Programming Practice

Prefix references to objects, such as Random objects, with obj.

The first statement declares objRandom as a reference of type Random and assigns it a Random object. A **reference** is a variable to which you assign an object. The new operator creates a new structure value or a new instance of an object in memory.

The second statement declares int variable intRandomNumber, then assigns to intRandomNumber the value returned by calling Random's Next method on object objRandom using the dot operator. The **Next** method generates a positive int value between zero and the largest possible int, which is the constant Int32.MaxValue (2,147,483,647). You can use the Next method to generate random values of type int or use the **NextDouble** method to generate random values of type double. The NextDouble method returns a positive double value between 0.0 and 1.0 (not including 1.0).

If the Next method were to produce truly random values, then every value in this range would have an equal chance (or probability) of being chosen when Next is called. However, the values returned by Next are actually **pseudorandom numbers**, a sequence of values produced by a complex mathematical calculation. This mathematical calculation comes close, but is not exactly random in choosing numbers.

The range of values produced by Next (that is, values between 0 and 2,147,483,647) often is different from the range needed in a particular application. For example, an application that simulates coin tossing might require only 0 for "heads" and 1 for "tails." An application that simulates the rolling of a six-sided die would require random ints from 1 to 6. Similarly, an application that randomly predicts the next type of spaceship (out of four possibilities) that flies across the horizon in a video game might require random ints from 1 to 4.

By passing an argument to the Next method[1] as follows

```
intValue = 1 + objRandom.Next( 6 );
```

you can produce integers in the range from 1 to 6. When a single argument is passed to Next, the values returned by Next will be in the range from 0 to (but not including) the value of that argument (that is, 5 in the preceding statement). You can change the range of numbers produced by adding 1 to the previous result, so that the return values are between 1 and 6, rather than 0 and 5. That new range, 1 to 6, corresponds nicely with the roll of a six-sided die, for example.

C# simplifies this process of setting the range of numbers by allowing the programmer to pass two arguments to Next. For example, the preceding statement also could be written as

```
intValue = objRandom.Next( 1, 7 )
```

Note that you must use 7 as the second argument to the Next method to produce integers in the range from 1 to 6. The first argument indicates the minimum value in the desired range; the second is equal to *one more than the maximum value desired*.

As with method Next, the range of values produced by method NextDouble (that is, values greater than or equal to 0.0 and less than 1.0) is also usually different from the range needed in a particular application. By multiplying the value returned from method NextDouble as follows

```
dblValue = 6 * objRandom.NextDouble();
```

you can produce double values in the range from 0.0 to 6.0 (not including 6.0). Figure 16.7 shows examples of the ranges returned by calls to methods Next and NextDouble.

---

1. In Tutorial 13, you learned that the number, type and order of arguments to a method must exactly match the method declaration. You may notice that the Next method of class Random is called using zero, one and two arguments. There is a sophisticated feature of C# called **method overloading** that allows multiple method declarations of the same name but with different numbers, types and/or order of arguments.

Method call	Resulting range
`objRandom.Next()`	0 to one less than `Int32.MaxValue`
`objRandom.Next( 30 )`	0 to 29
`10 + objRandom.Next( 10 )`	10 to 19
`objRandom.Next( 10, 20 )`	10 to 19
`objRandom.Next( 5, 100 )`	5 to 99
`objRandom.NextDouble()`	0.0 to less than 1.0
`8 * objRandom.NextDouble()`	0.0 to less than 8.0

Figure 16.7 `Next` and `NextDouble` method calls with corresponding ranges.

SELF-REVIEW

1. The expression _____ returns a number in the range from 8 to 300.
   a) `objRandom.Next( 8, 300 )`
   b) `objRandom.Next( 8, 301 )`
   c) `1 + objRandom.Next( 8, 300 )`
   d) None of the above.

2. The expression _____ returns a number in the range 15 to 35.
   a) `objRandom.Next( 15, 36 )`
   b) `objRandom.Next( 15, 35 )`
   c) `10 + objRandom.Next( 5, 26 )`
   d) Both a and c.

Answers: 1) b. 2) d.

16.3 Using Enumerations in the Craps Game Application

The following pseudocode describes the basic operation of the **Craps Game** application:

```
When the player clicks the Play Button:
     Roll the dice using random numbers
     Display images corresponding to the numbers on the rolled dice
     Calculate the sum of both dice

     Switch based on the sum of the two dice:

     Case where first roll is 7 or 11
          Disable the Roll Button
          Display the winning message

     Case where first roll is 2, 3 or 12
          Disable the Roll Button
          Display the losing message

     Case where none of the preceding Cases are true
          Set the value of the point to the sum of the dice
          Display point value
          Display message to roll again
          Display images for user's point
          Disable the Play Button
          Enable the Roll Button

When the player clicks the Roll Button:
     Roll the dice using random numbers
     Display images corresponding to the numbers on the rolled dice
     Calculate the sum of both dice

     If the player rolls the same value as the point
          Display the winning message
          Disable the Roll Button
          Enable the Play Button
```

Else If the player rolls a 7
    Display the losing message
    Disable the Roll Button
    Enable the Play Button

Now that you have test-driven the **Craps Game** application and studied its pseudocode representation, you will use an ACE table to help you convert the pseudocode to C#. Figure 16.8 lists the actions, controls and events that will help you complete your own version of this application.

Action/Control/Event (ACE) Table for the Craps Game Application

Action	Control/Object	Event
Label the application's controls	lblResult, fraPointDice-Group	Application is run
	btnPlay	Click
Roll the dice using random numbers	m_objRandom	
Display images corresponding to the numbers on the rolled dice	picDie1, picDie2	
Calculate the sum of both dice		
Switch based on sum:		
Case where first roll is 7 or 11 Disable the Roll Button	btnRoll	
Display the winning message	lblStatus	
Case where first roll is 2, 3 or 1 Disable the Roll Button	btnRoll	
Display the losing message	lblStatus	
Case where none of the preceding Cases are true Set the value of the point to the sum of the dice		
Display the point value	fraPointDice-Group	
Display message to roll again	lblStatus	
Display images for user's point	picPointDie1, picPointDie2	
Disable the Play Button	btnPlay	
Enable the Roll Button	btnRoll	
	btnRoll	Click
Roll the dice using random numbers	m_objRandom	
Display images corresponding to the numbers on the rolled dice	picDie1, picDie2	
Calculate the sum of both dice		
If the player rolls the same value as the point Display the winning message	lblStatus	
Disable the Roll Button	btnRoll	
Enable the Play Button	btnPlay	
If the player rolls a 7 Display the losing message	lblStatus	
Disable the Roll Button	btnRoll	
Enable the Play Button	btnPlay	

Figure 16.8 ACE table for the **Craps Game** application.

In the following boxes, you will create an application to simulate playing the game of Craps. You begin with the following box. The steps that follow show you how to add code to use the System.IO namespace. As you have already learned, C# has access to the Framework Class Library (FCL), which is a rich collection of classes that can be used to enhance applications. The FCL includes classes that provide methods for using files, graphics, multimedia and more. As you learned in Tutorial 5, these FCL classes are grouped (by functionality) in units called namespaces. The **System.IO** namespace provides classes and methods for accessing files (such as images and text) and directories (such as C:\SimplyCSP). You will need to use code to access image files for the **Craps Game** application; therefore, you use the System.IO namespace. Using a namespace (done with keyword using) allows you to easily access its members. By default, Visual Studio .NET references several namespaces in your code, but System.IO is not one of them. You will need to add the using statement (also called a using directive) for the System.IO namespace yourself.

Viewing the Craps Game Template Application	1. ***Copying the template to your working directory.*** Copy the C:\Examples\ Tutorial16\TemplateApplication\CrapsGame directory to your C:\SimplyCSP directory.

2. ***Opening the Craps Game application's template file.*** Double click Craps-Game.sln in the CrapsGame directory to open the application in Visual Studio .NET (Fig. 16.9).

Figure 16.9   Template **Craps Game** Form in design view.

3. ***Allowing image-file access.*** The application will display images; therefore, you need to import the System.IO namespace to allow access to methods to help you read image files. Select **View > Code**. Add using System.IO; (line 7) into your code (Fig. 16.10).

Using the System.IO namespace ——

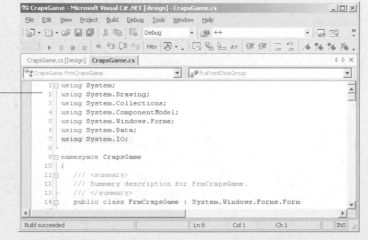

Figure 16.10   Adding a using directive to the **Craps Game** application.

4. ***Saving the project.*** Select **File > Save All** to save your modified code.

Notice that the numbers 2, 3, 7, 11 and 12 have special meanings during a game of Craps. Throughout the course of a Craps game, you will use these numbers (as constants) quite often. In this case, it would be helpful to create a group of related constants and assign them meaningful names for use in your application. C# allows you to accomplish this by using an **enumeration**. You will learn how to create constant identifiers (enumerations) that describe various significant dice combinations in Craps (such as SNAKE_EYES, TREY, CRAPS, LUCKY_SEVEN, YO_LEVEN and BOX_CARS). By providing descriptive identifiers for a group of related constants, enumerations enhance program readability and ensure that numbers are consistent throughout the application. You will learn how to use enumerations in the following box.

Introducing Enumerations and Declaring Instance Variables

1. ***Declaring an enumeration.*** Add lines 42–51 of Fig. 16.11 to your application after the control declarations. Enumerations begin with the keyword **enum** (line 43), followed by the name of the enumeration (DiceNames) and an opening left brace ({). The enumeration ends with a closing right brace (}) (line 51).

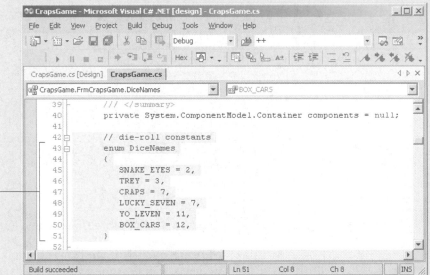

Declaring an enumeration

Figure 16.11 Enumeration DiceNames in the **Craps Game** application.

Enumerations are used in this application to make the code easier to read, especially for someone who is unfamiliar with the application. You can refer to the numbers using the enumeration constants and the member-access operator. For instance, use DiceNames.SNAKE_EYES for the number 2, DiceNames.TREY for the number 3, DiceNames.CRAPS and Dice-Names.LUCKY_SEVEN for the number 7, DiceNames.YO_LEVEN for the number 11 and DiceNames.BOX_CARS for the number 12. Notice that you can assign the same value to multiple enumeration constants, as you did in lines 47 and 48.

2. ***Declaring instance variables.*** Several methods will require the use of the same variables throughout the lifetime of the application. You will declare instance variables for this purpose. Add lines 53–59 of Fig. 16.12 below the enumeration declaration.

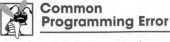

Good Programming Practice

Use enumerations to group related constants and enhance code readability.

Common Programming Error

An enumeration type can be specified after the enumeration name by using a colon (:) followed by byte, sbyte, int, uint, long, ulong, short or ushort. Enumerations use type int if no type is specified. Attempting to create enumeration values of other types, such as string, decimal and double, results in a syntax error.

(cont.)

In this application, you will need to access images that display the six faces of a die. For convenience, each file has a name that differs only by one number. For example, the image for the die face displaying 1 is named `die1.png`, and the image for the die face displaying 6 is named `die6.png`. Recall that `png` is an image-file name extension that is short for Portable Network Graphic. The images are stored in the `images` directory, in your project's `bin\Debug` directory. As such, the `string` `/images/die1.png` would correctly indicate the location of the die face displaying 1 relative to the `bin\Debug` directory. To help create a `string` representing the path to the image, strings `m_strFILE_PREFIX` (`/images/die`) and `m_strFILE_SUFFIX` (`.png`) are used (as constants) to store the prefix and suffix of the file name (lines 54–55).

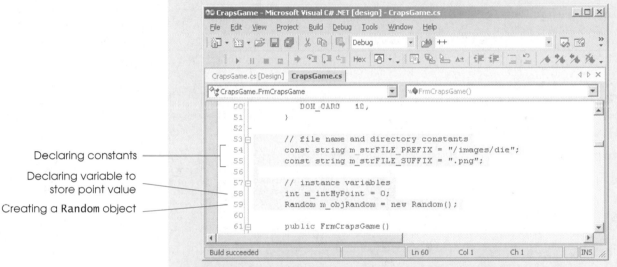

Declaring constants

Declaring variable to store point value

Creating a **Random** object

Figure 16.12 Instance variables added to the **Craps Game** application.

The game of Craps requires that you store the user's point, once established on the first roll, for the duration of the game. Therefore, variable `m_intMyPoint` (line 58 of Fig. 16.12) is declared as an `int` instance variable to store the value of the dice on the first roll. You will use the `Random` object referenced by `m_objRandom` (line 59) to "roll" the dice and generate those values.

3. *Saving the project.* Select **File > Save All** to save your modified code.

SELF-REVIEW

1. Use keyword _____ to define groups of related constants.
   a) `readonly`
   b) `enum`
   c) `constants`
   d) `enumeration`

2. Namespace _____ is used to access files and directories.
   a) `System.File`
   b) `System.FileDirectory`
   c) `System.FileAccess`
   d) `System.IO`

Answers: 1) b. 2) d.

16.4 Using Random Numbers in the Craps Game Application

Now that you have declared an enumeration and instance variables, you will add code to execute when the user clicks the **Craps Game** application's `Button`s. The following box explains how to add the code that executes when the user clicks the **Play** `Button`.

Coding the Play Button's Click Event Handler

1. *Creating the Play Button's Click event handler.* Return to the **Design View** to display the **Form**. Double click the **Play** Button to generate the **Play** Button's Click event handler and view the code file. (The **Play** Button is used to begin a new game of Craps.)

2. *Removing Images from a PictureBox and rolling dice.* Be sure to add the comment and break the header as shown in Fig. 16.13 so that the line numbers in your code match those presented in this tutorial. Begin coding the Click event handler by adding lines 218–227 from Fig. 16.13 into the btnPlay_Click event handler.

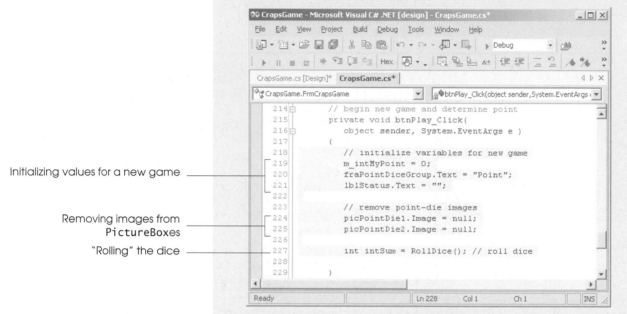

Initializing values for a new game

Removing images from PictureBoxes

"Rolling" the dice

Figure 16.13 btnPlay_Click event handler declaration.

Lines 219–221 initialize variables for a new game. Line 219 sets variable m_intMyPoint, the Craps game point value, to 0. Line 220 changes the text displayed on the GroupBox to Point, using the GroupBox's Text property. As you saw in the test-drive, the GroupBox's Text property will be used to display the point value. Finally, line 221 clears the value of the output Label because the user is starting a new game.

Lines 224–225 remove any images from the PictureBoxes used to display the point die. Though there are no images when the application is first run, if the user chooses to continue playing after completing a game, the images from the previous game must be cleared. Setting the Image property to keyword null indicates that there is no image to display. Keyword **null** is used to clear a reference's value, much as the empty string ("") is used to clear a string's value.

Line 227 declares the variable intSum and assigns to it the value returned by rolling the dice. This is accomplished by calling the RollDice method, which you will define later in this tutorial. The RollDice method will not only roll dice and return the sum of their values, but also will display the die images in the lower two PictureBoxes.

(cont.)(

3. ***Using a switch statement to determine the result of rolling the dice.*** Recall that if the player rolls 7 or 11 on the first roll, the player wins. However, if the player rolls 2, 3 or 12 on the first roll, the player loses. Add lines 229–247 of Fig. 16.14 to the `btnPlay_Click` event handler beneath the code you added in the previous step. Notice that after the closing right brace (}) of the `switch` statement (line 247), Visual Studio .NET indents your comments differently than our conventions. Move them back to their appropriate level of indentation, as in Fig. 16.14.

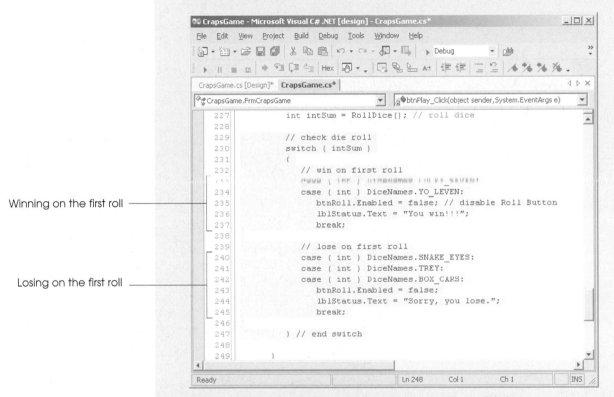

Winning on the first roll

Losing on the first roll

Figure 16.14   The `switch` statement in `btnPlay_Click`.

4. The first group of `cases` (lines 233–237) selects values 7 and 11, using the enumeration values `DiceNames.LUCKY_SEVEN` and `DiceNames.YO_LEVEN`. A cast operator is required to explicitly convert the enumeration values to `int`s. When you create an enumeration you are actually defining a new type — to access the enumeration values as `int`s, a case is needed. Recall that several `cases` can be grouped together using the fall-through technique on empty `cases`, such as the `case` in line 233. If the sum of the dice is 7 or 11, the code in lines 235–236 disables the **Roll** Button and displays "You win!!!" in the output Label `lblStatus`. If the dice add up to 2 (`Dice-Names.SNAKE_EYES`), 3 (`DiceNames.TREY`) or 12 (`DiceNames.BOX_CARS`), the body of the second group of `cases` executes (lines 240–245). This code disables the **Roll** Button and displays a message in Label `lblStatus` indicating that the player has lost.

5. ***Using the default case to continue the game.*** If the player did not roll a 2, 3, 7, 11 or 12, then the value of the dice becomes the point and the player must roll again. Add lines 247–256 of Fig. 16.15 within the `switch` statement to implement this rule. The first line of the `default case`'s body (line 249) sets the instance variable `m_intMyPoint` to the sum of the die values. Next, line 250 changes the text on the GroupBox, using its `Text` property to display the value of the current point. The Label `lblStatus` is changed to notify the user to roll again (line 251).

(cont.)

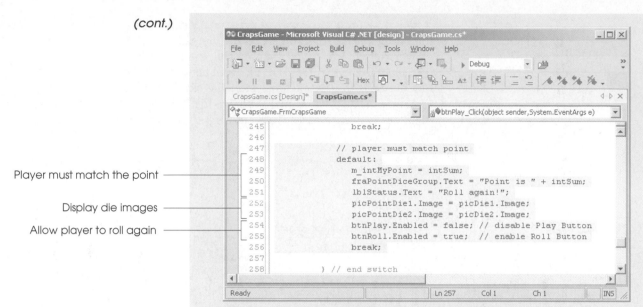

Player must match the point ——

Display die images ——

Allow player to roll again ——

Figure 16.15 The `default` statement in `btnPlay_Click`.

If the user must match the point, you display the die images corresponding to the result of the dice roll. In Tutorial 3, you learned how to insert an image into a `PictureBox` in the Windows Form Designer. To set the image for a `PictureBox`, you used its `Image` property. You can also use code to set this property as well. To display the die faces for the point in the Group-Box, you should set the `Image` property of the each `PictureBox` in the `GroupBox` to the same `Image` property value as its corresponding `Picture-Box` below the `GroupBox` (lines 252–253). Finally, the **Play** Button is disabled (line 254) and the **Roll** Button is enabled (line 255), limiting users to clicking the **Roll** Button for the rest of the game. The `break` statement (line 256) ends the `default` case.

6. ***Saving the project.*** Select **File > Save All** to save your modified code.

The **Roll** Button is enabled after the user clicks **Play**, so you must code an event handler for it. You define the event handler in the following box.

Coding the Roll Button's Click Event Handler	1. ***Generating the Roll Button's Click event handler.*** Return to the Windows Form Designer, and double click the **Roll** Button. This generates the **Roll** Button's `Click` event handler and opens the code window. Be sure to add the comments and break the header as shown in Fig. 16.16 so that the line numbers in your code match those presented in this tutorial. We will not be adding any more event handlers to this application, so you should now add a comment to the end of `btnPlay_Click`.
	2. ***Rolling the dice.*** The user clicks the **Roll** Button to try to match the point, which requires rolling dice. Add line 267 of Fig. 16.16 which will roll the dice, display the die images and store the sum of the dice in variable `intSum`. You will define method `RollDice` shortly.
	3. ***Determining the output of the roll.*** If the roll matches the point, the user wins and the game ends. However, if the user rolls a 7 (`DiceNames.CRAPS`), the user loses and the game ends. Add lines 269–282 of Fig. 16.17 into the `btnRoll_Click` event handler to incorporate this processing into your **Craps Game** application.

(cont.)

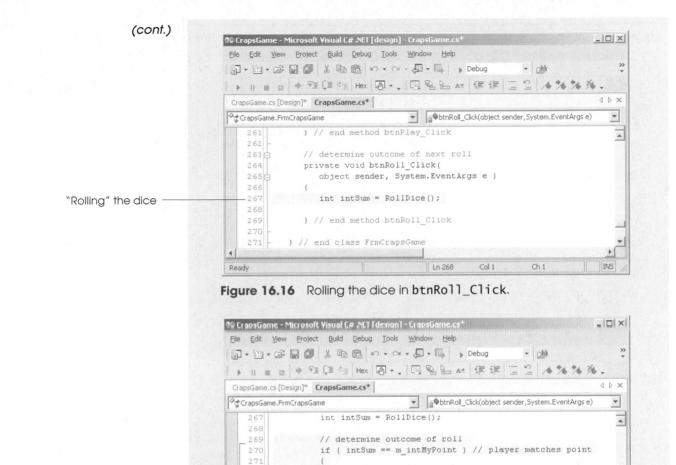

"Rolling" the dice

Figure 16.16   Rolling the dice in `btnRoll_Click`.

Display winning message

Display losing message

Figure 16.17   Determining the outcome of a roll.

Lines 270–275 determine whether the sum of the dice in the current roll matches the point. If the sum and point match, the application displays a winning message in Label `lblStatus`. It then allows the user to start a new game, by disabling the **Roll** Button and enabling the **Play** Button.

Lines 276–282 determine whether the sum of the dice in the current roll is 7 (`DiceNames.CRAPS`). If so, the application displays a message that the user has lost (in Label `lblStatus`) and ends the game by disabling the **Roll** Button and enabling the **Play** Button. If the player neither matches the point nor rolls a 7, then the player is allowed to roll again. The player rolls the dice again by clicking the **Roll** Button.

4. ***Saving the project.*** Select **File > Save All** to save your modified code.

In the following box, you add code into the application to simulate rolling dice and use code to display the dice in the appropriate `PictureBox`es.

Using Random Numbers to Simulate Rolling Dice

1. ***Creating a Random object and simulating die rolling.*** This application will roll and display dice many times as it runs. Therefore, it is a good idea to create two methods: one to roll the dice (`RollDice`) and one to display the dice (`DisplayDie`). Define method `RollDice` first, by adding lines 286–299 of Fig. 16.18.

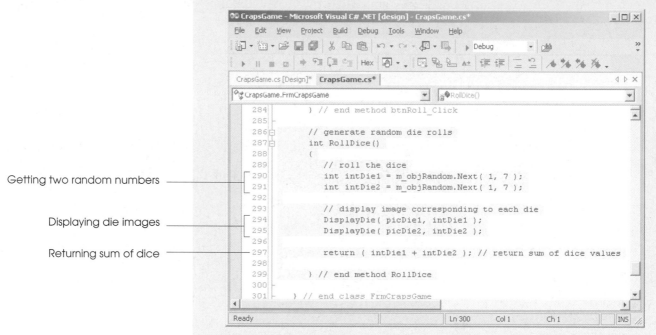

Getting two random numbers

Displaying die images

Returning sum of dice

Figure 16.18 `RollDice` method declaration.

This code sets the values of `intDie1` and `intDie2` to the values returned by `m_objRandom.Next( 1, 7 )`, which is a random number of type `int` between the values `1` to `6` (lines 290 and 291). Remember that the number returned is always less than the second argument.

The method then makes two calls to `DisplayDie` (lines 294 and 295), a method that displays the image of the die face corresponding to each number. The first parameter in `DisplayDie` is the `PictureBox` that will display the image, and the second parameter is the number that appears on the face of the die. You will define the `DisplayDie` method in *Step 2*. Finally, the method returns the sum of the values of the dice (line 297), which the application uses to determine the outcome of the Craps game.

2. ***Displaying the dice images.*** You will now define method `DisplayDie` to display the die images corresponding to the random numbers generated in method `RollDice`. Add lines 301–309 of Fig. 16.19 (after the `RollDice` method) to create the `DisplayDie` method.

Line 305 begins the statement that sets the `Image` property for the specified `PictureBox`. The `Image` property must be set using an object of type `Image`, so you must create an `Image` object.

The `Image` class contains a `FromFile` method to help create `Image` objects. **`Image.FromFile`** returns an `Image` object containing the image located at the path you specify. To specify the location, use the path (as a `String`) as the parameter to the `FromFile` method. In this case, you can begin by using the `Directory.GetCurrentDirectory` method (line 306). The **`Directory.Get-CurrentDirectory`** method (contained in the `System.IO` namespace) returns the location of the directory from which your application was loaded (the `bin\Debug` directory). In this case, `Directory.GetCurrentDirectory` will return the string `C:\SimplyCSP\CrapsGame\bin\Debug`.

(cont.)

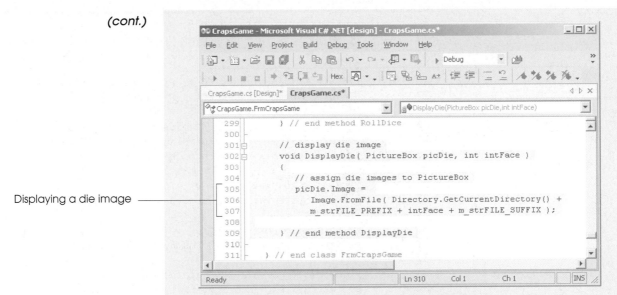

Displaying a die image

Figure 16.19 `DisplayDie` method declaration.

Now append `m strFILE PREFIX + intFace + m strFILE SUFFIX` to create the rest of the location of the file (line 307). If the value of `intFace` is 1, the expression would represent the string `/images/die1.png`. This is the location of the image of a die face showing 1. If you combine the value of `Directory.GetCurrentDirectory` with the expression mentioned earlier, the result is `C:\SimplyCSP\CrapsGame\bin\Debug\images\die1.png`, the location of the image on your computer. You can use Windows Explorer to verify that this is the correct location. This image is then displayed in the `PictureBox` by using its `Image` property.

3. ***Running the application.*** Select **Debug > Start** to run your completed application and enjoy the game!

4. ***Closing the application.*** Close your running application by clicking its close box.

5. ***Closing the IDE.*** Close Visual Studio .NET by clicking its close box.

Figure 16.20 presents the source code for the **Craps Game** application. The lines of code that contain new programming concepts that you learned in this tutorial are highlighted.

```
1   using System;
2   using System.Drawing;
3   using System.Collections;
4   using System.ComponentModel;
5   using System.Windows.Forms;
6   using System.Data;
7   using System.IO;
8
9   namespace CrapsGame
10  {
11      /// <summary>
12      /// Summary description for FrmCrapsGame.
13      /// </summary>
14      public class FrmCrapsGame : System.Windows.Forms.Form
15      {
```

Using the `System.IO` namespace

Figure 16.20   Craps Game application code. (Part 1 of 5.)

```
16        // GroupBox to display point dice
17        private System.Windows.Forms.GroupBox fraPointDiceGroup;
18
19        // PictureBoxes of point dice
20        private System.Windows.Forms.PictureBox picPointDie1;
21        private System.Windows.Forms.PictureBox picPointDie2;
22
23        // PictureBoxes of current dice
24        private System.Windows.Forms.PictureBox picDie1;
25        private System.Windows.Forms.PictureBox picDie2;
26
27        // Button to play a game
28        private System.Windows.Forms.Button btnPlay;
29
30        // Button to roll the dice
31        private System.Windows.Forms.Button btnRoll;
32
33        // Labels to display the status of the game
34        private System.Windows.Forms.Label lblResult;
35        private System.Windows.Forms.Label lblStatus;
36
37        /// <summary>
38        /// Required designer variable.
39        /// </summary>
40        private System.ComponentModel.Container components = null;
41
42        // die-roll constants
43        enum DiceNames
44        {
45            SNAKE_EYES = 2,
46            TREY = 3,
47            CRAPS = 7,
48            LUCKY_SEVEN = 7,
49            YO_LEVEN = 11,
50            BOX_CARS = 12,
51        }
52
53        // file name and directory constants
54        const string m_strFILE_PREFIX = "/images/die";
55        const string m_strFILE_SUFFIX = ".png";
56
57        // instance variables
58        int m_intMyPoint = 0;
59        Random m_objRandom = new Random();
60
61        public FrmCrapsGame()
62        {
63            //
64            // Required for Windows Form Designer support
65            //
66            InitializeComponent();
67
68            //
69            // TODO: Add any constructor code after InitializeComponent
70            // call
71            //
72        }
73
```

Declaring an enumeration — (lines 43–51)

Creating a **Random** object — (line 59)

Figure 16.20 Craps Game application code. (Part 2 of 5.)

```
74        /// <summary>
75        /// Clean up any resources being used.
76        /// </summary>
77        protected override void Dispose( bool disposing )
78        {
79           if( disposing )
80           {
81              if (components != null)
82              {
83                 components.Dispose();
84              }
85           }
86           base.Dispose( disposing );
87        }
88
89        // Windows Form Designer generated code
90
91        /// <summary>
92        /// The main entry point for the application.
93        /// </summary>
94        [STAThread]
95        static void Main()
96        {
97           Application.Run( new FrmCrapsGame() );
98        }
99
100       // begin new game and determine point
101       private void btnPlay_Click(
102          object sender, System.EventArgs e )
103       {
104          // initialize variables for new game
105          m_intMyPoint = 0;
106          fraPointDiceGroup.Text = "Point";
107          lblStatus.Text = "";
108
109          // remove point-die images
110          picPointDie1.Image = null;
111          picPointDie2.Image = null;
112
113          int intSum = RollDice(); // roll dice
114
115          // check die roll
116          switch ( intSum )
117          {
118             // win on first roll
119             case ( int ) DiceNames.LUCKY_SEVEN:
120             case ( int ) DiceNames.YO_LEVEN:
121                btnRoll.Enabled = false; // disable Roll Button
122                lblStatus.Text = "You win!!!";
123                break;
124
125             // lose on first roll
126             case ( int ) DiceNames.SNAKE_EYES:
127             case ( int ) DiceNames.TREY:
128             case ( int ) DiceNames.BOX_CARS:
129                btnRoll.Enabled = false;
130                lblStatus.Text = "Sorry, you lose.";
131                break;
```

Figure 16.20 Craps Game application code. (Part 3 of 5.)

```
132
133                   // player must match point
134                   default:
135                      m_intMyPoint = intSum;
136                      fraPointDiceGroup.Text = "Point is " + intSum;
137                      lblStatus.Text = "Roll again!";
138                      picPointDie1.Image = picDie1.Image;
139                      picPointDie2.Image = picDie2.Image;
140                      btnPlay.Enabled = false; // disable Play Button
141                      btnRoll.Enabled = true;  // enable Roll Button
142                      break;
143
144            } // end switch
145
146         } // end method btnPlay_Click
147
148         // determine outcome of next roll
149         private void btnRoll_Click(
150            object sender, System.EventArgs e )
151         {
152            int intSum = RollDice();
153
154            // determine outcome of roll
155            if ( intSum == m_intMyPoint ) // player matches point
156            {
157               lblStatus.Text = "You win!!!";
158               btnRoll.Enabled = false;
159               btnPlay.Enabled = true;
160            }
161            else if ( intSum ==
162               ( int ) DiceNames.CRAPS ) // player loses
163            {
164               lblStatus.Text = "Sorry, you lose.";
165               btnRoll.Enabled = false;
166               btnPlay.Enabled = true;
167            }
168
169         } // end method btnRoll_Click
170
171         // generate random die rolls
172         int RollDice()
173         {
174            // roll the dice
175            int intDie1 = m_objRandom.Next( 1, 7 );
176            int intDie2 = m_objRandom.Next( 1, 7 );
177
178            // display image corresponding to each die
179            DisplayDie( picDie1, intDie1 );
180            DisplayDie( picDie2, intDie2 );
181
182            return ( intDie1 + intDie2 ); // return sum of dice values
183
184         } // end method RollDice
185
186         // display die image
187         void DisplayDie( PictureBox picDie, int intFace )
188         {
```

Generating random numbers — (lines 175–176)

Figure 16.20 **Craps Game** application code. (Part 4 of 5.)

Using code to display an image ———

```
189          // assign die images to PictureBox
190          picDie.Image =
191            Image.FromFile( Directory.GetCurrentDirectory() +
192            m_strFILE_PREFIX + intFace + m_strFILE_SUFFIX );
193
194       } // end method DisplayDie
195
196    } // end class FrmCrapsGame
197  }
```

Figure 16.20 **Craps Game** application code. (Part 5 of 5.)

SELF-REVIEW

1. _____ returns a string that represents the location of the application file.

   a) `Directory.GetWorkingDirectory`   b) `Directory.GetDirectory`

   c) `Directory.GetCurrentDirectory`   d) `Directory.ActiveDirectory`

2. To clear the image in a `PictureBox`, set its Image property to _____.

   a) `""` (double quotes)   b) `null`

   c) `none`   d) `empty`

Answers: 1) c. 2) b.

16.5 Wrap-Up

In this tutorial, you created the **Craps Game** application to simulate playing the popular dice game called Craps. You learned about the Random class and how it can be used to generate random numbers by creating a Random object and calling method Next on it. You then learned how to specify the range of values within which random numbers should be generated by passing various arguments to method Next. You were also introduced to enumerations, which enhance program readability by using descriptive identifiers to represent constants in an application.

Using your knowledge of random-number generation and event handlers, you wrote code that added functionality to your **Craps Game** application. You used random-number generation to simulate the element of chance. In addition to "rolling dice" in code, you learned how to use a PictureBox to display an image by using code. You used the System.IO namespace to help access images located in a file.

In the next tutorial, you will learn how to use arrays, which allow you to use one name to store many values. You will apply your knowledge of random numbers and arrays to create a **Flag Quiz** application that tests your knowledge of various nations' flags.

SKILLS SUMMARY

Generating Random Numbers

- Create an object of class Random, and call this object's Next method. Use an argument to specify the maximum value for the random numbers.

Generating Random Numbers within a Specified Range

- Call the Random class's Next method with two arguments. The first argument represents the minimum possible value; the second argument represents one more than the maximum possible desired value.

Declaring Enumerations

- Begin an enumeration with keyword enum followed by the name of the enumeration and an opening left brace; then use a list (separated by commas) of descriptive names, and set each one to the value that you want it to represent. End the enumeration with a closing right brace.

KEY TERMS

Directory.GetCurrentDirectory—A method of class `Directory` in the `System.IO` namespace that returns a `String` containing the path to the directory that contains the application.

enum keyword—Begins an enumeration.

enumeration—A group of related, named constants.

Image.FromFile method—Returns an `Image` object containing the image located at the path you specify.

method overloading—Feature that allows multiple method declarations of the same name but with different numbers, types and/or order of arguments.

Next method of class Random—When called with no arguments, generates a positive `int` value between zero and the constant `Int32.MaxValue`.

NextDouble method of class Random—Generates a positive `double` value that is greater than or equal to 0.0 and less than 1.0.

null keyword—Used to clear a reference's value.

pseudorandom numbers—A sequence of values produced by a complex mathematical calculation that simulates random-number generation.

Random class—Contains methods to generate pseudorandom numbers.

reference—A variable to which you assign an object.

System.IO namespace—Contains methods to access files and directories.

CONTROLS, EVENTS, PROPERTIES & METHODS

Directory This class provides functionality to manipulate directories such as creating, moving, and navigating through them.

- *Method*

  `GetCurrentDirectory`—Returns the location of the directory from which the application was loaded.

Image This class provides functionality to manipulate images.

- *Method*

  `FromFile`—Used to specify the physical location (path) of the image.

Random This class is used to generate random numbers.

- *Methods*

  `Next`—When called with no arguments, generates a positive `int` value between zero and the largest possible `int`, which is the constant `Int32.MaxValue` (2,147,483,647).

  `NextDouble`—Generates a positive `double` value that is greater than or equal to 0.0 and less than 1.0.

MULTIPLE-CHOICE QUESTIONS

16.1 A Random object can generate pseudorandom numbers of type _____.

    a) `int`
    b) `decimal`
    c) `double`
    d) Both a and c.

16.2 A _____ is a group of related classes in the Framework Class Library.

    a) `classspace`
    b) `directory`
    c) `namespace`
    d) `cluster`

16.3 Object variable names should be prefixed with _____.

    a) `var`
    b) `obj`
    c) `ran`
    d) `ojt`

16.4 The Next method of class Random can be called using _____.

    a) one argument
    b) no arguments
    c) two arguments
    d) All of the above.

16.5 The statement _____ assigns `intValue` a random number in the range from 5 to 20.

a) `intValue = objRandom.Next(5, 21);` b) `intValue = objRandom.Next(4, 20);`

c) `intValue = objRandom.Next(5, 20);` d) `intValue = objRandom.Next(4, 21);`

16.6 The _____ method specifies the file from which an image is loaded.

a) `Random.Next`   b) `Image.FromFile`

c) `Directory.GetCurrentDirectory`   d) None of the above.

16.7 The `System.IO` namespace contains classes and methods to _____.

a) access files and directories   b) display graphics in an application

c) insert multimedia into an application   d) All of the above.

16.8 The values returned by the _____ method of class `Random` are actually pseudorandom numbers.

a) `NextRandom`   b) `Pseudorandom`

c) `Next`   d) `Pseudo`

16.9 When creating random numbers, the second argument passed to the `Next` method is _____.

a) equal to the maximum value you wish to be generated

b) equal to one more than the maximum value you wish to be generated

c) equal to one less than the maximum value you wish to be generated

d) equal to the minimum value you wish to be generated

16.10 A(n) _____ is a group of related, named constants.

a) namespace   b) variable

c) enumeration   d) None of the above.

EXERCISES

16.11 (*Guess the Number Application*) Develop an application that generates a random number and prompts the user to guess the number (Fig. 16.21). When the user clicks the **New Game** `Button`, the application chooses a number in the range 1 to 100 at random. The user enters guesses into the **Guess:** `TextBox` and clicks the **Enter** `Button`. If the guess is correct, the game ends, and the user can start a new game. If the guess is not correct, the application should indicate if the guess is higher or lower than the correct number.

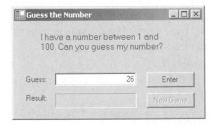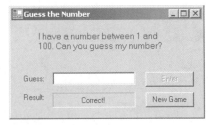

Figure 16.21   **Guess the Number** application.

a) *Copying the template to your working directory.* Copy the directory `C:\Examples\Tutorial16\Exercises\GuessNumber` to your `C:\SimplyCSP` directory.

b) *Opening the application's template file.* Double click `GuessNumber.sln` in the `GuessNumber` directory to open the application.

c) *Creating a Random object.* Create two instance variables. The first variable should store a `Random` object and the second variable should store a random-generated number.

d) *Adding a Load event handler for the Form.* Add a `Load` event handler for the `Form` that initializes the second instance variable to a random-generated number.

e) *Adding a Click event handler for the Enter Button.* Add a `Click` event handler for the **Enter** `Button` that retrieves the value entered by the user and compares that value to the random-generated number. If the guess is correct, display "`Correct!`" in the output `Label`. Then, disable the **Enter** `Button` and enable the **New Game** `Button`. If the user's guess is higher than the correct answer, display "Too high..." in the output Label. If the user's guess is lower than the correct answer, display "Too low..." in the output Label.

f) *Adding a Click event handler for the New Game Button.* Add a Click event handler for the **New Game** Button that generates a new random number for the instance variable. The event handler should then disable the **New Game** Button, enable the **Enter** Button and clear the **Result:** TextBox.

g) *Running the application.* Select **Debug > Start** to run your application. Enter guesses (clicking the **Enter** Button after each) until you have successfully determined the answer. Click the **New Game** Button and test the application again.

h) *Closing the application.* Close your running application by clicking its close box.

i) *Closing the IDE.* Close Visual Studio .NET by clicking its close box.

16.12 (*Dice Simulator Application*) Develop an application that simulates rolling two six-sided dice. Your application should have a **Roll** Button that, when clicked, displays two dice images corresponding to random numbers. It should also display the number of times each face has appeared. Your application should appear similar to Fig. 16.22.

Figure 16.22 **Dice Simulator** application.

a) *Copying the template to your working directory.* Copy the directory C:\Examples\ Tutorial16\Exercises\DiceSimulator to your C:\SimplyCSP directory.

b) *Opening the application's template file.* Double click DiceSimulator.sln in the DiceSimulator directory to open the application.

c) *Displaying the die image.* Create a method named DisplayDie that takes a PictureBox control as an argument. This method should generate a random number to simulate a die roll. Then, display the die image in the corresponding PictureBox control on the Form. The die image should correspond to the random number that was generated. To set the image, refer to the code presented in Fig. 16.20.

d) *Adding a Click event handler for the Roll Button.* Add a Click event handler for the **Roll** Button. Call method DisplayDie in this event handler to display the images for both dice.

e) *Displaying the frequency.* Add a method called DisplayFrequency that uses a switch statement to update the number of times each face has appeared. Create an enumeration for the dice faces which will be used in the switch statement.

f) *Running the application.* Select **Debug > Start** to run your application. Click the **Roll** Button several times. Each time, two die faces should be displayed at random. Verify after each roll that the appropriate face values on the left are incremented.

g) *Closing the application.* Close your running application by clicking its close box.

h) *Closing the IDE.* Close Visual Studio .NET by clicking its close box.

16.13 (*Lottery Picker Application*) A lottery commission offers four different lottery games to play: Three-number, Four-number, Five-number and Five-number + 1 lotteries. Each game has independent numbers. Develop an application that randomly picks numbers for all four games and displays the generated numbers in a GUI (Fig. 16.23). The games are played as follows:

- Three-number lotteries require players to choose three numbers in the range of 0–9.
- Four-number lotteries require players to choose four numbers, in the range of 0–9.
- Five-number lotteries require players to choose five numbers in the range of 1–39.
- Five-number + 1 lotteries require players to choose five numbers in the range of 1–49 and an additional number in the range of 1–42.

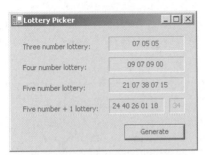

Figure 16.23   **Lottery Picker** application.

a) *Copying the template to your working directory.* Copy the directory C:\Examples\ Tutorial16\Exercises\LotteryPicker to your C:\SimplyCSP directory.

b) *Opening the application's template file.* Double click LotteryPicker.sln in the LotteryPicker directory to open the application.

c) *Generating random numbers.* Create a method that will generate the random numbers for all four games.

d) *Drawing numbers for the games.* Add code into your application to generate numbers for all four games. To make the applications simple, allow repetition of numbers.

e) *Running the application.* Select **Debug > Start** to run your application. Click the **Generate** Button multiple times. Make sure the values displayed are within the ranges described in the exercise description.

f) *Closing the application.* Close your running application by clicking its close box.

g) *Closing the IDE.* Close Visual Studio .NET by clicking its close box.

What does this code do? ▶   **16.14** What does this code do?

```
1   void PickRandomNumbers()
2   {
3      int intNumber1;
4      double dblNumber;
5      int intNumber2;
6      Random objRandom = new Random();
7
8      intNumber1 = objRandom.Next();
9      dblNumber = 5 * objRandom.NextDouble();
10     intNumber2 = objRandom.Next( 1, 10 );
11
12     lblInteger1.Text = Convert.ToString( intNumber1 );
13     lblDouble1.Text = Convert.ToString( dblNumber );
14     lblInteger2.Text = Convert.ToString( intNumber2 );
15
16   } // end method PickRandomNumbers
```

What's wrong with this code? ▶   **16.15** This method should assign a random decimal number (in the range 0 to `Int32.Max-Value`) to decimal decNumber. Find the error(s) in the following code.

```
1   void RandomDecimal()
2   {
3       decimal decNumber;
4       Random objRandom = new Random();
5
6       decNumber = objRandom.NextDouble();
7       lblDisplay.Text = Convert.ToString( decNumber );
8
9   } // end method RandomDecimal
```

Programming Challenge ▶   **16.16** (*Multiplication Teacher Application*)   Develop an application that helps children learn multiplication (Fig. 16.24). Use random-number generation to produce two positive one-digit integers that display in a question, such as "How much is 6 times 7?". The student should type the answer into a TextBox. If the answer is correct, then the application randomly displays one of three messages: "Very Good!", "Excellent!" or "Great Job!" in a Label and displays the next question. If the student is wrong, the Label displays the message "No. Please try again".

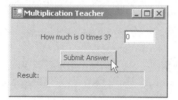 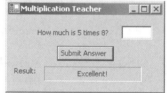

Figure 16.24   **Multiplication Teacher** application.

a) *Copying the template to your working directory.* Copy the directory `C:\Examples\Tutorial16\Exercises\MultiplicationTeacher` to your `C:\SimplyCSP` directory.

b) *Opening the application's template file.* Double click `MultiplicationTeacher.sln` in the `MultiplicationTeacher` directory to open the application.

c) *Generating the questions.* Add a method into your application to generate each new question.

d) *Determining whether the right answer was entered.* Add code into your application to call the method created in the previous step. After this method has been called, determine whether the student answered the question correctly, and display the appropriate message.

e) *Displaying a random message.* Add a method `GenerateOutput` that displays a random message congratulating the student for answering correctly. This method should be called if the student answered the question correctly.

f) *Running the application.* Select **Debug > Start** to run your application. Enter several correct answers and at least one incorrect answer. Verify that "No. Please try again" is displayed when you are incorrect, and one of the other responses is displayed at random when you are correct.

g) *Closing the application.* Close your running application by clicking its close box.

h) *Closing the IDE.* Close Visual Studio .NET by clicking its close box.

TUTORIAL 17

Objectives

In this tutorial, you will learn to:
- Create and initialize arrays.
- Store information in an array.
- Refer to individual elements of an array.
- Sort arrays.
- Use **ComboBox**es to display options in a drop-down list.
- Determine whether a specific character is in a `string`.
- Remove a character from a `string`.
- Convert a `string` to lowercase characters.

Outline

Flag Quiz Application

Introducing One-Dimensional Arrays and ComboBoxes

This tutorial introduces basic concepts and features of **data structures**. Data structures group together and organize related data. **Arrays** are data structures that consist of data items of the same type. You will learn how to create arrays and how to access the information that they contain. You also will learn how to sort a `string` array's information alphabetically.

This tutorial's **Flag Quiz** application also includes a `ComboBox` control. A `ComboBox` presents user options in a drop-down list. This will be the first time that you will add a `ComboBox` to an application, but you have used them many times before in the Visual Studio .NET environment. For example, you use a `ComboBox` to select the `TextAlign` property of a `Label`.

17.1 Test-Driving the Flag Quiz Application

You will now create an application that tests a student's knowledge of the flags of various countries. The application will use arrays to store information, such as the country names and `bool` values that determine if a country name has been previously selected by the application as a correct answer. This application must meet the following requirements:

Application Requirements

A geography teacher would like to quiz students on their knowledge of the flags of various countries. The teacher has asked you to write an application that displays a flag and allows the student to select the corresponding country from a list. The application should inform the user of whether the answer is correct and display the next flag. The application should display five flags randomly chosen from the flags of Australia, Brazil, China, Italy, Russia, South Africa, Spain and the United States. When the application is run, a given flag should be displayed only once.

You begin by test-driving the completed application. Then, you will learn the additional C# technologies you will need to create your own version of this application.

Test-Driving the Flag Quiz Application

1. ***Opening the completed application.*** Open the C:\Examples\Tutorial17\ CompletedApplication\FlagQuiz directory to locate the **Flag Quiz** application. Double click FlagQuiz.sln to open the application in Visual Studio .NET.

2. ***Running the Flag Quiz application.*** Select **Debug > Start** to run the application (Fig. 17.1). Note that you might see a different flag when you run the application, because the application randomly selects which flag to display.

PictureBox displays flag —————

————— ComboBox contains answers (country names)

Figure 17.1 **Flag Quiz** application's **Form**.

3. ***Selecting an answer.*** The ComboBox contains eight country names (we will discuss the ComboBox control shortly). One country name corresponds to the displayed flag and is the correct answer. The scrollbar allows you to browse through the ComboBox's drop-down list. Select an answer from the ComboBox, as shown in Fig. 17.2.

Answer being selected —————

————— Scrollbar in ComboBox's drop-down list

Figure 17.2 Selecting an answer from the ComboBox.

4. ***Submitting a correct answer.*** Click the **Submit** Button to check your answer. If it is correct, the message "Correct!" is displayed in an output Label (Fig. 17.3). Notice that the **Submit** Button is now disabled and that the **Next Flag** Button is enabled.

Figure 17.3 Submitting the correct answer.

5. ***Displaying the next flag.*** Click the **Next Flag** Button to display a different flag (Fig. 17.4). Notice that the **Submit** Button is now enabled, the **Next Flag** Button is disabled, the ComboBox displays **Australia** (the first country listed in the ComboBox) and the output Label is cleared.

Figure 17.4 Displaying the next flag.

(cont.)   6. ***Submitting an incorrect answer.*** To demonstrate the application's response, select an incorrect answer, then click **Submit** as in Fig. 17.5. The application displays "Sorry, incorrect." in the output Label.

Figure 17.5   Submitting an incorrect answer.

7. ***Finishing the quiz.*** After the application displays five flags and the user has submitted five answers, the quiz ends (Fig. 17.6). Notice that the two Buttons and the ComboBox are disabled.

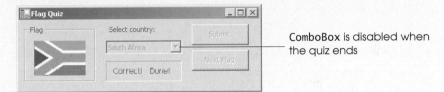

ComboBox is disabled when the quiz ends

Figure 17.6   Finishing the quiz.

8. ***Closing the application.*** Close your running application by clicking its close box.

9. ***Closing the IDE.*** Close Visual Studio .NET by clicking its close box.

17.2 Introducing Arrays

An array is a group of memory locations all containing data items of the same type. Array names follow the same conventions that apply to other identifiers. To refer to a particular location in an array, you specify the name of the array and the **position number** of the location, which is a value that indicates a specific location within an array. Position numbers begin at 0 (zero).

Figure 17.7 depicts an int array named intNetUnitsSold. This array contains 12 items, also called **elements**. Each array element represents the net number of "units sold" of a particular book in one month at a bookstore. For example, the value of element intNetUnitsSold[0] is the net sales of that book for January, the value of element intNetUnitsSold[1] is the net sales for February, etc.

Each array element is referred to by providing the name of the array followed by the position number of the element in square brackets ([]). The position numbers for the elements in an array begin with 0. Thus, the **zeroth element** of the intNetUnitsSold arrau is referred to as intNetUnitsSold[0], element 1 is referred to as intNetUnitsSold[1], element 6 is referred to as intNetUnitsSold[6] and so on. Element *i* of array intNetUnitsSold is referred to as intNetUnitsSold[i]. The position number in square brackets is called an **index** or a **subscript**. An index must be either zero, a positive integer or an integer expression that yields a positive result. If an application uses an expression as an index, the expression is evaluated first to determine the index. For example, if variable intValue1 is equal to 5, and variable intValue2 is equal to 6, then the statement

```
intNetUnitsSold[ intValue1 + intValue2 ] += 2;
```

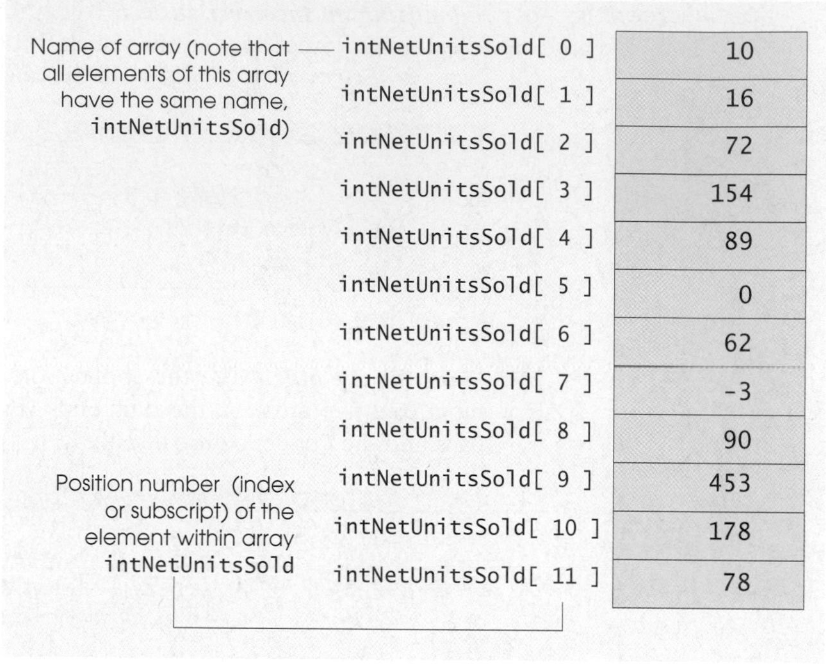

Name of array (note that — all elements of this array have the same name, intNetUnitsSold)	intNetUnitsSold[0]	10
	intNetUnitsSold[1]	16
	intNetUnitsSold[2]	72
	intNetUnitsSold[3]	154
	intNetUnitsSold[4]	89
	intNetUnitsSold[5]	0
	intNetUnitsSold[6]	62
	intNetUnitsSold[7]	-3
	intNetUnitsSold[8]	90
Position number (index or subscript) of the element within array intNetUnitsSold	intNetUnitsSold[9]	453
	intNetUnitsSold[10]	178
	intNetUnitsSold[11]	78

Figure 17.7 Array consisting of 12 elements.

adds 2 to array element intNetUnitsSold[11]. Note that an **indexed array name** (the array name followed by an index enclosed in parentheses)—like any other variable name—can be used on the left side of an assignment statement to place a new value into an array element.

Let's examine array intNetUnitsSold in Fig. 17.7 more closely. The name of the array is intNetUnitsSold. The 12 elements of the array are referred to with the names intNetUnitsSold[0] through intNetUnitsSold[11]. The value of intNetUnitsSold[0] is 10, the value of intNetUnitsSold[1] is 16, the value of intNetUnitsSold[2] is 72, the value of intNetUnitsSold[6] is 62 and the value of intNetUnitsSold[11] is 78. A positive value for an element in this array indicates that more books were sold than were returned. A negative value for an element in this array indicates that more books were returned than were sold. A value of zero indicates that the number of books sold was equal to the number of books returned.

Values stored in arrays can be used in various calculations and applications. For example, to determine the net units sold in the first three months of the year and store the result in variable intFirstQuarterUnits, we would write

```
intFirstQuarterUnits = intNetUnitsSold[ 0 ] + intNetUnitsSold[ 1 ] +
    intNetUnitsSold[ 2 ];
```

You will deal exclusively with **one-dimensional** arrays, such as intNetUnits-Sold, in this tutorial. The indexed array names of one-dimensional arrays use only one index. In the next tutorial, you will study two-dimensional arrays; their indexed array names use two indices.

SELF-REVIEW

1. The number that refers to a particular element of an array is called its _____.

    a) value   b) size

    c) indexed array name   d) index (or subscript)

2. The indexed array name of one-dimensional array decUnits's element 2 is _____.

    a) decUnits{ 2 }   b) decUnits[2]

    c) decUnits[0, 2]   d) decUnits(2)

Answers: 1) d. 2) b.

17.3 Declaring and Allocating Arrays

To declare an array, you provide the array's name and type. The following statement declares the array in Fig. 17.7:

```
int[] intNetUnitsSold;
```

The square brackets that follow the type indicate that `intNetUnitsSold` is an array. Arrays can be declared to contain any type. In an array of built-in types, every element of the array contains one value of the declared type. For example, every element of an `int` array contains an `int` value.

Before you can use an array, you must specify the size of the array and allocate memory for the array, using the `new` operator. Recall from Tutorial 16 that the `new` operator can be used to create an object. Arrays are represented as objects in C#, so they, too, must be allocated by using the `new` operator. The value stored in the array variable is actually a reference to the array object. To allocate memory for the array `intNetUnitsSold` after it has been declared, the statement

```
intNetUnitsSold = new int[ 13 ];
```

> **Common Programming Error**
>
> Attempting to access elements in the array by using an index outside the array bounds is a run-time error.

is used. **Array bounds** determine what indices can be used to access an element in the array. Here, the array bounds are 0 (which is implicit in the preceding statement) and 12 (one less than the number of elements in the array). Notice that the actual number of elements in the array (13) is specified in the allocation.

Arrays can be allocated in another way, illustrated by the following example:

```
int[] intSalesPerDay;
intSalesPerDay = { 0, 2, 3, 6, 1, 4, 5, 6 };
```

The braces (`{` and `}`) are called an **initializer list** and specify the initial values of the elements in the array. The initializer list contains a comma-separated list specifying the initial values of the elements in the array. The preceding example declares and allocates an array containing eight `int` values. C# can determine the array bounds from the number of elements in the initializer list. Thus, it is not necessary to specify the size of the array when an initializer list is present. Note that this type of declaration also does not require the `new` operator to create the array object; the compiler allocates memory for the object when it encounters an array declaration that includes an initializer list. An initializer list can be empty, in which case the array size would be 0.

When there is no initializer list (in other words, the `new` operator is used), the elements in the array are initialized to the default value for the array's type. These default values are 0 for numeric, built-in type variables (such as `int`), `false` for `bool` variables and `null` for references. Recall that keyword `null` denotes an empty reference (that is, a value indicating that a reference variable has not been assigned an object).

Often, the elements of an array are used in a calculation. The following box demonstrates declaring and initializing an array and accessing the array's elements.

Computing the Sum of an Array's Elements

1. **Copying the template to your working directory.** Copy the `C:\Examples\Tutorial17\TemplateApplication\SumArray` directory to your `C:\SimplyCSP` directory.

2. **Opening the Sum Array application's template file.** Double click `SumArray.sln` in the `SumArray` directory to open the application in Visual Studio .NET (Fig. 17.8).

3. **Adding the Sum Array Button's Click event handler.** Double click the **Sum Array** Button in design view to generate the empty event handler `btnSum_Click`.

(cont.)

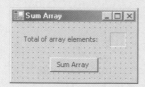

Figure 17.8 **Sum Array** application's **Form** in design view.

4. ***Combining the declaration and allocation of an array.*** Be sure to add the comments and break the header as shown in Fig. 17.9 so that the line numbers in your code match those presented in this tutorial. Then, add lines 120–124 of Fig. 17.9 to the event handler. Line 121 combines the declaration and allocation of an array into one statement.

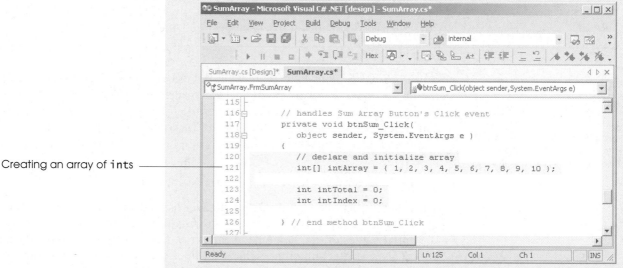

Creating an array of **ints**

Figure 17.9 Declaring an array in the event handler.

5. ***Calculating the sum.*** Add lines 126–135 (Fig. 17.10) to the event handler. The **for** loop (lines 127–132) retrieves each element's value (one at a time), which is added to **intTotal**. Line 135 displays the sum of the values of the array's elements.

Method **GetUpperBound** (line 128) returns the index of the last element in the array. Method **GetUpperBound** takes one argument, indicating a dimension of the array. We discuss arrays with two dimensions in Tutorial 18. For one-dimensional arrays, such as **intArray**, the argument passed to **GetUpperBound** is always 0, to indicate the first (and only) dimension (or row) of the array. In this case,

```
intArray.GetUpperBound( 0 )
```

returns 9.

Every array in C# "knows" its own length. The length (or the number of elements) of the array (10 in this case) is returned by the following expression:

```
intArray.Length
```

We could have set the upper bound in the **for** loop as

```
intArray.Length - 1
```

which returns 9. The value returned by method **GetUpperBound** is one less than the value of the array's **Length** property.

Error-Prevention Tip

Use method **GetUpperBound** when you need to find the largest index in an array. Using an actual numerical value for the upper bound instead could lead to errors if you change the number of array elements.

(cont.)

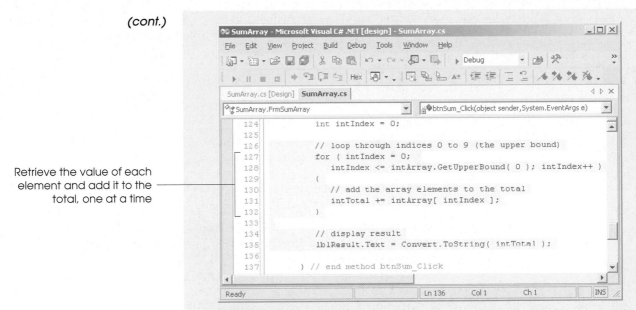

Retrieve the value of each element and add it to the total, one at a time

Figure 17.10 Calculating the sum of the values of an array's elements.

6. ***Running the application.*** Select **Debug > Start** to run your application. The result of adding the integers from 1 to 10, inclusive, is displayed (Fig. 17.11).

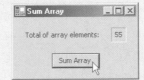

Figure 17.11 Displaying the sum of the values of an array's elements.

7. ***Closing the application.*** Close your running application by clicking its close box.

8. ***Closing the IDE.*** Close Visual Studio .NET by clicking its close box.

SELF-REVIEW

1. Arrays can be allocated using the _____ operator.
   a) declare
   b) create
   c) new
   d) allocate

2. An array's length is _____.
   a) one more than the array's last index
   b) one less than the array's last index
   c) the same as the array's last index
   d) returned by method GetUpperBound

Answers: 1) c. 2) a.

17.4 Constructing the Flag Quiz Application

Before you can begin building the **Flag Quiz** application, you will need to develop the application, using pseudocode and an ACE table. The following pseudocode describes the basic operation of the **Flag Quiz** application:

When the Form loads:
    Sort the country names alphabetically
    Place country names in the ComboBox
    Randomly select a flag
    Display the flag

When the user clicks the Submit Button:
    Retrieve the selected country name from the ComboBox

    If the selected value matches the correct answer
        Display "Correct!" in the Label
    Else
        Display "Sorry, incorrect." in the Label

    If five images have been displayed
        Append "Done!" to the Label's text
        Disable the Buttons and ComboBox
    Else
        Disable Submit Button
        Enable Next Flag Button

When the user clicks the Next Flag Button:
    Randomly select a flag that has not been chosen previously
    Display the new flag
    Clear the Label's text
    Set ComboBox to display its first item
    Update the number of flags shown
    Enable Submit Button
    Disable Next Flag Button

Now that you have test-driven the **Flag Quiz** application and studied its pseudocode representation, you will use an ACE table to help you convert the pseudocode to C#. Figure 17.12 lists the actions, controls and events that will help you complete your own version of this application.

Action/Control/Event (ACE) Table for the Flag Quiz Application

Action	Control/Class/Object	Event
Label the application's controls	`fraFlagGroupBox`, `lblChoose`	Application is run
	`FrmFlagQuiz`	Load
Sort the countries alphabetically	`Array`	
Place countries in the ComboBox	`cboOptions`	
Randomly select a flag	`objRandom`	
Display the flag	`picFlag`	
	`btnSubmit`	Click
Retrieve the selected country	`cboOptions`	
If selected value matches the correct answer Display "Correct!" in the Label	`lblFeedback`	
Else Display "Sorry, incorrect." in Label	`lblFeedback`	
If five images have been displayed Append "Done!" to Label's text	`lblFeedback`	
Disable the Buttons and ComboBox	`btnNext`, `btnSubmit`, `cboOptions`	
Else Disable Submit Button	`btnSubmit`	
Enable Next Flag Button	`btnNext`	

Figure 17.12 **Flag Quiz** application's ACE table. (Part 1 of 2.)

Action	Control/Class/Object	Event
	btnNext	Click
Randomly select a flag that has not been chosen previously	objRandom	
Display the new flag	picFlag	
Clear the Label's text	lblFeedback	
Set ComboBox to display first item	cboOptions	
Update the number of flags shown		
Enable Submit Button	btnSubmit	
Disable Next Flag Button	btnNext	

Figure 17.12 **Flag Quiz** application's ACE table. (Part 2 of 2.)

The following box shows you how to initialize the variables used in the application. In particular, the application requires two one-dimensional arrays.

Initializing Important Variables

1. ***Copying the template to your working directory.*** Copy the C:\Examples\ Tutorial17\TemplateApplication\FlagQuiz directory to your C:\ SimplyCSP directory.

2. ***Opening the Flag Quiz application's template file.*** Double click FlagQuiz.sln in the FlagQuiz directory to open the application in Visual Studio .NET.

3. ***Declaring the array of country names.*** Add lines 34–37 of Fig. 17.13 to the application. Lines 35–37 declare and initialize array m_strOptions. Each element is a string containing the name of a country. These lines assign the initializer list to the array, combining the declaration and initialization into one statement. The compiler allocates the size of the array (in this case, eight elements) to suit the number of items in the initializer list. Indent your code as shown in Fig. 17.13.

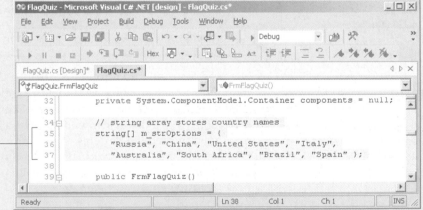

Creating an array of strings to store country names

Figure 17.13 string array that stores country names.

4. ***Declaring a bool array.*** The application should not display any flag more than once. The application uses random-number generation to pick a flag, so the same flag could be selected more than once—just as, when you roll a six-sided die many times, a die face could be repeated. You will use a bool array to keep track of which flags have been displayed. Add lines 39–40 of Fig. 17.14 to your code. Line 40 declares bool array m_blnUsed. You will initialize m_blnUsed shortly.

(cont.)

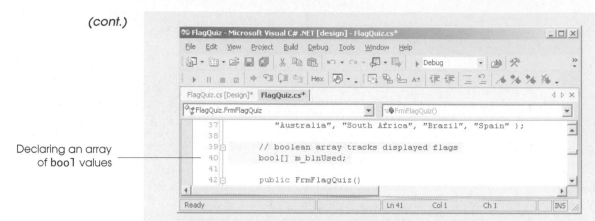

Declaring an array of **bool** values

Figure 17.14 **bool** array that keeps track of displayed flags.

5. *Initializing a counter and a variable to store the answer.* Add lines 42–44 of Fig. 17.15 to **FlagQuiz.cs**. The application ensures that only five flags are displayed by incrementing counter **m_intCount**, which is initialized to 1 (line 43). The correct answer (the name of the country whose flag is displayed) will be stored in **m_strCountry** (line 44).

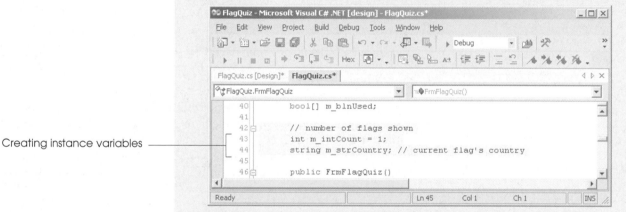

Creating instance variables

Figure 17.15 Instance variables, used throughout the application.

6. *Saving the project.* Select **File > Save All** to save your modified code.

GUI Design Tip

Each **ComboBox** should have a descriptive **Label** that describes the **ComboBox**'s contents.

Now you will add another control to the **Flag Quiz** application template. The **Flag Quiz** application allows students to select answers from a ComboBox. The **ComboBox** control combines a TextBox and a ListBox. A ComboBox usually appears as a TextBox with a down arrow to its right. The user can click the down arrow to display a list of predefined items. If a user chooses an item from this list, that item is displayed in the ComboBox. If the list contains more items than the drop-down list can display at one time, a vertical scrollbar appears. The following box shows you how to assign an array's elements to a ComboBox before the Form is displayed to users.

Adding and Customizing a ComboBox

1. *Adding a ComboBox to the Form.* Click the **FlagQuiz.cs [Design]** tab to display the application's Form (Fig. 17.16). Add a ComboBox to the Form by double clicking the

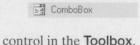

control in the **Toolbox**.

(cont.)

Figure 17.16   **Flag Quiz** template application's Form.

2. ***Customizing the ComboBox.*** Change the Name property of the ComboBox to cboOptions. Clear the ComboBox's Text property, and set the Location property to 136, 32. Leave the Size property at its default setting, 121, 21. The Form should look like Fig. 17.17.

Figure 17.17   ComboBox added to **Flag Quiz** application's Form.

Good Programming Practice

Prefix ComboBox control names with cbo.

GUI Design Tip

If a ComboBox's content should not be editable, set its DropDownStyle property to DropDownList.

3. ***Setting the appearance of ComboBox.*** Property **DropDownStyle** determines the ComboBox's appearance. Value **DropDownList** specifies that the ComboBox is not editable (the user cannot type text in its TextBox portion). You can click the arrow button to display a drop-down list from which you can select an item. In this style of ComboBox, if you press the key that corresponds to the first letter of an item in the ComboBox, that item is selected and displayed in the ComboBox's TextBox portion. Set the DropDownStyle property of the ComboBox to DropDownList. Finally, set the **MaxDropDownItems** property of cboOptions to 4, so that the drop-down list can display a maximum of four items at one time. A vertical scrollbar will be added to the drop-down list, to allow users to select the remaining items.

4. ***Rearranging and commenting the new control declaration.*** In code view, move the declaration for the cboOptions ComboBox from line 44 of your code to line 21 of Fig. 17.18. Modify the comment in line 19 as shown in Fig. 17.18.

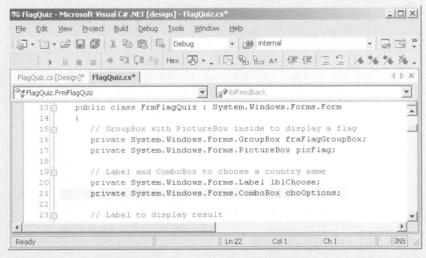

Figure 17.18   Rearranging and commenting the new control declaration.

(cont.)

5. ***Generating a Form Load event handler.*** The ComboBox should contain a list of country names when the Form is displayed. The Form's Load event occurs before the Form is displayed; as a result, you should add the items to the ComboBox in the Form's Load event handler. Double click the Form to generate the empty event handler FrmFlagQuiz_Load. Be sure to add the comments and break the header as shown in Fig. 17.19 so that the line numbers in your code match those presented in this tutorial.

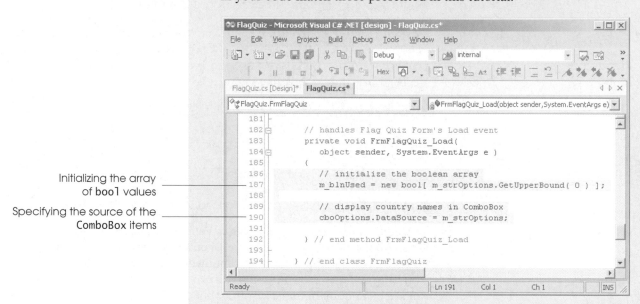

Initializing the array
of **bool** values

Specifying the source of the
ComboBox items

Figure 17.19 Assigning the **string** elements of an array to a **ComboBox**.

6. ***Initializing the bool array.*** Add lines 186–187 of Fig. 17.19 to FrmFlagQuiz_Load. Method GetUpperBound in line 187 returns array m_strOptions's largest index, which is used as the upper bound of m_blnUsed. Therefore, array m_blnUsed has the same size as m_strOptions. The elements of m_blnUsed correspond to the elements of m_strOptions; for example, m_blnUsed[0] specifies whether the flag corresponding to the country name of m_strOptions[0] (Russia) has been displayed. Recall that, by default, each uninitialized element in a bool array is false. The application will set an element of m_blnUsed to true if its corresponding flag has been displayed.

7. ***Displaying items in the ComboBox.*** Add lines 189–190 of Fig. 17.19 to the FrmFlagQuiz_Load method. ComboBox property **DataSource** specifies the source of the items displayed in the ComboBox. In this case, the source is array m_strOptions (discussed shortly).

8. ***Saving the project.*** Select **File > Save All** to save your modified code.

Recall that, to specify the image displayed in a PictureBox, you need to set its Image property to the image's file name. The flag images are stored in C:\SimplyCSP\FlagQuiz\bin\Debug\images. The name of each flag-image file is of the form *countryname*.png, where *countryname* has no white space. The following box shows how the application constructs the full path name needed to locate and display each flag.

Building a Flag-Image File's Path Name

1. *Creating a method to build the flag-image file's path name.* Add lines 194–198 of Fig. 17.20 to the **Flag Quiz** application after the FrmFlagQuiz_Load event handler. Method BuildPathName constructs a full path name for a flag-image file, beginning with the country name. The country name is retrieved from instance variable m_strCountry (the correct answer) and stored in local variable strOutput.

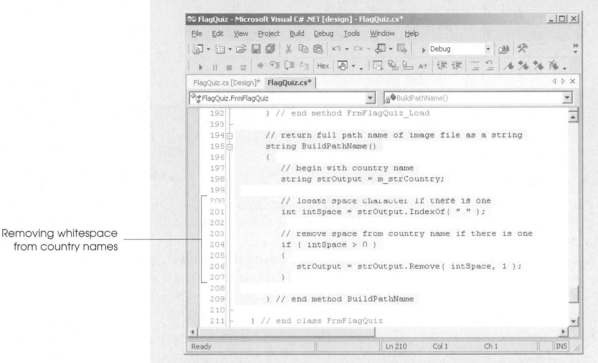

Removing whitespace from country names

Figure 17.20　Removing whitespace from the country name.

2. *Removing whitespace from the country name.* Some countries—for example, South Africa and the United States—have a space character in their names, but the flag-image file names do not allow whitespace characters. Add lines 200–209 of Fig. 17.20 to method BuildPathName. Line 201 uses String method **IndexOf** to assign to intSpace the index where the space character (" ") in the country name occurs. For instance, if strOutput were "South Africa", intSpace would be 5, because the space appears at index 5 of the name, counting from position zero. If the country does not have a space character, method IndexOf returns –1. Line 204 tests for whether intSpace is a positive number. In this application, method IndexOf returns a number greater than 0 if the country name is "South Africa" or "United States."

If a space is found, the **Remove** method is called to eliminate the space character (line 206). Method Remove receives an index as its first argument and the number of characters to remove as its second argument. For example, the words "South Africa" would become the word "SouthAfrica". Method Remove returns a copy of the string without the space character. The copy is assigned to variable strOutput. [*Note*: String methods, such as Remove, do not modify the string object for which they are called. The string object returned by these methods contains a modified copy of the string.]

3. *Ensuring that all characters are lowercase.* Add line 209 of Fig. 17.21 to method BuildPathName. Now that strOutput contains a country name without whitespace, line 209 invokes method **ToLower**, which returns a copy of the string with any uppercase letters in the name converted to lowercase. All the flag-image file names are in lowercase, for consistency.

(cont.)

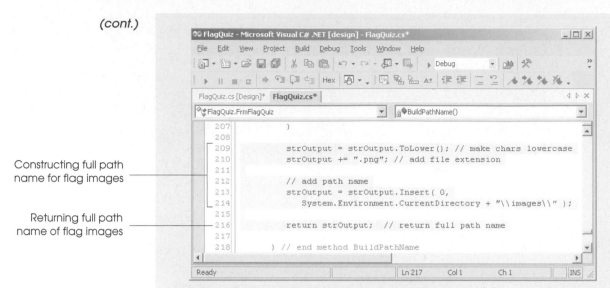

Figure 17.21   Building the flag-image file path name.

4. ***Adding the file extension.*** Add line 210 of Fig. 17.21 to method `Build-PathName`. The flag-image files are in PNG format. Line 210 appends the file extension `".png"` to `strOutput`.

5. ***Adding the fully qualified path name.*** Add lines 212–214 of Fig. 17.21 to method `BuildPathName`. The flag image files are stored in an `images` directory in the directory containing the application's executable. The `Current-Directory` property of class `System.Environment` (line 214) returns the directory from which the application executes as a fully qualified path name (for example, `C:\SimplyCSP\FlagQuiz\bin\Debug`). Method **Insert** combines this path name and `\images\` with *countryname*`.png`. Backslash (\) is an escape character, so the double backslash (\\) escape sequence is needed to insert a single backslash into the `string`. The first argument to `Insert` specifies at what index the `string` will be added, and the second argument is the `string` to insert. Method `Insert` returns a copy of the `string` with the inserted characters. This copy is assigned to `strOutput`.

6. ***Returning the full path name.*** Add line 216 of Fig. 17.21 to method `Build-PathName`. Line 216 returns the fully qualified path name of the specified country's flag image file.

7. ***Saving the project.*** Select **File > Save All** to save your modified code.

To ensure that the user is not asked the same question twice, a flag must be displayed no more than once when running the application. The application uses `bool` array `m_blnUsed` to track which flags have been displayed. The following box shows you how to ensure that the application displays a flag no more than once each time the application is run.

Selecting a Unique Flag to Display

1. ***Creating the GetUniqueRandomNumber method.*** Add lines 220–221 of Fig. 17.22 to the **Flag Quiz** application after method `BuildPathName`. Line 221 is the header for the `GetUniqueRandomNumber` method. `Get-UniqueRandomNumber` returns the index of a country name whose flag has not been displayed.

2. ***Generating a random index.*** Add line 223 of Fig. 17.22 to the method `GetUniqueRandomNumber`. To select the next flag to display, you create a reference, `objRandom` (line 223), to a Random object.

(cont.)

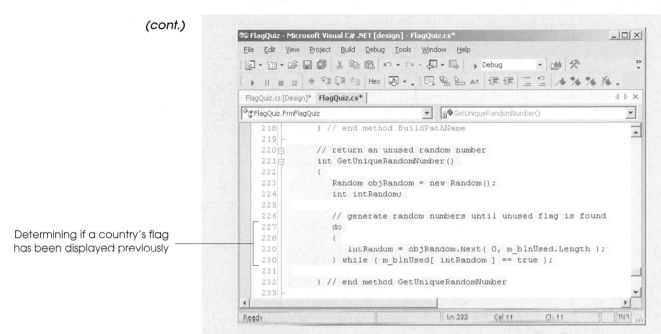

Determining if a country's flag
has been displayed previously

Figure 17.22   Generating a unique index.

3. ***Ensuring that each flag displays only once.*** Add lines 224–232 of Fig. 17.22 to `GetUniqueRandomNumber`. Method `Next` (line 229) of class `Random` generates a random index between `0` and `m_blnUsed.Length` (the number of country names). If the index has been selected previously, the element of `m_blnUsed` at the generated index is `true`. The do…while statement (lines 227–230) iterates until it finds a unique index (that is, until `m_blnUsed[ intRandom ]` is `false`).

4. ***Indicating that the index has been used.*** Add lines 232–233 of Fig. 17.23 to the `GetUniqueRandomNumber` method. Line 233 sets the element at the selected index of `m_blnUsed` to `true`. This indicates that the flag has been used. Checking the values in this array ensures that the index will not be used again in the application.

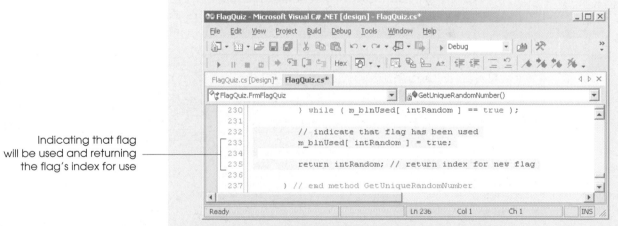

Indicating that flag
will be used and returning
the flag's index for use

Figure 17.23   Returning the unique index.

5. ***Returning the unique random number.*** Add line 235 of Fig. 17.23 to the `GetUniqueRandomNumber` method. Line 235 returns the unique random index.

6. ***Saving the project.*** Select **File > Save All** to save your modified code.

With the full path name and a unique flag selected, the application can display that flag. The following box shows how to display the selected flag.

Displaying a Flag

1. **Creating the *DisplayFlag* method.** Add lines 239–241 of Fig. 17.24 to the **Flag Quiz** application after method GetUniqueRandomNumber. Method DisplayFlag selects a random country name and displays that country's flag.

Getting index of unused flag ———

Retrieving the flag's corresponding country name ———

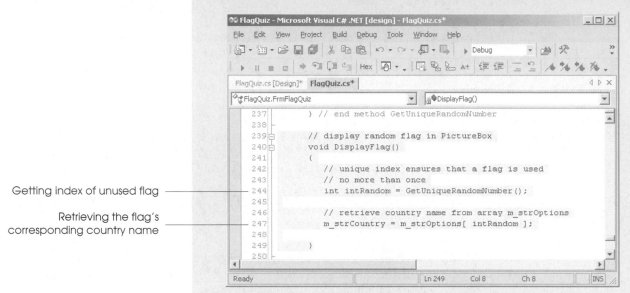

Figure 17.24 Choosing a random country name.

2. **Obtaining a unique index.** Add lines 242–244 of Fig. 17.24 to the DisplayFlag method. Line 244 invokes GetUniqueRandomNumber to find an index of a flag that has not been displayed during the application's execution and assigns it to intRandom.

3. **Retrieving a country name.** Add lines 246–249 of Fig. 17.24 to the DisplayFlag method. Line 247 assigns to m_strCountry the flag's corresponding country name at index intRandom of string array m_strOptions.

4. **Building the flag image's path name.** Add lines 249–250 of Fig. 17.25 to the DisplayFlag method. Line 250 invokes method BuildPathName. The method returns the flag image's path name, which is assigned to strPath.

Getting the path name of the flag and displaying the flag image ———

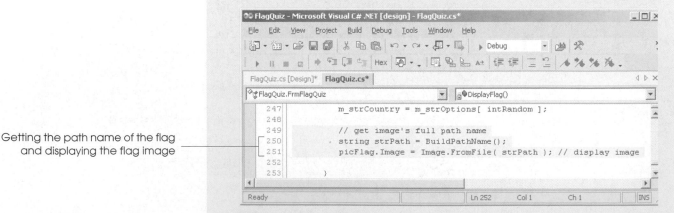

Figure 17.25 Displaying a flag image.

5. **Displaying the flag image.** Add line 251 of Fig. 17.25 to the DisplayFlag method. Line 251 sets PictureBox picFlag's Image property to the Image object returned by method Image.FromFile. Method Image.FromFile returns an Image object from the specified file.

(cont.)   6. ***Displaying a flag when the application is run.*** When the Form loads, the first flag image in the quiz is displayed. The Form Load event handler should invoke method DisplayFlag. Add line 192 of Fig. 17.26 to event handler FrmFlagQuiz_Load.

Displaying a flag when application is first run

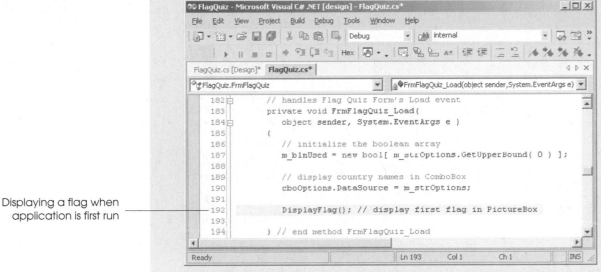

Figure 17.26   Displaying a flag when the Form is loaded.

7. ***Saving the project.*** Select **File > Save All** to save your modified code.

The user submits an answer by selecting a country name from the ComboBox, then clicking the **Submit** Button. The application displays whether the user's answer is correct. If the application is finished (that is, five flags have been displayed), the application informs the user that the quiz is done; otherwise, the application enables the user to view the next flag. The following box implements this functionality.

Processing a User's Answer

1. ***Adding the Submit Button's Click event handler.*** Return to design view and double click the **Submit** Button to generate the Click event handler btnSubmit_Click.

2. ***Retrieving the selected ComboBox item.*** Be sure to add the comments and break the header as shown in Fig. 17.27 so that the line numbers in your code match those presented in this tutorial (in addition, add the comment on line 256 to method DisplayFlag). Add lines 262–264 of Fig. 17.27 to the empty event handler. Lines 263–264 retrieve the user's answer, convert it to a string and assign it to strResponse. Property **SelectedValue** returns the value of the ComboBox's selected item. Method Convert.ToString converts the selected item to a string. Variable strResponse contains the selected country's name.

3. ***Verifying the user's answer.*** Add lines 266–274 of Fig. 17.27 to btnSubmit_Click. The if...else statement (lines 267–274) determines whether the user's response matches the correct answer. Line 269 displays "Correct!" in the Label if the user's response matches the correct answer. Otherwise, line 273 displays "Sorry, incorrect.".

4. ***Informing the user the quiz is over when five flags have been displayed.*** Add lines 276–288 of Fig. 17.28 to the btnSubmit_Click event handler. If five flags have been displayed (lines 277–278), the Label displays text informing the user that the quiz is over, and both Buttons are disabled. The ComboBox is also disabled, by setting its Enabled property to false.

(cont.)

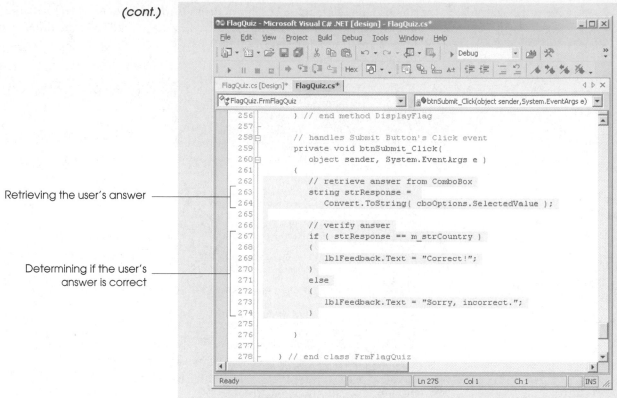

Retrieving the user's answer

Determining if the user's
answer is correct

Figure 17.27 Submit `Button` `Click` event handler.

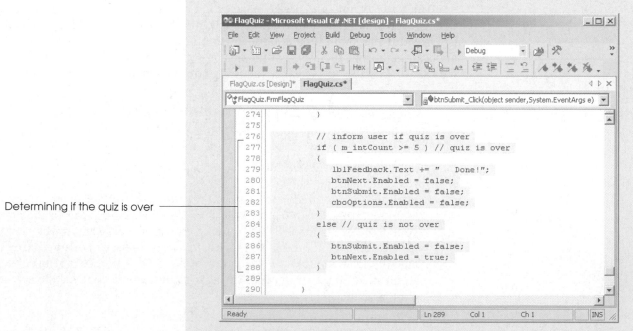

Determining if the quiz is over

Figure 17.28 Testing whether the quiz is finished.

5. ***Continuing the quiz while fewer than five flags have been shown.*** If the quiz is not finished (that is, m_intCount is less than 5), the application disables the **Submit** Button and enables the **Next Flag** Button (lines 286–287). The functionality of the **Next Flag** Button will be discussed shortly.

6. ***Saving the project.*** Select **File > Save All** to save your modified code.

The user requests the next flag in the quiz by clicking the **Next Flag** Button. The application then displays the next flag and increments the number of flags shown.

Displaying the Next Flag

1. *Adding the Next Flag Button's* `Click` *event handler to the application.* Return to design view and double click the **Next Flag** Button to generate the `Click` event handler `btnNext_Click`. Be sure to add the comments and break the header as shown in Fig. 17.29 so that the line numbers in your code match those presented in this tutorial. In addition, add the comment on line 291 to method `btnSubmit_Click`.

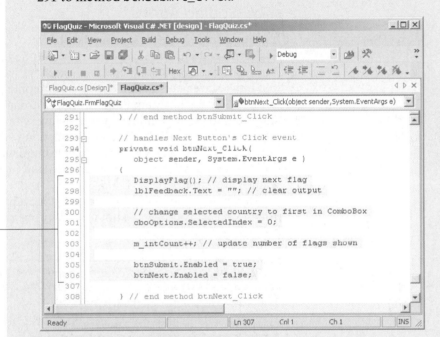

Displaying the next flag for the user to identify

Figure 17.29   Next Flag Button `Click` event handler.

2. *Displaying the next flag.* Add line 297 of Fig. 17.29 to the empty event handler. This line calls method `DisplayFlag` to place the next flag in the `PictureBox`.

3. *Clearing the previous results.* Add line 298 of Fig. 17.29 to `btnNext_Click` to clear the output `Label`, deleting the results of the previous question.

4. *Resetting the ComboBox.* Add lines 300–301 of Fig. 17.29 to `btnNext_Click`. Line 301 sets property **SelectedIndex** of ComboBox `cboOptions` to 0, the first item in the ComboBox's drop-down list.

5. *Updating the number of flags shown.* Add line 303 of Fig. 17.29 to `btnNext_Click` to update `m_intCount` to indicate that one more flag has been shown.

6. *Enabling the Submit Button and disabling the Next Flag Button.* Add lines 305–306 of Fig. 17.29 to `btnNext_Click`. Line 305 enables the **Submit** Button; line 306 disables the **Next Flag** Button. This is a visual reminder to the user that an answer must be submitted before another flag can be displayed.

7. *Saving the project.* Select **File > Save All** to save your modified code.

SELF-REVIEW 1. Property _____ specifies the source of the data displayed in the ComboBox.

    a) `ComboData`   b) `Source`

    c) `DataList`   d) `DataSource`

2. ComboBox property _____ is 0 when the first ComboBox item is selected.

    a) `SelectedIndex`   b) `SelectedValue`

    c) `Index`   d) `SelectedNumber`

Answers: 1) d. 2) a.

17.5 Sorting Arrays

Sorting data refers to arranging the data into some particular order, such as ascending or descending order. Sorting is one of the most popular computing capabilities. For example, a bank sorts checks by account number, so that it can prepare individual bank statements at the end of each month. Telephone companies sort account information by last name and, within last-name listings, by first name, to make it easy to find phone numbers. Virtually every organization must sort some data, and often, massive amounts of it. In this section, you learn how to sort the values in an array so that you can alphabetize the list of countries in the **Flag Quiz** application.

Users are able to find a country name in the ComboBox faster if the country names are alphabetized. [*Note*: Class ComboBox contains property `Sorted`, which, when set to `true`, sorts the items in the ComboBox alphabetically. This tutorial focuses on arrays, so we do not use this property.] The following box shows you how to sort an array.

Sorting an Array

   1.   ***Sorting the array of country names.*** Add line 191 of Fig. 17.30 to event handler `FrmFlagQuiz_Load`. Line 191 passes array `m_strOptions` to method **`Array.Sort`**, which sorts the values in the array into ascending alphabetical order. Note that this line is placed prior to the assigning of `m_strOptions` to property `DataSource`, so that the items in the ComboBox are displayed in alphabetical order.

Alphabetizing country names in the array

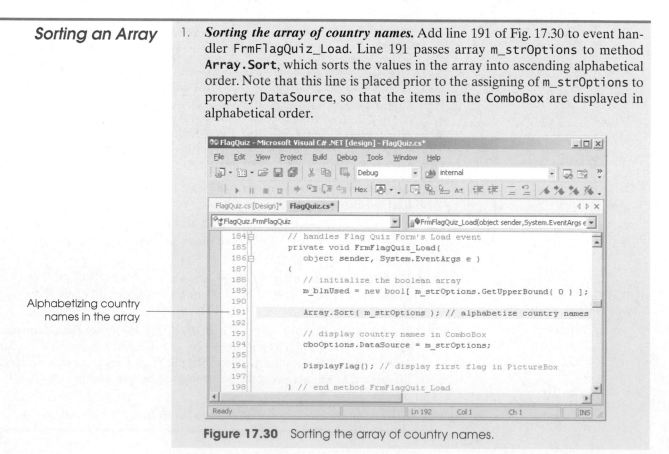

Figure 17.30   Sorting the array of country names.

(cont.) 2. **_Running the application._** Select **Debug > Start** to run your application. The country names should now be alphabetized. Enter different answers and make sure that the proper message is displayed based on whether the answer is correct. Make sure that after 5 answers have been entered, the text "Done!" is appended to the current message displayed.

3. **_Closing the application._** Close your running application by clicking its close box.

4. **_Closing the IDE._** Close Visual Studio .NET by clicking its close box.

Figure 17.31 presents the source code for the **Flag Quiz** application. The lines of code that contain new programming concepts that you learned in this tutorial are highlighted.

```
1    using System;
2    using System.Drawing;
3    using System.Collections;
4    using System.ComponentModel;
5    using System.Windows.Forms;
6    using System.Data;
7
8    namespace FlagQuiz
9    {
10      /// <summary>
11      /// Summary description for FrmFlagQuiz.
12      /// </summary>
13      public class FrmFlagQuiz : System.Windows.Forms.Form
14      {
15         // GroupBox with PictureBox inside to display a flag
16         private System.Windows.Forms.GroupBox fraFlagGroupBox;
17         private System.Windows.Forms.PictureBox picFlag;
18
19         // Label and ComboBox to choose a country name
20         private System.Windows.Forms.Label lblChoose;
21         private System.Windows.Forms.ComboBox cboOptions;
22
23         // Label to display result
24         private System.Windows.Forms.Label lblFeedback;
25
26         // Buttons to submit an answer and move to the next flag
27         private System.Windows.Forms.Button btnSubmit;
28         private System.Windows.Forms.Button btnNext;
29
30         /// <summary>
31         /// Required designer variable.
32         /// </summary>
33         private System.ComponentModel.Container components = null;
34
35         // string array stores country names
36         string[] m_strOptions = {
37            "Russia", "China", "United States", "Italy",
38            "Australia", "South Africa", "Brazil", "Spain" };
39
40         // boolean array tracks displayed flags
41         bool[] m_blnUsed;
42
```

Declaring and creating an array with an initializer list — (lines 36–38)

Declaring an array — (line 41)

Figure 17.31 **Flag Quiz** application code. (Part 1 of 4.)

```
43        // number of flags shown
44        int m_intCount = 1;
45        string m_strCountry; // current flag's country
46
47        public FrmFlagQuiz()
48        {
49           //
50           // Required for Windows Form Designer support
51           //
52           InitializeComponent();
53
54           //
55           // TODO: Add any constructor code after InitializeComponent
56           // call
57           //
58        }
59
60        /// <summary>
61        /// Clean up any resources being used.
62        /// </summary>
63        protected override void Dispose( bool disposing )
64        {
65           if( disposing )
66           {
67              if (components != null)
68              {
69                 components.Dispose();
70              }
71           }
72           base.Dispose( disposing );
73        }
74
75        // Windows Form Designer generated code
76
77        /// <summary>
78        /// The main entry point for the application.
79        /// </summary>
80        [STAThread]
81        static void Main()
82        {
83           Application.Run( new FrmFlagQuiz() );
84        }
85
86        // handles Flag Quiz Form's Load event
87        private void FrmFlagQuiz_Load(
88           object sender, System.EventArgs e )
89        {
90           // initialize the boolean array
91           m_blnUsed = new bool[ m_strOptions.GetUpperBound( 0 ) ];
92
93           Array.Sort( m_strOptions ); // alphabetize country names
94
95           // display country names in ComboBox
96           cboOptions.DataSource = m_strOptions;
97
98           DisplayFlag(); // display first flag in PictureBox
99
100       } // end method FrmFlagQuiz_Load
```

Creating a **bool** array with the **new** operator — *(line 91)*

Sorting an array — *(line 93)*

Displaying array elements in a ComboBox — *(line 96)*

Figure 17.31 Flag Quiz application code. (Part 2 of 4.)

```
101
102        // return full path name of image file as a string
103        string BuildPathName()
104        {
105           // begin with country name
106           string strOutput = m_strCountry;
107
108           // locate space character if there is one
109           int intSpace = strOutput.IndexOf( " " );
110
111           // remove space from country name if there is one
112           if ( intSpace > 0 )
113           {
114              strOutput = strOutput.Remove( intSpace, 1 );
115           }
116
117           strOutput = strOutput.ToLower(); // make chars lowercase
118           strOutput += ".png"; // add file extension
119
120           // add path name
121           strOutput = strOutput.Insert( 0,
122              System.Environment.CurrentDirectory + "\\images\\" );
123
124           return strOutput;   // return full path name
125
126        } // end method BuildPathName
127
128        // return an unused random number
129        int GetUniqueRandomNumber()
130        {
131           Random objRandom = new Random();
132           int intRandom;
133
134           // generate random numbers until unused flag is found
135           do
136           {
137              intRandom = objRandom.Next( 0, m_blnUsed.Length );
138           } while ( m_blnUsed[ intRandom ] == true );
139
140           // indicate that flag has been used
141           m_blnUsed[ intRandom ] = true;
142
143           return intRandom; // return index for new flag
144
145        } // end method GetUniqueRandomNumber
146
147        // display random flag in PictureBox
148        void DisplayFlag()
149        {
150           // unique index ensures that a flag is used
151           // no more than once
152           int intRandom = GetUniqueRandomNumber();
153
154           // retrieve country name from array m_strOptions
155           m_strCountry = m_strOptions[ intRandom ];
156
157           // get image's full path name
158           string strPath = BuildPathName();
```

Locating a space character in a **string** — 109

Removing a character from a **string** — 114

Converting a **string** to — 117

Inserting characters into a **string** — 121–122

Assigning a value to an array element — 141

Retrieving a value from an array — 155

Figure 17.31   Flag Quiz application code. (Part 3 of 4.)

```
159              picFlag.Image = Image.FromFile( strPath ); // display image
160
161          } // end method Display Flag
162
163          // handles Submit Button's Click event
164          private void btnSubmit_Click(
165              object sender, System.EventArgs e )
166          {
167              // retrieve answer from ComboBox
168              string strResponse =
169                  Convert.ToString( cboOptions.SelectedValue );
170
171              // verify answer
172              if ( strResponse == m_strCountry )
173              {
174                  lblFeedback.Text = "Correct!";
175              }
176              else
177              {
178                  lblFeedback.Text = "Sorry, incorrect.";
179              }
180
181              // inform user if quiz is over
182              if ( m_intCount >= 5 ) // quiz is over
183              {
184                  lblFeedback.Text += "    Done!";
185                  btnNext.Enabled = false;
186                  btnSubmit.Enabled = false;
187                  cboOptions.Enabled = false;
188              }
189              else // quiz is not over
190              {
191                  btnSubmit.Enabled = false;
192                  btnNext.Enabled = true;
193              }
194
195          } // end method btnSubmit_Click
196
197          // handles Next Button's Click event
198          private void btnNext_Click(
199              object sender, System.EventArgs e )
200          {
201              DisplayFlag(); // display next flag
202              lblFeedback.Text = ""; // clear output
203
204              // change selected country to first in ComboBox
205              cboOptions.SelectedIndex = 0;
206
207              m_intCount++; // update number of flags shown
208
209              btnSubmit.Enabled = true;
210              btnNext.Enabled = false;
211
212          } // end method btnNext_Click
213
214      } // end class FrmFlagQuiz
215  }
```

Converting the selected value from the **ComboBox** *into a* **string** — line 169

Disabling the **ComboBox** — line 187

Setting the selected **ComboBox** *item* — line 205

Figure 17.31   Flag Quiz application code. (Part 4 of 4.)

1. The process of ordering the elements of an array is called _____ the array.

    a) allocating   b) sorting

    c) declaring   d) initializing

2. Which of the following sorts array `dblAvgRainfall`?

    a) `Array( dblAvgRainfall ).Sort()`   b) `Sort.Array( dblAvgRainfall )`

    c) `Sort( dblAvgRainfall )`   d) `Array.Sort( dblAvgRainfall )`

Answers: 1) b. 2) d.

17.6 Wrap-Up

In this tutorial, you learned about data structures called arrays, which contain elements of the same type. You then learned how to create, initialize and access one-dimensional arrays. You created a simple application called **Sum Array**, which calculated the sum of the `int` values stored in an array. You studied pseudocode and an ACE table to help you begin creating the **Flag Quiz** application.

    In building the **Flag Quiz** application, you were introduced to the `ComboBox` control. You learned how to add a `ComboBox` to the `Form` and modify the `ComboBox`'s appearance. You then populated the `ComboBox` with data from an array. You reviewed how to display images in a `PictureBox` and how to generate random numbers by using an object of class `Random`.

    You were introduced to several new `String` methods, including method `Insert` (for inserting characters), method `Remove` (for removing characters), method `ToLower` (for converting uppercase letters to lowercase letters) and method `IndexOf` (for returning the index of a character in a `string`). You learned how to sort an array alphabetically by using method `Array.Sort`.

    In the next tutorial, you will learn how to create more sophisticated arrays with two dimensions and you will use them to implement a graphing application. You will see that two-dimensional arrays are like tables organized in rows and columns.

SKILLS SUMMARY

Declaring an Array

- Declare the array using the format:

    arrayType`[]` *arrayName*;

    where *arrayName* is the reference name of the array and *arrayType* is the type of data that will be stored in the array.

Creating an Array

- To create the array with default values, use the `new` operator as in the statement:

    arrayName = `new` *arrayType*`[` *arraySize* `]`;

    where *arraySize* is the number of elements in the array.

- To create the array with user-defined values, use an initializer list as in the statement:

    arrayName = `{` *arrayInitializerList* `}`;

    where *arrayInitializerList* is a comma-separated list of the items that will initialize the elements of the array.

Referring to Element *n* of an Array

- Use index *n*.
- Enclose the index in square brackets (`[]`) after the array name.

Obtaining the Length of an Array

- Use property `Length`.

Obtaining the Index of the Last Element in a One-Dimensional Array

- Invoke method `GetUpperBound` with 0 as its argument.

Combining TextBox Features With ListBox Features

- Use a ComboBox control.

Setting the Maximum Number of Drop-Down Items a ComboBox's List Displays

- Use property MaxDropDownItems.

Specifying the Source of Data Displayed in a ComboBox

- Use property DataSource.

Obtaining a User's Selection in a ComboBox

- Use property SelectedValue.

Sorting an Array

- Invoke method Array.Sort.

Determining Whether a string Contains a Specified Character

- Method IndexOf returns the index of a specified character in a string, or –1 if the character is not in the string.

Converting a string to Lowercase

- Method ToLower returns a copy of a string with all uppercase characters converted to lowercase.

Inserting Characters into a string

- Method Insert returns a copy of a string with characters added at a specified index.

Removing Characters from a string

- Method Remove returns a copy of the string with a specified number of characters removed.

KEY TERMS

array—A data structure containing data items of the same type.

array bounds—Integers that determine what indices can be used to access an element in the array. The lower bound is 0; the upper bound is the length of the array minus one.

Array.Sort method—Sorts the values of an array into ascending order.

ComboBox control—Combines a TextBox with a ListBox.

DataSource property of a ComboBox—Specifies the source of items listed in the ComboBox.

data structure—Groups together and organizes related data.

DropDownList value of DropDownStyle property—Specifies that a ComboBox is not editable.

DropDownStyle property of a ComboBox—Specifies the appearance of the ComboBox.

element—An item in an array.

GetUpperBound method—Returns the index of the last element in the array.

index—An array element's position number, also called a subscript. An index must be zero, a positive integer or an integer expression. If an application uses an expression as an index, the expression is evaluated first, to determine the index.

indexed array name—The array name followed by an index enclosed in parentheses. The indexed array name can be used on the left side of an assignment statement to place a new value into an array element. The indexed array name can be used in the right side of an assignment to retrieve the value of that array element.

IndexOf method—String method that accepts as an argument a character to search for in a string. The method returns the index of a specified character in a string. If the string does not contain the character, the method returns –1.

initializer list—Braces ({ and }) surrounding the initial values of the elements in the array.

Insert method—String method that inserts its second argument (a string) at the position specified by the first argument.

Length property—Contains the number of elements in an array.

MaxDropDownItems property of a ComboBox—Property of the ComboBox class that specifies how many items can be displayed in the drop-down list.

one-dimensional array—An array that uses only one index.

position number—A value that indicates a specific location within an array.

Remove method—String method that deletes a specified number of characters (the second argument) starting at the index specified by the first argument.

SelectedIndex property of a ComboBox—Specifies the index of the selected item.

SelectedValue property of a ComboBox—Specifies the selected item.

sorting—The process of ordering array elements in ascending or descending order.

ToLower method of class String—Creates a new string object that replaces every uppercase letter in a string with its lowercase equivalent.

zeroth element—The first element in an array.

GUI DESIGN GUIDELINES

ComboBoxes

■ Each ComboBox should have a descriptive Label that describes the ComboBox's contents.

■ If a ComboBox's content should not be editable, set its DropDownStyle property to Drop-DownList.

CONTROLS, EVENTS, PROPERTIES & METHODS

ComboBox Allows users to select from a drop-down list of options.

■ *In action*

■ *Properties*

DataSource—Specifies the source of items listed in a ComboBox.

DropDownStyle—Specifies a ComboBox's appearance.

Enabled—Specifies whether a user can select an item from the ComboBox.

Location—Specifies the location of the ComboBox control on the container control relative to the top-left corner.

MaxDropDownItems—Specifies the maximum number of items the ComboBox can display in its drop-down list.

Name—Specifies the name used to access the ComboBox control programmatically. The name should be prefixed with cbo.

SelectedIndex—Returns the index of the selected item, or –1 if no item is selected.

SelectedValue—Specifies the selected item.

Size—Specifies the height and width (in pixels) of the ComboBox control.

Array This data structure stores a fixed number of elements of the same type.

■ *Property*

Length—Specifies the number of elements in the array.

■ *Methods*

GetUpperBound—Returns the largest index of the array.

Sort—Orders an array's elements. An array of numerical values would be organized in ascending order and an array of strings would be organized in alphabetical order.

String The String class represents a series of characters treated as a single unit.

■ *Methods*

Format—Arranges the string in a specified format.

IndexOf—Returns the index of the specified character(s) in a string.

Insert—Returns a copy of the string for which it is called with the specified character(s) inserted.

Remove—Returns a copy of the string for which it is called with the specified character(s) removed.

ToLower—Returns a copy of the string for which it is called with any uppercase letters converted to lowercase letters.

MULTIPLE-CHOICE QUESTIONS

17.1 Arrays can be declared to hold values of _____.

a) type `double`
b) type `int`
c) type `string`
d) any type

17.2 The elements of an array are related by the fact that they have the same _____.

a) constant value
b) subscript
c) type
d) value

17.3 Method _____ returns the largest index in the array.

a) `GetUpperBound`
b) `GetUpperLimit`
c) `GetLargestIndex`
d) `GetUpperSubscript`

17.4 The first element in every array is the _____.

a) subscript
b) zeroth element
c) length of the array
d) smallest value in the array

17.5 Arrays _____.

a) are controls
b) always have one dimension
c) keep data in sorted order at all times
d) are objects

17.6 The initializer list can _____.

a) be used to determine the size of the array
b) contain a comma-separated list of initial values for the array elements
c) be empty
d) All of the above.

17.7 Which method call sorts array `strWords` in ascending order?

a) `Array.Sort( strWords )`
b) `strWords.SortArray()`
c) `Array.Sort( strWords, 1 )`
d) `Sort( strWords )`

17.8 The `ComboBox` control combines a `TextBox` with a _____ control.

a) `DateTimePicker`
b) `ListBox`
c) `NumericUpDown`
d) `Label`

17.9 To search for a period (.) in a `string` called `strTest`, call method _____.

a) `String.Search( strTest, "." )`
b) `String.IndexOf( strTest, "." )`
c) `strTest.IndexOf( "." )`
d) `strTest.Search( "." )`

17.10 Property _____ contains the size of an array.

a) `Elements`
b) `ArraySize`
c) `Length`
d) `Size`

EXERCISES

17.11 *(Enhanced Flag Quiz Application)* Enhance the **Flag Quiz** application by counting the number of questions that were answered correctly. After all the questions have been answered, display a message in a `Label` that describes how well the user performed, as in Fig. 17.32. The following table shows which messages to display:

Number of correct answers	Message
5	`Excellent!`
4	`Very good`
3	`Good`
2	`Poor`
1 or 0	`Fail`

Figure 17.32 Enhanced **Flag Quiz** application's GUI.

a) *Copying the template to your working directory.* Copy the directory C:\Examples\ Tutorial17\Exercises\FlagQuiz2 to your C:\SimplyCSP directory.

b) *Opening the application's template file.* Double click FlagQuiz.sln in the FlagQuiz2 directory to open the application.

c) *Adding a variable to count the number of correct answers.* Add an instance variable m_intNumberCorrect, and initialize it to 0. You will use this variable to count the number of correct answers submitted by the user.

d) *Counting the correct answers.* Increment m_intNumberCorrect in the **Submit** Button's event handler whenever the submitted answer is correct.

e) *Displaying the message.* Write a method DisplayMessage that displays a message in lblScore depending on the value of m_intNumberCorrect. Call this method from the **Submit** Button's event handler when the quiz is completed.

f) *Running the application.* Select **Debug > Start** to run your application. The finished application should behave as in Fig. 17.32. Run the application a few times and enter a different number of correct answers each time to verify that the correct feedback is displayed.

g) *Closing the application.* Close your running application by clicking its close box.

h) *Closing the IDE.* Close Visual Studio .NET by clicking its close box.

17.12 (*Salary Survey Application*) Use a one-dimensional array to solve the following problem: A company pays its salespeople on a commission basis. The salespeople receive $200 per week, plus 9% of their gross sales for that week. For example, a salesperson who grosses $5000 in sales in a week receives $200 plus 9% of $5000, a total of $650. Write an application (using an array of counters) that determines how many of the salespeople earned salaries in each of the following ranges (assuming that each salesperson's salary is truncated to an integer amount): $200–299, $300–399, $400–499, $500–599, $600–699, $700–799, $800–899, $900–999 and over $999.

Allow the user to enter the sales for each employee in a TextBox. The user should click the **Calculate** Button to calculate that salesperson's salary. When the user is done entering this information, clicking the **Show Totals** Button should display how many of the salespeople earned salaries in each of the above ranges. The finished application should behave like Fig. 17.33.

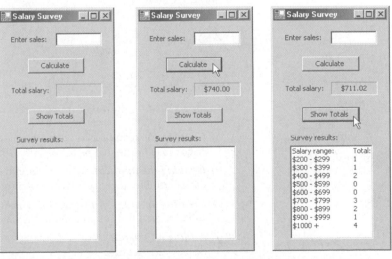

Figure 17.33 **Salary Survey** application's GUI.

a) *Copying the template to your working directory.* Copy the directory `C:\Examples\Tutorial17\Exercises\SalarySurvey` to your `C:\SimplyCSP` directory.

b) *Opening the application's template file.* Double click `SalarySurvey.sln` in the SalarySurvey directory to open the application.

c) *Creating an array of salary ranges.* Create a `string` array, and initialize it to contain the salary ranges (the `string`s displayed in the `ListBox`'s first column).

d) *Create an array that represents the number of salaries in each range.* Create an empty `int` array to store the number of employees who earn salaries in each range.

e) *Creating a Load event handler for the Form.* Write event handler `FrmSalarySurvey_Load`. Initialize the `int` array to contain default values.

f) *Creating an event handler for the Calculate Button.* Write event handler `btnCalculate_Click`. Obtain the user input from the **Enter sales:** TextBox. If the user enters a negative value, display a `MessageBox` asking for non-negative input and exit the event handler. Otherwise, calculate the commission due to the employee and add that amount to the base salary. Increment the element in array `decSalaries` that corresponds to the employee's salary range. Use a series of `if...else` statements to determine which element should be incremented. This event handler should also display the employee's salary in the **Total salary:** Label.

g) *Writing an event handler for the Show Totals Button.* Create event handler `btnShowTotals_Click` to display the salary distribution in the `ListBox`. Use a `for` statement to display the range (an element in `strSalaryRanges`) and the number of employees whose salary falls in that range (an element in `decSalaries`).

h) *Running the application.* Select **Debug > Start** to run your application. Enter several sales amounts using the **Calculate** Button. Click the **Show Totals** Button and verify that the proper amounts are displayed for each salary range, based on the salaries calculate from your input.

i) *Closing the application.* Close your running application by clicking its close box.

j) *Closing the IDE.* Close Visual Studio .NET by clicking its close box.

17.13 (*Cafeteria Survey Application*) Twenty students were asked to rate, on the scale from 1 to 10, the quality of the food in the student cafeteria, with 1 being "awful" and 10 being "excellent." Allow the user input to be entered using a ComboBox. Place the 20 responses in an `int` array, and determine the frequency of each rating. Display the frequencies as a histogram in a multiline, scrollable TextBox. Figure 17.34 demonstrates the completed application.

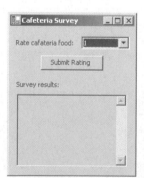

Figure 17.34 Cafeteria Survey GUI.

a) *Copying the template to your working directory.* Copy the directory `C:\Examples\Tutorial17\Exercises\CafeteriaSurvey` to your `C:\SimplyCSP` directory.

b) *Opening the application's template file.* Double click `CafeteriaSurvey.sln` in the CafeteriaSurvey directory to open the application.

c) *Creating an array of the possible ratings.* Create an array of 10 consecutive integers, called `m_intChoices` to contain the integers in the range 1–10, inclusive.

d) *Adding a ComboBox.* Add a ComboBox to the GUI as in Fig. 17.34. The ComboBox will display the possible ratings. Set property `DropDownStyle` to `DropDownList`. Rearrange and comment the new control declaration appropriately.

e) *Displaying the possible ratings when the application starts.* Write the event handler for the Load event so that the DataSource of the ComboBox is set to intChoices when the application starts.

f) *Creating an array to store the responses.* Create an int array of length 11 named m_intResponses. This will be used to store the number of responses in each of the 10 categories (element 0 will not be used).

g) *Counting the number of responses.* Create an int variable named m_intResponseCounter to keep track of how many responses have been input.

h) *Storing the responses.* Write the event handler btnSubmit_Click to increment m_intResponseCounter. Store the response in array m_intResponses. Call method DisplayHistogram to display the results.

i) *Creating method DisplayHistogram.* Add a header to the TextBox. Use nested for loops to display the ratings in the first column. The second column uses asterisks to indicate how many students surveyed submitted the corresponding rating.

j) *Running the application.* Select **Debug > Start** to run your application. Enter 20 responses using the **Submit Rating** Button. Verify that the resulting histogram displays the responses entered.

k) *Closing the application.* Close your running application by clicking its close box.

l) *Closing the IDE.* Close Visual Studio .NET by clicking its close box.

What does this code do? ▶ **17.14** Assume that intNumbers is an int array. What does intTempArray contain after the execution of the for statement?

```
1  int intLength = intNumbers.Length;
2  int[] intTempArray = new int[ intLength ];
3
4  intLength--;
5
6  for ( int intI = intLength; intI >= 0; intI-- )
7  {
8     intTempArray[ intI ] = intNumbers[ intLength - intI ];
9  }
```

What's wrong with this code? ▶ **17.15** The code that follows uses a for loop to sum the elements in an array. Find the error(s) in the following code:

```
1  int SumArray()
2  {
3     int intSum = 0;
4     int[] intNumbers = { 1, 2, 3, 4, 5, 6, 7, 8 };
5
6     for ( int intCounter = 0; intCounter <= intNumbers.Length;
7        intCounter++ )
8     {
9        intSum += intNumbers[ intCounter ];
10    }
11
12    return intSum;
13
14 } // end method SumArray
```

Programming Challenge ▶

17.16 (*Road Sign Test Application*) Write an application that will test the user's knowledge of road signs. Your application should display a random sign image and ask the user to select the sign name from a ComboBox. This application should look like Fig. 17.35. [*Hint*: The application is similar to the **Flag Quiz** application.] You can find the images in `C:\Examples\Tutorial17\Exercises\images`.

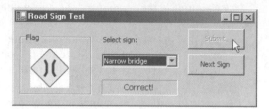

Figure 17.35   Road Sign Test GUI.

Objectives

In this tutorial, you will learn to:
- Understand the differences between one-dimensional and two-dimensional arrays.
- Declare and manipulate two-dimensional arrays.
- Understand the usefulness of two-dimensional arrays.
- Use RadioButtons to enable users to select exactly one option out of several.

Outline

Student Grades Application

Introducing Two-Dimensional Arrays and RadioButtons

In this tutorial, you will learn about two-dimensional arrays, which, like one-dimensional arrays, store multiple values. However, two-dimensional arrays allow you to store multiple rows of values. Also, you will learn about the RadioButton control, which you will employ to enable users to choose only one option out of many.

18.1 Test-Driving the Student Grades Application

In this tutorial, you will implement the **Student Grades** application by using a two-dimensional array. This application must meet the following requirements:

Application Requirements

A teacher issues three tests to a class of ten students. The grades on these tests are integers in the range from 0 to 100. The teacher has asked you to develop an application to keep track of each student's average and the average of the class as a whole. The teacher has also asked that there be a choice to view the grades as either numbers or letters. Letter grades should be calculated according to the grading system:

90–100	*A*
80–89	*B*
70–79	*C*
60–69	*D*
Below 60	*F*

The application should allow a user to input the student's name and three test grades, then compute each student's average and the class average. The application should display number grades by default.

The student's average is equal to the sum of the student's three grades divided by three. The class average is equal to the sum of all of the students' averages divided by the number of students in the class (ten in this case). You begin by test-driving the completed application. Then, you will learn the additional C# technologies you will need to create your own version of this application.

Test-Driving the Student Grades Application

1. ***Opening the completed application.*** Open the C:\Examples\ Tutorial18\CompletedApplication\StudentGrades directory to locate the **Student Grades** application. Double click StudentGrades.sln to open the application in Visual Studio .NET.

2. ***Running the Student Grades application.*** Select **Debug > Start** to run the application (Fig. 18.1).

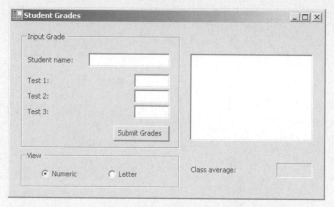

Figure 18.1 Running the completed **Student Grades** application.

3. ***Entering data.*** Type Gretta Green in the **Student Name:** TextBox. Type 87, 94 and 93 in the **Test 1:**, **Test 2:** and **Test 3:** TextBoxes, respectively (Fig. 18.2). Click the **Submit Grades** Button to display the data in the List-Box (Fig. 18.3).

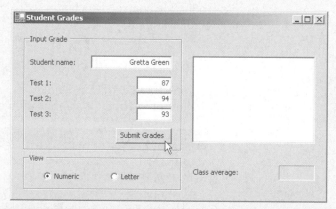

Figure 18.2 Inputting data to the **Student Grades** application.

Numeric RadioButton
selected as the default

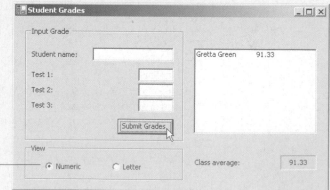

Figure 18.3 Displaying the student's numerical grade.

(cont.)   4. ***Changing the ListBox's appearance.*** Change the ListBox's appearance by clicking the white circle of the **Letter** RadioButton (Fig. 18.4). The ListBox will display the data using the letter grading system. Click the **Numeric** RadioButton to once again display the data in numeric form. (Fig. 18.3).

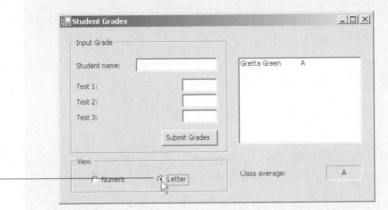

Select the **Letter** RadioButton

Figure 18.4 Displaying the student's resulting letter grade.

5. ***Closing the application.*** Close your running application by clicking its close box.

6. ***Closing the IDE.*** Close Visual Studio .NET by clicking its close box.

18.2 Two-Dimensional Rectangular Arrays

So far, you have studied one-dimensional arrays, which contain one sequence (or row) of values. In this section, we introduce **two-dimensional arrays** (often called **double-subscripted arrays**), which require two indices to identify particular elements. **Rectangular arrays** are two-dimensional arrays that are often used to represent **tables** of values consisting of information arranged in **rows** and **columns**. Each row is the same size and therefore has the same number of columns (hence, the term "rectangular"). To identify a particular table element, you must specify the two indices—by convention, the first identifies the element's row, and the second identifies the element's column. Figure 18.5 illustrates a two-dimensional rectangular array, intArray, which contains three rows and four columns. A rectangular two-dimensional array with *m* rows and *n* columns is called an ***m-by-n* array**; therefore, the array in Fig. 18.5 is a 3-by-4 array.

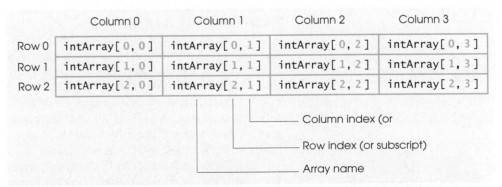

Figure 18.5 Two-dimensional rectangular array with three rows and four columns.

Every element in the intArray array is identified in Fig. 18.5 by an element name of the form intArray[intI, intJ], where intArray is the name of the array and intI and intJ are the indices that uniquely identify the row and column of each element in the intArray array. Notice that, because row numbers and column numbers in two-dimensional arrays each begin with zero, the names of the elements in the first row each have a first index of 0; the names of the elements in the last column each have a second index of 3 (Fig. 18.5).

Two-dimensional arrays are initialized much like one-dimensional arrays. For example, a two-dimensional rectangular array, `intNumbers`, with two rows and two columns could be declared and initialized with

```
int[,] intNumbers = new int[ 2, 2 ];
intNumbers[ 0, 0 ] = 1;
intNumbers[ 0, 1 ] = 2;
intNumbers[ 1, 0 ] = 3;
intNumbers[ 1, 1 ] = 4;
```

Notice that a comma (,) is required inside the square brackets following the data type to indicate that the array is two-dimensional. Alternatively, the preceding initialization could be written on one line using an initializer list:

```
int[,] intNumbers = { { 1, 2 }, { 3, 4 } };
```

The values in the initializer list are grouped by row using nested braces, with 1 and 2 initializing `intNumbers[ 0, 0 ]` and `intNumbers[ 0, 1 ]`, respectively, and 3 and 4 initializing `intNumbers[ 1, 0 ]` and `intNumbers[ 1, 1 ]`, respectively.

SELF-REVIEW

1. Arrays that use two indices are referred to as _____ arrays.

    a) single-subscripted   b) two-dimensional

    c) `double`   d) one-dimensional

2. The expression _____ creates an `int` array of two rows and five columns.

    a) `new int[ 2, 5 ]`   b) `new int[ 1, 5 ]`

    c) `new int[ 1, 4 ]`   d) `new int[ 2, 4 ]`

Answers: 1) b. 2) a.

18.3 Using RadioButtons

A **RadioButton** is a small white circle that either is blank or contains a smaller black dot. When a `RadioButton` is selected, a black dot appears in the circle. A `RadioButton` is known as a state button because it can be only in the "on" state or in the "off" state. (The other state button you have learned is the `CheckBox`, which was introduced in Tutorial 8.)

RadioButtons are similar to `CheckBoxes` in that they are state buttons, but `RadioButtons` normally appear as a group; only one `RadioButton` in the group can be selected at a time. Like car-radio preset buttons, which can select only one station at a time, `RadioButtons` are used to represent a set of mutually exclusive options. **Mutually exclusive options** are a set of options in which only one can be selected at a time. By default, all `RadioButtons` added directly to the `Form` become part of the same group. To separate `RadioButtons` into several groups, each `RadioButton` group must be in a different container (such as a `GroupBox`).

The `RadioButton` control's **Checked** property indicates whether the `RadioButton` is checked (contains a small black dot) or unchecked (blank). If the `RadioButton` is checked, the `Checked` property returns the `bool` value `true`. If the `RadioButton` is not checked, the `Checked` property returns `false`.

A `RadioButton` also generates an event when its checked state changes. Event **CheckedChanged** is generated when a `RadioButton` is either selected or deselected.

GUI Design Tip

Use RadioButtons when the user should choose only one option from a group.

GUI Design Tip

Always place each group of RadioButtons in a separate container (such as a GroupBox).

The following pseudocode describes the basic operation of the **Student Grades** application:

```
When the user clicks the Submit Grades Button:
    Retrieve the grades from the TextBoxes
    Add the student's name and test average to the arrays
    Display each student's name and test average in the ListBox
    Display the class's average in the Class average: TextBox
    Clear the student's name and test average from the TextBoxes

    If 10 students have been entered
        Disable the Submit Grades Button

When the user selects the Numeric RadioButton:
    Display each student's name and numeric average in the ListBox
    Display the class's numeric average in the Class average: TextBox

When the user selects the Letter RadioButton:
    Display each student's name and letter average in the ListBox
    Display the class's letter average in the Class average: TextBox
```

Your **Student Grades** application uses the RadioButton control's Checked-Changed event handler to update the ListBox when the user selects either letter grades or numeric grades for display. Now that you have test-driven the **Student Grades** application and studied its pseudocode representation, you will use an ACE table to help you convert the pseudocode to C#. Figure 18.6 lists the actions, controls and events that will help you complete your own version of this application.

	Action	Control/Object	Event
Action/Control/Event (ACE) Table for the Student Grades Application	Label the application's components	fraInputGrade, lblInputName, lblTest1, lblTest2, lblTest3, lblClassAverage, lblClassOutput	Application is run
		btnSubmit	Click
	Retrieve grades from the TextBoxes	txtName, txtTest1, txtTest2, txtTest3	
	Add the student's name and test average to the arrays	txtName, m_strStudents	
	Display each student's name and test average in the ListBox	lstNames	
	Display the class's average in the Class average: TextBox	lblClassOutput	
	Clear the student's name and test average from the TextBoxes	txtName, txtTest1, txtTest2, txtTest3	
	If 10 students have been entered		
	Disable the Submit Grades Button	btnSubmit	

Figure 18.6 ACE table for the **Student Grades** application. (Part 1 of 2.)

Action	Control/Object	Event
	radNumeric	CheckedChanged
Display each student's name and numeric average in the ListBox	lstNames	
Display the class's numeric average in the Class average: TextBox	lblClassOutput	
	radLetter	CheckedChanged
Display each students' name and letter average in the ListBox	lstNames	
Display the class's letter average in the Class average: TextBox	lblClassOutput	

Figure 18.6 ACE table for the **Student Grades** application. (Part 2 of 2.)

Now you will build your **Student Grades** application, using two-dimensional arrays and RadioButtons. The RadioButtons will allow the user to view the students' grades as letters or numbers.

Adding RadioButtons to the View GroupBox

1. ***Copying the template to your working directory.*** Copy the C:\Examples\ Tutorial18\TemplateApplication\StudentGrades directory to your C:\SimplyCSP directory.

2. ***Opening the Student Grades application's template file.*** Double click StudentGrades.sln in the StudentGrades directory to open the application in Visual Studio .NET.

3. ***Adding RadioButtons to the View GroupBox.*** Click the **View** GroupBox on the Form. Add a RadioButton to the GroupBox by double clicking the **RadioButton** control,

in the **Toolbox**. Repeat this process so that two RadioButtons have been added to the GroupBox. Notice that, as with CheckBoxes, each RadioButton control contains a label.

GUI Design Tip

Align groups of RadioButtons either horizontally or vertically.

Good Programming Practice

Prefix RadioButton controls with rad.

4. ***Customizing the RadioButtons.*** To align the RadioButtons horizontally, set the Location property of one RadioButton to 32, 24, and set the other RadioButton's Location property to 136, 24. Then, resize the RadioButton labels by setting each RadioButton's Size property to 80, 24. Rename the left RadioButton by changing its Name property to radNumeric and set its Text property to Numeric. Then, set the right RadioButton control's Name property to radLetter, and set its Text property to Letter. Set the Checked property of radNumeric to true. Your Form should now look similar to Fig. 18.7.

5. ***Saving the project.*** Select **File > Save All** to save your modified code.

(cont.)

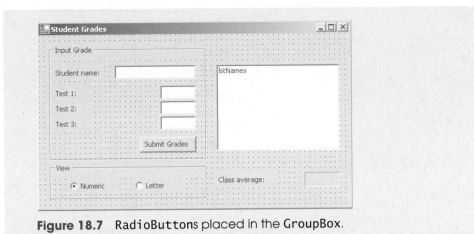

Figure 18.7 RadioButtons placed in the GroupBox.

Error-Prevention Tip

To avoid subtle logic errors, one RadioButton in a group should be selected by default, by setting its Checked property to true. This can be done using code or by setting the value using the **Properties** window.

SELF-REVIEW

1. The _____ property determines whether a RadioButton is selected.

   a) Selected   b) Clicked

   c) Checked   d) Enabled

2. The _____ event is raised when a RadioButton is either selected or deselected.

   a) CheckedChanged   b) Changed

   c) SelectedChanged   d) None of the above.

Answers: 1) c. 2) a.

18.4 Inserting Code into the Student Grades Application

Now that you have placed the controls on the Form, you are ready to write code to interact with the data given by the user. First you will declare a two-dimensional array to contain the student information.

Declaring a Two-Dimensional Array

1. ***Rearranging and commenting the control declarations.*** In code view, move the declarations for the two RadioButtons from lines 48–49 of your code to lines 36–37 of Fig. 18.8, and update the comment in lines 33–34.

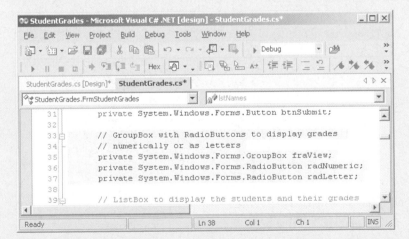

Figure 18.8 Rearranging and commenting the new control declarations.

(cont.)

2. *Declaring a two-dimensional array.* Add lines 54–55 of Fig. 18.9 to your code. Line 55 declares a 10-by-2 array of `strings` to contain the student information. The first column of `m_strStudents` will contain each student's name. The second column will contain each student's test average. Notice the `m_intStudentCount` instance variable (line 52), which contains the number of students entered by the user.

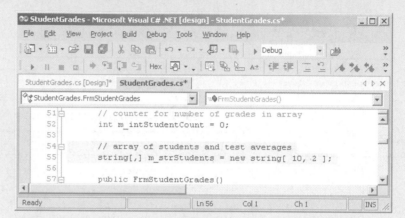

Figure 18.9 Declaring a two-dimensional array.

3. *Saving the project.* Select **File > Save All** to save your modified code.

The template code provides an incomplete version of the **Submit Grades** Button's `Click` event handler. You will now use the two-dimensional array that you declared in the previous box to finish this event handler.

Finishing the Submit Grades Button's Click Event Handler

1. *Adding the student information to the array.* Add lines 348–356 of Fig. 18.10 to your code. Line 350 adds the student's name to the first column of the two-dimensional the `m_strStudents` array. Lines 351–353 add the student's test average to the second column of the array. The `StudentAverage` method, which is provided in the template code, calculates the average based on the three test scores. By using the format control string `"{0:F}"`, the `String.Format` method converts the test average to a `string` with exactly two digits following the decimal point. This `string` is then stored in the array. Line 356 increments the number of students in the class.

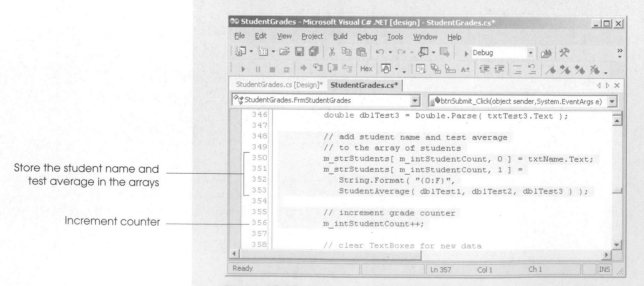

Store the student name and test average in the arrays

Increment counter

Figure 18.10 Storing the student information.

(cont.)   2. ***Displaying the output.*** Insert lines 358–366 of Fig. 18.11 into your code. Line 359 uses the Checked method of the RadioButton control to determine how the user would like the student's grades displayed. Line 361 calls the DisplayNumericGrades method, and line 365 calls the DisplayLetter-Grades method. These methods will be defined later in this tutorial.

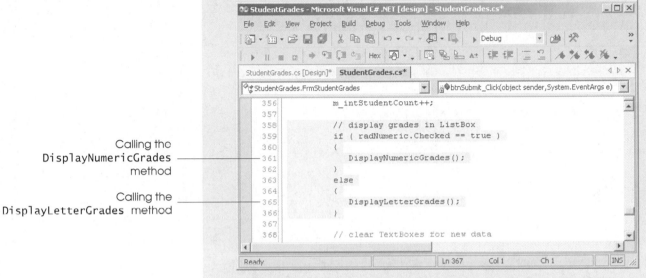

Calling the DisplayNumericGrades method

Calling the DisplayLetterGrades method

Figure 18.11   Displaying the output.

3. ***Disabling the Submit Grades Button.*** Insert lines 374–378 of Fig. 18.12 into your code. If 10 students have already been entered into the array, line 377 will disable the **Submit Grades** Button so that no more grades can be entered.

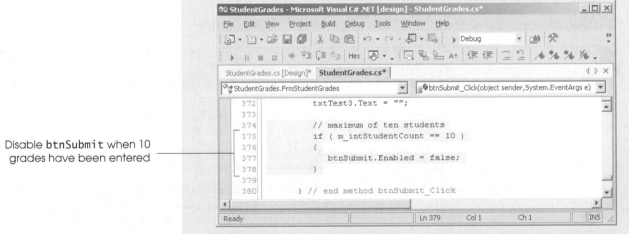

Disable btnSubmit when 10 grades have been entered

Figure 18.12   Application does not allow more than ten data entries.

4. ***Saving the project.*** Select **File > Save All** to save your modified code.

In the previous box, you called the DisplayNumericGrades and Display-LetterGrades methods, which are not yet defined, to display the appropriate data. Next, you will code the DisplayNumericGrades method.

Coding a Method to Display Numeric Grades

1. ***Coding the DisplayNumericGrades method.*** Add lines 382–407 of Fig. 18.13 below your btnSubmit_Click event handler. Line 386 uses the Clear method of ListBox property Items to clear the ListBox of all entries.

(cont.)

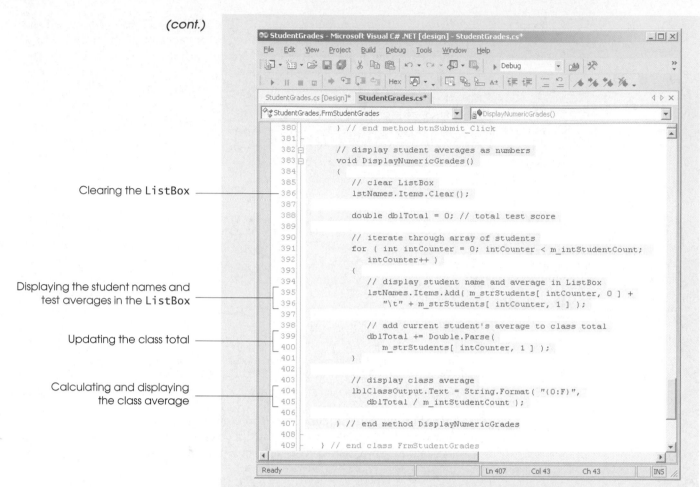

Clearing the ListBox

Displaying the student names and test averages in the ListBox

Updating the class total

Calculating and displaying the class average

Figure 18.13 `DisplayNumericGrades` method code.

The `for` loop in lines 391–401 iterates through the `m_strStudents` array, adding each student's name and test average to the `ListBox`. A tab character separates the student name from the test average. The `for` loop also uses `dblTotal` (declared in line 388) to sum the student averages (lines 399–400). Lines 404–405 use this sum to calculate and display the class average.

2. **Saving the project.** Select **File > Save All** to save your modified code.

You have now coded the `DisplayNumericGrades` method to output the students' averages and the class's average as numbers. Now you will code the `DisplayLetterGrades` method to output the same information as letter grades.

Coding a Method to Display Letter Grades	1. **Coding the `DisplayLetterGrades` method.** Add lines 409–435 of Fig. 18.14 below your `DisplayNumericGrades` method. This method's body is identical to `DisplayNumericGrades`' except for additional calls to the `ConvertToLetterGrade` method before the grades are displayed (lines 423 and 433). The `ConvertToLetterGrade` method, which is provided in the template code, takes a numeric grade (as a `double`) and returns the corresponding letter grade (as a `string`).
	2. **Saving the project.** Select **File > Save All** to save your modified code.

(cont.)

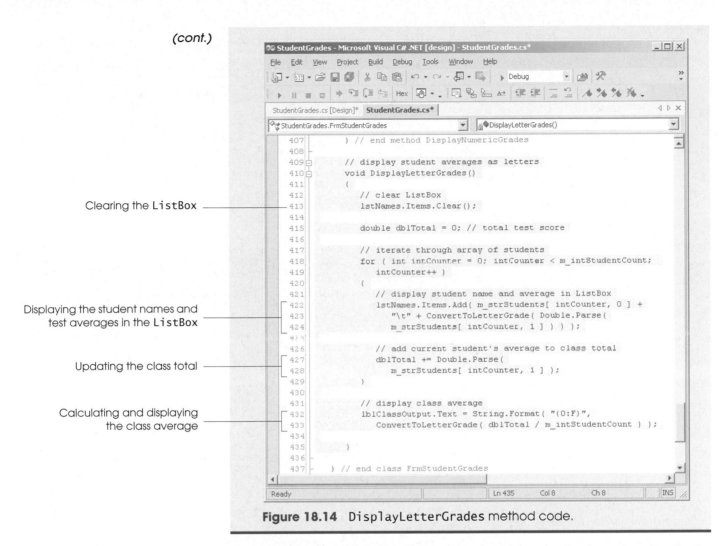

Clearing the `ListBox`

Displaying the student names and test averages in the `ListBox`

Updating the class total

Calculating and displaying the class average

Figure 18.14   `DisplayLetterGrades` method code.

You will now code event handlers to enhance the application's functionality by allowing the user to select whether the results will be presented as letter grades or numeric grades.

Coding Event Handlers for the RadioButtons

1. **Creating the radNumeric_CheckedChanged event handler.** In design view, double click the **Numeric** `RadioButton` to generate its `CheckedChanged` event handler. Add line 442 of Fig. 18.15 to the event handler. Line 442 calls the `DisplayNumericGrades` method. This method displays the student averages and class average as numeric grades. Be sure to add the comments in lines 436 and 438 and format the event handler as in Fig. 18.15.

2. **Creating the radLetter_CheckedChanged event handler.** In design view, double click the **Letter** `RadioButton` to generate its `CheckedChanged` event handler. Add line 451 of Fig. 18.16 to the event handler. Line 451 calls the `DisplayLetterGrades` method. This method displays the student averages and class average as letter grades. Be sure to add the comments in lines 445, 447 and 453 and format the event handler as in Fig. 18.16.

3. **Running the application.** Select **Debug > Start** to run your application. You can now select to view the grades as letters or numbers.

4. **Closing the application.** Close your running application by clicking its close box.

5. **Closing the IDE.** Close Visual Studio .NET by clicking its close box.

(cont.)

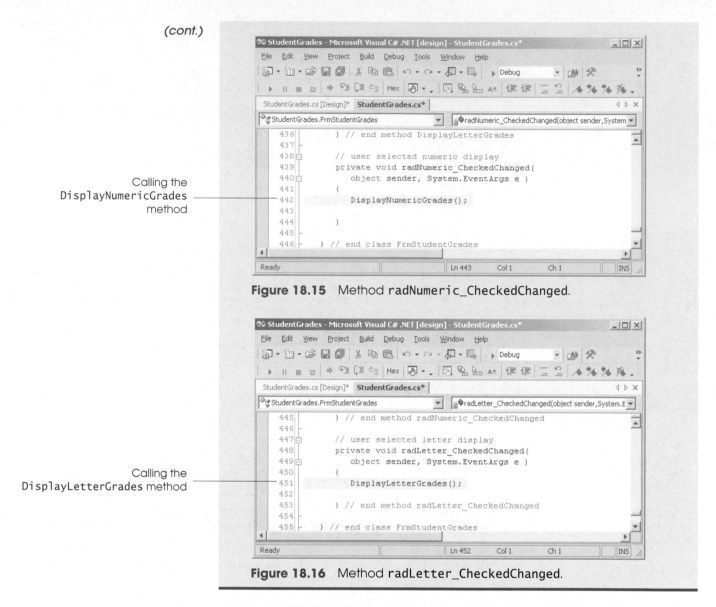

Calling the
DisplayNumericGrades
method

Figure 18.15 Method radNumeric_CheckedChanged.

Calling the
DisplayLetterGrades method

Figure 18.16 Method radLetter_CheckedChanged.

Figure 18.17 presents the source code for the **Student Grades** application. The lines of code that contain new programming concepts that you learned in this tutorial are highlighted.

```
1   using System;
2   using System.Drawing;
3   using System.Collections;
4   using System.ComponentModel;
5   using System.Windows.Forms;
6   using System.Data;
7
8   namespace StudentGrades
9   {
10     /// <summary>
11     /// Summary description for FrmStudentGrades.
12     /// </summary>
13     public class FrmStudentGrades : System.Windows.Forms.Form
14     {
```

Figure 18.17 **Student Grades** application code. (Part 1 of 5.)

```
15          // GroupBox to input grades
16          private System.Windows.Forms.GroupBox fraInputGrade;
17
18          // Label and TextBox to input a student name
19          private System.Windows.Forms.Label lblInputName;
20          private System.Windows.Forms.TextBox txtName;
21
22          // Labels and TextBoxes to enter three test scores
23          private System.Windows.Forms.Label lblTest1;
24          private System.Windows.Forms.TextBox txtTest1;
25          private System.Windows.Forms.Label lblTest2;
26          private System.Windows.Forms.TextBox txtTest2;
27          private System.Windows.Forms.Label lblTest3;
28          private System.Windows.Forms.TextBox txtTest3;
29
30          // Button to submit a student's grades
31          private System.Windows.Forms.Button btnSubmit;
32
33          // GroupBox with RadioButtons to display grades
34          // numerically or as letters
35          private System.Windows.Forms.GroupBox fraView;
36          private System.Windows.Forms.RadioButton radNumeric;
37          private System.Windows.Forms.RadioButton radLetter;
38
39          // ListBox to display the students and their grades
40          private System.Windows.Forms.ListBox lstNames;
41
42          // Labels to display the class average
43          private System.Windows.Forms.Label lblClassAverage;
44          private System.Windows.Forms.Label lblClassOutput;
45
46          /// <summary>
47          /// Required designer variable.
48          /// </summary>
49          private System.ComponentModel.Container components = null;
50
51          // counter for number of grades in array
52          int m_intStudentCount = 0;
53
54          // array of students and test averages
55          string[,] m_strStudents = new string[ 10, 2 ];
56
57          public FrmStudentGrades()
58          {
59             //
60             // Required for Windows Form Designer support
61             //
62             InitializeComponent();
63
64             //
65             // TODO: Add any constructor code after InitializeComponent
66             // call
67             //
68          }
69
70          /// <summary>
71          /// Clean up any resources being used.
72          /// </summary>
```

RadioButton control — (lines 36, 37)

Creating a two-dimensional array — (line 55)

Figure 18.17   Student Grades application code. (Part 2 of 5.)

```csharp
73          protected override void Dispose( bool disposing )
74          {
75             if( disposing )
76             {
77                if (components != null)
78                {
79                   components.Dispose();
80                }
81             }
82             base.Dispose( disposing );
83          }
84
85          // Windows Form Designer generated code
86
87          /// <summary>
88          /// The main entry point for the application.
89          /// </summary>
90          [STAThread]
91          static void Main()
92          {
93             Application.Run( new FrmStudentGrades() );
94          }
95
96          // convert a number to a letter grade
97          string ConvertToLetterGrade( double grade )
98          {
99             if ( grade >= 90 )
100            {
101               return "A";
102            }
103            else if ( grade >= 80 )
104            {
105               return "B";
106            }
107            else if ( grade >= 70 )
108            {
109               return "C";
110            }
111            else if ( grade >= 60 )
112            {
113               return "D";
114            }
115            else
116            {
117               return "F";
118            }
119
120         } // end method ConvertToLetterGrade
121
122         // returns student average
123         double StudentAverage(
124            double dblTest1, double dblTest2, double dblTest3 )
125         {
126            // return the average of 3 test scores
127            return ( ( dblTest1 + dblTest2 + dblTest3 ) / 3 );
128
129         } // end method StudentAverage
130
```

Figure 18.17   **Student Grades** application code. (Part 3 of 5.)

```
131        // handles Submit Button's Click event
132        private void btnSubmit_Click(
133           object sender, System.EventArgs e )
134        {
135           // extract user input
136           double dblTest1 = Double.Parse( txtTest1.Text );
137           double dblTest2 = Double.Parse( txtTest2.Text );
138           double dblTest3 = Double.Parse( txtTest3.Text );
139
140           // add student name and test average
141           // to the array of students
142           m_strStudents[ m_intStudentCount, 0 ] = txtName.Text;
143           m_strStudents[ m_intStudentCount, 1 ] =
144              String.Format( "{0:F}",
145              StudentAverage( dblTest1, dblTest2, dblTest3 ) );
146
147           // increment grade counter
148           m_intStudentCount++;
149
150           // display grades in ListBox
151           if ( radNumeric.Checked == true )
152           {
153              DisplayNumericGrades();
154           }
155           else
156           {
157              DisplayLetterGrades();
158           }
159
160           // clear TextBoxes for new data
161           txtName.Text = "";
162           txtTest1.Text = "";
163           txtTest2.Text = "";
164           txtTest3.Text = "";
165
166           // maximum of ten students
167           if ( m_intStudentCount == 10 )
168           {
169              btnSubmit.Enabled = false;
170           }
171
172        } // end method btnSubmit_Click
173
174        // display student averages as numbers
175        void DisplayNumericGrades()
176        {
177           // clear ListBox
178           lstNames.Items.Clear();
179
180           double dblTotal = 0; // total test score
181
182           // iterate through array of students
183           for ( int intCounter = 0; intCounter < m_intStudentCount;
184              intCounter++ )
185           {
186              // display student name and average in ListBox
187              lstNames.Items.Add( m_strStudents[ intCounter, 0 ] +
188                 "\t" + m_strStudents[ intCounter, 1 ] );
```

Assigning a value to a two-dimensional array — *(line 142)*

Using a format control string — *(lines 144–145)*

Using a RadioButton's Checked property — *(line 151)*

Accessing the elements of a two-dimensional array — *(lines 187–188)*

Figure 18.17   Student Grades application code. (Part 4 of 5.)

```
189
190                        // add current student's average to class total
191                        dblTotal += Double.Parse(
192                           m_strStudents[ intCounter, 1 ] );
193                     }
194
195                  // display class average
196                  lblClassOutput.Text = String.Format( "{0:F}",
197                     dblTotal / m_intStudentCount );
198
199               } // end method DisplayNumericGrades
200
201               // display student averages as letters
202               void DisplayLetterGrades()
203               {
204                  // clear ListBox
205                  lstNames.Items.Clear();
206
207                  double dblTotal = 0; // total test score
208
209                  // iterate through array of students
210                  for ( int intCounter = 0; intCounter < m_intStudentCount;
211                     intCounter++ )
212                  {
213                        // display student name and average in ListBox
214                        lstNames.Items.Add( m_strStudents[ intCounter, 0 ] +
215                           "\t" + ConvertToLetterGrade( Double.Parse(
216                           m_strStudents[ intCounter, 1 ] ) ) );
217
218                        // add current student's average to class total
219                        dblTotal += Double.Parse(
220                           m_strStudents[ intCounter, 1 ] );
221                     }
222
223                  // display class average
224                  lblClassOutput.Text = String.Format( "{0:F}",
225                     ConvertToLetterGrade( dblTotal / m_intStudentCount ) );
226
227               } // end method DisplayLetterGrades
228
229               // user selected numeric display
230               private void radNumeric_CheckedChanged(
231                  object sender, System.EventArgs e )
232               {
233                  DisplayNumericGrades();
234
235               } // end method radNumeric_CheckedChanged
236
237               // user selected letter display
238               private void radLetter_CheckedChanged(
239                  object sender, System.EventArgs e )
240               {
241                  DisplayLetterGrades();
242
243               } // end method radLetter_CheckedChanged
244
245            } // end class FrmStudentGrades
246  }
```

Creating a RadioButton's
CheckedChanged event handler

Figure 18.17   **Student Grades** application code. (Part 5 of 5.)

SELF-REVIEW
1. A container can contain _____ RadioButton(s).

a) exactly two   b) no more than one

c) no more than three   d) any number of

2. When one RadioButton in a container is selected, _____.

a) others can be selected at the same time   b) a logic error will occur

c) all others will be deselected   d) Both a and c.

Answers: 1.) d. 2.) c.

18.5 Wrap-Up

In this tutorial, you learned how to declare and assign values to a two-dimensional array. You used code to store user input in a two-dimensional array.

To help you complete the **Student Grades** application, you used RadioButtons. You learned that you must group related RadioButtons in separate containers. Initially, zero or one RadioButton in a container will be selected. Once a RadioButton has been selected, only one RadioButton can be selected at a time. You also learned that selecting or deselecting a RadioButton calls its CheckedChanged event handler.

In the next tutorial, you will learn about classes. (Recall that you have been using classes all along, from the Form class that represents the application's GUI to the Random class that you use to generate random numbers.) You will learn how to create your own classes for use in your applications.

SKILLS SUMMARY

Using Two-Dimensional Arrays

■ Declare a rectangular array to create a table of values (each row will contain the same number of columns).

Using a RadioButton

■ Use a RadioButton in an application to present the user with mutually exclusive options.

Selecting a RadioButton at Runtime

■ Click the white circle of the RadioButton. (A small black dot will appear inside the white circle.)

Determining Whether a RadioButton Is Selected

■ Access the RadioButton's Checked property.

Executing Code When a RadioButton's State Has Changed

■ Use the CheckedChanged event handler, which executes when a RadioButton is selected or deselected.

KEY TERMS

Checked property of RadioButton control—When true, displays a small black dot in the control. When false, the control displays an empty white circle.

CheckedChanged event—Raised when a RadioButton's state changes.

column—The second dimension of a two-dimensional array.

double-subscripted array—Contains multiple rows of values.

***m*-by-*n* array**—A two-dimensional array with *m* rows and *n* columns.

mutually exclusive options—A set of options in which only one can be selected at a time.

RadioButton control—Appears as a small white circle that is either blank (unchecked) or contains a smaller black dot (checked). Usually these controls appear in groups of two or more. Exactly one RadioButton in a group is selected at once.

rectangular array—A type of two-dimensional array that can represent tables of values consisting of information arranged in rows and columns. Each row contains the same number of columns.

row—In referring to an element of a two-dimensional array, the first index specifies the row.

table—A two-dimensional array used to contain information arranged in rows and columns.

two-dimensional array—A double-subscripted array that contains multiple rows of values.

GUI DESIGN GUIDELINES	**RadioButton** ■ Use RadioButtons when the user should choose only one option from a group. ■ Always place each group of RadioButtons in a separate container (such as a GroupBox). ■ Align groups of RadioButtons either horizontally or vertically.

CONTROLS, EVENTS, PROPERTIES & METHODS

RadioButton   ⊙ RadioButton   This component is used to enable users to select only one of several options.

■ *In action*

⊙ 3D Graph

■ *Event*

CheckedChanged—Raised when the control is either selected or deselected.

■ *Properties*

Checked—Set to true if the control is selected and false if it is not selected.

Location—Specifies the location of the RadioButton control on the container control relative to the top-left corner.

Name—Specifies the name used to access the RadioButton control programmatically. The name should be prefixed with rad.

Size—Specifies the height and width (in pixels) of the RadioButton control.

Text—Specifies the text displayed in the label to the right of the RadioButton.

MULTIPLE-CHOICE QUESTIONS

18.1 RadioButton controls should be prefixed with _____.

a) rad   b) rbn

c) btn   d) radbtn

18.2 A two-dimensional array in which each row contains the same number of columns is called a _____ array.

a) data   b) rectangular

c) tabular   d) All of the above.

18.3 In an *m*-by-*n* array, the *m* stands for _____.

a) the number of columns in the array   b) the total number of array elements

c) the number of rows in the array   d) the number of elements in each row

18.4 The _____ statement assigns an array of three columns and five rows to two-dimensional int array intArray.

a) intArray = new int[5, 3];   b) intArray = new int[4, 2];

c) intArray = new int[4, 3];   d) intArray = new int[5, 2];

18.5 A RadioButton is a type of _____ button.

a) check   b) change

c) state   d) action

18.6 Use a _____ to group RadioButtons on the Form.

a) GroupBox control   b) ComboBox control

c) ListBox control   d) None of the above.

18.7 The _____ event handler is invoked when selecting a RadioButton control.

a) Selected   b) CheckedChanged

c) ButtonChanged   d) CheckSelected

18.8 The _____ property is set to true when a RadioButton is selected.

    a) `Selected`   b) `Chosen`

    c) `On`   d) `Checked`

18.9 Two-dimensional arrays are often used to represent _____.

    a) a pie chart   b) distances

    c) lines   d) tables

18.10 The statement _____ assigns an array of three columns and three rows to two-dimensional `int` array `intArray`.

    a) `int[][] intArray = { { 1 2 3 } { 4 5 6 } { 7 8 9 } };`

    b) `int[,] intArray = new int( { { 1 2 3 } { 4 5 6 } { 7 8 9 } };`

    c) `int[,] intArray = { { 1 2 3 } { 4 5 6 } { 7 8 9 } };`

    d) `int[] intArray = { { 1 2 3 } { 4 5 6 } { 7 8 9 } } );`

EXERCISES

18.11 *(Food Survey Application)* A school cafeteria is giving an electronic survey to its students to improve their lunch menu. Create an application that will use a two-dimensional array to hold counters for the survey (Fig. 18.18). You will also provide RadioButtons for the students to indicate whether they like or dislike a particular food.

Figure 18.18 **Food Survey** application.

    a) *Copying the template to your working directory.* Copy the directory `C:\Examples\Tutorial18\Exercises\FoodSurvey` to your `C:\SimplyCSP` directory.

    b) *Opening the application's template file.* Double click `FoodSurvey.sln` in the FoodSurvey directory to open the application.

    c) *Adding RadioButtons to the Vote GroupBox.* Add two RadioButtons to the **Vote** GroupBox. Name one `radLike` and the other `radDislike`. Change their Text properties to `Like` and `Dislike`, respectively. Set the Checked property of `radLike` to `true`. Rearrange and comment the control declarations appropriately.

    d) *Declaring a two-dimensional int array.* Declare a two-dimensional `int` array named `m_intDisplay`, with 4 rows and 2 columns.

    e) *Creating event handler btnAdd_Click.* Generate the Click event handler for the **Add** Button. In the event handler, clear the ListBox, then add the header `"Food\t\tLike\t\tDislike"`. Create a local `int` variable `intIndex`. This variable should contain the index of the selected item in `cboFoods`.

    f) *Using a for loop to display the data.* Insert a `for` statement into the event handler to loop through each row in the `m_strFoods` array (rows 0–3). In the body of the loop, insert an `if` statement that checks if the `radLike` RadioButton is selected and if the variable `intIndex` is equal to the counter of your `for` statement. If both conditions are `true`, increment the counter in column 0 in the `m_intDisplay` array. Insert an `else if` statement that determines whether the `radDislike` RadioButton is selected and whether the variable `intIndex` is equal to the counter of your `for` statement. If both conditions are `true`, increment the counter in column 1 of the `m_intDisplay` array.

g) *Adding the current row to the ListBox.* Inside the for statement, add the current row to the ListBox. The counter variable of the for statement will be used as the index of the m_strFoods array. Use the "\t" escape sequence to align the results.

h) *Running the application.* Select **Debug > Start** to run your application. Choose either the **Like** or **Dislike** RadioButton. Click the **Add** Button and check to make sure all strings and numbers in the **Results** GroupBox are correct. Add several other selections to the **Food Survey** and make sure that the numbers are correct.

i) *Closing the application.* Close your running application by clicking its close box.

j) *Closing the IDE.* Close Visual Studio .NET by clicking its close box.

18.12 *(Sales Report Application)* A clothing manufacturer has asked you to create an application that will calculate the total sales of that manufacturer in a week. Sales values should be input separately for each clothing item, but the amount of sales for all five week days should be input at once. The application should calculate the total amount of sales for each item in the week and also calculate the total sales for the manufacturer for all the items in the week. Because the manufacturer is a small company, it will produce at most ten items in any week. The application is shown in Fig. 18.19.

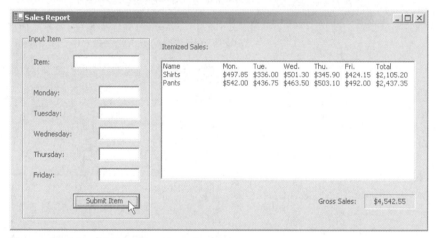

Figure 18.19 **Sales Report** application.

a) *Copying the template to your working directory.* Copy the directory C:\Examples\ Tutorial18\Exercises\SalesReport to your C:\SimplyCSP directory.

b) *Opening the application's template file.* Double click SalesReport.sln in the SalesReport directory to open the application.

c) *Declaring a two-dimensional int array.* Declare a two-dimensional decimal array named m_decItemSales, with 10 rows and 5 columns.

d) *Inputting data from the user.* Add code to the beginning of the btnSubmit_Click event handler to input the data from the user. Assign the item name to the one-dimensional m_intItemNames array, indexed with m_intItemCount (which stores the number of items added). Assign the daily sales data to the two-dimensional m_decItemSales array. The first index to this array should be m_intItemCount, and the second will range from 0 to 4. Finally, increment variable m_intItemCount to record that another item's sales data has been added.

e) *Iterating over all the items added.* Inside the DisplaySales method, after the strOutput variable has been declared, add code to begin a for statement. This for statement should iterate from 0 to m_intItemCount - 1. Declare the intItem variable as the for statement's counter. Insert code in this for statement to set strOutput to the item's name. Remember that the items' names are stored in string array m_strItemNames. Append two tab characters to format the output properly.

f) *Iterating over the days in the week.* Add code to initialize the decWeekTotal variable to 0. This variable keeps track of the total sales for each item over the course of the week. Add code to start a for statement. This for statement will iterate from 0 to 4, which is one less than the number of days in the work week. This is an example of a nested for statement, which is comparable to a nested if statement.

g) *Appending the daily sales and summing sales for the week.* Add code in this `for` statement to append the daily sales to `strOutput`. These sales are stored in the `m_decItemSales` array. This array must be accessed with the current item and the day of the week. The output is money, so use the `String.Format` method to format the value. Also append a tab character to format the output properly.

h) *Calculating the weekly sales.* Insert code to add the amount of the daily sales to the `decWeekTotal` variable. This variable stores the weekly sales for each item. Add a right brace to end the `for` statement started in *Step e*.

i) *Calculating the total sales and outputting an item's sales.* Insert code to add the weekly sales to the `decSalesTotal` variable. This variable keeps track of the total sales for all the items for the week. Add code to append the weekly sales to `strOutput`. The weekly sales are also stored as money, so use the `String.Format` method again. Then add `strOutput` to the `ListBox` using the Add method of `ListBox` property `Items`. Insert a right brace to end the `for` statement started in *Step e*.

j) *Running the application.* Select **Debug > Start** to run your application. Test your application to ensure that it runs correctly as in Fig. 18.19.

k) *Closing the application.* Close your running application by clicking its close box.

l) *Closing the IDE.* Close Visual Studio .NET by clicking its close box.

18.13 *(Profit Report Application)* The clothing manufacturer was so impressed with the **Sales Report** application you created for them (Exercise 18.12) they want you to create a **Profit Report** application as well. This application will be similar to the **Sales Report** application, but it will allow the user to input information as gains or losses. It should provide `RadioButton`s to allow the user to select whether a certain item is a gain or a loss (Fig. 18.20).

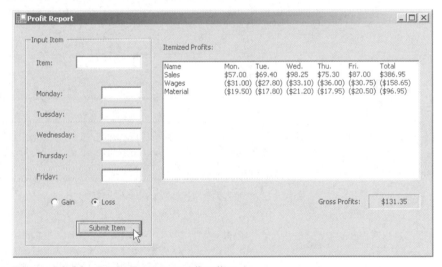

Figure 18.20 **Profit Report** application.

a) *Copying the template to your working directory.* Copy the directory `C:\Examples\Tutorial18\Exercises\ProfitReport` to your `C:\SimplyCSP` directory.

b) *Opening the application's template file.* Double click `ProfitReport.sln` in the `ProfitReport` directory to open the application.

c) *Modifying the template application.* Modify the template as you did in Exercise 18.12.

d) *Adding the Gain RadioButton.* Add a RadioButton to the **Input Item** GroupBox. Set its Name property to `radGain` and its Text property to Gain. Set its Size and Location properties so that the control appears as in Fig. 18.20. Set the RadioButton to be selected when the application starts (the default).

e) *Adding the Loss RadioButton.* Add a second RadioButton to the **Input Item** GroupBox. Set its Name property to `radLoss` and its Text property to Loss. Set its Size and Location properties so that the control appears as in Fig. 18.20. Rearrange and comment the control declarations appropriately.

f) *Testing which RadioButton was selected.* Add code to the `btnSubmit_Click` event handler to test which RadioButton was selected. If the **Gain** RadioButton was selected, add the input values to the array normally. If the **Loss** RadioButton was selected, add the input value to the array as negative values.

g) ***Running the application.*** Select **Debug > Start** to run your application. Test your application to ensure that it runs correctly as in Fig. 18.20.

h) ***Closing the application.*** Close your running application by clicking its close box.

i) ***Closing the IDE.*** Close Visual Studio .NET by clicking its close box.

What does this code do? ▶ **18.14** What is returned by the following code? Assume that GetStockPrices is a method that returns a 2-by-31 array, with the first row containing the stock price at the beginning of the day and the last row containing the stock price at the end of the day, for each day of the month.

```
1   int[] Mystery()
2   {
3      int[,] intPrices = new int[ 2, 31 ];
4
5      intPrices = GetStockPrices();
6
7      int[] intResult = new int[ 31 ];
8
9      for ( int intI = 0; intI < intResult.Length; intI++ )
10     {
11        intResult[ intI ] = intPrices[ 1, intI ] -
12           intPrices[ 0, intI ];
13     }
14
15     return intResult;
16
17  } // end method Mystery
```

What's wrong with this code? ▶ **18.15** Find the error(s) in the following code. The TwoDArrays method should create a two-dimensional array and initialize all its values to one.

```
1   int[,] TwoDArrays()
2   {
3      int[,] intArray = new int[ 4, 4 ];
4
5      // Assign 1 to all cell values
6      for ( int intI = 0; intI < 4; intI++ )
7      {
8         intArray[ intI, intI ] = 1;
9      }
10
11     return intArray;
12
13  } // end method TwoDArrays
```

Programming Challenge ▶ **18.16** (***Enhanced Lottery Picker***) A lottery commission offers four different lottery games to play: three-number, four-number, five-number and five-number + 1 lotteries. In Tutorial 16, your **Lottery Picker** application could select duplicate numbers for each lottery. In this exercise, you enhance the **Lottery Picker** to prevent duplicate numbers for the five-number and five-number + 1 lotteries (Fig. 18.21). According to this new requirement the games are now played as follows:

- Three-number lotteries require players to choose three numbers in the range 0–9.
- Four-number lotteries require players to choose four numbers, in the range 0–9.
- Five-number lotteries require players to choose five unique numbers in the range 1–39.
- Five-number + 1 lotteries require players to choose five unique numbers in the range 1–49 and an additional unique number in the range 1–42.

Figure 18.21 Enhanced **Lottery Picker** application.

a) *Copying the template to your working directory.* Copy the directory `C:\Examples\Tutorial18\Exercises\EnhancedLotteryPicker` to your `C:\SimplyCSP` directory.

b) *Opening the application's template file.* Double click `LotteryPicker.sln` in the `EnhancedLotteryPicker` directory to open the application.

c) *Declaring a two-dimensional array to maintain unique random numbers.* Declare the variable `m_blnNumbers` instance that stores a 2-by-50 `bool` array. You will use this array later in this exercise to test whether a lottery number has already been chosen.

d) *Initializing the array.* Each time the user clicks the **Generate** Button, the application should initialize the array by declaring its rows and setting the initial values. Write a `ClearArray` method that uses a `for` statement to assign each value in the `m_blnNumbers` array to `false`. Call the `ClearArray` method at the beginning of the **Generate** Button's `Click` event handler.

e) *Modifying the Generate method.* You will modify the `Generate` method to use the `bool` array to pick unique random numbers. Begin by writing a statement that generates a random number and assigns its value to an `int` variable `intNumber`.

f) *Determining whether the random number has already been selected.* Use an `if` statement to determine whether the maximum lottery number is equal to `40`. (This happens when the upper limit on the random number equals 40.) In this case, you will examine the first row of the array. To maintain unique numbers, you will set the value of the element in that row whose index equals the random number to `true` (indicating that it has been picked). For example, if the random number 34 has been picked, `m_blnNumbers[ 0, 34 ]` would contain the value `true`. To test whether a number has been picked, use a `while` statement inside the `if` statement to access that element of the array. If the array element's value is `true`, use the body of the loop to assign a new random number to `intNumber`. If the value in the array is `false`, use the condition in the `while` header to ignore the body of the loop. Just outside the `while`, include a statement that modifies the array to indicate that the number has now been picked.

g) *Completing the application.* Use a second `if` statement to determine whether the maximum lottery number is greater than 40. In this case, you will examine the second row of the array. Repeat the process in the previous step. Remember to return the value stored in `intNumber` at the end of the `Generate` method.

h) *Running the application.* Select **Debug > Start** to run your application. Click the **Generate** Button and check to make sure all numbers in both five number lotteries are unique. Do this several more times to make sure.

i) *Closing the application.* Close your running application by clicking its close box.

j) *Closing the IDE.* Close Visual Studio .NET by clicking its close box.

Microwave Oven Application

Building Your Own Classes and Objects

Objectives

In this tutorial, you will learn to:
- Create your own classes.
- Create and use objects of your own classes.
- Control access to instance variables.
- Use the `private` keyword.
- Create your own properties.
- Use the `Panel` control.
- Use `String` methods `PadLeft` and `Substring`.

Outline

In earlier tutorials, you used the following application-development methodology: You analyzed many typical problems that required an application to be built and determined what classes from the FCL were needed to implement each application. You then selected appropriate methods from these classes and created any necessary methods to complete each application.

You have now seen several FCL classes. Each GUI control is defined as a class. When you add a control to your application from the **Toolbox**, an object (also known as an instance) of that class is created (or **instantiated**) and added to your application. You have also seen FCL classes that are not GUI controls. The `String` and `Random` classes, for example, have been used to create `string` objects (for textual data) and `Random` objects (for generating random numbers), respectively. When you create and use an object of a class in an application, your application is known as a **client** of that class.

In this tutorial, you will learn to create and use your own classes (sometimes known as **programmer-defined classes**, or **programmer-defined types**). Creating your own classes is a key part of object-oriented programming (OOP). As with methods, classes can be reused. In the world of C# programming, applications are created by using a combination of FCL classes and methods and programmer-defined classes and methods. You have already created several methods in this book.

You will create a microwave-oven simulator where the user will enter an amount of time for the microwave to cook food. To handle the time data, you will create a class called `Time`. This class will store a number of minutes and seconds (which your **Microwave Oven** application will use to keep track of the remaining cook time) and provide properties whereby clients of this class can change the number of minutes and seconds.

19.1 Test-Driving the Microwave Oven Application

In this tutorial you will build your own class as you construct your **Microwave Oven** application. This application must meet the following requirements:

Application Requirements

*An electronics company is considering building microwave ovens. The company has asked you to develop an application to simulate a microwave oven. The oven will contain a keypad that allows the user to specify the microwave cooking time, which is displayed for the user. Once a time is entered, the user clicks the **Start Button** to begin the cooking process. The microwave's glass window changes color (from gray to yellow) to simulate the oven's light, which remains on while the food cooks, and a timer counts down one second at a time. Once the time expires, the color of the microwave's glass window returns to gray (indicating that the microwave's light is now off) and the microwave displays the text "Done!". The user can click the **Clear Button** at any time to stop the microwave and enter a new time. The user should be able to enter a number of minutes no larger than 59 and a number of seconds no larger than 59; otherwise, the invalid value will be set to zero.*

You begin by test-driving the completed application. Then, you will learn the additional C# technologies that you will need to create your own version of this application.

Test-Driving the Microwave Oven Application

1. **Opening the completed application.** Open the `C:\Examples\Tutorial19\ CompletedApplication\MicrowaveOven` directory to locate the **Microwave Oven** application. Double click `MicrowaveOven.sln` to open the application in Visual Studio .NET.

2. **Running the Microwave Oven application.** Select **Debug > Start** to run the application (Fig. 19.1). The application contains a large rectangle on the left (representing the microwave oven's glass window) and a keypad on the right, including a `Label` with the text **Microwave Oven**. The numeric `Buttons` are used to enter the cooking time, which will be displayed in the `Label` on the top right. Notice that the keypad `Buttons` appear flat, to give the application a more "real-world" appearance. To create this appearance, the **FlatStyle** property of each `Button` in the numeric keypad has been set to **Flat**. Similarly, the `Label`'s `BorderStyle` property has been set to **FixedSingle**.

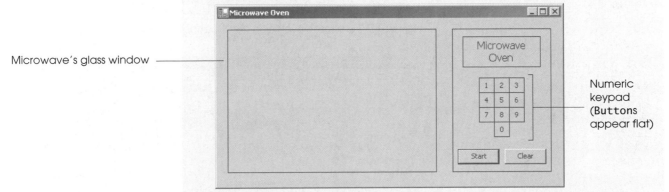

Microwave's glass window ——

Numeric keypad (`Buttons` appear flat)

Figure 19.1   Microwave Oven application's `Form`.

3. **Entering a time.** Click the following numeric `Buttons` in order: **1, 2, 3, 4** and **5**. Notice that you can enter no more than four digits (the first two for the minutes and the second two for the seconds)—any extra digits will not appear (Fig. 19.2). The number of minutes and the number of seconds must each be 59 or less. If the user enters an invalid number of minutes or seconds (such as 89), the invalid entry will be set to zero.

(cont.)

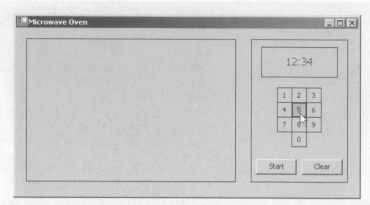

Figure 19.2 **Microwave Oven** application accepts only four digits.

4. *Entering invalid data.* Click the **Clear** Button to clear your input. Click the following numeric Buttons in order: **7, 2, 3** and **5** (Fig. 19.3). This input is invalid because the number of minutes, 72, is larger than the maximum allowed value, 59, so the number of minutes is reset to zero when the **Start** Button is clicked. Click the **Start** Button now. Notice that the number of minutes has been reset to **00** (Fig. 19.4). Also notice that the microwave oven's window has changed to yellow, to simulate the light that goes on inside the oven so that the user can watch the food cooking.

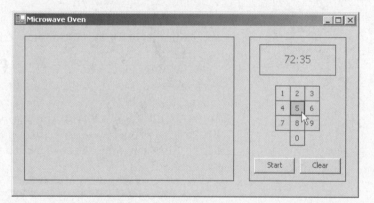

Figure 19.3 **Microwave Oven** application with invalid input.

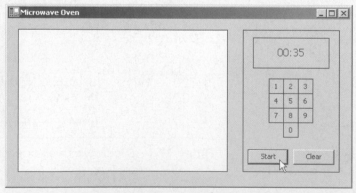

Figure 19.4 **Microwave Oven** application after invalid input has been entered and the **Start** Button has been clicked.

5. *Entering valid data.* Click the **Clear** Button to enter a new cooking time. Click Button **5** (to indicate 5 seconds); then, click **Start** (Fig. 19.5).

(cont.)

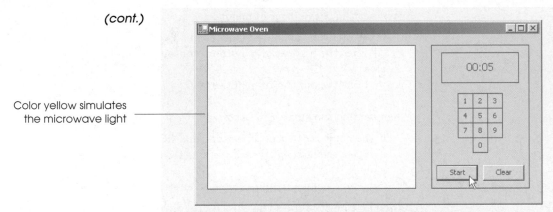

Color yellow simulates the microwave light

Figure 19.5 **Microwave Oven** application with a valid time entered and the inside light turned on (it's now cooking).

6. ***Viewing the application after the cooking time has expired.*** Wait five seconds. Notice that the display Label shows the time counting down by one each second. When the time has reached zero, the display Label changes to contain the text **Done!** and the microwave oven's window changes back to the same color as the Form (Fig. 19.6).

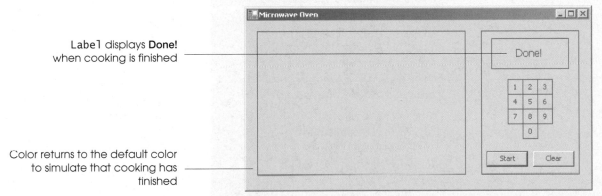

Label displays **Done!** when cooking is finished

Color returns to the default color to simulate that cooking has finished

Figure 19.6 **Microwave Oven** application after the cooking time has elapsed.

7. ***Closing the application.*** Close your application by clicking its close box.
8. ***Closing the IDE.*** Close Visual Studio .NET by clicking its close box.

19.2 Designing the Microwave Oven Application

In Tutorial 14, you learned to use GroupBoxes to group various controls. The **Microwave Oven** application also groups controls using a **Panel** control. The main difference between Panels and GroupBoxes is that GroupBoxes can display a caption and Panels cannot. The **Microwave Oven** application requires two Panels—one to contain the controls of the application, and the other to represent the microwave oven's glass window. The template application provided for you contains one of these Panels.

The **Microwave Oven** application contains a class (called Time) whose objects store the cooking time in minutes and seconds. All of the controls you have used (including the Form itself) are defined as classes. You will create the Time class before you complete the class for the **Microwave Oven**. The following pseudocode describes the basic operation of the Time class:

When the time object is created:
    Assign input to variables for number of minutes and number of seconds

GUI Design Tip

Use Panels to organize groups of related controls, where the purpose of those controls is obvious. If the purpose of the controls is not obvious, use a GroupBox in place of a Panel, because GroupBoxes can contain captions.

When setting the number of minutes:

    If the number of minutes is less than 60
        Set the number of minutes to specified value
    else
        Set the number of minutes to 0

When setting the number of seconds:

    If the number of seconds is less than 60
        Set the number of seconds to specified value
    else
        Set the number of seconds to 0

When an object of the `Time` class is created, the number of minutes and number of seconds will be initialized. Invalid data will cause both the number of minutes and number of seconds to be set to 0. The following pseudocode describes the basic operation of the **Microwave Oven** class:

When the user clicks a numeric Button:
    Display the formatted time

When the user clicks the Start Button:
    Store the minutes and seconds
    Display the formatted time
    Begin countdown—Start timer
    Turn the microwave light on

When the timer ticks (once per second):
    Decrease time by one second

    If new time is zero
        Stop the countdown
        Display text "Done!"
        Turn the microwave light off
    else
        Display new time

When the user clicks the Clear Button:
    Display text "Microwave Oven"
    Clear input
    Stop the countdown
    Turn the microwave light off

The user enters input by clicking the numeric `Button`s. Each time a numeric `Button` is clicked, the number on that `Button` is appended to the end of the cooking time that is displayed in the GUI's `Label`. At most, four digits can be displayed. After entering the cooking time, the user can click the **Start** `Button` to begin the cooking process or click the **Clear** `Button` and enter a new time. If the **Start** `Button` is clicked, a countdown using a `Timer` control begins, and the microwave oven's window changes to yellow, indicating that the microwave oven's light is on (so that the user can watch the food cook). Each second, the display is updated to show the remaining cooking time. When the countdown finishes, the display `Label` displays the text **Done!** and the microwave oven's "light" is turned off, by changing the window's color back to its default gray.

Now that you have test-driven the **Microwave Oven** application and studied its pseudocode representation, you will use an ACE table to help you convert the pseudocode to C#. Figure 19.7 lists the actions, controls and events that will help you complete your own version of this application.

Action/Control/Event (ACE) Table for the Microwave Oven Application

Action	Control/Object	Event
	bntOne, btnTwo, btnThree, btnFour, btnFive, btnSix, btnSeven, btnEight, btnNine, btnZero	Click
Display the formatted time	lblDisplay	
	btnStart	Click
Store the minutes and seconds	m_objTime	
Display the formatted time	lblDisplay	
Begin countdown—Start timer	tmrClock	
Turn microwave light on	pnlWindow	
	tmrClock	Tick
Decrease time by one second	m_objTime	
If new time is zero	m_objTime	
Stop the countdown	tmrClock	
Display text "Done!"	lblDisplay	
Turn microwave light off	pnlWindow	
else		
Display new time	lblDisplay	
	btnClear	Click
Display Text "Microwave Oven"	lblDisplay	
Clear input	m_strTime	
Stop the countdown	tmrClock	
Turn microwave light off	pnlWindow	

Figure 19.7   ACE table for the **Microwave Oven** application.

Input is sent to the application when the user clicks one of the numeric Buttons. Values are displayed in lblDisplay as they are entered. Once all input has been entered, the user clicks the **Start** Button to begin the countdown. The pnlWindow Panel's background color is set to yellow to simulate the microwave oven's light being turned on, and the tmrClock Timer will update lblDisplay each second during the countdown. To clear the input and start over, the user can click the **Clear** Button. In the following box, you begin creating your **Microwave Oven** application by adding the second Panel to the Form and viewing the template code.

Adding a Panel Control to the Microwave Oven Application

GUI Design Tip

Although it is possible to have a Panel without a border (by setting its BorderStyle to None), use borders on your Panels to improve readability and organization.

1. ***Copying the template to your working directory.*** Copy the C:\Examples\Tutorial19\TemplateApplication\MicrowaveOven directory to your C:\SimplyCSP directory.

2. ***Opening the Microwave Oven application's template file.*** Double click MicrowaveOven.sln in the MicrowaveOven directory to open the application in Visual Studio .NET.

3. ***Adding a Panel to the Form.*** Add a Panel control to the Form by double clicking the **Panel** control (☐ Panel) in the **Toolbox**. Name the control pnlWindow, as this Panel will represent your microwave oven's window. Set the Panel's Size property to 328, 224 and its Location property to 16, 16. Set the BorderStyle property to FixedSingle, to display a thin black rectangle surrounding your Panel.

(cont.)

Good Programming Practice

Use the pnl prefix when naming your Panel controls.

GUI Design Tip

A Panel can display scrollbars for use when the Panel is not large enough to display all of its controls at once. To increase readability, we suggest avoiding the use of scrollbars on Panels. If a Panel is not large enough to display all of its contents, increase the size of the Panel

4. **Rearranging and commenting the new control declaration.** In code view, locate the declaration for the pnlWindow Panel (line 40). Move this declaration above the rest of the control declarations, as in line 16 of Fig. 19.8. Add the comment in line 15.

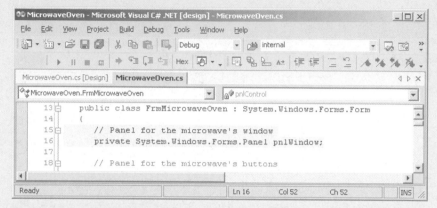

Figure 19.8 Rearranging and commenting the new control declaration.

5. **Viewing the template code.** Before you add more code to this application, take a few moments to examine the code provided. Line 45 of Fig. 19.9 declares the m_strTime variable, a string that will store user input. The template code also contains event handlers for the numeric Buttons' Click events. The user clicks a Button to append that Button's digit to the cooking time. Let's look closely at one of these event handlers (Fig. 19.10). Each event handler for the numeric keypad Buttons appends the current Button's number to m_strTime (line 292) and calls the DisplayTime method (line 293), which displays the remaining cooking time in the application's Label. There are ten of these event handlers—one for each digit from 0 to 9.

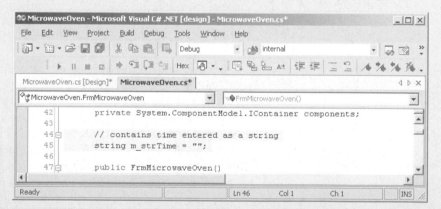

Figure 19.9 The m_strTime variable contains the user's input.

MicrowaveOven.cs contains four more methods that you will define in this tutorial. The first is the btnStart_Click event handler in lines 378–383 of Fig. 19.11. This event handler will be used to start the microwave oven's cooking process, which in this simulation consists of a time countdown and a change in the window's color to yellow, simulating the oven's light being on.

The btnClear_Click event handler (lines 385–390) will be used to clear the time entered. The **Clear** Button is used to change the time entered or terminate cooking early. The event handler resets the time to all zeros and displays the text **Microwave Oven**. The DisplayTime method (lines 392–396) will be used to display the cooking time as it is being entered. The tmrClock_Tick event handler (lines 398–403) will be used to change the application's Label during the countdown.

(cont.)

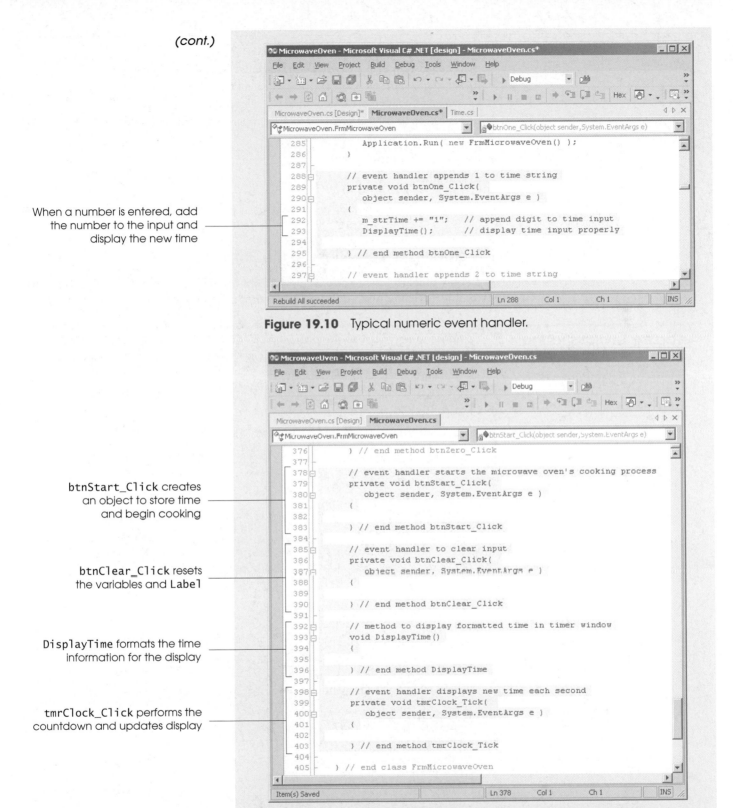

When a number is entered, add
the number to the input and
display the new time

Figure 19.10   Typical numeric event handler.

btnStart_Click creates
an object to store time
and begin cooking

btnClear_Click resets
the variables and **Label**

DisplayTime formats the time
information for the display

tmrClock_Click performs the
countdown and updates display

Figure 19.11   **Microwave Oven** application's remaining methods.

6. *Saving the project.* Select **File > Save All** to save your modified code.

SELF-REVIEW 1. A Panel is different from a GroupBox in that a _____.

a) GroupBox can be used to organize controls, whereas a Panel cannot

b) Panel contains a caption, whereas a GroupBox does not

c) GroupBox contains a caption, whereas a Panel does not

d) Panel can be used to organize controls, whereas a GroupBox cannot

2. Set the BorderStyle property of a Panel to _____, to display a thin black rectangle surrounding your Panel.

a) BlackRect b) SingleBlack

c) Single d) FixedSingle

Answers: 1) c. 2) d.

19.3 Adding a New Class to the Project

Next, you will learn how to add a class to your application. This class will be used to create objects that contain the time in minutes and seconds.

Adding a Class to the Microwave Oven Application

1. ***Adding a new class to the project.*** Select **Project > Add Class**. In the dialog that appears (Fig. 19.12), enter the class name (Time) in the **Name:** field, then click the **Open** Button. Note that the class name (ending with the .cs file extension) appears in the **Solution Explorer** below the project name (Fig. 19.13).

Select **Class** as a new item ——

Name of the new class ——

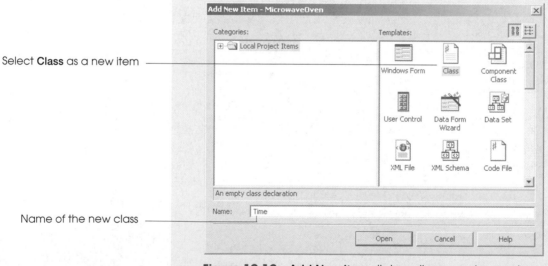

Figure 19.12 **Add New Item** dialog allows you to create a new class.

New file displayed in the **Solution Explorer** ——

Figure 19.13 **Solution Explorer** displaying the new class file.

(cont.)

2. ***Viewing the code that has been added to this class.*** If `Time.cs` does not open for you when it is created, double click the file in the **Solution Explorer**. Notice that several lines of code have been added for you (Fig. 19.14). Line 1 is a `using` directive, which tells the compiler which FCL classes can be accessed within the current file. By using the `namespace` keyword, line 3 places the `Time` class declaration within the `MicrowaveOven` namespace (Visual Studio .NET uses the project name as the default namespace). Grouping the `FrmMicrowaveOven` class and the `Time` class within the same namespace allows either class to use methods from the other class. In this application, the `FrmMicrowaveOven` class will use methods from the `Time` class.

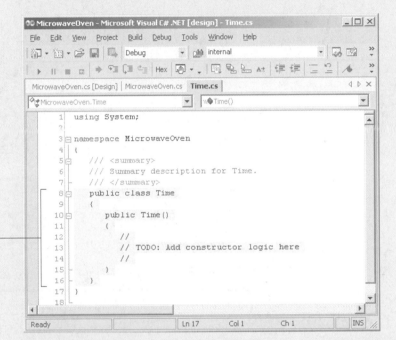

Default class declaration added by Visual Studio .NET

Figure 19.14 Default class declaration.

Line 8, which begins the `Time` class declaration, contains the `public` and `class` keywords, followed by the name of the class (in this case, `Time`). The `class` keyword indicates that what follows is a class declaration. You will learn about the `public` keyword in Section 19.7. An opening left brace (`{`) begins the class declaration (line 9), and a closing right brace (`}`) ends the class declaration (line 16). Any code placed between these braces form the class declaration's body. Any methods defined or variables declared in the body of a class are considered to be **members** of that class. The class declaration contains an empty method called a constructor (lines 10–15). You will create your own constructor in Section 19.4.

Good Programming Practice

Add comments at the beginning of programmer-defined classes to increase readability. The comments should indicate the name of the file that contains the class and the purpose of the class being defined.

3. ***Adding instance variables to your application.*** Add lines 1–2 of Fig. 19.15 to `Time.cs`, above the class declaration. You should add comments indicating the name and purpose of your class files. Add lines 13–15 to the `Time` class declaration.

Lines 14 and 15 declare each of the two `int` instance variables—`m_intMinute` and `m_intSecond`. The `Time` class will store a time value containing minutes and seconds—the value for minutes is stored in `m_intMinute` and the value for seconds is stored in `m_intSecond`. Recall from Tutorial 15 that our member-naming preference is to prefix an `m_` to each instance variable. Finally, be sure to add a comment on line 24 where the class declaration is terminated.

(cont.)

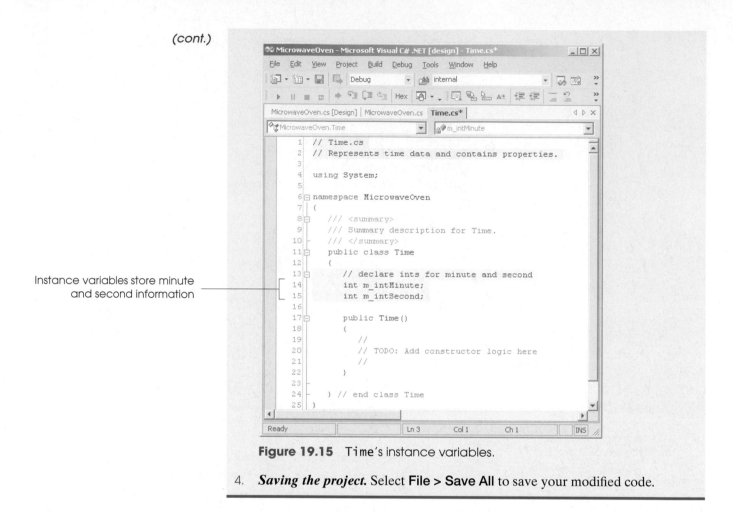

Instance variables store minute and second information

Figure 19.15 Time's instance variables.

4. **Saving the project.** Select **File > Save All** to save your modified code.

SELF-REVIEW

1. To add a class to a project in Visual Studio .NET, select _____.

    a) **File > Add Class**
                b) **File > Add File > Add Class**

    c) **Project > Add Class**
                d) **Project > Add File > Add Class**

2. A class declaration ends with a(n) _____.

    a) closing right brace (})
                b) `endclass` statement

    c) semicolon
                d) All of the above.

Answers: 1) c. 2) a.

19.4 Initializing Class Objects: Constructors

A class can contain methods as well as instance variables. You have already used the `Format` method from the `String` class and the `Next` method from the `Random` class. A **constructor** is a special method within a class declaration that is used to initialize a class's instance variables. In Tutorial 14, you learned how to use constructors to create objects. In the following box, you create a constructor for your `Time` class, allowing clients to create `Time` objects and initialize those objects' data.

Defining a Constructor

1. **Adding a constructor to a class.** Replace the empty constructor in lines 17–22 of Fig. 19.15 with lines 17–21 of Fig. 19.16 in the body of the `Time` class. The name of the constructor must be the class name (`Time`). Again, you will learn about the `public` keyword in Section 19.7.

(cont.)

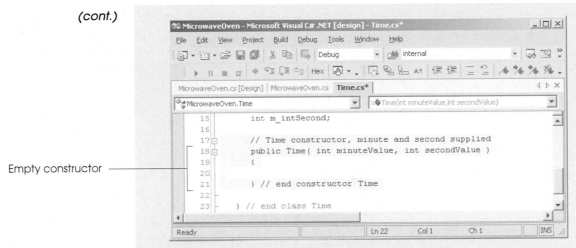

Figure 19.16   Empty constructor.

You write code for the constructor, which is invoked each time an object of that class is instantiated (created) using the **new** operator. This constructor method then performs the actions in its body, which you will add in the next few steps. A constructor's actions consist mainly of statements that initialize the class's instance variables.

Constructors can take arguments (you'll see how to provide arguments to constructors momentarily) but cannot return values. An important difference between constructors and other methods is that constructors cannot specify a return type. A class's instance variables can be initialized in the constructor or when those variables are declared in the class declaration. The m_intSecond variable, for instance, can be initialized where it is declared (line 15) or it can be initialized in Time's constructor.

2. ***Initializing variables in a constructor.*** Add lines 20–21 of Fig. 19.17 to the constructor. These lines initialize Time's instance variables to the values of the constructor's parameter variables (line 18 of Fig. 19.16). When an object is created in a client of a class, values are often specified for that object. A Time object can now be created with the statement

```
m_objTimeObject = new Time( 5, 3 );
```

This Time object will be created and the constructor will execute. The values 5 and 3 are assigned to the constructor's parameters, which will be used to initialize m_intSecond and m_intMinute.

Common Programming Error

Attempting to return a value from a constructor is a syntax error.

Error-Prevention Tip

Providing a constructor to ensure that every object is initialized with meaningful values can help eliminate logic errors.

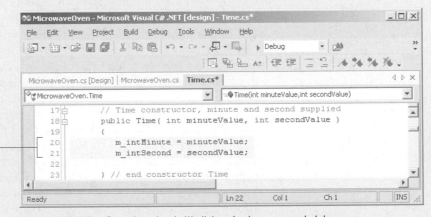

Figure 19.17   Constructor initializing instance variables.

(cont.)

3. ***Creating a Time object.*** After declaring the class, you can use it as a type (just as you would use int or double) in declarations. View Microwave-Oven.cs by selecting the **MicrowaveOven.cs** tab above the code editor. Add lines 47–48 of Fig. 19.18 to your application.

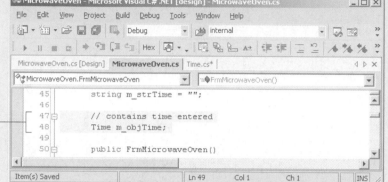

Declare m_objTime of the programmer-defined type Time

Figure 19.18 Declaring an object of type Time.

Notice the use of the class name, Time, as a type. Just as you can create many variables from a type, such as int, you can create many objects from class types. You can create your own class types as needed; this is one reason why C# is known as an **extensible language**—the language can be "extended" with new types.

4. ***Saving the project.*** Select **File > Save All** to save your modified code.

SELF-REVIEW

1. A(n) _____ language is one that can be "extended" with new types.

   a) data   b) extensible

   c) typeable   d) extended

2. Variables can be initialized _____.

   a) when they are declared   b) to their default values

   c) in a constructor   d) All of the above.

Answers: 1) b. 2) d.

19.5 Properties

Clients of a class usually want to manipulate that class's instance variables. For example, assume a class (Person) that stores information about a person, including age information (stored in int instance variable intAge). Clients who create an object of the Person class could want to modify intAge—perhaps incorrectly, by assigning a negative value to intAge, for example. Classes often provide **properties** to allow clients to access and modify instance variables safely. You have already seen and used several properties in previous tutorials. For instance, many GUI controls contain a Text property, used to retrieve or modify the text displayed by a control. When a value is to be assigned to a property, the code in that property declaration is executed. The code in that property typically checks the value to be assigned and rejects invalid data. In this tutorial, you learn how to create your own properties to help clients of a class read and modify the class's instance variables. You will create two properties, Minute and Second, for your Time class. Minute allows clients to access the m_intMinute variable safely, and Second allows clients to access the m_intSecond variable safely.

A property declaration actually consists of two **accessors**—method-like code units that handle the details of modifying and returning data. The **set** accessor allows clients to set (that is, assign values to) properties. For example, when the code

```
objTime.Minute = 35;
```

executes, the `set` accessor of the `Minute` property executes. A `set` accessor typically provides data-validation capabilities (such as range checking) to ensure that the value of each instance variable is set properly. In your **Microwave Oven** application, users can specify an amount of minutes only in the range 0 to 59. Values not in this range will be discarded by the `set` accessor, and `m_intMinute` will be assigned the value 0. The **get** accessor allows clients to get (that is, obtain the value of) a property. When the code

```
intMinuteValue = objTime.Minute;
```

executes, the `get` accessor of the `Minute` property executes (and returns the value of the `m_intMinute` instance variable).

Each property is typically defined to perform validity checking—to ensure that the data assigned to the property is valid. Keeping an object's data valid is also known as keeping that data in a **consistent state**. The `Minute` property keeps instance variable `m_intMinute` in a consistent state. In the following box, you create the `Minute` and `Second` properties for your `Time` class, defining `get` and `set` accessors for each.

Defining Properties

1. ***Adding the Minute property to the Time class.*** View `Time.cs` by selecting the **Time.cs** tab above the code editor. Add lines 25–38 of Fig. 19.19, then press *Enter* to add the `Minute` property to the `Time` class. The property declaration begins in line 26 with the `public` keyword (which will be discussed in Section 19.7), followed by a type (in this case, `int`), indicating the type of any value assigned to or read from this property. The property name (in this case, `Minute`) follows the type. Notice that no parentheses follow the property name. The lack of parentheses after the property name distinguishes a property from a method. A set of braces enclose the property declaration (lines 27 and 38). Notice that we have added a comment to this line, indicating the name of the property being terminated.

get accessor retrieves data ————

set accessor stores data ————

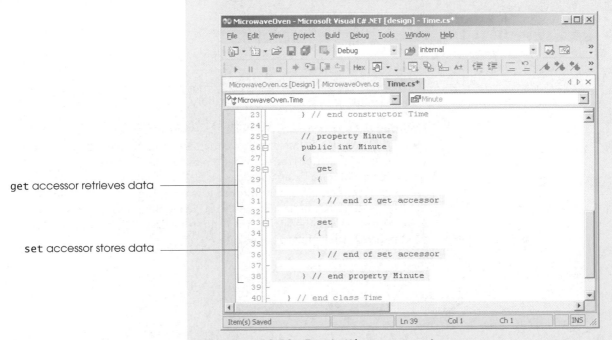

Figure 19.19 Empty `Minute` property.

(cont.)

The **get** keyword in line 28 indicates the beginning of this property's get accessor. A set of braces follow the get keyword (lines 29 and 31). Any code that you insert between these braces will make up the get accessor's body and will be executed when a client of this class attempts to read a value from the Minute property, such as with the code

```
intMinuteValue = objTime.Minute;
```

The **set** keyword in line 33 indicates the beginning of this property's set accessor. A set of braces follow the set keyword (lines 34 and 36). Any code that you insert between these braces will make up the set accessor's body and will be executed when a client of this class attempts to assign a value to the Minute property, such as with the code

Error-Prevention Tip

A property that sets the value of an instance variable should verify that the intended new value is correct. If it is not, the set accessor should place the instance variable into an appropriate consistent state.

```
objTime.Minute = 35;
```

The value assigned is stored in a special identifier named **value**. This identifier is used to access the value assigned to the Minute property. You will use the value identifier shortly.

2. *Defining the get accessor.* Add line 31 of Fig. 19.20 to your get accessor. Also add a comment (line 28) above the get accessor, to increase the clarity of your code. When the Minute property is referenced, you want your get accessor to return the value of m_intMinute just as you would return a value from a method, so you use the return keyword in line 31, followed by the m_intMinute identifier.

Returning data from a property ———

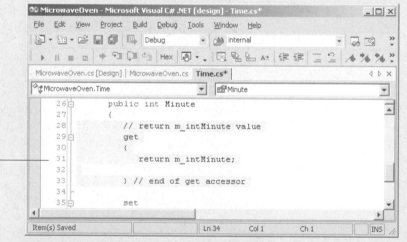

Figure 19.20   get accessor declaration.

3. *Defining the set accessor.* Add lines 38–46 of Fig. 19.21 to your set accessor. Also add a comment (line 35) above the set accessor, to increase the clarity of your code. When the Minute property is assigned a value, you want to test whether the value to be assigned is valid. You do not want to accept a minutes value greater than 59, a condition that is tested in line 39. If the number of minutes is valid, it will be assigned to m_intMinute in line 41. Otherwise, the value 0 will be assigned to m_intMinute in line 45. The value identifier is used to access the value to be assigned.

(cont.)

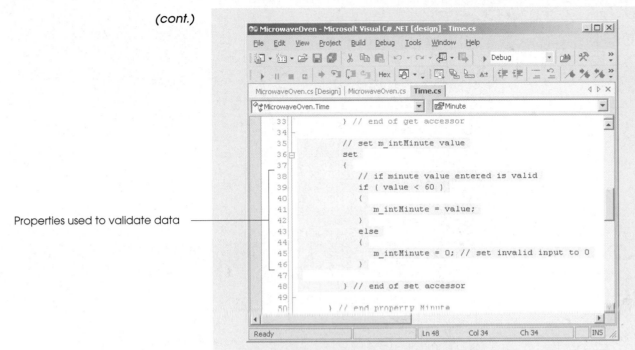

Properties used to validate data

Figure 19.21   set accessor declaration.

4. ***Adding the Second property to the Time class.*** Add lines 52–56 of Fig. 19.22 to your application.

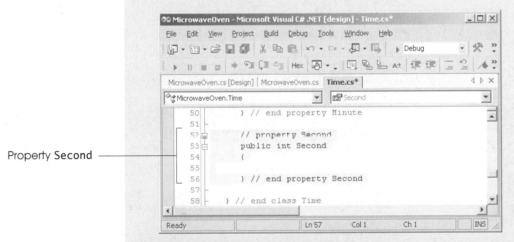

Property Second

Figure 19.22   Second property.

5. ***Defining the Second property's accessors.*** Add lines 55–75 of Fig. 19.23 to the Second property declaration. Notice that this property is similar to Minute, except that the m_intSecond variable is being modified and read, as opposed to the m_intMinute variable.

6. ***Assigning values to properties.*** Change lines 20–21 of Fig. 19.17 to lines 20–21 of Fig. 19.24. Now that you have defined properties to ensure that only valid data will be assigned to m_intMinute and m_intSecond, you can use these properties to safely initialize instance variables in the class's constructor.

7. ***Saving the project.*** Select **File > Save All** to save your modified code.

(cont.)

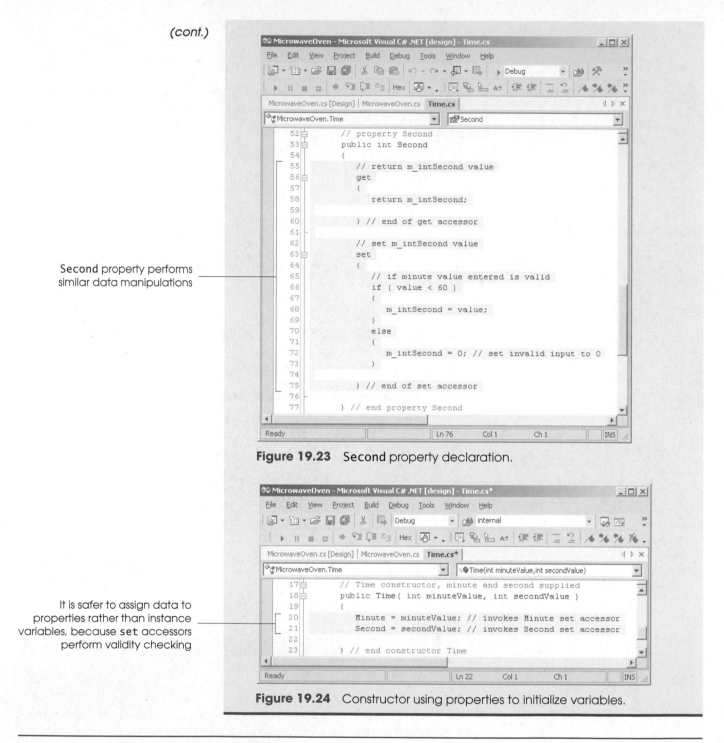

Second property performs
similar data manipulations

Figure 19.23 Second property declaration.

It is safer to assign data to
properties rather than instance
variables, because set accessors
perform validity checking

Figure 19.24 Constructor using properties to initialize variables.

SELF-REVIEW

1. A(n) _____ can ensure that a value is appropriate for a data member, before the data member is assigned that value.

    a) get accessor   b) access accessor

    c) modify accessor   d) set accessor

2. Properties can contain both _____ accessors.

    a) return and value   b) get and value

    c) get and set   d) return and set

Answers: 1) d. 2) c.

19.6 Completing the Microwave Oven Application

Now that you have completed your Time class, you will use an object of this class to maintain the cook time in your application. Follow the steps in the next box to add this functionality to your application.

Completing the Microwave Oven Application

1. ***Formatting user input.*** View MicrowaveOven.cs by selecting the **MicrowaveOven.cs** tab above the code editor. Add lines 385–389 of Fig. 19.25 to the btnStart_Click event handler.

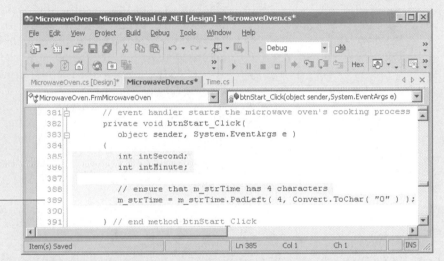

Ensure m_strTime has four characters for conversion purposes

Figure 19.25 Declaring variables for the second and minute values.

The intSecond and intMinute variables (lines 385–386) will be used to store the second and minute values entered by the user. Line 389 uses String method **PadLeft**, which appends characters to the beginning of a string based on that string's length. This method can be used to guarantee the length of a string—if that string has fewer characters than desired, the PadLeft method will add characters to the beginning of that string until the string has the proper number of characters. You want m_strTime to contain four characters (for example, "0325" rather than "325" for a time of "3:25", representing 3 minutes and 25 seconds). Having four digits makes the conversion to minutes and seconds easier. You can now simply convert the first two digits (03) to a minute value and the last two digits (25) to a second value. The first argument in the PadLeft call, 4, specifies the length that m_strTime will have after characters have been appended. If m_strTime already contains four or more characters, PadLeft will not have any effect. The second argument (the character 0) specifies the character that will be appended to the beginning of the string. Notice that specifying only "0" as the second argument will cause an error, as "0" is of type string. The PadLeft method expects the second argument to be a single character, which is of the char type. You obtain the character 0 by calling the **Convert.ToChar** method, which converts your string zero to a character zero. [*Note*: You could simply use the char value '0' instead of Convert.ToChar("0"). We use the latter to demonstrate the Convert.ToChar method.]

(cont.)

2. ***Converting user input to* ints.** Add lines 391–393 of Fig. 19.26 to event handler `btnStart_Click`. Line 392 calls the `Int32.Parse` method to convert the last two characters of `m_strTime` to an `int` and assign this value to `intSecond`. The last two characters are selected from `m_strTime` by using the **Substring** method. This is another `String` method, used to return only a portion of a `string` from `m_strTime`. The argument passed to `Substring`, 2, indicates that the subset of characters returned from this method should begin with the character at position 2, and continue until the end of the `string`. Remember that the character at position 2 is actually the third character in the `string`, because the position values of a `string` begin at 0. In the example `"0325"`, calling `Substring` with the argument 2 returns `"25"`. Line 403 selects the first two characters of `m_strTime`, converts the value to an `int`, and assigns this value to `intMinute`. The call to `Substring` on line 403 takes two arguments. The first argument, 0, indicates that the characters returned from this method start with the first character (at position 0) of `m_strTime`. The second argument, 2, indicates that only two characters from the starting position should be returned. In the example `"0325"`, calling `Substring` with the arguments 0 and 2 returns `"03"`.

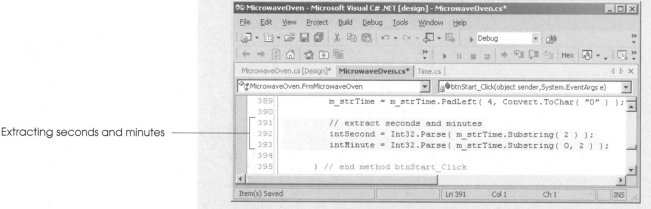

Extracting seconds and minutes

Figure 19.26 Forming the minute and second values from input.

3. ***Creating a* Time *object*.** Add lines 395–396 of Fig. 19.27 to `btnStart_Click`. Line 396 creates an object of the `Time` type. This is called **instantiation**. When the object is instantiated, the `new` operator allocates the memory in which the `Time` object will be stored; then, the `Time` constructor is called (with the values of `intMinute` and `intSecond` as arguments) to initialize the instance variables of the `Time` object. The constructor then returns a reference to the newly created object; this reference is assigned to `m_objTime`.

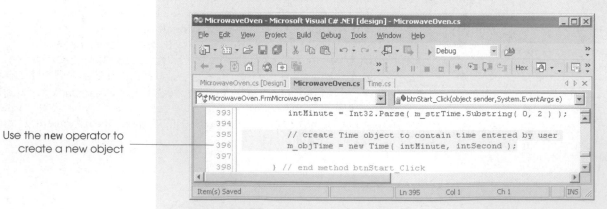

Use the **new** operator to create a new object

Figure 19.27 Creating a Time object.

(cont.)

Notice that, after you type new in line 396, *Intellisense* displays a window of available types. Notice that the new Time class will be displayed in the *Intellisense* window (Fig. 19.28). Your class has been added to the list of known types, demonstrating the extensibility of C#.

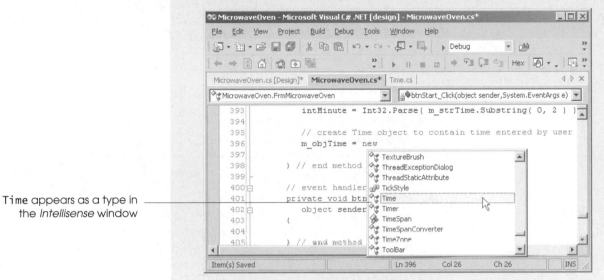

Time appears as a type in the *Intellisense* window

Figure 19.28 Time appearing as a type in an *Intellisense* window.

4. ***Accessing a Time object's properties.*** Add lines 398–399 of Fig. 19.29 to btnStart_Click. These lines use the newly created Time object and the String.Format method to display the cooking time properly. You want the resulting string to contain two digits (for the minute), a colon (:) and finally another two digits (for the second). For example, if the time entered was 3 minutes and 20 seconds, the string that will display for the user is "03:20".

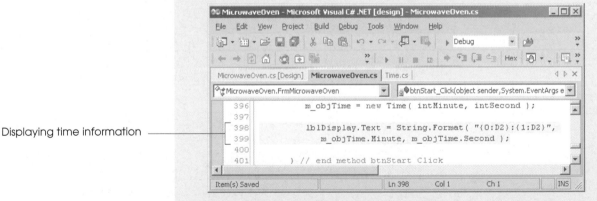

Displaying time information

Figure 19.29 Displaying time information with separating colon.

To achieve this result, you pass to the method the format control string "{0:D2}:{1:D2}", which indicates that arguments 0 and 1 (the first and second arguments after the format string argument) should take the format D2 (base 10 decimal number format using two digits) for display purposes—thus, 8 would be converted to 08. The colon between the braces } and { will be included in the output, separating the minutes from the seconds. The arguments after the format control string access m_objTime's minute and second values, using the Minute and Second properties. Notice that Time's properties appear in the *Intellisense* window (Fig. 19.30) when you try to access the object's members (using the dot operator). The *Intellisense* window also displays several methods that are generated by Visual Studio .NET when you create any class.

(cont.)

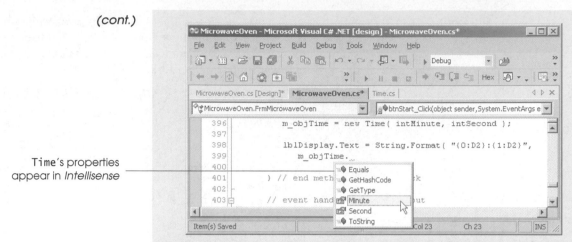

Time's properties appear in *Intellisense*

Figure 19.30 Properties of a programmer-defined type also appear in *Intellisense*.

5. ***Starting the cooking process.*** Add lines 401–405 of Fig. 19.31 to your application. Line 401 clears the user's input, so the user can enter new input at any time. Line 403 starts the `Timer` by setting its `Enabled` property to `true`. The `Timer`'s `Tick` event will now be raised each second. You will implement the event handler for this event shortly. Line 405 sets the `Panel`'s `BackColor` property to yellow to simulate the light inside the microwave oven. The color yellow is assigned to the `BackColor` property using the `Yellow` property of the **`Color`** structure. The `Color` structure contains several predefined colors as properties.

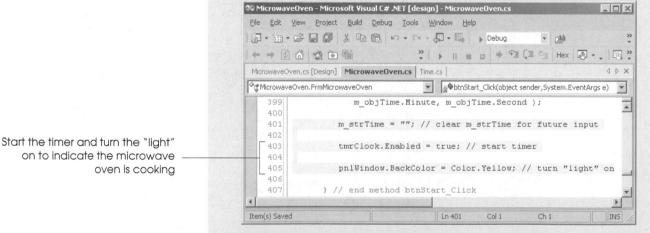

Start the timer and turn the "light" on to indicate the microwave oven is cooking

Figure 19.31 Starting the microwave oven countdown.

6. ***Clearing the cooking time.*** Add lines 413–418 of Fig. 19.32 to the `btnClear_Click` event handler. Line 414 sets the application's `Label` to **Microwave Oven**. Line 415 clears the input values stored in `m_strTime`, and line 416 resets the `Time` object to zero minutes and zero seconds. Line 417 disables the `Timer`, which stops the countdown. Line 418 sets the `Panel`'s background back to the `Panel`'s original color to simulate turning off the light inside the microwave oven. Notice that we set the `Panel`'s color using the **`SystemColors.Control`** property. This property contains the default background color for a `Panel` (and many other controls). When a `Panel` is added to a `Form`, its background takes on this default background color.

(cont.)

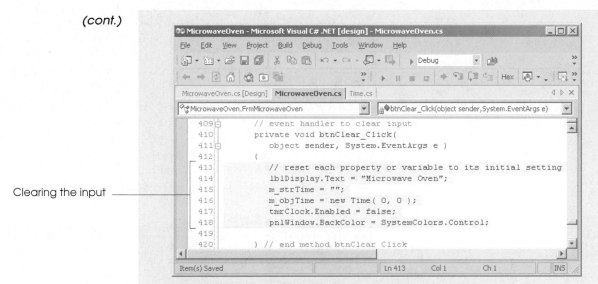

Clearing the input —

Figure 19.32 Clearing the **Microwave Oven** input.

7. ***Displaying data as it is being input.*** Add lines 425–434 of Fig. 19.33 to the `DisplayTime` method. This method will be called each time the user enters another digit for the cooking time. Lines 425–426 declare the `intSecond` and `intMinute` variables, which will store the current number of seconds and minutes. Line 428 declares `strDisplay`, which will store the user's current input in the proper display format. Lines 431–434 remove any extra digits entered by the user. (Recall that the user may enter a maximum of four digits.) Line 431 uses `String` property **Length**, which returns the number of characters in a `string`, to determine whether `m_strTime` has more than four digits.

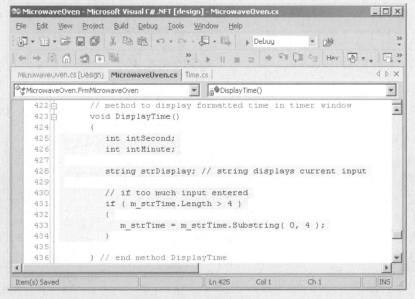

Figure 19.33 Modifying invalid user input.

(cont.)

If it does, line 433 uses `String` method `Substring` to remove the extra digits. The arguments (0 followed by 4) indicate that the substring returned should begin with the first character in `m_strTime` and continue for four characters. The result is assigned back to `m_strTime`, ensuring that any characters appended past the first four will be removed.

8. ***Completing the `DisplayTime` method.*** Add lines 436–444 of Fig. 19.34 to the `DisplayTime` method. These lines are similar to those of the `btnStart_Click` event handler. Line 436 appends zeros to the front of `m_strTime` if fewer than four digits were entered. Lines 439–440 use the `Substring` method to isolate the number of seconds and minutes currently entered. Lines 443–444 then use the `Format` method to display the input correctly.

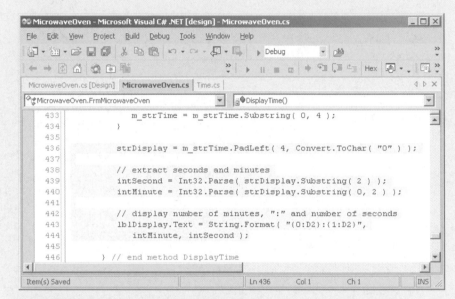

Figure 19.34 Displaying the current input.

9. ***Performing the countdown.*** Add lines 452–471 of Fig. 19.35 to the `tmrTimer_Tick` event handler. Remember that this event handler executes every second for as long as the `Timer` is enabled. Lines 453–468 modify the display `Label` once per second so that the time remaining is shown to the user.

   If the value of seconds is larger than zero (line 453), the number of seconds is decremented by one (line 455). If the value of seconds is zero but the value of minutes is greater than zero (line 457), the number of minutes is decremented by one (line 459) and the number of seconds is reset to 59 for the new minute (line 460). If the number of seconds is zero and the number of minutes is zero, the cooking process is stopped—the `Timer` is disabled (line 464), the display `Label` is set to `"Done!"` (line 465) and the window `Panel`'s background color is set back to its default background color (line 466).

10. ***Running the application.*** Select **Debug > Start** to run your application. Test your application to ensure that it runs correctly.

11. ***Closing the application.*** Close your running application by clicking its close box.

(cont.)

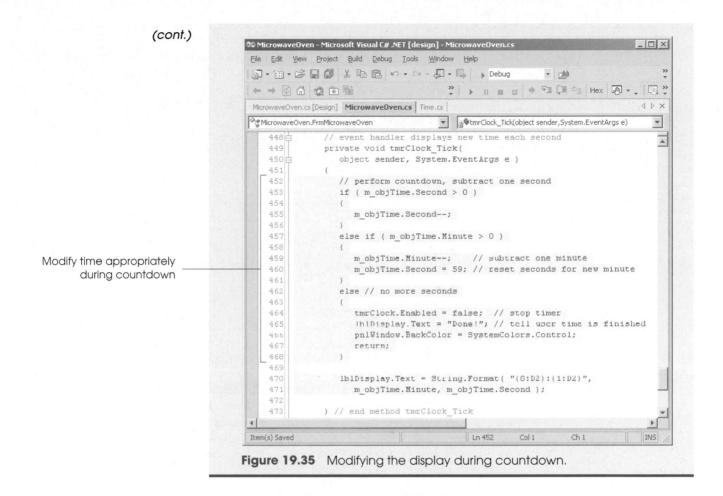

Modify time appropriately
during countdown

Figure 19.35 Modifying the display during countdown.

SELF-REVIEW

1. The _____ property returns the number of characters in a string.

   a) `Length`   b) `Size`

   c) `Char`   d) `Width`

2. The expression `strExample.Substring( 0, 7 )` returns the character(s) _____.

   a) that begin at position seven and run backward to position zero

   b) that begin at position zero and continue for seven characters

   c) at position zero and position seven   d) at position 0, repeated 7 times

Answers: 1) a. 2) b.

19.7 Controlling Access to Members

**Common
Programming Error**

Attempting to access a private class member from outside that class is a syntax error.

The **public** and **private** keywords are called **member-access modifiers**. You defined properties with member-access modifier `public` earlier in this tutorial. Class members that are declared with access modifier `public` are available to any `Time` object. The declaration of instance variables or properties with member-access modifier `private` makes them available only to methods, properties and events of the class. Attempting to access a class's `private` data from outside the class declaration is a syntax error. Normally, instance variables are declared `private`, whereas methods and properties are declared `public`. In the following box, you will declare this application's instance variables as `private`.

Controlling Access to Members

Good Programming Practice

Group all `private` class members in a class declaration, followed by all `public` class members. This helps enhance clarity and readability.

1. *Declaring Time's instance variables as private.* View `Time.cs` by selecting the **Time.cs** tab above the code editor. Precede the `int` type in lines 14 and 15 with the `private` keyword (as in Fig. 19.36), indicating that these instance variables are accessible only to members of the `Time` class. A class's `private` instance variables may be accessed only by methods, properties and events of that class.

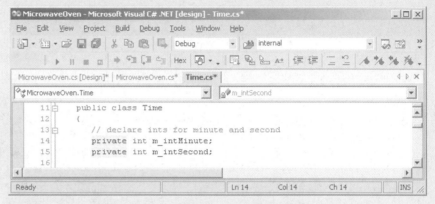

Figure 19.36 `Time`'s instance variables are `private`.

2. *Declaring FrmMicrowaveOven's instance variables as private.* View `MicrowaveOven.cs` by selecting the **MicrowaveOven.cs** tab above the code editor. Precede each type in lines 45 and 48 with the `private` keyword (as in Fig. 19.37), indicating that these instance variables are accessible only to members of the `FrmMicrowaveOven` class. When an object of the class contains such instance variables, only methods, properties and events of that object's class can access the variables.

Good Programming Practice

For clarity, every instance variable or property declaration should be preceded by a member-access modifier.

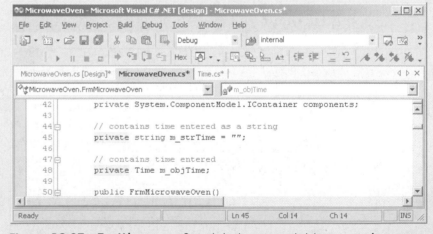

Figure 19.37 `FrmMicrowaveOven`'s instance variables are `private`.

Notice that the control variables (such as `pnlWindow`) you have created throughout this book have the `private` keyword automatically added to their declarations (as in line 16 of Fig. 19.8). You now know that this occurs because controls are specific to the `Form`'s class, and not the entire application, which includes class `Time`.

(cont.)

3. ***Setting the DisplayTime method as private.*** Add the `private` keyword to the beginning of the `DisplayTime` method header (line 423 of Fig. 19.38). As with variables, methods are declared `private` when they should only be accessible to other members of the current class. In this example only, the class that defines your **Microwave Oven** uses the `DisplayTime` method, so you should make this method `private`.

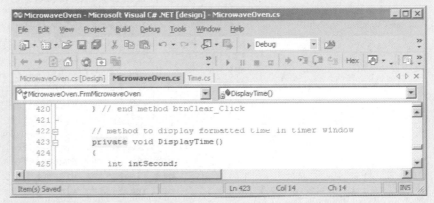

Figure 19.38   `FrmMicrowaveOven`'s methods are `private`.

Notice that the event handlers you have created throughout this book have the `private` keyword automatically added to their headers (as in line 289 of Fig. 19.10). You now know that this occurs because event handlers are specific to the Form's class, and not the entire application, which includes the `Time` class.

Software Design Tip

Declare all instance variables of a class as `private`. When necessary, provide `public` properties to set and get the values of `private` instance variables.

4. ***Running the application.*** Select **Debug > Start** to run your application. Notice that the application performs as it did in the previous box. This occurs because when instance variables are declared, they are by default `private` variables. For example, recall that the instance variables of `Time` did not appear in the *Intellisense* window of Fig. 19.30. These variables were `private` by default, and therefore not accessible outside of the `Time` class. Inaccessible variables do not appear in the *Intellisense* window. It is a good practice always to precede instance variables with a member-access modifier (usually `private`). Changing `DisplayTime` to be `private` did not affect the application either, because your code does not attempt to access this method from outside the class in which it is defined.

5. ***Closing the application.*** Close your running application by clicking its close box.

Figures 19.39 and 19.40 present the source code for the **Microwave Oven** application. The lines of code that contain new programming concepts that you learned in this tutorial are highlighted.

```
1   using System;
2   using System.Drawing;
3   using System.Collections;
4   using System.ComponentModel;
5   using System.Windows.Forms;
6   using System.Data;
7
8   namespace MicrowaveOven
9   {
```

Figure 19.39   **Microwave Oven** application code. (Part 1 of 6.)

```
10        /// <summary>
11        /// Summary description for FrmMicrowaveOven.
12        /// </summary>
13        public class FrmMicrowaveOven : System.Windows.Forms.Form
14        {
15           // Panel for the microwave's window
16           private System.Windows.Forms.Panel pnlWindow;
17
18           // Panel for the microwave's buttons
19           private System.Windows.Forms.Panel pnlControl;
20
21           // Label and Timer for the microwave's timer display
22           private System.Windows.Forms.Label lblDisplay;
23           private System.Windows.Forms.Timer tmrClock;
24
25           // Buttons of the microwave
26           private System.Windows.Forms.Button btnOne;
27           private System.Windows.Forms.Button btnTwo;
28           private System.Windows.Forms.Button btnThree;
29           private System.Windows.Forms.Button btnFour;
30           private System.Windows.Forms.Button btnFive;
31           private System.Windows.Forms.Button btnSix;
32           private System.Windows.Forms.Button btnSeven;
33           private System.Windows.Forms.Button btnEight;
34           private System.Windows.Forms.Button btnNine;
35           private System.Windows.Forms.Button btnZero;
36           private System.Windows.Forms.Button btnStart;
37           private System.Windows.Forms.Button btnClear;
38
39           /// <summary>
40           /// Required designer variable.
41           /// </summary>
42           private System.ComponentModel.IContainer components;
43
44           // contains time entered as a string
45           private string m_strTime = "";
46
47           // contains time entered
48           private Time m_objTime;
49
50           public FrmMicrowaveOven()
51           {
52              //
53              // Required for Windows Form Designer support
54              //
55              InitializeComponent();
56
57              //
58              // TODO: Add any constructor code after InitializeComponent
59              // call
60              //
61           }
62
63           /// <summary>
64           /// Clean up any resources being used.
65           /// </summary>
66           protected override void Dispose( bool disposing )
67           {
```

Declaring instance variable as `private` — line 45

Creating an object of a programmer-defined type — line 48

Figure 19.39   Microwave Oven application code. (Part 2 of 6.)

```
68              if( disposing )
69              {
70                 if (components != null)
71                 {
72                    components.Dispose();
73                 }
74              }
75              base.Dispose( disposing );
76           }
77
78           // Windows Form Designer generated code
79
80           /// <summary>
81           /// The main entry point for the application.
82           /// </summary>
83           [STAThread]
84           static void Main()
85           {
86              Application.Run( new FrmMicrowaveOven() );
87           }
88
89           // event handler appends 1 to time string
90           private void btnOne_Click(
91              object sender, System.EventArgs e )
92           {
93              m_strTime += "1";    // append digit to time input
94              DisplayTime();       // display time input properly
95
96           } // end method btnOne_Click
97
98           // event handler appends 2 to time string
99           private void btnTwo_Click(
100             object sender, System.EventArgs e )
101          {
102             m_strTime += "2";    // append digit to time input
103             DisplayTime();       // display time input properly
104
105          } // end method btnTwo_Click
106
107          // event handler appends 3 to time string
108          private void btnThree_Click(
109             object sender, System.EventArgs e )
110          {
111             m_strTime += "3";    // append digit to time input
112             DisplayTime();       // display time input properly
113
114          } // end method btnThree_Click
115
116          // event handler appends 4 to time string
117          private void btnFour_Click(
118             object sender, System.EventArgs e )
119          {
120             m_strTime += "4";    // append digit to time input
121             DisplayTime();       // display time input properly
122
123          } // end method btnFour_Click
124
125          // event handler appends 5 to time string
```

Figure 19.39 **Microwave Oven** application code. (Part 3 of 6.)

```
126      private void btnFive_Click(
127         object sender, System.EventArgs e )
128      {
129         m_strTime += "5";    // append digit to time input
130         DisplayTime();       // display time input properly
131
132      } // end method btnFive_Click
133
134      // event handler appends 6 to time string
135      private void btnSix_Click(
136         object sender, System.EventArgs e )
137      {
138         m_strTime += "6";    // append digit to time input
139         DisplayTime();       // display time input properly
140
141      } // end method btnSix_Click
142
143      // event handler appends 7 to time string
144      private void btnSeven_Click(
145         object sender, System.EventArgs e )
146      {
147         m_strTime += "7";    // append digit to time input
148         DisplayTime();       // display time input properly
149
150      } // end method btnSeven_Click
151
152      // event handler appends 8 to time string
153      private void btnEight_Click(
154         object sender, System.EventArgs e )
155      {
156         m_strTime += "8";    // append digit to time input
157         DisplayTime();       // display time input properly
158
159      } // end method btnEight_Click
160
161      // event handler appends 9 to time string
162      private void btnNine_Click(
163         object sender, System.EventArgs e )
164      {
165         m_strTime += "9";    // append digit to time input
166         DisplayTime();       // display time input properly
167
168      } // end method btnNine_Click
169
170      // event handler appends 0 to time string
171      private void btnZero_Click(
172         object sender, System.EventArgs e )
173      {
174         m_strTime += "0";    // append digit to time input
175         DisplayTime();       // display time input properly
176
177      } // end method btnZero_Click
178
179      // event handler starts the microwave oven's cooking process
180      private void btnStart_Click(
181         object sender, System.EventArgs e )
182      {
183         int intSecond;
```

Figure 19.39   Microwave Oven application code. (Part 4 of 6.)

```
184        int intMinute;
185
186        // ensure that m_strTime has 4 characters
187        m_strTime = m_strTime.PadLeft( 4, Convert.ToChar( "0" ) );
188
189        // extract seconds and minutes
190        intSecond = Int32.Parse( m_strTime.Substring( 2 ) );
191        intMinute = Int32.Parse( m_strTime.Substring( 0, 2 ) );
192
193        // create Time object to contain time entered by user
194        m_objTime = new Time( intMinute, intSecond );
195
196        lblDisplay.Text = String.Format( "{0:D2}:{1:D2}",
197           m_objTime.Minute, m_objTime.Second );
198
199        m_strTime = ""; // clear m_strTime for future input
200
201        tmrClock.Enabled = true; // start timer
202
203        pnlWindow.BackColor = Color.Yellow; // turn "light" on
204
205     } // end method btnStart_Click
206
207     // event handler to clear input
208     private void btnClear_Click(
209        object sender, System.EventArgs e )
210     {
211        // reset each property or variable to its initial setting
212        lblDisplay.Text = "Microwave Oven";
213        m_strTime = "";
214        m_objTime = new Time( 0, 0 );
215        tmrClock.Enabled = false;
216        pnlWindow.BackColor = SystemColors.Control;
217
218     } // end method btnClear_Click
219
220     // method to display formatted time in timer window
221     private void DisplayTime()
222     {
223        int intSecond;
224        int intMinute;
225
226        string strDisplay; // string displays current input
227
228        // if too much input entered
229        if ( m_strTime.Length > 4 )
230        {
231           m_strTime = m_strTime.Substring( 0, 4 );
232        }
233
234        strDisplay = m_strTime.PadLeft( 4, Convert.ToChar( "0" ) );
235
236        // extract seconds and minutes
237        intSecond = Int32.Parse( strDisplay.Substring( 2 ) );
238        intMinute = Int32.Parse( strDisplay.Substring( 0, 2 ) );
239
240        // display number of minutes, ":" and number of seconds
241        lblDisplay.Text = String.Format( "{0:D2}:{1:D2}",
242           intMinute, intSecond );
```

Creating a new object of a programmer-defined type — *(line 194)*

Accessing properties of a programmer-defined type — *(lines 196–197)*

Use the BackColor property to change the Panel's color — *(line 203)*

Use the SystemColors.Control propery to restore the default background color to the Panel — *(line 216)*

Declaring a method as private — *(line 221)*

The Length property returns number of characters in a string — *(line 229)*

The Substring method returns a subset of characters in a string — *(line 231)*

The PadLeft method appends characters to the beginning of a string — *(line 234)*

Figure 19.39 Microwave Oven application code. (Part 5 of 6.)

```
243
244        } // end method DisplayTime
245
246        // event handler displays new time each second
247        private void tmrClock_Tick(
248           object sender, System.EventArgs e )
249        {
250           // perform countdown, subtract one second
251           if  ( m_objTime.Second > 0 )
252           {
253              m_objTime.Second--;
254           }
255           else if ( m_objTime.Minute > 0 )
256           {
257              m_objTime.Minute--;    // subtract one minute
258              m_objTime.Second = 59; // reset seconds for new minute
259           }
260           else // no more seconds
261           {
262              tmrClock.Enabled = false;  // stop timer
263              lblDisplay.Text = "Done!"; // tell user time is finished
264              pnlWindow.BackColor = SystemColors.Control;
265              return;
266           }
267
268           lblDisplay.Text = String.Format( "{0:D2}:{1:D2}",
269              m_objTime.Minute, m_objTime.Second );
270
271        } // end method tmrClock_Tick
272
273     } // end class FrmMicrowaveOven
274  }
```

Figure 19.39 Microwave Oven application code. (Part 6 of 6.)

```
1  // Time.cs
2  // Represents time data and contains properties.
3
4  using System;
5
6  namespace MicrowaveOven
7  {
8  /// <summary>
9  /// Summary description for Time.
10 /// </summary>
11 public class Time
12 {
13     // declare ints for minute and second
14     private int m_intMinute;
15     private int m_intSecond;
16
17     // Time constructor, minute and second supplied
18     public Time( int minuteValue, int secondValue )
19     {
20        Minute = minuteValue; // invokes Minute set accessor
21        Second = secondValue; // invokes Second set accessor
22
23     } // end constructor Time
```

The **class** keyword used to declare a class → line 11

Constructor name must be the class name → line 18

Assign data to properties, rather than directly to instance variables → lines 20–21

Right brace ends constructor declaration → line 23

Figure 19.40 Class Time. (Part 1 of 2.)

```
24
25            // property Minute
26            public int Minute
27            {
28               // return m_intMinute value
29               get
30               {
31                  return m_intMinute;
32
33               } // end of get accessor
34
35               // set m_intMinute value
36               set
37               {
38                  // if minute value entered is valid
39                  if ( value < 60 )
40                  {
41                     m_intMinute = value;
42                  }
43                  else
44                  {
45                     m_intMinute = 0; // set invalid input to 0
46                  }
47
48               } // end of set accessor
49
50            } // end property Minute
51
52            // property Second
53            public int Second
54            {
55               // return m_intSecond value
56               get
57               {
58                  return m_intSecond;
59
60               } // end of get accessor
61
62               // set m_intSecond value
63               set
64               {
65                  // if minute value entered is valid
66                  if ( value < 60 )
67                  {
68                     m_intSecond = value;
69                  }
70                  else
71                  {
72                     m_intSecond = 0; // set invalid input to 0
73                  }
74
75               } // end of set accessor
76
77            } // end property Second
78
79         } // end class Time
80      }
```

get accessor returns data — line 58

set accessor modifies data — line 69

Right brace ends property declaration — line 77

Right brace ends class declaration — line 79

Figure 19.40   Class Time. (Part 2 of 2.)

SELF-REVIEW

1. Instance variable declarations can be preceded by which of the following keywords?

   a) `instance`
   b) `private`
   c) `public`
   d) Either b or c.

2. Instance variables are considered _____ by default.

   a) `private`
   b) `public`
   c) `two-dimensional`
   d) None of the above.

Answers: 1) d. 2) a.

19.8 Using the Debugger: The Autos and Locals Windows

Now you will enhance your knowledge of the debugger by studying the capabilities of the **Autos** and **Locals** windows. These windows allow you to view the values stored in an object's instance variables. In this section, you will learn how to view the contents of the `Time` object `m_objTime`'s instance variables to verify that your application is executing correctly. In the following box, you use these windows to examine the state of the `Time` object in the **Microwave Oven** application.

Using the Debugger: Using the Autos and Locals Windows

1. ***Viewing the application code.*** View `MicrowaveOven.cs` by selecting the `MicrowaveOven.cs` tab above the code editor.

2. ***Setting breakpoints.*** Set breakpoints at lines 453 and 466 by clicking in the margin indicator bar (Fig. 19.41). You can set breakpoints in your application to examine an object's instance variables at certain places during execution. In the **Microwave Oven** application, the `tmrClock`'s `Tick` event handler modifies the properties of `m_objTime`. Setting breakpoints at lines 453 and 466 allows you to suspend execution before and after certain properties have been modified, ensuring that data is being modified properly.

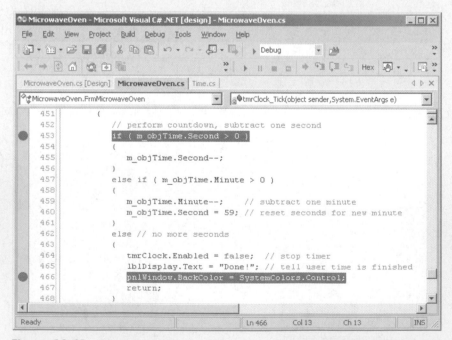

Figure 19.41 **Microwave Oven** application with breakpoints added.

3. ***Starting the debugger.*** Start the debugger by selecting **Debug > Start**.

(cont.)

4. ***Opening the Autos window.*** Open the **Autos** window (Fig. 19.42) by selecting **Debug > Windows > Autos** while the debugger is running. The **Autos window** allows you to view the contents of the properties used in the last statement that was executed. This allows you to verify that the previous statement executed correctly. The **Autos** window also lists the values in the next statement to be executed.

Figure 19.42   Empty **Autos** window.

5. ***Opening the Locals window.*** Open the **Locals** window (Fig. 19.43) by selecting **Debug > Windows > Locals** while the debugger is running. The **Locals window** allows you to view the state of the variables in the current scope. Recall that the scope of a variable's identifier is the portion of an application in which that identifier can be referenced. Because the Timer's Tick event is a method of the Form class, all of the instance variables and controls of the Form are viewable in the **Locals** window. This means that you will be able to view the values of the properties of m_objTime, because m_objTime is an instance variable of the Form class.

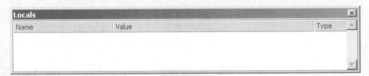

Figure 19.43   Empty **Locals** window.

6. ***Setting the time.*** Set the microwave oven's time to 01:01, then click the **Start** Button.

7. ***Using the Autos window.*** When execution halts at the breakpoint at line 453, view the **Autos** window (Fig. 19.44). If the **Autos** window is now hidden, reselect **Debug > Windows > Autos**. Notice that the **Autos** window lists m_objTime with the Second property of m_objTime just below. This property is listed because it will be used in the next statement (line 453). [*Note*: The e and sender variables are listed because they were used in the previous statement (the method header). The this keyword refers to the FrmMicrowaveOven object that was created in the main method. For the purposes of this tutorial, we are concerned only with m_objTime.] The Second property of m_objTime is listed along with its value (returned from the property's get accessor) and its type. Viewing the values stored in an object lets you verify that your application is manipulating these variables correctly.

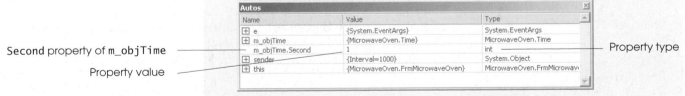

Figure 19.44   **Autos** window displaying the state of m_objTime.

(cont.)   8. ***Using the Locals window.*** While execution is still halted, look at the **Locals** window. If the **Locals** window is now hidden, reselect **Debug > Windows > Locals**. The **Locals** window lists all the variables in the scope of the Timer's Tick event handler. To view the contents of m_objTime, click the plus box next to the word **this**. Scroll down until you reach m_objTime, and click the plus box next to it. This will show all of the members of m_objTime, their current values and their types (Fig. 19.45). Notice that the values for minute and second are the same as they were in the **Autos** window.

Instance variables of m_objTime —

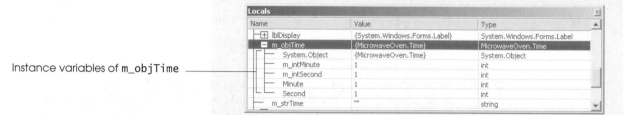

Figure 19.45   **Locals** window displaying the state of m_objTime.

9. ***Continuing application execution.*** Click the debug toolbar's Continue Button, and view the values of the m_objTime's members in both the **Autos** and **Locals** windows. Notice that the value for the amount of seconds (as represented by the m_intSecond variable and the Second property) is now shown in red, indicating that it has changed. Click the Continue Button again. Notice that both the amount of seconds and the amount of minutes have changed, so that the values of m_intSecond, m_intMinute and the Second and Minute properties are shown in red (Fig. 19.46 and Fig. 19.47).

Changed value shown in red —

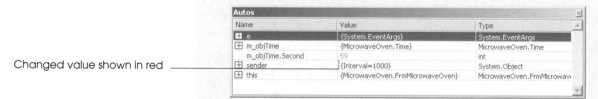

Figure 19.46   **Autos** window displaying the changed variables in red.

Changed values shown in red —

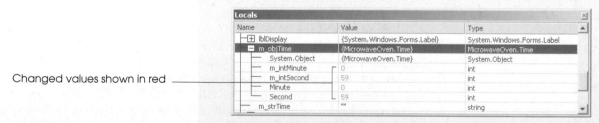

Figure 19.47   **Locals** window displaying the changed variables in red.

10. ***Changing the value of a variable.*** In the **Autos** window, double click the value for the Second property. Type 0, then press *Enter* to set the microwave oven's time to zero (Fig. 19.48). The **Autos** and **Locals** windows allow you to change the values of variables to verify that program execution is correct at certain points without having to run the application again for each value.

(cont.)

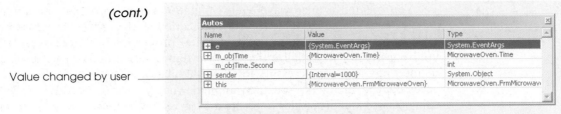

Figure 19.48   Changing the value of a variable in the **Autos** window.

Value changed by user

11. ***Continuing execution***. Click the Continue `Button`. Execution continues until the breakpoint at line 466 is reached.

12. ***Viewing the Autos and Locals window***. View the **Autos** window, and notice that the variables listed have now changed (Fig. 19.49). This happened because execution is now at a new statement that uses new variables. View the **Locals** window. Notice that the **Locals** window still lets you view the state of `m_objTime`.

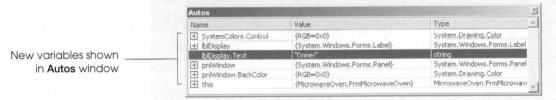

New variables shown in **Autos** window

Figure 19.49   New variables listed in the **Autos** window.

13. ***Stopping the debugger***. Click the Stop Debugging `Button` to end the debugging session.

14. ***Closing the application***. Close your running application by clicking its close box.

15. ***Closing the IDE***. Close Visual Studio .NET by clicking its close box.

In this section, you learned how to use the **Autos** and **Locals** windows to view the state of an object and verify that your application is running correctly.

SELF-REVIEW   1. The **Locals** window allows you to _____.

   a) change the value stored in an instance variable of an object
   b) view all of the variables in the current scope
   c) view the values stored in all of the variables in the current scope
   d) All of the above.

2. When a variable's value is changed, it becomes _____ in the **Autos** and **Locals** windows.

   a) red   b) italic
   c) blue   d) bold

Answers: 1) d. 2) a.

19.9 Wrap-Up

In previous tutorials, you used FCL classes and methods to add functionality to your applications. In this tutorial, you learned how to create your own classes, known as programmer-defined classes, to provide functionality not available in the FCL. In the world of C# programming, applications are created by using a combination of FCL classes and methods and programmer-defined classes and methods.

You created a microwave-oven simulator using a programmer-defined class called `Time`. You added a file to your application to create the `Time` class; you then added a constructor, instance variables and properties to that class. You defined your constructor to initialize the class's instance variables. For each property, you defined `get` and `set` accessors to allow the class's instance variables to be safely accessed and modified. You then applied what you have already learned about using classes and properties to create a `Time` object. You used the properties of the `Time` class to access and display the number of minutes and number of seconds that the user has specified as the microwave oven's cook time. You also learned how `Panel`s can organize controls (much like `GroupBox`es), and used a `Panel` to simulate the microwave oven's door. You concluded the tutorial by learning how to view an application's values using the debugger's **Autos** and **Locals** windows.

In the next tutorial, you will learn about collections. The FCL provides several collection classes, which enable you to store collections of data in an organized way. A collection can be thought of as a group of items. You will use collections to create a **Shipping Hub** application that stores information about several packages that are being shipped to various states. Each package will be defined by using a `Package` programmer-defined class. Several `Package` objects will be maintained by using collections.

SKILLS SUMMARY

Defining a Property

- Use the `public` keyword followed by the property's type and the property's name. Do not use parentheses following the property's name.
- Add the `get` and `set` accessors. The `get` accessor begins with the `get` keyword and a left brace and ends with a right brace. The `set` accessor begins with the `set` keyword and a left brace and ends with right brace.
- In the `get` accessor, provide code to return the requested data.
- In the `set` accessor, provide code to modify the relevant data. Be sure to do validity checking. Use the `value` identifier to access the value to be assigned.

Adding a Class File to Your Project

- Select **Project > Add Class**.
- In the **Add New Item** dialog, select **Class** and enter a name for the class.

Creating a Constructor

- Use the `public` keyword, followed by the name of the class and a set of parentheses enclosing any parameter variables for the constructor. Use braces to enclose the constructor declaration.
- Add code to initialize the object's data.

Adding a `Panel` to Your Application

- Double click the `Panel` control in the **Toolbox**, or drag the `Panel` control from the **Toolbox** to the **Form**. We recommend prefixing `Panel` names with `pnl`.

KEY TERMS

accessor—Method-like code units that handle the details of modifying and returning data.

Autos window—Allows you to view the contents of the properties used in the last statement that was executed in an application. This allows you to verify that the previous statement executed correctly and lists the values in the next statement to be executed.

client—When an application creates and uses an object of a class, that application is known as a client of that class.

Color structure—Contains several predefined colors as properties.

consistent state—A way to maintain the values of an object's instance variables such that those values are always valid.

constructor—A special class method that initializes a class's variables.

Convert.ToChar method—Converts data to type `char`.

extensible language—A language that can be "extended" with new data types. C# is an extensible language.

FixedSingle value of BorderStyle property—Specifies that the Label will display a thin, black border.

Flat value of FlatStyle property—Specifies that a Button will appear flat.

FlatStyle property of a Button—Determines whether the Button will appear flat or three-dimensional.

get accessor—Used to retrieve a value of an instance variable.

instantiate an object—Create an object of a class.

Length property of class String—Returns the number of characters in a string.

Locals window—Allows you to view the state of the variables in the current scope during debugging.

members of a class—Methods and variables declared within the body of a class.

member-access modifier—Keywords used to specify what members of a class that a client may access. Includes keywords public and private.

PadLeft method of class String—Adds characters to the beginning of the string until the length of a string equals the specified length.

Panel control—Used to group controls. Unlike GroupBoxes, Panels do not have captions.

private keyword—Member-access modifier that makes instance variables or methods accessible only to that class.

programmer-defined class (programmer-defined type)—Defined by a programmer, as opposed to a class predefined in the Framework Class Library.

property of a class—Contains accessors—portions of code that handle the details of modifying and returning data.

public keyword—Member-access modifier that makes instance variables or methods accessible wherever the application has a reference to that object.

set accessor—Provides data-validation capabilities to ensure that the value is set properly.

Substring method of class String—Returns characters from a string that correspond to the arguments passed by the user that indicate the start and the end positions within a string.

SystemColors.Control property—Returns the default color of several controls, including Panels.

value—Special identifier that allows access to the value to be assigned in a property's set accessor.

GUI DESIGN GUIDELINES

Panel

- Use Panels to organize groups of related controls where the purpose of those controls is obvious. If the purpose of the controls is not obvious, use a GroupBox in place of a Panel, because GroupBoxes can contain captions.

- A Panel can display scrollbars if that Panel is not large enough to display all of its controls at once. To increase readability, we suggest avoiding the use of scrollbars on Panels. If a Panel is not large enough to display all of its contents, increase the size of the Panel.

- Although it is possible to have a Panel without a border (by setting the BorderStyle property to None), use borders on your Panels to increase readability and organization.

CONTROLS, EVENTS, PROPERTIES & METHODS

Button   `ab| Button`   This control allows the user to raise an action or event.

- ***In action***

  `Calculate Total`

- ***Event***

  Click—Raised when the user clicks the Button.

■ *Properties*

Enabled—Determines whether the Button's event handler is executed when the Button is clicked.

FlatStyle—Determines whether the Button will appear flat or three-dimensional.

Flat—Specifies that a Button will appear flat.

Location—Specifies the location of the Button on the Form relative to the top-left corner.

Name—Specifies the name used to access the Button programmatically. The name should be prefixed with btn.

Size—Specifies the height and width (in pixels) of the Button.

Text—Specifies the text displayed on the Button.

■ *Method*

Focus—Transfers the focus of the application to the Button that calls it.

Convert The Convert class converts the value of a type to another type.

■ *Method*

ToChar—Converts a value into a character (of the char type).

Panel 　◻ Panel　 This control is used to organize various controls. Unlike the Group-Box control, the Panel control does not display a caption.

■ *In action*

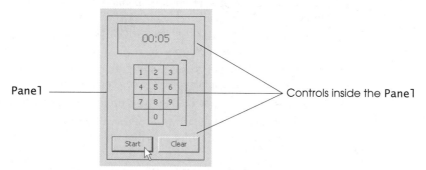

Panel ———————————————→ Controls inside the Panel

■ *Properties*

BackColor—Specifies the background color of the Panel.

BorderStyle—Specifies the Panel's border style.

　　None—Specifies that the Panel's will not display a border.

　　FixedSingle—Specifies that the Panel will display a thin, black border.

　　Fixed3D—Specifies that the Panel will display a three-dimensional border.

Location—Specifies the Panel's location on the Form.

Name—Specifies the name of the Panel. The name should be prefixed with pnl.

Size—Specifies the size of the Panel.

String The String class represents a series of characters treated as a single unit.

■ *Property*

Length—Returns the number of characters in the string.

■ *Methods*

Format—Arranges the string in a specified format.

IndexOf—Returns the index of the specified character(s) in a string.

Insert—Returns a copy of the string for which it is called with the specified character(s) inserted.

PadLeft—Inserts characters at the beginning of a string.

Remove—Returns a copy of the string for which it is called with the specified character(s) removed.

Substring—Returns a substring from a string.

ToLower—Returns a copy of the `string` for which it is called with any uppercase letters converted to lowercase letters.

SystemColors The `SystemColors` class contains color properties for the various Windows controls.

■ *Property*

Control—Returns the default color of several controls, including `Panels`.

MULTIPLE-CHOICE QUESTIONS

19.1 A `Button` appears flat if its _____ property is set to `Flat`.

a) `BorderStyle`
b) `FlatStyle`
c) `Style`
d) `BackStyle`

19.2 The _____ keyword introduces a class declaration.

a) `newclass`
b) `classdef`
c) `csclass`
d) `class`

19.3 The _____ operator is used to create an object.

a) `createobject`
b) `instantiate`
c) `create`
d) `new`

19.4 A `string` character is of the _____ type.

a) `char`
b) `stringcharacter`
c) `character`
d) `strcharacter`

19.5 The _____ is used to retrieve the value of an instance variable.

a) `get` accessor of a property
b) `retrieve` method of a class
c) `client` method of a class
d) `set` accessor of a property

19.6 When you add a new class to a project, the default namespace that contains the class in Visual Studio .NET is the name of the current _____.

a) file
b) project
c) method
d) variable

19.7 An important difference between constructors and other methods is that _____.

a) constructors cannot specify a return type
b) constructors cannot specify any parameters
c) other methods are implemented as `void` methods
d) constructors can assign values to instance variables

19.8 A class can yield many _____, just as a built-in type can yield many variables.

a) names
b) objects
c) values
d) types

19.9 The `set` accessor enables you to _____.

a) provide range checking
b) modify data
c) provide data validation
d) All of the above.

19.10 Instance variables declared `private` are not accessible _____.

a) outside the class
b) by other methods of the same class
c) by other members of the same class
d) inside the same class

EXERCISES

19.11 (*Triangle Creator Application*) Create an application that allows the user to enter the lengths for the three sides of a triangle as `ints`. The application should then determine whether the triangle is a right triangle (two sides of the triangle form a 90-degree angle), an equilateral triangle (all sides of equal length) or neither. The application's GUI is completed for you (Fig. 19.50). You must create a class to represent a triangle object and define the event handler for the **Create** Button.

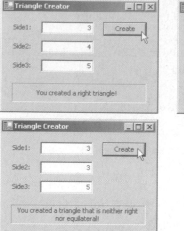

Figure 19.50 **Triangle Creator** application with all possible outputs.

a) *Copying the template to your working directory.* Copy the directory C:\Examples\ Tutorial19\Exercises\Triangle to your C:\SimplyCSP directory.

b) *Opening the application's template file.* Double click Triangle.sln in the Triangle directory to open the application.

c) *Creating the Triangle class.* Add a class to the project, and name it Triangle. This is where you will define the properties of the Triangle class.

d) *Defining the necessary properties.* Define a constructor that will take the lengths of the three sides of the triangle as arguments. Create three properties that enable clients to access and modify the lengths of the three sides. If the user enters a negative value, that side should be assigned the value zero.

e) *Adding additional features.* Create two more properties in the Triangle class: One determines whether the sides form a right triangle, the other an equilateral triangle. These properties are considered read-only, because you would naturally define only the get accessor. There is no simple set accessor that can make a triangle a right triangle or an equilateral triangle without first modifying the lengths of the triangle's sides. Therefore, simply omit the set accessor for this property.

f) *Adding code to the event handler.* Now that you have created your Triangle class, you can use it to create objects in your application. Double click the **Create** Button in **Design View** to generate the event handler. Create new variables to store the three lengths from the TextBoxes; then, use those values to create a new Triangle object.

g) *Displaying the result.* Use an if...else statement to determine if the triangle is a right triangle, an equilateral triangle or neither. Display the result in a Label.

h) *Running the application.* Select **Debug > Start** to run your application. Create various inputs until you have create an equilateral triangle, a right triangle and a triangle that is neither right nor equilateral. Verify that the proper output is displayed for each.

i) *Closing the application.* Close your running application by clicking its close box.

j) *Closing the IDE.* Close Visual Studio .NET by clicking its close box.

19.12 (*Modified Microwave Oven Application*) Modify the tutorial's **Microwave Oven** application to include an additional digit, which would represent the hour. Allow the user to enter up to 9 hours, 59 minutes and 59 seconds (Fig. 19.51).

a) *Copying the template to your working directory.* Copy the directory C:\Examples\ Tutorial19\Exercises\MicrowaveOven2 to your C:\SimplyCSP directory.

b) *Opening the application's template file.* Double click MicrowaveOven.sln in the MicrowaveOven2 directory to open the application.

c) *Adding the hour variable.* To allow the cooking time to include the hour digit, you will need to modify the Time class. Define a new private instance variable to represent the hour. Change the Time constructor to take as its first argument (now Time should have three arguments) the hour amount. You will also have to modify the **Start** Button event handler and the DisplayTime method to include an hour variable.

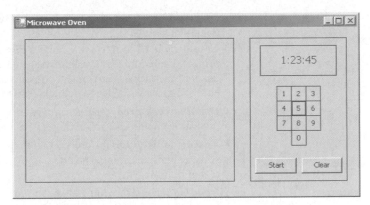

Figure 19.51 **Microwave Oven** application's GUI.

d) *Adding the Hour property.* Use the `Minute` and `Second` properties as your template to create the property for the hour. Remember, we are allowing an additional digit to represent the hour (hour < 10).

e) *Changing the padding amount.* Change the calls to the `PadLeft` method to be consistent with the new time format.

f) *Extracting the hour.* Add a call to the `Substring` method so that hour gets the first digit in the `m_strTime` string. Also, change the calls to the `Substring` method for minute and second so that they extract the proper digits from the `m_strTime` string.

g) *Accessing the first five digits.* Change the `if` statement from the `DisplayTime` method to take and display the first five digits entered by the user.

h) *Edit the Timer object.* Edit the `tmrClock_Tick` event handler to provide changes to hours and its corresponding minutes and seconds.

i) *Displaying the time.* Edit the format `string` so that the display `Label` includes the hour.

j) *Running the application.* Select **Debug > Start** to run your application. To ensure that your application works correctly, enter `1:00:10`, then click the **Start** Button. Watch as the microwave's timer counts down under one hour.

k) *Closing the application.* Close your running application by clicking its close box.

l) *Closing the IDE.* Close Visual Studio .NET by clicking its close box.

19.13 (*Account Information Application*) The local bank wants you to create an application that will allow them to view their clients' information. The interface is created for you; you need to implement the class (Fig. 19.52). Once the application is completed, the bank manager should be able to click the **Next** or **Previous** Button to run through each client's information. The information is stored in four arrays containing first names, last names, account numbers and account balances.

Figure 19.52 **Account Information** application GUI.

a) *Copying the template to your working directory.* Copy the directory C:\Examples\ Tutorial19\Exercises\AccountInformation to your C:\SimplyCSP directory.

b) *Opening the application's template file.* Double click AccountInformation.sln in the AccountInformation directory to open the application.

c) *Determining variables for the class.* Examine the code in AccountInformation.cs, including all the properties that the Client object uses to retrieve the information.

d) *Creating the Client class.* Create a new class, called Client. Add this class to the project. Define four private instance variables to represent each property value, to ensure that each Client object contains all the required information about each client. Use those variables to define a constructor.

e) *Defining each property.* Each private variable should have a corresponding property, allowing the user to set or get each private variable's value.

f) *Adding more information.* In the FrmAccountInformation_Load event handler, add two more accounts. Include names, account numbers and balances for each corresponding array.

g) *Running the application.* Select **Debug > Start** to run your application. Ensure that your application works correctly by using the **Next** and **Previous** Buttons to scroll through the different accounts.

h) *Closing the application.* Close your running application by clicking its close box.

i) *Closing the IDE.* Close Visual Studio .NET by clicking its close box.

What does this code do? ▶

19.14 What does the following code do? The first code listing contains the declaration of the Shape class. Each Shape object represents a closed shape with a number of sides. The second code listing contains a method (Mystery) created by a client of the Shape class. What does this method do?

```
1   public class Shape
2   {
3      private int m_intSides;
4
5      // constructor with number of sides
6      public Shape( int intSides )
7      {
8         Side = intSides;
9
10     } // end constructor Shape
11
12     // set and get side value
13     public int Side
14     {
15        // return m_intSides
16        get
17        {
18           return m_intSides;
19
20        } // end of get accessor
21
22        // set m_intSides
23        set
24        {
25           if ( value > 0 )
26           {
27              m_intSides = value;
28           }
29           else
30           {
31              m_intSides = 0;
32           }
33
34        } // end of set accessor
```

```
35
36      } // end property Side
37
38  } // end class Shape
```

```
1   public string Mystery( Shape objShape )
2   {
3      string strShape;
4
5      switch ( objShape.Side )
6      {
7         case 0:
8         case 1:
9         case 2: strShape = "Not a Shape";
10           break;
11
12        case 3: strShape = "Triangle";
13           break;
14
15        case 4: strShape = "Square";
16           break;
17
18        default: strShape = "Polygon";
19           break;
20      }
21
22      return strShape;
23
24  } // end method Mystery
```

What's wrong with this code? ▶ **19.15** Find the error(s) in the following code. The following method should create a new Shape object with intNumberSides sides. Assume the Shape class from Exercise 19.14 exists.

```
1   private void ManipulateShape( int intNumberSides )
2   {
3      Shape objShape = new Shape( 3 );
4      Shape.m_intSides = intNumberSides;
5
6   } // end method ManipulateShape
```

Using the Debugger ▶ **19.16** (*View Name Application*) The **View Name** application allows the user to enter the user's first and last name. When the user clicks the **View Name** Button, a MessageBox that displays the user's first and last name appears. The application creates an instance of the Name class. This class uses its property declarations to set the first-name and last-name instance variables. Copy the directory C:\Examples\Tutorial19\Exercises\Debugger\ ViewName to your C:\SimplyCSP directory. Open and run the application. While testing your application, you noticed that the MessageBox did not display the correct output. Use the debugger to find the logic error(s) in the application. The application with the correct output is displayed in Fig. 19.53.

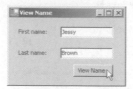 

Figure 19.53 **View Name** application with correct output.

Programming Challenge ▶ **19.17** (*DVD Burner Application*) Create an application that simulates a DVD burner. Users create a DVD with their choice of title and bonus materials. The GUI is provided for you (Fig. 19.54). You will create a class (DVDObject) to represent the DVD object and another class (Bonus) to represent bonus materials for a DVD object.

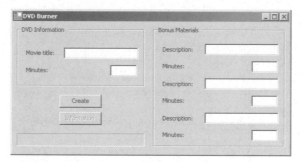

Figure 19.54 **DVD Burner** application's GUI.

a) *Copying the template to your working directory.* Copy the directory C:\Examples\ Tutorial19\Exercises\DVDBurner to your C:\SimplyCSP directory. Double click the DVDBurner.sln file in the DVDBurner directory to open the application in Visual Studio .NET.

b) *Opening the application's template file.* Double click DVDBurner.sln in the DVD-Burner directory to open the application.

c) *Creating the bonus material class.* Create a class named Bonus. The class's objects will each represent one bonus-material item on the DVD. Each Bonus object should have a name (description) and a length (in minutes). Use this tutorial's Time class as your guide in creating the properties for the name and length of each bonus material.

d) *Creating the DVD class.* Create a class, and name it DVDObject. This class contains the movie title and the length of the movie. The class should also include an array of three Bonus items.

e) *Creating the necessary variables.* Before you define the **Create** Button's event handler, create an DVDObject class instance variable. Inside the **Create** Button's event handler, create the necessary variables to store the information from the TextBoxes on the GUI. Also, this is where you need to create the array of Bonus objects to store the bonus materials.

f) *Adding bonus-material information.* Add the description and length of each bonus item to the Bonus array you created from the previous step.

g) *Creating a DVD object.* Use information about the movie, its title, length and the array of bonus materials to make your DVD object.

h) *Displaying the output.* The **Information** Button's Click event is already defined for you. Locate the event handler, add a string containing the complete information on the DVD object that you created earlier and display this string to a MessageBox.

i) *Running the application.* Select **Debug > Start** to run your application. Enter information for several DVDs. After information is entered for each, click the **Create** Button. Then, click the **Information** Button and verify that the information being displayed is correct for your newly created DVD.

j) *Closing the application.* Close your running application by clicking its close box.

k) *Closing the IDE.* Close Visual Studio .NET by clicking its close box.

Objectives

In this tutorial, you will learn to:
- Create and manipulate an `ArrayList` object.
- Set the `TabStop` and `TabIndex` properties of a control.
- Create an access key for a control.
- Use a `foreach` loop to iterate through an `ArrayList`.

Outline

Shipping Hub Application

Introducing Collections, the *foreach* Statement and Access Keys

Though most business can be conducted over phone lines or using e-mail messages, it is sometimes necessary to send documents using a shipping company. As the pace of business increases, it is essential that shipping companies develop an efficient means to transfer packages from one location to another. To accomplish this task, many shipping companies send packages to a central location (a hub) before the packages reach their final destination. In this tutorial, you will develop a **Shipping Hub** application to simulate package processing at a shipping warehouse. You will develop the application by using **collections**, which provide you with a quick and easy way to organize and manipulate the data used by your application. This tutorial focuses on the `ArrayList` collection, which includes the data storage capabilities of an array, but with much greater flexibility. You will also learn to use the `foreach` repetition statement to iterate through the objects in a collection.

20.1 Test-Driving the Shipping Hub Application

In this section, you will test-drive the **Shipping Hub** application. This application must meet the following requirements:

Application Requirements

*A shipping company receives packages at its headquarters, which functions as its shipping hub. After receiving the packages the company ships them to a distribution center in one of the following states; Alabama, Florida, Georgia, Kentucky, Mississippi, North Carolina, South Carolina, Tennessee, West Virginia or Virginia. The company needs an application to track the packages that pass through its shipping hub. The application generates a package ID number for each package that arrives at the shipping hub, when the user clicks the application's **Scan New** Button. Once a package has been scanned, the user should be able to enter the shipping address for the package. The user should be able to navigate through the list of scanned packages by using < BACK or NEXT > Buttons and by viewing a list of all packages destined for a particular state.*

489

This application stores a list of packages in an `ArrayList`. You will use the `foreach` repetition statement to access the objects stored in the `ArrayList`. You begin by test-driving the completed application. Then, you will learn the additional C# technologies that you will need to create your own version of this application.

Test-Driving the Shipping Hub Application

1. *Opening the completed application*. Open the `C:\Examples\Tutorial20\ CompletedApplication\ShippingHub` directory to locate the **Shipping Hub** application. Double click `ShippingHub.sln` to open the application in Visual Studio .NET.

2. *Running the Shipping Hub application*. Select **Debug > Start** to run the application (Fig. 20.1).

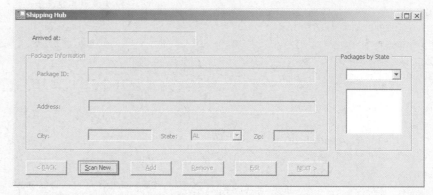

Figure 20.1 **Shipping Hub** application when first run.

3. *Scanning a new package*. Click the **Scan New** Button. The application displays a package ID number, enables the TextBoxes and allows the user to enter the package information (Fig. 20.2).

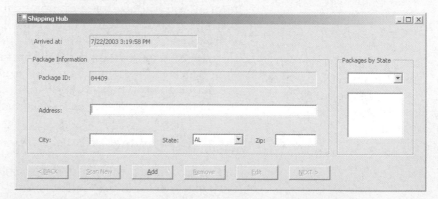

Figure 20.2 Scanning a new package.

4. *Using* **Tab**. Click in the **Address:** TextBox to transfer the focus of the application to that field so that you can enter data. Type `318 Some Street`, then press *Tab*. Notice that the cursor moves to the **City:** TextBox (Fig. 20.3).

5. *Adding a package to the list of packages*. Type `Point Pleasant` in the **City:** field, then press *Tab*. Select **WV** from the **State:** ComboBox, then press *Tab*. Type `25550` in the **Zip:** field, then click the **Add** Button to add the package to the application's `ArrayList`.

(cont.)

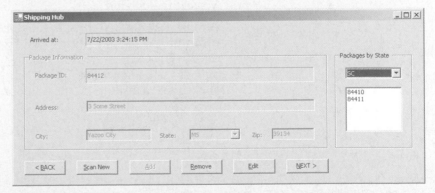

Cursor now appears
in the **City:** TextBox

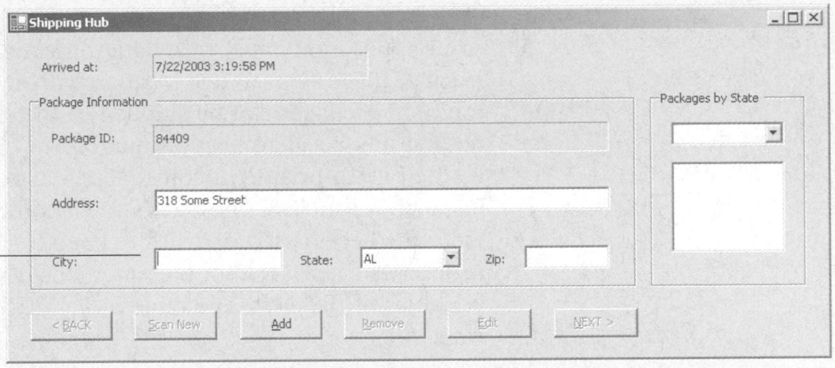

Figure 20.3   Pressing *Tab* moves the cursor to the next TextBox.

Note that you cannot enter more than five numbers in the **Zip:** field because the **Zip:** TextBox's MaxLength property is set to 5. The value in the **MaxLength** property determines the maximum number of characters that the user can enter into a TextBox. The values in the **State:** ComboBox were added using its Items property in the Windows Form Designer. When you open the template application, examine the values stored in the Items property to see how this is accomplished.

6. *Removing, editing and browsing packages*. The application's **NEXT >** and **< BACK** Buttons allow the user to navigate the list of packages. The **Remove** Button allows the user to delete packages, and the **Edit** Button allows the user to update a particular package's information. Experiment with the various Buttons by adding, removing and editing packages. We suggest using the following sample data:

   ■ 9 Some Road, Goose Creek, SC 29445

   ■ 234 Some Place, Tamassee, SC 29686

   ■ 46 Some Avenue, Mammoth Cave, KY 42259

   ■ 3 Some Street, Yazoo City, MS 39194

7. *Viewing all packages going to a state*. The ComboBox on the right side of the application allows the user to select a state. When a state is selected, all of the package ID numbers of packages destined for that state are displayed in the ListBox (Fig. 20.4). If the ListBox contains more package numbers than it can display, a vertical scrollbar will be added to the ListBox.

Figure 20.4   Viewing all packages going to South Carolina.

8. *Closing the application*. Close your running application by clicking its close box.

9. *Closing the IDE*. Close Visual Studio .NET by clicking its close box.

20.2 Package Class

Your application must store data retrieved from the packages' shipping information. Each package ships to one location with an address, city, state and zip code. However, multiple packages can be shipped to the same location, therefore each package will need a unique identification number to distinguish it from other packages. As you learned in Tutorial 19, a convenient way to group related information is by creating instances of a class. The Package class included with the template application provides the necessary properties to keep track of package information. It also provides properties to ensure that only methods of the Package class can access the instance variables of the class. The table in Fig. 20.5 describes the properties for the Package class.

Property	Description
Address	Provides access to instance variable m_strAddress, which represents the package's address as a string.
City	Provides access to instance variable m_strCity, which represents the package's city as a string.
State	Provides access to m_strState, which stores the package's state as a string. It uses the standard two-letter state abbreviations—for example, NC is used for North Carolina.
Zip	Provides access to m_intZip, which represents the zip code as a five-digit int.
PackageNumber	Provides access to m_intPackageNumber, which stores the package's identification number as a string.

Figure 20.5 Properties listing for the Package class.

The Package class must be added to the **Shipping Hub** application before objects of this class can be created. You will learn how to add the Package class to the **Shipping Hub** application in the following box.

Adding a Class to an Application

1. ***Copying the template to your working directory.*** Copy the C:\Examples\Tutorial20\TemplateApplication\ShippingHub directory to your C:\SimplyCSP directory.

2. ***Opening the Shipping Hub application's template file.*** Double click ShippingHub.sln in the ShippingHub directory to open the application in Visual Studio .NET.

3. ***Adding the Package class.*** In the **Solution Explorer**, right click the **ShippingHub** project. Select **Add > Add Existing Item...** from the context menu that appears. When the **Add Existing Item** dialog appears, select the Package.cs file, then click **Open**. The Package class is now included in the application and shown in the **Solution Explorer** (Fig. 20.6).

Package class added to the ShippingHub project

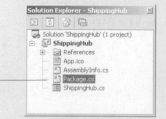

Figure 20.6 **Solution Explorer** with Package.cs added.

4. ***Saving the project.*** Select **File > Save All** to save your modified code.

20.3 Using the `TabIndex` and `TabStop` Properties

Many applications require users to enter information into multiple TextBoxes. It is awkward for users to have to select each TextBox using the mouse. It is often easier to allow the user to use *Tab* to navigate the controls on the Form. To ensure ease of use, the focus must be transferred to the proper control when *Tab* is pressed. The **TabIndex** property allows you to specify the order in which focus is transferred to controls when *Tab* is pressed. However, some controls, such as a read-only Text-Box, should not be selected using *Tab*. The **TabStop** property specifies whether the user can select the control using *Tab*. Setting this property to `false` prevents the control from being selected using *Tab*. You set both of these properties in the following box.

Setting the TabIndex and TabStop Properties

GUI Design Tip

Set a control's TabStop property to `true` only if the control is used to receive user input.

GUI Design Tip

Use the TabIndex property to define the logical order in which the user should enter data. Usually the order transfers the focus of the application from top to bottom and left to right.

1. **Opening ShippingHub.cs.** Double click `ShippingHub.cs` in the **Solution Explorer** to open the Form in design view. The **Shipping Hub** application requires that the user enter the package information into these TextBoxes. To ensure the user can easily enter the data, you should allow the user to press *Tab* to access the proper control.

2. **Setting the TabStop property.** The TabStop property defaults to `true` for controls that receive user input. Ensure that this is the case by setting the TabStop properties to `true` for the **Address:**, **City:** and **Zip:** TextBoxes, the **State:** and **Packages by State** ComboBoxes and the **Scan New** Button if they are not already set to `true`.

3. **Disabling the TabStop property.** Set the TabStop property for the other controls on the Form to `false`. The user should be given access only to certain controls; therefore, you must prevent *Tab* from transferring the focus to an improper control, such as a disabled TextBox.

4. **Using the Tab Order view in the Windows Form Designer.** To help visualize the tab order, Visual Studio .NET provides a view called **Tab Order**. To use the **Tab Order** view, select the Form by clicking it, then select **View > Tab Order**. White numbers indicating the TabIndex appear in blue boxes in the upper-left corner of the control (Fig. 20.7). The first time you click a control in this view, its TabIndex value will be set to 0, as displayed in the TabIndex box (Fig. 20.7). The control with TabIndex value 0 will receive the focus when an application begins running. Subsequent clicks will increment the value by one.

TabIndex box set to zero ————

TabIndex boxes (not modified) ————

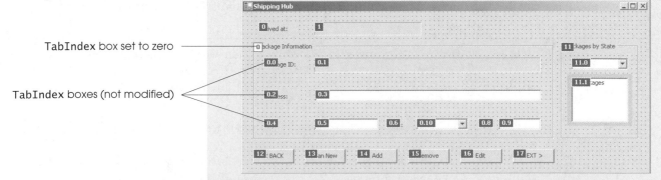

Figure 20.7 Setting the TabIndex properties using the **Tab Order** view of the **Shipping Hub** application.

(cont.)

Begin by clicking the **Package Information** GroupBox. Notice its value becomes 0 and the background of the surrounding box changes to white (Fig. 20.7). Then, click the **Address:** TextBox and notice that the value changes to 0.0. The first zero refers to the TabIndex of the container (in this case, the GroupBox), and the second zero refers to the TabIndex for that control within the container.

Continue setting the tab indices by clicking the **City:** TextBox, then the **State:** ComboBox and finally the **Zip:** TextBox. Complete setting the tab indices for the GroupBox by clicking each control in the GroupBox that has not been changed. Controls that have not been changed display a box with a blue background.

5. *Setting the TabIndex properties for the rest of the application.* Continue setting the TabIndex properties by clicking the **Scan New** Button. Then click the remaining unchanged controls in the order indicated in Fig. 20.8. Exit the **Tab Order** view by selecting **View > Tab Order**.

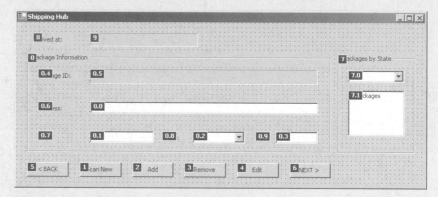

Figure 20.8 **Tab Order** view of the **Shipping Hub** application.

6. *Saving the project.* Select **File > Save All** to save your modified code.

Using the TabIndex and TabStop properties properly improves the speed at which the user enters data into an application. Most controls have TabIndex and TabStop properties. TabIndex values on a Form or within a GroupBox must be unique—two controls cannot receive the focus at the same time. By default, the first control added to the Form has a value of 0 for its TabIndex property. The second control added has a value of 1 for its TabIndex property. The third control has a value of 2 (one more than the last control's value) for its TabIndex property, and so on.

SELF-REVIEW

1. The _____ property specifies the order in which controls receive the focus when *Tab* is pressed.

    a) Text   b) TabStop
    c) Index   d) TabIndex

2. To prevent the focus from being transferred to a control using *Tab*, set the _____ property to _____.

    a) TabIndex, 0   b) TabStop, false
    c) TabControl, true   d) TabIndex, null

Answers: 1) d. 2) b.

20.4 Using Access Keys

Applications that require the user to enter a great deal of text data should provide users with the ability to enter data using only the keyboard. Setting the TabIndex and TabStop properties, for instance, helps the user enter data in a logical order. **Access keys** (or keyboard shortcuts) allow the user to perform an action on a control using the keyboard.

To specify an access key for a control, insert an & (ampersand) symbol in the Text property before the letter you wish to use as an access key. The & symbol is an escape character when used in a Text property. If you wish to use the *s* key as the access key on the **Scan New** Button, set its Text property to &Scan New (where &S is an escape sequence). You can specify many access keys in an application, but each letter used as an access key in a container must be unique. To use the access key, you must press and hold *Alt*, then press the access key character on the keyboard (release both keys after pressing the access key character). In this case of the **Scan New** Button, you would press and hold *Alt*, then press *S* (also written as *Alt+S*).

Access keys are often used on Button controls and on the MainMenu control, which will be introduced in Tutorial 22. If you wish to display an ampersand character on a control, you must type && in its Text property. Follow the steps in the next box to use access keys in your **Shipping Hub** application.

Creating Access Keys

GUI Design Tip

Use access keys to allow users to "click" a control using the keyboard.

Using the & symbol to create an access key (there is no space between & and S)

1. ***Creating an access key for the Scan New Button.*** Insert an & symbol before the letter S in the Text property of the **Scan New** Button (Fig. 20.9). Press *Enter* or click outside the field to update the property. Notice that the letter S is now underlined on the Button (Fig. 20.9). If the user presses *Alt* then *S* during execution, it will have the same effect as if the user "clicks" the **Scan New** Button. (The Click event will be raised.) Note that depending on your system configuration, you may need to press *Alt* to display the underline under the access key character.

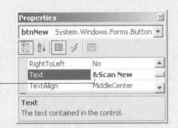
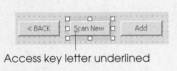

Access key letter underlined

Figure 20.9   Creating an access key.

2. ***Inserting access keys for the remaining Buttons.*** Use the Text properties of the remaining Buttons to create access keys. Precede the B on the **< BACK** Button with an ampersand. Repeat this process for the A on the **Add** Button, the R on the **Remove** Button, the E on the **Edit** Button and the N on the **NEXT >** Button.

3. ***Saving the project.*** Select **File > Save All** to save your modified code.

SELF-REVIEW

1. When creating an access key, the _____ the ampersand is underlined.

   a) character preceding   b) character following

   c) characters following   d) characters preceding

2. Press _____ then the underlined character on a Button to use an access key.

   a) *Control*   b) *Shift*

   c) *Alt*   d) *Tab*

Answers: 1) b. 2) c.

20.5 Collections

The .NET Framework provides several classes, called collections, which you can use to store groups of related objects. These classes provide methods to facilitate the storage and organization of your data without requiring any knowledge of the details of how the objects are being stored. This capability improves your application development time because you do not have to write code to organize your data efficiently—the methods in the collection classes are proven to be reliable and efficient.

In Tutorial 17 and Tutorial 18, you learned how to declare and use arrays in your applications. You may have noticed a limitation to arrays—once an array is declared, its size will not change to match its data set. This poses a problem if the number of items in an array will change over time.

The **ArrayList** class (a member of the **System.Collections** namespace) provides a convenient solution to this problem. The `ArrayList` collection provides all of the capabilities of an array, but also provides dynamic resizing capabilities. **Dynamic resizing** enables the `ArrayList` object to increase its size to accommodate new elements and to decrease its size when elements are removed.

> **Software Design Tip**
>
> Use an `ArrayList` to store a group of values when the number of elements in the group varies during the execution of an application.

SELF-REVIEW

1. Collections _____.
   a) force you to focus on how your data is stored
   b) speed up application development
   c) allow you to focus on the details of your application
   d) Both b and c.

2. One limitation of arrays is that _____.
   a) their size cannot change dynamically
   b) they can only store built-in types
   c) `strings` cannot be placed in them
   d) All of the above.

Answers: 1) d. 2) a.

20.6 Shipping Hub Application: Using the ArrayList Class

By now, you are familiar with designing GUIs and writing methods and event handlers. This tutorial's template file provides much of the application's functionality so that you may concentrate on using an `ArrayList`. You are encouraged to study the full source code at the end of the tutorial to understand how the application is implemented. The following pseudocode describes the basic operation of your **Shipping Hub** application:

        When the Form loads:
                Generate an initial package ID number
                Create an empty ArrayList

        When the user clicks the Scan New Button:
                Generate a unique package ID number
                Enable the TextBoxes, the ComboBox and the Add Button

        When the user clicks the Add Button:
                Retrieve the address, city, state and zip code values; disable the input
                        controls
                Add the package to the ArrayList
                Disable the TextBoxes and Buttons

                If the package's state is already displayed in the ComboBox
                        Add the package number to the ListBox
                Else
                        Update the state displayed in the ComboBox, then display the package
                                number for each package destined for that state in the ListBox

When the user clicks the < BACK Button:
    Display the previous package in the list

When the user clicks the NEXT > Button:
    Display the next package in the list

When the user clicks the Remove Button:
    Remove the package from the list

When the user clicks the Edit/Update Button:

    If the Button reads "Edit"
        Allow the user to modify the package's address information
        Change the Button to read "Update"
    Else
        Update the package's information in the list
        Disable the controls that allow user input, and change the Button to
read
          "Edit"

When the user chooses a different state in the ComboBox:
    Display the package number for each package destined for that state in the
    ListBox

The **Shipping Hub** application must store a list of packages through which the user can navigate using the **NEXT >** and **< BACK** Buttons. Each time the application runs, it must allow for any number of packages to be added. Using arrays, you would be limited by the number of values that you could store in the array. The ArrayList collection solves this problem by combining the functionality of an array with dynamic resizing capabilities.

Now that you have test-driven the **Shipping Hub** application and studied its pseudocode representation, you will use an ACE table to help you convert the pseudocode to C#. Figure 20.10 lists the actions, controls and events that you will help you complete your own version of this application.

Action/Control/Event (ACE) Table for the Shipping Hub Application	Action	Control/Class/Object	Event
	Label the application's controls	`fraAddress, fraListByState, lblArrived, lblPackageID, lblAddress, lblCity, lblState, lblZip`	Application is run
		`FrmShippingHub`	Load
	Generate an initial package ID number	`m_objRandom`	
	Create an empty ArrayList	`m_objList`	
		`btnNew`	Click
	Generate a unique package ID number	`m_objRandom`	
	Enable the TextBoxes, the ComboBox and the Add Button	`btnAdd, txtAddress, txtCity, cboState, txtZip`	

Figure 20.10 ACE table for the **Shipping Hub** application. (Part 1 of 2.)

Action	Control/Class/Object	Event
	`btnAdd`	`Click`
Retrieve the address, city, state and zip code values; disable the input controls	`txtAddress, txtCity, cboState, txtZip`	
Add the package to the ArrayList	`Package, m_objList`	
Disable the TextBoxes and Buttons	`btnAdd, txtAddress, txtCity, txtZip`	
If the package's state is already displayed in the ComboBox	`cboState`	
Add the package number to the ListBox	`lstPackages`	
Else	`cboState, lstPackages`	
Update the state displayed in the ComboBox, then display the package number for each package destined for that state in the ListBox		
	`btnBack`	`Click`
Display the previous package in the list	`txtAddress, txtCity, cboState, txtZip, lblArrivalTime, lblPackageNumber, m_objList`	
	`btnNext`	`Click`
Display the next package in the list	`txtAddress, txtCity, cboState, txtZip, lblArrivalTime, lblPackageNumber, m_objList`	
	`btnRemove`	`Click`
Remove the package from the list	`cboState, cboViewPackages, lstPackages, m_objList`	
	`btnEditUpdate`	`Click`
If the Button reads "Edit"	`btnEditUpdate`	
Allow the user to modify the package's address information	`txtAddress, txtCity, cboState, txtZip`	
Change the Button to read "Update"	`btnEditUpdate`	
Else	`m_objList`	
Update the package's information in the list		
Disable the controls that allow user input	`fraAddress`	
Change the Button to read "Edit"	`btnEditUpdate`	
	`cboViewPackages`	`Selected-Index-Changed`
Display the package number for each package destined for that state in the ListBox	`lstPackages, m_objList`	

Figure 20.10 ACE table for the **Shipping Hub** application. (Part 2 of 2.)

In this tutorial, you focus on the use of an `ArrayList` in the **Shipping Hub** application. You begin by creating an `ArrayList` object.

Creating a List of Packages

1. ***Declaring an ArrayList***. Add line 57 of Fig. 20.11 to your application to declare the `m_objList` `ArrayList`. The `ArrayList` class is located in the `System.Collections` namespace. Visual Studio .NET generates a `using` directive for this namespace for you.

Declaring an `ArrayList` reference

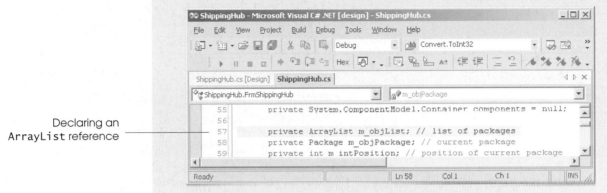

Figure 20.11 Declaring the `ArrayList` reference.

2. ***Initializing the ArrayList***. Add line 409 (Fig. 20.12) to the Form's **Load** event handler. This line uses the `new` operator to create a reference to an empty `ArrayList` object when the application loads. This reference is assigned to `m_objList`, the instance variable declared in *Step 1*. Notice that line 408 uses the `ComboBox`'s `Items` property to show the first state in the list. The **Items** property retrieves a collection of values stored in the `ComboBox`. Square brackets (`[]`) are then used to retrieve the value stored in the `ComboBox` at the specified index.

Creating the `ArrayList` reference

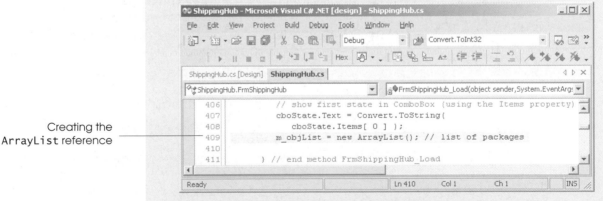

Figure 20.12 Creating an `ArrayList` object.

3. ***Saving the project***. Select **File > Save All** to save your modified code.

Now that you have created an `ArrayList` object, you will need to add code to allow the user to add packages to the `ArrayList`. To accomplish this, you will create a reference to an object of the `Package` class and use the `ArrayList`'s `Add` method to store the reference in the `ArrayList`. Recall that you already added the `Package` class to your application. You will now create packages and add them to your list.

Adding and Removing Packages

1. *Creating a package.* The user clicks the **Scan New** Button when a new package arrives at the shipping hub. When this occurs, the application should create a package number and allow the user to enter the shipping address. Add lines 417–419 of Fig. 20.13 into the **Scan New** Button's `Click` event handler. Line 417 increments `m_intPackageID` to ensure that all packages have a unique identification number. Lines 418–419 pass the package number as an argument to the constructor for the `Package` class. The value that you pass to the `Package` constructor can then be accessed using its `Package-Number` property. Note that line 418 uses the same reference, `m_objPackage`, many times to reference a new `Package` object. However, the previous `Package` object will not be destroyed each time the reference is changed. This is because each package reference is stored in the `ArrayList`.

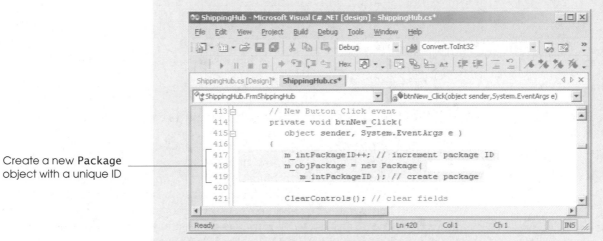

Create a new **Package** object with a unique ID

Figure 20.13   Creating a **Package** object.

2. *Displaying the package number and arrival time.* After the package has been "scanned," the application should display the new package's arrival time and package number to the user. Add lines 423–427 of Fig. 20.14 into your application. Lines 424–425 display the package identification number in a `Label`.

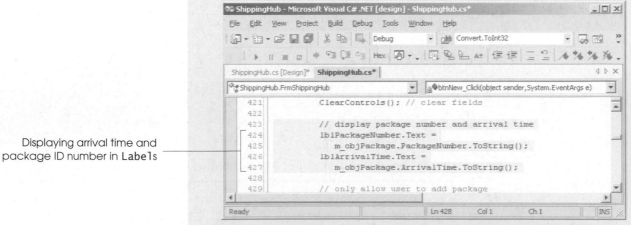

Displaying arrival time and package ID number in **Label**s

Figure 20.14   Displaying the package's number and arrival time.

(cont.)

The **ToString** method, which is defined for most objects and types, returns a value representing the object as text (of the **string** type). For instance, a **DateTime** structure's **ToString** method returns the date as a **string**, in the format 11/22/2003 9:34:00 AM. However, be aware that for many FCL classes, ToString merely returns the class name. The ToString method can be used as an alternative to the **Convert.ToString** method. Lines 426–427 display the arrival time (the current time) in a **Label**.

3. ***Adding a package to the ArrayList.*** To add the package to the **ArrayList** after entering the package's information, the user clicks the **Add** Button. Add line 443 of Fig. 20.15 to the **Add** Button's **Click** event handler.

Adding a **Package** object to an **ArrayList**

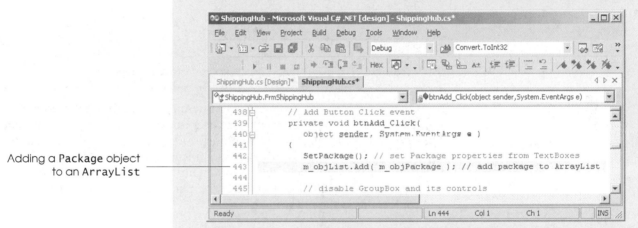

Figure 20.15   Adding a **Package** to the **ArrayList**.

This line stores the package information by adding the **Package** object to the **m_objList ArrayList** using the **ArrayList**'s **Add** method. Each time you add an object to the **ArrayList** by calling the **Add** method, the object is added to the end of the **ArrayList**. With arrays, you refer to a value's location by its index. Similarly, in an **ArrayList**, you refer to an object's location in the **ArrayList** as the object's index. Much like an array, the index of an object at the beginning of the **ArrayList** is zero and the index of an object at the end of the **ArrayList** is one less than the number of objects in the **ArrayList**.

4. ***Removing a package from the ArrayList.*** When the user selects a package and clicks the **Remove** Button, the application should remove the package from the **ArrayList**. The **ArrayList** class provides a simple way to remove objects from the **ArrayList**. Insert lines 509–510 (Fig. 20.16) into the **Remove** Button's **Click** event handler. Line 510 uses the **RemoveAt** method to remove a package from the **ArrayList**. The argument passed to the **RemoveAt** method is the index of the package in the **ArrayList**, contained in the **m_intPosition** variable. This variable keeps track of the position and is incremented or decremented each time the user clicks the **NEXT >** or **< BACK** Buttons.

If a package at index 3 is removed from the **ArrayList**, the package that was previously at index 4 will then be located at index 3. Whenever an object is removed from an **ArrayList**, the indices update accordingly. Notice that line 513 of Fig. 20.16 uses the **Count** property of the **ArrayList** class. The **Count** property returns the number of objects contained in the **ArrayList**.

5. ***Saving the project.*** Select **File > Save All** to save your modified code.

(cont.)

Removing the current package from the `ArrayList`

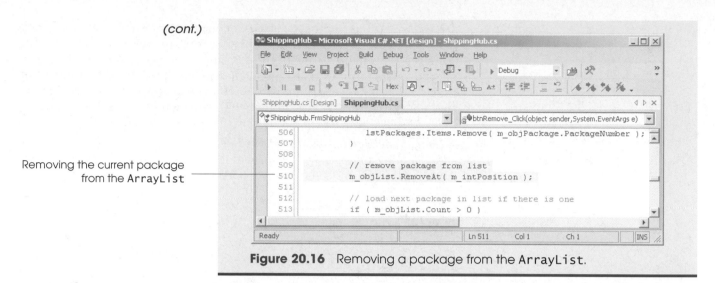

Figure 20.16 Removing a package from the `ArrayList`.

Once a package has been added to the `ArrayList`, the **Shipping Hub** application disables the `TextBox`es so that the user does not accidentally modify the package information. To allow users to modify any of the package information except for the arrival time and the package identification number, an **Edit** `Button` is provided. When the user clicks the **Edit** `Button`, its event handler should enable the controls that allow the user to modify the package data. You add functionality to accomplish this in the following box.

Updating Package Information

1. ***Changing the Edit Button's Text property***. Add lines 544–545 of Fig. 20.17 to your code. When the **Edit** `Button` is clicked, line 545 changes the text on the **Edit** `Button` to &Update (using U as the access key). This indicates that the user should click the same `Button`, which now is labelled **Update**, to submit changes to the package information.

Using code to change the text displayed on a `Button`

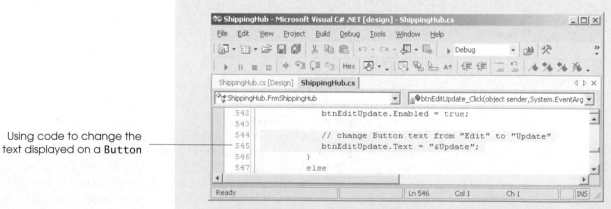

Figure 20.17 Changing the **Edit** `Button` to display **Update**.

(cont.)

2. *Updating the package data.* Insert lines 552–553 (Fig. 20.18) into the `btnEditUpdate_Click` event handler. When the user chooses to alter the package information, the package is removed from the `ArrayList`, and a new one with the updated address information is added. Line 552 removes the old `Package` object from the `ArrayList`. Line 553 uses the `ArrayList` class's `Insert` method to add the package to the `ArrayList`. The **Insert** method is like the Add method, but `Insert` allows you to specify the index in the `ArrayList` at which to insert the package. The first argument to the `Insert` method is the index at which to insert the package (in this case, `m_intPosition`), and the second argument contains the package to insert into the `ArrayList` (`m_objPackage`). Using the `Insert` method allows you to place the updated package object at the same index in the `ArrayList` as the package object you just removed. As with the `RemoveAt` method, the `Insert` method can change the indices in the `ArrayList`. Whenever an object is inserted into an `ArrayList`, the indices update accordingly.

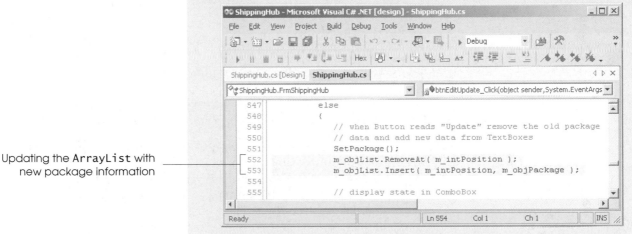

Updating the **ArrayList** with new package information

Figure 20.18   Removing and inserting a package to update data.

3. *Changing the Button's Text property to Edit.* After the user clicks the **Update** Button, the TextBoxes are once again disabled. The user's changes have been applied; therefore, you should reset the text on the **Update** Button to read **Edit**. Add lines 562–563 of Fig. 20.19 to the event handler to reset the text on the Button to **Edit**. Notice once again the use of the & to enable the Button's access key.

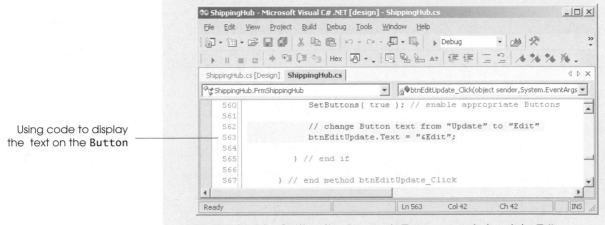

Using code to display the text on the **Button**

Figure 20.19   Setting the **Button**'s **Text** property back to **Edit**.

4. *Saving the project.* Select **File > Save All** to save your modified code.

The user navigates the ArrayList by clicking the **NEXT >** and **< BACK** Buttons. Each time the user chooses to view a different package in the ArrayList, the package information displayed in the Form's controls must be updated. To display a package's information, you must retrieve the information from the ArrayList that you created. You will learn how to do this in the following box.

Displaying a Package	1. **Retrieving package data.** Insert lines 583–584 from Fig. 20.20 into your application's LoadPackage method. To display the information, you retrieve the data from the ArrayList using square brackets ([]), just like an array. Line 568 assigns to m_objPackage the package stored at the m_intPosition index.

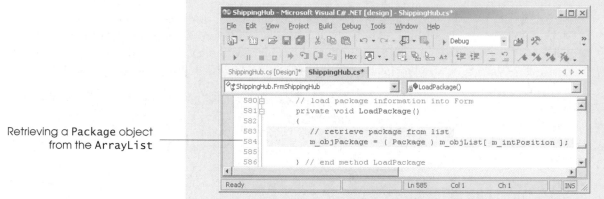

Retrieving a **Package** object from the **ArrayList**

Figure 20.20   Retrieving a package from the **ArrayList**.

Note that the code you inserted uses the cast operator to explicitly convert the object returned by the ArrayList to an object of the Package type. One of the many advantages of using an ArrayList is that it stores references to objects of the **object** type—which means that it can store *any* object you choose, from predefined objects (like a Random object) to programmer-defined objects (like a Package object). To use and access the properties and methods of a package returned from an ArrayList, you must explicitly convert it to a Package object.

2. **Displaying the package information.** Insert lines 586–594 of Fig. 20.21 into your application. These lines retrieve the package information from m_objPackage and display the data in the corresponding controls on the Form, using the ToString method.

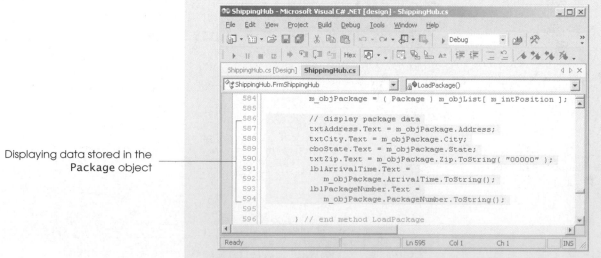

Displaying data stored in the **Package** object

Figure 20.21   Displaying the package data in the Form's controls.

3. **Saving the project.** Select **File > Save All** to save your modified code.

SELF-REVIEW

1. The _____ method of the `ArrayList` class can be used to add an object at a specific location in the `ArrayList`.

   a) `AddAt`   b) `Insert`

   c) `AddObjectAt`   d) `Add`

2. The **Shipping Hub** application uses an `ArrayList` because the `ArrayList` _____ class.

   a) can store a variable number of objects

   b) allows the addition and removal of packages

   c) allows the insertion of items into any index in the `ArrayList`

   d) All of the above.

Answers: 1) b. 2) d.

20.7 The foreach Repetition Statement

C# provides the **foreach** repetition statement for iterating through the values in an array or a collection. Instead of setting initial and final values for a counter variable, the `foreach` statement uses a control variable (a reference) that can reference each object in the collection. Assuming that you have created an `ArrayList`, `objArray-List`, that contains only `Package` objects, the code

```
foreach ( Package objPackage in objArrayList )
{
    lstPackages.Items.Add( objPackage.PackageNumber )
}
```

Good Programming Practice

Use a **foreach** repetition statement to iterate through values in an array or collection without using a counter variable.

adds each package's ID number to a `ListBox`. Beginning the `foreach` header is the the **foreach** keyword. The `foreach` statement requires both a collection type and an element. The **collection type** specifies the array or collection (in this case, the `ArrayList objArrayList`) through which you wish to iterate. The **element** is used to store a reference to a value in the collection type. If the `foreach` statement contains an element of the same type (or one that can be converted to the same type) as the collection type, the statement assigns the collection type's object to the element (in this case, `objPackage`). The body of the `foreach` statement is then executed. Keyword **in** separates the element from the collection type in the `foreach` header.

Common Programming Error

If the element in a **foreach** statement cannot be converted to the same type as the collection type's objects, a runtime error occurs. For example, if an `ArrayList` contained only `DateTime` values, declaring a reference to a `Package` object as the element would cause a runtime error.

As in the `for` statement, braces ({ and }) are required in a `foreach` statement to define a body of more than one line. For simplicity, we always use braces in our `foreach` statements. Notice that because the `foreach` statement does not require you to specify initial and final counter values, it simplifies access to groups of values. Unlike a counter in a `for` statement, however, the element in a `foreach` statement must be declared in the `foreach` header, as seen in the preceding example. The element in a `foreach` statement is read-only (it can be accessed but not modified), whereas a counter in a `for` statement can be both accessed and modified.

The UML activity diagram for the preceding `foreach` repetition statement is found in Fig. 20.22. Notice that it is similar to the UML diagram for the `for` statement in Tutorial 11. The only difference is that the `foreach` continues to execute the body until all elements in the array (or collection) have been accessed.

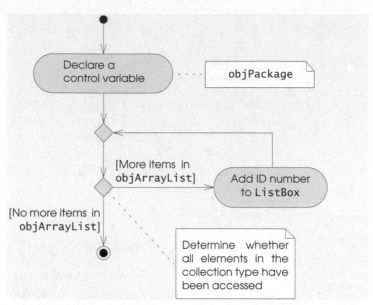

Figure 20.22 UML activity diagram for the **foreach** repetition statement.

When the user selects a state from the ComboBox, the application should display the package number for each package destined for that state. You will use the foreach statement in the **Shipping Hub** application to add this functionality.

Inserting a foreach Statement

1. ***Inserting a foreach statement.*** Add lines 643–647 of Fig. 20.23 to your application. Line 644 is the header for the foreach repetition statement. The header declares objViewPackage reference of the Package type. The loop will iterate through ArrayList m_objList, assigning the next element in the ArrayList (beginning with the first package object) to the objViewPackage reference before executing the body of the loop. When a new package is reached, the foreach body executes. Notice that you have added code to a ComboBox's SelectedIndexChanged event handler. The **SelectedIndexChanged** event is raised when the value selected in the ComboBox changes.

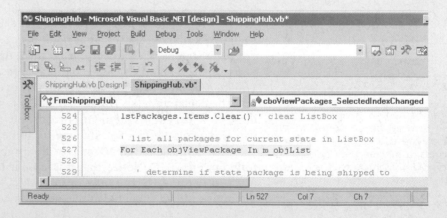

foreach header

Figure 20.23 Writing a foreach statement.

(cont.)   2. ***Determining a package's destination state.*** Insert lines 646–653 of Fig. 20.24 into the body of the `foreach` statement. These lines contain an `if` statement that tests each package's destination state against the state name displayed in the **Packages By State** ComboBox. If the two state names match, lines 651–652 display the package number in the `ListBox`.

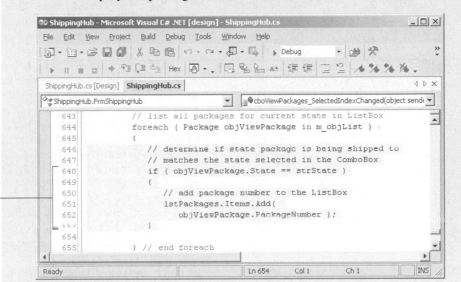

Displaying package ID numbers only for packages destined for the specified state

Figure 20.24   Displaying all packages going to the selected state.

3. ***Running the application.*** Select **Debug > Start** to run your application. Enter information for several packages going to the same state. Select that state in the **Packages by State** GroupBox and verify that correct packages are listed. Click the application's **Buttons** and make sure that you can remove, cycle through or modify the packages.

4. ***Closing the application.*** Close your running application by clicking its close box.

5. ***Closing the IDE.*** Close Visual Studio .NET by clicking its close box.

Figure 20.25 presents the source code for the **Shipping Hub** application. The lines of code that contain new programming concepts that you learned in this tutorial are highlighted.

```
1   using System;
2   using System.Drawing;
3   using System.Collections;
4   using System.ComponentModel;
5   using System.Windows.Forms;
6   using System.Data;
7
8   namespace ShippingHub
9   {
10     /// <summary>
11     /// Summary description for FrmShippingHub.
12     /// </summary>
13     public class FrmShippingHub : System.Windows.Forms.Form
14     {
15       // Labels for the arrival time
16       private System.Windows.Forms.Label lblArrived;
```

Figure 20.25   Shipping Hub application code. (Part 1 of 7.)

```
17          private System.Windows.Forms.Label lblArrivalTime;
18
19          // GroupBox for the package information
20          private System.Windows.Forms.GroupBox fraAddress;
21
22          // Labels for the package ID
23          private System.Windows.Forms.Label lblPackageID;
24          private System.Windows.Forms.Label lblPackageNumber;
25
26          // Labels, TextBoxes and ComboBox for the full address
27          private System.Windows.Forms.Label lblAddress;
28          private System.Windows.Forms.TextBox txtAddress;
29          private System.Windows.Forms.Label lblCity;
30          private System.Windows.Forms.TextBox txtCity;
31          private System.Windows.Forms.Label lblState;
32          private System.Windows.Forms.ComboBox cboState;
33          private System.Windows.Forms.Label lblZip;
34          private System.Windows.Forms.TextBox txtZip;
35
36          // GroupBox for choosing packages by state.
37          // contains a ComboBox and a ListBox for doing so.
38          private System.Windows.Forms.GroupBox fraListByState;
39          private System.Windows.Forms.ComboBox cboViewPackages;
40          private System.Windows.Forms.ListBox lstPackages;
41
42          // Buttons to go back one package, scan a new package,
43          // add a package, remove a package, edit an existing package
44          // and go forward one package.
45          private System.Windows.Forms.Button btnBack;
46          private System.Windows.Forms.Button btnNew;
47          private System.Windows.Forms.Button btnAdd;
48          private System.Windows.Forms.Button btnRemove;
49          private System.Windows.Forms.Button btnEditUpdate;
50          private System.Windows.Forms.Button btnNext;
51
52          /// <summary>
53          /// Required designer variable.
54          /// </summary>
55          private System.ComponentModel.Container components = null;
56
57          private ArrayList m_objList; // list of packages
58          private Package m_objPackage; // current package
59          private int m_intPosition; // position of current package
60          private Random m_objRandom; // random number for package ID
61          private int m_intPackageID; // individual package number
62
63          public FrmShippingHub()
64          {
65             //
66             // Required for Windows Form Designer support
67             //
68             InitializeComponent();
69
70             //
71             // TODO: Add any constructor code after InitializeComponent
72             // call
73             //
74          }
```

Figure 20.25 **Shipping Hub** application code. (Part 2 of 7.)

```
75
76          /// <summary>
77          /// Clean up any resources being used.
78          /// </summary>
79          protected override void Dispose( bool disposing )
80          {
81             if( disposing )
82             {
83                if (components != null)
84                {
85                   components.Dispose();
86                }
87             }
88             base.Dispose( disposing );
89          }
90
91          // Windows Form Designer generated code
92
93          /// <summary>
94          /// The main entry point for the application.
95          /// </summary>
96          [STAThread]
97          static void Main()
98          {
99             Application.Run( new FrmShippingHub() );
100         }
101
102         // Form Load event
103         private void FrmShippingHub_Load(
104            object sender, System.EventArgs e )
105         {
106            m_intPosition = 0; // set initial position to zero
107            m_objRandom = new Random(); // create new Random object
108            m_intPackageID = m_objRandom.Next(
109               1, 100000 ); // new package ID
110
111            // show first state in ComboBox (using the Items property)
112            cboState.Text = Convert.ToString(
113               cboState.Items[ 0 ] );
114            m_objList = new ArrayList(); // list of packages
115
116         } // end method FrmShippingHub_Load
117
118         // New Button Click event
119         private void btnNew_Click(
120            object sender, System.EventArgs e )
121         {
122            m_intPackageID++; // increment package ID
123            m_objPackage = new Package(
124               m_intPackageID ); // create package
125
126            ClearControls(); // clear fields
127
128            // display package number and arrival time
129            lblPackageNumber.Text =
130               m_objPackage.PackageNumber.ToString();
131            lblArrivalTime.Text =
132               m_objPackage.ArrivalTime.ToString();
```

Initially, there are no objects in the **ArrayList**, so set the position to zero

Use a **Random** object to generate a random number for package IDs

Figure 20.25 Shipping Hub application code. (Part 3 of 7.)

```
133
134            // only allow user to add package
135            fraAddress.Enabled = true; // disable GroupBox and controls
136            SetButtons( false ); // enable/disable Buttons
137            btnAdd.Enabled = true; // enable Add Button
138            btnNew.Enabled = false; // disable Scan New Button
139            txtAddress.Focus(); // transfer focus to txtAddress TextBox
140
141         } // end method btnNew_Click
142
143         // Add Button Click event
144         private void btnAdd_Click(
145            object sender, System.EventArgs e )
146         {
147            SetPackage(); // set Package properties from TextBoxes
148            m_objList.Add( m_objPackage ); // add package to ArrayList
149
150            // disable GroupBox and its controls
151            fraAddress.Enabled = false;
152            SetButtons( true ); // enable appropriate Buttons
153
154            // package cannot be added until Scan New is clicked
155            btnAdd.Enabled = false; // disable Add Button
156
157            // if package's state displayed, add ID to ListBox
158            if ( cboState.Text == cboViewPackages.Text )
159            {
160               lstPackages.Items.Add( m_objPackage.PackageNumber );
161            }
162
163            cboViewPackages.Text = m_objPackage.State; // list packages
164            btnNew.Enabled = true; // enable Scan New Button
165
166         } // end method btnAdd_Click
167
168         // Back Button Click event
169         private void btnBack_Click(
170            object sender, System.EventArgs e )
171         {
172            // move backward one package in the list
173            if ( m_intPosition > 0 )
174            {
175               m_intPosition--;
176            }
177            else // wrap to end of list
178            {
179               m_intPosition = m_objList.Count - 1;
180            }
181
182            LoadPackage(); // load package data from item in list
183
184         } // end method btnBack_Click
185
186         // Next Button Click event
187         private void btnNext_Click(
188            object sender, System.EventArgs e )
189         {
190            // move forward one package in the list
```

Display package ID numbers in `ListBox` if the state names match — (lines 158–161)

When the user clicks the **< BACK** Button, decrement the position. If the position was zero, set the position to the last object in the `ArrayList` — (lines 173–180)

Figure 20.25   **Shipping Hub** application code. (Part 4 of 7.)

When the user clicks the NEXT > Button, increment the position. If the position was the last object in the array, set the position to zero

```
191      if ( m_intPosition < m_objList.Count - 1 )
192      {
193          m_intPosition++;
194      }
195      else
196      {
197          m_intPosition = 0; // wrap to beginning of list
198      }
199
200      LoadPackage(); // load package data from item in list
201
202   } // end method btnNext_Click
203
204   // Remove Button Click Event
205   private void btnRemove_Click(
206      object sender, System.EventArgs e )
207   {
208      // remove ID from ListBox if state displayed
209      if ( cboState.Text == cboViewPackages.Text )
210      {
211          lstPackages.Items.Remove( m_objPackage.PackageNumber );
212      }
213
214      // remove package from list
215      m_objList.RemoveAt( m_intPosition );
216
217      // load next package in list if there is one
218      if ( m_objList.Count > 0 )
219      {
220          // if not at first position, go to previous one
221          if ( m_intPosition > 0 )
222          {
223              m_intPosition--;
224          }
225
226          LoadPackage(); //load package data from item in list
227      }
228      else
229      {
230          ClearControls(); // clear fields
231      }
232
233      SetButtons( true ); // enable appropriate Buttons
234
235   } // end method btnRemove_Click
236
237   // Edit Button Click event
238   private void btnEditUpdate_Click(
239      object sender, System.EventArgs e )
240   {
241      // when Button reads "Edit", allow user to
242      // edit package information only
243      if ( btnEditUpdate.Text == "&Edit" )
244      {
245          fraAddress.Enabled = true;
246          SetButtons( false );
247          btnEditUpdate.Enabled = true;
248
```

Load the next package, update m_intPosition as necessary

Figure 20.25   Shipping Hub application code. (Part 5 of 7.)

```
249                    // change Button text from "Edit" to "Update"
250                    btnEditUpdate.Text = "&Update";
251                 }
252                 else
253                 {
254                    // when Button reads "Update" remove the old package
255                    // data and add new data from TextBoxes
256                    SetPackage();
257                    m_objList.RemoveAt( m_intPosition );
258                    m_objList.Insert( m_intPosition, m_objPackage );
259
260                    // display state in ComboBox
261                    cboViewPackages.Text = m_objPackage.State;
262
263                    // when done, return to normal operating state
264                    fraAddress.Enabled = false; // disable GroupBox
265                    SetButtons( true ); // enable appropriate Buttons
266
267                    // change Button text from "Update" to "Edit"
268                    btnEditUpdate.Text = "&Edit";
269
270                 } // end if
271
272              } // end method btnEditUpdate_Click
273
274              // set package properties
275              private void SetPackage()
276              {
277                 m_objPackage.Address = txtAddress.Text;
278                 m_objPackage.City = txtCity.Text;
279                 m_objPackage.State =
280                    Convert.ToString( cboState.SelectedItem );
281                 m_objPackage.Zip = Int32.Parse( txtZip.Text );
282
283              } // end method SetPackage
284
285              // load package information into Form
286              private void LoadPackage()
287              {
288                 // retrieve package from list
289                 m_objPackage = ( Package ) m_objList[ m_intPosition ];
290
291                 // display package data
292                 txtAddress.Text = m_objPackage.Address;
293                 txtCity.Text = m_objPackage.City;
294                 cboState.Text = m_objPackage.State;
295                 txtZip.Text = m_objPackage.Zip.ToString( "00000" );
296                 lblArrivalTime.Text =
297                    m_objPackage.ArrivalTime.ToString();
298                 lblPackageNumber.Text =
299                    m_objPackage.PackageNumber.ToString();
300
301              } // end method LoadPackage
302
303              // clear all the input controls on the Form
304              private void ClearControls()
305              {
306                 txtAddress.Clear();
307                 txtCity.Clear();
```

Retrieve data from the user, and store it in the **Package** object — (lines 277–281)

Figure 20.25 Shipping Hub application code. (Part 6 of 7.)

```
308                txtZip.Clear();
309                cboState.SelectedText = "";
310                lblArrivalTime.Text = "";
311                lblPackageNumber.Text = "";
312
313          } // end method ClearControls
314
315          // enable/disable Buttons
316          private void SetButtons( bool blnState )
317          {
318                btnRemove.Enabled = blnState;
319                btnEditUpdate.Enabled = blnState;
320                btnNext.Enabled = blnState;
321                btnBack.Enabled = blnState;
322
323                // disable navigation if not multiple packages
324                if ( m_objList.Count < 1 )
325                {
326                   btnNext.Enabled = false;
327                   btnBack.Enabled = false;
328                }
329
330                // if no items, disable Remove and Edit/Update Buttons
331                if ( m_objList.Count == 0 )
332                {
333                   btnEditUpdate.Enabled = false;
334                   btnRemove.Enabled = false;
335                }
336
337          } // end method SetButtons
338
339          // event raised when user selects a new state in ComboBox
340          private void cboViewPackages_SelectedIndexChanged(
341             object sender, System.EventArgs e )
342          {
343             string strState =
344                Convert.ToString( cboViewPackages.SelectedItem );
345
346             lstPackages.Items.Clear(); // clear ListBox
347
348             // list all packages for current state in ListBox
349             foreach ( Package objViewPackage in m_objList)
350             {
351                // determine if state package is being shipped to
352                // matches the state selected in the ComboBox
353                if ( objViewPackage.State == strState )
354                {
355                   // add package number to the ListBox
356                   lstPackages.Items.Add(
357                      objViewPackage.PackageNumber );
358                }
359
360             } // end foreach
361
362          } // end method cboViewPackages_SelectedIndexChanged
363
364       } // end class FrmShippingHub
365 }
```

Enable or disable Buttons depending on value of blnState

Defining the SelectedIndexChanged event of a ComboBox

Figure 20.25 **Shipping Hub** application code. (Part 7 of 7.)

SELF-REVIEW 1. The collection type in a `foreach` repetition statement represents _____.

    a) the counter used for iteration   b) the reference used for iteration

    c) an array or collection through which to   d) the guard condition
       iterate

2. The _____ statement provides a convenient way to iterate through values in an array or collection.

    a) `while`   b) `for`

    c) `foreach`   d) None of the above.

Answers: 1) c. 2) c.

20.8 Wrap-Up

In this tutorial, you learned how to use the `TabStop` and `TabIndex` properties to enhance the **Shipping Hub** application's usability. You learned how to determine which controls receive the application's focus when *Tab* is pressed, using the `Tab-Stop` property. You then set the `TabIndex` property, to specify the order in which controls receive the focus of the application when *Tab* is pressed. To further enhance the user interface, you created access keys to allow the user to "click" But-tons in the **Shipping Hub** application by pressing *Alt*, then the access key for the particular `Button`.

    You learned about using the `ArrayList` collection. You used `ArrayList` meth-ods to add a `Package` object to an `ArrayList` and delete the package from a spe-cific index in an `ArrayList`. You then wrote code to insert a `Package` object into the `ArrayList` at a specific index. These methods helped you store, edit and navi-gate an `ArrayList` of packages in the **Shipping Hub** application.

    Finally, you learned about the `foreach` repetition statement. You declared a control variable for use in the loop and used that reference in the `foreach` state-ment to iterate through each element in a collection type (which can be an array or a collection). Then, you used the `foreach` statement to iterate through package objects in the `ArrayList` in your **Shipping Hub** application.

    In the next tutorial, you will learn about mouse events, which are events raised when the user moves or clicks the mouse. You will use these mouse events to allow the user to draw art on a `Form`.

SKILLS SUMMARY

Using the TabIndex and TabStop Properties

    ■ Set the `TabIndex` properties of controls on your `Form` using numbers to specify the order in which to transfer the focus of the application when the user presses *Tab*.

    ■ Set the `TabStop` property of a control to `false` if a control is not used by the user to input data. Set the `TabStop` property of a control to `true` if focus should be transferred to the control using *Tab*.

Creating Access Keys

    ■ Insert the & symbol in a control's `Text` property before the character you wish to use as an access key (keyboard shortcut).

Creating an ArrayList

    ■ Assign a reference to an `ArrayList` to an object of the `ArrayList` type using the `new` operator.

Using an ArrayList

    ■ Call `ArrayList` method `Add` on an `ArrayList` object to add the method's argument to the end of the `ArrayList`.

    ■ Call `ArrayList` method `RemoveAt` on an `ArrayList` object to remove the object from the `ArrayList` at the index specified by the method's argument.

■ Call ArrayList method Insert on an ArrayList object to add the object specified by the second argument to the ArrayList at the index specified by the first argument to the method.

Using a foreach Repetition Statement

■ Declare a reference of the same type as the elements you wish to access in a collection type (array or collection).

■ Specify the reference as the control variable in the foreach repetition statement and the array or collection through which you wish to iterate. The loop repeats and the body of the foreach repetition statement executes for each element in the collection type. The value accessed at the beginning of each iteration is stored in the element reference for the body of the loop.

Handling a ComboBox Control's SelectedIndexChanged Event

■ Double click the ComboBox control to generate the SelectedIndexChanged event handler.

KEY TERMS

access key—Keyboard shortcut that allows the user to perform an action on a control using the keyboard.

Add method of class ArrayList—Adds a specified object to the end of an ArrayList.

ArrayList class—Performs the same functionality as an array, but has resizing capabilities.

collection—A class used to store groups of related objects.

collection type of a foreach statement—Specifies the array or collection through which you wish to iterate.

Count property of class ArrayList—Returns the number of objects contained in the ArrayList.

dynamic resizing—A capability that allows certain objects (such as ArrayLists) to increase or decrease in size based on the addition or removal of elements from that object. Enables the ArrayList object to increase its size to accommodate new elements and to decrease its size when elements are removed.

element of a foreach statement—Used to store a reference to the current value of the collection being iterated.

foreach repetition statement—Used to iterate through elements in an array or collection.

Insert method of class ArrayList—Inserts a specified object into the specified location of an ArrayList.

Items property of ComboBox—Specifies the values the user can select from the ComboBox.

MaxLength property of TextBox—Specifies the maximum number of characters that can be input into a TextBox.

RemoveAt method of class ArrayList—Removes the object located at a specified location of an ArrayList.

SelectedIndexChanged event of ComboBox—Raised when a new value is selected in a ComboBox.

System.Collections namespace—Contains collection classes such as ArrayList.

Tab Order view—Used to set the TabIndex properties of a Form's controls.

TabIndex property—Specifies the order in which focus is transferred to controls on the Form when *Tab* is pressed.

TabStop property—Specifies whether a control can receive the focus when *Tab* is pressed.

ToString method—Returns a string representation of the object or type on which the method is called.

GUI DESIGN GUIDELINES

Overall Design

■ Set a control's TabStop property to true only if the control is used to receive user input.

■ Use the TabIndex property to define the logical order in which the user should enter data. Usually the order transfers the focus of the application from top to bottom and left to right.

■ Use access keys to allow users to "click" a control using the keyboard.

CONTROLS, EVENTS, PROPERTIES & METHODS

ArrayList This class is used to store a variable number of objects.

- *Property*

  Count—Returns the number of objects contained in the `ArrayList`.

- *Methods*

  Add—Adds an object to the `ArrayList` object.

  Insert—Adds an object to the `ArrayList` object at a specific index.

  RemoveAt—Removes an object from the `ArrayList` object at the specified index.

ComboBox This control allows users to select options from a drop-down list.

- *In action*

  Australia

- *Event*

  SelectedIndexChanged—Raised when a new value is selected in the `ComboBox`.

- *Properties*

  DataSource—Allows you to add items to the `ComboBox`.

  DropDownStyle—Determines the `ComboBox`'s style.

  Enabled—Determines whether the user can enter data (`true`) in the `ComboBox` or not (`false`).

  Items—Specifies the values the user can select from the `ComboBox`.

     Item—Retrieves the value at the specified index.

  Location—Specifies the location of the `ComboBox` control on its container control relative to the top-left corner.

  MaxDropDownItems—Determines the maximum number of items to be displayed when user clicks the drop-down arrow.

  Name—Specifies the name used to access the `ComboBox` control programmatically. The name should be prefixed with cbo.

  SelectedValue—Contains the item selected by the user.

  Text—Specifies the text displayed in the `ComboBox`.

TextBox This control allows the user to input data from the keyboard.

- *In action*

  0

- *Event*

  TextChanged—Raised when the text in the `TextBox` is changed.

- *Properties*

  Enabled—Determines whether the user can enter data (`true`) in the `TextBox` or not (`false`).

  Location—Specifies the location of the `TextBox` on its container control relative to the top-left corner.

  MaxLength—Specifies the maximum number of characters that can be input into the `TextBox`.

  Multiline—Specifies whether the `TextBox` is capable of displaying multiple lines of text.

  Name—Specifies the name used to access the `TextBox` programmatically. The name should be prefixed with txt.

  PasswordChar—Specifies the masking character to be used when displaying data in the `TextBox`.

ReadOnly—Determines whether the value of a TextBox can be changed.

ScrollBars—Specifies whether a multiline TextBox contains a scrollbar.

Size—Specifies the height and width (in pixels) of the TextBox.

Text—Specifies the text displayed in the TextBox.

TextAlign—Specifies how the text is aligned within the TextBox.

■ ***Method***

Focus—Transfers the focus of the application to the TextBox that calls it.

MULTIPLE-CHOICE QUESTIONS

20.1 _____ are specifically designed to store groups of values.

a) Collections

b) Properties

c) Accessors

d) None of the above.

20.2 _____ provides a quick and convenient way to navigate through controls on a Form.

a) *Tab*

b) *Enter*

c) *Caps Lock*

d) *Alt*

20.3 An ArrayList differs from an array in that an ArrayList can _____.

a) store objects of any type

b) resize dynamically

c) be accessed programmatically

d) All of the above.

20.4 The element in a foreach statement _____.

a) must be of type int

b) must be of (or convertible to) the same type as the collection or array type

c) must be of type ArrayList

d) None of the above.

20.5 The control that receives the focus the first time *Tab* is pressed has a TabIndex property set to _____.

a) First

b) 0

c) Next

d) 1

20.6 Users should be able to use *Tab* to transfer the focus to _____.

a) only Buttons

b) only TextBoxes

c) only controls that have an AcceptTab property

d) only the controls that receive user input

20.7 To ensure that the proper controls obtain the focus when *Tab* is pressed, use the _____.

a) TabIndex property

b) TabStop and TabIndex properties

c) TabStop property

d) Focus property

20.8 To add a value to the end of an ArrayList, call the _____ method.

a) Add

b) AddToEnd

c) AddAt

d) InsertAt

20.9 To remove a value from a specific index in the ArrayList, use the _____ method.

a) Remove

b) RemoveAt

c) Delete

d) DeleteAt

20.10 To display an ampersand character on a control, type _____ in its Text property.

a) &_

b) &

c) &&

d) _&

EXERCISES

20.11 (*Modified Salary Survey Application*) Modify the **Salary Survey** application you created in Exercise 17.12 by using a `foreach` loop to replace the `for` loop that is used in Tutorial 17 (Fig. 20.26).

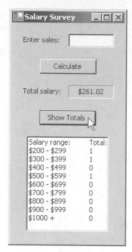

Figure 20.26 Modified **Salary Survey** application.

a) *Copying the template to your working directory.* Copy the directory `C:\Examples\Tutorial20\Exercises\SalarySurveyModified` to your `C:\SimplyCSP` directory.

b) *Opening the application's template file.* Double click `SalarySurvey.sln` in the `SalarySurveyModified` directory to open the application.

c) *Locating the event handler.* Double click the **Show Totals** Button to bring up the event handler. The code to handle the `Click` event should include two statements, one to clear the items in the `ListBox` and the other to add a header.

d) *Creating a counter variable.* The `foreach` loop allows you to loop through each element in a specified collection. The `for` loop from Exercise 17.12 handles the `string` (`m_strSalaryRanges`) and `int` (`m_intSalaries`) arrays. This presents a problem. You cannot loop through both of these arrays using the same element reference. (One is an `int`, and the other is a `string`.) To handle this you need to create a common counter variable, which you will use to loop through the indices of both arrays. This is possible because the lengths of both arrays are the same.

e) *Adding an element reference.* It does not matter which array you decide to use in this exercise, because these arrays are of the same length. Declare an element reference with the correct type.

f) *Create the foreach loop.* Use the new element reference that you have created along with the array of your choice to create the `foreach` loop statement.

g) *Adding text to the ListBox.* Add the statement to output to the `ListBox`—exactly the same as the one from Exercise 17.12. The only difference will be the name of the counter variable that you decide to use.

h) *Increment the counter variable.* To successfully loop through both arrays and output the data, you need to increment the counter variable. This ensures that the proper data is added to the `ListBox` through each iteration.

i) *Running the application.* Select **Debug > Start** to run your application. Enter several sales amounts using the **Calculate** Button. Click the **Show Totals** Button and verify that the proper amounts are displayed for each salary range, based on the salaries calculate from your input.

j) *Closing the application.* Close your running application by clicking its close box.

k) *Closing the IDE.* Close Visual Studio .NET by clicking its close box.

20.12 (*Modified Shipping Hub Application*) Modify the **Shipping Hub** application created in this tutorial, so that the user can double click a package in the `lstPackages` `ListBox`. When a package number is double clicked, the package's information should be displayed in a `MessageBox` (Fig. 20.27).

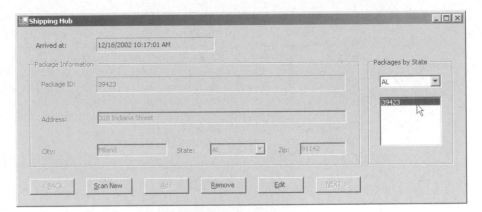

Figure 20.27 Modified **Shipping Hub** application.

a) *Copying the template to your working directory.* Copy the directory C:\Examples\
Tutorial20\Exercises\ShippingHubModified to your C:\SimplyCSP directory.

b) *Opening the application's template file.* Double click ShippingHub.sln in the
ShippingHubModified directory to open the application.

c) *Viewing the event handler.* Click **ShippingHub.cs** in the **Solution Explorer** and
select **View > Code**. Scroll to the end of code listing to locate the ListBox's Double-
Click event handler.

d) *Initializing necessary variables.* To loop through the packages in the ArrayList of
Packages, you need to create a reference of the Package type. It is also helpful to create a string variable to store the information about the given package. Write code in
the DoubleClick event handler to declare the strPackage string. A ListBox's
DoubleClick event is raised when the control is double clicked.

e) *Check whether the user has selected a valid item.* To determine whether the user has
selected a valid item (and not an empty element in the ListBox), write an if statement to make sure that the ListBox is not empty when the user selected an item.
[*Hint:* A SelectedIndex value of –1 means that no item is currently selected.]

f) *Writing a foreach loop.* Use the Package reference you declared in *Step d* to create
a foreach loop with the m_objList collection.

g) *Determining whether the current selected package is correct.* Insert an if statement
to determine whether the current object that is selected from the m_objList collection matches the selected item from the ListBox. Because the packages are listed in
the ListBox by their package number, use that information in your if statement.
Once the correct package is matched, store that package's information in the str-
Package string.

h) *Inserting the else block.* Make sure to notify the user if an invalid item has been
selected from the ListBox. If this occurs, add a message to the strPackage string
that will be displayed in the MessageBox.

i) *Displaying the MessageBox.* Call the MessageBox's Show method to display the text
you have added to the strPackage string. This displays either the information for
the package they have selected or the message telling them they have selected an
invalid package.

j) *Running the application.* Select **Debug > Start** to run your application. Add several
packages. In the **Packages by State** GroupBox, select a state for which there are
packages being sent. Double click one of the packages listed in the **Packages by
State** ListBox, and verify that the correct information is displayed in a MessageBox.

k) *Closing the application.* Close your running application by clicking its close box.

l) *Closing the IDE.* Close Visual Studio .NET by clicking its close box.

20.13 (*Controls Collection Application*) C# provides many different types of collections. One such collection is the `Controls` collection, which is used to provide access to all of the controls on a `Form`. Create an application that uses the `Controls` collection and a `foreach` loop to iterate through each control on the `Form`. As each control is encountered, add the control's name to a `ListBox`, and change the control's background color (in Fig. 20.28, `Color.Wheat` is used).

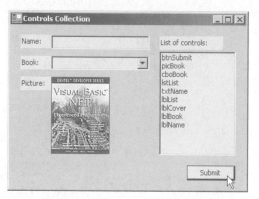

Figure 20.28 **Controls Collection** application.

a) *Copying the template to your working directory.* Copy the directory `C:\Examples\Tutorial20\Exercises\ControlsCollection` to your `C:\SimplyCSP` directory.

b) *Opening the application's template file.* Double click `ControlsCollection.sln` in the `ControlsCollection` directory to open the application.

c) *Generating an event handler.* Double click the **Submit** `Button` in design view to create an event handler for the click event.

d) *Declaring a control variable.* Declare a reference of the `Control` type. This reference represents each element in the `foreach` statement as it iterates through each `Control` on the `Form`.

e) *Clearing the `ListBox`.* To ensure that the information in the `ListBox` is updated each time the **Submit** `Button` is clicked, clear the `ListBox` of all items.

f) *Writing a `foreach` loop.* To create the `foreach` loop, use the control variable that you created to iterate through the `Form`'s `Controls` collection.

g) *Adding each control's name to the `ListBox`.* Use the `ListBox`'s `Add` method to insert the name of each control on the `Form`. Recall that a control's `Name` property contains the name of the control.

h) *Changing the control's background color.* Use the `Control`'s `BackColor` property to change the control's background color. Set the property to a new color using a member of the `Color` structure. [*Hint*: Type the word `Color` followed by the member-access operator to display a list of predefined colors using the *Intellisense* feature.] Note that the color of the `PictureBox` does not appear to change because its image displays in the control's foreground.

i) *Running the application.* Select **Debug > Start** to run your application. Click the **Submit** `Button`. Verify that the controls' background colors change, and that all the controls are listed in the **List of controls:** `ListBox`.

j) *Closing the application.* Close your running application by clicking its close box.

k) *Closing the IDE.* Close Visual Studio .NET by clicking its close box.

What does this code do? ▶	**20.14** What is the result of the following code?

```
1   ArrayList intList = new ArrayList();
2   string strOutput = "";
3
4   intList.Add( 1 );
5   intList.Add( 3 );
6   intList.Add( 5 );
7
8   foreach ( int intListItems in intList )
9   {
10      strOutput += ( " " + intListItems.ToString() );
11  }
12
13  MessageBox.Show( strOutput, "Mystery",
14      MessageBoxButtons.OK, MessageBoxIcon.Information );
```

What's wrong with this code? ▶ **20.15** This code should iterate through an array of Packages in the objList ArrayList and print each package's number in the lblDisplay Label. Assume objList has already been created and has had packages added to it. Find the error(s) in the following code.

```
1   foreach ( ArrayList objValue in objList )
2   {
3       lblDisplay.Text += ( " " + objValue.PackageNumber );
4   }
```

Programming Challenge ▶ **20.16** (***Enhanced Shipping Hub Application***) Enhance the **Shipping Hub** application created in Exercise 20.12 to allow the user to move a maximum of five packages from the warehouse to a truck for shipping (Fig. 20.29). If you have not completed Exercise 20.12, follow the steps in Exercise 20.12 before proceeding to the next step. If you have completed Exercise 20.12, copy the code you added to the lstPackages ListBox's DoubleClick event handler to the same event handler in this application before beginning the exercise.

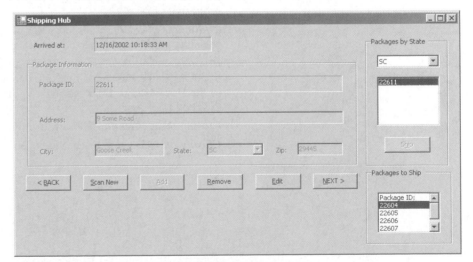

Figure 20.29 Enhanced **Shipping Hub** application.

a) ***Copying the template to your working directory.*** Copy the directory C:\Examples\ Tutorial20\Exercises\ShippingHubEnhanced to your C:\SimplyCSP directory.

b) *Opening the application's template file.* Double click ShippingHub.sln in the ShippingHubEnhanced directory to open the application.

c) *Enabling the Ship Button.* The **Ship** Button should not be enabled until a package is selected in the lstPackage ListBox. Double click the lstPackage ListBox from design view to define the event handler. Use the Button's Enabled property to enable the Button if the SelectedIndex of the ListBox is not -1. This means that when the user selects a package from the ListBox, the user can send the package to the truck by clicking the **Ship** Button. Also, insert a line of code after the foreach statement in the SelectedIndexChanged event handler to disable the **Ship** Button when a user chooses a different state.

d) *Defining the Ship Button's Click event.* Double click the **Ship** Button in **Design View** to define the Click event.

e) *Incrementing the counter.* Because you are only allowing five packages to be "shipped," declare an instance variable that will track how many packages have been placed onto the truck. Increment the variable each time the **Ship** Button is clicked.

f) *Creating temporary variables.* Create two temporary Package references to store the correct package's information. Use objTempPackage as the reference to the element in the collection type of a foreach statement, and the objTruckPackage as a reference to the package added to the truck.

g) *Using the if...else statement.* Use an if...else statement to allow packages to be placed onto the truck if the number of packages on the truck is less than five.

h) *Using the foreach loop.* Use a foreach loop to iterate through the values in m_objList. Each iteration should determine whether the current package is the one selected from the ListBox.

i) *Adding the package to the truck.* When the foreach loop has located the correct package, add that package to the truck by adding the reference to objTempPackage to the truck's ArrayList, m_objTruckList. Then assign the value in objTempPackage (the package sent to the truck) to objTruckPackage.

j) *Removing the package.* When the foreach loop completes, remove the package meant for the truck from m_objList and the lstPackages ListBox.

k) *Displaying the package in the ListBox.* Use a foreach loop that iterates through each package in the m_objTruckList ArrayList and displays each package in the lstTruck ListBox.

l) *Refreshing the GUI.* Call the ClearControls and SetButtons methods to clear the TextBoxes and enable the appropriate Buttons. Also, set the **Ship** Button's Enabled property to false.

m) *Coding the else block.* Display a MessageBox that notifies the user if the number of packages on the truck is already five. Then, disable the **Ship** Button.

n) *Running the application.* Select **Debug > Start** to run your application. Add several packages. In the **Packages by State** GroupBox, select several packages and add them to the **Packages to Ship** ListBox. Verify that you can add only 5 packages to this ListBox.

o) *Closing the application.* Close your running application by clicking its close box.

p) *Closing the IDE.* Close Visual Studio .NET by clicking its close box.

"Cat and Mouse" Painter Application

Introducing the Graphics Object and Mouse Events

Objectives

In this tutorial, you will learn to:
- Use mouse events to allow user interaction with an application.
- Handle MouseDown, MouseUp and MouseMove events.
- Use the Graphics object to draw circles on the Form.
- Determine which mouse button was pressed.

Outline

21.1 Test-Driving the Painter Application
21.2 Constructing the Painter Application
21.3 Using a Graphics Object
21.4 Handling the MouseDown Event
21.5 Handling the MouseUp Event
21.6 Handling the MouseMove Event
21.7 Distinguishing Between Mouse Buttons
21.8 Wrap-Up

The mouse is one of the computer's most important input devices. It is essential to the GUIs of Windows applications. With the mouse, the user can point to, click and drag items in applications. Clicking and releasing a mouse button are associated with events, as is moving the mouse. Every time you move the mouse, Windows interprets that event and redraws the mouse pointer as it moves across the screen.

In this tutorial, you create a **Painter** application that handles mouse events. The user clicks the left mouse button over the Form to enable drawing. By moving the mouse pointer over the Form with the left mouse button pressed, the user can create line drawings composed of small circles. In addition to learning how to draw a shape on the Form (a circle), you will learn how to set the shape's color. You will then learn how to stop drawing when the user releases the mouse button. You will also enable the user to erase a drawing by holding down the right mouse button.

21.1 Test-Driving the Painter Application

In this tutorial, you will create a **Painter** application. This application must meet the following requirements:

Application Requirements

The principal of an elementary school wants to introduce computers to children by appealing to their creative side. Many elementary-level applications test skills in mathematics, but the principal wishes to use an application that allows children to express their artistic skills. Develop an application to allow the student to "paint" on a Form, using the mouse. The application should draw when the user moves the mouse with the left mouse button held down and stop drawing when the left mouse button is released. The application draws many small blue-violet circles side-by-side to trace out lines, curves and shapes. An important part of any drawing application is the ability to erase mistakes or to clear the Form for more drawing room. The user can erase portions of the drawing by moving the mouse with the right mouse button held down.

523

You begin by test-driving the completed application. Then, you will learn the additional C# technologies that you will need to create your own version of this application.

Test-Driving the Painter Application

1. ***Opening the completed application***. Open the C:\Examples\Tutorial21\ CompletedApplication\Painter directory to locate the **Painter** application. Double click Painter.sln to open the application in Visual Studio .NET.

2. ***Running the Painter application***. Select **Debug > Start** to run the application (Fig. 21.1).

Figure 21.1 **Painter** application before drawing.

3. ***Drawing with the mouse***. To draw on the Form using the **Painter** application, press and hold down the left mouse button while the mouse pointer is anywhere over the Form (Fig. 21.2). To stop drawing, release the mouse button. Note that the application draws little blue-violet circles as you move the mouse while pressing the left mouse button. The size of these circles will vary depending on your display settings.

Drawing lines composed of small, colored circles ——

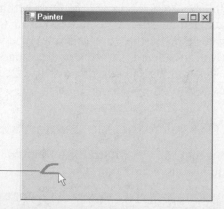

Figure 21.2 Drawing on the **Painter** application's Form.

4. ***Being creative***. Draw a cat and a computer mouse, as shown in Fig. 21.3. Be creative and have fun—your drawing need not look like the image shown.

5. ***Using the eraser***. Hold down the right mouse button and move the mouse pointer over part of your drawing. This "erases" the drawing wherever the mouse pointer comes into contact with the colored line (Fig. 21.4). You will see, when you add code to the application to erase, that you are actually drawing circles in the Form's background color.

(cont.)

Figure 21.3   Drawing a cat and a computer mouse on the Form.

Erasing by drawing circles
that are the same color
as the Form's background

Figure 21.4   Erasing part of the drawing.

6. ***Closing the application***. Close your running application by clicking its close box.

7. ***Closing the IDE***. Close Visual Studio .NET by clicking its close box.

21.2 Constructing the Painter Application

Before you begin building the **Painter** application, you should review the application's functionality. The following pseudocode describes the basic operation of the **Painter** application and what happens when the user moves the mouse pointer over the application's Form:

> When a mouse button is pressed:
>
> > If the left mouse button is pressed
> > > Enable user to draw
> > Else if the right mouse button is pressed
> > > Enable the user to erase
>
> When a mouse button is released:
> > Disable the user from drawing
> > Disable the user from erasing
>
> When the mouse is moved:
>
> > If the user is allowed to paint
> > > Draw a blue-violet circle at the position of the mouse pointer
> > Else If the user is allowed to erase
> > > "Erase" by drawing a circle at the position of the mouse pointer in the
> > > Form's background color

Now that you have test-driven the **Painter** application and studied its pseudocode representation, you will use an ACE table to help you convert the pseudocode to C#. Figure 21.5 lists the actions, controls and events that will help you complete your own version of this application.

Action/Control/Event (ACE) Table for the Painter Application

Action	Object/Class	Event
	FrmPainter	MouseDown
If the left mouse button is pressed	MouseEventArgs	
Enable user to draw		
Else if the right mouse button is pressed	MouseEventArgs	
Enable the user to erase		
	FrmPainter	MouseUp
Disable the user from drawing		
Disable the user from erasing		
	FrmPainter	MouseMove
If the user is allowed to paint Draw blue-violet circle at position of mouse pointer	m_objGraphic	
Else If the user is allowed to erase "Erase" by drawing a circle at the position of the mouse in the Form's background color	m_objGraphic	

Figure 21.5 Painter application's ACE table.

This tutorial starts by showing you how to use two mouse events—the event that occurs when you press a mouse button and the event that occurs when you release that mouse button. At first, your **Painter** application will draw a circle when the user presses or releases any mouse button. The circles drawn by pressing a mouse button will have a larger size than, and a different color from, the circles drawn by releasing the mouse button. Next, you will modify the application so that it draws when the user moves the mouse with a button pressed. If the user moves the mouse without pressing a mouse button, nothing will be drawn.

To complete the **Painter** application, you will need to add the eraser capability, which requires you to determine which mouse button the user presses. The last section of this tutorial will show you how to assign the drawing capability to the left mouse button and the eraser capability to the right mouse button.

21.3 Using a Graphics Object

Now that you have seen the pseudocode and ACE table, you are ready to begin building the **Painter** application. You will use a **Graphics** object to enable the user to draw on the Form. The Graphics class contains methods used for drawing text, lines, rectangles and other shapes. The following box shows you how to create the **Painter** application's Graphics object.

Creating a Graphics Object

1. *Copying the template to your working directory.* Copy the C:\Examples\ Tutorial21\TemplateApplication\Painter directory to your C:\SimplyCSP directory.

2. *Opening the Painter application's template file.* Double click the Painter.sln file to open the application in Visual Studio .NET.

(cont.) 3. ***Declaring a Graphics object.*** Add lines 23–24 of Fig. 21.6 into the **Painter** application. Line 24 declares Graphics reference m_objGraphic. Notice that the template already contains the declaration of the m_intDIAMETER constant (line 21). We will discuss this constant shortly.

Declaring a Graphics object ——————

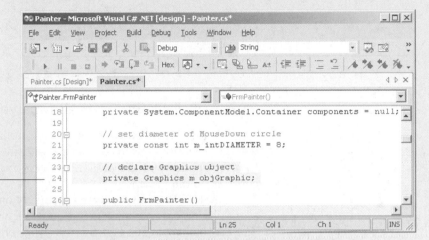

Figure 21.6   Declaring a Graphics object.

4. ***Creating a Graphics object.*** In design view, double click the Form to generate the FrmPainter_Load event handler. Be sure to add the comment and break the header as shown in Fig. 21.7 so that the line numbers in your code match those presented in this tutorial. Add lines 86–87 of Fig. 21.7 to the new event handler. The **CreateGraphics** method (which is a member of the Form class) creates a Graphics object with which you will draw shapes on the Form. Note that because you are writing code in the Form's class (FrmPainter), you do not need to use the member-access operator to access the Form's CreateGraphics method.

Creating a Graphics object ——————

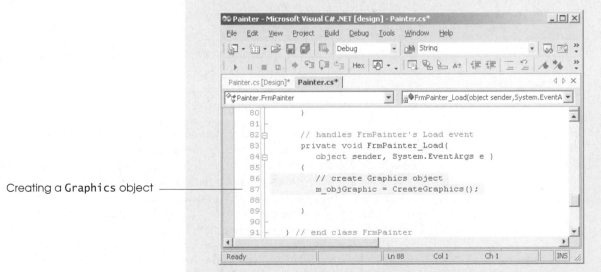

Figure 21.7   Creating a Graphics object.

The Graphics object could not be created at the same time it was declared because a class's methods (such as CreateGraphics) cannot be used in the declarations of a class's instance variables (such as objGraphics). For this reason, you create the Graphics object in the Form's Load event. Add a comment above the event handler, and break the event handler's header into two lines so that your line numbers are correct.

5. ***Saving the project.*** Select **File > Save All** to save your modified code.

SELF-REVIEW
1. To draw on a Form, use an object of the _____ class.
   a) Graphics   b) Drawing
   c) Paint   d) Sketch

2. The _____ method creates a Graphics object.
   a) GetGraphics   b) MakeGraphics
   c) CreateGraphics   d) InitializeGraphics

Answers: 1) a. 2) c.

21.4 Handling the MouseDown Event

This section begins our discussion of handling **mouse events**, which are generated when the mouse is used to interact with the Form or controls on the Form. In the **Painter** application, the mouse interacts exclusively with the Form. (There are no controls on the Form.)

A Form's **MouseDown** event occurs when a mouse button is pressed while the mouse pointer is over the Form. You will learn how to add a MouseDown event handler to your application in the following box. You will notice that, when you run your application after following the steps in this box, you can press any mouse button to draw a circle on the Form. When you add the eraser capability to the **Painter** application in Section 21.7, you will learn how to determine which mouse button was pressed.

Handling the MouseDown Event

1. ***Generating the MouseDown event handler.*** Switch to design view. To generate the MouseDown event handler, click the **Events** button in the **Properties** window (Fig. 21.8). Then, double click the MouseDown property.

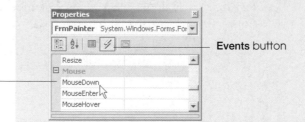

Double click MouseDown property ———

——— **Events** button

Figure 21.8   Creating a MouseDown event handler.

This generates the FrmPainter_MouseDown event handler. Be sure to add the comments and break the header as shown in Fig. 21.9 so that the line numbers in your code match those presented in this tutorial. The application invokes FrmPainter_MouseDown when the user generates the Form's Mouse-Down event by pressing a mouse button when the mouse pointer is over the FrmPainter Form. Notice that the second argument passed to the FrmPainter_MouseDown event handler is a variable of the **MouseEventArgs** type. This MouseEventArgs object (referenced by e) contains information about the MouseDown event, including the coordinates of the mouse pointer when the mouse button was pressed on the Form.

Note that the *x*- and *y*-coordinates of the MouseEventArgs object are relative to the top-left corner Form or control that raises the event. Point (0,0) represents the upper-left corner of the Form. If you wish to access the *x*-coordinate of the mouse, use the **X** property of the e reference. To access the *y*-coordinate of the mouse, use the **Y** property of the e reference, as in e.Y.

(cont.)

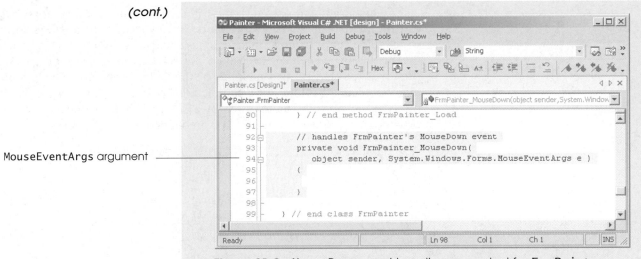

Figure 21.9   MouseDown event handler generated for FrmPainter.

2. ***Drawing on the Form whenever a mouse button is clicked.*** Add lines 96–99 of Fig. 21.10 to the MouseDown event handler. The **FillEllipse** method of the Graphics class draws an ellipse on the Form. Recall that you declared m_objGraphic as your Graphics reference earlier in this tutorial. Figure 21.11 shows a diagram of a general ellipse. The dotted rectangle is known as the ellipse's **bounding rectangle**. The bounding rectangle specifies an ellipse's height, width and location on the Form.

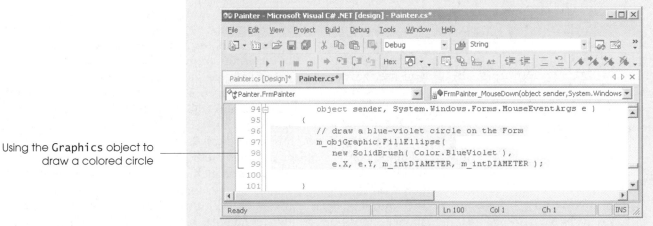

Figure 21.10   Adding code to the MouseDown event handler.

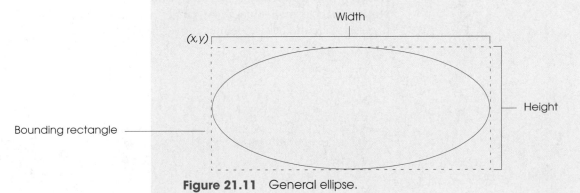

Figure 21.11   General ellipse.

(cont.)

The first argument passed to the FillEllipse method is a **brush**, which can be used to fill shapes with colors. In this case, the **SolidBrush** class, which fills a shape using a single color, is specified as the brush. The color of the brush is specified in the call to the constructor. The color you select (Color.BlueViolet) is a member of the Color structure, which contains many predefined colors. For a complete list of predefined colors in C#, simply type the word Color followed by a dot, and the *Intellisense* feature will provide a drop-down list of over 100 predefined colors (Fig. 21.12).

Type Color followed by a dot (.) to access *Intellisense*

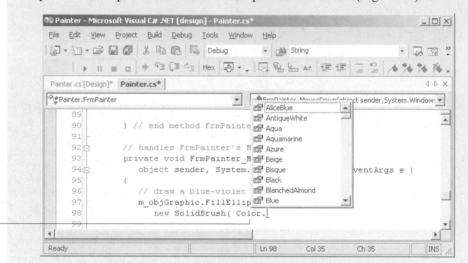

Figure 21.12   Selecting a color by using *Intellisense*.

The second and third arguments passed to the FillEllipse method specify the *x*- and *y*-coordinates of the upper-left corner of the bounding rectangle, relative to the upper-left corner of the Form. In this application, you use the *x*- and *y*- coordinates of the mouse (returned by the X and Y properties of MouseEventArgs reference e). The fourth and fifth arguments passed to the FillEllipse method (the m_intDIAMETER constant) specify the height and width of the bounding rectangle. An ellipse with equal width and height is a circle—this method call draws a blue-violet circle.

The Graphics object provides methods for drawing shapes other than ellipses. You will learn about these methods in Tutorial 26. Note that the *x*- and *y*-coordinates the Graphics object uses to draw a shape are relative to the control or Form that created it. In this case, the Graphics object draws shapes at positions relative to the Form.

3. ***Running the application***. Select **Debug > Start** to run your application. Notice that a small blue-violet circle is drawn when a mouse button is pressed while the mouse pointer is over the Form (Fig. 21.13).

Figure 21.13   Running the application.

(cont.)   4. ***Closing the application.*** Close your running application by clicking its close box.

SELF-REVIEW

1. To draw a solid shape, the FillEllipse method uses a _____.

   a) Pencil object   b) Marker object
   c) PaintBrush object   d) SolidBrush object

2. BlueViolet is a member of the _____ structure.

   a) SolidColor   b) FillColor
   c) Color   d) SystemColor

Answers: 1) d. 2) c.

21.5 Handling the MouseUp Event

Using the application, you can click anywhere on the Form and place a blue-violet circle. To enhance the application further, you will place a green circle on the Form when the user releases the mouse button. A Form's **MouseUp** event is generated when a mouse button is released and the pointer is over the Form. You will add this functionality in the following box.

Handling the MouseUp Event

1. ***Adding a second diameter.*** Add lines 23–24 of Fig. 21.14 to your application (above the initialization of the Graphics reference and below the initialization of the m_intDIAMETER constant). These lines declare a second constant that stores the diameter of a smaller circle. A circle with this diameter (in pixels) will be drawn whenever the user releases a mouse button.

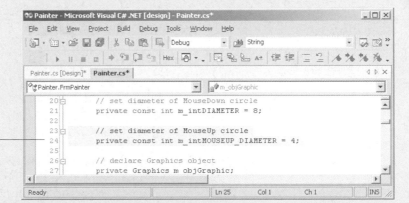

Using a constant to store a circle's diameter

Figure 21.14 Declaring a constant for use in the MouseUp event handler.

2. ***Adding the MouseUp event handler.*** Switch to design view and click the **Events** button in the **Properties** window, as you did in Fig. 21.8. Then, double click the MouseUp property. This creates an empty event handler called FrmPainter_MouseUp. Be sure to add the comments and modify the header as shown in Fig. 21.15 so that the line numbers in your code match those presented in this tutorial. This header is similar to the header for the MouseDown event handler (the only difference is that the word Down is changed to Up). The MouseUp event handler executes only when a mouse button is released.

(cont.)

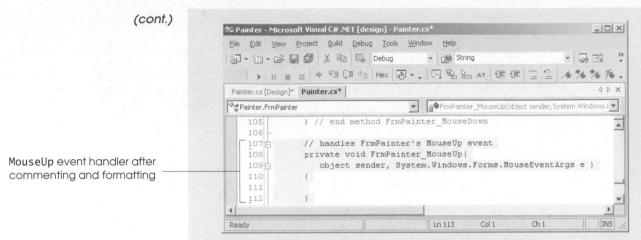

Figure 21.15 ⠀ Empty **MouseUp** event handler.

3. ***Drawing a circle when the user releases a mouse button.*** Add lines 111–113 of Fig. 21.16 to the **MouseUp** event handler to draw a circle at the position of the mouse pointer on the **Form** whenever the user releases the mouse button. The diameter of each "mouse up" circle is only half the diameter of the **BlueViolet** circles drawn by the **MouseDown** event handler that is called when a mouse button is pressed.

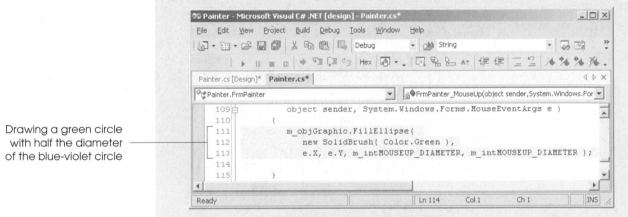

Figure 21.16 ⠀ **MouseUp** event handler code.

4. ***Running the application.*** Select **Debug > Start** to run your application (Fig. 21.17). Press and hold a mouse button, move the mouse pointer to a new location and release the button. Notice that a **BlueViolet** circle is drawn when you press any mouse button and that a **Green** circle is drawn when you release the mouse button.

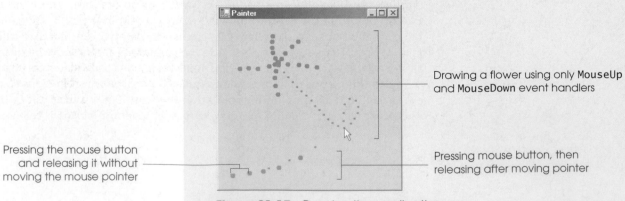

Figure 21.17 ⠀ Running the application.

(cont.) 5. ***Closing the application***. Close your running application by clicking its close box.

SELF-REVIEW

1. Releasing a mouse button generates a _____ event.
   a) `MouseRelease`   b) `MouseUp`
   c) `MouseOff`   d) `MouseClick`

2. The second and third arguments of the `FillEllipse` method specify the *x*- and *y*-coordinates of the _____.
   a) ellipse's center   b) bounding rectangle's lower-left corner
   c) bounding rectangle's upper-right corner   d) bounding rectangle's upper-left corner

   Answers: 1) b. 2) d.

21.6 Handling the MouseMove Event

Currently, the application allows you to draw only isolated circles when a mouse button is pressed or released. It does not yet allow you to draw more sophisticated shapes and designs. Next, you will enhance your application to provide more drawing capabilities. The application should continuously draw `BlueViolet` circles as long as the mouse is being dragged (that is, moved with a button pressed). If the mouse button is not pressed, moving the mouse across the `Form` should not draw anything. To add this functionality, you will begin by modifying your two event handlers.

Modifying the Painter Application

1. ***Adding a bool variable to specify whether a mouse button is pressed***. Delete the the `m_intMOUSEUP_DIAMETER` constant (lines 23–24 of Fig. 21.14) and add lines 20–21 of Fig. 21.18 to your application (above the initialization of `m_intDIAMETER`). This line declares and initializes the `bool` variable `m_blnShouldPaint`. The application must be able to determine whether a mouse button is pressed, because the application should draw on the `Form` only when the mouse button is held down.

Declaring and setting an instance variable to control painting

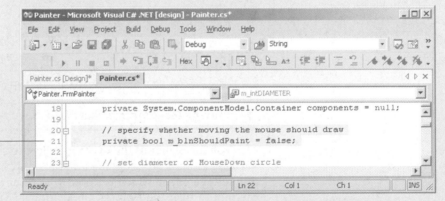

Figure 21.18 The `bool` instance variable `m_blnShouldPaint` is declared and set to `false`.

You will alter the `MouseDown` and `MouseUp` event handlers so that `m_blnShouldPaint` is `true` when any mouse button is held down and `false` when the mouse button is released. When the application is first loaded, it should not "paint" anything, so this instance variable is initialized to `false`.

(cont.)

2. *Altering the MouseDown event handler.* Remove the code inside the Mouse-Down event handler (lines 100–103), leaving just the method header and the set of braces. Add line 100 of Fig. 21.19 to the MouseDown event handler to set m_blnShouldPaint to true. This indicates that a mouse button is pressed.

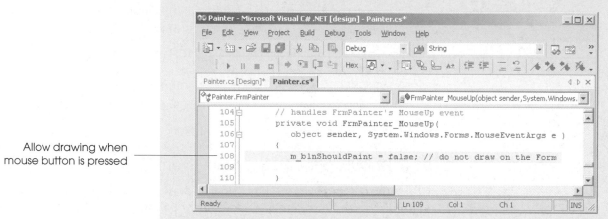

Allow drawing when mouse button is pressed

Figure 21.19 Setting m_blnShouldPaint to true.

3. *Altering the MouseUp event handler.* Remove the code inside the MouseUp event handler (lines 108–110), leaving just the method header and the set of braces. Add line 108 of Fig. 21.20 to set m_blnShouldPaint to false. This indicates that a mouse button has been released.

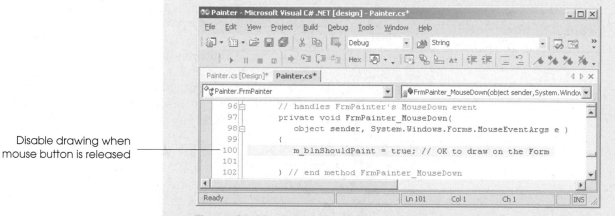

Disable drawing when mouse button is released

Figure 21.20 Setting m_blnShouldPaint to false.

4. *Saving the project.* Select **File > Save All** to save your modified code.

You have altered the event handlers to set the value of the m_blnShouldPaint variable to indicate whether a mouse button is pressed. Next, you will handle the **MouseMove** event, which is raised whenever the mouse moves. Whenever you move the mouse over the **Painter** application's Form, the application invokes the Mouse-Move event handler. You define the MouseMove event handler in the following box.

Adding the MouseMove Event Handler

1. *Adding the MouseMove event handler.* In design view, click the **Events** button in the **Properties** window, as you did in Fig. 21.8. Then, double click the MouseMove property. This generates the empty MouseMove event handler FrmPainter_MouseMove. Be sure to add the comments and break the header as shown in Fig. 21.21 so that the line numbers in your code match those presented in this tutorial.

(cont.)

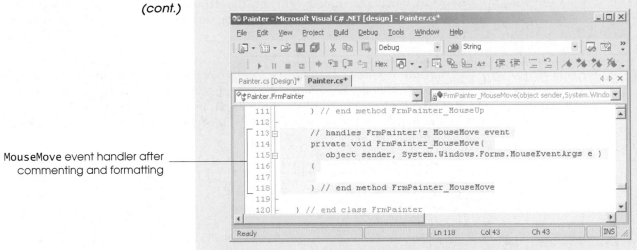

MouseMove event handler after commenting and formatting

Figure 21.21 MouseMove empty event handler.

2. ***Adding code to the MouseMove event handler.*** Add lines 117–123 of Fig. 21.22 to the MouseMove event handler. This event handler executes each time the mouse is moved. The `if` statement tests the value of `m_blnShouldPaint`. If this variable contains `true` (a mouse button is pressed), the `FillEllipse` method draws a `BlueViolet` circle on the Form. If `m_blnShouldPaint` contains `false` (no mouse button is pressed), then nothing is drawn.

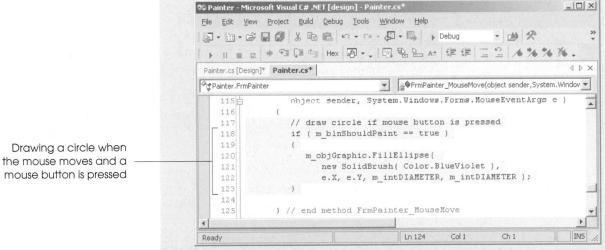

Drawing a circle when the mouse moves and a mouse button is pressed

Figure 21.22 MouseMove event handler draws circles on the Form if a mouse button is held down.

3. ***Running the application.*** Select **Debug > Start** to run your application. Try drawing various shapes and designs on the Form. Note that you can draw lines using any mouse button.

4. ***Closing the application.*** Close your running application by clicking its close box.

21.7 Distinguishing Between Mouse Buttons

Now that your application allows the user to draw using the mouse, you will add the code that allows the user to "erase" by moving the mouse over the drawing while pressing the right mouse button. You also will alter the application so that the user draws by moving the mouse with only the left mouse button pressed. To do this, you will need to determine which mouse button was pressed. You learn how to do this in the following box.

Distinguishing Between Mouse Buttons

1. ***Adding a bool variable to specify whether the application should erase while the mouse pointer is moving.*** Add lines 20–21 of Fig. 21.23 to your application (above the initialization of m_blnShouldPaint). The m_blnShouldErase instance variable specifies whether moving the mouse pointer should act like an eraser.

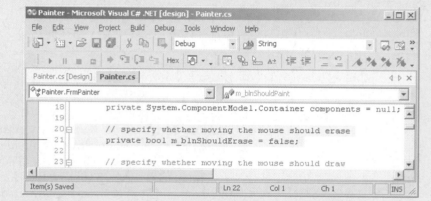

Declaring and setting an instance variable to control erasing

Figure 21.23 The bool instance variable m_blnShouldErase is declared and set to false.

2. ***Determining which mouse button was pressed.*** Replace the code in the FrmPainter_MouseDown event handler (line 104) with lines 104–113 of Fig. 21.24. The **Button** property of the MouseEventArgs object (referenced by e) specifies which mouse button was pressed. The **MouseButtons** enumeration defines constants that represent the mouse buttons.

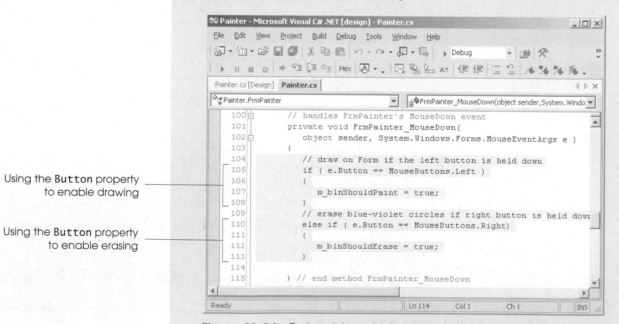

Using the **Button** property to enable drawing

Using the **Button** property to enable erasing

Figure 21.24 Determining which mouse button was pressed.

(cont.)   The three most common mouse buttons—**Right**, **Left** and **Middle**—are
included in MouseButtons. If the left mouse button was pressed (line 105),
line 107 sets m_blnShouldPaint to true, which indicates that dragging the
mouse should draw. If the right mouse button was pressed (line 110), line
112 sets m_blnShouldErase to true, which indicates that dragging the
mouse should erase any blue-violet circles touched by the mouse pointer.

Notice that only one of the variables can be true at one time. For example, if m_blnShouldPaint is true, then m_blnShouldErase is false. To
ensure this, both variables are set to false when the mouse button is
released. (See *Step 3*.)

3. ***Changing the MouseUp event handler.*** Add line 122 of Fig. 21.25 to the
FrmPainter_MouseUp event handler. The application should not erase or
draw when no mouse buttons are pressed. Line 122 sets m_blnShouldErase
to false to indicate that the mouse pointer should not act as an eraser. Note
that m_blnShouldPaint is also set to false.

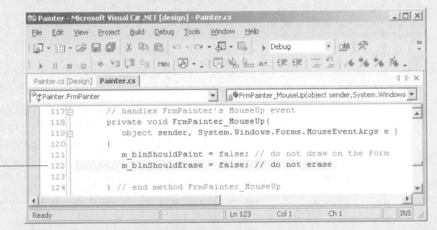

Disabling erasing when a
mouse button is released

Figure 21.25   Setting m_blnShouldErase to false when a mouse button is
released.

4. ***Drawing when the left mouse button is pressed.*** Replace the code in the
FrmPainter_MouseMove event handler with lines 130–142 of Fig. 21.26. If
m_blnShouldPaint is true (line 131), lines 133–135 draw a BlueViolet circle. Your changes to the MouseDown event handler make m_blnShouldPaint
true when the left mouse button is pressed. As a result, the application only
draws BlueViolet circles when the user drags the mouse while pressing the
left mouse button.

5. ***Erasing when the right mouse button is pressed.*** The MouseMove event handler does not actually erase anything. Instead, when m_blnShouldErase is
true (line 138 of Fig. 21.26), the FillEllipse method (lines 140–141)
draws a circle that is the same size as the BlueViolet circle and has the
same color as the Form's background. This allows the mouse pointer to act
like an eraser. Notice that the first argument to FillEllipse is BackColor.
Much like the CreateGraphics method, the BackColor property of the
Form can be accessed without the member-access operator. The BackColor
property returns the Form's background color as a Color value.

6. ***Running the application.*** Select **Debug > Start** to run your application. Try
drawing various shapes and designs on the Form, then try to erase them.

7. ***Closing the application.*** Close your running application by clicking its close
box.

8. ***Closing the IDE.*** Close Visual Studio .NET by clicking its close box.

(cont.)

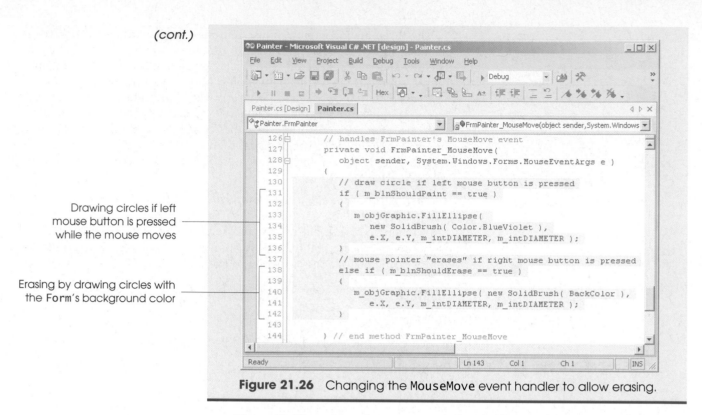

Drawing circles if left mouse button is pressed while the mouse moves

Erasing by drawing circles with the Form's background color

Figure 21.26   Changing the MouseMove event handler to allow erasing.

Figure 21.27 presents the source code for the **Painter** application. The lines of code that contain new programming concepts that you learned in this tutorial are highlighted.

```
1   using System;
2   using System.Drawing;
3   using System.Collections;
4   using System.ComponentModel;
5   using System.Windows.Forms;
6   using System.Data;
7
8   namespace Painter
9   {
10      /// <summary>
11      /// Summary description for FrmPainter.
12      /// </summary>
13      public class FrmPainter : System.Windows.Forms.Form
14      {
15         /// <summary>
16         /// Required designer variable.
17         /// </summary>
18         private System.ComponentModel.Container components = null;
19
20         // specify whether moving the mouse should erase
21         private bool m_blnShouldErase = false;
22
23         // specify whether moving the mouse should draw
24         private bool m_blnShouldPaint = false;
25
26         // set diameter of MouseDown circle
27         private const int m_intDIAMETER = 8;
28
```

Figure 21.27   **Painter** application code. (Part 1 of 3.)

```
29        // declare Graphics object
30        private Graphics m_objGraphic;
31
32        public FrmPainter()
33        {
34           //
35           // Required for Windows Form Designer support
36           //
37           InitializeComponent();
38
39           //
40           // TODO: Add any constructor code after InitializeComponent
41           // call
42           //
43        }
44
45        /// <summary>
46        /// Clean up any resources being used.
47        /// </summary>
48        protected override void Dispose( bool disposing )
49        {
50           if( disposing )
51           {
52              if (components != null)
53              {
54                 components.Dispose();
55              }
56           }
57           base.Dispose( disposing );
58        }
59
60        // Windows Form Designer generated code
61
62        /// <summary>
63        /// The main entry point for the application.
64        /// </summary>
65        [STAThread]
66        static void Main()
67        {
68           Application.Run( new FrmPainter() );
69        }
70
71        // handles FrmPainter's Load event
72        private void FrmPainter_Load(
73           object sender, System.EventArgs e )
74        {
75           // create Graphics object
76           m_objGraphic = CreateGraphics();
77
78        } // end method FrmPainter_Load
79
80        // handles FrmPainter's MouseDown event
81        private void FrmPainter_MouseDown(
82           object sender, System.Windows.Forms.MouseEventArgs e )
83        {
84           // draw on Form if the left button is held down
85           if ( e.Button == MouseButtons.Left )
86           {
```

The **Button** property specifies which button was pressed ———— 85

Figure 21.27 **Painter** application code. (Part 2 of 3.)

The **MouseButtons** enumeration specifies constants for the mouse button

```
87              m_blnShouldPaint = true;
88           }
89           // erase blue-violet circles if right button is held down
90           else if ( e.Button == MouseButtons.Right )
91           {
92              m_blnShouldErase = true;
93           }
94
95        } // end method FrmPainter_MouseDown
96
97        // handles FrmPainter's MouseUp event
98        private void FrmPainter_MouseUp(
99           object sender, System.Windows.Forms.MouseEventArgs e )
100       {
101          m_blnShouldPaint = false; // do not draw on the Form
102          m_blnShouldErase = false; // do not erase
103
104       } // end method FrmPainter_MouseUp
105
106       // handles FrmPainter's MouseMove event
107       private void FrmPainter_MouseMove(
108          object sender, System.Windows.Forms.MouseEventArgs e )
109       {
110          // draw circle if left mouse button is pressed
111          if ( m_blnShouldPaint == true )
112          {
113             m_objGraphic.FillEllipse(
114                new SolidBrush( Color.BlueViolet ),
115                e.X, e.Y, m_intDIAMETER, m_intDIAMETER );
116          }
117          // mouse pointer "erases" if right mouse button is pressed
118          else if ( m_blnShouldErase == true )
119          {
120             m_objGraphic.FillEllipse( new SolidBrush( BackColor ),
121                e.X, e.Y, m_intDIAMETER, m_intDIAMETER );
122          }
123
124       } // end method FrmPainter_MouseMove
125
126    } // end class FrmPainter
127 }
```

The **FillEllipse** method used to draw a **BlueViolet** ellipse

Create a **SolidBrush** with the Form's background color

Figure 21.27 **Painter** application code. (Part 3 of 3.)

SELF-REVIEW

1. Moving the mouse pointer generates a _____ event.

   a) MouseMove
   b) MousePositionChanged
   c) MouseMoved
   d) MouseChanged

2. The _____ enumeration specifies constants for the mouse buttons.

   a) MouseButtons
   b) Buttons
   c) MouseOptions
   d) ButtonOptions

Answers: 1) a. 2) a.

21.8 Wrap-Up

In this tutorial, you learned the essential elements of mouse event handling. You handled three common mouse events—MouseMove, MouseUp and MouseDown. You learned to create mouse event handlers associated with a Form. You generated these event handlers by double clicking the appropriate mouse event after clicking the **Events** button in the **Properties** window.

You used mouse events and a `Graphics` object in the **Painter** application. You invoked the `CreateGraphics` method to create a `Graphics` object. You used the `FillEllipse` method of the `Graphics` class to draw a solid circle on the `Form`. You learned how to use a `SolidBrush` object to draw a shape in a single, solid color. You used a member of the `Color` structure to specify the brush's color.

The **Painter** application uses mouse events to determine what the user wants to do. The user moves the mouse with the left mouse button held down to draw on the `Form`. Moving the mouse across the `Form` without pressing a button does not draw anything on the `Form`.

You learned to distinguish which mouse button was pressed. You used this to provide the **Painter** application with an eraser. When users move the mouse with the right mouse button pressed, the **Painter** application draws circles with the same background color as the `Form`.

To build the **Painter** application, you used `MouseEventArgs` objects, which are passed to mouse event handlers and provide information about mouse events. The X and Y properties of the `MouseEventArgs` object specify the *x*- and *y*-coordinates where the mouse event occurred. The `Button` property specifies which (if any) mouse button was pressed. You used constants defined by the `MouseButtons` enumeration to determine which button the `Button` property specified.

In the next tutorial, you will learn how to use event handlers that respond to user interactions with the keyboard. You will then build an application that uses keyboard events. The application will also teach you how to create menus and dialogs.

SKILLS SUMMARY

Raising Events with a Mouse

- Press a mouse's buttons and move the mouse to raise events.

Handling Mouse Events

- The `MouseEventArgs` class contains information about mouse events, such as the *x*- and *y*-coordinates where the mouse event occurred. Each mouse-event handler receives an object of class `MouseEventArgs` as an argument.
- Move the mouse to raise the `MouseMove` event.
- Press a mouse button to raise the `MouseDown` event.
- Release a mouse button to raise the `MouseUp` event.

Distinguishing Between Mouse Buttons

- The `Button` property of `MouseEventArgs` specifies which mouse button was pressed.
- The `MouseButtons` enumeration specifies the constants `Left`, `Right` and `Middle` for mouse buttons. These are used to determine which button was pressed.

Creating an Event Handler for a Mouse Event Associated with a Form

- Click the **Events** Button in the **Properties** window. Then, double click the name of the appropriate event in the **Properties** window.

Drawing on a Form

- Use `Graphics` methods to draw shapes on a `Form` or a control.
- Create a `Graphics` object (by invoking the `Form`'s `CreateGraphics` method) to access methods for drawing shapes.

Drawing a Solid Ellipse

- Use the `Graphics` method `FillEllipse` to draw a solid ellipse.
- Pass a `SolidBrush` object to the `FillEllipse` method to specify the shape's interior color.
- Specify the color, the height and width of the bounding rectangle and the coordinates of the bounding rectangle's upper-left corner. When the height and width of the bounding rectangle are equal, a circle is drawn.

KEY TERMS

bounding rectangle of ellipse—Specifies an ellipse's height, width and location.

brush—Used to fill shapes with colors.

Button property—The property of the MouseEventArgs class that specifies which (if any) mouse button is pressed.

CreateGraphics method—Creates a Graphics object on a Form or control.

FillEllipse method—The method of the Graphics class that draws an ellipse. This method takes as arguments a brush, a Color, the coordinates of the ellipse's bounding rectangle's upper-left corner and the width and height of the bounding rectangle.

Graphics class—Defines methods for drawing shapes.

Left value of MouseButtons enumeration—Used to represent the left mouse button.

Middle value of MouseButtons enumeration—Used to represent the middle mouse button.

mouse event—Generated when a user interacts with an application using the computer's mouse.

MouseButtons enumeration—Defines constants, such as Left, Right and Middle, to specify mouse buttons.

MouseDown event—Generated when a mouse button is pressed.

MouseEventArgs class—Specifies information about a mouse event.

MouseMove event—Generated when a mouse pointer is moved.

MouseUp event—Generated when the mouse button is released.

Right value of MouseButtons enumeration—Used to represent the right mouse button.

SolidBrush class—Defines a brush that draws with a single color.

X property—The property of the MouseEventArgs class that specifies the x-coordinate of the mouse event.

Y property—The property of the MouseEventArgs class that specifies the y-coordinate of the mouse event.

CONTROLS, EVENTS, PROPERTIES & METHODS

Form This class represents an application's GUI.

- *Events*

   Load—Raised when an application initially executes.

   MouseDown—Raised when a mouse button is clicked.

   MouseMove—Raised when the mouse pointer is moved.

   MouseUp—Raised when a mouse button is released.

- *Method*

   CreateGraphics—Creates a Graphics object.

- *Property*

   BackColor—Specifies the background color of the Form.

Graphics This class contains methods used to draw text, lines and shapes.

- *Method*

   FillEllipse—Draws a solid ellipse of a specified size and color at the specified location.

MouseEventArgs This class contains information about mouse events.

- *Properties*

   Button—Specifies which (if any) mouse button was pressed.

   X—Specifies the x-coordinate of the mouse event.

   Y—Specifies the y-coordinate of the mouse event.

MULTIPLE-CHOICE QUESTIONS

21.1 The *x*- and *y*-coordinates of the MouseEventArgs object are relative to _____.

a) the screen

b) the application

c) the Form or control that contains the control that raised the event

d) None of the above.

21.2 The _____ method of the Graphics class draws a solid ellipse.

a) FillEllipse

b) Ellipse

c) SolidEllipse

d) DrawEllipse

21.3 The _____ object passed to a mouse event handler contains information about the mouse event that was raised.

a) EventHandler

b) MouseEventHandler

c) MouseEventArgs

d) EventArgs

21.4 The _____ event is raised when a mouse button is pressed.

a) MousePress

b) MouseClick

c) MouseDown

d) MouseButtonDown

21.5 A _____ is used to fill a shape with color using a Graphics object.

a) painter

b) brush

c) paint bucket

d) marker

21.6 A _____ event is raised every time the mouse interacts with a control.

a) control

b) mouse pointer

c) mouse

d) user

21.7 The _____ property of MouseEventArgs specifies which mouse button was pressed.

a) Source

b) Button

c) WhichButton

d) ButtonPressed

21.8 The _____ class contains methods for drawing text, lines, rectangles and other shapes.

a) Pictures

b) Drawings

c) Graphics

d) Illustrations

21.9 An ellipse with its _____ is a circle.

a) height twice the length of its width

b) width set to zero

c) height half the length of its width

d) height equal to its width

21.10 The _____ method creates a Graphics object.

a) NewGraphics

b) CreateGraphics

c) PaintGraphics

d) InitializeGraphics

EXERCISES

21.11 *(Line Length Application)* The **Line Length** application should draw a straight black line on the Form and calculate the length of the line (Fig. 21.28). The line should begin at the coordinates where the mouse button is pressed and should stop at the point where the mouse button is released. The application should display the line's length (that is, the distance between the two endpoints) in the Label **Length =**. Use the following formula to calculate the line's length, where (x_1, y_1) is the first endpoint (the coordinates where the mouse button is pressed) and (x_2, y_2) is the second endpoint (the coordinates where the mouse button is released). To calculate the distance (or length) between the two points, use the following equation:

$$d = \sqrt{(x_1 - x_2)^2 + (y_1 - y_2)^2}$$

To draw a straight line, you need to use the DrawLine method on a Graphics object. When drawing lines, you should use a **Pen** object, which is an object used to specify characteristics of lines and curves. Use the following method call to draw a black line between the two points using a Graphics object reference objGraphic:

$$\text{objGraphic.DrawLine(new Pen(Color.Black), } x_1, y_1, x_2, y_2 \text{);}$$

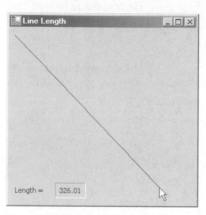

Figure 21.28 Line Length application.

a) *Copying the template to your working directory.* Copy the directory C:\Examples\ Tutorial21\Exercises\LineLength to your C:\SimplyCSP directory.

b) *Opening the application's template file.* Double click LineLength.sln in the Line-Length directory to open the application.

c) *Declaring instance variables.* Declare a reference to a Graphics object that you will use to draw a line. Then, declare four ints in which you will store the *x*- and *y*-coordinates of the two points.

d) *Adding a Load event handler.* Create a Load event handler. Add code to the Load event handler to initialize the Graphics object.

e) *Adding a MouseDown event handler.* Create a MouseDown event handler. Add code to the MouseDown event handler to store the coordinates of the first endpoint of the line.

f) *Creating the Distance method.* Define a method named Length that returns the distance between two endpoints as a double. The method should use the following statement to perform the line length calculation, where intXDistance is the difference between the *x*-coordinates of the two points and intYDistance is the difference between the *y*-coordinates of the two points:

```
Math.Sqrt( ( intXDistance * intXDistance ) +
    ( intYDistance * intYDistance ) );
```

g) *Adding a MouseUp event handler.* Create a MouseUp event handler. First store the coordinates of the line's second endpoint. Then, call the Length method to obtain the distance between the two endpoints (the line's length). Finally, display the line on the Form and the line's length in the **Length =** Label, as in Fig. 21.28.

h) *Running the application.* Select **Debug > Start** to run your application. Draw several lines and view their lengths. Verify that the length values are accurate.

i) *Closing the application.* Close your running application by clicking its close box.

j) *Closing the IDE.* Close Visual Studio .NET by clicking its close box.

21.12 *(Circle Painter Application)* The **Circle Painter** application should draw a blue circle with a randomly chosen size when the user presses a mouse button anywhere over the Form (Fig. 21.29). The application should randomly select a circle diameter in the range from 5 to 199, inclusive. To draw a blue circle with a given diameter (intDiameter), use the following statement:

```
objGraphic.DrawEllipse( new Pen( Color.Blue ), e.X, e.Y,
    intDiameter, intDiameter )
```

The DrawEllipse method, when passed a Pen (instead of a brush) as an argument, draws the outline of an ellipse. Recall that an ellipse is a circle if the height and width arguments are the same (in this case, the randomly selected intDiameter). Use the *x*- and *y*- coordinates of the MouseDown event as the *x*- and *y*- coordinates of the circle's bounding rectangle (that is, the second and third arguments to the DrawEllipse method). Notice that the first argument to the DrawEllipse method is a Pen object. See Exercise 21.11 for a description of Pen.

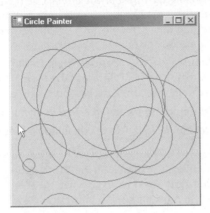

Figure 21.29   Circle Painter application.

a) **Copying the template to your working directory.** Copy the directory C:\Examples\ Tutorial21\Exercises\CirclePainter to your C:\SimplyCSP directory.

b) **Opening the application's template file.** Double click CirclePainter.sln in the CirclePainter directory to open the application.

c) **Adding a MouseDown event handler.** Create a MouseDown event handler. In the event handler, retrieve the *x*- and *y*-coordinates of the location of the mouse pointer when a mouse button was pressed. Then, generate a random number to use as the circle's diameter, using a Random object, and store it in a variable. Finally, call the DrawEllipse method on a reference to a Graphics object to draw a blue circle on the Form with the diameter generated by the Random object.

d) **Running the application.** Select **Debug > Start** to run your application. Draw several blue circles and make sure that they are of different sizes.

e) **Closing the application.** Close your running application by clicking its close box.

f) **Closing the IDE.** Close Visual Studio .NET by clicking its close box.

21.13 (*Advanced Circle Painter Application*) In this exercise, you will enhance the application you created in Exercise 21.12. The advanced **Circle Painter** application should draw blue circles with a randomly generated diameter when the user presses the left mouse button. When the user presses the right mouse button, the application should draw a red circle with a randomly generated diameter (Fig. 21.30).

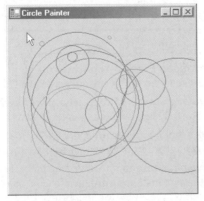

Figure 21.30   Advanced **Circle Painter** application.

a) *Copying the template to your working directory.* Copy the directory C:\Examples\ Tutorial21\Exercises\AdvancedCirclePainter to your C:\SimplyCSP directory.

b) *Opening the application's template file.* Double click CirclePainter.sln file in the AdvancedCirclePainter directory to open the application.

c) *Drawing the appropriate circle.* Use the Button property of MouseEventArgs reference e to determine which mouse button was pressed. Then, call the DrawEllipse method on a reference to a Graphics object to draw a blue circle on the Form if the left mouse button was clicked or a red circle if the right mouse button was clicked.

d) *Running the application.* Select **Debug > Start** to run your application. Draw several blue circles of different sizes using the left mouse button, then draw several red circles of different sizes using the right mouse button.

e) *Closing the application.* Close your running application by clicking its close box.

f) *Closing the IDE.* Close Visual Studio .NET by clicking its close box.

What does this code do? ▶ **21.14** Consider the example in Fig. 21.27. Suppose we change the MouseMove event handler to the code below. What happens when the user moves the mouse? Assume that the lblDisplay Label has been placed on the Form.

```
1   private void FrmPainter_MouseMove(
2       object sender, System.Windows.Forms.MouseEventArgs e )
3   {
4       lblDisplay.Text = "I'm at " + e.X + ", " + e.Y + ".";
5
6   } // end method FrmPainter_MouseMove
```

What's wrong with this code? ▶ **21.15** The following code should draw a BlueViolet circle of diameter 4 that corresponds to the movement of the mouse. Find the error(s) in the following code:

```
1   private void FrmPainter_MouseMove(
2       object sender, System.Windows.Forms.MouseEventArgs e )
3   {
4       if ( m_blnshouldPaint == true )
5       {
6           Graphics objGraphic = Graphics();
7
8           objGraphic.FillEllipse = (
9               new SolidBrush( Color.BlueViolet ), e.Y, e.X, 5, 4 );
10      }
11
12  } // end method FrmPainter_MouseMove
```

Programming Challenge ▶ **21.16** *(Advanced Painter Application)* Extend the Painter application to enable a user to change the size and color of the circles drawn (Fig. 21.31).

a) *Copying the template to your working directory.* Copy the directory C:\Examples\ Tutorial21\Exercises\AdvancedPainter to your C:\SimplyCSP directory.

b) *Opening the application's template file.* Double click AdvancedPainter.sln in the AdvancedPainter directory to open the application.

c) *Understanding the provided instance variables.* The template already provides you with four instance variables. The m_objBrushColor variable is a Color value that specifies the color of the brush used in the **Advanced Painter** application. The m_blnShouldPaint and m_blnShouldErase variables perform the same functions as in this tutorial's **Painter** application. The m_intDiameter variable stores the diameter of the circle to be drawn.

Figure 21.31 Advanced Painter application.

d) *Declaring an enumeration to store the circle diameter sizes.* Declare an enumeration Sizes to store the possible values of m_intDiameter. Set the SMALL constant to 4, MEDIUM to 8 and LARGE to 10.

e) *Adding event handlers for the Color RadioButtons.* The **Color** RadioButtons' event handlers should set m_objBrushColor to their specified colors (Color.Red, Color.Blue, Color.Green or Color.Black).

f) *Adding event handlers for the Size RadioButtons.* The **Size** RadioButtons' event handlers should set m_intDiameter to Sizes.SMALL (for the **Small** RadioButton), Sizes.MEDIUM (for the **Medium** RadioButton) or Sizes.LARGE (for the **Large** RadioButton).

g) *Adding a mouse event handler to a Panel.* To associate mouse events with the Panel, select pnlPainter from the **Class Name** ComboBox. Then, select the appropriate mouse event from the **Method Name** ComboBox.

h) *Coding the MouseDown and MouseUp event handlers.* The MouseUp and MouseDown event handlers behave exactly as they do in the **Painter** application.

i) *Coding the MouseMove event handler.* The MouseMove event handler behaves as the one in **Painter** application does. The color of the brush that draws the circle when m_blnShouldPaint is true is specified by m_objBrushColor. The eraser color is specified by the Panel's BackColor property.

j) *Running the application.* Select **Debug > Start** to run your application. Start drawing on the Panel using different brush sizes and colors. Use the right mouse button to erase part of your drawing.

k) *Closing the application.* Close your running application by clicking its close box.

l) *Closing the IDE.* Close Visual Studio .NET by clicking its close box.

22

Objectives

In this tutorial, you will learn to:
- Handle keyboard events.
- Create menus for your Windows applications.
- Use dialogs to display messages.
- Use the ShowDialog method of the **Font** and **Color** dialogs.
- Display the **Font** dialog to enable users to choose fonts.
- Display the **Color** dialog to enable users to choose colors.

Outline

22.1 Test-Driving the Typing Application
22.2 Analyzing the Typing Application
22.3 Keyboard Events
22.4 Menus
22.5 Wrap-Up

Typing Application

Introducing Keyboard Events, Menus and Dialogs

T ext editor applications enable you to perform a wide variety of tasks, from writing e-mails to creating business proposals. These applications often use menus and dialogs to help you customize the appearance of your documents. They also respond to keys pressed on the keyboard either by displaying characters or performing actions (such as accessing menus or dialogs). In this tutorial, you will learn how to handle **keyboard events**, which occur when keys on the keyboard are pressed and released. Handling keyboard events allows you to specify the action that the application should take when a key is pressed. You will then learn how to add menus to your application. By now, you are familiar with using the various menus and dialogs provided by Windows applications. You will learn to create menus, which group related commands and can allow the user to select various actions the application should take. Finally, you will learn about the **Font** and **Color** dialogs, which you will use to allow the user to change the appearance of text in the application.

22.1 Test-Driving the Typing Application

In this tutorial, you will create a **Typing** application to help students learn how to type. This application must meet the following requirements:

Application Requirements

A high-school course teaches students how to type. The instructor would like to use a Windows application that allows students to watch what they are typing on the screen without looking at the keyboard. You have been asked to create an application that displays what the student types. The application should display a virtual keyboard that highlights any key the student presses on the real keyboard. This application should also contain menu commands for selecting the font style and color of the text displayed, clearing the text displayed and inverting the background and foreground colors of the display.

This application allows the user to type text. As the user presses each key, the application highlights the corresponding key on the GUI and adds the character to a TextBox. The user can select the color and style of the characters the user types, invert the background and foreground colors and clear the TextBox. You will begin by test-driving the completed application. Then, you will learn the additional C# technologies that you will need to create your own version of this application.

Test-Driving the Typing Application

1. ***Opening the completed application.*** Open the C:\Examples\Tutorial22\ CompletedApplication\Typing directory to locate the **Typing** application. Double click Typing.sln to open the application in Visual Studio .NET.

2. ***Running the Typing application.*** Select **Debug > Start** to run the application. Type the sentence "Programming in C-Sharp is simple." Notice that as you type, the corresponding keys light up on the Form's virtual keyboard, and the text is displayed in the TextBox (Fig. 22.1).

Display menu

Virtual keyboard

Highlighted key

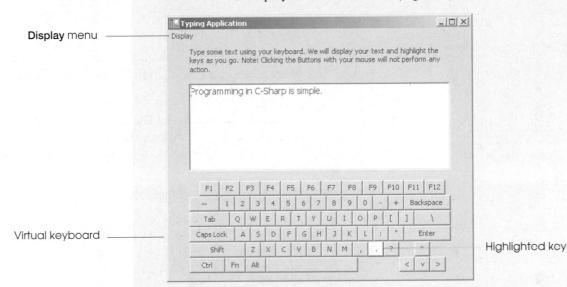

Figure 22.1   **Typing** application with key pressed.

3. ***Changing the font.*** Select **Display > Text > Font...** (Fig. 22.2) to open the **Font** dialog shown in Fig. 22.3. The **Font** dialog allows you to choose the font style that should be used to display the application's output. Select Tahoma from the **Font:** ComboBox, select Bold from the **Font style:** ComboBox and select 11 from the **Size:** ComboBox. Click the **OK** Button. Notice that the text you typed in *Step 2* is now bold.

Menu item

Submenu

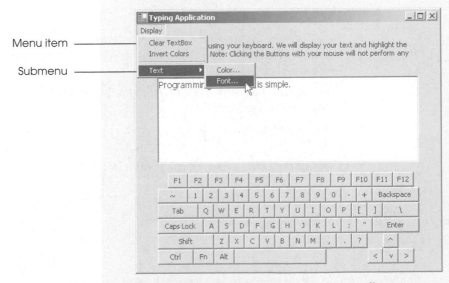

Figure 22.2   Selecting the **Font...** menu item.

(cont.)

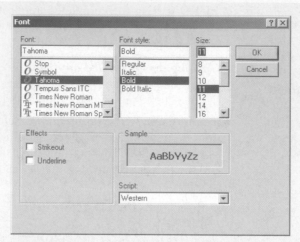

Figure 22.3 **Font** dialog displayed when **Display > Text > Font...** is selected.

4. *Changing the color of the font*. Select **Display > Text > Color...** to display the **Color** dialog (Fig. 22.4). This dialog is similar to the **Font** dialog, except that it allows you to choose the color of the text displayed. Select a color, then click **OK**.

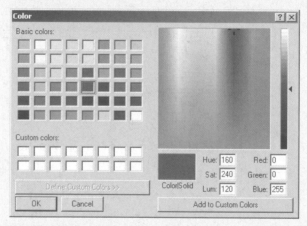

Figure 22.4 **Color** dialog displayed when **Display > Text > Color...** is selected.

5. *Inverting the background and foreground colors*. Select **Display > Invert Colors** (Fig. 22.5). This option allows you to swap the background and foreground colors, as in Fig. 22.6.

6. *Clearing the TextBox*. Select **Display > Clear TextBox** to remove all of the text from the TextBox.

7. *Closing the application*. Close your running application by clicking its close box.

8. *Closing the IDE*. Close Visual Studio .NET by clicking its close box.

(cont.)

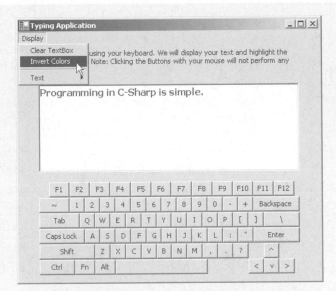

Figure 22.5   Selecting the **Invert Colors** menu item.

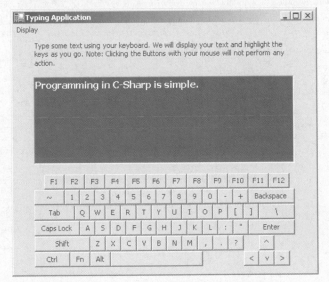

Figure 22.6   Output with the colors inverted.

22.2 Analyzing the Typing Application

Before you begin building the **Typing** application, you should analyze the application's components. The following pseudocode describes the basic operation of the **Typing** application:

> When the user presses a key:
> > Highlight the corresponding Button on the GUI
> > Display the key's value in the TextBox
>
> When the user releases a key:
> > Reset the corresponding Button's color to the Button's default color
>
> When the user selects the Color... menu item:
> > Display the Color dialog
> > Update the TextBox text's color
>
> When the user selects the Font... menu item:
> > Display the Font dialog
> > Update the TextBox text's font

When the user selects the Clear TextBox menu item:
　　Clear the TextBox

When the user selects the Invert Colors menu item:
　　Swap the TextBox's background and foreground colors

Now that you have test-driven the **Typing** application and studied its pseudocode representation, you will use an ACE table to help you convert the pseudocode to C#. Figure 22.7 lists the actions, controls and events that will help you complete your own version of this application. [*Note:* The number of Buttons is large and no Button events are used; therefore, the Buttons in the virtual keyboard are represented in the ACE table by the blanket term Button.]

Action/Control/Event (ACE) Table for the Typing Application

Action	Control	Event
Label the application's controls	lblPrompt	Application is run
	txtOutput	KeyPress, KeyDown
Highlight the corresponding Button on the GUI	keyboard Buttons	
Display the key's value in the TextBox	txtOutput	
	txtOutput	KeyUp
Reset the corresponding Button's color to the Button's default color	keyboard Buttons	
	mnuitmColor	Click
Display the Color dialog	dlgColorDialog	
Update the TextBox text's color	txtOutput	
	mnuitmFont	Click
Display the Font dialog	dlgFontDialog	
Update the TextBox text's font	txtOutput	
	mnuitmClear	Click
Clear the TextBox	txtOutput	
	mnuitmInvert	Click
Swap the TextBox's background and foreground colors	txtOutput	

Figure 22.7 ACE table for the **Typing** application.

22.3 Keyboard Events

This section introduces how to handle keyboard events, which are generated when keys on the keyboard are pressed and released. All keyboard events are raised using the control that currently has the focus. In the **Typing** application, these events are raised on the TextBox control. The first kind of keyboard event you will learn about is the **KeyDown** event, which is raised when a key is pressed. Since there are many keys on the keyboard, you will find that the template application provides much of the required code. In the following box, you will insert the remaining code to handle the event when the user presses a key.

Coding the KeyDown Event Handler

1. ***Copying the template to your working directory.*** Copy the C:\Examples\ Tutorial22\TemplateApplication\Typing directory to your C:\SimplyCSP directory.

2. ***Opening the Typing application's template file.*** Double click Typing.sln in the Typing directory to open the application in Visual Studio .NET.

(cont.)

3. *Adding the* **Backspace** *key case.* Add lines 926–933 from Fig. 22.8 to your code. These lines remove a character from the TextBox and highlight the **Backspace** Button when the *Backspace* key is pressed.

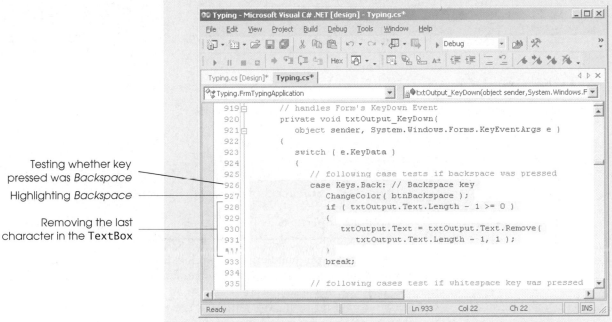

Testing whether key pressed was *Backspace*

Highlighting *Backspace*

Removing the last character in the TextBox

Figure 22.8 Removing a character when *Backspace* is pressed.

When a key is pressed, the KeyDown event is raised. As you have seen in previous tutorials, many event handlers are passed two arguments: sender and e. The **sender** object is the object (usually a GUI control) that raised the event (this is also known as the source of the event), and e contains data for the event. In this case, e (of the **KeyEventArgs** type) contains data about which key was pressed. The **KeyData** property of e (line 923) contains a value that represents which key was pressed.

C# provides the **Keys** enumeration to represent keyboard keys using meaningful names. Recall that enumerations are used to assign meaningful names to constant values. In this case, each value in the Keys enumeration is an int that represents a key. Keys.Back (line 926) is the Keys enumeration's representation of the *Backspace* key. Line 927 calls the ChangeColor method to highlight the **Backspace** Button. The ChangeColor method is provided for you in the template. The if statement on lines 928–932 tests whether there is text in the TextBox. If the TextBox contains text, lines 930–931 remove the last character from the TextBox. If the TextBox is empty, no action is performed.

When invoked, string method **Remove** deletes characters from a string. The first argument contains the index in the string at which to begin removing characters, and the second argument specifies the number of characters to remove. The string property **Length** returns the number of characters in the string. The position of the first character in a string is zero; therefore, you must subtract one from the value returned by the Length property to indicate the position of the last character. Use 1 as the second argument to indicate that you want to remove only one character.

4. *Adding the* **Enter** *key case.* Add lines 936–939 from Fig. 22.9 to the switch statement in the KeyDown event handler. Keys.Enter (line 936) represents the *Enter* key. Line 937 changes the color of the **Enter** key on the GUI, and line 938 inserts a new line in the TextBox.

(cont.)

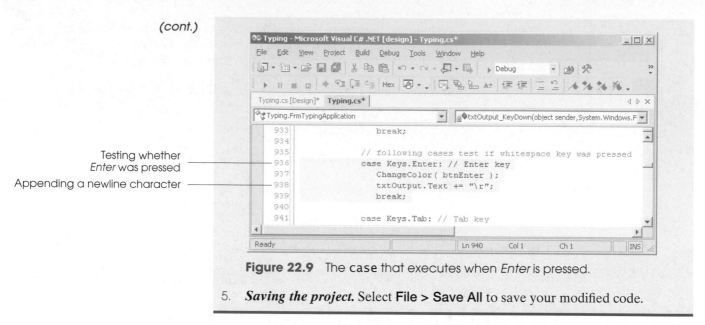

Testing whether *Enter* was pressed

Appending a newline character

Figure 22.9 The `case` that executes when *Enter* is pressed.

5. *Saving the project.* Select **File > Save All** to save your modified code.

The KeyDown event handler in this application does not test whether any of the letter keys were pressed. It is often inconvenient to use the KeyDown event handler for this purpose, because the KeyEventArgs object's KeyData property is case insensitive. If you try to handle letters in the KeyDown event handler, only uppercase letters will be recognized. This is not appropriate for the **Typing** application because the user should be able to type uppercase and lowercase letters. C# provides the **KeyPress** event handler, which can be used to recognize both uppercase and lowercase letters. You will learn how to use the KeyPress event handler in the following box.

Adding Code to the KeyPress Event Handler

1. *Writing the switch statement.* Add lines 1153–1154 of Fig. 22.10 to the KeyPress event handler. Line 1153 begins a `switch` statement that uses the uppercase equivalent of the pressed key for the controlling expression.

The key names in the Keys enumeration are in their uppercase form; therefore, the `case` statement must use the uppercase representation of the key that was pressed. The **Char** structure provides methods for manipulating individual characters. Char method **ToUpper** returns the uppercase representation of its argument. Note that the value returned by the ToUpper method does not alter the data in its argument.

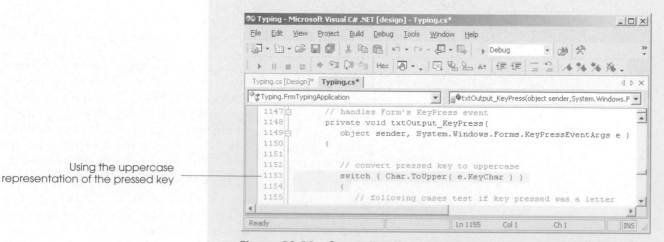

Using the uppercase representation of the pressed key

Figure 22.10 Converting the pressed key to an uppercase letter.

(cont.)

In this example, the argument that is passed to the ToUpper method uses the KeyChar property of e of **KeyPressEventArgs** type. The **KeyChar** property is similar to the KeyData property of the KeyEventArgs object, but contains only values representable as characters. While the KeyData property returns a Keys enumeration value, the KeyChar property returns a char. The difference is that the Keys value returned from the KeyChar property contains other information besides simply the key pressed, such as whether the *Shift* key was held down as well. Note that parameter e for the KeyDown and KeyPress event handlers are of different types. The KeyChar property can represent both uppercase and lowercase character values.

2. ***Inserting the* A *key case.*** Add lines 1156–1159 from Fig. 22.11 to the switch statement in the KeyPress event handler. These lines highlight the **A** Button in the application and display an **A** in the TextBox when the user presses the *A* key.

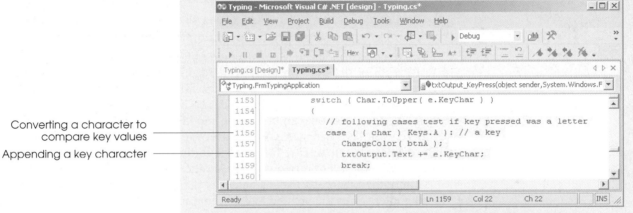

Converting a character to compare key values

Appending a key character

Figure 22.11   Performing actions when the *A* key is pressed.

Line 1156 compares the key pressed to the value Keys.A, which represents the *A* key. The Keys enumeration stores numeric values, but the key pressed by the user is passed to the KeyPress event handler as a character; therefore, the Keys enumeration value needs to be converted to a character before a comparison can be made. Line 1156 uses the cast operator to convert the enumeration value into a character. Line 1157 changes the color of the **A** Button on the GUI, and line 1158 adds either the "a" or "A" character, depending whether *Shift* was pressed, to the end of the text in the TextBox.

3. ***Inserting the* B *key case.*** Add lines 1161–1164 of Fig. 22.12 to the switch statement. These lines will highlight the **B** Button and add a B to the Text-Box when the user presses the *B* key. Notice that for each key pressed, its Button should be highlighted, and the correct output should be displayed in the TextBox.

(cont.)

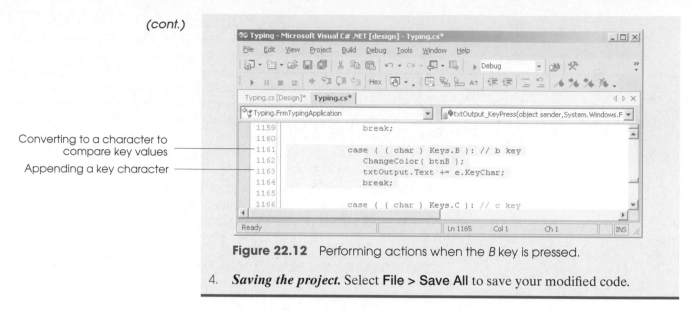

Converting to a character to compare key values

Appending a key character

Figure 22.12   Performing actions when the *B* key is pressed.

4. **Saving the project.** Select **File > Save All** to save your modified code.

You may be wondering why you could not just use the KeyPress event handler to test for all of the keys on the keyboard. Like the KeyDown event handler, the KeyPress event handler has its limitations. The KeyPress event handler cannot handle the modifier keys (*Ctrl*, *Shift* and *Alt*). **Modifier keys** do not display characters on the keyboard, but can be used to modify the way applications respond to a keyboard event. For instance, pressing the *Shift* key while pressing a letter in a text editor displays the uppercase form of the letter. You used the KeyDown event handler to handle the event raised when a modifier key is pressed. Another reason not to use only the KeyPress event handler is that the KeyChar property used in this event handler stores the pressed key as a character, requiring an explicit conversion of the Keys enumeration values before a comparison can be performed. It is more straightforward to compare the pressed key's numeric value against the numeric values stored in the Keys enumeration. The KeyData property used in the KeyDown event handler allows you to do this.

The **KeyUp** event is raised whenever a key is released by the user. It is raised regardless of whether the key pressed was handled by the KeyPress or the KeyDown event handler. The **Typing** application uses the KeyUp event handler to remove the highlight color from the Buttons on the GUI when the user releases a key. You will learn how to add the KeyUp event handler to your application in the following box.

Software Design Tip

Use the KeyPress event handler for letter key events. Use the KeyDown event handler for modifier, number and symbol key events.

Creating the KeyUp Event Handler

1. **Creating the KeyUp event handler.** To maintain clarity in the template application, an empty KeyUp event handler is provided for you. However, if you want to generate KeyUp, KeyDown or KeyPress event handlers for other controls, begin by selecting the control for which you wish to add the event handler. In design view, click on the txtOutput TextBox. In the **Properties** window, click the **Events** button. Then, double click the appropriate event handler from the **Properties** window, as shown in Fig. 22.13. When you double click an event name from the **Properties** window, that event handler is generated in your code.

2. **Writing code in the KeyUp event handler.** Add line 1294 of Fig. 22.14 to your application. The KeyUp event handler executes whenever a key is released; therefore, you need to change the color of the released Button back to that Button's default color. Line 1294 calls the ResetColor method, provided for you in the template, to perform this action.

(cont.)

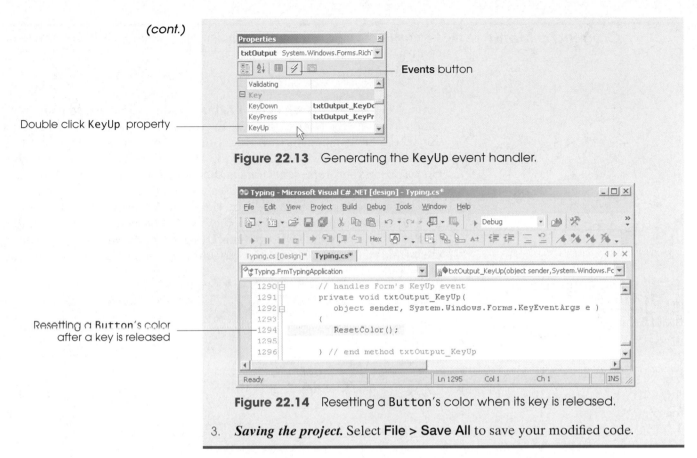

Figure 22.13   Generating the **KeyUp** event handler.

Figure 22.14   Resetting a **Button**'s color when its key is released.

3. ***Saving the project.*** Select **File > Save All** to save your modified code.

Now that you have added code that enables the user to see what they are typing by highlighting the corresponding **Button**s and displaying output in a **TextBox**, you must allow the user to alter the display. To do this, you will use the **MainMenu** control, which creates a menu that allows the user to select various options to format the **TextBox**.

SELF-REVIEW   1. A _____ event is raised when a key on the keyboard is pressed or released.

   a) keyboard   b) KeyDownEvent

   c) KeyChar   d) KeyUpEvent

2. The _____ event is raised when a key is released.

   a) KeyEventUp   b) KeyRelease

   c) KeyUp   d) None of the above.

Answers: 1) a. 2) c.

22.4 Menus

Menus allow you to group related commands for Windows applications. Although most menus and commands vary among applications, some—such as **Open** and **Save**—are common to many applications. Menus are an important part of GUIs because they organize commands without "cluttering" the GUI. In this section, you will learn how to enhance the **Typing** application by adding menus to allow the user to control how to display text in the **TextBox**. You will learn how to add menus to the **Typing** application.

Creating a Menu

1. *Creating a MainMenu control.* In design view, double click the MainMenu control,

in the **Windows Forms** tab of the **Toolbox** to add a MainMenu to your application (Fig. 22.15). Notice that, when you do this, a MainMenu control appears in the component tray. Recall that controls in the component tray are not part of the GUI. Also, on the top of your Form, a box that reads **Type Here** appears. This represents a **menu item**—a cell of text that the user can select in the MainMenu control. C# uses the **MenuItem** object to store these items. When you type text in the **Type Here** field, Visual Studio .NET creates a MenuItem. To edit the menu item, click the **MainMenu** icon in the component tray. This puts the IDE in **Menu Designer mode**, which allows you to create and edit menus. Change the Name property of the MainMenu control to mnuMainMenu.

Good Programming Practice

Prefix MainMenu controls with mnu.

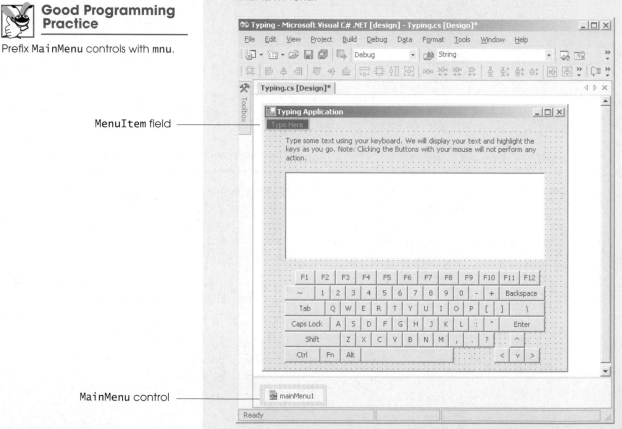

Figure 22.15   MainMenu control added to the **Typing** application.

2. *Creating the first menu item.* Click inside the **Type Here** box, type &Display then press *Enter*. This sets the text to be displayed in that menu item and indicates that the letter D is the access shortcut key. Then, change the Name property of the MenuItem to mnuitmDisplay. Notice that when you clicked the **Type Here** field, two more fields appeared (Fig. 22.16). The one on the right represents a new menu item that can be created to the right of the **Display** menu item. The field below the **Display** menu item represents a menu item that will appear when the **Display** menu item is selected. You will use the **Display** menu item to display all of the options that allow the user to customize the output displayed in the TextBox.

Good Programming Practice

Prefix MenuItem controls with mnuitm.

(cont.)

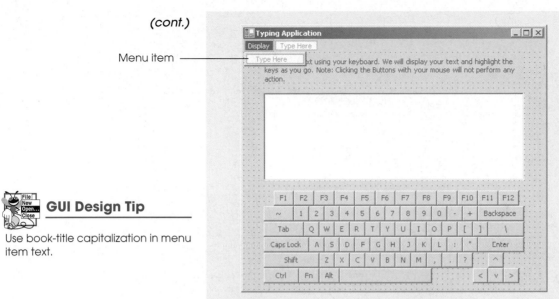

Menu item

Figure 22.16 Creating the **Display** menu.

 **GUI Design Tip**

Use book-title capitalization in menu item text.

3. *Creating additional menu items.* In the box that appeared below the **Display** menu, type &Clear TextBox. Name this menu item mnuitmClear by changing its Name property. Notice that once again, two more boxes appear. Every time you add an item to a menu these two boxes will appear (Fig. 22.17). Entering text in the box on the right turns the menu item on the left into a submenu. The box on the right is now a menu item of that submenu. A **submenu** is a menu within another menu. The box that appears on the bottom of the menu allows you to add another item to that menu. Type &Invert Colors in this box to add another menu item. Set the Name property of this menu item to mnuitmInvert.

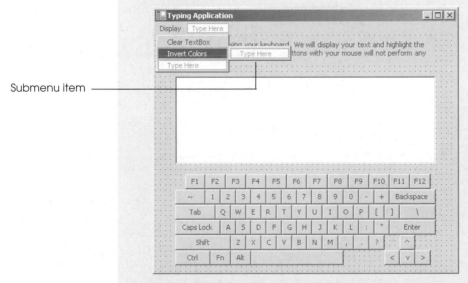

Submenu item

Figure 22.17 Adding items to the menu.

4. *Inserting a separator bar.* Right click the box that appears below the **Invert Colors** menu item, and select **Insert Separator** from the context menu that appears. Notice that a **separator bar**, which is a gray, recessed horizontal rule, appears below the **Invert Colors** menu item (Fig. 22.18). Separator bars are used to group submenus and menu items. A separator bar also can be created by typing a hyphen (–) in the Text property of a menu item. Set the Name property of this menu item to mnuitmBar.

GUI Design Tip

Use separator bars in a menu to group related menu items.

(cont.)

Separator bar ⎯⎯⎯⎯⎯⎯

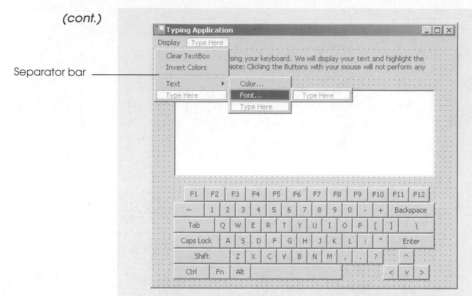

Figure 22.18 Adding a submenu to a menu item.

5. ***Creating a submenu.*** In the box under the separator bar, type **&Text**. This menu item will contain options to format the appearance of the text displayed in the **TextBox**. Set the **Name** property of this menu item to **mnuitm-Text**. All menu items can contain both menu items and submenus. Insert **&Color...** and **&Font...** as menu items in your submenu, naming them **mnuitmColor** and **mnuitmFont**, respectively. (Fig. 22.18)

GUI Design Tip

If clicking a menu item opens a dialog, an ellipsis (...) should follow the the menu item's text.

6. ***Rearranging and commenting the control declarations.*** In code view, locate the declarations for the new **MainMenu** and **MenuItem** controls. Move these declarations and add comments as shown in lines 107–125 of Fig. 22.19.

Figure 22.19 Rearranging and commenting the control declarations.

(cont.)

7. ***Running the application.*** Select **Debug > Start** to run your application, and select a menu item. Notice that nothing happens because you have not created event handlers for the menu items.

8. ***Closing the application.*** Close your application by clicking its close box.

For a menu item to perform some action when it is selected, an event handler must be added for that item to handle its **Click** event. The **Typing** application introduces the **Font** dialog and the **Color** dialog to allow the user to customize the appearance of what is being typed. Dialogs allow you to receive input from and display messages to the user. You will learn how to use the **Font** dialog in the following box.

Coding the Font...
MenuItem's Click Event
Handler

1. ***Creating an event handler.*** In design mode, double click the **Font...** menu item that you created to generate an event handler. Be sure to add the comments and break the header as shown in Fig. 22.20 so that the line numbers in your code match those presented in this tutorial.

Declarations for the
`FontDialog` and its result

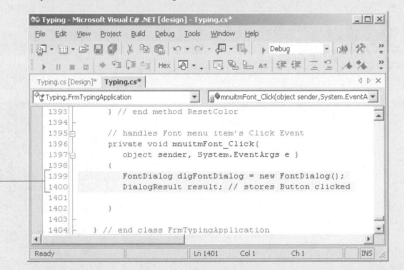

Figure 22.20   Declarations for the `FontDialog` and its `DialogResult`.

2. ***Declaring the dialog variables.*** Add lines 1399–1400 of Fig. 22.20 to your code. Line 1399 creates a new **FontDialog** object that will allow the user to select the font style to apply to the text. Line 1400 declares a variable of the `DialogResult` type that will store information indicating which **Button** the user clicked to exit the dialog.

Good Programming
Practice

Prefix references to dialogs with `dlg`.

3. ***Displaying the dialog.*** Add lines 1402–1403 from Fig. 22.21 to your event handler. These lines call the **ShowDialog** method to display the **Font** dialog.

Showing the dialog and
assigning the result

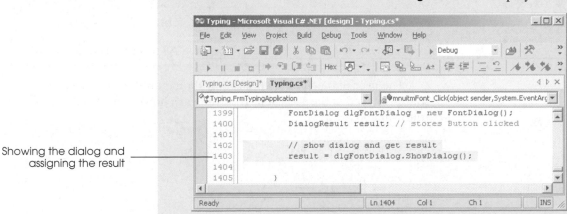

Figure 22.21   Opening the **Font** dialog.

(cont.)

4. ***Exiting the event handler if the user clicks Cancel.*** Add lines 1405–1409 from Fig. 22.22 to your application. These lines determine whether the user clicked the **Font** dialog's **Cancel** Button. Line 1406 compares the value stored in `result` with the enumeration value **`DialogResult.Cancel`**. **`DialogResult`** is an enumeration that contains values corresponding to standard dialog Button names. This provides a convenient way to determine which Button the user clicked. If the user clicks the **Cancel** Button, no action should take place and the method should exit using the `return` statement (line 1408).

Take no action if the user clicks the **Cancel** `Button`

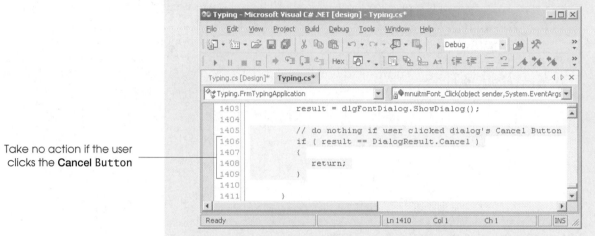

Figure 22.22   Exit the event handler if the user clicks **Cancel**.

5. ***Setting the font.*** Add lines 1411–1412 from Fig. 22.23 to give the text the style that the user selected from the `FontDialog`. This statement immediately updates the font displayed in the `txtOutput` TextBox.

Assigning the new font value

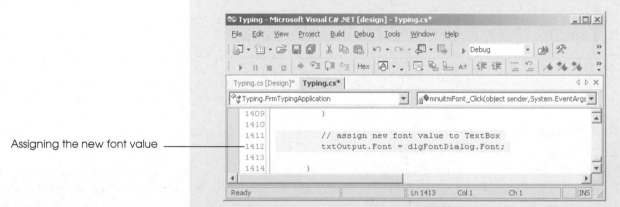

Figure 22.23   Changing the display font.

6. ***Saving the project.*** Select **File > Save All** to save your modified code.

The user of the **Typing** application should also be able to select the color of the font displayed in the TextBox. You will learn how to display the **Color** dialog in the following box.

Coding the Color...
MenuItem's Click Event
Handler

1. ***Creating an event handler.*** In the Windows Form Designer, double click the **Color...** menu item to generate a `Click` event handler.

2. ***Declaring the dialog variables.*** Be sure to add the comments and break the header as shown in Fig. 22.24 so that the line numbers in your code match those presented in this tutorial. Then, add lines 1421–1422 from Fig. 22.24 to your application. Line 1421 creates a new `ColorDialog` object that will allow the user to select the color of the text. Line 1422 declares a `DialogResult` variable to store the value of the `Button` clicked by the user.

Declarations for the
`ColorDialog` and its result

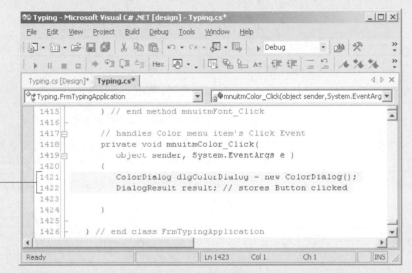

Figure 22.24   Declarations for the **Color** dialog and its `DialogResult`.

3. ***Setting the ColorDialog's open property.*** Add lines 1424–1425 from Fig. 22.25 to your application. The **ColorDialog** object allows you to specify which color options the dialog presents to the user of your application. To display the **Color** dialog shown in Fig. 22.4, the **FullOpen** option is set to `true` on line 1424. If this option is set to `false`, only the left half of the dialog will be displayed. Line 1425 opens the **Color** dialog using the `ShowDialog` method.

Displaying the `ColorDialog` with
a complete color selection

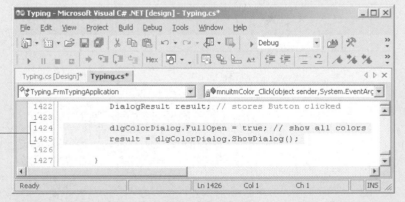

Figure 22.25   Displaying the **Color** dialog.

4. ***Setting the font color.*** Add lines 1427–1434 from Fig. 22.26 to your application. The `if` statement on lines 1428–1431 prevents the color from being changed if the user clicks **Cancel**. Line 1434 sets the text's color to the color the user selected in the **Color** dialog.

(cont.)

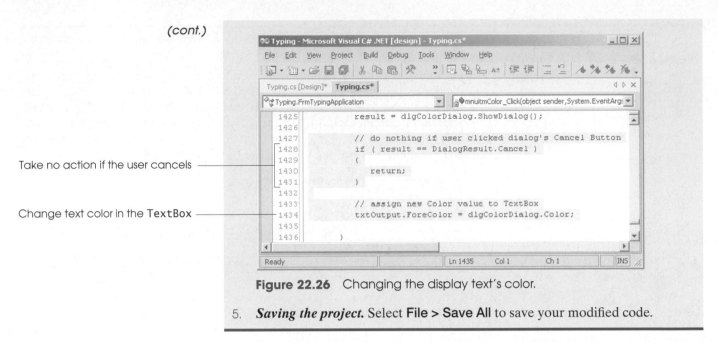

Take no action if the user cancels

Change text color in the `TextBox`

Figure 22.26 Changing the display text's color.

5. ***Saving the project.*** Select **File > Save All** to save your modified code.

The user should be able to clear all of the text in the `TextBox` using the **Clear TextBox** menu item. You will learn how to do this in the following box.

Clearing the TextBox

1. ***Creating an event handler.*** Double click the **Clear TextBox** menu item to generate the item's `Click` event handler.

2. ***Clearing the text.*** Be sure to add the comments and break the header as shown in Fig. 22.27 so that the line numbers in your code match those presented in this tutorial. Then, add line 1443 from Fig. 22.27 to your application. This line calls the `Clear` method to erase the text from the `TextBox`.

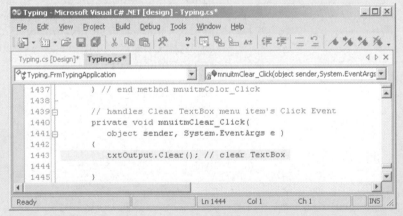

Figure 22.27 Calling the `Clear` method of the `TextBox` class to erase the text.

3. ***Saving the project.*** Select **File > Save All** to save your modified code.

The user should be able to swap the foreground and background colors of the `TextBox`. You will learn how to accomplish this in the following box.

Inverting Colors

1. *Creating an event handler*. Double click the **Invert Colors** menu item in design view. This creates an empty event handler for the **Invert Colors** menu item's `Click` event. Be sure to add the comments and break the header as shown in Fig. 22.28 so that the line numbers in your code match those presented in this tutorial.

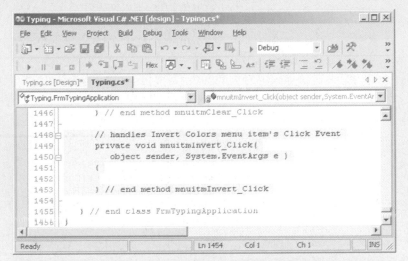

Figure 22.28   Empty event handler for **Invert Color** menu item.

2. *Inverting the colors*. Add lines 1452–1456 of Fig. 22.29 to your application. Line 1452 declares a `Color` variable. Recall that `Color` variables store color values. To swap colors, you must use a temporary variable to hold one of the colors that you want to swap. A **temporary variable** is used to store data when swapping values. Such a variable is no longer needed after the swap occurs. Without a temporary variable, you would lose the value of one color property (by reassigning its value) before you could assign its color to the other property.

Using a temporary variable
to swap color values

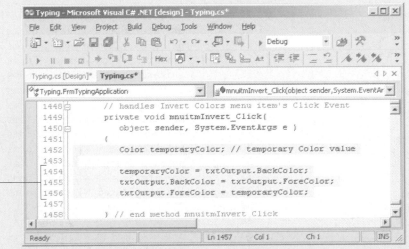

Figure 22.29   Swapping the background and foreground colors.

Line 1454 assigns the `Color` variable the background color of the `Text-Box`. Line 1455 then sets the background color to the foreground color. Finally, line 1456 assigns the text color the value stored in the temporary `Color` variable, which contains the `TextBox`'s background color from before the swap.

(cont.)

3. ***Running the application.*** Select **Debug > Start** to run your application. Enter text using your keyboard. The keys you press should be highlighted in the virtual keyboard on the Form. Use the menu to change the color of the text, then invert the colors of the text and the TextBox. Finally, use the menus to change the text's font, then clear the TextBox.

4. ***Closing the application.*** Close your running application by clicking its close box.

5. ***Closing the IDE.*** Close Visual Studio .NET by clicking its close box.

Figure 22.30 presents the source code for the **Typing** application. The lines of code that contain new programming concepts that you learned in this tutorial are highlighted.

```
1   using System;
2   using System.Drawing;
3   using System.Collections;
4   using System.ComponentModel;
5   using System.Windows.Forms;
6   using System.Data;
7
8   namespace Typing
9   {
10      /// <summary>
11      /// Summary description for FrmTypingApplication.
12      /// </summary>
13      public class FrmTypingApplication : System.Windows.Forms.Form
14      {
15         // Label displaying the prompt
16         private System.Windows.Forms.Label lblPrompt;
17
18         // RichTextBox displaying the user's key strokes
19         private System.Windows.Forms.RichTextBox txtOutput;
20
21         // Buttons representing the first row of keys
22         private System.Windows.Forms.Button btnF1;
23         private System.Windows.Forms.Button btnF2;
24         private System.Windows.Forms.Button btnF3;
25         private System.Windows.Forms.Button btnF4;
26         private System.Windows.Forms.Button btnF5;
27         private System.Windows.Forms.Button btnF6;
28         private System.Windows.Forms.Button btnF7;
29         private System.Windows.Forms.Button btnF8;
30         private System.Windows.Forms.Button btnF9;
31         private System.Windows.Forms.Button btnF10;
32         private System.Windows.Forms.Button btnF11;
33         private System.Windows.Forms.Button btnF12;
34
35         // Buttons representing the second row of keys
36         private System.Windows.Forms.Button btnTilde;
37         private System.Windows.Forms.Button btn1;
38         private System.Windows.Forms.Button btn2;
39         private System.Windows.Forms.Button btn3;
40         private System.Windows.Forms.Button btn4;
41         private System.Windows.Forms.Button btn5;
42         private System.Windows.Forms.Button btn6;
43         private System.Windows.Forms.Button btn7;
```

Figure 22.30 **Typing** application code. (Part 1 of 12.)

```
44          private System.Windows.Forms.Button btn8;
45          private System.Windows.Forms.Button btn9;
46          private System.Windows.Forms.Button btn0;
47          private System.Windows.Forms.Button btnHyphen;
48          private System.Windows.Forms.Button btnPlus;
49          private System.Windows.Forms.Button btnBackspace;
50
51          // Buttons representing the third row of keys
52          private System.Windows.Forms.Button btnTab;
53          private System.Windows.Forms.Button btnQ;
54          private System.Windows.Forms.Button btnW;
55          private System.Windows.Forms.Button btnE;
56          private System.Windows.Forms.Button btnR;
57          private System.Windows.Forms.Button btnT;
58          private System.Windows.Forms.Button btnY;
59          private System.Windows.Forms.Button btnU;
60          private System.Windows.Forms.Button btnI;
61          private System.Windows.Forms.Button btnO;
62          private System.Windows.Forms.Button btnP;
63          private System.Windows.Forms.Button btnLeftBrace;
64          private System.Windows.Forms.Button btnRightBrace;
65          private System.Windows.Forms.Button btnSlash;
66
67          // Buttons representing the fourth row of keys
68          private System.Windows.Forms.Button btnCaps;
69          private System.Windows.Forms.Button btnA;
70          private System.Windows.Forms.Button btnS;
71          private System.Windows.Forms.Button btnD;
72          private System.Windows.Forms.Button btnF;
73          private System.Windows.Forms.Button btnG;
74          private System.Windows.Forms.Button btnH;
75          private System.Windows.Forms.Button btnJ;
76          private System.Windows.Forms.Button btnK;
77          private System.Windows.Forms.Button btnL;
78          private System.Windows.Forms.Button btnColon;
79          private System.Windows.Forms.Button btnQuote;
80          private System.Windows.Forms.Button btnEnter;
81
82          // Buttons representing the fifth row of keys
83          private System.Windows.Forms.Button btnZ;
84          private System.Windows.Forms.Button btnX;
85          private System.Windows.Forms.Button btnC;
86          private System.Windows.Forms.Button btnV;
87          private System.Windows.Forms.Button btnB;
88          private System.Windows.Forms.Button btnN;
89          private System.Windows.Forms.Button btnM;
90          private System.Windows.Forms.Button btnComma;
91          private System.Windows.Forms.Button btnPeriod;
92          private System.Windows.Forms.Button btnQuestion;
93
94          // Buttons representing the sixth row of keys
95          private System.Windows.Forms.Button btnCtrlLeft;
96          private System.Windows.Forms.Button btnFn;
97          private System.Windows.Forms.Button btnAltLeft;
98          private System.Windows.Forms.Button btnSpace;
99
100         // Buttons representing the directional arrows
101         private System.Windows.Forms.Button btnUp;
```

Figure 22.30 Typing application code. (Part 2 of 12.)

```
102        private System.Windows.Forms.Button btnDown;
103        private System.Windows.Forms.Button btnLeft;
104        private System.Windows.Forms.Button btnRight;
105        private System.Windows.Forms.Button btnShiftLeft;
106
107        // MainMenu to organize commands
108        private System.Windows.Forms.MainMenu mnuMainMenu;
109
110        // MenuItem to serve as the menu header
111        private System.Windows.Forms.MenuItem mnuitmDisplay;
112
113        // MenuItem to clear the TextBox
114        private System.Windows.Forms.MenuItem mnuitmClear;
115
116        // MenuItem to invert the colors in the TextBox
117        private System.Windows.Forms.MenuItem mnuitmInvert;
118
119        // MenuItem to separate commands in menu
120        private System.Windows.Forms.MenuItem mnuitmBar;
121
122        // MenuItems to set text's color and font
123        private System.Windows.Forms.MenuItem mnuitmText;
124        private System.Windows.Forms.MenuItem mnuitmColor;
125        private System.Windows.Forms.MenuItem mnuitmFont;
126
127        /// <summary>
128        /// Required designer variable.
129        /// </summary>
130        private System.ComponentModel.Container components = null;
131
132        // reference to last Button pressed
133        private Button m_btnLastButton;
134
135        public FrmTypingApplication()
136        {
137           //
138           // Required for Windows Form Designer support
139           //
140           InitializeComponent();
141
142           //
143           // TODO: Add any constructor code after InitializeComponent
144           // call
145           //
146        }
147
148        /// <summary>
149        /// Clean up any resources being used.
150        /// </summary>
151        protected override void Dispose( bool disposing )
152        {
153           if( disposing )
154           {
155              if (components != null)
156              {
157                 components.Dispose();
158              }
159           }
```

Figure 22.30 Typing application code. (Part 3 of 12.)

```
160              base.Dispose( disposing );
161           }
162
163           // Windows Form Designer generated code
164
165           /// <summary>
166           /// The main entry point for the application.
167           /// </summary>
168           [STAThread]
169           static void Main()
170           {
171              Application.Run( new FrmTypingApplication() );
172           }
173
174           // handles Form's KeyDown Event
175           private void txtOutput_KeyDown(
176              object sender, System.Windows.Forms.KeyEventArgs e )
177           {
178              switch ( e.KeyData )
179              {
180                 // following case tests if backspace was pressed
181                 case Keys.Back: // Backspace key
182                    ChangeColor( btnBackspace );
183                    if ( txtOutput.Text.Length - 1 >= 0 )
184                    {
185                       txtOutput.Text = txtOutput.Text.Remove(
186                          txtOutput.Text.Length - 1, 1 );
187                    }
188                    break;
189
190                 // following cases test if whitespace key was pressed
191                 case Keys.Enter: // Enter key
192                    ChangeColor( btnEnter );
193                    txtOutput.Text += "\n";
194                    break;
195
196                 case Keys.Tab: // Tab key
197                    ChangeColor( btnTab );
198                    txtOutput.Text += "\t";
199                    break;
200
201                 case Keys.Space: // space bar
202                    ChangeColor( btnSpace );
203                    txtOutput.Text += " ";
204                    break;
205
206                 // following cases test if number key was pressed
207                 case Keys.D0: // 0 key
208                    ChangeColor( btn0 );
209                    txtOutput.Text += "0";
210                    break;
211
212                 case Keys.D1:
213                    ChangeColor( btn1 );
214                    txtOutput.Text += "1";
215                    break;
216
```

switch determines which key was pressed

Handling the case when the *Backspace* key is pressed

Handling the case when the *Enter* key is pressed

Figure 22.30 Typing application code. (Part 4 of 12.)

```
217                    case Keys.D2:
218                        ChangeColor( btn2 );
219                        txtOutput.Text += "2";
220                        break;
221
222                    case Keys.D3:
223                        ChangeColor( btn3 );
224                        txtOutput.Text += "3";
225                        break;
226
227                    case Keys.D4:
228                        ChangeColor( btn4 );
229                        txtOutput.Text += "4";
230                        break;
231
232                    case Keys.D5:
233                        ChangeColor( btn5 );
234                        txtOutput.Text += "5";
235                        break;
236
237                    case Keys.D6:
238                        ChangeColor( btn6 );
239                        txtOutput.Text += "6";
240                        break;
241
242                    case Keys.D7:
243                        ChangeColor( btn7 );
244                        txtOutput.Text += "7";
245                        break;
246
247                    case Keys.D8:
248                        ChangeColor( btn8 );
249                        txtOutput.Text += "8";
250                        break;
251
252                    case Keys.D9:
253                        ChangeColor( btn9 );
254                        txtOutput.Text += "9";
255                        break;
256
257                    // following cases test if one of the F keys was pressed
258                    case Keys.F1: // F1 key
259                        ChangeColor( btnF1 );
260                        break;
261
262                    case Keys.F2: // F2 key
263                        ChangeColor( btnF2 );
264                        break;
265
266                    case Keys.F3: // F3 key
267                        ChangeColor( btnF3 );
268                        break;
269
270                    case Keys.F4: // F4 key
271                        ChangeColor( btnF4 );
272                        break;
273
```

Figure 22.30 **Typing** application code. (Part 5 of 12.)

```
274                    case Keys.F5: // F5 key
275                        ChangeColor( btnF5 );
276                        break;
277
278                    case Keys.F6: // F6 key
279                        ChangeColor( btnF6 );
280                        break;
281
282                    case Keys.F7: // F7 key
283                        ChangeColor( btnF7 );
284                        break;
285
286                    case Keys.F8: // F8 key
287                        ChangeColor( btnF8 );
288                        break;
289
290                    case Keys.F9: // F9 key
291                        ChangeColor( btnF9 );
292                        break;
293
294                    case Keys.F10: // F10 key
295                        ChangeColor( btnF10 );
296                        break;
297
298                    case Keys.F11: // F11 key
299                        ChangeColor( btnF11 );
300                        break;
301
302                    case Keys.F12: // F12 key
303                        ChangeColor( btnF12 );
304                        break;
305
306                    // following cases test if a special
307                    // character key was pressed
308                    case Keys.OemOpenBrackets: // left square bracket
309                        ChangeColor( btnLeftBrace );
310                        txtOutput.Text += "[";
311                        break;
312
313                    case Keys.OemCloseBrackets: // right square bracket
314                        ChangeColor( btnRightBrace );
315                        txtOutput.Text += "]";
316                        break;
317
318                    case Keys.Oemplus: // plus sign
319                        ChangeColor( btnPlus );
320                        txtOutput.Text += "+";
321                        break;
322
323                    case Keys.OemMinus: // minus sign
324                        ChangeColor( btnHyphen );
325                        txtOutput.Text += "-";
326                        break;
327
328                    case Keys.Oemtilde: // tilde (~)
329                        ChangeColor( btnTilde );
330                        txtOutput.Text += "~";
331                        break;
```

Figure 22.30 Typing application code. (Part 6 of 12.)

```
332
333            case Keys.OemPipe: // backslash
334               ChangeColor( btnSlash );
335               txtOutput.Text += "\\";
336               break;
337
338            case Keys.OemSemicolon: // colon
339               ChangeColor( btnColon );
340               txtOutput.Text += ":";
341               break;
342
343            case Keys.OemQuotes: // quotation marks
344               ChangeColor( btnQuote );
345               txtOutput.Text += "\"";
346               break;
347
348            case Keys.OemPeriod: // period
349               ChangeColor( btnPeriod );
350               txtOutput.Text += ".";
351               break;
352
353            case Keys.Oemcomma: // comma
354               ChangeColor( btnComma );
355               txtOutput.Text += ",";
356               break;
357
358            case Keys.OemQuestion: // question mark
359               ChangeColor( btnQuestion );
360               txtOutput.Text += "?";
361               break;
362
363            case Keys.CapsLock: // Caps Lock key
364               ChangeColor( btnCaps );
365               break;
366
367            // following cases test if one of the
368            // arrow keys was pressed
369            case Keys.Down: // down arrow
370               ChangeColor( btnDown );
371               break;
372
373            case Keys.Up: // up arrow
374               ChangeColor( btnUp );
375               break;
376
377            case Keys.Left: // left arrow
378               ChangeColor( btnLeft );
379               break;
380
381            case Keys.Right: // right arrow
382               ChangeColor( btnRight );
383               break;
384
385            // following cases test if a modifier key was pressed
386            case ( ( Keys ) 65552 ): // Shift key
387               ChangeColor( btnShiftLeft );
388               break;
389
```

Figure 22.30 Typing application code. (Part 7 of 12.)

```
390                    case ( ( Keys ) 131089 ): // Control key
391                       ChangeColor( btnCtrlLeft );
392                       break;
393
394                    case ( ( Keys ) 262162 ): // Alt key
395                       ChangeColor( btnAltLeft );
396                       break;
397
398                 } // end switch e.KeyData
399
400              } // end method txtOutput_KeyDown
401
402              // handles Form's KeyPress event
403              private void txtOutput_KeyPress(
404                 object sender, System.Windows.Forms.KeyPressEventArgs e )
405              {
406
407                 // convert pressed key to uppercase
408                 switch ( Char.ToUpper( e.KeyChar ) )
409                 {
410                    // following cases test if key pressed was a letter
411                    case ( ( char ) Keys.A ): // a key
412                       ChangeColor( btnA );
413                       txtOutput.Text += e.KeyChar;
414                       break;
415
416                    case ( ( char ) Keys.B ): // b key
417                       ChangeColor( btnB );
418                       txtOutput.Text += e.KeyChar;
419                       break;
420
421                    case ( ( char ) Keys.C ): // c key
422                       ChangeColor( btnC );
423                       txtOutput.Text += e.KeyChar;
424                       break;
425
426                    case ( ( char ) Keys.D ): // d key
427                       ChangeColor( btnD );
428                       txtOutput.Text += e.KeyChar;
429                       break;
430
431                    case ( ( char ) Keys.E ): // e key
432                       ChangeColor( btnE );
433                       txtOutput.Text += e.KeyChar;
434                       break;
435
436                    case ( ( char ) Keys.F ): // f key
437                       ChangeColor( btnF );
438                       txtOutput.Text += e.KeyChar;
439                       break;
440
441                    case ( ( char ) Keys.G ): // g key
442                       ChangeColor( btnG );
443                       txtOutput.Text += e.KeyChar;
444                       break;
445
446                    case ( ( char ) Keys.H ): // h key
447                       ChangeColor( btnH );
```

Using the **KeyChar** property to determine which letter key was pressed *(line 408)*

Code executed when the *a* or *A* key is pressed *(lines 411–414)*

Code executed when the *b* or *B* key is pressed *(lines 416–419)*

Figure 22.30 Typing application code. (Part 8 of 12.)

```
448            txtOutput.Text += e.KeyChar;
449            break;
450
451         case ( ( char ) Keys.I ): // i key
452            ChangeColor( btnI );
453            txtOutput.Text += e.KeyChar;
454            break;
455
456         case ( ( char ) Keys.J ): // j key
457            ChangeColor( btnJ );
458            txtOutput.Text += e.KeyChar;
459            break;
460
461         case ( ( char ) Keys.K ): // k key
462            ChangeColor( btnK );
463            txtOutput.Text += e.KeyChar;
464            break;
465
466         case ( ( char ) Keys.L ): // l key
467            ChangeColor( btnL );
468            txtOutput.Text += e.KeyChar;
469            break;
470
471         case ( ( char ) Keys.M ): // m key
472            ChangeColor( btnM );
473            txtOutput.Text += e.KeyChar;
474            break;
475
476         case ( ( char ) Keys.N ): // n key
477            ChangeColor( btnN );
478            txtOutput.Text += e.KeyChar;
479            break;
480
481         case ( ( char ) Keys.O ): // o key
482            ChangeColor( btnO );
483            txtOutput.Text += e.KeyChar;
484            break;
485
486         case ( ( char ) Keys.P ): // p key
487            ChangeColor( btnP );
488            txtOutput.Text += e.KeyChar;
489            break;
490
491         case ( ( char ) Keys.Q ): // q key
492            ChangeColor( btnQ );
493            txtOutput.Text += e.KeyChar;
494            break;
495
496         case ( ( char ) Keys.R ): // r key
497            ChangeColor( btnR );
498            txtOutput.Text += e.KeyChar;
499            break;
500
501         case ( ( char ) Keys.S ): // s key
502            ChangeColor( btnS );
503            txtOutput.Text += e.KeyChar;
504            break;
505
```

Figure 22.30 Typing application code. (Part 9 of 12.)

```
506              case ( ( char ) Keys.T ): // t key
507                 ChangeColor( btnT );
508                 txtOutput.Text += e.KeyChar;
509                 break;
510
511              case ( ( char ) Keys.U ): // u key
512                 ChangeColor( btnU );
513                 txtOutput.Text += e.KeyChar;
514                 break;
515
516              case ( ( char ) Keys.V ): // v key
517                 ChangeColor( btnV );
518                 txtOutput.Text += e.KeyChar;
519                 break;
520
521              case ( ( char ) Keys.W ): // w key
522                 ChangeColor( btnW );
523                 txtOutput.Text += e.KeyChar;
524                 break;
525
526              case ( ( char ) Keys.X ): // x key
527                 ChangeColor( btnX );
528                 txtOutput.Text += e.KeyChar;
529                 break;
530
531              case ( ( char ) Keys.Y ): // y key
532                 ChangeColor( btnY );
533                 txtOutput.Text += e.KeyChar;
534                 break;
535
536              case ( ( char ) Keys.Z ): // z key
537                 ChangeColor( btnZ );
538                 txtOutput.Text += e.KeyChar;
539                 break;
540
541           } // end switch -- ends test for letters
542
543        } // end method txtOutput_KeyPress
544
545        // handles Form's KeyUp event
546        private void txtOutput_KeyUp(
547           object sender, System.Windows.Forms.KeyEventArgs e )
548        {
549           ResetColor();
550
551        } // end method txtOutput_KeyUp
552
553        // highlight Button passed as argument
554        private void ChangeColor( Button btnButton )
555        {
556           ResetColor();
557           btnButton.BackColor = Color.LightGoldenrodYellow;
558           m_btnLastButton = btnButton;
559
560        } // end method ChangeColor
561
```

Resets the Button's background color ——— (line 549)

Figure 22.30 Typing application code. (Part 10 of 12.)

```
562        // changes m_btnLastButton's color if it refers to a Button
563        private void ResetColor()
564        {
565           if ( m_btnLastButton != null )
566           {
567              m_btnLastButton.BackColor = SystemColors.Control;
568           }
569
570        } // end method ResetColor
571
572        // handles Font menu item's Click Event
573        private void mnuitmFont_Click(
574           object sender, System.EventArgs e )
575        {
576           FontDialog dlgFontDialog = new FontDialog();
577           DialogResult result; // stores Button clicked
578
579           // show dialog and get result
580           result = dlgFontDialog.ShowDialog();
581
582           // do nothing if user clicked dialog's Cancel Button
583           if ( result == DialogResult.Cancel )
584           {
585              return;
586           }
587
588           // assign new font value to TextBox
589           txtOutput.Font = dlgFontDialog.Font;
590
591        } // end method mnuitmFont_Click
592
593        // handles Color menu item's Click Event
594        private void mnuitmColor_Click(
595           object sender, System.EventArgs e )
596        {
597           ColorDialog dlgColorDialog = new ColorDialog();
598           DialogResult result; // stores Button clicked
599
600           dlgColorDialog.FullOpen = true; // show all colors
601           result = dlgColorDialog.ShowDialog();
602
603           // do nothing if user clicked dialog's Cancel Button
604           if ( result == DialogResult.Cancel )
605           {
606              return;
607           }
608
609           // assign new Color value to textbox
610           txtOutput.ForeColor = dlgColorDialog.Color;
611
612        } // end method mnuitmColor_Click
613
614        // handles Clear Textbox menu item's Click Event
615        private void mnuitmClear_Click(
616           object sender, System.EventArgs e )
617        {
618           txtOutput.Clear(); // clear TextBox
619
620        } // end method mnuitmClear_Click
```

Create the FontDialog and DialogResult variables

Display dialog and get the Button clicked to exit the dialog

Do nothing if the user clicks **Cancel** Button

Change the text's font to the value the user selected

Display the dialog and get the Button clicked to exit the dialog

Do nothing if the user clicks **Cancel** Button

Change the text's color to the value the user selected

Figure 22.30 Typing application code. (Part 11 of 12.)

```
621
622          // handles Invert Colors menu item's Click Event
623          private void mnuitmInvert_Click(
624             object sender, System.EventArgs e )
625          {
626             Color temporaryColor; // temporary Color value
627
628             temporaryColor = txtOutput.BackColor;
629             txtOutput.BackColor = txtOutput.ForeColor;
630             txtOutput.ForeColor = temporaryColor;
631
632          } // end method mnuitmInvert_Click
633
634       } // end class FrmTypingApplication
635 }
```

Swap the text color and the background color → (lines 628–630)

Figure 22.30   Typing application code. (Part 12 of 12.)

SELF-REVIEW

1. Menus can contain _____.
   a) commands that the user can select   b) submenus
   c) separator bars   d) All of the above.

2. _____ allow you to receive input from and display messages to users.
   a) Dialogs   b) Menus
   c) Separator bars d) Enumerations

Answers: 1) d. 2) a.

22.5 Wrap-Up

In this tutorial, you learned about keyboard events. You learned how to handle the event raised when the user presses a key on the keyboard by using the KeyDown and KeyPress events. You then learned how to use the KeyUp event handler to handle the event raised when the user releases a key.

You added menus to the **Typing** application. You learned that menus allow you to add controls to your application without cluttering the GUI. You also learned how to code a menu item's Click event handler to alter the displayed text in the **Typing** application. You learned how to display the **Color** and **Font** dialogs so the user could specify the font style and color of the text in the TextBox. You also learned how to use the DialogResult enumeration to determine which Button the user pressed to exit a dialog.

In the next tutorial, you will learn about the methods in the String class that allow you to manipulate strings. These methods will help you build a screen scraper application that can search text for a particular value.

SKILLS SUMMARY

Adding Keyboard Event Handlers to Your Application

- In design view, select the control for which you want to add the event handler.
- In the **Properties** window, click the **Events** button.
- Double click the appropriate event handler from the **Properties** window.

Executing Code When the User Presses a Letter Key on the Keyboard

- Use the KeyPress event handler.
- Use the KeyChar property to determine which key was pressed.
- Use the ToUpper method to convert the pressed key to an uppercase letter.
- Use a switch statement to perform an action depending on what key was pressed.
- Compare the pressed key to a Keys enumeration value in each case.

Executing Code When the User Presses a Key that is not a Letter

■ Use the KeyDown event handler.

■ Use the KeyData property to determine which key was pressed.

Executing Code When the User Releases a Key

■ Use the KeyUp event handler.

Adding Menus to Your Application

■ Select the MainMenu control from the tool bar.

■ Add menu items to the menu by typing the item names in the **Type Here** boxes that appear on the bottom of the menu.

■ Add submenus by typing menu item names in the **Type Here** boxes that appear to the right of the submenu's name.

■ Use a menu item's Click event handler to perform an action when that menu item is selected by the user.

Adding a Font Dialog to Your Application

■ Use the new operator to create a new FontDialog object.

■ Use a DialogResult variable to store the Button the user clicked to exit the dialog.

■ Use the ShowDialog method to display the dialog.

Adding a Color Dialog to Your Application

■ Use the new operator to create a new FontDialog object.

■ Use a DialogResult variable to store the Button the user clicked to exit the dialog.

■ Set the FullOpen option to true to provide the user with the full range of colors and to allow custom colors.

■ Use the ShowDialog keyword to display the dialog.

KEY TERMS

Cancel value of DialogResult enumeration—Used to determine whether the user clicked the **Cancel** Button of a dialog.

Char structure—Stores characters (such as letters and symbols).

Click event of class MenuItem—Generated when an item is clicked or a shortcut key is used.

ColorDialog class—Used to display a dialog containing color options to a user.

e event argument—Contains data for the event (such as KeyData).

FontDialog class—Used to display a dialog containing font options to a user and record the result.

FullOpen property of class ColorDialog—Property that, when true, enables the Color-Dialog to provide a full range of color options when displayed.

keyboard event—Raised when a key on the keyboard is pressed or released.

KeyChar property of class KeyPressEventArgs—Contains data about the key that raised the KeyPress event.

KeyData property of class KeyEventArgs—Contains data about the key that raised the KeyDown event.

KeyDown event—Generated when a key is initially pressed. Used to handle the event raised when a key that is not a letter key is pressed.

KeyEventArgs class—Stores information about special modifier keys.

KeyPress event—Generated when a key is pressed. Used to handle the event raised when a letter key is pressed.

KeyPressEventArgs class—Stores information about character keys.

Keys enumeration—Contains values representing keyboard keys.

KeyUp event—Generated when a key is released.

MainMenu control—Allows you to add menus to your application.

Menu Designer in Visual Studio .NET—Design mode in Visual Studio .NET that allows you to create and edit menus.

menu-access shortcut—*Alt* key shortcut that allows the user to combine the *Alt* key with another key to access a menu item.

menu item—A cell of text that the user can select in the `MainMenu` control.

MenuItem object—Represents menu items.

modifier key—Key such as *Shift*, *Alt* or *Control* that modifies the way that applications respond to a keyboard event.

sender event argument—Event argument that contains the object that raised the event (also called the source of the event).

separator bar—Bar placed in a menu to separate related menu items.

ShowDialog method of class FontDialog or ColorDialog—Displays the dialog on which it is called.

submenu—Menu within another menu.

temporary variable—Used to store data when swapping values.

Text property of class MenuItem—Specifies the menu item's text.

ToUpper method of structure Char—Returns the uppercase representation of the character passed as a parameter.

GUI DESIGN GUIDELINES

MainMenu

- Use book-title capitalization in menu item text.
- Use separator bars in a menu to group related menu items.
- If clicking a menu item opens a dialog, an ellipsis (…) should follow the menu item's text.

CONTROLS, EVENTS, PROPERTIES & METHODS

Char This structure stores characters, such as letters and symbols.

- *Method*

  ToUpper—Returns the uppercase equivalent of an alphabetic character.

ColorDialog　　`ColorDialog`　　This control allows the user to customize the color of what is being typed.

- *Properties*

  Color—Contains the color selected by the user. The default color is black.

  FullOpen—When `true`, displays an extended color palette. If this property is set to `false`, a dialog with less options is displayed.

- *Method*

  ShowDialog—Displays the **Color** dialog to the user.

FontDialog　　`FontDialog`　　This control allows the user to customize the font, size and style of what is being typed.

- *Method*

  ShowDialog—Displays the **Font** dialog to the user.

KeyEventArgs This class represents arguments passed to the `KeyPress` event handler.

- *Property*

  KeyData—Contains data about the key that raised the `KeyDown` event.

KeyPressEventArgs This class represents arguments passed to the `KeyPress` event handler.

- *Property*

  KeyChar—Contains data about the key that raised the `KeyPress` event.

MenuItem This class represents menu items.

■ *In action*

■ *Event*

Click—Raised when the user clicks a menu item or presses a shortcut key that represents an item.

TextBox   This control allows the user to input data from the keyboard.

■ *In action*

```
     0
```

■ *Events*

KeyDown—Raised when a key is pressed. KeyDown is case insensitive. It cannot recognize lowercase letters.

KeyPress—Raised when a key is pressed. KeyPress cannot handle modifier keys.

KeyUp—Raised when a key is released by the user.

TextChanged—Raised when the text in the TextBox is changed.

■ *Properties*

Enabled—Determines whether the user can enter data (true) in the TextBox or not (false).

Location—Specifies the location of the TextBox on the container control relative to the top-left corner.

MaxLength—Specifies the maximum number of characters that can be input into the TextBox.

Multiline—Specifies whether the TextBox is capable of displaying multiple lines of text.

Name—Specifies the name used to access the TextBox programmatically. The name should be prefixed with txt.

PasswordChar—Specifies the masking character to be used when displaying data in the TextBox.

ReadOnly—Determines whether the value of a TextBox can be changed.

ScrollBars—Specifies whether the TextBox contains a scrollbar.

Size—Specifies the height and width (in pixels) of the TextBox.

Text—Specifies the text displayed in the TextBox.

TextAlign—Specifies how the text is aligned within the TextBox.

■ *Method*

Focus—Transfers the focus of the application to the TextBox that calls it.

MULTIPLE-CHOICE QUESTIONS

22.1 When creating a menu, typing a _____ in front of a menu item name will create an access shortcut for that item.

a) &
b) !
c) $
d) #

22.2 *Alt*, *Shift* and *Control* are _____ keys.

a) modifier
b) ASCII
c) function
d) special

22.3 KeyChar is a property of _____.

a) KeyEventArgs
b) Key
c) KeyArgs
d) KeyPressEventArgs

22.4 Typing a hyphen (–) as a menu item's Text property will create a(n) _____.

a) separator bar   b) access shortcut

c) new submenu   d) keyboard shortcut

22.5 A _____ provides a group of related commands for Windows applications.

a) separator bar   b) hot key

c) menu   d) margin indicator bar

22.6 The _____ enumeration specifies key codes and modifiers.

a) Keyboard   b) Key

c) KeyboardTypes   d) Keys

22.7 The _____ event is raised when a key is pressed by the user.

a) KeyPress   b) KeyHeld

c) KeyDown   d) Both a and c.

22.8 Which of the following is not a keyboard event?

a) KeyPress   b) KeyDown

c) KeyUp   d) KeyClicked

22.9 Which of the following is not a structure?

a) Char   b) Color

c) String   d) DateTime

22.10 The _____ type allows you to determine which Button the user clicked to exit a dialog.

a) DialogButtons   b) DialogResult

c) Buttons   d) ButtonResult

EXERCISES

22.11 (***Enhanced Inventory Application with Keyboard Events***) Enhance the **Inventory** application that you developed in Tutorial 4 to prevent the user from entering input that is not a number. Use keyboard events to allow the user to press the number keys, the left and right arrows and the *Backspace* keys. If a key other than these is pressed, display a Message-Box instructing the user to enter a number (Fig. 22.31).

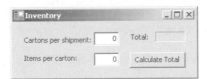 

Figure 22.31   Enhanced **Inventory** GUI.

a) ***Copying the template to your working directory.*** Copy the directory C:\Examples\ Tutorial22\Exercises\KeyEventInventory to your C:\SimplyCSP directory.

b) ***Opening the application's template file.*** Double click Inventory.sln in the KeyEventInventory directory to open the application.

c) ***Adding the KeyDown event handler for the first TextBox.*** Add an empty KeyDown event handler for the **Cartons per shipment:** TextBox.

d) ***Adding a switch statement.*** Add a switch statement to the KeyDown event handler that determines whether a number key, a left or right arrow or the *Backspace* key was pressed.

e) ***Adding the default statement.*** Add a default statement that will determine whether a key other than a valid one for this application was pressed. If an invalid key was pressed, display a MessageBox that instructs the user to enter a number.

f) ***Adding the KeyDown event handler for the second TextBox.*** Repeat *Steps c–e*, only this time create a KeyDown event handler for the **Items per carton:** TextBox. This event handler should perform the same functionality as the one for the **Cartons per shipment:** TextBox.

g) ***Running the application.*** Select **Debug > Start** to run your application. Try entering letters or pressing the up and down arrow keys in the TextBoxes. A MessageBox should be displayed. Enter valid input and click the **Calculate Total** Button. Verify that the correct output is displayed.

h) ***Closing the application.*** Close your running application by clicking its close box.

i) ***Closing the IDE.*** Close Visual Studio .NET by clicking its close box.

22.12 (*Bouncing Ball Application*) Write an application that allows the user to play a game, the goal of which is to prevent a bouncing ball from falling off the bottom of the Form. When the user presses the *S* key, a blue ball will bounce off the top, left and right sides (the "walls") of the Form. There should be a horizontal bar on the bottom of the Form, which serves as a paddle to prevent the ball from hitting the bottom of the Form. (The ball can bounce off the paddle, but not the bottom of the Form.) The user can move the paddle using the left and right arrow keys. If the ball hits the paddle, the ball should bounce up, and the game should continue. If the ball hits the bottom of the Form, the game should end. The paddle's width should decrease every 20 seconds to make the game more challenging. The GUI is provided for you (Fig. 22.32).

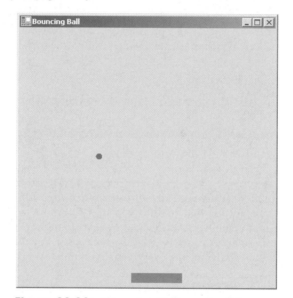

Figure 22.32   Bouncing Ball application.

a) ***Copying the template to your working directory.*** Copy the directory C:\Examples\Tutorial22\Exercises\BouncingBall to your C:\SimplyCSP directory.

b) ***Opening the application's template file.*** Double click BouncingBall.sln in the BouncingBall directory to open the application.

c) ***Creating the KeyDown event handler.*** Insert a KeyDown event handler for the Form.

d) ***Writing code to start the game.*** Write an if statement in the KeyDown event handler that tests whether the user presses the *S* key. You can use the KeyDown event handler for the *S* key in this case, because you do not care whether the user presses an uppercase *S* or a lowercase *S*. If the user presses the *S* key, start the two Timers that are provided in the template.

e) ***Inserting code to move the paddle left.*** Write an if statement that tests if the user pressed the left-arrow key and if the paddle's horizontal position is greater than zero. If the paddle's horizontal position equals zero, the left edge of the paddle is touching the left wall and the paddle should not be allowed to move farther to the left. If both the conditions in the if statement are true, decrease the paddle's *x*-coordinate by 10.

f) ***Inserting code to move the paddle right.*** Write an if statement that tests if the user pressed the right-arrow key and whether the paddle's *x*-coordinate is less than the width of the Form minus the width of the paddle. If the paddle's *x*-coordinate equals the Form's width minus the width of the paddle, the paddle's right edge is touching the right wall and the paddle should not be allowed to move farther to the right. If both the conditions in the if statement are true, increase the paddle's *x*-coordinate by 10.

g) *Running the application.* Select **Debug > Start** to run your application. Press the *S* key to begin the game and use the paddle to keep the bouncing ball from dropping off the Form. Continue doing this until 20 seconds have passed, and verify that the paddle is decreased in size at that time.

h) *Closing the application.* Close your running application by clicking its close box.

i) *Closing the IDE.* Close Visual Studio .NET by clicking its close box.

22.13 (*Modified Painter Application*) Modify the **Painter** application that you developed in Tutorial 21 to include menus that allow the user to select the size and color of the painted ellipses and the color of the Form (Fig. 22.33). (The menus replace the RadioButtons.) Also, add a multiline TextBox to allow the user to type text to accompany the painting. The user should be able to use menus to select the font style and color of the text and the background color of the TextBox.

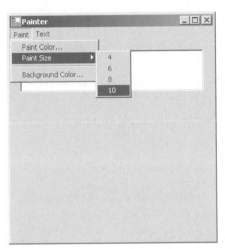 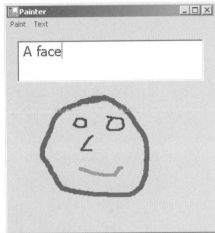

Figure 22.33   Modified **Painter** application.

a) *Copying the template to your working directory.* Copy the directory C:\Examples\ Tutorial22\Exercises\ModifiedPainter to your C:\SimplyCSP directory.

b) *Opening the application's template file.* Double click Painter.sln in the Modi- fiedPainter directory to open the application.

c) *Creating the menus.* Create two menus. The first one should be titled **Paint** and should contain a **Paint Color...** menu item, a **Paint Size** submenu that contains menu items **4**, **6**, **8** and **10**, a separator bar and a **Background Color...** menu item. The sec- ond menu should be titled **Text** and have **Text Color...** and **Font...** menu items, a sep- arator bar and a **TextBox Color...** menu item. Rearrange and comment the control declarations appropriately.

d) *Changing the paint color.* Add an event handler for the **Paint Color...** menu item. This event handler should display a **Color** dialog that allows the user to change the value stored in m_paintColor.

e) *Changing the paint size.* Add an event handler for each of the **Size** submenu's menu items. Each event handler should change the value stored in m_intDiamter to the value displayed on the menu (that is, clicking the **4** menu item will change the value of m_intDiameter to 4).

f) *Changing the background color.* Add an event handler for the **Background Color...** menu item. This event handler should display a **Color** dialog that allows the user to change the value stored in m_backgroundColor and also change the BackColor property of the Form. To change the background color of the Form, assign the value specifying the background color to BackColor. For instance, the statement BackColor = Color.White; changes the background color of the Form to white.

g) *Changing the text color.* Add an event handler for the **Text Color...** menu item. This event handler should display a **Color** dialog that allows the user to change the color of the text displayed in the TextBox.

h) *Changing the text style.* Add an event handler for the **Font...** menu item. This event handler should display a **Font** dialog that allows the user to change the style of the text displayed in the TextBox.

i) *Changing the TextBox's background color.* Add an event handler for the **TextBox Color...** menu item. This event handler should display a **Color** dialog that allows the user to change the background color of the TextBox.

j) *Running the application.* Select **Debug > Start** to run your application. Use the menus to draw shapes of various colors and brush sizes. Enter text to describe your drawing. Use the other menu options to change the color of the Form, the TextBox and the text in the TextBox.

k) *Closing the application.* Close your running application by clicking its close box.

l) *Closing the IDE.* Close Visual Studio .NET by clicking its close box.

What does this code do? ▶ **22.14** What is the result of the following code? Assume the Form contains a MainMenu control, with a MenuItem named mnuitmColor. Also assume the Form contains a Label called lblMystery.

```
1   private void mnuitmColor_Click( object sender, System.EventArgs e )
2   {
3      ColorDialog dlgColorDialog = new ColorDialog();
4      DialogResult result;
5
6      dlgColorDialog.FullOpen = true;
7
8      result = dlgColorDialog.ShowDialog();
9
10     if ( result == DialogResult.Cancel )
11     {
12        return;
13     }
14
15     lblMystery.BackColor = dlgColorDialog.Color;
16
17  } // end method mnuitmColor_Click
```

What's wrong with this code? ▶ **22.15** This code should allow a user to pick a font from a **Font** and set the text in txtDisplay to that font. Find the error(s) in the following code, assuming that a TextBox named txtDisplay exists on a Form, along with a MenuItem named mnuitmFont.

```
1   private void mnuitmFont_Click(
2      object sender, System.EventArgs e )
3   {
4      FontDialog dlgFontDialog;
5
6      dlgFontDialog = new FontDialog();
7      dlgFontDialog.ShowDialog();
8      txtDisplay.Font = dlgFontDialog.Font;
9
10  } // end method mnuitmFont_Click
```

Programming Challenge ▶ **22.16** (*Dvorak Keyboard Application*) Create an application that simulates the letters on the Dvorak keyboard. A Dvorak keyboard allows faster typing by placing the most commonly used keys in the most accessible locations. Use keyboard events to create an application similar to the **Typing** application, except that it simulates the Dvorak keyboard instead of the standard keyboard. The correct Dvorak key should be highlighted on the virtual keyboard and the correct character should be displayed in the TextBox. The keys and characters map as follows:

- On the top row, the *P* key of the Dvorak keyboard maps to the *R* key on a standard keyboard, and the *L* key of the Dvorak keyboard maps to the *P* key on a standard keyboard.

- On the middle row, the *A* key remains in the same position and the *S* key on the Dvorak keyboard maps to the semicolon key on the standard keyboard.

- On the bottom row, the *Q* key on the Dvorak keyboard maps to the *X* key on the standard keyboard and the *Z* key maps to the question mark key.

- All of the other keys on the Dvorak keyboard map to the locations shown in Fig. 22.34.

Figure 22.34   Dvorak Keyboard GUI.

a) ***Copying the template to your working directory.*** Copy the directory C:\Examples\ Tutorial22\Exercises\DvorakKeyboard to your C:\SimplyCSP directory.

b) ***Opening the application's template file.*** Double click DvorakKeyboard.sln in the DvorakKeyboard directory to open the application.

c) ***Creating the KeyPress event handler.*** Add a KeyPress event handler for the TextBox.

d) ***Creating a switch statement.*** Add a switch statement to the KeyPress event handler. The switch statement should test whether all of the letter keys on the Dvorak keyboard were pressed except for the *S, W, V* and *Z* keys. If a Dvorak key was pressed, highlight it on the GUI and display the character in the TextBox.

e) ***Creating a KeyDown event handler.*** Add a KeyDown event handler for the TextBox. The *S, W, V* and *Z* keys do not map to a letter key on the standard keyboard; therefore, a KeyDown event handler must be used to determine whether one of these keys was pressed.

f) ***Adding a switch statement.*** Add a switch statement to your KeyDown event handler that determines whether *S, W, V* or *Z* was pressed. If one of these keys was pressed, highlight the key, and add the character to the TextBox.

g) ***Running the application.*** Select **Debug > Start** to run your application. Use your keyboard to enter text. Verify that the text entered is correct based on the rules in the exercise description. Make sure the correct Buttons on the Form are highlighted as you enter text.

h) ***Closing the application.*** Close your running application by clicking its close box.

i) ***Closing the IDE.*** Close Visual Studio .NET by clicking its close box.

TUTORIAL 23

Objectives

In this tutorial, you will learn to:
- Create and manipulate `string` objects.
- Use properties and methods of class `String`.
- Search for substrings within `strings`.
- Extract substrings within `strings`.
- Replace substrings within `strings`.

Outline

Screen Scraping Application

Introducing *string* Processing

This tutorial introduces C#'s `string`-processing capabilities. The techniques presented in this tutorial can be used to create applications that process text. Earlier tutorials introduced the `String` class from the `System` namespace and several of its methods. In this tutorial, you will learn how to search `strings`, retrieve characters from `string` objects and replace characters in a `string`. You will create an application that uses these `string`-processing capabilities to manipulate a `string` containing **HTML** (**HyperText Markup Language**). HTML is a technology for describing Web content. Extracting desired information from the HTML that composes a Web page is called **screen scraping**. Applications that perform screen scraping can be used to extract specific information, such as weather conditions or stock prices, from Web pages so that the information can be formatted and manipulated more easily by computer applications. In this tutorial, you will create a simple **Screen Scraping** application.

23.1 Test-Driving the Screen Scraping Application

This application must meet the following requirements:

Application Requirements

*An online European auction house wants to expand its business to include bidders from the United States. However, all the auction house's Web pages currently display their prices in euros, not dollars. The auction house wants to generate separate Web pages for American bidders to display the prices of auction items in dollars. These new Web pages will be generated by using screen-scraping techniques on the already existing Web pages. You have been asked to build a prototype application to test the screen-scraping functionality. The application should search a sample string of HTML and extract information about the price of a specified auction item. For testing purposes, a **ComboBox** should be provided that contains auction items listed in the HTML. The selected item's amount must then be converted to dollars. For simplicity, assume that the exchange rate is one to one (that is, one euro is equivalent to one dollar). The price (in dollars) and sample HTML are displayed in Labels.*

The **Screen Scraping** application searches for the name of a specified auction item in a string of HTML. Users select the item for which to search from a ComboBox. The application then extracts and displays the price in dollars of this item. You begin by test-driving the completed application. Then, you will learn the additional C# technologies that you will need to create your own version of this application.

Test-Driving the Screen Scraping Application

1. ***Opening the completed application.*** Open the C:\Examples\ Tutorial23\CompletedApplication\ScreenScraping directory to locate the **Screen Scraping** application. Double click ScreenScraping.sln to open the application in Visual Studio .NET.

2. ***Running the Screen Scraping application.*** Select **Debug > Start** to run the application (Fig. 23.1). Notice that the HTML is displayed in a Label at the bottom of the Form.

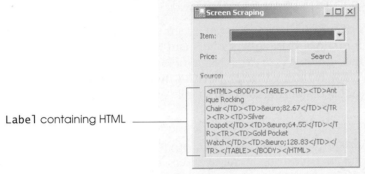

Label containing HTML

Figure 23.1   **Screen Scraping** application's Form.

3. ***Selecting an item name.*** The ComboBox contains three item names. Select an item name from the ComboBox as shown in Fig. 23.2.

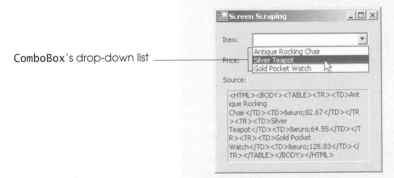

ComboBox's drop-down list

Figure 23.2   Selecting an item name from the ComboBox.

4. ***Searching for an item's price.*** Click the **Search** Button to display the price for the selected item. The extracted price is displayed in a Label (Fig. 23.3).

5. ***Closing the application.*** Close your running application by clicking its close box.

6. ***Closing the IDE.*** Close Visual Studio .NET by clicking its close box.

(cont.)

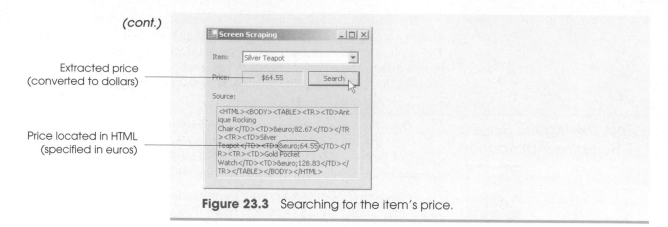

Extracted price
(converted to dollars)

Price located in HTML
(specified in euros)

Figure 23.3 Searching for the item's price.

23.2 Fundamentals of `strings`

A string is a series of **characters** treated as a single unit. These characters can be uppercase letters, lowercase letters, digits and various **special characters**, such as +, -, *, /, $ and others. A `string` is an object of class `String` in the `System` namespace. We write **string literals**, or **string constants** (often called **literal string objects**), as sequences of characters in double quotation marks, as follows:

```
"This is a string!"
```

You've already created and used `string`s in previous tutorials. You know that a declaration can assign a string literal to a `string` reference. For example, the declaration

```
string strColor = "blue";
```

initializes `string` reference `strColor` to refer to the `string` literal object `"blue"`. Like arrays, `string`s always know their own size. `String` property `Length` returns the length of the `string` (that is, the number of characters in the `string`). For example, the expression `strColor.Length` evaluates to 4 for the `string` `"blue"`.

The **string indexer** facilitates the retrieval of any character in the `string`. The `string` indexer returns the character at a specific position in the `string`. The indexer treats a `string` as an array of characters, taking an `int` argument specifying the index and returning the character at that index. As in arrays, the first element of a `string` is at index 0. For example, the following code

```
if ( strString1[ 0 ] == strString2[ 0 ] )
   lblMessage.Text = "The first characters are the same.";
```

compares the character at index 0 (that is, the first character) of `strString1` with the character at index 0 of `strString2`. As with arrays, the `string` indexer uses square brackets ([]) as the index operator.

In earlier tutorials, you used several methods of the `String` class to manipulate `string` objects. Figure 23.4 lists some of these methods. You will be introduced to new `String` methods later in this tutorial.

Method	Sample Expression Method Call (assume `strText == "My String"`)	Returns
`Insert( index, string )`	`strText.Insert( 9,"!" )`	`"My String!"`
`Remove( index, count )`	`strText.Remove( 2,1 )`	`"MyString"`
`ToLower()`	`strText.ToLower()`	`"my string"`
`ToUpper()`	`strText.ToUpper()`	`"MY STRING"`

Figure 23.4 String-class methods introduced in earlier tutorials.

Any `String` method that appears to modify a `string` actually returns a new `string` that contains the results. For example, `String` method `ToUpper` does not actually modify the original `string`, but instead returns a new `string` in which each lowercase letter has been converted to uppercase. This occurs because `strings` are **immutable** objects—that is, characters in `strings` cannot be changed after the `strings` are created.

SELF-REVIEW

1. The _____ property of the `String` class returns the number of characters in the `String`.

   a) `MaxChars`   b) `Length`
   c) `CharacterCount`   d) `TotalLength`

2. A `string` can be composed of _____.

   a) digits   b) lowercase letters
   c) special characters   d) All of the above.

Answers: 1) b. 2) d.

23.3 Analyzing the Screen Scraping Application

Before building the **Screen Scraping** application, you must analyze its components. The following pseudocode describes the basic operation of the **Screen Scraping** application.

> When the Form loads:
>   Display the HTML that contains the items' prices in a Label
>
> When the user clicks the Search Button:
>   Search the HTML for the item the user selected from the ComboBox
>   Extract the item's price
>   Convert the item's price from euros to dollars
>   Display the item's price in a Label

Now that you have test-driven the **Screen Scraping** application and studied its pseudocode representation, you will use an ACE table to help you convert the pseudocode to C#. Figure 23.5 lists the actions, controls and events that will help you complete your own version of this application.

Action/Control/Event (ACE) Table for the Screen Scraping Application

Action	Control/Object	Event

Label the application's controls	`lblItem,`
	`lblPrice,`
	`lblSource`
		Application is run

	`FrmScreenScraping`	Load
Display the HTML that contains the items' prices in a Label	`lblHTML`	
	`btnSearch`	Click
Search the HTML for the item the user selected from the ComboBox	`cboItems,` `strHTML`	
Extract the item's price	`strHTML`	
Convert the item's price from euros to dollars	`strHTML`	
Display the item's price in a Label	`lblResult,` `strHTML`	

Figure 23.5   ACE table for **Screen Scraping** application.

Now that you have analyzed the **Screen Scraping** application's components, you will learn about the String methods that you will use to construct the application.

23.4 Locating Substrings in strings

In many applications, it is necessary to search for a character or set of characters in a string. For example, a programmer creating a word-processing application would want to provide capabilities to allow users to search their documents. The String class provides methods to make it possible to search for specified **substrings** (or sequences of characters) in a string. In the following box, you begin building the **Screen Scraping** application.

Locating the Selected Item's Price

1. ***Copying the template to your working directory.*** Copy the C:\Examples\ Tutorial23\TemplateApplication\ScreenScraping directory to your C:\SimplyCSP directory.

2. ***Opening the Screen Scraping application's template file.*** Double click ScreenScraping.sln in the ScreenScraping directory to open the application in Visual Studio .NET.

3. ***Displaying the application's Form.*** Double click ScreenScraping.cs in the **Solution Explorer** to display the application's Form.

4. ***Creating a Click event handler for the Search Button.*** Double click the **Search** Button on the application's Form to generate the btnSearch_Click event handler. Be sure to add the comment and break the header as shown in Fig. 23.6 so that the line numbers in your code match those presented in this tutorial.

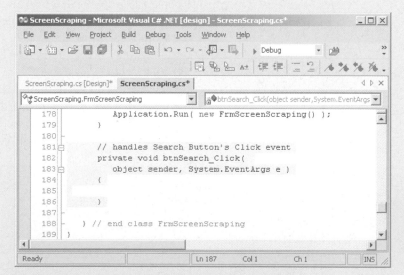

Figure 23.6 btnSearch_Click event handler.

5. ***Declaring three int variables and a string reference.*** Add lines 185–188 from Fig. 23.7 to the btnSearch_Click event handler. These lines declare intItemLocation, intPriceBegin and intPriceEnd variables and string reference strPrice.

(cont.)

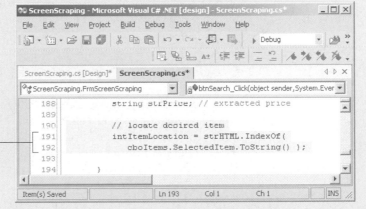

Figure 23.7 btnSearch_Click event handler declarations.

6. *Locating the specified item name.* Add lines 190–192 from Fig. 23.8 to the btnSearch_Click event handler. Lines 191–192 call String method **IndexOf** to locate the first occurrence of the specified item name in the HTML string (strHTML). There are three versions of IndexOf that search for substrings in a string. Lines 191–192 use the version of IndexOf that takes a single argument—the substring for which to search. (The specified item name is the SelectedItem of ComboBox, cboItems.)

Search for the SelectedItem in the string strHTML

Figure 23.8 Locating the desired item name.

You must first convert SelectedItem to a string, by using the ToString method, before passing the selected item to the IndexOf method. If IndexOf finds the specified substring (in this case, the item name), IndexOf returns the index at which the substring begins in the string. For example, a return value of 0 means that the substring begins at the first element (that is, the beginning) of the string. If IndexOf does not find the specified substring, IndexOf returns –1. The result is stored in intItemLocation.

7. *Locating the start of the price.* Add lines 194–196 from Fig. 23.9 to the btnSearch_Click event handler. Lines 195–196 locate the index at which the item's price begins. Lines 195–196 use a version of the IndexOf method that takes two arguments—the substring to search for and the starting index in the string at which the search should begin. The method does not examine any characters that occur prior to the starting index (specified by intItemLocation).

(cont.)

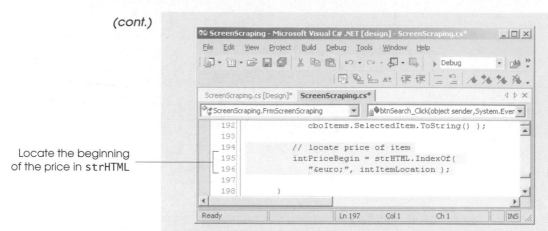

Locate the beginning
of the price in `strHTML`

Figure 23.9 Locating the desired item price.

The third version of the `IndexOf` method takes three arguments—the substring for which to search, the index at which to start searching and the number of characters to search. We do not use this version of `IndexOf` in the **Screen Scraping** application.

Because we know that the first price that follows the specified item name will be the desired price, we can begin our search at `intItemLocation`. The substring we search for is `"&euro;"`. This is the HTML representation of the euro symbol, which appears before every price value in the HTML `string` in this application. The index returned from the `IndexOf` method is stored in the `intPriceBegin` variable.

8. ***Locating the end of the price.*** Add line 197 from Fig. 23.10 to event handler `btnSearch_Click`. Line 197 finds the index at which the desired price ends. Line 197 calls the `IndexOf` method with the substring `"</TD>"` and the starting index, `intPriceBegin`. A `</TD>` tag directly follows every price (excluding any spaces) in the HTML `string`, so the index of the first `</TD>` tag after `intPriceBegin` marks the end of the current price.

The index returned from method `IndexOf` is stored in variable `intPriceEnd`. In the next box, we will use `intPriceBegin` and `intPriceEnd` to obtain the price from the `string` `strHTML`.

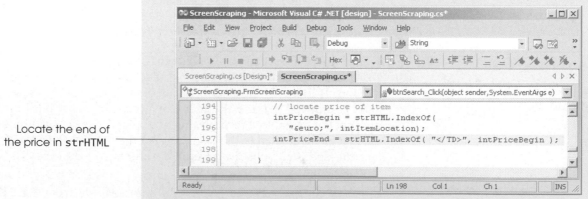

Locate the end of
the price in `strHTML`

Figure 23.10 Locating the end of the item's price.

9. ***Saving the project.*** Select **File > Save All** to save your modified code.

Another method that is similar to the `IndexOf` method is the **`LastIndexOf`** method. The `LastIndexOf` method locates the last occurrence of a substring in a `string`; it performs the search starting from the end of the `string` and searches toward the beginning of the `string`. If the `LastIndexOf` method finds the substring, `LastIndexOf` returns the starting index of the specified substring in the string; otherwise, `LastIndexOf` returns –1.

There are three versions of `LastIndexOf` that search for substrings in a string. The first version takes a single argument—the substring for which to search. The second version takes two arguments—the substring for which to search and the highest index from which to begin searching backward for the substring. The third version takes three arguments—the substring for which to search, the starting index from which to start searching backward and the number of characters to search. Figure 23.11 demonstrates the use of the three versions of `LastIndexOf`.

Method	Example Expression (assume strText = "My string is a long string")	Returns
IndexOf(*string*)	strText.IndexOf(`"ring"`)	5
IndexOf(*string, integer*)	strText.IndexOf(`"ring"`, 10)	22
IndexOf(*string, integer, integer*)	strText.IndexOf(`"ring"`, 10, 4)	–1
LastIndexOf(*string*)	strText.LastIndexOf(`"ring"`)	22
LastIndexOf(*string, integer*)	strText.LastIndexOf(`"ring"`, 3)	1
LastIndexOf(*string, integer, integer*)	strText.LastIndexOf(`"ring"`, 10, 8)	5

Figure 23.11   Demonstration of the `LastIndexOf` methods.

SELF-REVIEW

1. The _____ method locates the first occurrence of a substring.

   a) `IndexOf` b) `FirstIndexOf`

   c) `FindFirst` d) `Locate`

2. The third argument passed to the `LastIndexOf` method is _____.

   a) the starting index from which to start searching backward

   b) the starting index from which to start searching forward

   c) the length of the substring to locate

   d) the number of characters to search

Answers: 1) a. 2) d.

23.5 Extracting Substrings from `strings`

Once you've located a substring in a `string`, you might want to retrieve the substring from the `string`. The following box uses the **Substring** method to retrieve the price of the selected item from the HTML `string`.

Retrieving the Desired Item's Price

1. **Extracting the price.** Add lines 199–201 of Fig. 23.12 to the `btnSearch_Click` event handler. The `String` class provides two versions of the `Substring` method, each of which returns a new `string` object that contains a copy of a part of an existing `string` object.

   Lines 200–201 extract the price, using the version of the `Substring` method that takes two `int` arguments. The first argument (`intPriceBegin`), specifies the starting index from which the method copies characters from the original `string`. The second argument (`intPriceEnd - intPriceBegin`) specifies the length of the substring to be copied. The substring returned (`strPrice`) contains a copy of the specified characters from the original `string`. In this case, the substring returned is the item's price (in euros).

(cont.)

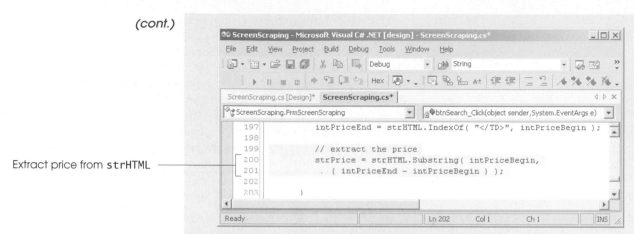

Extract price from `strHTML`

Figure 23.12 Retrieving the desired price.

The other version of the `Substring` method takes one `int` argument. The argument specifies the starting index from which the method copies characters in the original `string`. The substring returned contains a copy of the characters from the starting index to the end of the `string`. We do not use this version of `Substring` in the **Screen Scraping** application.

2. *Saving the project.* Select **File > Save All** to save your modified code.

SELF-REVIEW

1. The `Substring` method _____.
   a) accepts either one or two arguments
   b) returns a new `string` object
   c) creates a `string` object by copying part of an existing `string` object
   d) All of the above.

2. The second argument passed to the `Substring` method specifies _____.
   a) the last index of the `string` to copy
   b) the length of the substring to copy
   c) the index from which to begin copying backwards
   d) a character which, when reached, signifies that copying should stop

Answers: 1) d. 2) b.

23.6 Replacing Substrings in `strings`

You might want to replace certain characters in `strings`. The `String` class provides the **Replace** method to replace occurrences of one substring with a different substring. The `Replace` method takes two arguments—a `string` to replace in the original `string` and a `string` with which to replace all occurrences of the first argument. The `Replace` method returns a new `string` with the specified replacements. The original `string` remains unchanged. If there are no occurrences of the first argument in the `string`, the method returns the original `string`. The following box uses the `Replace` method to convert the extracted price from euros to dollars.

Converting the Price to Dollars

1. *Converting the price.* Add lines 203–204 of Fig. 23.13 to `btnSearch_Click`. Line 204 converts the extracted price from euros to dollars. For simplicity, we assume that dollars are equal to euros.

(cont.)

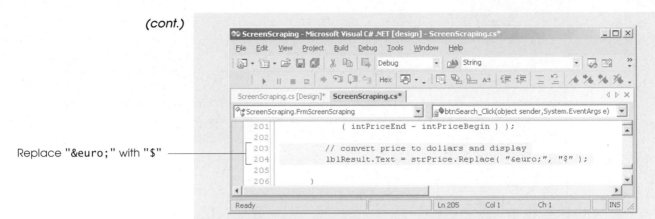

Figure 23.13 Converting the price to dollars.

Therefore, to perform the conversion, we need change only the name of the currency. Line 204 uses `String` method `Replace` to return a new `string` object, replacing every occurrence (one in this example) in `str-Price` of substring `"&euro;"` with substring `"$"`. Notice that we assign the value returned from the `Replace` method to `lblResult.Text` to display the text in dollars.

2. ***Saving the project.*** Select **File > Save All** to save your modified code.

The `Replace` method also is used when the `Form` for the **Screen Scraping** application first loads. The following box uses the `Replace` method to ensure that the HTML `string` displays correctly in a `Label`.

Displaying the HTML string

1. ***Creating a Load event handler for the Form.*** In design view, double click the Form to generate an empty `Load` event handler. This event handler will execute when the application runs. Be sure to add the comments and break the header as shown in Fig. 23.14 so that the line numbers in your code match those presented in this tutorial.

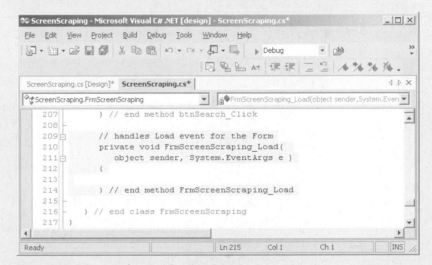

Figure 23.14 `Load` event for the `Form`.

Note: "Replace "€" with "$"" label points to line 204 in Figure 23.13.

(cont.)

2. ***Displaying the HTML string in a Label.*** Add lines 213–214 from Fig. 23.15 to the FrmScreenScraping_Load event handler. Line 214 calls String method Replace to replace every occurrence of "€" in the HTML string with "&€". As explained previously, the substring "€" is the HTML for the euro symbol. However, for this text to display in a Label correctly, we must prefix it with an additional ampersand (&) so the "e" in "euro" is not confused with an access shortcut. The value returned from the Replace method is displayed in the lblHTML Label.

Replace all occurrences of "&euro" with "&&euro"

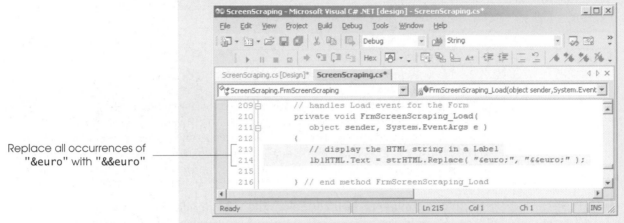

Figure 23.15 Displaying the HTML `string` in a `Label`.

3. ***Running the application.*** SSelect **Debug > Start** to run your application. Select the different items from the **Item** ComboBox, clicking the **Search** Button after each selection. Make sure that in each case, the proper price is extracted and displayed in dollar amounts.

4. ***Closing the application.*** Close your running application by clicking its close box.

5. ***Closing the IDE.*** Close Visual Studio .NET by clicking its close box.

SELF-REVIEW

1. If there are no occurrences of the substring in the `string`, the `Replace` method returns _____.

   a) 0   b) -1
   c) null   d) the original `string`

2. The `Replace` method takes _____ arguments.

   a) 0   b) 1
   c) 2   d) 3

Answer: 1) d. 2) c.

23.7 Other String Methods

The `String` class provides several additional methods that allow you to manipulate `strings`. Figure 23.16 lists some of these methods and provides a description of what each method does.

Method	Description	Sample Expression (assume strText == " My String")
EndsWith(*string*)	Returns true if a string ends with the argument *string*; otherwise, returns false.	strText.EndsWith("ing"); Returns: **true**
Join(*separator, array*)	Concatenates the elements in a string array, separated by the first argument. A new string containing the concatenated elements is returned.	string[] strArray = { "a", "b", "c" }; String.Join(";", strArray); Returns: "a;b;c"
Split()	Splits the words in a string whenever a space is reached.	string[] strArray = _ strText.Split(); Returns: "My" and "String" in an array of strings
StartsWith(*string*)	Returns true if a string starts with argument *string*; otherwise, returns false.	strText.StartsWith("Your"); Returns: **false**
Trim()	Removes any whitespace (that is, blank lines, spaces and tabs) from the beginning and end of a string.	strText.Trim(); Returns: "My String"

Figure 23.16   Description of other `String` methods.

Figure 23.17 presents the source code for the **Screen Scraping** application. The lines of code that contain new programming concepts that you learned in this tutorial are highlighted.

```
1   using System;
2   using System.Drawing;
3   using System.Collections;
4   using System.ComponentModel;
5   using System.Windows.Forms;
6   using System.Data;
7
8   namespace ScreenScraping
9   {
10     /// <summary>
11     /// Summary description for FrmScreenScraping.
12     /// </summary>
13     public class FrmScreenScraping : System.Windows.Forms.Form
14     {
15        // Label and ComboBox for choosing item
16        private System.Windows.Forms.Label lblItem;
17        private System.Windows.Forms.ComboBox cboItems;
18
```

Figure 23.17   **Screen Scraping** application code. (Part 1 of 3.)

```
19        // Labels for displaying price
20        private System.Windows.Forms.Label lblPrice;
21        private System.Windows.Forms.Label lblResult;
22
23        // Button for searching for price
24        private System.Windows.Forms.Button btnSearch;
25
26        // Labels to display HTML
27        private System.Windows.Forms.Label lblSource;
28        private System.Windows.Forms.Label lblHTML;
29
30        /// <summary>
31        /// Required designer variable.
32        /// </summary>
33        private System.ComponentModel.Container components = null;
34
35        // string of HTML to extract prices from
36        string strHTML = "<HTML><BODY><TABLE>" +
37           "<TR><TD>Antique Rocking Chair</TD>" +
38           "<TD>&&euro;82.67</TD></TR>" +
39           "<TR><TD>Silver Teapot</TD>" +
40           "<TD>&&euro;64.55</TD></TR>" +
41           "<TR><TD>Gold Pocket Watch</TD>" +
42           "<TD>&&euro;128.83</TD></TR>" +
43           "</TABLE></BODY></HTML>";
44
45        public FrmScreenScraping()
46        {
47           //
48           // Required for Windows Form Designer support
49           //
50           InitializeComponent();
51
52           //
53           // TODO: Add any constructor code after InitializeComponent
54           // call
55           //
56        }
57
58        /// <summary>
59        /// Clean up any resources being used.
60        /// </summary>
61        protected override void Dispose( bool disposing )
62        {
63           if( disposing )
64           {
65              if (components != null)
66              {
67                 components.Dispose();
68              }
69           }
70           base.Dispose( disposing );
71        }
72
73        // Windows Form Designer generated code
74
75        /// <summary>
76        /// The main entry point for the application.
```

Figure 23.17 Screen Scraping application code. (Part 2 of 3.)

```
 77             /// </summary>
 78             [STAThread]
 79             static void Main()
 80             {
 81                 Application.Run( new FrmScreenScraping() );
 82             }
 83
 84             // handles Search Button's Click event
 85             private void btnSearch_Click(
 86                 object sender, System.EventArgs e )
 87             {
 88                 int intItemLocation; // index of desired item
 89                 int intPriceBegin; // starting index of price
 90                 int intPriceEnd; // ending index of price
 91                 string strPrice; // extracted price
 92
 93                 // locate desired item
 94                 intItemLocation = strHTML.IndexOf(
 95                     cboItems.SelectedItem.ToString() );
 96
 97                 // locate price of item
 98                 intPriceBegin = strHTML.IndexOf(
 99                     "&euro;", intItemLocation );
100                 intPriceEnd = strHTML.IndexOf( "</TD>", intPriceBegin );
101
102                 // extract the price
103                 strPrice = strHTML.Substring( intPriceBegin,
104                     ( intPriceEnd - intPriceBegin ) );
105
106                 // convert price to dollars and display
107                 lblResult.Text = strPrice.Replace( "&euro;", "$" );
108
109             } // end method btnSearch_Click
110
111             // handles Load event for the Form
112             private void FrmScreenScraping_Load(
113                 object sender, System.EventArgs e )
114             {
115                 // display the HTML string in a Label
116                 lblHTML.Text = strHTML.Replace( "&euro;", "&&euro;" );
117
118             } // end method FrmScreenScraping_Load
119
120         } // end class ScreenScraping
121     }
```

Annotations (left margin):
- Search for the `SelectedItem` in the `strHTML` string → (lines 94–95)
- Locate the beginning of the price in `strHTML` → (lines 98–99)
- Locate the end of the price in `strHTML` → (line 100)
- Extract the price from `strHTML` → (lines 103–104)
- Replace `"&euro;"` with `"$"` → (line 107)
- Replace all occurrences of `"&euro"` with `"&&euro"` → (line 116)

Figure 23.17   Screen Scraping application code. (Part 3 of 3.)

SELF-REVIEW

1. The _____ method removes all whitespace characters that appear at the beginning and end of a string.

   a) RemoveSpaces   b) NoSpaces
   c) Trim   d) Truncate

2. The StartsWith method returns _____ if a string begins with the string text passed to StartsWith as an argument.

   a) true   b) false
   c) 1   d) the index of the substring

Answers: 1) c. 2) a.

23.8 Wrap-Up

In this tutorial, we introduced you to the `String` class from the `System` namespace. You learned how to create and manipulate `string` objects. You learned how to locate, retrieve and replace substrings in `strings`. You reviewed several methods from the `String` class and also learned additional methods. You applied your knowledge of `strings` in C# to create a simple **Screen Scraping** application that retrieved the price of an item from an HTML `string`.

In the next tutorial, you will learn how data is represented in a computer. You will be introduced to the concepts of files and streams. You will learn how to store data in sequential-access files.

SKILLS SUMMARY

Determining the Size of a `string`

- Use String property Length.

Locating Substrings in `strings`

- Use String method IndexOf to locate the first occurrence of a substring.
- Use String method LastIndexOf to locate the last occurrence of a substring.

Retrieving Substrings from `strings`

- Use String method Substring with one argument to obtain a substring that begins at the specified starting index and contains the remainder of the original `string`.
- Use String method Substring with two arguments to specify the starting index and the length of the substring.

Replacing Substrings in `strings`

- Use String method Replace to replace occurrences of one substring with another substring.
- The Replace method returns a new `string` containing the replacements.

Comparing Substrings to the Beginning or End of a `string`

- Use String method StartsWith to determine whether a `string` starts with a particular substring.
- Use String method EndsWith to determine whether a `string` ends with a particular substring.

Removing Whitespace from a `string`

- Use String method Trim to remove all whitespace characters that appear at the beginning and end of a `string`.

KEY TERMS

characters — Digits, letters and special symbols.

EndsWith method of class `String` — Determines if a `string` ends with a particular substring.

HTML (HyperText Markup Language) — A technology for describing Web content.

immutable — An object that cannot be changed after it is created. In C#, `strings` are immutable.

IndexOf method of class `String` — Returns the index of the first occurrence of a substring in a `String`. Returns -1 if the substring is not found.

Join method of class `String` — Concatenates the elements in a `String` array, separated by the first argument. A new `string` containing the concatenated elements is returned.

LastIndexOf method of class `String` — Returns the index of the last occurrence of a substring in a `string`. It returns -1 if the substring is not found.

literal string objects — A `string` constant written as a sequence of characters in double quotation marks (also called a string literal).

Replace method of class `String` — Returns a new `string` object in which every occurrence of a substring is replaced with a different substring.

screen scraping — The process of extracting desired information from the HTML that composes a Web page.

special characters—Characters that are neither digits or letters.

Split method of class String—Splits the words in a `string` whenever a space is reached.

StartsWith method of class String—Determines if a `string` starts with a particular substring.

string literal—A `String` constant written as a sequence of characters in double quotation marks (also called a literal `string` object).

substring—A sequence of characters in a `string`.

Substring method of class String—Returns a substring from a `string`.

ToLower method of class String—Creates a new `string` object that replaces every uppercase letter in a `String` with its lowercase equivalent.

ToUpper method of class String—Creates a new `string` object that replaces every lowercase letter in a `string` with its uppercase equivalent.

Trim method of class String—Removes all whitespace characters from the beginning and end of a `string`.

CONTROLS, EVENTS, PROPERTIES & METHODS

String The `String` class represents a series of characters treated as a single unit.

- *Property*

  `Length`—Returns the number of characters in the `string`.

- *Methods*

  `EndsWith`—Determines if a `string` ends with a particular substring.

  `Format`—Arranges the string in a specified format.

  `IndexOf`—Returns the index of the specified character(s) in a `string`.

  `Insert`—Returns a copy of the `string` for which it is called with the specified character(s) inserted.

  `LastIndexOf`—Returns the index of the last occurrence of a substring in a `string`. It returns `-1` if the substring is not found.

  `PadLeft`—Inserts characters at the beginning of a `string`.

  `Remove`—Returns a copy of the `string` for which it is called with the specified character(s) removed.

  `Replace`—Returns a new `string` object in which every occurrence of a substring is replaced with a different substring.

  `StartsWith`—Determines if a `string` starts with a particular substring.

  `Substring`—Returns a substring from a `string`.

  `ToLower`—Returns a copy of the `string` for which it is called with any uppercase letters converted to lowercase letters.

  `ToUpper`—Creates a new `string` object that replaces every lowercase letter in a `string` with its uppercase equivalent.

  `Trim`—Removes all whitespace characters from the beginning and end of a `string`.

MULTIPLE-CHOICE QUESTIONS

23.1 Extracting desired information from Web pages is called _____.

    a) Web crawling   b) screen scraping

    c) querying   d) redirection

23.2 If the `IndexOf` method does not find the specified substring, it returns _____.

    a) `false`   b) 0

    c) `-1`   d) None of the above.

23.3 The `String` class allows you to _____ strings.

    a) search   b) retrieve characters from

    c) replace characters in   d) All of the above.

23.4 _____ is a technology for describing Web content.

    a) The `String` class   b) A `string` literal

    c) HTML   d) A screen scraper

23.5 The `String` class is located in the _____ namespace.

    a) `String`   b) `System.Strings`

    c) `System.IO`   d) `System`

23.6 The _____ method creates a new `string` object by copying part of an existing `string` object.

    a) `StringCopy`   b) `Substring`

    c) `CopyString`   d) `CopySubString`

23.7 All `string` objects are _____.

    a) the same size

    b) always equal to each other

    c) preceded by at least one whitespace character

    d) immutable

23.8 The `IndexOf` method does not examine any characters that occur prior to the _____.

    a) starting index   b) first match

    c) last character of the `string`   d) None of the above.

23.9 The _____ method determines whether a `string` ends with a particular substring.

    a) `CheckEnd`   b) `StringEnd`

    c) `EndsWith`   d) `EndIs`

23.10 The `Trim` method removes all whitespace characters that appear _____ a `String`.

    a) in   b) at the beginning of

    c) at the end of   d) at the beginning and end of

EXERCISES

23.11 (*Supply Calculator Application*) Write an application that calculates the cost of all the supplies added to the user's shopping list (Fig. 23.18). The application should contain two `ListBox`es. The first `ListBox` contains all the supplies offered and their respective prices. Users should be able to select the desired supplies from the first `ListBox` and add them to the second `ListBox`. Provide a **Calculate** `Button` that displays the total price for the user's shopping list (the contents of the second `ListBox`).

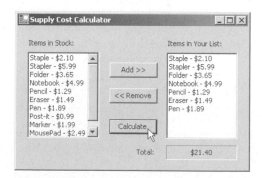

Figure 23.18 **Supply Calculator** application.

    a) *Copying the template to your working directory.* Copy the directory `C:\Examples\Tutorial23\Exercises\SupplyCalculator` to your `C:\SimplyCSP` directory.

    b) *Opening the application's template file.* Double click `SupplyCalculator.sln` in the `SupplyCalculator` directory to open the application.

    c) *Adding the Add >> Button's event handler.* Double click the **Add >>** `Button` to create an empty event handler. Add code to the event handler that adds the selected item from the first `ListBox` to the `lstStock` `ListBox`. Make sure to check that at least one item is selected in the first `ListBox` before attempting to add an item to the `lstStock` `ListBox`.

d) *Enabling the Buttons.* Once the user adds something to the lstStock ListBox, set the Enabled properties of the **<< Remove** and **Calculate** Buttons to true.

e) *Deselecting the items.* Once the items are added to the lstStock ListBox, make sure that those items are deselected in the lstSupply ListBox. Also, clear the **Total:** Label to indicate to the user that a new total price must be calculated.

f) *Adding the Remove Button's event handler.* Double click the **<< Remove** Button to create an empty event handler. Use a while loop to remove any selected items in the lstStock ListBox. Make sure to check that at least one item is selected before attempting to remove an item. [*Hint*: The lstStock.Items.RemoveAt(intIndex) method will remove the item located at intIndex from the lstStock ListBox.]

g) *Adding the Calculate Button's event handler.* Double click the **Calculate** Button to create an empty event handler. Use a for statement to loop through all the items in the lstStock ListBox. Convert each item from the ListBox into a string. Then, use the string method Substring to extract the price of each item.

h) *Displaying the total.* Convert the string representing each item's price to a decimal, and add this to the overall total (of type decimal). Remember to output the value in currency format.

i) *Running the application.* Select **Debug > Start** to run your application. Use the **Add >>** and **<< Remove** Buttons to add and remove items from the **Items in Your List:** ListBox. Click the **Calculate** Button and verify that the total price displayed is correct.

j) *Closing the application.* Close your running application by clicking its close box.

k) *Closing the IDE.* Close Visual Studio .NET by clicking its close box.

23.12 (*Encryption Application*) Write an application that encrypts a message from the user (Fig. 23.19). The application should be able to encrypt the message in two different ways—substitution cipher and a transposition cipher (both described below). The user should be able to enter the message in a TextBox and select the desired method of encryption. Display the encrypted message in a Label.

In a substitution cipher, every character in the English alphabet is represented by a different character in the substitution alphabet. Every time a letter occurs in the English sentence, it is replaced by the letter in the corresponding index of the substitution string. In a transposition cipher, two strings are created. The first new string contains all the characters at the even indices of the input string. The second new string contains all of the characters at the odd indices. The new strings are the encrypted text. For example a transposition cipher for the word "code" would be: "cd oe."

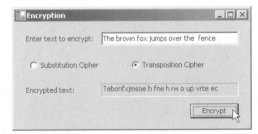

Figure 23.19 **Encryption** application.

a) *Copying the template to your working directory.* Copy the directory C:\Examples\Tutorial23\Exercises\Encryption to your C:\SimplyCSP directory.

b) *Opening the application's template file.* Double click Encryption.sln in the Encryption directory to open the application.

c) *Adding the Encrypt Button's event handler.* Double click the **Encrypt** Button to create an empty event handler.

d) *Determining the cipher method.* Use if...else statements to determine which method of encryption the user has selected and call the appropriate method.

e) *Locating the SubstitutionCipher method.* Locate the SubstitutionCipher method. The English and substitution alphabet strings have been defined for you in this method.

f) **Converting the text input to lowercase.** Add code to the SubstitutionCipher method that uses the ToLower method of the `string` class to make all the characters in the input `string` (txtPlainText.Text) lowercase.

g) **Performing the substitution encryption.** Use nested `for` loops to iterate through each character of the input `string`. When each character from the input `string` is found in the `string` holding the English alphabet, replace the character in the input `string` with the character located at the same index in the substitution `string`.

h) **Displaying the string.** Now that the `string` has been substituted with all the corresponding cipher characters, assign the cipher `string` to the `lblCipherText` Label.

i) **Locating the TranspositionCipher method.** Locate the TranspositionCipher method. Define three variables—a counter variable and two `strings` (each representing a word).

j) **Extracting the first word.** Use a `while` statement to retrieve all the "even" indices (starting from 0) from the input `string`. Increment the counter variable by 2 each time, and add the characters located at even indices to the first `string` created in *Step h*.

k) **Extracting the second word.** Use another `while` statement to retrieve all the "odd" indices (starting from 1) from the same input `string`. Increment the counter variable by 2, and add the characters at odd indices to the second `string` that you created in *Step h*.

l) **Outputting the result.** Add the two `strings` together with a space in between, and output the result to the `lblCipherText` Label.

m) **Running the application.** Select **Debug > Start** to run your application. Enter text into the **Enter text to encrypt:** TextBox. Select the **Substitution Cipher** RadioButton and click the **Encrypt** Button. Verify that the output is the properly encrypted text using the substitution cipher. Select the **Transposition Cipher** RadioButton and click the **Encrypt** Button. Verify that the output is the properly encrypted text using the transposition cipher.

n) **Closing the application.** Close your running application by clicking its close box.

o) **Closing the IDE.** Close Visual Studio .NET by clicking its close box.

23.13 (*Anagram Application*) Write an **Anagram** game that contains an array of preset words. The game should randomly select a word and scramble its letters. A Label displays the scrambled word for the user to guess. If the user guesses correctly, display a message, and repeat the process with a different word. If the guess is incorrect, display a message, and let the user try again (Fig. 23.20).

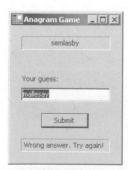

Figure 23.20 **Anagram** application.

a) **Copying the template to your working directory.** Copy the directory C:\Examples\Tutorial23\Exercises\Anagram to your C:\SimplyCSP directory.

b) **Opening the application's template file.** Double click Anagram.sln in the Anagram directory to open the application.

c) **Locating the GenerateAnagram method.** Locate the GenerateAnagram method. It is the first method after the FrmAnagram_Load event handler.

d) **Picking a random word.** Generate a random number to use as the index of the word in the m_strAnagram array. Retrieve the word from the m_strAnagram array, using the first random number as an index. Store the word in another `string` variable. Generate a second random number to store the index of a character to be moved.

e) *Generating the scrambled word.* Use a `for` statement to iterate through the word 20 times. Each time the loop executes, pass the second random number created in *Step d* to the `string` indexer. Append the character returned by the indexer to the end of the `string`, and remove it from its original position. Next, generate a new random number to move a different character during the next iteration of the loop. Remember to output the final word to the `lblAnagram` `Label`.

f) *Defining the Submit Button's event handler.* Double click the **Submit** `Button` to generate an empty event handler.

g) *Testing the user's input.* Use an `if...else` statement to determine whether the user's input matches the actual word. If the user is correct, clear and place the focus on the TextBox and generate a new word. Otherwise, select the user's text and place focus on the `TextBox`.

h) *Running the application.* Select **Debug > Start** to run your application. Submit correct answers and incorrect answers, and verify that the appropriate message is displayed each time.

i) *Closing the application.* Close your running application by clicking its close box.

j) *Closing the IDE.* Close Visual Studio .NET by clicking its close box.

What does this code do? ▶ **23.14** What is assigned to `strResult` when the following code executes?

```
1  string strWord1 = "CHORUS";
2  string strWord2 = "d i n o s a u r";
3  string strWord3 = "The theme is string.";
4  string strResult;
5
6  strResult = strWord1.ToLower();
7  strResult = strResult.Substring( 4 );
8  strWord2 = strWord2.Replace( " ", "" );
9  strWord2 = strWord2.Substring( 4, 4 );
10 strResult = strWord2 + strResult;
11
12 strWord3 = strWord3.Substring(
13     strWord3.IndexOf( " " ) + 1, 3 );
14
15 strResult = strWord3.Insert( 3, strResult );
```

What's wrong with this code? ▶ **23.15** This code should remove all commas from `strTest`. Find the error(s) in the following code.

```
1  string strTest = "Bug,2,Bug";
2  strTest = strTest.Replace( "" );
```

Programming Challenge ▶ **23.16** (*Pig Latin Application*) Write an application that encodes English language phrases into pig Latin (Fig. 23.21). Pig Latin is a form of coded language often used for amusement. Many variations exist in the methods used to form pig Latin phrases. For simplicity, use the following method to form the pig Latin words:

To form the pig Latin version of English-language phrase, the translation proceeds one word at a time. To translate an English word into a pig Latin word, place the first letter of the English word (if it is not a vowel) at the end of the English word and add the letters "ay." If the first letter of the English word is a vowel, place it at the end of the word and add "y." Using this method, the word "jump" becomes "umpjay", the word "the" becomes "hetay" and the word "ace" becomes "ceay." Blanks between words remain blanks.

Assume the following: The English phrase consists of words separated by blanks, there are no punctuation marks, and all words have two or more letters. Enable the user to input a sentence. The TranslateToPigLatin method should translate the sentence into pig Latin, word by word. [*Hint*: You will need to use the Join and Split methods of the String class demonstrated in Fig. 23.16 to form the pig Latin phrases].

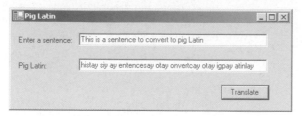

Figure 23.21   Pig Latin application.

a) ***Copying the template to your working directory.*** Copy the directory C:\Examples\ Tutorial23\Exercises\PigLatin to your C:\SimplyCSP directory.

b) ***Opening the application's template file.*** Double click PigLatin.sln in the PigLatin directory to open the application.

c) ***Splitting the sentence.*** Use the Split method on the string passed to the TranslateToPigLatin method. Assign the result of this operation to strWords.

d) ***Retrieving the word's first letter.*** Declare a for loop that iterates through your array of words. As you iterate through the array, store each word's first letter in strTemporary.

e) ***Determining the suffix.*** Use if...else statements to determine the suffix for each word. Store this suffix in strSuffix.

f) ***Generating new words.*** Generate the new words by arranging each word's pieces in the proper order.

g) ***Returning the new sentence.*** When the for loop finishes, use the Join method to combine all of the elements in strWords, and return the new pig Latin sentence.

h) ***Running the application.*** Select **Debug > Start** to run your application. Enter a sentence and click the **Translate** Button. Verify that the sentence is correctly converted into pig Latin.

i) ***Closing the application.*** Close your running application by clicking its close box.

j) ***Closing the IDE.*** Close Visual Studio .NET by clicking its close box.

Objectives

In this tutorial, you will learn to:
- Create, read from, write to and update files.
- Understand a computer's data hierarchy.
- Become familiar with sequential-access file processing.
- Use **StreamReader** and **StreamWriter** classes to read from and write to sequential-access files.
- Add and configure a **MonthCalendar** control.

Outline

Ticket Information Application

Introducing Sequential-Access Files

You have used variables and arrays to store data temporarily—the data is lost when a method or application terminates. When you want to store data for a longer period of time, you can use **files**, which are collections of data that are given a name, such as data.txt or Welcome.sln. Data in files exists even after the program that created the data terminates. Such data often is called **persistent data**. Computers store these files on **secondary storage media**, including magnetic disks (for example, the hard drive of your computer), optical disks (for instance, CD-ROMs or DVDs) and magnetic tapes (which are similar to music cassette tapes).

File processing, which includes creating, reading from, writing to and updating files, is an important capability of C#. It enables C# to support commercial applications that typically process massive amounts of persistent data. In this tutorial, you will learn about **sequential-access files**, which contain information that is read from a file in the order it was originally written to the file. You will learn how to create, open and write to a sequential-access file by building a **Write Event** application. This application allows the user to create or open a **text file** (a file containing human-readable characters) and to input the date, time and description of a community event (such as a concert or a sporting match).

You will then learn how to read data from a file by building the **Ticket Information** application. This application displays data from a file called calendar.txt created by the **Write Event** application.

24.1 Test-Driving the Ticket Information Application

Many communities and businesses use computer applications to allow their members and customers to view information about upcoming events, such as movies, concerts and sporting events. The **Write Event** application you will build in Section 24.4 writes the community event information to a sequential-access file. The **Ticket Information** application you will build in Section 24.5 displays the data stored in the file generated by the **Write Event** application. The **Ticket Information** application must meet the following requirements:

Application Requirements

A local town has asked you to write an application to allow its residents to view community events for the current month. Events taking place in the town include concerts, sporting events and movies. When the user selects a date, the application must indicate whether there are events scheduled for that day. The application must list the scheduled events and allow the user to select a listed event. When the user selects an event, the application must display the time and price and a brief description of the event. The community event information is stored in a sequential-access file named `calendar.txt`.

Your application will allow a user to select a date from a **MonthCalendar** control. Then, the application will open the `calendar.txt` file and read its contents to display information about events scheduled for the selected date. You begin by test-driving the completed application. Then, you will learn the additional C# technologies that you will need to create your own version of this application.

Test-Driving the Ticket Information Application

1. ***Opening the completed application.*** Open the C:\Examples\ Tutorial24\CompletedApplication\TicketInformation directory to locate the **Ticket Information** application. Double click `TicketInformation.sln` to open the application in Visual Studio .NET.

2. ***Running the Ticket Information application.*** Select **Debug > Start** to run the application (Fig. 24.1). The calendar will look different, depending on the date on which you test-drive this application. The calendar should reflect the day and month on which you actually run the application. The Month-Calendar control is similar to the DateTimePicker control (Tutorial 14), except that MonthCalendar allows you to select a range of dates, whereas the DateTimePicker allows you to select the time, but no more than one date. For simplicity, users of this application should select only one date. In addition, the application deals only with the current month, but the Month-Calendar control does allow the user to view calendars of previous or future months by using the arrow buttons.

Arrow buttons allow the user to scroll through months

MonthCalendar control

ComboBox lists any events

TextBox displays event details

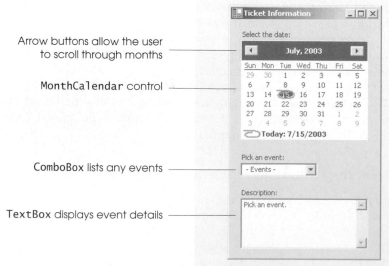

Figure 24.1 **Ticket Information** application's GUI.

(cont.)   3.   ***Getting event information.*** Select the 18th day of the current month in the MonthCalendar. Notice that the ComboBox displays the message "- No Events -" (Fig. 24.2). This is because there are no events scheduled for the 18th. Select the 19th day of the month. Notice that the ComboBox now displays "- Events -". Click the ComboBox to view the scheduled events and select **Comedy club**. The time, price and description of the event appear in the **Description:** TextBox (Fig. 24.2).

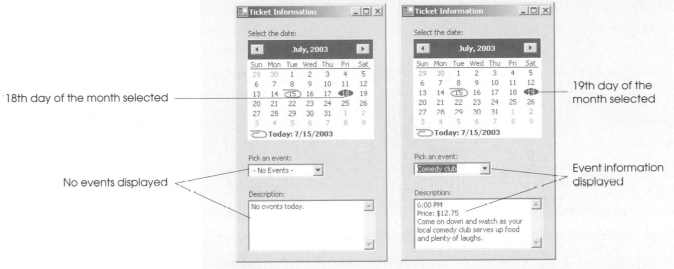

Figure 24.2   **Ticket Information** application displaying event information.

4.   ***Testing the application.*** Select other dates (such as 1, 12 and 30) and view the results.

5.   ***Closing the application.*** Close your running application by clicking its close box.

6.   ***Closing the IDE.*** Close Visual Studio .NET by clicking its close box.

SELF-REVIEW   1.   The _____ control allows a user to select a range of dates.

a) DateTimePicker   b) MonthCalender

c) ComboBox   d) TextBox

2.   The MonthCalendar control is similar to the _____ control.

a) DateTimePicker   b) ComboBox

c) TextBox   d) Timer

Answers: 1) b. 2) a.

24.2 Data Hierarchy

Data items processed by computers form a **data hierarchy** (Fig. 24.3) in which data items become larger and more complex in structure as they progress from bits to characters to fields to larger data structures.

Throughout this book, you have been manipulating data in your applications. The data has been in several forms: decimal digits (0, 1, 2, 3, 4, 5, 6, 7, 8 and 9), letters (A–Z and a–z) and special symbols ($, @, %, &, *, ( ), -, +, ", :, ?, / and many others). Digits, letters and special symbols are referred to as **characters**. The set of all characters used to write applications and represent data items on a particular computer is called that computer's **character set**.

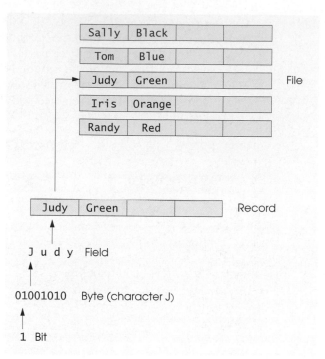

Figure 24.3 Data hierarchy.

The computer's character set is readable and understandable by humans. Ultimately, however, all data items processed by a computer are reduced to combinations of zeros and ones. The smallest data item that computers support is called a **bit**. "Bit" is short for "**binary digit**"—a digit that can be one of two values. Each data item, or bit, can be set only to the value 0 or the value 1. Computer circuitry performs various simple bit manipulations, such as examining the value of a bit, setting the value of a bit and reversing the value of a bit (from 1 to 0 or from 0 to 1). This approach has been adopted because it is simple and economical to build electronic devices that can assume two stable states—0 representing one state and 1 representing the other. It is remarkable that the extensive functions performed by computers involve only the most fundamental manipulations of 0s and 1s.

Because computers can process only 0s and 1s, every character in a computer's character set is represented as a pattern of 0s and 1s. **Bytes** are composed of 8 bits. Characters in C# are **Unicode**® characters, which are composed of 2 bytes. Programming with data in the low-level form of bits is difficult, so programmers create applications and data items with characters, and computers manipulate and process these characters as patterns of bits.

Just as characters are composed of bits, **fields** are composed of characters. A field is a group of characters that conveys some meaning. For example, a field consisting of uppercase and lowercase letters can represent a person's name.

Typically, a **record** (which usually is represented as a `class` in C#) is a collection of several related fields (called member variables in C#). In a payroll system, for example, a record for a particular employee might include the following fields:

1. Employee identification number
2. Name
3. Address
4. Hourly pay rate
5. Number of exemptions claimed
6. Year-to-date earnings
7. Amount of taxes withheld

Thus, a record is a group of related fields. In the preceding example, each field is associated with the same employee. A file is a group of related records. A company's payroll file normally contains one record for each employee. Hence, a payroll file for a small company might contain only 22 records, whereas a payroll file for a large company might contain 100,000 records. It is not unusual for a company to have many files, some containing millions, billions or even trillions of characters of information.

To facilitate the retrieval of specific records from a file, at least one field in each record is chosen as a **record key**. A record key identifies a record as belonging to a particular person or entity and distinguishes that record from all other records. Therefore, the record key must be unique. In the payroll record just described, the employee identification number normally would be chosen as the record key because each employee's identification number is different.

There are many ways to organize records in a file. The most common type of organization is called a sequential-access file, in which records typically are stored in order by a record-key field. In a payroll file, records usually are placed in order by employee identification number. The first employee record in the file contains the lowest employee identification number, and subsequent records contain increasingly higher employee identification numbers.

Most businesses use many different files to store data. For example, a company might have payroll files, accounts receivable files (listing money due from clients), accounts payable files (listing money due to suppliers), inventory files (listing facts about all the items handled by the business) and many other types of files. Sometimes, a group of related files is called a **database**. A collection of programs designed to create and manage databases is called a **database management system** (DBMS). You will learn about databases in Tutorial 25.

SELF-REVIEW

1. The smallest data item a computer can process is called a _____.

    a) database   b) byte

    c) file   d) bit

2. A _____ is a group of related records.

    a) file   b) field

    c) bit   d) byte

Answers: 1) d. 2) a.

24.3 Files and Streams

C# actually views each file as a sequential **stream** of bytes (Fig. 24.4). When a file is opened, C# creates an object and associates a stream with that object.

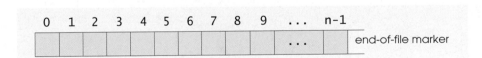

Figure 24.4 C#'s conceptual view of an *n*-byte file.

To perform file processing in C#, the System.IO namespace must be referenced. This namespace includes declarations of stream classes such as **StreamReader** (for text input from a file) and **StreamWriter** (for text output to a file).

Common Programming Error

Having a StreamReader and StreamWriter object open for the same file at the same time causes an error because both objects are attempting to access the same file.

24.4 Writing to a File: Creating the Write Event Application

An important aspect of the **Ticket Information** application is its ability to read data sequentially from a file. You will need to create the file from which the **Ticket Infor-**

mation application will read its data. Therefore, before you create the **Ticket Infor-mation** application, you must learn how to write to a file sequentially.

The **Write Event** application should enable the user to create a new file or open an existing file. The user might want to create a new file for events or update an existing file by adding more event information. You will add this functionality in the following box.

Adding a Dialog to Open or Create a File	1. ***Copying the template to your working directory.*** Copy the C:\Examples\ Tutorial24\TemplateApplication\WriteEvent directory to your C:\SimplyCSP directory.

2. ***Opening the Write Event application's template file.*** Double click WriteEvent.sln in the WriteEvent directory to open the application in Visual Studio .NET.

3. ***Adding a dialog to the Form.*** The application uses the **OpenFileDialog** control to customize the **Open** dialog. To add an OpenFileDialog component to the application, double click the OpenFileDialog control

in the **Windows Forms** tab of the **Toolbox**. Change the control's Name property to objOpenFileDialog. Change its **FileName** property to calen-dar.txt, which will be the default file name displayed in the **Open** dialog. [*Note:* This is the name of the file from which the **Ticket Information** appli-cation retrieves information.] The **Open** dialog normally allows the user to open only existing files, but you also want the user to be able to create a file. For this reason, set the **CheckFileExists** property to false so that the **Open** dialog allows the user to specify a new file name. If the user specifies a file that does not exist, the file is created and opened. Figure 24.5 shows the application in design view after the OpenFileDialog control has been added and renamed.

OpenFileDialog control —

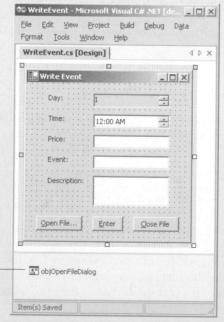

Figure 24.5 OpenFileDialog added and renamed.

(cont.)   4. ***Rearranging and commenting the new control declaration.*** In code view, move the declaration for the `OpenFileDialog` control from line 43 of your code to line 45 of Fig. 24.6, then add the comment in line 44.

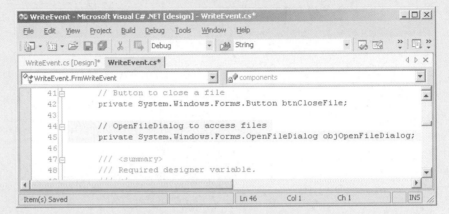

Figure 24.6   Rearranging and commenting the new control declaration.

5. ***Saving the project.*** Select **File > Save All** to save your modified code.

The **Write Event** application stores the user-input information in a text file. It expects the user to open or create a file with the extension `.txt`. If the user does not do so, the application displays an error message. The following box guides you through adding this functionality.

Determining Whether a File Name Is Valid

1. ***Adding the header for the CheckValidity method.*** Add lines 272–276 of Fig. 24.7 to the application. The `CheckValidity` method receives a file name as a `string` and returns a `bool` value. If the file name is valid, the method returns `true`. Otherwise, the method returns `false`.

CheckValidity method header —

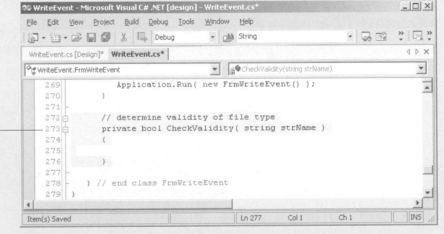

Figure 24.7   Method `CheckValidity` header.

2. ***Displaying a MessageBox to indicate an invalid file name.*** Add lines 275–282 of Fig. 24.8 to the `CheckValidity` method. `String` method `EndsWith` (line 276) returns `false` if `strName` does not end with `.txt`, the extension that indicates a text file. Lines 278–280 display a `MessageBox` informing the user that the application expects a text (`.txt`) file.

(cont.)

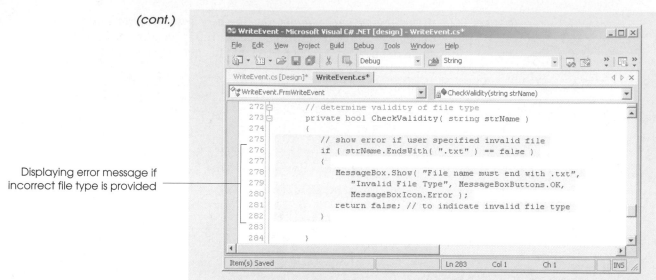

Displaying error message if incorrect file type is provided

Figure 24.8 Displaying an error message indicating an invalid file name.

3. *Receiving a valid file name.* Add lines 284–291 of Fig. 24.9 to the `if` statement. If a valid file name is entered, the `CheckValidity` method should return `true`. The GUI should indicate that the user cannot create or open another file but may enter data into the file or close the file. For this reason, line 287 disables the **Open File...** `Button`, while lines 288–289 enable the **Enter** and **Close File** `Buttons`, respectively. The method returns `true` (line 290) to indicate that the user entered a valid file name.

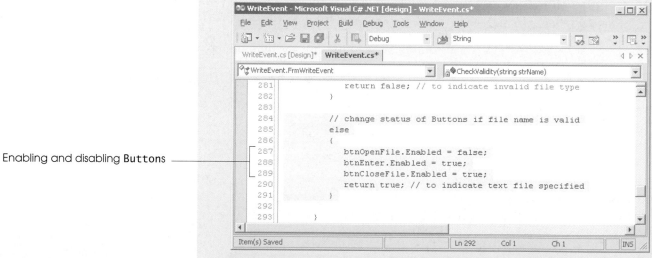

Enabling and disabling `Buttons`

Figure 24.9 Changing the GUI's appearance if a valid file name is entered.

4. *Saving the project.* Select **File > Save All** to save your modified code.

You have added the `OpenFileDialog` control to allow users to open a file and a method that determines whether the user has entered a valid file name. Now you will add code that associates the specified file with a stream.

Creating a StreamWriter Object

1. *Referencing the `System.IO` namespace to enable file processing.* To easily access the classes and methods that will enable you to perform file processing with sequential-access files, you must reference the `System.IO` namespace. Accordingly, add line 7 of Fig. 24.10.

(cont.)

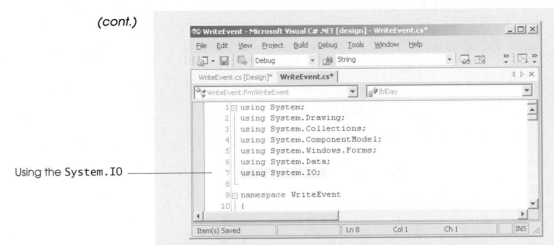

Figure 24.10   System.IO namespace referenced from the Frm-WriteEvent class.

Using the System.IO

2. ***Declaring a StreamWriter variable.*** The System.IO namespace includes the StreamWriter class, which is used to create objects for writing text to a file. You will use a StreamWriter to write data into the file created or opened by the user. Add line 53 of Fig. 24.11 to the FrmWriteEvent class declaration to declare the variable that will be assigned a StreamWriter object.

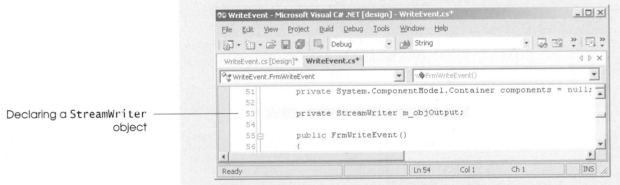

Declaring a StreamWriter object

Figure 24.11   Declaring a StreamWriter object.

3. ***Creating the Open File... Button's Click event handler.*** In design view, double click the **Open File...** Button on the **Write Event** application's Form (Fig. 24.12) to create the empty btnOpenFile_Click event handler.

4. ***Displaying the Open dialog.*** Be sure to add the comments and break the header as shown in Fig. 24.13 so that the line numbers in your code match those presented in this tutorial. Then, add lines 303–304 of Fig. 24.13 to the event handler. When the user clicks the **Open File...** Button, the **Show-Dialog** method of the OpenFileDialog control displays the **Open** dialog to allow the user to open a file (line 304). If the user specifies a file that does not exist, it will be created. The user can use the default file name (calendar.txt) or specify another file name. Line 304 assigns the return value of the ShowDialog method to a DialogResult variable named result.

(cont.)

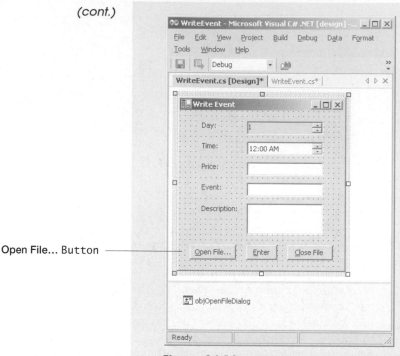

Figure 24.12 **Write Event** application **Form** in design view.

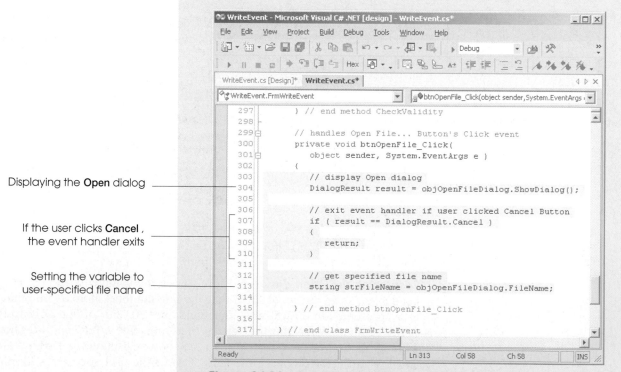

Figure 24.13 Displaying the **Open** dialog and retrieving the result.

5. *Exiting event handler if the user clicks the Cancel Button.* Add lines 306–310 of Fig. 24.13 to the event handler. The value of the `DialogResult` variable specifies whether the user clicked the **Cancel** Button in the **Open** dialog. If the user did so, the event handler exits (line 309). At this point, the user can still open or create a file by clicking the enabled **Open File...** Button again.

(cont.)

6. ***Retrieving the file name.*** Add lines 312–313 of Fig. 24.13 to the event handler. The **FileName** property of OpenFileDialog specifies the file name that the user selected (line 313). The application stores the path and file name in strFileName. The file name will be tested to determine whether it is valid then, it will be used to initialize the StreamWriter object.

7. ***Checking for a valid file type.*** Add lines 315–317 of Fig. 24.14 to the event handler. Line 316 invokes the CheckValidity method (which you defined in the previous box) to determine whether the specified file is a text file (that is, the file name ends with ".txt").

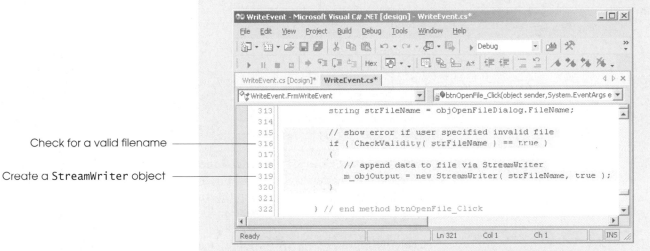

Check for a valid filename

Create a StreamWriter object

Figure 24.14   Validating the filename and initializing a StreamWriter object.

8. ***Initializing a StreamWriter object.*** Add lines 318–320 of Fig. 24.14 to the event handler. The call to the StreamWriter constructor (line 319) creates StreamWriter object m_objOutput, which will be used to write to the new file specified by the user. Notice that the StreamWriter constructor takes two arguments. The first indicates the name of the file (specified by the strFileName variable) to which you will write information. The second is a bool value that determines whether the StreamWriter will append information to the end of the file. You pass value true so that any information written to the file will be appended to the end of the file.

9. ***Saving the project.*** Select **File > Save All** to save your modified code.

Now that the application can open a file, the user can input information that will be written to that file. In the following box, you will add code that makes the **Enter** Button's Click event handler write the data to the text file.

Common Programming Error

When you open an existing file by invoking the StreamWriter constructor with a false second argument, data previously contained in the file will be lost.

Writing Information to a Sequential-Access File

1. ***Clearing user input from the TextBoxes and resetting the NumericUpDown control.*** Add lines 324–332 of Fig. 24.15 to the application below the btnOpenFile_Click event handler. After the user's input is processed, the **Enter** Button's Click event handler will invoke the ClearUserInput method to clear the TextBoxes and to reset the NumericUpDown control's value to 1 (the first day of the month).

2. ***Creating the btnEnter_Click event handler.*** In design view, double click the **Enter** Button to add the btnEnter_Click event handler.

(cont.)

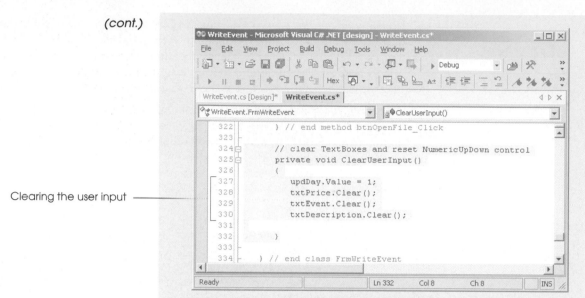

Clearing the user input

Figure 24.15 Clearing the user input.

3. *Defining the btnEnter_Click event handler.* Be sure to add the comments and break the header as shown in Fig. 24.16 so that the line numbers in your code match those presented in this tutorial. Then, add lines 339–345 of Fig. 24.16 to the event handler. Lines 340–344 write the user input line-by-line to the file by using the StreamWriter's **WriteLine** method. The WriteLine method writes its argument to the file, followed by a newline character. The information is written to the file in the following order: day of the event, time, price, event name and description. Each piece of information is written on a separate line of the file. Line 345 invokes the ClearUserInput method that you defined in *Step 1* of this box.

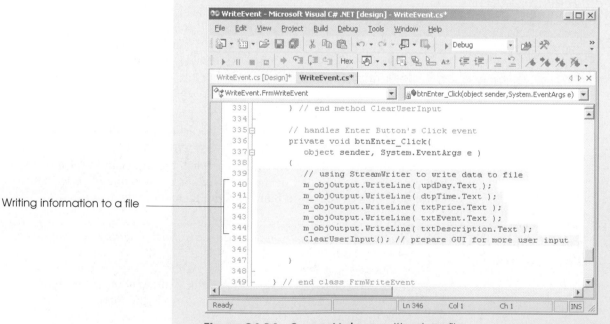

Writing information to a file

Figure 24.16 StreamWriter writing to a file.

4. *Saving the project.* Select **File > Save All** to save your modified code.

You should close the connection to the file after you have finished processing it. This allows other methods or applications to view and modify it. You will add this capability to the **Close File** Button's `Click` event handler in the following box.

Closing the
StreamWriter

1. ***Creating the `btnClose_Click` event handler.*** Double click the **Close File** Button of the **Write Event** application's Form. The `btnClose_Click` event handler appears in the `WriteEvent.cs` file.

2. ***Defining the `btnClose_Click` event handler.*** Be sure to add the comments and break the header as shown in Fig. 24.17 so that the line numbers in your code match those presented in this tutorial. Then, add lines 354–359 of Fig. 24.17 to the event handler. Line 354 uses the `StreamWriter`'s **Close** method to close the stream. Line 357 re-enables the **Open File...** Button in case the user would like to create or update another sequential-access file. Lines 358–359 disable the **Enter** and **Close File** Buttons because users should not be able to click these Buttons when a file is not open.

Closing the `StreamWriter` object ———

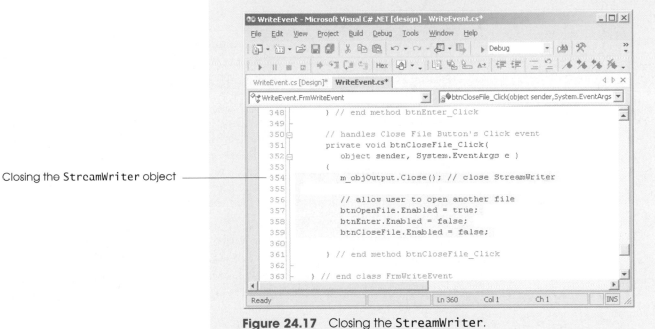

Figure 24.17   Closing the `StreamWriter`.

3. ***Saving the project.*** Select **File > Save All** to save your modified code.

You have now successfully created the **Write Event** application. You will test this application to see how it works and will view the file contents in the following box.

Writing Event
Information to a File

1. ***Running the application.*** Select **Debug > Start** to run your application (Fig. 24.18)

Figure 24.18   **Write Event** application running.

(cont.)

2. ***Creating a file.*** Click the **Open File...** Button to create the file to which you will write. The **Open** dialog (Fig. 24.19) appears. Browse to the directory `C:\Examples\Tutorial24\TemplateApplication\TicketInformation\bin\Debug`. [*Note*: An existing `calendar.txt` file should appear in the **Open** dialog.] The file name `calendar.txt` should be displayed in the **File name:** field. Click the **Open** Button to open the existing `calendar.txt` file.

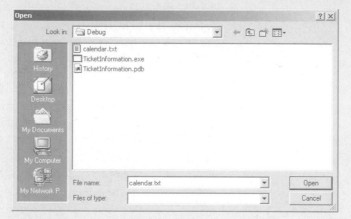

Figure 24.19   **Open** dialog displaying the contents of the template **Ticket Information** application's **Debug** directory.

3. ***Inputting event information***. In the **Day:** NumericUpDown control, select 4 to indicate that the event is scheduled on the fourth day of the month. Enter 2:30 PM in the **Time:** DateTimePicker. Type 12.50 in the **Price:** TextBox. Enter Arts and Crafts Fair in the **Event:** TextBox. In the **Description:** TextBox, enter the information Take part in creating various types of arts and crafts at this fair. Click the **Enter** Button to add this event's information to the `calendar.txt` file.

4. ***Inputting more event information.*** Write more event information to the file by repeating *Step 3* with your own sets of events.

5. ***Closing the file.*** When you have entered all the events you wish, click the **Close File** Button. This closes the `calendar.txt` file and prevents any more events from being written.

6. ***Closing the application.*** Close your running application by clicking its close box.

7. ***Opening and closing the sequential-access file.*** Use Visual Studio .NET to open `calendar.txt`. Select **File > Open > File...** to display the **Open** dialog. Select the `calendar.txt` file and click **Open**. Scroll down towards the bottom of the file. The information you entered in *Step 3* should appear in the file, similar to Fig. 24.20. Select **File > Close** to close the `calendar.txt` file.

Day and time of event, ticket price, event name and description —

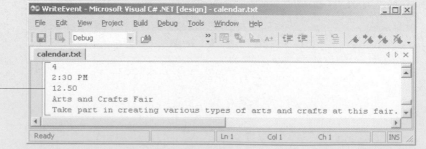

Figure 24.20   Sequential-access file generated by **Write Event** application.

8. ***Closing the IDE.*** Close Visual Studio .NET by clicking its close box.

Figure 24.21 presents the source code for the **Write Event** application. The lines of code that contain new programming concepts that you learned in this tutorial are highlighted.

```
1    using System;
2    using System.Drawing;
3    using System.Collections;
4    using System.ComponentModel;
5    using System.Windows.Forms;
6    using System.Data;
7    using System.IO;
8
9    namespace WriteEvent
10   {
11       /// <summary>
12       /// Summary description for FrmWriteEvent.
13       /// </summary>
14       public class FrmWriteEvent : System.Windows.Forms.Form
15       {
16          // Label and NumericUpDown to choose day
17          private System.Windows.Forms.Label lblDay;
18          private System.Windows.Forms.NumericUpDown updDay;
19
20          // Label and DateTimePicker to choose time
21          private System.Windows.Forms.Label lblTime;
22          private System.Windows.Forms.DateTimePicker dtpTime;
23
24          // Label and TextBox to input price
25          private System.Windows.Forms.Label lblPrice;
26          private System.Windows.Forms.TextBox txtPrice;
27
28          // Label and TextBox to input event
29          private System.Windows.Forms.Label lblEvent;
30          private System.Windows.Forms.TextBox txtEvent;
31
32          // Label and TextBox to input description
33          private System.Windows.Forms.Label lblDescription;
34          private System.Windows.Forms.TextBox txtDescription;
35
36          // Button to open an existing file
37          private System.Windows.Forms.Button btnOpenFile;
38
39          // Button to write data to the file
40          private System.Windows.Forms.Button btnEnter;
41
42          // Button to close a file
43          private System.Windows.Forms.Button btnCloseFile;
44
45          // OpenFileDialog to access files
46          private System.Windows.Forms.OpenFileDialog objOpenFileDialog;
47
48          /// <summary>
49          /// Required designer variable.
50          /// </summary>
51          private System.ComponentModel.Container components = null;
52
53          private StreamWriter m_objOutput;
54
```

Using the `System.IO` — line 7

`StreamWriter` that will write text to a file — line 53

Figure 24.21   Write Event application code. (Part 1 of 4.)

```
55        public FrmWriteEvent()
56        {
57           //
58           // Required for Windows Form Designer support
59           //
60           InitializeComponent();
61
62           //
63           // TODO: Add any constructor code after InitializeComponent
64           // call
65           //
66        }
67
68        /// <summary>
69        /// Clean up any resources being used.
70        /// </summary>
71        protected override void Dispose( bool disposing )
72        {
73           if( disposing )
74           {
75              if (components != null)
76              {
77                 components.Dispose();
78              }
79           }
80           base.Dispose( disposing );
81        }
82
83        // Windows Form Designer generated code
84
85        /// <summary>
86        /// The main entry point for the application.
87        /// </summary>
88        [STAThread]
89        static void Main()
90        {
91           Application.Run( new FrmWriteEvent() );
92        }
93
94        // determine validity of file type
95        private bool CheckValidity( string strName )
96        {
97           // show error if user specified invalid file
98           if ( strName.EndsWith( ".txt" ) == false )
99           {
100              MessageBox.Show( "File name must end with .txt",
101                 "Invalid File Type", MessageBoxButtons.OK,
102                 MessageBoxIcon.Error );
103              return false; // to indicate invalid file type
104           }
105
106           // change status of Buttons if file name is valid
107           else
108           {
109              btnOpenFile.Enabled = false;
110              btnEnter.Enabled = true;
111              btnCloseFile.Enabled = true;
```

Figure 24.21 Write Event application code. (Part 2 of 4.)

```
112              return true; // to indicate text file specified
113           }
114
115        } // end method CheckValidity
116
117        // handles Open File... Button's Click event
118        private void btnOpenFile_Click(
119           object sender, System.EventArgs e )
120        {
121           // display Open dialog
122           DialogResult result = objOpenFileDialog.ShowDialog();
123
124           // exit event handler if user clicked Cancel Button
125           if ( result == DialogResult.Cancel )
126           {
127              return;
128           }
129
130           // get specified file name
131           string strFileName = objOpenFileDialog.FileName;
132
133           // show error if user specified invalid file
134           if ( CheckValidity( strFileName ) == true )
135           {
136              // append data to file via StreamWriter
137              m_objOutput = new StreamWriter( strFileName, true );
138           }
139
140        } // end method btnOpenFile_Click
141
142        // clear TextBoxes and reset NumericUpDown control
143        private void ClearUserInput()
144        {
145           updDay.Value = 1;
146           txtPrice.Clear();
147           txtEvent.Clear();
148           txtDescription.Clear();
149
150        } // end method ClearUserInput
151
152        // handles Enter Button's Click event
153        private void btnEnter_Click(
154           object sender, System.EventArgs e )
155        {
156           // using StreamWriter to write data to file
157           m_objOutput.WriteLine( updDay.Text );
158           m_objOutput.WriteLine( dtpTime.Text );
159           m_objOutput.WriteLine( txtPrice.Text );
160           m_objOutput.WriteLine( txtEvent.Text );
161           m_objOutput.WriteLine( txtDescription.Text );
162           ClearUserInput(); // prepare GUI for more user input
163
164        } // end method btnEnter_Click
165
166        // handles Close File Button's Click event
167        private void btnCloseFile_Click(
168           object sender, System.EventArgs e )
169        {
```

Labels in margin:
- Retrieve the user input from the **Open** dialog (line 122)
- Storing filename entered by user (line 131)
- Create a **StreamWriter** object to associate a stream with the user-specified text file (line 137)
- Append data to the end of the file (lines 157–161)

Figure 24.21   **Write Event** application code. (Part 3 of 4.)

Closing the file's
associated stream

```
170            m_objOutput.Close(); // close StreamWriter
171
172        // allow user to open another file
173        btnOpenFile.Enabled = true;
174        btnEnter.Enabled = false;
175        btnCloseFile.Enabled = false;
176
177    } // end method btnCloseFile_Click
178
179  } // end class FrmWriteEvent
180 }
```

Figure 24.21   **Write Event** application code. (Part 4 of 4.)

24.5 Building the Ticket Information Application

Now that you have created the **Write Event** application to enable a user to write community-event information to a sequential-access text file, you will create the **Ticket Information** application you test-drove at the beginning of the tutorial. First you need to analyze the application. The following pseudocode describes the basic operation of the **Ticket Information** application:

> When the Form loads:
> > Display the current day's events
>
> When the user selects a date on the calendar:
> > Display the selected day's events
>
> When the user selects an event from the Pick an event: ComboBox:
> > Retrieve index of selected item in the Pick an event: ComboBox
> > Display event information in the Description: TextBox
>
> When method CreateEventList is called:
> > Extract data for the current day from calendar.txt
> > Clear the Pick an event: ComboBox
> >
> > If events are scheduled for that day
> > > Add each event to the Pick an event: ComboBox
> > > DIsplay "- Events -" in the Pick an event: ComboBox
> > > Display "Pick an event." in the Description: TextBox
> > Else
> > > DIsplay "- No Events -" in the Pick an event: ComboBox
> > > Display "No events today." in the Description: TextBox
>
> When method ExtractData is called:
> > Retrieve the selected date from the calendar
> > Open calendar.txt file for reading
> > Read the first line of the file
> >
> > While there are events left in the file and the number of events is less than 10
> >
> > > If the current event is for the day selected by the user
> > > > Store the event information
> > > > Increment the number of events for the selected day
> > > Else
> > > > Move to the beginning of the next record in the file
> > > Read the next line of the file

Now that you have test-driven the **Ticket Information** application and studied its pseudocode representation, you will use an ACE table to help you convert the pseudocode to C#. Figure 24.22 lists the actions, controls and events that you will help you complete your own version of this application.

Action/Control/Event (ACE) Table for the Ticket Information Application

Action	Control/Object	Event/Method
Label the application's controls	lblDay, lblTime lblPrice, lblEvent, lblDescription	Application is run
	FrmEvents	Load
Display the current day's events		
	mvwDate	DateChanged
Display the selected day's events		
	cboEvent	Selected-IndexChanged
Retrieve index of selected item in the Pick an event: ComboBox	cboEvent	
Display event information in the Description: TextBox	txtDescription	
		Create-EventList
Extract data for the current day		
Clear the Pick an event: ComboBox	cboEvent	
If events are scheduled for that day 　Add each event to the Pick an event: ComboBox	cboEvent, m_strData	
Display "- Events -" in the Pick an event: ComboBox	cboEvent	
Display "No events today." in the Description: TextBox	txtDescription	
Else 　Display "- No Events -" in the Pick an event: ComboBox	cboEvent	
Display "No events today." in the Description: TextBox	txtDescription	
		ExtractData
Retrieve the selected date from the calendar	mvwDate	
Open calendar.txt file for reading	objInput	
Read the first line of the file	objInput	
While there are events left in the file and the number of events is less than 10	objInput	
If the current event is for the day selected by the user 　　Store the event information	m_strData, strLine, objInput	
Increment the number of events for the selected day		
Else 　　Move to the beginning of the next record in the file	objInput	
Read the next line of the file	objInput	

Figure 24.22 ACE table for the **Ticket Information** application.

The **Ticket Information** application allows the user to view the information for a specific date by selecting the date from a MonthCalendar control. The following box guides you through configuring the MonthCalendar control.

Adding a MonthCalendar Control

1. *Copying the template to your working directory.* Copy the C:\Examples\ Tutorial24\TemplateApplication\TicketInformation directory to your C:\SimplyCSP directory.

2. *Opening the Ticket Information application's template file.* Double click TicketInformation.sln in the TicketInformation directory to open the application in Visual Studio .NET. The template Form in design view looks like Fig. 24.23. The template also provides the empty methods CreateEventList and ExtractData. You will add code to these methods later.

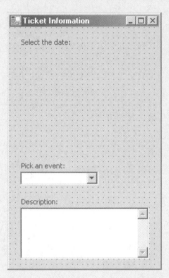

Figure 24.23 MonthCalendar template application's Form.

3. *Add a MonthCalendar control to the Form.* Double click the MonthCalendar control

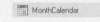

in the **Windows Form** tab of the **Toolbox**. Click the MonthCalendar control on the Form. The **Properties** window should display the control's properties. Change the Name property to mvwDate. Set the Location of the MonthCalendar control to 16, 32.

4. *Rearranging and commenting the new control declaration.* In code view, move the declaration for the OpenFileDialog control from line 25 of your code to line 17 of Fig. 24.24, and update the comment in line 15.

5. *Saving the project.* Select **File > Save All** to save your modified code.

Good Programming Practice

Prefix the names of MonthCalendar controls with mvw.

(cont.)

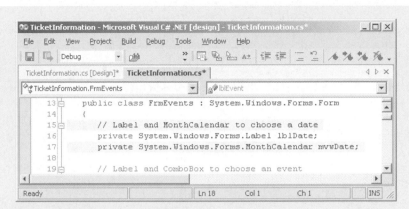

Figure 24.24   Rearranging and commenting the new control declaration.

Now that you have added the `MonthCalendar` control, you can begin writing code for the **Ticket Information** application. For this application, you will create two methods named `CreateEventList` and `ExtractData`. The template for this application provides the method headers for both `CreateEventList` and `ExtractData`. You will define these methods later in this tutorial. Before adding any functionality to the application, you will reference `System.IO` and create two instance variables in the following box.

Beginning to Build the Ticket Information Application

1. *Referencing the System.IO namespace.* You must reference the `System.IO` namespace to allow the application to easily use the `StreamReader` class to read information from a sequential-access file. Accordingly, add line 7 of Fig. 24.25 before the class declaration.

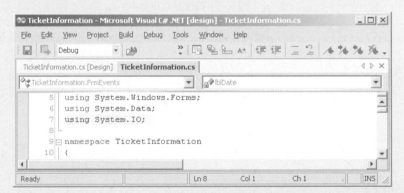

Figure 24.25   `System.IO` namespace referenced from `FrmEvents`.

2. *Adding instance variables.* Add lines 33–37 of Fig. 24.26 to the application. To keep track of information, you will store the event information read from the file in the `m_strData` array (line 34) and the number of events for a specified day in `m_intNumberOfEvents` (line 37). For simplicity, the `m_strData` array is initialized with ten rows of five items each (allowing up to ten total events per day).

3. *Saving the project.* Select **File > Save All** to save your modified code.

(cont.)

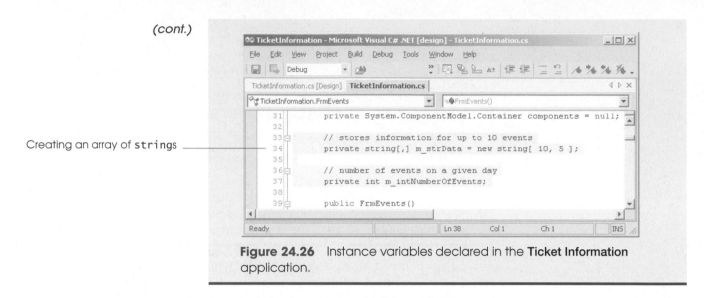

Creating an array of `strings`

Figure 24.26 Instance variables declared in the **Ticket Information** application.

When you run the **Ticket Information** application, by default, the current day should be selected in the `MonthCalendar` control. The application should show the list of the day's events in the `ComboBox`. Recall that, if there are no events for the day, the `ComboBox` displays `"- No Events -"`. In the following box, you will invoke a method from the Form's `Load` event handler to set the display in the `ComboBox` appropriately.

Handling the Form's Load Event

1. ***Defining the Form's Load event.*** Double click the Form in design view to generate the `FrmEvents_Load` event handler. Be sure to add the comments and break the header as shown in Fig. 24.27 so that the line numbers in your code match those presented in this tutorial. Then, add lines 172–173 of Fig. 24.27 to the event handler. Line 173 invokes the `CreateEventList` method. You will soon add code to `CreateEventList` to populate the `ComboBox` with any events scheduled for the current day.

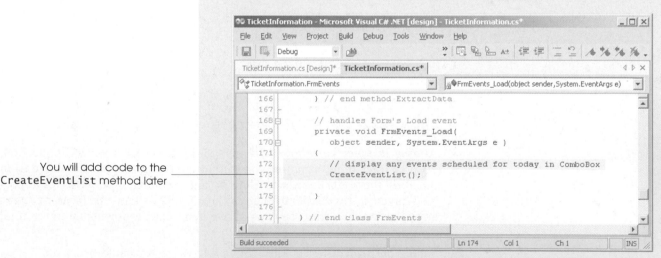

You will add code to the `CreateEventList` method later

Figure 24.27 Load event handler calling method `CreateEventList`.

2. ***Saving the project.*** Select **File > Save All** to save your modified code.

When the user selects a date in the `MonthCalendar` control, the **DateChanged** event is raised. You add code to the event handler that invokes the `CreateEventList` method in the following box.

Handling the
MonthCalendar's
DateChanged Event

1. *Creating the* **MonthCalendar's** *DateChanged event handler.* In design view, double click the MonthCalendar to generate the empty event handler mvwDate_DateChanged.

2. *Invoking the* **CreateEventList** *method.* Be sure to add the comments and break the header as shown in Fig. 24.28 so that the line numbers in your code match those presented in this tutorial. Then, add lines 182–183 of Fig. 24.28 to the mvwDate_DateChanged event handler. Line 183 invokes the Create-EventList method, which you will define in the next box.

Calling the
CreateEventList method

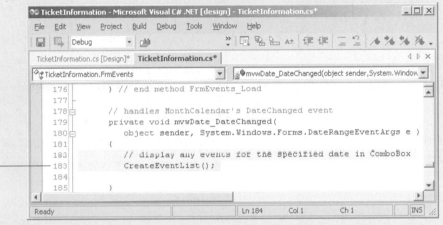

Figure 24.28 MonthCalendar's DateChanged event handler.

3. *Saving the project.* Select **File > Save All** to save your modified code.

The application invokes the CreateEventList method during the Form's Load event and the MonthCalendar's DateChanged event. The CreateEventList method will populate the ComboBox with event names if there are any events for the date the user chooses, or it will indicate that the event list is empty if there are no events for that day. You define this functionality in the following box.

Defining the
CreateEventList
Method

1. *Setting variables and clearing the* **ComboBox** *in the* **CreateEventList** *method.* Add lines 159–166 of Fig. 24.29 to the CreateEventList method. The CreateEventList method first declares a counter, intCount (line 159), that will be used to iterate through the events. Line 163 invokes the Extract-Data method, passing the DateTime that is currently selected in the Month-Calendar. This date is specified by the MonthCalendar control's **SelectionStart** property. You will define the ExtractData method in the next box. The ExtractData method will store event information in the m_strData array and assign the number of events scheduled for the specified date to m_intNumberOfEvents. The Items.Clear method removes any events currently displayed in the ComboBox (line 166).

2. *Setting events displayed in the* **ComboBox.** Add lines 168–188 of Fig. 24.30 to the CreateEventList method. If there are events scheduled for the chosen day (line 169), then the for statement iterates through the m_strData array and adds the name of each event to the ComboBox (lines 171–176). The CreateEventList method informs the user that there are events scheduled for the specified day by using the Text properties of the ComboBox and Text-Box (lines 179–180). If there are events for the chosen day, then the ComboBox displays "- Events -" and the TextBox displays "Pick an event.". If there are no events for the chosen day, the ComboBox displays "- No Events -" and the TextBox displays "No events today." (lines 186–187).

(cont.)

You will add code to the
ExtractData method in the next
box

Figure 24.29 `CreateEventList` modified to call the `ExtractData` method and clear the **ComboBox**.

Extracting an event name
from array and displaying
it in the **ComboBox**

Indicating that events are
scheduled for the day

Indicating that no events are
scheduled for the day

Figure 24.30 Displaying the events scheduled for the specified day.

3. **Saving the project.** Select **File > Save All** to save your modified code.

As described in *Step 1* of the previous box, the ExtractData method uses a variable of the DateTime type (dtmDay) as its only parameter. The ExtractData method assigns the information about any events scheduled for that day to the m_strData array and assigns the number of events for that day to the m_intNumberOfEvents variable. You define the ExtractData method in the following box.

Reading a Sequential-Access File

1. ***Adding variables to the ExtractData method.*** Add lines 196–201 of Fig. 24.31 to the ExtractData method. The DateTime selected in the MonthCalendar control is passed to the ExtractData method as the dtmDay parameter. The intChosenDay variable (line 197) stores the day selected using Day property of the DateTime variable dtmDay. The intFileDay variable (line 198) will store the day of the event read from the file. The intLineNumbers variable (line 199) will store the number of lines to skip between events in the file. The ExtractData method will assign the number of events scheduled for the specified date to the m_intNumberOfEvents variable, which is initialized to 0 in line 201.

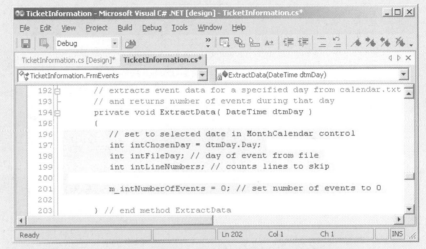

Figure 24.31 ExtractData method's variable declarations.

2. ***Using a StreamReader to read from the file.*** Add lines 203–208 of Fig. 24.32 to the method. To read from the file, ExtractData creates a new StreamReader object (lines 204–205), passing the name of the file to be read ("calendar.txt"). Recall that you wrote information to this file using the **Write Event** application earlier in this tutorial. [*Note*: Because the data file is in the same directory as the application's executable (C:\SimplyCSP\TicketInformation\bin\Debug), you do not need to use the full path name.]

The **ReadLine** method (line 208) of the StreamReader reads a line of characters up to and including a newline character from the specified stream (objInput) and returns the characters as a string. Line 208 assigns the first line of the file to strLine.

Creating a StreamReader object to read the calendar.txt file

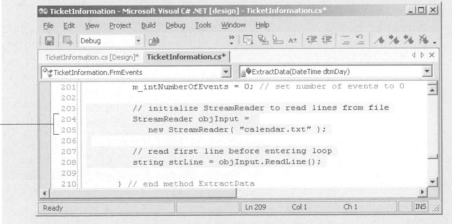

Figure 24.32 Using StreamReader to read data from a sequential-access file.

(cont.)

3. ***Extracting the day from an event in the file.*** Add lines 210–216 of Fig. 24.33 to the `ExtractData` method. The `while` statement determines whether there is more information to read in the file (lines 211–212). This condition ensures that the end of the file has not been reached, at which point looping should stop. This is done by using the `StreamReader` object's **Peek** method, which returns `-1` if there are no more characters to read in the file (that is, the end of the file has been reached). The condition also ensures that no more than 10 events for the specified day are read from the file (that is, `m_intNumberOfEvents` is less than 10). This constraint is necessary due to the fixed size of the `m_strData` array. If these conditions are met, the body of the `while` statement executes. Line 214 converts the line read from the file (that is, the day of the event) to an `int` and assigns that value to `intFileDay`. The first time the loop executes, `strLine` contains the first line in the file.

Verify that the end of the file has not been reached and less than 10 events are stored in the array

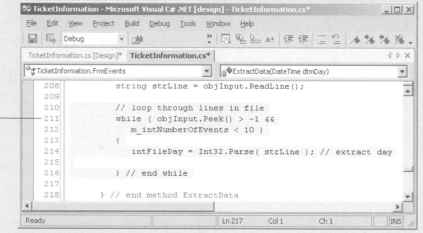

Figure 24.33 Extracting the day from an event entry in the file.

4. ***Reading event information from the sequential-access file.*** Add lines 216–240 of Fig. 24.34 to the `ExtractData` method's `while` statement. The `while` statement reads each event sequentially from the file. If the day of the event read from the file (`intFileDay`) and the specified day (`intChosenDay`) are the same (line 218), then the event information (day, time, ticket price, name and description) is read from the file and is stored in the `m_strData` array (lines 220–228).

Recall that when you created the **Write Event** application, each piece of data (day, time, price, event and description) was written to `calendar.txt` on a separate line, so the event data is retrieved using the `ReadLine` method. Each event for the chosen day is placed in its own row of the array (indicated by `m_intNumberOfEvents`), and each piece of event information is placed in its own column of the array. Line 229 increments `m_intNumberOfEvents` to indicate that an event has been scheduled for that date.

If `intFileDay` and the selected day do not match, then the `Stream-Reader` skips to the next event, using a `for` loop (lines 234–236). Line 240 then reads the next line in the file that contains an event's date. This entire process is repeated until the end of the file is reached or until 10 events have been added to the `m_strData` array.

5. ***Saving the project.*** Select **File > Save All** to save your modified code.

(cont.)

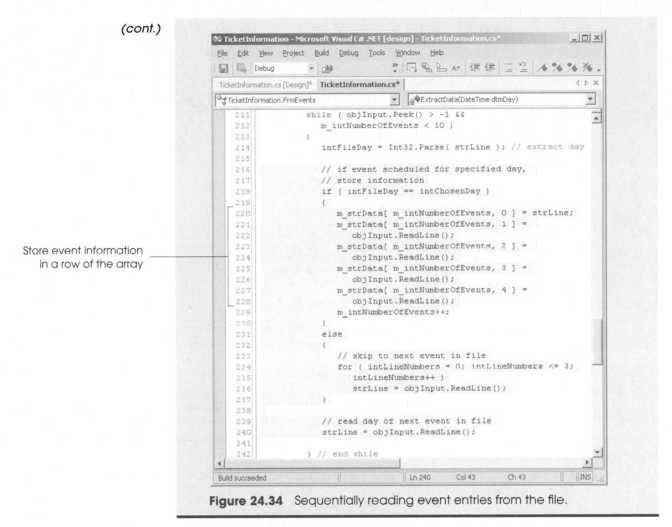

Store event information
in a row of the array

Figure 24.34 Sequentially reading event entries from the file.

The ComboBox displays the names of any events scheduled for the date specified in the MonthCalendar control. When the user selects the community event from the ComboBox, the SelectedIndexChanged event is raised and the description of the community event is displayed in the TextBox. The following box explains how to add this functionality.

Handling the **SelectedIndex- Changed** *Event*	1. ***Creating the ComboBox's*** ***SelectedIndexChanged*** ***event handler.*** In design view, double click the ComboBox to generate the empty event handler cboEvent_SelectedIndexChanged.
	2. ***Displaying event information.*** Be sure to add the comments and break the header as shown in Fig. 24.35 so that the line numbers in your code match those presented in this tutorial. Then, add lines 269–277 of Fig. 24.35 to the event handler. When the user selects an event in the ComboBox, the cboEvent_SelectedIndexChanged event handler displays information about the event in the txtDescription TextBox. The SelectedIndex property of the ComboBox returns the index number of the selected event, which is equivalent to the row number of the event in the m_strData array.
	The event handler appends descriptive text, newline characters, the time the event starts (lines 270–271), the ticket price (lines 273–274) and the event's description (lines 276–277) to the TextBox's Text property. Add comments before and after the event handler (lines 265 and 279), and add a comment to the end of the mvwDate_DateChanged event handler (line 263).

(cont.)

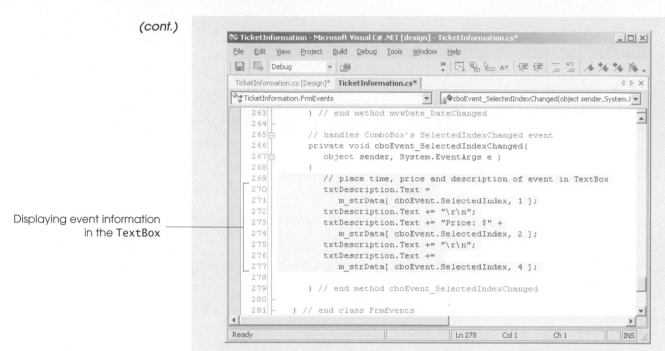

Displaying event information in the TextBox

Figure 24.35 cboEvent_SelectedIndexChanged defined to display event information.

3. **Running the application.** Select **Debug > Start** to run your application. Select various days of the current month until you find a day with events listed. Select an event from the ComboBox to ensure that your application works correctly.

4. **Closing the application.** Close your running application by clicking its close box.

5. **Closing the IDE.** Close Visual Studio .NET by clicking its close box.

Figure 24.36 presents the source code for the **Ticket Information** application. The lines of code that contain new programming concepts that you learned in this tutorial are highlighted.

```
1   using System;
2   using System.Drawing;
3   using System.Collections;
4   using System.ComponentModel;
5   using System.Windows.Forms;
6   using System.Data;
7   using System.IO;
8
9   namespace TicketInformation
10  {
11      /// <summary>
12      /// Summary description for FrmEvents.
13      /// </summary>
14      public class FrmEvents : System.Windows.Forms.Form
15      {
16          // Label and MonthCalendar to choose a date
17          private System.Windows.Forms.Label lblDate;
18          private System.Windows.Forms.MonthCalendar mvwDate;
```

Using the System.IO

Figure 24.36 Ticket Information application code. (Part 1 of 5.)

```
19
20        // Label and ComboBox to choose an event
21        private System.Windows.Forms.Label lblEvent;
22        private System.Windows.Forms.ComboBox cboEvent;
23
24        // Label and TextBox to input a description
25        private System.Windows.Forms.Label lblDescription;
26        private System.Windows.Forms.TextBox txtDescription;
27
28        /// <summary>
29        /// Required designer variable.
30        /// </summary>
31        private System.ComponentModel.Container components = null;
32
33        // stores information for up to 10 events
34        private string[,] m_strData = new string[ 10, 5 ];
35
36        // number of events on a given day
37        private int m_intNumberOfEvents;
38
39        public FrmEvents()
40        {
41           //
42           // Required for Windows Form Designer support
43           //
44           InitializeComponent();
45
46           //
47           // TODO: Add any constructor code after InitializeComponent
48           // call
49           //
50        }
51
52        /// <summary>
53        /// Clean up any resources being used.
54        /// </summary>
55        protected override void Dispose( bool disposing )
56        {
57           if( disposing )
58           {
59              if (components != null)
60              {
61                 components.Dispose();
62              }
63           }
64           base.Dispose( disposing );
65        }
66
67        // Windows Form Designer generated code
68
69        /// <summary>
70        /// The main entry point for the application.
71        /// </summary>
72        [STAThread]
73        static void Main()
74        {
75           Application.Run( new FrmEvents() );
76        }
```

Figure 24.36   **Ticket Information** application code. (Part 2 of 5.)

```
77
78            // populates ComboBox with current day's events (if any)
79            private void CreateEventList()
80            {
81               int intCount; // counter
82
83               // stores event information in array m_strData
84               // and assigns number of events to m_intNumberOfEvents
85               ExtractData( mvwDate.SelectionStart );
86
87               // remove any items in ComboBox
88               cboEvent.Items.Clear();
89
90               // add each new event name to ComboBox
91               if ( m_intNumberOfEvents > 0 )
92               {
93                  for ( intCount = 0; intCount < m_intNumberOfEvents;
94                     intCount++ )
95                  {
96                     // extract and display event name
97                     cboEvent.Items.Add( m_strData[ intCount, 3 ] );
98                  }
99
100                  // inform user that events are scheduled
101                  cboEvent.Text = " - Events - ";
102                  txtDescription.Text = "Pick an event.";
103               }
104
105               // inform user that no events are scheduled
106               else
107               {
108                  cboEvent.Text = " - No Events - ";
109                  txtDescription.Text = "No events today.";
110               }
111
112            } // end method CreateEventList
113
114            // extracts event data for a specified day from calendar.txt
115            // and returns number of events during that day
116            private void ExtractData( DateTime dtmDay )
117            {
118               // set to selected date in MonthCalendar control
119               int intChosenDay = dtmDay.Day;
120               int intFileDay; // day of event from file
121               int intLineNumbers; // counts lines to skip
122
123               m_intNumberOfEvents = 0; // set number of events to 0
124
125               // initialize StreamReader to read lines from file
126               StreamReader objInput =
127                  new StreamReader( "calendar.txt" );
128
129               // read first line before entering loop
130               string strLine = objInput.ReadLine();
131
132               // loop through lines in file
133               while ( objInput.Peek() > -1 &&
134                  m_intNumberOfEvents < 10 )
135               {
```

Creating a `StreamReader` object ⟶ (lines 126–127)

Using the `ReadLine` method to read the first line of the file ⟶ (line 130)

Ensuring that the end of the file has not been reached ⟶ (lines 133–134)

Figure 24.36 Ticket Information application code. (Part 3 of 5.)

```
136              intFileDay = Int32.Parse( strLine ); // extract day
137
138              // if event scheduled for specified day,
139              // store information
140              if ( intFileDay == intChosenDay )
141              {
142                 m_strData[ m_intNumberOfEvents, 0 ] = strLine;
143                 m_strData[ m_intNumberOfEvents, 1 ] =
144                    objInput.ReadLine();
145                 m_strData[ m_intNumberOfEvents, 2 ] =
146                    objInput.ReadLine();
147                 m_strData[ m_intNumberOfEvents, 3 ] =
148                    objInput.ReadLine();
149                 m_strData[ m_intNumberOfEvents, 4 ] =
150                    objInput.ReadLine();
151                 m_intNumberOfEvents++;
152              }
153              else
154              {
155                 // skip to next event in file
156                 for ( intLineNumbers = 0; intLineNumbers <= 3;
157                    intLineNumbers++ )
158                    strLine = objInput.ReadLine();
159              }
160
161              // read day of next event in file
162              strLine = objInput.ReadLine();
163
164           } // end while
165
166        } // end method ExtractData
167
168        // handles Form's Load event
169        private void FrmEvents_Load(
170           object sender, System.EventArgs e )
171        {
172           // display any events scheduled for today in ComboBox
173           CreateEventList();
174
175        } // end method FrmEvents_Load
176
177        // handles MonthCalendar's DateChanged event
178        private void mvwDate_DateChanged(
179           object sender, System.Windows.Forms.DateRangeEventArgs e )
180        {
181           // display any events for the specified date in ComboBox
182           CreateEventList();
183
184        } // end method mvwDate_DateChanged
185
186        // handles ComboBox's SelectedIndexChanged event
187        private void cboEvent_SelectedIndexChanged(
188           object sender, System.EventArgs e )
189        {
190           // place time, price and description of event in TextBox
191           txtDescription.Text =
192              m_strData[ cboEvent.SelectedIndex, 1 ];
193           txtDescription.Text += "\r\n";
```

Reading information from a file and storing the data in an array

Using the **ReadLine** method to skip to the next event in the file

Using the **ReadLine** method to read the day of the next event

Handling a MonthCalendar's DateChanged event

Figure 24.36   Ticket Information application code. (Part 4 of 5.)

```
194              txtDescription.Text += "Price: $" +
195                 m_strData[ cboEvent.SelectedIndex, 2 ];
196              txtDescription.Text += "\r\n";
197              txtDescription.Text +=
198                 m_strData[ cboEvent.SelectedIndex, 4 ];
199
200           } // end method cboEvent_SelectedIndexChanged
201
202        } // end class FrmEvents
203  }
```

Figure 24.36 **Ticket Information** application code. (Part 5 of 5.)

24.6 Wrap-Up

In this tutorial, you learned how to store data in sequential-access files. Data in files is called persistent data because the data is maintained after the application that generates the data terminates. Computers store files on secondary storage devices.

Sequential-access files store data items in the order that they are written to the file. They are part of the data hierarchy in which computers process data items. These files are composed of records, which are collections of related fields. Fields are made up of characters, which are composed of bytes. Bytes are composed of the smallest data items that computers can support—bits.

You learned how C# views each file as a sequential stream of bytes with an end-of-file marker. You learned how to create a sequential-access file in the **Write Event** application by associating a StreamWriter object with a specified file name. You used StreamWriter to add information to that file. After creating a file of community events with the **Write Event** application, you developed the **Ticket Information** application, which uses a StreamReader object to read information from that file sequentially. The user selects a date in the **Ticket Information** application's Month-Calendar control and extracts event information from a sequential-access file about any events scheduled for the specified date.

In the next tutorial, you will be introduced to databases, which were briefly mentioned earlier in this tutorial. Databases provide another common mechanism for maintaining persistent data.

SKILLS SUMMARY

Displaying the Open Dialog

- Add an OpenFileDialog object to your application by double clicking the OpenFileDialog tab in the **Toolbox**.
- Invoke the OpenFileDialog's ShowDialog method.

Retrieving the Filename From the Open Dialog

- Use the FileName property of the OpenFileDialog object.

Writing to a Sequential-Access File

- Reference the System.IO namespace.
- Create a StreamWriter object by passing two arguments to the constructor: the name of the file to open for writing and a bool value that determines whether information will be appended to the file.
- Use the WriteLine method of StreamWriter to write information to the file.

Reading from a Sequential-Access File

- Reference the System.IO namespace.
- Create a StreamReader object by passing the name of the file to open for reading to the constructor.
- Use the ReadLine method of StreamReader to read information from the file.

Adding a MonthCalendar Control

■ Double click the MonthCalendar control's tab in the **Toolbox** to add a MonthCalendar to the application.

Handling a MonthCalendar Control's DateChanged Event

■ Double click the MonthCalendar control to generate the DateChanged event handler.

■ The SelectionStart property returns the first (or only) date selected.

KEY TERMS

bit—Short for "binary digit," a bit is a digit that can assume one of two values.

byte—Eight bits.

character—A digit, letter or special symbol (characters in C# are Unicode characters, which are composed of 2 bytes).

character set—The set of all characters used to write applications and represent data items on a particular computer. C# uses the Unicode character set.

CheckFileExists property of class OpenFileDialog—Enables the user to display a warning if a specified file does not exist.

database—A group of related files.

database management system (DBMS)—A collection of programs designed to create and manage databases.

data hierarchy—A collection of data items processed by computers that become larger and more complex in structure as you progress from bits to characters to fields to larger data structures.

DateChanged event of MonthCalendar control—Raised when a new date (or a range of dates) is selected.

field—A group of characters that conveys some meaning. For example, a field consisting of uppercase and lowercase letters can represent a person's name.

file—Collection of data that is assigned a name. Files are used for long-term persistence of large amounts of data, even after the program that created the data terminates.

FileName property of class OpenFileDialog—Specifies the file name displayed in the dialog.

MonthCalendar control—Control that displays a calendar from which a user can select a range of dates.

Peek method of the class StreamReader—Returns the next character to be read or –1 if there are no more characters to read in the file (that is, the end of the file has been reached).

persistent data—Data maintained in files.

ReadLine method of the StreamReader class—Reads a line from a file and returns it as a string.

record—A collection of related fields. Usually a class in C# composed of several fields (called member variables in C#).

record key—Identifies a record and distinguishes that record from all other records.

secondary storage media—Devices such as magnetic disks, optical disks and magnetic tapes on which computers store files.

SelectionStart property of MonthCalendar control—Returns the first (or only) date selected.

sequential-access file—Contains data that is read in the order that it was written to the file.

StreamReader class—Provides methods for reading information from a file.

StreamWriter class—Provides methods for writing information to a file.

text file—A file containing human-readable characters.

Unicode—A character set containing characters that are composed of 2 bytes. Characters are represented in C# using the Unicode character set.

WriteLine method of StreamWriter class—Writes a string and a line terminator to a file.

CONTROLS, EVENTS, PROPERTIES & METHODS

ComboBox This control allows users to select options from a drop-down list.

- ■ *In action*

    Australia

- ■ *Event*

    SelectedIndexChanged—Raised when a new value is selected in the ComobBox.

- ■ *Properties*

    DataSource—Allows you to add items to the ComboBox.

    DropDownStyle—Determines the ComboBox's style.

    Enabled—Determines whether the user can enter data (true) in the ComboBox or not (false).

    Items—Specifies the values the user can select from the ComboBox.

    Item—Retrieves the value at the specified index.

    Location—Specifies the location of the ComboBox control on its container control relative to the top-left corner.

    MaxDropDownItems—Determines the maximum number of items to be displayed when user clicks the drop-down arrow.

    Name—Specifies the name used to access the ComboBox control programmatically. The name should be prefixed with cbo.

    SelectedIndex—Specifies the index of the item selected.

    SelectedValue—Contains the item selected by the user.

    Text—Specifies the text displayed in the ComboBox.

- ■ *Methods*

    Items.Add—Adds an item to the ComboBox.

    Items.Clear—Deletes all the values in the ComboBox.

MonthCalendar MonthCalendar This control displays a calendar from which the user can select a date or a range of dates.

- ■ *In action*

- ■ *Event*

    DateChanged—Raised when a new date (or a range of dates) is selected.

- ■ *Properties*

    Location—Specifies the location of the MonthCalendar control on the Form.

    Name—Specifies the name used to access the properties of the MonthCalendar control in program code. The name should be prefixed with mvw.

    SelectionStart—Returns the first (or only) date selected.

OpenFileDialog OpenFileDialog This object enables an application to use the **Open** dialog.

- ■ *Properties*

    CheckFileExists—Enables the user to display a warning if a specified file does not exist.

FileName—Sets the default file name displayed in the dialog. It can also be used to retrieve the name of the user-entered file.

Name—Specifies the name that will be used to reference the control's properties and methods. Use prefix obj when naming an OpenFileDialog object.

- *Method*

ShowDialog—Displays the **Open** dialog and returns the result of the user interaction with the dialog.

StreamWriter This class is used to write data to a file.

- *Methods*

Close—Used to close the stream.

WriteLine—Writes the data specified in its argument, followed by a newline character.

StreamReader This class is used to read data from a file.

- *Methods*

Close—Closes the stream.

ReadLine—Reads a line of data from a particular file.

MULTIPLE-CHOICE QUESTIONS

24.1 Data maintained in a file is called _____.

a) persistent data   b) bits

c) secondary data   d) databases

24.2 Methods from the _____ class can be used to write data to a file.

a) StreamReader   b) FileWriter

c) StreamWriter   d) WriteFile

24.3 The _____ namespace provides the classes and methods that you need to use to perform file processing.

a) System.IO   b) System.Files

c) System.Stream   d) System.Windows.Forms

24.4 Sometimes a group of related files is called a _____.

a) field   b) database

c) collection   d) byte

24.5 A(n) _____ allows the user to select a file to open.

a) CreateFileDialog   b) OpenFileDialog

c) MessageBox   d) None of the above.

24.6 Digits, letters and special symbols are referred to as _____.

a) constants   b) ints

c) strings   d) characters

24.7 The _____ method reads a line from a file.

a) ReadLine   b) Read

c) ReadAll   d) ReadToNewline

24.8 A _____ contains information that is read in the order it was written to the file.

a) sequential-access file   b) text file

c) StreamReader   d) StreamWriter

24.9 The smallest data item that a computer can support is called a _____.

a) character set   b) character

c) special symbol   d) bit

24.10 Methods from the _____ class can be used to read data from a file.

a) `StreamWriter` b) `FileReader`

c) `StreamReader` d) `ReadFile`

EXERCISES

24.11 (*Birthday Saver Application*) Create an application to store people's names and birthdays in a file (Fig. 24.37). The user creates a file and inputs each person's first name, last name and birthday on the Form. The information is then written to the file.

Figure 24.37 **Birthday Saver** application's GUI.

a) *Copying the template to your working directory.* Copy the directory `C:\Examples\ Tutorial24\Exercises\BirthdaySaver` to your `C:\SimplyCSP` directory.

b) *Opening the application's template file.* Double click `BirthdaySaver.sln` in the `BirthdaySaver` directory to open the application.

c) *Adding and customizing an `OpenFileDialog` component.* Add an `OpenFileDialog` component to the Form. Change its `Name` property to `objOpenFileDialog`. Set the `CheckFileExists` property to `false`. Rearrange and comment the control declaration appropriately.

d) *Referencing namespace `System.IO`.* Reference `System.IO` to allow file processing.

e) *Declaring a `StreamWriter` object.* Declare a `StreamWriter` object that can be used throughout the entire class.

f) *Defining the Open File... Button's `Click` event handler.* Double click the **Open File...** `Button` to create the `btnOpen_Click` event handler. Write code to display the **Open** dialog. If the user clicks the **Cancel** `Button` in the dialog, then the event handler should perform no further actions. Otherwise, determine whether the user provided a file name that has the `.txt` extension (indicating a text file). If the user did not, display a `MessageBox` asking the user to select an appropriate file. If the user specified a valid file name, perform *Step g*.

g) *Initializing the `StreamWriter`.* Initialize the `StreamWriter` in the event handler `btnOpenFile_Click`, passing the user-input file name as an argument. Allow the user to append information to the file by passing the `bool` value `true` as the second argument to the `StreamWriter`.

h) *Defining the Enter Button's `Click` event handler.* Double click the **Enter** `Button` to create the `btnEnter_Click` event handler. This event handler should write the entire name of the person on one line in the file. Then the person's birthday should be written on the next line in the file. Finally, the `TextBox`es on the Form should be cleared, and the `DateTimePicker`'s value should be set back to the current date.

i) *Defining the Close File Button's `Click` event handler.* Double click the **Close File** `Button` to create the `btnClose_Click` event handler. Close the `StreamWriter` connection in this event handler.

j) *Running the application.* Select **Debug > Start** to run your application. Open a file by clicking the **Open File...** `Button`. After a file has been opened, use the input fields provided to enter birthday information. After each person's name and birthday are typed in, click the **Enter** `Button`. When you are finished, close the file by clicking the **Close File** `Button`. Browse to the file and ensure that its contents contain the birthday information that you entered.

k) *Closing the application.* Close your running application by clicking its close box.

l) *Closing the IDE.* Close Visual Studio .NET by clicking its close box.

24.12 (*Photo Album Application*) Create an application to display images for the user, as shown in Fig. 24.38. This application should display the current image in a large `PictureBox` and display the previous and next images in smaller PictureBoxes. A description of the book represented by the large image should be displayed in a multiline TextBox. The application should use the Directory class's methods to facilitate the displaying of the images.

Figure 24.38   Photo Album application GUI.

a) *Copying the template to your working directory.* Copy the directory C:\Examples\ Tutorial24\Exercises\PhotoAlbum to your C:\SimplyCSP directory.

b) *Opening the application's template file.* Double click PhotoAlbum.sln in the PhotoAlbum directory to open the application.

c) *Creating instance variables.* Create the m_intCurrent instance variable to represent the current image that is displayed, and set its value to 0. Create the m_strLargeImage array (to store the path names of five large images), the m_strSmallImage array (to store the path names of five small images) and the m_strDescriptions array (to store the descriptions of the five books represented by the images).

d) *Defining the RetrieveData method.* Create a method named RetrieveData to store the path names of the larger images in m_strLargeImages and the path names of the smaller images in m_strSmallImage. Use the Directory class's GetCurrentDirectory method to determine the directory path for the images\large and images\small directories. The books.txt sequential-access file stores the file name of each image. The file is organized such that the file names of the small and large images are on the first line. These files have similar names. The small image's file name ends with _thumb.jpg (that is, *filename*_thumb.jpg), while the large image's file name ends with _large.jpg (that is, *filename*_large.jpg). The description of the book, which should be stored in the m_strDescriptions array, follows the file name.

e) *Defining the DisplayPicture method.* Create a method named DisplayPicture to display the current image in the large PictureBox and to display the previous and next images in the smaller PictureBoxes.

f) *Using if...else in the DisplayPicture method.* Use an if...else statement to display the images on the Form. If the int instance variable is 0, display the image of the first book. Also, display the next book's image in the next image PictureBox. However, because there is no previous image, nothing should be displayed in the previous image PictureBox, and the **Previous Image** Button should be disabled. If the last image is displayed in the large PictureBox, then disable the **Next Image** Button, and do not display anything in the next image PictureBox. Otherwise, all three PictureBoxes should display their corresponding images, and the **Previous Image** and **Next Image** Buttons should be enabled.

g) *Defining the FrmPhotoAlbum_Load event handler.* Double click the Form to create the FrmPhotoAlbum_Load event handler. Invoke the RetrieveData and DisplayPicture methods in this event handler.

h) *Defining the btnPrevious_Click event handler.* Double click the **Previous Image** Button to create the btnPrevious_Click event handler. In this event handler, decrease the int instance variable by 1 and invoke the DisplayPicture method.

i) *Defining the btnNext_Click event handler.* Double click the **Next Image** Button to create the btnNext_Click event handler. In this event handler, increment the int instance variable by 1 and invoke the DisplayPicture method.

j) *Running the application.* Select **Debug > Start** to run your application. Click the **Previous Image** and **Next Image** Buttons to ensure that the proper images and descriptions are displayed.

k) *Closing the application.* Close your running application by clicking its close box.

l) *Closing the IDE.* Close Visual Studio .NET by clicking its close box.

24.13 (*Car Reservation Application*) Create an application to allow a user to reserve a car for the specified day (Fig. 24.39). The small car reservation company can rent out only four cars per day. Let the application allow the user to specify a certain day. If four cars have already been reserved for that day, then indicate to the user that no vehicles are available.

Figure 24.39 CarReservation application's GUI.

a) *Copying the template to your working directory.* Copy the directory C:\Examples\Tutorial24\Exercises\CarReservation to your C:\SimplyCSP directory.

b) *Opening the application's template file.* Double click CarReservation.sln in the CarReservation directory to open the application.

c) *Adding a MonthCalendar control to the Form.* Drag and drop a MonthCalendar control on the Form. Set the Location property of the control to 16, 32. Rearrange and comment the new control declaration appropriately.

d) *Referencing the System.IO namespace.* Reference the System.IO namespace to allow file processing.

e) *Defining the FrmReserve_Load event handler.* Double click the Form to create the FrmReserve_Load event handler.

f) *Defining the NumberOfReservations method.* Create a method named NumberOfReservations that takes one argument of the DateTime type. The method should create a StreamReader that reads from the reservations.txt file. Use a while statement to allow the StreamReader to search through the entire reservations.txt file to see how many cars have been rented for the day selected by the user. The method should close the StreamReader connection and return the number of cars rented for the day selected.

g) *Defining the CheckReservations method.* Create a method named CheckReservations. This method should invoke the NumberOfReservations method, passing it the user-selected day as an argument. The CheckReservations method should then retrieve the number returned by NumberOfReservations and determine if four cars have been rented for that day. If four cars have been rented, display a message dialog to the user stating that no cars are available that day for rental. If fewer than four cars have been rented for that day, create a StreamWriter object, passing reservations.txt as the first argument and true as the second argument. Write the day and the user's name to the reservations.txt file, and display a message dialog to the user stating that a car has been reserved.

h) *Defining the btnReserve_Click event handler.* Double click the **Reserve Car** Button to create the btnReserve_Click event handler. In this event handler, invoke the CheckReservations method and clear the **Name:** TextBox.

i) *Running the application.* Select **Debug > Start** to run your application. Enter several reservations, including four reservations for the same day. Enter a reservation for a day that already has four reservations to ensure that a message dialog will be displayed.

j) *Closing the application.* Close your running application by clicking its close box. Open reservations.txt to ensure that the proper data has been stored (based on the reservations entered in *Step i*).

k) *Closing the IDE.* Close Visual Studio .NET by clicking its close box.

What does this code do? ▶   **24.14** What is the result of the following code?

```
1   string strPath1 = "oldfile.txt";
2   string strPath2 = "newfile.txt";
3   string strLine;
4
5   StreamWriter objStreamWriter;
6   objStreamWriter = new StreamWriter( strPath2 );
7
8   StreamReader objStreamReader;
9   objStreamReader = new StreamReader( strPath1 );
10
11  while ( objStreamReader.Peek() > -1 )
12  {
13      strLine = objStreamReader.ReadLine();
14      objStreamWriter.WriteLine( strLine );
15  }
16
17  objStreamWriter.Close();
18  objStreamReader.Close();
```

What's wrong with this code? ▶   **24.15** Find the error(s) in the following code, which is supposed to read a line from somefile.txt, convert the line to uppercase and then append it to somefile.txt.

```
1   string strPath = "somefile.txt";
2   string strContents;
3
4   StreamWriter objStreamWriter;
5   objStreamWriter = new StreamWriter( strPath, true );
6
7   StreamReader objStreamReader;
8   objStreamReader = new StreamReader( strPath );
9
10  strContents = objStreamReader.ReadLine();
11
12  strContents = strContents.ToUpper();
13
14  objStreamWriter.Write( strContents );
15
16  objStreamReader.Close();
17  objStreamWriter.Close();
```

Programming Challenge ▶ **24.16** (*File Scrape Application*) Create an application, similar to the screen scraping application of Tutorial 23, that opens a user-specified file and searches the file for the price of a book, returning it to the user (Fig. 24.40). [*Hints*: You will need to use the ReadToEnd method of the StreamReader class to retrieve the entire contents of the files. The book price appears, for example, in the sample booklist.htm file as Our Price: $59.99.]

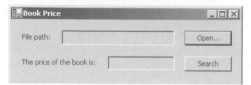

Figure 24.40 **File Scrape** application GUI.

a) *Copying the template to your working directory.* Copy the directory C:\Examples\ Tutorial24\Exercises\FileScrape directory to your C:\SimplyCSP directory. Notice that two HTML files—booklist.htm and bookpool.htm—are provided for you.

b) *Opening the application's template file.* Double click FileScrape.sln in the File-Scrape directory to open the application.

c) *Adding and customizing an OpenFileDialog component.* Add an OpenFileDialog component to the Form. Change its Name property to objOpenFileDialog. Set the CheckFileExists property to false. Rearrange and comment the control declaration appropriately.

d) *Creating an event handler.* Create an event handler for the **Open...** Button that allows the user to select a file to search for prices.

e) *Creating a second event handler.* Create an event handler for the **Search** Button. This event handler should search the specified HTML file for the book price. When the price is found, display it in the output Label.

f) *Running the application.* Select **Debug > Start** to run your application. Click the **Open...** Button and select one of the .htm files provided in the FileScrape directory. Click the **Search** Button and view the price of the book. For booklist.htm, the price should be $59.99, and for bookpool.htm, the price should be $39.50.

g) *Closing the application.* Close your running application by clicking its close box.

h) *Closing the IDE.* Close Visual Studio .NET by clicking its close box.

Objectives

In this tutorial, you will learn to:
- Connect to databases.
- View the contents of an Access database.
- Add database controls to Windows **Forms**.
- Use the **Server Explorer** window.
- Use the **Query Builder** dialog.
- Read information from and update information in databases.

Outline

ATM Application

Introducing Database Programming

I n the last tutorial, you learned how to create sequential-access files and how to search through such files to locate information. Sequential-access files are inappropriate for so-called **instant-access applications**, in which information must be located immediately. Popular instant-access applications include airline-reservation systems, banking systems, point-of-sale systems, automated teller machines (ATMs) and other transaction-processing systems that require rapid access to specific data. The bank at which an individual has an account might have hundreds of thousands or even millions of other customers; however, when that individual uses an ATM, the appropriate account is checked for sufficient funds in seconds. This type of instant access is made possible by databases. Individual database records can be accessed directly (and quickly) without sequentially searching through large numbers of other records, as is required with sequential-access files. In this tutorial, you will be introduced to databases and the part of Microsoft .NET—called **ADO .NET**—used for interacting with databases. You will learn about databases and ADO .NET as you create this tutorial's **ATM** application.

25.1 Test-Driving the ATM Application

Many banks offer ATMs to provide their customers with quick and easy access to their bank accounts. When customers use these machines, their account information is updated immediately to reflect the actions they perform (for example, withdrawals). This application must meet the following requirements:

Application Requirements

A local bank has asked you to create a prototype automated teller machine (ATM) application to access a database that contains fictitious customer records. Each record consists of an account number, Personal Identification Number (PIN), first name and balance amount. For testing purposes, valid account numbers will be provided in a ComboBox. The ATM application should allow the user to log in to an account by providing a valid PIN. Once logged in, the user can view the account balance and withdraw money from the account (if the account contains sufficient funds). If money is withdrawn, the application should update the database.

Your **ATM** application will allow the user to enter a PIN number. If the user provides a correct PIN, then the ATM will retrieve information about the requested account, such as the account holder's name and balance, from the database. If the PIN entered is invalid, a message is displayed asking the user to re-enter the PIN. You begin by test-driving the completed application. Then, you will learn the additional C# technologies that you will need to create your own version of this application.

Test-Driving the ATM Application

1. *Opening the completed application.* Open the `C:\Examples\Tutorial25\ CompletedApplication\ATM` directory to locate the **ATM** application. Double click `ATM.sln` to open the application in Visual Studio .NET.

2. *Running the ATM application.* Select **Debug > Start** to run the application (Fig. 25.1). Note that the **OK, Balance, Withdraw** and **Done** Buttons are disabled.

Displays instructions and messages to the user

Keypad for entering the PIN and withdrawal amount

Disabled **Buttons**

ComboBox that displays account numbers

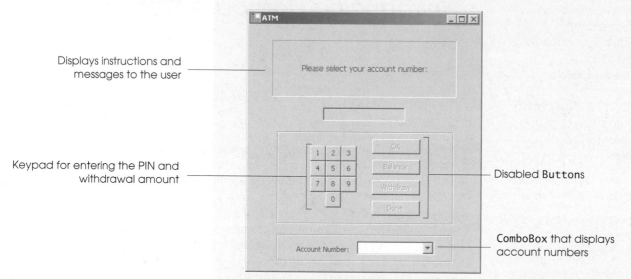

Figure 25.1 **ATM** application `Form`.

3. *Selecting an account number.* The `Label` at the top of the ATM displays a message informing the user to select an account number. Use the `ComboBox` at the bottom of the `Form` to choose an account number. Select account number 12548693. Notice that the `Label` now prompts the user to provide a PIN (Fig. 25.2). The **Done** Button has also been enabled, allowing the user to restart the ATM transaction.

4. *Entering a PIN.* Use the keypad to input the PIN number 1234. As you enter the PIN number, your entry is displayed as an *, to conceal the input. The **OK** Button should be enabled now. Click **OK**. The `Label` at the top of the ATM displays a welcome message telling the user to select a transaction (Fig. 25.3). Notice that the **Balance** and **Withdraw** Buttons have been enabled, allowing the user to perform these types of transactions.

5. *Viewing balance information.* Click the **Balance** Button to view the account balance. The amount displays in the `Label` at the top of the `Form`.

6. *Withdrawing money from the account.* Click the **Withdraw** Button to perform a withdrawal. The `Label` at the top of the `Form` asks you to input the amount you want to withdraw. Use the keypad to input 20 for the amount. Click **OK**. The `Label` displays your new account balance after deducting the 20 dollars (Fig. 25.4).

(cont.)

Asterisk is displayed in the
`TextBox` for each keypad
`Button` pressed for the PIN

Account number
selected

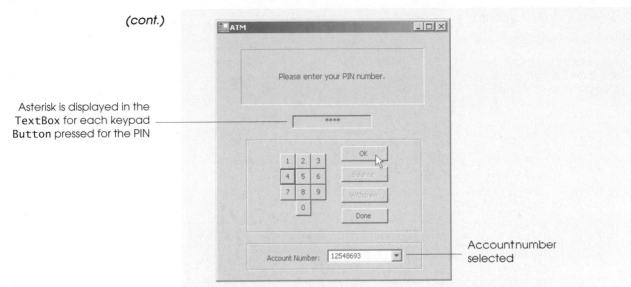

Figure 25.2 Providing PIN for the selected account.

Welcome message displays in the
`Label` when the use enters the
correct PIN

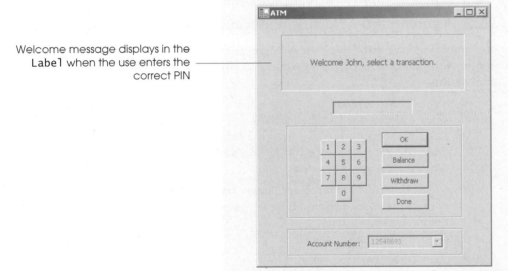

Figure 25.3 ATM displaying a welcome message.

7. ***Ending the transaction.*** Click the **Done** `Button` to complete the ATM transaction. The transaction ends, and the `Label` prompts for the next customer's account number. The **Balance**, **Withdraw** and **OK** `Buttons` are disabled.

8. ***Checking on whether the account information has been updated.*** Click the running application's close box to terminate the application. Repeat *Steps 2–5* to check the balance of the same account. Notice that the balance amount reflects the withdrawal you performed in *Step 6*. This shows that the account balance has been updated.

9. ***Closing the application.*** Close your running application by clicking its close box.

10. ***Closing the IDE.*** Close Visual Studio .NET by clicking its close box.

(cont.)

New balance displays in
the **Label** after the user
performs a withdrawal

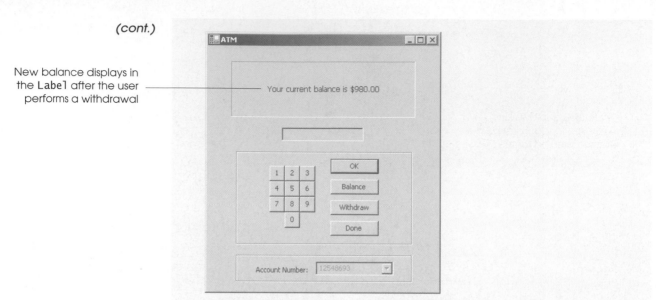

Figure 25.4 **ATM** application displaying the balance after the withdrawal.

25.2 Planning the ATM Application

Now that you have test-driven the **ATM** application, you will begin by analyzing the application. The following pseudocode describes the basic operation of the **ATM** application.

```
When the Form is loaded:
    Open a connection to the database
    Read the account numbers from the database
    Store the account numbers in the ComboBox
    Close the database connection

When the user selects an account number from the ComboBox:
    Prompt the user to enter a PIN
    Enable the Done Button
    Clear the TextBox for the PIN

When the user enters the PIN:
    Append the number to the PIN

When the text in the TextBox changes:
    Enable the OK Button

When the user clicks the OK Button to submit the PIN:

Search the database for the account number's corresponding account
    information

    If the user provided a correct PIN
        Enable the Balance and Withdraw Buttons
        Disable the ComboBox
        Display the user's name and prompt the user to select a transaction
    Else
        Prompt the user to enter a valid PIN

    Clear the TextBox

When the user clicks the Balance Button:
    Display the balance

When the user clicks the Withdraw Button:
    Prompt the user to enter the withdrawal amount
```

When the user clicks the OK Button to submit the withdrawal amount:
    If the withdrawal amount is less than the balance
        Calculate the new balance and update the database
    Else
        Indicate that the amount is too large
    Clear the withdrawal amount

When the user clicks the Done Button:
    Disable the OK, Balance, Withdraw and Done Buttons
    Enable the ComboBox
    Display instructions for the next customer

Now that you have test-driven the **ATM** application and studied its pseudocode representation, you will use an ACE table to help you convert the pseudocode to C#. Figure 25.5 lists the actions, controls and events that will help you complete your own version of this application.

Action/Control/Event (ACE) Table for the ATM Application

Action	Control/Object	Event
	FrmATM	Load
Open connection to the database	objOleDbConnection	
Read account numbers from database	objReader	
Store account numbers in ComboBox	cboAccountNumbers	
Close the database connection	objOleDbConnection	
	cboAccountNumbers	SelectedIndexChanged
Prompt the user to enter a PIN	lblDisplay	
Enable the Done Button	btnDone	
Clear the TextBox for the PIN	txtInput	
	btnOne, btnTwo, btnThree, btnFour, btnFive, btnSix, btnSeven, btnEight, btnNine	Click
Append the number to the PIN		
	txtInput	TextChanged
Enable the OK Button	btnOK	
	btnOK	Click
Search the database for the account number's corresponding account information	objOleDbConnection, objSelectAccountData	

If the user provided a correct PIN
    Enable the Balance and
    Withdraw Buttons
	btnBalance, btnWithdraw	

Disable the ComboBox	cboAccountNumbers	
Display the user's name and prompt the user to select a transaction	lblDisplay	

Else
    Prompt the user to enter a
    valid PIN
	lblDisplay	

Clear the TextBox	txtInput	
	btnBalance	Click
Display the balance	lblDisplay	

Figure 25.5   ACE table for the **ATM** application. (Part 1 of 2.)

Action	Control/Object	Event
	btnWithdraw	Click
Prompt the user to enter the withdrawal amount	lblDisplay	
	btnOK	Click

If the withdrawal amount is less than the balance
    Calculate the new balance and
    update the database
	objOleDbConnection,
	objUpdateBalance,
	lblDisplay	

Else Indicate that amount is too large	lblDisplay	
Clear the withdrawal amount	txtInput	
	btnDone	Click
Disable the OK, Balance, Withdraw and Done Buttons	btnOk, btnBalance, btnWithdraw, btnDone	
Enable the ComboBox	cboAccountNumbers	
Display instructions for the next customer	lblDisplay	

Figure 25.5 ACE table for the **ATM** application. (Part 2 of 2.)

25.3 Creating Database Connections

In this tutorial, you use Visual Studio .NET's **Server Explorer** window to connect to a database. A database is an organized collection of data. Many different strategies exist for organizing data in databases to allow easy access to and manipulation of the data. A database management system (DBMS) enables you to access and store data without worrying about how the data is organized. In this tutorial, you use a Microsoft Access database. You connect to the database in the following box.

Adding a Database Connection to the ATM Application

1. *Copying the template to your working directory.* Copy the C:\Examples\ Tutorial25\TemplateApplication\ATM directory to your C:\SimplyCSP directory.

2. *Opening the ATM application's template file.* Double click ATM.sln in the ATM directory to open the application in Visual Studio .NET.

3. *Displaying the Server Explorer window.* Select **View > Server Explorer** to display the **Server Explorer** window.

4. *Adding a database connection.* To access and manipulate data in a database, you must first establish a connection to the database. Click the **Server Explorer** window's Connect to Database Button (Fig. 25.6) to display the **Data Link Properties** dialog (Fig. 25.7). [*Note*: The contents of your **Server Explorer** window may differ slightly.]

(cont.)

Click the Connect to
Database **Button**

Figure 25.6   **Server Explorer** window.

5.   ***Selecting the type of database to access.*** Click the **Provider** tab in the **Data Link Properties** dialog, then select the **Microsoft Jet 4.0 OLE DB Provider** item in the **OLE DB Provider(s)** box as in Fig. 25.7. This selection corresponds to a Microsoft Access database. Click **Next >>**. [*Note*: The number of items displayed in Fig. 25.7 might vary on your system.]

Provider tab

Select this provider

Click to continue

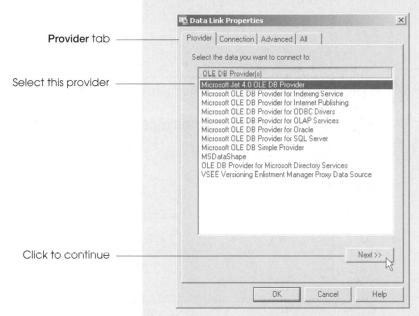

Figure 25.7   **Provider** tab in the **Data Link Properties** dialog.

6.   ***Specifying the database connection.*** Before you can manipulate the database, you must first use Visual Studio .NET to connect to the database. After clicking **Next >>**, you are brought to the **Connection** tab of the **Data Link Properties** dialog (Fig. 25.8). Here, you create a **connection object** for the Visual Studio .NET IDE. A connection object maintains a connection to a database. Click the ellipsis (**...**) **Button** to the right of the **Select or enter a database name:** field, shown in Fig. 25.8, to display the **Select Access Database** dialog (Fig. 25.9).

7.   ***Using the Select Access Database dialog.*** In the **Select Access Database** dialog, select the db_ATM.mdb database in the C:\SimplyCSP\ATM directory, as in Fig. 25.9. Click **Open**. You will be redirected back to the **Connection** tab of the **Data Link Properties** dialog.

(cont.)

Connection tab —

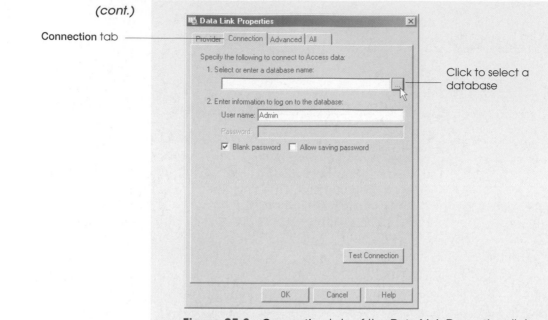

Figure 25.8 **Connection** tab of the **Data Link Properties** dialog.

Select the db_ATM.mdb file —

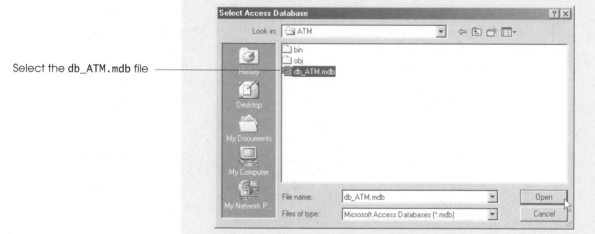

Figure 25.9 **Select Access Database** dialog.

8. *Testing the database connection.* Notice that the path of the database is now displayed in the **Select or enter a database name:** field (Fig. 25.10). The database that you will be using does not require a password to access its information. Under the **Enter information to log on to the database:** section, make sure the **Blank password** CheckBox is checked. Also make sure that the **User name:** TextBox contains Admin.

    Click the **Test Connection** Button. The **Microsoft Data Link** dialog will appear, indicating a successful connection (Fig. 25.10). However, if the connection fails, make sure that you followed all the instructions in *Steps 5–8*. Click the **Microsoft Data Link** dialog's **OK** Button to close the dialog. Click **OK** to close the **Data Link Properties** dialog.

(cont.)

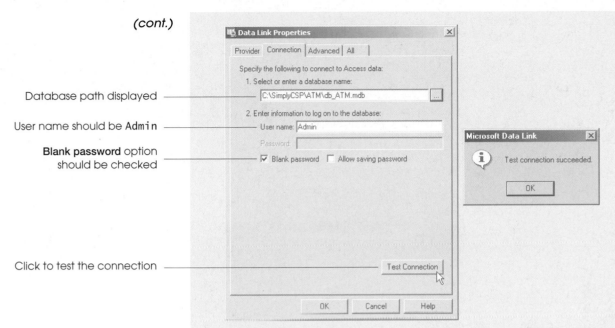

Database path displayed

User name should be Admin

Blank password option
should be checked

Click to test the connection

Figure 25.10   **Connection** tab containing selected database path.

9. ***Viewing the database connection in the Server Explorer window.*** Notice
    that a data connection to the db_ATM.mdb database appears in the **Server**
    Explorer window (Fig. 25.11). You will use the **Server Explorer**'s data con-
    nection to add a data connection to the **ATM** application in the next step.
    [*Note*: As well as displaying the connection to db_ATM.mdb, your system
    may display data from previous connections or data about your network
    connection.]

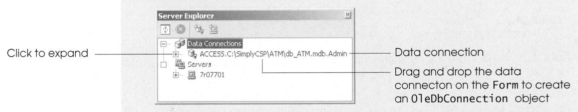

Click to expand

Data connection

Drag and drop the data
connecton on the **Form** to create
an **OleDbConnection** object

Figure 25.11   Database connection shown in the **Server Explorer** window.

10. ***Adding the database-connection object to the Form.*** Select the data con-
    nection in the **Server Explorer** window, and drag and drop it on the **Form**.
    A message dialog will be displayed asking if the database's password
    should be included in the source code (Fig. 25.12). Because this database
    does not include a password, click the **Don't include password** Button.
    An ADO .NET **OleDbConnection** object appears in the component tray
    (Fig. 25.13). You now have established a connection between the **ATM**
    application and the db_ATM.mdb database. The **OleDbConnection** object
    maintains a connection to the database. Class **OleDbConnection** provides
    methods, such as **Open** and **Close**, which allow you to open and close the
    connection to the database. You will use these methods shortly.

(cont.)

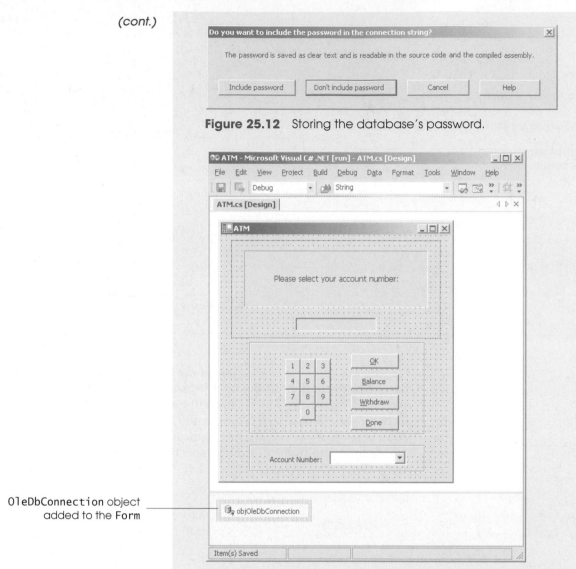

Figure 25.12 Storing the database's password.

OleDbConnection object added to the Form

Figure 25.13 OleDbConnection object added to the Form.

Notice that the data connection (Fig. 25.11) displays the exact, or absolute, path of the database. In this case, the database connection references a database in the C:\SimplyCSP\ATM directory. This is known as an **absolute path**. If the database is moved, the application will not run. In this case, you can reset the connection by selecting the **ConnectionString** property of the OleDbConnection object (which includes information needed to open a connection to a database), selecting **<New Connection...>** and specifying the new directory in the dialog that appears. [*Note:* The Connection-String property of the completed application has been modified so that it can be run from any location.]

11. ***Setting the OleDbConnection object's properties.*** Click the OleDbConnection object to view its properties in the **Properties** window. Change the name to objOleDbConnection.

12. ***Saving the project.*** Select **File > Save All** to save your modified code.

Now that you have established a connection to the database by using the **Server Explorer** window, you will need to understand how the db_ATM.mdb database organizes its data. You will use the **Server Explorer** window to view the database information in the Visual Studio .NET IDE. You will learn about the database in the following box.

Understanding the **db_ATM.mdb** *Database Structure*	1. ***Viewing the*** `AccountInformation` ***table of the*** **db_ATM.mdb** ***database.*** Expand the **Access.C:\SimplyCSP\ATM\db_ATM.mdb.Admin** node in the **Server Explorer**, then expand the **Tables** node to display the **AccountInformation** node (Fig. 25.14). `AccountInformation` is a table in the db_ATM.mdb database. A **table** is used to store related information in rows and columns. Relational databases, such as Microsoft Access, are composed of one or more tables. Right click the **AccountInformation** node, and select **Retrieve Data from Table** (Fig. 25.14). The contents of the `AccountInformation` table display in Visual Studio .NET (Fig. 25.15).

Click to display the **Tables** node

Right click the
AccountInformation node

Select to view the table's
contents

Figure 25.14 Viewing the `AccountInformation` table.

Columns (fields)

Rows (records)

Collectively, rows and
columns form a table

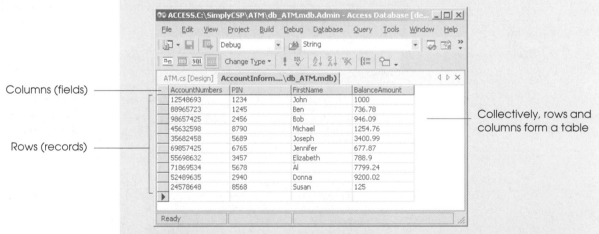

Figure 25.15 `AccountInformation` table's content.

2. ***Understanding the database.*** Figure 25.15 displays the entire database (because it consists of one table) used in the **ATM** application. This table contains ten rows and four columns. In Microsoft Access, a record is a table row and a field is a table column. For example, in this table, the row containing the 12548693, 1234, John and 1000 is considered a single record, and the `AccountNumber`, `PIN`, `FirstName` and `BalanceAmount` columns are fields that represent the data in each record.

(cont.)

In addition to rows and columns, a table should contain a **primary key**, which is a column (or combination of columns) that contains unique values that are used to distinguish rows from one another. In this table, the AccountNumber column is the primary key for referencing the data. Because no two account numbers are the same, the AccountNumber column can act as the primary key.

3. *Closing the AccountInformation window.* Right click the **AccountInformation** tab, then select **Close**.

Now that you have established a connection to the database and examined the contents of the database, you will add three **data command objects** to the Form. These objects will be used to retrieve information from and update information in the database. You create these objects in the following box.

Adding Data Command Objects to the Form

1. *Adding a data command object to the Form.* Select the **Data** tab in the **Toolbox**. Drag and drop an ADO .NET **OleDbCommand** control from the **Data** tab onto the Form to create a data command object. You will use this particular data command object to retrieve information from the database.

2. *Setting the Name and Connection properties of the data command object.* Set the Name property of the OleDbCommand object to objSelectAccount. Because the OleDbCommand object will interact with the database, it must be provided with an existing data connection. Select the OleDbCommand's Connection property. Click the down-arrow Button that appears next to the Connection property field. Expand the **Existing** node and select the name of the connection object (objOleDbConnection) you created earlier in this tutorial (as in Fig. 25.16).

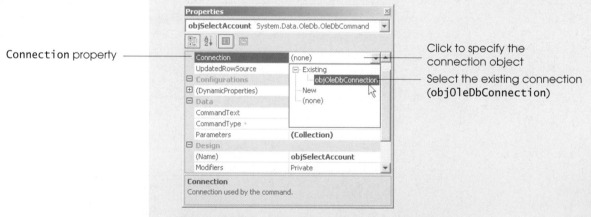

Figure 25.16 Properties of objSelectAccount.

3. *Setting the CommandText property of the data command object.* Select the CommandText property of the data command object (objSelectAccount) in the **Properties** window. Click the ellipsis (...) Button that appears next to the CommandText property field. The **Query Builder** and **Add Table** dialogs appear (Fig. 25.17). **Query Builder** is a Visual Studio .NET tool that allows you to specify the commands that retrieve information from and modify information in databases.

(cont.)

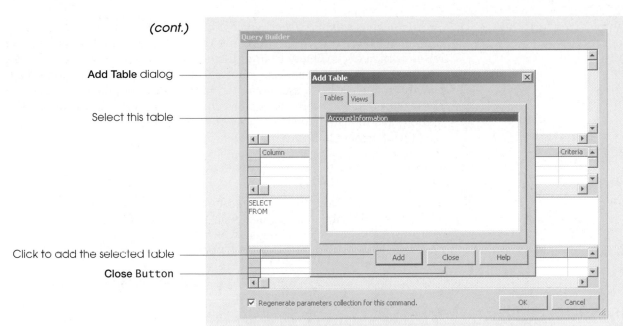

Add Table dialog

Select this table

Click to add the selected table

Close Button

Figure 25.17   **Query Builder** and **Add Table** dialogs.

4. ***Adding a table to the Query Builder.*** Notice that the AccountInformation table name appears in the **Add Table** dialog. The **Add Table** dialog
   displays all of the database's tables. This table appears in the dialog because
   you set the OleDbConnection object's Connection property, which connects to the db_ATM.mdb database (*Step 2*). Select AccountInformation in
   the **Tables** tab of the **Add Table** dialog, and click the **Add** Button. Notice
   that a window containing the AccountInformation table's columns now
   appears in the **Query Builder** dialog (Fig. 25.18). Click the **Close** Button in
   the **Add Table** dialog.

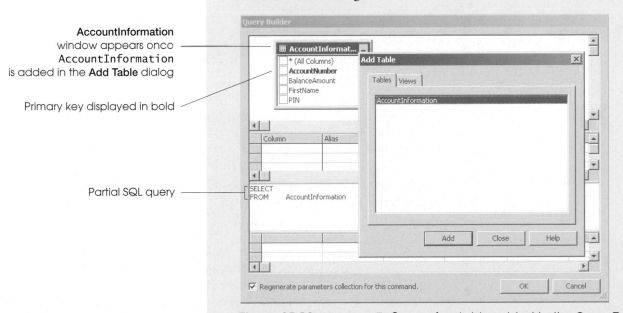

AccountInformation
window appears once
AccountInformation
is added in the **Add Table** dialog

Primary key displayed in bold

Partial SQL query

Figure 25.18   AccountInformation table added to the **Query Builder**
dialog.

(cont.)

5. ***Specifying the columns from which to retrieve data.*** You want this data command object to retrieve information from the database. Notice that the lower portion of the **Query Builder** dialog contains the words **SELECT**, **FROM** and `AccountInformation`. This represents the **SQL (Structured Query Language)** code that will be used to select information from the database. SQL is a language used to perform database queries (requests for specified information) and to manipulate data. The `FROM AccountInformation` portion of the SQL statement indicates that the information you will select will be from the database's `AccountInformation` table.

In the **AccountInformation** window of the **Query Builder**, place a checkmark in the **AccountNumber** CheckBox. Notice that `AccountNumber` appears in the table beneath the **AccountInformation** window (Fig. 25.19). The `AccountNumber` column also appears next to the SELECT keyword. This indicates that the data command object will retrieve the data from the `Account-Number` column in the database. Click **OK** in the **Query Builder** dialog.

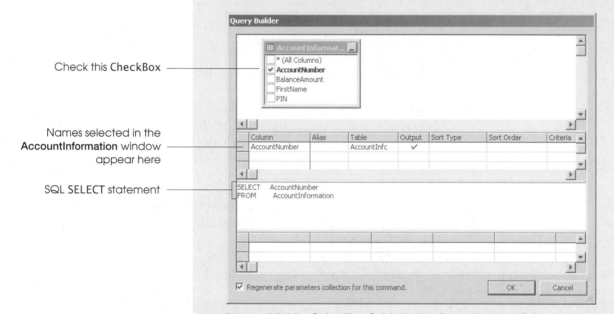

Check this **CheckBox**

Names selected in the **AccountInformation** window appear here

SQL **SELECT** statement

Figure 25.19 Selecting fields in the **Query Builder** dialog.

6. ***Adding another data command object.*** Add another data command object to the Form. Set its Name property to `objSelectAccountData` and set the `Connection` property to the connection object `objOleDbConnection`. Click the ellipsis (…) Button that appears next to the CommandText property field to display the **Add Table** and **Query Builder** dialogs.

7. ***Adding a table to the Query Builder.*** Add the `AccountInformation` table to the **Query Builder** dialog and click the **Add Table** dialog's **Close** Button.

8. ***Specifying the columns from which to retrieve data.*** You want this data command object to retrieve information from the database as well. In the **AccountInformation** window of the **Query Builder**, place a check mark in the **PIN, BalanceAmount** and **FirstName** CheckBoxes. These names appear in the table beneath the **AccountInformation** window. The names PIN, `BalanceAmount` and `FirstName` columns also should appear next to the SELECT keyword to indicate that the data command object will retrieve the data from these three columns in the database.

(cont.) 9. ***Specifying where to retrieve the information.*** Check the **AccountNumber** CheckBox in the **AccountInformation** window of the **Query Builder** dialog. AccountNumber appears in the table below the **AccountInformation** window, and the word AccountNumber has been added to the SELECT statement. In the **Criteria** column of the AccountNumber row, type =?. Notice that the words WHERE (AccountNumber=?) have been added to the end of the SQL statement (Fig. 25.20). The **WHERE** clause specifies the selection criteria for the query (in this case, the AccountNumber column having a specific value). The **criteria** of the command indicates from which specific row data will be retrieved or manipulated. The (AccountNumber=?) portion of the statement indicates that the application will search for the AccountNumber value (which you do not yet know, because the user provides it when the application runs) in the database.

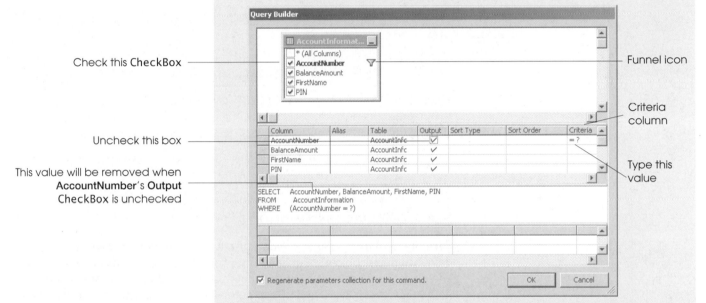

Figure 25.20 WHERE SQL keyword added to the SQL statement.

Also notice that a funnel icon appears to the right of the **AccountNumber** CheckBox in the **AccountInformation** window. This funnel icon indicates that you have specified a value in the **Criteria** column of the AccountNumber row. In the **Output** column, uncheck the **AccountNumber**'s CheckBox to remove AccountNumber from the SELECT statement. This means the result of the SELECT statement should not contain the AccountNumber column. We do this because we only want the account number, balance amount, first name and pin number to be returned from the statement. Notice that the **Account-Number** CheckBox in the **AccountInformation** window has been unchecked as well. The SQL statement should now look like the statement in Fig. 25.21. This SQL statement will retrieve the PIN, BalanceAmount and FirstName values from the AccountInformation table, where the AccountNumber value equals a value that you will specify shortly. Click the **OK** Button to accept the SQL statement, and close the **Query Builder** dialog.

10. ***Creating a parameter.*** After clicking the **OK** Button in the **Query Builder** dialog, the **Microsoft Development Environment** dialog (Fig. 25.22) should appear, asking if you want to apply a new parameter configuration. Click the **Yes** Button to create a parameter. This dialog appears only when you need to specify a value to complete the SQL statement (which is why it did not appear when you created the SQL statement for the first data command object).

(cont.)

AccountNumber CheckBox
is now unchecked

Complete SELECT statement

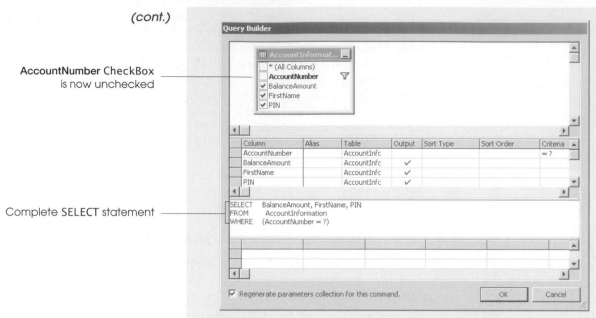

Figure 25.21 Complete SQL SELECT statement.

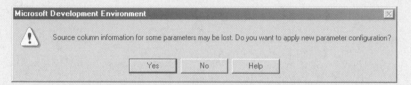

Figure 25.22 Microsoft Development Environment dialog.

11. *Viewing the Parameters property of the data command object.* Select the data command object's **Parameters** property in the **Properties** window, and click the ellipsis (…) Button that appears in the **Parameters** property field (Fig. 25.23). The **OleDbParameter Collection Editor** dialog appears (Fig. 25.24). Notice that an AccountNumber parameter appears in the collection. Although you do not need to change any settings in this dialog, you will use the AccountNumber parameter in the code file to specify the value that will replace the ? in the SQL statement (created in *Step 9*). You will write C# code to specify the value for this parameter, because you will not know the AccountNumber value until the user selects it from the ComboBox in the application's GUI. Click **OK** to close the dialog.

Parameters property

Click to view the collection

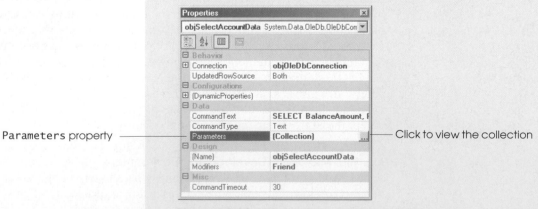

Figure 25.23 Parameters property field of a data command object.

(cont.)

AccountNumber parameter

Parameter name which you
will use in C# code to
complete the SQL statement

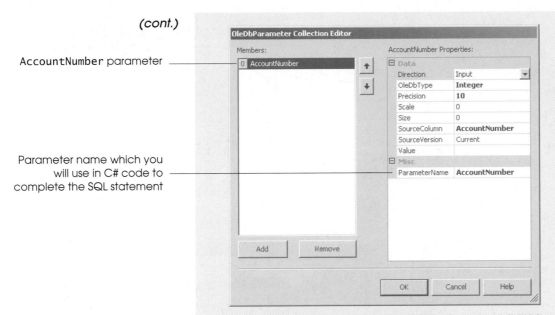

Figure 25.24   OleDbParameter Collection Editor dialog.

12. ***Adding a third data command object.*** Drag and drop another OleDbCom-
    mand object on the Form. Name the object objUpdateBalance, and set the
    Connection property to objOleDbConnection. The command objects
    should appear in the component tray as in Fig. 25.25. Repeat *Steps 3–4* of
    this box to display the **Query Builder** dialog.

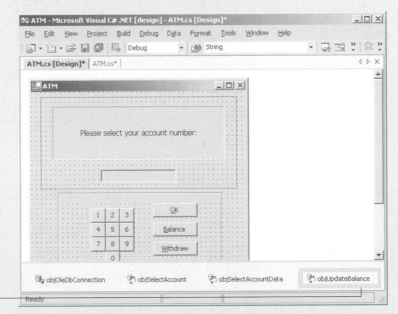

OleDbCommand object

Figure 25.25   OleDbCommands displayed in the component tray.

13. ***Changing the command to update the database.*** After you have added the
    AccountInformation table to the **Query Builder** dialog, right click the
    Column column in the table beneath the **AccountInformation** window
    (Fig. 25.26). Select **Change Type > Update**. Notice that the SELECT state-
    ment in the lower portion of the **Query Builder** dialog has been changed to
    an **UPDATE** statement. You will use an UPDATE statement to modify (that is,
    update) data in the database.

(cont.)

Right click the `Column`

Select this to create
an UPDATE statement

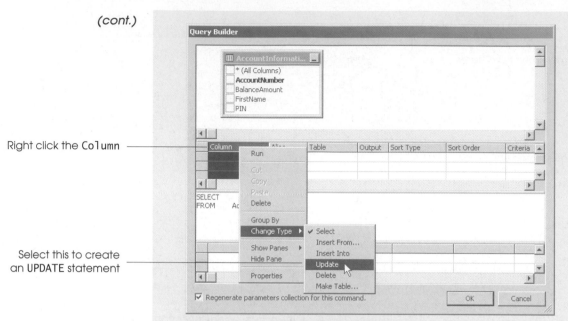

Figure 25.26   Specifying an UPDATE statement.

14. ***Specifying a value to update.*** Check the **BalanceAmount** CheckBox in the
AccountInformation window. Notice that the `BalanceAmount` column
name appears in the UPDATE statement after the SQL SET keyword. In the
New Value column of the table beneath the **AccountInformation** window,
type ? to indicate that the new value is not yet known. The SQL statement
in the **Query Builder** dialog now appears as Fig. 25.27. This indicates that
the `BalanceAmount` column in the `AccountInformation` table will be
updated to a new value that you will specify when the application runs.

Check this **CheckBox**

New Value column

Type in this value

This expression appears

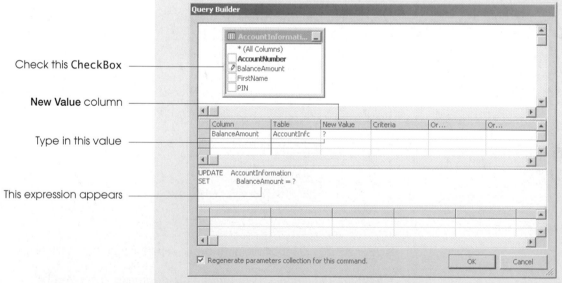

Figure 25.27   Specifying the `BalanceAmount` column in the UPDATE statement.

(cont.)

15. ***Specifying which account to update.*** Specify which account to update by checking the **AccountNumber** CheckBox in the **AccountInformation** window. In the table beneath the **AccountInformation** window, type =? in the **Criteria** field of the AccountNumber row to indicate that the account number to update is not yet known. Because we are not modifying the account number, uncheck the **AccountNumber** CheckBox in the **AccountInformation** window to remove the AccountNumber value from the SET clause of the SQL statement. The UPDATE statement should now appear as shown in Fig. 25.28. This SQL statement will update the BalanceAmount to a value that you will specify by writing C# code. Click the **Yes** Button to dismiss the **Query Builder** dialog and click **OK** in the **Microsoft Development Environment** dialog to create parameters.

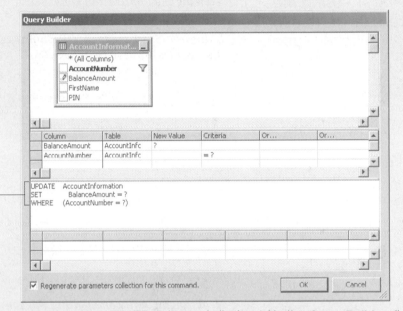

Complete UPDATE command with parameters

Figure 25.28   UPDATE statement displayed in the **Query Builder** dialog.

16. ***Viewing the Parameters property.*** View the parameters created for this data command as you did in *Step 11.* Notice that there are two parameters: BalanceAmount and Original_AccountNumber. The parameter name Original_AccountNumber was created by Visual Studio .NET. This value will represent the AccountNumber value that will be specified when the user selects an account number from the ComboBox. You will use both these parameters in the code file shortly.

17. ***Saving the project.*** Select **File > Save All** to save your modified code.

SELF-REVIEW

1. The _____ object maintains a connection to the database.

   a) OleDbCommand   b) OleDbAdapter

   c) OleDbConnection   d) None of the above.

2. You can specify the value of a parameter by using the Parameters property of an _____ object.

   a) OleDbCommand   b) OleDbConnection

   c) OleDbParameter   d) None of the above.

Answers: 1) c. 2) a.

25.4 Programming the ATM Application

When you view the code file (ATM.cs), notice that code has been provided for you. This code defines the basic ATM functionality; however, you will be defining the FrmATM_Load event handler and the RetrieveAccountInformation and Update-Balance methods that will access the database. The empty FrmATM_Load event handler and method headers have been provided for you. Your task will be to code their functionality. Now that you have established a connection to the db_ATM.mdb database and have created data command objects, you will write the necessary code to complete the application. You reference an ADO .NET namespace from the application in the following box to provide access to the OleDb database objects.

Using the
System.Data.OleDb
Namespace

1. **Viewing the application code.** Select **View > Code** to display the **ATM** application code file.

2. **Using the System.Data.OleDb namespace.** Add line 7 of Fig. 25.29 to use the System.Data.OleDb namespace. Using this namespace will allow you to easily perform database processing.

Using namespace
System.Data.OleDb

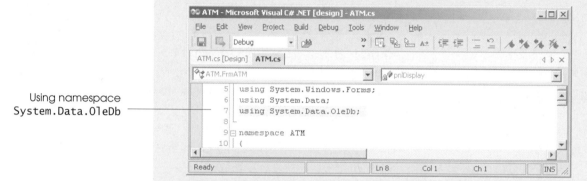

Figure 25.29 System.Data.OleDb used by ATM.cs.

3. **Rearranging and commenting the control declarations.** Locate the declarations for the four controls you added to the Form. Move these declarations, and add comments so that they appear as in lines 49–61 of Fig. 25.30.

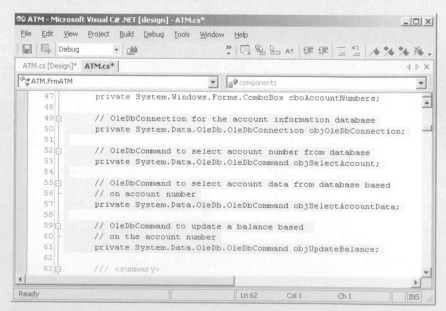

Figure 25.30 Rearranging and commenting the control declarations.

4. **Saving the project.** Select **File > Save All** to save your modified code.

Now you will define the FrmATM_Load event handler to fill the ComboBox with a list of account numbers from the database. This will allow the user to select an existing account number when the **ATM** application is executed. You do this in the following box.

Displaying Existing Account Numbers in the ComboBox

1. *Connecting to the database.* Locate the FrmATM_Load event handler near the bottom of the code file. Add lines 645–649 of Fig. 25.31 to the FrmATM_Load event handler. Because the OleDbConnection object's connection to the database is not open by default, you must open it. Line 645 opens the connection to the database by invoking the Open method of the OleDbConnection object. Lines 648–649 create an **OleDbDataReader** object (called a **data reader** object) and assign it to the objReader reference. Data readers are used to read data from a database. These objects only retrieve data and cannot modify data. The data reader is created by invoking the **ExecuteReader** method for the object referenced by objSelectAccount (an OleDbCommand object). This method executes the SQL statement and makes the result of the query available in the data reader.

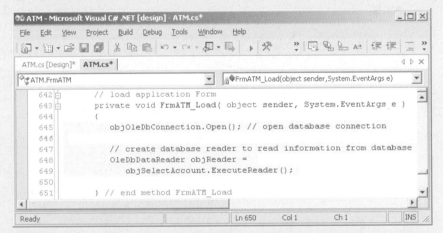

Figure 25.31   Opening the connection to the database and creating a data reader.

2. *Filling the ComboBox with account numbers.* Add lines 651–658 of Fig. 25.32 to the FrmATM_Load event handler. Lines 652–656 are a while statement that fills the ComboBox with account numbers. Line 652 invokes the data reader object's **Read** method to begin reading information from the database. You must call the Read method to position the data reader to the table's first row. Lines 654–655 retrieve the value stored in the AccountNumber column and add it to the ComboBox. To retrieve the data from the database, you simply provide the name of the column (in double quotes) in square brackets after the reference name of the data reader. Thus, the objReader["AccountNumber"] expression retrieves the value stored in the AccountNumber column. Accessing data this way makes use of indexers. An **indexer** is a special property that allows array-style indexed access to lists of elements. Some objects (such as OleDbDataReader objects) contain data that can be manipulated as a list of elements. Indexers provide an easy way for programmers to access these elements. With arrays, elements are accessed by using an integer subscript. Indexers can be created to accept integer and non-integer subscripts. In this example, the subscript is a string that specifies the name of the column where we want to retrieve data from. The while statement will continue to execute as long as the data reader has information to read. Line 658 invokes the Close method of OleDbConnection to close the database connection.

(cont.)

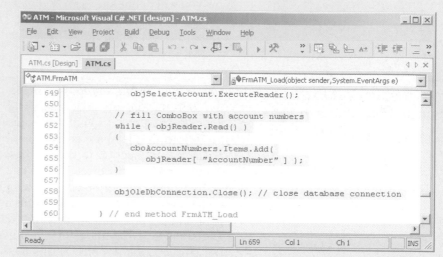

Figure 25.32 Filling the **ComboBox** with account numbers.

3. **Saving the project.** Select **File > Save All** to save your modified code.

Now you are ready to define the `RetrieveAccountInformation` method, which will be used to determine whether the PIN number provided by the user is valid. You create this method in the following box.

Retrieving Account Information from the Database

1. **Connecting to the database.** Locate the method header for `RetrieveAccountInformation` near the bottom of the code file. Add lines 665–670 of Fig. 25.33 to the `RetrieveAccountInformation` method. Lines 667–668 set the `AccountNumber` parameter value of the `objSelectAccountData` data command to the value of `cboAccountNumbers.SelectedItem` (the account number selected by the user). This statement completes the SQL query by providing the missing piece of information—the account number. This will set the command to perform a `SELECT` query on the `AccountInformation` table of the database. The `PIN`, `BalanceAmount` and `FirstName` values associated with the provided account number (specified through the `ComboBox`) are selected from the database. Line 670 opens a connection to the database by invoking the `Open` method of the `OleDbConnection` object.

Setting the **AccountNumber** parameter value of the command object

Opening the database connection

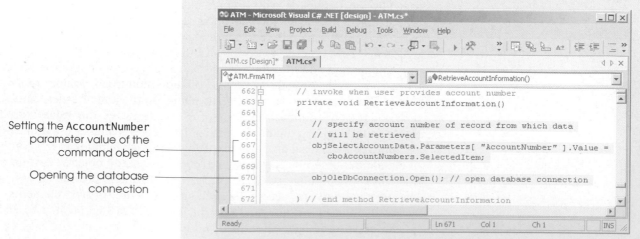

Figure 25.33 Specifying the **AccountNumber** parameter value of the data command object and connecting to the database.

(cont.)

2. **Creating and using a data reader.** You are now ready to read information from the database. Add lines 672–688 of Fig. 25.34 to the Retrieve-AccountInformation method. Lines 673–674 create an OleDbDataReader object and assign it to the objReader reference. Line 676 invokes the data reader object's Read method to begin reading information from the database. Recall that the Read method must be called to position the data reader to the table's first row.

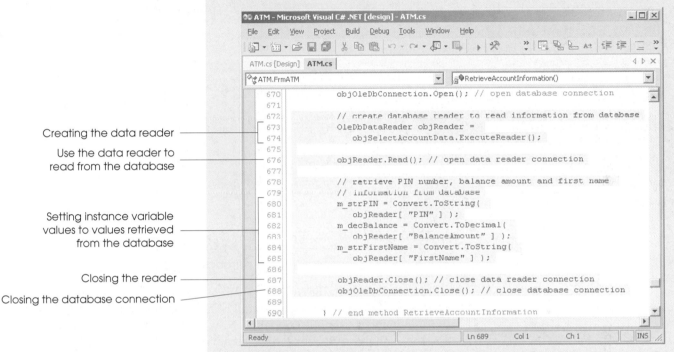

Figure 25.34 OleDbDataReader for reading a row's data.

Lines 680–685 set the m_strPIN, m_decBalance and m_strFirstName instance variables to the PIN number, balance amount and first name stored in the database for the requested account, respectively. Each account number is unique, so we know there is only one row from which this information is being read. The data reader returns items as objects, so conversions are needed before the assignments in lines 680–685 can be performed. Convert methods ToDecimal and ToString are used to convert the information retrieved from the database to a decimal and a string, respectively.

Line 687 invokes the reader's Close method to close the data reader connection. While the data reader is being used, the connection object is busy and cannot be used for any other actions, besides closing the connection. Calling the Close method of the data reader allows the data connection to be used for other operations. You did not need to call this method when you filled the ComboBox because you used the while statement, which kept the data reader open until no more data could be read. Line 688 uses the Close method of OleDbConnection to close the database connection.

3. **Saving the project.** Select **File > Save All** to save your modified code.

After defining the RetrieveAccountInformation method, you will need to create the UpdateBalance method. This method is invoked if the user-requested withdrawal amount can be deducted from the account balance. The UpdateBalance method updates the account balance in the database by writing to the database. You define this method in the following box.

Updating the Balance Amount in the Database

1. ***Connecting to the database and creating an update statement.*** Locate the `UpdateBalance` method. Add lines 695–702 of Fig. 25.35 to the `UpdateBalance` method. Lines 696–697 set a value for the `BalanceAmount` parameter of the `objUpdateBalance` data command object equal to the value of the `m_decBalance` variable. The value stored in this variable reflects any withdrawals made by the user.

Specifying `objUpdateBalance`'s `BalanceAmount` parameter value

Specifying `objUpdateBalance`'s `Original_AccountNumber` parameter value

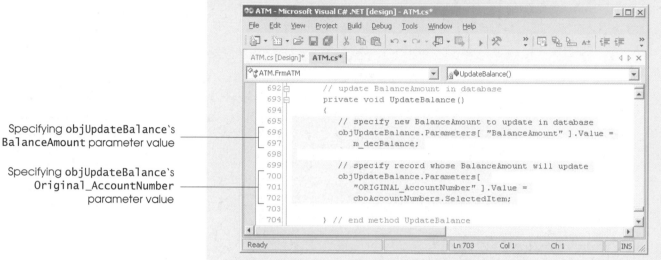

Figure 25.35 Connecting to the database to update a column.

Lines 700–702 set the `Original_AccountNumber` parameter value of the `objUpdateBalance` data command object to the value of the selected account number from the `ComboBox`. Now the UPDATE statement you created for the `objUpdateBalance` data command object is complete. The SQL statement will update the `BalanceAmount` column for the row containing the `AccountNumber` column value of the selected account. The new value of the `BalanceAmount` for that row will be set to the value of `m_decBalance`.

2. ***Executing the update statement.*** Add lines 704–709 of Fig. 25.36 to the `UpdateBalance` method. Line 704 opens the connection to the database. Line 707 executes the update statement by using the **ExecuteNonQuery** method of the `objUpdateBalance` data command object. The database has now been updated. Line 709 closes the database connection by using the `Close` method.

Opening the database connection

Executing the UPDATE command

Closing the database connection

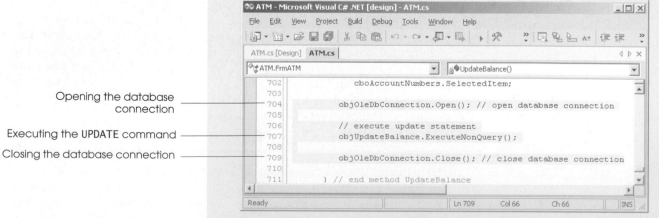

Figure 25.36 Executing an UPDATE statement before closing the database connection.

(cont.)

3. ***Running the application.*** Select **Debug > Start** to run your application. Select an account number from the application's ComboBox. Enter the correct PIN number for that account (this can be found in the database) and click the **OK** Button. Perform a withdrawal and view the modified balance. Click the **Done** Button, then select the same account and enter the correct PIN number. Click the **Balance** Button to verify that the new balance has been retained.

4. ***Closing the application.*** Close your running application by clicking its close box.

5. ***Closing the IDE.*** Close Visual Studio .NET by clicking its close box.

Figure 25.37 presents the source code for the **ATM** application. The lines of code that contain new programming concepts that you learned in this tutorial are highlighted.

Using the `System.Data.OleDb` namespace

```
1    using System;
2    using System.Drawing;
3    using System.Collections;
4    using System.ComponentModel;
5    using System.Windows.Forms;
6    using System.Data;
7    using System.Data.OleDb;
8
9    namespace ATM
10   {
11      /// <summary>
12      /// Summary description for FrmATM.
13      /// </summary>
14      public class FrmATM : System.Windows.Forms.Form
15      {
16         // Panel with Label and TextBox inside to display
17         // instructions and messages to the user
18         private System.Windows.Forms.Panel pnlDisplay;
19         private System.Windows.Forms.Label lblDisplay;
20         private System.Windows.Forms.TextBox txtInput;
21
22         // GroupBox containing Buttons
23         private System.Windows.Forms.GroupBox fraButtons;
24
25         // Buttons for entering PIN and withdrawal amount
26         private System.Windows.Forms.Button btnZero;
27         private System.Windows.Forms.Button btnOne;
28         private System.Windows.Forms.Button btnTwo;
29         private System.Windows.Forms.Button btnThree;
30         private System.Windows.Forms.Button btnFour;
31         private System.Windows.Forms.Button btnFive;
32         private System.Windows.Forms.Button btnSix;
33         private System.Windows.Forms.Button btnSeven;
34         private System.Windows.Forms.Button btnEight;
35         private System.Windows.Forms.Button btnNine;
36
37         // Buttons to take an action
38         private System.Windows.Forms.Button btnOK;
39         private System.Windows.Forms.Button btnBalance;
40         private System.Windows.Forms.Button btnWithdraw;
41         private System.Windows.Forms.Button btnDone;
```

Figure 25.37 **ATM** application code. (Part 1 of 8.)

```
42
43      // GroupBox with Label and ComboBox inside for choosing
44      // an account number
45      private System.Windows.Forms.GroupBox fraAccountNumber;
46      private System.Windows.Forms.Label lblAccountNumber;
47      private System.Windows.Forms.ComboBox cboAccountNumbers;
48
49      // OleDbConnection for the account information database
50      private System.Data.OleDb.OleDbConnection objOleDbConnection;
51
52      // OleDbCommand to select account number from database
53      private System.Data.OleDb.OleDbCommand objSelectAccount;
54
55      // OleDbCommand to select account data from database based
56      // on account number
57      private System.Data.OleDb.OleDbCommand objSelectAccountData;
58
59      // OleDbCommand to update a balance based
60      // on the account number
61      private System.Data.OleDb.OleDbCommand objUpdateBalance;
62
63      /// <summary>
64      /// Required designer variable.
65      /// </summary>
66      private System.ComponentModel.Container components = null;
67
68      // variable to store user-entered PIN number
69      private string m_strUserPIN;
70
71      // variables to store account balance and user's first name
72      private decimal m_decBalance;
73      private string m_strFirstName;
74      private string m_strPIN;
75
76      // variable to indicate action being performed
77      private string m_strAction = "Account";
78
79      public FrmATM()
80      {
81         //
82         // Required for Windows Form Designer support
83         //
84         InitializeComponent();
85
86         //
87         // TODO: Add any constructor code after InitializeComponent
88         // call
89         //
90      }
91
92      /// <summary>
93      /// Clean up any resources being used.
94      /// </summary>
95      protected override void Dispose( bool disposing )
96      {
97         if( disposing )
98         {
99            if (components != null)
100           {
```

Figure 25.37 **ATM** application code. (Part 2 of 8.)

```
101                    components.Dispose();
102              }
103           }
104        base.Dispose( disposing );
105     }
106
107     // Windows Form Designer generated code
108
109     /// <summary>
110     /// The main entry point for the application.
111     /// </summary>
112     [STAThread]
113     static void Main()
114     {
115        Application.Run( new FrmATM() );
116     }
117
118     // invoke when 0 Button is clicked
119     private void btnZero_Click(
120        object sender, System.EventArgs e )
121     {
122        InputNumber( "0" ); // invoke method with argument 0
123
124     } // end method btnZero_Click
125
126     // invoke when 1 Button is clicked
127     private void btnOne_Click(
128        object sender, System.EventArgs e )
129     {
130        InputNumber( "1" ); // invoke method with argument 1
131
132     } // end method btnOne_Click
133
134     // invoke when 2 Button is clicked
135     private void btnTwo_Click(
136        object sender, System.EventArgs e )
137     {
138        InputNumber( "2" ); // invoke method with argument 2
139
140     } // end method btnTwo_Click
141
142     // invoke when 3 Button is clicked
143     private void btnThree_Click(
144        object sender, System.EventArgs e )
145     {
146        InputNumber( "3" ); // invoke method with argument 3
147
148     } // end method btnThree_Click
149
150     // invoke when 4 Button is clicked
151     private void btnFour_Click(
152        object sender, System.EventArgs e )
153     {
154        InputNumber( "4" ); // invoke method with argument 4
155
156     } // end method btnFour_Click
157
```

Figure 25.37   ATM application code. (Part 3 of 8.)

```
158        // invoke when 5 Button is clicked
159        private void btnFive_Click(
160           object sender, System.EventArgs e )
161        {
162           InputNumber( "5" ); // invoke method with argument 5
163
164        } // end method btnFive_Click
165
166        // invoke when 6 Button is clicked
167        private void btnSix_Click(
168           object sender, System.EventArgs e )
169        {
170           InputNumber( "6" ); // invoke method with argument 6
171
172        } // end method btnSix_Click
173
174        // invoke when 7 Button is clicked
175        private void btnSeven_Click(
176           object sender, System.EventArgs e )
177        {
178           InputNumber( "7" ); // invoke method with argument 7
179
180        } // end method btnSeven_Click
181
182        // invoke when 8 Button is clicked
183        private void btnEight_Click(
184           object sender, System.EventArgs e )
185        {
186           InputNumber( "8" ); // invoke method with argument 8
187
188        } // end method btnEight_Click
189
190        // invoke when 9 Button is clicked
191        private void btnNine_Click(
192           object sender, System.EventArgs e )
193        {
194           InputNumber( "9" ); // invoke method with argument 9
195
196        } // end method btnNine_Click
197
198        // determines what text will display in TextBox
199        private void InputNumber( string strNumber )
200        {
201           // if user is entering PIN number display * to
202           // conceal PIN entry; store entered PIN in variable
203           if ( m_strAction == "PIN" )
204           {
205              txtInput.Text += "*";
206              m_strUserPIN += strNumber;
207           }
208           else // otherwise display number
209           {
210              txtInput.Text += strNumber;
211           }
212
213        } // end method InputNumber
214
```

Figure 25.37   **ATM** application code. (Part 4 of 8.)

```
215        // invoke when OK Button is clicked
216        private void btnOK_Click(
217           object sender, System.EventArgs e )
218        {
219           // determine what action to perform
220           switch ( m_strAction )
221           {
222              // if user provided PIN number
223              case "PIN":
224
225                 RetrieveAccountInformation(); // invoke method
226
227                 // determine if PIN number is within valid range
228                 if ( m_strUserPIN == m_strPIN )
229                 {
230                    // enable Buttons and disable ComboBox
231                    btnBalance.Enabled = true;
232                    btnWithdraw.Enabled = true;
233                    cboAccountNumbers.Enabled = false;
234
235                    // display status to user
236                    lblDisplay.Text = "Welcome " + m_strFirstName +
237                       ", select a transaction.";
238
239                    // change action to indicate that no user-action
240                    // is expected
241                    m_strAction = "NoAction";
242                 }
243                 else
244                 {
245                    // indicate that incorrect PIN was provided
246                    lblDisplay.Text =
247                       "Sorry, PIN number is incorrect."
248                       + "Please re-enter the PIN number.";
249
250                    // clear user's previous PIN entry
251                    m_strUserPIN = "";
252                 }
253
254                 txtInput.Clear(); // clear TextBox
255                 break;
256
257              // if user provided withdrawal amount
258              case "Withdrawal":
259
260                 // invoke Withdrawal method with decimal argument
261                 Withdrawal( Convert.ToDecimal( txtInput.Text ) );
262                 txtInput.Clear();
263                 m_strAction = "NoAction";
264                 break;
265
266           } // end switch
267
268        } // end method btnOK_Click
269
270        // invoked when Withdraw Button is clicked
271        private void btnWithdraw_Click(
272           object sender, System.EventArgs e )
273        {
```

Figure 25.37   ATM application code. (Part 5 of 8.)

```
274          // display message to user
275          lblDisplay.Text =
276             "Enter the amount you would like to withdraw.";
277
278          // change action to indicate user will
279          // provide withdrawal amount
280          m_strAction = "Withdrawal";
281
282       } // end method btnWithdraw_Click
283
284       // determine new balance amount
285       private void Withdrawal( decimal decWithdrawAmount )
286       {
287          // determine if amount can be withdrawn
288          if ( decWithdrawAmount <= m_decBalance )
289          {
290             // determine new balance amount after withdrawal
291             m_decBalance -= decWithdrawAmount;
292
293             UpdateBalance(); // invoke method to update database
294
295             // display balance information to user
296             lblDisplay.Text = "Your current balance is " +
297                String.Format( "{0:C}", m_decBalance );
298          }
299          else
300          {
301             // indicate amount cannot be withdrawn
302             lblDisplay.Text = "The withdrawal amount is too large."
303                + " Select Withdraw and enter a different amount.";
304          }
305
306       } // end method WithDrawal
307
308       // invoked when Balance Button is clicked
309       private void btnBalance_Click(
310          object sender, System.EventArgs e )
311       {
312          // display user's balance
313          lblDisplay.Text = "Your current balance is " +
314             String.Format( "{0:C}", m_decBalance );
315
316       } // end method btnBalance_Click
317
318       // invoked when Done Button is clicked
319       private void btnDone_Click(
320          object sender, System.EventArgs e )
321       {
322          lblDisplay.Text = "Please select your account number.";
323
324          // change action to indicate that user will
325          // provide account number
326          m_strAction = "Account";
327          m_strUserPIN = "";
328
329          txtInput.Clear(); // clear TextBox
330          btnOK.Enabled = false; // disable OK Button
331          btnBalance.Enabled = false; // disable Balance Button
```

Figure 25.37 **ATM** application code. (Part 6 of 8.)

```
332                 btnWithdraw.Enabled = false; // disable Withdraw Button
333                 btnDone.Enabled = false; // disable Done Button
334                 cboAccountNumbers.Enabled = true; // enable ComboBox
335                 cboAccountNumbers.Text = ""; // clear selected account
336
337           } // end method btnDone_Click
338
339           // invoke when user inputs information in TextBox
340           private void txtInput_TextChanged(
341               object sender, System.EventArgs e )
342           {
343               btnOK.Enabled = true; // enable OK Button
344
345           } // end method txtInput_TextChanged
346
347           // invoke when selection is made in ComboBox
348           private void cboAccountNumbers_SelectedIndexChanged(
349               object sender, System.EventArgs e )
350           {
351               // change action to indicate that user will
352               // provide account number
353               m_strAction = "PIN";
354
355               // prompt user to enter PIN number
356               lblDisplay.Text = "Please enter your PIN number.";
357               btnDone.Enabled = true; // enable Done Button;
358               txtInput.Clear(); // clear TextBox
359
360           } // end method cboAccountNumbers_SelectedIndexChanged
361
362           // load application Form
363           private void FrmATM_Load( object sender, System.EventArgs e )
364           {
365               objOleDbConnection.Open(); // open database connection
366
367               // create database reader to read information from database
368               OleDbDataReader objReader =
369                   objSelectAccount.ExecuteReader();
370
371               // fill ComboBox with account numbers
372               while ( objReader.Read() )
373               {
374                   cboAccountNumbers.Items.Add(
375                       objReader[ "AccountNumber" ] );
376               }
377
378               objOleDbConnection.Close(); // close database connection
379
380           } // end method FrmATM_Load
381
382           // invoke when user provides account number
383           private void RetrieveAccountInformation()
384           {
385               // specify account number of row from which data
386               // will be retrieved
387               objSelectAccountData.Parameters[ "AccountNumber" ].Value =
388                   cboAccountNumbers.SelectedItem;
389
```

Opens a database connection ──── 365

Creates a data reader ──── 368–369

Fills the **ComboBox** with account numbers ──── 374

Closes the database connection ──── 378

Sets the **AccountNumber** parameter of **objSelectAccountData** ──── 387–388

Figure 25.37   ATM application code. (Part 7 of 8.)

Opens a database connection
```
390    objOleDbConnection.Open(); // open database connection
391
```

```
392    // create database reader to read information from database
```
Creates a data reader
```
393    OleDbDataReader objReader =
394        objSelectAccountData.ExecuteReader();
395
```
Reads with the data reader
```
396    objReader.Read(); // open data reader connection
397
```

```
398    // retrieve PIN number, balance amount and first name
399    // information from database
```
Sets instance variables to read data from database
```
400    m_strPIN = Convert.ToString(
401        objReader[ "PIN" ] );
402    m_decBalance = Convert.ToDecimal(
403        objReader[ "BalanceAmount" ] );
404    m_strFirstName = Convert.ToString(
405        objReader[ "FirstName" ] );
406
```
Closes the data reader
```
407    objReader.Close(); // close data reader connection
```
Closes the database connection
```
408    objOleDbConnection.Close(); // close database connection
409
```

```
410    } // end method RetrieveAccountInformation
411
```

```
412    // update BalanceAmount in database
413    private void UpdateBalance()
414    {
415        // specify new BalanceAmount to update in database
```
Sets the BalanceAmount parameter of objUpdateBalance
```
416        objUpdateBalance.Parameters[ "BalanceAmount" ].Value =
417            m_decBalance;
418
```

```
419        // specify row whose BalanceAmount will update
```
Sets the parameter of objUpdateBalance
```
420        objUpdateBalance.Parameters[
421            "Original_AccountNumber" ].Value =
422            cboAccountNumbers.SelectedItem;
423
```
Opens the database connection
```
424    objOleDbConnection.Open(); // open database connection
425
```

```
426    // execute update statement
```
Executes the UPDATE statement
```
427    objUpdateBalance.ExecuteNonQuery();
428
```
Closes the database connection
```
429    objOleDbConnection.Close(); // close database connection
430
```

```
431    } // end method UpdateBalance
432
```

```
433    } // end class FrmATM
434 }
```

Figure 25.37 **ATM** application code. (Part 8 of 8.)

SELF-REVIEW

1. The _____ method opens the connection to the database.

    a) Open   b) Start

    c) Connect   d) None of the above.

2. While a _____ is being used, the connection object is busy and cannot be used for any other actions, besides closing the connection to the database.

    a) data command object   b) connection object

    c) database   d) data reader.

Answers: 1) a. 2) d.

25.5 Wrap-Up

In this tutorial, you learned that a database is an organized collection of data and that database management systems provide mechanisms for storing and organizing data in a format consistent with that of a database. You then examined the contents of the Microsoft Access database that was used in the **ATM** application. While examining the db_ATM.mdb database, you learned that a field in a database table is a column and that a record is an entire table row. You also learned that each record must contain a primary key, which is used to distinguish one row from another.

After learning about the Access database, you used ADO .NET objects to communicate with the database. You learned how to create a connection to the database by using the **Server Explorer** and also how to create data command objects by using the **Toolbox**. You then were introduced to the database objects, which you used in the **ATM** application. You learned about connection objects, which are used to establish connections to databases, and about data command objects, that allow you to access and manipulate database data. By creating the data command objects, you learned how to use Visual Studio .NET's **Query Builder** tool to build Structured Query Language (SQL) statements. These statements allowed you to retrieve and update information in the database. Using **Query Builder**, you created SELECT and UPDATE statements. You also learned about data readers that allowed you to retrieve information from a database.

In the next tutorial, you will learn about graphics. In particular, you will learn about coordinate systems and how to create colors and draw shapes. You will then use the concepts and techniques presented in the tutorial to create an application that can draw and print payroll checks.

SKILLS SUMMARY

Adding a Database Connection by Using the Server Explorer Window

- Click the Connect to Database Button to display the **Data Link Properties** dialog.
- Click the **Provider** tab in the **Data Link Properties** dialog.
- Select **Microsoft Jet 4.0 OLE DB Provider** in the **OLE DB Provider(s)** box.
- Click **Next**; then, click the ellipsis (...) Button next to the **Select or enter a database name:** field.
- Choose the desired database, then click **Open**.
- Click the **Test Connection** Button. Click **OK** in the dialog that appears; then, click **OK** in the **Data Link Properties** dialog.

Adding a Connection Object to the Form

- Select the desired database connection in the **Server Explorer** window.
- Drag and drop the connection on the Form.

Adding a Data Command Object to the Form

- Select the OleDbCommand icon from the **Data** tab in the **Toolbox**.
- Drag and drop the icon on the Form.
- Select the Connection property in the **Properties** window, and specify the name of the connection object created for the Form previously.
- Select the CommandText property, then click the ellipsis Button to display the **Add Table** and **Query Builder** dialogs.
- Add a table to the **Query Builder** dialog by using the **Add Table** dialog.
- Set the desired command statement by right clicking the **Column** field and selecting **Change Type**.
- Check desired field CheckBoxes, and use the **Criteria** column if necessary.

Opening the Database Connection

- Use the Open method of the connection object.

Closing the Database Connection
■ Use the Close method of the connection object.

Using a Data Reader
■ Invoke the ExecuteReader method of the data command object to create the data reader object.
■ Invoke the data reader object's Read method.
■ Retrieve the necessary information.
■ Invoke the data reader object's Close method to close the data reader.

KEY TERMS

absolute path—The complete, exact location of a document.

ADO .NET—Part of Microsoft .NET that is used to interact with databases.

Close method of class OleDbConnection—Closes the connection to the database.

Close method of class OleDbDataReader—Closes the data reader.

connection object—Used to establish a connection to a database.

ConnectionString property of class OleDbConnection—Specifies information needed to open a connection to a database.

criteria of WHERE clause—Indicates from which specific row data will be retrieved or manipulated.

data command object—Executes commands that retrieve or modify data in a database.

data reader—Reads data from a database.

ExecuteReader method of OleDbCommand object—Executes an SQL statement and makes the result of the query available in the data reader.

ExecuteNonQuery method of OleDbCommand object—Executes an SQL statement and returns the number of rows modified.

FROM SQL keyword—Specifies table from which to get data.

indexer—A special property that allows array-style indexed access to lists of elements.

instant-access application—Application where a particular row of information must be located immediately.

OleDbCommand object—Used to execute an SQL statement on a database.

OleDbDataReader object—Used to read data from a database. Also known as a data reader object.

Open method of class OleDbConnection—Opens the connection to the database.

Parameters property of class OleDbCommand—Specifies an unknown value for the SQL statement.

primary key—Column (or combination of columns) in a database table that contains unique values used to distinguish rows from one another.

Query Builder—Visual Studio .NET tool that allows you to specify the statements that retrieve information from and modify information in databases.

Read method of class OleDbDataReader—Retrieves information from the data reader.

SELECT SQL keyword—Used to request specified information from a database.

Structured Query Language (SQL)—Language often used by relational databases to perform queries and manipulate data in relational databases.

table—Used to store related information in rows and columns.

UPDATE SQL keyword—Used to modify data in a database table.

WHERE SQL keyword—Specifies criteria that determine the rows to retrieve.

CONTROLS, EVENTS, PROPERTIES & METHODS

OleDbConnection ⟨ OleDbConnection ⟩ This object establishes a connection to a database.

■ *Property*

ConnectionString—Specifies information needed to open a connection to a database.

■ *Methods*

Close—Closes the connection to the database.

Open—Opens the connection to the database.

OleDbCommand   OleDbCommand   This object is used to execute a command on a database.

■ *Properties*

CommandText—Specifies an SQL statement.

Connection—Specifies the connection to a database.

Parameters—Specifies an unknown value for the SQL statement.

■ *Methods*

ExecuteNonQuery—Executes nonquery command statements such as UPDATEs.

ExecuteReader—Creates a data reader by executing a database query.

OleDbDataReader This object is used to read data from a database.

■ *Methods*

Read—Retrieves information from the data reader.

Close—Closes the data reader.

MULTIPLE-CHOICE QUESTIONS

25.1 A _____ provides mechanisms for storing and organizing data in a manner that is consistent with a database's format.

    a) relational database   b) connection object

    c) data command   d) database management system

25.2 In Microsoft Access, an entire row in a database table is known as a _____.

    a) record   b) field

    c) column   d) primary key

25.3 A primary key is used to _____.

    a) create rows in a database   b) identify fields in a database

    c) distinguish between rows in a table   d) read information from a database

25.4 A data command object allows you to _____.

    a) connect to a database   b) read information from a database

    c) execute a command to retrieve or   d) create a database
       modify database data

25.5 A data reader can _____.

    a) retrieve information from a database   b) modify information stored in a database

    c) establish a connection to a database   d) close a connection to a database

25.6 In a SELECT statement, what follows the SELECT keyword?

    a) the name of the table   b) the name of the field(s)

    c) the name of the database   d) the criteria that the row must meet

25.7 What does the following SELECT statement do?

```
SELECT Age FROM People WHERE LastName = 'Purple'
```

    a) It selects the age of the person (or people) with the last name Purple from the People table.

    b) It selects the value Purple from the Age table of the People database.

    c) It selects the age of the person with the last name Purple from the People database.

    d) It selects the People field from the Age table with the LastName value Purple.

25.8 The SQL _____ modifies information in a database.

    a) `SELECT` statement   b) `MODIFY` statement

    c) `CHANGE` statement   d) `UPDATE` statement

25.9 Assuming the account number is 2, which of the following statements modifies the PIN field in the Accounts table?

    a) `SELECT PIN FROM Accounts WHERE AccountNumber = 2`

    b) `SELECT Accounts FROM AccountNumber = 2 WHERE PIN`

    c) `UPDATE Accounts SET PIN=1243 WHERE AccountNumber = 2`

    d) `UPDATE PIN=1243 SET AccountNumber = 2 WHERE Accounts`

25.10 A _____ is an organized collection of data.

    a) row   b) database

    c) data reader   d) primary key

EXERCISES

25.11 *(Stock Portfolio Application)* A stockbroker wants an application that will display a client's stock portfolio (Fig. 25.38). All the companies that the user holds stock in should be displayed in a ComboBox when the application is loaded. When the user selects a company from the ComboBox and clicks the **Stock Information** Button, the stock information for that company should be displayed in Labels.

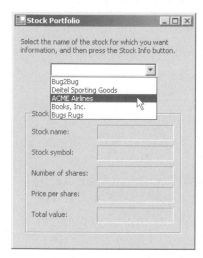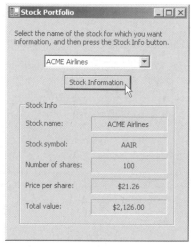

Figure 25.38   **Stock Portfolio** application.

    a) *Copying the template to your working directory.* Copy the directory `C:\Examples\Tutorial25\Exercises\StockPortfolio` to your `C:\SimplyCSP` directory.

    b) *Opening the application's template file.* Double click `StockPortfolio.sln` in the StockPortfolio directory to open the application.

    c) *Copying the database to your working directory.* Copy the `stocks.mdb` database from your `C:\Examples\Tutorial25\Exercises\Databases` directory to your `C:\SimplyCSP\StockPortfolio` directory.

    d) *Adding a data connection to the Server Explorer.* Click the Connect to Database icon in the **Server Explorer**, and add a data connection to the `stock.mdb` database. Add an `OleDbConnection` object to the Form.

    e) *Adding command objects to the Form.* Add two command objects to the Form, and set both their Connection properties to the database connection object. Name the command objects `objSelectStockNameCommand` and `objSelectStockInformationCommand`. The first object will be used to retrieve the name of a stock, and the second item will be used to retrieve all of a stock's information, based on the name of the stock. Rearrange and comment the control declarations appropriately.

    f) *Setting the command objects' CommandText properties.* Select the `objSelectStockNameCommand` object, then click the ellipsis Button that appears to the right of the CommandText property in the **Properties** window. In the **Query Builder**, select **stockName** from the **stocks** table, and click **OK**. Select the objSelectStockInformationCommand, and open the **Query Builder**, as you did for objSelectStockNameCommand. This time, select the **stockSymbol**, **shares** and **price** items from the **stocks** table. Then, select the **stockName** item and provide it with the =? criteria value. Finally, uncheck the **stockName** item from the **stocks** table. Click **OK** to dismiss the **Query Builder**.

g) *Adding a Load event to the Form.* Add a Load event handler for the Form. Add code to this event handler to open a connection to the database. Use the objSelectStockNameCommand to retrieve the StockNames, and add them to the ComboBox.

h) *Adding a Click event handler for the btnStockInformation Button.* Add a Click event handler for the **Stock Information** Button. Add code to the event handler that passes the SelectedItem to the StockData method as a string. Then, close the connection.

i) *Defining the StockData method.* Create a StockData method that takes a string representing the name of the stock as an argument. Connect to the database, and retrieve the information for the stock passed as an argument. Display the information in the corresponding Labels and close the connection to the database. Call the ComputeTotalValueString method, which you define in the next step, to calculate the total value.

j) *Defining the ComputeTotalValueString method.* Create the ComputeTotalValueString method to compute the total value by multiplying the number of shares by the price per share.

k) *Running the application.* Select **Debug > Start** to run your application. Select various stock companies from the ComboBox, and click the **Stock Information** Button to display a company's information.

l) *Closing the application.* Close your running application by clicking its close box.

m) *Closing the IDE.* Close Visual Studio .NET by clicking its close box.

25.12 *(Restaurant Bill Calculator Application)* A restaurant wants you to develop an application that calculates a table's bill (Fig. 25.39). The application should display all the menu items from the restaurant's database in four ComboBoxes. Each ComboBox should contain a category of food offered by the restaurant (**Beverage, Appetizer, Main course** and **Dessert**). The user can choose from one of these ComboBoxes to add an item to a table's bill. When the table is finished ordering, the user can click the **Calculate Bill** Button to display the **Subtotal:, Tax:** and **Total:** for the table.

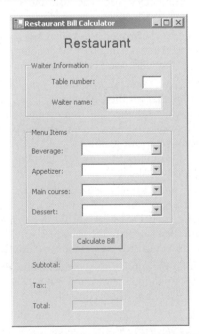
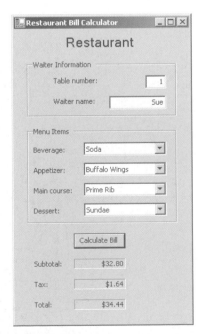

Figure 25.39 Restaurant Bill Calculator application.

a) *Copying the template to your working directory.* Copy the directory `C:\Examples\Tutorial25\Exercises\RestaurantBillCalculator` to your `C:\SimplyCSP` directory.

b) *Opening the application's template file.* Double click `RestaurantBillCalculator.sln` in the `RestaurantBillCalculator` directory to open the application.

c) *Copying the database to your working directory.* Copy the `menu.mdb` database from `C:\Examples\Tutorial25\Exercises\Databases` to your `C:\SimplyCSP\RestaurantBillCalculator` directory.

d) *Adding a data connection to the Server Explorer.* Click the Connect to Database icon in the **Server Explorer**, and add a data connection to the `menu.mdb` database. Add an `OleDbConnection` object to the Form.

e) *Adding command objects to the Form.* Add two command objects to the Form, and set both their `Connection` properties to the database connection object. Name the command objects `objSelectNameCommand` and `objSelectPriceCommand`. The first object will be used to retrieve the name of a menu item, based on category (for example, appetizer). The second command object will be used to retrieve a menu item's price, based on the item's name. Rearrange and comment the control declarations appropriately.

f) *Setting the command objects' CommandText properties.* Select the `objSelectNameCommand` object, and open the **Query Builder**. Add the **menu** table and select the **name** and **category** items. Provide the **category** item with the `=?` criteria value, and deselect **category** in the **menu** table. Click **OK**. Select the `objSelectPriceCommand`, and open the **Query Builder**. This time, select the items marked **price** and **name** from the **menu** table. Provide the **name** item with the `=?` criteria value. Finally, uncheck the **name** item in the **menu** table. Click **OK** to dismiss the **Query Builder**.

g) *Adding a Load event to the Form.* Create the Load event handler for the Form. Add code to the event handler that opens a connection to the database. Call the `LoadCategory` method four times, each time passing a different category and ComboBox as arguments. Close the connection to the database.

h) *Coding the LoadCategory method.* Create a the `LoadCategory` method that takes a `string` representing the Category to load and the name of the ComboBox to add items to as arguments. Because the Form's Load event handler is calling this method before it closes the connection to the database, the connection should still be open. Create a data reader to read all the items from the database for the specified Category, using `objSelectNameCommand`. Close the reader before exiting the method, so that a new reader can be created when the method is invoked again.

i) *Adding a SelectedIndexChanged event handler for the ComboBoxes.* Add a `SelectedIndexChanged` event handler for all the ComboBoxes. Add code to the event handler that adds the `string` representation of the `SelectedItem` to the `ArrayList`.

j) *Adding a Click event handler for the btnCalculateBill Button.* Add a Click event handler for the **Calculate Bill** Button. Add code to the event handler to ensure that a table number and waiter name have been entered. If one of these fields is empty, display a `MessageBox` informing the user that both fields must contain information. The event handler should then call the `CalculateSubtotal` method to calculate the subtotal of the bill. Display the subtotal, tax and total of the bill in the appropriate Labels.

k) *Coding the CalculateSubtotal method.* The `CalculateSubtotal` method should open a connection to the database and retrieve the `Price` field for all the menu items in the `m_objBillItems` ArrayList (using `objSelectPriceCommand`). This method should then calculate the total price of all the items in the `ArrayList` and return this value as a `decimal`. Remember to close the connection to the database.

l) *Running the application.* Select **Debug > Start** to run your application. Enter the bill information as shown in Fig. 25.39 and click the **Calculate** Button to ensure that your application works correctly.

m) *Closing the application.* Close your running application by clicking its close box.

n) *Closing the IDE.* Close Visual Studio .NET by clicking its close box.

25.13 *(Airline Reservation Application)* An airline company wants you to develop an application that displays flight information stored in their database (Fig. 25.40). The database contains two tables—one containing information about the flights and the other containing passenger information. The user should be able to choose a flight number from a ComboBox. When the **View Flight Information** Button is clicked, the application should display the date of the flight, the flight's departure and arrival cities and the names of the passengers scheduled to take the flight.

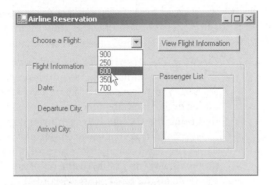

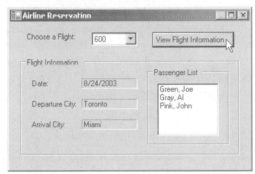

Figure 25.40 **Airline Reservation** application.

a) *Copying the template to your working directory.* Copy the directory `C:\Examples\Tutorial25\Exercises\AirlineReservation` to your `C:\SimplyCSP` directory.

b) *Opening the application's template file.* Double click `AirlineReservation.sln` in the `AirlineReservation` directory to open the application.

c) *Copying the database to your working directory.* Copy the `reservations.mdb` database from `C:\Examples\Tutorial25\Exercises\Databases` to your `C:\SimplyCSP\AirlineReservation` directory.

d) *Adding a data connection to the Server Explorer.* Click the Connect to Database icon in the **Server Explorer**, and add a data connection to the `reservations.mdb` database. Add an `OleDbConnection` object to the Form.

e) *Adding command objects to the Form.* Add three command objects to the Form, and set all their `Connection` properties to the database connection object. Name the command objects `objSelectFlightNumberCommand` (used to retrieve flight numbers), `objSelectFlightInformationCommand` (used to retrieve information about a flight based on the flight's number) and `objSelectPassengerInformationCommand` (used to retrieve information about a flight's passengers based on the flight's number). Rearrange and comment the control declarations appropriately.

f) *Setting the command objects' CommandText properties.* Select the `objSelectFlightNumberCommand` object, and open the **Query Builder**. Select **FlightNumber** from the **flights** table, and click **OK**. Select the `objSelectFlightInformationCommand`, and open the **Query Builder**. This time, select the **Date**, **DepartureCity** and **ArrivalCity** items from the **flights** table. This action causes all items from the table to be returned. Then, select the **FlightNumber** item, and provide it with the `=?` criteria value. Finally, uncheck the **FlightNumber** item from the **flights** table. Click **OK** to dismiss the **Query Builder**. Select the `objSelectPassengerInformationCommand`, and open the **Query Builder**. Select the **LastName** and **FirstName** items from the **reser-**

vations table. Then, select the **FlightNumber** item, and provide it with the **=?** criteria value. Finally, uncheck the **FlightNumber** item from the **reservations** table. Click **OK** to dismiss the **Query Builder**.

g) *Adding a Load event to the Form.* Create a Load event handler for the Form that opens a connection to the database. Retrieve all the FlightNumbers from the Flights table in the reservations.mdb database (using objSelectFlightNumber-Command), then add those FlightNumbers to the ComboBox.

h) *Adding a Click event handler for the btnViewFlightInformation Button.* Add a Click event handler for the **View Flight Information** Button. Add code to the event handler to pass the SelectedItem to the DisplayFlightInformation method.

i) *Defining the DisplayFlightInformation method.* The DisplayFlightInformation method should take as an argument a string representing the flight number chosen. You will need to define two readers in this method to read from the two tables in the database. Once you open the connection to the database, create a reader that reads the specified flight information from the flights table (using objSelect-FlightInformationCommand). Display the flight information in the correct Label. Close this reader, and create a second reader that reads passenger information from the reservations table (using objPassengerInformationCommand). Retrieve from the table all the passengers scheduled to take the specified flight. Clear any old items from the ListBox, and display passengers' names in the ListBox.

j) *Running the application.* Select **Debug > Start** to run your application. Select various flight numbers from the ComboBox, and click the **View Flight Information** Button to display a flight's information.

k) *Closing the application.* Close your running application by clicking its close box.

l) *Closing the IDE.* Close Visual Studio .NET by clicking its close box.

What does this code do? ▶ **25.14** What does the following code do?

```
1   int m_intAge;
2   objSelectAgeData.Parameters[ "Name" ].Value = "Bob";
3
4   objOleDbConnection.Open();
5
6   OleDbDataReader objReader =
7      objSelectAgeData.ExecuteReader();
8
9   objReader.Read();
10
11  m_intAge = Convert.ToInt32( objReader[ "Age" ] );
12
13  objReader.Close();
14  objOleDbConnection.Close();
```

What's wrong with this code? ▶ **25.15** Find the error(s) in the following code. This method should modify the Age field of strUserName.

```
1   objUpdateAge[ "Age" ].Value = intAge;
2
3   objUpdateAge.Parameters[ "Original_NAME" ].Value =
4      strUserName;
5
6   objUpdateAge.ExecuteNonQuery();
7
8   objOleDbConnection.Close();
9   objUpdateAge[ "Age" ].Value = intAge;
```

Programming Challenge ▶

25.16 (Enhanced Restaurant Bill Calculator Application) Modify the application you developed in Exercise 25.12 to keep track of multiple table bills at the same time. The user should be able to calculate a bill for a table and save that table's subtotal and waiter's name. The user should also be able to retrieve that information at a later time. [*Hint*: This database contains two tables—one for the menu items, as before, and another for all the tables in the restaurant.] Sample outputs are shown in Fig. 25.41.

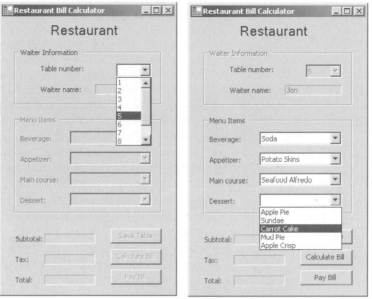

Figure 25.41 Enhanced **Restaurant Bill Calculator** application's GUI.

a) *Copying the template to your working directory.* Copy the directory C:\Examples\ Tutorial25\Exercises\RestaurantBillCalculatorEnhanced to your C:\SimplyCSP directory.

b) *Opening the application's template file.* Double click RestaurantBillCalculator.sln in the RestaurantBillCalculatorEnhanced directory to open the application.

c) *Copying the database to your working directory.* Copy the menu2.mdb database from C:\Examples\Tutorial25\Exercises\Databases to your C:\SimplyCSP\RestaurantBillCalculatorEnhanced directory.

d) *Adding a data connection to the Server Explorer.* Click the Connect to Database icon in the **Server Explorer**, and add a data connection to the menu2.mdb database. Add an OleDbConnection object to the Form.

e) *Adding command objects to the Form.* Add five command objects to the Form, and set their Connection properties to the database connection object. Name the command objects objSelectNameCommand, objSelectPriceCommand, objSelectTableNumberCommand, objSelectTableInfoCommand and objUpdateSubtotalCommand. Rearrange and comment the control declarations appropriately.

f) *Setting the command objects' CommandText properties.* Set the CommandText properties of objSelectNameCommand and objSelectPriceCommand as you did in Exercise 25.12. Set objSelectTableNumberCommand to retrieve table numbers from the **tables** table. Set objSelectTableInfoCommand to retrieve the name of the waiter and the subtotal of a table, based on that table's number. Set objUpdateSubtotalCommand to modify the subtotal for a table, also based on that table's number. [*Note*: For the last command object, you will need to change the type of query in the **Query Builder**, as you did earlier in this tutorial.]

g) *Copying your existing code.* Copy the code for the application you created in Exercise 25.12 into the template application for this exercise. Place this code before the ResetForm method. Disregard any syntax errors that may appear in the **Task List** at this point.

h) *Adding an instance variable.* Add an instance variable (after the declaration of m_objBillItems) called m_decSubtotal that will hold the subtotal for each table when it is loaded in the application.

i) *Modifying the btnCalculateBill_Click and CalculateSubtotal methods.* Remove the portion of the btnCalculateBill_Click event handler that checked for a table number and waiter name—this information will be displayed shortly. Modify the CalculateSubtotal method to update the table's subtotal based on the table's previous subtotal and any new items selected.

j) *Creating a method.* Create the LoadTables method that reads the table numbers from the database and adds them to the **Table number**: ComboBox. This method should be called in FrmRestaurantBillCalculator_Load directly after the connection to the database is opened.

k) *Adding an event handler.* Add an event handler for the **Table number**: ComboBox. When a table is selected from the ComboBox, that table's data should be loaded from the database.

l) *Creating an event handler for the Save Table Button.* Create an event handler for the **Save Table** Button. This event handler should calculate the subtotal for the selected table. The event handler should then call the UpdateTable method, passing the subtotal and table number as arguments. Finally, call the ResetForm method to reset the data displayed in the GUI.

m) *Creating an event handler for the Pay Bill Button.* Create an event handler for the **Pay Bill** Button. This event handler should retrieve the current table number and call the UpdateTable method, passing a subtotal of 0 (for new customers) and table number as arguments. Finally, call the ResetForm method to reset the data displayed in the GUI.

n) *Creating method UpdateTable.* Create an UpdateTable method that takes the subtotal and table number as arguments. This method should save the table data in the database.

o) *Running the application.* Select **Debug > Start** to run your application. Enter bill information for several tables. Ensure that your application works correctly by testing each of the three Buttons on various tables.

p) *Closing the application.* Close your running application by clicking its close box.

q) *Closing the IDE.* Close Visual Studio .NET by clicking its close box.

Objectives

In this tutorial, you will learn to:
- Draw two-dimensional shapes.
- Control the colors and patterns of filled shapes.
- Use `Graphics` objects.
- Draw shapes on an object.
- Create an application to write checks.

Outline

Check Writer Application

Introducing Graphics and Printing

In this tutorial, you will learn about C#'s tools for drawing two-dimensional shapes and for controlling colors and fonts. C# supports graphics that allow you to visually enhance Windows applications. To build the **Check Writer** application, you will take advantage of the GDI+ Application Programming Interface (API). An **API** is an interface used by a program to access the operating system and various services on the computer. **GDI+** is a graphics API that provides classes for creating and manipulating two-dimensional vector graphics, fonts and images. A **vector graphic** is not represented as a grid of pixels, but is instead represented by a set of mathematical properties called vectors, which describe a graphic's dimensions, attributes and position. Using the GDI+ API, you can create robust graphics without worrying about the specific details of graphics hardware.

The Framework Class Library contains many sophisticated drawing capabilities as part of the `System.Drawing` namespace and the other namespaces that comprise GDI+. Specifically, the `System.Drawing.Printing` namespace will be used in the **Check Writer** application to specify how the check will be printed on the page.

As you will see, GDI+ graphics capabilities will help you preview and print a check using the **Check Writer** application. To complete the application, you will learn some more powerful drawing capabilities, such as changing the styles of lines used to draw shapes and controlling the colors of filled shapes. You will also learn how to specify a text style using fonts.

26.1 Test-Driving the Check Writer Application

Before test-driving the completed **Check Writer** application, you should understand the purpose of the application. This application must meet the following requirements:

> **Application Requirements**
>
> *A local business is responsible for distributing paychecks to its employees. The human resources department needs a way to generate and print the paychecks. You have been asked to create an application to allow the human resources department to input all information necessary for a valid check, including the employee's name, the date, the amount that the employee should be paid and the company's address information. Your application should graphically draw the check so that it can be printed.*

This application prints a paycheck. The user inputs the check number, the date, the numeric amount of the check, the employee's name, the amount of the check written in words and the company's address information. The user can press the **Preview** `Button`, which displays the format of the check. The user can then press the **Print** `Button` if the format is acceptable, causing the check to print from the printer. You begin by test-driving the completed application. Then, you will learn the additional C# technologies that you will need to create your own version of this application.

Test-Driving the Check Writer Application

1. ***Opening the completed application.*** Open the `C:\Examples\Tutorial26\CompletedApplication\CheckWriter` directory to locate the **Check Writer** application. Double click `CheckWriter.sln` to open the application in Visual Studio .NET.

2. ***Running the Check Writer application.*** Select **Debug > Start** to run the application (Fig. 26.1).

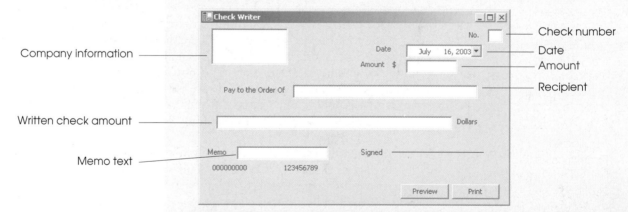

Figure 26.1 **Check Writer** application displaying an empty check.

3. ***Providing inputs for the company information.*** In the company information TextBox, type `The Company`. Press *Enter* to proceed to the next line of the TextBox. Type `123 Fake Street`. Press *Enter* to proceed to the third line of the TextBox. Type `AnyTown, MA 11111`.

4. ***Providing values for the remaining information.*** For the **No.** field, input the check number `100`. Leave the **Date** field (represented by a `DateTimePicker` control) as today's date, which is the default. Input `1,000.00` as the check amount. Enter `John Smith` as the recipient, and type `One Thousand and 00/100` in the TextBox to the left of **Dollars**. In the **Memo** field, type `Paycheck`. The check should appear as shown in Fig. 26.2.

(cont.)

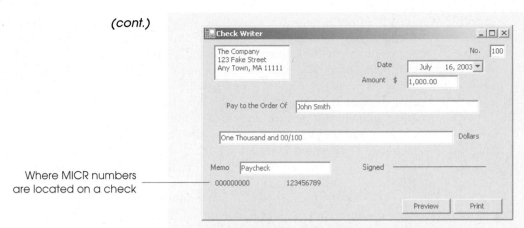

Figure 26.2   **Check Writer** application displaying a completed check.

5. You may have noticed that at the bottom left side of all bank checks is a string of numbers and symbols. These are called Magnetic Ink Character Recognition (MICR) numbers. MICR numbers are broken into three components. The first nine digits are the bank's routing number, followed by the account number and then the check number. Banks have special machines that read these numbers and route the check to the appropriate account. Using the MICR font, you can create MICR numbers in your check-writing application. To download the MICR font, visit `http://www.newfreeware.com/publishers/1561/`. We do not use the MICR font in the application provided with the book.

6. ***Previewing the check.*** Click the **Preview** Button. A **Print preview** dialog appears, displaying the completed check as shown in Fig. 26.3. This dialog is actually a control of the `PrintPreviewDialog` type, which is used to display how a document appears before it is printed.

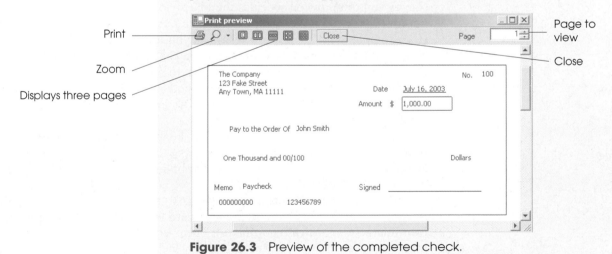

Figure 26.3   Preview of the completed check.

(cont.)

The **Print preview** dialog contains several toolbar `Buttons`. The first `Button` is the print `Button` (🖨), which allows users to print the document. The next `Button` (🔍) zooms in and out, allowing users to view the document at different sizes. The next five `Buttons` allow users to specify the number of pages that can be displayed in the dialog at one time. Users can view 1, 2, 3, 4 or 6 pages at a time in the dialog box. The **Close** `Button` closes the dialog box. Finally, the rightmost control in the dialog box allows users to specify which page of the document they wish to view. The `PrintPreviewDialog` control is discussed in detail in Section 26.4. The document that displays in this dialog box is the `PrintDocument`, an object that you will create when coding the application.

Click **Close** to close the **Print preview** dialog. [*Note*: Printing or previewing the document is not possible when there is no printer installed on your computer. Previewing the document is possible, however, if printers are installed but not connected.]

7. ***Printing the check.*** To print the check, your computer must be connected to a printer. Click the **Print** `Button`. The check prints from the default printer of your computer.

8. ***Closing the application.*** Close your running application by clicking its close box.

9. ***Closing the IDE.*** Close Visual Studio .NET by clicking its close box.

26.2 GDI+ Introduction

This section introduces the graphics classes and structures used in this tutorial and discusses GDI+ graphics programming. Graphics typically consist of lines, shapes, colors and text drawn on the background of a control.

Objects of the `Pen` and `Brush` classes affect the appearances of the lines and shapes you draw. A **Pen** specifies the line style used to draw a shape (for example, line thickness, solid lines, dashed lines, etc.). A **Brush** specifies how to fill a shape (for example, solid color or pattern). As you learned in Tutorial 21, the `Graphics` class contains methods used for drawing. The drawing methods of the `Graphics` class usually require a `Pen` or `Brush` object to render a specified shape.

The `Color` structure contains predefined colors that can be used for the graphics in an application. The `Color` structure also contains methods that allow users to create new colors.

Objects of the `Font` class affect the appearance of text. The **Font** class contains properties (such as **Bold**, **Italic** and **Size**) that describe font characteristics. The **FontFamily** class contains methods for obtaining font information (such as **GetName** and **GetType**).

GDI+ uses a **coordinate system** (Fig. 26.4) to identify every point on the screen. A coordinate pair has both an ***x*-coordinate** (the **horizontal coordinate**) and a ***y*-coordinate** (the **vertical coordinate**). The *x*-coordinate is the horizontal distance from zero at the left of the drawing area, which increases as you move to the right. The *y*-coordinate is the vertical distance from zero at the top of the drawing area, which increases as you move down.

The ***x*-axis** defines every horizontal coordinate, and the ***y*-axis** defines every vertical coordinate. Programmers position text and shapes on the screen by specifying their (x, y) coordinates. The upper-left corner of a GUI component (such as a `Panel` or the `Form`) has the coordinates $(0, 0)$. In the diagram in Fig. 26.4, the red point at position (x, y) is x pixels from the left of position $(0, 0)$ along the *x*-axis and y pixels from the top of position $(0, 0)$ along the *y*-axis. Coordinate units are measured in pixels, which are the smallest units of resolution on a computer monitor.

Portability Tip

Different computer monitors have different resolutions, so the density of pixels on various monitors will vary. This may cause graphics to appear in different sizes on different monitors.

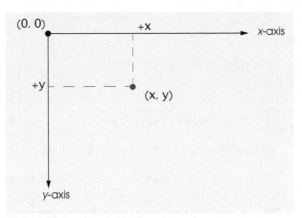

Figure 26.4   GDI+ coordinate system.

SELF-REVIEW

1. The _____ class contains properties that describe font characteristics.

   a) `Font`   b) `GDIFont`
   c) `SystemFont`   d) `FontStyle`

2. The _____ corner of a GUI component has the coordinate $(0, 0)$.

   a) lower-left   b) upper-right
   c) upper-left   d) lower-right

Answers: 1) a. 2) c.

26.3 Constructing the Check Writer Application

Now that you have learned about the features that you will use in your **Check Writer** application, you need to analyze the application. The following pseudocode describes the basic operation of the **Check Writer** application:

> When the user clicks the Preview Button:
>   Retrieve input from the user
>   Display the check in a Print preview dialog
>
> When the user clicks the Print Button:
>   Retrieve input from the user
>   Print the check on the printer

You will now use an ACE table to help you convert the pseudocode to C#. Figure 26.5 lists the actions, controls and events that will help you complete your own version of this application.

Action/Control/Event (ACE) Table for the Check Writer Application

Action	Control/Object	Event
Label the application's controls	`lblNumber, lblDate, lblAmount, lblPayee, lblDollars, lblMemo, lblSigned`	Application is run
	`btnPreview`	`Click`
Retrieve input from the user	`txtNumber, dtpDate, txtAmount, txtPayee, txtPayment, txtMemo, txtPayer`	
Display the check in a Print preview dialog	`objPreview`	

Figure 26.5   ACE table for the **Check Writer** application. (Part 1 of 2.)

Action	Control/Object	Event
	btnPrint	Click
Retrieve input from the user	txtNumber, dtpDate, txtAmount, txtPayee, txtPayment, txtMemo, txtPayer	
Print the check on the printer	objPrintDocument	

Figure 26.5 ACE table for the **Check Writer** application. (Part 2 of 2.)

Now that you understand the **Check Writer** application, you can begin to create it. A template application is provided that contains many of the GUI's controls. You might notice that the application does not follow some GUI design guidelines. This is because the controls must be placed near, or sometimes overlapping, one another for the printed check to appear correctly. You begin writing code for this application by creating a PrintPreviewDialog object in the following box.

Adding a PrintPreviewDialog in the Check Writer Application

1. *Copying the template to your working directory.* Copy the C:\Examples\Tutorial26\TemplateApplication\CheckWriter directory to your C:\SimplyCSP directory.

2. *Opening the Check Writer application's template file.* Double click CheckWriter.sln in the CheckWriter directory to open the application in Visual Studio .NET.

3. *Adding the PrintPreviewDialog.* In the **Toolbox**, locate the **PrintPreviewDialog** control

   PrintPreviewDialog

   in the **Windows Forms** group; double click the control to add it to the Form. The control should appear in the component tray as shown in Fig. 26.6.

Added PrintPreviewDialog —

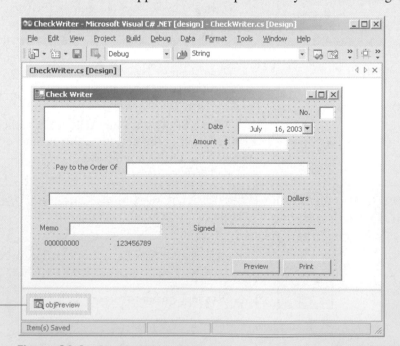

Figure 26.6 **Check Writer** application in **Design** view with PrintPreviewDialog.

(cont.)

The `PrintPreviewDialog` control uses a dialog to allow users to view documents of different sizes, print a document and display multiple pages of a document before printing. Click the `PrintPreviewDialog` object that you just created and change its `Name` property to `objPreview`. This object has a **Document** property that specifies the document to preview. The document must be a `PrintDocument` object, which will be discussed later in the tutorial. For now, do not specify the document.

4. ***Running the application.*** Select **Debug > Start** to run your application (Fig. 26.7). Click the **Preview** Button, then click the **Print** Button. Currently, the application does nothing because you have not yet added event handlers for the Buttons. You will add functionality to the application in the next series of boxes.

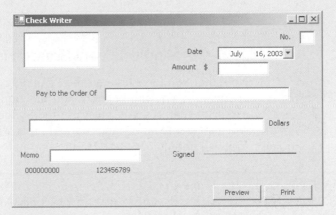

Figure 26.7   Running template application.

5. ***Closing the application.*** Close your running application by clicking its close box.

SELF-REVIEW

1. Use a _____ control to preview a document before it is printed.

    a) `PrintDialog`   b) `PrintPreviewDialog`
    c) `PrintPreviewControl`   d) `PrintDocument`

2. A `PrintPreviewDialog` object has a _____ property that specifies the document to preview.

    a) `Preview`   b) `PreviewDocument`
    c) `View`   d) `Document`

Answers: 1) b. 2) d.

26.4 PrintPreviewDialogs and PrintDocuments

In the **Check Writer** application, you use an object of the `PrintPreviewDialog` class. As previously mentioned, this object displays a dialog that will show a document as it will appear when it is printed. Recall that the dialog object contains the `Document` property, which allows you to specify the document to preview, and that the object specified in the `Document` property must be of the `PrintDocument` type. `PrintPreviewDialog` also contains the **UseAntiAlias** property, which makes the text in the dialog appear smoother on the screen. To accomplish this, set the `UseAntiAlias` property to `true`. The `PrintPreviewDialog`'s **ShowDialog** method displays the preview dialog. You will use this method later in the application.

The **PrintDocument** object allows you to specify how to print a specified document. The object can raise a **PrintPage** event, which occurs when the data required to print the current page is needed (that is, when the **Print** method is called). You can define this object's `PrintPage` event handler to specify what you want to print. The `Print` method uses a `Graphics` object to print the document. You will use the `Print` method later in the program.

SELF-REVIEW

1. The object in the `Document` property must be of the _____ type.
   a) `PrintPreviewDialog` b) `PrintDocument`
   c) `PrintPreviewControl` d) `PrintDialog`

2. The _____ method of the `PrintDocument` object uses a graphics object to print the document.
   a) `Graphics` b) `Document`
   c) `Print` d) None of the above.

Answers: 1) b. 2) c.

26.5 Creating an Event Handler for the Check Writer Application

Now that you have created the `PrintPreviewDialog` object in the **Check Writer** application, you can begin to add functionality to the application. Before you can use print features, you must use the `System.Drawing.Printing` namespace. You will also create an instance variable that will be used by several different methods. You will implement these features in the following box.

Using a Namespace and Declaring an Instance Variable

1. ***Using the System.Drawing.Printing namespace.*** Select **View > Code** to view the CheckWriter.cs code. Add line 7 before `namespace Check-Writer`, as shown in Fig. 26.8, to use the **System.Drawing.Printing** namespace. This statement allows your applications to easily access all services related to printing. After you add this namespace, the application can use `PrintDocument` objects. The namespace also enables access to the `PrintPageEventArgs.Graphics` property, which you will use to draw the graphics that will appear on the printed page.

Using namespace
`System.Drawing.Printing`

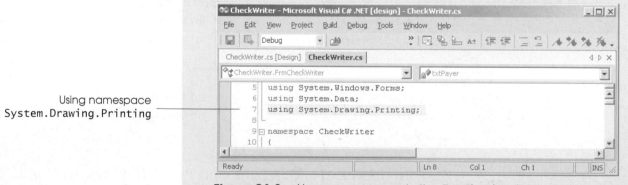

Figure 26.8 Use a namespace in the `FrmCheckWriter` class.

2. ***Rearranging and commenting the new control declaration.*** Move the declaration for the `PrintPreviewDialog` control from line 56 of your code to line 58 of Fig. 26.9, then add the comment in line 57.

3. ***Declaring the instance variable.*** Add line 65 (Fig. 26.10) to the application. This statement declares a `Font` reference named `m_objFont` that you will use shortly to reference a font object. Reference `m_objFont` will be used to specify the text font.

4. ***Saving the project.*** Select **File > Save All** to save your modified code.

(cont.)

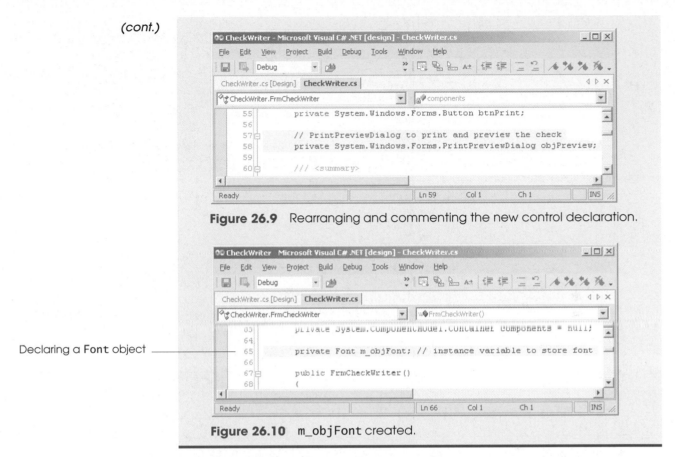

Figure 26.9 Rearranging and commenting the new control declaration.

Declaring a **Font** object

Figure 26.10 m_objFont created.

Now that you have added a using directive to the **Check Writer** application and declared the Font reference, you can write code to enable printing and previewing. You will begin by defining the objPrintDocument_PrintPage method, which will specify what to print. When printing the check, you want the printed document to resemble the application's Form. This can be done using a foreach statement that draws the contents of each control in a Graphics object. You can then print the check using this Graphics object. You will begin writing code to perform these actions in the following box.

Defining an Event Handler to Print Pages

1. ***Creating the objPrintDocument_PrintPage method.*** Add lines 331–336 of Fig. 26.11 to your code. These lines create the event handler for the Print-Page event. You need to type these lines to create the event handler because the PrintDocument object has not yet been created. You will create this object later in this tutorial.

2. ***Declaring the variables.*** Add lines 335–343 from Fig. 26.12 to the event handler. Lines 335–336 declare float variables that represent the *x*- and *y*-coordinates where controls appear on the Form. The **float** type stores floating-point values. A float is similar to a double, but is less precise and requires less memory. Lines 339 and 342 declare float variables that specify the coordinates of the left and top margins of the page to be printed. These values are determined by using the **MarginBounds.Left** and **MarginBounds.Top** properties of the PrintPageEventArgs object (e from line 333) that is passed when the PrintPage event is raised. Line 343 declares string variable strLine, which will be used to store text from the controls.

(cont.)

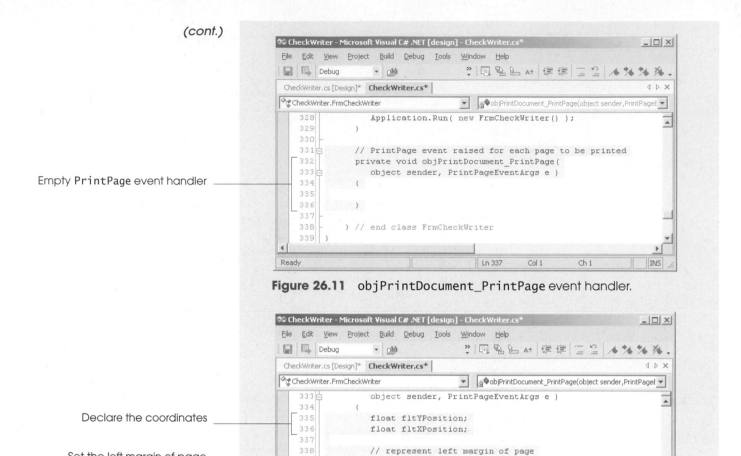

Figure 26.11 objPrintDocument_PrintPage event handler.

Empty PrintPage event handler

Declare the coordinates

Set the left margin of page

Set the top margin of page

Figure 26.12 Variables created for objPrintDocument_PrintPage.

3. *Iterating through the controls on the Form.* Add lines 345–349 from Fig. 26.13 to the method. This foreach statement iterates through each control on the Form to print the check. Line 346 declares a **Control** reference (an object that represents a control on the Form) to be the control variable in your foreach statement. The **this** keyword references the current object—in this case, the Form. You will define the body of this foreach statement in the next box.

4. *Drawing the check's border.* Add lines 351–353 from Fig. 26.14 into the event handler. The Form's border is not contained in a control; therefore, you must use a Graphics object to draw a rectangle around the check to be printed. These lines of code draw the rectangle.

To draw the rectangle around the check, use the PrintPageEventArgs object (e from line 333 of Fig. 26.12) that is passed when the PrintPage event is raised. The Graphics property of this object allows you to specify what you want to print. By calling the **DrawRectangle** method on the Graphics object, you can specify the properties of the **rectangle** structure.

(cont.)

Declaring a `foreach` statement ——

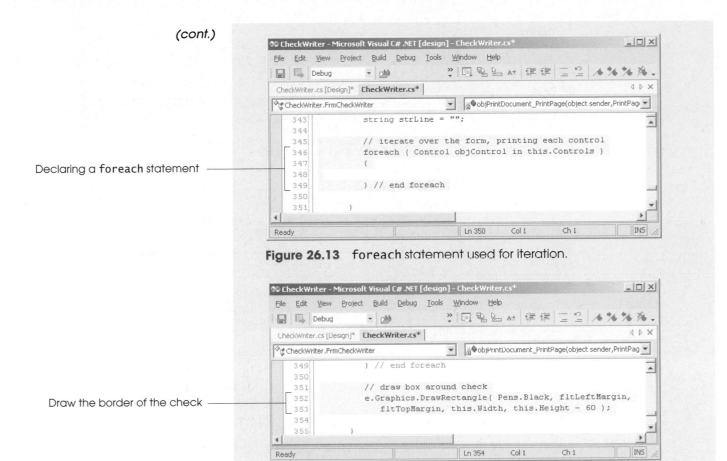

Figure 26.13 `foreach` statement used for iteration.

Draw the border of the check ——

Figure 26.14 Event handler `objPrintDocument_PrintPage` modified to draw border of check.

The first argument you pass to the method is the `Pens.Black` object. This is a `Pen` object that uses a black color to draw the rectangle's border. The second argument specifies the *x*-coordinate that defines the left side of the rectangle you wish to draw. Use the `fltLeftMargin` variable that you created in *Step 2* to represent the position of the left margin of the page on which the check will print. This value ensures that the rectangle will align with the left margin.

The third argument in the method call specifies the *y*-coordinate that defines the top of the rectangle. Use the `fltTopMargin` variable that you created in *Step 2* to represent the position of the top margin of the page on which the check will print. Together, the *x*- and *y*-coordinates in the second and third arguments define the upper left corner of the rectangle.

The fourth and fifth arguments specify the width and height of the rectangle. The width is set to `this.Width`, which returns the width of the Form. The height, on the other hand, is set to `this.Height - 60`. This value is the height of the Form minus 60 pixels. You subtract 60 pixels because you do not want to print the Buttons on the bottom of the Form. These Buttons were created to allow users to print and preview the checks. (They were not intended to be printed on the checks.)

5. ***Indicating that there are no more pages to print.*** Add lines 355–356 from Fig. 26.15 to the method. Line 356 indicates that there are no more pages to print by setting the event argument's **HasMorePages** property to `false`.

6. ***Saving the project.*** Select **File > Save All** to save your modified code.

(cont.)

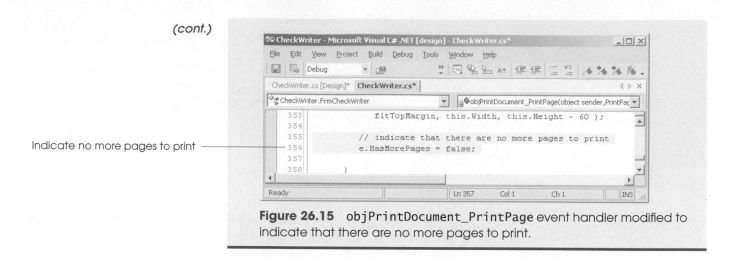

Indicate no more pages to print ——————

Figure 26.15 `objPrintDocument_PrintPage` event handler modified to indicate that there are no more pages to print.

SELF-REVIEW

1. Using the `System._____` namespace gives you access to print-related functions.

   a) `Windows`   b) `Printing`
   c) `Drawing.Printing`   d) `Drawing`

2. The _____ keyword references the current object.

   a) `this`   b) `current`
   c) `form`   d) None of the above.

Answers: 1) c. 2) a.

26.6 Graphics Objects: Colors, Lines and Shapes

A **Graphics** object controls how information is drawn. In addition to providing methods for drawing various shapes, `Graphics` objects contain methods for font manipulation, color manipulation and other graphics-related actions. You can draw on many controls, such as `Labels` and `Buttons`, which have their own drawing areas. To draw on a control, first obtain a `Graphics` object for that control by invoking the control's `CreateGraphics` method as in

```
Graphics objGraphics = pnlDisplay.CreateGraphics();
```

Now you can use the methods provided in the `Graphics` class to draw on the `pnl-Display` Panel. You will see many `Graphics` methods throughout this tutorial.

Colors

Colors can enhance a program's appearance and help convey meaning. For example, a red traffic light indicates stop, while yellow indicates caution and green indicates go. The `Color` structure defines methods and constants used to manipulate colors.

Every color can be created from a combination of alpha, red, green and blue components called **ARGB value**. The alpha value determines the **opacity** (amount of transparency) of the color. For example, the alpha value 0 specifies a transparent color, and the value 255 specifies an opaque color. Alpha values between 0 and 255 (inclusive) result in a blending of the color's RGB value with that of any background color, causing a semitransparent effect. All three RGB components are bytes that represent integer values in the range 0–255. The first number in the RGB value defines the amount of red in the color, the second defines the amount of green and the third defines the amount of blue. The larger the value for a particular color, the greater the amount of that particular color. C# enables you to choose from almost 17 million colors. If a particular computer monitor cannot display all of these colors, it displays the color closest to the one specified or attempts to imitate it using **dithering** (using small dots of existing colors to form a pattern that simulates

Good Programming Practice

When working with color, keep in mind that many people are color-blind or have varying difficulties perceiving and distinguishing colors.

the desired color). Figure 26.16 summarizes some predefined `Color` constants. You can also find a list of various RGB values and their corresponding colors at `http://www.pitt.edu/~nisg/cis/web/cgi/rgb.html`.

Constant	RGB value	Constant	RGB value
Color.Orange	255, 200, 0	Color.White	255, 255, 255
Color.Pink	255, 175, 175	Color.Gray	128, 128, 128
Color.Cyan	0, 255, 255	Color.DarkGray	64, 64, 64
Color.Magenta	255, 0, 255	Color.Red	255, 0, 0
Color.Yellow	255, 255, 0	Color.Green	0, 255, 0
Color.Black	0, 0, 0	Color.Blue	0, 0, 255

Figure 26.16 `Color` structure constants and their RGB values.

You can use pre-existing colors, or you can create your own by using the **FromArgb** method. The following demonstrates how to create a color:

```
Color colorSilver;
colorSilver = Color.FromArgb( 192, 192, 192 );
```

These statements create a silver color and assign it to the `colorSilver` variable. Now you can use `colorSilver` whenever you need a silver color. The `Color` method `FromArgb` is used to create this color and other colors by specifying the RGB values as arguments. When passed three arguments, this method sets the alpha value to 255 (that is, opaque). Alternatively, you can call the `FromArgb` method with four arguments, where the first argument specifies the alpha value, and the remaining three arguments specify the amount of red, green and blue in a color.

Drawing Lines, Rectangles and Ovals

This section presents several `Graphics` methods for drawing lines, rectangles and ovals. To draw shapes and `strings`, you must specify the types of `Brushes` and `Pens` to use. A `Pen`, which functions much like an ordinary pen, is used to specify characteristics such as the color and width of the shape's lines. Most drawing methods require a `Pen` object. To fill the interior of objects, you must specify a `Brush`. All classes derived from the abstract `Brush` class define objects that fill the interiors of shapes with color patterns or images. For example, a `SolidBrush` specifies a single `Color` that fills the interior of a shape. The following statement creates a `Solid-Brush` with the color orange:

```
SolidBrush objBrush = new SolidBrush( Color.Orange );
```

Many drawing methods have multiple versions. When employing methods that draw outlined hollow shapes, use versions that take a `Pen` argument. When employing methods that draw shapes filled with colors, patterns or images, use versions that take a `Brush` argument. Many of these methods require `x`, `y`, `width` and `height` arguments. The `x` and `y` arguments represent the shape's upper-left corner coordinate. The `width` and `height` arguments represent the width and height of the shape in pixels, respectively. Figure 26.17 summarizes several `Graphics` methods and their parameters.

Graphics Drawing Methods and Descriptions

Note: Many of these methods have multiple versions.

`DrawLine( Pen p, float x1, float y1, float x2, float y2 )`
Draws a line from the point (x1, y1) to the point (x2, y2). The Pen determines the color, style and width of the line.

`DrawRectangle( Pen p, float x, float y, float width, float height )`
Draws a rectangle of the specified width and height. The top-left corner of the rectangle is at the point (x, y). The Pen determines the rectangle's color, style and border width.

`FillRectangle( Brush b, float x, float y, float width, float height )`
Draws a solid rectangle of the specified width and height. The top-left corner of the rectangle is at the point (x, y). The Brush determines the fill pattern inside the rectangle.

`DrawEllipse( Pen p, float x, float y, float width, float height )`
Draws an ellipse inside a rectangular area of the specified width and height. The top-left corner of the rectangular area is at the point (x, y), and the Pen determines the color, style and border width of the ellipse.

`FillEllipse( Brush b, float x, float y, float width, float height )`
Draws a filled ellipse inside a rectangular area of the specified width and height. The top-left corner of the rectangular area is at the point (x, y), and the Brush determines the pattern inside the ellipse.

Figure 26.17 `Graphics` methods that draw lines, rectangles and ovals.

1. The RGB value of a `Color` represents _____.
   a) the index number of a color
   b) the amount of red, green and blue in a color
   c) the thickness of the drawing object
   d) the type of shape to draw

2. The _____ method is used to draw solid rectangles.
   a) `DrawRectangle`   b) `FillRectangle`
   c) `SolidRectangle`   d) `OpaqueRectangle`

Answers: 1) b. 2) b.

26.7 Printing Each Control of the Check Writer Application

Recall earlier that you created the empty `foreach` statement, in *Step 3* of the previous box, to iterate through all the controls on the Form. Now you will write code for the body of the `foreach` statement to print all controls on the Form, except for the Buttons. You do this in the following box.

Iterating through All the Objects of the Form to Print Each Control	1. ***Checking for Buttons.*** In the body of the `foreach` statement of `objPrintDocument_PrintPage`, add lines 348–352 of Fig. 26.18. Adding this `if` statement determines whether the current control is a Button. If the control is not a Button, then the body of the `if` statement executes. However, if the control is a Button, the `foreach` statement continues to the next control on the Form.

(cont.)

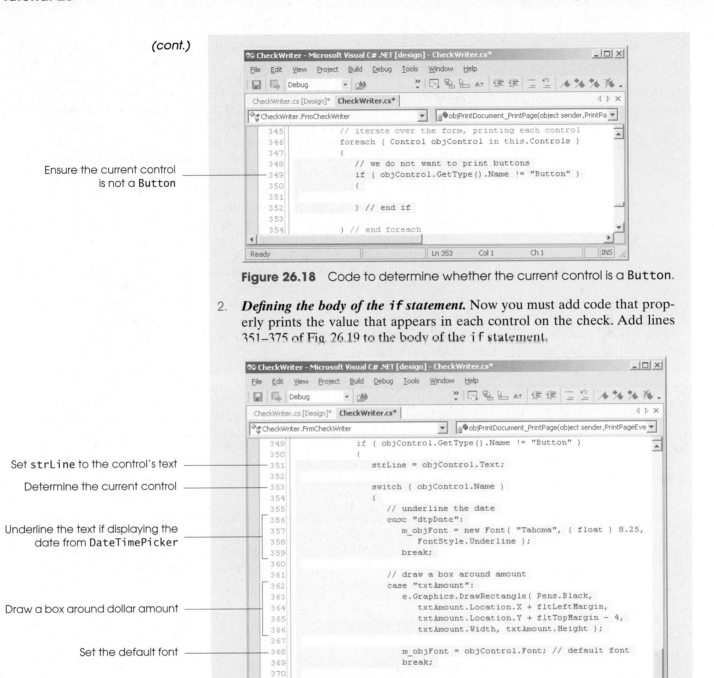

Ensure the current control is not a **Button**

Figure 26.18 Code to determine whether the current control is a **Button**.

2. ***Defining the body of the if statement.*** Now you must add code that properly prints the value that appears in each control on the check. Add lines 351–375 of Fig. 26.19 to the body of the **if** statement.

Set **strLine** to the control's text

Determine the current control

Underline the text if displaying the date from **DateTimePicker**

Draw a box around dollar amount

Set the default font

Figure 26.19 **switch** statement to print controls.

(cont.)

Line 351 sets the `strLine` variable that you created earlier to `objControl.Text`. This property contains the value contained in the control's `Text` property (text displayed to the user or entered by the user). The `switch` statement (lines 353–375) specifies how each control prints. The controlling expression is set to the value `objControl.Name`. This is the `Name` property of the control. You can use the `Name` property to select specific controls that need to be treated differently when printed.

The first `case` (lines 356–359) determines what happens when the current control is the `dtpDate DateTimePicker`. This `case` sets the `m_objFont` reference to the font style of the date—an underlined Tahoma font, with a size of `8.25` (the same size as the text in the control). The cast operator converts `8.25` from the `double` type to the `float` type. So, the date on the check will be underlined and will appear in `8.25` points in Tahoma font. Fonts are discussed in detail later in this tutorial.

The second `case` (lines 362–369) executes if the control is the `txtAmount TextBox`. This `case` draws the box that surrounds the decimal amount of the check. `DrawRectangle` (a `Graphics` method) is invoked by using the `e.Graphics` property. The outline of the rectangle prints in black, indicated by `Pens.Black`. The *x*- and *y*-coordinates are specified by adding the Text-Box's (*x-y*) location on the `Form` to the `fltLeftMargin` and `fltTopMargin` variables, respectively. Recall that we begin printing the check at the corner of the top and left margins. Adding the margin values to the `Location` properties ensures that the `txtAmount TextBox` prints in the same position as it appears on the `Form`. (Line 365 subtracts four points of space to center the box on the text.) Line 368 sets the font of the text to draw to the same value as the font used to display text in the control.

The `default` case (lines 371–373) executes for all the other controls. This `case` sets the `m_objFont` font style to the same value as the font used to display text in the control. Line 375 ends the `switch` statement.

3. ***Setting the positions of the text of each control.*** Add lines 377–383 from Fig. 26.20 to the body of the `if` statement. Line 378 sets the `fltXPosition` variable to `fltLeftMargin + objControl.Location.X`. By adding the *x*-coordinate of the current control (represented by `objControl.Location.X`) to the left margin, you ensure that the check will not draw outside the margins of the page.

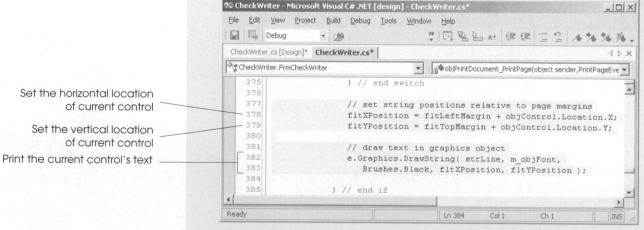

Set the horizontal location of current control

Set the vertical location of current control

Print the current control's text

Figure 26.20 Code to set the `string` positions of the controls.

(cont.)

Line 379 performs a similar operation, setting `fltYPosition` to the sum of the top margin and *y*-coordinate of the control's location. Lines 382–383 call the DrawString method on the `e.Graphics` property. The **DrawString** method draws the specified `string` of text in the `Graphics` object. The first argument is the `string` to draw, in this case `strLine`. Recall earlier that you set `strLine` to the `Text` property of the current control. The second argument is the font, which is specified by `m_objFont`. The third argument specifies a `Brush`. You pass the value `Brushes.Black`, which creates a black brush object to draw the text. The fourth and fifth arguments are the *x*- and *y*-coordinates where the first character of the `string` prints. Use the `fltXPosition` and `fltYPosition` variables that you set in lines 378–379 to print the text at the correct location on the page.

4. ***Saving the project.*** Select **File > Save All** to save your modified code.

SELF-REVIEW 1. The _____ method draws a specified `string` of text.

    a) `String`   b) `PrintString`

    c) `DrawString`   d) `Draw`

2. Typing `Brushes.Black` _____.

    a) obtains a black `Brush` object   b) retrieves the color of a brush

    c) paints the screen black   d) creates a `Pen` object

Answers: 1) c. 2) a.

26.8 Font Class

In the **Check Writer** application, you used a `Font` object to specify the style of the text printed on a page. This section introduces the methods and constants contained in the `Font` class. Note that once a `Font` has been created, its properties cannot be modified. That means that if you require a different `Font`, you must create a new `Font` object with the appropriate settings. There are many versions of the `Font` constructor for creating custom `Font`s to help you do this. Some properties of the `Font` class are summarized in Fig. 26.21.

Property	Description
`Bold`	Sets a font to a bold font style if value is set to `true`.
`FontFamily`	Represents the `FontFamily` of the `Font` (a grouping structure to organize fonts with similar properties).
`Height`	Represents the height of the font.
`Italic`	Sets a font to an italic font style if value is set to `true`.
`Name`	Sets the font's name to the specified `string`.
`Size`	Represents a `float` value indicating the current font size measured in design units. (Design units are any specified units of measurement for the font.)
`SizeInPoints`	Represents a `float` value indicating the current font size measured in points.
`Strikeout`	Sets a font to the strikeout font style if value is set to `true` (for example, ~~Deitel~~).
`Underline`	Sets a font to the underline font style if the value is set to `true`.

Figure 26.21 `Font` class read-only properties.

Common Programming Error

Specifying a font that is not available on a system is a logic error. If this occurs, that system's default font will be used instead.

Note that the Size property returns the font size as measured in **design units**, whereas SizeInPoints returns the font size as measured in points (a common measurement). The Size property can be specified in a variety of ways, such as inches or millimeters. Some versions of the Font constructor accept a Graphics-Unit argument—an enumeration that allows users to specify the unit of measurement used to describe the font size. Members of the GraphicsUnit enumeration include Point (1/72 inch), Display (1/75 inch), Document (1/300 inch), Millimeter, Inch and Pixel. If this argument is provided, the Size property contains the size of the font as measured in the specified design unit, and the SizeInPoints property contains the size of the font in points. For example, if you create a Font having size 1 and specify that GraphicsUnit.Inch will be used to measure the font, the Size property will be 1, and the SizeInPoints property will be 72 because there are 72 points in an inch. If you create a new Font object without specifying a GraphicsUnit, the default measurement for the font size is Graphics-Unit.Point (thus, the Size and SizeInPoints properties will be equal). [*Note*: There is no way to change the properties of a Font object—to use a different font, you must create a new Font object.]

The Font class has a number of constructors. Most require a **font name**, which is a string representing a font currently supported by the system. Common fonts include *SansSerif* and *Serif*. Constructors also require the **font size** as an argument. Lastly, Font constructors usually require a **font style**, specified by an element of the **FontStyle** enumeration: Fontstyle.Bold, Fontstyle.Italic, Fontstyle.Regular, Fontstyle.Strikeout and Fontstyle.Underline.

SELF-REVIEW

1. The most common measurement of font size is _____.

   a) points b) inches

   c) pixels d) millimeters

2. _____ is an example of a font style.

   a) Bold b) Italic

   c) StrikeOut d) All of the above.

Answers: 1) a. 2) d.

26.9 Previewing and Printing the Check

After defining how objects are printed in the objPrintDocument_PrintPage event handler, you must define what occurs when each Button is clicked. You begin with the btnPrint_Click event handler to specify the functionality when clicking the **Print** Button. You will write this event handler in the following box.

Defining the **btnPrint_Click** *Event Handler*

1. *Creating the **btnPrint_Click** event handler.* In the Windows Form Designer, double click the **Print** Button. The btnPrint_Click event handler appears in the CheckWriter.cs file.

2. *Creating a **PrintDocument** object.* Be sure to add the comments and break the header as shown in Fig. 26.22 so that the line numbers in your code match those presented in this tutorial. Then, add lines 403–404 of Fig. 26.22 to the event handler. The PrintDocument object is used to help print the check.

(cont.)

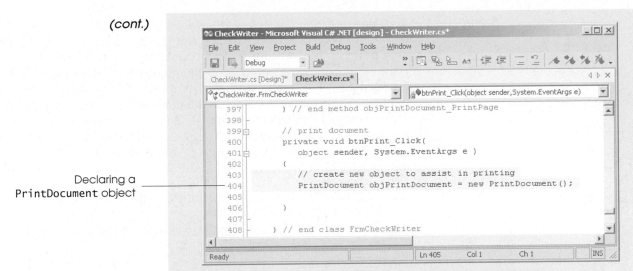

Declaring a
`PrintDocument` object

Figure 26.22 Code that creates the `PrintDocument` object.

3. ***Specifying the PrintPage event handler.*** Add lines 406–408 of Fig. 26.23 to the event handler. These lines specify the event handler called when the PrintPage event is raised. Lines 407–408 use the += operator to associate the `PrintPage` event of the `objPrintDocument` object with an event handler represented by an object of type `PrintPageEventHandler`. The event-handling method (`objPrintDocument_PrintPage`) is specified as the argument to the `PrintPageEventHandler` constructor. This indicates that the `objPrintDocument_PrintPage` event handler that you created earlier in this tutorial should be executed when the `PrintPage` event of `objPrint-Document` is raised. Normally, we specify an event handler by double-clicking a control in design view, or by double-clicking an event in the **Properties** window. Because our `PrintDocument` was not added visually (using the **Toolbox**), we must specify it's event handlers programmatically.

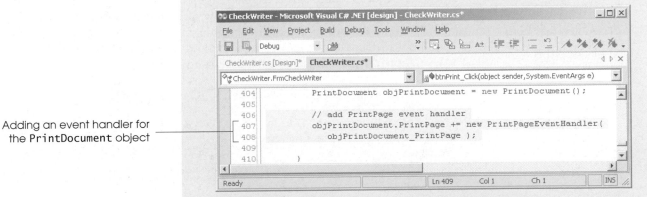

Adding an event handler for
the `PrintDocument` object

Figure 26.23 Code that adds an event handler to the `PrintDocument` object.

You can think of the reference to `PrintPageEventHandler` on line 407 as a constructor that creates a reference to an event handler (the `objPrintDocument_PrintPage` event handler that you created earlier in this tutorial). Line 407 uses the `new` operator to create this reference and uses the += operator to associate the `PrintPage` event of the `objPrint-Document` object with the event handler.

(cont.)

4. **Verifying that the user has a printer installed.** Add lines 410–415 of Fig. 26.24 to the btnPrint_Click event handler. Line 411 uses the **PrinterSettings.InstalledPrinters.Count** property to determine how many printers the user has installed on the computer. If there are no printers installed (that is, if the Count property returns 0), the user cannot print or preview the document. Line 413 in the body of the if statement displays an error message by calling the ErrorMessage method, which you will define in the next box. Line 414 exits the event handler using the return keyword. [*Note:* If the user has printers installed, but none of them are connected to the machine at runtime, errors will occur.]

Take no action if there are no printers installed

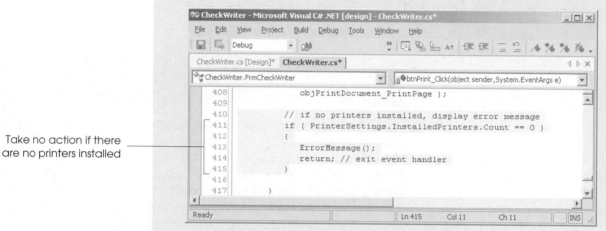

Figure 26.24 Exiting the event handler if no printers are installed.

5. **Printing the document.** Add lines 417–418 of Fig. 26.25 to the btnPrint_Click event handler. Line 418 calls the Print method of the PrintDocument object. The Print method, in turn, raises the PrintPage event each time it needs output for printing. Your PrintPage event handler then executes and uses a Graphics object to draw. The Graphics object is obtained from the Graphics property of the PrintPageEventArgs class. In this case, the PrintPageEventArgs object was passed as the e argument. The objPrintDocument_PrintPage method uses this PrintPageEventArgs' Graphics object to call the DrawRectangle and DrawString methods.

Printing the check

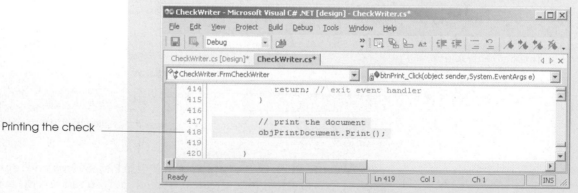

Figure 26.25 btnPrint_Click event handler modified to print the document.

6. **Saving the project.** Select **File > Save All** to save your modified code.

Now that you have defined the btnPrint_Click method, you will complete the application by coding the Click event handler for the **Preview** Button. When this Button is clicked, a dialog appears allowing users to preview the check before printing it. You will create the btnPreview_Click event handler to enable this feature in the following box.

Defining the btnPreview_Click Event Handler	1. ***Creating the btnPreview_Click event handler.*** In the Windows Form Designer, double click the **Preview** Button. The btnPreview_Click event handler appears in the CheckWriter.cs file.
	2. ***Creating the PrintDocument object and adding the PrintPage handler.*** Be sure to add the comments and break the header as shown in Fig. 26.26 so that the line numbers in your code match those presented in this tutorial. Then, add lines 427–432 of Fig. 26.26 to the event handler. As in event handler btnPrint_Click, line 428 creates a new PrintDocument object named objPrintDocument. Lines 431–432 specify that the PrintDocument object's PrintPage event handler is the objPrintDocument_PrintPage method.

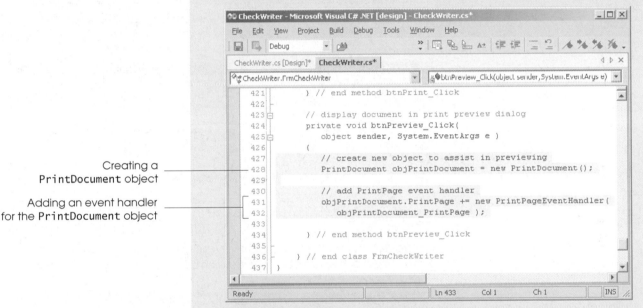

Creating a
PrintDocument object

Adding an event handler
for the PrintDocument object

Figure 26.26   btnPreview_Click event handler modified to create PrintDocument and add PrintPage event handler.

3. ***Verifying that the user has a printer.*** Add lines 434–439 of Fig. 26.27 to the btnPreview_Click event handler. These lines of code are exactly the same as the code from *Step 4* of the previous box. An error message is displayed if there are no installed printers.

4. ***Specifying the PrintPreviewDialog object's Document property.*** Add line 441 of Fig. 26.28 to the event handler. Recall earlier that, when you created the PrintPreviewDialog object, you learned that its Document property specifies the document to preview. This property requires that its value be of the PrintDocument type, the same class you use to print the check. This line sets objPreview's Document property to objPrintDocument (the Print-Document you created in line 428 of Fig. 26.26).

5. ***Showing the Print preview dialog.*** Add line 442 of Fig. 26.29 to the event handler. This line invokes the PrintPreviewDialog object's ShowDialog method to display the **Print preview** dialog that displays how the PrintDocument will appear when printed. To display the document, the PrintPreviewControl of the PrintPreviewDialog raises the PrintPage event. Rather than using the Graphics object to print a page using your printer, the PrintPreviewDialog uses the Graphics object to display the page on the screen.

(cont.)

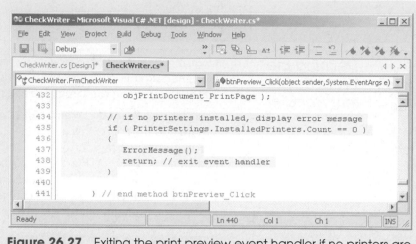

Figure 26.27 Exiting the print preview event handler if no printers are installed.

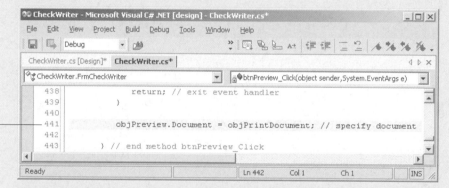

Setting the document to preview

Figure 26.28 `btnPreview_Click` event handler modified to set the `PrintPreviewDialog` object's **Document** property.

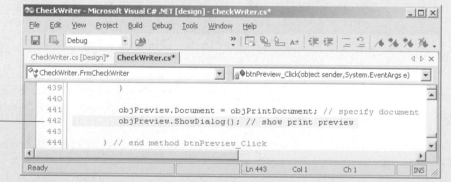

Displaying the preview dialog

Figure 26.29 `btnPreview_Click` event handler modified to show preview dialog.

6. ***Defining the ErrorMessage method.*** Add lines 446–454 from Fig. 26.30 into your application. Lines 449–452 display an error message to the user indicating that printing and print previewing the check is not possible if there are no printers installed on the computer.

7. ***Running the application.*** Select **Debug > Start** to run your application. Enter the information for check and click the **Preview** Button. The check should be displayed in the print preview. Use the **Print** Button to print the check. Verify that the check prints out to your default printer (if you have a printer set up).

(cont.)

Method to display error message ———

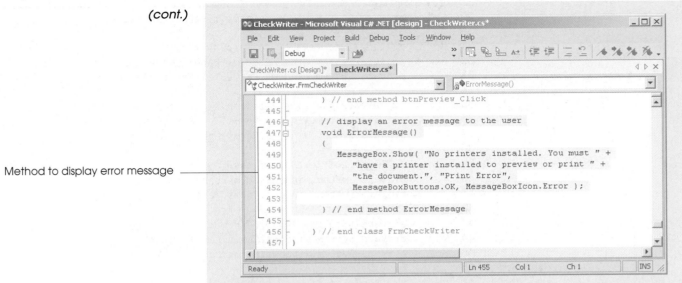

Figure 26.30   Displaying an error message when no printers are installed.

8. ***Closing the application.*** Close your running application by clicking its close box.

9. ***Closing the IDE.*** Close Visual Studio .NET by clicking its close box.

Figure 26.31 presents the source code for the **Check Writer** application. The lines of code that contain new programming concepts that you learned in this tutorial are highlighted.

```
1   using System;
2   using System.Drawing;
3   using System.Collections;
4   using System.ComponentModel;
5   using System.Windows.Forms;
6   using System.Data;
7   using System.Drawing.Printing;
8
9   namespace CheckWriter
10  {
11     /// <summary>
12     /// Summary description for FrmCheckWriter.
13     /// </summary>
14     public class FrmCheckWriter : System.Windows.Forms.Form
15     {
16        // Label to display payer information
17        private System.Windows.Forms.TextBox txtPayer;
18
19        // Label and TextBox to display number of check
20        private System.Windows.Forms.Label lblNumber;
21        private System.Windows.Forms.TextBox txtNumber;
22
23        // Label and DateTimePicker to display date of check
24        private System.Windows.Forms.Label lblDate;
25        private System.Windows.Forms.DateTimePicker dtpDate;
26
27        // Label and TextBox to display check amount
28        private System.Windows.Forms.Label lblAmount;
```

Figure 26.31   **Check Writer** application code. (Part 1 of 5.)

```
29        private System.Windows.Forms.TextBox txtAmount;
30
31        // Label and TextBox to display recipient
32        private System.Windows.Forms.Label lblPayee;
33        private System.Windows.Forms.TextBox txtPayee;
34
35        // TextBox and Label to display written check amount
36        private System.Windows.Forms.TextBox txtPayment;
37        private System.Windows.Forms.Label lblDollars;
38
39        // Label and TextBox to display memo text
40        private System.Windows.Forms.Label lblMemo;
41        private System.Windows.Forms.TextBox txtMemo;
42
43        // Labels to display MICR numbers
44        private System.Windows.Forms.Label lblABA;
45        private System.Windows.Forms.Label lblAccount;
46
47        // Labels to display signature
48        private System.Windows.Forms.Label lblSigned;
49        private System.Windows.Forms.Label lblUnderline;
50
51        // Button to preview the check
52        private System.Windows.Forms.Button btnPreview;
53
54        // Button to print the check
55        private System.Windows.Forms.Button btnPrint;
56
57        // PrintPreviewDialog to print and preview the check
58        private System.Windows.Forms.PrintPreviewDialog objPreview;
59
60        /// <summary>
61        /// Required designer variable.
62        /// </summary>
63        private System.ComponentModel.Container components = null;
64
65        private Font m_objFont; // instance variable to store font
66
67        public FrmCheckWriter()
68        {
69            //
70            // Required for Windows Form Designer support
71            //
72            InitializeComponent();
73
74            //
75            // TODO: Add any constructor code after InitializeComponent
76            // call
77            //
78        }
79
80        /// <summary>
81        /// Clean up any resources being used.
82        /// </summary>
83        protected override void Dispose( bool disposing )
84        {
85            if( disposing )
86            {
```

Instance variable to store the font —— 65

Figure 26.31 **Check Writer** application code. (Part 2 of 5.)

```
 87                           if (components != null)
 88                           {
 89                               components.Dispose();
 90                           }
 91                       }
 92                       base.Dispose( disposing );
 93                   }
 94
 95                   // Windows Form Designer generated code
 96
 97                   /// <summary>
 98                   /// The main entry point for the application.
 99                   /// </summary>
100                   [STAThread]
101                   static void Main()
102                   {
103                       Application.Run( new FrmCheckWriter() );
104                   }
105
106                   // PrintPage event raised for each page to be printed
107                   private void objPrintDocument_PrintPage(
108                       object sender, PrintPageEventArgs e )
109                   {
110                       float fltYPosition;
111                       float fltXPosition;
112
113                       // represent left margin of page
114                       float fltLeftMargin = e.MarginBounds.Left;
115
116                       // represent top margin of page
117                       float fltTopMargin = e.MarginBounds.Top;
118                       string strLine = "";
119
120                       // iterate over the form, printing each control
121                       foreach ( Control objControl in this.Controls )
122                       {
123                           // we do not want to print buttons
124                           if ( objControl.GetType().Name != "Button" )
125                           {
126                               strLine = objControl.Text;
127
128                               switch ( objControl.Name )
129                               {
130                                   // underline the date
131                                   case "dtpDate":
132                                       m_objFont = new Font( "Tahoma", ( float ) 8.25,
133                                           FontStyle.Underline );
134                                       break;
135
136                                   // draw a box around amount
137                                   case "txtAmount":
138                                       e.Graphics.DrawRectangle( Pens.Black,
139                                           txtAmount.Location.X + fltLeftMargin,
140                                           txtAmount.Location.Y + fltTopMargin - 4,
141                                           txtAmount.Width, txtAmount.Height );
142
143                                       m_objFont = objControl.Font; // default font
144                                       break;
```

Event handler indicating what to print → (lines 107–108)

Variable to store the left margin value → (line 114)

Variable to store the right margin value → (line 117)

Looping through each control on the **Form** → (line 121)

Underlining text → (lines 132–133)

Drawing a box around the text → (lines 138–141)

Using the control's font → (line 143)

Figure 26.31 Check Writer application code. (Part 3 of 5.)

```
145
146                             default:
147                                 m_objFont = objControl.Font; // default font
148                                 break;
149
150                         } // end switch
151
152                         // set string positions relative to page margins
153                         fltXPosition = fltLeftMargin + objControl.Location.X;
154                         fltYPosition = fltTopMargin + objControl.Location.Y;
155
156                         // draw text in graphics object
157                         e.Graphics.DrawString( strLine, m_objFont,
158                             Brushes.Black, fltXPosition, fltYPosition );
159
160                     } // end if
161
162                 } // end foreach
163
164                 // draw box around check
165                 e.Graphics.DrawRectangle( Pens.Black, fltLeftMargin,
166                     fltTopMargin, this.Width, this.Height - 60 );
167
168                 // indicate that there are no more pages to print
169                 e.HasMorePages = false;
170
171             } // end method objPrintDocument_PrintPage
172
173             // print document
174             private void btnPrint_Click(
175                 object sender, System.EventArgs e )
176             {
177                 // create new object to assist in printing
178                 PrintDocument objPrintDocument = new PrintDocument();
179
180                 // add PrintPage event handler
181                 objPrintDocument.PrintPage += new PrintPageEventHandler(
182                     objPrintDocument_PrintPage );
183
184                 // if no printers installed, display error message
185                 if ( PrinterSettings.InstalledPrinters.Count == 0 )
186                 {
187                     ErrorMessage();
188                     return; // exit event handler
189                 }
190
191                 // print the document
192                 objPrintDocument.Print();
193
194             } // end method btnPrint_Click
195
196             // display document in print preview dialog
197             private void btnPreview_Click(
198                 object sender, System.EventArgs e )
199             {
200                 // create new object to assist in previewing
201                 PrintDocument objPrintDocument = new PrintDocument();
202
```

Labels (left margin annotations):
- Printing text → lines 157–158
- Drawing a box around the check → lines 165–166
- Indicating that there are no more pages → line 169
- Create a **PrintDocument** object → line 178
- Add an event handler for the **PrintDocument** object → lines 181–182
- Display an error message if no printers are installed → line 187
- Print the check → line 192
- Create a **PrintDocument** object → line 201

Figure 26.31   **Check Writer** application code. (Part 4 of 5.)

```
                              203      // add PrintPage event handler
Add an event handler for     204      objPrintDocument.PrintPage += new PrintPageEventHandler(
the PrintDocument object      205         objPrintDocument_PrintPage );
                              206
                              207      // if no printers installed, display error message
                              208      if ( PrinterSettings.InstalledPrinters.Count == 0 )
                              209      {
Display an error message     210         ErrorMessage();
if no printers are installed  211         return; // exit event handler
                              212      }
                              213
                              214      objPreview.Document = objPrintDocument; // specify document
Show preview in dialog        215      objPreview.ShowDialog(); // show print preview
                              216
                              217   } // end method btnPreview_Click
                              218
                              219   // display an error message to the user
                              220   void ErrorMessage()
                              221   {
                              222      MessageBox.Show( "No printers installed. You must " +
                              223         "have a printer installed to preview or print " +
                              224         "the document.", "Print Error",
                              225         MessageBoxButtons.OK, MessageBoxIcon.Error );
                              226
                              227   } // end method ErrorMessage
                              228
                              229   } // end class FrmCheckWriter
                              230 }
```

Figure 26.31   Check Writer application code. (Part 5 of 5.)

SELF-REVIEW

1. The _____ property determines how many printers the user has installed on the computer.
   a) `PrinterSettings.NumberOfPrinters`
   b) `PrinterSettings.InstalledPrinters.Count`
   c) `PrinterSettings.InstalledPrinters.Length`
   d) `PrinterSettings.Count`

2. The _____ object contains the `PrintPage` event.
   a) `PrintDocument`   b) `PrintPreviewDialog`
   c) `PrintPreviewControl`   d) `PrintDialog`

Answers: 1) b. 2) a.

26.10 Wrap-Up

In this tutorial, you were introduced to the topic of graphics and printing. You created a **Check Writer** application, which allows you to enter data in a check and print it using the printer installed on your computer. You learned how to use the Graphics object and its members. While building the **Check Writer** application, you used these concepts to draw shapes and `strings` using graphics objects such as Pens and Brushes. You also learned how to use code to create fonts to apply to text you wish to display or print.

You also learned about several new classes, including `PrintPreviewDialog`, `PrintPreviewControl` and `PrintDocument`. You used the `PrintDocument` class to create a `PrintDocument` object. You then used its `PrintPage` event to execute code that draws and prints the check when the user clicks the **Print** Button. You also added a `PrintPreviewDialog` in your application, allowing the user to pre-view a check before printing it.

In the next tutorial, you will learn how to use multimedia in your applications. In particular, you will be introduced to Microsoft Agent, a technology used to add three-dimensional, animated characters to a program. You will use this technology to create a phone book application.

SKILLS SUMMARY

Printing a Rectangle

- Use the `PrintPageEventArgs` object's `Graphics` property.
- Use the `Graphics` property to invoke the `DrawRectangle` or `FillRectangle` method.
- Specify the five parameters: A `Brush` (or `Pen`) object, the *x*-coordinate, the *y*-coordinate, the width and the height.

Printing a `String`

- Use the `PrintPageEventArgs` object's `Graphics` property.
- Use the `Graphics` property to invoke the `DrawString` method.
- Specify the five parameters: the string to print, the font style, the `Brush` object, the *x*-coordinate and the *y*-coordinate.

Associating a `PrintPage` Event with a Defined Event Handler

- Use *objectName*`.PrintPage += new PrintPageEventHandler(` *eventHandlerName* `);` where *objectName* represents the name of the object with which the event will be associated and *eventHandlerName* represents the name of the defined event handler to be associated with the `PrintPage` event.

Printing a Document

- Create a new `PrintDocument` object.
- Define the `PrintDocument`'s `PrintPage` event handler to specify what to print.
- Use the `PrintDocument` to invoke the `Print` method.

Displaying a Print Preview Dialog

- Create a `PrintPreviewDialog` object.
- Specify the `PrintDocument` to preview in the `PrintPreviewDialog`'s `Document` property.
- Invoke the `PrintPreviewDialog`'s `ShowDialog` method.

KEY TERMS

API (application programming interface)—Used by a program to access the operating system and various services on the computer.

ARGB values—A combination of alpha, red, green and blue components from which every color is created.

Brush object—Used to specify drawing parameters when drawing solid shapes.

Control reference—An object that represents a control on the `Form`.

coordinate system—A scheme for identifying every possible point on the computer screen.

design units—Any specified units of measurement for a font.

dithering—Process that uses small dots of existing colors to form a pattern that simulates a desired color.

Document property—Property of the `PrintPreviewDialog` that allows you to specify the document that will be displayed in the dialog.

DrawRectangle method of the Graphics class—Draws the outline of a rectangle of a specified size and color at a specified location.

DrawString method—`Graphics` method that draws a specified `string`.

float type—Stores floating-point values. A `float` is similar to a `double`, but is less precise and requires less memory.

Font class—Contains properties that define unique fonts.

FontFamily class—Contains methods, such as `GetName` and `GetType`, for obtaining font information.

FromArgb method of the Color class—Creates a new Color object from RGB and alpha values.

GDI+—An application programming interface (API) that provides classes for creating two-dimensional vector graphics.

GetName method of the Font class—Returns the name of the Font object.

GetType method of the Font class—Returns the type of the Font object.

Graphics object—Draws two-dimensional images.

HasMorePages property of the PrintPageEventArgs class—Specifies if there are more pages to print. When False, the PrintPage event is no longer raised.

Image class—Used to store and manipulate images from various file formats.

MarginBounds.Left property of the PrintPageEventArgs class—Specifies the left margin of a printed page.

MarginBounds.Top property of the PrintPageEventArgs class—Specifies the top margin of a printed page.

opacity—Amount of transparency of the color.

Pen object—Used to specify drawing parameters when drawing shape outlines.

Print method—PrintDocument method used to print a document.

PrintDocument class—Allows users to describe how to print a document.

PrintPage event—Occurs when the data required to print the current page is needed.

PrintPreviewDialog class—Previews a document before it prints in a dialog box.

PrinterSettings.InstalledPrinters.Count property—Determines how many printers the user has installed on the computer.

Rectangle structure—Enables you to define rectangular shapes and their dimensions.

ShowDialog method of class PrintPreviewDialog—Used to display the PrintPreview-Dialog to the user.

System.Drawing.Printing namespace—Allows your applications to access all services related to printing.

this keyword—References the current object.

UseAntiAlias property—Property of class PrintPreviewDialog that makes the text in the PrintPreviewDialog appear smoother on the screen.

vector graphics—Graphics created by a set of mathematical properties called vectors, which include the graphics' dimensions, attributes and positions.

***x*-axis**—Describes every horizontal coordinate.

***x*-coordinate**—Horizontal distance (increasing to the right) from the left of the drawing area.

***y*-axis**—Describes every vertical coordinate.

***y*-coordinate**—Vertical distance (increasing downward) from the top of the drawing area.

CONTROLS, EVENTS, PROPERTIES & METHODS

Font   This class is used to define the font face, size and style of text throughout an application.

■ *Properties*

Bold—Sets the weight of the text.

Italic—Sets the angle of the text.

Size—Sets the size of the text.

FontFamily—Contains a FontFamily object, which is used to store font face information.

FontSyle—Specifies the style applied to a Font object.

Graphics   The class that contains methods used to draw text, lines and shapes.

■ *Methods*

DrawLine—Draws a line of a specified size and color.

DrawEllipse—Draws the outline of an ellipse of a specified size and color at a specified location.

DrawRectangle—Draws the outline of a rectangle of a specified size and color at a specified location.

DrawString—Draws a string in a specified font and color at a specified position.

FillEllipse—Draws a solid ellipse of a specified size and color at the specified location.

FillRectangle—Draws a solid rectangle of a specified size and color at the specified location.

PrintDocument This class allows you to specify how to print a document.

- *Event*

  PrintPage—Raised when data required to print a page is needed.

- *Method*

  Print—Uses a Graphics object to print a page.

PrinterSettings This class stores information about the system's printer settings.

- *Property*

  Count—Returns the number of printers installed on the system.

PrintPageEventArgs This class contains data passed to a PrintPage event.

- *Properties*

  HasMorePages—Specifies if there are more pages to print. When false, the PrintPage event is no longer raised.

  MarginBounds—Specifies the margin of the printed page.

    Left—Specifies the left margin of the page.

    Top—Specifies the top margin of the page.

PrintPreviewDialog 🔲 PrintPreviewDialog   This control is used to display how a document will look when it is printed.

- *Properties*

  Document—Specifies the document that the control will preview. The document must be of the PrintDocument type.

  Name—Specifies the name used to access the PrintPreviewDialog control programmatically. The name should be prefixed with obj.

  UseAntiAlias—Specifies whether the dialog will display a smoothed image.

- *Method*

  ShowDialog—Used to display the PrintPreviewDialog to the user.

MULTIPLE-CHOICE QUESTIONS

26.1 The RGB value (0, 0, 255) represents _____.

   a) Color.Red   b) Color.Green

   c) Color.Blue   d) Color.Yellow

26.2 The _____ property of the PrintPreviewDialog object makes text appear smoother.

   a) AntiAlias   b) UseAntiAlias

   c) Alias   d) UseAlias

26.3 Use a _____ object to allow users to preview a document before it is printed.

   a) PrintPreviewDialog   b) PrintDocument

   c) Print   d) PrintPreviewControl

26.4 The _____ event occurs when the data required to print the current page is needed.

   a) OnPaint   b) Print

   c) Document   d) PrintPage

26.5 To display the preview dialog of the _____ object, call the ShowDialog method.

   a) `PrintPreviewDialog`   b) `PrintDocument`

   c) `PrintDialog`   d) Both a and b.

26.6 Set the _____ property to `false` to indicate that there are no more pages to print.

   a) `Document`   b) `HasMorePages`

   c) `TerminatePrint`   d) Both a and b.

26.7 The Print method of class `PrintDocument` sends a _____ object to the printer for printing.

   a) `Graphics`   b) `PrintDocument`

   c) `PrintPreviewDialog`   d) `Brush`

26.8 The _____ keyword references the current object.

   a) `me`   b) `class`

   c) `this`   d) `property`

26.9 Opacity is the _____ value of a color.

   a) red   b) transparency

   c) dithering   d) bluc

26.10 Design units are used to specify the _____ of a Font.

   a) `Size`   b) `Name`

   c) `FontFamily`   d) `Style`

EXERCISES

26.11 (*Check Writer Modified to Print Background Images*) Modify the **Check Writer** application to display and print a background for the check. The GUI should look similar to Fig. 26.32. Users can select a background image. The image should appear in the **Print preview** dialog box and also should print as a background to the check.

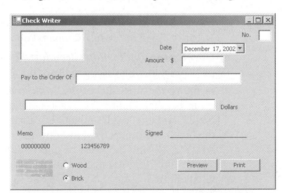

Figure 26.32   Modified **Check Writer** GUI.

   a) *Copying the template to your working directory.* Copy the directory `C:\Examples\Tutorial26\Exercises\ModifiedCheckWriter` to your `C:\SimplyCSP` directory.

   b) *Opening the application's template file.* Double click `CheckWriter.sln` in the `ModifiedCheckWriter` directory to open the application.

   c) *Adding an instance variable.* Add an instance variable of the `string` type that will contain the name of the background image.

   d) *Defining the Load event handler.* Double click an empty area of the Form to create its Load event handler. Define the event handler to initialize the `string` instance variable to "wood.jpg". Set the Image property of the PictureBox to this image. [*Hint*: use the FromFile method of the Image class.]

   e) *Defining the CheckedChanged event handler.* Double click the **Wood** RadioButton to create its CheckedChanged event handler. Define the event handler to notify the application when users have made a background selection. If the **Wood** RadioButton is selected, then a preview of the wooden background should display in the picPreview PictureBox. Otherwise, if the **Brick** RadioButton is selected, then a preview of the brick background should display in the picPreview PictureBox.

f) *Running the application.* Select **Debug > Start** to run your application. Fill out the information for a check. Preview and print the check with each background to ensure that your application works correctly.

g) *Closing the application.* Close your running application by clicking its close box.

h) *Closing the IDE.* Close Visual Studio .NET by clicking its close box.

26.12 (*Company Logo Application*) Develop a **Company Logo** application that allows users to design a company logo (Fig. 26.33).

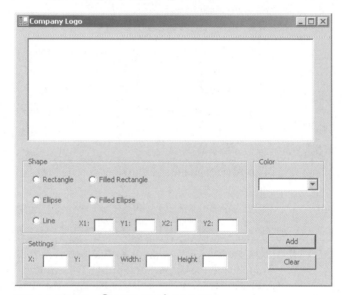

Figure 26.33 **Company Logo** GUI.

a) *Copying the template to your working directory.* Copy the directory C:\Examples\ Tutorial26\Exercises\CompanyLogo to your C:\SimplyCSP directory.

b) *Opening the application's template file.* Double click CompanyLogo.sln in the CompanyLogo directory to open the application.

c) *Defining the Add Button's Click event handler.* Create the **Add** Button's Click event handler. Define the event handler so that the shape the user specifies is drawn on the PictureBox. Use the CreateGraphics method on the PictureBox to retrieve the Graphics object used to draw on the PictureBox. [*Note*: The TextBoxes labelled **X1:**, **Y1:**, **X2:** and **Y2:** must be filled out to draw a line. The TextBoxes labelled **X:**, **Y:**, **Width:** and **Height:** must be filled out to draw a rectangle, filled rectangle, ellipse, or filled ellipse.]

d) *Defining the Clear Button's Click event handler.* Create the **Clear** Button's Click event handler, and define it so that the PictureBox is cleared. [*Hint*: To clear the entire PictureBox, use the PictureBox's Invalidate method. The Invalidate method is often used to refresh (update) the graphics of a control. By using the Invalidate method without specifying a graphic to draw, the PictureBox clears.] Also ensure that all TextBoxes are cleared when the **Clear** Button is clicked.

e) *Running the application.* Select **Debug > Start** to run your application. Draw each shape, using various colors, and test the **Add** and **Clear** Buttons to ensure that your application works correctly.

f) *Closing the application.* Close your running application by clicking its close box.

g) *Closing the IDE.* Close Visual Studio .NET by clicking its close box.

26.13 (*Letterhead Application*) Create a **Letterhead** application that allows users to design stationery for company documents (Fig. 26.34). Allow users to specify the image that will serve as the letterhead.

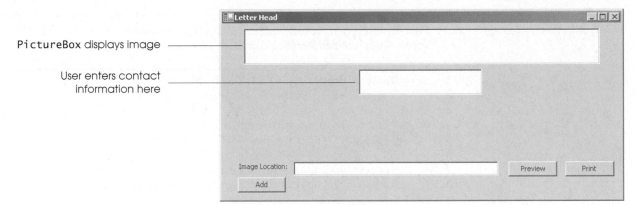

PictureBox displays image ⎯⎯⎯

User enters contact
information here ⎯⎯⎯

Figure 26.34 Letterhead GUI.

a) *Copying the template to your working directory.* Copy the C:\Examples\ Tutorial26\Exercises\Letterhead directory to your C:\SimplyCSP directory.

b) *Opening the application's template file.* Double click Letterhead.sln in the Letterhead directory to open the application.

c) *Creating a PrintPreviewDialog control.* Add a PrintPreviewDialog control to allow users to preview the letterhead before it is printed. Rearrange and comment the control declaration appropriately.

d) *Defining the PrintPage event handler.* Allow users to print the document by defining the PrintPage event handler as you did in the **Check Writer** application.

e) *Defining the btnPrint_Click event handler.* The btnPrint_Click event handler should tell the PrintDocument where to find the PrintPage event handler, as in the **Check Writer** application, and print the document.

f) *Defining the btnPreview_Click event handler.* The btnPreview_Click event handler should tell the PrintDocument where to find the PrintPage event handler, as in the **Check Writer** application, and then show the preview dialog.

g) *Defining the btnAdd_Click event handler.* The btnAdd_Click event handler should set the PictureBox's. Image property to the value entered in the TextBox. [*Hint*: use the FromFile method of the Image class.] If no value was entered, display an error message.

h) *Running the application.* Select **Debug > Start** to run your application. The Letterhead.png image file, located in C:\Examples\Tutorial26\Exercises\Images, has been provided for you to test the application's letterhead image capability. Preview and print the letterhead to ensure that your application works correctly.

i) *Closing the application.* Close your running application by clicking its close box.

j) *Closing the IDE.* Close Visual Studio .NET by clicking its close box.

What does this code do? ▶ **26.14** What is the result of the following code? Assume that objOutput_PrintPage is defined.

```
1   private void btnPrint_Click(
2      object sender, System.EventArgs e )
3   {
4      PrintDocument objOutput = new PrintDocument();
5
6      // add PrintPage event handler
7      objOutput.PrintPage += new PrintPageEventHandler(
8         objOutput_PrintPage );
9
10     objOutput.Print();
11
12  } // end method btnPrint_Click
```

What's wrong with this code? ▶ **26.15** Find the error(s) in the following code. This is the definition for a `Click` event handler for a `Button`. This event handler should draw a filled rectangle on a `PictureBox` control.

```
1   private void btnDrawImage_Click(
2       object sender, System.EventArgs e)
3   {
4       // create an orange colored brush
5       SolidBrush objBrush = new SolidBrush( Orange );
6
7       // create a Graphics object to draw on the PictureBox
8       Graphics objGraphics = picPictureBox.AcquireGraphics();
9
10      // draw a filled rectangle
11      objGraphics.FillRectangle( objBrush, 2, 3, 40, 30 );
12
13  } // end method btnDrawImage_Click
```

Programming Challenge ▶ **26.16** (*Screen Saver Application*) Develop an application that simulates a screen saver. This application should add random-colored, random-sized, solid and hollow shapes at different positions of the screen. Copy the C:\Exercises\Tutorial26\ScreenSaver directory, and place it in your C:\SimplyCSP directory. The design of the Form has been created, which consists of a black Form and a Timer control. In the ScreenSaver.cs code view, the DisplayShape method has been provided, and the Timer's tick event handler has already been defined for you.

You must write the rest of the DisplayShape method code. Create the Graphics object from the Form using the Form's CreateGraphics method, and specify random colors, sizes and positions for the filled and hollow shapes that will be displayed on the screen. The width and height of the shapes should be no larger than 100 pixels.

26.17 (*Screen Saver Enhancement Application*) Enhance the **Screen Saver** application from Exercise 26.16 by modifying the Timer control's Tick event handler. Add code to this event handler so that after a specified amount of time, the screen should clear the displayed shapes. After the screen clears, random shapes should continue to display. Also, use the Color.FromArgb method so that you can specify random opacity (alpha values) for the colors. You should pass four arguments to this method. The first argument is the alpha value, the second is the red value, the third is the green value and the fourth is the blue value.

Objectives

In this tutorial, you will learn to:
- Download the components necessary to run Microsoft Agent.
- Enhance Windows applications using multimedia.
- Create applications that interact with users.
- Use Microsoft Agent in a C# application.

Outline

Phone Book Application

Introducing Multimedia Using Microsoft Agent

When computers were first introduced, they were large and expensive and were used primarily to perform arithmetic calculations. **Multimedia** applications, which use a variety of media, including graphics, animation, video and sound, were made impractical by the high cost and slow speed of computers. However, today's affordable, ultrafast processors are making multimedia-based applications commonplace. As the market for multimedia explodes, users are purchasing computers with faster processors, larger amounts of memory and wider communications bandwidths needed to support multimedia applications.

Users are seeing exciting new three-dimensional multimedia applications that interact with the user by means of animation, audio and video. Multimedia programming is an entertaining and innovative field, but one that presents many challenges. C# enables you to include such multimedia presentations in your applications.

In this tutorial, you will explore the **Microsoft Agent** technology, which uses entertaining, animated three-dimensional cartoon characters to interact with the application user. You will create a **Phone Book** application that uses one of the predefined Agent characters.

27.1 Microsoft Agent

In this tutorial, you will create a **Phone Book** application that displays people's phone numbers, using Microsoft Agent to interact with users and enhance the application. This application must meet the following requirements:

> ### Application Requirements
>
> *A software company's customer service department is responsible for calling clients. They need a quick way to access their clients' phone numbers and have asked you to develop an application that stores and retrieves the names and numbers of their clients. The service-department employees want an application that employs multimedia (using the Microsoft Agent character, Peedy the Parrot) to allow them to retrieve the phone numbers by speaking the clients' names and also by selecting clients' names with the mouse.*

Microsoft Agent is a technology used to add **interactive animated characters** to Windows applications or Web pages. Microsoft Agent characters can speak (by using voice synthesis) and respond to user input (by using speech recognition). Microsoft employs its Agent technology in such applications as Word, Excel and PowerPoint, where they help users understand how to use the application.

The Microsoft Agent control provides you with access to four predefined characters—*Genie* (a genie), *Merlin* (a wizard), *Peedy* (a parrot) and *Robby* (a robot). Each character contains unique animations that you can use in their applications to illustrate different instructions and actions. For instance, the Peedy character-animation set includes several flying animations which you can use to move Peedy across the screen. Microsoft provides basic information on Agent technology at:

> www.microsoft.com/msagent/default.asp

Microsoft Agent technology enables users to interact with applications and Web pages by using speech. When the user speaks into a microphone, the control uses a **speech-recognition engine**, an application that translates vocal sound input from a microphone into a language that the computer understands. The Microsoft Agent control also uses a text-to-speech engine, which allows the Microsoft Agent characters to speak lines of text. A **text-to-speech engine** is an application that translates typed words into sound, which users hear through headphones or speakers connected to a computer. Microsoft provides speech-recognition and text-to-speech engines for several languages at

> www.microsoft.com/products/msagent/downloads/user.asp

SELF-REVIEW

1. A _____ translates typed words into sound.

   a) speech-recognition engine   b) text-to-speech engine
   c) character-animation set   d) All of the above.

2. The application that translates vocal sound input from a microphone to a language understood by the computer is called the _____.

   a) speech-recognition engine   b) text-to-speech engine
   c) character-animation set   d) All of the above.

Answers: 1) b. 2) a.

27.2 Downloading Microsoft Agent Components

Microsoft Agent characters can be used as visual aids for applications. These Agents also allow users to speak to, listen to and interact with the characters. This tutorial demonstrates how to use the Microsoft Agent characters to build the **Phone Book** application. To run this tutorial's application, you must download and install the Agent control, speech-recognition engine, text-to-speech engine and Peedy character definition from the Microsoft Agent Web site. Begin by visiting:

> www.microsoft.com/products/msagent/downloads/user.asp

This page (Fig. 27.1) displays a list of Microsoft Agent downloads. The first component you need to download is the Agent character file. Click the **Microsoft Agent character files** link (Fig. 27.1).

Clicking this link directs users to the location where the Microsoft Agent character files can be downloaded (Fig. 27.2). Select the Peedy character from the drop-down list and click the **Download selected character** link. Save the file Peedy.exe to your computer, and install the Peedy character files by double clicking this file. [*Note:* You will need to download and install the other characters as well to complete this tutorial's exercises.]

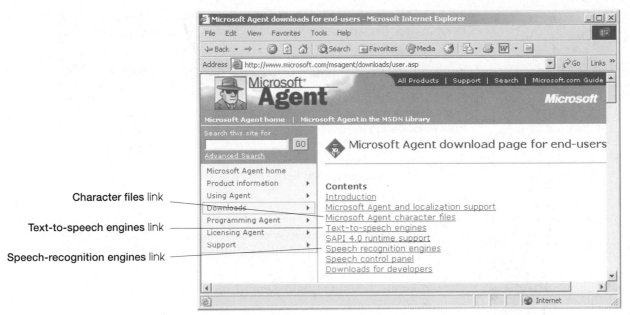

Character files link

Text-to-speech engines link

Speech-recognition engines link

Figure 27.1   Microsoft Web page containing Agent-related downloads.

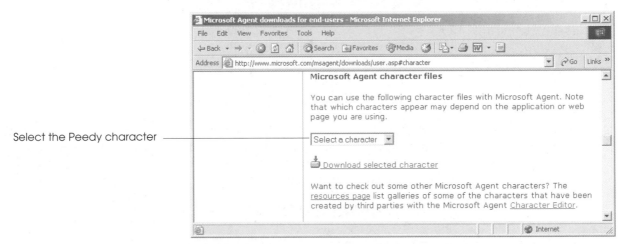

Select the Peedy character

Figure 27.2   Location for downloading the Microsoft Agent character.

Next, you should download the text-to-speech engine. Return to the **Microsoft Agent Downloads Contents** list by scrolling to the top of the current page, and click the **Text-to-speech engines** link. Click the ComboBox to display the dropdown list, and select the engine that supports American English. Click the **Download selected engine** link to save the file tv_enua.exe. Double click this file once it has been downloaded to install the text-to-speech engine. You may need to restart your machine after this installation.

You must also download the speech-recognition engine. Return to the **Microsoft Agent Downloads Contents** list by scrolling to the top of the current page, and click the **Speech recognition engines** link. Click the **Download the Microsoft Speech Recognition Engine** link to save the file actcnc.exe. Double click this file once it has been downloaded to install the speech-recognition engine. The installation process will walk you through the configuration of your microphone. Once you have downloaded and installed all of the components, you are ready to use Microsoft Agent.

[*Note*: Windows XP users may need to download an additional file for speech components to function correctly. If you find in the next box that your agents do not speak, return to the **Microsoft Agent Downloads Contents** list by scrolling to the top of the current page, and click the **SAPI runtime support** link. Click the **Down-**

load the Microsoft SAPI 4.0a runtime binaries link to save the file spchapi.exe. Double click this file once it has been downloaded to install support binaries.]

27.3 Test-Driving the Phone Book Application

Recall that you will be creating the **Phone Book** application to allow users to search for a phone number using an interactive Microsoft Agent character. Your **Phone Book** application, which you build in the next section, will contain people's names and phone numbers for the customer-service department. You begin by test-driving the application. Then, you will learn the additional C# technologies that you will need to create your own version of this application.

Test-Driving the Phone Book Application

1. ***Opening the completed application.*** Open the C:\Examples\Tutorial27\ CompletedApplication\PhoneBook directory to locate the **Phone Book** application. Double click PhoneBook.sln to open the application in Visual Studio .NET.

2. ***Running the Phone Book application.*** Select **Debug > Start** to run the application (Fig. 27.3).

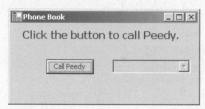

Figure 27.3 **Phone Book** application Form.

3. ***Calling Peedy.*** Click the **Call Peedy** Button to display Peedy. Peedy flies onto the screen into a position beneath the Form, waves and speaks the instructions shown in Fig. 27.4. When he is finished speaking, Peedy goes into a resting position (Fig. 27.5).

ComboBox disabled until Peedy arrives

Figure 27.4 Peedy appears after the **Call Peedy** Button is clicked.

Figure 27.5 Peedy in a resting pose.

(cont.) 4. ***Using the ComboBox to select a name.*** After Peedy appears on the screen, the ComboBox is enabled. Select the name Howard from the list (Fig. 27.6). Notice that the **Call Peedy** Button is disabled, as Peedy is already on the screen. After Howard is selected, Peedy executes several animations. He first appears to be thinking (Fig. 27.7), then tells you Howard's number (Fig. 27.8), then smiles for the user (Fig. 27.9).

Disabled **Call Peedy** Button ⎯⎯⎯⎯⎯

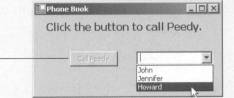

Figure 27.6   Selecting a name from the **ComboBox**.

Figure 27.7   Peedy thinking.

Figure 27.8   Peedy communicates Howard's phone number.

Figure 27.9   Peedy smiles after speaking the phone number.

5. ***Providing a voice command.*** Press the *Scroll Lock* key. A box appears beneath Peedy (called a **status box**) that displays information about Peedy's actions. The status box states that Peedy is listening for your command, as in Fig. 27.10. Speak the name John into your microphone.

Figure 27.10   Peedy listening for a voice command.

If Peedy hears and understands your command, the status box displays the command he heard, as in Fig. 27.11. Otherwise, you must repeat the command clearly, so Peedy can understand.

(cont.)

-- Peedy is not listening --
Heard "John"

Figure 27.11 Peedy heard the voice command.

When Peedy successfully hears your command, he gestures as if he is thinking about your request, then displays John's phone number (Fig. 27.12). You will have noticed that Peedy performs several gestures during this application. You will learn how to control these gestures later in the tutorial.

John's phone number is (555) 555-9876.

Figure 27.12 Peedy displays the requested phone number.

6. ***Viewing the context menu.*** Right click Peedy and notice that a context menu appears (Fig. 27.13). Selecting one of the names (**John**, **Jennifer** or **Howard**) will cause the same actions to occur as when a name was chosen from the ComboBox.

Commands in pop-up window —————

Open Voice Commands Window
Hide
John
Jennifer
Howard

Figure 27.13 Context menu window.

7. ***Closing the application.*** Close your running application by clicking its close box.

8. ***Closing the IDE.*** Close Visual Studio .NET by clicking its close box.

SELF-REVIEW

1. The _____ displays information about the Microsoft Agent character's actions.
   a) balloon
   b) status box
   c) help window
   d) text window

2. You must press the _____ key for Peedy to listen to your voice commands.
   a) *Shift*
   b) *Number Lock*
   c) *Scroll Lock*
   d) *Insert*

Answers: 1) b. 2) c.

27.4 Constructing the Phone Book Application

Now that you have test-driven the **Phone Book** application, you need to analyze the application, using pseudocode. The Microsoft Agent character Peedy helps users search for a specific telephone number. The user can click the ComboBox to select a name and retrieve the specified telephone numbers. However, thanks to the enhancement of the Microsoft Agent character, the user also can communicate verbally with Peedy. The user can retrieve a phone number simply by pressing the *Scroll Lock* key and speaking the name of a person into a microphone connected to the computer. Peedy listens for a name, and if he recognizes it, displays and speaks the number to the user. The following pseudocode describes the basic operation of the **Phone Book** application.

```
When the Form loads:
       Display names in the ComboBox
       Load Peedy the Parrot character into the Agent control
       Obtain Peedy the Parrot from the Agent control's Characters property
       Add names as commands for Peedy the Parrot

When the user clicks the Call Peedy Button:
       Display Peedy the Parrot and have the parrot speak the instructions
       Enable ComboBox containing people's names
       Disable the Call Peedy Button

When the user selects a name from the ComboBox:
       Have Peedy the Parrot speak the name and phone number of the person
              selected by the user

When the user speaks a name to Peedy the Parrot:
       Have Peedy the Parrot speak the name and phone number of the person
              selected by the user

When Peedy the Parrot hides:
       Disable ComboBox containing people's names
       Enable the Call Peedy Button
```

Now that you have test-driven the **Phone Book** application and studied its pseudocode representation, you will use an ACE table to help you convert the pseudocode to C#. Figure 27.14 lists the actions, controls and events that you will help you complete your own version of this application.

Action/Control/Event (ACE) Table for the Phone Book Application	**Action**	**Control/Object**	**Event**
	Label the application's controls	`lblInformation`	Application is run
		`FrmPhoneBook`	Load
	Display names in the ComboBox	`cboName,` `m_strNameList`	
	Load Peedy the Parrot character into the Microsoft Agent control	`objMainAgent`	
	Obtain Peedy the Parrot from the Agent control's Characters property	`objMainAgent,` `m_objMSpeaker`	
	Add names as commands for Peedy the Parrot	`m_objMSpeaker,` `m_strNameList`	
		`btnCall`	Click
	Display Peedy the Parrot and have the parrot speak the instructions	`m_objMSpeaker`	
	Enable ComboBox containing people's names	`cboName`	
	Disable the Call Peedy Button	`btnCall`	

Figure 27.14 ACE table for the **Phone Book** application. (Part 1 of 2.)

Action	Control/Object	Event
	cboName	Selected-IndexChanged
Have Peedy the Parrot speak the name and phone number of the person selected by the user	cboName, m_strNameList, m_strNumberList, m_objMSpeaker	
	objMainAgent	Command
Have Peedy the Parrot speak the name and phone number of the person selected by the user	cboName, m_strNameList, m_strNumberList, m_objMSpeaker	
	objMainAgent	HideEvent
Enable ComboBox containing people's names	cboName	
Disable the Call Peedy Button	btnCall	

Figure 27.14 ACE table for the **Phone Book** application. (Part 2 of 2.)

Now that you understand the purpose of the **Phone Book** application, you will begin to create it. In the following box, you will add the Microsoft Agent control to your **Toolbox**.

Customizing the Toolbox for the Phone Book Application

1. *Copying the template to your working directory.* Copy the C:\Examples\ Tutorial27\TemplateApplication\PhoneBook directory to your C:\SimplyCSP directory.

2. *Opening the Phone Book application's template file.* Double click Phone-Book.sln in the PhoneBook directory to open the application in Visual Studio .NET.

3. *Adding the Microsoft Agent to the Toolbox.* Before you begin designing the Form, you must make the Microsoft Agent accessible. To do this, you must add the Microsoft Agent control to the **Toolbox** window. Select **Tools > Add/Remove Items...**, as in Fig. 27.15. The **Customize Toolbox** dialog appears (Fig. 27.16). Select the **COM Components** tab and search for the **Microsoft Agent Control 2.0** item. Then, click its CheckBox to select the control as in Fig. 27.16. Click the **OK** Button. The Agent control now appears in the **Windows Forms** group in the **Toolbox**, as in Fig. 27.17.

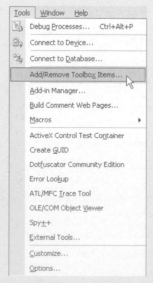

Figure 27.15 **Tools** menu.

(cont.)

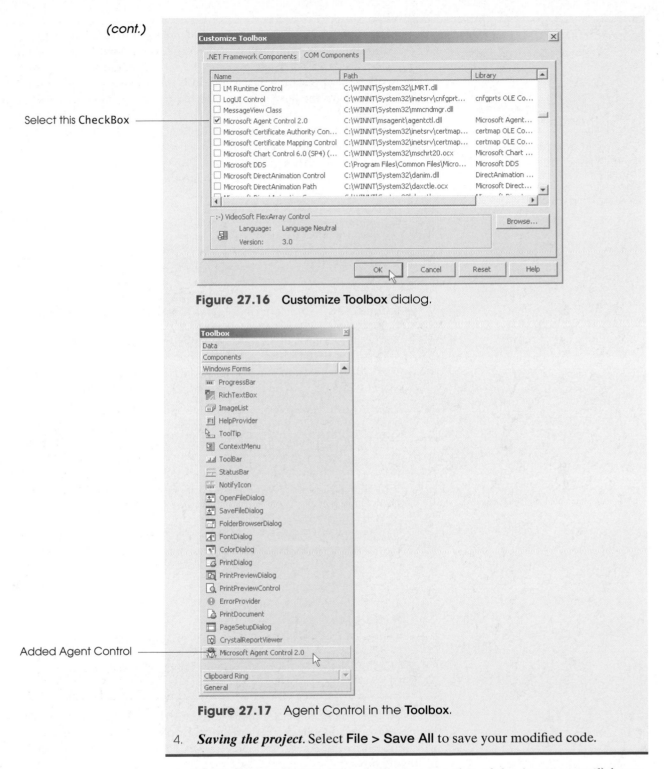

Figure 27.16   **Customize Toolbox** dialog.

Figure 27.17   Agent Control in the **Toolbox**.

4. ***Saving the project.*** Select **File > Save All** to save your modified code.

The visual design of the Form (with the exception of the Agent control) is provided in the template application. The next step after adding the Microsoft Agent control to the **Toolbox** is to place a Microsoft Agent control on the Form.

Adding the Microsoft Agent Control to the Application

Good Programming Practice

Controls in a container should not overlap. Place your controls so that they are clearly separated from one another, making the design of your application a clean one.

1. *Placing the Microsoft Agent control on the Form.* To meet the application requirements, you must add a Microsoft Agent control to your Form, which will be used to display and manage the actions of the Microsoft Agent characters in your application. Drag and drop the Microsoft Agent control from the **Toolbox** onto the Form. Change the Microsoft Agent control's Name property from the default (axAgent1) to objMainAgent. Change the Microsoft Agent control's Location property to 16, 48 (Fig. 27.18). Because the control icon is not visible when the application runs, the location on the Form does not affect the application's appearance. However, it is good practice to place the control so that it is not overlapping another control on the Form.

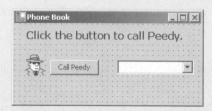

Figure 27.18 Form format of **Phone Book**.

Though you set the Agent control's Location property in this step, you will write code later that will determine where the Agent character appears when the application is running. As you saw in the test drive, the Microsoft Agent character can be displayed outside the application's Form.

2. *Running the application.* Select **Debug > Start** to run your application (Fig. 27.19). The **Call Peedy** Button will be used to make the Agent (in this case, Peedy) appear on the screen. However, clicking the Button does not cause any action to take place yet, because the Button's Click event handler has not been defined. Notice that the ComboBox next to the **Call Peedy** Button is disabled. You will use code to enable and fill the ComboBox with names shortly.

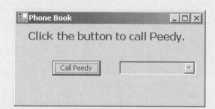

Figure 27.19 **Phone Book** Form with no functionality.

3. *Closing the application.* Close your running application by clicking its close box.

Now that you have placed the Agent control on the application's Form, you will define the event handlers for the **Phone Book** application. These event handlers will define how the Agent responds to user actions. You begin writing code in the following box.

Using Code to Display the Peedy Agent Character

1. *Rearranging and commenting the new control declaration.* Go to code view. Move the declaration for the Microsoft Agent control from line 23 of your code to line 25 of Fig. 27.20, then add the comment in line 24.

(cont.)

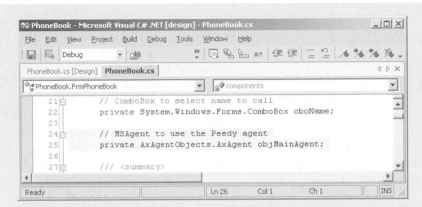

Figure 27.20 Rearranging and commenting the new control declaration.

2. ***Declaring instance variables.*** Add lines 32–40 of Fig. 27.21 in your code to declare the instance variables you will use in several event handlers. In addition to the Microsoft Agent objMainAgent object that manages all the application's characters, you also need an object to represent the current character (sometimes referred to as the speaker). In this example, the current character will always be Peedy the Parrot. Line 32 declares a variable to represent this Agent character. The m_objMSpeaker variable is declared as an **AgentObjects.IAgentCtlCharacter** object.

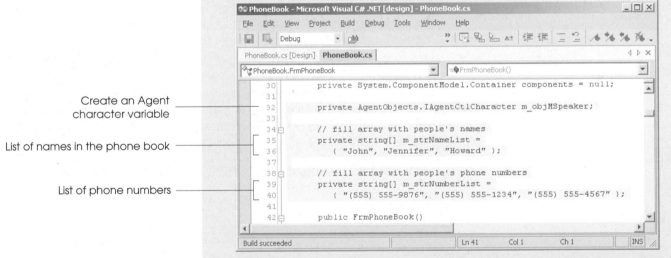

Create an Agent character variable

List of names in the phone book

List of phone numbers

Figure 27.21 Declaring and creating arrays in the **Phone Book** application.

The m_strNameList and m_strNumberList arrays are then declared and filled. The m_strNameList array (lines 35–36) stores the names of people in the phone book (John, Jennifer and Howard), and the m_strNumberList array (lines 39–40) stores the corresponding phone number for each person ((555) 555-9876, (555) 555-1234 and (555) 555-4567).

3. ***Writing code that executes when the application loads.*** The next step in creating the **Phone Book** application is to use the Form's Load event to execute code before the application becomes available to the user. Double click the Form in the Windows Form Designer to generate the Load event handler, and enter code view. Be sure to add the comment and break the header as shown in Fig. 27.22 so that the line numbers in your code match those presented in this tutorial. Then, add lines 147–154 to the Load event handler.

(cont.)

Declaring a counter variable ⸺

Adding names to the ComboBox ⸺

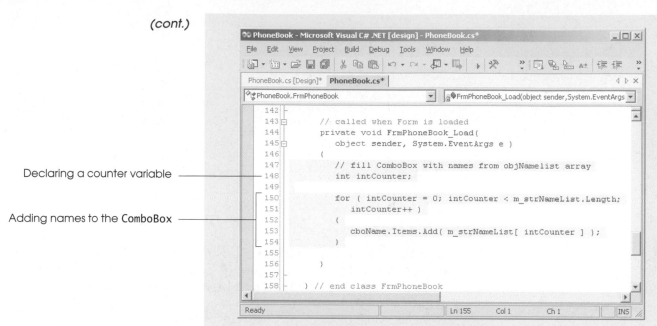

Figure 27.22 Adding items to the **ComboBox**.

The `intCounter` variable (line 148) is used to iterate through the `m_strNameList` array in the `for` statement (lines 150–154). This statement fills the **ComboBox** with the contact names that are stored in the `m_strNameList` array. This allows the user to select names by using the **ComboBox** instead of speaking the name to Peedy.

4. ***Initializing the Peedy Agent character.*** Add lines 156–159 of Fig. 27.23 to the event handler. Line 157 loads the Peedy character into `objMainAgent`. The first argument of the `Load` method is a `string` used to represent the Agent character being loaded. In this case, use the `"Peedy"` `string`. The second argument is a `string` representing the file where the character is defined (`"Peedy.acs"`).

Loading the Peedy character ⸺

Assigning Peedy to the Agent character variable ⸺

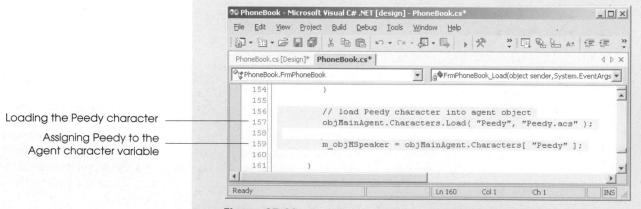

Figure 27.23 Loading the Microsoft Agent character.

Several characters can be loaded into a Microsoft Agent control. In this example, however, we will only be using Peedy the Parrot, so no more characters will be loaded. Line 159 assigns the loaded character to `m_objMSpeaker`. The character is accessed using the **Characters** property of our Microsoft Agent control. This property contains a collection of characters that have been loaded into the Microsoft Agent control.

(cont.)

The `m_objMSpeaker` variable can now be used to reference the Peedy Agent character. It is not necessary to create a separate object of the `AgentObjects.IAgentCtlCharacter` type—the Peedy character can be accessed with the expression `objMainAgent.Characters[ "Peedy" ]`. We have created `m_objMSpeaker` to increase application clarity. If any other characters had been loaded into the Microsoft Agent control, they can be accessed by replacing the `string` `"Peedy"` with the name of the character to be accessed.

![Bee icon] **Good Programming Practice**

Use a variable as an alternative reference to an object when the full reference to the object is long. This improves code readability.

5. ***Inserting commands in the Agent Commands context menu.*** Add lines 161–169 of Fig. 27.24 to your event handler. This code uses the same counter from the previous step in its `for` statement (lines 162–169). The header of the `for` statement resets the counter variable's value to 0. Then, the `for` statement adds names from the `m_strNameList` to the Peedy character as voice-enabled commands. The list of valid commands for a character is stored in the **Commands** property of the `AgentObjects.IAgentCtlCharacter` object.

Creating commands so that Peedy can recognize names when spoken

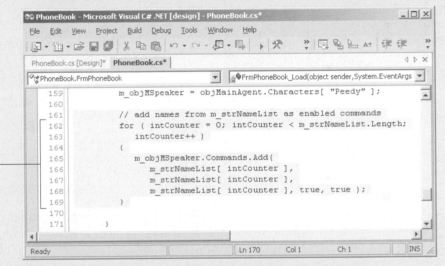

Figure 27.24 Adding commands to Peedy's context menu.

The **Add** method of the **Commands** property adds a new command to the command list. The Add method takes five arguments. The first three arguments are `string`s and the last two are `bool` values. The first argument identifies the command name. This value enables access to the command from your application. The second argument is a `string` that appears in a context menu when the user right clicks Peedy. The third `string` represents the word(s) for which Peedy listens when users make a verbal request. The fourth argument indicates whether the command is enabled. If so, the Agent character will respond to the spoken command. The final argument specifies whether the command is visible in the **Commands** context menu, which you have already seen in Fig. 27.13.

In this example, you set the first three arguments to the same value in the `m_strNameList` array and set the last two arguments to `true` for each name. Now Peedy understands users if they speak any of the names found in the `m_strNameList` array—John, Jennifer or Howard.

A **Command** event is raised when the user selects the command from the **Commands** pop-up window or speaks the command into a microphone. Command events are handled by the **Command** event handler of the Microsoft Agent control (`objMainAgent`, in this example).

(cont.)

6. ***Defining the btnCall_Click event handler.*** After defining the Form's Load event, you must create an event handler for the **Call Peedy** Button. When this Button is clicked, Peedy should appear and interact with the user. To create the Button's **Click** event handler, double click the **Call Peedy** Button in the Windows Form Designer. Be sure to add the comments and break the header as shown in Fig. 27.25 so that the line numbers in your code match those presented in this tutorial. Then, add lines 178–183 of Fig. 27.25 to your code.

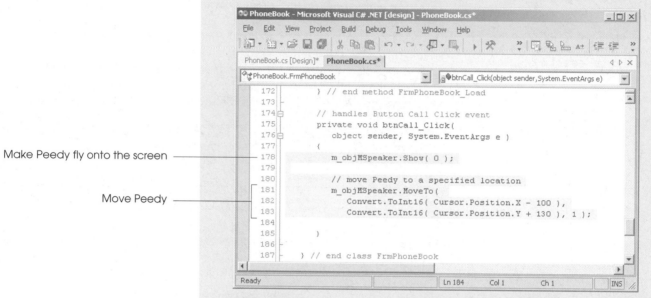

Make Peedy fly onto the screen

Move Peedy

```
172        } // end method FrmPhoneBook_Load
173
174        // handles Button Call Click event
175        private void btnCall_Click(
176            object sender, System.EventArgs e )
177        {
178            m_objMSpeaker.Show( 0 );
179
180            // move Peedy to a specified location
181            m_objMSpeaker.MoveTo(
182                Convert.ToInt16( Cursor.Position.X - 100 ),
183                Convert.ToInt16( Cursor.Position.Y + 130 ), 1 );
184
185        }
186
187    } // end class FrmPhoneBook
```

Figure 27.25 Displaying the Microsoft Agent character.

Line 178 uses the **Show** method to display Peedy on the screen. Specifying 0 as the argument makes Peedy fly onto the screen and land at his default location (towards the top left of the screen). However, if 1 is passed to the method, Peedy's image pops onto the screen at his default location (without the flying animation).

After the Show method is called, Peedy appears at (or flies to) the default position on the screen. The command in lines 181–183 causes Peedy to move to a new location. These lines use the **MoveTo** method of the m_objMSpeaker Agent object. The MoveTo method takes three arguments. The first two are an *x*-coordinate and a *y*-coordinate, both of the **short** type. The short type is similar to the int type, but short variables occupy less space in memory and therefore cannot hold larger int values. **Convert.ToInt16** converts the value of Cursor.Position.X - 100 from an int value to a short value, where **Cursor.Position.X** contains the current position of the mouse pointer. We have subtracted 100 to specify a position that is 100 pixels to the left of the mouse pointer. The same was done for the *y*-coordinate. In this case, the method moves the Agent character 100 pixels to the left and 130 pixels below the mouse pointer at the time the **Call Peedy** Button is clicked. This keeps Peedy near the application's Form. The third argument of the MoveTo method is Peedy's speed. This argument dictates the amount of time, in milliseconds, between frames in Peedy's animation.

GUI Design Tip

Locate the Microsoft Agent character near the application's Form.

(cont.)

7. ***Coding Peedy's greeting.*** Add lines 185–195 of Fig. 27.26 to your Click event handler. Line 185 uses the **Play** method to command Peedy to perform an action. This method plays the character animation specified by the string argument that is passed. In this line, Peedy's Wave animation is played—he waves hello to the user. [*Note*: We use only a few of the Peedy character's available animations. To see a listing of the available animations, please visit msdn.microsoft.com/library/default.asp?url=/library/en-us/msagent/peedylst_53xw.asp.]

Make Peedy wave ────────

Make Peedy speak instructions ────

Make Peedy rest ────

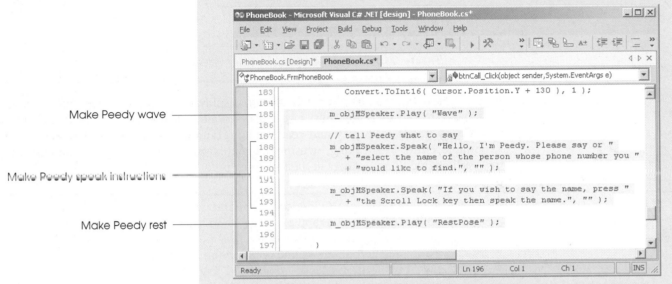

Figure 27.26   Code that defines Microsoft Agent's actions when Peedy first appears on the screen.

Lines 188–193 call the **Speak** method twice to specify what Peedy says. The first argument passed to the Speak method contains the string that Peedy speaks by using the computer's speakers. This string also appears in a conversation bubble above his head. You have already seen an example of this in Fig. 27.4. In this example, you provide the instructions for using the **Phone Book** application. [*Note*: The second argument to the Speak method is a string specifying the location of an audio file to be played. You pass the empty string so that no file will be played.] After Peedy displays the instructions, he is positioned in his rest pose (Fig. 27.5) by passing string "RestPose" (line 195) to the Play method.

8. ***Enabling and disabling controls.*** Now that you have made the Agent character available by clicking the **Call Peedy** Button, you should disable the Button and allow the ComboBox to be used. Add lines 197–198 of Fig. 27.27 to your Click event handler. These lines set the **Call Peedy** Button's Enabled property to false and cboName's Enabled property to true while the Agent character is shown. Recall that the ComboBox is disabled by default. You disable the **Call Peedy** Button because Peedy is on the screen at this point.

9. ***Saving the project.*** Select **File > Save All** to save your modified code.

GUI Design Tip

Use Microsoft Agent character gestures to indicate actions the user should take, or a response to an action the user has already taken.

(cont.)

Enable the **ComboBox** and
disable the **Call Peedy** Button

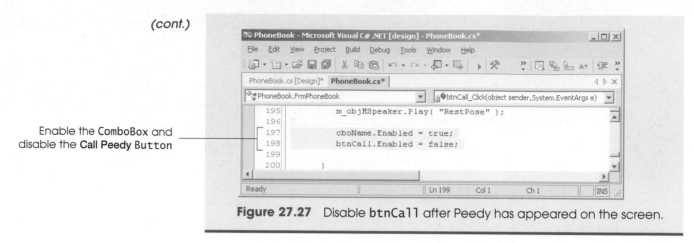

Figure 27.27 Disable `btnCall` after Peedy has appeared on the screen.

Now that you have written code to display Peedy on the screen and have him speak to the user, you must insert code to allow Peedy to respond to user input. Peedy needs to display and read a phone number when the user selects a valid name, either by speaking, by using the context menu or by using the ComboBox. You will enable these features in the following box.

Completing the Phone Book Application

1. **Defining the objMainAgent_Command event handler.** The event handler `objMainAgent_Command` executes when the Command event is raised. Recall that this happens when a user speaks a command to the Agent character by using the microphone (while pressing the *Scroll Lock* key). The event is also raised if the user selects a command from Peedy's context menu. You can generate the event handler by clicking the **Events** Button in the **Properties** window, then double clicking the **Command** event. Be sure to add the comments and break the header as shown in Fig. 27.28 so that the line numbers in your code match those presented in this tutorial. Then, add lines 207–209 of Fig. 27.28 to this event handler.

Retrieve user input

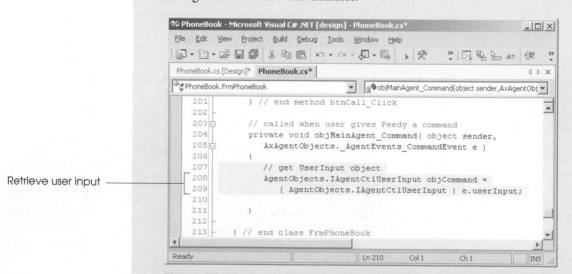

Figure 27.28 Event handler `objMainAgent_Command` defined.

Lines 208–209 declare the `objCommand` variable, which stores values of the **AgentObjects.IAgentCtlUserInput** type. This object is used to retrieve the commands that users give Peedy. Notice that you use the cast operator to convert the user input to the `AgentObjects.IAgentCtlUserInput` type. You do this to access the name of the command the Agent received.

(cont.)   2. ***Interpreting user input and displaying a phone number.*** Add lines 211–228 of Fig. 27.29 to your code. Line 211 creates a counter variable that is used in a `for` statement (lines 216–228). The body of this statement contains an `if` statement (lines 219–227). The code inside the `if` statement executes if the user's command matches one of the voice-enabled commands you added earlier by using the `m_strNameList` array.

Declaring a counter variable ——

Peedy thinks and speaks the
telephone number, if found ——

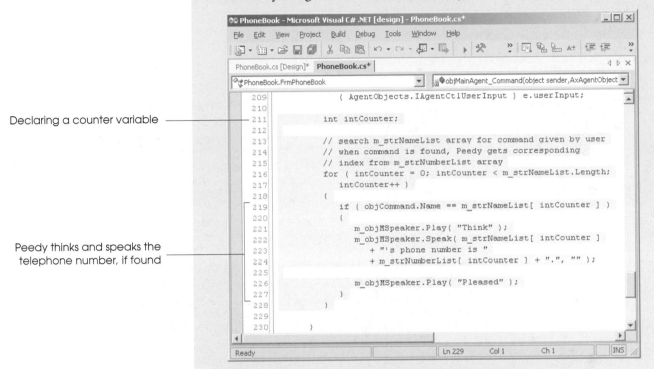

Figure 27.29   Finding the spoken or selected name.

Using the counter variable, the `for` statement iterates through each index of the array, comparing the command name (for example, `John`) to the name in the array. If the names match, the body of the `if` statement plays Peedy's `Think` animation (line 221) and uses Peedy to speak and display the requested phone number (lines 222–224). After speaking the phone number, Peedy smiles (the `Pleased` animation played in line 226).

3. ***Creating the `cboName_SelectedIndexChanged` event handler.*** You must now write code to display a phone number if the user chooses a name from the `cboName` ComboBox. Double click the `cboName` ComboBox in the Windows Form Designer to generate the `cboName_SelectedIndexChanged` event handler, and enter code view. Be sure to add the comments and break the header as shown in Fig. 27.30 so that the line numbers in your code match those presented in this tutorial. Then, add lines 237–254 in Fig. 27.30 to the event handler.

This ComboBox allows users who are unable to access the voice-recognition engines to use the application. Much as in the `Command` event handler, lines 241–254 search the array for a `string` that matches the selected item in the ComboBox. If a match is found, then Peedy's `Think` animation plays (Fig. 27.7), and the phone number is provided. After Peedy states the number, his `Pleased` animation plays, indicating that he is content with his ability to provide the user with the correct phone number (Fig. 27.9).

The `cboName_SelectedIndexChanged` method executes code similar to the `objMainAgent_Command` event handler. The only difference is that the `Command` method is invoked by verbal requests (or by using the context menu), whereas this method is invoked by selecting items in the `cboName`.

(cont.)

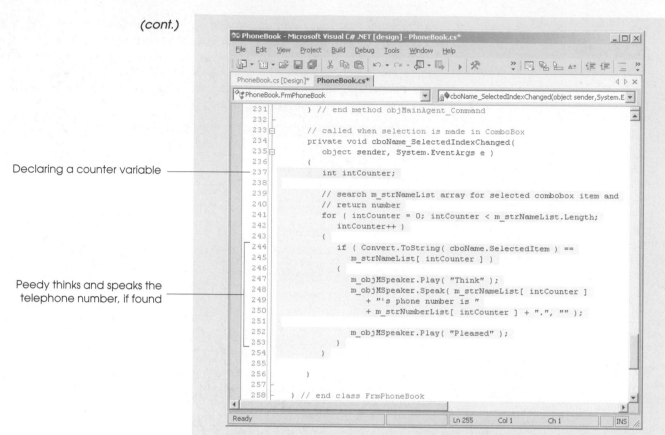

Declaring a counter variable

Peedy thinks and speaks the telephone number, if found

Figure 27.30 `cboName_SelectedIndexChanged` event handler defined.

4. ***Resetting the application's controls when Peedy is hidden.*** You might have noticed that you can choose **Hide** from Peedy's context menu (when you right click Peedy). When the user hides the Peedy character, you should enable the **Call Peedy** `Button` to allow the user to make Peedy reappear. Also, to prevent the user from selecting a name from the `ComboBox` while Peedy is hidden, you should disable the `ComboBox`. When the user selects **Hide**, a `HideEvent` is raised. To generate the `HideEvent` event handler, click the **Events** `Button` in the **Properties** window, then double click the **HideEvent** event. Be sure to add the comments and break the header as shown in Fig. 27.31 so that the line numbers in your code match those presented in this tutorial. Then, add lines 263–264 of Fig. 27.31 to the event handler. These lines enable the **Call Peedy** `Button` and disable the `ComboBox`.

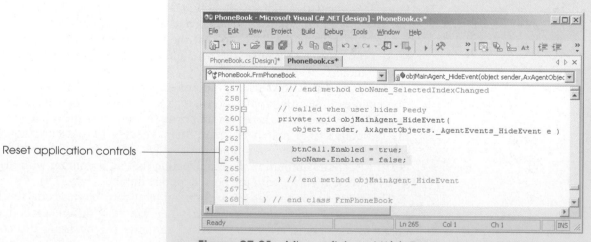

Reset application controls

Figure 27.31 Microsoft Agent `HideEvent` event handler.

(cont.)

5. ***Running the application.*** Select **Debug > Start** to run your application. Click the **Call Peedy** Button to display the Peedy Microsoft Agent character. Use Peedy to determine the phone numbers stored in the application.

6. ***Closing the application.*** Close your running application by clicking its close box.

7. ***Closing the IDE.*** Close Visual Studio .NET by clicking its close box.

Figure 27.32 presents the source code for the **Phone Book** application. The lines of code that contain new programming concepts that you learned in this tutorial are highlighted.

```
1   using System;
2   using System.Drawing;
3   using System.Collections;
4   using System.ComponentModel;
5   using System.Windows.Forms;
6   using System.Data;
7
8   namespace PhoneBook
9   {
10     /// <summary>
11     /// Summary description for FrmPhoneBook.
12     /// </summary>
13     public class FrmPhoneBook : System.Windows.Forms.Form
14     {
15        // Label displays instructions
16        private System.Windows.Forms.Label lblInstructions;
17
18        // Button calls Peedy
19        private System.Windows.Forms.Button btnCall;
20
21        // ComboBox to select name to call
22        private System.Windows.Forms.ComboBox cboName;
23
24        // MSAgent to use the Peedy agent
25        private AxAgentObjects.AxAgent objMainAgent;
26
27        /// <summary>
28        /// Required designer variable.
29        /// </summary>
30        private System.ComponentModel.Container components = null;
31
32        private AgentObjects.IAgentCtlCharacter m_objMSpeaker;
33
34        // fill array with people's names
35        private string[] m_strNameList =
36           { "John", "Jennifer", "Howard" };
37
38        // fill array with people's phone numbers
39        private string[] m_strNumberList =
40           { "(555) 555-9876", "(555) 555-1234", "(555) 555-4567" };
41
42        public FrmPhoneBook()
43        {
44           //
45           // Required for Windows Form Designer support
46           //
```

Variable to hold the Microsoft Agent character — *(pointing to line 32)*

Figure 27.32   Phone Book application code. (Part 1 of 4.)

```
47              InitializeComponent();
48
49              //
50              // TODO: Add any constructor code after InitializeComponent
51              // call
52              //
53          }
54
55          /// <summary>
56          /// Clean up any resources being used.
57          /// </summary>
58          protected override void Dispose( bool disposing )
59          {
60              if( disposing )
61              {
62                  if (components != null)
63                  {
64                      components.Dispose();
65                  }
66              }
67              base.Dispose( disposing );
68          }
69
70          // Windows Form Designer generated code
71
72          /// <summary>
73          /// The main entry point for the application.
74          /// </summary>
75          [STAThread]
76          static void Main()
77          {
78              Application.Run( new FrmPhoneBook() );
79          }
80
81          // called when Form is loaded
82          private void FrmPhoneBook_Load(
83              object sender, System.EventArgs e )
84          {
85              // fill ComboBox with names from objNamelist array
86              int intCounter;
87
88              for ( intCounter = 0; intCounter < m_strNameList.Length;
89                  intCounter++ )
90              {
91                  cboName.Items.Add( m_strNameList[ intCounter ] );
92              }
93
94              // load Peedy character into agent object
95              objMainAgent.Characters.Load( "Peedy", "Peedy.acs" );
96
97              m_objMSpeaker = objMainAgent.Characters[ "Peedy" ];
98
99              // add names from m_strNameList as enabled commands
100             for ( intCounter = 0; intCounter < m_strNameList.Length;
101                 intCounter++ )
102             {
```

Loading Peedy — 95

Assigning the Peedy
character to m_objMSpeaker — 97

Figure 27.32 Phone Book application code. (Part 2 of 4.)

```
103              m_objMSpeaker.Commands.Add(
104                 m_strNameList[ intCounter ],
105                 m_strNameList[ intCounter ],
106                 m_strNameList[ intCounter ], true, true );
107           }
108
109        } // end method FrmPhoneBook_Load
110
111        // handles Call Button Click event
112        private void btnCall_Click(
113           object sender, System.EventArgs e )
114        {
115           m_objMSpeaker.Show( 0 );
116
117           // move Peedy to a specified location
118           m_objMSpeaker.MoveTo(
119              Convert.ToInt16( Cursor.Position.X - 100 ),
120              Convert.ToInt16( Cursor.Position.Y + 130 ), 1 );
121
122           m_objMSpeaker.Play( "Wave" );
123
124           // tell Peedy what to say
125           m_objMSpeaker.Speak( "Hello, I'm Peedy. Please say or "
126              + "select the name of the person whose phone number you "
127              + "would like to find.", "" );
128
129           m_objMSpeaker.Speak( "If you wish to say the name, press "
130              + "the Scroll Lock key then speak the name.", "" );
131
132           m_objMSpeaker.Play( "RestPose" );
133
134           cboName.Enabled = true;
135           btnCall.Enabled = false;
136
137        } // end method btnCall_Click
138
139        // called when user gives Peedy a command
140        private void objMainAgent_Command( object sender,
141           AxAgentObjects._AgentEvents_CommandEvent e )
142        {
143           // get UserInput object
144           AgentObjects.IAgentCtlUserInput objCommand =
145              ( AgentObjects.IAgentCtlUserInput ) e.userInput;
146
147           int intCounter;
148
149           // search m_strNameList array for command given by user
150           // when command is found, Peedy gets corresponding
151           // index from m_strNumberList array
152           for ( intCounter = 0; intCounter < m_strNameList.Length;
153              intCounter++ )
154           {
155              if ( objCommand.Name == m_strNameList[ intCounter ] )
156              {
157                 m_objMSpeaker.Play( "Think" );
158                 m_objMSpeaker.Speak( m_strNameList[ intCounter ]
159                    + "'s phone number is "
160                    + m_strNumberList[ intCounter ] + ".", "" );
```

Adding commands for the Peedy character — (lines 103–106)

Showing Peedy — (line 115)

Moving Peedy — (line 119)

Peedy waving — (line 122)

Peedy speaking instructions and resting — (lines 125–132)

Command event handler header — (lines 140–141)

Converting user input to the **AgentObjects. IAgentCtlUserInput** type — (lines 144–145)

Figure 27.32 Phone Book application code. (Part 3 of 4.)

```
161
162                      m_objMSpeaker.Play( "Pleased" );
163                   }
164             }
165
166       } // end method objMainAgent_Command
167
168       // called when selection is made in ComboBox
169       private void cboName_SelectedIndexChanged(
170          object sender, System.EventArgs e )
171       {
172          int intCounter;
173
174          // search m_strNameList array for selected ComboBox item and
175          // return number
176          for ( intCounter = 0; intCounter < m_strNameList.Length;
177             intCounter++ )
178          {
179             if ( Convert.ToString( cboName.SelectedItem ) ==
180                m_strNameList[ intCounter ] )
181             {
182                m_objMSpeaker.Play( "Think" );
183                m_objMSpeaker.Speak( m_strNameList[ intCounter ]
184                   + "'s phone number is "
185                   + m_strNumberList[ intCounter ] + ".", "" );
186
187                m_objMSpeaker.Play( "Pleased" );
188             }
189          }
190
191       } // end method cboName_SelectedIndexChanged
192
193       // called when user hides Peedy
194       private void objMainAgent_HideEvent(
195          object sender, AxAgentObjects._AgentEvents_HideEvent e )
196       {
197          btnCall.Enabled = true;
198          cboName.Enabled = false;
199
200       } // end method objMainAgent_HideEvent
201
202    } // end class FrmPhoneBook
203 }
```

HideEvent event handler header — lines 194–195

Figure 27.32 **Phone Book** application code. (Part 4 of 4.)

SELF-REVIEW

1. The _____ event is called when the user hides Peedy.
   a) Hide
   b) Away
   c) Command
   d) HideEvent

2. Use the _____ method to relocate the Microsoft Agent character on the screen.
   a) Move
   b) Relocate
   c) MoveTo
   d) Place

Answers: 1) d. 2) c.

27.5 Wrap-Up

In this tutorial, you were introduced to Microsoft Agent and learned how it can be used to enhance software applications. You learned what Microsoft Agent is used for and how to download all the necessary components. You then wrote code to use a Microsoft Agent character, Peedy the Parrot.

Using Peedy, you created an application that interacts with the user by listening to the user's commands and answers using speech. You used the Show and MoveTo methods to show Peedy and move him on the screen. You also used Peedy's Speak method to speak instructions and phone numbers to the user. You then learned how to control Peedy's gestures, such as Wave and Think, not only to entertain the user but also to signal visually what the application is doing.

Tutorials 28–31 present you with a Web-based bookstore application case study. You will learn how to build an application that can be accessed by using a Web browser. In Tutorial 28, you will be introduced to the concept of a multi-tier application and you will take your first steps toward building a three-tier application, which you will complete in the subsequent tutorials.

SKILLS SUMMARY

Displaying the Microsoft Agent to Users
- Load the desired Microsoft Agent, using the Characters.Load method.
- Call the Microsoft Agent object's Show method.

Allowing Verbal Communication with the Agent
- Add voice-enabled commands, using the Microsoft Agent's Commands.Add method.
- Define the Command event handler.

Causing the Agent to Speak
- Call the Microsoft Agent's Speak method.
- Specify the string that Microsoft Agent should speak.

Causing Agent to Perform Actions
- Call the Microsoft Agent character's Play method.
- Specify the animation that Microsoft Agent should display.

KEY TERMS

Add method of the Commands property—Adds a command to a Microsoft Agent character.

AgentObjects.IAgentCtlCharacter object—References a Microsoft Agent character.

AgentObjects.IAgentCtlUserInput object—Stores the user input retrieved from a Microsoft Agent character.

Characters property of the Microsoft Agent control—Used to access a specific Microsoft Agent character.

Command event of the Microsoft Agent control—Raised when a user speaks a command to a Microsoft Agent character or selects a command from a character's context menu.

Commands property of class IAgentCtlCharacter—Sets which commands the Microsoft Agent character can understand as input from the user.

Convert.ToInt16 method—Converts data to type short.

Cursor.Position property—Property containing the *x*- and *y*-coordinates of the mouse cursor on the screen (in pixels).

HideEvent event—Event raised when a Microsoft Agent character is hidden.

IAgentCtlCharacter object—References a Microsoft Agent character.

IAgentCtlUserInput object—Stores the user input retrieved from a Microsoft Agent character.

interactive animated characters—The Microsoft Agent technology adds such characters to Windows applications and Web pages. These characters can interact with the user through mouse clicks and microphone input.

Microsoft Agent—Adds interactive animated characters to Windows applications and Web pages.

MoveTo method—Relocates the Microsoft Agent character on the screen.

multimedia—The use of various media, such as sound, video and animation, to create content in an application.

Play method—Plays a Microsoft Agent character animation.

short type—Holds small integer values.

Show method—Displays a Microsoft Agent character on the screen.

Speak method—Has the Microsoft Agent character speak text to the user.

speech-recognition engine—Translates vocal sound input from a microphone into a language that the computer understands.

status box—A box that appears below a Microsoft agent character that displays information about the character's actions.

text-to-speech engine—Application that translates typed words into spoken sound that users hear through headphones or speakers connected to a computer.

GUI DESIGN GUIDELINES

Microsoft Agent Control

■ Locate the Microsoft Agent character near the application's Form.

■ Use Microsoft Agent character gestures to indicate actions the user should take, or a response to an action the user has already taken.

CONTROLS, EVENTS, PROPERTIES & METHODS

Convert The Convert class converts the value of a type to another type.

■ *Method*

ToInt16—Converts the value from another type to type short.

IAgentCtlCharacter   This class is used to represent the Agent character that is used in the application.

■ *Property*

Commands—Contains the commands the character will recognize.

■ *Methods*

Show—Displays the character on the screen.

MoveTo—Moves the character to a specified location on the screen.

Play—Plays character animations.

Speak—Specifies the text to be spoken by the character.

Commands.Add—Adds a new command to the command list for the Agent object.

IAgentCtlUserInput   This class is used to retrieve commands from users.

■ *Property*

Name—Retrieves the name of the command given by the user.

Microsoft Agent Control   🕵 Control   This control is used to create and manipulate the multimedia features of a Microsoft Agent character.

■ *In action*

■ *Events*

Command—Raised when a user gives the Microsoft Agent character a verbal command or selects an option from the character's context menu.

HideEvent—Raised when a user hides the Microsoft Agent character.

■ *Property*

Location—Specifies the location of the Microsoft Agent control on the Form.

■ *Method*
    `Characters.Load`—Loads a character into the Microsoft Agent control.

MULTIPLE-CHOICE QUESTIONS

27.1 The _____ method is used to specify what the Microsoft Agent will say.
a) Speak	b) Say
c) Command	d) Voice

27.2 The _____ method is used to activate a Microsoft Agent character's animation.
a) Show	b) Play
c) Speak	d) Appear

27.3 The MoveTo method takes three arguments. What do the first two arguments represent?
a) The direction in which the Agent should move (left, right, up, down).
b) The name of the character and its position.
c) The *x*-coordinate and *y*-coordinate of the location to which the Agent should move.
d) The name of the character and the direction of movement.

27.4 Which method of `IAgentCtlCharacter` displays the Microsoft Agent character on the screen?
a) Play	b) Show
c) Speak	d) Appear

27.5 Use the _____ event handler to execute code when users click **Hide** in the Agent character context menu.
a) Hide	b) HideEvent
c) Command	d) Disappear

27.6 The Add method of the Commands property _____.
a) adds a new command to the command list
b) joins two commands together
c) displays the Commands pop-up window
d) Both a and c

27.7 The _____ event handler controls what occurs when users speak to the Agent.
a) Command	b) ClickEvent
c) Click	d) SelectedIndexChanged

27.8 _____ specifies the *x*-coordinate of the mouse cursor on the screen.
a) Cursor.Location.X	b) Cursor.Position.X
c) Mouse.Location.X	d) Mouse.Position.X

27.9 Specifying _____ as a parameter to Peedy's Play method causes him to smile.
a) "Think"	b) "Smile"
c) "Pleased"	d) "Happy"

27.10 Specifying _____ as a parameter to Peedy's Play method causes him to rest.
a) "RestPose"	b) "Rest"
c) "Think"	d) "Pose"

EXERCISES

27.11 (*Appointment Book Application Using Microsoft Agent*) Write an application that allows users to add appointments to an appointment book that uses Microsoft Agent (Fig. 27.33). When users speak a person's name, Merlin returns the time and date of the appointment that users have with that person. If users say "Today," Merlin returns a list of the users' appointments for the day.

    a) *Copying the template to your working directory.* Copy the directory `C:\Examples\Tutorial27\Exercises\AppointmentBook` to your `C:\SimplyCSP` directory.

Figure 27.33 Appointment Book GUI.

b) ***Opening the application's template file.*** Double click `AppointmentBook.sln` in the `AppointmentBook` directory to open the application.

c) ***Downloading the Merlin Microsoft Agent.*** Download the `Merlin.acs` character file from the Microsoft Web site.

d) ***Adding the Agent Control to the Form.*** Add the Microsoft Agent control to the Form. Rearrange and comment the control declaration appropriately.

e) ***Creating instance variables.*** Create three instance variables of the `ArrayList` type to store the date, time and person with which the user has an appointment. Create an instance variable of the `AgentObjects.IAgentCtlCharacter` type (as you did in the **Phone Book** application).

f) ***Defining the `FrmAppointments_Load` event handler.*** Load Merlin's character file, display him on the screen and add the Today command to the command list.

g) ***Defining the `btnAdd_Click` event handler.*** Define this event handler so that the information provided by the user is added to its corresponding `ArrayList`. The **Appointment With:** `TextBox` input should be added to the `ArrayList` containing the names of people with whom the user has an appointment. The input for the appointment date and time should also be added to their respective `ArrayLists`. Display an error message if the user leaves the **Appointment With:** or the **Appointment Time:** `TextBox` empty.

h) ***Adding voice-enabled commands.*** Within the `btnAdd_Click` event handler, add a voice-enabled command to allow a user to speak the name of the person with whom the user has an appointment to the command list. This allows a user to check whether there is an appointment with someone by speaking the person's name. The command should also appear in the `Commands` context menu.

i) ***Defining the Agent's Command event handler.*** As you did in the **Phone Book** application, define what occurs when a user speaks or selects a command. If the user specifies the Today command, Merlin should tell the user the names of all the people with whom the user has an appointment today. If the user specifies a specific name, Merlin should state the time and date at which the user has an appointment with this person. If the user did not schedule any appointments, Merlin should inform the user that no appointments were scheduled.

j) ***Running the application.*** Select **Debug > Start** to run your application. Add several appointments to ensure that your application runs correctly as in Fig. 27.33.

k) ***Closing the application.*** Close your running application by clicking its close box.

l) ***Closing the IDE.*** Close Visual Studio .NET by clicking its close box.

27.12 *(Craps Game Application Enhancement Using Microsoft Agent)* Modify the **Craps Game** application from Tutorial 16 to include a Microsoft Agent character (Fig. 27.34).

a) ***Copying the template to your working directory.*** Copy the directory `C:\Examples\Tutorial27\Exercises\CrapsGameEnhancement` to your `C:\SimplyCSP` directory.

b) ***Opening the application's template file.*** Double click `CrapsGame.sln` in the `CrapsGameEnhancement` directory to open the application.

c) ***Downloading the Genie Microsoft Agent.*** Download the `Genie.acs` character file from the Microsoft Web site.

d) ***Adding the Agent control to the Form.*** Add the Microsoft Agent control to the Form. Rearrange and comment the control declaration appropriately.

e) ***Creating an instance variable.*** Create an instance variable of the `AgentObjects.IAgentCtlCharacter` type (as you did in the **Phone Book** application).

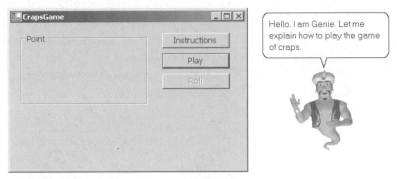

Figure 27.34 Enhanced **Craps Game** GUI.

f) *Defining the FrmCrapsGame_Load event handler.* Load Genie's character file, and display him on the screen.

g) *Modifying the btnPlay_Click event handler.* Add code to the btnPlay_Click event handler to control the Agent. When the user wins the game, Genie should play his Pleased animation and congratulate the user. If the user loses, Genie should play his Confused animation and say that the user lost. If the user neither wins nor loses, Genie should tell the user to roll again. Make sure to reset him to his RestPose after he plays any animation.

h) *Defining the btnRoll_Click event handler.* Add code to the btnRoll_Click event handler to control the Agent. If users "make their point," Genie should play his Pleased animation and state that the user won. If the user rolls a 7, Genie should play his Confused animation and say that the user lost. Otherwise, Genie should tell the user to roll again.

i) *Defining the btnInstructions_Click event handler.* Define the event handler btnInstructions_Click to make Genie introduce himself to the user. Genie should then explain the rules to the game of craps.

j) *Running the application.* Select **Debug > Start** to run your application. Play several games to ensure that your application runs correctly. Also be sure to test the **Instructions** Button.

k) *Closing the application.* Close your running application by clicking its close box.

l) *Closing the IDE.* Close Visual Studio .NET by clicking its close box.

27.13 (*Security Panel Application Enhancement Using Microsoft Agent*) Modify the **Security Panel** application from Tutorial 12 to include Microsoft Agent (Fig. 27.35).

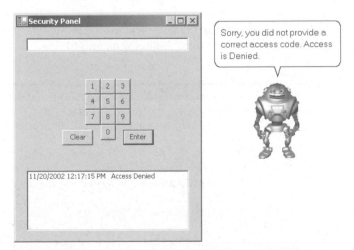

Figure 27.35 Enhanced **Security Panel** application.

a) *Copying the template to your working directory.* Copy the directory C:\Examples\ Tutorial27\Exercises\SecurityPanelEnhancement to your C:\SimplyCSP directory.

b) *Opening the application's template file.* Double click SecurityPanel.sln in the SecurityPanelEnhancement directory to open the application.

c) *Downloading the Robby Microsoft Agent.* Download the Robby.acs character file from the Microsoft Web site.

d) *Adding the Agent control to the Form.* Add the Microsoft Agent control to the Form.

e) *Creating an instance variable.* Create an instance variable of the AgentObjects.IAgentCtlCharacter type (as you did in the **Phone Book** application). Rearrange and comment the control declarations appropriately.

f) *Defining the FrmSecurityPanel_Load event handler.* Load Robby's character file, and display him on the screen. Command Robby to tell users to input their access codes.

g) *Modifying the btnEnter_Click event handler.* Add code to the btnEnter_Click event handler to use the Microsoft Agent. If the user enters a valid access code, Robby should welcome the user and state the type of employee that the access code represents. If the access code is invalid, then Robby should state that an invalid code was provided and that access is denied.

h) *Running the application.* Select **Debug > Start** to run your application. Enter various correct and incorrect codes to ensure that your application runs correctly.

i) *Closing the application.* Close your running application by clicking its close box.

j) *Closing the IDE.* Close Visual Studio .NET by clicking its close box.

What does this code do? ▶ **27.14** After the user clicks the **Call** Button, what does the following event handler do?

```
1   private void btnCall_Click(
2       object sender, System.EventArgs e )
3   {
4       objMainAgent.Characters.Load( "Genie","Genie.acs" );
5
6       objMSpeaker = objMainAgent.Characters[ "Genie" ];
7
8       objMSpeaker.Show( 0 );
9
10      objMSpeaker.Speak( "Hello, I'm Genie the special agent!", "" );
11
12  } // end method btnCall_Click
```

What's wrong with this code? ▶ **27.15** Find the error(s) in the following code. The event handler should have an agent object appear and say, "Hello, my name is Merlin." This should happen when the user clicks the **Call** Button.

```
1   private void btnCall_Click( object sender, System.EventArgs e )
2   {
3       AgentObjects.IAgentCtlCharacter objMSpeaker;
4
5       objMainAgent.Characters.Load( "Merlin", "Merlin.acs" );
6
7       objMSpeaker = objMainAgent.Characters[ "Merlin.acs" ];
8
9       objMSpeaker.Show( 0 );
10
11      objMSpeaker.Play( "Hello, my name is Merlin", "" );
12
13  } // end method btnCall_Click
```

Programming Challenge ▶

27.16 (*Car Payment Calculator Application Enhancement Using Microsoft Agent*) Enhance the **Car Payment Calculator** application from Tutorial 9 to use the Microsoft Agent Robby. When the application is run, Robby should appear on the screen and wave to users. He should then explain what the application does. After users have entered information into each field of the **Car Payment Calculator** and clicked the **Calculate** Button, Robby should speak the calculated payment amounts and the number of months for which they were calculated. Copy the directory C:\Examples\Tutorial27\Exercises\CarPaymentCalculator-Enhancement to your C:\SimplyCSP directory. Double click the CarPaymentCalculator.sln file to open the application in Visual Studio .NET.

28 TUTORIAL

Objectives

Outline

Bookstore Application: Web Applications

Introducing Internet Information Services

In previous tutorials, you used C# to develop Windows applications. These applications contained a GUI with which the user interacted. You can also use Visual Studio .NET to create **Web applications.** These applications, also known as Web-based applications, use C# in combination with Microsoft's **ASP .NET technology** to create Web content (data that can be viewed in a Web browser such as Internet Explorer). This Web content includes HTML (HyperText Markup Language) documents and images.

In this tutorial, you will learn important Web-development concepts in the context of the **Bookstore** application. This application consists of two Web pages. The first page displays a list of books. After selecting a book, the user clicks a Button, which directs the browser to a second Web page. Information about the selected book is then retrieved from a database and displayed for the user. The second Web page also contains a Button that, when clicked, directs the Web browser back to the first Web page, allowing the user to select a different book. Before you create this application, you will be introduced to fundamental Web development concepts that are required to understand the **Bookstore** application. You will then test-drive the **Bookstore** application. In Tutorials 29–31, you will analyze the pseudocode and ACE table and develop the **Bookstore** application.

28.1 Multi-Tier Architecture

Web applications are **multi-tier applications**, sometimes referred to as **n-tier applications**. Multi-tier applications divide functionality into separate **tiers** (that is, logical groupings of functionality). The separate tiers of an application can be located on the same computer or on separate computers distributed across any computer network, including the Internet. Figure 28.1 illustrates the basic structure of a multi-tier application.

The **information tier** (also called the **data tier** or the **bottom tier**) maintains data for the application. The information tier for the **Bookstore** application is represented by a database that contains product information, such as book titles, author names, publication dates and edition numbers. The database also contains ISBN numbers, book descriptions and prices.

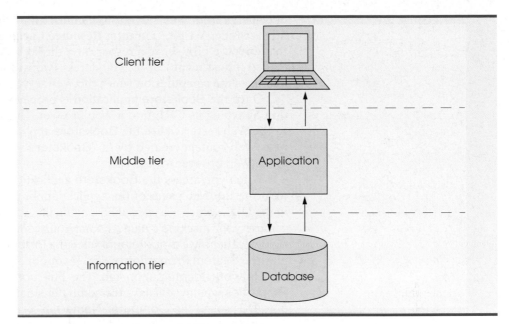

Figure 28.1   Three-tier application model.

The **middle tier** controls interactions between application clients (such as Web browsers) and application data in the information tier. In the **Bookstore** application, the middle-tier code determines which book was selected and which book's information is retrieved from the database. The middle-tier code also determines how the selected book's data will be displayed. The middle tier processes client requests (for example, a request to view a book's information) from the top tier, which we define shortly, and retrieves data from the database (author names, prices, descriptions, etc.) in the information tier. The middle tier then processes the data and presents the content to the client. In other words, the middle tier represents the functionality of the Web application.

The **client tier**, or **top tier**, is the application's user interface, which is typically a Web browser. In the **Bookstore** application, the client tier is represented by the pages displayed in the Web browser. The user interacts directly with this application through the client tier (browser) by entering text, selecting from a list, clicking **Buttons**, etc. The browser reports the user's actions to the middle tier, which processes the information. The middle tier can also make requests to and retrieve data from the information tier. The client then displays to the user the data retrieved by the middle tier from the information tier.

SELF-REVIEW

1. A database is located in the _____ tier.
   a) top
   b) middle
   c) bottom
   d) client

2. The role of the middle tier is to _____.
   a) display the application's user interface
   b) provide a database for the application
   c) control the interaction between the client and information tiers
   d) control the interaction between the client and the user interface

Answers: 1) c. 2) c.

28.2 Web Servers

A **Web server** is specialized software that responds to client (Web browser) requests by providing requested resources (such as HTML documents). To request documents from Web servers, users must know the locations at which those documents reside. A **URL** (**Uniform Resource Locator**) can be thought of as an address that directs a browser to a resource on the Web. A URL contains a computer name (called a **host name**) or an IP address (we will discuss IP addresses shortly) that identifies the computer on which the Web server resides.

Once the **Bookstore** application is properly set up, users can run the application by typing its URL into a Web browser. This action is translated into a request to the Web server where the **Bookstore** application resides. The Web server sends back Web content created by the **Bookstore** application. This content is displayed in the Web browser for the user.

When you access the **Bookstore** application, you provide a URL in a browser to locate the Web pages of the application. In this tutorial, you will use `localhost` in the URL, which is a special host name that identifies the local computer. You also can use your machine's name. [*Note:* Your computer's name can be determined by right clicking **My Computer** and selecting **Properties** from the context menu to display the **System Properties** dialog. If your operating system is Windows 2000, click the **Network Identification** tab. The **Full computer name:** field in the **System Properties** window displays the computer's name. If your operating system is Windows XP, select the **Computer Name** tab. The **Full computer name:** field in the **Computer Name** tab displays the computer name.]

A **host** is a computer that stores and maintains resources such as Web pages, databases and multimedia files. In the case of the **Bookstore** application, the host is your computer. A **domain** represents a group of **hosts** on the Internet; it combines with a host name (for example, www for World Wide Web) and a **top-level domain** (**TLD**) to form a **fully qualified domain name** (**FQDN**), which provides a user-friendly way to identify a site on the Internet. In a fully qualified domain name, the TLD often describes the type of organization that owns the domain. For example, the com TLD usually refers to a commercial business, the org TLD usually refers to a nonprofit organization and the edu TLD usually refers to an educational institution. In addition, each country has its own TLD, such as cn for China, et for Ethiopia, om for Oman and us for the United States.

Each fully qualified domain name corresponds to a numeric address called an **IP** (**Internet Protocol**) **address**, which is much like the street address of a house. Just as people use street addresses to locate houses or businesses in a city, computers use IP addresses to locate other computers on the Internet. A **domain name system** (**DNS**) **server** is a computer that maintains a database of host names and their corresponding IP addresses. The process of translating fully qualified domain names to IP addresses is called a **DNS lookup**. For example, to access the Deitel Web site, type the fully qualified domain name `www.deitel.com` into a Web browser. The DNS lookup translates `www.deitel.com` into the IP address of the Deitel Web server (that is, `63.110.43.82`). The IP address of `localhost` is always `127.0.0.1`.

SELF-REVIEW

1. A _____ is a computer that stores and maintains resources.

   a) host   b) IP address

   c) domain name   d) domain name system

2. A DNS lookup is a _____.

   a) translation of an IP address to a domain name

   b) translation of a fully qualified domain name to an IP address

   c) translation of a fully qualified domain name to a host name

   d) search for a domain name

Answers: 1) a. 2) b.

28.3 Internet Information Services (IIS)

Microsoft **Internet Information Services (IIS)** is the Web server you will use to respond to client requests. IIS must be installed on your machine before you can create Web applications using Visual Studio .NET. To determine if IIS is installed, you should read Appendix G. [*Note:* If you encounter problems setting up IIS, please visit www.deitel.com/books/csharpSimply1/index.html. This site contains frequently asked questions (FAQs) from our readers and an errata list. If you cannot find the solution to your problem there, please e-mail us at deitel@deitel.com and we will respond promptly.]

Before you can test-drive the completed application you must specify initial settings for the **Bookstore** application.

Specifying Initial Settings for the Bookstore Application

1. ***Copying the Bookstore application files to IIS's root directory.*** Copy the C:\Examples\Tutorial28\CompletedApplication\Bookstore directory to IIS's root directory, which is usually C:\Inetpub\wwwroot (Fig. 28.2). [*Note*: The directory names and file names in the wwwroot directory may be different on your computer.]

Figure 28.2   Bookstore directory in IIS's root directory.

2. ***Opening IIS.*** If your operating system is Windows 2000, begin by going to the Windows **Start** menu and selecting **Settings > Control Panel** to display the **Control Panel** dialog. Double click the **Administrative Tools** icon, then double click the **Internet Services Manager** icon to display the **Internet Information Services** dialog (Fig. 28.3). If your operating system is Windows XP, go to the Windows **Start** menu and select **Control Panel**. Click the **Switch to Classic View** link in the upper-left portion of the **Control Panel** dialog to display its contents. Double click the **Administrative Tools** icon, and then double click the **Internet Information Services** icon to display the **Internet Information Services** dialog.

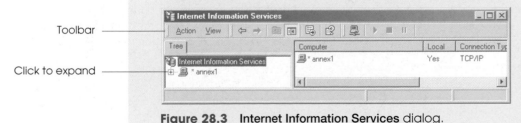

Figure 28.3   Internet Information Services dialog.

(cont.)

3. ***Viewing the Default Web Site.*** Beneath the name **Internet Information Services** (on the **Tree** tab in Windows 2000) is the name of your computer (on which IIS has been installed). Our computer's name is **annex1**. Your computer's name will be different. Expand this node by clicking the plus box. The default sites (Windows 2000 only) set up by IIS should be displayed (Fig. 28.4). The default sites that display in the left pane may differ on your screen. In Windows XP, a node named **Web Sites** appears (Fig. 28.5). Recall that the theme used for the appearance of windows and dialogs is set to **Windows Classic**. The appearance of your windows and dialogs may be different. Expand the **Web Sites** node to display the **Default Web Site** node.

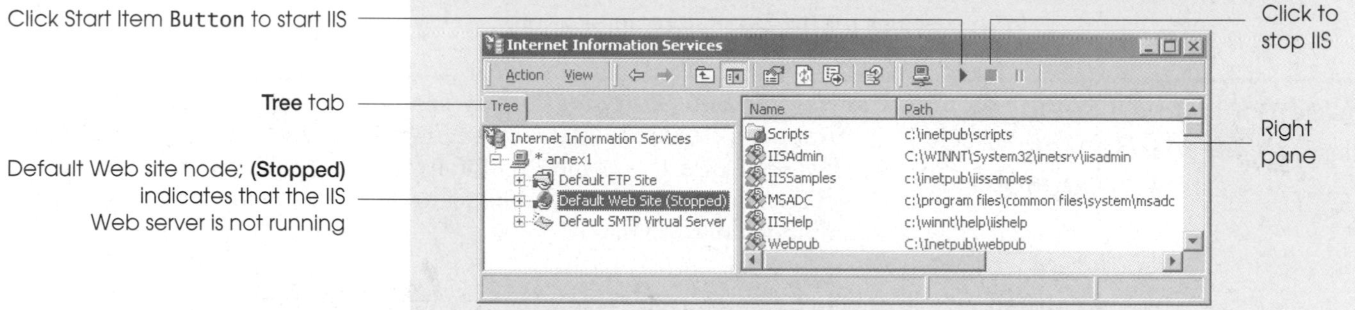

Click Start Item **Button** to start IIS ——

Click to stop IIS

Tree tab ——

Right pane

Default Web site node; **(Stopped)** indicates that the IIS Web server is not running

Figure 28.4 Starting IIS on a computer running Windows 2000.

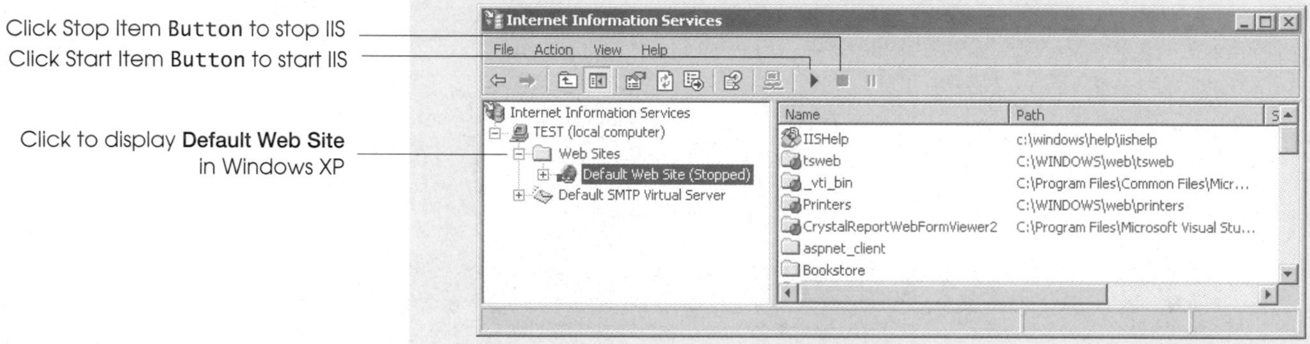

Click Stop Item **Button** to stop IIS
Click Start Item **Button** to start IIS

Click to display **Default Web Site** in Windows XP

Figure 28.5 Location of **Default Web Site** on a Windows XP computer.

In both Windows 2000 and Windows XP, you will be using only the **Default Web Site**. If no text appears next to **Default Web Site**, this means that IIS is started and you can proceed to *Step 4*. However, if the text **(Stopped)** appears (Fig. 28.4), you need to start IIS. To start IIS in either Windows 2000 or Windows XP, select the **Default Web Site** entry and click the Start Item **Button** in the toolbar. IIS will then start allowing IIS to respond to client requests. [*Note*: The contents of the right pane may be different on your system.]

4. ***Opening the Bookstore Properties dialog.*** Click **Default Web Site** in the left pane to display the contents of your Web site in the right pane. Right click **Bookstore** in the right pane, and select **Properties** (Fig. 28.6). This option opens the **Bookstore Properties** dialog (Fig. 28.7).

(cont.)

Click Default Web Site to display the Web site's contents in the right pane

Right click this directory

Contents of **Default Web Site**

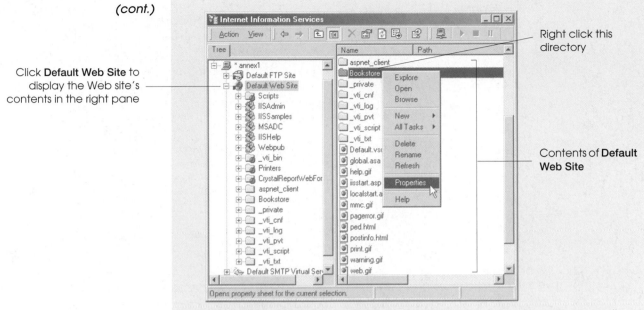

Figure 28.6 `Bookstore` directory in the **Internet Information Services** dialog.

Directory tab

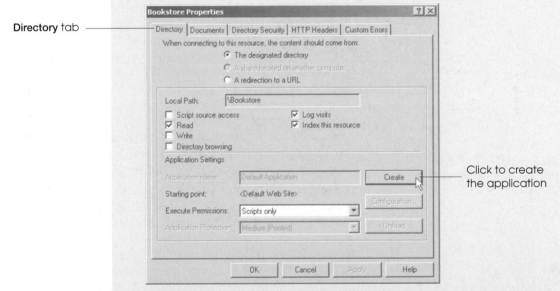

Click to create the application

Figure 28.7 **Properties** of the `Bookstore` directory.

5. ***Setting IIS to recognize the Bookstore application.*** To successfully run the application, IIS must recognize the **Bookstore** as a Web application. In the **Directory** tab, click the **Create** Button (Fig. 28.7). The dialog should now look like Fig. 28.8. Click the **OK** Button. This directory is now recognized by IIS as a Web application with the name **Bookstore**. Close the **Internet Information Services** dialog.

Common Programming Error

Failure to configure IIS to recognize a directory as an application results in an error that prevents the Web application's start page from loading in a Web browser.

(cont.)

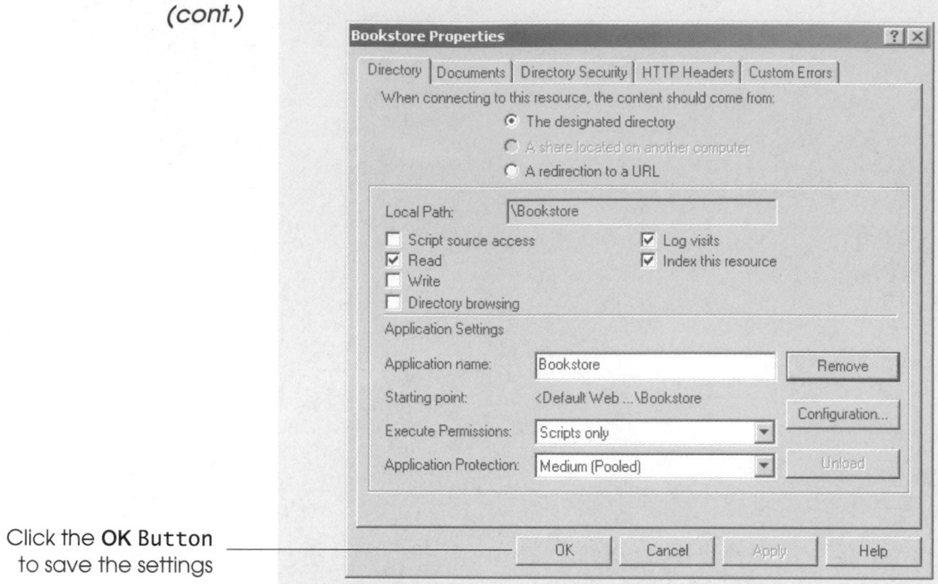

Click the **OK** Button
to save the settings

Figure 28.8 **Bookstore Properties** dialog after clicking **Create** in Fig. 28.7.

6. ***Adding the Databases directory to the wwwroot directory.*** Open a Windows Explorer window, and navigate to the wwwroot directory. Copy the `C:\Examples\Tutorial28\Databases` directory to the wwwroot directory. This directory contains the database that will be used for the application. This database contains information about various books.

   [*Note:* The remaining steps in this box cover security settings that are required for directories in the NTFS file system. If your system uses the FAT32 file system, you can skip *Steps 7–12*. To determine which file system you are using, open Windows Explorer and right click the C: drive, then select **Properties**. In the dialog that appears, select the **General** tab. The file system will be displayed in the **File system:** field. If you are using the NTFS file system, proceed with *Step 7*. If you are using the FAT32 file system, you may skip the remaining steps in this box.]

7. ***Changing the settings of the Databases directory.*** Your application will need to open and retrieve information from the database stored in the `Databases` directory. You must change some settings of this directory. If your operating system is Windows 2000, complete all the instructions presented in *Step 8* and move on to the next section. (*Steps 9–12* do not apply to Windows 2000.) If your operating system is Windows XP skip *Step 8* and complete the remaining steps (*9–12*) of this box.

8. ***(Windows 2000 only) Changing the security settings of the Databases directory in the Windows Explorer.*** Right click the `Databases` directory that you placed in the wwwroot directory, and select **Properties** (Fig. 28.9). This option opens the **Databases Properties** dialog (Fig. 28.10). You now need to change the security settings of this directory. Select the **Security** tab. Make sure that the **Allow inheritable permissions from parent to propagate to this object** CheckBox is checked. Now click the **Add...** Button (Fig. 28.11). [*Note:* The contents of the **Name** box of the **Security** tab may differ on your computer.]

(cont.)

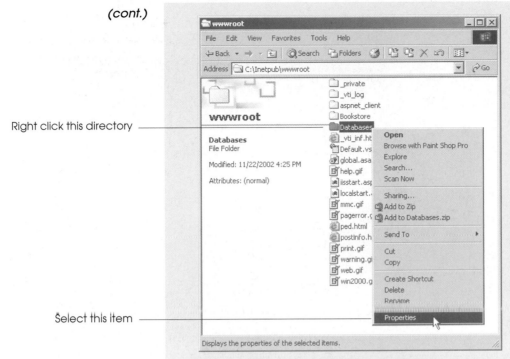

Figure 28.9   Selecting the **Properties** item.

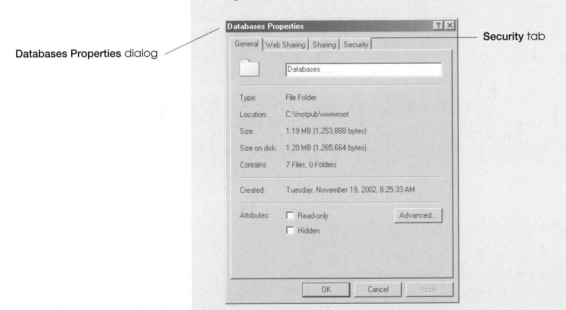

Figure 28.10   **Databases Properties** dialog.

A **Select Users or Groups** dialog (Fig. 28.12) appears, where you can specify the users or groups of users who can access the directory. Make sure that the **Look in:** drop-down list at the top of the dialog displays your computer name. If it does not, search for your computer name in the drop-down list, and select it. Locate the **ASPNET** user in the **Name** box. Double click the **ASPNET** user so that it is added to the bottom half of the dialog. The **ASPNET** user represents a user that is configured to run ASP .NET Web applications with the minimum amount of access privileges. Click the **OK** Button.

(cont.)

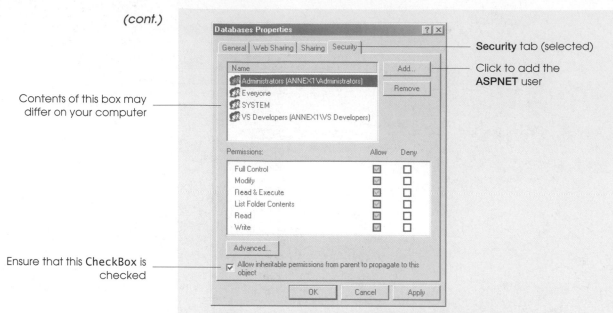

Security tab (selected)

Click to add the **ASPNET** user

Contents of this box may differ on your computer

Ensure that this **CheckBox** is checked

Figure 28.11   **Security** tab for the `Databases` directory.

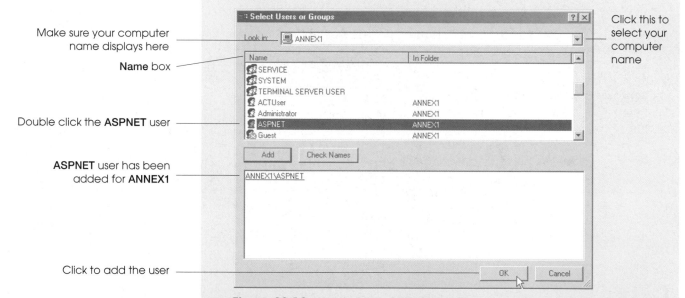

Make sure your computer name displays here

Name box

Double click the **ASPNET** user

ASPNET user has been added for **ANNEX1**

Click to add the user

Click this to select your computer name

Figure 28.12   Adding the **ASPNET** user.

You are then returned to the **Databases Properties** dialog (Fig. 28.13). Select the **ASPNET** user you added from the **Name** box, and check the **Write CheckBox** in the **Allow** column of the **Permissions:** box to give the **ASPNET** user permission to write to the `Databases` directory (Fig. 28.13). Any application that opens an Access database writes a **lock file** in the directory to indicate that the database is in use. Only one lock file can be written at a time. Therefore, only one application can modify the database at a time. Giving the **ASPNET** user write permission enables the ASP .NET application to write a lock file in this directory when the application opens the database. Click the **OK** Button to close the **Databases Properties** dialog.

Common Programming Error

Failure to give the **ASPNET** user write permission to the directory containing the database will cause an error when the application executes. The application will not be able to open the database.

(cont.)

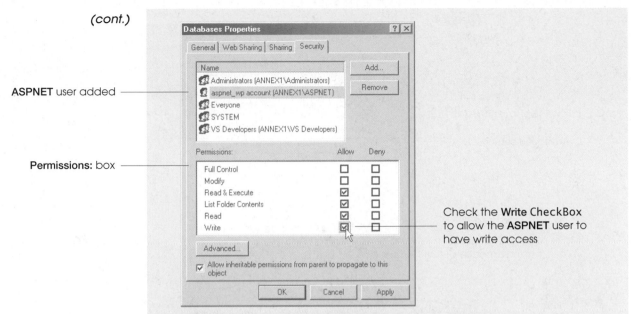

ASPNET user added

Permissions: box

Check the **Write** CheckBox
to allow the **ASPNET** user to
have write access

Figure 28.13   Giving the **ASPNET** user write permission.

9. *(Windows XP Only) Displaying the Security tab of the Databases directory.* In the `wwwroot` directory, select **Tools > Folder Options...** (Fig. 28.14) to open the **Folder Options** dialog (Fig. 28.15). Select the **View** tab, and make sure that the **Use simple file sharing (Recommended)** CheckBox at the bottom of the **Advanced settings:** box is unchecked. You need to make sure this box is unchecked to ensure that the **Security** tab will be displayed in the **Databases Properties** dialog, which you access in the next step. If you changed any of the settings, click **Apply** and then **OK** to save the changes.

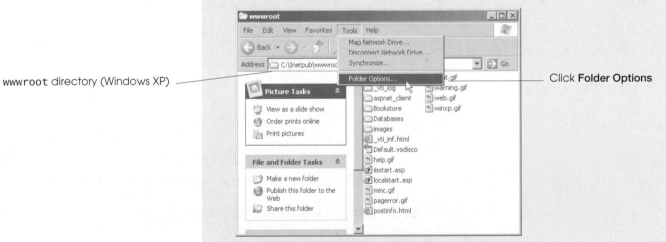

wwwroot directory (Windows XP)

Click **Folder Options**

Figure 28.14   Displaying the **Folder Options** dialog.

10. *(Windows XP Only) Displaying the Databases Properties dialog.* Right click the `Databases` directory, and select **Properties**. The **Databases Properties** dialog appears. Click the **Security** tab; then, click the **Advanced** Button to display the **Advanced Security Settings for Databases** dialog. Make sure that the **Inherit from parent the permission entries that apply to child objects. Include these with entries explicitly defined here.** CheckBox contains a check mark. Click the **OK** Button to return to the **Database Properties** dialog. Click the **Add...** Button to add a user to the directory (Fig. 28.16). The **Select Users or Groups** dialog appears (Fig. 28.17).

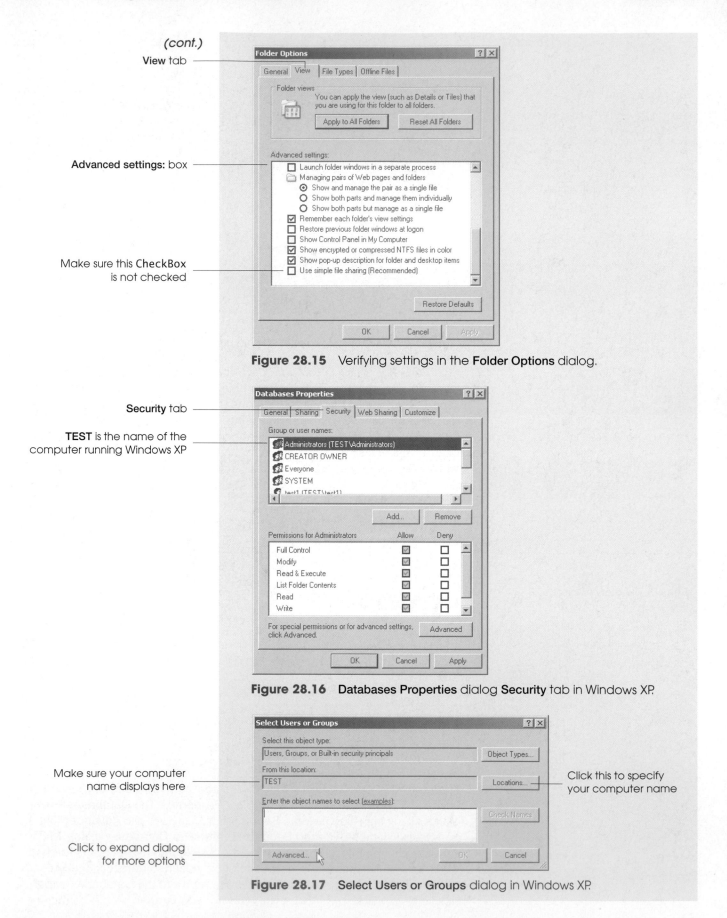

(cont.)

View tab

Advanced settings: box

Make sure this **CheckBox**
is not checked

Figure 28.15   Verifying settings in the **Folder Options** dialog.

Security tab

TEST is the name of the
computer running Windows XP

Figure 28.16   **Databases Properties** dialog **Security** tab in Windows XP.

Make sure your computer
name displays here

Click this to specify
your computer name

Click to expand dialog
for more options

Figure 28.17   **Select Users or Groups** dialog in Windows XP.

(cont.)

11. ***(Windows XP Only) Adding a new user to the Databases directory.*** In the **Select Users or Groups** dialog, make sure that the **From this location:** field contains your computer name. If it does not, click the **Locations...** Button, select your computer name from the **Location:** box and click the **OK** Button to accept the changes. In the **Select Users or Groups** dialog, click the **Advanced...** Button. This dialog expands to provide more options (Fig. 28.18). Click the **Find Now** Button, select the **ASPNET** user name and click **OK** (Fig. 28.19). The **ASPNET** user represents a user that is configured to run ASP .NET Web applications with the minimum amount of access privileges. The **ASPNET** user should now be displayed in the **Select Users or Groups** dialog (Fig. 28.20). Click **OK**.

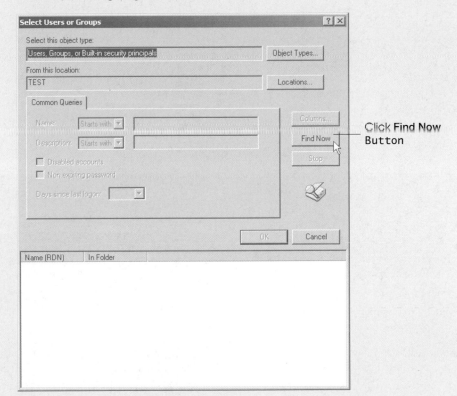

Figure 28.18   Expanded **Select Users or Groups** dialog.

12. ***(Windows XP Only) Giving the ASPNET user write permissions.*** The **ASP-NET** user should appear in the **Security** tab of the **Databases Properties** dialog. Select the **ASPNET** user, and check the **Write** CheckBox in the **Allow** column to give the user write permission (Fig. 28.21). Any application that opens an Access database writes a **lock file** in the directory to indicate that the database is in use. Only one lock file can be written at a time. Therefore, only one application can modify the database at a time. Giving the **ASPNET** user write permission enables the ASP .NET application to write a lock file in this directory when the application opens the database. Click the **OK** Button to close the **Databases Properties** dialog.

(cont.)

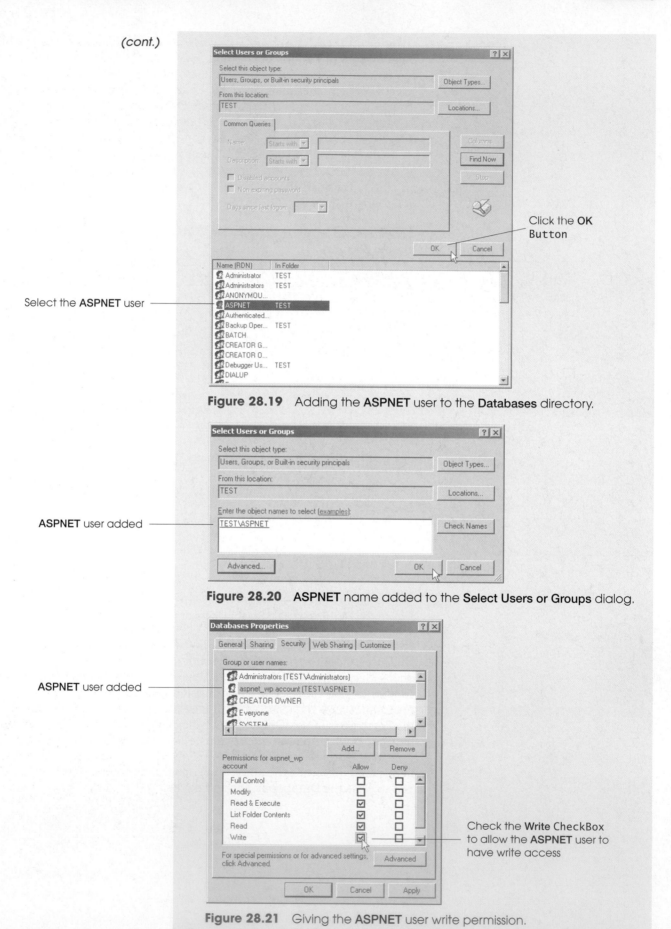

Select the **ASPNET** user ──────

Click the **OK** Button

Figure 28.19 Adding the **ASPNET** user to the **Databases** directory.

ASPNET user added ──────

Figure 28.20 **ASPNET** name added to the **Select Users or Groups** dialog.

ASPNET user added ──────

Check the **Write CheckBox** to allow the **ASPNET** user to have write access

Figure 28.21 Giving the **ASPNET** user write permission.

SELF-REVIEW 1. The _____ user represents a user that is configured to run ASP .NET Web applications with the minimum amount of access privileges.

    a) **TEST**   b) **WEB**

    c) **ASPNET**   d) **ASPX**

2. To start IIS in the **Internet Information Services** dialog, you must select _____ and click the Start Item **Button**.

    a) the Web application's directory   b) **Default Web Site**

    c) Both a and b.   d) None of the above.

Answers: 1) c. 2) b.

28.4 Test-Driving the Bookstore Application

In the next three tutorials, you will build a **Bookstore** application that displays book information to users upon request. This application must meet the following requirements:

> **Application Requirements**
>
> *A bookstore employee receives e-mails from customers asking for information pertaining to the books the store provides online. Responding to the numerous e-mails can be a tedious and time-consuming task. The employee has asked you to create a Web application that allows users to view information about various books online. This information includes the author, price, ISBN number, edition number, copyright date and a brief description of the book.*

The **Bookstore** application you create uses ASP .NET and is designed to allow users to view various pieces of information about the books offered by the store. You begin by test-driving the completed application. Then, in Tutorials 29–31, you will learn the additional C# technologies that you will need to create your own version of this application.

Test-Driving the Web-Based Bookstore Application

1. ***Opening the completed application.*** Open the C:\InetPub\wwwroot\ Bookstore directory to locate the **Bookstore** application. Double click Bookstore.sln to open the application in Visual Studio .NET.

    When you open the application, you may receive the error message in Fig. 28.22. If this occurs, open the **Command Prompt** window by selecting **Start > Programs > Accessories > Command Prompt**. Change directories by typing cd C:*WindowsDirectory*\Microsoft.NET\Framework\v1.1.4322 then pressing *Enter*, where *WindowsDirectory* is normally **WINDOWS** or **WINNT**. Then, type aspnet_regiis /i and press *Enter* to set up ASP .NET version 1.1.

Figure 28.22 Error message for ASP .NET version 1.1.

(cont.)

2. ***Setting the start page.*** The start page is the first page that loads when the application is run. To specify the start page, right click the Books.aspx file in the **Solution Explorer**, and select **Set As Start Page** (Fig. 28.23). Files with the extension **.aspx** (usually referred to as **Web Forms**, **Web Form Pages** or **ASPX pages**) contain the Web page's GUI. The Web Form file represents the Web page that is sent to the client browser. [*Note*: From this point onward, we refer to Web Form files as ASPX pages.] A Web application can contain several ASPX pages. In this example, Books.aspx displays the available books to the user. The BookInformation.aspx page displays information about the book selected. You must set Books.aspx to appear first because you do not know in which book the user is interested until the user makes a selection from the Books.aspx page.

Right click the Books.aspx page

Select this option to
set the start page

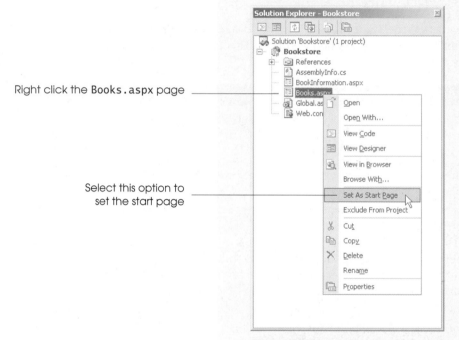

Figure 28.23 Setting Books.aspx as the Web application's start page.

3. ***Running the Bookstore application.*** Select **Debug > Start** to run the application. The Books.aspx page appears in Internet Explorer as shown in Fig. 28.24. [*Note*: If you are unable to run the project, make sure that you have followed all of the instructions for copying files, starting IIS and setting the Database directory's properties.] This page displays a ListBox containing the available books. Although this ListBox looks similar to the ListBox control you have used in Windows applications, this ListBox is actually a **Web control** (also called an **ASP .NET server control**). Programmers customize ASPX pages by adding Web controls, such as Labels, TextBoxes and Buttons. As you will learn, Web controls look similar to their Windows application counterparts.

Internet Explorer and its HTML content represent the client tier. In Tutorial 29, you will add Web controls, such as Labels to display text, a ListBox to display the list of available books, Buttons to load a different page and a Table to display information on a particular book.

(cont.)

Location of `Books.aspx` page ——

`Label` controls ——

`ListBox` control containing the available books ——

`Button` control ——

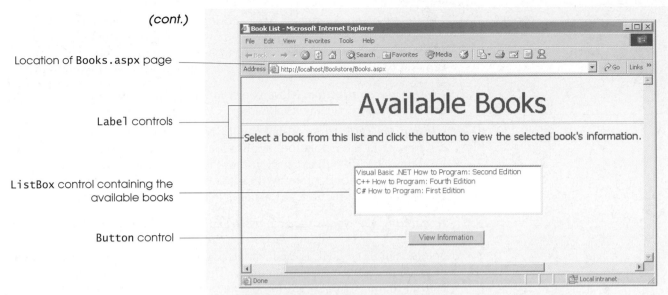

Figure 28.24   Page that displays a list of available books.

The books displayed in the `ListBox` are retrieved from a database. The database, named **db_bookstore.mdb**, is the information tier of this three-tier application. Although only the book titles are displayed in the List-Box, the database includes other information, such as the authors and prices of the books. In Tutorial 30, you will examine the application's information tier and learn how to connect to the database to access the data.

4. ***Selecting a book.*** Select **C++ How To Program: Fourth Edition** from the book list, and click the **View Information** `Button`. The `BookInformation.aspx` page appears (Fig. 28.25). This page displays the title, author and an image of the selected book. This page also contains a table that lists the selected book's price, ISBN number, edition number and copyright date, as well as a description of the book.

Location of the `BookInformation.aspx` page ——

`Table` Web control ——

When clicked, this `Button` returns the user to `Books.aspx` ——

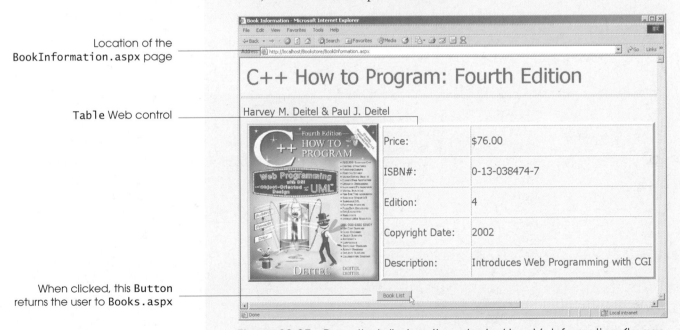

Figure 28.25   Page that displays the selected book's information. (Image courtesy of Deitel & Associates, Inc.)

(cont.)

5. ***Returning to Books.aspx.*** After viewing a book's information, users can decide whether they wish to view another book's information. The bottom of this page contains a **Book List** Button that, when clicked, redirects the browser back to the Books.aspx page to redisplay the list of book titles.

6. ***Closing the application.*** Close your running application (in this case, Internet Explorer) by clicking its close box.

7. ***Closing the IDE.*** Close Visual Studio .NET by clicking its close box. You have now run the **Bookstore** application from Visual Studio .NET on your local machine. In the next step, you will request the Books.aspx Web page, using only Internet Explorer. With real-world ASP .NET applications, clients are browsers that request ASPX pages that reside on remote Web servers.

8. ***Requesting the Books.aspx page from Internet Explorer.*** Open Internet Explorer, and enter the URL http://localhost/Bookstore/ Books.aspx. The URL is the location of the Books.aspx page of the **Book-store** application on your computer. The Books.aspx ASPX page should load in the browser. Select a book, and click the Button to verify that the **Bookstore** application behaves properly.

9. ***Closing the application.*** Close your running application (in this case, Internet Explorer) by clicking its close box.

10. ***Removing the completed application from the IIS's root directory.*** Now you will need to remove the completed application from IIS's root directory before you begin developing the application. You cannot have two applications with the same name in the wwwroot directory. Therefore, you must delete the completed application so that you can create the **Bookstore** application from scratch over the next three tutorials. Stop IIS by clicking the Stop Item Button (the filled square next to the Start Item Button) in the **Internet Information Services** dialog. Right click Bookstore in the right pane, and select **Delete** to remove the completed **Bookstore** application from IIS's root directory (Fig. 28.26). [*Note*: In some cases, Windows may not let you delete this directory until after you restart your computer.]

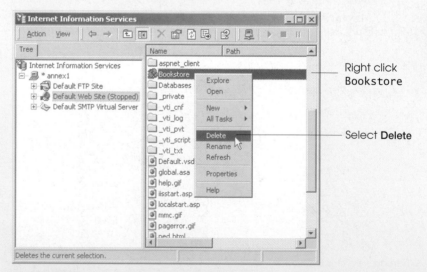

Figure 28.26 Deleting the Bookstore directory from IIS's root directory.

Notice that this example uses all three tiers of a three-tier application. The information tier is the database from which the application retrieves information.

The middle tier is the code that controls what occurs when users interact with the Web pages. The client tier is represented by the Web pages from which the user views and selects books.

SELF-REVIEW   1. Web controls also are called _____.

a) ASP .NET server controls   b) ASP controls

c) HTML controls   d) None of the above.

2. In real-world ASP .NET applications, typically clients are _____ that request ASPX pages that reside on remote Web servers.

a) Web Form pages   b) Web controls

c) Web browsers   d) None of the above.

Answers: 1) a. 2) c.

28.5 Wrap-Up

In this tutorial, you learned about the components of a three-tier application. You were introduced to the information tier, which maintains the data for the application. You then learned about the client tier, which displays the application's user interface, and the middle tier, which provides the communication between the information and client tiers. Next, you were introduced to Microsoft Internet Information Services (IIS), which is used for serving Web content such as ASP .NET Web pages. You then test-drove the three-tier **Bookstore** application. In doing this, you learned how to start and stop IIS and how to run ASP .NET Web-based applications. You were also introduced to ASPX pages, and you learned that Web controls are used to customize these pages.

In the next tutorial, you will create the user interface for this application. You will design the Web pages that display the book list and book information. You will then proceed to Tutorial 30, **Bookstore** Application: Information Tier. This tutorial describes the database used in the application and provides a step-by-step discussion of how the application connects to the database. Discussion of the **Bookstore** application will conclude with Tutorial 31, **Bookstore** Application: Middle Tier. In this tutorial, you will write the functionality for the **Bookstore** application.

SKILLS SUMMARY

Starting IIS in Windows 2000

- Go to the Windows **Start** menu, and select **Settings > Control Panel**.
- Double click **Administrative Tools**, then double click **Internet Services Manager** to display the **Internet Information Services** dialog.
- Click the plus box next to your computer name's node to display the default sites set up by IIS.
- Click **Default Web Site** in the left pane.
- Click the Start Item **Button** in the toolbar. (This is required only if the **Default Web Site** is stopped.)

Starting IIS in Windows XP

- Go to the Windows **Start** menu, and select **Control Panel**.
- In the **Control Panel** dialog, click the **Switch to Classic View** link.
- Double click **Administrative Tools**, then double click **Internet Information Services** to display the **Internet Information Services** dialog.
- Click the plus box next to your computer name's node to display the **Web Sites** node.
- Click the **Web Sites** node to display the **Default Web Site** node.
- Click **Default Web Site** in the left pane.
- Click the Start Item **Button** in the toolbar. (This is required only if the **Default Web Site** is stopped.)

Stopping IIS in Windows 2000

- Go to the Windows **Start** menu, and select **Settings > Control Panel**.
- Double click **Administrative Tools**, then double click **Internet Services Manager** to display the **Internet Information Services** dialog.
- Click the plus box next to your computer name's node to display the default sites set up by IIS.
- Click **Default Web Site** in the left pane.
- Click the Stop Item `Button` in the toolbar.

Stopping IIS in Windows XP

- Go to the Windows **Start** menu, and select **Control Panel**.
- In the **Control Panel** dialog, click the **Switch to Classic View** link.
- Double click **Administrative Tools**, then double click **Internet Information Services** to display the **Internet Information Services** dialog.
- Click the plus box next to your computer name's node to display the **Web Sites** node.
- Click the **Web Sites** node to display the **Default Web Site** node.
- Click **Default Web Site** in the left pane.
- Click the Stop Item `Button` in the toolbar.

Setting up a Web Application on Your Machine

- Place the Web application's project directory in your Web server's root directory (usually `C:\Inetpub\wwwroot`).
- Start IIS.
- Click **Default Web Site** in the **Internet Information Services** dialog to display the contents of the directory in the right pane.
- Right click the desired project's directory, then select **Properties**.
- Click the **Create** `Button`; then, click **OK**.
- Open the application, then right click the start page in the **Solution Explorer** window.
- Select **Set As Start Page**.

Enabling Web Applications to Use Access Databases in Windows 2000

- Search for the directory containing the database in the wwwroot directory; right click the name of the directory, and select **Properties**.
- Select the **Security** tab.
- Make sure that the **Allow inheritable permissions from parent to propagate to this object** `CheckBox` is checked, and click the **Add** `Button`.
- Double click the **ASPNET** user, and click the **OK** `Button`.
- Give the **ASPNET** user write permission by selecting the **ASPNET** user and checking the **Write** `CheckBox` in the **Allow** column.
- Click **OK** to accept the settings.

Enabling Web Applications to Use Access Databases in Windows XP

- Select **Tools > Folder Options…** in the wwwroot directory.
- Click the **View** tab; then, make sure that the **Use simple file sharing (Recommended)** `CheckBox` in the **Advanced settings:** tab of the **Folder Options** dialog does not contain a checkmark.
- If you changed any settings, click **OK** to accept the changes.
- Search for the directory containing the database in the wwwroot directory; right click the name of the directory, and select **Properties**.
- Select the **Security** tab, then click the **Add** `Button`.
- Click the **Advanced…** `Button` to display more options in the **Select Users or Groups** dialog.
- Click the **Find Now** `Button`.
- Double click the **ASPNET** user, and click the **OK** `Button`.

- Click the **OK** Button again to add **ASPNET** as a user.
- Give the **ASPNET** user write permission by selecting the **ASPNET** user and checking the **Write** CheckBox in the **Allow** column.
- Click **OK** to accept the settings.

Testing the Web Application on localhost, Using Visual Studio .NET

- Open the application in Visual Studio .NET.
- Select **Debug > Start** to run the application.

Testing the Web Application on localhost, Using Internet Explorer

- Open an Internet Explorer browser.
- Type the URL http://localhost/*nameOfProject*/*nameOfStartPage*, where *nameOf-Project* is the name of the project directory and *nameOfStartPage* is the name of the first ASPX page that loads when the application is run.
- Press *Enter* to run the application.

KEY TERMS

ASP .NET technology—Can be combined with C# to create web applications.

ASPX page—File ending in .aspx that specifies the GUI of a Web page using Web controls. Also called a Web Form or Web Form Page.

bottom tier—The tier (also known as the information tier, or the data tier) containing the application data of a multi-tier application—typically implemented as a database.

client tier—The user interface of a multi-tier application (also called the top tier).

data tier—The tier (also known as the information tier, or the bottom tier) containing the application data of a multi-tier application—typically implemented as a database.

DNS lookup—Process that translates domain names to IP addresses.

domain—Represents a group of hosts on the Internet.

domain name system (DNS) server—Computer that maintains a database of host names and their corresponding IP addresses.

fully qualified domain name (FQDN)—Host name combined with a domain and top-level domain that provides a user-friendly way to identify a site on the Internet.

host—A computer that stores and maintains resources, such as Web pages, databases and multimedia files.

host name—Name of a computer where resources reside.

information tier—Tier containing the application data; typically implemented as a database. Also called the bottom tier or database tier.

Internet Information Services (IIS)—A Microsoft Web server.

IP address—Unique address used to locate a computer on the Internet.

lock file—File which ensures that only one program at a time manipulates an Access database.

localhost—Host name that identifies the local computer.

middle tier—Tier that controls interaction between the client and information tiers.

multi-tier (*n*-tier) application—Application that divides functionality into separate tiers. Typically, each tier performs a specific function.

top-level domain (TLD)—Usually describes the type of organization that owns the domain name.

top tier—Tier containing the application's user interface. Also called the client tier.

uniform resource locator (URL)—Address that can be used to direct a browser to a resource on the Web.

Web applications—Applications that create web content.

Web controls—Controls, such as TextBoxes and Buttons, that are used to customize ASPX pages. Also called an ASP .NET server control.

Web server—Specialized software that responds to client requests by providing resources.

MULTIPLE-CHOICE QUESTIONS

28.1 ASPX pages have the _____ extension.

a) `.html`

b) `.wbform`

c) `.csaspx`

d) `.aspx`

28.2 _____ applications divide functionality into separate tiers.

a) *n*-tier

b) Multi-tier

c) Both a and b.

d) None of the above.

28.3 All tiers of a multi-tier application _____.

a) must be located on the same computer

b) must be located on different computers

c) can be located on the same computer or on different computers

d) must be arranged so that the client and middle tier are on the same computer and the information tier is on a different computer

28.4 The client tier interacts with the _____ tier to access information from the _____ tier.

a) middle; information

b) information; middle

c) information; bottom

d) bottom; information

28.5 A _____ is specialized software that responds to client requests by providing resources.

a) host

b) host name

c) DNS server

d) Web server

28.6 A(n) _____ can be thought of as an address that is used to direct a browser to a resource on the Web.

a) middle tier

b) ASPX page

c) URL

d) query string

28.7 A _____ represents a group of _____ on the Internet.

a) domain; hosts

b) host; domain names

c) host name; hosts

d) None of the above.

28.8 _____ is a Web server.

a) IIS

b) `localhost`

c) Visual Studio .NET

d) `wwwroot`

28.9 A _____ is a Web server that is located on a computer across a network, such as the Internet.

a) `localhost`

b) local Web server

c) remote Web server

d) None of the above.

28.10 The _____ tier is the application's user interface.

a) middle

b) client

c) bottom

d) information

EXERCISES

28.11 (*Phone Book Application*) Over the next three tutorials, you will create a **Phone Book** application. This phone book should be a Web-based version of the **Phone Book** application created in Tutorial 27. [*Note*: This Web application will not use Microsoft Agent.] The **Phone Book** application should consist of two ASPX pages, named PhoneBook and Phone-Number. The PhoneBook page displays a DropDownList (a Web control similar to a ComboBox Windows Form control) that contains the names of several people. The names are retrieved from the db_Phone.mdb database. When a name is selected and the **Get Number** Button is clicked, the client browser is redirected to the PhoneNumber page. The telephone number of the selected name should be retrieved from a database and displayed in a Label on the

PhoneNumber page. For this exercise, you need only organize the components (the Phone-Book and PhoneNumber ASPX pages, the db_Phone.mdb database and the code that performs the specified functionality) of this Web application into separate tiers. Decide which components belong in which tiers. You will begin building the solution, using Visual Studio .NET, in the next tutorial.

28.12 (*US State Facts Application*) Over the next three tutorials, you will create a **US State Facts** application. This application is designed to allow users to review their knowledge about specific U.S. states. This application should consist of two ASPX pages. The first page (named States) should display a ListBox containing 10 different state names. These state names are stored in the db_StateFacts.mdb database. The user should be allowed to select a state name and click a Button to retrieve information about the selected state from the database. The information should be displayed on a different ASPX page (named State-Facts). The StateFacts page should display an image of the state flag and list the state capital, state flower, state tree and state bird (retrieved from the database) in a Table. You will be provided with images of the state flags. For this exercise, you need only organize the components (the States and StateFacts ASPX pages, the db_StateFacts.mdb database and the code that performs the specified functionality) of this Web application into separate tiers. Decide which components belong in which tiers. You will begin building the solution, using Visual Studio .NET, in the next tutorial.

28.13 (*Road Sign Review Application*) Over the next three tutorials, you will create a **Road Sign Review** application. The **Road Sign Review** application should consist of two ASPX pages. This application displays road signs for users to review and allows them to schedule a driving test. The first page (named RoadSigns) should display 15 road signs in a Table. You will be provided images of the road signs. When the mouse pointer is moved over a sign, the name of the sign will appear in a tooltip in the Web browser window. The table should display the images by retrieving their information from the db_RoadSigns.mdb database. This page also will contain two TextBoxes and a Button to allow users to provide their information to register for a driving test. When users click the **Register** Button, the second page (RoadTestRegistered) displays information confirming that the user has registered for a driving test. For this exercise, you need only organize the components (the RoadSigns and RoadTestRegistered ASPX pages, the db_RoadSigns.mdb database and the code that performs the specified functionality) of this Web application into separate tiers. Decide which components belong in which tiers. You will begin building the solution, using Visual Studio .NET, in the next tutorial.

Objectives

In this tutorial, you will learn to:
- Create an **ASP .NET Web Application** project.
- Create and design ASPX pages.
- Use Web controls.
- Reposition controls using the `style` attribute.

Outline

Bookstore Application: Client Tier

Introducing Web Controls

In this tutorial, you will create the client tier (user interface) of your three-tier **Bookstore** application, using visual-programming techniques. You will begin by creating the application's project—an ASP .NET Web application. Then, you will learn about Web controls by creating the application's GUI.

29.1 Analyzing the Bookstore Application

Now that you have taken the three-tier **Bookstore** application for a test-drive (in Tutorial 28), you need to analyze the application components. The following pseudocode describes the basic operation of the **Bookstore** application:

> When the Books page is requested:
>   Retrieve the book titles from the database
>   Display book titles in a ListBox
>
> When the user selects a book title from the ListBox and clicks the View Information Button:
>   Retrieve the selected book
>   Store the selected book in a variable
>   Redirect the user to the BookInformation page
>
> When the BookInformation page is requested:
>   Display the book title in a Label
>   Retrieve the selected book's information from a database
>   Display the authors in a Label
>   Display the cover art in an image
>   Display the remaining information in a Table
>
> When the user presses the Book List Button on the BookInformation page:
>   Redirect the client browser back to the Books page

Now that you have test-driven the **Bookstore** application and studied its pseudocode representation, you will use an ACE table to help you convert the pseudocode to C#. Figure 29.1 lists the actions, controls and events that will help you complete your own version of this application.

Action/Control/Event (ACE) Table for the Web-Based Bookstore Application

Action	Control/Class/Object	Event
Label the Books page	lblAvailable, lblInstructions	Application is run
	Page	Load (for Books.aspx)
Retrieve the book titles from the database	objOleDbConnection, objSelectTitles, objReader	
Display book titles in a ListBox	lstBookTitles	
	btnInformation	Click
Retrieve the selected book	lstBookTitles	
Store the selected book in a variable	Session	
Redirect the user to the BookInformation page	Response	
	Page	Load (for Book- Information.aspx)
Display the book title in a Label	lblBookTitle	
Retrieve the selected book's information from a database	objOleDbConnection, objSelectBookData, objReader	
Display the authors in a Label	lblAuthors	
Display the cover art in an image	imgBook	
Display the remaining information in a Table	tblBook	
	btnBookList	Click
Redirect the client browser back to the Books page	Response	

Figure 29.1   ACE table for the Web-based **Bookstore** application.

29.2 Creating ASPX Pages

Now that you have been introduced to IIS and three-tier, Web-based application concepts, you will begin creating the **Bookstore** application that you test-drove in the last tutorial. Before you begin to create the GUI for the **Bookstore** application, you need to set Visual Studio .NET to display line numbers for the ASPX page.

Configuring Visual Studio .NET to Display Line Numbers For ASPX Pages

1. ***Opening the* Options *dialog.*** Open Visual Studio .NET. Select **Tools > Options...** to display the **Options** dialog.

2. ***Enabling line numbers to be displayed.*** Click **Text Editor** in the left pane of the **Options** dialog; then, click **HTML/XML**. Click **General**, and check the **Line Numbers** CheckBox (Fig. 29.2). Click the **OK** Button to save the settings and close the **Options** dialog.

(cont.)

Text Editor (clicked)

HTML/XML (clicked)

General (selected)

Line numbers CheckBox
(checked)

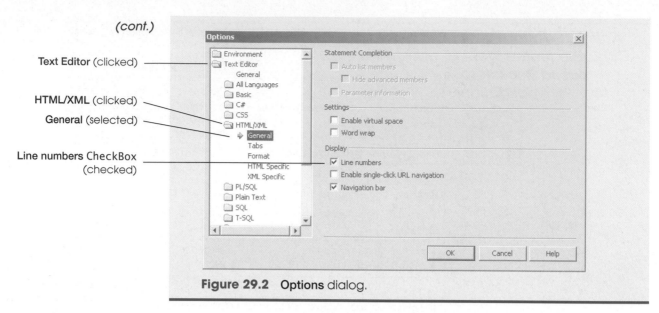

Figure 29.2 **Options** dialog.

Now that you have configured Visual Studio .NET to display line numbers for the ASPX page, you can begin creating the **Bookstore** application. This Web-based application allows users to view information about books they select. After viewing a book's information, users can return to the page containing the list of books and select another book. You will create the **ASP .NET Web Application** project for the **Bookstore** in the following box.

Creating an ASP .NET Web Application

1. **Starting IIS.** IIS must be running on the server machine (localhost, in this case) for you to be able to create ASP .NET Web applications in Visual Studio .NET. Start IIS as demonstrated in *Step 3* of the box, *Specifying Initial Settings for the Bookstore Application*, in Tutorial 28.

2. **Creating the project.** In Visual Studio .NET, select **File > New > Project...** to display the **New Project** dialog (Fig. 29.3). In this dialog, select **Visual C# Projects** in the **Project Types:** pane and **ASP .NET Web Application** in the **Templates:** pane. Notice that the **Name:** TextBox for the project name is disabled. Specify the name and location of the project in the **Location:** TextBox. The default value in this TextBox is http://localhost/WebApplication1. The files for this application will be stored in a directory called WebApplication1, located at http://localhost. Recall that this location is really IIS's root directory (usually C:\Inetpub\wwwroot).

Visual C# Projects selected
in the Project Types: pane

Type http://localhost/
Bookstore in this TextBox

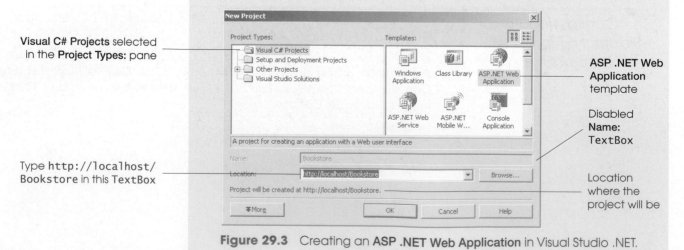

ASP .NET Web
Application
template

Disabled
Name:
TextBox

Location
where the
project will be

Figure 29.3 Creating an **ASP .NET Web Application** in Visual Studio .NET.

(cont.)

Change WebApplication1 to Bookstore. If the Bookstore directory does not yet exist at http://localhost, it will be created for you. Below the **Location:** TextBox, the text "**Project will be created at http://local-host/Bookstore.**" appears. Click **OK** to create the project. The **Create New Web** dialog displays next, while Visual Studio .NET creates the Web site on the server (Fig. 29.4).

Figure 29.4   Visual Studio .NET creating the **Bookstore** application.

3. *Examining the project files.* The **Solution Explorer** window for the **Bookstore** application is shown in Fig. 29.5. As with Windows applications, Visual Studio .NET creates several files for each new **ASP .NET Web Application** project. WebForm1.aspx is the default name for the ASPX page.

Project name ⎯⎯⎯⎯⎯⎯⎯⎯⎯⎯

Default ASPX page name ⎯⎯⎯⎯⎯

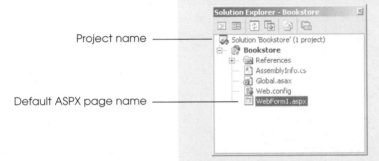

Figure 29.5   **Solution Explorer** window for the **Bookstore** solution.

4. *Viewing the Toolbox.* ASPX pages can be customized by using Web controls. These types of controls are used for ASPX pages in a manner similar to how Windows controls are used for Windows Forms. You will be using these controls to create the user interface of your **Bookstore** application. Web controls are located in the **Web Forms** tab of the **Toolbox**. Select **View > Toolbox**, then click the **Web Forms** tab. Figure 29.6 shows the **Web Forms** controls listed in the **Toolbox**. The left part of the figure displays the beginning of the **Web Forms** controls list, and the right part of the figure displays the remaining **Web Forms** controls. Notice that some of the control icons, such as Label, TextBox and Button, are the same as the Windows controls presented earlier in the book. Although some of these control names appear the same, the functionality provided by **Web Forms** controls is different, and they can be used only with ASPX pages.

5. *Viewing the ASPX page in Design mode.* When you create a Web application, an ASPX page will be displayed in the Web Form Designer (Fig. 29.7). [*Note*: We do not apply a Lucida font to the word "Form" (in "Web Form Designer"), because Web Forms are not instances of the Form class.]

(cont.)

Web Forms tab

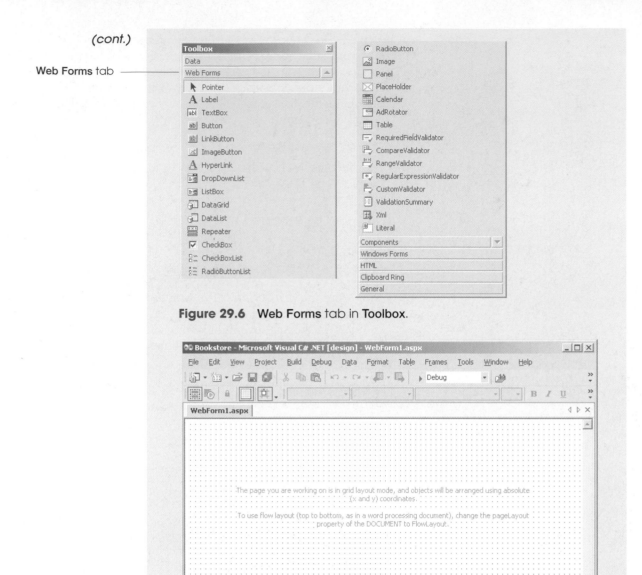

Figure 29.6 **Web Forms** tab in **Toolbox**.

HTML Button

Design Button (selected)

Figure 29.7 **Design** mode of Web Form Designer.

Unlike the Windows Form Designer, the Web Form Designer contains two different viewing modes. The first mode is the **Design mode**. Figure 29.7 shows the ASPX page displayed in **Design** mode for WebForm1.aspx. It consists of a grid on which you drag and drop components, such as Buttons and Labels, from the **Toolbox**. If the **Design** mode for the ASPX page does not display, click the **Design** Button, in the lower left corner of the Web Form Designer. **Design** mode should be used when you want to visually create the ASPX page's GUI by dragging and dropping Web controls onto the ASPX page.

(cont.)

6. ***Switching to HTML mode.*** The Web Form Designer also can display the ASPX page in **HTML mode** (Fig. 29.8). Click the **HTML** Button. ASPX pages are defined using a combination of HTML and ASP .NET markup. **ASP .NET markup** is the set of instructions processed on the Web server's machine. ASP .NET markup is often converted into HTML and sent to a browser client as part of a response to a client request. When you click the **HTML** Button in the Web Form Designer, the Web Form Designer switches to **HTML** mode. You use **HTML** mode when you wish to view your ASPX page's markup. You also can use this mode to edit the markup. When you click the **Design** Button, the Web Form Designer switches to **Design** mode. Although you will not be writing markup to create Web controls for this ASPX page, you will be using it to set the locations of the Web controls. [*Note*: Your markup may look different from that in Fig. 29.8—we have modified the code slightly for presentation purposes.]

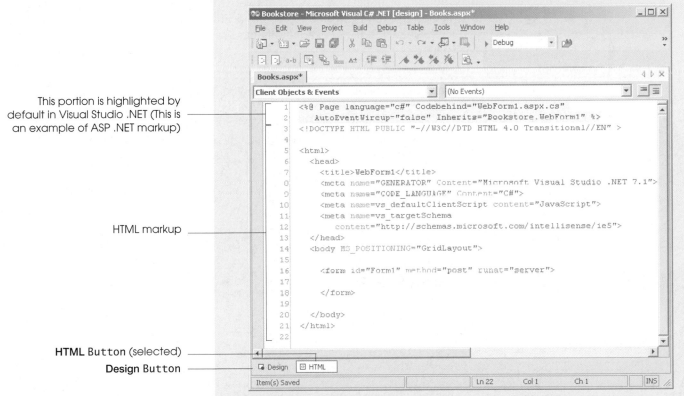

This portion is highlighted by default in Visual Studio .NET (This is an example of ASP .NET markup)

HTML markup

HTML Button (selected)

Design Button

Figure 29.8   **HTML** mode of Web Form Designer.

7. ***Saving the solution file to your Bookstore directory.*** By default, Visual Studio .NET saves solution files for ASP .NET Web applications in a separate directory. For easy access, you will save the solution file to your Bookstore directory located in the wwwroot directory. Click on **Solution 'Bookstore' (1 project)** in the **Solution Explorer**, then select **File > Save Bookstore.sln As…** to display the **Save File As** dialog.

[*Note*: A **Microsoft Development Environment** dialog may appear first asking if you would like to save your changes. No changes should have been made so far, so if this dialog appears, we suggest you click the **No** Button and undo any of your changes. If you would instead like to save the changes you've made, click the **Yes** Button to dismiss this dialog.] In this dialog, navigate to the wwwroot directory, and save the solution file in the Bookstore directory.

SELF-REVIEW 1. _____ mode allows you to view the ASPX page's markup.

    a) **HTML**   b) **Design**

    c) Web control   d) Markup

2. Some Web control names are the same as Windows control names, _____.

    a) because their functionality is the same

    b) but the functionality provided by Web controls is different

    c) because both Web controls and Windows controls can be used in Web applications

    d) None of the above.

Answers: 1) a. 2) b.

29.3 Designing the Books.aspx Page

This **Bookstore** application consists of two ASPX pages, which you create one at a time. The first page of the **Bookstore** application will be named Books.aspx. This page will display the list of available books. You design the first ASPX page in the following box.

Creating the
Books.aspx Page

1. **Renaming the ASPX page.** After you have viewed the contents of the default ASPX page (WebForm1.aspx), you will want to give this ASPX page a meaningful name. Select the WebForm1.aspx file in the **Solution Explorer** window. Change the **File Name** property in the **Properties** window from WebForm1.aspx to Books.aspx (Fig. 29.9).

Change the File's Name property value to Books.aspx →

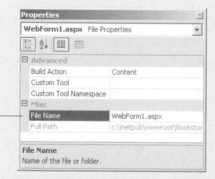

Figure 29.9 Setting the **File Name** property of the ASPX page.

Good Programming Practice

Change the ASPX page's name to a unique and meaningful name for easy identification. The name you choose must end with the .aspx extension for the page to be identified as an ASPX page.

Now click the Web Form Designer. The properties of the ASPX page should display in the **Properties** window. Notice that ASPX pages are listed with the identifier **DOCUMENT** in the Component Object Box (Fig. 29.10), because they do not have individual names. Select the **title** property, and change WebForm1 to Book List. This step sets the text that is displayed in the requesting browser's title bar.

Component Object Box displays **DOCUMENT** for ASPX pages →

title property changed to Book List →

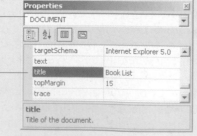

Figure 29.10 The title property of Books.aspx.

(cont.)

2. ***Changing the background color of the ASPX page.*** Now you are ready to begin creating the GUI. Make sure you are in **Design** mode. First, we will change the **bgColor** property of the Books.aspx page so that the background color of Books.aspx is set to light blue. Select bgColor in the **Properties** window, then click the ellipsis (...) Button to display the **Color Picker** dialog (Fig. 29.11). Click the **Web Palette** tab, and select light blue, as shown in Fig. 29.11. Click the **OK** Button. The background color of the Books.aspx page is now light blue.

Web Palette tab

Light-blue color box (selected)

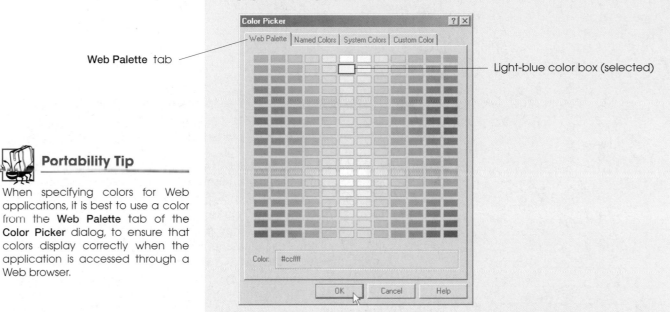

Figure 29.11   Light blue selected in the **Color Picker** dialog.

3. ***Creating a Label.*** Next, click the **Label** Web control from the **Web Forms** tab of the **Toolbox**. Drag and drop the control

onto the Books.aspx page. The Label should appear on the ASPX page (Fig. 29.12). Select the Label to view its properties in the **Properties** window. Select the ID property, and change Label1 to lblAvailable. The **ID property** is used to identify controls, much like the Name property in Windows controls. Now change the Label's Text property from Label to Available Books. Set the Label's font size by setting Size, under the Font property, to XX-Large (Fig. 29.13). Set the Label's font to Tahoma by clicking the down arrow next to the Name property (also under the Font property) and selecting Tahoma from the list that appears. To display the words correctly in the Label, you will need to set the height and width of the control. Set the Height property of the Label to 56px, and set the Width to 335px (where **px** stands for pixels).

Label Web control

Figure 29.12   Label control displayed in the ASPX page.

Portability Tip

When specifying colors for Web applications, it is best to use a color from the **Web Palette** tab of the **Color Picker** dialog, to ensure that colors display correctly when the application is accessed through a Web browser.

Good Programming Practice

Web controls with similar names and functionality to those of Windows controls should be given the same prefixes recommended in earlier tutorials. For example, prefix the Label Web control with lbl.

(cont.)

Font property node (expanded) ——

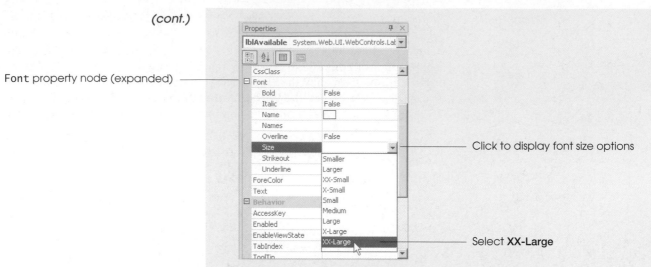

Click to display font size options

Select **XX-Large**

Figure 29.13 Setting the font size of the Label control.

4. ***Positioning the Label.*** Place the Label in the top center of the page. To set the exact location of the Label, switch to **HTML** mode. Notice that lines 15–20 of Fig. 29.14 (`<asp:label id="lblAvailable"...>`) have been added to the markup. [*Note*: Your markup may look different from that in Fig. 29.15—we have modified the code slightly for presentation purposes. For example, some of the meta elements may appear in a different order.] Line 16 contains the style attribute, as shown in Fig. 29.14. Set the LEFT: portion of the **style** attribute value to 295px and the TOP: portion of the attribute value to 16px. These values specify that the Label will be positioned 295 pixels from the left side of the page and 16 pixels down from the upper left corner of the ASPX page. Switch back into **Design** mode. The Label should now be repositioned on the page (Fig. 29.15).

TOP portion of the style attribute value

LEFT portion of the style attribute value

style attribute

HTML Button (selected)

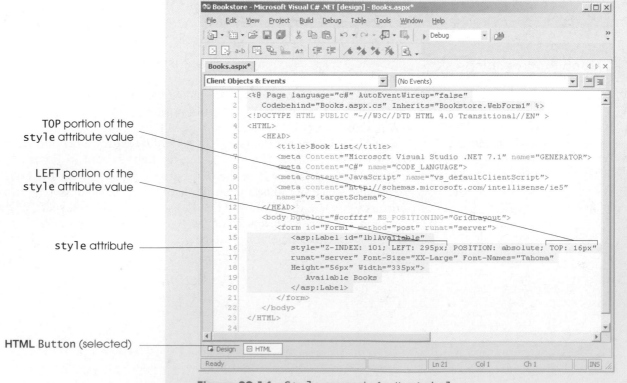

Figure 29.14 Style property for the Label.

(cont.)

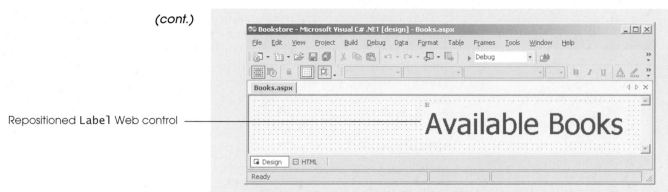

Figure 29.15   Complete `Label` displayed in **Design** mode.

Repositioned `Label` Web control

5. *Creating a horizontal rule.* Click the **HTML** tab in the **Toolbox**. Drag and drop the **Horizontal Rule** control

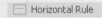

and place it beneath the `lblAvailable` `Label`. A **Horizontal Rule** control provides a horizontal line on a Web page. You use it to separate content on your ASPX page. The **Horizontal Rule** control is a type of HTML control. **HTML control**s correspond to standard HTML elements (in this case, a horizontal rule element). In this case study, we ask you to assume that a control is a Web control, unless we explicitly tell you that it is an HTML control.

In the **Properties** window, set the `id` property of the **Horizontal Rule** control to `hrzBooks`. Next, click the `style` property value in the **Properties** window. Click the ellipsis (**...**) `Button` that appears in the `style` field. The **Style Builder** dialog appears (Fig. 29.16). Click the **Position** Tab in the left pane of the dialog. Set the **Top:** value to 80px, the **Left:** value to 8px, the **Height:** value to 4px and the **Width:** value to 150%. Click **OK**. These settings position the **Horizontal Rule** control 80 pixels from the upper left corner of the page and 8 pixels from the left side of the page. The height of the control is now 4 pixels. Setting the width to 150% ensures that the horizontal rule extends to the entire width of the page.

Good Programming Practice

When naming a **Horizontal Rule** control, use the prefix `hrz` followed by a word that describes the control's use.

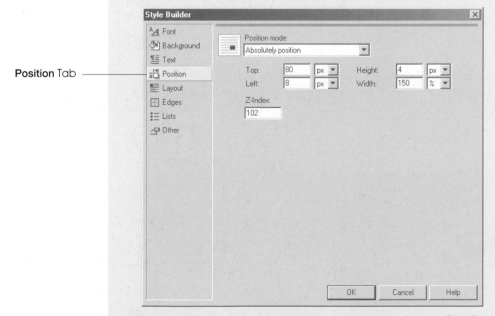

Position Tab

Figure 29.16   **Style Builder** dialog for the `Horizontal Rule` control.

(cont.)

6. ***Creating another Label.*** After the horizontal rule is in place, create another Label control (found in the **Web Forms** tab in the **Toolbox**). Change the ID of the Label to lblInstructions. In the **Properties** window, change the Text property to Select a book from this list and click the button to view the selected book's information. Then, set the font size to Medium and the font name to Tahoma. Set the height to 18px and the width to 699px. Switch to **HTML** mode and reposition the Label control as you did in *Step 4*. However, set the LEFT: portion of the style attribute value to 93px and the TOP: portion of the attribute value to 95px.

7. ***Creating a ListBox.*** Switch to **Design** mode. The next control you will place on this page is a ListBox. The ListBox will contain a list of the available books offered by the bookstore. In the next two tutorials, you will retrieve information from the database to populate the ListBox with book titles. Drag and drop the ListBox control,

     🔲 ListBox

and place it below lblInstructions. Change the ID property of the List-Box to lstBookTitles. In the **Properties** window, set the Height to 100 pixels and the Width to 330 pixels. In **HTML** mode, set the LEFT: portion of the style attribute value of the ListBox to 286px and the TOP: portion of the attribute value to 155px.

8. ***Adding a Button control.*** The final control you will add to the page is a **Button** (found in the **Web Forms** tab in the **Toolbox**). Switch to **Design** mode. Drag and drop the Button control,

     ab Button

onto the ASPX page. Change the Button's ID to btnInformation, and change its Text property to View Information. Set its Width to 130 pixels in the **Properties** window. Then, switch to **HTML** mode. Change the LEFT: portion of the style attribute value to 380px and the TOP: portion to 270px. The Books.aspx page should look like Fig. 29.17. [*Note*: Unbound appears in the ListBox because no items have been added to it.]

ListBox control ———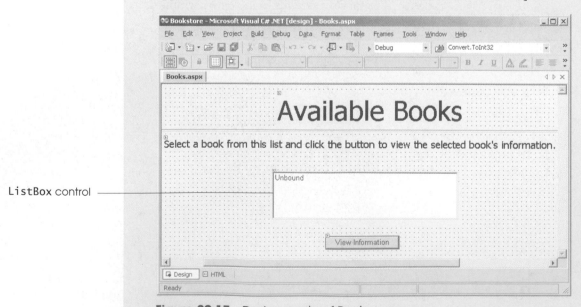

Figure 29.17   **Design** mode of Books.aspx.

9. ***Saving the project.*** Select **File > Save All** to save your modified code.

SELF-REVIEW 1. Use the _____ property to change the name of a **Web Forms** control.

    a) `Text`   b) `Name`

    c) `ID`   d) `Value`

2. The **Horizontal Rule** control is a(n) _____ control.

    a) **Web Forms**   b) **HTML**

    c) **Data**   d) **Windows Forms**

Answers: 1) c. 2) b.

29.4 Designing the BookInformation Page

Now that you have designed the `Books.aspx` page, you will design the `BookInformation.aspx` page, which displays the information about the book that was selected from the `ListBox`. You create this page in the following box.

Creating the
BookInformation Page

1. ***Creating a new ASPX page.*** Select **File > Add New Item...**, to display the **Add New Item - Bookstore** dialog (Fig. 29.18). Select **Web Form** in the **Templates:** pane, and rename the ASPX page to `BookInformation.aspx`, using the **Name:** TextBox. Click the **Open** Button. A new ASPX page named `BookInformation.aspx` appears in the **Solution Explorer** window.

Web Form template ——

Change this to
`BookInformation.aspx` ——

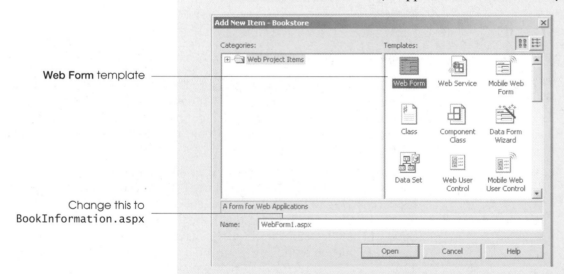

Figure 29.18 Add New Item - Bookstore dialog.

Now click the Web Form Designer. The properties of the ASPX page should display in the **Properties** window. Select the title property, and change `BookInformation` to `Book Information` (insert a space between the words).

2. ***Changing the background color.*** If the file does not open in **Design** mode, switch to **Design** mode at this time. Change the background color of this page to light blue as you did in *Step 2* of the box, *Creating the Books.aspx Page*.

3. ***Creating the `lblBookTitle` Label.*** Create a new `Label` by double clicking the `Label` tab in the **Web Forms** tab of the **Toolbox**. This `Label` will display the title of the book selected by the user. Because you do not yet know what book title will be selected, clear the `Text` property of this `Label`. The `Text` property will be set in Tutorial 31.

(cont.)

Change the ID property of the Label to lblBookTitle, set the font size to XX-Large and set the ForeColor to Blue. The **ForeColor** property specifies the color of the text that displays on the Label. To set the ForeColor, select the ForeColor property in the **Properties** window, and click the down arrow that appears in the ForeColor field. Click the **Web** tab and select Blue to set the forecolor (Fig. 29.19). Set the height to 60px and the width to 1100px. In **HTML** mode, set the LEFT: portion of the style attribute value of the Label to 20px and the TOP: portion of the attribute value to 15px.

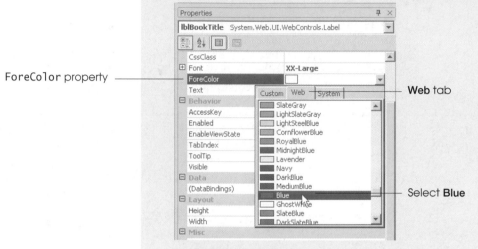

ForeColor property

Web tab

Select Blue

Figure 29.19 Setting a Label's ForeColor property.

4. **Creating the horizontal rule.** Switch to **Design** mode. Drag and drop a **Horizontal Rule** control beneath the lblBookTitle Label. Set the id property to hrzBookInformation; then, change the style property, setting the **Top:** value to 90px, the **Left:** value to 0px, the **Height:** value to 4px and the **Width:** value to 150%.

5. **Creating the lblAuthors Label.** After adding the **Horizontal Rule** control, create another Label. Name the Label lblAuthors, and change its Font property's Size to Large. Set the height of the Label to 34px and the width to 989px. Clear the text for this Label, because you do not know which book will be selected. You will set this text in Tutorial 31. In **HTML** mode, set the LEFT: portion of the style attribute value to 20 and the TOP: portion to 110.

6. **Creating the Image control.** Switch to **Design** mode. Now you must add the **Image control** that displays the cover of the selected book. Drag and drop the Image control,

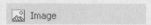

from the **Web Forms** tab in the **Toolbox** window. Change the Image control's ID property to imgBook. Set the Height and Width properties to 360 and 300 pixels, respectively. Specify the BorderStyle as **Outset** and set the **BorderWidth** to 5 pixels. The **BorderStyle** property specifies the type of border that displays around the Image. Setting BorderStyle to Outset gives the Image a raised-control appearance. The BorderWidth property specifies the width of the border of the Image control. Setting BorderWidth to 5 causes the border to be 5 pixels thick. Switch to **HTML** mode. Set the LEFT: portion of the style attribute value of the Image to 20px and the TOP: portion to 150px. In Tutorial 31, you will specify the image that will be displayed.

Good Programming Practice

When naming an Image Web control, use the prefix img followed by a word that describes what the Image will display.

(cont.)   7. ***Creating the btnBookList Button.*** Switch to **Design** mode. Add a Button to the page. Set the Button's ID to btnBookList, and set its Text to Book List. In the **Properties** window, set the Width property to 80 pixels. Switch to **HTML** mode; then, change the LEFT: portion of the style attribute value of the Button to 325px and the TOP: portion to 550px. Switch to **Design** mode. The design of the Bookinformation.aspx page should look like Fig. 29.20.

Image Web control ——

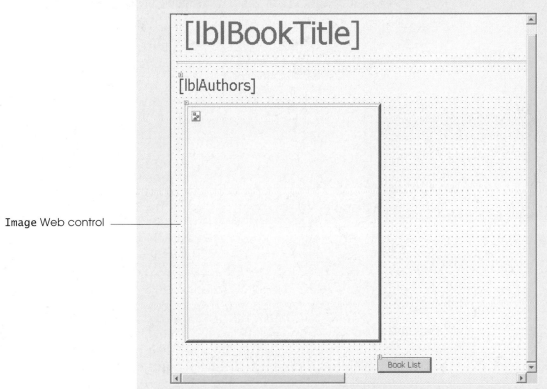

Figure 29.20   Design of the BookInformation.aspx page without the Table.

8. ***Saving the project.*** Select **File > Save All** to save your modified code.

You are now ready to add the **Table** control to the page. The Table is perhaps the most significant control on this page, because it will display the book information in a structured manner. You add the Table in the following box.

<hr />

Adding the Table Control

Good Programming Practice

When naming a Table control, use the prefix tbl followed by a word that describes what information the Table will display.

1. ***Creating the Table control.*** From the **Web Forms** tab of the **Toolbox**, drag and drop the Table control,

 Table

onto the page. In the **Properties** window, change the ID of the Table to tblBook, set the BorderStyle to Outset and change the BorderWidth to 5 pixels. Also, change the **GridLines** property to value Both. The GridLines property displays separators between the cells (known as cell borders) in the Table. Setting GridLines to Both displays both horizontal and vertical separators between each cell. In **HTML** mode, set the LEFT: portion of the style attribute value of the Table to 335px and change the TOP: portion to 150px.

(cont.)   2. ***Creating rows in the Table.*** Switch to **Design** mode. You now must create rows for the Table. To do so, select the **Rows** property in the **Properties** window. Click the ellipsis (**...**) Button to the right of the Rows property. A **TableRow Collection Editor** dialog appears. Add five rows to the table by clicking the **Add Button** five times (Fig. 29.21). Leave the dialog open so you can customize the Table's rows in the next few steps.

Five **TableRow**s added by the user

Members: pane

Click to add rows to the table

Cells property

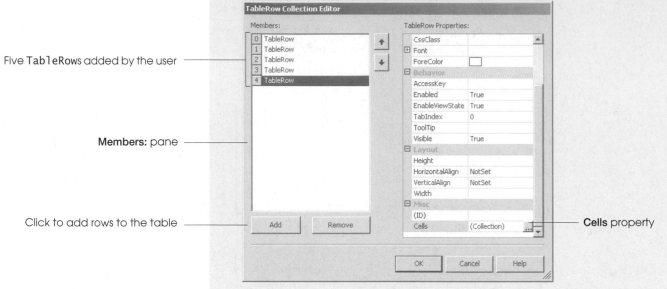

Figure 29.21   **TableRow Collection Editor** dialog for the Table control.

3. ***Creating cells in the Table.*** Table rows contain cells that display data. You will now create each individual cell in each table row. Select TableRow 0 in the **Members:** pane. Go to the **TableRow Properties** pane, and click the ellipsis (**...**) Button to the right of the **Cells** property to display the **TableCell Collection Editor** dialog (Fig. 29.22). Add two cells to the row by clicking **Add** twice. Select TableCell 0, and set the Font property's Size to Large. Change the TableCell's Height property to 70 pixels and Width property to 200 pixels, and specify the Text property as Price:. Select the second TableCell in the **Members:** box, and set the Font property's Size to Large. Click **OK** in the **TableCell Collection Editor** to accept the settings.

Two **TableCell**s added by the user

Add **TableCell**s by clicking **Add**

Font property

Text property

Height property

Width property

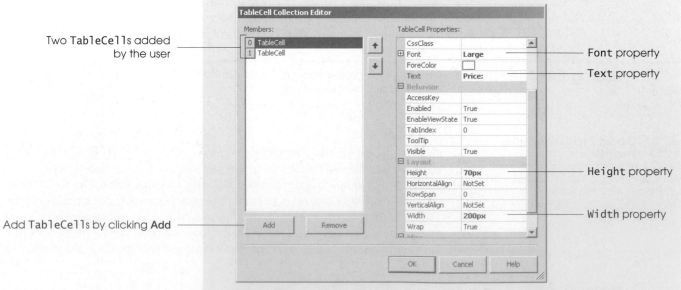

Figure 29.22   **TableCell Collection Editor** dialog of the Table control.

(cont.)

4. **Placing text into Table cells.** Notice that you set only the font size for the second TableCell. We have not yet set the Text property of the second TableCell because the information that will be displayed in this TableCell is currently unknown. You will specify the information that will be displayed in this TableCell in Tutorial 31. Perform *Step 3* on the rest of the Table-Rows and TableCells, changing the text in the first cells of each row to ISBN#:, Edition:, Copyright Date: and Description:, respectively. Click **OK** in the **TableRow Collection Editor** when you are finished. Your BookInformation.aspx page will look like Fig. 29.23.

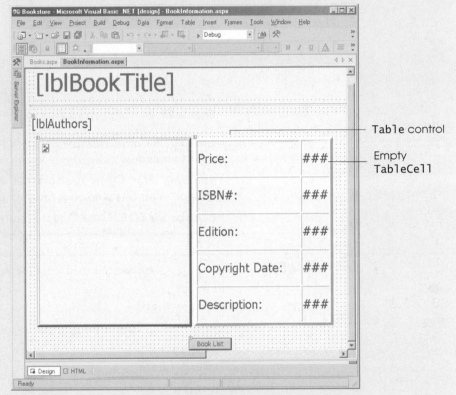

Figure 29.23   Design of the BookInformation.aspx page.

5. **Saving the project.** Select **File > Save All** to save your modified code.

Now that you have completed the user interface design, you will run the application. You have specified only the **Bookstore** application's user interface—therefore, it does not have any functionality. You test the application in the following box.

Running the Bookstore Application

1. **Running the application.** Select **Debug > Start** to run your application (Fig. 29.24). The Books.aspx page appears, because the first page you create in an ASP .NET application (in this case, Books.aspx) automatically will be set as the start page. Notice that the ListBox does not yet contain any book titles. This is because you have not yet set up the database connections to retrieve the information. Click the **View Information** Button. Notice that nothing happens. Currently, you have specified only the visual aspects of the page. Thus, users are not forwarded to BookInformation.aspx when the **View Information** Button is clicked.

(cont.)

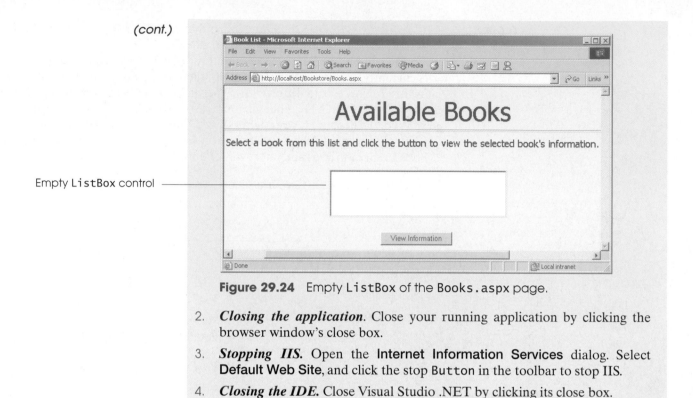

Empty ListBox control

Figure 29.24 Empty `ListBox` of the `Books.aspx` page.

2. *Closing the application.* Close your running application by clicking the browser window's close box.

3. *Stopping IIS.* Open the **Internet Information Services** dialog. Select **Default Web Site**, and click the stop `Button` in the toolbar to stop IIS.

4. *Closing the IDE.* Close Visual Studio .NET by clicking its close box.

SELF-REVIEW

1. The _____ property is used to set the width of an `Image` control's border.

   a) `Width`   b) `BorderStyle`

   c) `BorderWidth`   d) None of the above.

2. Use the _____ property to display cell borders between `TableCells` in a `Table`.

   a) `GridLines`   b) `BorderStyle`

   c) `BorderWidth`   d) `Separator`

Answers: 1) c. 2) a.

29.5 Wrap-Up

In this tutorial, you created the ASPX pages for your three-tier **Bookstore** application. You learned how to create an ASP .NET Web application and how to add Web controls to the ASPX pages. In doing so, you were introduced to the two different modes offered by Visual Studio .NET: **Design** mode and **HTML** mode. You learned that **Design** mode is used to create the user interface by dragging and dropping Web controls on the ASPX page, while **HTML** mode allows you to view and edit the page's markup.

When you added Web controls to the ASPX page, you learned how to set the exact position of the controls by using the `style` attribute in **HTML** mode. You positioned these controls by specifying the `LEFT:` and `TOP:` portions of the `style` attribute values. The Web controls you used in this tutorial included `Labels`, `Buttons`, `ListBoxes`, `Images` and `Tables`. You also set the `Image` control's `BorderStyle` property to `Outset`, which gave the `Image` a raised appearance.

In the next tutorial, you will access the database, or information tier, of the application, which contains information about the books in the bookstore. You will use **Query Builder** to create the necessary SQL statements. You also will create a database connection and data command objects. After you have created these database components, Tutorial 31 will enable you to create the middle tier of the bookstore, which specifies the functionality of the ASPX pages.

SKILLS SUMMARY

Creating an ASP .NET Web Application

- Select **File > New > Project**.
- Select **Visual C# Projects** in the left pane.
- Select the **ASP .NET Web Application** icon from the **Templates:** pane in the **New Project** dialog.
- Rename the application, then click **OK**.

Adding an ASPX Page to a Web Application

- Right click the project name in the **Solution Explorer**; then, select **Add > Add New Item...** to display the **Add New Item** dialog.
- Select the **Web Form** icon in the **Templates:** box, and rename the ASPX page in the **Name:** TextBox.
- Click **Open** to add the new ASPX page to the Web Application.

Creating a `Table` Web Control

- Drag and drop the `Table` control from the **Web Forms** tab of the **Toolbox** onto the page.
- Click the ellipsis (...) Button in the **Rows** property of the **Properties** window.
- Click the **Add** Button to add rows to the `Table`.
- Click the ellipsis (...) Button in the **Cells** property of the **Properties** window within the **TableRow Collection Editor** dialog.
- Click the **Add** Button to add cells to the `TableRows`.

Setting a Web Control's Location

- Switch to **HTML** mode.
- Use the `LEFT:` portion of the Web control's `style` attribute to specify the number of pixels that the Web control will be located from the left side of the Web page.
- Use the `TOP:` portion of the Web control's `style` attribute to specify the number of pixels that the Web control will be located from the top of the Web page.

Changing to Design Mode

- Click the **Design** mode Button beneath the ASPX page in the Web Form Designer.

Changing to HTML Mode

- Click the **HTML** mode Button beneath the ASPX page in the Web Form Designer.

KEY TERMS

ASP .NET markup—The set of instructions processed on the Web server's machine. An ASPX page is made up of HTML and ASP .NET markup.

bgColor property of an ASPX page—Specifies an ASPX page's background color.

BorderStyle property of a Web control—Specifies a Web control's border type.

BorderWidth property of a Web control—Specifies the width of a Web control's border.

Button Web control—Allows users to perform an action.

Cells property of the Table Web control—Allows programmers to create and access `TableCells` in a `Table`.

Design mode—Displays the ASPX page's GUI at design time.

ForeColor property of Label Web control—Specifies font color for text on a `Label` control.

GridLines property of the Table Web control—Specifies the format in which table cell separators are displayed.

Horizontal Rule HTML control—Displays a line to separate controls on an ASPX page.

HTML controls—Correspond to HTML elements.

HTML mode—Displays the ASPX page's markup at design time.

ID property of a Web control—Specifies the name of a Web control.

Image Web control—Displays an image in an ASPX page.

Label Web control—Displays text on an ASPX page.

ListBox Web control—Displays a list of items.

Outset value of BorderStyle property—Gives an Image Web control a raised appearance.

px—Specifies that the size is measured in pixels.

Rows property of the Table Web control—Allows programmers to create and access table rows.

Size property of a Web control—Allows you to specify the size of a Web control.

style attribute—Allows you to specify the position of a Web control.

Table Web control—Displays a table in an ASPX page.

Text property of a Web control—Specifies the text that displays on a Web control.

title property of an ASPX page—Specifies the page's title.

Width property of a Web control—Allows you to specify the width of a Web control.

CONTROLS, EVENTS, PROPERTIES & METHODS	**ASPX page** The page on which controls are dropped to design the GUI.

■ *Properties*

bgColor—Specifies the ASPX page's background color.

title—Specifies the page's title.

Button 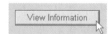 This control allows the user to raise an action or event.

■ *In action*

View Information

■ *Properties*

ID—Specifies the name used to access the Button programmatically. The name should be prefixed with btn.

Text—Specifies the text displayed on the Button.

Width—Specifies the width of the Button.

Horizontal Rule   Horizontal Rule   This control displays a line on the ASPX page. It is usually used to separate different areas of the ASPX page.

■ *In action*

■ *Properties*

id—Specifies the name of the **Horizontal Rule** control. The name should be prefixed with hrz.

Style—Allows you to specify where to position the **Horizontal Rule** control on the ASPX page.

Image   Image   This control displays an image on the ASPX page.

■ *In action*

■ *Properties*

BorderStyle—Specifies the appearance of the Image's border.

BorderWidth—Specifies the width of the Image's border.

Height—Specifies the height of the Image control.

ID—Specifies the name used to access the Image control programmatically. The name should be prefixed with img.

Width—Specifies the width of the Image control.

Label   This control displays text on the ASPX page that the user cannot modify.

■ *In action*

Books

■ *Properties*

ForeColor—Specifies font color for text on a Label control.

Height—Specifies the height of the Label.

ID—Specifies the name used to access the Label programmatically. The name should be prefixed with lbl.

Name (under the expanded Font property in the **Solution Explorer**)—Specifies the name of the font used for the Label's text.

Size (under the expanded Font property in the **Solution Explorer**)—Specifies the size of the Label's text.

Text—Specifies the text displayed on the Label.

Width—Specifies the width of the Label.

ListBox   ☷ ListBox   This control allows the user to view and select from multiple items in a list.

■ *In action*

Visual Basic .NET How to Program: Second Edition
C++ How to Program: Fourth Edition
Java How to Program: Fourth Edition

■ *Properties*

Height—Specifies the height of the ListBox.

ID—Specifies the name used to access the ListBox control programmatically. The name should be prefixed with lst.

Width—Specifies the width of the ListBox.

Table   ▦ Table   This control is usually used to organize data in a spreadsheet format.

■ *In action*

Price:	$76.00
ISBN#:	0-13-029363-6
Edition:	2
Copyright Date:	2002
Description:	Microsoft Visual Basic .NET

■ *Properties*

BorderStyle—Specifies the appearance of the Table's border.

BorderWidth—Specifies the width of the Table's border.

Cells—Retrieves or sets the value in the specified table cell.

GridLines—Specifies the format in which table cell separators are displayed.

ID—Specifies the name used to access the Table control programmatically. The name should be prefixed with tbl.

Rows—Retrieves or sets the value in the specified table cell.

MULTIPLE-CHOICE QUESTIONS

29.1 You change the _____ property of the ASPX page to specify the color that displays in the background of the page.

a) BackColor

b) bgColor

c) BackgroundColor

d) Color

29.2 Button, Label and Table controls for ASPX pages can be accessed from the _____ tab.

a) **Web Forms**

b) **Components**

c) **Data**

d) Both a and b.

29.3 The _____ attribute specifies the position of a Web control on an ASPX page.

a) position

b) location

c) style

d) coordinate

29.4 Unlike the Windows Form Designer, the Web Form Designer _____.

a) does not provide two viewing modes

b) provides two viewing modes

c) allows you to design the graphical user interface

d) does not allow you to design the user interface

29.5 The BorderStyle property of the Image control _____.

a) specifies the color of the border

b) specifies the type of border that displays around the Image control

c) specifies the width of the border

d) Both a and b.

29.6 Setting the BorderStyle property to Outset makes a control appear _____.

a) raised

b) with a bold border

c) with the specified border width

d) with the specified border color

29.7 Every _____ of a Table Web control can contain one or more _____.

a) TableRow; TableColumns

b) TableColumn; TableRows

c) TableRow; TableCells

d) TableCell; TableRows

29.8 For you to create an **ASP .NET Web Application** project, _____ must be running.

a) IIS

b) Microsoft Access

c) Microsoft Word

d) Internet Explorer

29.9 The _____ mode allows you to create the ASPX page's GUI by dragging and dropping controls on the page.

a) **HTML**

b) **Design**

c) **Visual**

d) **GUI**

29.10 To specify the position of a Web control, set the _____ and _____ values of the _____ attribute.

a) X, Y, style

b) X, Y, position

c) TOP, LEFT, style

d) TOP, LEFT, position

EXERCISES

*[Note: In these exercises, we may ask you to set an ASPX page as the application's start page, meaning that this page will appear first when the application is run. You can set an ASPX page as the start page by right clicking the file in the **Solution Explorer** and selecting **Set As Start Page**.]*

29.11 (***Phone Book Application: GUI***) Create the user interface for the **Phone Book** application. The design for the two pages for this application is displayed in Fig. 29.25.

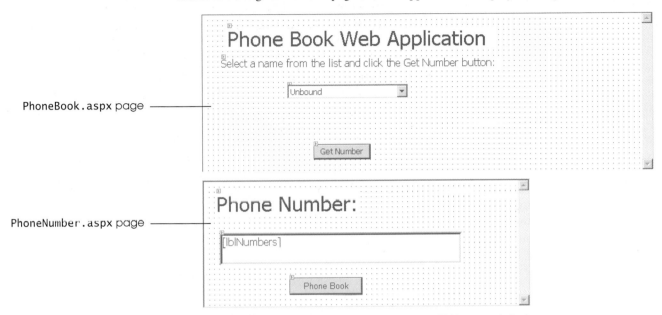

PhoneBook.aspx page ———

PhoneNumber.aspx page ———

Figure 29.25 Phone Book application ASPX pages' design.

a) ***Creating an ASP .NET Web application.*** Create an ASP .NET Web application, and name it PhoneBook. Rename the ASPX page to PhoneBook.aspx, and set Phone-Book.aspx as the start page.

b) ***Changing the background color.*** Change the background color of your ASPX page (PhoneBook.aspx) to the light-yellow **Web Palette** color (located in the sixth column of the 12th row) by using the bgColor property as demonstrated in this tutorial. Change the title of the ASPX page to Phone Book.

c) ***Adding a Label.*** Create a Label, set the font size to X-Large and change the Text property to Phone Book Web Application. Set the LEFT: portion of the style attribute value to 40px and the TOP: portion to 17px. Name the control lblPhoneBook.

d) ***Adding another Label.*** Create another Label, and set the Text property to Select a name from the list and click the Get Number Button. Set the LEFT: portion of the style attribute value to 30px and the TOP: portion to 65px. Name this Web control lblInstructions.

e) ***Adding a DropDownList Web control.*** Create a DropDownList Web control by dragging and dropping it from the **Toolbox** onto the ASPX page. The DropDownList Web control looks similar to the ComboBox Windows Form control. Set the width to 190px, and set the LEFT: portion of the style attribute value to 134px and the TOP: portion to 108px. Name the DropDownList cboNames.

f) ***Adding a Button.*** Create a Button, set its width to 90px and change the Text property to Get Number. Set the LEFT: portion of the style attribute value to 175px and the TOP: portion to 200px. Name the Web control btnGet.

g) ***Adding another ASPX page to the Phone Book application.*** Add another ASPX page to the **Phone Book** application, name it PhoneNumber.aspx and change the background to the light-yellow color. Change the title property to Phone Number.

h) ***Adding a Label to PhoneNumber.aspx.*** Create a Label and name it lblPhoneNumber. Set the font size to X-Large and change the Text property to Phone Number:. Set the LEFT: portion of the style attribute value to 20px and the TOP: portion to 15px.

i) *Adding another Label.* Create another Label, set its BorderStyle to Inset and set its height and width to 50px and 380px, respectively. Clear the text of the Label. Name the Label lblNumbers, and set the LEFT: portion of the style attribute value to 25px and the TOP: portion to 80px.

j) *Adding a Button to the PhoneNumber.aspx page.* Create a Button, set its width to 115px and change the Text property to Phone Book. Set the LEFT: portion of the style attribute value to 135px and the TOP: portion to 150px. Name the Button btnPhoneBook.

k) *Saving the solution file.* Save the solution file to the PhoneBook directory located in the root directory of your Web server, as you did in *Step 8* of the box, *Creating an ASP .NET Web Application.*

29.12 (*US State Facts Application: GUI*) Create the user interface for the **US State Facts** application. The design for the two pages of this application is displayed in Fig. 29.26.

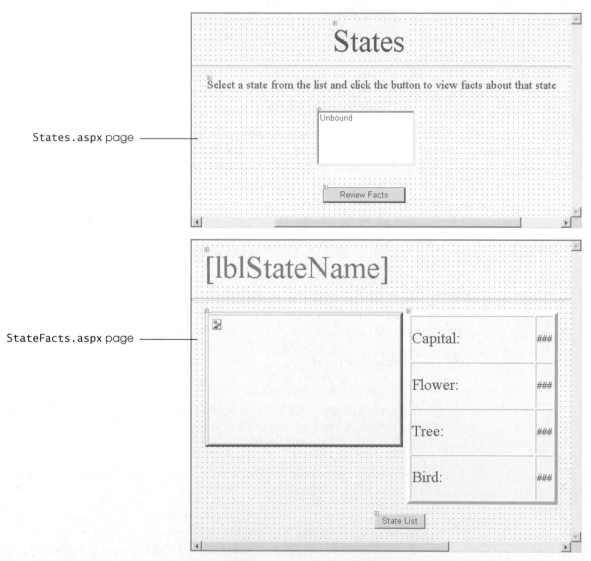

States.aspx page

StateFacts.aspx page

Figure 29.26 **US State Facts** application ASPX pages' design.

a) *Creating an ASP .NET Web application.* Create a new ASP .NET Web application, and name it USStateFacts. Rename the first ASPX page to States.aspx, and set States.aspx as the start page.

b) *Changing the background color.* Change the background color of the States.aspx page to the light-blue **Web Palette** color (located in the sixth column of the second row) by using the bgColor property as demonstrated in this tutorial. Change the title property of the ASPX page to States.

c) *Adding a Label to States.aspx*. Create a Label Web control, and place it on the page. Set the font size to XX-Large, and change the Text property to States. Change the LEFT: portion of its style attribute value to 390px, and set the TOP: portion to 15px. Name the Web control lblStates.

d) *Adding a horizontal rule to States.aspx*. Create a horizontal rule, place it on the ASPX page and set its width to 150%. When setting its position, change the TOP: value to 80px, set the LEFT: value to 0px and specify the Height: as 4px. Name the horizontal rule hrzStates.

e) *Adding another Label to States.aspx*. Create another Label, and place it beneath the horizontal rule. Change the font size to Medium, and set the Text property to Select a state from the list and click the button to view facts about that state. Change the LEFT: portion of its style attribute value to 195px, and set the TOP: portion to 100px. Name this Web control lblInstructions.

f) *Adding a ListBox to States.aspx*. Create a ListBox, and place it on the ASPX page. Set its Height property to 100px and its Width property to 155px. Set the LEFT: portion of the style attribute value to 365px and the TOP: portion to 150px. Name the ListBox lstStates.

g) *Adding a Button to States.aspx*. Create a Button, and place it on the page. Set its Text property to Review Facts and its Width property to 130px. Change the LEFT: portion of the style attribute value to 375px and the TOP: portion to 270px. Name the Button btnFacts.

h) *Adding another ASPX page to the US State Facts application*. Add another ASPX page to the **US State Facts** application, name it StateFacts.aspx and change the background color to light blue.

i) *Adding a Label to StateFacts.aspx*. Create a Label, name it lblStateName, set its font size to XX-Large and change its ForeColor property to Blue. Clear the Label's text. Set its position by setting the LEFT: portion of the style attribute value to 20px and the TOP: portion to 15px.

j) *Adding a horizontal rule*. Place the horizontal rule beneath the Label and set its TOP: position to 90px, its LEFT: position to 0px and its Height: to 4px. Change the width to 150%. Name the horizontal rule hrzStateFacts.

k) *Adding an Image control to StateFacts.aspx*. Create an Image control, and set its BorderStyle to Outset. Change the BorderWidth to 5px. Set its height to 200px and its width to 300px. Set the position of the Image by changing the LEFT: portion of the style attribute value to 20px and the TOP: portion to 110px. Name the Web control imgFlag.

l) *Adding a Table to StateFacts.aspx*. Create a Table with four rows and two columns. Set the BorderStyle to Outset, the BorderWidth to 5px and GridLines to Both. Set the height and width of each TableCell of the first column to 70px and 200px, respectively, and set the Font property's Size to Large. Set the Text property of the cells in the first column to Capital:, Flower:, Tree: and Bird:, respectively. Change the LEFT: portion of the style attribute value to 335px and the TOP: portion to 110px. Name the Table control tblState.

m) *Adding a Button to StateFacts.aspx*. Create a Button, change its text to State List and change the LEFT: portion of the style attribute value to 285px and the TOP: portion to 425px. Name the Button control btnStateList.

n) *Saving the solution file*. Save the solution file to the USStateFacts directory located in the root directory of your Web server, as you did in *Step 8* of the box, *Creating an ASP .NET Web Application*.

29.13 (*Road Sign Review Application: GUI*) Create the user interface for the **Road Sign Review** application. The design for the two pages of this application is displayed in Fig. 29.27.

a) *Creating an ASP .NET Web application*. Create a new ASP .NET Web application, and name it **RoadSignReview**. Change the name of the existing ASPX page to Road-Signs.aspx, and set RoadSigns.aspx as the start page.

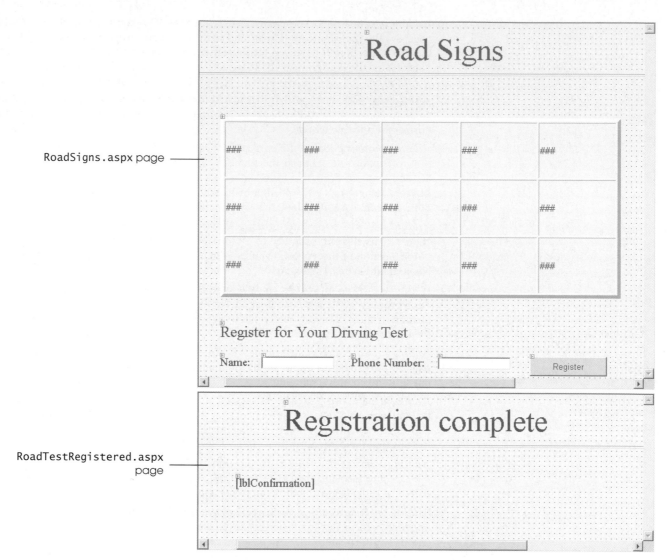

RoadSigns.aspx page —

RoadTestRegistered.aspx page —

Figure 29.27 Road Signs application ASPX pages' design.

b) *Changing the background color.* Change the background color of RoadSigns.aspx to the light-green **Web Palette** color (located in the sixth column of the 14th row) by using the bgColor property as demonstrated in this tutorial. Change the title of the ASPX page to RoadSigns.

c) *Adding a Label to RoadSigns.aspx.* Create a Label, and set its font size to XX-Large. Change the Text property to Road Signs. Set its position by changing the style attribute value's LEFT: portion to 295px and the TOP: portion to 16px. Name the Label control lblRoadSigns.

d) *Adding a horizontal rule to RoadSigns.aspx.* Create a horizontal rule. Set its width to 150%, and set the TOP: position to 80px, the LEFT: position to 0px and the height to 4px. Name the horizontal rule hrzRoadSigns.

e) *Adding a Table to RoadSigns.aspx.* Create a Table with three rows and five columns. Set the BorderStyle to Outset, the BorderWidth to 5px and the GridLines property to Both. Also, set the Table's Height property to 279px and Width property to 626px. Set each row's height to 50px and each TableCell's width to 20px. Change the style attribute value by setting LEFT: to 70px and TOP: to 150px. Name the Table control tblRoadSigns.

f) *Adding a Label to RoadSigns.aspx.* Create a Label, and set its font size to Large. Change the Text property to Register for Your Driving Test. Set its position by changing the style attribute value's LEFT: portion to 70px and TOP: portion to 470px. Name the Web control lblRegister.

g) *Adding a Label and TextBox to RoadSigns.aspx.* Create a Label and set its text to Name:. Set its font size to Medium, and change its position to LEFT: 70px and TOP: 520px. Name the Label control lblName. Create a TextBox, and place it next to the **Name:** Label. Set its height to 20px and width to 115px. Change the position to LEFT: 135px and TOP: 520px. Name the TextBox control txtName.

h) *Adding another Label and TextBox pair to RoadSigns.aspx.* Create a Label and set its text to Phone Number:. Set its font size to Medium, and change its position to LEFT: 275px and TOP: 520px. Name the Label control lblPhoneNumber. Create a TextBox, and place it next to the **Phone Number:** Label. Set its height to 20px and width to 115px. Change its position to LEFT: 410px and TOP: 520px. Name the TextBox control txtPhoneNumber.

i) *Adding a Button to RoadSigns.aspx.* Create a Button, set its Text to Register, and change its height and width to 30px and 120px, respectively. Change the position of the Button by setting the LEFT: portion of the style attribute value to 555px and the TOP: portion to 520px. Name the Button control btnRegister.

j) *Adding another ASPX page to the Road Sign Review application.* Add another ASPX page to the application, name it RoadTestRegistered.aspx and change the background color to light green.

k) *Adding a Label to RoadTestRegistered.aspx.* Create a Label, setting its font size to XX-Large and its Text property to Registration Complete. Change its position by setting the LEFT: portion of its style attribute value to 200px and the TOP: portion to 15px. Name the Label control lblRegistration.

l) *Adding a horizontal rule to RoadTestRegistered.aspx.* Create a horizontal rule. Set its width to 150%, the TOP: position to 80px, the LEFT: position to 0px and the height to 4px. Name the horizontal rule hrzRoadTestRegistered.

m) *Adding another Label to RoadTestRegistered.aspx.* Create a Label, name it lblConfirmation and set its font size to Medium. Delete the Text property value, leaving it blank. Change its position by setting the LEFT: portion of its style attribute value to 125px and the TOP: portion to 130px.

n) *Saving the solution file.* Save the solution file to the RoadSignReview directory located in the root directory of your Web server, as you did in *Step 8* of the box, *Creating an ASP .NET Web Application.*

TUTORIAL 30

Bookstore Application: Information Tier

Examining the Database and Creating Database Components

This tutorial focuses on the Web application's information tier, where the application's data resides. In your **Bookstore** application, the information tier is represented by a Microsoft Access database, db_bookstore.mdb, that stores each book's information. Before you begin this tutorial, you should be familiar with the database concepts presented in Tutorial 25.

In this tutorial, you will create the objects that your application will need to connect to the database. You also will define the SQL statements that will retrieve data from that database. Actually, the information tier consists solely of the db_bookstore.mdb database. The connection objects and data command objects created in this tutorial are actually part of the middle tier, as they perform the functionality of retrieving data from the database. You create these objects here because they interact with the information tier and do not require any programming. You will complete the **Bookstore** application by creating the middle tier in the next tutorial.

30.1 Reviewing the **Bookstore** Application

You have taken the three-tier **Bookstore** application for a test-drive (in Tutorial 28) and have designed the GUI by using Web controls and an HTML control. Now you are ready to create the database components for the application. Before you begin, you should review the pseudocode and the ACE table (Fig. 30.1) for this application:

When the Books page is requested:
    Retrieve the book titles from the database
    Display book titles in a ListBox

When the user selects a book title from the ListBox and clicks the View Information Button:
    Retrieve the selected book
    Store the selected book in a variable
    Redirect the user to the BookInformation page

When the BookInformation page is requested:
        Display the book title in a Label
        Retrieve the selected book's information from a database
        Display the authors in a Label
        Display the cover art in an image
        Display the remaining information in a Table

When the user presses the Book List Button on the BookInformation page:
        Redirect the client browser back to the Books page

Action/Control/Event (ACE) Table for the Web-Based Bookstore Application

Action	Control/Class/Object	Event
Label the Books page	lblAvailable, lblInstructions	Application is run
	Page	Load (for Books.aspx)
Retrieve the book titles from the database	objOleDbConnection, objSelectTitles, objReader	
Display book titles in a ListBox	lstBookTitles	
	btnInformation	Click
Retrieve the selected book	lstBookTitles	
Store the selected book in a variable	Session	
Redirect the user to the BookInformation page	Response	
	Page	Load (for Book-Information.aspx)
Display the book title in a Label	lblBookTitle	
Retrieve the selected book's information from a database	objOleDbConnection, objSelectBookData, objReader	
Display the authors in a Label	lblAuthors	
Display the cover art in an image	imgBook	
Display the remaining information in a Table	tblBook	
	btnBookList	Click
Redirect the client browser back to the Books page	Response	

Figure 30.1 ACE table for the Web-based **Bookstore** application.

In this tutorial, you will be creating the objects that are used to retrieve information from the database, including the objects that connect to the database and the objects that execute the command statements.

30.2 Information Tier: Database

The information tier maintains all of the data needed for an application. The database that stores this data might contain product data, such as a description, price and quantity in stock, and customer data, such as a name and shipping information.

Databases are an integral part of real-world applications, because they provide the ability to update data in real time. As soon as a piece of data is entered into the database, it is accessible to users and applications with the proper authorization. Because data is stored electronically, it can be accessed and manipulated much faster than paper copies. Most databases are relational databases—databases where the data is organized in tables. A variety of database products (used to build and modify databases) from Microsoft and other vendors exist, ranging from personal products like Microsoft Access to enterprise products such as Oracle, Sybase and Microsoft SQL Server 2000. Database products also can be used to generate reports from information in a database.

The **Bookstore** application stores the books' data in a Microsoft Access database (db_bookstore.mdb). This data is retrieved from the database by using C# code and ADO .NET objects. The database contains one table, named Products, that stores each book's information.

The Products table contains nine fields (columns): productID, title, authors, copyrightDate, edition, isbn, coverart, description and price. These fields contain an ID number, the title, authors, copyright date, edition number, ISBN number (a unique number used to reference a book), image name, description and price of each book, respectively. Figure 30.2 displays the Products table of db_bookstore.mdb, using the **Server Explorer** window.

Products table of the
db_bookstore.mdb database

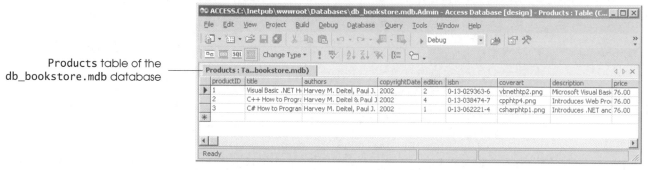

Figure 30.2   Products table of the db_bookstore.mdb database.

SELF-REVIEW   1. Once data is entered into a database, _____.

a) the data is immediately accessible to users and applications

b) users must wait until the system reboots to access the data

c) all applications using the database must manually be updated

d) None of the above.

2. Databases are an integral part of real-world applications because they provide the ability to _____.

a) store information that cannot be altered

b) update data in real time

c) execute applications

d) None of the above.

Answers: 1) a. 2) b.

30.3 Using the Server Explorer and Query Builder in ASPX Pages

Before you begin programming this application's middle tier, you must set up the database connections that retrieve data from the database. Recall that you used the **Server Explorer** window and the **Query Builder** tool in Tutorial 25. You will use these IDE features again to create a database connection and to generate SQL statements to request book information. You add the database connection and data command objects in the following box.

Adding Database Components to the Books Page

1. *Starting IIS.* Make sure that IIS is running for the **Default Web Site**. If it is not running, start it in the **Internet Information Services** dialog, by selecting **Default Web Site** in the left pane and clicking the Start Item **Button**.

2. *Opening the Bookstore application.* Open the `C:\InetPub\wwwroot\Bookstore` directory to locate the **Bookstore** application. Double click `Bookstore.sln` to open the application in Visual Studio .NET.

3. *Using the Server Explorer window to add a connection to the database.* You must set up a connection to the database before accessing its data. You will use ADO .NET objects to accomplish this task. This connection will allow you to read information about a book from the database. Select **View > Server Explorer** to display the **Server Explorer** window. Click the Connect to Database icon (Fig. 30.3) to display the **Data Link Properties** dialog.

Connect to Database icon

Figure 30.3 Connecting to the database in the **Server Explorer** window.

4. *Specifying provider settings.* You now need to specify the provider of the database software you are using. Click the **Provider** tab to display a list of providers. Because you are using a Microsoft Access database, select the **Microsoft Jet 4.0 OLE DB Provider**, and click the **Next >>** Button (Fig. 30.4). [*Note:* The number of items and the names of the **OLE DB Provider(s)** displayed in the **Provider** tab may be different on your system.]

Provider tab

Select this provider

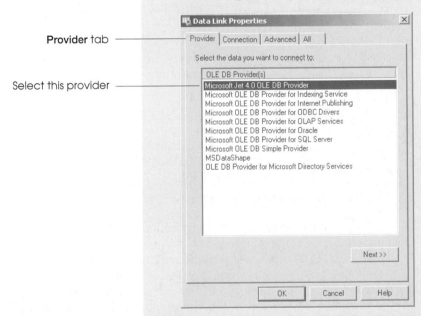

Figure 30.4 **Data Link Properties** dialog's **Provider** tab.

(cont.)

5. *Specifying connection settings.* When you click **Next >>**, the **Connection** tab (Fig. 30.5) of the **Data Link Properties** dialog is displayed. You are now ready to specify db_bookstore.mdb as the database. Click the ellipsis (...) Button next to the **Select or enter a database name:** TextBox. The **Select Access Database** dialog appears as in Fig. 30.6. Locate db_bookstore.mdb in the C:\InetPub\wwwroot\Databases directory, and click **Open**.

Connection tab ——

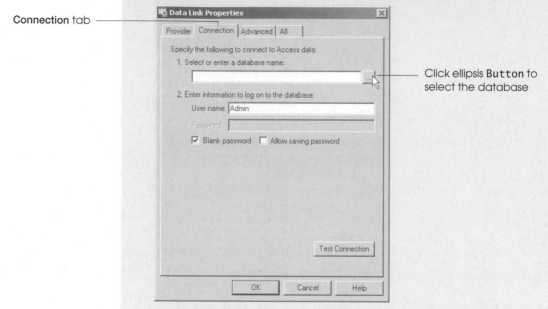

Click ellipsis Button to select the database

Figure 30.5   **Data Link Properties** dialog's **Connection** tab.

Select db_bookstore.mdb database (this may display as db_bookstore, depending on your Windows settings) ——

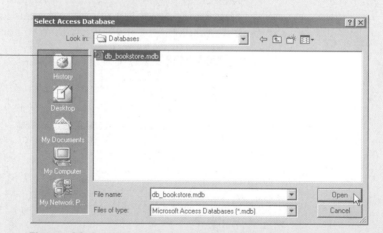

Figure 30.6   **Select Access Database** dialog.

6. *Testing the connection.* Before proceeding to the next step, you ensure that the connection is set up properly. The path of the database should now display in the **Select or enter a database name:** TextBox (Fig. 30.7). The database that you will be using does not require a password to access its information. Make sure the **Blank password** CheckBox, under the **Enter information to log on to the database:** section, is checked. (We do this because the application's database is not password protected.) Click the **Test Connection** Button to test the database connection. The **Microsoft Data Link** dialog should appear, confirming a successful connection. If the connection failed, you should make sure you followed all the instructions from *Steps 2–5* in this box. Click **OK** to close the **Microsoft Data Link** dialog. Click **OK** in the **Data Link Properties** dialog. The db_bookstore.mdb connection has now been added to the **Server Explorer** window.

(cont.)

Location of the database ——————

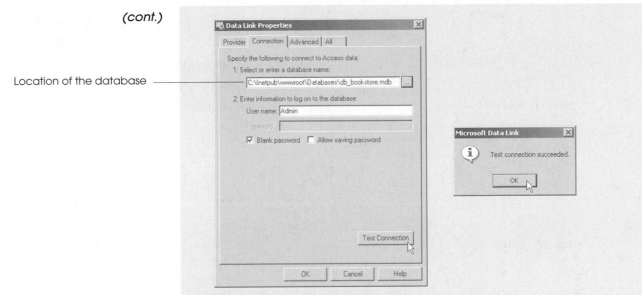

Figure 30.7   Testing the database connection.

7. ***Adding a data connection object to the ASPX page.*** Double click `Books.aspx` in the **Solution Explorer** window to display the `Books.aspx` page. From the **Server Explorer** window, drag and drop the `db_bookstore.mdb` connection node on the `Books.aspx` page. A message dialog will be displayed asking if the database's password should be included in the source code. Because this database does not include a password, click the **Don't include password** Button. An `OleDbConnection` object appears in the component tray. Rename the connection object `objOleDbConnection`. Recall that a connection object is used to maintain a connection to the database.

8. ***Adding a data command object to the ASPX page.*** From the **Data** tab of the **Toolbox**, drag and drop an `OleDbCommand` object on the ASPX page. Recall that the `OleDbCommand` object allows you to specify SQL statements to retrieve information from the database. Rename the `OleDbCommand` object to `objSelectTitles`. Set the `Connection` property of the data command object to the connection object you created for this page, `objOleDbConnection`. To do this, click the down-arrow Button that appears next to the `Connection` property field. Expand the **Existing** node and select the name of the connection object (`objOleDbConnection`) that you created in *Step 6*. You are now ready to create the SQL statements that will retrieve data from the database. Select the `CommandText` property, and click the ellipsis (...) Button that appears next to the `CommandText` field. The **Query Builder** and **Add Table** dialogs appear (Fig. 30.8).

9. ***Adding the Products table to the Query Builder dialog.*** Before you can use the **Query Builder** dialog, you must select a database table. In the **Add Table** dialog, select `Products`, then click the **Add** Button. Click **Close** to close the **Add Table** dialog.

10. ***Selecting information from the database.*** You are ready to retrieve the values from the `title` field of the `Products` table. In the **Query Builder** dialog, check the `title` CheckBox in the `Products` window. Your SELECT statement should look like the one displayed in Fig. 30.9. This statement will retrieve the `title` field values from the `Products` table of the database. You will later use this information to populate the ListBox in the `Books.aspx` page. Click **OK** to close the **Query Builder** dialog.

(cont.)

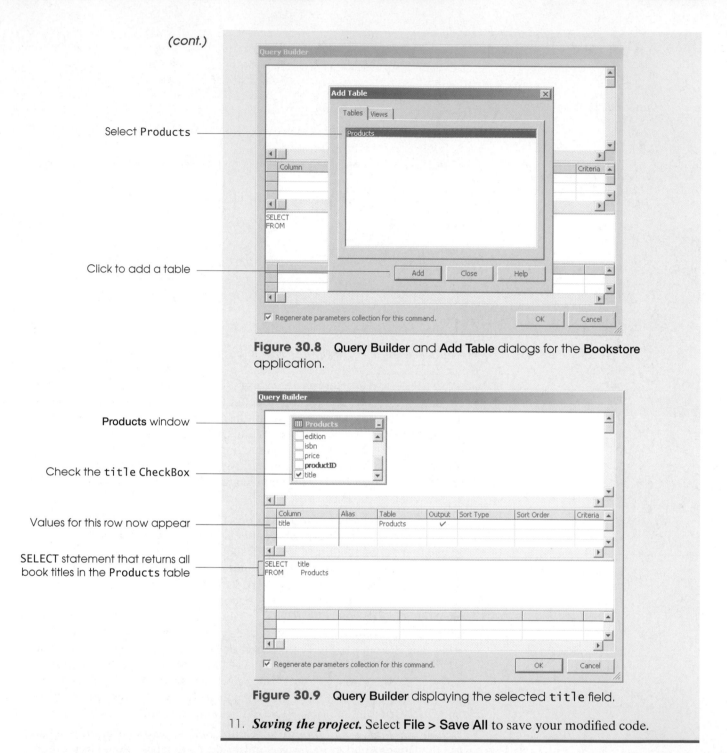

Select **Products**

Click to add a table

Figure 30.8 **Query Builder** and **Add Table** dialogs for the **Bookstore** application.

Products window

Check the `title` CheckBox

Values for this row now appear

SELECT statement that returns all book titles in the **Products** table

Figure 30.9 **Query Builder** displaying the selected `title` field.

11. *Saving the project.* Select **File > Save All** to save your modified code.

Now that you have added database connection and command objects to the `Books.aspx` page, you will do the same for the `BookInformation.aspx` page. The `CommandText` property for the data command object of this page will differ from that of the `Books.aspx` page. In the `BookInformation.aspx` page, you will use the `Parameters` property of the data command object because you do not yet know which record to retrieve—this will be determined when the user selects a book. You will specify the record in the middle tier of the application, which you will program in Tutorial 31. For now you will set the database connections and data command objects in the following box.

*Adding Database
Components to the
BookInformation Page*

1. *Adding a data connection object to the ASPX page.* From the **Server Explorer** window, drag and drop the db_bookstore.mdb connection node on the BookInformation.aspx page. Again, a message dialog will be displayed asking if the database's password should be included in the source code. Click the **Don't include password** Button. An OleDbConnection object appears in the component tray. Rename the connection object to objOleDbConnection.

2. *Adding a data command object to the ASPX page.* From the **Data** tab of the **Toolbox**, drag and drop an OleDbCommand object on the ASPX page. Rename the OleDbCommand object to objSelectBookData. Set the Connection property of the data command object to the connection object you created for this page, objOleDbConnection. Select the CommandText property, and click the ellipsis (...) Button that appears next to the CommandText field. The **Query Builder** and **Add Table** dialogs appear (Fig. 30.10).

Add Table dialog ——————

Add this table ——————

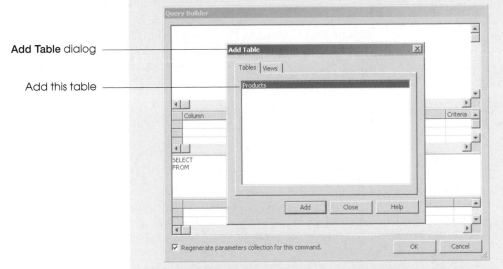

Figure 30.10   **Query Builder** and **Add Table** dialogs.

3. *Adding the Products table.* In the **Add Table** dialog, select Products, then click the **Add** Button. Click **Close** to close the **Add Table** dialog.

4. *Selecting the fields to retrieve from the database.* Check the authors, copyrightDate, coverart, description, edition, isbn, price and title CheckBoxes in the Products window of the **Query Builder** dialog. Notice that the field names appear after the SELECT keyword in the SELECT statement, as well as in the table beneath the Products window (Fig. 30.11).

5. *Specifying the record from which information will be retrieved.* In the table beneath the Products window, type =? in the **Criteria** field of the title row (Fig. 30.12) to indicate that you do not know the record from which the information will be retrieved. Recall that a funnel will appear to the right of the title CheckBox, which indicates that a value will be retrieved from the field (title) according to the specified criteria.

6. *Completing the SELECT statement.* Click the check in the **Output** column of the title row to remove the title field name from the SELECT portion of the SQL statement. You do this because you do not want to retrieve the title information—the title is used only to locate the appropriate record. The complete SELECT statement should look like the one in Fig. 30.13. Click **OK**. The **Microsoft Development Environment** dialog (Fig. 30.14) appears, asking if you want to apply a new parameter configuration. Click the **Yes** Button to create a title parameter.

(cont.)

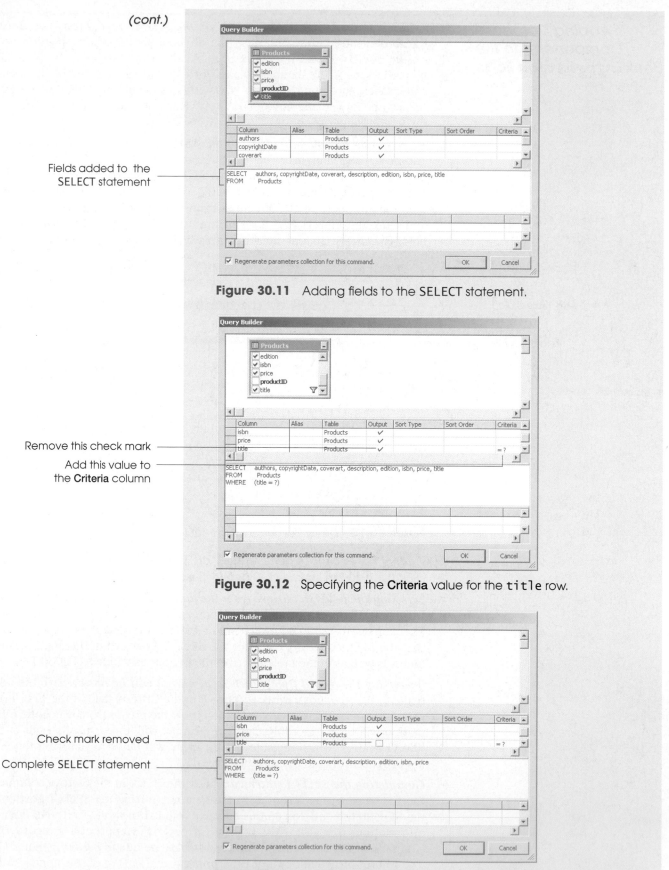

Fields added to the SELECT statement

Figure 30.11   Adding fields to the SELECT statement.

Remove this check mark

Add this value to the **Criteria** column

Figure 30.12   Specifying the **Criteria** value for the `title` row.

Check mark removed

Complete SELECT statement

Figure 30.13   Removing the `title` field from the SELECT portion of the SQL statement.

(cont.)

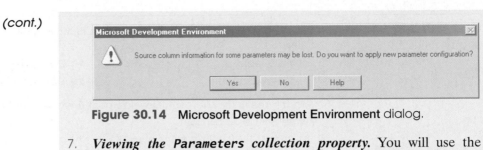

Figure 30.14 **Microsoft Development Environment** dialog.

7. ***Viewing the Parameters collection property.*** You will use the `title` parameter you created in *Step 5* of this box in the next tutorial to specify the record from which you will retrieve information. In this step, you will verify that the parameter was created correctly. Select the `Parameters` property in the **Properties** window of `objSelectBookData`. Click the ellipsis (...) `Button` that appears next to the `Parameters` (Fig. 30.15) field to view the collection of parameters. The **OleDbParameter Collection Editor** dialog appears (Fig. 30.16). This dialog displays the parameters of the data command object. Notice that there is only one parameter, named `title`. Click **OK** to close the dialog.

Parameters property —— 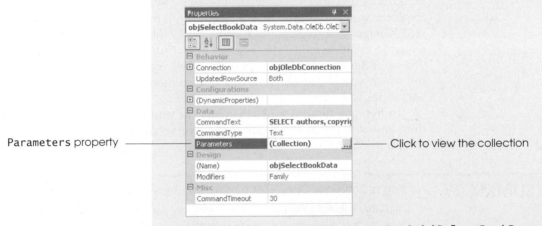 —— Click to view the collection

Figure 30.15 **Parameters** property of `objSelectBookData`.

`title` parameter created —— 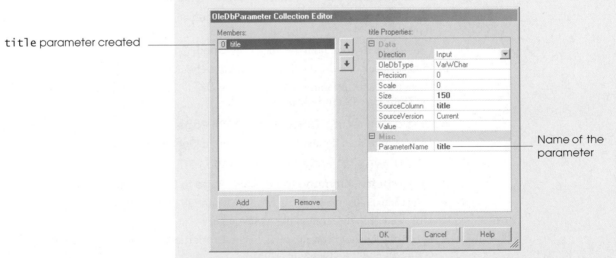 —— Name of the parameter

Figure 30.16 **OleDbParameter Collection Editor** dialog.

8. ***Saving the project.*** Select **File > Save All** to save your modified code.

9. ***Closing the IDE.*** Close Visual Studio .NET by clicking its close box.

SELF-REVIEW

1. The _____ dialog allows you to select a database table to add to the **Query Builder** dialog.

   a) **Add Table**   b) **Database**

   c) **Database Table**   d) **Data Link Properties**

2. Clicking **Yes** in the **Microsoft Development Environment** dialog after using the **Query Builder** dialog _____.

   a) creates the `OleDbCommand` object   b) creates the SQL statement

   c) creates parameter items in the `Parameters` property   d) None of the above.

Answers: 1) a. 2) c.

30.4 Wrap-Up

In this tutorial, you were introduced to the information tier of the three-tier, Web-based **Bookstore** application. You examined the contents of the db_bookstore.mdb database. You accessed the information tier of the **Bookstore** application by creating database connection objects and data command objects. You used the **Server Explorer** window and the **Query Builder** tool to add a database connection to your ASPX pages and to create SQL statements for the data command objects, respectively. In creating the `OleDbCommand` object for the BookInformation.aspx page, you used the `Parameters` property, because you did not know the title of the book for which you would be retrieving information. You will specify the value of this parameter when you program the middle tier.

In the next tutorial, you will create the middle tier of your **Bookstore** application. You will add code to your application to control what data from the database will be displayed on the ASPX page.

SKILLS SUMMARY

Adding a Database Connection Using the Server Explorer Window

- Click the Connect to Database icon to display the **Data Link Properties** dialog.
- Click the **Provider** tab in the **Data Link Properties** dialog.
- Select **Microsoft Jet 4.0 OLE DB Provider** in the **OLE DB Provider(s)** box.
- Click **Next >>**; then, click the ellipsis (**...**) Button next to the **Select or enter a database name:** field.
- Choose the desired database, then click **Open**.
- Place a check mark in the **Blank password** CheckBox.
- Click the **Test Connection** Button. Click **OK** in the dialog that appears; then, click **OK** in the **Data Link Properties** dialog.

Adding a Connection Object to the ASPX Page

- Select the desired database connection in the **Server Explorer** window.
- Drag and drop the connection on the ASPX page.

Adding a Data Command to the ASPX Page to Select Information

- Select the `OleDbCommand` icon from the **Data** tab in the **Toolbox**.
- Drag and drop the icon on the ASPX page.
- Select the `Connection` property in the **Properties** window, and specify the name of the connection object created previously.
- Select the `CommandText` property, then click the ellipsis Button to access the **Query Builder** tool.
- Add a table to the **Query Builder** dialog by using the **Add Table** dialog.
- Check desired-field CheckBoxes, and use the **Criteria** columns if necessary.

MULTIPLE-CHOICE QUESTIONS

30.1 _____ is an example of a database product.

a) Microsoft Access

b) Microsoft SQL Server

c) Oracle

d) All of the above.

30.2 An advantage of using information in a database is that _____.

a) the data can be updated in real time

b) information that changes need be updated only in one location

c) Both a and b.

d) None of the above.

30.3 When a funnel appears to the right of a field's CheckBox in the **Query Builder** dialog, it indicates that _____.

a) information will be updated in the specified field

b) a value will be retrieved from that field according to specified criteria

c) the field will not be included in the SQL statement

d) None of the above.

30.4 The Parameters property of _____ contains a collection of parameters.

a) OleDbConnection

b) OleDbDataConnection

c) OleDbDataCommand

d) OleDbCommand

30.5 The _____ can be used to create an OleDbConnection.

a) **Server Explorer** window

b) **Query Builder** tool

c) Both a and b.

d) None of the above.

30.6 You use the _____ object to create SQL statements for retrieving data from a database.

a) OleDbConnection

b) OleDbDataReader

c) OleDbCommand

d) None of the above.

30.7 The _____ is used when creating SQL statements visually for the OleDBCommand object's CommandText property.

a) **Server Explorer** window

b) **Query Builder** tool

c) Both a and b.

d) None of the above.

30.8 You use the _____ object to open a connection to the database.

a) OleDbConnection

b) OleDbDataReader

c) OleDbCommand

d) None of the above.

30.9 You use the _____ property of the OleDbCommand object to specify values for information that is not known in advance.

a) Connection

b) Parameters

c) Field

d) Name

30.10 Another name for the database tier is _____.

a) the information tier

b) the bottom tier

c) Both a and b.

d) None of the above.

EXERCISES

30.11 (*Phone Book Application: Database*) Create the database connections and data command objects for the **Phone Book** application by using the **Server Explorer** window and the **Query Builder** tool.

a) *Opening the application.* Open the **Phone Book** application that you created in Tutorial 29.

b) *Copying the db_Phone.mdb database to the Databases directory.* Copy the C:\Examples\Tutorial30\Exercises\Databases\db_Phone.mdb database to the Databases directory in IIS's wwwroot directory.

c) *Using Server Explorer to add a connection to the database.* In the **Server Explorer** window, add a connection to the db_Phone.mdb database. Drag and drop the connection object on the PhoneBook.aspx page. Name the connection object objOleDbConnection.

d) *Using Query Builder for the PhoneBook.aspx page.* Add an OleDbCommand to the PhoneBook.aspx page. Set the Connection property to the OleDbConnection object you added to the ASPX page, and use **Query Builder** to set the CommandText property of the OleDbCommand. This command should retrieve all the names of the people from the database. Name this command object objSelectNames.

e) *Adding a connection to the database to the PhoneNumber.aspx page.* Using the **Server Explorer** window, drag and drop a database connection object on the Phone-Number.aspx page. Name this connection object objOleDbConnection.

f) *Using Query Builder for PhoneBook.aspx.* Add an OleDbCommand to the PhoneNumber.aspx page. Set the Connection property to the OleDbConnection object you added to the ASPX page, and use **Query Builder** to set the CommandText property of the OleDbCommand. This configuration should retrieve the phone number of the person whose name will be selected from the DropDownList in the PhoneBook.aspx page by the user. You need to set the criteria to specify which person's phone number will be retrieved from the database. Name this command object objSelectPhoneNumber.

g) *Saving the project.* Select **File > Save All** to save your modified code.

30.12 (*US State Facts Application: Database*) Create the database connections and data command objects for the **US State Facts** application by using the **Server Explorer** window and the **Query Builder** tool.

a) *Opening the application.* Open the **US State Facts** application that you created in Tutorial 29.

b) *Copying the db_StateFacts.mdb database to the Databases directory.* Copy the C:\Examples\Tutorial30\Exercises\Databases\db_StateFacts.mdb database to the Databases directory in IIS's wwwroot directory.

c) *Using Server Explorer to add a connection to the database.* In the **Server Explorer** window, add a connection to the db_StateFacts.mdb database. Drag and drop the connection object on the States.aspx page. Name this connection object objOleDbConnection.

d) *Using Query Builder for the States.aspx page.* Add an OleDbCommand to the States.aspx page. Set the Connection property to the OleDbConnection object you added to the ASPX page, and use **Query Builder** to set the CommandText property of the OleDbCommand. This command should retrieve the names of the states from the **name** field of the states table in the database. Name this command object objSelectNames.

e) *Adding a connection to the database to the StateFacts.aspx page.* Using the **Server Explorer** window, drag and drop a database connection object on the database on the StateFacts.aspx page. Name this connection object objOleDbConnection.

f) *Using Query Builder for StateFacts.aspx.* Add an OleDbCommand to the StateFacts.aspx page. Set the Connection property to the OleDbConnection object you added to the ASPX page, and use **Query Builder** to set the CommandText property of the OleDbCommand. This configuration should retrieve all the information from the states table of the database about the state selected by the user. You need to set the criteria to specify which state's information will be retrieved from the database. Name this command object objSelectStateInformation.

g) *Saving the project.* Select **File > Save All** to save your modified code.

30.13 (*Road Sign Review Application: Database*) Create the database connections and data command objects for the **Road Sign Review** application by using the **Server Explorer** window and the **Query Builder** tool.

a) *Opening the application.* Open the **Road Sign Review** application that you created in Tutorial 29.

b) *Copying the db_RoadSigns.mdb database to the Databases directory.* Copy the C:\Examples\Tutorial30\Exercises\Databases\db_RoadSigns.mdb database to the Databases directory in IIS's wwwroot directory.

c) *Using Server Explorer to add a connection to the database.* In the **Server Explorer** window, add a connection to the db_RoadSigns.mdb database. Drag and drop the connection object on the RoadSigns.aspx page. Name this command object objOleDbConnection.

d) *Using Query Builder for the RoadSigns.aspx page.* Add an OleDbCommand to the RoadSigns.aspx page. Set the Connection property to the OleDbConnection object that you added to the ASPX page, and use **Query Builder** to set the CommandText property of the OleDbCommand. This configuration should retrieve all the information about all the road signs from the signs table of the database. You will not need to specify criteria for this exercise, because all the information from the database needs to be retrieved. Name this command object objSelectSignInformation.

e) *Saving the project.* Select **File > Save All** to save your modified code.

Objectives

In this tutorial, you will learn to:
- Write the functionality for the middle tier, using C# code.
- Modify code-behind files in a Web application.
- Specify parameters of **OleDbCommand** objects.

Outline

Bookstore Application: Middle Tier

Introducing Code-Behind Files

I n earlier tutorials, you built the client tier and created connections to the information tier of the **Bookstore** application. Using the Visual Studio .NET IDE, you were able to design the user interface of this Web-based application. In this tutorial, you will learn about the middle tier and complete the **Bookstore** application by programming the middle tier's functionality. Recall that the middle tier is responsible for interacting with the client and information tiers. The middle tier accepts user requests for data from the client tier, retrieves the data from the information tier (that is, the database) and responds to the client's requests with HTML documents, containing the requested data.

31.1 Reviewing the **Bookstore** Application

You have taken the three-tier **Bookstore** application for a test-drive (in Tutorial 28) and have created the Web controls and database components for the application. Now you will need to write code to specify the functionality of the **Bookstore** application. Before you begin to write the code, you should review the pseudocode and the ACE table (Fig. 31.1) for this application:

When the Books page is requested:
    Retrieve the book titles from the database
    Display book titles in a ListBox

When the user selects a book title from the ListBox and clicks the View Information Button:
    Retrieve the selected book
    Store the selected book in a variable
    Redirect the user to the BookInformation page

When the BookInformation page is requested:
    Display the book title in a Label
    Retrieve the selected book's information from a database
    Display the authors in a Label
    Display the cover art in an image
    Display the remaining information in a Table

When the user presses the Book List Button on the BookInformation page:
Redirect the client browser back to the Books page

Action/Control/Event (ACE) Table for the Web-Based Bookstore Application

Action	Control/Class/Object	Event
Label the Books page	lblAvailable, lblInstructions	Application is run
	Page	Load (for Books.aspx)
Retrieve the book titles from the database	objOleDbConnection, objSelectTitles, objReader	
Display book titles in a ListBox	lstBookTitles	
	btnInformation	Click
Retrieve the selected book	lstBookTitles	
Store the selected book in a variable	Session	
Redirect the user to the BookInformation page	Response	
	Page	Load (for Book-Information.aspx)
Display the book title in a Label	lblBookTitle	
Retrieve the selected book's information from a database	objOleDbConnection, objSelectBookData, objReader	
Display the authors in a Label	lblAuthors	
Display the cover art in an image	imgBook	
Display the remaining information in a Table	tblBook	
	btnBookList	Click
Redirect the client browser back to the Books page	Response	

Figure 31.1   ACE table for the Web-based **Bookstore** application.

In this tutorial, you will implement the interaction between the user interface and the database of the **Bookstore** application. This means that you will write the code that determines which image will be displayed by the Image control and which information will be retrieved from the database and displayed in the Table control. You also will write the code that redirects the client browser to another page when a Button is clicked.

31.2 Programming the Books Page's Code-Behind File

Although you have designed your **Bookstore** application's GUI and have added database connections, the **Bookstore** currently does not have any other functionality. You will now begin programming your application. You start with the Books.aspx page in the following box.

Defining the Page_Load Event Handler for the Books Page

1. ***Starting IIS.*** Make sure that IIS is running for the **Default Web Site**. If it is not running, start it in the **Internet Information Services** dialog, by selecting **Default Web Site** in the left pane and clicking the Start Item Button.

(cont.)   2. ***Opening the Bookstore application.*** Open the `C:\InetPub\wwwroot\`
`Bookstore` directory to locate the **Bookstore** application. Double click
`Bookstore.sln` to open the application in Visual Studio .NET.

3. ***Displaying the code-behind file in the Solution Explorer window.*** Every
ASPX page created in Visual Studio .NET has a corresponding class written
in a .NET language, such as C#. This class includes event handlers, initialization code, methods and other supporting code and represents the middle tier
of your application. The C# file that contains this class is called the **code-
behind file** and provides the ASPX page's functionality. It has the file extension `.aspx.cs`. Click the Show All Files **Button** (Fig. 31.2) in the toolbar of
the **Solution Explorer**. Click the plus box next to `Books.aspx` to display the
code-behind file, `Books.aspx.cs` (Fig. 31.2).

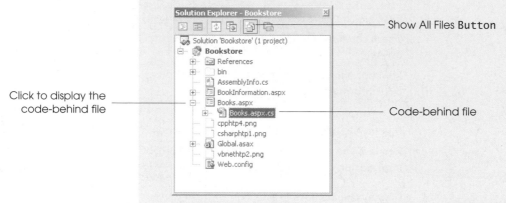

Show All Files **Button**

Click to display the
code-behind file

Code-behind file

Figure 31.2   Code-behind file for the `Books.aspx` ASPX page.

4. ***Viewing the code-behind file.*** Figure 31.3 displays `Books.aspx.cs`—the
code-behind file for `Books.aspx`.

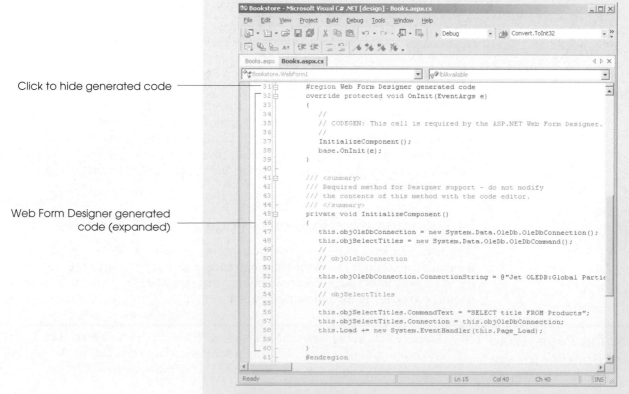

Click to hide generated code

Web Form Designer generated
code (expanded)

Figure 31.3   `Books.aspx.cs` code-behind file containing code generated
by Visual Studio .NET.

(cont.)
Recall that Visual Studio .NET generates this code-behind file when the project is created; we have reformatted it for presentation purposes. To view this file, double click Books.aspx.cs in the **Solution Explorer** window. [*Note*: You also can right click Books.aspx and select **View Code** to view the code-behind file.] Click the plus box of Web Form Designer generated code to display the generated code. Click the minus box of #region to hide the generated code.

5. ***Changing the class name.*** Change the class name in lines 15 and 17 from WebForm1 to Books (Fig. 31.4). Line 17 indicates that this class inherits from the Page class. The **Page** class defines the basic functionality for an ASPX page, much as the Form class defines the basic functionality for a Windows application Form. The Page class is located in the System.Web.UI namespace. The Page class provides properties, methods and events that are useful for creating Web-based applications.

Change the class name to Books

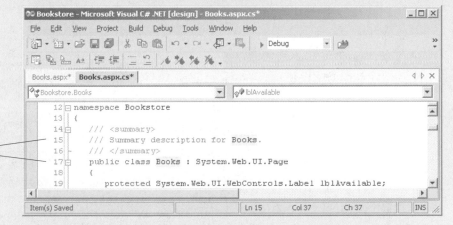

Figure 31.4   Changing the application's class name.

6. ***Using a namespace.*** To use database-related objects, you will need to use the System.Data.OleDb namespace. Add line 11 of Fig. 31.5 before the Books class declaration.

Using namespace
System.Data.OleDb

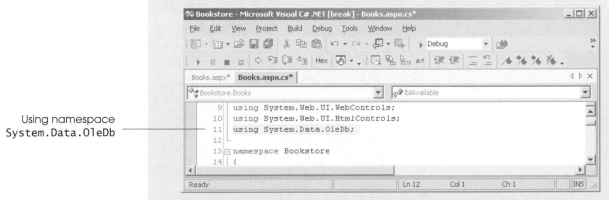

Figure 31.5   Using namespace System.Data.OleDb.

7. ***Rearranging and commenting the control declarations.*** Rearrange and comment the control declarations as shown in lines 20–37 of Fig. 31.6.

(cont.)

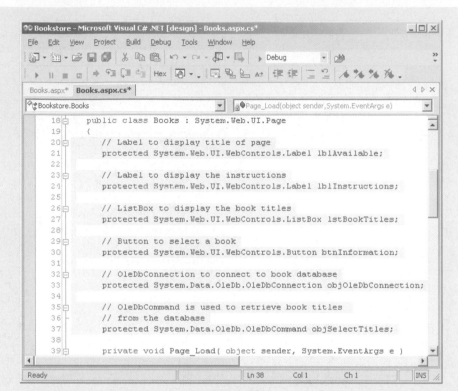

Figure 31.6 Rearranging and commenting the control declarations.

8. *Defining the Page_Load event handler.* **Page_Load** is an event handler that executes any processing necessary to display the page. This event handler is created for you when the ASPX page is created, although it has no code. Add lines 41–46 of Fig. 31.7 to the **Page_Load** event handler. [*Note:* Initially, the **Page_Load** event handler contains a comment telling us to add code to initialize the page. Remove this comment from the event handler, as that code is being added in this step and the next step.] Line 41 opens the connection to the database by invoking the **OleDbConnection** method **Open**. Line 44 creates a data reader by invoking the **ExecuteReader** method of the data command object (**objSelectTitles**) you created in Tutorial 30. Note that we have added spaces inside the event handler's argument list in line 39 and added the comment in line 46 for clarity.

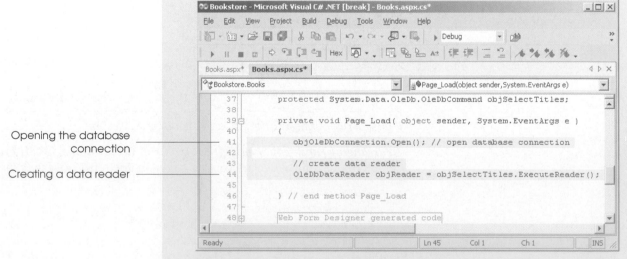

Figure 31.7 Opening the database connection and creating a reader.

(cont.)

The **Load** event (which causes the execution of Page_Load) for a Web page is similar to the Load event for a Windows Form. You put code in the Load event handler that is needed to initialize the page or the objects the page uses.

9. ***Using the data reader.*** Add lines 46–54 of Fig. 31.8 to the Page_Load event handler. Lines 47–52 define a while statement that starts the data reader by invoking the Read method. The while statement will terminate when there is no more data to read. Lines 50–51 add the values stored in the database's title field to the ListBox. The title field values will continue to be added to the ListBox until there are no more title field values to read. Line 54 closes the connection to the database by invoking the Close method of the OleDbConnection class.

Begin reading, using the data reader

Adding book titles from the database to the ListBox

Closing database connection

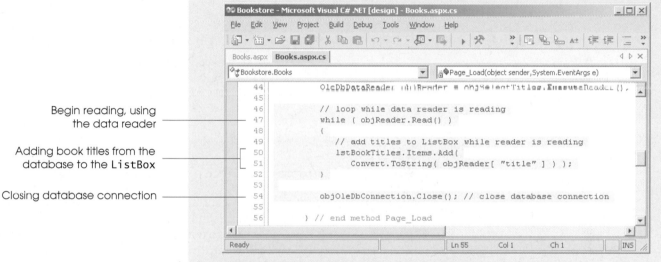

Figure 31.8   Reading data from a database.

10. ***Saving the project.*** Select **File > Save All** to save your modified code.

Next, you will define the btnInformation_Click event handler. This event handler is invoked when the user clicks the **View Information** Button. The event handler determines the selected book and redirects the client browser to the Book-Information page. You create the event handler in the following box.

Defining the Click Event Handler for the Books Page

1. ***Creating the Click event handler.*** Switch to **Design** mode. Double click the btnInformation Button control. The btnInformation_Click event handler should appear in the Books.aspx.cs file.

2. ***Adding code to the Click event handler.*** Be sure to add the comments and break the header as shown in Fig. 31.9 so that the line numbers in your code match those presented in this tutorial. Then, add lines 95–106 of Fig. 31.9 to the event handler. Lines 96–99 determine if the user selected a book title. You use the ListBox's SelectedItem property to determine if a book has been selected. The **SelectedItem** property specifies the item that is selected from the ListBox. If the user does not select an item, no value is specified in the SelectedItem property (which is what line 96 checks).

If a book title has not been selected, the first title in the ListBox will be set as the default selection. This is accomplished by using the ListBox's SelectedIndex property. The **SelectedIndex** property specifies the index of the selected item. You set the first title in the ListBox as the default selection by setting this property to 0 (line 98), which is the index number of the first item.

(cont.)

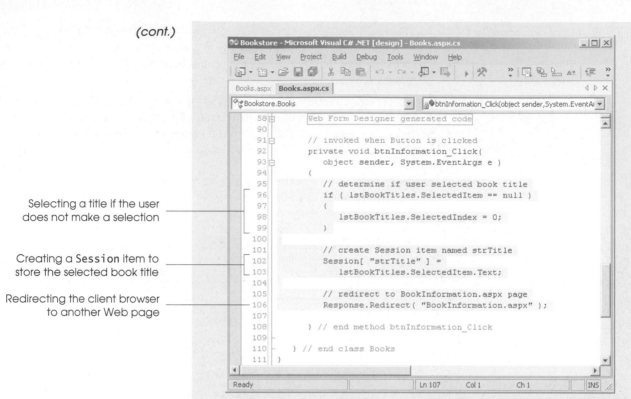

Selecting a title if the user does not make a selection

Creating a `Session` item to store the selected book title

Redirecting the client browser to another Web page

Figure 31.9   `btnInformation_Click` event handler declaration.

Values are not maintained across different ASPX pages. This means that values stored in instance variables cannot be passed from page to page. However, ASP .NET provides a **Session** object for sharing values among ASPX pages. Lines 102–103 allow information to be maintained across the **Bookstore** application's ASPX pages by adding a **key-value pair** to the `Session` object. A key-value pair associates a value with a corresponding name (key) which identifies the value. In this case, the key is the name `strTitle`, and the value is the title of the selected book, which is determined by `lstBookTitles.SelectedItem.Text`. The storage of key-value pairs across Web pages is made possible by **session state**, which is ASP .NET's built-in support for tracking data. Session state enables the current user's information (including the book the user selected) to be maintained across a browser session. The square brackets in line 102 indicate that session keys are stored in a collection.

When the user selects a book, the title of the selected book is set as the value of the `strTitle` key. This information is added to the `Session` object so that it may be used in the `BookInformation` page. After the `strTitle` key has been provided with a value, the page redirects the client browser by calling `Response.Redirect` (line 106). The **Response** object is a predefined ASP .NET object that provides methods for responding to clients. **Redirect** is one of the `Response` object's methods, which is used to specify the Web page to which the client browser will be redirected.

3. ***Saving the project.*** Select **File > Save All** to save your modified code.

Before you begin to program the `BookInformation.aspx.cs` code-behind file, you need to place images of the book covers in the `Bookstore` directory. The `BookInformation.aspx` page will display the cover image of the selected book. You will learn how to place the images in the following box.

<table>
<tr><td>

Adding Images to the
Bookstore Directory

</td><td>

1. ***Locating the images.*** Locate the C:\Examples\Tutorial31\Images directory, which contains images of the book covers.

2. ***Placing the images in the Bookstore directory.*** Copy the three images csharphtp1.png, cpphtp4.png and vbnethtp2.png, then paste them into the Bookstore directory that is located in the wwwroot directory on your computer. These image files will be used when you program the BookInformation.aspx page.

</td></tr>
</table>

SELF-REVIEW

1. The _____ class defines the basic functionality for an ASPX page.

   a) Form   b) WebForm

   c) Page   d) None of the above.

2. The Page class is located in the _____ namespace.

   a) System.Web.UI   b) System.Data

   c) System.WebForm   d) System.OleDb

Answers: 1) c. 2) a.

31.3 Programming the BookInformation Page's Code-Behind File

The next ASPX page in this application is BookInformation.aspx. This ASPX page displays information about the book the user selected. In the following box, you will add the code to the Page_Load event handler of the BookInformation.aspx page so that you may retrieve the requested book's information from the database.

<table>
<tr><td>

Defining the Page_Load
Event Handler for the
BookInformation Page

</td><td>

1. ***Changing the class name.*** Double click BookInformation.aspx in the **Solution Explorer** window to view the BookInformation.aspx page. Select **View > Code** to view the code-behind file BookInformation.aspx.cs. Make sure that the class name is BookInformation (Fig. 31.10).

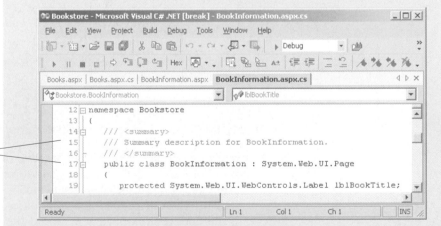

Class name should be
BookInformation

Figure 31.10   Changing the name of the class.

2. ***Using a namespace.*** To use database-related objects, you will need to use the System.Data.OleDb namespace. Add line 11 of Fig. 31.11 before the BookInformation class declaration.

</td></tr>
</table>

(cont.)

Using the `System.Data.OleDb` namespace

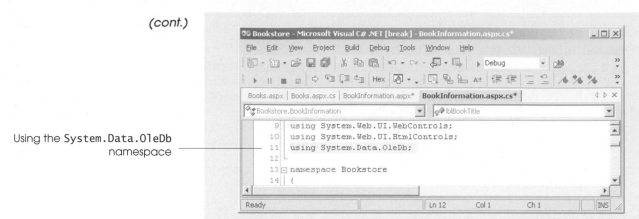

Figure 31.11 Using the `System.Data.OleDb` namespace.

3. ***Rearranging and commenting the control declarations.*** Rearrange and comment the control declarations as shown in lines 20–40 of Fig. 31.12.

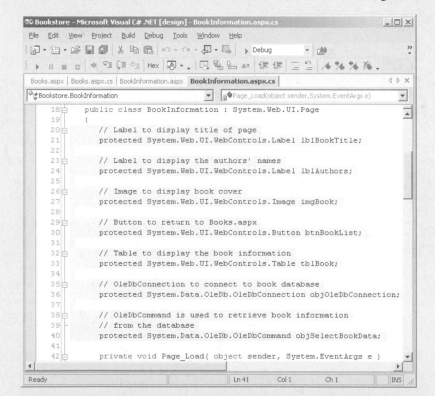

Figure 31.12 Rearranging and commenting the control declarations.

4. ***Setting a parameter value and opening the database connection.*** Add lines 44–52 of Fig. 31.13 to the `Page_Load` event handler of the `BookInforma-tion.aspx` page. Lines 45–46 sets the `Text` property of the `lblBookTitle` `Label` to the title of the selected book, using the `Session` item. Recall that in the `Books.aspx` page, you stored the title of the selected book in the `Session` item with the `strTitle` key. Lines 49–50 set the `title` parameter of the `objSelectBookData` command object to the title of the selected book, which is stored in the `Text` property of the `lblBookTitle` `Label`. Line 52 opens the connection to the database by invoking the `Open` method. Note that we have added spaces inside the event handler's argument list in line 42 and added the comment in line 54 for clarity.

(cont.)

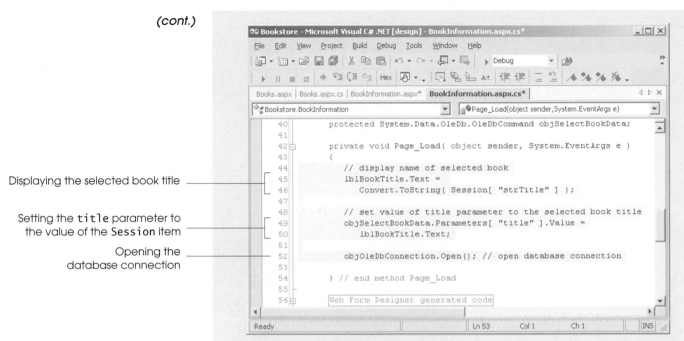

Figure 31.13 Page_Load event handler modified to set a parameter value and open a database connection.

5. *Creating the data reader.* Add lines 54–58 of Fig. 31.14 to the Page_Load event handler. Lines 55–56 create the data reader (of the OleDbData-Reader type) by invoking the ExecuteReader method of the objSelect-BookData command object. Line 58 invokes the data reader's Read method to start the data reader. Your query (specified using data command objects) from the previous tutorial will be executed, returning information about the user's selected book.

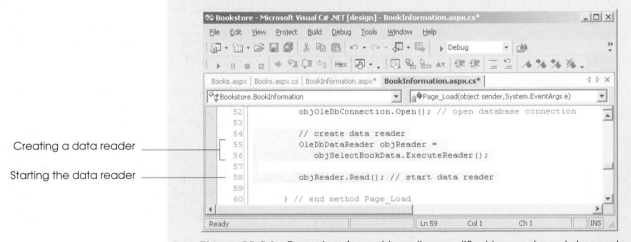

Figure 31.14 Page_Load event handler modified to create a data reader.

6. *Using the data reader.* Add lines 60–66 of Fig. 31.15 to the Page_Load event handler. Lines 61–66 retrieve data from the database. [*Note*: The OleDbDa-taReader can read, but not modify, information from the database.] Lines 61–62 set the lblAuthors Label's text to the authors of the selected book, specified by objReader["authors"]. Line 62 retrieves the value found in the authors field. Remember that the reader is retrieving the information specified by the SQL statement of the objSelectBookData data command object. The SQL statement specified only that the selected book and its book information should be retrieved from the database.

(cont.)

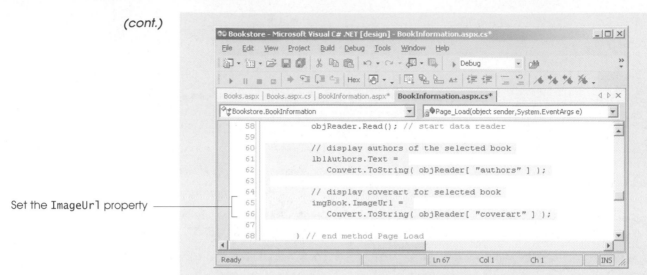

Set the `ImageUrl` property ——

Figure 31.15   Displaying book authors and cover image.

Lines 65–66 set the `Image` control's `ImageUrl` property to the name of the selected book's cover image, which is specified by using the value of `objReader[ "coverart" ]`.

7. *Displaying book information in the Table.* Add lines 68–89 of Fig. 31.16 to the `Page_Load` event handler. Lines 68–86 display the book information in the `Table` (`tblBook`). Recall that you created a table with five rows that contain two cells each. The second cell in the first row is given the value of the selected book's price. This task is accomplished by using the `Rows` and `Cells` properties. For example, lines 69–70 specify the row number by using property `Rows` of the `Table` control and specifying 0 for the first row. The `Cells` property of `Rows` is then used to specify the second cell in the row by using the value 1. Next, the `Text` property of `Cells` is used to set the text that will display in the second cell of the first row in the `Table`. The `Text` property is assigned the value of the data read by the data reader (`objReader[ "price" ]`), which is converted to a `string` (recall that the data reader returns items of the `object` type). The rest of the book's information is displayed in the same manner. The second cell in the second row contains the value of the ISBN number. The second cell in the third row displays the edition number. The fourth row contains the copyright date and the fifth row contains the selected book's description.

Line 88 closes the data reader, and line 89 closes the database connection by calling the `Close` method. When this application is run, the information is displayed in the format shown in Fig. 31.17.

8. *Saving the project.* Select **File > Save All** to save your modified code.

(cont.)

Display book information in the **Table**

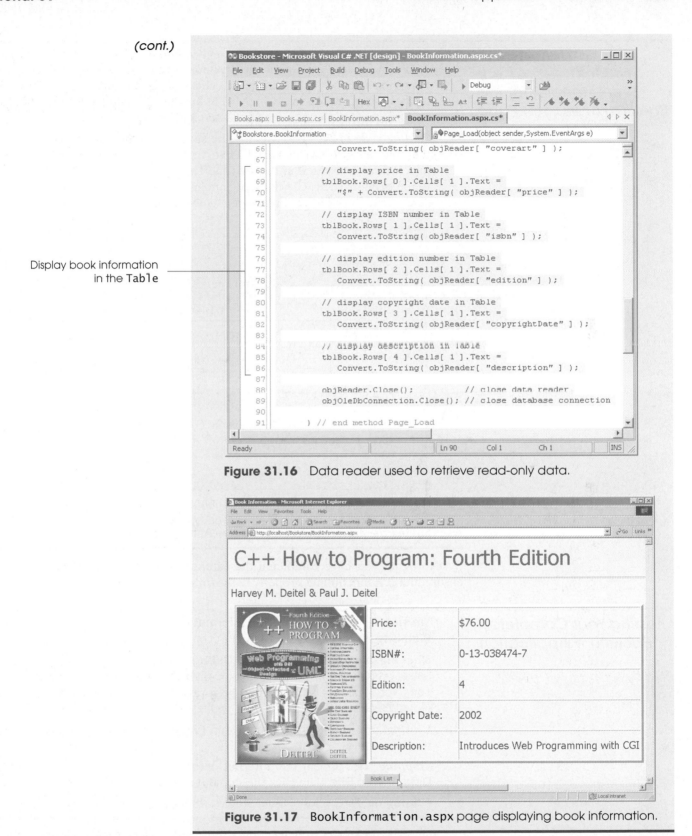

```
66              Convert.ToString( objReader[ "coverart" ] );
67
68         // display price in Table
69         tblBook.Rows[ 0 ].Cells[ 1 ].Text =
70            "$" + Convert.ToString( objReader[ "price" ] );
71
72         // display ISBN number in Table
73         tblBook.Rows[ 1 ].Cells[ 1 ].Text =
74            Convert.ToString( objReader[ "isbn" ] );
75
76         // display edition number in Table
77         tblBook.Rows[ 2 ].Cells[ 1 ].Text =
78            Convert.ToString( objReader[ "edition" ] );
79
80         // display copyright date in Table
81         tblBook.Rows[ 3 ].Cells[ 1 ].Text =
82            Convert.ToString( objReader[ "copyrightDate" ] );
83
84         // display description in Table
85         tblBook.Rows[ 4 ].Cells[ 1 ].Text =
86            Convert.ToString( objReader[ "description" ] );
87
88         objReader.Close();         // close data reader
89         objOleDbConnection.Close(); // close database connection
90
91      } // end method Page_Load
```

Figure 31.16 Data reader used to retrieve read-only data.

Figure 31.17 **BookInformation.aspx** page displaying book information.

The final event handler you define in the **BookInformation.aspx** page is the **btnBookList_Click** event handler. This event handler allows the user to return to the list of available books. You create this event handler in the following box.

<table>
<tr>
<td>

*Defining the
btnBookList_Click
Event Handler for the
BookInformation Page*

</td>
<td>

1. ***Creating the btnBookList_Click event handler.*** Now you are ready to define the event handler for the btnBookList Button. Select the BookInformation.aspx page, then double click the **Book List** Button. This step creates the btnBookList_Click event handler. This Button is used to redirect the client browser to the Books.aspx page.

2. ***Adding code to the event handler.*** Be sure to add the comments and break the header as shown in Fig. 31.18 so that the line numbers in your code match those presented in this tutorial. Then, add lines 132–133 of Fig. 31.18 to the btnBookList_Click event handler. Line 133 redirects the user to the Books.aspx page by calling Response.Redirect.

</td>
</tr>
</table>

Redirecting to the
Books.aspx page

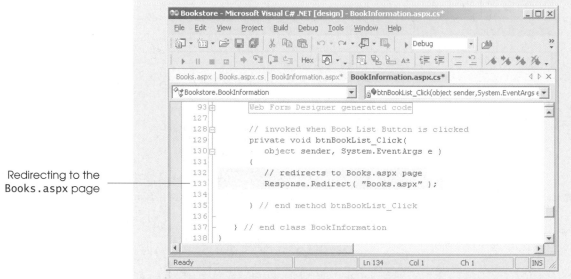

Figure 31.18 Declaration of the btnBookList_Click event handler.

3. ***Saving the project.*** Select **File > Save All** to save your modified code.

Now that you have completed the **Bookstore** application, you will test it to ensure that it is functioning properly in the following box.

<table>
<tr>
<td>

*Testing Your Completed
Bookstore Application*

</td>
<td>

1. ***Starting IIS.*** Open the **Internet Information Services** dialog, select **Default Web Site** and click the Start Item Button to start IIS.

2. ***Running the application.*** Select **Debug > Start** to run your application. Select a book title from the ListBox, then click the **View Information** Button. Notice that this application performs the same functions as the completed **Bookstore** application that you test-drove in Tutorial 28.

3. ***Closing the application.*** Close your running application by clicking the browser window's close box.

4. ***Stopping IIS.*** Open the **Internet Information Services** dialog. Select **Default Web Site**, then click the stop Button in the toolbar to stop IIS.

5. ***Closing the IDE.*** Close Visual Studio .NET by clicking its close box.

</td>
</tr>
</table>

Figures 31.19 and 31.20 present the source code for the Books.aspx and BookInformation.aspx pages of the **Bookstore** application, respectively. The lines of code that contain new programming concepts that you learned in this tutorial are highlighted.

```
1   using System;
2   using System.Collections;
3   using System.ComponentModel;
4   using System.Data;
5   using System.Drawing;
6   using System.Web;
7   using System.Web.SessionState;
8   using System.Web.UI;
9   using System.Web.UI.WebControls;
10  using System.Web.UI.HtmlControls;
11  using System.Data.OleDb;
12
13  namespace Bookstore
14  {
15     /// <summary>
16     /// Summary description for Books.
17     /// </summary>
18     public class Books : System.Web.UI.Page
19     {
20        // Label to display title of page
21        protected System.Web.UI.WebControls.Label lblAvailable;
22
23        // Label to display the instructions
24        protected System.Web.UI.WebControls.Label lblInstructions;
25
26        // ListBox to display the book titles
27        protected System.Web.UI.WebControls.ListBox lstBookTitles;
28
29        // Button to select a book
30        protected System.Web.UI.WebControls.Button btnInformation;
31
32        // OleDbConnection to connect to book database
33        protected System.Data.OleDb.OleDbConnection objOleDbConnection;
34
35        // OleDbCommand is used to retrieve book titles
36        // from the database
37        protected System.Data.OleDb.OleDbCommand objSelectTitles;
38
39        private void Page_Load( object sender, System.EventArgs e )
40        {
41           objOleDbConnection.Open(); // open database connection
42
43           // create data reader
44           OleDbDataReader objReader = objSelectTitles.ExecuteReader();
45
46           // loop while data reader is reading
47           while ( objReader.Read() )
48           {
49              // add titles to ListBox while reader is reading
50              lstBookTitles.Items.Add(
51                 Convert.ToString( objReader[ "title" ] ) );
52           }
53
54           objOleDbConnection.Close(); // close database connection
55
56        } // end method Page_Load
57
58        // Web Form Designer generated code
```

Defining the Page_Load event handler → (line 39)

Figure 31.19 Books.aspx page code. (Part 1 of 2.)

```
59
60            // invoked when Button is clicked
61            private void btnInformation_Click(
62               object sender, System.EventArgs e )
63            {
64               // determine if user selected book title
65               if ( lstBookTitles.SelectedItem == null )
66               {
67                  lstBookTitles.SelectedIndex = 0;
68               }
69
70               // create Session item named strTitle
71               Session[ "strTitle" ] =
72                  lstBookTitles.SelectedItem.Text;
73
74               // redirect to BookInformation.aspx page
75               Response.Redirect( "BookInformation.aspx" );
76
77            } // end method btnInformation_Click
78
79         } // end class Books
80      }
```

Determining if the user made a selection from ListBox

Creating a Session item

Redirecting client browsers to the BookInformation.aspx page

Figure 31.19 Books.aspx page code. (Part 2 of 2.)

```
1    using System;
2    using System.Collections;
3    using System.ComponentModel;
4    using System.Data;
5    using System.Drawing;
6    using System.Web;
7    using System.Web.SessionState;
8    using System.Web.UI;
9    using System.Web.UI.WebControls;
10   using System.Web.UI.HtmlControls;
11   using System.Data.OleDb;
12
13   namespace Bookstore
14   {
15      /// <summary>
16      /// Summary description for BookInformation.
17      /// </summary>
18      public class BookInformation : System.Web.UI.Page
19      {
20         // Label to display title of page
21         protected System.Web.UI.WebControls.Label lblBookTitle;
22
23         // Label to display the authors' names
24         protected System.Web.UI.WebControls.Label lblAuthors;
25
26         // Image to display book cover
27         protected System.Web.UI.WebControls.Image imgBook;
28
29         // Button to return to Books.aspx
30         protected System.Web.UI.WebControls.Button btnBookList;
31
32         // Table to display the book information
33         protected System.Web.UI.WebControls.Table tblBook;
```

Figure 31.20 BookInformation.aspx page code. (Part 1 of 3.)

Defining the `Page_Load`
event handler

Using a `Session` item to
retrieve parameter value

Using a `Session` item to
set a parameter value

Setting the `ImageUrl`
property of an `Image`

Using the `Rows` property of `Table`
and the `Cells` property of `Rows`

```
34
35          // OleDbConnection to connect to book database
36          protected System.Data.OleDb.OleDbConnection objOleDbConnection;
37
38          // OleDbCommand is used to retrieve book information
39          // from the database
40          protected System.Data.OleDb.OleDbCommand objSelectBookData;
41
42          private void Page_Load( object sender, System.EventArgs e )
43          {
44             // display name of selected book
45             lblBookTitle.Text =
46                Convert.ToString( Session[ "strTitle" ] );
47
48             // set value of title parameter to the selected book title
49             objSelectBookData.Parameters[ "title" ].Value =
50                lblBookTitle.Text;
51
52             objOleDbConnection.Open(); // open database connection
53
54             // create data reader
55             OleDbDataReader objReader =
56                objSelectBookData.ExecuteReader();
57
58             objReader.Read(); // start data reader
59
60             // display authors of the selected book
61             lblAuthors.Text =
62                Convert.ToString( objReader[ "authors" ] );
63
64             // display coverart for selected book
65             imgBook.ImageUrl =
66                Convert.ToString( objReader[ "coverart" ] );
67
68             // display price in Table
69             tblBook.Rows[ 0 ].Cells[ 1 ].Text =
70                "$" + Convert.ToString( objReader[ "price" ] );
71
72             // display ISBN number in Table
73             tblBook.Rows[ 1 ].Cells[ 1 ].Text =
74                Convert.ToString( objReader[ "isbn" ] );
75
76             // display edition number in Table
77             tblBook.Rows[ 2 ].Cells[ 1 ].Text =
78                Convert.ToString( objReader[ "edition" ] );
79
80             // display copyright date in Table
81             tblBook.Rows[ 3 ].Cells[ 1 ].Text =
82                Convert.ToString( objReader[ "copyrightDate" ] );
83
84             // display description in Table
85             tblBook.Rows[ 4 ].Cells[ 1 ].Text =
86                Convert.ToString( objReader[ "description" ] );
87
88             objReader.Close();              // close data reader
89             objOleDbConnection.Close(); // close database connection
90
91          } // end method Page_Load
```

Figure 31.20 `BookInformation.aspx` page code. (Part 2 of 3.)

```
92
93          // Web Form Designer generated code
94
95          // invoked when Book List Button is clicked
96          private void btnBookList_Click(
97             object sender, System.EventArgs e )
98          {
99             // redirects to Books.aspx page
100            Response.Redirect( "Books.aspx" );
101
102         } // end method btnBookList_Click
103
104      } // end class BookInformation
105   }
```

Redirecting client browsers to the Books.aspx page

Figure 31.20 BookInformation.aspx page code. (Part 3 of 3.)

SELF-REVIEW

1. A(n) _____ reads data from a database.

   a) OleDbDataReader   b) OleDbConnection

   c) Query Builder   d) DataSet

2. To specify the third cell in the second row of a Table control called tableName, type _____.

   a) tableName.Rows[2].Cells[3]   b) tableName.Rows[1].Cells[2]

   c) tableName.Cells[3].Rows[2]   d) tableName.Cells[2].Rows[1]

Answers: 1) a. 2) b.

31.4 Internet and Web Resources

Please take a moment to visit each of these sites briefly. To save typing time, use the hot links on the enclosed CD or at www.deitel.com.

www.asp.net
This Microsoft site overviews ASP .NET and provides ASP .NET tutorials. This site also includes the IBuySpy e-commerce storefront example that uses ASP .NET and links to Web sites where users can purchase books.

www.asp101.com/aspplus
This site overviews ASP .NET and includes articles, code examples and links to ASP .NET resources.

www.411asp.net
This resource site provides users with ASP .NET tutorials and code samples. The community pages allow users to ask questions, answer questions and post messages.

www.aspfree.com
This site provides free ASP .NET demos and source code. The site also provides a list of articles on various topics and a frequently asked questions (FAQs) page.

31.5 Wrap-Up

In this tutorial, you programmed the middle tier of your three-tier **Bookstore** application. By defining methods and event handlers, you specified the actions that execute when the user interacts with ASPX pages. You learned about Session objects and how they are used to maintain values across ASPX pages. You also learned about the Response.Redirect method, which allows you to redirect the client browser to other ASPX pages.

After learning about Sessions and Response.Redirect, you used them in the **Bookstore** application. You began with the first ASPX page of the application, Books.aspx. This page retrieved the book titles from the database and displayed them in a ListBox control when the ASPX page was loaded. You did this by defining the Page_Load event handler. You then defined the actions that would occur when the user clicks the **View Information** Button. In the Click event handler, you created a Session item to store the title of the book selected by the user. You also used the Response.Redirect method in the Click event handler to direct users from the Books.aspx page to the BookInformation.aspx page.

You then defined the BookInformation.aspx page. You defined the Page_Load event handler to display the information about the selected book. Recall that you used the value stored in the Session item to determine the book title selected by the user. You then created a data reader to retrieve the selected book's information and displayed it in the Table control. Through programming, you were able to control the flow of data from the information tier to the client tier, completing the three-tier **Bookstore** application. You also learned about ASP .NET resources available on the Web.

In the next tutorial, you will learn how to handle exceptions, which are indications of problems occurring during application execution. You will use exception handling to verify user input.

SKILLS SUMMARY

Accessing the Code-Behind File

- Click the Show All Files Button in the **Solution Explorer** window.
- Click the plus box next to the desired ASPX page to display the corresponding code-behind file name.
- Double click the code-behind file name to view the code-behind file.

Creating and Using a Session Item

- Type Session["*nameOfKey*"], where *nameOfKey* represents the key in a key-value pair. Assign this item a value in an assignment statement.
- Use Session["*nameOfKey*"] to retrieve the item's value.

Redirecting the Client Browser to Another Web Page

- Type Redirect.Response("*URLOfPage*"), where *URLOfPage* represents the URL of the page to which the client browser redirects.

KEY TERMS

code-behind file—C# file that contains a class that provides an ASPX page's functionality.

key-value pair—Associates a value with a corresponding key, which is used to identify the value.

Load event of the Page class—Raised when the ASPX page is loaded, causes the Page_Load event handler to be executed.

Page class—Defines the basic functionality for an ASPX page.

Page_Load event handler—Executes any processing necessary to display a Web page.

Response object—A predefined ASP .NET object that provides methods for responding to clients.

Response.Redirect—Method used to redirect the client browser to another Web page.

SelectedIndex property of ListBox Web control—Returns the index of the selected item.

SelectedItem property of ListBox Web control—Returns the value of the selected item.

session state—ASP .NET's built-in support for tracking data.

Session object—Maintained across several Web pages containing a collection of items (key-value pairs). This variable is specific to each user.

CONTROLS, EVENTS, PROPERTIES & METHODS

ASPX page   Page on which controls are dropped to design the GUI.

- *Event*

  Load—Raised when the ASPX page is created.

- *Properties*

  bgColor—Specifies the Web Form's background color.

  title—Specifies the page's title.

Image   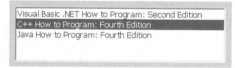   This control displays an image on the ASPX page.

- *In action*

- *Properties*

  BorderStyle—Specifies the appearance of the Image's border.

  BorderWidth—Specifies the width of the Image's border.

  Height—Specifies the height of the Image control.

  ID—Specifies the name used to access the Image control programmatically. The name should be prefixed with img.

  ImageUrl—Specifies the location of the image file.

  Width—This property specifies the width of the Image control.

ListBox   ListBox   This control allows the user to view and select from multiple items in a list.

- *In action*

  > Visual Basic .NET How to Program: Second Edition
  > C++ How to Program: Fourth Edition
  > Java How to Program: Fourth Edition

- *Properties*

  Height—Specifies the height of the ListBox.

  ID—Specifies the name used to access the ListBox control programmatically. The name should be prefixed with lst.

  SelectedIndex—Returns the index of the selected item in the ListBox.

  SelectedItem—Returns the value of the selected item in the ListBox.

  Width—Specifies the width of the ListBox.

Response   This class provides methods for responding to clients.

- *Method*

  Redirect—Redirects the client browser to the specified location.

MULTIPLE-CHOICE QUESTIONS

31.1 The Page_Load event handler _____.
a) redirects the client browser to different Web pages
b) defines the functionality when a Button is clicked
c) executes any processing necessary to display a Web page
d) defines the functionality when a Web control is selected

31.2 The Response.Redirect method _____.
a) refreshes the current Web page
b) sends the client browser to a specified Web page
c) responds to user input
d) responds to the click of a Button

31.3 Session items are used in the **Bookstore** application because _____.
a) variables in ASP .NET Web applications must be created as Session items
b) values need to be shared among Web pages
c) Session items are simpler to create than instance variables
d) Both a and b.

31.4 Session state is used for _____ in ASP .NET.
a) tracking user-specific data   b) running an application
c) using a database   d) None of the above.

31.5 The file extension for an ASPX code-behind file written in C# is _____.
a) .asp   b) .aspx
c) .aspx.cs   d) .code

31.6 The Response object is a predefined ASP .NET object that _____.
a) connects to a database
b) retrieves information from a database
c) creates Web controls
d) provides methods for responding to client requests

31.7 The Response.Redirect method takes a(n) _____ as an argument.
a) URL   b) int value
c) bool value   d) OleDbConnection object

31.8 The _____ property specifies the image that an Image control displays.
a) ImageGIF   b) ImageUrl
c) Image   d) Display

31.9 The C# file that contains the ASPX page's corresponding class is called the _____.
a) ASPX file   b) code-behind file
c) class file   d) None of the above.

31.10 Information can be maintained across Web pages by adding a _____ to the Session object.
a) key-value pair   b) number
c) database connection object   d) None of the above.

EXERCISES

31.11 (*Phone Book Application: Functionality*) Define the middle tier for the **Phone Book** application (Fig. 31.21).

a) *Opening the application*. Open the **Phone Book** application that you created in Tutorial 29 and continued to develop in Tutorial 30.

b) *Using System.Data.OleDb in PhoneBook.aspx.cs*. Use the System.Data.OleDb namespace in PhoneBook.aspx.cs.

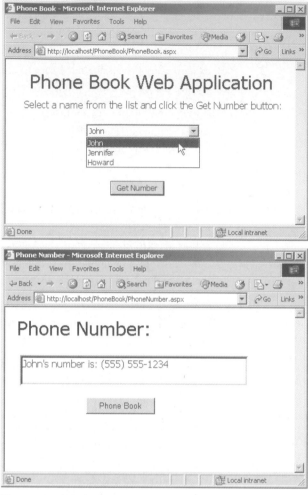

Figure 31.21   **Phone Book** application.

c) *Rearranging and commenting the control declarations.* Organize the control declarations as they appear on the Web Form. Add a comment above each declaration.

d) *Defining the Page_Load event handler of PhoneBook.aspx page.* Use the Open method to open the connection to the database. Create a data reader to read the information specified by the data command object.

e) *Populating the DropDownList with names.* Add a while statement to PhoneBook.aspx's Page_Load method. This loop should add to the DropDownList each person's name read by the data reader.

f) *Closing the reader and connection.* Close the data reader and the connection to the database by invoking their Close methods.

g) *Creating the Get Number Button's Click event handler for the PhoneBook.aspx page.* Double click the **Get Number** Button to create the Button's Click event handler.

h) *Creating a Session item.* In the Click event handler, create a Session item to store the selected name.

i) *Redirecting to the PhoneNumber.aspx page.* In the Click event handler, use the Response.Redirect method to redirect the client browser to the PhoneNumber.aspx page.

j) *Using System.Data.OleDb in PhoneNumber.aspx.cs.* Use the System.Data.OleDb namespace in PhoneNumber.aspx.cs.

k) *Rearranging and commenting the control declarations.* Organize the control declarations as they appear on the Web Form. Add a comment above each declaration.

l) *Defining the Page_Load event handler for the PhoneNumber.aspx page.* Use the Open method to open the connection to the database. Access the Session item to retrieve the selected name. Specify this name as the parameter value for the OleDb-Command object. Create a data reader to read the information specified by the data command object.

m) *Displaying the selected name and phone number.* In the Page_Load event handler, read the desired phone number from the data reader. Display the selected name and corresponding phone number in the lblNumbers Label.

n) *Closing the reader and connection.* Close the data reader and the connection to the database by invoking their Close methods.

o) *Creating the Phone Book Button's Click event handler for the PhoneNumber.aspx page.* Double click the **Phone Book** Button to create the Button's Click event handler.

p) *Redirecting to the PhoneBook.aspx page.* In the Click event handler, use method Response.Redirect to redirect the client browser to the PhoneBook.aspx page.

q) *Running the application.* Select **Debug > Start** to run your application. Select a name from the ComboBox, then click the **Get Number** Button. Confirm that the information is displayed correctly on the PhoneNumber.aspx page. Click the **Phone Book** Button to return to the PhoneBook.aspx page. Test the other two entries in the ComboBox to ensure that your application works correctly.

r) *Closing the application.* Close your running application by clicking the browser window's close box.

s) *Closing the IDE.* Close Visual Studio .NET by clicking its close box.

31.12 (*US State Facts Application: Functionality*) Define the middle tier for the **US State Facts** application (Fig. 31.22).

a) *Opening the application.* Open the **US State Facts** application that you created in Tutorial 29 and continued to develop in Tutorial 30.

b) *Copying the FlagImages directory to your project directory.* Copy the C:\Examples\ Tutorial31\Exercises\Images\FlagImages directory to the USStateFacts directory.

c) *Using System.Data.OleDb in States.aspx.cs.* Use the System.Data.OleDb namespace in States.aspx.cs before the class declaration.

d) *Rearranging and commenting the control declarations.* Organize the control declarations as they appear on the Web Form. Add a comment above each declaration.

e) *Defining the Page_Load event handler for the States.aspx page.* Use the Open method to open the connection to the database. Create a data reader to read the information specified by the data command object.

f) *Populating the ListBox with state names in the States.aspx page.* Add a while statement to States.aspx's Page_Load method. This loop should add to the List-Box the name of each state read by the data reader.

g) *Creating a Button's Click event handler for the States.aspx page.* Double click the **Review Facts** Button to create the Button's Click event handler.

h) *Creating a Session item.* Create a Session item in the Click event handler and assign it to the state name that the user selects from the ListBox.

i) *Redirecting to the StateFacts.aspx page.* In the Click event handler, use the Redirect.Response method to redirect the client browser to the StateFacts.aspx page.

j) *Using System.Data.OleDb in StateFacts.aspx.cs.* Use the System.Data.OleDb namespace in StateFacts.aspx.cs.

k) *Rearranging and commenting the control declarations.* Organize the control declarations as they appear on the Web Form. Add a comment above each declaration.

l) *Defining the Page_Load event handler of StateFacts.aspx page.* Use the Open method to open the connection to the database. Access the Session object to retrieve the selected state name. Specify this name as a parameter value for the Ole-DbCommand object. Create a data reader to read the information specified by the data command object.

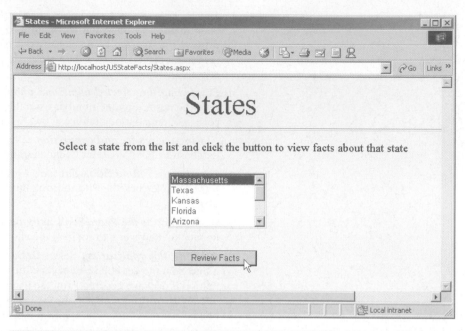

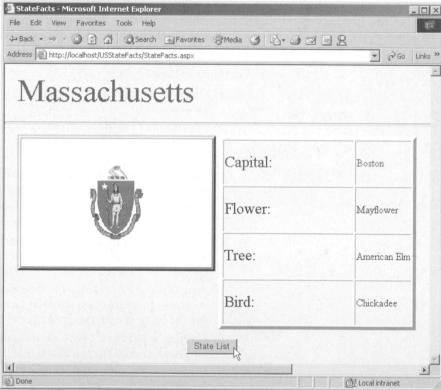

Figure 31.22 US State Facts application.

m) *Displaying the state facts in the Table.* In the Page_Load event handler, use the data reader to retrieve the desired state's facts. Display the selected state's name in the lblStateName Label. Set the ImageUrl property of the Image control to the location of the selected state's flag image. Display the name of the state capital, flower, tree and bird in the Table on the StateFacts.aspx page.

n) *Closing the connection.* Close the connection to the database by invoking the Close method.

o) *Creating the State List Button's Click event handler for the StateFacts.aspx page.* Double click the **State List** Button to create the Button's Click event handler.

p) *Redirecting to the States.aspx page.* In the Click event handler use the Redirect.Response method to redirect the client browser to the States.aspx page.

q) *Running the application.* Select **Debug > Start** to run your application. Select a state from the ComboBox, then click the **Review Facts** Button. Confirm that the information is displayed correctly on the StateFacts.aspx page. Click the **State List** Button to return to the States.aspx page. Test several other entries in the ComboBox to ensure that your application works correctly.

r) *Closing the application.* Close your running application by clicking the browser window's close box.

s) *Closing the IDE.* Close Visual Studio .NET by clicking its close box.

31.13 (*Road Sign Review Application: Functionality*) Define the middle tier for the **Road Sign Review** application (Fig. 31.23).

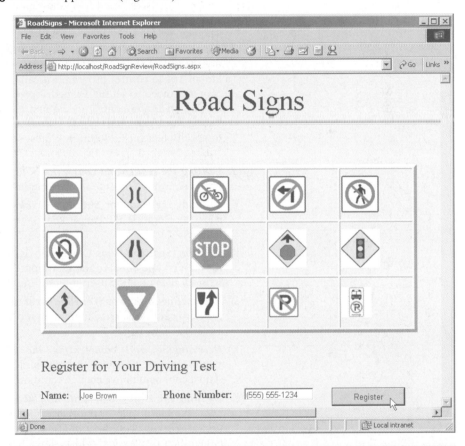

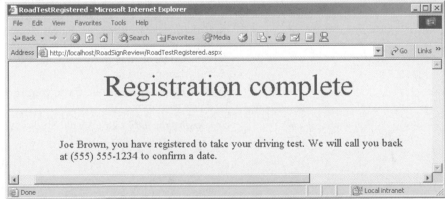

Figure 31.23   Road Sign Review application.

a) *Opening the application.* Open the **Road Sign Review** application that you created in Tutorial 29 and continued to develop in Tutorial 30.

b) *Copying the SignImages directory to your project directory.* Copy the `C:\Examples\Tutorial31\Exercises\Images\SignImages` directory to the RoadSignReview directory.

c) *Using System.Data.OleDb in RoadSigns.aspx.cs.* Use the `System.Data.OleDb` namespace in RoadSigns.aspx.cs.

d) *Rearranging and commenting the control declarations.* Organize the control declarations as they appear on the Web Form. Add a comment above each declaration.

e) *Defining the Page_Load event handler for the RoadSigns.aspx page.* Use the `Open` method to open the connection to the database. Create a data reader to read the information specified by the data command object.

f) *Populating the Table with sign images in the RoadSigns.aspx page.* Add a `while` statement to RoadSigns.aspx's Page_Load method. This loop should display an image of the sign and display the sign name in the `ToolTip` property. This property specifies the text that displays in a tooltip box when the mouse hovers over the `Image`. The sign image and name should be retrieved using the data reader. To display an `Image` in a cell of the `Table`, you need to create an `Image` control, specify a cell and use the cell's `Controls.Add` method to add an image to that cell. For example, to create an `Image` control programmatically, type `Image imgImageName = new Image()`. You then need to set the `ImageUrl` property to the location of the desired image. To display an `Image` control in the first cell of the first row, you would write the line `Table.Rows[ 0 ].Cells[ 0 ].Controls.Add( imgImageName )`. Also, if you wish to specify text for a tooltip, you must set the cell's `ToolTip` property—for example, `Table.Rows[ 0 ].Cells[ 0 ].ToolTip = "This is a tooltip"`.

g) *Closing the reader and connection.* Close the data reader and the connection to the database by invoking their `Close` methods.

h) *Creating the Register Button's Click event handler for RoadSigns.aspx.* Double click the **Register** Button of RoadSigns.aspx to create the Button's `Click` event handler.

i) *Creating Session items.* Create two `Session` items in the `Click` event handler, then set the first one equal to the user input for the **Name:** TextBox. The second `Session` item should equal the user input for the **Phone Number:** TextBox.

j) *Redirecting to the RoadTestRegistered.aspx page.* In the `Click` event handler, use the `Redirect.Response` method to redirect the client browser to the RoadTestRegistered.aspx page.

k) *Rearranging and commenting the control declarations in RoadTestRegistered.aspx.cs.* Organize the control declarations as they appear on the Web Form. Add a comment above each declaration.

l) *Defining the Page_Load method of RoadTestRegistered.aspx page.* Use the `Session` items to display a confirmation to the user about the user's registration information. Display the confirmation using the `lblConfirmation` Label. Display the user's name, then display text which states that the user will be contacted shortly at the phone number provided. This information should be displayed in a `Label`.

m) *Running the application.* Select **Debug > Start** to run your application. Type your name and phone number in the appropriate TextBoxes, then click the **Register** Button. Confirm that the information is displayed correctly on the RoadTestRegistered.aspx page.

n) *Closing the application.* Close your running application by clicking the browser window's close box.

o) *Closing the IDE.* Close Visual Studio .NET by clicking its close box.

TUTORIAL 32

Objectives

In this tutorial, you will learn to:
- Understand exception handling.
- Use the `try`, `catch` and `finally` blocks and the `throw` statement to handle exceptions.

Outline

32.1 Test-Driving the Enhanced Car Payment Calculator Application

32.2 Introduction to Exception Handling

32.3 Exception Handling in C#

32.4 Constructing the Enhanced Car Payment Calculator Application

32.5 Wrap-Up

Enhanced Car Payment Calculator Application

Introducing Exception Handling

In this tutorial, you will learn about **exception handling**. An **exception** is an indication of a problem that occurs during an application's execution. The name "exception" comes from the fact that, although a problem can occur, the problem occurs infrequently—if the "rule" is that a statement normally executes correctly, then the "exception to the rule" is that a problem occurs. Exception handling enables you to create applications that can resolve (or handle) exceptions during application execution. In many cases, handling an exception allows an application to continue executing as if no problem had been encountered.

This tutorial begins with a test-drive of the **Enhanced Car Payment Calculator** application, then overviews exception handling concepts and demonstrates basic exception handling techniques. You will learn the specifics of exception handling with the `try`, `catch` and `finally` blocks.

32.1 Test-Driving the Enhanced Car Payment Calculator Application

In this tutorial, you will enhance the **Car Payment Calculator** application from Tutorial 9 by adding exception handling statements. This application must meet the following requirements:

Application Requirements

*A bank wishes to prevent users from entering incorrect data on their car loans. Although the application you developed in Tutorial 9 calculates a result when incorrect data is entered, this result does not correctly represent the user's input. Alter the **Car Payment Calculator** application to allow users to enter only Integers in the **Price:** TextBox and **Down payment:** TextBox. Similarly, users should be allowed to enter only `double` values in the **Annual interest rate:** TextBox. If the user enters anything besides an `int` for the price or down payment, or a `double` for the interest rate, a message dialog should be displayed instructing the user to input proper data. The interest rate should be entered such that an input of 5 is equal to 5%.*

The original **Car Payment Calculator** application used the `Int32.Parse` and `Double.Parse` methods to set the values of the variables used in the application. This ensured that the payment calculation was always performed using numeric values. The `Int32.Parse` method converts its `string` argument to a value of the `int` type. The `Double.Parse` method converts its `string` argument to a value of the `double` type. However, as discussed in Tutorial 5, a user may enter invalid input. The `string` passed to the `Int32.Parse` method must be a `string` of digits only. Otherwise, an error will occur, and the application will not execute correctly. You will add exception handling to the **Car Payment Calculator** application so that when invalid input is entered, the user will be asked to enter valid input and the application will not calculate monthly payments. If the user provides valid input, the application should calculate the monthly payments for a car when financed for 24, 36, 48 and 60 months. Users input the car price, the down payment and the annual interest rate. You begin by test-driving the completed application. Then, you will learn the additional C# technologies you will need to create your own version of this application.

Test-Driving the Enhanced Car Payment Calculator Application

1. **Opening the completed application.** Open the `C:\Examples\Tutorial32\CompletedApplication\EnhancedCarPaymentCalculator` directory to locate the **Enhanced Car Payment Calculator** application. Double click `EnhancedCarPaymentCalculator.sln` to open the application in Visual Studio .NET.

2. **Running the Enhanced Car Payment Calculator application.** Select **Debug > Start** to run the application (Fig. 32.1).

Figure 32.1 Running the completed **Enhanced Car Payment Calculator** application.

3. **Entering an invalid value in the Down payment: TextBox.** Enter 16900 in the **Price:** TextBox, 6000.50 in the **Down payment:** TextBox and 7.5 in the **Annual interest rate:** TextBox. The Form appears as in Fig. 32.2.

4. **Attempting to calculate the monthly payment amounts.** Click the **Calculate** Button to attempt to calculate the monthly payment. Notice that an error message dialog (Fig. 32.3) appears.

5. **Entering non-numeric data in the Down payment: TextBox.** Click the **OK** Button to dismiss the message dialog. Change the value 6000.50 in the **Down payment:** TextBox to 600p. The Form appears as in Fig. 32.4. Click the **Calculate** Button to attempt to display the monthly payment in the TextBox. The message dialog shown in Fig. 32.3 appears again (a non-numeric character like p cannot be entered when an `int` is expected).

(cont.)

Figure 32.2   Entering an invalid value in the **Down payment:** TextBox.

Displaying a message when an exception is thrown

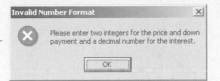

Figure 32.3   Message dialog displayed when incorrect input is entered.

Figure 32.4   Entering non-numeric data in the **Down Payment:** TextBox.

6. ***Entering non-numeric data in the Annual interest rate: TextBox.*** Click the **OK** Button to dismiss the message dialog. Change the value 600p in the **Down payment:** TextBox to 6000. Enter 7.5% in the **Annual interest rate:** TextBox. The Form appears as in Fig. 32.5. Click the **Calculate** Button to attempt to calculate the monthly payment. The message dialog shown in Fig. 32.3 appears again (7.5 is the correct input; entering the % character is incorrect).

7. ***Correcting the input.*** Click the **OK** Button to dismiss the message dialog. Change the value 7.5% in the **Annual interest rate:** TextBox to 7.5, and click the **Calculate** Button to display the monthly payments (Fig. 32.6).

8. ***Closing the application.*** Close your running application by clicking its close box.

9. ***Closing the IDE.*** Close Visual Studio .NET by clicking its close box.

(cont.)

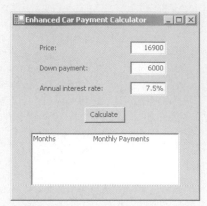

Figure 32.5 Entering non-numeric data in the **Annual interest rate:** TextBox.

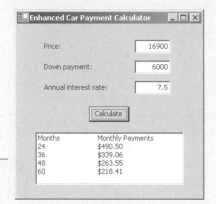

Results displayed only when valid input is entered

Figure 32.6 Displaying monthly payments after input is corrected.

32.2 Introduction to Exception Handling

Application logic frequently tests conditions that determine how application execution should proceed. Consider the following pseudocode:

Perform a task

If the preceding task did not execute correctly
    Perform error processing

Perform the next task

If the preceding task did not execute correctly
    Perform error processing

...

In this pseudocode, you begin by performing a task. Then, you test whether the task executed correctly. If not, you perform error processing. Otherwise, you continue with the next task. Although this form of error checking works, intermixing application logic with error-handling logic can make the application difficult to read, modify, maintain and debug—especially in large applications. In fact, if potential problems occur infrequently, intermixing application and error-handling logic can degrade an application's performance, because the application must explicitly test for errors after each task to determine whether the next task can be performed.

Exception handling enables you to remove error-handling code from the code that implements your application's logic, which improves application clarity and enhances modifiability. You can decide to handle only the exceptions you choose—all exceptions, all exceptions of a certain type or all exceptions in a group of related types. Such flexibility reduces the likelihood that errors will be overlooked, thereby making an application more robust.

A method **throws an exception** if a problem occurs during method execution but the method is unable to correct the problem. There is no guarantee that there will be an **exception handler**—code that executes when the application detects an exception—to process that kind of exception. If there is, the exception handler catches and handles the exception. An **uncaught exception**—an exception that does not have an exception handler—might cause application execution to terminate.

SELF-REVIEW

1. A(n) _____ is called when the application detects an exception.
   a) exception code
   b) exception processor
   c) exception handler
   d) None of the above.

2. A method will _____ an exception if a problem occurs during method execution but the method is unable to correct the problem.
   a) throw
   b) catch
   c) return
   d) None of the above.

Answers: 1) c. 2) a.

32.3 Exception Handling in C#

C# provides **try blocks** to enable exception handling. A `try` block consists of the `try` keyword followed by a block of code in which exceptions might occur. The purpose of the `try` block is to contain statements that might cause exceptions and statements that should not execute if an exception occurs.

At least one **catch block** (also called an exception handler) or a **finally block** must appear immediately after the `try` block. Each `catch` block can specify a parameter that identifies the type of exception the exception handler can process. The parameter enables the `catch` block to interact with the caught exception object. A `catch` block that does not specify a parameter can catch all exception types. A parameterless `catch` block should be placed after all other `catch` blocks. After the last `catch` block, an optional `finally` block provides code that always executes, whether or not an exception occurs.

If an exception occurs in a `try` block, the `try` block terminates immediately. As with any other block of code, when a `try` block terminates, local variables declared in the block go out of scope. Next, the application searches for the first `catch` block (immediately following the `try` block) that can process the type of exception that occurred. The application locates the matching `catch` by comparing the thrown exception's type with each `catch` block's exception-parameter type. A match occurs if the type of the exception matches the `catch` block's parameter type. When a match occurs, the code associated with the matching `catch` block executes. When a `catch` block finishes processing, local variables declared within the `catch` block (as well as the `catch`'s parameter) go out of scope. Any remaining `catch` blocks that correspond to the `try` block are ignored, and execution resumes at the first line of code after the last `catch` block if there is no `finally` block. Otherwise, execution resumes at the `finally` block.

If there is no `catch` block that matches the exception thrown in the corresponding `try` block, the execution resumes at the corresponding `finally` block (if it exists). After the `finally` block executes, the exception is passed to the method that called the current method, which then attempts to handle the exception. If the calling method does not handle the exception, the exception is again passed to the previous method in the call chain. If the exception goes unhandled, C# will display a dialog providing the user with information about the exception. The user can then choose to exit or continue running the application, although the application may not execute correctly due to the exception.

If no exceptions occur in a `try` block, the application ignores the `catch` block(s) for that `try` block. Application execution resumes with the next statement after the last `catch` block if there is no `finally` block. Otherwise, execution resumes at the `finally` block. A `finally` block (if one is present) will execute whether or not an exception is thrown in the corresponding `try` block or any of its corresponding `catch` blocks.

It is possible that a `catch` block might decide that it either cannot process that exception or can only partially process the exception. In such cases, the exception handler can defer the handling (or perhaps a portion of it) to another `catch` block. The handler achieves this by **rethrowing the exception** using the **throw** statement

```
throw exceptionReference;
```

where *exceptionReference* is the parameter for the exception in the `catch` block. When a rethrow occurs, the next enclosing `try` block (if any), which is normally in the calling method, detects the rethrown exception and attempts to catch it.

SELF-REVIEW

1. The _____ (if there is one) is always executed regardless of whether an exception occurs.

   a) `catch` block   b) `finally` block
   c) both `catch` and `finally` blocks   d) None of the above.

2. If no exceptions occur in a `try` block, the application ignores the _____ for that block.

   a) `finally` block   b) `return` statement
   c) `catch` block(s)   d) None of the above.

   Answers: 1) b. 2) c.

32.4 Constructing the Enhanced Car Payment Calculator Application

Now that you have been introduced to exception handling, you will construct your **Enhanced Car Payment Calculator** application. The following pseudocode describes the basic operation of the **Enhanced Car Payment Calculator** application:

> When the user clicks the Calculate Button:
>   Clear the ListBox of any previous text
>
>   Try
>   Get the car price from the Price: TextBox
>   Get the down payment from the Down payment: TextBox
>   Get the annual interest rate from the Annual interest rate: TextBox
>   Calculate the loan amount (price minus down payment)
>   Calculate the monthly interest rate (annual interest rate divided by 1200)
>   Calculate and display the monthly payments for 2, 3, 4 and 5 years
>
>   Catch
>   Display the error message dialog

Now that you have test-driven the **Enhanced Car Payment Calculator** application and studied its pseudocode representation, you will use an ACE table to help you convert the pseudocode to C#. Figure 32.7 lists the actions, controls and events that will help you complete your own version of this application.

<table>
<tr><td rowspan="10">Action/Control/Event
(ACE) Table for the
Enhanced Car Payment
Calculator Application
</td><td colspan="3"></td></tr>
</table>

Action	Control/Class/Object	Event

Label all the application's components	`lblStickerPrice,`
	`lblDownPayment,`
	`lblInterest`
		Application is run

	`btnCalculate`	Click
Try Clear the ListBox of any previous text	`lstPayments`	
Get the car price from the **Price:** TextBox	`txtStickerPrice`	
Get the down payment from the **Down payment:** TextBox	`txtDownPayment`	
Get the annual interest rate from the **Annual interest rate:** TextBox	`txtInterest`	
Calculate the loan amount		
Calculate the monthly interest rate		
Calculate and display the monthly payments	`lstPayments`	
Catch Display the error message dialog	`MessageBox`	

Figure 32.7   Enhanced Car Payment Calculator application ACE table.

Now that you've analyzed the **Enhanced Car Payment Calculator** application's components, you will learn how to place exception handling in your application's code.

Handling a FormatException

1. ***Copying the template to your working directory.*** Copy the `C:\Examples\Tutorial32\TemplateApplication\EnhancedCarPaymentCalculator` directory to your `C:\SimplyCSP` directory.

2. ***Opening the Enhanced Car Payment Calculator application's template file.*** Double click `EnhancedCarPaymentCalculator.sln` in the EnhancedCarPaymentCalculator directory to open the application in Visual Studio .NET. Open the `EnhancedCarPaymentCalculator.cs` file in code view.

3. ***Studying the code.*** View lines 202–204 of Fig. 32.8. Lines 202–203 read the `int` values from the **Down payment:** and **Price:** TextBoxes, respectively. Line 204 reads a `double` value from the **Annual interest rate:** TextBox. These three statements explicitly convert the data in the TextBoxes to `int` and `double` values, using the `Int32.Parse` and `Double.Parse` methods. However, these statements do not ensure that the input strings are formatted correctly, which could cause errors in your application.

   The `Int32.Parse` method throws a `FormatException` if it cannot convert its argument to an `int`. The **FormatException** class represents exceptions that occur when a method is passed an argument that is of the wrong type (and cannot be implicitly converted to the correct type). The `Double.Parse` method performs in a similar manner by throwing a `FormatException` if it cannot convert its argument to a `double`.

(cont.)

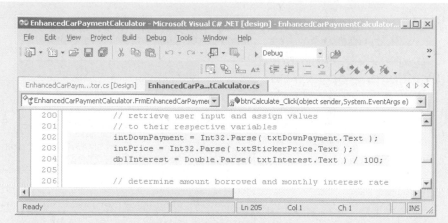

Figure 32.8 Int32.Parse and Double.Parse do not ensure that data is in the correct format.

4. ***Causing a FormatException.*** Select **Debug > Start** to run your application. Enter the input of Fig. 32.4 and click the **Calculate** Button. The dialog in Fig. 32.9 will appear, informing you of the type of exception that has occurred. Click the **Continue** Button to close the application. [*Note:* Sometimes clicking the **Continue** Button when an exception has occurred will cause the application to keep running, possibly incorrectly. When this happens, we suggest you close the application and modify it to handle the exception (as we will demonstrate shortly)].

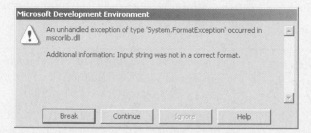

Figure 32.9 Unhandled FormatException from invalid input.

5. ***Adding a try block to your application.*** Add lines 200–202 of Fig. 32.10 to your application. Then, add line 235 of Fig. 32.11 to your application. The try keyword followed by an opening left brace (lines 201–202) begins the try block, and a closing right brace (line 235) ends the try block. The code contained between these braces is the code that might throw an exception (lines 205–207 of your code) and code that you do not want to execute if an exception occurs. Notice that the right brace (}) in line 237 is underlined, indicating a syntax error. Adding the try keyword to your application creates a syntax error until a corresponding catch or finally block is added to the application. You will add a catch block, which will fix the error in line 237, in the next step.

6. ***Adding a catch block to your application.*** Add lines 237–241 of Fig. 32.12 to your application. The catch keyword designates the beginning of a catch block. Line 238 specifies that this catch block will execute if a FormatException is thrown. This code will execute if the user enters invalid input in one of the TextBoxes. Notice that the right brace in line 243 is no longer underlined because adding a catch block fixed the error on that line. Line 241 ends the catch block and the entire try…catch statement.

(cont.)

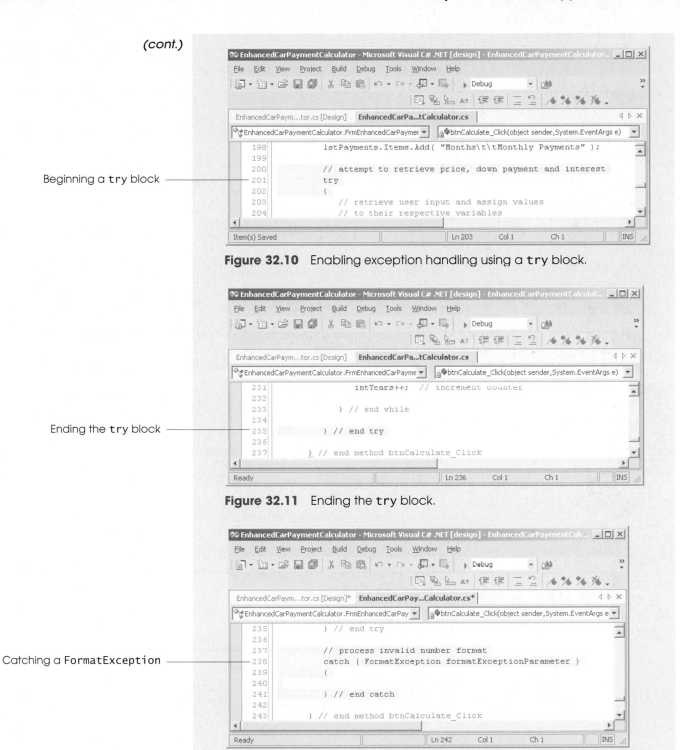

Figure 32.10 Enabling exception handling using a **try** block.

Beginning a **try** block

Figure 32.11 Ending the **try** block.

Ending the **try** block

Figure 32.12 Handling a **FormatException**.

Catching a **FormatException**

7. ***Displaying an error message to the user.*** Add lines 240–245 of Fig. 32.13 to the **catch** handler. These lines display a **MessageBox** to the user, instructing the user to enter valid input. Notice that the **MessageBoxIcon.Error** icon is used, because an exception is an error that occurs during the execution of the application.

(cont.)

Displaying a message when the `catch` block executes

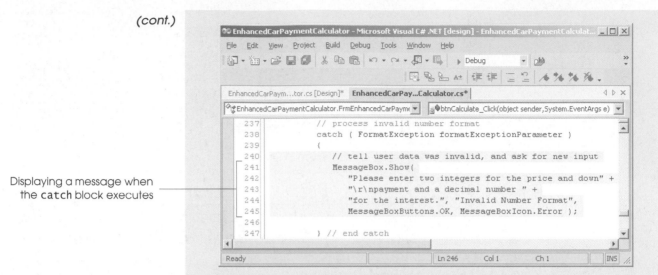

Figure 32.13 Displaying a message dialog to the user.

8. ***Running the application***. Select **Debug > Start** to run your application. Note that the compiler warns you that the `formatExceptionParameter` variable is declared but never used. This warning will appear whenever you declare a variable that is never again used in the application. This enables programmers to create cleaner code by not declaring unnecessary variables. To remove the variable's declaration, the variable name could simply be removed from line 238, as in

```
catch ( FormatException )
```

The application will work the same. We have left the variable in this example for demonstration purposes.

9. ***Closing the application***. Close your running application by clicking its close box.

10. ***Closing the IDE***. Close Visual Studio .NET by clicking its close box.

Figure 32.14 presents the source code for the **Enhanced Car Payment Calculator** application. The lines of code that contain new programming concepts that you learned in this tutorial are highlighted.

```
1  using System;
2  using System.Drawing;
3  using System.Collections;
4  using System.ComponentModel;
5  using System.Windows.Forms;
6  using System.Data;
7
8  namespace EnhancedCarPaymentCalculator
9  {
10    /// <summary>
11    /// Summary description for FrmEnhancedCarPayment.
12    /// </summary>
13    public class FrmEnhancedCarPayment : System.Windows.Forms.Form
14    {
15      // Label and TextBox for sticker price
16      private System.Windows.Forms.Label lblStickerPrice;
17      private System.Windows.Forms.TextBox txtStickerPrice;
```

Figure 32.14 Enhanced Car Payment Calculator application code. (Part 1 of 4.)

```
18
19          // Label and TextBox for down payment
20          private System.Windows.Forms.Label lblDownPayment;
21          private System.Windows.Forms.TextBox txtDownPayment;
22
23          // Label and textbox for interest rate
24          private System.Windows.Forms.TextBox txtInterest;
25          private System.Windows.Forms.Label lblInterest;
26
27          // Button to calculate total cost
28          private System.Windows.Forms.Button btnCalculate;
29
30          // ListBox to display total cost
31          private System.Windows.Forms.ListBox lstPayments;
32
33          /// <summary>
34          /// Required designer variable.
35          /// </summary>
36          private System.ComponentModel.Container components = null;
37
38          public FrmEnhancedCarPayment()
39          {
40             //
41             // Required for Windows Form Designer support
42             //
43             InitializeComponent();
44
45             //
46             // TODO: Add any constructor code after InitializeComponent
47             // call
48             //
49          }
50
51          /// <summary>
52          /// Clean up any resources being used.
53          /// </summary>
54          protected override void Dispose( bool disposing )
55          {
56             if( disposing )
57             {
58                if (components != null)
59                {
60                   components.Dispose();
61                }
62             }
63             base.Dispose( disposing );
64          }
65
66          // Windows Form Designer generated code
67
68          /// <summary>
69          /// The main entry point for the application.
70          /// </summary>
71          [STAThread]
72          static void Main()
73          {
74             Application.Run( new FrmEnhancedCarPayment() );
75          }
```

Figure 32.14   Enhanced Car Payment Calculator application code. (Part 2 of 4.)

```
76
77          // handles Calculate Button's Click event
78          private void btnCalculate_Click(
79             object sender, System.EventArgs e )
80          {
81             int intYears = 2;                  // repetition counter
82             int intMonths = 0;                 // payment period
83             int intPrice = 0;                  // car price
84             int intDownPayment = 0;            // down payment
85             double dblInterest = 0;            // interest rate
86             decimal decMonthlyPayment = 0;     // monthly payment
87             int intLoanAmount = 0;             // cost after down payment
88             double dblMonthlyInterest = 0;     // monthly interest rate
89
90             // remove text displayed in ListBox
91             lstPayments.Items.Clear();
92
93             // add header to ListBox
94             lstPayments.Items.Add( "Months\t\tMonthly Payments" );
95
96             // attempt to retrieve price, down payment and interest
97             try
98             {
99                // retrieve user input and assign values
100               // to their respective variables
101               intDownPayment = Int32.Parse( txtDownPayment.Text );
102               intPrice = Int32.Parse( txtStickerPrice.Text );
103               dblInterest = Double.Parse( txtInterest.Text ) / 100;
104
105               // determine amount borrowed and monthly interest rate
106               intLoanAmount = intPrice - intDownPayment;
107               dblMonthlyInterest = dblInterest / 12;
108
109               // loop four times
110               while ( intYears <= 5 )
111               {
112                  // calculate payment period
113                  intMonths = 12 * intYears;
114
115                  // calculate monthly payment using FCL Math.Pow
116                  // method for raising to a power
117                  decMonthlyPayment = ( decimal )
118                     ( intLoanAmount * dblMonthlyInterest *
119                     Math.Pow( 1 + dblMonthlyInterest, intMonths ) /
120                     ( Math.Pow( 1 + dblMonthlyInterest, intMonths )
121                     - 1 ) );
122
123                  // display payment value
124                  lstPayments.Items.Add( intMonths + "\t\t" +
125                     String.Format( "{0:C}", decMonthlyPayment ) );
126
127                  intYears++;  // increment counter
128
129               } // end while
130
131            } // end try
132
```

Beginning the try block — (lines 97–98)

Exceptions may be thrown — (lines 101–103)

Ending the try block — (line 131)

Figure 32.14 Enhanced Car Payment Calculator application code. (Part 3 of 4.)

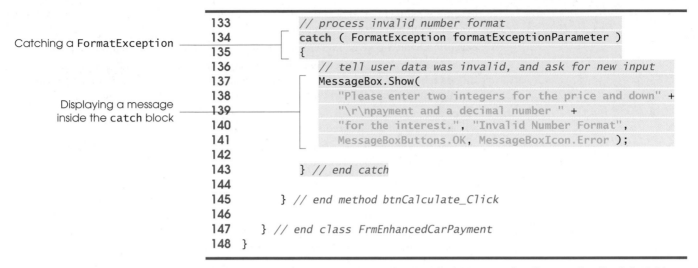

Catching a FormatException

Displaying a message inside the **catch** block

```
133        // process invalid number format
134    catch ( FormatException formatExceptionParameter )
135    {
136        // tell user data was invalid, and ask for new input
137        MessageBox.Show(
138            "Please enter two integers for the price and down" +
139            "\r\npayment and a decimal number " +
140            "for the interest.", "Invalid Number Format",
141            MessageBoxButtons.OK, MessageBoxIcon.Error );
142
143    } // end catch
144
145    } // end method btnCalculate_Click
146
147    } // end class FrmEnhancedCarPayment
148 }
```

Figure 32.14 Enhanced Car Payment Calculator application code. (Part 4 of 4.)

SELF-REVIEW

1. If you are attempting to catch multiple errors, you may use several _____ blocks after the _____ block.

   a) `try`, `catch`   b) `catch`, `try`

   c) `finally`, `try`   d) None of the above.

2. The exception you wish to handle should be declared as a parameter of the _____ block.

   a) `try`   b) `catch`

   c) `finally`   d) None of the above.

Answers: 1) b. 2) b.

32.5 Wrap-Up

In this tutorial, you learned exception handling concepts and when to use exception handling in C#. You learned how to use a `try` block with `catch` blocks to handle exceptions in your applications. You learned that an optional `finally` block contains code that should always execute. You also learned that the `throw` statement can be used to rethrow an exception that cannot be handled in the `catch` block. Next, you applied your knowledge of exception handling in C# to enhance your **Car Payment Calculator** application to check for input errors. You used a `try` block to enclose the statements that might throw `FormatExceptions` and a `catch` block to handle the `FormatExceptions`.

SKILLS SUMMARY

Handling an Exception

- Enclose in a `try` block code that might generate an exception and any code that should not execute if an exception occurs.

- Follow the `try` block with one or more `catch` blocks. Each `catch` block is an exception handler that specifies the type of exception it can handle.

- Follow the `catch` blocks with an optional `finally` block that contains code that should always execute.

KEY TERMS

catch block—Also called an exception handler, this block executes when code within the corresponding `try` block in the application detects an exceptional situation and throws an exception of the type the `catch` block declares.

exception—An indication of a problem that occurs during an application's execution.

exception handler—A block that executes when the application detects an exceptional situation and throws an exception.

exception handling—Dealing with problems that occur during application execution.

finally block—An optional block of code that follows the last catch block in a sequence of catch blocks or the try block if there are no catches. The finally block provides code that always executes, whether or not an exception occurs.

FormatException class—An exception of this type is thrown when a method cannot convert its argument to a desired numeric type, such as int or double.

rethrow the exception—The catch block can defer the exception handling (or perhaps a portion of it) to another catch block by using the throw keyword.

throw statement—Used to rethrow an exception in a catch block.

throws an exception—A method throws an exception if a problem occurs while the method is executing.

try block—A block containing statements that might cause exceptions and statements that should not execute if an exception occurs.

uncaught exception—An exception that does not have an exception handler. Uncaught exceptions might terminate application execution.

MULTIPLE-CHOICE QUESTIONS

32.1 Dealing with exceptional situations as an application executes is called _____.
a) exception detection
b) exception handling
c) exception resolution
d) exception debugging

32.2 A(n) _____ is always followed by at least one catch block or a finally block.
a) if statement
b) event handler
c) try block
d) None of the above.

32.3 The method call Int32.Parse("123.4a") will throw a(n) _____.
a) FormatException
b) ParsingException
c) DivideByZeroException
d) None of the above.

32.4 If no exceptions are thrown in a try block, _____.
a) the catch block(s) are skipped
b) all catch blocks are executed
c) an error occurs
d) the default exception is thrown

32.5 A(n) _____ is an exception that does not have an exception handler, and therefore might cause the application to terminate execution.
a) uncaught block
b) uncaught exception
c) error handler
d) thrower

32.6 A try block can have _____ associated with it.
a) only one catch block
b) several finally blocks
c) one or more catch blocks
d) None of the above.

32.7 The _____ statement is used to rethrow an exception from inside a catch block.
a) rethrow
b) throw
c) try
d) catch

32.8 The exception you wish to handle should be declared as a parameter of the _____ block.
a) try
b) catch
c) finally
d) None of the above.

32.9 A finally block is located _____.
a) after the try block, but before each catch block
b) before the try block
c) after the try block and the try block's corresponding catch blocks
d) Either b or c.

32.10 A _____ is executed if an exception is thrown from a `try` block or if no exception is thrown.

a) `catch` block

b) `finally` block

c) exception handler

d) All of the above.

EXERCISES

32.11 (*Enhanced Miles Per Gallon Application*) Modify the **Miles Per Gallon** application (Exercise 13.13) to use exception handling to process the `FormatExceptions` that occur when converting the `strings` in the `TextBoxes` to `doubles` (Fig. 32.15). The original application allowed the user to input the number of miles driven and the number of gallons used for a tank of gas to determine the number of miles the user was able to drive on one gallon of gas.

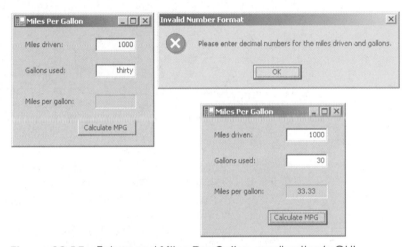

Figure 32.15 Enhanced **Miles Per Gallon** application's GUI.

a) *Copying the template to your working directory.* Copy the directory `C:\Examples\Tutorial32\Exercises\EnhancedMilesPerGallon` to your `C:\SimplyCSP` directory.

b) *Opening the application's template file.* Double click `MilesPerGallon.sln` in the `EnhancedMilesPerGallon` directory to open the application.

c) *Adding a try block.* Find the `btnCalculateMPG_Click` event handler. Enclose all of the code in this event handler in a `try` block.

d) *Adding a catch block.* After the `try` block you added in *Step c*, add a `catch` block to handle any `FormatExceptions` that may occur in the `try` block. Inside the `catch` block, add code to display an error message dialog.

e) *Running the application.* Select **Debug > Start** to run your application. Enter invalid data as shown in Fig. 32.15 and click the **Calculate MPG** Button. A Message-Box should appear asking you to enter valid input. Enter valid input and click the **Calculate MPG** Button again. Verify that the correct output is displayed.

f) *Closing the application.* Close your running application by clicking its close box.

g) *Closing the IDE.* Close Visual Studio .NET by clicking its close box.

32.12 (*Enhanced Prime Numbers Application*) Modify the **Prime Numbers** application (Exercise 13.17) to use exception handling to process the `FormatExceptions` that occur when converting the `strings` in the `TextBoxes` to `ints` (Fig. 32.16). The original application took two numbers (representing a lower bound and an upper bound) and determined all of the prime numbers within the specified bounds, inclusive. An `int` greater than 1 is said to be prime if it is divisible by only 1 and itself. For example, 2, 3, 5 and 7 are prime numbers, but 4, 6, 8 and 9 are not.

a) *Copying the template to your working directory.* Copy the directory `C:\Examples\Tutorial32\Exercises\EnhancedPrimeNumbers` to your `C:\SimplyCSP` directory.

b) *Opening the application's template file.* Double click `PrimeNumbers.sln` in the `EnhancedPrimeNumbers` directory to open the application.

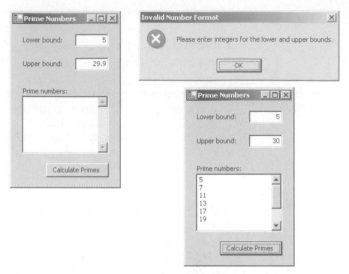

Figure 32.16 Enhanced **Prime Numbers** application's GUI.

c) *Adding a try block*. Find the btnCalculatePrimes_Click event handler. Enclose all the code following the variable declarations in a try block.

d) *Adding a catch block*. Add a catch block that catches any FormatExceptions that may occur in the try block you added to btnCalculatePrimes_Click in *Step c*. Inside the catch block, add code to display an error message dialog.

e) *Running the application.* Select **Debug > Start** to run your application. Enter invalid data as shown in Fig. 32.16 and click the **Calculate Primes** Button. A MessageBox should appear asking you to enter valid input. Enter valid input and click the **Calculate Primes** Button again. Verify that the correct output is displayed.

f) *Closing the application.* Close your running application by clicking its close box.

g) *Closing the IDE.* Close Visual Studio .NET by clicking its close box.

32.13 (*Enhanced Letterhead Designer Application*) Modify the **Letterhead** application (Exercise 26.13) to use exception handling to process the FileNotFoundException that may occur when the user specifies the image that will serve as the letterhead (Fig. 32.17). We will define what a FileNotFoundException is shortly. The application should still allow users to design stationery for company documents.

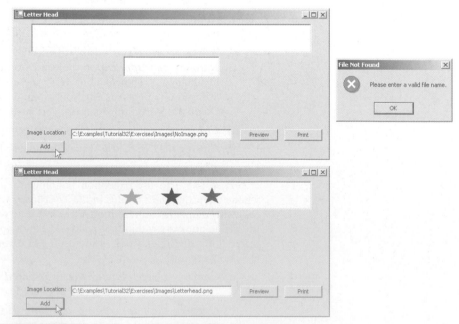

Figure 32.17 Enhanced **Letterhead** application.

a) *Copying the template to your working directory.* Copy the directory C:\Examples\ Tutorial32\Exercises\EnhancedLetterhead to your C:\SimplyCSP directory.

b) *Opening the application's template file.* Double click Letterhead.sln in the EnhancedLetterhead directory to open the application.

c) *Adding a try block to the btnAdd_Click event handler.* Find the btnAdd_Click event handler. Enclose the body of btnAdd_Click in a try block.

d) *Adding a catch block to the btnAdd_Click event handler.* Add a catch block that catches any FileNotFoundExceptions that may occur in the try block that you added in *Step c.* A **FileNotFoundException** is thrown when you attempt to access a file that does not exist. Inside the catch block, add code to display an error message dialog.

e) *Running the application.* Select **Debug > Start** to run your application. Enter an incorrect path for your image, and ensure that a MessageBox appears indicating the invalid input.

f) *Closing the application.* Close your running application by clicking its close box.

g) *Closing the IDE.* Close Visual Studio .NET by clicking its close box.

What does this code do? ▶ **32.14** What does the following code do, assuming that dblValue1 and dblValue2 are both declared as doubles?

```
1   try
2   {
3       dblValue1 = Double.Parse( txtInput1.Text );
4       dblValue2 = Double.Parse( txtInput2.Text );
5
6       txtOutput.Text = Convert.ToString( dblValue1 * dblValue2 );
7   }
8
9   catch ( FormatException formatExceptionParameter )
10  {
11      MessageBox.Show(
12          "Please enter decimal values.",
13          "Invalid Number Format",
14          MessageBoxButtons.OK, MessageBoxIcon.Error );
15  }
```

What's wrong with this code? ▶ **32.15** The following code should add integers from two TextBoxes and display the result in txtResult. Assume that intValue1 and intValue2 are declared as ints. Find the error(s) in the following code:

```
1   try
2   {
3       intValue1 = Int32.Parse( txtInput1.Text );
4       intValue2 = Int32.Parse( txtInput2.Text );
5
6       txtOutput.Text = Convert.ToString( intValue1 + intValue2 );
7
8       catch ( )
9       {
10          MessageBox.Show(
11              "Please enter valid ints.",
12              "Invalid Number Format",
13              MessageBoxButtons.OK, MessageBoxIcon.Error );
14      }
15  }
```

Programming Challenge ▶

32.16 (*Enhanced Vending Machine Application*) The **Vending Machine** application from Tutorial 3 has been modified to use exception handling to process the IndexOutOfRangeExceptions that occur when selecting items out of the range 0 through 7 (Fig. 32.18). This type of exception will be defined shortly. To get a snack, the user must type the number of the desired snack in the TextBox, then press the **Dispense Snack:** Button. The name of the snack is displayed in the output Label.

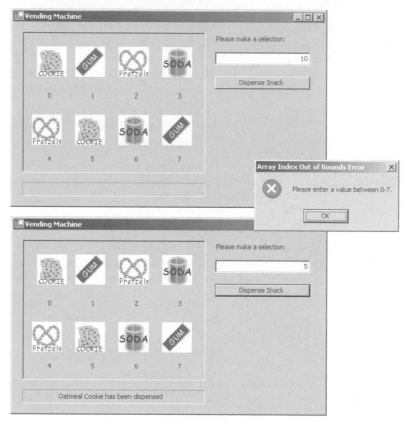

Figure 32.18 Enhanced **Vending Machine** application.

a) *Copying the template to your working directory.* Copy the directory C:\Examples\ Tutorial32\Exercises\EnhancedVendingMachine to your C:\SimplyCSP directory.

b) *Opening the application's template file.* Double click VendingMachine.sln in the EnhancedVendingMachine directory to open the application.

c) *Adding a try block.* Find the btnDispense_Click event handler. Enclose all of the code in the event handler in a try block.

d) *Adding a catch block.* Add a catch block that catches any FormatExceptions that may occur in the try block that you added to btnDispense_Click in *Step c*. Inside the catch block, add code to display an error message dialog.

e) *Adding a second catch block.* Immediately following the catch block you added in *Step c*, add a second catch block to catch any IndexOutOfRangeExceptions that may occur. An **IndexOutOfRangeException** occurs when the application attempts to access an array with an invalid index. Inside the catch block, add code to display an error message dialog.

f) *Running the application.* Select **Debug > Start** to run your application. Make an out of range selection (for instance, 32) and click the **Dispense Snack** Button. Verify that the proper MessageBox is displayed for the invalid input. Enter letters for a selection and click the **Dispense Snack** Button. Verify that the proper MessageBox is displayed for the invalid input.

g) *Closing the application.* Close your running application by clicking its close box.

h) *Closing the IDE.* Close Visual Studio .NET by clicking its close box.

Operator Precedence Chart

Operators are shown in decreasing order of precedence from top to bottom with each level of precedence separated by a horizontal line. C# operators associate from left to right. Parentheses may be used to increase the precedence of an expression or group several terms together.

Operator	Type
.	member access
[]	element access
()	method call
++	postfix increment
--	postfix decrement
new	object creation
typeof	typeof
checked	checked
unchecked	unchecked
!	logical negation
+	unary plus
-	unary minus
++	prefix increment
--	prefix decrement
~	unary bitwise complement
(*type*)	unary cast
*	multiplication
/	division
%	remainder
+	addition
-	subtraction
<<	left shift
>>	right shift

Figure A.1   Operator list (in order of operator precedence). (Part 1 of 2.)

Operator	Type
<	relational less than
<=	relational less than or equal to
>	relational greater than
>=	relational greater than or equal to
is	type comparison
as	conversion
==	relational is equal to
!=	relational is not equal to
&	bitwise AND
^	logical exclusive OR
|	bitwise inclusive OR
&&	logical AND
||	logical inclusive OR
?:	conditional
=	assignment
*=	multiplication and assignment
/=	division and assignment
%=	modulus and assignment
+=	addition and assignment
-=	subtraction and assignment
<<=	left shift assignment
>>=	right shift assignment
&=	logical AND assignment
^=	logical exclusive OR assignment
|=	logical inclusive OR assignment

Figure A.1   Operator list (in order of operator precedence). (Part 2 of 2.)

ASCII Character Set

The digits in the left column of Fig. B.1 are the left digits of the decimal equivalent (0–127) of the character code, and the digits in the top row of Fig. B.1 are the right digits of the character code. For example, the character code for "F" is 70, and the character code for "&" is 38.

Most users of this book are interested in the ASCII character set used to represent English characters on many computers. The ASCII character set is a subset of the Unicode® character set used by C# to represent characters from most of the world's languages.

	0	1	2	3	4	5	6	7	8	9
0	nul	soh	stx	etx	eot	enq	ack	bel	bs	ht
1	nl	vt	ff	cr	so	si	dle	dc1	dc2	dc3
2	dc4	nak	syn	etb	can	em	sub	esc	fs	gs
3	rs	us	sp	!	"	#	$	%	&	'
4	(	)	*	+	,	-	.	/	0	1
5	2	3	4	5	6	7	8	9	:	;
6	<	=	>	?	@	A	B	C	D	E
7	F	G	H	I	J	K	L	M	N	O
8	P	Q	R	S	T	U	V	W	X	Y
9	Z	[	\	]	^	_	'	a	b	c
10	d	e	f	g	h	i	j	k	l	m
11	n	o	p	q	r	s	t	u	v	w
12	x	y	z	{	|	}	~	del		

Figure B.1   ASCII character set.

GUI Design Guidelines

This appendix contains a complete list of the GUI design guidelines presented at the end of each tutorial. The guidelines are organized by tutorial; within each tutorial section, they are organized by control.

Tutorial 3: Welcome Application (Introduction to Visual Programming)

Overall Design

■ Use colors in your applications, but not to the point of distracting the user.

Forms

■ Choose short and descriptive Form titles. Capitalize words that are not articles, prepositions or conjunctions. Do not use punctuation.

■ Use **Tahoma** font to improve readability for controls that display text.

Labels

■ Use Labels to display text that users cannot change.

■ Ensure that all Label controls are large enough to display their text.

PictureBoxes

■ Use PictureBoxes to enhance GUIs with graphics that users cannot change.

■ Images should fit inside their PictureBoxes. This can be achieved by setting Picture-Box property SizeMode to StretchImage.

Tutorial 4: Designing the Inventory Application (Introducing TextBoxes and Buttons)

Overall Design

■ Leave at least two grid units between each group of controls on the Form.

■ Use a control's Location property to precisely specify its position on the Form.

■ Place an application's output below and/or to the right of the Form's input controls.

Buttons

■ Buttons are labelled using their Text property. These labels should use book-title capitalization and be as short as possible while still being meaningful to the user.

- Buttons should be stacked downward from the top right of a Form or arranged on the same line starting from the bottom right of a Form.

Forms

- Changing the Form's title allows users to identify the application's purpose.

- Form titles should use book-title capitalization.

- When sizing a Form, leave approximately two grid units of space between the edges of the Form and the controls that you will later add. This ensures that there is a uniform border around the Form. A grid unit is the distance between two adjacent dots on the Form in design view.

- Change the Form's font to Tahoma to be consistent with Microsoft's recommended font for Windows.

Labels

- A Label used to describe the purpose of a control should use sentence-style capitalization and end with a colon. These types of Labels are called descriptive Labels.

- A Label can be used to display output to the user.

- Place each descriptive Label either above or to the left of the control (for instance, a TextBox) that it identifies.

- A descriptive Label should have the same height as the TextBox it describes if the controls are arranged horizontally.

- A descriptive Label and the control it identifies should be left-aligned if they are arranged vertically.

- Align the left sides of a group of descriptive Labels if the Labels are arranged vertically.

- The TextAlign property of a descriptive Label should be set to MiddleLeft to ensure that text within groups of Labels align.

- The TextAlign property of a Label that displays the results of calculations should be set to MiddleCenter to distinguish the value from values in descriptive Labels.

- Output Labels should be distinguished from descriptive Labels by setting the BorderStyle property to Fixed3D and the TextAlign property to MiddleCenter.

- If several output Labels are arranged vertically to display numbers used in a mathematical calculation (such as in an invoice), set the TextAlign property of these Labels to MiddleRight.

- A descriptive Label and the control it identifies should be top-aligned if they are arranged horizontally.

TextBoxes

- Use TextBoxes to input data from the keyboard.

- Each TextBox should have a descriptive Label indicating the input expected from the user.

- Make TextBoxes wide enough for their expected inputs.

Tutorial 7: Wage Calculator Application (Introducing Algorithms, Pseudocode and Program Control)

Overall Design

- Format all monetary amounts using the C (currency) format specifier.

TextBox

- When using multiple TextBoxes vertically, align the TextBoxes on their right sides, and where possible make the TextBoxes the same size. Left-align the descriptive Labels for such TextBoxes.

Tutorial 8: Dental Payment Application (Introducing CheckBoxes and Message Dialogs)

CheckBoxes

- A CheckBox's label should be descriptive and as short as possible. When a CheckBox label contains more than one word, use book-title capitalization.

■ Align groups of CheckBoxes either horizontally or vertically.

Message Dialogs

■ Text displayed in a dialog should be descriptive and as short as possible.

Tutorial 9: Car Payment Calculator Application (*Introducing the* `while` *Repetition Statement*)

ListBox

■ A ListBox should be large enough to display all of its contents or large enough that scrollbars may be used easily.

■ Use headers in a ListBox when you are displaying tabular data. Adding headers improves readability by indicating the information that will be displayed in the ListBox.

Tutorial 10: Class Average Application (*Introducing the* `do...while` *Repetition Statement*)

Button

■ Disable Buttons when function should not be available to the user.

■ Enable a disabled Button when its function should be available to the user once again.

Tutorial 11: Interest Calculator Application (*Introducing the* `for` *Repetition Statement*)

TextBox

■ If a TextBox will display multiple lines of output, set the Multiline property to true and left-align the output by setting the TextAlign property to Left.

■ If a multiline TextBox will display many lines of output, limit the TextBox height and use a vertical scrollbar to allow users to view additional lines of output.

NumericUpDown

■ A NumericUpDown control should follow the same GUI Design Guidelines as a TextBox.

■ Use a NumericUpDown control to limit the range of user input.

Tutorial 12: Security Panel Application (*Introducing* `switch` *Multiple Selection Statement*)

Overall Design

■ If your GUI is modeling a real-world object, its design should mimic the physical appearance of the object.

TextBox

■ Mask passwords and other sensitive pieces of information in TextBoxes.

Tutorial 14: Shipping Time Application (*Using DateTimes and Timers*)

DateTimePicker

■ Use a DateTimePicker to retrieve date and time information from the user.

■ Each DateTimePicker should have a corresponding descriptive Label.

■ If the user should specify a time of day or a date and time, set the DateTimePicker's ShowUpDown property to true. If the user should specify a date, set the DateTimePicker's ShowUpDown property to false to allow the user to select a day from the month calendar.

GroupBox

■ GroupBox titles should be concise and should use book-title capitalization.

■ Use GroupBoxes to group related controls on the Form visually.

Tutorial 17: Flag Quiz Application (Introducing One-Dimensional Arrays and ComboBoxes)

ComboBoxes

- ■ Each ComboBox should have a descriptive Label that describes the ComboBox's contents.
- ■ If a ComboBox's content should not be editable, set its DropDownStyle property to Drop-DownList.

Tutorial 18: Student Grades Application (Introducing Two-Dimensional Arrays and RadioButtons)

RadioButton

- ■ Use RadioButtons when the user should choose only one option from a group.
- ■ Always place each group of RadioButtons in a separate container (such as a GroupBox).
- ■ Align groups of RadioButtons either horizontally or vertically.

Tutorial 19: Microwave Oven Application (Building Your Own Classes and Objects)

Panel

- ■ Use Panels to organize groups of related controls where the purpose of those controls is obvious. If the purpose of the controls is not obvious, use a GroupBox in place of a Panel, because GroupBoxes can contain captions.
- ■ A Panel can display scrollbars if that Panel is not large enough to display all of its controls at once. To increase readability, we suggest avoiding the use of scrollbars on Panels. If a Panel is not large enough to display all of its contents, increase the size of the Panel.
- ■ Although it is possible to have a Panel without a border (by setting the BorderStyle property to None), use borders on your Panels to increase readability and organization.

Tutorial 20: Shipping Hub Application (Introducing Collections, the foreach Statement and Access Keys)

Overall Design

- ■ Set a control's TabStop property to true only if the control is used to receive user input.
- ■ Use the TabIndex property to define the logical order in which the user should enter data. Usually the order transfers the focus of the application from top to bottom and left to right.
- ■ Use access keys to allow users to "click" a control using the keyboard.

Tutorial 22: Typing Application (Introducing Keyboard Events, Menus and Dialogs)

MainMenu

- ■ Use book-title capitalization in menu item text.
- ■ Use separator bars in a menu to group related menu items.
- ■ If clicking a menu item opens a dialog, an ellipsis (…) should follow the menu item's text.

Tutorial 27: Phone Book Application (Introducing Multimedia Using Microsoft Agent)

Microsoft Agent Control

- ■ Locate the Microsoft Agent character near the application's Form.
- ■ Use Microsoft Agent character gestures to indicate actions the user should take, or a response to an action the user has already taken.

APPENDIX

Visual Studio .NET Windows Form Designer Tools

This book presents some 20 different controls available in Visual Studio .NET. In all, there are 47 items available to you by default in the **Toolbox**. This appendix contains a chart (Fig. D.1) indicating the purpose and usage of each of these controls. A list of Web resources can be found after the chart.

Icon	Item	Purpose	Usage
	Pointer	Allows you to select and modify elements in the IDE. The pointer is not a control.	Used to navigate a GUI.
	Button	Allows users to indicate that an action should be performed.	Most commonly used to execute code when clicked.
	CheckBox	Allows the user to select or deselect an option.	Becomes checked when selected and unchecked when deselected.
	CheckedList-Box	Provides the user with a checkable list of items.	Much like a CheckBox, but all options are contained in a format similar to that of a ListBox.
	ColorDialog	Allows the user to display the Windows **Color** dialog.	Retrieve the user's color selection in an application.
	ComboBox	Provides a short list of items in a drop-down menu.	Allow the user to view, enter new text in or search with a search string from multiple items in a list.
	ContextMenu	Displays a menu of programmer-defined options when the user right-clicks an object.	Provide additional options or features as a shortcut.

Figure D.1 Visual Studio .NET Windows Form Designer Tools. (Part 1 of 4.)

Icon	Item	Purpose	Usage
	DataGrid	Displays data within a chart.	Represent ADO .NET data in a scrollable chart.
	DateTime-Picker	Allows users to choose the date and time.	Display or allow the selection of a time and date.
	DomainUpDown	Displays string values, using the up and down arrows.	Select strings from an object collection.
	ErrorProvider	Displays errors regarding a control to the user.	Inform the user if there is an error associated with the control.
	Folder-BrowserDialog	Displays a dialog that enables the user to browse and select a folder.	Enables the browsing and selection of a folder (not files).
	FontDialog	Displays a font dialog that includes all available fonts installed on the computer.	Used to retrieve a user-specified font format and size in an application.
	GroupBox	Allows controls to be grouped together.	Organize related controls separately from the rest of the Form.
	HelpProvider	Provides additional help features for a specific control.	Create additional help features for a control.
	HScrollBar	A horizontal scrollbar.	Allow users to view text or graphics that may be too large to display horizontally in a control.
	ImageList	A manageable list of images.	Store a list of images for use in other controls, such as a ListView or menu.
	Label	Displays text to the user.	Identify specific items on the Form or display general-purpose text.
	LinkLabel	Similar to a Label control but can include hyperlinks.	Display a hyperlink label that, when clicked, will open a file or Web page.
	ListBox	Provides a list of items.	Allow the user to view and select from multiple items in a list.
	ListView	Displays a group of items with identifiable icons.	Display a list of items (such as files) much like Windows Explorer.
	MainMenu	Creates a menu object on a Form.	Allow users to select options from menus, adding functionality to the application.
	MonthCalendar	Allows the user to select the date and time from a calendar that displays one month at a time.	Retrieve the user's date selection from a calendar.

Figure D.1 Visual Studio .NET Windows **Form** Designer Tools. (Part 2 of 4.)

Icon	Item	Purpose	Usage
	NotifyIcon	Creates icons that are displayed in a status area, usually while an action is performed in the background.	Remind the user that a certain process is running in the background of the application.
	NumericUpDown	Contains a number that is increased or decreased by clicking the up or down arrows.	Allow the user to specify a number in programmer-defined increments.
	OpenFile-Dialog	Displays a dialog to assist the user in selecting a file.	Retrieve user's file-name selection.
	PageSetup-Dialog	Displays a dialog to allow the user to change a document's page properties.	Allow the user to modify the page settings and printer options.
	Panel	Similar to a GroupBox, but can include a scrollbar.	Group controls separately on the Form.
	PictureBox	Displays images.	Allow users to view graphics in an application.
	PrintDialog	Allows the user to select a printer and printing options.	Shown to retrieve user selection for printing options.
	PrintDocument	Executes the printing process.	Accessed to print documents.
	PrintPreview-Control	Allows the user to preview a document before printing it.	Display a preview of the document.
	PrintPreview-Dialog	A dialog used to display a PrintPreviewControl.	Display a print-preview dialog.
	ProgressBar	Displays a visual representation of the progress of an action or set of actions.	Inform the user of the completeness of an operation.
	RadioButton	Provides the user with a list of options from which only one or none can be selected.	Allow the users to select at most one of several options.
	RichTextBox	Creates a TextBox control with advanced text-editing capabilities.	Allow the user to perform more sophisticated editing beyond the features of a TextBox.
	SaveFile-Dialog	Assists the user in selecting a location in which to save a file.	Allow files to be saved.
	Splitter	Allows the user to resize a docked control within an application.	Enable the user to change the size of a control.
	StatusBar	Display useful information regarding the Form or objects in the application.	Notify the user of information not intended for the body of a Form.

Figure D.1   Visual Studio .NET Windows **Form** Designer Tools. (Part 3 of 4.)

Icon	Item	Purpose	Usage
	TabControl	Displays available tab pages in which you can place other controls.	Allow multiple tab pages on a **Form**.
|abl|	TextBox	Accepts user input from the keyboard. Can also be used to display text.	Used to retrieve user input from the keyboard.
	Timer	Performs an action at programmer-specified intervals. A Timer is not visible to the user.	Allow the action of an event through a specific amount of time.
	ToolBar	Contains icons representing specific commands.	Provide the user with options in a toolbar.
	ToolTip	Display text information about an object when the mouse cursor is over it.	Display additional information to the user.
	TrackBar	Allow the user to set a value from a specified range.	Similar to the scrollbar, but includes a range of values.
	TreeView	Displays a tree structure of objects, using nodes.	Display a hierarchical representation of a collection of objects.
	VScrollBar	Allow the user to view text or graphics that may be too large to display vertically in a control.	Enable a vertical scrollbar in the control.

Figure D.1   Visual Studio .NET Windows **Form** Designer Tools. (Part 4 of 4.)

D.1 Internet and Web Resources

A great way to learn about controls not covered in this book is to use them. Several Web sites provide information to help you get started. The following sites should help you as you explore new features of Visual Studio .NET:

msdn.microsoft.com/library/default.asp?url=/library/en-us/vbcon/ html/vbconSelectingWFCClientControl.asp
This site provides documentation for the most commonly used Windows **Form** controls, grouped by function.

dotnet247.com/247reference/guide/48.aspx
This site provides articles describing features and usage of common controls in .NET. You will also find links to discussions of more advanced topics in .NET.

msdn.microsoft.com/library/default.asp?url=/library/en-us/vbcon/ html/vboricontrolsforwinforms.asp
This Web page provides a more technical description of controls you can use on a Windows **Form**.

Controls, Events, Properties & Methods

This appendix contains a listing of controls and predefined classes used in the text. Each control or class includes a description of its purpose, as well as explanations of events, properties and methods related to that control or class, as covered in the text.

Tutorial 1: Graphing Application (Introducing Computers, the Internet and C#)

No new elements.

Tutorial 2: Welcome Application (Introducing the Visual Studio® .NET IDE)

No new elements.

Tutorial 3: Welcome Application (Introduction to Visual Programming)

Label   A Label   This control displays on the Form text that the user cannot modify.

■ *In action*

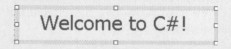

■ *Properties*

Text—Specifies the text displayed on the Label.

Font—Specifies the font name, style and size of the text displayed in the Label.

TextAlign—Determines how the text is aligned within the Label.

PictureBox   PictureBox   This control displays an image on the Form.

■ *In action*

■ *Properties*

Image—Specifies the file path of the image.

SizeMode—Specifies how an image is displayed in the PictureBox.

Size—Specifies the height and width (in pixels) of the PictureBox.

Tutorial 4: Designing the Inventory Application (Introducing TextBoxes and Buttons)

Button   Button   This control allows the user to raise an action or event.

■ *In action*

Calculate Total

■ *Properties*

Name—Specifies the name used to access the Button programmatically. The name should be prefixed with btn.

Size—Specifies the height and width (in pixels) of the Button.

Text—Specifies the text displayed on the Button.

Label   A Label   This control displays text that the user cannot modify.

■ *In action*

Total:

■ *Properties*

BorderStyle—Specifies the appearance of the Label's border.

Font—Specifies the font name, style and size of the text displayed in the Label.

Location—Specifies the location of the Label on the Form relative to the Form's top-left corner.

Name—Specifies the name used to access the Label programatically (i.e., in a program). The name should be prefixed with lbl.

Size—Specifies the height and width (in pixels) of the Label.

Text—Specifies the text displayed in the Label.

TextAlign—Determines how the text is aligned within the Label.

TextBox   TextBox   This control allows the user to input data from the keyboard.

■ *In action*

■ *Properties*

Name—Specifies the name used to access the TextBox programmatically. The name should be prefixed with txt.

Size—Specifies the height and width (in pixels) of the TextBox.

Text—Specifies the text displayed in the TextBox.

TextAlign—Specifies how the text is aligned within the TextBox.

Tutorial 5: Completing the Inventory Application (Introducing Programming)

Button   `ab|  Button`   This control allows the user to raise an action or event.

- ■ *In action*

    Calculate Total

- ■ *Event*

    Click—Raised when the user clicks the Button.

- ■ *Properties*

    Location—Specifies the location of the Button on the Form relative to the top-left corner.

    Name—Specifies the name used to access the Button programmatically. The name should be prefixed with btn.

    Size—Specifies the height and width (in pixels) of the Button.

    Text—Specifies the text displayed on the Button.

Convert Class containing methods to change between types.

- ■ *Method*

    ToString—Converts its argument into a value of type string.

Int32 Class that represents an integer.

- ■ *Methods*

    Parse—Converts the given string of characters to a value of type int.

Tutorial 6: Enhancing the Inventory Application (Introducing Variables, Memory Concepts and Arithmetic)

TextBox   `ab|  TextBox`   This control allows the user to input data from the keyboard.

- ■ *In action*

- ■ *Event*

    TextChanged—Raised when the text in the TextBox is changed.

- ■ *Properties*

    Location—Specifies the location of the Label on the Form relative to the top-left corner.

    Name—Specifies the name used to access the TextBox programmatically. The name should be prefixed with txt.

    Size—Specifies the height and width (in pixels) of the TextBox.

    Text—Specifies the text displayed in the TextBox.

    TextAlign—Specifies how the text is aligned within the TextBox.

Tutorial 7: Wage Calculator Application (Introducing Algorithms, Pseudocode and Program Control)

Decimal Represents a monetary value.

- ■ *Method*

Parse—Converts the given string of characters to a value of type `decimal`.

Double Represents a floating-point number (one with a decimal point).

■ *Method*

Parse—Converts the given string of characters to a value of type `double`.

String Represents a series of characters treated as a single unit.

■ *Method*

Format—Arranges the string of characters in a specified format.

Tutorial 8: Dental Payment Application (Introducing CheckBoxes and Message Dialogs)

CheckBox   ☑ CheckBox   This control allows the user to select an option.

■ *In action*

☑ Cleaning
☐ Cavity Filling

■ *Properties*

Checked—Specifies whether the CheckBox is checked (`true`) or unchecked (`false`).

Location—Specifies the location of the CheckBox on the Form.

Name—Specifies the name used to access the CheckBox control programmatically. The name should be prefixed with chk.

Text—Specifies the text displayed next to the CheckBox.

Tutorial 9: Car Payment Calculator Application (Introducing the `while` Repetition Statement)

Math The Math class performs mathematical operations.

■ *Method*

Pow—Raises a given base (first argument) to a given exponent (second argument) and returns the result as a `double`.

ListBox   ▤ ListBox   This control allows the user to view and select from items in a list.

■ *In action*

Months	Monthly Payments
24	$490.50
36	$339.06
48	$263.55
60	$218.41

■ *Properties*

Items—Returns an object that contains the items displayed in the ListBox.

Location—Specifies the location of the ListBox on the Form.

Name—Specifies the name used to access the properties of the ListBox programatically. The name should be prefixed with lst.

Size—Specifies the height and width (in pixels) of the ListBox.

■ *Methods*

Items.Add—Adds an item to the Items property.

Items.Clear—Deletes all the values in the ListBox's Items property.

Tutorial 10: Class Average Application (Introducing the do...while Repetition Statement)

Button This control allows the user to raise an action or event.

■ *In action*

> Calculate Total

■ *Event*

Click—Raised when the user clicks the Button.

■ *Properties*

Enabled—Determines whether the Button's event handler executes when the Button is clicked.

Location—Specifies the location of the Button on the Form relative to the top-left corner.

Name—Specifies the name used to access the Button programmatically. The name should be prefixed with btn.

Size—Specifies the height and width (in pixels) of the Button.

Text—Specifies the text displayed on the Button.

■ *Method*

Focus—Transfers the focus of the application to the Button that calls it.

ListBox ListBox This control allows the user to view and select from items in a list.

■ *In action*

Months	Monthly Payments
24	$490.50
36	$339.06
48	$263.55
60	$218.41

■ *Properties*

Items—Returns an object that contains the items displayed in the ListBox.

Items.Count—Returns the number of items in the ListBox.

Location—Specifies the location of the ListBox on the Form relative to the top-left corner.

Name—Specifies the name used to access the ListBox programmatically. The name should be prefixed with lst.

Size—Specifies the height and width (in pixels) of the ListBox.

■ *Methods*

Items.Add—Adds an item to the Items property.

Items.Clear—Deletes all the values in the ListBox's Items property.

TextBox TextBox This control allows the user to input data from the keyboard.

■ *In action*

■ *Event*

TextChanged—Raised when the text in the TextBox is changed.

■ *Properties*

Location—Specifies the location of the TextBox on the Form relative to the top-left corner.

Name—Specifies the name used to access the TextBox programmatically. The name should be prefixed with txt.

Size—Specifies the height and width (in pixels) of the TextBox.

Text—Specifies the text displayed in the TextBox.

TextAlign—Specifies how the text is aligned within the TextBox.

■ *Methods*

Clear—Removes the text in the TextBox.

Focus—Transfers the focus of the application to the TextBox that calls it.

Tutorial 11: Interest Calculator Application (Introducing the for Repetition Statement)

NumericUpDown  This control allows you to specify maximum and minimum numeric input values.

■ *In action*

■ *Properties*

Increment—Specifies by how much the current number in the NumericUpDown control changes when the user clicks the control's up (for incrementing) or down (for decrementing) arrow.

Location—Specifies the location of the NumericUpDown control on the Form relative to the top-left corner.

Maximum—Determines the maximum input value in a particular NumericUpDown control.

Minimum—Determines the minimum input value in a particular NumericUpDown control.

Name—Specifies the name used to access the NumericUpDown control programmatically. The name should be prefixed with upd.

ReadOnly—Determines whether the input value can be typed by the user.

Size—Specifies the height and width (in pixels) of the NumericUpDown control.

TextAlign—Specifies how the text is aligned within the NumericUpDown control.

TextBox labl TextBox This control allows the user to input data from the keyboard.

■ *In action*

■ *Event*

TextChanged—Raised when the text in the TextBox is changed.

■ *Properties*

Location—Specifies the location of the TextBox on the Form relative to the top-left corner.

Multiline—Specifies whether the TextBox is capable of displaying multiple lines of text.

Name—Specifies the name used to access the TextBox programmatically. The name should be prefixed with txt.

ReadOnly—Determines whether the value of a TextBox can be changed.

ScrollBars—Specifies whether a TextBox has a scrollbar and, if so, of what type. By default, the ScrollBars property set to None. Setting the value to Vertical places a scrollbar along the right side of the TextBox.

Size—Specifies the height and width (in pixels) of the TextBox.

Text—Specifies the text displayed in the TextBox.

TextAlign—Specifies how the text is aligned within the TextBox.

■ *Method*

Focus—Transfers the focus of the application to the TextBox that calls it.

Tutorial 12: Security Panel Application (Introducing the `switch` Multiple-Selection Statement)

TextBox [abl TextBox]   This control allows the user to input data from the keyboard.

■ *In action*

> [0]

■ *Event*

TextChanged—Raised when the text in the TextBox is changed.

■ *Properties*

Enabled—Determines whether the user can enter data (true) in the TextBox or not (false).

Location—Specifies the location of the TextBox on the Form relative to the top-left corner.

Multiline—Specifies whether the TextBox is capable of displaying multiple lines of text.

Name—Specifies the name used to access the TextBox programmatically. The name should be prefixed with txt.

PasswordChar—Specifies the masking character to be used when displaying data in the TextBox.

ReadOnly—Determines whether the value of a TextBox can be changed.

ScrollBars—Specifies whether the TextBox contains a scrollbar.

Size—Specifies the height and width (in pixels) of the TextBox.

Text—Specifies the text displayed in the TextBox.

TextAlign—Specifies how the text is aligned within the TextBox.

■ *Method*

Focus—Transfers the focus of the application to the TextBox that calls it.

Tutorial 13: Enhancing the Wage Calculator Application (Introducing Methods)

Math This class provides methods used to perform common arithmetic calculations.

■ *Methods*

Min—Returns the smaller of two numeric values.

Max—Returns the larger of two numeric values.

Pow—Raises a given base (first argument) to a given exponent (second argument) and returns the result as a double.

Sqrt—Returns the square root of a numeric value.

Tutorial 14: Shipping Time Application (Using DateTimes and Timers)

DateTime This structure provides properties and methods to store and manipulate date and time information.

■ *Properties*

Day—Returns the day stored in a DateTime variable.

Hour—Returns the hour stored in a DateTime variable.

Month—Returns the month stored in a DateTime variable.

Now—Returns the system's current date and time.

Year—Returns the year stored in a DateTime variable.

■ *Methods*

AddDays—Creates a new DateTime value that is the specified number of days later (or earlier) in time.

AddHours—Creates a new DateTime value that is the specified number of hours later (or earlier) in time.

AddMinutes—Creates a new DateTime value that is the specified number of minutes later (or earlier) in time.

ToLongDateString—Returns a string containing the date in the format "Wednesday, October 30, 2002."

ToShortTimeString—Returns a string containing the time in the format "4:00 PM."

DateTimePicker   ▦ DateTimePicker   This control is used to retrieve date and time information from the user.

■ *In action*

DateTimePicker using default format

■ *Event*

ValueChanged—Raised when the Value property is changed.

■ *Properties*

CustomFormat—Sets which format string to use when displaying the date and/or time.

Format—Specifies the format in which the date and time are displayed on the control.

    Long—Specifies that the date should be displayed in the format "Monday, December 09, 2002."

    Short—Specifies that the date should be displayed in the format "12/9/2002."

    Time—Specifies that the time should be displayed in the format "8:39:53 PM."

    Custom—Allows the programmer to specify a custom format in which to display the date and/or time.

Hour—Stores the hour in the DateTimePicker control.

Location—Specifies the location of the DateTimePicker control on its container relative to the container's top-left corner.

MinDate—Specifies the minimum date and/or time that can be selected when using this control.

MaxDate—Specifies the maximum date and/or time that can be selected when using this control.

Name—Specifies the name used to access the DateTimePicker control programmatically. The name should be prefixed with dtp.

ShowUpDown—Specifies whether the up-down arrows are displayed on the control for time values (true). If false, a down arrow is displayed for accessing a drop-down calendar.

Value—Stores the date and/or time in the DateTimePicker control.

GroupBox   ⬚ GroupBox   This control groups related controls visually.

■ *In action*

■ *Properties*

Name—Specifies the name used to access the GroupBox control programmatically. The name should be prefixed with fra.

Location—Specifies the location of the GroupBox control on the Form.

Size—Specifies the height and width (in pixels) of the GroupBox control.

Text—Specifies the text displayed on the GroupBox.

Timer This control wakes up at specified intervals of time to execute code in its Tick event handler.

- ■ *Event*

  Tick—Raised after the number of milliseconds specified in the Interval property has elapsed.

- ■ *Properties*

  Enabled—Determines whether the Timer is running (true). The default is false.

  Interval—Determines the time interval between Tick events.

  Name—Specifies the name used to access the Timer control programmatically. The name should be prefixed with tmr.

Tutorial 15: Fund Raiser Application (Introducing Scope and Pass-by-Reference)

No new elements.

Tutorial 16: Craps Game Application (Introducing Random-Number Generation)

Directory This class provides functionality to manipulate directories such as creating, moving, and navigating through them.

- ■ *Method*

  GetCurrentDirectory—Returns the location of the directory from which the application was loaded.

Image This class provides functionality to manipulate images.

- ■ *Method*

  FromFile—Used to specify the physical location (path) of the image.

Random This class is used to generate random numbers.

- ■ *Methods*

  Next—When called with no arguments, generates a positive int value between zero and the largest possible int, which is the constant Int32.MaxValue (2,147,483,647).

  NextDouble—Generates a positive double value that is greater than or equal to 0.0 and less than 1.0.

Tutorial 17: Flag Quiz Application (Introducing One-Dimensional Arrays and ComboBoxes)

ComboBox Allows users to select from a drop-down list of options.

- ■ *In action*

Australia ▼
Australia
Brazil
China
Italy

- ■ *Properties*

  DataSource—Specifies the source of items listed in a ComboBox.

  DropDownStyle—Specifies a ComboBox's appearance.

  Enabled—Specifies whether a user can select an item from the ComboBox.

`Location`—Specifies the location of the `ComboBox` control on the container control relative to the top-left corner.

`MaxDropDownItems`—Specifies the maximum number of items the `ComboBox` can display in its drop-down list.

`Name`—Specifies the name used to access the `ComboBox` control programmatically. The name should be prefixed with `cbo`.

`SelectedIndex`—Returns the index of the selected item, or –1 if no item is selected.

`SelectedValue`—Specifies the selected item.

`Size`—Specifies the height and width (in pixels) of the `ComboBox` control.

Array This data structure stores a fixed number of elements of the same type.

- *Property*

`Length`—Specifies the number of elements in the array.

- *Methods*

`GetUpperBound`—Returns the largest index of the array.

`Sort`—Orders an array's elements. An array of numerical values would be organized in ascending order and an array of `strings` would be organized in alphabetical order.

String The `String` class represents a series of characters treated as a single unit.

- *Methods*

`Format`—Arranges the `string` in a specified format.

`IndexOf`—Returns the index of the specified character(s) in a `string`.

`Insert`—Returns a copy of the `string` for which it is called with the specified character(s) inserted.

`Remove`—Returns a copy of the `string` for which it is called with the specified character(s) removed.

`ToLower`—Returns a copy of the `string` for which it is called with any uppercase letters converted to lowercase letters.

Tutorial 18: Student Grades Application (Introducing Two-Dimensional Arrays and RadioButtons)

RadioButton   This component is used to enable users to select only one of several options.

- *In action*

- *Event*

`CheckedChanged`—Raised when the control is either selected or deselected.

- *Properties*

`Checked`—Set to `true` if the control is selected and `false` if it is not selected.

`Location`—Specifies the location of the `RadioButton` control on the container control relative to the top-left corner.

`Name`—Specifies the name used to access the `RadioButton` control programmatically. The name should be prefixed with `rad`.

`Size`—Specifies the height and width (in pixels) of the `RadioButton` control.

`Text`—Specifies the text displayed in the label to the right of the `RadioButton`.

Tutorial 19: Microwave Oven Application (Building Your Own Classes and Objects)

Button   This control allows the user to raise an action or event.

- ■ *In action*

- ■ *Event*

    Click—Raised when the user clicks the Button.

- ■ *Properties*

    Enabled—Determines whether the Button's event handler is executed when the Button is clicked.

    FlatStyle—Determines whether the Button will appear flat or three-dimensional.

    Flat—Specifies that a Button will appear flat.

    Location—Specifies the location of the Button on the Form relative to the top-left corner.

    Name—Specifies the name used to access the Button programmatically. The name should be prefixed with btn.

    Size—Specifies the height and width (in pixels) of the Button.

    Text—Specifies the text displayed on the Button.

- ■ *Method*

    Focus—Transfers the focus of the application to the Button that calls it.

Convert The Convert class converts the value of a type to another type.

- ■ *Method*

    ToChar—Converts a value into a character (of the char type).

Panel ☐ Panel This control is used to organize various controls. Unlike the Group-Box control, the Panel control does not display a caption.

- ■ *In action*

Panel ————————— 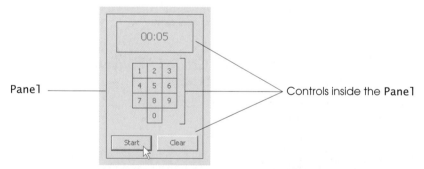 ————————> Controls inside the Panel

- ■ *Properties*

    BackColor—Specifies the background color of the Panel.

    BorderStyle—Specifies the Panel's border style.

    None—Specifies that the Panel's will not display a border.

    FixedSingle—Specifies that the Panel will display a thin, black border.

    Fixed3D—Specifies that the Panel will display a three-dimensional border.

    Location—Specifies the Panel's location on the Form.

    Name—Specifies the name of the Panel. The name should be prefixed with pnl.

    Size—Specifies the size of the Panel.

String The String class represents a series of characters treated as a single unit.

- ■ *Property*

    Length—Returns the number of characters in the string.

- ■ *Methods*

    Format—Arranges the string in a specified format.

    IndexOf—Returns the index of the specified character(s) in a string.

Insert—Returns a copy of the `string` for which it is called with the specified character(s) inserted.

PadLeft—Inserts characters at the beginning of a `string`.

Remove—Returns a copy of the `string` for which it is called with the specified character(s) removed.

Substring—Returns a substring from a `string`.

ToLower—Returns a copy of the `string` for which it is called with any uppercase letters converted to lowercase letters.

SystemColors The `SystemColors` class contains color properties for the various Windows controls.

- *Property*

  Control—Returns the default color of several controls, including `Panel`s.

Tutorial 20: Shipping Hub Application (Introducing Collections, the foreach Statement and Access Keys)

ArrayList This class is used to store a variable number of objects.

- *Property*

  Count—Returns the number of objects contained in the `ArrayList`.

- *Methods*

  Add—Adds an object to the `ArrayList` object.

  Insert—Adds an object to the `ArrayList` object at a specific index.

  RemoveAt—Removes an object from the `ArrayList` object at the specified index.

ComboBox   This control allows users to select options from a drop-down list.

- *In action*

- *Event*

  SelectedIndexChanged—Raised when a new value is selected in the ComboBox.

- *Properties*

  DataSource—Allows you to add items to the ComboBox.

  DropDownStyle—Determines the ComboBox's style.

  Enabled—Determines whether the user can enter data (`true`) in the ComboBox.

  Items—Specifies the values the user can select from the ComboBox.

     Item—Retrieves the value at the specified index.

  Location—Specifies the location of the ComboBox control on its container control relative to the top-left corner.

  MaxDropDownItems—Determines the maximum number of items to be displayed when user clicks the drop-down arrow.

  Name—Specifies the name used to access the ComboBox control programmatically. The name should be prefixed with `cbo`.

  SelectedValue—Contains the item selected by the user.

  Text—Specifies the text displayed in the ComboBox.

TextBox abl TextBox   This control allows the user to input data from the keyboard.

- *In action*

  0

- ■ *Event*

  TextChanged—Raised when the text in the TextBox is changed.

- ■ *Properties*

  Enabled—Determines whether the user can enter data (true) in the TextBox or not (false).

  Location—Specifies the location of the TextBox on its container control relative to the top-left corner.

  MaxLength—Specifies the maximum number of characters that can be input into the TextBox.

  Multiline—Specifies whether the TextBox is capable of displaying multiple lines of text.

  Name—Specifies the name used to access the TextBox programmatically. The name should be prefixed with txt.

  PasswordChar—Specifies the masking character to be used when displaying data in the TextBox.

  ReadOnly—Determines whether the value of a TextBox can be changed.

  ScrollBars—Specifies whether a multiline TextBox contains a scrollbar.

  Size—Specifies the height and width (in pixels) of the TextBox.

  Text—Specifies the text displayed in the TextBox.

  TextAlign—Specifies how the text is aligned within the TextBox.

- ■ *Method*

  Focus—Transfers the focus of the application to the TextBox that calls it.

Tutorial 21: "Cat and Mouse" Painter Application (Introducing the Graphics Object and Mouse Events)

Form This class represents an application's GUI.

- ■ *Events*

  Load—Raised when an application initially executes.

  MouseDown—Raised when a mouse button is clicked.

  MouseMove—Raised when the mouse pointer is moved.

  MouseUp—Raised when a mouse button is released.

- ■ *Method*

  CreateGraphics—Creates a Graphics object.

- ■ *Property*

  BackColor—Specifies the background color of the Form.

Graphics This class contains methods used to draw text, lines and shapes.

- ■ *Method*

  FillEllipse—Draws a solid ellipse of a specified size and color at the specified location.

MouseEventArgs This class contains information about mouse events.

- ■ *Properties*

  Button—Specifies which (if any) mouse button was pressed.

  X—Specifies the *x*-coordinate of the mouse event.

  Y—Specifies the *y*-coordinate of the mouse event.

Tutorial 22: Typing Application (Introducing Keyboard Events, Menus and Dialogs)

Char This structure stores characters, such as letters and symbols.

- ■ *Method*

  ToUpper—Returns the uppercase equivalent of an alphabetic character.

ColorDialog   ColorDialog   This control allows the user to customize the
color of what is being typed.

■ *Properties*

Color—Contains the color selected by the user. The default color is black.

FullOpen—When true, displays an extended color palette. If this property is set to
false, a dialog with less options is displayed.

■ *Method*

ShowDialog—Displays the **Color** dialog to the user.

FontDialog   FontDialog   This control allows the user to customize the
font, size and style of what is being typed.

■ *Method*

ShowDialog—Displays the **Font** dialog to the user.

KeyEventArgs This class represents arguments passed to the KeyPress event handler.

■ *Property*

KeyData—Contains data about the key that raised the KeyDown event.

KeyPressEventArgs This class represents arguments passed to the KeyPress event handler.

■ *Property*

KeyChar—Contains data about the key that raised the KeyPress event.

MenuItem This class represents menu items.

■ *In action*

![File Format menu with About highlighted and Exit below]

■ *Event*

Click—Raised when the user clicks a menu item or presses a shortcut key that represents
an item.

TextBox   abl TextBox   This control allows the user to input data from the
keyboard.

■ *In action*

![TextBox showing 0]

■ *Events*

KeyDown—Raised when a key is pressed. KeyDown is case insensitive. It cannot recognize
lowercase letters.

KeyPress—Raised when a key is pressed. KeyPress cannot handle modifier keys.

KeyUp—Raised when a key is released by the user.

TextChanged—Raised when the text in the TextBox is changed.

■ *Properties*

Enabled—Determines whether the user can enter data (true) in the TextBox (false).

Location—Specifies the location of the TextBox on the container control relative to the
top-left corner.

MaxLength—Specifies the maximum number of characters that can be input into the
TextBox.

Multiline—Specifies whether the TextBox is capable of displaying multiple lines of text.

Name—Specifies the name used to access the TextBox programmatically. The name should be prefixed with txt.

PasswordChar—Specifies the masking character to be used when displaying data in the TextBox.

ReadOnly—Determines whether the value of a TextBox can be changed.

ScrollBars—Specifies whether the TextBox contains a scrollbar.

Size—Specifies the height and width (in pixels) of the TextBox.

Text—Specifies the text displayed in the TextBox.

TextAlign—Specifies how the text is aligned within the TextBox.

- *Method*

Focus—Transfers the focus of the application to the TextBox that calls it.

Tutorial 23: Screen Scraping Application (Introducing string Processing)

String The String class represents a series of characters treated as a single unit.

- *Property*

Length—Returns the number of characters in the string.

- *Methods*

EndsWith—Determines if a string ends with a particular substring.

Format—Arranges the string in a specified format.

IndexOf—Returns the index of the specified character(s) in a string.

Insert—Returns a copy of the string for which it is called with the specified character(s) inserted.

LastIndexOf—Returns the index of the last occurrence of a substring in a string. It returns -1 if the substring is not found.

PadLeft—Inserts characters at the beginning of a string.

Remove—Returns a copy of the string for which it is called with the specified character(s) removed.

Replace—Returns a new string object in which every occurrence of a substring is replaced with a different substring.

StartsWith—Determines if a string starts with a particular substring.

Substring—Returns a substring from a string.

ToLower—Returns a copy of the string for which it is called with any uppercase letters converted to lowercase letters.

ToUpper—Creates a new string object that replaces every lowercase letter in a string with its uppercase equivalent.

Trim—Removes all whitespace characters from the beginning and end of a string.

Tutorial 24: Ticket Information Application (Introducing Sequential-Access Files)

ComboBox    ComboBox   This control allows users to select options from a drop-down list.

- *In action*

Australia

- *Event*

SelectedIndexChanged—Raised when a new value is selected in the ComobBox.

- *Properties*

DataSource—Allows you to add items to the ComboBox.

DropDownStyle—Determines the ComboBox's style.

Enabled—Determines whether the user can enter data (true) in the ComboBox (false).

Items—Specifies the values the user can select from the ComboBox.

    Item—Retrieves the value at the specified index.

Location—Specifies the location of the ComboBox control on its container control relative to the top-left corner.

MaxDropDownItems—Determines the maximum number of items to be displayed when user clicks the drop-down arrow.

Name—Specifies the name used to access the ComboBox control programmatically. The name should be prefixed with cbo.

SelectedIndex—Specifies the index of the item selected.

SelectedValue—Contains the item selected by the user.

Text—Specifies the text displayed in the ComboBox.

■ *Methods*

Items.Add—Adds an item to the ComboBox.

Items.Clear—Deletes all the values in the ComboBox.

MonthCalendar　⊞ MonthCalendar　This control displays a calendar from which the user can select a date or a range of dates.

■ *In action*

■ *Event*

DateChanged—Raised when a new date (or a range of dates) is selected.

■ *Properties*

Location—Specifies the location of the MonthCalendar control on the Form.

Name—Specifies the name used to access the properties of the MonthCalendar control in program code. The name should be prefixed with mvw.

SelectionStart—Returns the first (or only) date selected.

OpenFileDialog　🗐 OpenFileDialog　This object enables an application to use the **Open** dialog.

■ *Properties*

CheckFileExists—Enables the user to display a warning if a specified file does not exist.

FileName—Sets the default file name displayed in the dialog. It can also be used to retrieve the name of the user-entered file.

Name—Specifies the name that will be used to reference the control's properties and methods. Use prefix obj when naming an OpenFileDialog object.

■ *Method*

ShowDialog—Displays the **Open** dialog and returns the result of the user interaction with the dialog.

StreamWriter This class is used to write data to a file.

■ *Methods*

Close—Used to close the stream.

WriteLine—Writes the data specified in its argument, followed by a newline character.

StreamReader This class is used to read data from a file.

- *Methods*

    Close—Closes the stream.

    ReadLine—Reads a line of data from a particular file.

Tutorial 25: ATM Application (Introducing Database Programming)

OleDbConnection   `OleDbConnection`   This object establishes a connection to a database.

- *Property*

    ConnectionString—Specifies information needed to open a connection to a database.

- *Methods*

    Close—Closes the connection to the database.

    Open—Opens the connection to the database.

OleDbCommand   `OleDbCommand`   This object is used to execute a command on a database.

- *Properties*

    CommandText—Specifies an SQL statement.

    Connection—Specifies the connection to a database.

    Parameters—Specifies an unknown value for the SQL statement.

- *Methods*

    ExecuteNonQuery—Executes nonquery command statements such as UPDATEs.

    ExecuteReader—Creates a data reader by executing a database query.

OleDbDataReader This object is used to read data from a database.

- *Methods*

    Read—Retrieves information from the data reader.

    Close—Closes the data reader.

Tutorial 26: CheckWriter Application (Introducing Graphics and Printing)

Font This class is used to define the font face, size and style of text throughout an application.

- *Properties*

    Bold—Sets the weight of the text.

    Italic—Sets the angle of the text.

    Size—Sets the size of the text.

    FontFamily—Contains a FontFamily object, which is used to store font face information.

    FontSyle—Specifies the style applied to a Font object.

Graphics The class that contains methods used to draw text, lines and shapes.

- *Methods*

    DrawLine—Draws a line of a specified size and color.

    DrawEllipse—Draws the outline of an ellipse of a specified size and color at a specified location.

    DrawRectangle—Draws the outline of a rectangle of a specified size and color at a specified location.

    DrawString—Draws a string in a specified font and color at a specified position.

FillEllipse—Draws a solid ellipse of a specified size and color at the specified location.

FillRectangle—Draws a solid rectangle of a specified size and color at the specified location.

PrintDocument   This class allows you to specify how to print a document.

- *Event*

  PrintPage—Raised when data required to print a page is needed.

- *Method*

  Print—Uses a Graphics object to print a page.

PrinterSettings   This class stores information about the system's printer settings.

- *Property*

  Count—Returns the number of printers installed on the system.

PrintPageEventArgs   This class contains data passed to a PrintPage event.

- *Properties*

  HasMorePages—Specifies if there are more pages to print. When false, the PrintPage event is no longer raised.

  MarginBounds—Specifies the margin of the printed page.

      Left—Specifies the left margin of the page.

      Top—Specifies the top margin of the page.

PrintPreviewDialog   PrintPreviewDialog   This control is used to display how a document will look when it is printed.

- *Properties*

  Document—Specifies the document that the control will preview. The document must be of the PrintDocument type.

  Name—Specifies the name used to access the PrintPreviewDialog control programmatically. The name should be prefixed with obj.

  UseAntiAlias—Specifies whether the dialog will display a smoothed image.

- *Method*

  ShowDialog—Used to display the PrintPreviewDialog to the user.

Tutorial 27: Phone Book Application (Introducing Multimedia Using Microsoft Agent)

Convert   The Convert class converts the value of a type to another type.

- *Method*

  ToInt16—Converts the value from another type to type short.

IAgentCtlCharacter   This class is used to represent the Agent character that is used in the application.

- *Property*

  Commands—Contains the commands the character will recognize.

- *Methods*

  Show—Displays the character on the screen.

  MoveTo—Moves the character to a specified location on the screen.

  Play—Plays character animations.

  Speak—Specifies the text to be spoken by the character.

  Commands.Add—Adds a new command to the command list for the Agent object.

IAgentCtlUserInput This class is used to retrieve commands from users.

- *Property*

  Name—Retrieves the name of the command given by the user.

Microsoft Agent Control   Control This control is used to create and manipulate the multimedia features of a Microsoft Agent character.

- *In action*

- *Events*

  Command—Raised when a user gives the Microsoft Agent character a verbal command or selects an option from the character's context menu.

  HideEvent—Raised when a user hides the Microsoft Agent character.

- *Property*

  Location—Specifies the location of the Microsoft Agent control on the Form.

- *Method*

  Characters.Load—Loads a character into the Microsoft Agent control.

Tutorial 28: Bookstore Application: Web Applications (Introducing Internet Information Services)

No new elements.

Tutorial 29: Bookstore Application: Client Tier (Introducing Web Controls)

ASPX page The page on which controls are dropped to design the GUI.

- *Properties*

  bgColor—Specifies the ASPX page's background color.

  title—Specifies the page's title.

Button ab] Button This control allows the user to raise an action or event.

- *In action*

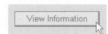

- *Properties*

  ID—Specifies the name used to access the Button programmatically. The name should be prefixed with btn.

  Text—Specifies the text displayed on the Button.

  Width—Specifies the width of the Button.

Horizontal Rule ▭ Horizontal Rule This control displays a line on the ASPX page. It is usually used to separate different areas of the ASPX page.

- *In action*

- *Properties*

    id—Specifies the name of the **Horizontal Rule** control. The name should be prefixed with hrz.

    Style—Allows you to specify where to position the **Horizontal Rule** control on the ASPX page.

Image    Image   This control displays an image on the ASPX page.

- *In action*

- *Properties*

    BorderStyle—Specifies the appearance of the Image's border.

    BorderWidth—Specifies the width of the Image's border.

    Height—Specifies the height of the Image control.

    ID—Specifies the name used to access the Image control programmatically. The name should be prefixed with img.

    Width—Specifies the width of the Image control.

Label   A Label   This control displays text on the ASPX page that the user cannot modify.

- *In action*

Books

- *Properties*

    ForeColor—Specifies font color for text on a Label control.

    Height—Specifies the height of the Label.

    ID—Specifies the name used to access the Label programmatically. The name should be prefixed with lbl.

    Name (under the expanded Font property in the **Solution Explorer**)—Specifies the name of the font used for the Label's text.

    Size (under the expanded Font property in the **Solution Explorer**)—Specifies the size of the Label's text.

    Text—Specifies the text displayed on the Label.

    Width—Specifies the width of the Label.

ListBox   ListBox   This control allows the user to view and select from multiple items in a list.

- *In action*

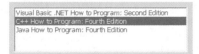

- *Properties*

    Height—Specifies the height of the ListBox.

ID—Specifies the name used to access the ListBox control programmatically. The name should be prefixed with lst.

Width—Specifies the width of the ListBox.

Table   ▦ Table   This control is usually used to organize data in a spreadsheet format.

■ *In action*

Price:	$76.00
ISBN#:	0-13-029363-6
Edition:	2
Copyright Date:	2002
Description:	Microsoft Visual Basic .NET

■ *Properties*

BorderStyle—Specifies the appearance of the Table's border.

BorderWidth—Specifies the width of the Table's border.

Cells—Retrieves or sets the value in the specified table cell.

GridLines—Specifies the format in which table cell separators are displayed.

ID—Specifies the name used to access the Table control programmatically. The name should be prefixed with tbl.

Rows—Retrieves or sets the value in the specified table cell.

Tutorial 30: Bookstore Application: Information Tier (Examining Database and Create Database Components)

No new elements.

Tutorial 31: Bookstore Application: Middle Tier (Introducing Code Behind Files)

No new elements.

Tutorial 32: Enhanced Car Payment Calculator Application (Introducing Exception Handling)

No new elements.

Keyword Chart

This table contains a complete listing of C# keywords (Fig. F.1). Many of these keywords are discussed throughout the text.

C# Keywords			
abstract	as	base	bool
break	byte	case	catch
char	checked	class	const
continue	decimal	default	delegate
do	double	else	enum
event	explicit	extern	false
finally	fixed	float	for
foreach	goto	if	implicit
in	int	interface	internal
is	lock	long	namespace
new	null	object	operator
out	override	params	private
protected	public	readonly	ref
return	sbyte	sealed	short
sizeof	stackalloc	static	string
struct	switch	this	throw
true	try	typeof	uint
ulong	unchecked	unsafe	ushort
using	virtual	volatile	void
while			

Figure F.1 C# keywords.

Internet Information Services (IIS) Setup Instructions

To create Web applications using Visual Studio .NET, Internet Information Services (IIS) needs to be installed on your computer. This appendix will guide you through the installation of IIS on computers using either the Windows 2000 or the Windows XP Professional Edition operating system. [***Note*: IIS cannot be installed on computers using Windows XP Home Edition.]** For Web applications to compile and execute correctly, IIS must be installed before Visual Studio .NET is installed. It is recommended that you follow the steps to determine whether IIS is installed on your computer. If IIS is not installed on your computer and Visual Studio .NET is, you will need to uninstall Visual Studio .NET before continuing with the IIS installation. Once IIS is installed, you will need to reinstall Visual Studio .NET. [*Note*: If you are working in a lab environment and are prompted for a Windows CD, contact your system administrator for assistance.]

Alternatively, you can update your installation of Visual Studio. NET to recognize ASP .NET by using the ASP .NET IIS Registration Tool. For more information on this process visit:

```
msdn.microsoft.com/library/default.asp?url=/library/en-us/cptools/
html/cpgrfaspnetiisregistrationtoolaspnet_regiisexe.asp
```

G.1 Installing IIS

This section will show you how to determine whether IIS is installed on a computer using the Windows 2000 and Windows XP operating systems. If IIS is not installed, this section will guide you through the installation process.

To begin, open the **Control Panel** by selecting **Start > Settings > Control Panel** in Windows 2000 or **Start > Control Panel** in Windows XP. When the **Control Panel** window opens, double click the **Add/Remove Programs** icon (Fig. G.1) in Windows 2000 or the **Add or Remove Programs** link (Fig. G.2) in Windows XP.

The **Add/Remove Programs** window lists all of the programs that are currently installed on your computer (Fig. G.3). The names and number of items on your computer will be different from those in the figure. In the left column of the

Add/Remove Programs window, click the **Add/Remove Windows Components** icon (Fig. G.3) to display the **Windows Components Wizard**.

Click **Add/Remove Programs** icon to display programs installed on your comptuer

Figure G.1   Clicking the **Add/Remove Programs** icon in the **Control Panel** in Windows 2000.

Click **Add or Remove Programs** link to display programs installed on your comptuer

Figure G.2   Clicking the **Add or Remove Programs** link in the **Control Panel** in Windows XP. (The contents of your **Control Panel** may differ.)

Add/Remove Programs window helps you manage all programs on your computer

Figure G.3   Clicking the **Add/Remove Windows Components** icon.

The **Windows Components Wizard** (Fig. G.4) displays a list of Windows components that can be added to or removed from your computer. Scroll down to the **Internet Information Services (IIS)** component's CheckBox. If there is a check mark in this CheckBox, IIS is already installed, and you can click **Cancel** to exit the wizard. If the CheckBox is empty (Fig. G.4), click in the CheckBox (Fig. G.5), and click the **Next >** Button.

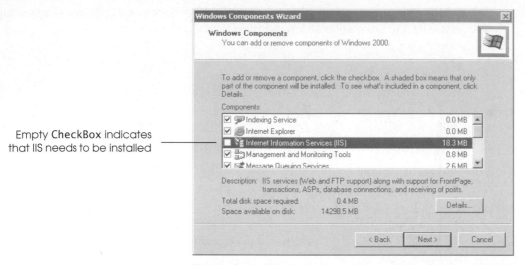

Empty **CheckBox** indicates that IIS needs to be installed

Figure G.4   **Windows Components Wizard** without IIS installed.

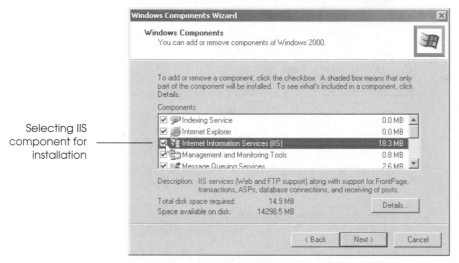

Selecting IIS component for installation

Figure G.5   Clicking the **Internet Information Services** CheckBox to install IIS.

Clicking **Next >** will begin the installation process and display the screen shown in Fig. G.6.

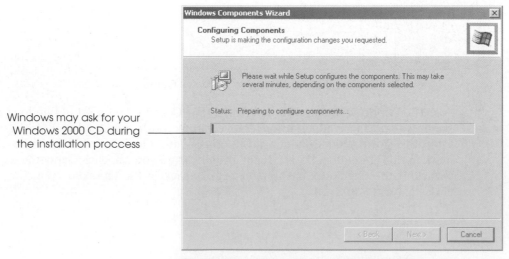

Windows may ask for your Windows 2000 CD during the installation proccess

Figure G.6   IIS installing on Windows 2000.

To install IIS, Windows may need to copy files from the Windows 2000 or Windows XP CD. If prompted, insert the CD and click **OK** to continue with the installation. When a dialog informs you that the installation is finished, click **Finish** to complete the installation and close the **Windows Components Wizard** (Fig. G.7).

This dialog appears after a successful installation

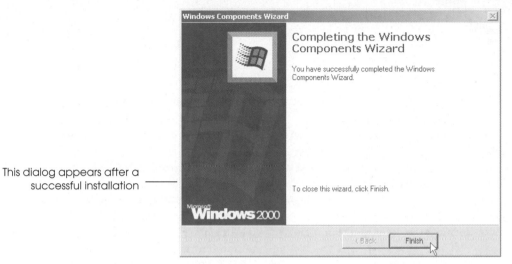

Figure G.7   Clicking **Finish** to complete the IIS installation.

GLOSSARY

Symbols

&& (logical AND) operator—Used to ensure that two conditions are *both* true before choosing a certain path of execution. Performs short-circuit evaluation.

|| (logical inclusive OR) operator—Used to ensure that either *or* both of two conditions are `true` in an application before a certain path of execution is chosen.

^ (logical exclusive OR) operator—Evaluates to `true` if and only if one of its operands results in `true` and the other results in `false`.

! (logical NOT, or logical negation) operator—Reverses the meaning of a condition: A `true` condition, when logically negated, becomes `false`, and a `false` condition, when logically negated, becomes `true`.

A

absolute path—The complete, exact location of a document.

access key—Keyboard shortcut that allows the user to perform an action on a control using the keyboard.

accessor—Method-like code units that handle the details of modifying and returning data.

ACE (Action/Control/Event) table—A program development tool you can use to relate GUI events with the actions that should be performed in response to those events.

action/decision model of programming—A model representing control statements as UML activity diagrams with rounded rectangles, indicating *actions* to be performed, and diamond symbols, indicating *decisions* to be made.

action expression (in the UML)—Used in an action state within a UML activity diagram to specify a particular action to perform.

action state—An action to perform in a UML activity diagram that is represented by an action-state symbol.

action-state symbol—A rectangle with its left and right sides replaced with arcs curving outward that represents an action to perform in a UML activity diagram.

Active Server Pages .NET (ASP .NET)—.NET software that helps programmers create applications for the Web.

active tab—The tab of the document currently displayed in the IDE.

active window—The window that is currently being used—sometimes referred to as the window that has the focus.

activity diagram—A UML diagram that models the activity (also called the workflow) of a portion of a software system.

Add method of class ArrayList—Adds a specified object to the end of an `ArrayList`.

Add method of the Commands property—Adds a command to a Microsoft Agent character.

Add method of the Items control property—Adds an item to a `ListBox` control.

ADO .NET—Part of Microsoft .NET that is used to interact with databases.

AgentObjects.IAgentCtlCharacter object—References a Microsoft Agent character.

AgentObjects.IAgentCtlUserInput object—Stores the user input retrieved from a Microsoft Agent character.

algorithm—A procedure for solving a problem, specifying the actions to be executed and the order in which these actions are to be executed.

alphabetic icon—The icon in the **Properties** window that, when clicked, sorts properties alphabetically.

API (application programming interface)—Used by a program to access the operating system and various services on the computer.

APPLICATION-DRIVEN approach—Provides step-by-step instructions for creating and interacting with useful, real-world computer applications.

ARGB values—A combination of alpha, red, green and blue components from which every color is created.

argument—Inputs to the method that provide information that the method needs to perform its task.

arithmetic and logic unit (ALU)—The "manufacturing" section of the computer that performs calculations such as addition, subtraction, multiplication and division. It also makes decisions, allowing the computer to perform such tasks as determining whether two items stored in memory are equal.

arithmetic operators—The operators +, -, *, /, and %.

array—A data structure containing data items of the same type.

array bounds—Integers that determine what indices can be used to access an element in the array. The lower bound is 0; the upper bound is the length of the array minus one.

ArrayList class—Performs the same functionality as an array, but has resizing capabilities.

Array.Sort method—Sorts the values of an array into ascending order.

ASP .NET technology—Can be combined with C# to create web applications.

ASP .NET markup—The set of instructions processed on the Web server's machine. An ASPX page is made up of HTML and ASP .NET markup.

ASPX page—File ending in .aspx that specifies the GUI of a Web page using Web controls. Also called a Web Form or Web Form Page.

assembler—Translator programs that convert assembly-language programs to machine language at computer speeds.

assembly language—A type of programming language that uses English-like abbreviations to represent the fundamental operations on the computer. Assembly language is easier for a human to understand than machine language, but harder to understand than a high-level language.

assignment operator (=)—Sets its left operand to the value of its right operand.

assignment statement—A unit of code that copies one value to another. An assignment statement contains an "equals"-sign (=) operator that causes the value of its right operand to be copied to its left operand.

assignment operators—Operators used to abbreviate assignment statements.

attributes—Information about an object, such as its size, color and weight.

Auto Hide—A space-saving IDE feature used for windows such as **Toolbox**, **Properties** and **Dynamic Help** that hides a window until the mouse pointer is placed on the hidden window's tab.

Autos window—Allows you to view the contents of the properties used in the last statement that was executed in an application. This allows you to verify that the previous statement executed correctly and lists the values in the next statement to be executed.

B

BackColor property of a Form—Specifies the Form's background color.

bandwidth—The information-carrying capacity of communications lines.

bgColor property of an ASPX page—Specifies an ASPX page's background color.

binary operator—Requires two operands.

bit—Short for "binary digit," a bit is a digit that can assume one of two values.

block—A group of code statements.

block scope—Variables declared inside control statements, such as a for statement, or methods have block scope. Block scope begins at the identifier's declaration and ends at the block's closing right brace.

book-title capitalization—A style that capitalizes the first letter of each word in the text (for example, **Calculate Total**).

bool type—Has the value true or false.

BorderStyle property of the Label control—Specifies a Label's border style, which allows you to visually distinguish one control from another. This property can be set to None (no border), FixedSingle (a single dark line as a border), or Fixed3D (giving the Label a "sunken" appearance).

BorderStyle property of a Web control—Specifies a Web control's border type.

BorderWidth property of a Web control—Specifies the width of a Web control's border.

bottom tier—The tier (also known as the information tier, or the data tier) containing the application data of a multi-tier application—typically implemented as a database.

bounding rectangle of ellipse—Specifies an ellipse's height, width and location.

break mode—The IDE mode when application execution is suspended. This mode is entered through the debugger.

breakpoint—A statement where execution is to suspend, indicated by a solid maroon circle.

break statement—Required at the end of each case. This statement immediately terminates the switch, and program control continues with the next statement after the switch.

brush—Used to fill shapes with colors.

Brush object—Used to specify drawing parameters when drawing solid shapes.

bug—A flaw that causes an application to run incorrectly.

built-in type—A type (also known as a primitive data type) already defined in C#, such as an int.

Button control—Used to command the application to perform an action.

Button property—The property of the MouseEventArgs class that specifies which (if any) mouse button is pressed.

Button Web control—Allows users to perform an action.

byte—Eight bits.

C

C# programming (Visual C#) language—A visual, object-oriented, event-driven programming language designed for Microsoft's .NET platform.

call-by-reference—*See* pass-by-reference.

call-by-value—*See* pass-by-value.

callee—The method being called.

caller—The method that calls another method.

Cancel value of DialogResult enumeration—Used to determine whether the user clicked the **Cancel** Button of a dialog.

case label—Precedes the statements that will execute if the switch's controlling expression matches the expression for a specific case.

case sensitive—The instance where two words that are spelled identically are treated differently if the capitalization of the two words differs.

cast operator—Explicitly converts a variable from one type to another.

catch block—Also called an exception handler, this block executes when code within the corresponding try block in the application detects an exceptional situation and throws an exception of the type the catch block declares.

categorized icon—The icon in the **Properties** window that, when clicked, sorts properties categorically.

Cells property of the Table Web control—Allows programmers to create and access TableCells in a Table.

central processing unit (CPU)—The part of the computer's hardware responsible for supervising the operation of the other sections of the computer.

Char structure—Stores characters (such as letters and symbols).

char type—Used to store character values.

character—A digit, letter or special symbol (characters in C# are Unicode characters, which are composed of 2 bytes).

character set—The set of all characters used to write applications and represent data items on a particular computer. C# uses the Unicode character set.

character constant—Another name for a character literal.

character literal—The value of a variable of type char, it is represented by a character within single quotes, such as 'A', 'd', '*', '.' and the like.

Characters property of the Microsoft Agent control—Used to access a specific Microsoft Agent character.

CheckBox control—A small white square GUI element that either is blank or contains a check mark.

CheckBox label—The text that appears alongside a CheckBox.

CheckedChanged event—Raised when a RadioButton's state changes.

Checked property of the CheckBox control—Specifies whether the CheckBox is checked (true) or unchecked (false).

Checked property of RadioButton control—When true, displays a small black dot in the control. When false, the control displays an empty white circle.

CheckFileExists property of class OpenFileDialog—Enables the user to display a warning if a specified file does not exist.

class—Represents a group of related objects. A class specifies the general format of its objects; the properties and actions available to an object depend on its class. An object is to its class much as a house is to its blueprint.

class body—The main section of the class declaration, following the class header and enclosed by braces.

class declaration—The code that belongs to a class, beginning with keyword class.

class keyword—Used to begin a class declaration.

class name—The identifier used to identify the name of a class in code.

class scope—Enables all methods in the same class to access all instance variables declared in that class. Begins at the opening left brace of the class declaration and terminates at closing right brace.

Clear method of class TextBox—Removes text in a TextBox.

Clear method of the Items control property—Deletes all values in a ListBox's control.

Click event—Raised when a user clicks a control.

Click event of class MenuItem—Generated when an item is clicked or a shortcut key is used.

client—When an application creates and uses an object of a class, that application is known as a client of that class.

client tier—The user interface of a multi-tier application (also called the top tier).

close box—The icon that, when clicked, closes a window.

Close method of class OleDbConnection—Closes the connection to the database.

Close method of class OleDbDataReader—Closes a data reader.

ColorDialog class—Used to display a dialog containing color options to a user.

code-behind file—C# file that contains a class that provides an ASPX page's functionality.

code editor—The window displaying code in the IDE.

code view—Displays the code in an editor window.

collapsed code—Code within a region that has been hidden by clicking on a minus box.

collection—A class used to store groups of related objects.

collection type of a foreach statement—Specifies the array or collection through which you wish to iterate.

Color structure—Contains several predefined colors as properties.

column—The second dimension of a two-dimensional array.

ComboBox control—Combines a TextBox with a ListBox.

Command event of the Microsoft Agent control—Raised when a user speaks a command to a Microsoft Agent character or selects a command from a character's context menu.

Commands property of class IAgentCtlCharacter—Sets which commands the Microsoft Agent character can understand as input from the user.

comment—A line of code that follows a double slash (//) or any code that falls between the delimiters /* and */. A comment is inserted to improve an application's readability.

comparison operators—*See* relational operators.

compilation error—Errors that prevent an application from compiling successfully.

compiler—A translator program that converts high-level-language programs into machine language.

component object box—The ComboBox at the top of the **Properties** window that allows you to select the Form or control object whose properties you want set.

component tray—The area below the Windows Form Designer that contains controls, such as Timers, that are not part of the graphical user interface.

computer—A device capable of performing computations and making logical decisions at speeds millions and even billions of times faster than the speeds at which human beings carry out those same tasks.

computer program—A set of instructions that guides a computer through an orderly series of actions.

computer programmer—A person who writes computer programs in programming languages.

condition—An expression with a true or false value that is used to make a decision.

connection object—Used to establish a connection to a database.

ConnectionString property of OleDbConnection—Specifies information needed to open a connection to a database.

consistent state—A way to maintain the values of an object's instance variables such that those values are always valid.

const keyword—Declares a constant, which is a variable whose value cannot be changed after its initial declaration.

constant—A variable whose value cannot be changed after its initial declaration.

constant expression—A value that cannot be changed. A case label consists of the keyword case followed by a constant expression. This constant expression must be a character literal or an integer literal.

constructor—A special class method that initializes a class's variables.

container—An object that contains controls.

Contents... command—Displays a categorized table of contents in which help articles are organized by topic.

Continue Button—Executes any statements between the next executable statement and the next breakpoint or the end of the current event handler, whichever comes first.

control—A reusable GUI component, such as a GroupBox, RadioButton and Panel.

Control reference—An object that represents a control on the Form.

control statement—An application component that specifies the order in which statements execute (also known as the flow of control).

control-statement nesting—Placing one control statement in the body of another control statement.

control-statement stacking—A set of control statements in sequence. The exit point of one control statement is connected to the entry point of the next control statement in sequence.

control variable—A variable used to control the number of iterations of a counter-controlled loop.

controlling expression—The expression in a switch statement whose value is compared sequentially with each case until either a match occurs, the default case is executed or the right brace is reached.

Convert.ToChar method—Converts data to type char.

Convert.ToInt16 method—Converts data to type short.

Convert.ToString method—Converts its arguments to a string of characters.

coordinate system—A scheme for identifying every possible point on the computer screen.

Count property of ArrayList—Returns the number of objects contained in the ArrayList.

Count property of Items—Returns the number of ListBox item.

counter—A variable often used to determine the number of times a block of statements in a loop will execute.

counter-controlled repetition—A technique (also called definite repetition) that uses a counter variable to determine the number of times that a block of statements will execute.

CreateGraphics method—Creates a Graphics object on a Form or control.

criteria of WHERE clause—Indicates from which specific row data will be retrieved or manipulated.

currency format—Used to display values as monetary amounts.

Cursor.Position property—Property containing the *x*- and *y*-coordinates of the mouse cursor on the screen (in pixels).

CustomFormat property of a DateTimePicker control—Contains the format string used to display the date and/or time when the Format property is set to Custom.

D

data command object—Executes commands that retrieve or modify data in a database.

data hierarchy—A collection of data items processed by computers that become larger and more complex in structure as you progress from bits to characters to fields to larger data structures.

data reader—Reads data from a database.

data structure—Groups together and organizes related data.

data tier—The tier (also known as the information tier, or the bottom tier) containing the application data of a multi-tier application—typically implemented as a database.

database—A group of related files.

database management system (DBMS)—A collection of programs designed to create and manage databases.

DateChanged event of MonthCalendar control—Raised when a new date (or a range of dates) is selected.

DataSource property of a ComboBox—Specifies the source of items listed in the ComboBox.

DateTime structure—A structure whose properties can be used to store and display date and time information.

DateTimePicker control—Retrieves date and time information from the user.

debugger—Software that allows you to analyze the behavior of an application to determine that it is executing correctly.

debugging—The process of fixing errors in an application.

declaration—A statement that reports the existence of a variable to the compiler.

decimal type—Used to store monetary amounts.

Decimal.Parse method—Converts a given string of characters to a value of type decimal.

decision symbol—The diamond-shaped symbol in a UML activity diagram that indicates that a decision is to be made.

default case—The optional case whose statements execute if the switch's controlling expression does not match any of the cases' values.

default properties—Provide the initial characteristics of an object.

definite repetition—*See* counter-controlled repetition.

descriptive Label—Used to describe another control on the Form. This helps users understand a control's purpose.

design view (design mode)—IDE view that allows you to create applications using Visual Studio .NET's windows, toolbars and menu bar.

Design mode—Displays the ASPX page's GUI at design time.

design units—Any specified units of measurement for a font.

dialog (message dialog)—A window that displays messages to users and gathers input from users.

diamond—A symbol (also known as the decision symbol) in a UML activity diagram; that indicates that a decision is to be made.

Directory.GetCurrentDirectory—Method of class Directory in namespace System.IO that returns a String containing the path to the directory that contains the application.

dismiss—Synonym for close.

dithering—Process that uses small dots of existing colors to form a pattern that simulates a desired color.

divide-and-conquer technique—Constructing large applications from small, manageable pieces to make development and maintenance of large applications easier.

DNS lookup—Process that translates domain names to IP addresses.

do...while repetition statement—Control statement that executes a set of statements while the loop-continuation condition is true; the condition is tested after the loop executes.

Document property—Property of the PrintPreviewDialog that allows you to specify the document that will be displayed in the dialog.

domain—Represents a group of hosts on the Internet.

domain name system (DNS) server—Computer that maintains a database of host names and their corresponding IP addresses.

dot operator—*See* member access operator.

dotted line—A UML activity diagram symbol that connects each UML-style note with the element that the note describes.

Double.Parse method—Converts the given string of characters to a value of type double.

double slash (//)—Denotes a single-line comment.

double-subscripted array—Contains multiple rows of values.

double-selection statement—A statement, such as if...else, that selects between two different actions or sequences of actions.

double type—Stores floating-point values.

DrawRectangle method of class Graphics—Draws the outline of a rectangle of a specified size and color at a specified location.

DrawString method—Graphics method that draws a specified string.

DropDownList value of DropDownStyle property—Specifies that a ComboBox is not editable.

DropDownStyle property of a ComboBox—Specifies a ComboBox's appearance.

dynamic help—A help option that provides links to articles that apply to the current content (that is, the item selected with the mouse pointer).

dynamic resizing—A capability that allows certain objects (such as ArrayLists) to increase or decrease in size based on the addition or removal of elements from that object. Enables the ArrayList object to increase its size to accommodate new elements and to decrease its size when elements are removed.

E

e event argument—Contains data for the event (such as KeyData).

element—An item in an array.

element of a foreach statement—Used to store a reference to the current value of the collection being iterated.

empty case—A case with no statements.

empty string—Does not contain any characters.

Enabled property—Specifies whether a control, such as a Button, appears enabled (true) or disabled (false).

Enabled property of a TextBox—Determines whether a TextBox will respond to user input.

EndsWith method of class String—Determines if a string ends with a particular substring.

enum keyword—Begins an enumeration.

enumeration—A group of related, named constants.

equality operator—Operator that compares two values. Returns true if the two values are equal; otherwise, returns false.

escape character—The backslash (\) character that is used to form escape sequences.

escape sequence—The backslash (\) and the character next to it, when used within a string, represent a special character, such as a newline (\n) or a tab (\t).

event—A user action that can trigger an event handler.

event-driven program—Responds to user-initiated events such as mouse clicks and keystrokes.

event handler—A section of code that is executed (called) when a certain event is raised (occurs).

expanded code—Viewed by clicking a plus box.

exception—An indication of a problem that occurs during an application's execution.

exception handler—A block that executes when the application detects an exceptional situation and throws an exception.

exception handling—Dealing with problems that occur during application execution.

executable statement—Actions that are performed when the corresponding C# application is run.

ExecuteReader method of OleDbCommand object—Executes an SQL statement and makes the result of the query available in the data reader.

ExecuteNonQuery method of OleDbCommand object—Executes an SQL statement and returns the number of rows modified.

explicit conversion—A conversion from one type to another requiring additional code, such as a cast operator.

extensible language—A language that can be "extended" with new data types. C# is an extensible language.

F

fall through—Occurs when program control follows an empty case in a switch statement by continuing with another case rather than exiting the switch statement.

false keyword—A bool value that represents a condition that is false.

field—A group of characters that conveys some meaning. For example, a field consisting of uppercase and lowercase letters can represent a person's name.

file—Collection of data that is assigned a name. Files are used for long-term persistence of large amounts of data, even after the program that created the data terminates.

FileName property of class OpenFileDialog—Specifies the file name displayed in the dialog.

FillEllipse method—The method of the Graphics class that draws an ellipse. This method takes as arguments a brush, a Color, the coordinates of the ellipse's bounding rectangle's upper-left corner and the width and height of the bounding rectangle.

final state—Represented by a solid circle surrounded by a hollow circle in a UML activity diagram—the end of the workflow after a program performs its activities.

final value of a control variable—The last value a control variable will hold before a counter-controlled loop terminates.

finally block—An optional block of code that follows the last catch block in a sequence of catch blocks or the try block if there are no catches. The finally block provides code that always executes, whether or not an exception occurs.

FixedSingle value of BorderStyle property—Specifies that the Label will display a thin, black border.

Flat value of FlatStyle property—Specifies that a Button will appear flat.

FlatStyle property of a Button—Determines whether the Button will appear flat or three-dimensional.

float type—Stores floating-point values. A float is similar to a double, but is less precise and requires less memory.

floating-point division (/)—Incorporates numbers after decimal points (no rounding occurs).

focus—Designates the window currently in use.

Focus method—Transfers the focus of the application to the control, on which the method is called.

Font class—Contains properties that define unique fonts.

FontDialog class—Used to display a dialog containing font options to a user and record the result.

FontFamily class—Contains methods, such as GetName and GetType, for obtaining font information.

for header—The first line of a for repetition statement. The for header specifies all four essential elements for the counter-controlled repetition of a for repetition statement.

for keyword—Begins the for statement.

for repetition statement—Handles the details of counter-controlled repetition. The for statement uses all four elements essential to counter-controlled repetition in one line of code (the name of a control variable, the initial value, the increment or decrement value and the condition to test for the final value) in one line of code.

foreach repetition statement—Used to iterate through elements in an array or collection.

ForeColor property of Label Web control—Specifies font color for text on a Label control.

Form—The object that represents the Windows application's graphical user interface (GUI).

format control string—A string that specifies how data should be formatted.

Format property of DateTimePicker—Specifies a predefined or custom format with which to display the date and/or time.

format specifier—Code that specifies the type of format that should be applied to a string for output.

FormatException class—An exception of this type is thrown when a method cannot convert its argument to a desired numeric type, such as int or double.

Framework Class Library (FCL)—.NET's "prepackaged" classes and methods for performing common mathematical calculations, string manipulations, character manipulations, error checking, input/output operations and many other useful operations.

FROM SQL keyword—Specifies table from which to get data.

FromArgb method of the Color class—Creates a new Color object from RGB and alpha value.

FullOpen property of class ColorDialog—Property that, when true, enables the ColorDialog to provide a full range of color options when displayed.

fully qualified domain name (FQDN)—Host name combined with a domain and top-level domain that provides a user-friendly way to identify a site on the Internet.

functionality—The actions an application can execute.

G

GDI+—An application programming interface (API) that provides classes for creating two-dimensional vector graphics.

get accessor—Used to retrieve a value of an instance variable.

GetName method of the Font class—Returns the name of the Font object.

GetType method of the Font class—Returns the type of the Font object.

GetUpperBound method—Returns the index of the last element in the array.

graphical user interface (GUI)—The visual part of an application with which users interact.

Graphics class—Defines methods for drawing shapes.

Graphics object—Draws two-dimensional images.

grid—The dots on the background of a Form that are used to align controls placed on the Form.

GridLines property of the Table Web control—Specifies the format in which table cell separators are displayed.

grid unit—The space between two adjacent horizontal (or vertical) dots on the Form in design view.

GroupBox control—Groups related controls visually.

guard condition—An expression contained in square brackets above or next to the arrows leading from a decision symbol in a UML activity diagram that determines whether workflow continues along a path.

H

hardware—The various devices that make up a computer, including the keyboard, screen, mouse, hard drive, memory, CD-ROM and processing units.

HasMorePages property of PrintPageEventArgs—Specifies if there are more pages to print. When False, the PrintPage event is no longer raised.

header—A line of text in that clarifies what information is being displayed.

Height property—This property, a member of the Size property, indicates the height of the Form or one of its controls in pixels.

HideEvent event—Event raised when a Microsoft Agent character is hidden.

high-level language—A type of programming language in which a single program statement accomplishes a substantial task. High-level languages use instructions that look almost like everyday English and that contain common mathematical notations.

Horizontal Rule HTML control—Displays a line to separate controls on an ASPX page.

host—A computer that stores and maintains resources, such as Web pages, databases and multimedia files.

host name—Name of a computer where resources reside.

HTML controls—Correspond to HTML elements.

HTML mode—Displays the ASPX page's markup at design time.

HyperText Markup Language (HTML)—A language for marking up information to share over the World Wide Web via hyperlinked text documents..

I

IAgentCtlCharacter object—References a Microsoft Agent character.

IAgentCtlUserInput object—Stores the user input retrieved from a Microsoft Agent character.

icon—The graphical representation of commands in the Visual Studio .NET IDE.

ID property of a Web control—Specifies the name of a Web control.

identifier—A series of characters consisting of letters, digits and underscores used to name program units such as classes, controls and variables.

if selection statement—Performs an action (or sequence of actions) based on a condition. This is also called a single-selection statement.

if...else selection statement—Performs an action (or sequence of actions) if a condition is `true` and performs a different action (or sequence of actions) if the condition is `false`. This is also called a double-selection statement.

Image class—Used to store and manipulate images from various file formats.

Image.FromFile method—Returns an `Image` object containing the image located at the path you specify.

Image property of a PictureBox control—Indicates the file name of the image displayed in a `PictureBox`.

Image Web control—Displays an image in an ASPX page.

immutable—An object that cannot be changed after it is created. In C#, `string`s are immutable.

implicit conversion—A conversion from one type to another performed by C# without any additional code.

increment (or decrement) of a control variable—The amount by which the control variable's value changes during each iteration of the loop.

Increment property of NumericUpDown control—Specifies by how much the current number in the `NumericUpDown` control changes when the user clicks the control's up (for incrementing) or down (for decrementing) arrow.

index—An array element's position number, also called a subscript. An index must be zero, a positive integer or an integer expression. If an application uses an expression as an index, the expression is evaluated first, to determine the index.

Index... command—Displays an alphabetized list of topics through which you can browse.

indexed array name—The array name followed by an index enclosed in parentheses. The indexed array name can be used on the left side of an assignment statement to place a new value into an array element. The indexed array name can be used in the right side of an assignment to retrieve the value of that array element.

IndexOf method—`String` method that accepts as an argument a character to search for in a `string`. The method returns the index of a specified character in a `string`. If the `string` does not contain the character, the method returns –1.

IndexOf method of class String—Returns the index of the first occurrence of a substring in a `String`. Returns –1 if the substring is not found.

indexer—A special property that allows array-style indexed access to lists of elements.

infinite loop—An error in which a repetition statement never terminates.

information tier—Tier containing the application data; typically implemented as a database. Also called the bottom tier or database tier.

initial state—The beginning of the workflow in a UML activity diagram before the program performs the modeled activities.

initial value of a control variable—The value of a control variable will hold when counter-controlled repetition begins.

initializer list—Braces ({ and }) surrounding the initial values of the elements in the array.

instance variable—Declared inside a class but outside any method of that class. Instance variables have class scope.

input—Data entered by the user into an application by typing at the keyboard, by clicking the mouse buttons and in a variety of other ways.

input unit—The "receiving" section of the computer that obtains information (data and computer programs) from various input devices, such as the keyboard and the mouse.

instant-access application—Application where a particular row of information must be located immediately.

Insert method—`String` method that inserts its second argument (a `string`) at the position specified by the first argument.

Insert method of class ArrayList—Inserts a specified object into the specified location of an `ArrayList`.

instantiate an object—Create an object of a class.

int type—Stores integer values.

Int32.Parse method—Converts a string of characters to an integer value.

integer—A whole number, such as 919, –11, 0 and 138624.

integer division (/)—Ignores numbers after decimal points (rounding occurs).

integrated development environment (IDE)—A software tool that enables programmers to write, run, test and debug programs quickly and conveniently.

IntelliSense **feature**—A Visual Studio .NET feature that aids the programmer during development by providing windows listing available class members and pop-up descriptions for those members.

interactive animated characters—The Microsoft Agent technology adds such characters to Windows applications and Web pages.

These characters can interact with the user through mouse clicks and microphone input.

internal Web browser—The Web browser (Internet Explorer) included in Visual Studio .NET, with which you can browse the Web.

Internet—A worldwide computer network. Most people today access the Internet through the World Wide Web.

Internet Information Services (IIS)—A Microsoft Web server.

Interval property of a Timer control—Specifies the number of milliseconds between each Tick event.

invoke—Cause a method to perform its designated task.

IP address—Unique address used to locate a computer on the Internet.

Items property of ListBox—Returns an object containing all the values in the ListBox.

Items property of ComboBox—Specifies the values the user can select from the ComboBox.

J

Join method of class String—Concatenates the elements in a String array, separated by the first argument. A new string containing the concatenated elements is returned.

K

keyboard event—Raised when a key on the keyboard is pressed or released.

KeyChar property of class KeyPressEventArgs—Contains data about the key that raised the KeyPress event.

KeyData property of class KeyEventArgs—Contains data about the key that raised the KeyDown event.

KeyDown event—Generated when a key is initially pressed. Used to handle the event raised when a key that is not a letter key is pressed.

KeyEventArgs class—Stores information about special modifier keys.

KeyPress event—Generated when a key is pressed. Used to handle the event raised when a letter key is pressed.

KeyPressEventArgs class—Stores information about character keys.

Keys enumeration—Contains values representing keyboard keys.

KeyUp event—Generated when a key is released.

key-value pair—Associates a value with a corresponding key, which is used to identify the value.

keyword—A word in code reserved for a specific purpose. These words appear in blue in the IDE and cannot be used as identifiers.

L

Label control—Displays text the user cannot modify.

Label Web control—Displays text on an ASPX page.

LastIndexOf method of class String—Returns the index of the last occurrence of a substring in a string. It returns -1 if the substring is not found.

left brace ({)—The symbol that denotes the beginning of a block of code.

left operand—Value on the left side of an operand.

Left value of MouseButtons enumeration—Used to represent the left mouse button.

Length property—Contains the number of elements in an array.

Length property of class String—Returns the number of characters in a string.

ListBox control—Allows the user to view items in a list. Items can be added to or removed from the list programmatically.

ListBox Web control—Displays a list of items.

literal string objects—A string constant written as a sequence of characters in double quotation marks (also called a string literal).

LIVE-CODE approach—Shows dozens of complete, working C# applications and depicts their outputs.

Load event—Raised when an application initially executes.

Load event of the Page class—Raised when the ASPX page is loaded, causes the Page_Load event handler to be executed.

localhost—Host name that identifies the local computer.

local variable—Declared inside a block, such as a method or a for statement. Local variables have block scope.

Locals window—Allows you to view the state of the variables in the current scope during debugging.

location bar—The ComboBox in Visual Studio .NET where you can enter the name of a Web site to visit.

location in computer's memory—Stores a variable.

Location property of a control—Specifies the location of the upper-left corner of a control. This property is used to place a control on the Form precisely.

lock file—File which ensures that only one program at a time manipulates an Access database.

logic error—A problem that does not prevent the application from compiling successfully, but does cause the application to produce erroneous results.

logical operators—Operators (for example, &&, ||, ^ and !) that can be used to form complex conditions by combining simple ones.

loop—Another name for a repetition statement.

loop-continuation condition—In a repetition statement (such as a while statement), enables repetition to continue while the condition is true and that causes repetition to terminate when the condition becomes false.

M

machine dependent—Can be used on only one type of computer.

machine language—A computer's natural language, generally consisting of streams of numbers that instruct the computer how to perform its most elementary operations.

Main method—The required starting point in a C# application.

MainMenu control—Allows you to add menus to your application.

margin indicator bar—A margin in the IDE where breakpoints are displayed.

MarginBounds.Left property (PrintPageEventArgs)—The left margin of a printed page.

MarginBounds.Top property (PrintPageEventArgs)—The top margin of a printed page.

masking—Hiding text such as passwords or other sensitive pieces of information that should not be observed by other people as they are typed. Masking is achieved by using the PasswordChar property of the TextBox for which you would like to hide data. The actual data entered is retained in the TextBox's Text property.

masking character—Used to replace each character displayed in a TextBox when the TextBox's data is masked for privacy.

Math.Pow method—Raises a given base to a given exponent and returns the result as a double value.

MaxDate property of DateTimePicker—Maximum allowed date.

Math.Sqrt method—Returns the square root of a numeric value.

MaxDropDownItems property of a ComboBox—Specifies how many items can be displayed in the drop-down list.

Maximum property of NumericUpDown control—Determines the maximum input value in a particular NumericUpDown control.

MaxLength property of TextBox—Specifies the maximum number of characters that can be input into a TextBox.

***m*-by-*n* array**—A two-dimensional array with *m* rows and *n* columns.

members of a class—Methods and variables declared within the body of a class.

member access operator—Also known as the dot operator (.), allows programmers to access a control's properties using code.

member-access modifier—Keywords used to specify what members of a class that a client may access. Includes keywords public and private.

memory unit—The rapid-access, relatively low-capacity "warehouse" section of the computer, which stores data temporarily while an application is running.

menu—A group of related commands.

Menu Designer in Visual Studio .NET—Design mode in Visual Studio .NET that allows you to create and edit menus.

menu-access shortcut—*Alt* key shortcut that allows the user to combine the *Alt* key with another key to access a menu item.

menu item—A cell of text that the user can select in the MainMenu control.

MenuItem object—Represents menu items.

merge symbol—In the UML, this symbol joins two flows of activity into one flow of activity.

MessageBox class—Provides a method for displaying message dialogs.

MessageBoxButtons constants—Identifiers that specify Buttons that can be displayed in a MessageBox dialog.

MessageBoxIcon constants—Identifiers that specify icons that can be displayed in a MessageBox dialog.

MessageBox.Show method—Displays a message dialog.

method—A set of instructions for performing a particular task.

method body—The declarations and statements that appear between the set of braces that follow the method header. The method body contains C# code that performs actions, generally by manipulating or interacting with the parameters from the parameter list.

method call—Invokes a method, specifying the method name and providing information (arguments) that the callee (the method being called) requires to perform its task.

method declaration—The method header, body and braces surrounding the body.

method header—The first line of a method (including the return type, the method name and the parameter list).

method name—Follows the return type in a method header and distinguishes one method from another. A method name can be any valid identifier.

method overloading—Feature that allows multiple method declarations of the same name but with different numbers, types and/or order of arguments.

Microsoft Agent—Adds interactive animated characters to Windows applications and Web pages.

Microsoft .NET—Microsoft's vision for using the Internet and the Web in the development, engineering and use of software. .NET includes tools such as Visual Studio .NET and programming languages such as C#.

Microsoft Developer Network (MSDN)—An online library that contains articles, downloads and tutorials on technologies of interest to Visual Studio .NET developers.

Middle value of MouseButtons enumeration—Used to represent the middle mouse button.

middle tier—Tier that controls interaction between the client and information tiers.

MinDate property of DateTimePicker—Minimum allowed date.

Minimum property of NumericUpDown control—Determines the minimum input value in a particular NumericUpDown control.

minus box—The icon that, when clicked, collapses a node.

modifier key—Key such as *Shift*, *Alt* or *Control* that modifies the way that applications respond to a keyboard event.

MonthCalendar control—Control that displays a calendar from which a user can select a range of dates.

mouse event—Generated when a user interacts with an application using the computer's mouse.

mouse pointer—Used to navigate the IDE and to manipulate the Form and its controls.

MouseButtons enumeration—Defines constants, such as Left, Right and Middle, to specify mouse buttons.

MouseDown event—Generated when a mouse button is pressed.

MouseEventArgs class—Specifies information about a mouse event.

MouseMove event—Generated when a mouse pointer is moved.

MouseUp event—Generated when the mouse button is released.

MoveTo method—Relocates the Microsoft Agent character on the screen.

multiple-selection statement—Selects from among many different actions or sequences of actions.

multiplication operator—The asterisk (*) used to multiply its two operands, producing their product as a result.

Multiline TextBox control—Provides the ability to enter or display multiple lines of text. If the text exceeds the size of the TextBox, the control can be set to display a scrollbar.

Multiline property of TextBox control—Specifies whether the TextBox is capable of displaying multiple lines of text. If the value of the property is true, the TextBox may contain multiple lines of text; if the value of the property is false, the TextBox can contain only one line of text.

multimedia—The use of various media, such as sound, video and animation, to create content in an application.

multi-tier (*n*-tier) application—Application that divides functionality into separate tiers. Typically, each tier performs a specific function.

mutually exclusive options—A set of options in which only one can be selected at a time.

N

name of a control variable—Identifier used to reference the control variable of a loop.

name of a variable—The identifier used in an application to access or modify a variable's value.

Name property of a control—Specifies the name used to access the control programmatically.

namespace—Classes in the FCL are organized by functionality into these directory-like entities.

namespace keyword—Used to group classes within the specified namespace.

narrowing conversion—Changes a value's type to a smaller type. Loss of data can occur. C# requires narrowing conversions to be performed explicitly.

nested (embedded) parentheses—Located within another set of parentheses.

nested statement—A control statement placed inside another control statement.

.NET Framework—Microsoft-provided software that executes applications, provides the Framework Class Library (FCL) and supplies many other programming capabilities.

newline character—Special character that indicates when text should continue on the next line.

new operator—Returns a reference to a newly created object.

Next method of class Random—When called with no arguments, generates a positive int value between zero and the constant Int32.MaxValue.

NextDouble method of Random—Generates a positive double value that is greater than or equal to 0.0 and less than 1.0.

node—An item that can be expanded or collapsed.

nondestructive process—Does not overwrite a value.

nonvolatile—Retaining information even when the computer is powered off. Secondary storage is nonvolatile.

note—An explanatory remark (represented by a rectangle with a folded upper-right corner) describing the purpose of a symbol in a UML activity diagram.

Now property of DateTime statement—The current system time and date.

null keyword—Used to clear a reference's value.

NumericUpDown control—Allows you to specify maximum and minimum numeric input values. Also allows you to specify an increment (or decrement) when the user clicks the up (or down) arrow.

O

object-oriented programming (OOP)—A way of programming that uses objects as reusable components modelling items in the real world. Object-oriented programs are often easier to understand, correct and modify than programs developed with previous techniques.

objects—Reusable software components that model items in the real world.

object technology—A packaging scheme for creating meaningful software units. The units are large and are focused on particular application areas. There are date objects, time objects, paycheck objects and file objects, among others.

off-by-one error—Occurs when a loop executes for one more or one fewer iterations than is necessary.

OleDbCommand object—Used to execute an SQL statement on a database.

OleDbDataReader object—Used to read data from a database. Also known as a data reader object.

one-dimensional array—An array that uses only one index.

opacity—Amount of transparency of the color.

Open method of class OleDbConnection—Opens the connection to the database.

operand—An expression subject to an operator.

out keyword—Passes an uninitialized parameter by reference.

outlined code—Collapsed code that is represented by ellipses.

output—Instructions and other information displayed by an application for users to read in the application's GUI.

output Label—Used to display calculation results.

output unit—The section of the computer that takes information the computer has processed and places it on various output devices, making the information available for use outside the computer.

Outset value of BorderStyle property—Gives an Image Web control a raised appearance.

P

PadLeft method of class String—Adds characters to the beginning of the string until the length of a string equals the specified length.

Page class—Defines the basic functionality for an ASPX page.

Page_Load event handler—Executes any processing necessary to display a Web page.

palette—A set of colors.

Panel control—Used to group controls. Unlike GroupBoxes, Panels do not have captions.

Parameter Info feature of Visual Studio .NET—Provides the programmer with information about methods and their arguments.

parameter list—A comma-separated list in which the method declares each parameter variable's name and type.

parameter variable—Declared in a method's parameter list that can be used in the body of the method.

Parameters property of OleDbCommand—Specifies a value for an SQL statement.

pass-by-reference—When an argument is passed by reference, the called method can access and modify the caller's original data directly. Keywords `ref` and `out` indicate pass-by-reference (also called call-by-reference).

pass-by-value—When an argument is passed by value, the application makes a copy of the argument's value and passes that copy to the called method. With pass-by-value, changes to the called method's copy do not affect the original variable's value. By default, C# uses pass-by-value (also called call-by-value).

PasswordChar property of a TextBox—A property that specifies the masking character for a `TextBox`.

Peek method of StreamReader—Returns the next character to be read or -1 if there are no more characters to read in the file (that is, the end of the file has been reached).

Pen object—Used to specify drawing parameters when drawing shape outlines.

persistent data—Data maintained in files.

PictureBox control—Displays an image.

pin (pushpin) icon—An icon that enables or disables the Auto Hide feature.

pixel—A tiny point on your computer screen that displays a color.

plus box—An icon that, when clicked, expands a node.

position number—A value that indicates a specific location within an array.

postfix increment and decrement operators—Operators `++` and `--`, when they appear to the right of the operand. Causes the operand's value to be used in the expression in which the operand appears, after which the value of the operand is incremented or decremented by 1.

prefix increment and decrement operators—Operators `++` and `--`, when they appear to the left of the operand. Causes the operand's value to be incremented or decremented by 1, after which the operand's value is used in the expression in which the operand appears.

primary key—Column (or combination of columns) in a database table that contains unique values used to distinguish rows from one another.

Print method of class PrintDocument—Method used to print a document.

PrintDocument class—Allows users to describe how to print a document.

PrintPage event—Occurs when the data required to print the current page is needed.

PrintPreviewDialog class—Previews a document before it prints in a dialog box.

PrinterSettings.InstalledPrinters.Count—Determines how many printers the user has installed on the computer.

private keyword—Member-access modifier that makes instance variables or methods accessible only to that class.

procedural programming language— Focuses on actions (verbs) rather than things or objects (nouns). Examples include Fortran, Pascal, BASIC and C.

program control—The task of ordering an application's statements in the correct order.

programmer-defined class (programmer-defined type)—Defined by a programmer, as opposed to a class predefined in the Framework Class Library.

programmer-defined method—Created by a programmer to meet the unique needs of a particular application.

project—A group of related files that make up an application.

properties—Object attributes, such as size, color and weight.

Properties window—The window that displays the properties for a `Form` or control object.

property of a class—Contains accessors—portions of code that handle the details of modifying and returning data.

pseudocode—An informal language that helps programmers develop algorithms.

pseudorandom numbers—A sequence of values produced by a complex mathematical calculation that simulates random-number generation.

public keyword—Member-access modifier that makes instance variables or methods accessible wherever the application has a reference to that object.

px—Specifies that the size is measured in pixels.

Q

Query Builder—Visual Studio .NET tool that allows you to specify the statements that retrieve information from and modify information in databases.

Quick Info **box**—Displays a variable's name and value when the mouse pointer is placed over the variable name.

R

RadioButton control—Appears as a small white circle that is either blank (unchecked) or contains a smaller black dot (checked). Usually these controls appear in groups of two or more. Exactly one `RadioButton` in a group is selected at once.

raise—Causes to occur (refers to an event).

Random class—Contains methods to generate pseudorandom numbers.

Read method of class OleDbDataReader—Retrieves information from the data reader.

ReadLine method of the StreamReader class—Reads a line from a file and returns it as a `string`.

ReadOnly property of a NumericUpDown control—Determines whether the input value can be typed by the user.

Rectangle structure—Enables you to define rectangular shapes and their dimensions.

rectangular array—A type of two-dimensional array that can represent tables of values consisting of information arranged in rows and columns. Each row contains the same number of columns.

record—A collection of related fields. Usually a `class` in C# composed of several fields (called member variables in C#).

record key—Identifies a record and distinguishes that record from all other records.

redundant parentheses—Unnecessary parentheses that are included to make an expression easier to read.

ref keyword—Passes an initialized parameter by reference.

reference—A variable to which you assign an object.

region—A portion of code that can be collapsed or expanded.

relational operators—Operators < (less than), > (greater than), <= (less than or equal to) and >= (greater than or equal to) that compare two values.

remainder operator (%)—Yields the remainder after division.

RemoveAt method of ArrayList—Removes the object located at a specified location of an ArrayList.

repetition statement—Allows the programmer to specify that an action or sequence of actions should be repeated, depending on the value of a condition.

Replace method of class String—Returns a new string object in which every occurrence of a substring is replaced with a different substring.

reserved word—See keyword.

Response object—A predefined ASP .NET object that provides methods for responding to clients.

Response.Redirect—Method used to redirect the client browser to another Web page.

rethrow the exception—The catch block can defer the exception handling (or perhaps a portion of it) to another catch block by using the throw keyword.

return statement—Sends a value back to the method's caller.

return type—Type of the result returned from method.

RGB value—The amount of red, green and blue needed to create a color.

right brace (})—The symbol that denotes the end of a block of code.

Right value of MouseButtons enumeration—Used to represent the right mouse button.

right operand—Value on the right side of an operand.

row—In referring to an element of a two-dimensional array, the first index specifies the row.

Rows property of the Table Web control—Allows programmers to create and access table rows.

rules of operator precedence—Determine the sequence in which operations in arithmetic expressions are applied.

run mode—An IDE mode indicating that the application is running (executing).

runtime error—Has its effect at execution time.

S

scope—The portion of an application in which an identifier (such as a variable name) can be referenced. Some identifiers can be referenced throughout an application; others can be referenced only from limited portions of an application (such as within a single method or block).

screen scraping—The process of extracting desired information from the HTML that composes a Web page.

ScrollBars property of TextBox control—Specifies whether a TextBox has a scrollbar and, if so, of what type. By default, the ScrollBars property set to None. Setting the value to Vertical places a scrollbar along the right side of the TextBox.

Search... command—Allows you to find help articles based on search keywords.

secondary storage media—Devices such as magnetic disks, optical disks and magnetic tapes on which computers store files.

secondary storage unit—Long-term, high-capacity "warehousing" section of the computer. Secondary memory takes longer to access information in primary memory but is less expensive and is nonvolatile.

SELECT SQL keyword—Used to request specified information from a database.

SelectedIndex property of a ComboBox—Specifies the index of the selected item.

SelectedIndex property of ListBox Web control—Returns the index of the selected item.

SelectedIndexChanged event of ComboBox—Raised when a new value is selected in a ComboBox.

SelectedItem property of ListBox Web control—Returns the value of the selected item.

SelectedValue property of a ComboBox—Specifies the selected item.

selection statement—Selects among alternative courses of action.

SelectionStart property of MonthCalendar control—Returns the first (or only) date selected.

semicolon (;)—A character used to terminate each statement in an application.

sender event argument—Event argument that contains the object that raised the event (also called the source of the event).

sentence-style capitalization—A style that capitalizes the first letter of the first word in the text. Every other letter in the text is lowercase, unless it is the first letter of a proper noun.

separator bar—Bar placed in a menu to separate related menu items.

sequence statement—Built into C#—unless directed to act otherwise, the computer executes C# statements sequentially.

sequential-access file—Contains data that is read in the order that it was written to the file.

sequential execution—Statements in an application are executed one after another in the order in which they are written.

set accessor—Provides data-validation capabilities to ensure that the value is set properly.

Session object—Maintained across several Web pages containing a collection of items (key-value pairs). This variable is specific to each user.

session state—ASP .NET's built-in support for tracking data.

short type—Holds small integer values.

short-circuit evaluation—The evaluation of the right operand in && and || expressions occurs only if the first condition meets the criteria for the condition.

Show method—Displays a Microsoft Agent character on the screen.

ShowDialog method of FontDialog or ColorDialog—Displays the dialog on which it is called.

ShowDialog method of class PrintPreviewDialog—Displays the PrintPreviewDialog to the user.

ShowUpDown property of a DateTimePicker control—When true, allows the user to specify the time using up and down arrows.

simple condition—Contains one expression.

single-entry/single-exit control statement—A control statement that has one entry point and one exit point. All C# control statements are single-entry/single-exit control statements.

single-selection statement—A control statement that selects or ignores a single action or sequence of actions.

size of a variable—The amount of memory required to store the variable.

Size property of a control—Specifies the height and width, in pixels, of the Form or one of its controls.

Size property of a Web control—Allows you to specify the size of a Web control.

SizeMode property of a PictureBox control—Specifies how an image is displayed in a PictureBox.

sizing handle—Square that, when enabled, can be used to resize the Form or one of its controls.

small circles (in the UML)—The solid circle in an activity diagram represents the activity's initial state and the solid circle surrounded by a hollow circle represents the activity's final state.

software—The set of applications that run on computers.

software reuse—An approach to software development that enables programmers to avoid "reinventing the wheel" by taking advantage of existing pieces of software, helping them develop new applications faster.

solid circle (in the UML)—Symbol that represents the activity's initial state.

SolidBrush class—Defines a brush that draws with a single color.

solution—Contains one or more projects.

Solution Explorer—A window that provides access to all the files in a solution.

sorting—The process of ordering array elements in ascending or descending order.

Speak method—Has the Microsoft Agent character speak text to the user.

special characters—Characters that are neither digits or letters.

speech-recognition engine—Translates vocal sound input from a microphone into a language that the computer understands.

Split method of class String—Splits the words in a string whenever a space is reached.

Start Page—The initial page displayed when Visual Studio .NET is opened.

StartsWith method of class String—Determines if a string starts with a particular substring.

state button—Can be in the on/off (true/false) state.

statement—A unit of code that, when compiled and executed, performs an action.

status box—A box that appears below a Microsoft agent character that displays information about the character's actions.

Step Into Button—Executes the next statement in the application. If the next statement to execute is a method call, control is transferred to the called method.

Step Over Button—Executes the next statement in the application. If the next statement to execute is a method call, the called method executes in its entirety.

Stop Debugging Button—Ends the debugging session and returns the IDE to design mode.

straight-line form—The way arithmetic expressions must be typed in your code.

StreamReader class—Provides methods for reading information from a file.

StreamWriter class—Provides methods for writing information to a file.

StretchImage—The value of PictureBox property SizeMode that scales an image to fill the PictureBox.

string literal—A String constant written as a sequence of characters in double quotation marks (also called a literal string object).

string type—Contains a series of characters (letters, numbers, etc.).

string-concatenation operator (+)—Combines (or concatenates) its two operands into one string of characters.

String.Format method—Formats a string.

structured programming—A technique for organizing program control that helps you develop applications that are easy to understand, debug and modify.

Structured Query Language (SQL)—Language often used by relational databases to perform queries and manipulate data in relational databases.

style attribute—Allows you to specify the position of a Web control.

submenu—Menu within another menu.

substring—A sequence of characters in a string.

Substring method of class String—Returns characters from a string that correspond to the arguments passed by the user that indicate the start and the end positions within a string.

switch statement—Multiple-selection statement used to make a decision by comparing an expression to a series of values.

syntax—Specifies how a statement must be formed to execute without syntax errors.

syntax error—An error that occurs when program statements violate the grammatical rules of a programming language.

System.Collections namespace—Contains collection classes such as ArrayList.

System.Drawing.Printing namespace—Allows your applications to access all services related to printing.

System.IO namespace—Contains methods to access files and directories.

SystemColors.Control property—Returns the default color of several controls, including Panels.

T

Tab Order view—Used to set the TabIndex properties of a Form's controls.

TabIndex property—Specifies the order in which focus is transferred to controls on the **Form** when *Tab* is pressed.

table—A two-dimensional array used to contain information arranged in rows and columns.

Table Web control—Displays a table in an ASPX page.

TabStop property—Specifies whether a control can receive the focus when *Tab* is pressed.

Tahoma font—The Microsoft-recommended font for use in Windows applications.

TCP/IP—The set of protocols forming the foundation of today's Internet. Transmission Control Protocol (TCP) ensures that messages, consisting of pieces called "packets," are properly routed from sender to receiver and that those messages arrive intact. Internet Protocol (IP) enables many different networks to communicate with each other.

template—Building blocks for different types of C# applications.

temporary variable—Used to store data when swapping values.

text file—A file containing human-readable characters.

text formatting—Modifying the appearance of text for display purposes.

Text property of a control—Specifies the text displayed by the **Form** or a **Label**.

Text property of a Web control—Specifies the text that displays on a Web control.

Text property of class MenuItem—Specifies the menu item's text.

text-to-speech engine—Application that translates typed words into spoken sound that users hear through headphones or speakers connected to a computer.

TextAlign property of a control—Specifies how text is aligned within a **Label**.

TextBox control—Used to retrieve user input from the keyboard.

TextChanged event—Occurs when the text in a **TextBox** changes.

this keyword—References the current object.

throw statement—Used to rethrow an exception in a **catch** block.

throws an exception—A method throws an exception if a problem occurs while the method is executing.

Tick event of a Timer control—Raised after the number of milliseconds specified in the **Interval** property has elapsed.

Timer control—Wakes up at specified intervals to execute code in its **Tick** event handler.

title bar—Contains text that identifies a window or dialog.

title property of an ASPX page—Specifies the page's title.

ToLongDateString method of type DateTime—Returns a **string** containing the date in the format "Thursday, August 14, 2003".

ToLower method of class String—Creates a new **string** object that replaces every uppercase letter in a **string** with its lowercase equivalent.

tool tip—The description of an icon that appears when the mouse pointer is held over that icon for a few seconds.

toolbar—A bar that contains **Buttons** that execute commands.

toolbar icon—A picture on a toolbar **Button**.

Toolbox—A window that contains controls used to customize **Forms**.

Tools menu—Contains commands for accessing additional IDE tools and options that enable customization of the IDE.

top tier—Tier containing the application's user interface. Also called the client tier.

top-level domain (TLD)—Usually describes the type of organization that owns the domain name.

ToShortTimeString method of DateTime—Returns a **string** containing the time in the format "10:00 AM".

ToString method—Returns a **string** representation of the object or type on which the method is called.

ToUpper method of class String—Creates a new **string** object that replaces every lowercase letter in a **string** with its uppercase equivalent.

ToUpper method of structure Char—Returns the uppercase representation of the character passed as a parameter.

transfer of control—Occurs when an executed statement does not directly follow the previously executed statement in the written application.

transferring the focus—Selecting a control in an application.

transition—A change from one action state to another, represented by transition arrows in a UML activity diagram.

transition arrow (in the UML)—Symbol that represents a transition.

Trim method of class String—Removes all whitespace characters from the beginning and end of a **string**.

true keyword—A **bool** value that represents a condition that is true.

truth table—Displays the boolean result of a logical operator for all possible combinations of **true** and **false** values for its operands.

try block—A block containing statements that might cause exceptions and statements that should not execute if an exception occurs.

two-dimensional array—A double-subscripted array that contains multiple rows of values.

type of a variable—Specifies the kind of data that can be stored in a variable and the range of values that can be stored.

U

UML (Unified Modeling Language)—An industry standard for modeling software systems graphically.

uncaught exception—An exception that does not have an exception handler. Uncaught exceptions might terminate application execution.

Unicode—A character set containing characters that are composed of 2 bytes. Characters are represented in C# using the Unicode character set.

uniform resource locator (URL)—Address that can be used to direct a browser to a resource on the Web.

UPDATE SQL keyword—Used to modify data in a database table.

UseAntiAlias property of class PrintPreviewDialog—Specifies whether the text in the **PrintPreviewDialog** appears smoother on the screen.

using directive—Provides access to classes from the specified namespace.

V

value—Special identifier that allows access to the value to be assigned in a property's set accessor.

value of a variable—The piece of data that is stored in a variable's location in memory.

Value property of a DateTimePicker—Stores the date and time in a DateTimePicker control.

ValueChanged event of a DateTimePicker—Raised when a user selects a new day or time.

variable—A location in the computer's memory where a value can be stored for use by an application.

vector graphics—Graphics created by a set of mathematical properties called vectors, which include the graphics' dimensions, attributes and positions.

Vertical value of ScrollBars property—Places a scrollbar along the right side of a TextBox when assigned to property ScrollBars.

visual programming with C#—Instead of writing detailed program statements, the programmer uses Visual Studio .NET's graphical user interface to conveniently drag and drop predefined objects into place, and to label and resize them. Visual Studio .NET writes much of the C# program, saving the programmer considerable effort.

Visual Studio .NET—An integrated development environment (IDE) for developing C# and other .NET applications.

void keyword—Used in place of the return type to indicate that a method will return no value.

volatile memory—Memory that is erased when the machine is powered off. Primary memory is volatile.

W

watch—An expression or variable that is added to the **Watch** window.

Watch window—A Visual Studio .NET window that allows you to view variable values as an application is being debugged.

Web applications—Applications that create web content.

Web controls—Controls, such as TextBoxes and Buttons, that are used to customize ASPX pages. Also called an ASP .NET server control.

Web-safe colors—Colors that display the same on different computers.

Web server—Specialized software that responds to client requests by providing resources.

Web services—Reusable pieces of Web-based software available on the Internet.

WHERE SQL keyword—Specifies criteria that determine the rows to retrieve.

while repetition statement—A control statement that executes a set of body statements while its loop-continuation condition is true.

white space—A tab, space or newline.

widening conversion—Changes a value's type to a larger type. C# allows widening conversions to be performed implicitly.

Width property—This property, a member of the Size property, indicates the width of the Form or one of its controls, in pixels.

Width property of a Web control—Allows you to specify the width of a Web control.

Windows application—A program that displays a GUI.

Windows Form Designer—The Visual Studio .NET interface for designing GUIs.

workflow—The activity of a portion of a software system.

World Wide Web (WWW)—A communications system that allows computer users to locate and view multimedia documents (such as documents with text, graphics, animations, audios and videos).

World Wide Web Consortium (W3C)—A forum through which qualified individuals and companies cooperate to develop and standardize technologies for the World Wide Web.

WriteLine method of StreamWriter class—Writes a string and a line terminator to a file.

X

x-axis—Describes every horizontal coordinate.

x-coordinate—Horizontal distance (increasing to the right) from the left of the drawing area.

X property—The property of the MouseEventArgs class that specifies the x-coordinate of the mouse event.

Y

y-axis—Describes every vertical coordinate.

y-coordinate—Vertical distance (increasing downward) from the top of the drawing area.

Y property—The property of the MouseEventArgs class that specifies the y-coordinate of the mouse event.

yellow arrow of debugger—Indicates that the current line contains the next statement to execute.

Z

zeroth element—The first element in an array.

End User License Agreement

PRENTICE HALL LICENSE AGREEMENT AND LIMITED WARRANTY

READ THE FOLLOWING TERMS AND CONDITIONS CAREFULLY BEFORE OPENING THIS SOFTWARE PACKAGE. THIS LEGAL DOCUMENT IS AN AGREEMENT BETWEEN YOU AND PRENTICE-HALL, INC. (THE "COMPANY"). BY OPENING THIS SEALED SOFTWARE PACKAGE, YOU ARE AGREEING TO BE BOUND BY THESE TERMS AND CONDITIONS. IF YOU DO NOT AGREE WITH THESE TERMS AND CONDITIONS, DO NOT OPEN THE SOFTWARE PACKAGE. PROMPTLY RETURN THE UNOPENED SOFTWARE PACKAGE AND ALL ACCOMPANYING ITEMS TO THE PLACE YOU OBTAINED THEM FOR A FULL REFUND OF ANY SUMS YOU HAVE PAID.

1.   GRANT OF LICENSE: In consideration of your purchase of this book, and your agreement to abide by the terms and conditions of this Agreement, the Company grants to you a nonexclusive right to use and display the copy of the enclosed software program (hereinafter the "SOFTWARE") on a single computer (i.e., with a single CPU) at a single location so long as you comply with the terms of this Agreement. The Company reserves all rights not expressly granted to you under this Agreement.

2.   OWNERSHIP OF SOFTWARE: You own only the magnetic or physical media (the enclosed media) on which the SOFTWARE is recorded or fixed, but the Company and the software developers retain all the rights, title, and ownership to the SOFTWARE recorded on the original media copy(ies) and all subsequent copies of the SOFTWARE, regardless of the form or media on which the original or other copies may exist. This license is not a sale of the original SOFTWARE or any copy to you.

3.   COPY RESTRICTIONS: This SOFTWARE and the accompanying printed materials and user manual (the "Documentation") are the subject of copyright. The individual programs on the media are copyrighted by the authors of each program. Some of the programs on the media include separate licensing agreements. If you intend to use one of these programs, you must read and follow its accompanying license agreement. You may not copy the Documentation or the SOFTWARE, except that you may make a single copy of the SOFTWARE for backup or archival purposes only. You may be held legally responsible for any copying or copyright infringement which is caused or encouraged by your failure to abide by the terms of this restriction.

4.   USE RESTRICTIONS: You may not network the SOFTWARE or otherwise use it on more than one computer or computer terminal at the same time. You may physically transfer the SOFTWARE from one computer to another provided that the SOFTWARE is used on only one computer at a time. You may not distribute copies of the SOFTWARE or Documentation to others. You may not reverse engineer, disassemble, decompile, modify, adapt, translate, or create derivative works based on the SOFTWARE or the Documentation without the prior written consent of the Company.

5.   TRANSFER RESTRICTIONS: The enclosed SOFTWARE is licensed only to you and may not be transferred to any one else without the prior written consent of the Company. Any unauthorized transfer of the SOFTWARE shall result in the immediate termination of this Agreement.

6.   TERMINATION: This license is effective until terminated. This license will terminate automatically

without notice from the Company and become null and void if you fail to comply with any provisions or limitations of this license. Upon termination, you shall destroy the Documentation and all copies of the SOFTWARE. All provisions of this Agreement as to warranties, limitation of liability, remedies or damages, and our ownership rights shall survive termination.

7.   MISCELLANEOUS: This Agreement shall be construed in accordance with the laws of the United States of America and the State of New York and shall benefit the Company, its affiliates, and assignees.

8.   LIMITED WARRANTY AND DISCLAIMER OF WARRANTY: The Company warrants that the SOFTWARE, when properly used in accordance with the Documentation, will operate in substantial conformity with the description of the SOFTWARE set forth in the Documentation. The Company does not warrant that the SOFTWARE will meet your requirements or that the operation of the SOFTWARE will be uninterrupted or error-free. The Company warrants that the media on which the SOFTWARE is delivered shall be free from defects in materials and workmanship under normal use for a period of thirty (30) days from the date of your purchase. Your only remedy and the Company's only obligation under these limited warranties is, at the Company's option, return of the warranted item for a refund of any amounts paid by you or replacement of the item. Any replacement of SOFTWARE or media under the warranties shall not extend the original warranty period. The limited warranty set forth above shall not apply to any SOFTWARE which the Company determines in good faith has been subject to misuse, neglect, improper installation, repair, alteration, or damage by you. EXCEPT FOR THE EXPRESSED WARRANTIES SET FORTH ABOVE, THE COMPANY DISCLAIMS ALL WARRANTIES, EXPRESS OR IMPLIED, INCLUDING WITHOUT LIMITATION, THE IMPLIED WARRANTIES OF MERCHANTABILITY AND FITNESS FOR A PARTICULAR PURPOSE. EXCEPT FOR THE EXPRESS WARRANTY SET FORTH ABOVE, THE COMPANY DOES NOT WARRANT, GUARANTEE, OR MAKE ANY REPRESENTATION REGARDING THE USE OR THE RESULTS OF THE USE OF THE SOFTWARE IN TERMS OF ITS CORRECTNESS, ACCURACY, RELIABILITY, CURRENTNESS, OR OTHERWISE.

IN NO EVENT, SHALL THE COMPANY OR ITS EMPLOYEES, AGENTS, SUPPLIERS, OR CONTRACTORS BE LIABLE FOR ANY INCIDENTAL, INDIRECT, SPECIAL, OR CONSEQUENTIAL DAMAGES ARISING OUT OF OR IN CONNECTION WITH THE LICENSE GRANTED UNDER THIS AGREEMENT, OR FOR LOSS OF USE, LOSS OF DATA, LOSS OF INCOME OR PROFIT, OR OTHER LOSSES, SUSTAINED AS A RESULT OF INJURY TO ANY PERSON, OR LOSS OF OR DAMAGE TO PROPERTY, OR CLAIMS OF THIRD PARTIES, EVEN IF THE COMPANY OR AN AUTHORIZED REPRESENTATIVE OF THE COMPANY HAS BEEN ADVISED OF THE POSSIBILITY OF SUCH DAMAGES. IN NO EVENT SHALL LIABILITY OF THE COMPANY FOR DAMAGES WITH RESPECT TO THE SOFTWARE EXCEED THE AMOUNTS ACTUALLY PAID BY YOU, IF ANY, FOR THE SOFTWARE.

SOME JURISDICTIONS DO NOT ALLOW THE LIMITATION OF IMPLIED WARRANTIES OR LIABILITY FOR INCIDENTAL, INDIRECT, SPECIAL, OR CONSEQUENTIAL DAMAGES, SO THE ABOVE LIMITATIONS MAY NOT ALWAYS APPLY. THE WARRANTIES IN THIS AGREEMENT GIVE YOU SPECIFIC LEGAL RIGHTS AND YOU MAY ALSO HAVE OTHER RIGHTS WHICH VARY IN ACCORDANCE WITH LOCAL LAW.

ACKNOWLEDGMENT

YOU ACKNOWLEDGE THAT YOU HAVE READ THIS AGREEMENT, UNDERSTAND IT, AND AGREE TO BE BOUND BY ITS TERMS AND CONDITIONS. YOU ALSO AGREE THAT THIS AGREEMENT IS THE COMPLETE AND EXCLUSIVE STATEMENT OF THE AGREEMENT BETWEEN YOU AND THE COMPANY AND SUPERSEDES ALL PROPOSALS OR PRIOR AGREEMENTS, ORAL, OR WRITTEN, AND ANY OTHER COMMUNICATIONS BETWEEN YOU AND THE COMPANY OR ANY REPRESENTATIVE OF THE COMPANY RELATING TO THE SUBJECT MATTER OF THIS AGREEMENT.

Should you have any questions concerning this Agreement or if you wish to contact the Company for any reason, please contact in writing at the address below.

Robin Short
Prentice Hall PTR
One Lake Street
Upper Saddle River, New Jersey 07458

The DEITEL®
Suite of Products...

INTRODUCING THE NEW SIMPLY SERIES

The Deitels are pleased to announce the new *Simply Series*. These books take an engaging new approach to teaching programming languages from the ground up. The pedagogy of this series combines the DEITEL® signature *LIVE-CODE Approach* with an *APPLICATION-DRIVEN Tutorial Approach* to teaching programming with outstanding pedagogical features that help students learn.

Simply Visual Basic®.NET
An APPLICATION-DRIVEN
Tutorial Approach

Visual Studio .NET 2002 Version:
©2003, 830 pp., paper (0-13-140553-5)

Visual Studio .NET 2003 Version:
©2004, 960 pp., paper (0-13-142640-0)

Simply Visual Basic® .NET An APPLICATION-DRIVEN Tutorial Approach guides readers through building real-world applications that incorporate Visual Basic .NET programming fundamentals. Using a step-by-step tutorial approach, readers begin learning the basics of programming and each successive tutorial builds on the readers' previously learned concepts while introducing new programming features. Learn GUI design, controls, methods, functions, data types, control statements, procedures, arrays, object-oriented programming, strings and characters, sequential files and more in this comprehensive introduction to Visual Basic .NET. We also include higher-end topics such as database programming, multimedia and graphics and Web applications development. If you're using Visual Studio® .NET 2002, choose the Visual Studio .NET 2002 version; or, if you're moving to Visual Studio .NET 2003, you can use the updated edition with updated screen captures and line numbers.

Simply Java™ Programming
An APPLICATION-DRIVEN
Tutorial Approach

©2004, 900 pp., paper
(0-13-142648-6)

Simply Java™ Programming An APPLICATION-DRIVEN Tutorial Approach guides readers through building real-world applications that incorporate Java programming fundamentals. Using a step-by-step tutorial approach, readers begin learning the basics of programming and each successive tutorial builds on the readers' previously learned concepts while introducing new programming features. Learn GUI design, components, methods, event-handling, types, control statements, arrays, object-oriented programming, exception-handling, strings and characters, sequential files and more in this comprehensive introduction to Java. We also include higher-end topics such as database programming, multimedia, graphics and Web applications development.

Simply C#
An APPLICATION-DRIVEN
Tutorial Approach

©2004, 850 pp., paper
(0-13-142641-9)

Simply C# An APPLICATION-DRIVEN Tutorial Approach guides readers through building real-world applications that incorporate C# programming fundamentals. Using a step-by-step tutorial approach, readers begin learning the basics of programming and each successive tutorial builds on the readers' previously learned concepts while introducing new programming features. Learn GUI design, controls, methods, functions, data types, control statements, procedures, arrays, object-oriented programming, strings and characters, sequential files and more in this comprehensive introduction to C#. We also include higher-end topics such as database programming, multimedia and graphics and Web applications development.

Simply C++
An APPLICATION-DRIVEN
Tutorial Approach

©2004, 800 pp., paper
(0-13-142660-5)

For information about *Simply C++ An APPLICATION-DRIVEN Tutorial Approach* and other *Simply Series* books under development, visit **www.deitel.com**. You may also sign up for the *DEITEL® BUZZ ONLINE* at **www.deitel.com/newsletter/subscribe.html** for monthly updates on the entire DEITEL® publishing program.

Sign up now for the new DEITEL® BUZZ ONLINE newsletter at:
w w w . d e i t e l . c o m / n e w s l e t t e r / s u b s c r i b e . h t m l

HOW TO PROGRAM BOOKS

The Deitels' acclaimed *How to Program Series* has achieved its success largely due to the innovative pedagogy used to teach key programming concepts. Their signature *LIVE-CODE Approach,* icon-identified programming tips and comprehensive exercises form the backbone of a series of books that has taught over one million students the craft of programming.

C++ How to Program Fourth Edition

BOOK / CD-ROM

©2003, 1400 pp., paper
(0-13-038474-7)

The world's best-selling C++ textbook is now even better! Designed for beginning through intermediate courses, this comprehensive, practical intro-duction to C++ includes hundreds of hands-on exercises and uses 267 *LIVE-CODE* programs to demonstrate C++'s powerful capabilities. This edition includes a new chapter—Web Programming with CGI—that provides everything readers need to begin developing their own Web-based applications that will run on the Internet!

Java™ How to Program Fifth Edition

BOOK / CD-ROM

©2003, 1500 pp., paper
(0-13-101621-0)

The Deitels' new Fifth Edition of *Java™ How to Program* is now even better! It now includes a tuned treatment of object-oriented program-ming; coverage of Java 1.4's new I/O APIs; new chapters on JDBC, servlets and JSP; an updated, optional case study on object-oriented design with version 1.4 of the UML; and a new code highlighting feature that makes it easier for readers to locate important program segments.

Visual Basic® .NET How to Program Second Edition

BOOK / CD-ROM

©2002, 1400 pp., paper
(0-13-029363-6)

This book provides a compre-hensive introduction to the next version of Visual Basic—Visual Basic .NET—featuring extensive updates and increased functionality. *Visual Basic .NET How to Program, Second Edition* covers introductory programming techniques as well as more advanced topics, featuring ASP .NET, ADO .NET, Web services and developing Web-based applications. This book also includes extensive coverage of XML.

Visual C++ .NET® How To Program

BOOK / CD-ROM

©2004, 1400 pp., paper (0-13-437377-4)

Written by the authors of the world's best-selling introductory/intermediate C and C++ textbooks, this comprehensive book thoroughly examines Visual C++® .NET. *Visual C++® .NET How to Program* begins with a strong founda-tion in the introductory and intermediate programming principles students will need in industry, including fundamental topics such as arrays, functions and control structures. Readers learn the concepts of object-oriented programming, including how to create reusable software components with classes and assemblies. The text then explores such essential topics as networking, databases, XML and multimedia. Graphical user interfaces are also extensively covered, giving students the tools to build compelling and fully interactive programs using the "drag-and-drop" techniques provided by the latest version of Visual Studio .NET, Visual Studio .NET 2003.

Advanced Java™ 2 Platform How to Program

BOOK / CD-ROM

©2002, 1811 pp., paper (0-13-089560-1)

Expanding on the world's best-selling Java textbook—*Java™ How to Program*—*Advanced Java™ 2 Platform How To Program* presents advanced Java topics for developing sophisticated, user-friendly GUIs; significant, scalable enterprise appli-cations; wireless applications and distributed systems. Primarily based on Java 2 Enterprise Edition (J2EE), this textbook integrates tech-nologies such as XML, JavaBeans, security, JDBC™, JavaServer Pages (JSP™), servlets, Remote Method Invocation (RMI), Enterprise JavaBeans™ (EJB) and design patterns into a production-quality system that allows developers to benefit from the leverage and platform inde-pendence Java 2 Enterprise Edition provides. The book also features the development of a complete, end-to-end e-business solution using advanced Java technologies.

C# How to Program

BOOK / CD-ROM

©2002, 1568 pp., paper (0-13-062221-4)

C# How to Program provides a comprehensive introduction to Microsoft's new object-oriented language. C# builds on the skills already mastered by countless C++ and Java programmers, enabling them to create powerful Web applications and components—ranging from XML-based Web services on Microsoft's .NET platform to middle-tier business objects and system-level applications.

C How to Program
Fourth Edition

BOOK / CD-ROM

©2004, 1255 pp., paper (0-13-142644-3)

The new Fourth Edition of *C How to Program*—the world's best-selling C text—is designed for introductory through intermediate courses as well as programming languages survey courses. This comprehensive text is aimed at readers with little or no programming experience through intermediate audiences. Highly practical in approach, it introduces fundamental notions of structured programming and software engineering and gets up to speed quickly.

Getting Started with Microsoft® Visual C++™ 6 with an Introduction to MFC

BOOK / CD-ROM

©2000, 163 pp., paper (0-13-016147-0)

Internet & World Wide Web How to Program
Second Edition

BOOK / CD-ROM

©2002, 1428 pp., paper (0-13-030897-8)

Internet & World Wide Web How to Program, Second Edition offers a thorough treatment of programming concepts that yield visible or audible results in Web pages and Web-based applications. This book discusses effective Web-based design, server- and client-side scripting, multi-tier Web-based applications development, ActiveX® controls and electronic commerce essentials.

Wireless Internet & Mobile Business How to Program

©2002, 1292 pp., paper (0-13-062226-5)

Wireless Internet & Mobile Business How to Program offers a thorough treatment of both the management and technical aspects of wireless Internet applications development, including coverage of current practices and future trends.

Python How to Program

BOOK / CD-ROM

©2002, 1376 pp., paper (0-13-092361-3)

Python How to Program provides a comprehensive introduction to Python—a powerful object-oriented programming language with clear syntax and the ability to bring together various technologies quickly and easily.

e-Business & e-Commerce for Managers

©2001, 794 pp., cloth (0-13-032364-0)

This comprehensive overview of building and managing e-businesses explores topics such as the decision to bring a business online, choosing a business model, accepting payments, marketing strategies and security, as well as many other important issues (such as career resources).

XML How to Program

BOOK / CD-ROM

©2001, 934 pp., paper (0-13-028417-3)

This book is a comprehensive guide to programming in XML. It teaches how to use XML to create customized tags and includes chapters that address markup languages for science and technology, multimedia, commerce and many other fields.

Perl How to Program

BOOK / CD-ROM

©2001, 1057 pp., paper (0-13-028418-1)

This comprehensive guide to Perl programming emphasizes the use of the Common Gateway Interface (CGI) with Perl to create powerful, dynamic multi-tier Web-based client/server applications.

e-Business & e-Commerce How to Program

BOOK / CD-ROM

©2001, 1254 pp., paper (0-13-028419-X)

e-Business & e-Commerce How to Program explores programming technologies for developing Web-based e-business and e-commerce solutions, and covers e-business and e-commerce models and business issues.

Visual Basic® 6 How to Program

BOOK / CD-ROM

©1999, 1015 pp., paper (0-13-456955-5)

Visual Basic® 6 How to Program was developed in cooperation with Microsoft to cover important topics such as graphical user interfaces (GUIs), multimedia, object-oriented programming, networking, database programming, Script®, COM/DCOM and ActiveX®.

Sign up now for the new *Deitel® Buzz Online* newsletter at:
www·deitel·com/newsletter/subscribe·html

The DEITEL® DEVELOPER SERIES

Deitel & Associates is recognized worldwide for its best-selling *How to Program Series* of books for college and university students and its signature *LIVE-CODE Approach* to teaching programming languages. Now, for the first time, Deitel & Associates brings its proven teaching methods to a new series of books specifically designed for professionals.

THREE TYPES OF BOOKS FOR THREE DISTINCT AUDIENCES:

A Technical Introduction

A Technical Introduction books provide programmers, technical managers, project managers and other technical professionals with introductions to broad new technology areas.

A Programmer's Introduction

A Programmer's Introduction books offer focused treatments of programming fundamentals for practicing programmers. These books are also appropriate for novices.

For Experienced Programmers

For Experienced Programmers books are for experienced programmers who want a detailed treatment of a programming language or technology. These books contain condensed introductions to programming language fundamentals and provide extensive intermediate level coverage of high-end topics.

Java™ Web Services for Experienced Programmers

©2003, 700 pp., paper (0-13-046134-2)

Java™ Web Services for Experienced Programmers provides the experienced Java programmer with 103 *LIVE-CODE* examples and covers industry standards including XML, SOAP, WSDL and UDDI. Learn how to build and integrate Web services using the Java API for XML RPC, the Java API for XML Messaging, Apache Axis and the Java Web Services Developer Pack.

Web Services A Technical Introduction

©2003, 400 pp., paper (0-13-046135-0)

Web Services: A Technical Introduction familiarizes programmers, technical managers and project managers with key Web services concepts, including what Web services are and why they are revolutionary. The book covers the business case for Web services, the latest Web-services standards and Web services implementations in .NET and Java.

ORDER INFORMATION

SINGLE COPY SALES:
Visa, Master Card, American Express, Checks, or Money Orders only
Toll-Free: 800-643-5506; Fax: 800-835-5327

GOVERNMENT AGENCIES:
Prentice Hall Customer Service
(#GS-02F-8023A)
Tel: 201-767-5994; Fax: 800-445-6991

COLLEGE PROFESSORS:
For desk or review copies, please visit us on the World Wide Web at www.prenhall.com

CORPORATE ACCOUNTS:
Quantity, Bulk Orders totaling 10 or more books. Purchase orders only — No credit cards.
Tel: 201-236-7156; Fax: 201-236-7141
Toll-Free: 800-382-3419

CANADA:
Pearson Technology Group Canada
10 Alcorn Avenue, suite #300
Toronto, Ontario, Canada M4V 3B2
Tel: 416-925-2249; Fax: 416-925-0068
E-mail: phcinfo.pubcanada@pearsoned.com

UK/IRELAND:
Pearson Education
Edinburgh Gate
Harlow, Essex CM20 2JE UK
Tel: 01279 623928; Fax: 01279 414130
E-mail: enq.orders@pearsoned-ema.com

EUROPE, MIDDLE EAST & AFRICA:
Pearson Education
P.O. Box 75598
1070 AN Amsterdam, The Netherlands
Tel: 31 20 5755 800; Fax: 31 20 664 5334
E-mail: amsterdam@pearsoned-ema.com

ASIA:
Pearson Education Asia
317 Alexandra Road #04-01
IKEA Building
Singapore 159965
Tel: 65 476 4688; Fax: 65 378 0370

JAPAN:
Pearson Education
Nishi-Shinjuku, KF Building 101
8-14-24 Nishi-Shinjuku, Shinjuku-ku
Tokyo, Japan 160 0023
Tel: 81 3 3365 9001; Fax: 81 3 3365 9009

INDIA:
Pearson Education Indian Liaison Office
90 New Raidhani Enclave, Ground Floor
Delhi 110 092, India
Tel: 91 11 2059850 & 2059851
Fax: 91 11 2059852

AUSTRALIA:
Pearson Education Australia
Unit 4, Level 2
14 Aquatic Drive
Frenchs Forest, NSW 2086, Australia
Tel: 61 2 9454 2200; Fax: 61 2 9453 0089
E-mail: marketing@pearsoned.com.au

NEW ZEALAND/FIJI:
Pearson Education
46 Hillside Road
Auckland 10, New Zealand
Tel: 649 444 4968; Fax: 649 444 4957
E-mail: sales@pearsoned.co.nz

SOUTH AFRICA:
Pearson Education
P.O. Box 12122
Mill Street
Cape Town 8010 South Africa
Tel: 27 21 686 6356; Fax: 27 21 686 4590

LATIN AMERICA:
Pearson Education Latinoamerica
815 NW 57th Street Suite 484
Miami, FL 33158
Tel: 305 264 8344; Fax: 305 264 7933

www·deitel·com   www·prenhall·com/deitel
www·InformIT·com/deitel

PEARSON PTR

interactive

We make it click.

Complete Training Courses

Each complete package includes the corresponding *How to Program Series* textbook and interactive multimedia Windows-based CD-ROM *Cyber Classroom*. *Complete Training Courses* are perfect for anyone interested in Web and e-commerce programming. They are affordable resources for college students and professionals learning programming for the first time or reinforcing their knowledge.

Intuitive Browser-Based Interface

You'll love the *Complete Training Courses'* browser-based interface, designed to be easy and accessible to anyone who's ever used a Web browser. Every *Complete Training Course* features the full text, illustrations and program listings of its corresponding *How to Program* textbook—all in full color—with full-text searching and hyperlinking.

Further Enhancements to the Deitels' Signature *LIVE-CODE* Approach

Every code sample from the main text can be found in the interactive, multimedia, CD-ROM-based *Cyber Classrooms* included in the *Complete Training Courses*. Syntax coloring of code is included for the *How to Program* books that are published in full color. Even the two-color books use effective syntax shading. The *Cyber Classroom* products are always in full color.

Audio Annotations

Hours of detailed, expert audio descriptions of thousands of lines of code help reinforce concepts.

Easily Executable Code

With one click of the mouse, you can execute the code or save it to your hard drive to manipulate using the programming environment of your choice. With selected *Complete Training Courses*, you can also load all of the code into a development environment such as Microsoft® Visual Studio .NET, enabling you to modify and execute the programs with ease.

Abundant Self-Assessment Material

Practice exams test your understanding of key concepts with hundreds of test questions and answers in addition to those found in the main text. The textbook includes hundreds of programming exercises, while the *Cyber Classrooms* include answers to about half the exercises.

www.phptr.com/phptrinteractive

Sign up now for the new *DEITEL® BUZZ ONLINE* newsletter at:
www.deitel.com/newsletter/subscribe.html

BOOK/MULTIMEDIA PACKAGES

The Complete C++ Training Course, Fourth Edition

(0-13-100252-X)

The Complete e-Business & e-Commerce Programming Training Course

(0-13-089549-0)

The Complete Java™ Training Course, Fifth Edition

(0-13-101766-7)

The Complete Perl Training Course

(0-13-089552-0)

The Complete Visual Basic® .NET Training Course, Second Edition

(0-13-042530-3)

The Complete Visual Basic® 6 Training Course

(0-13-082929-3)

The Complete C# Training Course

(0-13-064584-2)

The Complete Python Training Course

(0-1.3-067374-9)

The Complete Internet & World Wide Web Programming Training Course, Second Edition

(0-13-089550-4)

The Complete Wireless Internet & Mobile Business Programming Training Course

(0-13-062335-0)

The Complete XML Programming Training Course

(0-13-089557-1)

All of these ISBNs are retail ISBNs. College and university instructors should contact your local Prentice Hall representative or write to cs@prenhall.com *for the corresponding student edition ISBNs.*

The Deitels are the authors of best-selling Java™, C++, C#, C, Visual Basic® and Internet and World Wide Web books and multimedia packages.

Corporate Training Delivered Worldwide

Deitel & Associates, Inc. provides intensive, lecture-and-laboratory courses to organizations worldwide. The programming courses use our signature *Live-Code Approach*, presenting complete working programs.

Deitel & Associates, Inc. has trained over one million students and professionals worldwide through corporate training courses, public seminars, university teaching, *How to Program Series* textbooks, *Deitel® Developer Series* textbooks, *Simply Series* textbooks, *Cyber Classroom Series* multimedia packages, *Complete Training Course Series* textbook and multimedia packages, broadcast-satellite courses and Web-based training.

Educational Consulting

Deitel & Associates, Inc. offers complete educational consulting services for corporate training programs and professional schools including:

- Curriculum design and development
- Preparation of Instructor Guides
- Customized courses and course materials
- Design and implementation of professional training certificate programs
- Instructor certification
- Train-the-trainers programs
- Delivery of software-related corporate training programs

Visit our Web site for more information on our corporate training curriculum and to purchase our training products.

www.deitel.com/training

Would you like to review upcoming publications?

If you are a professor or senior industry professional interested in being a reviewer of our forthcoming publications, please contact us by email at deitel@deitel.com. Insert "Content Reviewer" in the subject heading.

Are you interested in a career in computer education, publishing and training?

We offer a limited number of full-time positions available for college graduates in computer science, information systems, information technology, management information systems, English and communications, marketing, multimedia technology and other areas. Please check our Web site for the latest job postings or contact us by e-mail at deitel@deitel.com. Insert "Full-time Job" in the subject heading.

Are you a Boston-area college student looking for an internship?

We have a limited number of competitive summer positions and 20-hr./week school-year opportunities for computer science, English and business majors. Students work at our worldwide headquarters west of Boston. We also offer full-time internships for students taking a semester off from school. This is an excellent opportunity for students looking to gain industry experience and earn money to pay for school. Please contact us by e-mail at deitel@deitel.com. Insert "Internship" in the subject heading.

Would you like to explore contract training opportunities with us?

Deitel & Associates, Inc. is looking for contract instructors to teach software-related topics at our clients' sites in the United States and worldwide. Applicants should be experienced professional trainers or college professors. For more information, please visit www.deitel.com and send your resume to Abbey Deitel at abbey.deitel@deitel.com.

Are you a training company in need of quality course materials?

Corporate training companies worldwide use our *Complete Training Course Series* book and multimedia packages, our *Web-Based Training Series* courses and our *Deitel® Developer Series* books in their classes. We have extensive ancillary instructor materials for each of our products. For more details, please visit www.deitel.com or contact us by email at deitel@deitel.com.

Sign up now for the new *Deitel® Buzz Online* newsletter at:
www.deitel.com/newsletter/subscribe.html

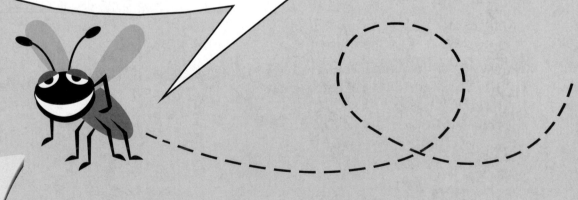